The Editors

RICHARD M. SCAMMON is director of the Elections Research Center in Washington. He has served as director of the Census in the Kennedy administration, as a delegate to the U.N. General Assembly and as a member of the National Bipartisan Commission on Central America.

One of the nation's leading authorities on elections in this country and overseas, he is senior elections consultant to NBC News. He was chairman of the President's Commission on Registration and Voting Participation and has acted as an official election observer in West Germany, the U.S.S.R., the Dominican Republic, Vietnam and El Salvador and as a technical adviser during Egyptian-Israeli-U.S. discussions of electoral arrangements for the West Bank and Gaza Strip.

He is a trustee of the National Council on Public Polls, a member of the board of directors of the International Foundation for Electoral Systems and serves on the Editorial Boards of *Electoral Studies, World Affairs,* and *Public Opinion.*

ALICE V. McGILLIVRAY has been associated with the Elections Research Center for many years and is responsible for much of the work in this volume. She attended Auburn University in Alabama and received her B.A. from George Washington University and M.A. from American University in Washington, D.C.

AMERICA AT THE POLLS 2 brings together in one reference volume the basic county-by-county statistics of U.S. Presidential elections for the years 1968-1984. From Richard Nixon's victory in the turbulent 1968 election to Ronald Reagan's landslide re-election in 1984, the book details American political behavior for five Presidential contests.

Historical figures summarize the popular and Electoral College votes from 1920 through 1984, followed by tables of the state-by-state Presidential vote for those years. A brief note lists all candidates and their national vote.

A chapter for each state contains statewide votes as well as a county outline map and the detailed county-by-county vote for President 1968-1984. A special note section gives a breakdown of the state's minor party vote.

Percentages and pluralities are presented for every state and every county to provide a comprehensive, authoritative reference volume.

AMERICA AT THE POLLS 2

A HANDBOOK OF AMERICAN
PRESIDENTIAL ELECTION
STATISTICS 1968-1984

COMPILED AND EDITED BY

RICHARD M. SCAMMON

and

ALICE V. McGILLIVRAY

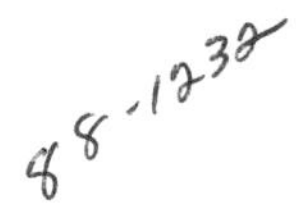

ELECTIONS RESEARCH CENTER

CONGRESSIONAL QUARTERLY WASHINGTON 1988

1321 Connecticut Ave. N.W., Washington, D.C. 20036

Copies available from: Congressional Quarterly Inc., 1414 22nd St. N.W., Washington, D.C. 20037

Printed in the United States of America

Library of Congress Catalog Card Number: 87-33221
International Standard Book Number: 0-87187-452-0

CONTENTS

INTRODUCTION i

UNITED STATES 1
President 1920-1984
Electoral College 1920-1984
State-by-State, President 1920-1984

STATE CHAPTERS

Alabama 36
Alaska 49
Arizona 60
Arkansas 66
California 79
Colorado 87
Connecticut 100
Delaware 105
Florida 110
Georgia 123
Hawaii 141
Idaho 146
Illinois 154
Indiana 167
Iowa 180
Kansas 193
Kentucky 206
Louisiana 219
Maine 232
Maryland 238
Massachusetts 244
Michigan 250
Minnesota 263
Mississippi 276
Missouri 289
Montana 302
Nebraska 310
Nevada 323
New Hampshire 329
New Jersey 334
New Mexico 340
New York 348
North Carolina 356
North Dakota 369
Ohio 377
Oklahoma 390
Oregon 403
Pennsylvania 411
Rhode Island 424
South Carolina 429
South Dakota 437
Tennessee 450
Texas 463
Utah 491
Vermont 499
Virginia 505
Washington 523
West Virginia 531
Wisconsin 539
Wyoming 552

District of Columbia 558

PRESIDENTIAL PRIMARIES

1984 565
1980 572
1976 579
1972 586
1968 591

INTRODUCTION

When the first AMERICA AT THE POLLS was published in 1965, it covered Presidential voting in the United States from 1920 through 1964—from the post-war election of Warren G. Harding to the landslide win of Lyndon B. Johnson in 1964. The new AMERICA AT THE POLLS 2 has been prepared to update through 1984 the county-by-county vote detail for President carried in the first study.

Drawing both from the earlier work and from more recent publications in the Elections Research Center's AMERICA VOTES series, AMERICA AT THE POLLS 2 details county-by-county the Presidential voting for each state—total vote, major party vote (including George Wallace in 1968), total minor party vote, percentages and pluralities.

In addition to the standard county-by-county data, the user will find popular and Electoral College voting data for President back to 1920 on a national and state-wide basis. Population data and county outline maps are included in each state section. As in other Center publications, note commentaries detail the breakdown of "other" category voting in each state, list changes in county organizational arrangements and detail other special aspects of the vote reporting as may be required. The minor party candidates are listed in each state under the ballot designation used in that state, though the national tables give the normal designation used nationally by the party involved.

Finally, since the development of Presidential primary voting has been so substantial in the past several decades, a summary of Presidential preference primary elections by state and candidate has been included for the five elections covered.

The basic data for AMERICA AT THE POLLS 2 have been provided by the state election authorities across the nation, and to them and to others who helped in putting together this volume goes the gratitude of the Editors. Since the assembling of any mass of data of this size will involve some errors, it is hoped users noting such will communicate them to the Center for adjustment in subsequent volumes. For interpretations of material, the Editors assume sole responsibility.

Richard M. Scammon
Alice V. McGillivray

Washington, D. C.
November, 1987

UNITED STATES

POPULAR VOTE FOR PRESIDENT 1920 TO 1984

Year	Total Vote	Republican Vote	Republican Candidate	Democratic Vote	Democratic Candidate	Other Vote	Plurality	Percentage Total Vote Rep.	Total Vote Dem.	Major Vote Rep.	Major Vote Dem.
1984	92,652,842	54,455,075	Reagan, Ronald	37,577,185	Mondale, Walter F.	620,582	16,877,890 R	58.8%	40.6%	59.2%	40.8%
1980	86,515,221	43,904,153	Reagan, Ronald	35,483,883	Carter, Jimmy	7,127,185	8,420,270 R	50.7%	41.0%	55.3%	44.7%
1976	81,555,889	39,147,793	Ford, Gerald R.	40,830,763	Carter, Jimmy	1,577,333	1,682,970 D	48.0%	50.1%	48.9%	51.1%
1972	77,718,554	47,169,911	Nixon, Richard M.	29,170,383	McGovern, George S.	1,378,260	17,999,528 R	60.7%	37.5%	61.8%	38.2%
1968	73,211,875	31,785,480	Nixon, Richard M.	31,275,166	Humphrey, Hubert H.	10,151,229	510,314 R	43.4%	42.7%	50.4%	49.6%
1964	70,644,592	27,178,188	Goldwater, Barry M.	43,129,566	Johnson, Lyndon B.	336,838	15,951,378 D	38.5%	61.1%	38.7%	61.3%
1960	68,838,219	34,108,157	Nixon, Richard M.	34,226,731	Kennedy, John F.	503,331	118,574 D	49.5%	49.7%	49.9%	50.1%
1956	62,026,908	35,590,472	Eisenhower, Dwight D.	26,022,752	Stevenson, Adlai E.	413,684	9,567,720 R	57.4%	42.0%	57.8%	42.2%
1952	61,550,918	33,936,234	Eisenhower, Dwight D.	27,314,992	Stevenson, Adlai E.	299,692	6,621,242 R	55.1%	44.4%	55.4%	44.6%
1948	48,793,826	21,991,291	Dewey, Thomas E.	24,179,345	Truman, Harry S.	2,623,190	2,188,054 D	45.1%	49.6%	47.6%	52.4%
1944	47,976,670	22,017,617	Dewey, Thomas E.	25,612,610	Roosevelt, Franklin D.	346,443	3,594,993 D	45.9%	53.4%	46.2%	53.8%
1940	49,900,418	22,348,480	Willkie, Wendell	27,313,041	Roosevelt, Franklin D.	238,897	4,964,561 D	44.8%	54.7%	45.0%	55.0%
1936	45,654,763	16,684,231	Landon, Alfred M.	27,757,333	Roosevelt, Franklin D.	1,213,199	11,073,102 D	36.5%	60.8%	37.5%	62.5%
1932	39,758,759	15,760,684	Hoover, Herbert C.	22,829,501	Roosevelt, Franklin D.	1,168,574	7,068,817 D	39.6%	57.4%	40.8%	59.2%
1928	36,805,951	21,437,277	Hoover, Herbert C.	15,007,698	Smith, Alfred E.	360,976	6,429,579 R	58.2%	40.8%	58.8%	41.2%
1924	29,095,023	15,719,921	Coolidge, Calvin	8,386,704	Davis, John W.	4,988,398	7,333,217 R	54.0%	28.8%	65.2%	34.8%
1920	26,768,613	16,153,115	Harding, Warren G.	9,133,092	Cox, James M.	1,482,406	7,020,023 R	60.3%	34.1%	63.9%	36.1%

For detail of other vote see note section included with each U.S. summary table that follows.

ELECTORAL COLLEGE VOTE 1920 TO 1984

Year	Total	Republican	Democratic	Other
1984	538	525	13	—
1980	538	489	49	—
1976	538	240	297	1 REAGAN
1972	538	520	17	1 LIBERTARIAN
1968	538	301	191	46 AIP
1964	538	52	486	—
1960	537	219	303	15 BYRD
1956	531	457	73	1 JONES
1952	531	442	89	—
1948	531	189	303	39 SR
1944	531	99	432	—
1940	531	82	449	—
1936	531	8	523	—
1932	531	59	472	—
1928	531	444	87	—
1924	531	382	136	13 PROGRESSIVE
1920	531	404	127	—

PRESIDENT 1984

In New York the Republican figures include Conservative votes and the Democratic figures include Liberal votes.

In Minnesota, the Republican candidates appear of the ballot as Independent-Republican, the Democratic as Democratic-Farmer-Labor. In many states various non-major party candidates appeared on the ballot with variations of the party designations given here, were listed as "Independent" or "Non-Party", or were carried with entirely different party labels.

The Workers World candidate for President was Gavrielle Holmes in Ohio and Rhode Island; in several states minor party Vice-Presidential candidates were different from those listed below.

The full list of candidates for President and Vice-President was:

54,455,075	Ronald Reagan and George Bush, Republican.
37,577,185	Walter F. Mondale and Geraldine A. Ferraro, Democratic.
228,314	David Bergland and James A. Lewis, Libertarian.
78,807	Lyndon H. LaRouche and Billy M. Davis, Independent.
72,200	Sonia Johnson and Richard Walton, Citizens.
66,336	Bob Richards and Maureen Salaman, Populist.
46,868	Dennis L. Serrette and Nancy Ross, Alliance.
36,386	Gus Hall and Angela Davis, Communist.
24,706	Mel Mason and Matilde Zimmermann, Socialist Workers.
17,985	Larry Holmes and Gloria LaRiva, Workers World.
13,161	Delmar Dennis and Traves Brownlee, American.
10,801	Ed Winn and Helen Halyard, Workers League.
4,242	Earl F. Dodge and Warren C. Martin, Prohibition.
1,486	John B. Anderson and Grace Pierce, National Unity.
892	Gerald Baker and Ferris Alger, Big Deal.
825	Arthur J. Lowery and Raymond L. Garland, United Sovreign Citizens.

The candidates listed above are those who appeared on the ballot in at least one state. Where identified by state authorities, write-in votes for minor party candidates are credited to their total above and listed in the individual state note sections. In addition to the votes listed, 13,623 scattered write-in votes were reported from various states and 3,950 votes were cast for "None of these Candidates" in Nevada.

UNITED STATES

PRESIDENT 1984

State	Electoral Vote			Total	Republican	Democratic	Other	Plurality	Percentage			
									Total Vote		Major Vote	
	Rep.	Dem.	Other	Vote					Rep.	Dem.	Rep.	Dem.
Alabama	9			1,441,713	872,849	551,899	16,965	320,950 R	60.5%	38.3%	61.3%	38.7%
Alaska	3			207,605	138,377	62,007	7,221	76,370 R	66.7%	29.9%	69.1%	30.9%
Arizona	7			1,025,897	681,416	333,854	10,627	347,562 R	66.4%	32.5%	67.1%	32.9%
Arkansas	6			884,406	534,774	338,646	10,986	196,128 R	60.5%	38.3%	61.2%	38.8%
California	47			9,505,423	5,467,009	3,922,519	115,895	1,544,490 R	57.5%	41.3%	58.2%	41.8%
Colorado	8			1,295,380	821,817	454,975	18,588	366,842 R	63.4%	35.1%	64.4%	35.6%
Connecticut	8			1,466,900	890,877	569,597	6,426	321,280 R	60.7%	38.8%	61.0%	39.0%
Delaware	3			254,572	152,190	101,656	726	50,534 R	59.8%	39.9%	60.0%	40.0%
Florida	21			4,180,051	2,730,350	1,448,816	885	1,281,534 R	65.3%	34.7%	65.3%	34.7%
Georgia	12			1,776,120	1,068,722	706,628	770	362,094 R	60.2%	39.8%	60.2%	39.8%
Hawaii	4			335,846	185,050	147,154	3,642	37,896 R	55.1%	43.8%	55.7%	44.3%
Idaho	4			411,144	297,523	108,510	5,111	189,013 R	72.4%	26.4%	73.3%	26.7%
Illinois	24			4,819,088	2,707,103	2,086,499	25,486	620,604 R	56.2%	43.3%	56.5%	43.5%
Indiana	12			2,233,069	1,377,230	841,481	14,358	535,749 R	61.7%	37.7%	62.1%	37.9%
Iowa	8			1,319,805	703,088	605,620	11,097	97,468 R	53.3%	45.9%	53.7%	46.3%
Kansas	7			1,021,991	677,296	333,149	11,546	344,147 R	66.3%	32.6%	67.0%	33.0%
Kentucky	9			1,369,345	821,702	539,539	8,104	282,163 R	60.0%	39.4%	60.4%	39.6%
Louisiana	10			1,706,822	1,037,299	651,586	17,937	385,713 R	60.8%	38.2%	61.4%	38.6%
Maine	4			553,144	336,500	214,515	2,129	121,985 R	60.8%	38.8%	61.1%	38.9%
Maryland	10			1,675,873	879,918	787,935	8,020	91,983 R	52.5%	47.0%	52.8%	47.2%
Massachusetts	13			2,559,453	1,310,936	1,239,606	8,911	71,330 R	51.2%	48.4%	51.4%	48.6%
Michigan	20			3,801,658	2,251,571	1,529,638	20,449	721,933 R	59.2%	40.2%	59.5%	40.5%
Minnesota		10		2,084,449	1,032,603	1,036,364	15,482	3,761 D	49.5%	49.7%	49.9%	50.1%
Mississippi	7			941,104	582,377	352,192	6,535	230,185 R	61.9%	37.4%	62.3%	37.7%
Missouri	11			2,122,783	1,274,188	848,583	12	425,605 R	60.0%	40.0%	60.0%	40.0%
Montana	4			384,377	232,450	146,742	5,185	85,708 R	60.5%	38.2%	61.3%	38.7%
Nebraska	5			652,090	460,054	187,866	4,170	272,188 R	70.6%	28.8%	71.0%	29.0%
Nevada	4			286,667	188,770	91,655	6,242	97,115 R	65.8%	32.0%	67.3%	32.7%
New Hampshire	4			389,066	267,051	120,395	1,620	146,656 R	68.6%	30.9%	68.9%	31.1%
New Jersey	16			3,217,862	1,933,630	1,261,323	22,909	672,307 R	60.1%	39.2%	60.5%	39.5%
New Mexico	5			514,370	307,101	201,769	5,500	105,332 R	59.7%	39.2%	60.3%	39.7%
New York	36			6,806,810	3,664,763	3,119,609	22,438	545,154 R	53.8%	45.8%	54.0%	46.0%
North Carolina	13			2,175,361	1,346,481	824,287	4,593	522,194 R	61.9%	37.9%	62.0%	38.0%
North Dakota	3			308,971	200,336	104,429	4,206	95,907 R	64.8%	33.8%	65.7%	34.3%
Ohio	23			4,547,619	2,678,560	1,825,440	43,619	853,120 R	58.9%	40.1%	59.5%	40.5%
Oklahoma	8			1,255,676	861,530	385,080	9,066	476,450 R	68.6%	30.7%	69.1%	30.9%
Oregon	7			1,226,527	685,700	536,479	4,348	149,221 R	55.9%	43.7%	56.1%	43.9%
Pennsylvania	25			4,844,903	2,584,323	2,228,131	32,449	356,192 R	53.3%	46.0%	53.7%	46.3%
Rhode Island	4			410,492	212,080	197,106	1,306	14,974 R	51.7%	48.0%	51.8%	48.2%
South Carolina	8			968,529	615,539	344,459	8,531	271,080 R	63.6%	35.6%	64.1%	35.9%
South Dakota	3			317,867	200,267	116,113	1,487	84,154 R	63.0%	36.5%	63.3%	36.7%
Tennessee	11			1,711,994	990,212	711,714	10,068	278,498 R	57.8%	41.6%	58.2%	41.8%
Texas	29			5,397,571	3,433,428	1,949,276	14,867	1,484,152 R	63.6%	36.1%	63.8%	36.2%
Utah	5			629,656	469,105	155,369	5,182	313,736 R	74.5%	24.7%	75.1%	24.9%
Vermont	3			234,561	135,865	95,730	2,966	40,135 R	57.9%	40.8%	58.7%	41.3%
Virginia	12			2,146,635	1,337,078	796,250	13,307	540,828 R	62.3%	37.1%	62.7%	37.3%
Washington	10			1,883,910	1,051,670	807,352	24,888	244,318 R	55.8%	42.9%	56.6%	43.4%
West Virginia	6			735,742	405,483	328,125	2,134	77,358 R	55.1%	44.6%	55.3%	44.7%
Wisconsin	11			2,211,689	1,198,584	995,740	17,365	202,844 R	54.2%	45.0%	54.6%	45.4%
Wyoming	3			188,968	133,241	53,370	2,357	79,871 R	70.5%	28.2%	71.4%	28.6%
Dist. of Col.		3		211,288	29,009	180,408	1,871	151,399 D	13.7%	85.4%	13.9%	86.1%
United States	525	13	—	92,652,842	54,455,075	37,577,185	620,582	16,877,890 R	58.8%	40.6%	59.2%	40.8%

PRESIDENT 1980

In New York the Republican figures include Conservative votes and in a number of states candidates appeared on the ballot with variants of the party designations listed below, without any party designation, or with entirely different party names.

In several cases, Vice-Presidential nominees were different from those listed for most states and the Socialist Workers party nominee for President varied from state to state.

43,904,153	Ronald Reagan and George Bush, Republican.
35,483,883	Jimmy Carter and Walter F. Mondale, Democratic.
5,720,060	John B. Anderson and Patrick J. Lucey, Independent.
921,299	Edward E. Clark and David Koch, Libertarian.
234,294	Barry Commoner and LaDonna Harris, Citizens.
45,023	Gus Hall and Angela Davis, Communist.
41,268	John R. Rarick and Eileen M. Shearer, American Independent.
38,737	Clifton DeBerry and Matilde Zimmermann, Socialist Workers.
32,327	Ellen McCormack and Carroll Driscoll, Right to Life.
18,116	Maureen Smith and Elizabeth Barron, Peace and Freedom.
13,300	Deirdre Griswold and Larry Holmes, Workers World.
7,212	Benjamin C. Bubar and Earl F. Dodge, Statesman.
6,898	David McReynolds and Diane Drufenbrock, Socialist.
6,647	Percy L. Greaves and Frank L. Varnum, American.
6,272	Andrew Pulley and Matilde Zimmermann, Socialist Workers.
4,029	Richard Congress and Matilde Zimmermann, Socialist Workers.
3,694	Kurt Lynen and Harry Kieve, Middle Class.
1,718	Bill Gahres and J. F. Loughlin, Down With Lawyers.
1,555	Frank W. Shelton and George E. Jackson, American.
923	Martin E. Wendelken with no Vice-Presidential candidate, Independent.
296	Harley McLain and Jewelie Goeller, Natural Peoples.

In addition to these votes, 13,185 scattered write-in votes were reported from various states, 6,139 votes were cast in Minnesota for American party electors without designated national nominees, and 4,193 votes were cast for "None of these Candidates" in Nevada.

State-by-state vote details will be found in the individual state note sections and a supplementary state-by-state national table follows for all "other" candidates polling over 100,000 votes. An asterisk by the vote denotes write-in.

UNITED STATES

PRESIDENT 1980

State	Electoral Vote Rep.	Electoral Vote Dem.	Electoral Vote Other	Total Vote	Republican	Democratic	Other	Plurality	Percentage Total Vote Rep.	Percentage Total Vote Dem.	Percentage Major Vote Rep.	Percentage Major Vote Dem.
Alabama	9			1,341,929	654,192	636,730	51,007	17,462 R	48.8%	47.4%	50.7%	49.3%
Alaska	3			158,445	86,112	41,842	30,491	44,270 R	54.3%	26.4%	67.3%	32.7%
Arizona	6			873,945	529,688	246,843	97,414	282,845 R	60.6%	28.2%	68.2%	31.8%
Arkansas	6			837,582	403,164	398,041	36,377	5,123 R	48.1%	47.5%	50.3%	49.7%
California	45			8,587,063	4,524,858	3,083,661	978,544	1,441,197 R	52.7%	35.9%	59.5%	40.5%
Colorado	7			1,184,415	652,264	367,973	164,178	284,291 R	55.1%	31.1%	63.9%	36.1%
Connecticut	8			1,406,285	677,210	541,732	187,343	135,478 R	48.2%	38.5%	55.6%	44.4%
Delaware	3			235,900	111,252	105,754	18,894	5,498 R	47.2%	44.8%	51.3%	48.7%
Florida	17			3,686,930	2,046,951	1,419,475	220,504	627,476 R	55.5%	38.5%	59.1%	40.9%
Georgia		12		1,596,695	654,168	890,733	51,794	236,565 D	41.0%	55.8%	42.3%	57.7%
Hawaii		4		303,287	130,112	135,879	37,296	5,767 D	42.9%	44.8%	48.9%	51.1%
Idaho	4			437,431	290,699	110,192	36,540	180,507 R	66.5%	25.2%	72.5%	27.5%
Illinois	26			4,749,721	2,358,049	1,981,413	410,259	376,636 R	49.6%	41.7%	54.3%	45.7%
Indiana	13			2,242,033	1,255,656	844,197	142,180	411,459 R	56.0%	37.7%	59.8%	40.2%
Iowa	8			1,317,661	676,026	508,672	132,963	167,354 R	51.3%	38.6%	57.1%	42.9%
Kansas	7			979,795	566,812	326,150	86,833	240,662 R	57.9%	33.3%	63.5%	36.5%
Kentucky	9			1,294,627	635,274	616,417	42,936	18,857 R	49.1%	47.6%	50.8%	49.2%
Louisiana	10			1,548,591	792,853	708,453	47,285	84,400 R	51.2%	45.7%	52.8%	47.2%
Maine	4			523,011	238,522	220,974	63,515	17,548 R	45.6%	42.3%	51.9%	48.1%
Maryland		10		1,540,496	680,606	726,161	133,729	45,555 D	44.2%	47.1%	48.4%	51.6%
Massachusetts	14			2,524,298	1,057,631	1,053,802	412,865	3,829 R	41.9%	41.7%	50.1%	49.9%
Michigan	21			3,909,725	1,915,225	1,661,532	332,968	253,693 R	49.0%	42.5%	53.5%	46.5%
Minnesota		10		2,051,980	873,268	954,174	224,538	80,906 D	42.6%	46.5%	47.8%	52.2%
Mississippi	7			892,620	441,089	429,281	22,250	11,808 R	49.4%	48.1%	50.7%	49.3%
Missouri	12			2,099,824	1,074,181	931,182	94,461	142,999 R	51.2%	44.3%	53.6%	46.4%
Montana	4			363,952	206,814	118,032	39,106	88,782 R	56.8%	32.4%	63.7%	36.3%
Nebraska	5			640,854	419,937	166,851	54,066	253,086 R	65.5%	26.0%	71.6%	28.4%
Nevada	3			247,885	155,017	66,666	26,202	88,351 R	62.5%	26.9%	69.9%	30.1%
New Hampshire	4			383,990	221,705	108,864	53,421	112,841 R	57.7%	28.4%	67.1%	32.9%
New Jersey	17			2,975,684	1,546,557	1,147,364	281,763	399,193 R	52.0%	38.6%	57.4%	42.6%
New Mexico	4			456,971	250,779	167,826	38,366	82,953 R	54.9%	36.7%	59.9%	40.1%
New York	41			6,201,959	2,893,831	2,728,372	579,756	165,459 R	46.7%	44.0%	51.5%	48.5%
North Carolina	13			1,855,833	915,018	875,635	65,180	39,383 R	49.3%	47.2%	51.1%	48.9%
North Dakota	3			301,545	193,695	79,189	28,661	114,506 R	64.2%	26.3%	71.0%	29.0%
Ohio	25			4,283,603	2,206,545	1,752,414	324,644	454,131 R	51.5%	40.9%	55.7%	44.3%
Oklahoma	8			1,149,708	695,570	402,026	52,112	293,544 R	60.5%	35.0%	63.4%	36.6%
Oregon	6			1,181,516	571,044	456,890	153,582	114,154 R	48.3%	38.7%	55.6%	44.4%
Pennsylvania	27			4,561,501	2,261,872	1,937,540	362,089	324,332 R	49.6%	42.5%	53.9%	46.1%
Rhode Island		4		416,072	154,793	198,342	62,937	43,549 D	37.2%	47.7%	43.8%	56.2%
South Carolina	8			894,071	441,841	430,385	21,845	11,456 R	49.4%	48.1%	50.7%	49.3%
South Dakota	4			327,703	198,343	103,855	25,505	94,488 R	60.5%	31.7%	65.6%	34.4%
Tennessee	10			1,617,616	787,761	783,051	46,804	4,710 R	48.7%	48.4%	50.1%	49.9%
Texas	26			4,541,636	2,510,705	1,881,147	149,784	629,558 R	55.3%	41.4%	57.2%	42.8%
Utah	4			604,222	439,687	124,266	40,269	315,421 R	72.8%	20.6%	78.0%	22.0%
Vermont	3			213,299	94,628	81,952	36,719	12,676 R	44.4%	38.4%	53.6%	46.4%
Virginia	12			1,866,032	989,609	752,174	124,249	237,435 R	53.0%	40.3%	56.8%	43.2%
Washington	9			1,742,394	865,244	650,193	226,957	215,051 R	49.7%	37.3%	57.1%	42.9%
West Virginia		6		737,715	334,206	367,462	36,047	33,256 D	45.3%	49.8%	47.6%	52.4%
Wisconsin	11			2,273,221	1,088,845	981,584	202,792	107,261 R	47.9%	43.2%	52.6%	47.4%
Wyoming	3			176,713	110,700	49,427	16,586	61,273 R	62.6%	28.0%	69.1%	30.9%
Dist. of Col.		3		175,237	23,545	131,113	20,579	107,568 D	13.4%	74.8%	15.2%	84.8%
United States	489	49	—	86,515,221	43,904,153	35,483,883	7,127,185	8,420,270 R	50.7%	41.0%	55.3%	44.7%

PRESIDENT 1976

In Washington, one Republican elector voted in the Electoral College for Ronald Reagan for President and Robert Dole for Vice-President.

In New York the Republican figures include Conservative votes and the Democratic figures include Liberal votes; in Vermont the Democratic figures include votes cast on the Independent Vermonters party ticket.

In a number of states candidates appeared on the ballot with variants of the party designations listed below and in several cases with entirely different party names.

The ballot designations for electors for Eugene J. McCarthy for President varied from state to state, as did the names of Vice-Presidential candidates running with him. In New Jersey, the Maddox Vice-Presidential candidate was Edmund O. Matzal.

The full list of candidates for President and Vice-President was:

40,830,763	Jimmy Carter and Walter F. Mondale, Democratic.
39,147,793	Gerald R. Ford and Robert Dole, Republican.
756,691	Eugene J. McCarthy with various Vice-Presidential candidates, Independent.
173,011	Roger L. MacBride and David D. Bergland, Libertarian.
170,531	Lester G. Maddox and William D. Dyke, American Independent.
160,773	Thomas J. Anderson and Rufus Shackelford, American.
91,314	Peter Camejo and Willie Mae Reid, Socialist Workers.
58,992	Gus Hall and Jarvis Tyner, Communist.
49,024	Margaret Wright and Benjamin Spock, People's.
40,043	Lyndon H. LaRouche and R. W. Evans, United States Labor.
15,934	Benjamin C. Bubar and Earl F. Dodge, Prohibition.
9,616	Julius Levin and Constance Blomen, Socialist Labor.
6,038	Frank P. Zeidler and J. Q. Brisben, Socialist.
361	Ernest L. Miller and Roy N. Eddy, Restoration.
36	Frank Taylor and Henry Swan, United American.

In addition to these votes, 39,861 scattered write-in votes were reported from various states and 5,108 votes were cast for "None of these Candidates" in Nevada.

UNITED STATES

PRESIDENT 1976

State	Electoral Vote			Total					Percentage			
									Total Vote		Major Vote	
	Rep.	Dem.	Other	Vote	Republican	Democratic	Other	Plurality	Rep.	Dem.	Rep.	Dem.
Alabama		9		1,182,850	504,070	659,170	19,610	155,100 D	42.6%	55.7%	43.3%	56.7%
Alaska	3			123,574	71,555	44,058	7,961	27,497 R	57.9%	35.7%	61.9%	38.1%
Arizona	6			742,719	418,642	295,602	28,475	123,040 R	56.4%	39.8%	58.6%	41.4%
Arkansas		6		767,535	267,903	498,604	1,028	230,701 D	34.9%	65.0%	35.0%	65.0%
California	45			7,867,117	3,882,244	3,742,284	242,589	139,960 R	49.3%	47.6%	50.9%	49.1%
Colorado	7			1,081,554	584,367	460,353	36,834	124,014 R	54.0%	42.6%	55.9%	44.1%
Connecticut	8			1,381,526	719,261	647,895	14,370	71,366 R	52.1%	46.9%	52.6%	47.4%
Delaware		3		235,834	109,831	122,596	3,407	12,765 D	46.6%	52.0%	47.3%	52.7%
Florida		17		3,150,631	1,469,531	1,636,000	45,100	166,469 D	46.6%	51.9%	47.3%	52.7%
Georgia		12		1,467,458	483,743	979,409	4,306	495,666 D	33.0%	66.7%	33.1%	66.9%
Hawaii		4		291,301	140,003	147,375	3,923	7,372 D	48.1%	50.6%	48.7%	51.3%
Idaho	4			344,071	204,151	126,549	13,371	77,602 R	59.3%	36.8%	61.7%	38.3%
Illinois	26			4,718,914	2,364,269	2,271,295	83,350	92,974 R	50.1%	48.1%	51.0%	49.0%
Indiana	13			2,220,362	1,183,958	1,014,714	21,690	169,244 R	53.3%	45.7%	53.8%	46.2%
Iowa	8			1,279,306	632,863	619,931	26,512	12,932 R	49.5%	48.5%	50.5%	49.5%
Kansas	7			957,845	502,752	430,421	24,672	72,331 R	52.5%	44.9%	53.9%	46.1%
Kentucky		9		1,167,142	531,852	615,717	19,573	83,865 D	45.6%	52.8%	46.3%	53.7%
Louisiana		10		1,278,439	587,446	661,365	29,628	73,919 D	46.0%	51.7%	47.0%	53.0%
Maine	4			483,216	236,320	232,279	14,617	4,041 R	48.9%	48.1%	50.4%	49.6%
Maryland		10		1,439,897	672,661	759,612	7,624	86,951 D	46.7%	52.8%	47.0%	53.0%
Massachusetts		14		2,547,558	1,030,276	1,429,475	87,807	399,199 D	40.4%	56.1%	41.9%	58.1%
Michigan	21			3,653,749	1,893,742	1,696,714	63,293	197,028 R	51.8%	46.4%	52.7%	47.3%
Minnesota		10		1,949,931	819,395	1,070,440	60,096	251,045 D	42.0%	54.9%	43.4%	56.6%
Mississippi		7		769,361	366,846	381,309	21,206	14,463 D	47.7%	49.6%	49.0%	51.0%
Missouri		12		1,953,600	927,443	998,387	27,770	70,944 D	47.5%	51.1%	48.2%	51.8%
Montana	4			328,734	173,703	149,259	5,772	24,444 R	52.8%	45.4%	53.8%	46.2%
Nebraska	5			607,668	359,705	233,692	14,271	126,013 R	59.2%	38.5%	60.6%	39.4%
Nevada	3			201,876	101,273	92,479	8,124	8,794 R	50.2%	45.8%	52.3%	47.7%
New Hampshire	4			339,618	185,935	147,635	6,048	38,300 R	54.7%	43.5%	55.7%	44.3%
New Jersey	17			3,014,472	1,509,688	1,444,653	60,131	65,035 R	50.1%	47.9%	51.1%	48.9%
New Mexico	4			418,409	211,419	201,148	5,842	10,271 R	50.5%	48.1%	51.2%	48.8%
New York		41		6,534,170	3,100,791	3,389,558	43,821	288,767 D	47.5%	51.9%	47.8%	52.2%
North Carolina		13		1,678,914	741,960	927,365	9,589	185,405 D	44.2%	55.2%	44.4%	55.6%
North Dakota	3			297,188	153,470	136,078	7,640	17,392 R	51.6%	45.8%	53.0%	47.0%
Ohio		25		4,111,873	2,000,505	2,011,621	99,747	11,116 D	48.7%	48.9%	49.9%	50.1%
Oklahoma	8			1,092,251	545,708	532,442	14,101	13,266 R	50.0%	48.7%	50.6%	49.4%
Oregon	6			1,029,876	492,120	490,407	47,349	1,713 R	47.8%	47.6%	50.1%	49.9%
Pennsylvania		27		4,620,787	2,205,604	2,328,677	86,506	123,073 D	47.7%	50.4%	48.6%	51.4%
Rhode Island		4		411,170	181,249	227,636	2,285	46,387 D	44.1%	55.4%	44.3%	55.7%
South Carolina		8		802,583	346,149	450,807	5,627	104,658 D	43.1%	56.2%	43.4%	56.6%
South Dakota	4			300,678	151,505	147,068	2,105	4,437 R	50.4%	48.9%	50.7%	49.3%
Tennessee		10		1,476,345	633,969	825,879	16,497	191,910 D	42.9%	55.9%	43.4%	56.6%
Texas		26		4,071,884	1,953,300	2,082,319	36,265	129,019 D	48.0%	51.1%	48.4%	51.6%
Utah	4			541,198	337,908	182,110	21,180	155,798 R	62.4%	33.6%	65.0%	35.0%
Vermont	3			187,765	102,085	80,954	4,726	21,131 R	54.4%	43.1%	55.8%	44.2%
Virginia	12			1,697,094	836,554	813,896	46,644	22,658 R	49.3%	48.0%	50.7%	49.3%
Washington	8		1	1,555,534	777,732	717,323	60,479	60,409 R	50.0%	46.1%	52.0%	48.0%
West Virginia		6		750,964	314,760	435,914	290	121,154 D	41.9%	58.0%	41.9%	58.1%
Wisconsin		11		2,104,175	1,004,987	1,040,232	58,956	35,245 D	47.8%	49.4%	49.1%	50.9%
Wyoming	3			156,343	92,717	62,239	1,387	30,478 R	59.3%	39.8%	59.8%	40.2%
Dist. of Col.		3		168,830	27,873	137,818	3,139	109,945 D	16.5%	81.6%	16.8%	83.2%
United States	240	297	1	81,555,889	39,147,793	40,830,763	1,577,333	1,682,970 D	48.0%	50.1%	48.9%	51.1%

PRESIDENT 1972

In Virginia one Republican elector voted in the Electoral College for the Libertarian candidates for President and Vice-President.

In New York the Republican figures include Conservative votes and the Democratic figures include Liberal votes. In Alabama the Democratic figures include votes cast on the National Democratic Party of Alabama ticket, and in South Carolina include United Citizens Party votes.

In certain states candidates appeared on the ballot under party names other than those used below; for the Socialist Workers party the votes listed for Jenness and Pulley were actually cast for substitute candidates (Reed and DeBerry) or without named candidates in several states.

The Democratic Vice-Presidential candidate originally was Senator Thomas F. Eagleton; on his withdrawal shortly after the party convention, R. Sargent Shriver was named by the Democratic National Committee as candidate.

The full list of candidates for President and Vice-President was:

47,169,911	Richard M. Nixon and Spiro T. Agnew, Republican.
29,170,383	George S. McGovern and R. Sargent Shriver, Democratic.
1,099,482	John G. Schmitz and Thomas J. Anderson, American.
78,756	Benjamin Spock and Julius Hobson, People's.
66,677	Linda Jenness and Andrew Pulley, Socialist Workers.
53,814	Louis Fisher and Genevieve Gunderson, Socialist Labor.
25,595	Gus Hall and Jarvis Tyner, Communist.
13,505	E. Harold Munn and Marshall E. Uncapher, Prohibition.
3,673	John Hospers and Theodora Nathan, Libertarian.
1,743	John V. Mahalchik and Irving Homer, America First.
220	Gabriel Green and Daniel Fry, Universal.

In addition to the above, 34,795 scattered votes were reported from various states.

Vice-President Agnew resigned in October 1973 and Representative Gerald R. Ford of Michigan was nominated by President Nixon to fill the vacancy. In November (Senate) and December (House of Representatives) this action was approved by Congress.

In August 1974 President Nixon resigned and was succeeded by Vice-President Ford. In the same month Nelson A. Rockefeller, former Governor of New York, was nominated to be Vice-President and was confirmed by Congress in December 1974.

UNITED STATES

PRESIDENT 1972

State	Electoral Vote Rep.	Electoral Vote Dem.	Electoral Vote Other	Total Vote	Republican	Democratic	Other	Plurality	Percentage Total Vote Rep.	Percentage Total Vote Dem.	Percentage Major Vote Rep.	Percentage Major Vote Dem.
Alabama	9			1,006,111	728,701	256,923	20,487	471,778 R	72.4%	25.5%	73.9%	26.1%
Alaska	3			95,219	55,349	32,967	6,903	22,382 R	58.1%	34.6%	62.7%	37.3%
Arizona	6			622,926	402,812	198,540	21,574	204,272 R	64.7%	31.9%	67.0%	33.0%
Arkansas	6			651,320	448,541	199,892	2,887	248,649 R	68.9%	30.7%	69.2%	30.8%
California	45			8,367,862	4,602,096	3,475,847	289,919	1,126,249 R	55.0%	41.5%	57.0%	43.0%
Colorado	7			953,884	597,189	329,980	26,715	267,209 R	62.6%	34.6%	64.4%	35.6%
Connecticut	8			1,384,277	810,763	555,498	18,016	255,265 R	58.6%	40.1%	59.3%	40.7%
Delaware	3			235,516	140,357	92,283	2,876	48,074 R	59.6%	39.2%	60.3%	39.7%
Florida	17			2,583,283	1,857,759	718,117	7,407	1,139,642 R	71.9%	27.8%	72.1%	27.9%
Georgia	12			1,174,772	881,496	289,529	3,747	591,967 R	75.0%	24.6%	75.3%	24.7%
Hawaii	4			270,274	168,865	101,409		67,456 R	62.5%	37.5%	62.5%	37.5%
Idaho	4			310,379	199,384	80,826	30,169	118,558 R	64.2%	26.0%	71.2%	28.8%
Illinois	26			4,723,236	2,788,179	1,913,472	21,585	874,707 R	59.0%	40.5%	59.3%	40.7%
Indiana	13			2,125,529	1,405,154	708,568	11,807	696,586 R	66.1%	33.3%	66.5%	33.5%
Iowa	8			1,225,944	706,207	496,206	23,531	210,001 R	57.6%	40.5%	58.7%	41.3%
Kansas	7			916,095	619,812	270,287	25,996	349,525 R	67.7%	29.5%	69.6%	30.4%
Kentucky	9			1,067,499	676,446	371,159	19,894	305,287 R	63.4%	34.8%	64.6%	35.4%
Louisiana	10			1,051,491	686,852	298,142	66,497	388,710 R	65.3%	28.4%	69.7%	30.3%
Maine	4			417,042	256,458	160,584		95,874 R	61.5%	38.5%	61.5%	38.5%
Maryland	10			1,353,812	829,305	505,781	18,726	323,524 R	61.3%	37.4%	62.1%	37.9%
Massachusetts		14		2,458,756	1,112,078	1,332,540	14,138	220,462 D	45.2%	54.2%	45.5%	54.5%
Michigan	21			3,489,727	1,961,721	1,459,435	68,571	502,286 R	56.2%	41.8%	57.3%	42.7%
Minnesota	10			1,741,652	898,269	802,346	41,037	95,923 R	51.6%	46.1%	52.8%	47.2%
Mississippi	7			645,963	505,125	126,782	14,056	378,343 R	78.2%	19.6%	79.9%	20.1%
Missouri	12			1,855,803	1,153,852	697,147	4,804	456,705 R	62.2%	37.6%	62.3%	37.7%
Montana	4			317,603	183,976	120,197	13,430	63,779 R	57.9%	37.8%	60.5%	39.5%
Nebraska	5			576,289	406,298	169,991		236,307 R	70.5%	29.5%	70.5%	29.5%
Nevada	3			181,766	115,750	66,016		49,734 R	63.7%	36.3%	63.7%	36.3%
New Hampshire	4			334,055	213,724	116,435	3,896	97,289 R	64.0%	34.9%	64.7%	35.3%
New Jersey	17			2,997,229	1,845,502	1,102,211	49,516	743,291 R	61.6%	36.8%	62.6%	37.4%
New Mexico	4			386,241	235,606	141,084	9,551	94,522 R	61.0%	36.5%	62.5%	37.5%
New York	41			7,165,919	4,192,778	2,951,084	22,057	1,241,694 R	58.5%	41.2%	58.7%	41.3%
North Carolina	13			1,518,612	1,054,889	438,705	25,018	616,184 R	69.5%	28.9%	70.6%	29.4%
North Dakota	3			280,514	174,109	100,384	6,021	73,725 R	62.1%	35.8%	63.4%	36.6%
Ohio	25			4,094,787	2,441,827	1,558,889	94,071	882,938 R	59.6%	38.1%	61.0%	39.0%
Oklahoma	8			1,029,900	759,025	247,147	23,728	511,878 R	73.7%	24.0%	75.4%	24.6%
Oregon	6			927,946	486,686	392,760	48,500	93,926 R	52.4%	42.3%	55.3%	44.7%
Pennsylvania	27			4,592,106	2,714,521	1,796,951	80,634	917,570 R	59.1%	39.1%	60.2%	39.8%
Rhode Island	4			415,808	220,383	194,645	780	25,738 R	53.0%	46.8%	53.1%	46.9%
South Carolina	8			673,960	477,044	186,824	10,092	290,220 R	70.8%	27.7%	71.9%	28.1%
South Dakota	4			307,415	166,476	139,945	994	26,531 R	54.2%	45.5%	54.3%	45.7%
Tennessee	10			1,201,182	813,147	357,293	30,742	455,854 R	67.7%	29.7%	69.5%	30.5%
Texas	26			3,471,281	2,298,896	1,154,289	18,096	1,144,607 R	66.2%	33.3%	66.6%	33.4%
Utah	4			478,476	323,643	126,284	28,549	197,359 R	67.6%	26.4%	71.9%	28.1%
Vermont	3			186,947	117,149	68,174	1,624	48,975 R	62.7%	36.5%	63.2%	36.8%
Virginia	11		1	1,457,019	988,493	438,887	29,639	549,606 R	67.8%	30.1%	69.3%	30.7%
Washington	9			1,470,847	837,135	568,334	65,378	268,801 R	56.9%	38.6%	59.6%	40.4%
West Virginia	6			762,399	484,964	277,435		207,529 R	63.6%	36.4%	63.6%	36.4%
Wisconsin	11			1,852,890	989,430	810,174	53,286	179,256 R	53.4%	43.7%	55.0%	45.0%
Wyoming	3			145,570	100,464	44,358	748	56,106 R	69.0%	30.5%	69.4%	30.6%
Dist. of Col.		3		163,421	35,226	127,627	568	92,401 D	21.6%	78.1%	21.6%	78.4%
United States	520	17	1	77,718,554	47,169,911	29,170,383	1,378,260	17,999,528 R	60.7%	37.5%	61.8%	38.2%

PRESIDENT 1968

In North Carolina one Republican elector voted in the Electoral College for the American Independent candidates for President and Vice-President.

In New York the Democratic figure includes Liberal votes and in Alabama the Democratic vote is the total of the Alabama Independent Democratic and National Democratic Party of Alabama vote. In certain states candidates appeared under variants of the party name used below and in most states the Vice-Presidential candidate of the American Independent party was listed as Marvin Griffin rather than Curtis E. LeMay.

The full list of candidates for President and Vice-President was:

31,785,480	Richard M. Nixon and Spiro T. Agnew, Republican.
31,275,166	Hubert H. Humphrey and Edmund S. Muskie, Democratic.
9,906,473	George C. Wallace and Curtis E. LeMay, American Independent.
52,588	Henning A. Blomen and George S. Taylor, Socialist Labor.
47,133	Dick Gregory, Peace and Freedom, with various Vice-Presidential candidates.
41,388	Fred Halstead and Paul Boutelle, Socialist Workers.
36,563	Eldridge Cleaver, Peace and Freedom, with various Vice-Presidential candidates.
25,552	Eugene J. McCarthy, under various titles and written-in, but without indication of Vice-Presidential candidates.
15,123	E. Harold Munn and Rolland E. Fisher, Prohibition.
1,519	Ventura Chavez and Adelicio Moya, People's Constitutional.
1,075	Charlene Mitchell and Michael Zagarell, Communist.
142	James Hensley and Roscoe B. MacKenna, Universal.
34	Richard K. Troxell and Merle Thayer, Constitution.
17	Kent M. Soeters and James P. Powers, Berkeley Defense Group.

In the vote listed above for Eldridge Cleaver, two states are included (California and Utah) in which only the party Vice-Presidential candidate appeared on the ballot.

In addition to these votes, 12,430 were cast for elector tickets for which there were no formal Presidential or Vice-Presidential candidates, and 11,192 scattered votes were reported from various states.

UNITED STATES

PRESIDENT 1968

State	Electoral Vote Rep.	Electoral Vote Dem.	Electoral Vote AIP	Total Vote	Republican	Democratic	AIP	Other	Plurality	Percentage Total Vote Rep.	Percentage Total Vote Dem.	Percentage Total Vote AIP
Alabama			10	1,049,922	146,923	196,579	691,425	14,995	494,846 A	14.0%	18.7%	65.9%
Alaska	3			83,035	37,600	35,411	10,024		2,189 R	45.3%	42.6%	12.1%
Arizona	5			486,936	266,721	170,514	46,573	3,128	96,207 R	54.8%	35.0%	9.6%
Arkansas			6	619,969	190,759	188,228	240,982		50,223 A	30.8%	30.4%	38.9%
California	40			7,251,587	3,467,664	3,244,318	487,270	52,335	223,346 R	47.8%	44.7%	6.7%
Colorado	6			811,199	409,345	335,174	60,813	5,867	74,171 R	50.5%	41.3%	7.5%
Connecticut		8		1,256,232	556,721	621,561	76,650	1,300	64,840 D	44.3%	49.5%	6.1%
Delaware	3			214,367	96,714	89,194	28,459		7,520 R	45.1%	41.6%	13.3%
Florida	14			2,187,805	886,804	676,794	624,207		210,010 R	40.5%	30.9%	28.5%
Georgia			12	1,250,266	380,111	334,440	535,550	165	155,439 A	30.4%	26.7%	42.8%
Hawaii		4		236,218	91,425	141,324	3,469		49,899 D	38.7%	59.8%	1.5%
Idaho	4			291,183	165,369	89,273	36,541		76,096 R	56.8%	30.7%	12.5%
Illinois	26			4,619,749	2,174,774	2,039,814	390,958	14,203	134,960 R	47.1%	44.2%	8.5%
Indiana	13			2,123,597	1,067,885	806,659	243,108	5,945	261,226 R	50.3%	38.0%	11.4%
Iowa	9			1,167,931	619,106	476,699	66,422	5,704	142,407 R	53.0%	40.8%	5.7%
Kansas	7			872,783	478,674	302,996	88,921	2,192	175,678 R	54.8%	34.7%	10.2%
Kentucky	9			1,055,893	462,411	397,541	193,098	2,843	64,870 R	43.8%	37.6%	18.3%
Louisiana			10	1,097,450	257,535	309,615	530,300		220,685 A	23.5%	28.2%	48.3%
Maine		4		392,936	169,254	217,312	6,370		48,058 D	43.1%	55.3%	1.6%
Maryland		10		1,235,039	517,995	538,310	178,734		20,315 D	41.9%	43.6%	14.5%
Massachusetts		14		2,331,752	766,844	1,469,218	87,088	8,602	702,374 D	32.9%	63.0%	3.7%
Michigan		21		3,306,250	1,370,665	1,593,082	331,968	10,535	222,417 D	41.5%	48.2%	10.0%
Minnesota		10		1,588,506	658,643	857,738	68,931	3,194	199,095 D	41.5%	54.0%	4.3%
Mississippi			7	654,509	88,516	150,644	415,349		264,705 A	13.5%	23.0%	63.5%
Missouri	12			1,809,502	811,932	791,444	206,126		20,488 R	44.9%	43.7%	11.4%
Montana	4			274,404	138,835	114,117	20,015	1,437	24,718 R	50.6%	41.6%	7.3%
Nebraska	5			536,851	321,163	170,784	44,904		150,379 R	59.8%	31.8%	8.4%
Nevada	3			154,218	73,188	60,598	20,432		12,590 R	47.5%	39.3%	13.2%
New Hampshire	4			297,298	154,903	130,589	11,173	633	24,314 R	52.1%	43.9%	3.8%
New Jersey	17			2,875,395	1,325,467	1,264,206	262,187	23,535	61,261 R	46.1%	44.0%	9.1%
New Mexico	4			327,350	169,692	130,081	25,737	1,840	39,611 R	51.8%	39.7%	7.9%
New York		43		6,791,688	3,007,932	3,378,470	358,864	46,422	370,538 D	44.3%	49.7%	5.3%
North Carolina	12		1	1,587,493	627,192	464,113	496,188		131,004 R	39.5%	29.2%	31.3%
North Dakota	4			247,882	138,669	94,769	14,244	200	43,900 R	55.9%	38.2%	5.7%
Ohio	26			3,959,698	1,791,014	1,700,586	467,495	603	90,428 R	45.2%	42.9%	11.8%
Oklahoma	8			943,086	449,697	301,658	191,731		148,039 R	47.7%	32.0%	20.3%
Oregon	6			819,622	408,433	358,866	49,683	2,640	49,567 R	49.8%	43.8%	6.1%
Pennsylvania		29		4,747,928	2,090,017	2,259,405	378,582	19,924	169,388 D	44.0%	47.6%	8.0%
Rhode Island		4		385,000	122,359	246,518	15,678	445	124,159 D	31.8%	64.0%	4.1%
South Carolina	8			666,978	254,062	197,486	215,430		38,632 R	38.1%	29.6%	32.3%
South Dakota	4			281,264	149,841	118,023	13,400		31,818 R	53.3%	42.0%	4.8%
Tennessee	11			1,248,617	472,592	351,233	424,792		47,800 R	37.8%	28.1%	34.0%
Texas		25		3,079,216	1,227,844	1,266,804	584,269	299	38,960 D	39.9%	41.1%	19.0%
Utah	4			422,568	238,728	156,665	26,906	269	82,063 R	56.5%	37.1%	6.4%
Vermont	3			161,404	85,142	70,255	5,104	903	14,887 R	52.8%	43.5%	3.2%
Virginia	12			1,361,491	590,319	442,387	321,833	6,952	147,932 R	43.4%	32.5%	23.6%
Washington		9		1,304,281	588,510	616,037	96,990	2,744	27,527 D	45.1%	47.2%	7.4%
West Virginia		7		754,206	307,555	374,091	72,560		66,536 D	40.8%	49.6%	9.6%
Wisconsin	12			1,691,538	809,997	748,804	127,835	4,902	61,193 R	47.9%	44.3%	7.6%
Wyoming	3			127,205	70,927	45,173	11,105		25,754 R	55.8%	35.5%	8.7%
Dist. of Col.		3		170,578	31,012	139,566			108,554 D	18.2%	81.8%	
United States	301	191	46	73,211,875	31,785,480	31,275,166	9,906,473	244,756	510,314 R	43.4%	42.7%	13.5%

PRESIDENT 1964

In New York the Democratic figure includes Liberal votes.

The full list of candidates for President and Vice-President was:

43,129,566	Lyndon B. Johnson and Hubert H. Humphrey, Democratic.
27,178,188	Barry M. Goldwater and William E. Miller, Republican.
45,219	Eric Hass and Henning A. Blomen, Socialist Labor.
32,720	Clifton DeBerry and Edward Shaw, Socialist Workers.
23,267	E. Harold Munn and Mark R. Shaw, Prohibition.
6,953	John Kasper and J. B. Stoner, National States Rights.
5,060	Joseph B. Lightburn and T. C. Billings, Constitution.
19	James Hensley and John O. Hopkins, Universal.

In addition, 210,732 votes were cast in Alabama for an unpledged Democratic elector ticket and 12,868 scattered votes were reported from various states.

UNITED STATES

PRESIDENT 1964

State	Electoral Vote			Total Vote	Republican	Democratic	Other	Plurality	Percentage			
									Total Vote		Major Vote	
	Rep.	Dem.	Other						Rep.	Dem.	Rep.	Dem.
Alabama	10			689,818	479,085		210,733	268,353 R	69.5%		100.0%	
Alaska		3		67,259	22,930	44,329		21,399 D	34.1%	65.9%	34.1%	65.9%
Arizona	5			480,770	242,535	237,753	482	4,782 R	50.4%	49.5%	50.5%	49.5%
Arkansas		6		560,426	243,264	314,197	2,965	70,933 D	43.4%	56.1%	43.6%	56.4%
California		40		7,057,586	2,879,108	4,171,877	6,601	1,292,769 D	40.8%	59.1%	40.8%	59.2%
Colorado		6		776,986	296,767	476,024	4,195	179,257 D	38.2%	61.3%	38.4%	61.6%
Connecticut		8		1,218,578	390,996	826,269	1,313	435,273 D	32.1%	67.8%	32.1%	67.9%
Delaware		3		201,320	78,078	122,704	538	44,626 D	38.8%	60.9%	38.9%	61.1%
Florida		14		1,854,481	905,941	948,540		42,599 D	48.9%	51.1%	48.9%	51.1%
Georgia	12			1,139,335	616,584	522,556	195	94,028 R	54.1%	45.9%	54.1%	45.9%
Hawaii		4		207,271	44,022	163,249		119,227 D	21.2%	78.8%	21.2%	78.8%
Idaho		4		292,477	143,557	148,920		5,363 D	49.1%	50.9%	49.1%	50.9%
Illinois		26		4,702,841	1,905,946	2,796,833	62	890,887 D	40.5%	59.5%	40.5%	59.5%
Indiana		13		2,091,606	911,118	1,170,848	9,640	259,730 D	43.6%	56.0%	43.8%	56.2%
Iowa		9		1,184,539	449,148	733,030	2,361	283,882 D	37.9%	61.9%	38.0%	62.0%
Kansas		7		857,901	386,579	464,028	7,294	77,449 D	45.1%	54.1%	45.4%	54.6%
Kentucky		9		1,046,105	372,977	669,659	3,469	296,682 D	35.7%	64.0%	35.8%	64.2%
Louisiana	10			896,293	509,225	387,068		122,157 R	56.8%	43.2%	56.8%	43.2%
Maine		4		380,965	118,701	262,264		143,563 D	31.2%	68.8%	31.2%	68.8%
Maryland		10		1,116,457	385,495	730,912	50	345,417 D	34.5%	65.5%	34.5%	65.5%
Massachusetts		14		2,344,798	549,727	1,786,422	8,649	1,236,695 D	23.4%	76.2%	23.5%	76.5%
Michigan		21		3,203,102	1,060,152	2,136,615	6,335	1,076,463 D	33.1%	66.7%	33.2%	66.8%
Minnesota		10		1,554,462	559,624	991,117	3,721	431,493 D	36.0%	63.8%	36.1%	63.9%
Mississippi	7			409,146	356,528	52,618		303,910 R	87.1%	12.9%	87.1%	12.9%
Missouri		12		1,817,879	653,535	1,164,344		510,809 D	36.0%	64.0%	36.0%	64.0%
Montana		4		278,628	113,032	164,246	1,350	51,214 D	40.6%	58.9%	40.8%	59.2%
Nebraska		5		584,154	276,847	307,307		30,460 D	47.4%	52.6%	47.4%	52.6%
Nevada		3		135,433	56,094	79,339		23,245 D	41.4%	58.6%	41.4%	58.6%
New Hampshire		4		288,093	104,029	184,064		80,035 D	36.1%	63.9%	36.1%	63.9%
New Jersey		17		2,847,663	964,174	1,868,231	15,258	904,057 D	33.9%	65.6%	34.0%	66.0%
New Mexico		4		328,645	132,838	194,015	1,792	61,177 D	40.4%	59.0%	40.6%	59.4%
New York		43		7,166,275	2,243,559	4,913,102	9,614	2,669,543 D	31.3%	68.6%	31.3%	68.7%
North Carolina		13		1,424,983	624,844	800,139		175,295 D	43.8%	56.2%	43.8%	56.2%
North Dakota		4		258,389	108,207	149,784	398	41,577 D	41.9%	58.0%	41.9%	58.1%
Ohio		26		3,969,196	1,470,865	2,498,331		1,027,466 D	37.1%	62.9%	37.1%	62.9%
Oklahoma		8		932,499	412,665	519,834		107,169 D	44.3%	55.7%	44.3%	55.7%
Oregon		6		786,305	282,779	501,017	2,509	218,238 D	36.0%	63.7%	36.1%	63.9%
Pennsylvania		29		4,822,690	1,673,657	3,130,954	18,079	1,457,297 D	34.7%	64.9%	34.8%	65.2%
Rhode Island		4		390,091	74,615	315,463	13	240,848 D	19.1%	80.9%	19.1%	80.9%
South Carolina	8			524,779	309,048	215,723	8	93,325 R	58.9%	41.1%	58.9%	41.1%
South Dakota		4		293,118	130,108	163,010		32,902 D	44.4%	55.6%	44.4%	55.6%
Tennessee		11		1,143,946	508,965	634,947	34	125,982 D	44.5%	55.5%	44.5%	55.5%
Texas		25		2,626,811	958,566	1,663,185	5,060	704,619 D	36.5%	63.3%	36.6%	63.4%
Utah		4		401,413	181,785	219,628		37,843 D	45.3%	54.7%	45.3%	54.7%
Vermont		3		163,089	54,942	108,127	20	53,185 D	33.7%	66.3%	33.7%	66.3%
Virginia		12		1,042,267	481,334	558,038	2,895	76,704 D	46.2%	53.5%	46.3%	53.7%
Washington		9		1,258,556	470,366	779,881	8,309	309,515 D	37.4%	62.0%	37.6%	62.4%
West Virginia		7		792,040	253,953	538,087		284,134 D	32.1%	67.9%	32.1%	67.9%
Wisconsin		12		1,691,815	638,495	1,050,424	2,896	411,929 D	37.7%	62.1%	37.8%	62.2%
Wyoming		3		142,716	61,998	80,718		18,720 D	43.4%	56.6%	43.4%	56.6%
Dist. of Col.		3		198,597	28,801	169,796		140,995 D	14.5%	85.5%	14.5%	85.5%
United States	52	486	—	70,644,592	27,178,188	43,129,566	336,838	15,951,378 D	38.5%	61.1%	38.7%	61.3%

PRESIDENT 1960

Senator Harry Flood Byrd received 15 votes for President in the Electoral College; these were the votes of 6 of the 11 Democratic electors in Alabama, all 8 unpledged Democratic electors in Mississippi, and one of the 8 Republican electors in Oklahoma. The Alabama and Mississippi electors also cast 14 votes for Senator Strom Thurmond for Vice-President; the single Oklahoma elector voted for Senator Barry M. Goldwater for Vice-President.

In New York the Democratic figure includes Liberal votes.

The full list of candidates for President and Vice-President was:

34,226,731	John F. Kennedy and Lyndon B. Johnson, Democratic.
34,108,157	Richard M. Nixon and Henry Cabot Lodge, Republican.
47,522	Eric Hass and Georgia Cozzini, Socialist Labor.
46,203	Rutherford L. Decker and E. Harold Munn, Prohibition.
44,977	Orval E. Faubus and John G. Crommelin, National States Rights.
40,165	Farrell Dobbs and Myra Tanner Weiss, Socialist Workers.
18,162	Charles L. Sullivan and Merritt B. Curtis, Constitution.
8,708	J. Bracken Lee and Kent H. Courtney, Conservative.
4,204	C. Benton Coiner and Edward J. Silverman, Conservative.
1,767	Lar Daly and B. M. Miller, Tax Cut.
1,485	Clennon King and Reginald Carter, Independent Afro-American.
1,401	Merritt B. Curtis and B. M. Miller, Constitution.

In addition, 169,572 votes were cast in Louisiana for Independent electors and 116,248 in Mississippi for an unpledged Democratic elector ticket. 539 votes were cast in Michigan for an Independent American ticket and 2,378 scattered votes were reported from various states.

UNITED STATES

PRESIDENT 1960

State	Electoral Vote Rep.	Electoral Vote Dem.	Electoral Vote Other	Total Vote	Republican	Democratic	Other	Plurality	Percentage Total Vote Rep.	Percentage Total Vote Dem.	Percentage Major Vote Rep.	Percentage Major Vote Dem.
Alabama		5	6	570,225	237,981	324,050	8,194	86,069 D	41.7%	56.8%	42.3%	57.7%
Alaska	3			60,762	30,953	29,809		1,144 R	50.9%	49.1%	50.9%	49.1%
Arizona	4			398,491	221,241	176,781	469	44,460 R	55.5%	44.4%	55.6%	44.4%
Arkansas		8		428,509	184,508	215,049	28,952	30,541 D	43.1%	50.2%	46.2%	53.8%
California	32			6,506,578	3,259,722	3,224,099	22,757	35,623 R	50.1%	49.6%	50.3%	49.7%
Colorado	6			736,236	402,242	330,629	3,365	71,613 R	54.6%	44.9%	54.9%	45.1%
Connecticut		8		1,222,883	565,813	657,055	15	91,242 D	46.3%	53.7%	46.3%	53.7%
Delaware		3		196,683	96,373	99,590	720	3,217 D	49.0%	50.6%	49.2%	50.8%
Florida	10			1,544,176	795,476	748,700		46,776 R	51.5%	48.5%	51.5%	48.5%
Georgia		12		733,349	274,472	458,638	239	184,166 D	37.4%	62.5%	37.4%	62.6%
Hawaii		3		184,705	92,295	92,410		115 D	50.0%	50.0%	50.0%	50.0%
Idaho	4			300,450	161,597	138,853		22,744 R	53.8%	46.2%	53.8%	46.2%
Illinois		27		4,757,409	2,368,988	2,377,846	10,575	8,858 D	49.8%	50.0%	49.9%	50.1%
Indiana	13			2,135,360	1,175,120	952,358	7,882	222,762 R	55.0%	44.6%	55.2%	44.8%
Iowa	10			1,273,810	722,381	550,565	864	171,816 R	56.7%	43.2%	56.7%	43.3%
Kansas	8			928,825	561,474	363,213	4,138	198,261 R	60.4%	39.1%	60.7%	39.3%
Kentucky	10			1,124,462	602,607	521,855		80,752 R	53.6%	46.4%	53.6%	46.4%
Louisiana		10		807,891	230,980	407,339	169,572	176,359 D	28.6%	50.4%	36.2%	63.8%
Maine	5			421,767	240,608	181,159		59,449 R	57.0%	43.0%	57.0%	43.0%
Maryland		9		1,055,349	489,538	565,808	3	76,270 D	46.4%	53.6%	46.4%	53.6%
Massachusetts		16		2,469,480	976,750	1,487,174	5,556	510,424 D	39.6%	60.2%	39.6%	60.4%
Michigan		20		3,318,097	1,620,428	1,687,269	10,400	66,841 D	48.8%	50.9%	49.0%	51.0%
Minnesota		11		1,541,887	757,915	779,933	4,039	22,018 D	49.2%	50.6%	49.3%	50.7%
Mississippi			8	298,171	73,561	108,362	116,248	7,886 U	24.7%	36.3%	40.4%	59.6%
Missouri		13		1,934,422	962,221	972,201		9,980 D	49.7%	50.3%	49.7%	50.3%
Montana	4			277,579	141,841	134,891	847	6,950 R	51.1%	48.6%	51.3%	48.7%
Nebraska	6			613,095	380,553	232,542		148,011 R	62.1%	37.9%	62.1%	37.9%
Nevada		3		107,267	52,387	54,880		2,493 D	48.8%	51.2%	48.8%	51.2%
New Hampshire	4			295,761	157,989	137,772		20,217 R	53.4%	46.6%	53.4%	46.6%
New Jersey		16		2,773,111	1,363,324	1,385,415	24,372	22,091 D	49.2%	50.0%	49.6%	50.4%
New Mexico		4		311,107	153,733	156,027	1,347	2,294 D	49.4%	50.2%	49.6%	50.4%
New York		45		7,291,079	3,446,419	3,830,085	14,575	383,666 D	47.3%	52.5%	47.4%	52.6%
North Carolina		14		1,368,556	655,420	713,136		57,716 D	47.9%	52.1%	47.9%	52.1%
North Dakota	4			278,431	154,310	123,963	158	30,347 R	55.4%	44.5%	55.5%	44.5%
Ohio	25			4,161,859	2,217,611	1,944,248		273,363 R	53.3%	46.7%	53.3%	46.7%
Oklahoma	7		1	903,150	533,039	370,111		162,928 R	59.0%	41.0%	59.0%	41.0%
Oregon	6			776,421	408,060	367,402	959	40,658 R	52.6%	47.3%	52.6%	47.4%
Pennsylvania		32		5,006,541	2,439,956	2,556,282	10,303	116,326 D	48.7%	51.1%	48.8%	51.2%
Rhode Island		4		405,535	147,502	258,032	1	110,530 D	36.4%	63.6%	36.4%	63.6%
South Carolina		8		386,688	188,558	198,129	1	9,571 D	48.8%	51.2%	48.8%	51.2%
South Dakota	4			306,487	178,417	128,070		50,347 R	58.2%	41.8%	58.2%	41.8%
Tennessee	11			1,051,792	556,577	481,453	13,762	75,124 R	52.9%	45.8%	53.6%	46.4%
Texas		24		2,311,084	1,121,310	1,167,567	22,207	46,257 D	48.5%	50.5%	49.0%	51.0%
Utah	4			374,709	205,361	169,248	100	36,113 R	54.8%	45.2%	54.8%	45.2%
Vermont	3			167,324	98,131	69,186	7	28,945 R	58.6%	41.3%	58.6%	41.4%
Virginia	12			771,449	404,521	362,327	4,601	42,194 R	52.4%	47.0%	52.8%	47.2%
Washington	9			1,241,572	629,273	599,298	13,001	29,975 R	50.7%	48.3%	51.2%	48.8%
West Virginia		8		837,781	395,995	441,786		45,791 D	47.3%	52.7%	47.3%	52.7%
Wisconsin	12			1,729,082	895,175	830,805	3,102	64,370 R	51.8%	48.0%	51.9%	48.1%
Wyoming	3			140,782	77,451	63,331		14,120 R	55.0%	45.0%	55.0%	45.0%
United States	219	303	15	68,838,219	34,108,157	34,226,731	503,331	118,574 D	49.5%	49.7%	49.9%	50.1%

PRESIDENT 1956

One of the 11 Democratic electors chosen in Alabama cast his Electoral College vote for Walter B. Jones and Herman Talmadge rather than for the national Democratic candidates.

The Republican figure in Mississippi includes votes cast for two elector tickets. In New York the Democratic figure includes Liberal votes.

The full list of candidates for President and Vice-President was:

35,590,472	Dwight D. Eisenhower and Richard M. Nixon, Republican.
26,022,752	Adlai E. Stevenson and Estes Kefauver, Democratic.
111,178	T. Coleman Andrews and Thomas H. Werdel, States Rights.
44,450	Eric Hass and Georgia Cozzini, Socialist Labor.
41,937	Enoch A. Holtwick and Edwin M. Cooper, Prohibition.
7,797	Farrell Dobbs and Myra Tanner Weiss, Socialist Workers.
2,657	Harry Flood Byrd and William E. Jenner, States Rights.
2,126	Darlington Hoopes and Samuel H. Friedman, Socialist.
1,829	Henry B. Krajewski and Anne Marie Yezo, American Third Party.
8	Gerald L. K. Smith and Charles F. Robertson, Christian Nationalist.

In addition, 196,318 votes were cast in Alabama, Louisiana, Mississippi, and South Carolina for Independent electors or for States Rights elector tickets not officially pledged to any candidate, and 5,384 scattered votes were reported from various states.

UNITED STATES

PRESIDENT 1956

State	Electoral Vote Rep.	Electoral Vote Dem.	Electoral Vote Other	Total Vote	Republican	Democratic	Other	Plurality	Percentage Total Vote Rep.	Percentage Total Vote Dem.	Percentage Major Vote Rep.	Percentage Major Vote Dem.
Alabama		10	1	496,861	195,694	280,844	20,323	85,150 D	39.4%	56.5%	41.1%	58.9%
Alaska												
Arizona	4			290,173	176,990	112,880	303	64,110 R	61.0%	38.9%	61.1%	38.9%
Arkansas		8		406,572	186,287	213,277	7,008	26,990 D	45.8%	52.5%	46.6%	53.4%
California	32			5,466,355	3,027,668	2,420,135	18,552	607,533 R	55.4%	44.3%	55.6%	44.4%
Colorado	6			657,074	394,479	257,997	4,598	136,482 R	60.0%	39.3%	60.5%	39.5%
Connecticut	8			1,117,121	711,837	405,079	205	306,758 R	63.7%	36.3%	63.7%	36.3%
Delaware	3			177,988	98,057	79,421	510	18,636 R	55.1%	44.6%	55.3%	44.7%
Florida	10			1,125,762	643,849	480,371	1,542	163,478 R	57.2%	42.7%	57.3%	42.7%
Georgia		12		669,655	222,778	444,688	2,189	221,910 D	33.3%	66.4%	33.4%	66.6%
Hawaii												
Idaho	4			272,989	166,979	105,868	142	61,111 R	61.2%	38.8%	61.2%	38.8%
Illinois	27			4,407,407	2,623,327	1,775,682	8,398	847,645 R	59.5%	40.3%	59.6%	40.4%
Indiana	13			1,974,607	1,182,811	783,908	7,888	398,903 R	59.9%	39.7%	60.1%	39.9%
Iowa	10			1,234,564	729,187	501,858	3,519	227,329 R	59.1%	40.7%	59.2%	40.8%
Kansas	8			866,243	566,878	296,317	3,048	270,561 R	65.4%	34.2%	65.7%	34.3%
Kentucky	10			1,053,805	572,192	476,453	5,160	95,739 R	54.3%	45.2%	54.6%	45.4%
Louisiana	10			617,544	329,047	243,977	44,520	85,070 R	53.3%	39.5%	57.4%	42.6%
Maine	5			351,706	249,238	102,468		146,770 R	70.9%	29.1%	70.9%	29.1%
Maryland	9			932,827	559,738	372,613	476	187,125 R	60.0%	39.9%	60.0%	40.0%
Massachusetts	16			2,348,506	1,393,197	948,190	7,119	445,007 R	59.3%	40.4%	59.5%	40.5%
Michigan	20			3,080,468	1,713,647	1,359,898	6,923	353,749 R	55.6%	44.1%	55.8%	44.2%
Minnesota	11			1,340,005	719,302	617,525	3,178	101,777 R	53.7%	46.1%	53.8%	46.2%
Mississippi		8		248,104	60,685	144,453	42,966	83,768 D	24.5%	58.2%	29.6%	70.4%
Missouri		13		1,832,562	914,289	918,273		3,984 D	49.9%	50.1%	49.9%	50.1%
Montana	4			271,171	154,933	116,238		38,695 R	57.1%	42.9%	57.1%	42.9%
Nebraska	6			577,137	378,108	199,029		179,079 R	65.5%	34.5%	65.5%	34.5%
Nevada	3			96,689	56,049	40,640		15,409 R	58.0%	42.0%	58.0%	42.0%
New Hampshire	4			266,994	176,519	90,364	111	86,155 R	66.1%	33.8%	66.1%	33.9%
New Jersey	16			2,484,312	1,606,942	850,337	27,033	756,605 R	64.7%	34.2%	65.4%	34.6%
New Mexico	4			253,926	146,788	106,098	1,040	40,690 R	57.8%	41.8%	58.0%	42.0%
New York	45			7,095,971	4,345,506	2,747,944	2,521	1,597,562 R	61.2%	38.4%	61.3%	38.7%
North Carolina		14		1,165,592	575,062	590,530		15,468 D	49.3%	50.7%	49.3%	50.7%
North Dakota	4			253,991	156,766	96,742	483	60,024 R	61.7%	38.1%	61.8%	38.2%
Ohio	25			3,702,265	2,262,610	1,439,655		822,955 R	61.1%	38.9%	61.1%	38.9%
Oklahoma	8			859,350	473,769	385,581		88,188 R	55.1%	44.9%	55.1%	44.9%
Oregon	6			736,132	406,393	329,204	535	77,189 R	55.2%	44.7%	55.2%	44.8%
Pennsylvania	32			4,576,503	2,585,252	1,981,769	9,482	603,483 R	56.5%	43.3%	56.6%	43.4%
Rhode Island	4			387,609	225,819	161,790		64,029 R	58.3%	41.7%	58.3%	41.7%
South Carolina		8		300,583	75,700	136,372	88,511	47,863 D	25.2%	45.4%	35.7%	64.3%
South Dakota	4			293,857	171,569	122,288		49,281 R	58.4%	41.6%	58.4%	41.6%
Tennessee	11			939,404	462,288	456,507	20,609	5,781 R	49.2%	48.6%	50.3%	49.7%
Texas	24			1,955,168	1,080,619	859,958	14,591	220,661 R	55.3%	44.0%	55.7%	44.3%
Utah	4			333,995	215,631	118,364		97,267 R	64.6%	35.4%	64.6%	35.4%
Vermont	3			152,978	110,390	42,549	39	67,841 R	72.2%	27.8%	72.2%	27.8%
Virginia	12			697,978	386,459	267,760	43,759	118,699 R	55.4%	38.4%	59.1%	40.9%
Washington	9			1,150,889	620,430	523,002	7,457	97,428 R	53.9%	45.4%	54.3%	45.7%
West Virginia	8			830,831	449,297	381,534		67,763 R	54.1%	45.9%	54.1%	45.9%
Wisconsin	12			1,550,558	954,844	586,768	8,946	368,076 R	61.6%	37.8%	61.9%	38.1%
Wyoming	3			124,127	74,573	49,554		25,019 R	60.1%	39.9%	60.1%	39.9%
United States	457	73	1	62,026,908	35,590,472	26,022,752	413,684	9,567,720 R	57.4%	42.0%	57.8%	42.2%

PRESIDENT 1952

The Republican figure in South Carolina includes votes cast for two elector tickets; in Mississippi the Republican total is the vote cast for an Independent elector ticket "pledged to vote for the nominees of the National Republican Party". In New York the Democratic figure includes Liberal votes.

The full list of candidates for President and Vice-President was:

33,936,234	Dwight D. Eisenhower and Richard M. Nixon, Republican.
27,314,992	Adlai E. Stevenson and John J. Sparkman, Democratic.
140,023	Vincent Hallinan and Charlotta Bass, Progressive.
72,949	Stuart Hamblen and Enoch A. Holtwick, Prohibition.
30,267	Eric Hass and Stephen Emery, Socialist Labor.
20,203	Darlington Hoopes and Samuel H. Friedman, Socialist.
10,312	Farrell Dobbs and Myra Tanner Weiss, Socialist Workers.
4,203	Henry B. Krajewski and Frank Jenkins, Poor Man's Party.

In addition, 17,205 votes were cast for various elector tickets filed on behalf of General Douglas MacArthur, including Christian Nationalist (with Jack B. Tenney as candidate for Vice-President), Constitution (with Vivien Kellems), and America First (with Senator Harry Flood Byrd). In California, Missouri, and Texas the MacArthur vote was cast for two elector tickets. 4,530 scattered votes were reported from various states.

UNITED STATES

PRESIDENT 1952

State	Electoral Vote			Total Vote	Republican	Democratic	Other	Plurality	Percentage			
									Total Vote		Major Vote	
	Rep.	Dem.	Other						Rep.	Dem.	Rep.	Dem.
Alabama		11		426,120	149,231	275,075	1,814	125,844 D	35.0%	64.6%	35.2%	64.8%
Alaska												
Arizona	4			260,570	152,042	108,528		43,514 R	58.3%	41.7%	58.3%	41.7%
Arkansas		8		404,800	177,155	226,300	1,345	49,145 D	43.8%	55.9%	43.9%	56.1%
California	32			5,141,849	2,897,310	2,197,548	46,991	699,762 R	56.3%	42.7%	56.9%	43.1%
Colorado	6			630,103	379,782	245,504	4,817	134,278 R	60.3%	39.0%	60.7%	39.3%
Connecticut	8			1,096,911	611,012	481,649	4,250	129,363 R	55.7%	43.9%	55.9%	44.1%
Delaware	3			174,025	90,059	83,315	651	6,744 R	51.8%	47.9%	51.9%	48.1%
Florida	10			989,337	544,036	444,950	351	99,086 R	55.0%	45.0%	55.0%	45.0%
Georgia		12		655,785	198,961	456,823	1	257,862 D	30.3%	69.7%	30.3%	69.7%
Hawaii												
Idaho	4			276,254	180,707	95,081	466	85,626 R	65.4%	34.4%	65.5%	34.5%
Illinois	27			4,481,058	2,457,327	2,013,920	9,811	443,407 R	54.8%	44.9%	55.0%	45.0%
Indiana	13			1,955,049	1,136,259	801,530	17,260	334,729 R	58.1%	41.0%	58.6%	41.4%
Iowa	10			1,268,773	808,906	451,513	8,354	357,393 R	63.8%	35.6%	64.2%	35.8%
Kansas	8			896,166	616,302	273,296	6,568	343,006 R	68.8%	30.5%	69.3%	30.7%
Kentucky		10		993,148	495,029	495,729	2,390	700 D	49.8%	49.9%	50.0%	50.0%
Louisiana		10		651,952	306,925	345,027		38,102 D	47.1%	52.9%	47.1%	52.9%
Maine	5			351,786	232,353	118,806	627	113,547 R	66.0%	33.8%	66.2%	33.8%
Maryland	9			902,074	499,424	395,337	7,313	104,087 R	55.4%	43.8%	55.8%	44.2%
Massachusetts	16			2,383,398	1,292,325	1,083,525	7,548	208,800 R	54.2%	45.5%	54.4%	45.6%
Michigan	20			2,798,592	1,551,529	1,230,657	16,406	320,872 R	55.4%	44.0%	55.8%	44.2%
Minnesota	11			1,379,483	763,211	608,458	7,814	154,753 R	55.3%	44.1%	55.6%	44.4%
Mississippi		8		285,532	112,966	172,566		59,600 D	39.6%	60.4%	39.6%	60.4%
Missouri	13			1,892,062	959,429	929,830	2,803	29,599 R	50.7%	49.1%	50.8%	49.2%
Montana	4			265,037	157,394	106,213	1,430	51,181 R	59.4%	40.1%	59.7%	40.3%
Nebraska	6			609,660	421,603	188,057		233,546 R	69.2%	30.8%	69.2%	30.8%
Nevada	3			82,190	50,502	31,688		18,814 R	61.4%	38.6%	61.4%	38.6%
New Hampshire	4			272,950	166,287	106,663		59,624 R	60.9%	39.1%	60.9%	39.1%
New Jersey	16			2,418,554	1,373,613	1,015,902	29,039	357,711 R	56.8%	42.0%	57.5%	42.5%
New Mexico	4			238,608	132,170	105,661	777	26,509 R	55.4%	44.3%	55.6%	44.4%
New York	45			7,128,239	3,952,813	3,104,601	70,825	848,212 R	55.5%	43.6%	56.0%	44.0%
North Carolina		14		1,210,910	558,107	652,803		94,696 D	46.1%	53.9%	46.1%	53.9%
North Dakota	4			270,127	191,712	76,694	1,721	115,018 R	71.0%	28.4%	71.4%	28.6%
Ohio	25			3,700,758	2,100,391	1,600,367		500,024 R	56.8%	43.2%	56.8%	43.2%
Oklahoma	8			948,984	518,045	430,939		87,106 R	54.6%	45.4%	54.6%	45.4%
Oregon	6			695,059	420,815	270,579	3,665	150,236 R	60.5%	38.9%	60.9%	39.1%
Pennsylvania	32			4,580,969	2,415,789	2,146,269	18,911	269,520 R	52.7%	46.9%	53.0%	47.0%
Rhode Island	4			414,498	210,935	203,293	270	7,642 R	50.9%	49.0%	50.9%	49.1%
South Carolina		8		341,087	168,082	173,004	1	4,922 D	49.3%	50.7%	49.3%	50.7%
South Dakota	4			294,283	203,857	90,426		113,431 R	69.3%	30.7%	69.3%	30.7%
Tennessee	11			892,553	446,147	443,710	2,696	2,437 R	50.0%	49.7%	50.1%	49.9%
Texas	24			2,075,946	1,102,878	969,228	3,840	133,650 R	53.1%	46.7%	53.2%	46.8%
Utah	4			329,554	194,190	135,364		58,826 R	58.9%	41.1%	58.9%	41.1%
Vermont	3			153,557	109,717	43,355	485	66,362 R	71.5%	28.2%	71.7%	28.3%
Virginia	12			619,689	349,037	268,677	1,975	80,360 R	56.3%	43.4%	56.5%	43.5%
Washington	9			1,102,708	599,107	492,845	10,756	106,262 R	54.3%	44.7%	54.9%	45.1%
West Virginia		8		873,548	419,970	453,578		33,608 D	48.1%	51.9%	48.1%	51.9%
Wisconsin	12			1,607,370	979,744	622,175	5,451	357,569 R	61.0%	38.7%	61.2%	38.8%
Wyoming	3			129,253	81,049	47,934	270	33,115 R	62.7%	37.1%	62.8%	37.2%
United States	442	89	—	61,550,918	33,936,234	27,314,992	299,692	6,621,242 R	55.1%	44.4%	55.4%	44.6%

PRESIDENT 1948

The electoral votes of Alabama, Louisiana, Mississippi, and South Carolina were cast for the States Rights nominees. In addition, one of the 12 Democratic electors chosen in Tennessee cast his Electoral College vote for the States Rights nominees rather than for the national Democratic candidates.

In Alabama the Democratic electors were pledged to the States Rights candidates. There were no national Democratic electors on the ballot in that state.

The Republican figure in Mississippi includes votes cast for two elector tickets. In New York the Democratic figure includes Liberal votes.

The full list of candidates for President and Vice-President was:

24,179,345	Harry S. Truman and Alben W. Barkley, Democratic.
21,991,291	Thomas E. Dewey and Earl Warren, Republican.
1,176,125	Strom Thurmond and Fielding L. Wright, States Rights.
1,157,326	Henry A. Wallace and Glen H. Taylor, Progressive.
139,572	Norman Thomas and Tucker P. Smith, Socialist.
103,900	Claude A. Watson and Dale H. Learn, Prohibition.
29,241	Edward A. Teichert and Stephen Emery, Socialist Labor.
13,614	Farrell Dobbs and Grace Carlson, Socialist Workers.

In addition, 3,412 scattered votes were reported from various states.

UNITED STATES

PRESIDENT 1948

State	Electoral Vote Rep.	Electoral Vote Dem.	Electoral Vote Other	Total Vote	Republican	Democratic	Other	Plurality	Percentage Total Vote Rep.	Percentage Total Vote Dem.	Percentage Major Vote Rep.	Percentage Major Vote Dem.
Alabama			11	214,980	40,930		174,050	130,513 SR	19.0%		100.0%	
Alaska												
Arizona		4		177,065	77,597	95,251	4,217	17,654 D	43.8%	53.8%	44.9%	55.1%
Arkansas		9		242,475	50,959	149,659	41,857	98,700 D	21.0%	61.7%	25.4%	74.6%
California		25		4,021,538	1,895,269	1,913,134	213,135	17,865 D	47.1%	47.6%	49.8%	50.2%
Colorado		6		515,237	239,714	267,288	8,235	27,574 D	46.5%	51.9%	47.3%	52.7%
Connecticut	8			883,518	437,754	423,297	22,467	14,457 R	49.5%	47.9%	50.8%	49.2%
Delaware	3			139,073	69,588	67,813	1,672	1,775 R	50.0%	48.8%	50.6%	49.4%
Florida		8		577,643	194,280	281,988	101,375	87,708 D	33.6%	48.8%	40.8%	59.2%
Georgia		12		418,844	76,691	254,646	87,507	169,511 D	18.3%	60.8%	23.1%	76.9%
Hawaii												
Idaho		4		214,816	101,514	107,370	5,932	5,856 D	47.3%	50.0%	48.6%	51.4%
Illinois		28		3,984,046	1,961,103	1,994,715	28,228	33,612 D	49.2%	50.1%	49.6%	50.4%
Indiana	13			1,656,212	821,079	807,831	27,302	13,248 R	49.6%	48.8%	50.4%	49.6%
Iowa		10		1,038,264	494,018	522,380	21,866	28,362 D	47.6%	50.3%	48.6%	51.4%
Kansas	8			788,819	423,039	351,902	13,878	71,137 R	53.6%	44.6%	54.6%	45.4%
Kentucky		11		822,658	341,210	466,756	14,692	125,546 D	41.5%	56.7%	42.2%	57.8%
Louisiana			10	416,336	72,657	136,344	207,335	67,946 SR	17.5%	32.7%	34.8%	65.2%
Maine	5			264,787	150,234	111,916	2,637	38,318 R	56.7%	42.3%	57.3%	42.7%
Maryland	8			596,748	294,814	286,521	15,413	8,293 R	49.4%	48.0%	50.7%	49.3%
Massachusetts		16		2,107,146	909,370	1,151,788	45,988	242,418 D	43.2%	54.7%	44.1%	55.9%
Michigan	19			2,109,609	1,038,595	1,003,448	67,566	35,147 R	49.2%	47.6%	50.9%	49.1%
Minnesota		11		1,212,226	483,617	692,966	35,643	209,349 D	39.9%	57.2%	41.1%	58.9%
Mississippi			9	192,190	5,043	19,384	167,763	148,154 SR	2.6%	10.1%	20.6%	79.4%
Missouri		15		1,578,628	655,039	917,315	6,274	262,276 D	41.5%	58.1%	41.7%	58.3%
Montana		4		224,278	96,770	119,071	8,437	22,301 D	43.1%	53.1%	44.8%	55.2%
Nebraska	6			488,940	264,774	224,165	1	40,609 R	54.2%	45.8%	54.2%	45.8%
Nevada		3		62,117	29,357	31,291	1,469	1,934 D	47.3%	50.4%	48.4%	51.6%
New Hampshire	4			231,440	121,299	107,995	2,146	13,304 R	52.4%	46.7%	52.9%	47.1%
New Jersey	16			1,949,555	981,124	895,455	72,976	85,669 R	50.3%	45.9%	52.3%	47.7%
New Mexico		4		187,063	80,303	105,464	1,296	25,161 D	42.9%	56.4%	43.2%	56.8%
New York	47			6,177,337	2,841,163	2,780,204	555,970	60,959 R	46.0%	45.0%	50.5%	49.5%
North Carolina		14		791,209	258,572	459,070	73,567	200,498 D	32.7%	58.0%	36.0%	64.0%
North Dakota	4			220,716	115,139	95,812	9,765	19,327 R	52.2%	43.4%	54.6%	45.4%
Ohio		25		2,936,071	1,445,684	1,452,791	37,596	7,107 D	49.2%	49.5%	49.9%	50.1%
Oklahoma		10		721,599	268,817	452,782		183,965 D	37.3%	62.7%	37.3%	62.7%
Oregon	6			524,080	260,904	243,147	20,029	17,757 R	49.8%	46.4%	51.8%	48.2%
Pennsylvania	35			3,735,348	1,902,197	1,752,426	80,725	149,771 R	50.9%	46.9%	52.0%	48.0%
Rhode Island		4		327,702	135,787	188,736	3,179	52,949 D	41.4%	57.6%	41.8%	58.2%
South Carolina			8	142,571	5,386	34,423	102,762	68,184 SR	3.8%	24.1%	13.5%	86.5%
South Dakota	4			250,105	129,651	117,653	2,801	11,998 R	51.8%	47.0%	52.4%	47.6%
Tennessee		11	1	550,283	202,914	270,402	76,967	67,488 D	36.9%	49.1%	42.9%	57.1%
Texas		23		1,249,577	303,467	824,235	121,875	520,768 D	24.3%	66.0%	26.9%	73.1%
Utah		4		276,306	124,402	149,151	2,753	24,749 D	45.0%	54.0%	45.5%	54.5%
Vermont	3			123,382	75,926	45,557	1,899	30,369 R	61.5%	36.9%	62.5%	37.5%
Virginia		11		419,256	172,070	200,786	46,400	28,716 D	41.0%	47.9%	46.1%	53.9%
Washington		8		905,058	386,314	476,165	42,579	89,851 D	42.7%	52.6%	44.8%	55.2%
West Virginia		8		748,750	316,251	429,188	3,311	112,937 D	42.2%	57.3%	42.4%	57.6%
Wisconsin		12		1,276,800	590,959	647,310	38,531	56,351 D	46.3%	50.7%	47.7%	52.3%
Wyoming		3		101,425	47,947	52,354	1,124	4,407 D	47.3%	51.6%	47.8%	52.2%
United States	189	303	39	48,793,826	21,991,291	24,179,345	2,623,190	2,188,054 D	45.1%	49.6%	47.6%	52.4%

PRESIDENT 1944

The Republican figures in Georgia, Mississippi and South Carolina include votes cast for two elector tickets. The Democratic figure in Mississippi includes votes cast for two elector tickets and in New York includes American Labor and Liberal votes.

In South Carolina an uncommitted Southern Democratic elector ticket ran in second place ahead of the Republican candidates.

The full list of candidates for President and Vice-President was:

25,612,610	Franklin D. Roosevelt and Harry S. Truman, Democratic.
22,017,617	Thomas E. Dewey and John W. Bricker, Republican.
79,003	Norman Thomas and Darlington Hoopes, Socialist.
74,799	Claude A. Watson and Andrew Johnson, Prohibition.
45,191	Edward A. Teichert and Arla A. Albaugh, Socialist Labor.
1,780	Gerald L. K. Smith and Harry Romer, American First.

In addition, 135,444 votes were cast in Texas for a Texas Regulars elector ticket and 7,799 in South Carolina for an uncommitted Southern Democratic elector ticket. There were 2,447 scattered votes reported from various states.

UNITED STATES

PRESIDENT 1944

State	Electoral Vote Rep.	Electoral Vote Dem.	Electoral Vote Other	Total Vote	Republican	Democratic	Other	Plurality	Percentage Total Vote Rep.	Percentage Total Vote Dem.	Percentage Major Vote Rep.	Percentage Major Vote Dem.
Alabama		11		244,743	44,540	198,918	1,285	154,378 D	18.2%	81.3%	18.3%	81.7%
Alaska												
Arizona		4		137,634	56,287	80,926	421	24,639 D	40.9%	58.8%	41.0%	59.0%
Arkansas		9		212,954	63,551	148,965	438	85,414 D	29.8%	70.0%	29.9%	70.1%
California		25		3,520,875	1,512,965	1,988,564	19,346	475,599 D	43.0%	56.5%	43.2%	56.8%
Colorado	6			505,039	268,731	234,331	1,977	34,400 R	53.2%	46.4%	53.4%	46.6%
Connecticut		8		831,990	390,527	435,146	6,317	44,619 D	46.9%	52.3%	47.3%	52.7%
Delaware		3		125,361	56,747	68,166	448	11,419 D	45.3%	54.4%	45.4%	54.6%
Florida		8		482,803	143,215	339,377	211	196,162 D	29.7%	70.3%	29.7%	70.3%
Georgia		12		328,129	59,900	268,187	42	208,287 D	18.3%	81.7%	18.3%	81.7%
Hawaii												
Idaho		4		208,321	100,137	107,399	785	7,262 D	48.1%	51.6%	48.3%	51.7%
Illinois		28		4,036,061	1,939,314	2,079,479	17,268	140,165 D	48.0%	51.5%	48.3%	51.7%
Indiana	13			1,672,091	875,891	781,403	14,797	94,488 R	52.4%	46.7%	52.9%	47.1%
Iowa	10			1,052,599	547,267	499,876	5,456	47,391 R	52.0%	47.5%	52.3%	47.7%
Kansas	8			733,776	442,096	287,458	4,222	154,638 R	60.2%	39.2%	60.6%	39.4%
Kentucky		11		867,924	392,448	472,589	2,887	80,141 D	45.2%	54.5%	45.4%	54.6%
Louisiana		10		349,383	67,750	281,564	69	213,814 D	19.4%	80.6%	19.4%	80.6%
Maine	5			296,400	155,434	140,631	335	14,803 R	52.4%	47.4%	52.5%	47.5%
Maryland		8		608,439	292,949	315,490		22,541 D	48.1%	51.9%	48.1%	51.9%
Massachusetts		16		1,960,665	921,350	1,035,296	4,019	113,946 D	47.0%	52.8%	47.1%	52.9%
Michigan		19		2,205,223	1,084,423	1,106,899	13,901	22,476 D	49.2%	50.2%	49.5%	50.5%
Minnesota		11		1,125,504	527,416	589,864	8,224	62,448 D	46.9%	52.4%	47.2%	52.8%
Mississippi		9		180,234	11,613	168,621		157,008 D	6.4%	93.6%	6.4%	93.6%
Missouri		15		1,571,697	761,175	807,356	3,166	46,181 D	48.4%	51.4%	48.5%	51.5%
Montana		4		207,355	93,163	112,556	1,636	19,393 D	44.9%	54.3%	45.3%	54.7%
Nebraska	6			563,126	329,880	233,246		96,634 R	58.6%	41.4%	58.6%	41.4%
Nevada		3		54,234	24,611	29,623		5,012 D	45.4%	54.6%	45.4%	54.6%
New Hampshire		4		229,625	109,916	119,663	46	9,747 D	47.9%	52.1%	47.9%	52.1%
New Jersey		16		1,963,761	961,335	987,874	14,552	26,539 D	49.0%	50.3%	49.3%	50.7%
New Mexico		4		152,225	70,688	81,389	148	10,701 D	46.4%	53.5%	46.5%	53.5%
New York		47		6,316,790	2,987,647	3,304,238	24,905	316,591 D	47.3%	52.3%	47.5%	52.5%
North Carolina		14		790,554	263,155	527,399		264,244 D	33.3%	66.7%	33.3%	66.7%
North Dakota	4			220,182	118,535	100,144	1,503	18,391 R	53.8%	45.5%	54.2%	45.8%
Ohio	25			3,153,056	1,582,293	1,570,763		11,530 R	50.2%	49.8%	50.2%	49.8%
Oklahoma		10		722,636	319,424	401,549	1,663	82,125 D	44.2%	55.6%	44.3%	55.7%
Oregon		6		480,147	225,365	248,635	6,147	23,270 D	46.9%	51.8%	47.5%	52.5%
Pennsylvania		35		3,794,793	1,835,054	1,940,479	19,260	105,425 D	48.4%	51.1%	48.6%	51.4%
Rhode Island		4		299,276	123,487	175,356	433	51,869 D	41.3%	58.6%	41.3%	58.7%
South Carolina		8		103,382	4,617	90,601	8,164	82,802 D	4.5%	87.6%	4.8%	95.2%
South Dakota	4			232,076	135,365	96,711		38,654 R	58.3%	41.7%	58.3%	41.7%
Tennessee		12		510,692	200,311	308,707	1,674	108,396 D	39.2%	60.4%	39.4%	60.6%
Texas		23		1,150,334	191,423	821,605	137,306	630,182 D	16.6%	71.4%	18.9%	81.1%
Utah		4		248,319	97,891	150,088	340	52,197 D	39.4%	60.4%	39.5%	60.5%
Vermont	3			125,361	71,527	53,820	14	17,707 R	57.1%	42.9%	57.1%	42.9%
Virginia		11		388,485	145,243	242,276	966	97,033 D	37.4%	62.4%	37.5%	62.5%
Washington		8		856,328	361,689	486,774	7,865	125,085 D	42.2%	56.8%	42.6%	57.4%
West Virginia		8		715,596	322,819	392,777		69,958 D	45.1%	54.9%	45.1%	54.9%
Wisconsin	12			1,339,152	674,532	650,413	14,207	24,119 R	50.4%	48.6%	50.9%	49.1%
Wyoming	3			101,340	51,921	49,419		2,502 R	51.2%	48.8%	51.2%	48.8%
United States	99	432	—	47,976,670	22,017,617	25,612,610	346,443	3,594,993 D	45.9%	53.4%	46.2%	53.8%

PRESIDENT 1940

The Republican figures in Connecticut, Georgia, Mississippi and South Carolina include votes cast for two or three elector tickets. In New York the Democratic figure includes American Labor votes.

The full list of candidates for President and Vice-President was:

27,313,041	Franklin D. Roosevelt and Henry A. Wallace, Democratic.
22,348,480	Wendell Willkie and Charles L. McNary, Republican.
116,410	Norman Thomas and Maynard C. Krueger, Socialist.
58,708	Roger Babson and Edgar V. Moorman, Prohibition.
46,259	Earl Browder and James W. Ford, Communist.
14,892	John W. Aiken and Aaron M. Orange, Socialist Labor.

In addition, 545 votes were cast in North Dakota for the individual candidacy of Alfred Knutson and 2,083 scattered votes were reported from various states.

UNITED STATES

PRESIDENT 1940

State	Electoral Vote Rep.	Electoral Vote Dem.	Electoral Vote Other	Total Vote	Republican	Democratic	Other	Plurality	Percentage Total Vote Rep.	Percentage Total Vote Dem.	Percentage Major Vote Rep.	Percentage Major Vote Dem.
Alabama		11		294,219	42,184	250,726	1,309	208,542 D	14.3%	85.2%	14.4%	85.6%
Alaska												
Arizona		3		150,039	54,030	95,267	742	41,237 D	36.0%	63.5%	36.2%	63.8%
Arkansas		9		200,429	42,122	157,213	1,094	115,091 D	21.0%	78.4%	21.1%	78.9%
California		22		3,268,791	1,351,419	1,877,618	39,754	526,199 D	41.3%	57.4%	41.9%	58.1%
Colorado	6			549,004	279,576	265,554	3,874	14,022 R	50.9%	48.4%	51.3%	48.7%
Connecticut		8		781,502	361,819	417,621	2,062	55,802 D	46.3%	53.4%	46.4%	53.6%
Delaware		3		136,374	61,440	74,599	335	13,159 D	45.1%	54.7%	45.2%	54.8%
Florida		7		485,640	126,158	359,334	148	233,176 D	26.0%	74.0%	26.0%	74.0%
Georgia		12		312,686	46,495	265,194	997	218,699 D	14.9%	84.8%	14.9%	85.1%
Hawaii												
Idaho		4		235,168	106,553	127,842	773	21,289 D	45.3%	54.4%	45.5%	54.5%
Illinois		29		4,217,935	2,047,240	2,149,934	20,761	102,694 D	48.5%	51.0%	48.8%	51.2%
Indiana	14			1,782,747	899,466	874,063	9,218	25,403 R	50.5%	49.0%	50.7%	49.3%
Iowa	11			1,215,432	632,370	578,802	4,260	53,568 R	52.0%	47.6%	52.2%	47.8%
Kansas	9			860,297	489,169	364,725	6,403	124,444 R	56.9%	42.4%	57.3%	42.7%
Kentucky		11		970,163	410,384	557,322	2,457	146,938 D	42.3%	57.4%	42.4%	57.6%
Louisiana		10		372,305	52,446	319,751	108	267,305 D	14.1%	85.9%	14.1%	85.9%
Maine	5			320,840	163,951	156,478	411	7,473 R	51.1%	48.8%	51.2%	48.8%
Maryland		8		660,104	269,534	384,546	6,024	115,012 D	40.8%	58.3%	41.2%	58.8%
Massachusetts		17		2,026,993	939,700	1,076,522	10,771	136,822 D	46.4%	53.1%	46.6%	53.4%
Michigan	19			2,085,929	1,039,917	1,032,991	13,021	6,926 R	49.9%	49.5%	50.2%	49.8%
Minnesota		11		1,251,188	596,274	644,196	10,718	47,922 D	47.7%	51.5%	48.1%	51.9%
Mississippi		9		175,824	7,364	168,267	193	160,903 D	4.2%	95.7%	4.2%	95.8%
Missouri		15		1,833,729	871,009	958,476	4,244	87,467 D	47.5%	52.3%	47.6%	52.4%
Montana		4		247,873	99,579	145,698	2,596	46,119 D	40.2%	58.8%	40.6%	59.4%
Nebraska	7			615,878	352,201	263,677		88,524 R	57.2%	42.8%	57.2%	42.8%
Nevada		3		53,174	21,229	31,945		10,716 D	39.9%	60.1%	39.9%	60.1%
New Hampshire		4		235,419	110,127	125,292		15,165 D	46.8%	53.2%	46.8%	53.2%
New Jersey		16		1,972,552	945,475	1,016,808	10,269	71,333 D	47.9%	51.5%	48.2%	51.8%
New Mexico		3		183,258	79,315	103,699	244	24,384 D	43.3%	56.6%	43.3%	56.7%
New York		47		6,301,596	3,027,478	3,251,918	22,200	224,440 D	48.0%	51.6%	48.2%	51.8%
North Carolina		13		822,648	213,633	609,015		395,382 D	26.0%	74.0%	26.0%	74.0%
North Dakota	4			280,775	154,590	124,036	2,149	30,554 R	55.1%	44.2%	55.5%	44.5%
Ohio		26		3,319,912	1,586,773	1,733,139		146,366 D	47.8%	52.2%	47.8%	52.2%
Oklahoma		11		826,212	348,872	474,313	3,027	125,441 D	42.2%	57.4%	42.4%	57.6%
Oregon		5		481,240	219,555	258,415	3,270	38,860 D	45.6%	53.7%	45.9%	54.1%
Pennsylvania		36		4,078,714	1,889,848	2,171,035	17,831	281,187 D	46.3%	53.2%	46.5%	53.5%
Rhode Island		4		321,152	138,654	182,181	317	43,527 D	43.2%	56.7%	43.2%	56.8%
South Carolina		8		99,830	4,360	95,470		91,110 D	4.4%	95.6%	4.4%	95.6%
South Dakota	4			308,427	177,065	131,362		45,703 R	57.4%	42.6%	57.4%	42.6%
Tennessee		11		522,823	169,153	351,601	2,069	182,448 D	32.4%	67.3%	32.5%	67.5%
Texas		23		1,124,437	212,692	909,974	1,771	697,282 D	18.9%	80.9%	18.9%	81.1%
Utah		4		247,819	93,151	154,277	391	61,126 D	37.6%	62.3%	37.6%	62.4%
Vermont	3			143,062	78,371	64,269	422	14,102 R	54.8%	44.9%	54.9%	45.1%
Virginia		11		346,608	109,363	235,961	1,284	126,598 D	31.6%	68.1%	31.7%	68.3%
Washington		8		793,833	322,123	462,145	9,565	140,022 D	40.6%	58.2%	41.1%	58.9%
West Virginia		8		868,076	372,414	495,662		123,248 D	42.9%	57.1%	42.9%	57.1%
Wisconsin		12		1,405,522	679,206	704,821	21,495	25,615 D	48.3%	50.1%	49.1%	50.9%
Wyoming		3		112,240	52,633	59,287	320	6,654 D	46.9%	52.8%	47.0%	53.0%
United States	82	449	—	49,900,418	22,348,480	27,313,041	238,897	4,964,561 D	44.8%	54.7%	45.0%	55.0%

PRESIDENT 1936

The Republican figures in Delaware, Mississippi, and South Carolina include votes cast for two elector tickets. In New York the Democratic figure includes American Labor votes.

The full list of candidates for President and Vice-President was:

27,757,333	Franklin D. Roosevelt and John N. Garner, Democratic.
16,684,231	Alfred M. Landon and Frank Knox, Republican.
892,267	William Lemke and Thomas C. O'Brien, Union.
187,833	Norman Thomas and George A. Nelson, Socialist.
80,171	Earl Browder and James W. Ford, Communist.
37,677	D. Leigh Colvin and Claude A. Watson, Prohibition.
12,829	John W. Aiken and Emil F. Teichert, Socialist Labor.
1,598	William Dudley Pelley and Willard W. Kemp, Christian.

In addition, 824 scattered votes were reported from various states.

UNITED STATES

PRESIDENT 1936

State	Electoral Vote Rep.	Electoral Vote Dem.	Electoral Vote Other	Total Vote	Republican	Democratic	Other	Plurality	Percentage Total Vote Rep.	Percentage Total Vote Dem.	Percentage Major Vote Rep.	Percentage Major Vote Dem.
Alabama		11		275,744	35,358	238,196	2,190	202,838 D	12.8%	86.4%	12.9%	87.1%
Alaska												
Arizona		3		124,163	33,433	86,722	4,008	53,289 D	26.9%	69.8%	27.8%	72.2%
Arkansas		9		179,431	32,049	146,765	617	114,716 D	17.9%	81.8%	17.9%	82.1%
California		22		2,638,882	836,431	1,766,836	35,615	930,405 D	31.7%	67.0%	32.1%	67.9%
Colorado		6		488,685	181,267	295,021	12,397	113,754 D	37.1%	60.4%	38.1%	61.9%
Connecticut		8		690,723	278,685	382,129	29,909	103,444 D	40.3%	55.3%	42.2%	57.8%
Delaware		3		127,603	57,236	69,702	665	12,466 D	44.9%	54.6%	45.1%	54.9%
Florida		7		327,436	78,248	249,117	71	170,869 D	23.9%	76.1%	23.9%	76.1%
Georgia		12		293,170	36,943	255,363	864	218,420 D	12.6%	87.1%	12.6%	87.4%
Hawaii												
Idaho		4		199,617	66,256	125,683	7,678	59,427 D	33.2%	63.0%	34.5%	65.5%
Illinois		29		3,956,522	1,570,393	2,282,999	103,130	712,606 D	39.7%	57.7%	40.8%	59.2%
Indiana		14		1,650,897	691,570	934,974	24,353	243,404 D	41.9%	56.6%	42.5%	57.5%
Iowa		11		1,142,737	487,977	621,756	33,004	133,779 D	42.7%	54.4%	44.0%	56.0%
Kansas		9		865,507	397,727	464,520	3,260	66,793 D	46.0%	53.7%	46.1%	53.9%
Kentucky		11		926,214	369,702	541,944	14,568	172,242 D	39.9%	58.5%	40.6%	59.4%
Louisiana		10		329,778	36,791	292,894	93	256,103 D	11.2%	88.8%	11.2%	88.8%
Maine	5			304,240	168,823	126,333	9,084	42,490 R	55.5%	41.5%	57.2%	42.8%
Maryland		8		624,896	231,435	389,612	3,849	158,177 D	37.0%	62.3%	37.3%	62.7%
Massachusetts		17		1,840,357	768,613	942,716	129,028	174,103 D	41.8%	51.2%	44.9%	55.1%
Michigan		19		1,805,098	699,733	1,016,794	88,571	317,061 D	38.8%	56.3%	40.8%	59.2%
Minnesota		11		1,129,975	350,461	698,811	80,703	348,350 D	31.0%	61.8%	33.4%	66.6%
Mississippi		9		162,142	4,467	157,333	342	152,866 D	2.8%	97.0%	2.8%	97.2%
Missouri		15		1,828,635	697,891	1,111,043	19,701	413,152 D	38.2%	60.8%	38.6%	61.4%
Montana		4		230,502	63,598	159,690	7,214	96,092 D	27.6%	69.3%	28.5%	71.5%
Nebraska		7		608,023	247,731	347,445	12,847	99,714 D	40.7%	57.1%	41.6%	58.4%
Nevada		3		43,848	11,923	31,925		20,002 D	27.2%	72.8%	27.2%	72.8%
New Hampshire		4		218,114	104,642	108,460	5,012	3,818 D	48.0%	49.7%	49.1%	50.9%
New Jersey		16		1,820,437	720,322	1,083,850	16,265	363,528 D	39.6%	59.5%	39.9%	60.1%
New Mexico		3		169,135	61,727	106,037	1,371	44,310 D	36.5%	62.7%	36.8%	63.2%
New York		47		5,596,398	2,180,670	3,293,222	122,506	1,112,552 D	39.0%	58.8%	39.8%	60.2%
North Carolina		13		839,475	223,294	616,141	40	392,847 D	26.6%	73.4%	26.6%	73.4%
North Dakota		4		273,716	72,751	163,148	37,817	90,397 D	26.6%	59.6%	30.8%	69.2%
Ohio		26		3,012,660	1,127,855	1,747,140	137,665	619,285 D	37.4%	58.0%	39.2%	60.8%
Oklahoma		11		749,740	245,122	501,069	3,549	255,947 D	32.7%	66.8%	32.8%	67.2%
Oregon		5		414,021	122,706	266,733	24,582	144,027 D	29.6%	64.4%	31.5%	68.5%
Pennsylvania		36		4,138,105	1,690,300	2,353,788	94,017	663,488 D	40.8%	56.9%	41.8%	58.2%
Rhode Island		4		310,278	125,031	164,338	20,909	39,307 D	40.3%	53.0%	43.2%	56.8%
South Carolina		8		115,437	1,646	113,791		112,145 D	1.4%	98.6%	1.4%	98.6%
South Dakota		4		296,452	125,977	160,137	10,338	34,160 D	42.5%	54.0%	44.0%	56.0%
Tennessee		11		477,086	147,055	328,083	1,948	181,028 D	30.8%	68.8%	30.9%	69.1%
Texas		23		849,701	104,661	739,952	5,088	635,291 D	12.3%	87.1%	12.4%	87.6%
Utah		4		216,679	64,555	150,248	1,876	85,693 D	29.8%	69.3%	30.1%	69.9%
Vermont	3			143,689	81,023	62,124	542	18,899 R	56.4%	43.2%	56.6%	43.4%
Virginia		11		334,590	98,336	234,980	1,274	136,644 D	29.4%	70.2%	29.5%	70.5%
Washington		8		692,338	206,892	459,579	25,867	252,687 D	29.9%	66.4%	31.0%	69.0%
West Virginia		8		829,945	325,358	502,582	2,005	177,224 D	39.2%	60.6%	39.3%	60.7%
Wisconsin		12		1,258,560	380,828	802,984	74,748	422,156 D	30.3%	63.8%	32.2%	67.8%
Wyoming		3		103,382	38,739	62,624	2,019	23,885 D	37.5%	60.6%	38.2%	61.8%
United States	8	523	—	45,654,763	16,684,231	27,757,333	1,213,199	11,073,102 D	36.5%	60.8%	37.5%	62.5%

PRESIDENT 1932

The Republican figure in Mississippi includes votes cast for two elector tickets.

The full list of candidates for President and Vice-President was:

22,829,501	Franklin D. Roosevelt and John N. Garner, Democratic.
15,760,684	Herbert C. Hoover and Charles Curtis, Republican.
884,649	Norman Thomas and James H. Maurer, Socialist.
103,253	William Z. Foster and James W. Ford, Communist.
81,872	William D. Upshaw and Frank S. Regan, Prohibition.
53,247	William H. Harvey and Frank Hemenway, Liberty.
34,043	Verne L. Reynolds and John W. Aiken, Socialist Labor.
7,431	Jacob S. Coxey and Julius J. Reiter, Farmer-Labor.
1,645	John Zahnd and Florence Garvin, National.
740	James R. Cox and Victor C. Tisdal, Jobless.

In addition, 157 votes were cast for a Jacksonian elector ticket in Texas and 9 in Arizona for an Arizona Progressive Democratic Ticket. There were 1,528 scattered votes reported from various states.

UNITED STATES

PRESIDENT 1932

State	Electoral Vote Rep.	Electoral Vote Dem.	Electoral Vote Other	Total Vote	Republican	Democratic	Other	Plurality	Percentage Total Vote Rep.	Percentage Total Vote Dem.	Percentage Major Vote Rep.	Percentage Major Vote Dem.
Alabama		11		245,303	34,675	207,910	2,718	173,235 D	14.1%	84.8%	14.3%	85.7%
Alaska												
Arizona		3		118,251	36,104	79,264	2,883	43,160 D	30.5%	67.0%	31.3%	68.7%
Arkansas		9		216,569	27,465	186,829	2,275	159,364 D	12.7%	86.3%	12.8%	87.2%
California		22		2,266,972	847,902	1,324,157	94,913	476,255 D	37.4%	58.4%	39.0%	61.0%
Colorado		6		457,696	189,617	250,877	17,202	61,260 D	41.4%	54.8%	43.0%	57.0%
Connecticut	8			594,183	288,420	281,632	24,131	6,788 R	48.5%	47.4%	50.6%	49.4%
Delaware	3			112,901	57,073	54,319	1,509	2,754 R	50.6%	48.1%	51.2%	48.8%
Florida		7		276,943	69,170	206,307	1,466	137,137 D	25.0%	74.5%	25.1%	74.9%
Georgia		12		255,590	19,863	234,118	1,609	214,255 D	7.8%	91.6%	7.8%	92.2%
Hawaii												
Idaho		4		186,520	71,312	109,479	5,729	38,167 D	38.2%	58.7%	39.4%	60.6%
Illinois		29		3,407,926	1,432,756	1,882,304	92,866	449,548 D	42.0%	55.2%	43.2%	56.8%
Indiana		14		1,576,927	677,184	862,054	37,689	184,870 D	42.9%	54.7%	44.0%	56.0%
Iowa		11		1,036,687	414,433	598,019	24,235	183,586 D	40.0%	57.7%	40.9%	59.1%
Kansas		9		791,978	349,498	424,204	18,276	74,706 D	44.1%	53.6%	45.2%	54.8%
Kentucky		11		983,059	394,716	580,574	7,769	185,858 D	40.2%	59.1%	40.5%	59.5%
Louisiana		10		268,804	18,853	249,418	533	230,565 D	7.0%	92.8%	7.0%	93.0%
Maine	5			298,444	166,631	128,907	2,906	37,724 R	55.8%	43.2%	56.4%	43.6%
Maryland		8		511,054	184,184	314,314	12,556	130,130 D	36.0%	61.5%	36.9%	63.1%
Massachusetts		17		1,580,114	736,959	800,148	43,007	63,189 D	46.6%	50.6%	47.9%	52.1%
Michigan		19		1,664,765	739,894	871,700	53,171	131,806 D	44.4%	52.4%	45.9%	54.1%
Minnesota		11		1,002,843	363,959	600,806	38,078	236,847 D	36.3%	59.9%	37.7%	62.3%
Mississippi		9		146,034	5,180	140,168	686	134,988 D	3.5%	96.0%	3.6%	96.4%
Missouri		15		1,609,894	564,713	1,025,406	19,775	460,693 D	35.1%	63.7%	35.5%	64.5%
Montana		4		216,479	78,078	127,286	11,115	49,208 D	36.1%	58.8%	38.0%	62.0%
Nebraska		7		570,135	201,177	359,082	9,876	157,905 D	35.3%	63.0%	35.9%	64.1%
Nevada		3		41,430	12,674	28,756		16,082 D	30.6%	69.4%	30.6%	69.4%
New Hampshire	4			205,520	103,629	100,680	1,211	2,949 R	50.4%	49.0%	50.7%	49.3%
New Jersey		16		1,630,063	775,684	806,630	47,749	30,946 D	47.6%	49.5%	49.0%	51.0%
New Mexico		3		151,606	54,217	95,089	2,300	40,872 D	35.8%	62.7%	36.3%	63.7%
New York		47		4,688,614	1,937,963	2,534,959	215,692	596,996 D	41.3%	54.1%	43.3%	56.7%
North Carolina		13		711,498	208,344	497,566	5,588	289,222 D	29.3%	69.9%	29.5%	70.5%
North Dakota		4		256,290	71,772	178,350	6,168	106,578 D	28.0%	69.6%	28.7%	71.3%
Ohio		26		2,609,728	1,227,319	1,301,695	80,714	74,376 D	47.0%	49.9%	48.5%	51.5%
Oklahoma		11		704,633	188,165	516,468		328,303 D	26.7%	73.3%	26.7%	73.3%
Oregon		5		368,751	136,019	213,871	18,861	77,852 D	36.9%	58.0%	38.9%	61.1%
Pennsylvania	36			2,859,021	1,453,540	1,295,948	109,533	157,592 R	50.8%	45.3%	52.9%	47.1%
Rhode Island		4		266,170	115,266	146,604	4,300	31,338 D	43.3%	55.1%	44.0%	56.0%
South Carolina		8		104,407	1,978	102,347	82	100,369 D	1.9%	98.0%	1.9%	98.1%
South Dakota		4		288,438	99,212	183,515	5,711	84,303 D	34.4%	63.6%	35.1%	64.9%
Tennessee		11		390,273	126,752	259,473	4,048	132,721 D	32.5%	66.5%	32.8%	67.2%
Texas		23		874,382	98,218	771,109	5,055	672,891 D	11.2%	88.2%	11.3%	88.7%
Utah		4		206,578	84,795	116,750	5,033	31,955 D	41.0%	56.5%	42.1%	57.9%
Vermont	3			136,980	78,984	56,266	1,730	22,718 R	57.7%	41.1%	58.4%	41.6%
Virginia		11		297,942	89,637	203,979	4,326	114,342 D	30.1%	68.5%	30.5%	69.5%
Washington		8		614,814	208,645	353,260	52,909	144,615 D	33.9%	57.5%	37.1%	62.9%
West Virginia		8		743,774	330,731	405,124	7,919	74,393 D	44.5%	54.5%	44.9%	55.1%
Wisconsin		12		1,114,814	347,741	707,410	59,663	359,669 D	31.2%	63.5%	33.0%	67.0%
Wyoming		3		96,962	39,583	54,370	3,009	14,787 D	40.8%	56.1%	42.1%	57.9%
United States	59	472	—	39,758,759	15,760,684	22,829,501	1,168,574	7,068,817 D	39.6%	57.4%	40.8%	59.2%

PRESIDENT 1928

The Republican figures in Georgia, Mississippi, and South Carolina include votes cast for two or three elector tickets; in Pennsylvania the Communist total includes votes cast for two elector tickets.

The full list of candidates for President and Vice-President was:

21,437,277	Herbert C. Hoover and Charles Curtis, Republican.
15,007,698	Alfred E. Smith and Joseph T. Robinson, Democratic.
265,583	Norman Thomas and James H. Maurer, Socialist.
46,896	William Z. Foster and Benjamin Gitlow, Communist.
21,586	Verne L. Reynolds and Jeremiah D. Crowley, Socialist Labor.
20,101	William F. Varney and James A. Edgerton, Prohibition.
6,390	Frank E. Webb and L. R. Tillman, Farmer-Labor.

In addition, 420 scattered votes were reported from various states.

UNITED STATES

PRESIDENT 1928

State	Electoral Vote			Total					Percentage			
									Total Vote		Major Vote	
	Rep.	Dem.	Other	Vote	Republican	Democratic	Other	Plurality	Rep.	Dem.	Rep.	Dem.
Alabama		12		248,981	120,725	127,796	460	7,071 D	48.5%	51.3%	48.6%	51.4%
Alaska												
Arizona	3			91,254	52,533	38,537	184	13,996 R	57.6%	42.2%	57.7%	42.3%
Arkansas		9		197,726	77,784	119,196	746	41,412 D	39.3%	60.3%	39.5%	60.5%
California	13			1,796,656	1,162,323	614,365	19,968	547,958 R	64.7%	34.2%	65.4%	34.6%
Colorado	6			392,242	253,872	133,131	5,239	120,741 R	64.7%	33.9%	65.6%	34.4%
Connecticut	7			553,118	296,641	252,085	4,392	44,556 R	53.6%	45.6%	54.1%	45.9%
Delaware	3			104,602	68,860	35,354	388	33,506 R	65.8%	33.8%	66.1%	33.9%
Florida	6			252,068	145,860	101,764	4,444	44,096 R	57.9%	40.4%	58.9%	41.1%
Georgia		14		231,592	101,800	129,604	188	27,804 D	44.0%	56.0%	44.0%	56.0%
Hawaii												
Idaho	4			151,541	97,322	52,926	1,293	44,396 R	64.2%	34.9%	64.8%	35.2%
Illinois	29			3,107,489	1,769,141	1,313,817	24,531	455,324 R	56.9%	42.3%	57.4%	42.6%
Indiana	15			1,421,314	848,290	562,691	10,333	285,599 R	59.7%	39.6%	60.1%	39.9%
Iowa	13			1,009,189	623,570	379,011	6,608	244,559 R	61.8%	37.6%	62.2%	37.8%
Kansas	10			713,200	513,672	193,003	6,525	320,669 R	72.0%	27.1%	72.7%	27.3%
Kentucky	13			940,521	558,064	381,070	1,387	176,994 R	59.3%	40.5%	59.4%	40.6%
Louisiana		10		215,833	51,160	164,655	18	113,495 D	23.7%	76.3%	23.7%	76.3%
Maine	6			262,170	179,923	81,179	1,068	98,744 R	68.6%	31.0%	68.9%	31.1%
Maryland	8			528,348	301,479	223,626	3,243	77,853 R	57.1%	42.3%	57.4%	42.6%
Massachusetts		18		1,577,823	775,566	792,758	9,499	17,192 D	49.2%	50.2%	49.5%	50.5%
Michigan	15			1,372,082	965,396	396,762	9,924	568,634 R	70.4%	28.9%	70.9%	29.1%
Minnesota	12			970,976	560,977	396,451	13,548	164,526 R	57.8%	40.8%	58.6%	41.4%
Mississippi		10		151,568	27,030	124,538		97,508 D	17.8%	82.2%	17.8%	82.2%
Missouri	18			1,500,845	834,080	662,684	4,081	171,396 R	55.6%	44.2%	55.7%	44.3%
Montana	4			194,108	113,300	78,578	2,230	34,722 R	58.4%	40.5%	59.0%	41.0%
Nebraska	8			547,128	345,745	197,950	3,433	147,795 R	63.2%	36.2%	63.6%	36.4%
Nevada	3			32,417	18,327	14,090		4,237 R	56.5%	43.5%	56.5%	43.5%
New Hampshire	4			196,757	115,404	80,715	638	34,689 R	58.7%	41.0%	58.8%	41.2%
New Jersey	14			1,549,381	926,050	616,517	6,814	309,533 R	59.8%	39.8%	60.0%	40.0%
New Mexico	3			118,077	69,708	48,211	158	21,497 R	59.0%	40.8%	59.1%	40.9%
New York	45			4,405,626	2,193,344	2,089,863	122,419	103,481 R	49.8%	47.4%	51.2%	48.8%
North Carolina	12			635,150	348,923	286,227		62,696 R	54.9%	45.1%	54.9%	45.1%
North Dakota	5			239,845	131,419	106,648	1,778	24,771 R	54.8%	44.5%	55.2%	44.8%
Ohio	24			2,508,346	1,627,546	864,210	16,590	763,336 R	64.9%	34.5%	65.3%	34.7%
Oklahoma	10			618,427	394,046	219,174	5,207	174,872 R	63.7%	35.4%	64.3%	35.7%
Oregon	5			319,942	205,341	109,223	5,378	96,118 R	64.2%	34.1%	65.3%	34.7%
Pennsylvania	38			3,150,612	2,055,382	1,067,586	27,644	987,796 R	65.2%	33.9%	65.8%	34.2%
Rhode Island		5		237,194	117,522	118,973	699	1,451 D	49.5%	50.2%	49.7%	50.3%
South Carolina		9		68,605	5,858	62,700	47	56,842 D	8.5%	91.4%	8.5%	91.5%
South Dakota	5			261,857	157,603	102,660	1,594	54,943 R	60.2%	39.2%	60.6%	39.4%
Tennessee	12			353,192	195,388	157,143	661	38,245 R	55.3%	44.5%	55.4%	44.6%
Texas	20			717,733	372,324	344,542	867	27,782 R	51.9%	48.0%	51.9%	48.1%
Utah	4			176,603	94,618	80,985	1,000	13,633 R	53.6%	45.9%	53.9%	46.1%
Vermont	4			135,191	90,404	44,440	347	45,964 R	66.9%	32.9%	67.0%	33.0%
Virginia	12			305,364	164,609	140,146	609	24,463 R	53.9%	45.9%	54.0%	46.0%
Washington	7			500,840	335,844	156,772	8,224	179,072 R	67.1%	31.3%	68.2%	31.8%
West Virginia	8			642,752	375,551	263,784	3,417	111,767 R	58.4%	41.0%	58.7%	41.3%
Wisconsin	13			1,016,831	544,205	450,259	22,367	93,946 R	53.5%	44.3%	54.7%	45.3%
Wyoming	3			82,835	52,748	29,299	788	23,449 R	63.7%	35.4%	64.3%	35.7%
United States	444	87	—	36,805,951	21,437,277	15,007,698	360,976	6,429,579 R	58.2%	40.8%	58.8%	41.2%

PRESIDENT 1924

Wisconsin's 13 electoral votes were cast for the Progressive nominees, and in eleven other states in the Midwest and West the Progressive candidates ran second. In several states the Progressive total includes votes cast for two or three elector tickets.

The full list of candidates for President and Vice-President was:

15,719,921	Calvin Coolidge and Charles G. Dawes, Republican.
8,386,704	John W. Davis and Charles W. Bryan, Democratic.
4,832,532	Robert M. LaFollette and Burton K. Wheeler, Progressive.
56,292	Herman P. Faris and Marie Caroline Brehm, Prohibition.
34,174	Frank T. Johns and Verne L. Reynolds, Socialist Labor.
33,360	William Z. Foster and Benjamin Gitlow, Communist.
24,340	Gilbert O. Nations and Leander L. Pickett, American.
2,948	William J. Wallace and John C. Lincoln, Commonwealth Land.

In addition, 4,752 scattered votes were reported from various states.

UNITED STATES

PRESIDENT 1924

State	Electoral Vote Rep.	Electoral Vote Dem.	Electoral Vote Other	Total Vote	Republican	Democratic	Progressive	Other	Plurality	Percentage Total Vote Rep.	Percentage Total Vote Dem.	Percentage Total Vote Prog.
Alabama		12		164,563	42,823	113,138	8,040	562	70,315 D	26.0%	68.8%	4.9%
Alaska												
Arizona	3			73,961	30,516	26,235	17,210		4,281 R	41.3%	35.5%	23.3%
Arkansas		9		138,540	40,583	84,790	13,167		44,207 D	29.3%	61.2%	9.5%
California	13			1,281,778	733,250	105,514	424,649	18,365	308,601 R	57.2%	8.2%	33.1%
Colorado	6			342,261	195,171	75,238	69,946	1,906	119,933 R	57.0%	22.0%	20.4%
Connecticut	7			400,396	246,322	110,184	42,416	1,474	136,138 R	61.5%	27.5%	10.6%
Delaware	3			90,885	52,441	33,445	4,979	20	18,996 R	57.7%	36.8%	5.5%
Florida		6		109,158	30,633	62,083	8,625	7,817	31,450 D	28.1%	56.9%	7.9%
Georgia		14		166,635	30,300	123,262	12,687	386	92,962 D	18.2%	74.0%	7.6%
Hawaii												
Idaho	4			147,690	69,791	23,951	53,948		15,843 R	47.3%	16.2%	36.5%
Illinois	29			2,470,067	1,453,321	576,975	432,027	7,744	876,346 R	58.8%	23.4%	17.5%
Indiana	15			1,272,390	703,042	492,245	71,700	5,403	210,797 R	55.3%	38.7%	5.6%
Iowa	13			976,770	537,458	160,382	274,448	4,482	263,010 R	55.0%	16.4%	28.1%
Kansas	10			662,456	407,671	156,320	98,461	4	251,351 R	61.5%	23.6%	14.9%
Kentucky	13			813,843	396,758	375,593	38,465	3,027	21,165 R	48.8%	46.2%	4.7%
Louisiana		10		121,951	24,670	93,218		4,063	68,548 D	20.2%	76.4%	
Maine	6			192,192	138,440	41,964	11,382	406	96,476 R	72.0%	21.8%	5.9%
Maryland	8			358,630	162,414	148,072	47,157	987	14,342 R	45.3%	41.3%	13.1%
Massachusetts	18			1,129,837	703,476	280,831	141,225	4,305	422,645 R	62.3%	24.9%	12.5%
Michigan	15			1,160,419	874,631	152,359	122,014	11,415	722,272 R	75.4%	13.1%	10.5%
Minnesota	12			822,146	420,759	55,913	339,192	6,282	81,567 R	51.2%	6.8%	41.3%
Mississippi		10		112,442	8,494	100,474	3,474		91,980 D	7.6%	89.4%	3.1%
Missouri	18			1,310,095	648,488	574,962	83,996	2,649	73,526 R	49.5%	43.9%	6.4%
Montana	4			174,425	74,138	33,805	66,124	358	8,014 R	42.5%	19.4%	37.9%
Nebraska	8			463,559	218,985	137,299	105,681	1,594	81,686 R	47.2%	29.6%	22.8%
Nevada	3			26,921	11,243	5,909	9,769		1,474 R	41.8%	21.9%	36.3%
New Hampshire	4			164,769	98,575	57,201	8,993		41,374 R	59.8%	34.7%	5.5%
New Jersey	14			1,088,054	676,277	298,043	109,028	4,706	378,234 R	62.2%	27.4%	10.0%
New Mexico	3			112,830	54,745	48,542	9,543		6,203 R	48.5%	43.0%	8.5%
New York	45			3,263,939	1,820,058	950,796	474,913	18,172	869,262 R	55.8%	29.1%	14.6%
North Carolina		12		481,608	190,754	284,190	6,651	13	93,436 D	39.6%	59.0%	1.4%
North Dakota	5			199,081	94,931	13,858	89,922	370	5,009 R	47.7%	7.0%	45.2%
Ohio	24			2,016,296	1,176,130	477,887	358,008	4,271	698,243 R	58.3%	23.7%	17.8%
Oklahoma		10		527,828	225,756	255,798	46,274		30,042 D	42.8%	48.5%	8.8%
Oregon	5			279,488	142,579	67,589	68,403	917	74,176 R	51.0%	24.2%	24.5%
Pennsylvania	38			2,144,850	1,401,481	409,192	307,567	26,610	992,289 R	65.3%	19.1%	14.3%
Rhode Island	5			210,115	125,286	76,606	7,628	595	48,680 R	59.6%	36.5%	3.6%
South Carolina		9		50,755	1,123	49,008	623	1	47,885 D	2.2%	96.6%	1.2%
South Dakota	5			203,868	101,299	27,214	75,355		25,944 R	49.7%	13.3%	37.0%
Tennessee		12		301,030	130,831	159,339	10,666	194	28,508 D	43.5%	52.9%	3.5%
Texas		20		657,054	130,794	483,381	42,879		352,587 D	19.9%	73.6%	6.5%
Utah	4			156,990	77,327	47,001	32,662		30,326 R	49.3%	29.9%	20.8%
Vermont	4			102,917	80,498	16,124	5,964	331	64,374 R	78.2%	15.7%	5.8%
Virginia		12		223,603	73,328	139,717	10,369	189	66,389 D	32.8%	62.5%	4.6%
Washington	7			421,549	220,224	42,842	150,727	7,756	69,497 R	52.2%	10.2%	35.8%
West Virginia	8			583,662	288,635	257,232	36,723	1,072	31,403 R	49.5%	44.1%	6.3%
Wisconsin			13	840,827	311,614	68,115	453,678	7,420	142,064 P	37.1%	8.1%	54.0%
Wyoming	3			79,900	41,858	12,868	25,174		16,684 R	52.4%	16.1%	31.5%
United States	382	136	13	29,095,023	15,719,921	8,386,704	4,832,532	155,866	7,333,217 R	54.0%	28.8%	16.6%

PRESIDENT 1920

The Republican figure in South Carolina includes votes cast for two elector tickets; the figure in Florida is the vote cast for the one elector candidate who ran on both Republican tickets in that state. In Washington, the total vote for minor party candidates exceeded that for the Democratic candidates, but the Democratic total was greater than that for any one of the minor party nominees.

The full list of candidates for President and Vice-President was:

16,153,115	Warren G. Harding and Calvin Coolidge, Republican.
9,133,092	James M. Cox and Franklin D. Roosevelt, Democratic.
915,490	Eugene V. Debs and Seymour Stedman, Socialist.
265,229	Parley P. Christensen and Max S. Hayes, Farmer-Labor.
189,339	Aaron S. Watkins and D. Leigh Colvin, Prohibition.
48,098	James Ferguson and William J. Hough, American.
30,594	William W. Cox and August Gillhaus, Socialist Labor.
5,833	Robert C. Macauley and Richard C. Barnum, Single Tax.

In addition, 27,309 votes were cast in Texas for a Black-and-Tan Republican elector ticket and 514 scattered votes were reported from various states.

UNITED STATES

PRESIDENT 1920

State	Electoral Vote Rep.	Electoral Vote Dem.	Electoral Vote Other	Total Vote	Republican	Democratic	Other	Plurality	Percentage Total Vote Rep.	Percentage Total Vote Dem.	Percentage Major Vote Rep.	Percentage Major Vote Dem.
Alabama		12		233,951	74,719	156,064	3,168	81,345 D	31.9%	66.7%	32.4%	67.6%
Alaska												
Arizona	3			66,803	37,016	29,546	241	7,470 R	55.4%	44.2%	55.6%	44.4%
Arkansas		9		183,871	72,316	106,427	5,128	34,111 D	39.3%	57.9%	40.5%	59.5%
California	13			943,463	624,992	229,191	89,280	395,801 R	66.2%	24.3%	73.2%	26.8%
Colorado	6			292,053	173,248	104,936	13,869	68,312 R	59.3%	35.9%	62.3%	37.7%
Connecticut	7			365,518	229,238	120,721	15,559	108,517 R	62.7%	33.0%	65.5%	34.5%
Delaware	3			94,875	52,858	39,911	2,106	12,947 R	55.7%	42.1%	57.0%	43.0%
Florida		6		145,684	44,853	90,515	10,316	45,662 D	30.8%	62.1%	33.1%	66.9%
Georgia		14		149,558	42,981	106,112	465	63,131 D	28.7%	71.0%	28.8%	71.2%
Hawaii												
Idaho	4			138,281	91,351	46,930		44,421 R	66.1%	33.9%	66.1%	33.9%
Illinois	29			2,094,714	1,420,480	534,395	139,839	886,085 R	67.8%	25.5%	72.7%	27.3%
Indiana	15			1,262,974	696,370	511,364	55,240	185,006 R	55.1%	40.5%	57.7%	42.3%
Iowa	13			894,959	634,674	227,804	32,481	406,870 R	70.9%	25.5%	73.6%	26.4%
Kansas	10			570,243	369,268	185,464	15,511	183,804 R	64.8%	32.5%	66.6%	33.4%
Kentucky		13		918,636	452,480	456,497	9,659	4,017 D	49.3%	49.7%	49.8%	50.2%
Louisiana		10		126,397	38,539	87,519	339	48,980 D	30.5%	69.2%	30.6%	69.4%
Maine	6			197,840	136,355	58,961	2,524	77,394 R	68.9%	29.8%	69.8%	30.2%
Maryland	8			428,443	236,117	180,626	11,700	55,491 R	55.1%	42.2%	56.7%	43.3%
Massachusetts	18			993,718	681,153	276,691	35,874	404,462 R	68.5%	27.8%	71.1%	28.9%
Michigan	15			1,048,411	762,865	233,450	52,096	529,415 R	72.8%	22.3%	76.6%	23.4%
Minnesota	12			735,838	519,421	142,994	73,423	376,427 R	70.6%	19.4%	78.4%	21.6%
Mississippi		10		82,351	11,576	69,136	1,639	57,560 D	14.1%	84.0%	14.3%	85.7%
Missouri	18			1,332,140	727,252	574,699	30,189	152,553 R	54.6%	43.1%	55.9%	44.1%
Montana	4			179,006	109,430	57,372	12,204	52,058 R	61.1%	32.1%	65.6%	34.4%
Nebraska	8			382,743	247,498	119,608	15,637	127,890 R	64.7%	31.3%	67.4%	32.6%
Nevada	3			27,194	15,479	9,851	1,864	5,628 R	56.9%	36.2%	61.1%	38.9%
New Hampshire	4			159,092	95,196	62,662	1,234	32,534 R	59.8%	39.4%	60.3%	39.7%
New Jersey	14			910,251	615,333	258,761	36,157	356,572 R	67.6%	28.4%	70.4%	29.6%
New Mexico	3			105,412	57,634	46,668	1,110	10,966 R	54.7%	44.3%	55.3%	44.7%
New York	45			2,898,513	1,871,167	781,238	246,108	1,089,929 R	64.6%	27.0%	70.5%	29.5%
North Carolina		12		538,649	232,819	305,367	463	72,548 D	43.2%	56.7%	43.3%	56.7%
North Dakota	5			205,786	160,082	37,422	8,282	122,660 R	77.8%	18.2%	81.1%	18.9%
Ohio	24			2,021,653	1,182,022	780,037	59,594	401,985 R	58.5%	38.6%	60.2%	39.8%
Oklahoma	10			485,678	243,840	216,122	25,716	27,718 R	50.2%	44.5%	53.0%	47.0%
Oregon	5			238,522	143,592	80,019	14,911	63,573 R	60.2%	33.5%	64.2%	35.8%
Pennsylvania	38			1,851,248	1,218,215	503,202	129,831	715,013 R	65.8%	27.2%	70.8%	29.2%
Rhode Island	5			167,981	107,463	55,062	5,456	52,401 R	64.0%	32.8%	66.1%	33.9%
South Carolina		9		66,808	2,610	64,170	28	61,560 D	3.9%	96.1%	3.9%	96.1%
South Dakota	5			182,237	110,692	35,938	35,607	74,754 R	60.7%	19.7%	75.5%	24.5%
Tennessee	12			428,036	219,229	206,558	2,249	12,671 R	51.2%	48.3%	51.5%	48.5%
Texas		20		486,109	114,658	287,920	83,531	173,262 D	23.6%	59.2%	28.5%	71.5%
Utah	4			145,828	81,555	56,639	7,634	24,916 R	55.9%	38.8%	59.0%	41.0%
Vermont	4			89,961	68,212	20,919	830	47,293 R	75.8%	23.3%	76.5%	23.5%
Virginia		12		231,000	87,456	141,670	1,874	54,214 D	37.9%	61.3%	38.2%	61.8%
Washington	7			398,715	223,137	84,298	91,280	138,839 R	56.0%	21.1%	72.6%	27.4%
West Virginia	8			509,936	282,007	220,785	7,144	61,222 R	55.3%	43.3%	56.1%	43.9%
Wisconsin	13			701,281	498,576	113,422	89,283	385,154 R	71.1%	16.2%	81.5%	18.5%
Wyoming	3			56,253	35,091	17,429	3,733	17,662 R	62.4%	31.0%	66.8%	33.2%
United States	404	127	—	26,768,613	16,153,115	9,133,092	1,482,406	7,020,023 R	60.3%	34.1%	63.9%	36.1%

ALABAMA

POPULAR VOTE FOR PRESIDENT 1920 TO 1984

		Republican		Democratic				Percentage			
								Total Vote		Major Vote	
Year	Total Vote	Vote	Candidate	Vote	Candidate	Other Vote	Plurality	Rep.	Dem.	Rep.	Dem.
1984	1,441,713	872,849	Reagan, Ronald	551,899	Mondale, Walter F.	16,965	320,950 R	60.5%	38.3%	61.3%	38.7%
1980	1,341,929	654,192	Reagan, Ronald	636,730	Carter, Jimmy	51,007	17,462 R	48.8%	47.4%	50.7%	49.3%
1976	1,182,850	504,070	Ford, Gerald R.	659,170	Carter, Jimmy	19,610	155,100 D	42.6%	55.7%	43.3%	56.7%
1972	1,006,111	728,701	Nixon, Richard M.	256,923	McGovern, George S.	20,487	471,778 R	72.4%	25.5%	73.9%	26.1%
1968 **	1,049,922	146,923	Nixon, Richard M.	196,579	Humphrey, Hubert H.	706,420	494,846 A	14.0%	18.7%	42.8%	57.2%
1964 **	689,818	479,085	Goldwater, Barry M.		Johnson, Lyndon B.	210,733	268,353 R	69.5%		100.0%	
1960	570,225	237,981	Nixon, Richard M.	324,050	Kennedy, John F.	8,194	86,069 D	41.7%	56.8%	42.3%	57.7%
1956	496,861	195,694	Eisenhower, Dwight D.	280,844	Stevenson, Adlai E.	20,323	85,150 D	39.4%	56.5%	41.1%	58.9%
1952	426,120	149,231	Eisenhower, Dwight D.	275,075	Stevenson, Adlai E.	1,814	125,844 D	35.0%	64.6%	35.2%	64.8%
1948 **	214,980	40,930	Dewey, Thomas E.		Truman, Harry S.	174,050	130,513 SR	19.0%		100.0%	
1944	244,743	44,540	Dewey, Thomas E.	198,918	Roosevelt, Franklin D.	1,285	154,378 D	18.2%	81.3%	18.3%	81.7%
1940	294,219	42,184	Willkie, Wendell	250,726	Roosevelt, Franklin D.	1,309	208,542 D	14.3%	85.2%	14.4%	85.6%
1936	275,744	35,358	Landon, Alfred M.	238,196	Roosevelt, Franklin D.	2,190	202,838 D	12.8%	86.4%	12.9%	87.1%
1932	245,303	34,675	Hoover, Herbert C.	207,910	Roosevelt, Franklin D.	2,718	173,235 D	14.1%	84.8%	14.3%	85.7%
1928	248,981	120,725	Hoover, Herbert C.	127,796	Smith, Alfred E.	460	7,071 D	48.5%	51.3%	48.6%	51.4%
1924	164,563	42,823	Coolidge, Calvin	113,138	Davis, John W.	8,602	70,315 D	26.0%	68.8%	27.5%	72.5%
1920	233,951	74,719	Harding, Warren G.	156,064	Cox, James M.	3,168	81,345 D	31.9%	66.7%	32.4%	67.6%

In 1968 other vote was 691,425 American Independent (Wallace); 10,960 American Independent of Alabama; 4,022 Prohibition and 13 scattered. In 1964 and 1948 the national Democratic candidates were not represented on the ballot. In 1964 other vote was 210,732 Unpledged Democratic and 1 scattered. In 1948 other vote was 171,443 States Rights; 1,522 Progressive and 1,085 Prohibition.

ELECTORAL COLLEGE VOTE 1920 TO 1984

Year	Total	Republican	Democratic	Other
1984	9	9	—	—
1980	9	9	—	—
1976	9	—	9	—
1972	9	9	—	—
1968	10	—	—	10 AIP
1964	10	10	—	—
1960 **	11	—	5	6 BYRD
1956 **	11	—	10	1 JONES
1952	11	—	11	—
1948	11	—	—	11 SR
1944	11	—	11	—
1940	11	—	11	—
1936	11	—	11	—
1932	11	—	11	—
1928	12	—	12	—
1924	12	—	12	—
1920	12	—	12	—

In 1960 six of the eleven Democratic electors voted in the Electoral College for Harry Flood Byrd and Strom Thurmond rather than for the national Democratic candidates. In 1956 one of the eleven Democratic electors voted in the Electoral College for Walter B. Jones and Herman Talmadge rather than for the national Democratic candidates.

ALABAMA

LAUDERDALE
LIMESTONE
MADISON
JACKSON
COLBERT
LAWRENCE
FRANKLIN
MORGAN
MARSHALL
DE KALB
MARION
WINSTON
CULLMAN
CHEROKEE
BLOUNT
ETOWAH
LAMAR
FAYETTE
WALKER
ST. CLAIR
CALHOUN
CLEBURNE
JEFFERSON
TALLADEGA
PICKENS
TUSCALOOSA
SHELBY
CLAY
RANDOLPH
BIBB
COOSA
CHAMBERS
GREENE
CHILTON
TALLAPOOSA
HALE
SUMTER
PERRY
AUTAUGA
ELMORE
LEE
MACON
DALLAS
RUSSELL
MARENGO
MONTGOMERY
LOWNDES
BULLOCK
CHOCTAW
WILCOX
BARBOUR
PIKE
BUTLER
CLARKE
CRENSHAW
MONROE
HENRY
CONECUH
DALE
WASHINGTON
COFFEE
COVINGTON
HOUSTON
ESCAMBIA
GENEVA
MOBILE
BALDWIN

ALABAMA

PRESIDENT 1984

1980 Census Population	County	Total Vote	Republican	Democratic	Other	Rep.-Dem. Plurality	Percentage Total Vote Rep.	Total Vote Dem.	Major Vote Rep.	Major Vote Dem.
32,259	AUTAUGA	11,917	8,350	3,366	201	4,984 R	70.1%	28.2%	71.3%	28.7%
78,556	BALDWIN	33,045	24,964	7,272	809	17,692 R	75.5%	22.0%	77.4%	22.6%
24,756	BARBOUR	10,161	5,459	4,591	111	868 R	53.7%	45.2%	54.3%	45.7%
15,723	BIBB	5,687	3,487	2,167	33	1,320 R	61.3%	38.1%	61.7%	38.3%
36,459	BLOUNT	12,482	8,508	3,738	236	4,770 R	68.2%	29.9%	69.5%	30.5%
10,596	BULLOCK	5,299	1,697	3,537	65	1,840 D	32.0%	66.7%	32.4%	67.6%
21,680	BUTLER	8,709	4,941	3,641	127	1,300 R	56.7%	41.8%	57.6%	42.4%
119,761	CALHOUN	38,082	23,291	12,752	2,039	10,539 R	61.2%	33.5%	64.6%	35.4%
39,191	CHAMBERS	13,463	8,024	5,302	137	2,722 R	59.6%	39.4%	60.2%	39.8%
18,760	CHEROKEE	6,319	3,225	3,029	65	196 R	51.0%	47.9%	51.6%	48.4%
30,612	CHILTON	12,678	8,243	3,924	511	4,319 R	65.0%	31.0%	67.7%	32.3%
16,839	CHOCTAW	7,349	3,960	3,373	16	587 R	53.9%	45.9%	54.0%	46.0%
27,702	CLARKE	10,811	6,282	4,452	77	1,830 R	58.1%	41.2%	58.5%	41.5%
13,703	CLAY	5,033	3,432	1,456	145	1,976 R	68.2%	28.9%	70.2%	29.8%
12,595	CLEBURNE	4,623	3,259	1,238	126	2,021 R	70.5%	26.8%	72.5%	27.5%
38,533	COFFEE	15,118	10,558	4,370	190	6,188 R	69.8%	28.9%	70.7%	29.3%
54,519	COLBERT	21,032	9,530	11,008	494	1,478 D	45.3%	52.3%	46.4%	53.6%
15,884	CONECUH	6,336	3,538	2,737	61	801 R	55.8%	43.2%	56.4%	43.6%
11,377	COOSA	4,379	2,585	1,781	13	804 R	59.0%	40.7%	59.2%	40.8%
36,850	COVINGTON	13,883	9,944	3,812	127	6,132 R	71.6%	27.5%	72.3%	27.7%
14,110	CRENSHAW	5,272	3,261	1,904	107	1,357 R	61.9%	36.1%	63.1%	36.9%
61,642	CULLMAN	23,126	14,782	7,989	355	6,793 R	63.9%	34.5%	64.9%	35.1%
47,821	DALE	13,692	10,319	3,215	158	7,104 R	75.4%	23.5%	76.2%	23.8%
53,981	DALLAS	20,718	9,585	10,955	178	1,370 D	46.3%	52.9%	46.7%	53.3%
53,658	DE KALB	19,349	12,098	7,212	39	4,886 R	62.5%	37.3%	62.7%	37.3%
43,390	ELMORE	16,077	11,694	4,198	185	7,496 R	72.7%	26.1%	73.6%	26.4%
38,440	ESCAMBIA	12,724	8,694	3,853	177	4,841 R	68.3%	30.3%	69.3%	30.7%
103,057	ETOWAH	38,781	19,243	19,074	464	169 R	49.6%	49.2%	50.2%	49.8%
18,809	FAYETTE	7,201	4,654	2,533	14	2,121 R	64.6%	35.2%	64.8%	35.2%
28,350	FRANKLIN	10,027	5,304	4,601	122	703 R	52.9%	45.9%	53.5%	46.5%
24,253	GENEVA	9,011	6,308	2,330	373	3,978 R	70.0%	25.9%	73.0%	27.0%
11,021	GREENE	5,209	1,361	3,675	173	2,314 D	26.1%	70.6%	27.0%	73.0%
15,604	HALE	6,056	2,691	3,289	76	598 D	44.4%	54.3%	45.0%	55.0%
15,302	HENRY	6,236	3,952	2,231	53	1,721 R	63.4%	35.8%	63.9%	36.1%
74,632	HOUSTON	27,485	20,834	6,488	163	14,346 R	75.8%	23.6%	76.3%	23.7%
51,407	JACKSON	14,572	6,730	7,635	207	905 D	46.2%	52.4%	46.8%	53.2%
671,324	JEFFERSON	266,547	158,362	107,506	679	50,856 R	59.4%	40.3%	59.6%	40.4%
16,453	LAMAR	5,867	3,943	1,910	14	2,033 R	67.2%	32.6%	67.4%	32.6%
80,546	LAUDERDALE	28,659	15,354	12,907	398	2,447 R	53.6%	45.0%	54.3%	45.7%
30,170	LAWRENCE	9,494	4,466	4,866	162	400 D	47.0%	51.3%	47.9%	52.1%
76,283	LEE	26,161	16,757	9,077	327	7,680 R	64.1%	34.7%	64.9%	35.1%
46,005	LIMESTONE	14,010	8,423	5,410	177	3,013 R	60.1%	38.6%	60.9%	39.1%
13,253	LOWNDES	5,252	1,629	3,567	56	1,938 D	31.0%	67.9%	31.4%	68.6%
26,829	MACON	9,499	1,543	7,857	99	6,314 D	16.2%	82.7%	16.4%	83.6%
196,966	MADISON	78,142	50,428	26,889	825	23,539 R	64.5%	34.4%	65.2%	34.8%
25,047	MARENGO	10,213	5,261	4,811	141	450 R	51.5%	47.1%	52.2%	47.8%
30,041	MARION	10,713	6,771	3,918	24	2,853 R	63.2%	36.6%	63.3%	36.7%
65,622	MARSHALL	20,391	12,330	7,704	357	4,626 R	60.5%	37.8%	61.5%	38.5%
364,980	MOBILE	130,959	81,923	47,252	1,784	34,671 R	62.6%	36.1%	63.4%	36.6%
22,651	MONROE	9,756	5,917	3,725	114	2,192 R	60.6%	38.2%	61.4%	38.6%
197,038	MONTGOMERY	75,005	43,328	31,206	471	12,122 R	57.8%	41.6%	58.1%	41.9%
90,231	MORGAN	35,543	24,103	11,324	116	12,779 R	67.8%	31.9%	68.0%	32.0%
15,012	PERRY	6,408	2,600	3,731	77	1,131 D	40.6%	58.2%	41.1%	58.9%
21,481	PICKENS	8,296	4,685	3,586	25	1,099 R	56.5%	43.2%	56.6%	43.4%
28,050	PIKE	9,953	6,231	3,541	181	2,690 R	62.6%	35.6%	63.8%	36.2%
20,075	RANDOLPH	7,515	4,940	2,439	136	2,501 R	65.7%	32.5%	66.9%	33.1%
47,356	RUSSELL	14,452	6,654	7,610	188	956 D	46.0%	52.7%	46.6%	53.4%
41,205	ST. CLAIR	14,654	10,408	4,000	246	6,408 R	71.0%	27.3%	72.2%	27.8%
66,298	SHELBY	28,068	21,858	5,884	326	15,974 R	77.9%	21.0%	78.8%	21.2%
16,908	SUMTER	6,993	2,493	4,478	22	1,985 D	35.6%	64.0%	35.8%	64.2%

ALABAMA

PRESIDENT 1984

1980 Census Population	County	Total Vote	Republican	Democratic	Other	Rep.-Dem. Plurality	Percentage Total Vote Rep.	Percentage Total Vote Dem.	Percentage Major Vote Rep.	Percentage Major Vote Dem.
73,826	TALLADEGA	23,020	14,067	8,490	463	5,577 R	61.1%	36.9%	62.4%	37.6%
38,676	TALLAPOOSA	13,666	9,045	4,458	163	4,587 R	66.2%	32.6%	67.0%	33.0%
137,541	TUSCALOOSA	44,739	28,075	16,066	598	12,009 R	62.8%	35.9%	63.6%	36.4%
68,660	WALKER	23,753	12,852	10,591	310	2,261 R	54.1%	44.6%	54.8%	45.2%
16,821	WASHINGTON	7,543	4,434	3,081	28	1,353 R	58.8%	40.8%	59.0%	41.0%
14,755	WILCOX	5,022	2,337	2,663	22	326 D	46.5%	53.0%	46.7%	53.3%
21,953	WINSTON	9,478	6,845	2,624	9	4,221 R	72.2%	27.7%	72.3%	27.7%
3,893,888	TOTAL	1,441,713	872,849	551,899	16,965	320,950 R	60.5%	38.3%	61.3%	38.7%

ALABAMA

PRESIDENT 1980

1980 Census Population	County	Total Vote	Republican	Democratic	Other	Rep.-Dem. Plurality	Percentage Total Vote Rep.	Total Vote Dem.	Major Vote Rep.	Major Vote Dem.
32,259	AUTAUGA	11,063	6,292	4,295	476	1,997 R	56.9%	38.8%	59.4%	40.6%
78,556	BALDWIN	28,353	18,652	8,448	1,253	10,204 R	65.8%	29.8%	68.8%	31.2%
24,756	BARBOUR	9,001	4,171	4,458	372	287 D	46.3%	49.5%	48.3%	51.7%
15,723	BIBB	5,623	2,491	3,097	35	606 D	44.3%	55.1%	44.6%	55.4%
36,459	BLOUNT	12,724	6,819	5,656	249	1,163 R	53.6%	44.5%	54.7%	45.3%
10,596	BULLOCK	5,637	1,446	3,960	231	2,514 D	25.7%	70.3%	26.7%	73.3%
21,680	BUTLER	8,368	3,810	4,156	402	346 D	45.5%	49.7%	47.8%	52.2%
119,761	CALHOUN	35,541	17,475	17,017	1,049	458 R	49.2%	47.9%	50.7%	49.3%
39,191	CHAMBERS	11,899	4,864	6,649	386	1,785 D	40.9%	55.9%	42.2%	57.8%
18,760	CHEROKEE	6,438	2,482	3,764	192	1,282 D	38.6%	58.5%	39.7%	60.3%
30,612	CHILTON	11,477	6,615	4,706	156	1,909 R	57.6%	41.0%	58.4%	41.6%
16,839	CHOCTAW	6,580	2,859	3,680	41	821 D	43.4%	55.9%	43.7%	56.3%
27,702	CLARKE	10,663	5,059	5,249	355	190 D	47.4%	49.2%	49.1%	50.9%
13,703	CLAY	5,747	2,764	2,858	125	94 D	48.1%	49.7%	49.2%	50.8%
12,595	CLEBURNE	4,526	2,389	2,050	87	339 R	52.8%	45.3%	53.8%	46.2%
38,533	COFFEE	13,399	6,760	6,140	499	620 R	50.5%	45.8%	52.4%	47.6%
54,519	COLBERT	20,013	6,619	12,550	844	5,931 D	33.1%	62.7%	34.5%	65.5%
15,884	CONECUH	6,181	2,948	3,102	131	154 D	47.7%	50.2%	48.7%	51.3%
11,377	COOSA	4,209	1,714	2,383	112	669 D	40.7%	56.6%	41.8%	58.2%
36,850	COVINGTON	13,608	7,014	6,305	289	709 R	51.5%	46.3%	52.7%	47.3%
14,110	CRENSHAW	5,256	2,478	2,704	74	226 D	47.1%	51.4%	47.8%	52.2%
61,642	CULLMAN	22,240	10,212	11,525	503	1,313 D	45.9%	51.8%	47.0%	53.0%
47,821	DALE	12,573	7,247	4,936	390	2,311 R	57.6%	39.3%	59.5%	40.5%
53,981	DALLAS	18,147	7,647	9,770	730	2,123 D	42.1%	53.8%	43.9%	56.1%
53,658	DE KALB	18,690	9,673	8,820	197	853 R	51.8%	47.2%	52.3%	47.7%
43,390	ELMORE	15,190	8,688	5,947	555	2,741 R	57.2%	39.2%	59.4%	40.6%
38,440	ESCAMBIA	12,053	6,513	5,148	392	1,365 R	54.0%	42.7%	55.9%	44.1%
103,057	ETOWAH	37,806	16,177	20,790	839	4,613 D	42.8%	55.0%	43.8%	56.2%
18,809	FAYETTE	6,789	3,315	3,389	85	74 D	48.8%	49.9%	49.4%	50.6%
28,350	FRANKLIN	10,763	4,448	6,136	179	1,688 D	41.3%	57.0%	42.0%	58.0%
24,253	GENEVA	9,628	4,747	4,703	178	44 R	49.3%	48.8%	50.2%	49.8%
11,021	GREENE	4,538	1,034	3,474	30	2,440 D	22.8%	76.6%	22.9%	77.1%
15,604	HALE	5,979	2,074	3,583	322	1,509 D	34.7%	59.9%	36.7%	63.3%
15,302	HENRY	5,879	2,813	2,973	93	160 D	47.8%	50.6%	48.6%	51.4%
74,632	HOUSTON	23,238	14,884	7,848	506	7,036 R	64.1%	33.8%	65.5%	34.5%
51,407	JACKSON	14,203	4,897	8,776	530	3,879 D	34.5%	61.8%	35.8%	64.2%
671,324	JEFFERSON	259,512	132,612	113,069	13,831	19,543 R	51.1%	43.6%	54.0%	46.0%
16,453	LAMAR	6,186	2,778	3,366	42	588 D	44.9%	54.4%	45.2%	54.8%
80,546	LAUDERDALE	27,243	10,467	15,379	1,397	4,912 D	38.4%	56.5%	40.5%	59.5%
30,170	LAWRENCE	8,742	2,456	6,112	174	3,656 D	28.1%	69.9%	28.7%	71.3%
76,283	LEE	21,972	10,982	9,606	1,384	1,376 R	50.0%	43.7%	53.3%	46.7%
46,005	LIMESTONE	13,384	4,574	8,180	630	3,606 D	34.2%	61.1%	35.9%	64.1%
13,253	LOWNDES	5,329	1,524	3,577	228	2,053 D	28.6%	67.1%	29.9%	70.1%
26,829	MACON	8,774	1,259	7,028	487	5,769 D	14.3%	80.1%	15.2%	84.8%
196,966	MADISON	65,072	30,604	30,469	3,999	135 R	47.0%	46.8%	50.1%	49.9%
25,047	MARENGO	9,660	4,048	5,178	434	1,130 D	41.9%	53.6%	43.9%	56.1%
30,041	MARION	10,738	5,182	5,450	106	268 D	48.3%	50.8%	48.7%	51.3%
65,622	MARSHALL	19,933	8,159	10,854	920	2,695 D	40.9%	54.5%	42.9%	57.1%
364,980	MOBILE	116,992	67,515	46,180	3,297	21,335 R	57.7%	39.5%	59.4%	40.6%
22,651	MONROE	9,072	4,615	4,262	195	353 R	50.9%	47.0%	52.0%	48.0%
197,038	MONTGOMERY	66,504	35,745	28,018	2,741	7,727 R	53.7%	42.1%	56.1%	43.9%
90,231	MORGAN	29,271	13,214	14,703	1,354	1,489 D	45.1%	50.2%	47.3%	52.7%
15,012	PERRY	6,522	2,262	4,208	52	1,946 D	34.7%	64.5%	35.0%	65.0%
21,481	PICKENS	8,182	3,582	4,504	96	922 D	43.8%	55.0%	44.3%	55.7%
28,050	PIKE	9,991	5,220	4,417	354	803 R	52.2%	44.2%	54.2%	45.8%
20,075	RANDOLPH	7,094	3,279	3,378	437	99 D	46.2%	47.6%	49.3%	50.7%
47,356	RUSSELL	13,500	4,485	8,123	892	3,638 D	33.2%	60.2%	35.6%	64.4%
41,205	ST. CLAIR	13,654	7,768	5,236	650	2,532 R	56.9%	38.3%	59.7%	40.3%
66,298	SHELBY	23,267	14,957	7,396	914	7,561 R	64.3%	31.8%	66.9%	33.1%
16,908	SUMTER	7,199	2,104	5,015	80	2,911 D	29.2%	69.7%	29.6%	70.4%

ALABAMA

PRESIDENT 1980

1980 Census Population	County	Total Vote	Republican	Democratic	Other	Rep.-Dem. Plurality	Percentage Total Vote Rep.	Percentage Total Vote Dem.	Percentage Major Vote Rep.	Percentage Major Vote Dem.
73,826	TALLADEGA	20,641	9,902	10,159	580	257 D	48.0%	49.2%	49.4%	50.6%
38,676	TALLAPOOSA	13,603	5,958	7,260	385	1,302 D	43.8%	53.4%	45.1%	54.9%
137,541	TUSCALOOSA	40,720	19,750	19,103	1,867	647 R	48.5%	46.9%	50.8%	49.2%
68,660	WALKER	22,828	8,795	13,616	417	4,821 D	38.5%	59.6%	39.2%	60.8%
16,821	WASHINGTON	6,625	3,045	3,520	60	475 D	46.0%	53.1%	46.4%	53.6%
14,755	WILCOX	7,261	2,280	4,951	30	2,671 D	31.4%	68.2%	31.5%	68.5%
21,953	WINSTON	8,436	4,981	3,368	87	1,613 R	59.0%	39.9%	59.7%	40.3%
3,893,888	TOTAL	1,341,929	654,192	636,730	51,007	17,462 R	48.8%	47.4%	50.7%	49.3%

ALABAMA

PRESIDENT 1976

1970 Census Population	County	Total Vote	Republican	Democratic	Other	Rep.-Dem. Plurality	Percentage Total Vote Rep.	Percentage Total Vote Dem.	Percentage Major Vote Rep.	Percentage Major Vote Dem.
24,460	AUTAUGA	9,338	4,512	4,640	186	128 D	48.3%	49.7%	49.3%	50.7%
59,382	BALDWIN	22,967	13,256	9,191	520	4,065 R	57.7%	40.0%	59.1%	40.9%
22,543	BARBOUR	8,690	3,758	4,730	202	972 D	43.2%	54.4%	44.3%	55.7%
13,812	BIBB	4,474	1,591	2,850	33	1,259 D	35.6%	63.7%	35.8%	64.2%
26,853	BLOUNT	10,978	4,233	6,645	100	2,412 D	38.6%	60.5%	38.9%	61.1%
11,824	BULLOCK	5,092	1,482	3,536	74	2,054 D	29.1%	69.4%	29.5%	70.5%
22,007	BUTLER	7,208	2,909	4,271	28	1,362 D	40.4%	59.3%	40.5%	59.5%
103,092	CALHOUN	32,700	11,763	20,466	471	8,703 D	36.0%	62.6%	36.5%	63.5%
36,356	CHAMBERS	11,848	5,488	6,164	196	676 D	46.3%	52.0%	47.1%	52.9%
15,606	CHEROKEE	6,256	1,492	4,668	96	3,176 D	23.8%	74.6%	24.2%	75.8%
25,180	CHILTON	10,385	4,725	5,550	110	825 D	45.5%	53.4%	46.0%	54.0%
16,589	CHOCTAW	6,972	3,033	3,911	28	878 D	43.5%	56.1%	43.7%	56.3%
26,724	CLARKE	9,006	4,126	4,737	143	611 D	45.8%	52.6%	46.6%	53.4%
12,636	CLAY	4,858	1,883	2,946	29	1,063 D	38.8%	60.6%	39.0%	61.0%
10,996	CLEBURNE	3,981	1,436	2,490	55	1,054 D	36.1%	62.5%	36.6%	63.4%
34,872	COFFEE	12,651	4,683	7,844	124	3,161 D	37.0%	62.0%	37.4%	62.6%
49,632	COLBERT	16,842	4,471	11,996	375	7,525 D	26.5%	71.2%	27.2%	72.8%
15,645	CONECUH	4,980	1,812	3,086	82	1,274 D	36.4%	62.0%	37.0%	63.0%
10,662	COOSA	3,766	1,196	2,533	37	1,337 D	31.8%	67.3%	32.1%	67.9%
34,079	COVINGTON	12,224	4,977	7,081	166	2,104 D	40.7%	57.9%	41.3%	58.7%
13,188	CRENSHAW	5,266	1,801	3,372	93	1,571 D	34.2%	64.0%	34.8%	65.2%
52,445	CULLMAN	20,055	6,899	12,961	195	6,062 D	34.4%	64.6%	34.7%	65.3%
52,938	DALE	11,531	4,996	6,346	189	1,350 D	43.3%	55.0%	44.0%	56.0%
55,296	DALLAS	16,361	7,144	8,866	351	1,722 D	43.7%	54.2%	44.6%	55.4%
41,981	DE KALB	16,437	6,597	9,759	81	3,162 D	40.1%	59.4%	40.3%	59.7%
33,535	ELMORE	13,508	6,551	6,646	311	95 D	48.5%	49.2%	49.6%	50.4%
34,906	ESCAMBIA	11,157	4,934	5,957	266	1,023 D	44.2%	53.4%	45.3%	54.7%
94,144	ETOWAH	35,750	10,333	25,020	397	14,687 D	28.9%	70.0%	29.2%	70.8%
16,252	FAYETTE	6,287	2,165	4,076	46	1,911 D	34.4%	64.8%	34.7%	65.3%
23,933	FRANKLIN	9,721	3,345	6,279	97	2,934 D	34.4%	64.6%	34.8%	65.2%
21,924	GENEVA	8,739	2,663	5,983	93	3,320 D	30.5%	68.5%	30.8%	69.2%
10,650	GREENE	3,818	903	2,900	15	1,997 D	23.7%	76.0%	23.7%	76.3%
15,888	HALE	5,394	2,034	3,236	124	1,202 D	37.7%	60.0%	38.6%	61.4%
13,254	HENRY	5,234	2,052	3,144	38	1,092 D	39.2%	60.1%	39.5%	60.5%
56,574	HOUSTON	19,738	10,672	8,787	279	1,885 R	54.1%	44.5%	54.8%	45.2%
39,202	JACKSON	15,325	3,913	10,989	423	7,076 D	25.5%	71.7%	26.3%	73.7%
644,991	JEFFERSON	217,090	113,590	99,531	3,969	14,059 R	52.3%	45.8%	53.3%	46.7%
14,335	LAMAR	5,724	1,739	3,860	125	2,121 D	30.4%	67.4%	31.1%	68.9%
68,111	LAUDERDALE	23,185	7,226	15,549	410	8,323 D	31.2%	67.1%	31.7%	68.3%
27,281	LAWRENCE	8,284	1,415	6,810	59	5,395 D	17.1%	82.2%	17.2%	82.8%
61,268	LEE	18,737	9,884	8,427	426	1,457 R	52.8%	45.0%	54.0%	46.0%
41,699	LIMESTONE	12,000	2,997	8,803	200	5,806 D	25.0%	73.4%	25.4%	74.6%
12,897	LOWNDES	5,462	1,621	3,732	109	2,111 D	29.7%	68.3%	30.3%	69.7%
24,841	MACON	7,449	1,387	5,915	147	4,528 D	18.6%	79.4%	19.0%	81.0%
186,540	MADISON	57,287	20,959	35,497	831	14,538 D	36.6%	62.0%	37.1%	62.9%
23,819	MARENGO	8,755	3,841	4,731	183	890 D	43.9%	54.0%	44.8%	55.2%
23,788	MARION	9,303	3,036	6,244	23	3,208 D	32.6%	67.1%	32.7%	67.3%
54,211	MARSHALL	20,100	6,006	13,696	398	7,690 D	29.9%	68.1%	30.5%	69.5%
317,308	MOBILE	105,876	53,835	50,264	1,777	3,571 R	50.8%	47.5%	51.7%	48.3%
20,883	MONROE	7,263	3,476	3,669	118	193 D	47.9%	50.5%	48.6%	51.4%
167,790	MONTGOMERY	54,733	29,360	24,641	732	4,719 R	53.6%	45.0%	54.4%	45.6%
77,316	MORGAN	25,986	9,058	16,547	381	7,489 D	34.9%	63.7%	35.4%	64.6%
15,388	PERRY	6,683	2,164	4,486	33	2,322 D	32.4%	67.1%	32.5%	67.5%
20,326	PICKENS	6,786	2,969	3,776	41	807 D	43.8%	55.6%	44.0%	56.0%
25,038	PIKE	9,889	4,363	5,387	139	1,024 D	44.1%	54.5%	44.7%	55.3%
18,331	RANDOLPH	6,044	2,286	3,539	219	1,253 D	37.8%	58.6%	39.2%	60.8%
45,394	RUSSELL	12,592	4,150	8,077	365	3,927 D	33.0%	64.1%	33.9%	66.1%
27,956	ST. CLAIR	10,869	4,877	5,653	339	776 D	44.9%	52.0%	46.3%	53.7%
38,037	SHELBY	16,629	9,035	7,197	397	1,838 R	54.3%	43.3%	55.7%	44.3%
16,974	SUMTER	5,689	2,191	3,457	41	1,266 D	38.5%	60.8%	38.8%	61.2%

ALABAMA

PRESIDENT 1976

1970 Census Population	County	Total Vote	Republican	Democratic	Other	Rep.-Dem. Plurality	Percentage Total Vote Rep.	Total Vote Dem.	Major Vote Rep.	Major Vote Dem.
65,280	TALLADEGA	17,608	6,425	10,577	606	4,152 D	36.5%	60.1%	37.8%	62.2%
33,840	TALLAPOOSA	13,163	5,237	7,614	312	2,377 D	39.8%	57.8%	40.8%	59.2%
116,029	TUSCALOOSA	37,006	16,021	20,275	710	4,254 D	43.3%	54.8%	44.1%	55.9%
56,246	WALKER	23,710	7,389	16,232	89	8,843 D	31.2%	68.5%	31.3%	68.7%
16,241	WASHINGTON	5,670	2,171	3,471	28	1,300 D	38.3%	61.2%	38.5%	61.5%
16,303	WILCOX	5,565	1,824	3,723	18	1,899 D	32.8%	66.9%	32.9%	67.1%
16,654	WINSTON	7,868	3,710	4,134	24	424 D	47.2%	52.5%	47.3%	52.7%
3,444,175	TOTAL	1,182,850	504,070	659,170	19,610	155,100 D	42.6%	55.7%	43.3%	56.7%

ALABAMA

PRESIDENT 1972

1970 Census Population	County	Total Vote	Republican	Democratic	Other	Rep.-Dem. Plurality	Percentage Total Vote Rep.	Percentage Total Vote Dem.	Percentage Major Vote Rep.	Percentage Major Vote Dem.
24,460	AUTAUGA	7,140	5,367	1,593	180	3,774 R	75.2%	22.3%	77.1%	22.9%
59,382	BALDWIN	18,375	15,104	2,923	348	12,181 R	82.2%	15.9%	83.8%	16.2%
22,543	BARBOUR	7,029	4,985	1,846	198	3,139 R	70.9%	26.3%	73.0%	27.0%
13,812	BIBB	4,248	3,332	837	79	2,495 R	78.4%	19.7%	79.9%	20.1%
26,853	BLOUNT	8,173	6,486	1,582	105	4,904 R	79.4%	19.4%	80.4%	19.6%
11,824	BULLOCK	4,591	2,178	2,321	92	143 D	47.4%	50.6%	48.4%	51.6%
22,007	BUTLER	6,128	4,685	1,401	42	3,284 R	76.5%	22.9%	77.0%	23.0%
103,092	CALHOUN	26,471	20,364	5,832	275	14,532 R	76.9%	22.0%	77.7%	22.3%
36,356	CHAMBERS	11,003	8,716	2,076	211	6,640 R	79.2%	18.9%	80.8%	19.2%
15,606	CHEROKEE	4,422	3,179	1,182	61	1,997 R	71.9%	26.7%	72.9%	27.1%
25,180	CHILTON	8,867	7,349	1,356	162	5,993 R	82.9%	15.3%	84.4%	15.6%
16,589	CHOCTAW	5,030	3,055	1,934	41	1,121 R	60.7%	38.4%	61.2%	38.8%
26,724	CLARKE	7,414	5,256	2,031	127	3,225 R	70.9%	27.4%	72.1%	27.9%
12,636	CLAY	4,474	3,948	507	19	3,441 R	88.2%	11.3%	88.6%	11.4%
10,996	CLEBURNE	4,014	3,420	581	13	2,839 R	85.2%	14.5%	85.5%	14.5%
34,872	COFFEE	11,336	9,076	2,160	100	6,916 R	80.1%	19.1%	80.8%	19.2%
49,632	COLBERT	16,564	11,215	4,811	538	6,404 R	67.7%	29.0%	70.0%	30.0%
15,645	CONECUH	4,296	3,214	1,042	40	2,172 R	74.8%	24.3%	75.5%	24.5%
10,662	COOSA	3,461	2,672	773	16	1,899 R	77.2%	22.3%	77.6%	22.4%
34,079	COVINGTON	10,881	9,278	1,547	56	7,731 R	85.3%	14.2%	85.7%	14.3%
13,188	CRENSHAW	4,294	3,129	1,085	80	2,044 R	72.9%	25.3%	74.3%	25.7%
52,445	CULLMAN	18,091	14,390	3,571	130	10,819 R	79.5%	19.7%	80.1%	19.9%
52,938	DALE	10,038	8,346	1,594	98	6,752 R	83.1%	15.9%	84.0%	16.0%
55,296	DALLAS	14,280	8,644	5,427	209	3,217 R	60.5%	38.0%	61.4%	38.6%
41,981	DE KALB	13,237	9,434	3,759	44	5,675 R	71.3%	28.4%	71.5%	28.5%
33,535	ELMORE	10,590	8,461	1,891	238	6,570 R	79.9%	17.9%	81.7%	18.3%
34,906	ESCAMBIA	9,591	7,883	1,598	110	6,285 R	82.2%	16.7%	83.1%	16.9%
94,144	ETOWAH	28,581	20,851	7,372	358	13,479 R	73.0%	25.8%	73.9%	26.1%
16,252	FAYETTE	5,094	4,240	836	18	3,404 R	83.2%	16.4%	83.5%	16.5%
23,933	FRANKLIN	7,812	5,877	1,840	95	4,037 R	75.2%	23.6%	76.2%	23.8%
21,924	GENEVA	6,938	5,851	1,049	38	4,802 R	84.3%	15.1%	84.8%	15.2%
10,650	GREENE	4,735	1,404	3,235	96	1,831 D	29.7%	68.3%	30.3%	69.7%
15,888	HALE	4,828	2,859	1,779	190	1,080 R	59.2%	36.8%	61.6%	38.4%
13,254	HENRY	4,291	3,414	853	24	2,561 R	79.6%	19.9%	80.0%	20.0%
56,574	HOUSTON	15,124	12,622	2,358	144	10,264 R	83.5%	15.6%	84.3%	15.7%
39,202	JACKSON	9,410	6,202	2,985	223	3,217 R	65.9%	31.7%	67.5%	32.5%
644,991	JEFFERSON	198,528	135,095	57,288	6,145	77,807 R	68.0%	28.9%	70.2%	29.8%
14,335	LAMAR	4,075	3,283	766	26	2,517 R	80.6%	18.8%	81.1%	18.9%
68,111	LAUDERDALE	20,108	14,410	5,112	586	9,298 R	71.7%	25.4%	73.8%	26.2%
27,281	LAWRENCE	5,863	4,433	1,416	14	3,017 R	75.6%	24.2%	75.8%	24.2%
61,268	LEE	15,441	11,571	3,622	248	7,949 R	74.9%	23.5%	76.2%	23.8%
41,699	LIMESTONE	8,452	6,188	2,079	185	4,109 R	73.2%	24.6%	74.9%	25.1%
12,897	LOWNDES	4,661	1,990	2,559	112	569 D	42.7%	54.9%	43.7%	56.3%
24,841	MACON	5,845	1,931	3,636	278	1,705 D	33.0%	62.2%	34.7%	65.3%
186,540	MADISON	52,984	38,899	13,108	977	25,791 R	73.4%	24.7%	74.8%	25.2%
23,819	MARENGO	7,926	5,156	2,645	125	2,511 R	65.1%	33.4%	66.1%	33.9%
23,788	MARION	6,942	5,927	986	29	4,941 R	85.4%	14.2%	85.7%	14.3%
54,211	MARSHALL	16,238	12,090	3,894	254	8,196 R	74.5%	24.0%	75.6%	24.4%
317,308	MOBILE	85,634	62,639	20,694	2,301	41,945 R	73.1%	24.2%	75.2%	24.8%
20,883	MONROE	6,890	5,155	1,636	99	3,519 R	74.8%	23.7%	75.9%	24.1%
167,790	MONTGOMERY	49,197	35,353	12,723	1,121	22,630 R	71.9%	25.9%	73.5%	26.5%
77,306	MORGAN	23,553	18,100	5,004	449	13,096 R	76.8%	21.2%	78.3%	21.7%
15,388	PERRY	5,699	2,800	2,718	181	82 R	49.1%	47.7%	50.7%	49.3%
20,326	PICKENS	6,046	4,071	1,933	42	2,138 R	67.3%	32.0%	67.8%	32.2%
25,038	PIKE	7,422	5,690	1,624	108	4,066 R	76.7%	21.9%	77.8%	22.2%
18,331	RANDOLPH	5,892	4,427	1,330	135	3,097 R	75.1%	22.6%	76.9%	23.1%
45,394	RUSSELL	9,043	6,034	2,644	365	3,390 R	66.7%	29.2%	69.5%	30.5%
27,956	ST. CLAIR	8,710	6,952	1,538	220	5,414 R	79.8%	17.7%	81.9%	18.1%
38,037	SHELBY	11,558	9,390	1,859	309	7,531 R	81.2%	16.1%	83.5%	16.5%
16,974	SUMTER	5,461	2,686	2,737	38	51 D	49.2%	50.1%	49.5%	50.5%

ALABAMA

PRESIDENT 1972

1970 Census Population	County	Total Vote	Republican	Democratic	Other	Rep.-Dem. Plurality	Percentage Total Vote Rep.	Percentage Total Vote Dem.	Percentage Major Vote Rep.	Percentage Major Vote Dem.
65,280	TALLADEGA	17,455	12,763	4,567	125	8,196 R	73.1%	26.2%	73.6%	26.4%
33,840	TALLAPOOSA	10,843	8,535	2,113	195	6,422 R	78.7%	19.5%	80.2%	19.8%
116,029	TUSCALOOSA	30,179	21,172	8,272	735	12,900 R	70.2%	27.4%	71.9%	28.1%
56,246	WALKER	18,507	14,581	3,724	202	10,857 R	78.8%	20.1%	79.7%	20.3%
16,241	WASHINGTON	4,392	3,282	1,096	14	2,186 R	74.7%	25.0%	75.0%	25.0%
16,303	WILCOX	5,945	2,641	3,254	50	613 D	44.4%	54.7%	44.8%	55.2%
16,654	WINSTON	5,771	4,971	779	21	4,192 R	86.1%	13.5%	86.5%	13.5%
3,444,165	TOTAL	1,006,111	728,701	256,923	20,487	471,778 R	72.4%	25.5%	73.9%	26.1%

ALABAMA

PRESIDENT 1968

1960 Census Population	County	Total Vote	Republican	Democratic	AIP	Other	Plurality	Percentage		
								Rep.	Dem.	AIP
18,739	AUTAUGA	7,782	606	1,553	5,523	100	3,970 A	7.8%	20.0%	71.0%
49,088	BALDWIN	18,404	2,154	1,821	14,167	262	12,013 A	11.7%	9.9%	77.0%
24,700	BARBOUR	7,946	386	1,898	5,491	171	3,593 A	4.9%	23.9%	69.1%
14,357	BIBB	4,673	263	652	3,746	12	3,094 A	5.6%	14.0%	80.2%
25,449	BLOUNT	9,086	2,013	331	6,536	206	4,523 A	22.2%	3.6%	71.9%
13,462	BULLOCK	4,347	190	1,964	2,161	32	197 A	4.4%	45.2%	49.7%
24,560	BUTLER	7,361	500	1,240	5,601	20	4,361 A	6.8%	16.8%	76.1%
95,878	CALHOUN	26,775	3,061	4,146	19,211	357	15,065 A	11.4%	15.5%	71.7%
37,828	CHAMBERS	10,636	1,082	1,358	7,885	311	6,527 A	10.2%	12.8%	74.1%
16,303	CHEROKEE	5,685	343	462	4,773	107	4,311 A	6.0%	8.1%	84.0%
25,693	CHILTON	8,902	1,602	566	6,611	123	5,009 A	18.0%	6.4%	74.3%
17,870	CHOCTAW	6,093	176	1,641	4,250	26	2,609 A	2.9%	26.9%	69.8%
25,738	CLARKE	8,626	488	1,717	6,168	253	4,451 A	5.7%	19.9%	71.5%
12,400	CLAY	5,044	706	256	4,048	34	3,342 A	14.0%	5.1%	80.3%
10,911	CLEBURNE	3,995	485	160	3,314	36	2,829 A	12.1%	4.0%	83.0%
30,583	COFFEE	10,766	682	1,071	8,885	128	7,814 A	6.3%	9.9%	82.5%
46,506	COLBERT	15,621	1,727	2,291	11,341	262	9,050 A	11.1%	14.7%	72.6%
17,762	CONECUH	5,346	186	1,151	3,828	181	2,677 A	3.5%	21.5%	71.6%
10,726	COOSA	3,811	330	623	2,830	28	2,207 A	8.7%	16.3%	74.3%
35,631	COVINGTON	13,128	831	791	11,419	87	10,588 A	6.3%	6.0%	87.0%
14,909	CRENSHAW	5,480	209	726	4,513	32	3,787 A	3.8%	13.2%	82.4%
45,572	CULLMAN	17,265	4,964	1,115	11,063	123	6,099 A	28.8%	6.5%	64.1%
31,066	DALE	9,705	607	862	8,109	127	7,247 A	6.3%	8.9%	83.6%
56,667	DALLAS	16,636	1,246	6,516	8,798	76	2,282 A	7.5%	39.2%	52.9%
41,417	DE KALB	14,859	5,314	1,274	8,144	127	2,830 A	35.8%	8.6%	54.8%
30,524	ELMORE	11,812	801	1,745	9,038	228	7,293 A	6.8%	14.8%	76.5%
33,511	ESCAMBIA	10,765	680	1,492	8,474	119	6,982 A	6.3%	13.9%	78.7%
96,980	ETOWAH	31,186	4,351	4,613	21,416	806	16,803 A	14.0%	14.8%	68.7%
16,148	FAYETTE	6,238	827	676	4,683	52	3,856 A	13.3%	10.8%	75.1%
21,988	FRANKLIN	9,096	2,524	588	5,909	75	3,385 A	27.7%	6.5%	65.0%
22,310	GENEVA	8,581	284	380	7,871	46	7,491 A	3.3%	4.4%	91.7%
13,600	GREENE	3,969	180	2,229	1,555	5	674 D	4.5%	56.2%	39.2%
19,537	HALE	5,260	266	2,003	2,934	57	931 A	5.1%	38.1%	55.8%
15,286	HENRY	5,292	84	955	4,233	20	3,278 A	1.6%	18.0%	80.0%
50,718	HOUSTON	16,536	974	1,488	13,872	202	12,384 A	5.9%	9.0%	83.9%
36,681	JACKSON	10,908	1,191	1,022	8,504	191	7,313 A	10.9%	9.4%	78.0%
634,864	JEFFERSON	205,034	39,752	55,845	106,233	3,204	50,388 A	19.4%	27.2%	51.8%
14,271	LAMAR	5,925	364	302	5,229	30	4,865 A	6.1%	5.1%	88.3%
61,622	LAUDERDALE	18,883	2,952	2,166	13,467	298	10,515 A	15.6%	11.5%	71.3%
24,501	LAWRENCE	7,529	580	650	6,253	46	5,603 A	7.7%	8.6%	83.1%
49,754	LEE	13,136	2,366	2,803	7,721	246	4,918 A	18.0%	21.3%	58.8%
36,513	LIMESTONE	10,375	870	889	8,430	186	7,541 A	8.4%	8.6%	81.3%
15,417	LOWNDES	3,263	234	1,127	1,822	80	695 A	7.2%	34.5%	55.8%
26,717	MACON	6,381	257	4,450	1,619	55	2,831 D	4.0%	69.7%	25.4%
117,348	MADISON	51,953	13,213	8,004	29,823	913	16,610 A	25.4%	15.4%	57.4%
27,098	MARENGO	9,154	457	3,479	5,185	33	1,706 A	5.0%	38.0%	56.6%
21,837	MARION	8,403	1,492	365	6,415	131	4,923 A	17.8%	4.3%	76.3%
48,018	MARSHALL	16,680	2,725	955	12,742	258	10,017 A	16.3%	5.7%	76.4%
314,301	MOBILE	91,936	10,509	18,615	61,673	1,139	43,058 A	11.4%	20.2%	67.1%
22,372	MONROE	7,324	375	1,673	5,217	59	3,544 A	5.1%	22.8%	71.2%
169,210	MONTGOMERY	46,531	6,746	12,088	27,202	495	15,114 A	14.5%	26.0%	58.5%
60,454	MORGAN	22,277	3,043	1,878	16,841	515	13,798 A	13.7%	8.4%	75.6%
17,358	PERRY	5,553	308	2,457	2,768	20	311 A	5.5%	44.2%	49.8%
21,882	PICKENS	6,328	321	1,434	4,549	24	3,115 A	5.1%	22.7%	71.9%
25,987	PIKE	8,341	658	1,565	6,038	80	4,473 A	7.9%	18.8%	72.4%
19,477	RANDOLPH	6,804	839	666	5,103	196	4,264 A	12.3%	9.8%	75.0%
46,351	RUSSELL	11,245	704	2,707	7,584	250	4,877 A	6.3%	24.1%	67.4%
25,388	ST. CLAIR	9,697	1,635	869	7,050	143	5,415 A	16.9%	9.0%	72.7%
32,132	SHELBY	10,770	1,706	1,105	7,736	223	6,030 A	15.8%	10.3%	71.8%
20,041	SUMTER	4,807	303	2,336	2,158	10	178 D	6.3%	48.6%	44.9%

ALABAMA

PRESIDENT 1968

1960 Census Population	County	Total Vote	Republican	Democratic	AIP	Other	Plurality	Percentage Rep.	Percentage Dem.	Percentage AIP
65,495	TALLADEGA	18,756	1,935	3,099	13,505	217	10,406 A	10.3%	16.5%	72.0%
35,007	TALLAPOOSA	11,821	1,205	1,331	9,043	242	7,712 A	10.2%	11.3%	76.5%
109,047	TUSCALOOSA	28,371	3,822	5,556	18,611	382	13,055 A	13.5%	19.6%	65.6%
54,211	WALKER	19,385	2,628	1,971	14,416	370	11,788 A	13.6%	10.2%	74.4%
15,372	WASHINGTON	5,683	200	902	4,545	36	3,643 A	3.5%	15.9%	80.0%
18,739	WILCOX	4,435	237	1,658	2,511	29	853 A	5.3%	37.4%	56.6%
14,858	WINSTON	5,527	2,174	258	3,032	63	858 A	39.3%	4.7%	54.9%
3,266,740	TOTAL	1,049,922	146,923	196,579	691,425	14,995	494,846 A	14.0%	18.7%	65.9%

ALABAMA

ELECTION NOTES

1984 Other vote was 9,504 Bergland (Libertarian); 4,671 Hall (Independent); 1,401 Richards (Independent); 730 Mason (Independent); 659 Serrette (Independent).

1980 Other vote was 16,481 Anderson (Independent); 15,010 Rarick (Conservative); 13,318 Clark (Libertarian); 1,743 Bubar (Statesman); 1,629 Hall (Communist); 1,303 DeBerry (Socialist Workers); 1,006 McReynolds (Socialist); 517 Commoner (Citizens).

1976 Other vote was 9,198 Maddox (Conservative); 6,669 Bubar (Prohibition); 1,954 Hall (Independent); 1,481 MacBride (Libertarian); 99 McCarthy (write-in); 70 Anderson (write-in); 1 Camejo (write-in); 1 LaRouche (write-in); 137 scattered write-in. The state-wide total for the other vote column includes these 308 write-in votes not reported by county.

1972 Other vote was 11,928 Schmitz (Conservative); 8,559 Munn (Prohibition). The Democratic candidate was also the nominee of the National Democratic Party of Alabama and 37,815 of his votes were received as the NDPA candidate. In Fayette county the votes for the Conservative and Prohibition candidates were omitted from the original canvass, but are included here.

1968 Other vote was 10,960 American Independent of Alabama (favorable to Wallace, but not recognized by him); 4,022 Munn (Prohibition); 13 scattered write-in. Of the six Presidential elector slates, the regular Democratic ticket was pledged to Wallace and two separate groups of electors were pledged to Humphrey. These two separate tickets were the Alabama Independent Democratic (142,435) and the National Democratic Party of Alabama (54,144) and the vote listed as Democratic for President in the county-by-county table is the combined vote of these two elector tickets.

ALASKA

POPULAR VOTE FOR PRESIDENT 1960 TO 1984

Year	Total Vote	Republican Vote	Republican Candidate	Democratic Vote	Democratic Candidate	Other Vote	Plurality	Percentage Total Vote Rep.	Percentage Total Vote Dem.	Percentage Major Vote Rep.	Percentage Major Vote Dem.
1984	207,605	138,377	Reagan, Ronald	62,007	Mondale, Walter F.	7,221	76,370 R	66.7%	29.9%	69.1%	30.9%
1980	158,445	86,112	Reagan, Ronald	41,842	Carter, Jimmy	30,491	44,270 R	54.3%	26.4%	67.3%	32.7%
1976	123,574	71,555	Ford, Gerald R.	44,058	Carter, Jimmy	7,961	27,497 R	57.9%	35.7%	61.9%	38.1%
1972	95,219	55,349	Nixon, Richard M.	32,967	McGovern, George S.	6,903	22,382 R	58.1%	34.6%	62.7%	37.3%
1968	83,035	37,600	Nixon, Richard M.	35,411	Humphrey, Hubert H.	10,024	2,189 R	45.3%	42.6%	51.5%	48.5%
1964	67,259	22,930	Goldwater, Barry M.	44,329	Johnson, Lyndon B.		21,399 D	34.1%	65.9%	34.1%	65.9%
1960	60,762	30,953	Nixon, Richard M.	29,809	Kennedy, John F.		1,144 R	50.9%	49.1%	50.9%	49.1%

Alaska was formally admitted to statehood in January 1959.

ELECTORAL COLLEGE VOTE 1960 TO 1984

Year	Total	Republican	Democratic	Other
1984	3	3	—	—
1980	3	3	—	—
1976	3	3	—	—
1972	3	3	—	—
1968	3	3	—	—
1964	3	—	3	—
1960	3	3	—	—

ALASKA

1984

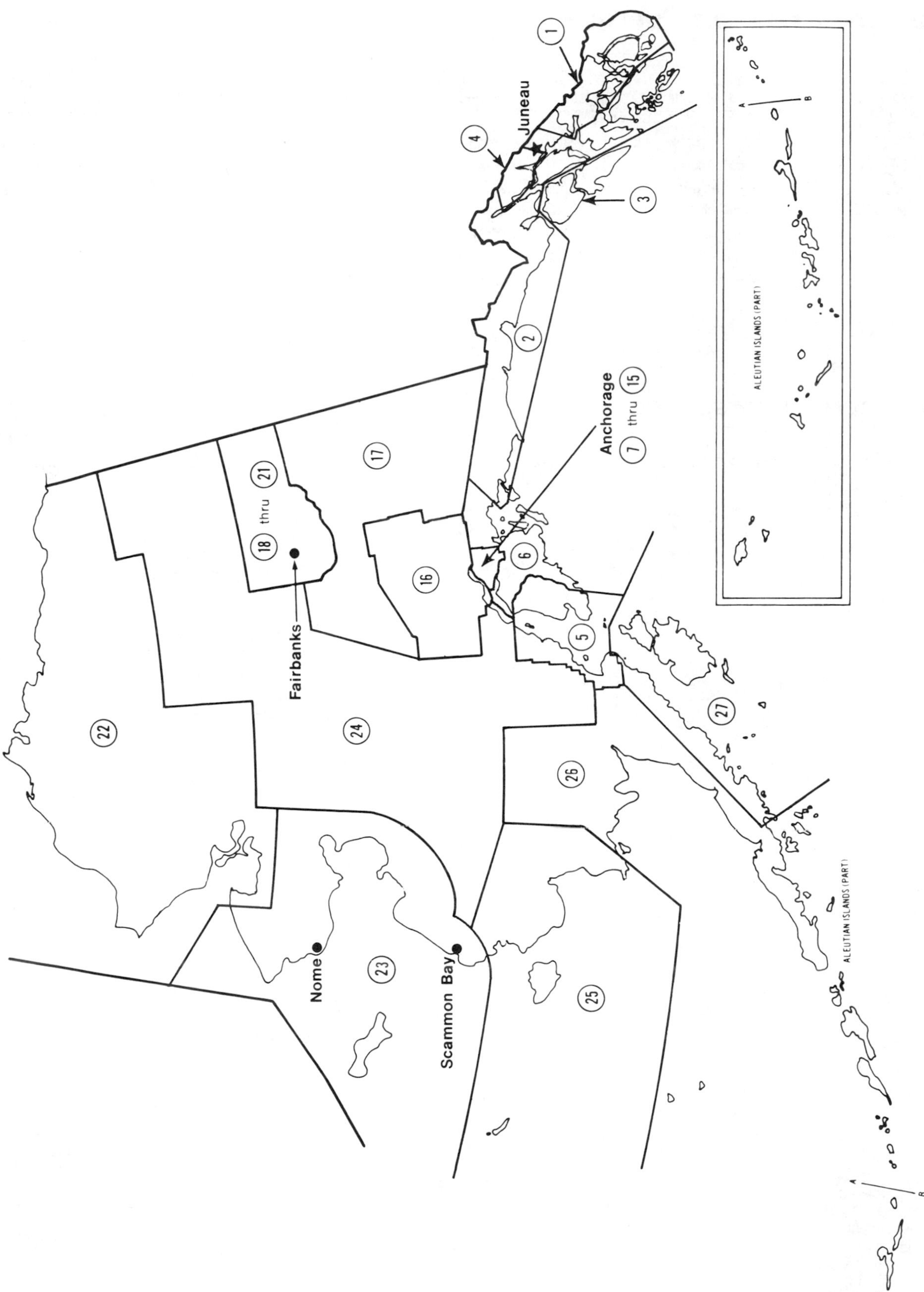

1
4
Juneau
3
2
Anchorage
7 thru 15
17
18 thru 21
16
6
5
Fairbanks
22
24
27
26
23
Nome
Scammon Bay
25
ALEUTIAN ISLANDS (PART)
ALEUTIAN ISLANDS (PART)
A
B
A
B

ALASKA

1976-1980

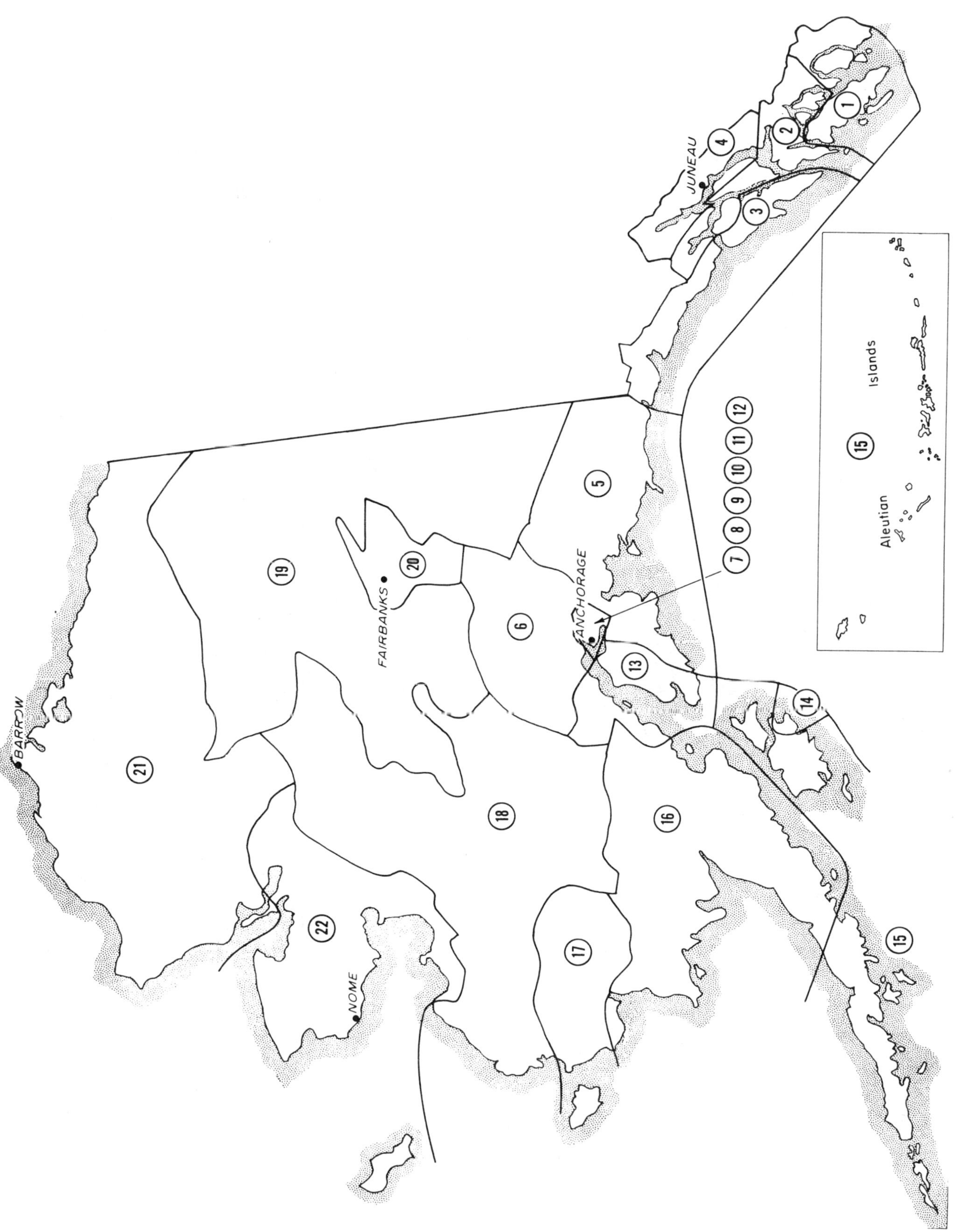

ALASKA

1972

JUNEAU
ANCHORAGE
FAIRBANKS
BARROW
NOME
Aleutian
Islands
1
2
3
4
5
6
7
8
9
10
11
12
13
14
15
16
17
18
19
20

ALASKA

1968

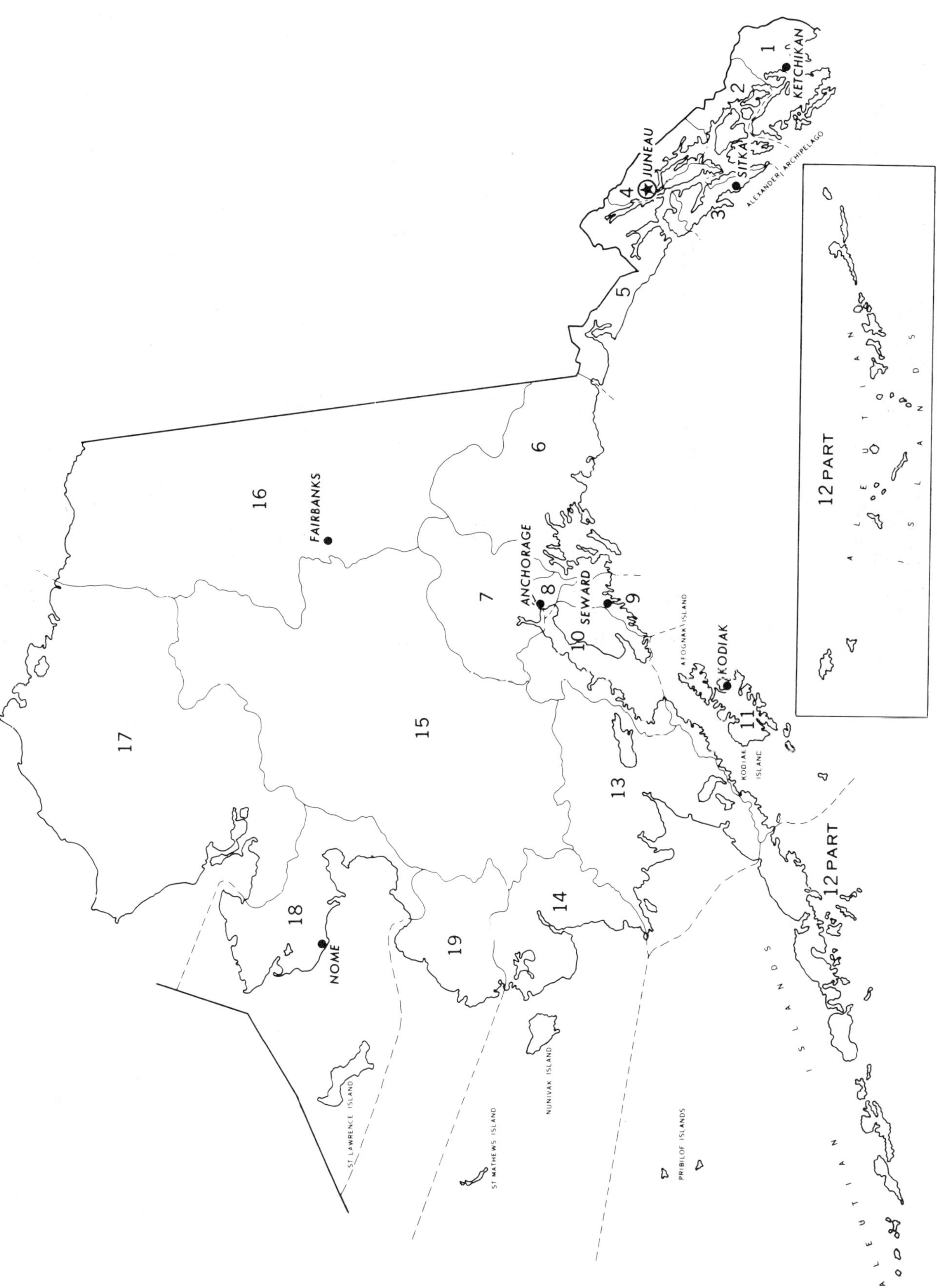

1
2
3
4
5
6
7
8
9
10
11
12 PART
12 PART
13
14
15
16
17
18
19
KETCHIKAN
SITKA
JUNEAU
ALEXANDER ARCHIPELAGO
FAIRBANKS
ANCHORAGE
SEWARD
KODIAK
AFOGNAK ISLAND
KODIAK ISLAND
NOME
NUNIVAK ISLAND
ST LAWRENCE ISLAND
ST MATHEWS ISLAND
PRIBILOF ISLANDS
ALEUTIAN ISLANDS

ALASKA

PRESIDENT 1984

1980 Census Population	District	Total Vote	Republican	Democratic	Other	Rep.-Dem. Plurality	Percentage Total Vote Rep.	Total Vote Dem.	Major Vote Rep.	Major Vote Dem.
17,940	DISTRICT 1	8,406	5,256	2,937	213	2,319 R	62.5%	34.9%	64.2%	35.8%
9,301	DISTRICT 2	4,664	2,645	1,857	162	788 R	56.7%	39.8%	58.8%	41.2%
9,266	DISTRICT 3	4,236	2,540	1,561	135	979 R	60.0%	36.9%	61.9%	38.1%
19,528	DISTRICT 4	12,939	7,322	5,293	324	2,029 R	56.6%	40.9%	58.0%	42.0%
19,068	DISTRICT 5	11,627	8,188	2,896	543	5,292 R	70.4%	24.9%	73.9%	26.1%
9,267	DISTRICT 6	4,298	2,883	1,261	154	1,622 R	67.1%	29.3%	69.6%	30.4%
8,853	DISTRICT 7	6,154	4,363	1,539	252	2,824 R	70.9%	25.0%	73.9%	26.1%
18,202	DISTRICT 8	11,660	8,603	2,752	305	5,851 R	73.8%	23.6%	75.8%	24.2%
18,005	DISTRICT 9	11,818	8,361	3,186	271	5,175 R	70.7%	27.0%	72.4%	27.6%
17,686	DISTRICT 10	10,955	7,634	3,034	287	4,600 R	69.7%	27.7%	71.6%	28.4%
17,958	DISTRICT 11	8,121	5,176	2,621	324	2,555 R	63.7%	32.3%	66.4%	33.6%
18,170	DISTRICT 12	9,754	5,348	4,063	343	1,285 R	54.8%	41.7%	56.8%	43.2%
18,907	DISTRICT 13	9,004	6,106	2,616	282	3,490 R	67.8%	29.1%	70.0%	30.0%
19,031	DISTRICT 14	10,575	7,465	2,843	267	4,622 R	70.6%	26.9%	72.4%	27.6%
18,561	DISTRICT 15	12,113	8,993	2,749	371	6,244 R	74.2%	22.7%	76.6%	23.4%
17,725	DISTRICT 16	13,548	9,942	2,935	671	7,007 R	73.4%	21.7%	77.2%	22.8%
9,112	DISTRICT 17	5,012	3,793	1,014	205	2,779 R	75.7%	20.2%	78.9%	21.1%
9,300	DISTRICT 18	6,072	4,858	967	247	3,891 R	80.0%	15.9%	83.4%	16.6%
8,934	DISTRICT 19	6,141	3,880	1,905	356	1,975 R	63.2%	31.0%	67.1%	32.9%
18,320	DISTRICT 20	9,924	6,538	2,914	472	3,624 R	65.9%	29.4%	69.2%	30.8%
9,247	DISTRICT 21	6,347	3,629	2,433	285	1,196 R	57.2%	38.3%	59.9%	40.1%
9,030	DISTRICT 22	3,492	2,075	1,319	98	756 R	59.4%	37.8%	61.1%	38.9%
9,388	DISTRICT 23	3,816	2,165	1,546	105	619 R	56.7%	40.5%	58.3%	41.7%
9,549	DISTRICT 24	3,911	2,321	1,473	117	848 R	59.3%	37.7%	61.2%	38.8%
9,698	DISTRICT 25	3,964	2,004	1,825	135	179 R	50.6%	46.0%	52.3%	47.7%
9,479	DISTRICT 26	4,366	3,019	1,216	131	1,803 R	69.1%	27.9%	71.3%	28.7%
9,592	DISTRICT 27	4,688	3,270	1,252	166	2,018 R	69.8%	26.7%	72.3%	27.7%
369,117	TOTAL	207,605	138,377	62,007	7,221	76,370 R	66.7%	29.9%	69.1%	30.9%

ALASKA

PRESIDENT 1980

1980 Census Population	District	Total Vote	Republican	Democratic	Other	Rep.-Dem. Plurality	Percentage Total Vote Rep.	Percentage Total Vote Dem.	Percentage Major Vote Rep.	Percentage Major Vote Dem.
15,138	DISTRICT 1	6,112	3,473	1,772	867	1,701 R	56.8%	29.0%	66.2%	33.8%
7,804	DISTRICT 2	3,368	1,612	1,256	500	356 R	47.9%	37.3%	56.2%	43.8%
8,742	DISTRICT 3	3,920	2,019	1,354	547	665 R	51.5%	34.5%	59.9%	40.1%
22,143	DISTRICT 4	11,489	5,345	3,899	2,245	1,446 R	46.5%	33.9%	57.8%	42.2%
10,702	DISTRICT 5	4,794	2,847	973	974	1,874 R	59.4%	20.3%	74.5%	25.5%
17,739	DISTRICT 6	8,176	5,008	1,316	1,852	3,692 R	61.3%	16.1%	79.2%	20.8%
27,827	DISTRICT 7	8,427	4,311	2,620	1,496	1,691 R	51.2%	31.1%	62.2%	37.8%
40,976	DISTRICT 8	12,605	7,432	2,860	2,313	4,572 R	59.0%	22.7%	72.2%	27.8%
12,337	DISTRICT 9	4,521	2,363	1,164	994	1,199 R	52.3%	25.7%	67.0%	33.0%
28,385	DISTRICT 10	12,388	7,659	2,778	1,951	4,881 R	61.8%	22.4%	73.4%	26.6%
37,511	DISTRICT 11	15,966	9,741	3,308	2,917	6,433 R	61.0%	20.7%	74.6%	25.4%
25,981	DISTRICT 12	12,009	7,450	2,456	2,103	4,994 R	62.0%	20.5%	75.2%	24.8%
22,241	DISTRICT 13	10,091	6,170	1,806	2,115	4,364 R	61.1%	17.9%	77.4%	22.6%
8,757	DISTRICT 14	2,983	1,473	844	666	629 R	49.4%	28.3%	63.6%	36.4%
9,472	DISTRICT 15	1,862	832	710	320	122 R	44.7%	38.1%	54.0%	46.0%
6,830	DISTRICT 16	2,286	869	1,083	334	214 D	38.0%	47.4%	44.5%	55.5%
8,790	DISTRICT 17	2,744	720	1,623	401	903 D	26.2%	59.1%	30.7%	69.3%
8,322	DISTRICT 18	2,386	769	1,327	290	558 D	32.2%	55.6%	36.7%	63.3%
9,168	DISTRICT 19	4,349	2,255	1,168	926	1,087 R	51.9%	26.9%	65.9%	34.1%
55,756	DISTRICT 20	22,999	11,673	5,310	6,016	6,363 R	50.8%	23.1%	68.7%	31.3%
8,152	DISTRICT 21	2,373	1,010	1,022	341	12 D	42.6%	43.1%	49.7%	50.3%
7,708	DISTRICT 22	2,597	1,081	1,193	323	112 D	41.6%	45.9%	47.5%	52.5%
400,481	TOTAL	158,445	86,112	41,842	30,491	44,270 R	54.3%	26.4%	67.3%	32.7%

ALASKA

PRESIDENT 1976

1970 Census Population	District	Total Vote	Republican	Democratic	Other	Rep.-Dem. Plurality	Percentage Total Vote Rep.	Total Vote Dem.	Major Vote Rep.	Major Vote Dem.
	DISTRICT 1	5,216	2,994	1,983	239	1,011 R	57.4%	38.0%	60.2%	39.8%
	DISTRICT 2	2,595	1,423	1,022	150	401 R	54.8%	39.4%	58.2%	41.8%
	DISTRICT 3	3,006	1,710	1,152	144	558 R	56.9%	38.3%	59.7%	40.3%
	DISTRICT 4	8,903	5,252	3,214	437	2,038 R	59.0%	36.1%	62.0%	38.0%
	DISTRICT 5	3,638	2,071	1,307	260	764 R	56.9%	35.9%	61.3%	38.7%
	DISTRICT 6	4,775	2,882	1,486	407	1,396 R	60.4%	31.1%	66.0%	34.0%
	DISTRICT 7	7,444	4,105	2,935	404	1,170 R	55.1%	39.4%	58.3%	41.7%
	DISTRICT 8	9,369	5,412	3,368	589	2,044 R	57.8%	35.9%	61.6%	38.4%
	DISTRICT 9	4,627	2,561	1,726	340	835 R	55.3%	37.3%	59.7%	40.3%
	DISTRICT 10	10,070	6,837	2,839	394	3,998 R	67.9%	28.2%	70.7%	29.3%
	DISTRICT 11	10,834	6,588	3,568	678	3,020 R	60.8%	32.9%	64.9%	35.1%
	DISTRICT 12	9,533	6,381	2,700	452	3,681 R	66.9%	28.3%	70.3%	29.7%
	DISTRICT 13	6,652	4,057	2,099	496	1,958 R	61.0%	31.6%	65.9%	34.1%
	DISTRICT 14	2,382	1,380	856	146	524 R	57.9%	35.9%	61.7%	38.3%
	DISTRICT 15	1,335	746	538	51	208 R	55.9%	40.3%	58.1%	41.9%
	DISTRICT 16	2,033	1,063	876	94	187 R	52.3%	43.1%	54.8%	45.2%
	DISTRICT 17	2,310	1,074	1,149	87	75 D	46.5%	49.7%	48.3%	51.7%
	DISTRICT 18	1,812	942	804	66	138 R	52.0%	44.4%	54.0%	46.0%
	DISTRICT 19	3,610	1,893	1,415	302	478 R	52.4%	39.2%	57.2%	42.8%
	DISTRICT 20	19,096	10,306	6,706	2,084	3,600 R	54.0%	35.1%	60.6%	39.4%
	DISTRICT 21	2,048	749	1,229	70	480 D	36.6%	60.0%	37.9%	62.1%
	DISTRICT 22	2,286	1,129	1,086	71	43 R	49.4%	47.5%	51.0%	49.0%
302,173	TOTAL	123,574	71,555	44,058	7,961	27,497 R	57.9%	35.7%	61.9%	38.1%

ALASKA

PRESIDENT 1972

1970 Census Population	District	Total Vote	Republican	Democratic	Other	Rep.-Dem. Plurality	Percentage Total Vote Rep.	Percentage Total Vote Dem.	Percentage Major Vote Rep.	Percentage Major Vote Dem.
11,717	DISTRICT 1	4,315	2,529	1,526	260	1,003 R	58.6%	35.4%	62.4%	37.6%
7,522	DISTRICT 2	2,490	1,386	967	137	419 R	55.7%	38.8%	58.9%	41.1%
7,558	DISTRICT 3	3,030	1,549	1,393	88	156 R	51.1%	46.0%	52.7%	47.3%
15,768	DISTRICT 4	7,457	4,277	2,968	212	1,309 R	57.4%	39.8%	59.0%	41.0%
7,435	DISTRICT 5	2,915	1,689	903	323	786 R	57.9%	31.0%	65.2%	34.8%
7,670	DISTRICT 6	3,636	2,384	849	403	1,535 R	65.6%	23.3%	73.7%	26.3%
38,818	DISTRICT 7	7,857	4,527	2,854	476	1,673 R	57.6%	36.3%	61.3%	38.7%
23,102	DISTRICT 8	8,402	5,275	2,454	673	2,821 R	62.8%	29.2%	68.2%	31.8%
38,595	DISTRICT 9	10,045	6,759	2,501	785	4,258 R	67.3%	24.9%	73.0%	27.0%
23,310	DISTRICT 10	10,632	6,882	2,854	896	4,028 R	64.7%	26.8%	70.7%	29.3%
14,770	DISTRICT 11	4,844	2,686	1,337	821	1,349 R	55.5%	27.6%	66.8%	33.2%
7,568	DISTRICT 12	1,900	1,117	727	56	390 R	58.8%	38.3%	60.6%	39.4%
7,352	DISTRICT 13	488	293	178	17	115 R	60.0%	36.5%	62.2%	37.8%
7,361	DISTRICT 14	1,956	1,042	843	71	199 R	53.3%	43.1%	55.3%	44.7%
7,671	DISTRICT 15	2,238	919	1,235	84	316 D	41.1%	55.2%	42.7%	57.3%
7,635	DISTRICT 16	2,004	902	1,004	98	102 D	45.0%	50.1%	47.3%	52.7%
45,664	DISTRICT 17	14,315	7,672	5,535	1,108	2,137 R	53.6%	38.7%	58.1%	41.9%
7,419	DISTRICT 18	2,038	1,202	640	196	562 R	59.0%	31.4%	65.3%	34.7%
7,666	DISTRICT 19	2,334	1,114	1,155	65	41 D	47.7%	49.5%	49.1%	50.9%
7,660	DISTRICT 20	2,323	1,145	1,044	134	101 R	49.3%	44.9%	52.3%	47.7%
302,173	TOTAL	95,219	55,349	32,967	6,903	22,382 R	58.1%	34.6%	62.7%	37.3%

ALASKA

PRESIDENT 1968

1960 Census Population	District	Total Vote	Republican	Democratic	AIP	Other	Plurality	Percentage Rep.	Dem.	AIP
	DISTRICT 1	4,539	2,151	1,871	517		280 R	47.4%	41.2%	11.4%
	DISTRICT 2	1,880	940	828	112		112 R	50.0%	44.0%	6.0%
	DISTRICT 3	2,497	1,110	1,236	151		126 D	44.5%	49.5%	6.0%
	DISTRICT 4	5,664	2,532	2,767	365		235 D	44.7%	48.9%	6.4%
	DISTRICT 5	1,372	590	646	136		56 D	43.0%	47.1%	9.9%
	DISTRICT 6	1,795	878	635	282		243 R	48.9%	35.4%	15.7%
	DISTRICT 7	2,318	1,075	893	350		182 R	46.4%	38.5%	15.1%
	DISTRICT 8	30,669	13,833	13,005	3,831		828 R	45.1%	42.4%	12.5%
	DISTRICT 9	908	371	449	88		78 D	40.9%	49.4%	9.7%
	DISTRICT 10	4,280	1,671	1,717	892		46 D	39.0%	40.1%	20.8%
	DISTRICT 11	2,095	986	862	247		124 R	47.1%	41.1%	11.8%
	DISTRICT 12	851	419	363	69		56 R	49.2%	42.7%	8.1%
	DISTRICT 13	1,244	591	553	100		38 R	47.5%	44.5%	8.0%
	DISTRICT 14	2,119	835	1,147	137		312 D	39.4%	54.1%	6.5%
	DISTRICT 15	2,117	964	848	305		116 R	45.5%	40.1%	14.4%
	DISTRICT 16	12,175	5,743	4,569	1,863		1,174 R	47.2%	37.5%	15.3%
	DISTRICT 17	1,845	785	962	98		177 D	42.5%	52.1%	5.3%
	DISTRICT 18	1,896	849	943	104		94 D	44.8%	49.7%	5.5%
	DISTRICT 19	897	274	559	64		285 D	30.5%	62.3%	7.1%
	NEW RESIDENT	1,874	1,003	558	313		445 R	53.5%	29.8%	16.7%
226,167	TOTAL	83,035	37,600	35,411	10,024		2,189 R	45.3%	42.6%	12.1%

ALASKA

Data for Alaska are carried by election districts. Included are four election district maps, with election years noted, so the user can relate data to geography. Population by districts excludes non-resident military and their dependents and figures are not available except for the years 1972, 1980 and 1984.

ELECTION NOTES

1984 Other vote was 6,378 Bergland (Libertarian); 843 scattered write-in.

1980 Other vote was 18,479 Clark (Libertarian); 11,155 Anderson (Independent); 857 scattered write-in. Clark, the Libertarian candidate, ran second in District 6.

1976 Other vote was 6,785 MacBride (Libertarian); 1,176 scattered write-in.

1972 Other vote was Schmitz (American Independent).

1968 Wallace on the ballot as Independent.

ARIZONA

POPULAR VOTE FOR PRESIDENT 1920 TO 1984

Year	Total Vote	Republican Vote	Republican Candidate	Democratic Vote	Democratic Candidate	Other Vote	Plurality	Percentage Total Vote Rep.	Percentage Total Vote Dem.	Percentage Major Vote Rep.	Percentage Major Vote Dem.
1984	1,025,897	681,416	Reagan, Ronald	333,854	Mondale, Walter F.	10,627	347,562 R	66.4%	32.5%	67.1%	32.9%
1980	873,945	529,688	Reagan, Ronald	246,843	Carter, Jimmy	97,414	282,845 R	60.6%	28.2%	68.2%	31.8%
1976	742,719	418,642	Ford, Gerald R.	295,602	Carter, Jimmy	28,475	123,040 R	56.4%	39.8%	58.6%	41.4%
1972	622,926	402,812	Nixon, Richard M.	198,540	McGovern, George S.	21,574	204,272 R	64.7%	31.9%	67.0%	33.0%
1968	486,936	266,721	Nixon, Richard M.	170,514	Humphrey, Hubert H.	49,701	96,207 R	54.8%	35.0%	61.0%	39.0%
1964	480,770	242,535	Goldwater, Barry M.	237,753	Johnson, Lyndon B.	482	4,782 R	50.4%	49.5%	50.5%	49.5%
1960	398,491	221,241	Nixon, Richard M.	176,781	Kennedy, John F.	469	44,460 R	55.5%	44.4%	55.6%	44.4%
1956	290,173	176,990	Eisenhower, Dwight D.	112,880	Stevenson, Adlai E.	303	64,110 R	61.0%	38.9%	61.1%	38.9%
1952	260,570	152,042	Eisenhower, Dwight D.	108,528	Stevenson, Adlai E.		43,514 R	58.3%	41.7%	58.3%	41.7%
1948	177,065	77,597	Dewey, Thomas E.	95,251	Truman, Harry S.	4,217	17,654 D	43.8%	53.8%	44.9%	55.1%
1944	137,634	56,287	Dewey, Thomas E.	80,926	Roosevelt, Franklin D.	421	24,639 D	40.9%	58.8%	41.0%	59.0%
1940	150,039	54,030	Willkie, Wendell	95,267	Roosevelt, Franklin D.	742	41,237 D	36.0%	63.5%	36.2%	63.8%
1936	124,163	33,433	Landon, Alfred M.	86,722	Roosevelt, Franklin D.	4,008	53,289 D	26.9%	69.8%	27.8%	72.2%
1932	118,251	36,104	Hoover, Herbert C.	79,264	Roosevelt, Franklin D.	2,883	43,160 D	30.5%	67.0%	31.3%	68.7%
1928	91,254	52,533	Hoover, Herbert C.	38,537	Smith, Alfred E.	184	13,996 R	57.6%	42.2%	57.7%	42.3%
1924 **	73,961	30,516	Coolidge, Calvin	26,235	Davis, John W.	17,210	4,281 R	41.3%	35.5%	53.8%	46.2%
1920	66,803	37,016	Harding, Warren G.	29,546	Cox, James M.	241	7,470 R	55.4%	44.2%	55.6%	44.4%

In 1924 Other vote was Progressive.

ELECTORAL COLLEGE VOTE 1920 TO 1984

Year	Total	Republican	Democratic	Other
1984	7	7	—	—
1980	6	6	—	—
1976	6	6	—	—
1972	6	6	—	—
1968	5	5	—	—
1964	5	5	—	—
1960	4	4	—	—
1956	4	4	—	—
1952	4	4	—	—
1948	4	—	4	—
1944	4	—	4	—
1940	3	—	3	—
1936	3	—	3	—
1932	3	—	3	—
1928	3	3	—	—
1924	3	3	—	—
1920	3	3	—	—

ARIZONA

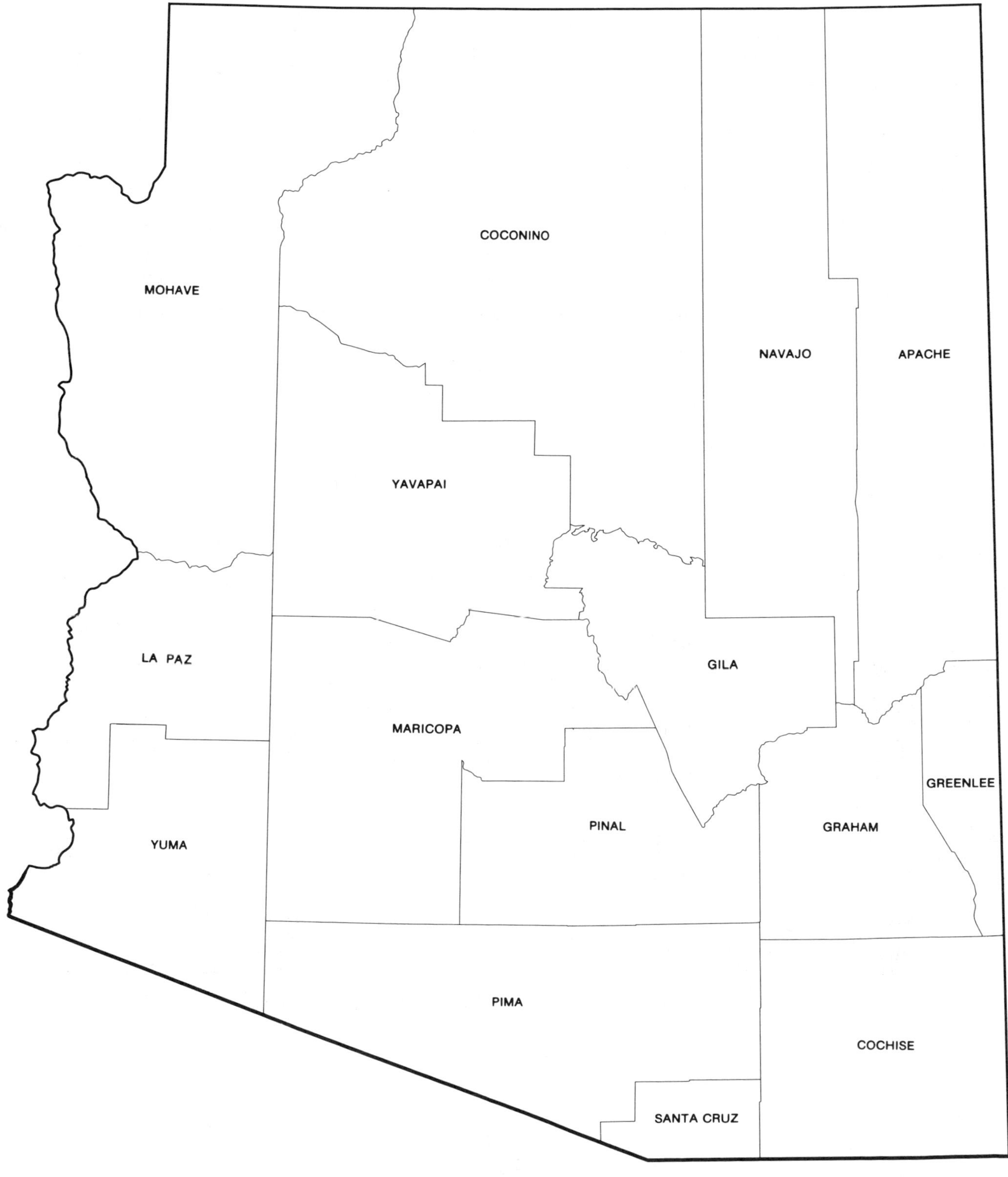
COCONINO
MOHAVE
NAVAJO
APACHE
YAVAPAI
LA PAZ
GILA
MARICOPA
GREENLEE
YUMA
PINAL
GRAHAM
PIMA
COCHISE
SANTA CRUZ

ARIZONA

PRESIDENT 1984

1980 Census Population	County	Total Vote	Republican	Democratic	Other	Rep.-Dem. Plurality	Percentage Total Vote Rep.	Percentage Total Vote Dem.	Percentage Major Vote Rep.	Percentage Major Vote Dem.
52,108	APACHE	13,032	5,638	7,277	117	1,639 D	43.3%	55.8%	43.7%	56.3%
85,686	COCHISE	26,355	16,405	9,671	279	6,734 R	62.2%	36.7%	62.9%	37.1%
75,008	COCONINO	29,735	17,581	11,528	626	6,053 R	59.1%	38.8%	60.4%	39.6%
37,080	GILA	15,249	8,543	6,509	197	2,034 R	56.0%	42.7%	56.8%	43.2%
22,862	GRAHAM	8,416	5,247	3,080	89	2,167 R	62.3%	36.6%	63.0%	37.0%
11,406	GREENLEE	3,785	1,801	1,963	21	162 D	47.6%	51.9%	47.8%	52.2%
12,557	LA PAZ	4,313	2,757	1,502	54	1,255 R	63.9%	34.8%	64.7%	35.3%
1,509,052	MARICOPA	572,273	411,902	154,833	5,538	257,069 R	72.0%	27.1%	72.7%	27.3%
55,865	MOHAVE	25,072	17,364	7,436	272	9,928 R	69.3%	29.7%	70.0%	30.0%
67,629	NAVAJO	19,578	11,379	8,017	182	3,362 R	58.1%	40.9%	58.7%	41.3%
531,443	PIMA	217,612	123,830	91,585	2,197	32,245 R	56.9%	42.1%	57.5%	42.5%
90,918	PINAL	28,619	16,464	11,923	232	4,541 R	57.5%	41.7%	58.0%	42.0%
20,459	SANTA CRUZ	6,389	3,855	2,463	71	1,392 R	60.3%	38.6%	61.0%	39.0%
68,145	YAVAPAI	34,988	24,802	9,609	577	15,193 R	70.9%	27.5%	72.1%	27.9%
77,997	YUMA	20,481	13,848	6,458	175	7,390 R	67.6%	31.5%	68.2%	31.8%
2,718,215	TOTAL	1,025,897	681,416	333,854	10,627	347,562 R	66.4%	32.5%	67.1%	32.9%

ARIZONA

PRESIDENT 1980

1980 Census Population	County	Total Vote	Republican	Democratic	Other	Rep.-Dem. Plurality	Percentage Total Vote Rep.	Percentage Total Vote Dem.	Percentage Major Vote Rep.	Percentage Major Vote Dem.
52,108	APACHE	10,595	5,991	3,917	687	2,074 R	56.5%	37.0%	60.5%	39.5%
85,686	COCHISE	22,445	13,351	7,028	2,066	6,323 R	59.5%	31.3%	65.5%	34.5%
75,008	COCONINO	26,199	14,613	7,832	3,754	6,781 R	55.8%	29.9%	65.1%	34.9%
37,080	GILA	13,399	7,405	5,068	926	2,337 R	55.3%	37.8%	59.4%	40.6%
22,862	GRAHAM	7,961	4,765	2,801	395	1,964 R	59.9%	35.2%	63.0%	37.0%
11,406	GREENLEE	3,782	1,537	2,043	202	506 D	40.6%	54.0%	42.9%	57.1%
	LA PAZ									
1,509,052	MARICOPA	486,834	316,287	119,752	50,795	196,535 R	65.0%	24.6%	72.5%	27.5%
55,865	MOHAVE	20,054	13,809	4,900	1,345	8,909 R	68.9%	24.4%	73.8%	26.2%
67,629	NAVAJO	16,882	10,790	5,110	982	5,680 R	63.9%	30.3%	67.9%	32.1%
531,443	PIMA	187,057	93,055	64,418	29,584	28,637 R	49.7%	34.4%	59.1%	40.9%
90,918	PINAL	23,258	12,195	9,207	1,856	2,988 R	52.4%	39.6%	57.0%	43.0%
20,459	SANTA CRUZ	5,340	2,674	2,089	577	585 R	50.1%	39.1%	56.1%	43.9%
68,145	YAVAPAI	28,994	19,823	6,664	2,507	13,159 R	68.4%	23.0%	74.8%	25.2%
90,554	YUMA	21,145	13,393	6,014	1,738	7,379 R	63.3%	28.4%	69.0%	31.0%
2,718,215	TOTAL	873,945	529,688	246,843	97,414	282,845 R	60.6%	28.2%	68.2%	31.8%

ARIZONA

PRESIDENT 1976

1970 Census Population	County	Total Vote	Republican	Democratic	Other	Rep.-Dem. Plurality	Percentage Total Vote Rep.	Total Vote Dem.	Major Vote Rep.	Major Vote Dem.
32,304	APACHE	10,327	3,447	6,583	297	3,136 D	33.4%	63.7%	34.4%	65.6%
61,910	COCHISE	19,883	9,921	9,281	681	640 R	49.9%	46.7%	51.7%	48.3%
48,326	COCONINO	21,418	11,036	9,450	932	1,586 R	51.5%	44.1%	53.9%	46.1%
29,255	GILA	11,962	5,136	6,440	386	1,304 D	42.9%	53.8%	44.4%	55.6%
16,578	GRAHAM	6,958	3,659	3,050	249	609 R	52.6%	43.8%	54.5%	45.5%
10,330	GREENLEE	4,247	1,532	2,601	114	1,069 D	36.1%	61.2%	37.1%	62.9%
	LA PAZ									
968,487	MARICOPA	418,841	258,262	144,613	15,966	113,649 R	61.7%	34.5%	64.1%	35.9%
25,857	MOHAVE	14,640	7,601	6,504	535	1,097 R	51.9%	44.4%	53.9%	46.1%
47,559	NAVAJO	14,560	6,796	7,323	441	527 D	46.7%	50.3%	48.1%	51.9%
351,667	PIMA	155,061	77,264	71,214	6,583	6,050 R	49.8%	45.9%	52.0%	48.0%
68,579	PINAL	20,604	9,354	10,595	655	1,241 D	45.4%	51.4%	46.9%	53.1%
13,966	SANTA CRUZ	4,738	2,312	2,265	161	47 R	48.8%	47.8%	50.5%	49.5%
36,837	YAVAPAI	21,600	12,998	7,685	917	5,313 R	60.2%	35.6%	62.8%	37.2%
60,827	YUMA	17,880	9,324	7,998	558	1,326 R	52.1%	44.7%	53.8%	46.2%
1,772,482	TOTAL	742,719	418,642	295,602	28,475	123,040 R	56.4%	39.8%	58.6%	41.4%

ARIZONA

PRESIDENT 1972

1970 Census Population	County	Total Vote	Republican	Democratic	Other	Rep.-Dem. Plurality	Percentage Total Vote Rep.	Total Vote Dem.	Major Vote Rep.	Major Vote Dem.
32,304	APACHE	6,750	3,394	3,145	211	249 R	50.3%	46.6%	51.9%	48.1%
61,910	COCHISE	18,299	11,706	6,023	570	5,683 R	64.0%	32.9%	66.0%	34.0%
48,326	COCONINO	17,389	10,611	6,250	528	4,361 R	61.0%	35.9%	62.9%	37.1%
29,255	GILA	10,372	5,673	4,295	404	1,378 R	54.7%	41.4%	56.9%	43.1%
16,578	GRAHAM	5,943	3,575	1,863	505	1,712 R	60.2%	31.3%	65.7%	34.3%
10,330	GREENLEE	3,858	1,758	2,013	87	255 D	45.6%	52.2%	46.6%	53.4%
	LA PAZ									
968,487	MARICOPA	353,000	244,593	95,135	13,272	149,458 R	69.3%	27.0%	72.0%	28.0%
25,857	MOHAVE	9,801	6,755	2,588	458	4,167 R	68.9%	26.4%	72.3%	27.7%
47,559	NAVAJO	11,572	6,999	4,003	570	2,996 R	60.5%	34.6%	63.6%	36.4%
351,667	PIMA	131,997	73,154	56,223	2,620	16,931 R	55.4%	42.6%	56.5%	43.5%
68,579	PINAL	17,559	10,584	6,404	571	4,180 R	60.3%	36.5%	62.3%	37.7%
13,966	SANTA CRUZ	4,079	2,137	1,866	76	271 R	52.4%	45.7%	53.4%	46.6%
36,837	YAVAPAI	17,201	12,277	3,977	947	8,300 R	71.4%	23.1%	75.5%	24.5%
60,827	YUMA	15,106	9,596	4,755	755	4,841 R	63.5%	31.5%	66.9%	33.1%
1,772,482	TOTAL	622,926	402,812	198,540	21,574	204,272 R	64.7%	31.9%	67.0%	33.0%

ARIZONA

PRESIDENT 1968

1960 Census Population	County	Total Vote	Republican	Democratic	AIP	Other	Plurality	Percentage Rep.	Dem.	AIP
30,438	APACHE	4,198	2,092	1,668	402	36	424 R	49.8%	39.7%	9.6%
55,039	COCHISE	16,711	7,619	6,597	2,393	102	1,022 R	45.6%	39.5%	14.3%
41,857	COCONINO	11,392	6,765	3,504	1,049	74	3,261 R	59.4%	30.8%	9.2%
25,745	GILA	9,706	3,610	4,831	1,222	43	1,221 D	37.2%	49.8%	12.6%
14,045	GRAHAM	4,929	2,327	1,726	859	17	601 R	47.2%	35.0%	17.4%
11,509	GREENLEE	3,751	1,026	2,434	276	15	1,408 D	27.4%	64.9%	7.4%
	LA PAZ									
663,510	MARICOPA	274,651	162,262	86,204	24,941	1,244	76,058 R	59.1%	31.4%	9.1%
7,736	MOHAVE	6,212	3,208	2,109	883	12	1,099 R	51.6%	34.0%	14.2%
37,994	NAVAJO	9,012	4,596	2,930	1,438	48	1,666 R	51.0%	32.5%	16.0%
265,660	PIMA	97,766	49,479	39,786	7,221	1,280	9,693 R	50.6%	40.7%	7.4%
62,673	PINAL	16,246	6,883	7,409	1,869	85	526 D	42.4%	45.6%	11.5%
10,808	SANTA CRUZ	3,533	1,702	1,557	242	32	145 R	48.2%	44.1%	6.8%
28,912	YAVAPAI	14,196	8,296	3,989	1,837	74	4,307 R	58.4%	28.1%	12.9%
46,235	YUMA	14,633	6,856	5,770	1,941	66	1,086 R	46.9%	39.4%	13.3%
1,302,161	TOTAL	486,936	266,721	170,514	46,573	3,128	96,207 R	54.8%	35.0%	9.6%

ARIZONA

The county of LaPaz was formed from the northern half of Yuma county after a vote on May 25, 1982 by the people of this region to form a new county. LaPaz became the fifteenth county in Arizona on January 1, 1983.

ELECTION NOTES

1984 Other vote was 10,585 Bergland (Libertarian); 18 Johnson (write-in); 3 Winn (write-in); 21 scattered write-in.

1980 Other vote was 76,952 Anderson (Independent); 18,784 Clark (Libertarian); 1,100 DeBerry (Socialist Workers); 551 Commoner (write-in); 25 Hall (write-in); 2 Griswold (write-in).

1976 Other vote was 19,229 McCarthy (Independent); 7,647 MacBride (Libertarian); 928 Camejo (Socialist Workers); 564 Anderson (write-in); 85 Maddox (write-in); 22 Taylor (write-in).

1972 Other vote was 21,208 Schmitz (American Independent); 366 no Presidential candidate indicated (Socialist Workers). Socialist Workers votes in Pima and Yavapai counties are omitted in the data table due to a confusion in the structure of the ballot which permitted over-voting for individual Socialist Workers electors on many thousands of ballots. With the canvassed over-vote for individual electors in Pima and Yavapai counties included, the state-wide Socialist Workers vote would be 30,945.

1968 Wallace on the ballot as American Independent. Other vote was 2,751 McCarthy (New Party); 217 Cleaver (Peace and Freedom); 85 Halstead (Socialist Workers); 75 Blomen (Socialist Labor).

ARKANSAS

POPULAR VOTE FOR PRESIDENT 1920 TO 1984

Year	Total Vote	Republican Vote	Republican Candidate	Democratic Vote	Democratic Candidate	Other Vote	Plurality	Percentage Total Vote Rep.	Percentage Total Vote Dem.	Percentage Major Vote Rep.	Percentage Major Vote Dem.
1984	884,406	534,774	Reagan, Ronald	338,646	Mondale, Walter F.	10,986	196,128 R	60.5%	38.3%	61.2%	38.8%
1980	837,582	403,164	Reagan, Ronald	398,041	Carter, Jimmy	36,377	5,123 R	48.1%	47.5%	50.3%	49.7%
1976	767,535	267,903	Ford, Gerald R.	498,604	Carter, Jimmy	1,028	230,701 D	34.9%	65.0%	35.0%	65.0%
1972	651,320	448,541	Nixon, Richard M.	199,892	McGovern, George S.	2,887	248,649 R	68.9%	30.7%	69.2%	30.8%
1968 **	619,969	190,759	Nixon, Richard M.	188,228	Humphrey, Hubert H.	240,982	50,223 A	30.8%	30.4%	50.3%	49.7%
1964	560,426	243,264	Goldwater, Barry M.	314,197	Johnson, Lyndon B.	2,965	70,933 D	43.4%	56.1%	43.6%	56.4%
1960	428,509	184,508	Nixon, Richard M.	215,049	Kennedy, John F.	28,952	30,541 D	43.1%	50.2%	46.2%	53.8%
1956	406,572	186,287	Eisenhower, Dwight D.	213,277	Stevenson, Adlai E.	7,008	26,990 D	45.8%	52.5%	46.6%	53.4%
1952	404,800	177,155	Eisenhower, Dwight D.	226,300	Stevenson, Adlai E.	1,345	49,145 D	43.8%	55.9%	43.9%	56.1%
1948 **	242,475	50,959	Dewey, Thomas E.	149,659	Truman, Harry S.	41,857	98,700 D	21.0%	61.7%	25.4%	74.6%
1944	212,954	63,551	Dewey, Thomas E.	148,965	Roosevelt, Franklin D.	438	85,414 D	29.8%	70.0%	29.9%	70.1%
1940	200,429	42,122	Willkie, Wendell	157,213	Roosevelt, Franklin D.	1,094	115,091 D	21.0%	78.4%	21.1%	78.9%
1936	179,431	32,049	Landon, Alfred M.	146,765	Roosevelt, Franklin D.	617	114,716 D	17.9%	81.8%	17.9%	82.1%
1932	216,569	27,465	Hoover, Herbert C.	186,829	Roosevelt, Franklin D.	2,275	159,364 D	12.7%	86.3%	12.8%	87.2%
1928	197,726	77,784	Hoover, Herbert C.	119,196	Smith, Alfred E.	746	41,412 D	39.3%	60.3%	39.5%	60.5%
1924	138,540	40,583	Coolidge, Calvin	84,790	Davis, John W.	13,167	44,207 D	29.3%	61.2%	32.4%	67.6%
1920	183,871	72,316	Harding, Warren G.	106,427	Cox, James M.	5,128	34,111 D	39.3%	57.9%	40.5%	59.5%

In 1968 other vote was American (Wallace). In 1948 other vote was 40,068 States Rights; 1,037 Socialist; 751 Progressive and 1 Prohibition.

ELECTORAL COLLEGE VOTE 1920 TO 1984

Year	Total	Republican	Democratic	Other
1984	6	6	—	—
1980	6	6	—	—
1976	6	—	6	—
1972	6	6	—	—
1968	6	—	—	6 AIP
1964	6	—	6	—
1960	8	—	8	—
1956	8	—	8	—
1952	8	—	8	—
1948	9	—	9	—
1944	9	—	9	—
1940	9	—	9	—
1936	9	—	9	—
1932	9	—	9	—
1928	9	—	9	—
1924	9	—	9	—
1920	9	—	9	—

ARKANSAS

BENTON
CARROLL
BOONE
MARION
BAXTER
FULTON
RANDOLPH
CLAY
WASHINGTON
MADISON
NEWTON
SEARCY
STONE
IZARD
SHARP
LAWRENCE
GREENE
CRAIGHEAD
MISSISSIPPI
INDEPENDENCE
CRAWFORD
FRANKLIN
JOHNSON
POPE
VAN BUREN
CLEBURNE
JACKSON
POINSETT
SEBASTIAN
LOGAN
CONWAY
FAULKNER
WHITE
WOODRUFF
CROSS
CRITTENDEN
ST. FRANCIS
SCOTT
YELL
PERRY
PULASKI
LONOKE
PRAIRIE
MONROE
LEE
POLK
MONTGOMERY
GARLAND
SALINE
PHILLIPS
HOWARD
HOT SPRING
GRANT
JEFFERSON
ARKANSAS
PIKE
SEVIER
CLARK
DALLAS
CLEVELAND
LINCOLN
DESHA
LITTLE RIVER
HEMPSTEAD
NEVADA
OUACHITA
CALHOUN
BRADLEY
DREW
MILLER
COLUMBIA
UNION
ASHLEY
CHICOT
LAFAYETTE

ARKANSAS

PRESIDENT 1984

1980 Census Population	County	Total Vote	Republican	Democratic	Other	Rep.-Dem. Plurality	Percentage Total Vote Rep.	Percentage Total Vote Dem.	Percentage Major Vote Rep.	Percentage Major Vote Dem.
24,175	ARKANSAS	8,008	4,804	3,153	51	1,651 R	60.0%	39.4%	60.4%	39.6%
26,538	ASHLEY	9,089	5,675	3,373	41	2,302 R	62.4%	37.1%	62.7%	37.3%
27,409	BAXTER	15,564	10,870	4,528	166	6,342 R	69.8%	29.1%	70.6%	29.4%
78,115	BENTON	32,010	24,296	7,306	408	16,990 R	75.9%	22.8%	76.9%	23.1%
26,067	BOONE	11,567	7,961	3,356	250	4,605 R	68.8%	29.0%	70.3%	29.7%
13,803	BRADLEY	5,017	2,690	2,313	14	377 R	53.6%	46.1%	53.8%	46.2%
6,079	CALHOUN	2,535	1,474	1,058	3	416 R	58.1%	41.7%	58.2%	41.8%
16,203	CARROLL	7,390	5,041	2,263	86	2,778 R	68.2%	30.6%	69.0%	31.0%
17,793	CHICOT	5,927	2,502	3,407	18	905 D	42.2%	57.5%	42.3%	57.7%
23,326	CLARK	8,853	4,185	4,638	30	453 D	47.3%	52.4%	47.4%	52.6%
20,616	CLAY	7,105	3,767	3,279	59	488 R	53.0%	46.2%	53.5%	46.5%
16,909	CLEBURNE	9,008	5,769	3,172	67	2,597 R	64.0%	35.2%	64.5%	35.5%
7,868	CLEVELAND	3,165	1,773	1,378	14	395 R	56.0%	43.5%	56.3%	43.7%
26,644	COLUMBIA	10,285	6,526	3,680	79	2,846 R	63.5%	35.8%	63.9%	36.1%
19,505	CONWAY	8,836	5,049	3,742	45	1,307 R	57.1%	42.3%	57.4%	42.6%
63,239	CRAIGHEAD	22,343	14,047	8,035	261	6,012 R	62.9%	36.0%	63.6%	36.4%
36,892	CRAWFORD	12,701	9,551	3,071	79	6,480 R	75.2%	24.2%	75.7%	24.3%
49,499	CRITTENDEN	13,934	6,663	6,520	751	143 R	47.8%	46.8%	50.5%	49.5%
20,434	CROSS	6,635	3,917	2,701	17	1,216 R	59.0%	40.7%	59.2%	40.8%
10,515	DALLAS	4,472	2,361	2,035	76	326 R	52.8%	45.5%	53.7%	46.3%
19,760	DESHA	5,878	2,696	2,918	264	222 D	45.9%	49.6%	48.0%	52.0%
17,910	DREW	6,073	3,407	2,638	28	769 R	56.1%	43.4%	56.4%	43.6%
46,192	FAULKNER	19,043	11,595	7,169	279	4,426 R	60.9%	37.6%	61.8%	38.2%
14,705	FRANKLIN	6,843	4,382	2,399	62	1,983 R	64.0%	35.1%	64.6%	35.4%
9,975	FULTON	4,223	2329	1864	30	465 R	55.2%	44.1%	55.5%	44.5%
70,531	GARLAND	33,958	21,213	11,484	1,261	9,729 R	62.5%	33.8%	64.9%	35.1%
13,008	GRANT	5,353	3,167	2,148	38	1,019 R	59.2%	40.1%	59.6%	40.4%
30,744	GREENE	11,000	6,179	4,730	91	1,449 R	56.2%	43.0%	56.6%	43.4%
23,635	HEMPSTEAD	8,268	4,904	3,327	37	1,577 R	59.3%	40.2%	59.6%	40.4%
26,819	HOT SPRING	11,546	5,629	5,836	81	207 D	48.8%	50.5%	49.1%	50.9%
13,459	HOWARD	4,832	3,079	1,746	7	1,333 R	63.7%	36.1%	63.8%	36.2%
30,147	INDEPENDENCE	11,911	7,428	4,415	68	3,013 R	62.4%	37.1%	62.7%	37.3%
10,768	IZARD	5,136	2,726	2,346	64	380 R	53.1%	45.7%	53.7%	46.3%
21,646	JACKSON	7,981	3,901	4,038	42	137 D	48.9%	50.6%	49.1%	50.9%
90,718	JEFFERSON	32,909	14,514	18,082	313	3,568 D	44.1%	54.9%	44.5%	55.5%
17,423	JOHNSON	7,827	4,720	3,056	51	1,664 R	60.3%	39.0%	60.7%	39.3%
10,213	LAFAYETTE	4,007	2,290	1,695	22	595 R	57.1%	42.3%	57.5%	42.5%
18,447	LAWRENCE	6,676	4,039	2,594	43	1,445 R	60.5%	38.9%	60.9%	39.1%
15,539	LEE	4,717	2,101	2,541	75	440 D	44.5%	53.9%	45.3%	54.7%
13,369	LINCOLN	4,272	1,860	2,406	6	546 D	43.5%	56.3%	43.6%	56.4%
13,952	LITTLE RIVER	5,295	3,155	2,090	50	1,065 R	59.6%	39.5%	60.2%	39.8%
20,144	LOGAN	8,969	5,663	3,206	100	2,457 R	63.1%	35.7%	63.9%	36.1%
34,518	LONOKE	13,142	8,425	4,636	81	3,789 R	64.1%	35.3%	64.5%	35.5%
11,373	MADISON	5,703	3,516	2,133	54	1,383 R	61.7%	37.4%	62.2%	37.8%
11,334	MARION	5,524	3,545	1,945	34	1,600 R	64.2%	35.2%	64.6%	35.4%
37,766	MILLER	13,088	8,302	4,686	100	3,616 R	63.4%	35.8%	63.9%	36.1%
59,517	MISSISSIPPI	17,766	10,180	7,548	38	2,632 R	57.3%	42.5%	57.4%	42.6%
14,052	MONROE	4,971	2,508	2,413	50	95 R	50.5%	48.5%	51.0%	49.0%
7,771	MONTGOMERY	3,757	2,221	1,497	39	724 R	59.1%	39.8%	59.7%	40.3%
11,097	NEVADA	4,152	2,352	1,783	17	569 R	56.6%	42.9%	56.9%	43.1%
7,756	NEWTON	4,173	2,749	1,414	10	1,335 R	65.9%	33.9%	66.0%	34.0%
30,541	OUACHITA	13,089	6,700	5,858	531	842 R	51.2%	44.8%	53.4%	46.6%
7,266	PERRY	3,480	2,047	1,404	29	643 R	58.8%	40.3%	59.3%	40.7%
34,772	PHILLIPS	10,723	4,686	5,946	91	1,260 D	43.7%	55.5%	44.1%	55.9%
10,373	PIKE	4,118	2,665	1,443	10	1,222 R	64.7%	35.0%	64.9%	35.1%
27,032	POINSETT	9,587	5,622	3,906	59	1,716 R	58.6%	40.7%	59.0%	41.0%
17,007	POLK	7,386	5,181	2,101	104	3,080 R	70.1%	28.4%	71.1%	28.9%
39,021	POPE	15,855	10,667	5,082	106	5,585 R	67.3%	32.1%	67.7%	32.3%
10,140	PRAIRIE	3,876	2,407	1,437	32	970 R	62.1%	37.1%	62.6%	37.4%
340,613	PULASKI	133,418	77,651	54,237	1,530	23,414 R	58.2%	40.7%	58.9%	41.1%

ARKANSAS

PRESIDENT 1984

1980 Census Population	County	Total Vote	Republican	Democratic	Other	Rep.-Dem. Plurality	Percentage Total Vote Rep.	Total Vote Dem.	Major Vote Rep.	Major Vote Dem.
16,834	RANDOLPH	5,733	3,188	2,507	38	681 R	55.6%	43.7%	56.0%	44.0%
30,858	ST. FRANCIS	10,322	5,378	4,866	78	512 R	52.1%	47.1%	52.5%	47.5%
53,161	SALINE	19,297	11,709	6,977	611	4,732 R	60.7%	36.2%	62.7%	37.3%
9,685	SCOTT	4,709	3,066	1,609	34	1,457 R	65.1%	34.2%	65.6%	34.4%
8,847	SEARCY	4,201	2,819	1,313	69	1,506 R	67.1%	31.3%	68.2%	31.8%
95,172	SEBASTIAN	36,817	27,595	8,688	534	18,907 R	75.0%	23.6%	76.1%	23.9%
14,060	SEVIER	5,271	3,302	1,942	27	1,360 R	62.6%	36.8%	63.0%	37.0%
14,607	SHARP	6,930	4,392	2,492	46	1,900 R	63.4%	36.0%	63.8%	36.2%
9,022	STONE	4,045	2,325	1,654	66	671 R	57.5%	40.9%	58.4%	41.6%
48,573	UNION	18,759	12,333	6,208	218	6,125 R	65.7%	33.1%	66.5%	33.5%
13,357	VAN BUREN	6,659	4,060	2,529	70	1,531 R	61.0%	38.0%	61.6%	38.4%
100,494	WASHINGTON	36,698	24,993	11,319	386	13,674 R	68.1%	30.8%	68.8%	31.2%
50,835	WHITE	19,435	12,566	6,603	266	5,963 R	64.7%	34.0%	65.6%	34.4%
11,222	WOODRUFF	3,759	1,675	2,055	29	380 D	44.6%	54.7%	44.9%	55.1%
17,026	YELL	6,802	4,051	2,679	72	1,372 R	59.6%	39.4%	60.2%	39.8%
2,286,435	TOTAL	884,406	534,774	338,646	10,986	196,128 R	60.5%	38.3%	61.2%	38.8%

ARKANSAS

PRESIDENT 1980

1980 Census Population	County	Total Vote	Republican	Democratic	Other	Rep.-Dem. Plurality	Percentage Total Vote Rep.	Total Vote Dem.	Major Vote Rep.	Major Vote Dem.
24,175	ARKANSAS	7,985	3,409	4,303	273	894 D	42.7%	53.9%	44.2%	55.8%
26,538	ASHLEY	8,748	3,960	4,552	236	592 D	45.3%	52.0%	46.5%	53.5%
27,409	BAXTER	15,147	9,684	4,789	674	4,895 R	63.9%	31.6%	66.9%	33.1%
78,115	BENTON	29,440	18,830	9,231	1,379	9,599 R	64.0%	31.4%	67.1%	32.9%
26,067	BOONE	12,088	6,778	4,576	734	2,202 R	56.1%	37.9%	59.7%	40.3%
13,803	BRADLEY	4,890	1,650	3,139	101	1,489 D	33.7%	64.2%	34.5%	65.5%
6,079	CALHOUN	2,396	896	1,438	62	542 D	37.4%	60.0%	38.4%	61.6%
16,203	CARROLL	7,728	4,273	2,977	478	1,296 R	55.3%	38.5%	58.9%	41.1%
17,793	CHICOT	5,776	2,239	3,445	92	1,206 D	38.8%	59.6%	39.4%	60.6%
23,326	CLARK	9,153	2,743	6,122	288	3,379 D	30.0%	66.9%	30.9%	69.1%
20,616	CLAY	7,330	3,091	3,985	254	894 D	42.2%	54.4%	43.7%	56.3%
16,909	CLEBURNE	8,355	4,042	4,021	292	21 R	48.4%	48.1%	50.1%	49.9%
7,868	CLEVELAND	3,058	1,124	1,856	78	732 D	36.8%	60.7%	37.7%	62.3%
26,644	COLUMBIA	9,967	5,259	4,445	263	814 R	52.8%	44.6%	54.2%	45.8%
19,505	CONWAY	9,189	4,145	4,698	346	553 D	45.1%	51.1%	46.9%	53.1%
63,239	CRAIGHEAD	21,456	11,010	9,231	1,215	1,779 R	51.3%	43.0%	54.4%	45.6%
36,892	CRAWFORD	12,899	8,542	3,948	409	4,594 R	66.2%	30.6%	68.4%	31.6%
49,499	CRITTENDEN	13,823	6,248	7,022	553	774 D	45.2%	50.8%	47.1%	52.9%
20,434	CROSS	6,492	2,895	3,471	126	576 D	44.6%	53.5%	45.5%	54.5%
10,515	DALLAS	4,539	1,596	2,838	105	1,242 D	35.2%	62.5%	36.0%	64.0%
19,760	DESHA	6,037	2,057	3,748	232	1,691 D	34.1%	62.1%	35.4%	64.6%
17,910	DREW	6,184	2,272	3,757	155	1,485 D	36.7%	60.8%	37.7%	62.3%
46,192	FAULKNER	17,073	7,544	8,528	1,001	984 D	44.2%	50.0%	46.9%	53.1%
14,705	FRANKLIN	6,426	3,448	2,716	262	732 R	53.7%	42.3%	55.9%	44.1%
9,975	FULTON	4,257	2,101	2,037	119	64 R	49.4%	47.9%	50.8%	49.2%
70,531	GARLAND	29,717	15,739	12,515	1,463	3,224 R	53.0%	42.1%	55.7%	44.3%
13,008	GRANT	5,276	2,007	3,078	191	1,071 D	38.0%	58.3%	39.5%	60.5%
30,744	GREENE	10,841	4,514	5,996	331	1,482 D	41.6%	55.3%	42.9%	57.1%
23,635	HEMPSTEAD	8,628	3,852	4,671	105	819 D	44.6%	54.1%	45.2%	54.8%
26,819	HOT SPRINGS	10,817	3,561	6,897	359	3,336 D	32.9%	63.8%	34.1%	65.9%
13,459	HOWARD	5,064	2,386	2,564	114	178 D	47.1%	50.6%	48.2%	51.8%
30,147	INDEPENDENCE	11,125	5,076	5,683	366	607 D	45.6%	51.1%	47.2%	52.8%
10,768	IZARD	5,254	2,266	2,750	238	484 D	43.1%	52.3%	45.2%	54.8%
21,646	JACKSON	8,081	3,191	4,651	239	1,460 D	39.5%	57.6%	40.7%	59.3%
90,718	JEFFERSON	30,046	10,697	17,292	2,057	6,595 D	35.6%	57.6%	38.2%	61.8%
17,423	JOHNSON	7,636	3,619	3,709	308	90 D	47.4%	48.6%	49.4%	50.6%
10,213	LAFAYETTE	3,776	1,756	1,947	73	191 D	46.5%	51.6%	47.4%	52.6%
18,447	LAWRENCE	6,963	3,245	3,547	171	302 D	46.6%	50.9%	47.8%	52.2%
15,539	LEE	4,876	1,711	3,103	62	1,392 D	35.1%	63.6%	35.5%	64.5%
13,369	LINCOLN	3,849	1,243	2,517	89	1,274 D	32.3%	65.4%	33.1%	66.9%
13,952	LITTLE RIVER	5,024	2,272	2,631	121	359 D	45.2%	52.4%	46.3%	53.7%
20,144	LOGAN	8,913	4,511	4,098	304	413 R	50.6%	46.0%	52.4%	47.6%
34,518	LONOKE	11,585	5,619	5,605	361	14 R	48.5%	48.4%	50.1%	49.9%
11,373	MADISON	5,835	3,180	2,434	221	746 R	54.5%	41.7%	56.6%	43.4%
11,334	MARION	5,356	3,059	2,046	251	1,013 R	57.1%	38.2%	59.9%	40.1%
37,766	MILLER	12,921	6,770	5,996	155	774 R	52.4%	46.4%	53.0%	47.0%
59,517	MISSISSIPPI	16,417	7,170	8,908	339	1,738 D	43.7%	54.3%	44.6%	55.4%
14,052	MONROE	4,829	2,027	2,686	116	659 D	42.0%	55.6%	43.0%	57.0%
7,771	MONTGOMERY	3,612	1,585	1,878	149	293 D	43.9%	52.0%	45.8%	54.2%
11,097	NEVADA	4,440	1,697	2,631	112	934 D	38.2%	59.3%	39.2%	60.8%
7,756	NEWTON	4,033	2,423	1,436	174	987 R	60.1%	35.6%	62.8%	37.2%
30,541	OUACHITA	12,208	4,329	7,152	727	2,823 D	35.5%	58.6%	37.7%	62.3%
7,266	PERRY	3,186	1,459	1,606	121	147 D	45.8%	50.4%	47.6%	52.4%
34,772	PHILLIPS	11,146	4,270	6,642	234	2,372 D	38.3%	59.6%	39.1%	60.9%
10,373	PIKE	4,097	1,916	2,094	87	178 D	46.8%	51.1%	47.8%	52.2%
27,032	POINSETT	9,180	4,040	4,894	246	854 D	44.0%	53.3%	45.2%	54.8%
17,007	POLK	6,824	3,993	2,617	214	1,376 R	58.5%	38.3%	60.4%	39.6%
39,021	POPE	14,230	7,217	6,364	649	853 R	50.7%	44.7%	53.1%	46.9%
10,140	PRAIRIE	3,895	1,855	1,928	112	73 D	47.6%	49.5%	49.0%	51.0%
340,613	PULASKI	112,937	52,125	54,839	5,973	2,714 D	46.2%	48.6%	48.7%	51.3%

ARKANSAS

PRESIDENT 1980

1980 Census Population	County	Total Vote	Republican	Democratic	Other	Rep.-Dem. Plurality	Percentage Total Vote Rep.	Percentage Total Vote Dem.	Percentage Major Vote Rep.	Percentage Major Vote Dem.
16,834	RANDOLPH	5,929	2,579	3,070	280	491 D	43.5%	51.8%	45.7%	54.3%
30,858	ST. FRANCIS	10,487	4,485	5,816	186	1,331 D	42.8%	55.5%	43.5%	56.5%
53,161	SALINE	19,555	8,330	10,368	857	2,038 D	42.6%	53.0%	44.6%	55.4%
9,685	SCOTT	4,626	2,228	2,236	162	8 D	48.2%	48.3%	49.9%	50.1%
8,847	SEARCY	4,183	2,459	1,536	188	923 R	58.8%	36.7%	61.6%	38.4%
95,172	SEBASTIAN	36,879	23,403	10,141	3,335	13,262 R	63.5%	27.5%	69.8%	30.2%
14,060	SEVIER	5,497	2,502	2,854	141	352 D	45.5%	51.9%	46.7%	53.3%
14,607	SHARP	6,416	3,420	2,774	222	646 R	53.3%	43.2%	55.2%	44.8%
9,022	STONE	3,975	1,793	1,968	214	175 D	45.1%	49.5%	47.7%	52.3%
48,573	UNION	17,063	9,401	6,852	810	2,549 R	55.1%	40.2%	57.8%	42.2%
13,357	VAN BUREN	6,292	3,090	2,968	234	122 R	49.1%	47.2%	51.0%	49.0%
100,494	WASHINGTON	35,421	20,788	12,276	2,357	8,512 R	58.7%	34.7%	62.9%	37.1%
50,835	WHITE	17,313	8,079	8,750	484	671 D	46.7%	50.5%	48.0%	52.0%
11,222	WOODRUFF	3,756	1,204	2,452	100	1,248 D	32.1%	65.3%	32.9%	67.1%
17,026	YELL	7,137	3,187	3,702	248	515 D	44.7%	51.9%	46.3%	53.7%
2,286,435	TOTAL	837,582	403,164	398,041	36,377	5,123 R	48.1%	47.5%	50.3%	49.7%

ARKANSAS

PRESIDENT 1976

1970 Census Population	County	Total Vote	Republican	Democratic	Other	Rep.-Dem. Plurality	Percentage Total Vote Rep.	Total Vote Dem.	Major Vote Rep.	Major Vote Dem.
23,347	ARKANSAS	8,120	2,480	5,640		3,160 D	30.5%	69.5%	30.5%	69.5%
24,976	ASHLEY	8,354	3,092	5,253	9	2,161 D	37.0%	62.9%	37.1%	62.9%
15,319	BAXTER	11,651	5,885	5,766		119 R	50.5%	49.5%	50.5%	49.5%
50,476	BENTON	24,017	12,670	11,289	58	1,381 R	52.8%	47.0%	52.9%	47.1%
19,073	BOONE	9,347	3,959	5,388		1,429 D	42.4%	57.6%	42.4%	57.6%
12,778	BRADLEY	4,701	1,134	3,567		2,433 D	24.1%	75.9%	24.1%	75.9%
5,573	CALHOUN	2,514	495	2,014	5	1,519 D	19.7%	80.1%	19.7%	80.3%
12,301	CARROLL	6,650	2,804	3,791	55	987 D	42.2%	57.0%	42.5%	57.5%
18,164	CHICOT	5,495	1,621	3,868	6	2,247 D	29.5%	70.4%	29.5%	70.5%
21,537	CLARK	8,479	1,816	6,641	22	4,825 D	21.4%	78.3%	21.5%	78.5%
18,771	CLAY	7,557	1,893	5,664		3,771 D	25.0%	75.0%	25.0%	75.0%
10,349	CLEBURNE	7,731	1,992	5,726	13	3,734 D	25.8%	74.1%	25.8%	74.2%
6,605	CLEVELAND	2,966	646	2,320		1,674 D	21.8%	78.2%	21.8%	78.2%
25,952	COLUMBIA	9,001	4,287	4,708	6	421 D	47.6%	52.3%	47.7%	52.3%
16,805	CONWAY	8,629	2,177	6,443	9	4,266 D	25.2%	74.7%	25.3%	74.7%
52,068	CRAIGHEAD	20,053	6,213	13,840		7,627 D	31.0%	69.0%	31.0%	69.0%
25,677	CRAWFORD	10,710	4,764	5,946		1,182 D	44.5%	55.5%	44.5%	55.5%
48,106	CRITTENDEN	13,465	5,202	8,249	14	3,047 D	38.6%	61.3%	38.7%	61.3%
19,783	CROSS	6,137	1,909	4,198	30	2,289 D	31.1%	68.4%	31.3%	68.7%
10,022	DALLAS	4,286	1,012	3,266	8	2,254 D	23.6%	76.2%	23.7%	76.3%
18,761	DESHA	5,600	1,372	4,228		2,856 D	24.5%	75.5%	24.5%	75.5%
15,157	DREW	5,480	1,730	3,750		2,020 D	31.6%	68.4%	31.6%	68.4%
31,572	FAULKNER	15,343	3,904	11,423	16	7,519 D	25.4%	74.5%	25.5%	74.5%
11,301	FRANKLIN	5,676	1,973	3,703		1,730 D	34.8%	65.2%	34.8%	65.2%
7,699	FULTON	3,715	1,038	2,670	7	1,632 D	27.9%	71.9%	28.0%	72.0%
54,131	GARLAND	26,170	10,394	15,707	69	5,313 D	39.7%	60.0%	39.8%	60.2%
9,711	GRANT	4,844	1,047	3,797		2,750 D	21.6%	78.4%	21.6%	78.4%
24,765	GREENE	10,192	2,690	7,495	7	4,805 D	26.4%	73.5%	26.4%	73.6%
19,308	HEMPSTEAD	8,256	2,859	5,397		2,538 D	34.6%	65.4%	34.6%	65.4%
21,963	HOT SPRINGS	9,996	2,187	7,809		5,622 D	21.9%	78.1%	21.9%	78.1%
11,412	HOWARD	4,782	1,575	3,207		1,632 D	32.9%	67.1%	32.9%	67.1%
22,723	INDEPENDENCE	9,998	2,878	7,116	4	4,238 D	28.8%	71.2%	28.8%	71.2%
7,381	IZARD	4,722	1,394	3,328		1,934 D	29.5%	70.5%	29.5%	70.5%
20,452	JACKSON	8,239	1,783	6,456		4,673 D	21.6%	78.4%	21.6%	78.4%
85,329	JEFFERSON	29,035	8,034	21,001		12,967 D	27.7%	72.3%	27.7%	72.3%
13,630	JOHNSON	7,217	2,173	5,044		2,871 D	30.1%	69.9%	30.1%	69.9%
10,018	LAFAYETTE	3,809	1,467	2,342		875 D	38.5%	61.5%	38.5%	61.5%
16,320	LAWRENCE	6,882	1,708	5,167	7	3,459 D	24.8%	75.1%	24.8%	75.2%
18,884	LEE	5,038	1,574	3,463	1	1,889 D	31.2%	68.7%	31.2%	68.8%
12,913	LINCOLN	3,744	699	3,045		2,346 D	18.7%	81.3%	18.7%	81.3%
11,194	LITTLE RIVER	4,573	1,431	3,142		1,711 D	31.3%	68.7%	31.3%	68.7%
16,789	LOGAN	8,294	2,909	5,313	72	2,404 D	35.1%	64.1%	35.4%	64.6%
26,249	LONOKE	10,299	2,522	7,761	16	5,239 D	24.5%	75.4%	24.5%	75.5%
9,453	MADISON	5,428	2,502	2,926		424 D	46.1%	53.9%	46.1%	53.9%
7,000	MARION	5,024	2,045	2,979		934 D	40.7%	59.3%	40.7%	59.3%
33,385	MILLER	11,580	4,737	6,821	22	2,084 D	40.9%	58.9%	41.0%	59.0%
62,060	MISSISSIPPI	16,328	6,009	10,292	27	4,283 D	36.8%	63.0%	36.9%	63.1%
15,657	MONROE	4,848	1,285	3,556	7	2,271 D	26.5%	73.3%	26.5%	73.5%
5,821	MONTGOMERY	3,344	924	2,420		1,496 D	27.6%	72.4%	27.6%	72.4%
10,111	NEVADA	4,269	1,163	3,101	5	1,938 D	27.2%	72.6%	27.3%	72.7%
5,844	NEWTON	3,481	1,641	1,840		199 D	47.1%	52.9%	47.1%	52.9%
30,896	OUACHITA	11,699	2,753	8,946		6,193 D	23.5%	76.5%	23.5%	76.5%
5,634	PERRY	3,142	832	2,310		1,478 D	26.5%	73.5%	26.5%	73.5%
40,046	PHILLIPS	11,117	3,342	7,774	1	4,432 D	30.1%	69.9%	30.1%	69.9%
8,711	PIKE	4,066	1,234	2,822	10	1,588 D	30.3%	69.4%	30.4%	69.6%
26,822	POINSETT	9,566	2,726	6,835	5	4,109 D	28.5%	71.5%	28.5%	71.5%
13,297	POLK	5,966	2,432	3,505	29	1,073 D	40.8%	58.7%	41.0%	59.0%
28,607	POPE	12,732	4,348	8,355	29	4,007 D	34.2%	65.6%	34.2%	65.8%
10,249	PRAIRIE	3,649	813	2,836		2,023 D	22.3%	77.7%	22.3%	77.7%
287,189	PULASKI	101,475	37,690	63,541	244	25,851 D	37.1%	62.6%	37.2%	62.8%

ARKANSAS

PRESIDENT 1976

1970 Census Population	County	Total Vote	Republican	Democratic	Other	Rep.-Dem. Plurality	Percentage Total Vote Rep.	Total Vote Dem.	Major Vote Rep.	Major Vote Dem.
12,645	RANDOLPH	6,122	1,571	4,551		2,980 D	25.7%	74.3%	25.7%	74.3%
30,799	ST. FRANCIS	10,520	3,639	6,851	30	3,212 D	34.6%	65.1%	34.7%	65.3%
36,107	SALINE	16,138	4,123	12,008	7	7,885 D	25.5%	74.4%	25.6%	74.4%
8,207	SCOTT	4,314	1,427	2,880	7	1,453 D	33.1%	66.8%	33.1%	66.9%
7,731	SEARCY	3,834	1,767	2,067		300 D	46.1%	53.9%	46.1%	53.9%
79,237	SEBASTIAN	33,397	17,665	15,698	34	1,967 R	52.9%	47.0%	52.9%	47.1%
11,272	SEVIER	4,877	1,468	3,391	18	1,923 D	30.1%	69.5%	30.2%	69.8%
8,233	SHARP	5,683	2,151	3,532		1,381 D	37.8%	62.2%	37.8%	62.2%
6,838	STONE	3,747	1,014	2,718	15	1,704 D	27.1%	72.5%	27.2%	72.8%
45,428	UNION	16,182	7,918	8,257	7	339 D	48.9%	51.0%	49.0%	51.0%
8,275	VAN BUREN	5,628	1,624	4,004		2,380 D	28.9%	71.1%	28.9%	71.1%
77,370	WASHINGTON	29,834	14,132	15,610	92	1,478 D	47.4%	52.3%	47.5%	52.5%
39,253	WHITE	16,168	4,756	11,412		6,656 D	29.4%	70.6%	29.4%	70.6%
11,566	WOODRUFF	3,893	848	3,040	5	2,192 D	21.8%	78.1%	21.8%	78.2%
14,208	YELL	7,717	1,932	5,785		3,853 D	25.0%	75.0%	25.0%	75.0%
1,923,295	TOTAL	767,535	267,903	498,604	1,028	230,701 D	34.9%	65.0%	35.0%	65.0%

ARKANSAS

PRESIDENT 1972

1970 Census Population	County	Total Vote	Republican	Democratic	Other	Rep.-Dem. Plurality	Percentage Total Vote Rep.	Total Vote Dem.	Major Vote Rep.	Major Vote Dem.
23,347	ARKANSAS	7,113	5,225	1,849	39	3,376 R	73.5%	26.0%	73.9%	26.1%
24,976	ASHLEY	7,203	5,506	1,680	17	3,826 R	76.4%	23.3%	76.6%	23.4%
15,319	BAXTER	9,431	6,754	2,677		4,077 R	71.6%	28.4%	71.6%	28.4%
50,476	BENTON	18,778	14,621	4,083	74	10,538 R	77.9%	21.7%	78.2%	21.8%
19,073	BOONE	7,362	5,484	1,862	16	3,622 R	74.5%	25.3%	74.7%	25.3%
12,778	BRADLEY	4,614	3,218	1,368	28	1,850 R	69.7%	29.6%	70.2%	29.8%
5,573	CALHOUN	2,020	1,298	707	15	591 R	64.3%	35.0%	64.7%	35.3%
12,301	CARROLL	5,086	3,565	1,401	120	2,164 R	70.1%	27.5%	71.8%	28.2%
18,164	CHICOT	4,333	2,858	1,469	6	1,389 R	66.0%	33.9%	66.1%	33.9%
21,537	CLARK	6,960	4,173	2,741	46	1,432 R	60.0%	39.4%	60.4%	39.6%
18,771	CLAY	6,314	4,381	1,933		2,448 R	69.4%	30.6%	69.4%	30.6%
10,349	CLEBURNE	4,274	2,870	1,400	4	1,470 R	67.2%	32.8%	67.2%	32.8%
6,605	CLEVELAND	2,571	1,837	734		1,103 R	71.5%	28.5%	71.5%	28.5%
25,952	COLUMBIA	8,023	5,801	2,193	29	3,608 R	72.3%	27.3%	72.6%	27.4%
16,805	CONWAY	7,205	4,187	3,009	9	1,178 R	58.1%	41.8%	58.2%	41.8%
52,068	CRAIGHEAD	17,155	11,312	5,843		5,469 R	65.9%	34.1%	65.9%	34.1%
25,677	CRAWFORD	8,566	6,974	1,520	72	5,454 R	81.4%	17.7%	82.1%	17.9%
48,106	CRITTENDEN	11,217	7,971	3,246		4,725 R	71.1%	28.9%	71.1%	28.9%
19,783	CROSS	5,143	3,743	1,221	179	2,522 R	72.8%	23.7%	75.4%	24.6%
10,022	DALLAS	3,554	2,152	1,402		750 R	60.6%	39.4%	60.6%	39.4%
18,761	DESHA	5,058	3,385	1,665	8	1,720 R	66.9%	32.9%	67.0%	33.0%
15,157	DREW	8,285	6,124	2,161		3,963 R	73.9%	26.1%	73.9%	26.1%
31,572	FAULKNER	11,350	6,746	4,604		2,142 R	59.4%	40.6%	59.4%	40.6%
11,301	FRANKLIN	4,930	3,678	1,252		2,426 R	74.6%	25.4%	74.6%	25.4%
7,699	FULTON	2,990	2,030	960		1,070 R	67.9%	32.1%	67.9%	32.1%
54,131	GARLAND	21,112	15,602	5,207	303	10,395 R	73.9%	24.7%	75.0%	25.0%
9,711	GRANT	3,581	2,414	1,147	20	1,267 R	67.4%	32.0%	67.8%	32.2%
24,765	GREENE	8,391	6,128	2,263		3,865 R	73.0%	27.0%	73.0%	27.0%
19,308	HEMPSTEAD	7,010	4,963	2,047		2,916 R	70.8%	29.2%	70.8%	29.2%
21,963	HOT SPRINGS	8,333	5,378	2,872	83	2,506 R	64.5%	34.5%	65.2%	34.8%
11,412	HOWARD	3,751	2,682	1,069		1,613 R	71.5%	28.5%	71.5%	28.5%
22,723	INDEPENDENCE	7,721	5,076	2,630	15	2,446 R	65.7%	34.1%	65.9%	34.1%
7,381	IZARD	3,114	2,001	1,108	5	893 R	64.3%	35.6%	64.4%	35.6%
20,452	JACKSON	6,288	4,196	2,092		2,104 R	66.7%	33.3%	66.7%	33.3%
85,329	JEFFERSON	27,260	16,888	10,346	26	6,542 R	62.0%	38.0%	62.0%	38.0%
13,630	JOHNSON	6,152	4,107	2,045		2,062 R	66.8%	33.2%	66.8%	33.2%
10,018	LAFAYETTE	3,421	2,460	952	9	1,508 R	71.9%	27.8%	72.1%	27.9%
16,320	LAWRENCE	5,732	3,981	1,751		2,230 R	69.5%	30.5%	69.5%	30.5%
18,884	LEE	5,481	3,540	1,907	34	1,633 R	64.6%	34.8%	65.0%	35.0%
12,913	LINCOLN	3,433	2,318	1,115		1,203 R	67.5%	32.5%	67.5%	32.5%
11,194	LITTLE RIVER	3,641	2,550	1,091		1,459 R	70.0%	30.0%	70.0%	30.0%
16,789	LOGAN	6,950	4,964	1,956	30	3,008 R	71.4%	28.1%	71.7%	28.3%
26,249	LONOKE	7,835	5,298	2,504	33	2,794 R	67.6%	32.0%	67.9%	32.1%
9,453	MADISON	5,261	3,372	1,889		1,483 R	64.1%	35.9%	64.1%	35.9%
7,000	MARION	3,497	2,331	1,108	58	1,223 R	66.7%	31.7%	67.8%	32.2%
33,385	MILLER	11,210	8,355	2,855		5,500 R	74.5%	25.5%	74.5%	25.5%
62,060	MISSISSIPPI	14,627	10,931	3,544	152	7,387 R	74.7%	24.2%	75.5%	24.5%
15,657	MONROE	4,566	2,897	1,578	91	1,319 R	63.4%	34.6%	64.7%	35.3%
5,821	MONTGOMERY	2,281	1,555	688	38	867 R	68.2%	30.2%	69.3%	30.7%
10,111	NEVADA	3,692	2,513	1,179		1,334 R	68.1%	31.9%	68.1%	31.9%
5,844	NEWTON	2,755	1,924	831		1,093 R	69.8%	30.2%	69.8%	30.2%
30,896	OUACHITA	10,562	6,620	3,931	11	2,689 R	62.7%	37.2%	62.7%	37.3%
5,634	PERRY	2,262	1,445	810	7	635 R	63.9%	35.8%	64.1%	35.9%
40,046	PHILLIPS	10,586	6,235	4,283	68	1,952 R	58.9%	40.5%	59.3%	40.7%
8,711	PIKE	3,143	2,316	798	29	1,518 R	73.7%	25.4%	74.4%	25.6%
26,822	POINSETT	8,998	7,010	1,908	80	5,102 R	77.9%	21.2%	78.6%	21.4%
13,297	POLK	4,823	3,609	1,120	94	2,489 R	74.8%	23.2%	76.3%	23.7%
28,607	POPE	10,244	6,917	3,302	25	3,615 R	67.5%	32.2%	67.7%	32.3%
10,249	PRAIRIE	3,059	2,186	873		1,313 R	71.5%	28.5%	71.5%	28.5%
287,189	PULASKI	91,468	57,576	33,611	281	23,965 R	62.9%	36.7%	63.1%	36.9%

ARKANSAS

PRESIDENT 1972

1970 Census Population	County	Total Vote	Republican	Democratic	Other	Rep.-Dem. Plurality	Percentage Total Vote Rep.	Percentage Total Vote Dem.	Percentage Major Vote Rep.	Percentage Major Vote Dem.
12,645	RANDOLPH	4,103	2,578	1,525		1,053 R	62.8%	37.2%	62.8%	37.2%
30,799	ST. FRANCIS	8,631	5,692	2,674	265	3,018 R	65.9%	31.0%	68.0%	32.0%
36,107	SALINE	12,527	7,972	4,503	52	3,469 R	63.6%	35.9%	63.9%	36.1%
8,207	SCOTT	3,195	2,424	771		1,653 R	75.9%	24.1%	75.9%	24.1%
7,731	SEARCY	4,016	3,163	853		2,310 R	78.8%	21.2%	78.8%	21.2%
79,237	SEBASTIAN	31,047	25,219	5,770	58	19,449 R	81.2%	18.6%	81.4%	18.6%
11,272	SEVIER	3,613	2,526	1,048	39	1,478 R	69.9%	29.0%	70.7%	29.3%
8,233	SHARP	3,840	2,677	1,154	9	1,523 R	69.7%	30.1%	69.9%	30.1%
6,838	STONE	2,952	1,989	958	5	1,031 R	67.4%	32.5%	67.5%	32.5%
45,428	UNION	15,543	11,925	3,531	87	8,394 R	76.7%	22.7%	77.2%	22.8%
8,275	VAN BUREN	4,235	2,622	1,594	19	1,028 R	61.9%	37.6%	62.2%	37.8%
77,370	WASHINGTON	24,701	17,523	7,108	70	10,415 R	70.9%	28.8%	71.1%	28.9%
39,253	WHITE	12,941	8,701	4,161	79	4,540 R	67.2%	32.2%	67.6%	32.4%
11,566	WOODRUFF	3,222	1,989	1,183	50	806 R	61.7%	36.7%	62.7%	37.3%
14,208	YELL	4,979	3,310	1,669		1,641 R	66.5%	33.5%	66.5%	33.5%
1,923,295	TOTAL	651,320	448,541	199,892	2,887	248,649 R	68.9%	30.7%	69.2%	30.8%

ARKANSAS

PRESIDENT 1968

1960 Census Population	County	Total Vote	Republican	Democratic	AIP	Other	Plurality	Percentage Rep.	Dem.	AIP
23,355	ARKANSAS	7,600	1,806	2,019	3,775		1,756 A	23.8%	26.6%	49.7%
24,220	ASHLEY	7,906	1,470	2,035	4,401		2,366 A	18.6%	25.7%	55.7%
9,943	BAXTER	6,866	3,401	1,952	1,513		1,449 R	49.5%	28.4%	22.0%
36,272	BENTON	16,228	8,104	4,088	4,036		4,016 R	49.9%	25.2%	24.9%
16,116	BOONE	7,425	3,349	1,907	2,169		1,180 R	45.1%	25.7%	29.2%
14,029	BRADLEY	4,805	802	1,457	2,546		1,089 A	16.7%	30.3%	53.0%
5,991	CALHOUN	2,190	287	688	1,215		527 A	13.1%	31.4%	55.5%
11,284	CARROLL	5,068	2,596	1,298	1,174		1,298 R	51.2%	25.6%	23.2%
18,990	CHICOT	5,647	865	2,595	2,187		408 D	15.3%	46.0%	38.7%
20,950	CLARK	7,151	1,642	2,733	2,776		43 A	23.0%	38.2%	38.8%
21,258	CLAY	6,358	2,410	1,663	2,285		125 R	37.9%	26.2%	35.9%
9,059	CLEBURNE	4,160	1,301	1,202	1,657		356 A	31.3%	28.9%	39.8%
6,944	CLEVELAND	2,470	312	407	1,751		1,344 A	12.6%	16.5%	70.9%
26,400	COLUMBIA	8,246	1,916	2,487	3,843		1,356 A	23.2%	30.2%	46.6%
15,430	CONWAY	6,491	1,973	2,560	1,958		587 D	30.4%	39.4%	30.2%
47,303	CRAIGHEAD	15,527	5,047	3,738	6,742		1,695 A	32.5%	24.1%	43.4%
21,318	CRAWFORD	7,218	2,723	1,578	2,917		194 A	37.7%	21.9%	40.4%
47,564	CRITTENDEN	10,586	2,454	3,475	4,657		1,182 A	23.2%	32.8%	44.0%
19,551	CROSS	5,704	1,093	1,555	3,056		1,501 A	19.2%	27.3%	53.6%
10,522	DALLAS	3,647	672	1,253	1,722		469 A	18.4%	34.4%	47.2%
20,770	DESHA	5,716	972	2,270	2,474		204 A	17.0%	39.7%	43.3%
15,213	DREW	4,671	1,040	1,324	2,307		983 A	22.3%	28.3%	49.4%
24,303	FAULKNER	10,922	2,791	3,756	4,375		619 A	25.6%	34.4%	40.1%
10,213	FRANKLIN	4,593	1,333	1,149	2,111		778 A	29.0%	25.0%	46.0%
6,657	FULTON	3,297	1,198	1,019	1,080		118 R	36.3%	30.9%	32.8%
46,697	GARLAND	20,284	7,674	5,655	6,955		719 R	37.8%	27.9%	34.3%
8,294	GRANT	3,673	627	852	2,194		1,342 A	17.1%	23.2%	59.7%
25,198	GREENE	8,077	2,859	2,197	3,021		162 A	35.4%	27.2%	37.4%
19,661	HEMPSTEAD	7,241	1,783	2,322	3,136		814 A	24.6%	32.1%	43.3%
21,893	HOT SPRINGS	8,056	1,780	2,137	4,139		2,002 A	22.1%	26.5%	51.4%
10,878	HOWARD	4,007	1,286	1,061	1,660		374 A	32.1%	26.5%	41.4%
20,048	INDEPENDENCE	7,841	2,782	2,289	2,770		12 R	35.5%	29.2%	35.3%
6,766	IZARD	2,988	931	948	1,109		161 A	31.2%	31.7%	37.1%
22,843	JACKSON	6,932	1,356	2,051	3,525		1,474 A	19.6%	29.6%	50.9%
81,373	JEFFERSON	24,038	4,860	9,125	10,053		928 A	20.2%	38.0%	41.8%
12,421	JOHNSON	5,107	1,667	1,747	1,693		54 D	32.6%	34.2%	33.2%
11,030	LAFAYETTE	3,584	672	1,208	1,704		496 A	18.8%	33.7%	47.5%
17,267	LAWRENCE	6,214	1,788	1,613	2,813		1,025 A	28.8%	26.0%	45.3%
21,001	LEE	4,876	834	2,135	1,907		228 D	17.1%	43.8%	39.1%
14,447	LINCOLN	3,781	488	1,209	2,084		875 A	12.9%	32.0%	55.1%
9,211	LITTLE RIVER	3,310	745	1,092	1,473		381 A	22.5%	33.0%	44.5%
15,957	LOGAN	6,499	2,341	1,998	2,160		181 R	36.0%	30.7%	33.2%
24,551	LONOKE	7,693	1,677	2,014	4,002		1,988 A	21.8%	26.2%	52.0%
9,068	MADISON	4,922	2,320	1,574	1,028		746 R	47.1%	32.0%	20.9%
6,041	MARION	3,252	1,385	990	877		395 R	42.6%	30.4%	27.0%
31,686	MILLER	10,653	2,662	2,929	5,062		2,133 A	25.0%	27.5%	47.5%
70,174	MISSISSIPPI	15,509	4,369	4,993	6,147		1,154 A	28.2%	32.2%	39.6%
17,327	MONROE	4,993	804	1,783	2,406		623 A	16.1%	35.7%	48.2%
5,370	MONTGOMERY	2,526	885	649	992		107 A	35.0%	25.7%	39.3%
10,700	NEVADA	3,921	840	1,308	1,773		465 A	21.4%	33.4%	45.2%
5,963	NEWTON	2,886	1,467	852	567		615 R	50.8%	29.5%	19.6%
31,641	OUACHITA	11,843	2,209	4,603	5,031		428 A	18.7%	38.9%	42.5%
4,927	PERRY	2,290	740	634	916		176 A	32.3%	27.7%	40.0%
43,997	PHILLIPS	11,472	2,154	5,039	4,279		760 D	18.8%	43.9%	37.3%
7,864	PIKE	3,295	1,104	656	1,535		431 A	33.5%	19.9%	46.6%
30,834	POINSETT	7,886	2,140	1,672	4,074		1,934 A	27.1%	21.2%	51.7%
11,981	POLK	5,196	2,094	1,290	1,812		282 R	40.3%	24.8%	34.9%
21,177	POPE	8,666	3,319	2,578	2,769		550 R	38.3%	29.7%	32.0%
10,515	PRAIRIE	3,582	693	875	2,014		1,139 A	19.3%	24.4%	56.2%
242,980	PULASKI	80,150	26,709	27,597	25,844		888 D	33.3%	34.4%	32.2%

ARKANSAS

PRESIDENT 1968

1960 Census Population	County	Total Vote	Republican	Democratic	AIP	Other	Plurality	Percentage Rep.	Percentage Dem.	Percentage AIP
12,520	RANDOLPH	4,214	1,237	1,367	1,610		243 A	29.4%	32.4%	38.2%
33,303	ST. FRANCIS	9,146	1,608	3,284	4,254		970 A	17.6%	35.9%	46.5%
28,956	SALINE	11,294	2,614	3,111	5,569		2,458 A	23.1%	27.5%	49.3%
7,297	SCOTT	3,400	1,162	1,000	1,238		76 A	34.2%	29.4%	36.4%
8,124	SEARCY	3,359	1,909	724	726		1,183 R	56.8%	21.6%	21.6%
66,685	SEBASTIAN	27,042	12,073	6,320	8,649		3,424 R	44.6%	23.4%	32.0%
10,156	SEVIER	3,847	1,217	1,129	1,501		284 A	31.6%	29.3%	39.0%
6,319	SHARP	3,460	1,136	1,025	1,299		163 A	32.8%	29.6%	37.5%
6,294	STONE	2,664	987	698	979		8 R	37.0%	26.2%	36.7%
49,518	UNION	17,198	4,919	4,426	7,853		2,934 A	28.6%	25.7%	45.7%
7,228	VAN BUREN	3,698	1,325	1,149	1,224		101 R	35.8%	31.1%	33.1%
55,797	WASHINGTON	21,863	10,640	6,131	5,092		4,509 R	48.7%	28.0%	23.3%
32,745	WHITE	12,139	3,887	3,198	5,054		1,167 A	32.0%	26.3%	41.6%
13,954	WOODRUFF	3,629	625	1,270	1,734		464 A	17.2%	35.0%	47.8%
11,940	YELL	5,281	1,819	1,513	1,949		130 A	34.4%	28.6%	36.9%
1,786,272	TOTAL	619,969	190,759	188,228	240,982		50,223 A	30.8%	30.4%	38.9%

ARKANSAS

ELECTION NOTES

1984 Other vote was 2,221 Bergland (Libertarian); 1,890 LaRouche (Independent); 1,499 Hall (People Before Profits); 1,461 Richards (Populist); 1,291 Serrette (Independent Alliance); 960 Johnson (Citizen's Group); 842 Dodge (Prohibition); 822 Lowery (United Sovereign Citizens).

1980 Other vote was 22,468 Anderson (Anderson Coalition); 8,970 Clark (Libertarian); 2,345 Commoner (Citizens); 1,350 Bubar (Statesman); 1,244 Hall (People Before Profits).

1976 Other vote was 639 McCarthy (write-in); 389 Anderson (write-in).

1972 Other vote was Schmitz (write-in). Although the data indicate a possible discrepancy in both the Republican and Democratic vote in Drew county, the official state canvass figures are used here.

1968 Wallace on the ballot as American. Due to an undercount in Jefferson county, early unamended canvass gave the state-wide totals as 189,062 Republican; 184,901 Democratic; 235,627 American. The Democratic vote in Little River county was amended from 1,095.

CALIFORNIA

POPULAR VOTE FOR PRESIDENT 1920 TO 1984

	Total	Republican		Democratic		Other		Percentage			
								Total Vote		Major Vote	
Year	Vote	Vote	Candidate	Vote	Candidate	Vote	Plurality	Rep.	Dem.	Rep.	Dem.
1984	9,505,423	5,467,009	Reagan, Ronald	3,922,519	Mondale, Walter F.	115,895	1,544,490 R	57.5%	41.3%	58.2%	41.8%
1980	8,587,063	4,524,858	Reagan, Ronald	3,083,661	Carter, Jimmy	978,544	1,441,197 R	52.7%	35.9%	59.5%	40.5%
1976	7,867,117	3,882,244	Ford, Gerald R.	3,742,284	Carter, Jimmy	242,589	139,960 R	49.3%	47.6%	50.9%	49.1%
1972	8,367,862	4,602,096	Nixon, Richard M.	3,475,847	McGovern, George S.	289,919	1,126,249 R	55.0%	41.5%	57.0%	43.0%
1968	7,251,587	3,467,664	Nixon, Richard M.	3,244,318	Humphrey, Hubert H.	539,605	223,346 R	47.8%	44.7%	51.7%	48.3%
1964	7,057,586	2,879,108	Goldwater, Barry M.	4,171,877	Johnson, Lyndon B.	6,601	1,292,769 D	40.8%	59.1%	40.8%	59.2%
1960	6,506,578	3,259,722	Nixon, Richard M.	3,224,099	Kennedy, John F.	22,757	35,623 R	50.1%	49.6%	50.3%	49.7%
1956	5,466,355	3,027,668	Eisenhower, Dwight D.	2,420,135	Stevenson, Adlai E.	18,552	607,533 R	55.4%	44.3%	55.6%	44.4%
1952	5,141,849	2,897,310	Eisenhower, Dwight D.	2,197,548	Stevenson, Adlai E.	46,991	699,762 R	56.3%	42.7%	56.9%	43.1%
1948	4,021,538	1,895,269	Dewey, Thomas E.	1,913,134	Truman, Harry S.	213,135	17,865 D	47.1%	47.6%	49.8%	50.2%
1944	3,520,875	1,512,965	Dewey, Thomas E.	1,988,564	Roosevelt, Franklin D.	19,346	475,599 D	43.0%	56.5%	43.2%	56.8%
1940	3,268,791	1,351,419	Willkie, Wendell	1,877,618	Roosevelt, Franklin D.	39,754	526,199 D	41.3%	57.4%	41.9%	58.1%
1936	2,638,882	836,431	Landon, Alfred M.	1,766,836	Roosevelt, Franklin D.	35,615	930,405 D	31.7%	67.0%	32.1%	67.9%
1932	2,266,972	847,902	Hoover, Herbert C.	1,324,157	Roosevelt, Franklin D.	94,913	476,255 D	37.4%	58.4%	39.0%	61.0%
1928	1,796,656	1,162,323	Hoover, Herbert C.	614,365	Smith, Alfred E.	19,968	547,958 R	64.7%	34.2%	65.4%	34.6%
1924 **	1,281,778	733,250	Coolidge, Calvin	105,514	Davis, John W.	443,014	308,601 R	57.2%	8.2%	87.4%	12.6%
1920	943,463	624,992	Harding, Warren G.	229,191	Cox, James M.	89,280	395,801 R	66.2%	24.3%	73.2%	26.8%

In 1924 other vote was 424,649 Progressive and 18,365 Prohibition.

ELECTORAL COLLEGE VOTE 1920 TO 1984

Year	Total	Republican	Democratic	Other
1984	47	47	—	—
1980	45	45	—	—
1976	45	45	—	—
1972	45	45	—	—
1968	40	40	—	—
1964	40	—	40	—
1960	32	32	—	—
1956	32	32	—	—
1952	32	32	—	—
1948	25	—	25	—
1944	25	—	25	—
1940	22	—	22	—
1936	22	—	22	—
1932	22	—	22	—
1928	13	13	—	—
1924	13	13	—	—
1920	13	13	—	—

CALIFORNIA

DEL NORTE
SISKIYOU
MODOC
HUMBOLDT
TRINITY
SHASTA
LASSEN
TEHAMA
PLUMAS
MENDOCINO
GLENN
BUTTE
SIERRA
NEVADA
COLUSA
YUBA
LAKE
SUTTER
PLACER
EL DORADO
YOLO
SONOMA
NAPA
ALPINE
SACRAMENTO
AMADOR
SOLANO
CALAVERAS
MARIN
TUOLUMNE
CONTRA COSTA
SAN JOAQUIN
MONO
SAN FRANCISCO
ALAMEDA
SAN MATEO
STANISLAUS
MARIPOSA
SANTA CLARA
MERCED
MADERA
SANTA CRUZ
FRESNO
INYO
SAN BENITO
MONTEREY
KINGS
TULARE
SAN LUIS OBISPO
KERN
SAN BERNARDINO
SANTA BARBARA (PART)
VENTURA (PART)
LOS ANGELES (PART)
VENTURA (PART)
SANTA BARBARA (PART)
ORANGE
RIVERSIDE
SANTA BARBARA (PART)
LOS ANGELES (PART)
VENTURA (PART)
SAN DIEGO
IMPERIAL

CALIFORNIA

PRESIDENT 1984

1980 Census Population	County	Total Vote	Republican	Democratic	Other	Rep.-Dem. Plurality	Percentage Total Vote Rep.	Total Vote Dem.	Major Vote Rep.	Major Vote Dem.
1,105,379	ALAMEDA	480,874	192,408	282,041	6,425	89,633 D	40.0%	58.7%	40.6%	59.4%
1,097	ALPINE	466	264	194	8	70 R	56.7%	41.6%	57.6%	42.4%
19,314	AMADOR	11,363	6,986	4,188	189	2,798 R	61.5%	36.9%	62.5%	37.5%
143,851	BUTTE	71,964	45,381	25,421	1,162	19,960 R	63.1%	35.3%	64.1%	35.9%
20,710	CALAVERAS	11,877	7,632	4,081	164	3,551 R	64.3%	34.4%	65.2%	34.8%
12,791	COLUSA	5,188	3,388	1,725	75	1,663 R	65.3%	33.2%	66.3%	33.7%
656,380	CONTRA COSTA	316,318	172,331	140,994	2,993	31,337 R	54.5%	44.6%	55.0%	45.0%
18,217	DEL NORTE	6,841	3,996	2,696	149	1,300 R	58.4%	39.4%	59.7%	40.3%
85,812	EL DORADO	42,478	27,583	14,312	583	13,271 R	64.9%	33.7%	65.8%	34.2%
514,621	FRESNO	192,936	104,757	86,315	1,864	18,442 R	54.3%	44.7%	54.8%	45.2%
21,350	GLENN	8,632	6,020	2,488	124	3,532 R	69.7%	28.8%	70.8%	29.2%
108,514	HUMBOLDT	53,891	27,832	25,217	842	2,615 R	51.6%	46.8%	52.5%	47.5%
92,110	IMPERIAL	22,301	13,829	8,237	235	5,592 R	62.0%	36.9%	62.7%	37.3%
17,895	INYO	8,338	5,863	2,360	115	3,503 R	70.3%	28.3%	71.3%	28.7%
403,089	KERN	145,744	94,776	49,567	1,401	45,209 R	65.0%	34.0%	65.7%	34.3%
73,738	KINGS	20,848	13,364	7,324	160	6,040 R	64.1%	35.1%	64.6%	35.4%
36,366	LAKE	19,831	10,874	8,648	309	2,226 R	54.8%	43.6%	55.7%	44.3%
21,661	LASSEN	8,761	5,352	3,254	155	2,098 R	61.1%	37.1%	62.2%	37.8%
7,477,503	LOS ANGELES	2,612,914	1,424,113	1,158,912	29,889	265,201 R	54.5%	44.4%	55.1%	44.9%
63,116	MADERA	23,241	13,954	8,994	293	4,960 R	60.0%	38.7%	60.8%	39.2%
222,568	MARIN	116,050	56,887	57,533	1,630	646 D	49.0%	49.6%	49.7%	50.3%
11,108	MARIPOSA	6,518	3,989	2,399	130	1,590 R	61.2%	36.8%	62.4%	37.6%
66,738	MENDOCINO	31,422	16,369	14,407	646	1,962 R	52.1%	45.9%	53.2%	46.8%
134,560	MERCED	42,477	24,997	17,012	468	7,985 R	58.8%	40.0%	59.5%	40.5%
8,610	MODOC	4,310	2,995	1,219	96	1,776 R	69.5%	28.3%	71.1%	28.9%
8,577	MONO	3,677	2,659	962	56	1,697 R	72.3%	26.2%	73.4%	26.6%
290,444	MONTEREY	97,470	55,710	40,733	1,027	14,977 R	57.2%	41.8%	57.8%	42.2%
99,199	NAPA	45,561	26,322	18,599	640	7,723 R	57.8%	40.8%	58.6%	41.4%
51,645	NEVADA	31,768	19,809	11,198	761	8,611 R	62.4%	35.2%	63.9%	36.1%
1,932,709	ORANGE	850,077	635,013	206,272	8,792	428,741 R	74.7%	24.3%	75.5%	24.5%
117,247	PLACER	60,427	38,035	21,294	1,098	16,741 R	62.9%	35.2%	64.1%	35.9%
17,340	PLUMAS	9,228	5,224	3,837	167	1,387 R	56.6%	41.6%	57.7%	42.3%
663,166	RIVERSIDE	287,202	182,324	102,043	2,835	80,281 R	63.5%	35.5%	64.1%	35.9%
783,381	SACRAMENTO	368,841	204,922	159,128	4,791	45,794 R	55.6%	43.1%	56.3%	43.7%
25,005	SAN BENITO	9,380	5,695	3,554	131	2,141 R	60.7%	37.9%	61.6%	38.4%
895,016	SAN BERNARDINO	342,705	222,071	116,454	4,180	105,617 R	64.8%	34.0%	65.6%	34.4%
1,861,846	SAN DIEGO	769,267	502,344	257,029	9,894	245,315 R	65.3%	33.4%	66.2%	33.8%
678,974	SAN FRANCISCO	286,972	90,219	193,278	3,475	103,059 D	31.4%	67.4%	31.8%	68.2%
347,342	SAN JOAQUIN	137,213	81,795	53,846	1,572	27,949 R	59.6%	39.2%	60.3%	39.7%
155,435	SAN LUIS OBISPO	76,950	49,035	26,946	969	22,089 R	63.7%	35.0%	64.5%	35.5%
587,329	SAN MATEO	260,631	135,185	122,268	3,178	12,917 R	51.9%	46.9%	52.5%	47.5%
298,694	SANTA BARBARA	142,320	89,314	51,243	1,763	38,071 R	62.8%	36.0%	63.5%	36.5%
1,295,071	SANTA CLARA	526,639	288,638	229,865	8,136	58,773 R	54.8%	43.6%	55.7%	44.3%
188,141	SANTA CRUZ	92,147	41,652	49,091	1,404	7,439 D	45.2%	53.3%	45.9%	54.1%
115,715	SHASTA	53,127	33,041	19,298	788	13,743 R	62.2%	36.3%	63.1%	36.9%
3,073	SIERRA	1,896	1,078	781	37	297 R	56.9%	41.2%	58.0%	42.0%
39,732	SISKIYOU	18,101	10,544	7,130	427	3,414 R	58.3%	39.4%	59.7%	40.3%
235,203	SOLANO	94,798	51,678	41,982	1,138	9,696 R	54.5%	44.3%	55.2%	44.8%
299,681	SONOMA	149,657	76,447	71,295	1,915	5,152 R	51.1%	47.6%	51.7%	48.3%
265,900	STANISLAUS	93,985	55,665	37,459	861	18,206 R	59.2%	39.9%	59.8%	40.2%
52,246	SUTTER	20,323	14,477	5,535	311	8,942 R	71.2%	27.2%	72.3%	27.7%
38,888	TEHAMA	18,455	11,586	6,527	342	5,059 R	62.8%	35.4%	64.0%	36.0%
11,858	TRINITY	5,935	3,544	2,218	173	1,326 R	59.7%	37.4%	61.5%	38.5%
245,738	TULARE	79,943	51,066	28,065	812	23,001 R	63.9%	35.1%	64.5%	35.5%
33,928	TUOLUMNE	18,051	10,485	7,283	283	3,202 R	58.1%	40.3%	59.0%	41.0%
529,174	VENTURA	220,462	151,383	66,550	2,529	84,833 R	68.7%	30.2%	69.5%	30.5%
113,374	YOLO	50,853	24,329	25,879	645	1,550 D	47.8%	50.9%	48.5%	51.5%
49,733	YUBA	15,397	9,780	5,339	278	4,441 R	63.5%	34.7%	64.7%	35.3%
23,667,902	TOTAL	9,505,423	5,467,009	3,922,519	115,895	1,544,490 R	57.5%	41.3%	58.2%	41.8%

CALIFORNIA

PRESIDENT 1980

1980 Census Population	County	Total Vote	Republican	Democratic	Other	Rep.-Dem. Plurality	Percentage Total Vote Rep.	Percentage Total Vote Dem.	Percentage Major Vote Rep.	Percentage Major Vote Dem.
1,105,379	ALAMEDA	417,617	158,531	201,720	57,366	43,189 D	38.0%	48.3%	44.0%	56.0%
1,097	ALPINE	461	254	133	74	121 R	55.1%	28.9%	65.6%	34.4%
19,314	AMADOR	9,670	5,401	3,191	1,078	2,210 R	55.9%	33.0%	62.9%	37.1%
143,851	BUTTE	66,012	38,188	19,520	8,304	18,668 R	57.9%	29.6%	66.2%	33.8%
20,710	CALAVERAS	10,275	6,054	3,076	1,145	2,978 R	58.9%	29.9%	66.3%	33.7%
12,791	COLUSA	4,995	2,897	1,605	493	1,292 R	58.0%	32.1%	64.3%	35.7%
656,380	CONTRA COSTA	287,545	144,112	107,398	36,035	36,714 R	50.1%	37.3%	57.3%	42.7%
18,217	DEL NORTE	6,987	4,016	2,338	633	1,678 R	57.5%	33.5%	63.2%	36.8%
85,812	EL DORADO	36,449	21,238	10,765	4,446	10,473 R	58.3%	29.5%	66.4%	33.6%
514,621	FRESNO	161,386	82,515	65,254	13,617	17,261 R	51.1%	40.4%	55.8%	44.2%
21,350	GLENN	8,312	5,386	2,227	699	3,159 R	64.8%	26.8%	70.7%	29.3%
108,514	HUMBOLDT	48,712	24,047	17,133	7,532	6,914 R	49.4%	35.2%	58.4%	41.6%
92,110	IMPERIAL	21,579	12,068	7,961	1,550	4,107 R	55.9%	36.9%	60.3%	39.7%
17,895	INYO	8,027	5,201	2,080	746	3,121 R	64.8%	25.9%	71.4%	28.6%
403,089	KERN	122,121	72,842	41,097	8,182	31,745 R	59.6%	33.7%	63.9%	36.1%
73,738	KINGS	19,021	10,531	7,299	1,191	3,232 R	55.4%	38.4%	59.1%	40.9%
36,366	LAKE	16,654	8,934	5,978	1,742	2,956 R	53.6%	35.9%	59.9%	40.1%
21,661	LASSEN	8,198	4,464	2,941	793	1,523 R	54.5%	35.9%	60.3%	39.7%
7,477,503	LOS ANGELES	2,440,185	1,224,533	979,830	235,822	244,703 R	50.2%	40.2%	55.6%	44.4%
63,116	MADERA	19,780	10,599	7,783	1,398	2,816 R	53.6%	39.3%	57.7%	42.3%
222,568	MARIN	108,507	49,678	39,231	19,598	10,447 R	45.8%	36.2%	55.9%	44.1%
11,108	MARIPOSA	5,608	3,082	1,889	637	1,193 R	55.0%	33.7%	62.0%	38.0%
66,738	MENDOCINO	28,224	12,432	10,784	5,008	1,648 R	44.0%	38.2%	53.5%	46.5%
134,560	MERCED	36,996	18,043	15,886	3,067	2,157 R	48.8%	42.9%	53.2%	46.8%
8,610	MODOC	4,000	2,579	1,046	375	1,533 R	64.5%	26.2%	71.1%	28.9%
8,577	MONO	3,421	2,132	865	424	1,267 R	62.3%	25.3%	71.1%	28.9%
290,444	MONTEREY	86,794	47,452	29,086	10,256	18,366 R	54.7%	33.5%	62.0%	38.0%
99,199	NAPA	44,035	23,632	14,898	5,505	8,734 R	53.7%	33.8%	61.3%	38.7%
51,645	NEVADA	26,261	15,207	7,605	3,449	7,602 R	57.9%	29.0%	66.7%	33.3%
1,932,709	ORANGE	780,212	529,797	176,704	73,711	353,093 R	67.9%	22.6%	75.0%	25.0%
117,247	PLACER	51,440	28,179	17,311	5,950	10,868 R	54.8%	33.7%	61.9%	38.1%
17,340	PLUMAS	8,161	4,182	2,911	1,068	1,271 R	51.2%	35.7%	59.0%	41.0%
663,166	RIVERSIDE	243,278	145,642	76,650	20,986	68,992 R	59.9%	31.5%	65.5%	34.5%
783,381	SACRAMENTO	322,120	153,721	130,031	38,368	23,690 R	47.7%	40.4%	54.2%	45.8%
25,005	SAN BENITO	7,602	4,054	2,749	799	1,305 R	53.3%	36.2%	59.6%	40.4%
895,016	SAN BERNARDINO	289,812	172,957	91,790	25,065	81,167 R	59.7%	31.7%	65.3%	34.7%
1,861,846	SAN DIEGO	716,866	435,910	195,410	85,546	240,500 R	60.8%	27.3%	69.0%	31.0%
678,974	SAN FRANCISCO	254,028	80,967	133,184	39,877	52,217 D	31.9%	52.4%	37.8%	62.2%
347,342	SAN JOAQUIN	116,863	64,718	41,551	10,594	23,167 R	55.4%	35.6%	60.9%	39.1%
155,435	SAN LUIS OBISPO	69,527	38,631	20,508	10,388	18,123 R	55.6%	29.5%	65.3%	34.7%
587,329	SAN MATEO	238,637	116,491	87,335	34,811	29,156 R	48.8%	36.6%	57.2%	42.8%
298,694	SANTA BARBARA	128,995	69,629	40,650	18,716	28,979 R	54.0%	31.5%	63.1%	36.9%
1,295,071	SANTA CLARA	477,003	229,048	166,995	80,960	62,053 R	48.0%	35.0%	57.8%	42.2%
188,141	SANTA CRUZ	85,804	37,347	32,346	16,111	5,001 R	43.5%	37.7%	53.6%	46.4%
115,715	SHASTA	47,418	27,547	15,364	4,507	12,183 R	58.1%	32.4%	64.2%	35.8%
3,073	SIERRA	1,718	855	651	212	204 R	49.8%	37.9%	56.8%	43.2%
39,732	SISKIYOU	16,738	9,331	5,664	1,743	3,667 R	55.7%	33.8%	62.2%	37.8%
235,203	SOLANO	80,676	40,919	30,952	8,805	9,967 R	50.7%	38.4%	56.9%	43.1%
299,681	SONOMA	125,985	60,722	45,596	19,667	15,126 R	48.2%	36.2%	57.1%	42.9%
265,900	STANISLAUS	84,186	41,595	33,683	8,908	7,912 R	49.4%	40.0%	55.3%	44.7%
52,246	SUTTER	18,557	11,778	5,103	1,676	6,675 R	63.5%	27.5%	69.8%	30.2%
38,888	TEHAMA	15,457	9,140	4,832	1,485	4,308 R	59.1%	31.3%	65.4%	34.6%
11,858	TRINITY	5,546	3,048	1,734	764	1,314 R	55.0%	31.3%	63.7%	36.3%
245,738	TULARE	70,846	41,317	25,155	4,374	16,162 R	58.3%	35.5%	62.2%	37.8%
33,928	TUOLUMNE	16,063	8,810	5,449	1,804	3,361 R	54.8%	33.9%	61.8%	38.2%
529,174	VENTURA	190,650	114,930	56,311	19,409	58,619 R	60.3%	29.5%	67.1%	32.9%
113,374	YOLO	49,690	19,603	21,527	8,560	1,924 D	39.5%	43.3%	47.7%	52.3%
49,733	YUBA	14,111	7,942	4,896	1,273	3,046 R	56.3%	34.7%	61.9%	38.1%
23,667,902	TOTAL	8,587,063	4,524,858	3,083,661	978,544	1,441,197 R	52.7%	35.9%	59.5%	40.5%

CALIFORNIA

PRESIDENT 1976

1970 Census Population	County	Total Vote	Republican	Democratic	Other	Rep.-Dem. Plurality	Percentage Total Vote Rep.	Total Vote Dem.	Major Vote Rep.	Major Vote Dem.
1,073,184	ALAMEDA	407,681	155,280	235,988	16,413	80,708 D	38.1%	57.9%	39.7%	60.3%
484	ALPINE	447	225	189	33	36 R	50.3%	42.3%	54.3%	45.7%
11,821	AMADOR	8,018	3,699	4,037	282	338 D	46.1%	50.3%	47.8%	52.2%
101,969	BUTTE	54,854	28,400	24,203	2,251	4,197 R	51.8%	44.1%	54.0%	46.0%
13,585	CALAVERAS	7,528	3,695	3,607	226	88 R	49.1%	47.9%	50.6%	49.4%
12,430	COLUSA	5,182	2,733	2,340	109	393 R	52.7%	45.2%	53.9%	46.1%
558,389	CONTRA COSTA	256,534	126,598	123,742	6,194	2,856 R	49.3%	48.2%	50.6%	49.4%
14,580	DEL NORTE	5,478	2,481	2,789	208	308 D	45.3%	50.9%	47.1%	52.9%
43,833	EL DORADO	26,154	12,472	12,763	919	291 D	47.7%	48.8%	49.4%	50.6%
413,053	FRESNO	150,805	72,533	74,958	3,314	2,425 D	48.1%	49.7%	49.2%	50.8%
17,521	GLENN	7,773	4,094	3,501	178	593 R	52.7%	45.0%	53.9%	46.1%
99,692	HUMBOLDT	43,372	18,034	23,500	1,838	5,466 D	41.6%	54.2%	43.4%	56.6%
74,492	IMPERIAL	21,262	10,618	10,244	400	374 R	49.9%	48.2%	50.9%	49.1%
15,571	INYO	6,706	3,905	2,635	166	1,270 R	58.2%	39.3%	59.7%	40.3%
329,162	KERN	110,961	58,023	50,567	2,371	7,456 R	52.3%	45.6%	53.4%	46.6%
64,610	KINGS	16,642	8,263	8,061	318	202 R	49.7%	48.4%	50.6%	49.4%
19,548	LAKE	12,285	5,462	6,374	449	912 D	44.5%	51.9%	46.1%	53.9%
14,960	LASSEN	6,998	3,007	3,801	190	794 D	43.0%	54.3%	44.2%	55.8%
7,032,075	LOS ANGELES	2,459,077	1,174,926	1,221,893	62,258	46,967 D	47.8%	49.7%	49.0%	51.0%
41,519	MADERA	14,892	6,844	7,625	423	781 D	46.0%	51.2%	47.3%	52.7%
206,038	MARIN	101,715	53,425	43,590	4,700	9,835 R	52.5%	42.9%	55.1%	44.9%
6,015	MARIPOSA	4,317	2,012	2,093	212	81 D	46.6%	48.5%	49.0%	51.0%
51,101	MENDOCINO	21,509	9,784	10,653	1,072	869 D	45.5%	49.5%	47.9%	52.1%
104,629	MERCED	32,208	14,842	16,637	729	1,795 D	46.1%	51.7%	47.1%	52.9%
7,469	MODOC	3,744	1,917	1,733	94	184 R	51.2%	46.3%	52.5%	47.5%
4,016	MONO	2,721	1,600	1,025	96	575 R	58.8%	37.7%	61.0%	39.0%
250,071	MONTEREY	80,153	40,896	36,849	2,408	4,047 R	51.0%	46.0%	52.6%	47.4%
79,140	NAPA	40,205	20,839	18,048	1,318	2,791 R	51.8%	44.9%	53.6%	46.4%
26,346	NEVADA	16,881	8,170	7,926	785	244 R	48.4%	47.0%	50.8%	49.2%
1,420,386	ORANGE	657,433	408,632	232,246	16,555	176,386 R	62.2%	35.3%	63.8%	36.2%
77,306	PLACER	40,311	18,154	21,026	1,131	2,872 D	45.0%	52.2%	46.3%	53.7%
11,707	PLUMAS	6,563	2,884	3,429	250	545 D	43.9%	52.2%	45.7%	54.3%
459,074	RIVERSIDE	198,558	97,774	96,228	4,556	1,546 R	49.2%	48.5%	50.4%	49.6%
631,498	SACRAMENTO	275,876	123,110	144,203	8,563	21,093 D	44.6%	52.3%	46.1%	53.9%
18,226	SAN BENITO	6,680	3,398	3,122	160	276 R	50.9%	46.7%	52.1%	47.9%
684,072	SAN BERNARDINO	228,885	113,265	109,636	5,984	3,629 R	49.5%	47.9%	50.8%	49.2%
1,357,854	SAN DIEGO	633,795	353,302	263,654	16,839	89,648 R	55.7%	41.6%	57.3%	42.7%
715,674	SAN FRANCISCO	256,888	103,561	133,733	19,594	30,172 D	40.3%	52.1%	43.6%	56.4%
290,208	SAN JOAQUIN	101,361	50,277	48,733	2,351	1,544 R	49.6%	48.1%	50.8%	49.2%
105,690	SAN LUIS OBISPO	54,298	27,785	24,926	1,587	2,859 R	51.2%	45.9%	52.7%	47.3%
556,234	SAN MATEO	231,741	117,338	102,896	11,507	14,442 R	50.6%	44.4%	53.3%	46.7%
264,324	SANTA BARBARA	119,844	60,922	55,018	3,904	5,904 R	50.8%	45.9%	52.5%	47.5%
1,064,714	SANTA CLARA	443,138	219,188	208,023	15,927	11,165 R	49.5%	46.9%	51.3%	48.7%
123,790	SANTA CRUZ	73,969	31,872	37,772	4,325	5,900 D	43.1%	51.1%	45.8%	54.2%
77,640	SHASTA	37,854	17,273	19,200	1,381	1,927 D	45.6%	50.7%	47.4%	52.6%
2,365	SIERRA	1,576	680	841	55	161 D	43.1%	53.4%	44.7%	55.3%
33,225	SISKIYOU	14,615	7,070	7,060	485	10 R	48.4%	48.3%	50.0%	50.0%
169,941	SOLANO	61,644	26,136	33,682	1,826	7,546 D	42.4%	54.6%	43.7%	56.3%
204,885	SONOMA	105,952	50,555	50,353	5,044	202 R	47.7%	47.5%	50.1%	49.9%
194,506	STANISLAUS	73,465	32,937	38,448	2,080	5,511 D	44.8%	52.3%	46.1%	53.9%
41,935	SUTTER	16,131	8,745	6,966	420	1,779 R	54.2%	43.2%	55.7%	44.3%
29,517	TEHAMA	13,635	6,110	6,990	535	880 D	44.8%	51.3%	46.6%	53.4%
7,615	TRINITY	4,356	1,989	2,172	195	183 D	45.7%	49.9%	47.8%	52.2%
188,322	TULARE	58,441	31,864	25,551	1,026	6,313 R	54.5%	43.7%	55.5%	44.5%
22,169	TUOLUMNE	13,003	6,104	6,492	407	388 D	46.9%	49.9%	48.5%	51.5%
376,430	VENTURA	155,401	82,670	68,529	4,202	14,141 R	53.2%	44.1%	54.7%	45.3%
91,788	YOLO	43,317	18,376	23,533	1,408	5,157 D	42.4%	54.3%	43.8%	56.2%
44,736	YUBA	12,285	5,496	6,451	338	955 D	44.7%	52.5%	46.0%	54.0%
19,953,134	TOTAL	7,867,117	3,882,244	3,742,284	242,589	139,960 R	49.3%	47.6%	50.9%	49.1%

CALIFORNIA

PRESIDENT 1972

1970 Census Population	County	Total Vote	Republican	Democratic	Other	Rep.-Dem. Plurality	Percentage Total Vote Rep.	Total Vote Dem.	Major Vote Rep.	Major Vote Dem.
1,073,184	ALAMEDA	471,195	201,862	259,254	10,079	57,392 D	42.8%	55.0%	43.8%	56.2%
484	ALPINE	576	366	195	15	171 R	63.5%	33.9%	65.2%	34.8%
11,821	AMADOR	6,616	3,533	2,705	378	828 R	53.4%	40.9%	56.6%	43.4%
101,969	BUTTE	50,028	28,819	18,401	2,808	10,418 R	57.6%	36.8%	61.0%	39.0%
13,585	CALAVERAS	6,779	4,119	2,268	392	1,851 R	60.8%	33.5%	64.5%	35.5%
12,430	COLUSA	4,717	2,715	1,810	192	905 R	57.6%	38.4%	60.0%	40.0%
558,389	CONTRA COSTA	256,884	139,044	111,718	6,122	27,326 R	54.1%	43.5%	55.4%	44.6%
14,580	DEL NORTE	5,648	2,927	2,156	565	771 R	51.8%	38.2%	57.6%	42.4%
43,833	EL DORADO	20,905	11,330	8,654	921	2,676 R	54.2%	41.4%	56.7%	43.3%
413,053	FRESNO	156,719	79,051	72,682	4,986	6,369 R	50.4%	46.4%	52.1%	47.9%
17,521	GLENN	7,743	4,569	2,681	493	1,888 R	59.0%	34.6%	63.0%	37.0%
99,692	HUMBOLDT	45,763	22,345	21,132	2,286	1,213 R	48.8%	46.2%	51.4%	48.6%
74,492	IMPERIAL	22,849	14,178	7,982	689	6,196 R	62.1%	34.9%	64.0%	36.0%
15,571	INYO	7,159	4,873	2,006	280	2,867 R	68.1%	28.0%	70.8%	29.2%
329,162	KERN	119,193	71,686	41,937	5,570	29,749 R	60.1%	35.2%	63.1%	36.9%
64,610	KINGS	18,595	10,509	7,274	812	3,235 R	56.5%	39.1%	59.1%	40.9%
19,548	LAKE	11,750	6,477	4,715	558	1,762 R	55.1%	40.1%	57.9%	42.1%
14,960	LASSEN	7,122	3,618	3,134	370	484 R	50.8%	44.0%	53.6%	46.4%
7,032,075	LOS ANGELES	2,830,370	1,549,717	1,189,977	90,676	359,740 R	54.8%	42.0%	56.6%	43.4%
41,519	MADERA	14,892	7,835	6,580	477	1,255 R	52.6%	44.2%	54.4%	45.6%
206,038	MARIN	103,883	54,123	47,414	2,346	6,709 R	52.1%	45.6%	53.3%	46.7%
6,015	MARIPOSA	3,779	2,122	1,487	170	635 R	56.2%	39.3%	58.8%	41.2%
51,101	MENDOCINO	21,814	11,128	9,435	1,251	1,693 R	51.0%	43.3%	54.1%	45.9%
104,629	MERCED	32,648	17,737	13,914	997	3,823 R	54.3%	42.6%	56.0%	44.0%
7,469	MODOC	3,565	2,085	1,271	209	814 R	58.5%	35.7%	62.1%	37.9%
4,016	MONO	2,799	1,872	828	99	1,044 R	66.9%	29.6%	69.3%	30.7%
250,071	MONTEREY	82,408	47,004	32,545	2,859	14,459 R	57.0%	39.5%	59.1%	40.9%
79,140	NAPA	39,261	23,403	14,529	1,329	8,874 R	59.6%	37.0%	61.7%	38.3%
26,346	NEVADA	14,638	8,004	5,693	941	2,311 R	54.7%	38.9%	58.4%	41.6%
1,420,386	ORANGE	656,653	448,291	176,847	31,515	271,444 R	68.3%	26.9%	71.7%	28.3%
77,306	PLACER	36,945	18,597	16,911	1,437	1,686 R	50.3%	45.8%	52.4%	47.6%
11,707	PLUMAS	6,360	2,952	3,057	351	105 D	46.4%	48.1%	49.1%	50.9%
459,074	RIVERSIDE	186,404	108,120	71,591	6,693	36,529 R	58.0%	38.4%	60.2%	39.8%
631,498	SACRAMENTO	288,221	141,218	137,287	9,716	3,931 R	49.0%	47.6%	50.7%	49.3%
18,226	SAN BENITO	6,881	3,961	2,582	338	1,379 R	57.6%	37.5%	60.5%	39.5%
684,072	SAN BERNARDINO	242,256	144,689	85,986	11,581	58,703 R	59.7%	35.5%	62.7%	37.3%
1,357,854	SAN DIEGO	601,137	371,627	206,455	23,055	165,172 R	61.8%	34.3%	64.3%	35.7%
715,674	SAN FRANCISCO	304,770	127,461	170,882	6,427	43,421 D	41.8%	56.1%	42.7%	57.3%
290,208	SAN JOAQUIN	111,469	61,646	44,062	5,761	17,584 R	55.3%	39.5%	58.3%	41.7%
105,690	SAN LUIS OBISPO	51,033	28,566	20,779	1,688	7,787 R	56.0%	40.7%	57.9%	42.1%
556,234	SAN MATEO	256,297	135,377	109,745	11,175	25,632 R	52.8%	42.8%	55.2%	44.8%
264,324	SANTA BARBARA	121,541	67,075	50,609	3,857	16,466 R	55.2%	41.6%	57.0%	43.0%
1,064,714	SANTA CLARA	457,293	237,334	208,506	11,453	28,828 R	51.9%	45.6%	53.2%	46.8%
123,790	SANTA CRUZ	69,759	34,799	32,336	2,624	2,463 R	49.9%	46.4%	51.8%	48.2%
77,640	SHASTA	35,603	16,618	17,214	1,771	596 D	46.7%	48.3%	49.1%	50.9%
2,365	SIERRA	1,324	629	658	37	29 D	47.5%	49.7%	48.9%	51.1%
33,225	SISKIYOU	14,696	7,563	6,434	699	1,129 R	51.5%	43.8%	54.0%	46.0%
169,941	SOLANO	57,965	31,314	24,766	1,885	6,548 R	54.0%	42.7%	55.8%	44.2%
204,885	SONOMA	105,434	57,697	43,746	3,991	13,951 R	54.7%	41.5%	56.9%	43.1%
194,506	STANISLAUS	76,867	39,521	35,005	2,341	4,516 R	51.4%	45.5%	53.0%	47.0%
41,935	SUTTER	16,372	10,224	5,409	739	4,815 R	62.4%	33.0%	65.4%	34.6%
29,517	TEHAMA	12,424	6,054	5,175	1,195	879 R	48.7%	41.7%	53.9%	46.1%
7,615	TRINITY	3,681	1,868	1,621	192	247 R	50.7%	44.0%	53.5%	46.5%
188,322	TULARE	60,150	36,048	21,775	2,327	14,273 R	59.9%	36.2%	62.3%	37.7%
22,169	TUOLUMNE	10,856	5,894	4,596	366	1,298 R	54.3%	42.3%	56.2%	43.8%
376,430	VENTURA	150,805	95,310	49,307	6,188	46,003 R	63.2%	32.7%	65.9%	34.1%
91,788	YOLO	42,738	17,969	23,694	1,075	5,725 D	42.0%	55.4%	43.1%	56.9%
44,736	YUBA	11,630	6,623	4,435	572	2,188 R	56.9%	38.1%	59.9%	40.1%
19,953,134	TOTAL	8,367,862	4,602,096	3,475,847	289,919	1,126,249 R	55.0%	41.5%	57.0%	43.0%

CALIFORNIA

PRESIDENT 1968

1960 Census Population	County	Total Vote	Republican	Democratic	AIP	Other	Plurality	Percentage		
								Rep.	Dem.	AIP
905,670	ALAMEDA	407,349	153,285	219,545	28,426	6,093	66,260 D	37.6%	53.9%	7.0%
397	ALPINE	253	150	83	20		67 R	59.3%	32.8%	7.9%
9,990	AMADOR	5,390	2,269	2,440	660	21	171 D	42.1%	45.3%	12.2%
62,030	BUTTE	39,211	22,225	12,887	3,891	208	9,338 R	56.7%	32.9%	9.9%
10,289	CALAVERAS	5,832	3,042	2,134	643	13	908 R	52.2%	36.6%	11.0%
12,075	COLUSA	4,577	2,361	1,858	344	14	503 R	51.6%	40.6%	7.5%
409,030	CONTRA COSTA	218,917	97,486	101,668	18,330	1,433	4,182 D	44.5%	46.4%	8.4%
17,771	DEL NORTE	5,168	2,387	2,236	495	50	151 R	46.2%	43.3%	9.6%
29,390	EL DORADO	15,241	7,468	6,054	1,676	43	1,414 R	49.0%	39.7%	11.0%
365,945	FRESNO	137,396	59,901	65,153	11,292	1,050	5,252 D	43.6%	47.4%	8.2%
17,245	GLENN	7,138	3,848	2,466	808	16	1,382 R	53.9%	34.5%	11.3%
104,892	HUMBOLDT	36,214	16,719	16,476	2,759	260	243 R	46.2%	45.5%	7.6%
72,105	IMPERIAL	20,446	10,818	7,481	2,100	47	3,337 R	52.9%	36.6%	10.3%
11,684	INYO	6,687	3,641	2,314	714	18	1,327 R	54.4%	34.6%	10.7%
291,984	KERN	115,832	53,990	49,284	12,309	249	4,706 R	46.6%	42.5%	10.6%
49,954	KINGS	18,101	7,796	8,643	1,640	22	847 D	43.1%	47.7%	9.1%
13,786	LAKE	9,111	4,464	3,777	838	32	687 R	49.0%	41.5%	9.2%
13,597	LASSEN	6,218	2,553	2,930	712	23	377 D	41.1%	47.1%	11.5%
6,038,771	LOS ANGELES	2,657,982	1,266,480	1,223,251	151,050	17,201	43,229 R	47.6%	46.0%	5.7%
60,468	MADERA	14,303	6,229	6,932	1,120	22	703 D	43.6%	48.5%	7.8%
146,820	MARIN	82,755	41,422	36,278	3,801	1,254	5,144 R	50.1%	43.8%	4.6%
5,064	MARIPOSA	2,997	1,496	1,187	302	12	309 R	49.9%	39.6%	10.1%
51,059	MENDOCINO	17,904	8,305	7,935	1,554	110	370 R	46.4%	44.3%	8.7%
90,446	MERCED	28,349	11,595	14,453	2,248	53	2,858 D	40.9%	51.0%	7.9%
8,308	MODOC	3,267	1,713	1,264	284	6	449 R	52.4%	38.7%	8.7%
2,213	MONO	1,758	1,130	465	156	7	665 R	64.3%	26.5%	8.9%
198,351	MONTEREY	67,124	33,670	28,261	4,800	393	5,409 R	50.2%	42.1%	7.2%
65,890	NAPA	32,612	14,270	14,762	3,476	104	492 D	43.8%	45.3%	10.7%
20,911	NEVADA	11,794	6,061	4,607	1,078	48	1,454 R	51.4%	39.1%	9.1%
703,925	ORANGE	498,707	314,905	148,869	33,034	1,899	166,036 R	63.1%	29.9%	6.6%
56,998	PLACER	29,144	12,427	14,050	2,574	93	1,623 D	42.6%	48.2%	8.8%
11,620	PLUMAS	5,611	2,097	2,961	529	24	864 D	37.4%	52.8%	9.4%
306,191	RIVERSIDE	157,670	83,414	61,146	12,432	678	22,268 R	52.9%	38.8%	7.9%
502,778	SACRAMENTO	233,246	97,177	118,769	16,269	1,031	21,592 D	41.7%	50.9%	7.0%
15,396	SAN BENITO	6,229	2,961	2,809	447	12	152 R	47.5%	45.1%	7.2%
503,591	SAN BERNARDINO	223,616	111,974	89,418	21,187	1,037	22,556 R	50.1%	40.0%	9.5%
1,033,011	SAN DIEGO	464,863	261,540	167,669	33,340	2,314	93,871 R	56.3%	36.1%	7.2%
742,855	SAN FRANCISCO	299,947	100,970	177,509	17,332	4,136	76,539 D	33.7%	59.2%	5.8%
249,989	SAN JOAQUIN	98,589	47,293	42,073	8,923	300	5,220 R	48.0%	42.7%	9.1%
81,044	SAN LUIS OBISPO	37,881	19,420	15,828	2,416	217	3,592 R	51.3%	41.8%	6.4%
444,387	SAN MATEO	225,668	98,654	106,519	14,720	5,775	7,865 D	43.7%	47.2%	6.5%
168,962	SANTA BARBARA	93,420	50,068	37,565	5,083	704	12,503 R	53.6%	40.2%	5.4%
642,315	SANTA CLARA	358,367	163,446	173,511	18,754	2,656	10,065 D	45.6%	48.4%	5.2%
84,219	SANTA CRUZ	49,944	25,365	20,492	3,465	622	4,873 R	50.8%	41.0%	6.9%
59,468	SHASTA	29,230	11,821	14,510	2,815	84	2,689 D	40.4%	49.6%	9.6%
2,247	SIERRA	1,193	548	559	85	1	11 D	45.9%	46.9%	7.1%
32,885	SISKIYOU	13,732	6,334	6,260	1,088	50	74 R	46.1%	45.6%	7.9%
134,597	SOLANO	50,952	17,683	27,271	5,810	188	9,588 D	34.7%	53.5%	11.4%
147,375	SONOMA	78,059	38,088	33,587	5,875	509	4,501 R	48.8%	43.0%	7.5%
157,294	STANISLAUS	65,063	29,573	31,316	3,973	201	1,743 D	45.5%	48.1%	6.1%
33,380	SUTTER	14,545	8,665	4,624	1,228	28	4,041 R	59.6%	31.8%	8.4%
25,305	TEHAMA	10,999	5,198	4,565	1,216	20	633 R	47.3%	41.5%	11.1%
9,706	TRINITY	3,307	1,426	1,433	432	16	7 D	43.1%	43.3%	13.1%
168,403	TULARE	56,189	29,314	22,180	4,580	115	7,134 R	52.2%	39.5%	8.2%
14,404	TUOLUMNE	9,119	4,330	3,913	865	11	417 R	47.5%	42.9%	9.5%
199,138	VENTURA	116,261	59,705	47,794	8,234	528	11,911 R	51.4%	41.1%	7.1%
65,727	YOLO	28,960	11,123	15,833	1,742	262	4,710 D	38.4%	54.7%	6.0%
33,859	YUBA	11,150	5,371	4,461	1,296	22	910 R	48.2%	40.0%	11.6%
15,717,204	TOTAL	7,251,587	3,467,664	3,244,318	487,270	52,335	223,346 R	47.8%	44.7%	6.7%

CALIFORNIA

ELECTION NOTES

1984 Other vote was 49,951 Bergland (Libertarian); 39,265 Richards (American Independent); 26,297 Johnson (Peace and Freedom); 16 Serrette (write-in); 366 scattered write-in. The state-wide total for the other vote column includes these 382 write-in votes not reported by county.

1980 Other vote was 739,833 Anderson (Independent); 148,434 Clark (Libertarian); 61,063 Commoner (Independent); 18,116 Smith (Peace and Freedom); 9,856 Rarick (American Independent); 847 Hall (write-in); 231 Pulley (write-in); 87 Greaves (write-in); 36 Bubar (write-in); 15 Griswold (write-in); 26 scattered write-in. The state-wide total for the other vote column includes these 1,242 write-in votes not reported by county.

1976 Other vote was 58,412 McCarthy (write-in); 56,388 MacBride (Independent); 51,098 Maddox (American Independent); 41,731 Wright (Peace and Freedom); 17,259 Camejo (Independent); 12,766 Hall (Independent); 4,565 Anderson (write-in); 222 Levin (write-in); 34 Bubar (write-in); 26 Miller (write-in); 14 Taylor (write-in); 74 scattered write-in.

1972 Other vote was 232,554 Schmitz (American Independent); 55,167 Spock (Peace and Freedom); 980 Hospers (write-in); 574 Jenness (write-in); 373 Hall (write-in); 197 Fisher (write-in); 53 Munn (write-in); 21 Green (write-in).

1968 Wallace on the ballot as American Independent. Other vote was 27,707 no Presidential candidate indicated but pledged to Peggy Terry for Vice-President (Peace and Freedom); 20,721 McCarthy (write-in); 3,230 Gregory (write-in); 341 Blomen (write-in); 260 Mitchell (write-in); 59 Munn (write-in); 17 Soeters (write-in).

COLORADO

POPULAR VOTE FOR PRESIDENT 1920 TO 1984

								Percentage			
	Total	Republican		Democratic		Other		Total Vote		Major Vote	
Year	Vote	Vote	Candidate	Vote	Candidate	Vote	Plurality	Rep.	Dem.	Rep.	Dem.
1984	1,295,380	821,817	Reagan, Ronald	454,975	Mondale, Walter F.	18,588	366,842 R	63.4%	35.1%	64.4%	35.6%
1980	1,184,415	652,264	Reagan, Ronald	367,973	Carter, Jimmy	164,178	284,291 R	55.1%	31.1%	63.9%	36.1%
1976	1,081,554	584,367	Ford, Gerald R.	460,353	Carter, Jimmy	36,834	124,014 R	54.0%	42.6%	55.9%	44.1%
1972	953,884	597,189	Nixon, Richard M.	329,980	McGovern, George S.	26,715	267,209 R	62.6%	34.6%	64.4%	35.6%
1968	811,199	409,345	Nixon, Richard M.	335,174	Humphrey, Hubert H.	66,680	74,171 R	50.5%	41.3%	55.0%	45.0%
1964	776,986	296,767	Goldwater, Barry M.	476,024	Johnson, Lyndon B.	4,195	179,257 D	38.2%	61.3%	38.4%	61.6%
1960	736,236	402,242	Nixon, Richard M.	330,629	Kennedy, John F.	3,365	71,613 R	54.6%	44.9%	54.9%	45.1%
1956	657,074	394,479	Eisenhower, Dwight D.	257,997	Stevenson, Adlai E.	4,598	136,482 R	60.0%	39.3%	60.5%	39.5%
1952	630,103	379,782	Eisenhower, Dwight D.	245,504	Stevenson, Adlai E.	4,817	134,278 R	60.3%	39.0%	60.7%	39.3%
1948	515,237	239,714	Dewey, Thomas E.	267,288	Truman, Harry S.	8,235	27,574 D	46.5%	51.9%	47.3%	52.7%
1944	505,039	268,731	Dewey, Thomas E.	234,331	Roosevelt, Franklin D.	1,977	34,400 R	53.2%	46.4%	53.4%	46.6%
1940	549,004	279,576	Willkie, Wendell	265,554	Roosevelt, Franklin D.	3,874	14,022 R	50.9%	48.4%	51.3%	48.7%
1936	488,685	181,267	Landon, Alfred M.	295,021	Roosevelt, Franklin D.	12,397	113,754 D	37.1%	60.4%	38.1%	61.9%
1932	457,696	189,617	Hoover, Herbert C.	250,877	Roosevelt, Franklin D.	17,202	61,260 D	41.4%	54.8%	43.0%	57.0%
1928	392,242	253,872	Hoover, Herbert C.	133,131	Smith, Alfred E.	5,239	120,741 R	64.7%	33.9%	65.6%	34.4%
1924 **	342,261	195,171	Coolidge, Calvin	75,238	Davis, John W.	71,852	119,933 R	57.0%	22.0%	72.2%	27.8%
1920	292,053	173,248	Harding, Warren G.	104,936	Cox, James M.	13,869	68,312 R	59.3%	35.9%	62.3%	37.7%

In 1924 other vote was 69,946 Progressive; 966 Prohibition; 562 Communist and 378 Socialist Labor.

ELECTORAL COLLEGE VOTE 1920 TO 1984

Year	Total	Republican	Democratic	Other
1984	8	8	—	—
1980	7	7	—	—
1976	7	7	—	—
1972	7	7	—	—
1968	6	6	—	—
1964	6	—	6	—
1960	6	6	—	—
1956	6	6	—	—
1952	6	6	—	—
1948	6	—	6	—
1944	6	6	—	—
1940	6	6	—	—
1936	6	—	6	—
1932	6	—	6	—
1928	6	6	—	—
1924	6	6	—	—
1920	6	6	—	—

COLORADO

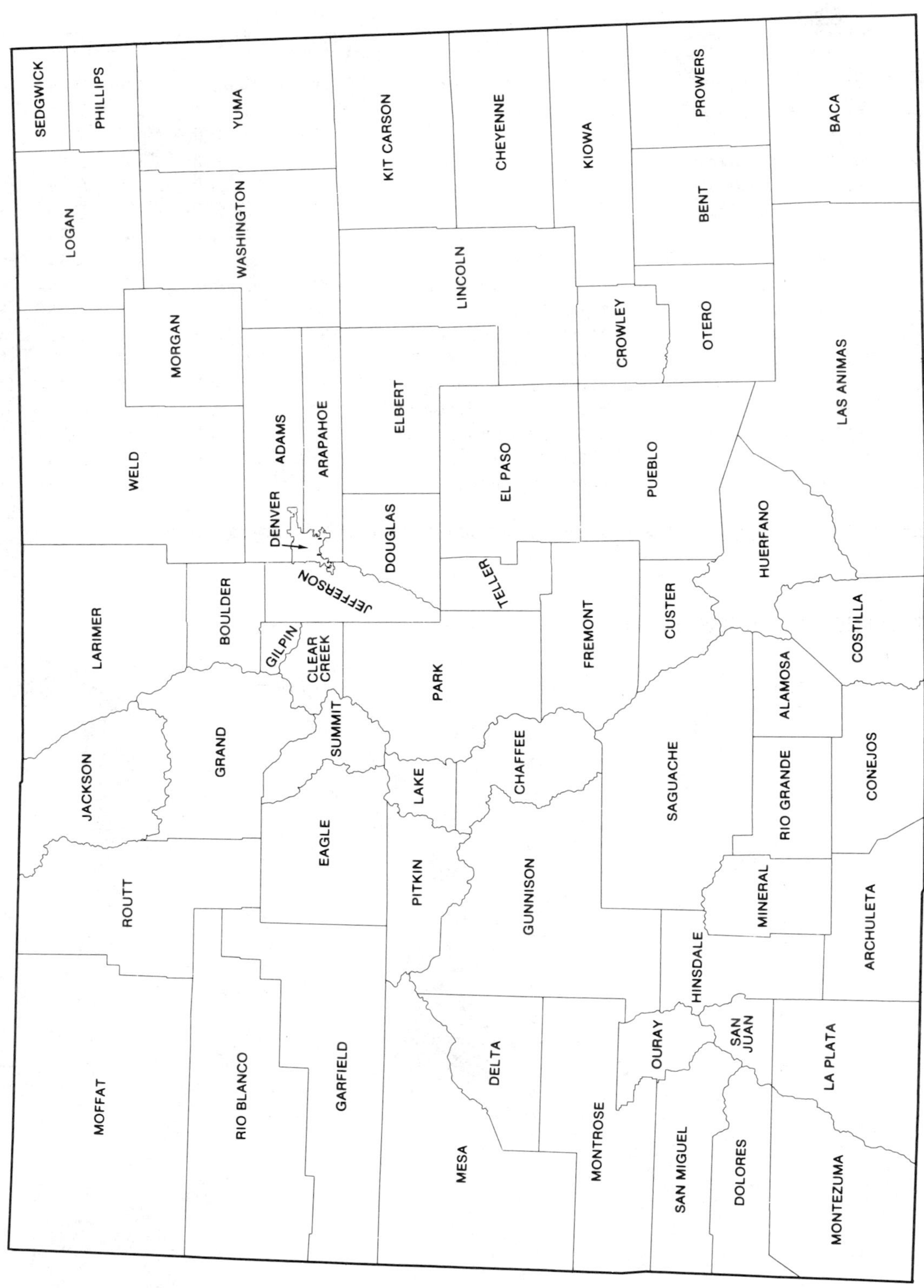
SEDGWICK
PHILLIPS
YUMA
KIT CARSON
CHEYENNE
KIOWA
PROWERS
BACA
LOGAN
WASHINGTON
LINCOLN
BENT
MORGAN
CROWLEY
OTERO
LAS ANIMAS
ADAMS
ARAPAHOE
ELBERT
WELD
EL PASO
PUEBLO
DENVER
DOUGLAS
HUERFANO
JEFFERSON
TELLER
LARIMER
BOULDER
FREMONT
CUSTER
COSTILLA
GILPIN
CLEAR CREEK
PARK
ALAMOSA
GRAND
SUMMIT
CHAFFEE
SAGUACHE
JACKSON
LAKE
RIO GRANDE
CONEJOS
EAGLE
ROUTT
PITKIN
GUNNISON
MINERAL
ARCHULETA
HINSDALE
OURAY
SAN JUAN
LA PLATA
DELTA
MOFFAT
RIO BLANCO
GARFIELD
MESA
MONTROSE
SAN MIGUEL
DOLORES
MONTEZUMA

COLORADO

PRESIDENT 1984

1980 Census Population	County	Total Vote	Republican	Democratic	Other	Rep.-Dem. Plurality	Percentage Total Vote Rep.	Total Vote Dem.	Major Vote Rep.	Major Vote Dem.
245,944	ADAMS	91,511	55,092	35,285	1,134	19,807 R	60.2%	38.6%	61.0%	39.0%
11,799	ALAMOSA	4,711	2,953	1,720	38	1,233 R	62.7%	36.5%	63.2%	36.8%
293,621	ARAPAHOE	149,555	107,556	39,891	2,108	67,665 R	71.9%	26.7%	72.9%	27.1%
3,664	ARCHULETA	2,163	1,557	584	22	973 R	72.0%	27.0%	72.7%	27.3%
5,419	BACA	2,509	1,903	580	26	1,323 R	75.8%	23.1%	76.6%	23.4%
5,945	BENT	2,199	1,314	859	26	455 R	59.8%	39.1%	60.5%	39.5%
189,625	BOULDER	97,238	53,535	42,195	1,508	11,340 R	55.1%	43.4%	55.9%	44.1%
13,227	CHAFFEE	5,550	3,680	1,779	91	1,901 R	66.3%	32.1%	67.4%	32.6%
2,153	CHEYENNE	1,218	892	307	19	585 R	73.2%	25.2%	74.4%	25.6%
7,308	CLEAR CREEK	3,292	2,151	1,089	52	1,062 R	65.3%	33.1%	66.4%	33.6%
7,794	CONEJOS	3,247	1,669	1,553	25	116 R	51.4%	47.8%	51.8%	48.2%
3,071	COSTILLA	1,631	621	997	13	376 D	38.1%	61.1%	38.4%	61.6%
2,988	CROWLEY	1,527	993	517	17	476 R	65.0%	33.9%	65.8%	34.2%
1,528	CUSTER	1,093	832	241	20	591 R	76.1%	22.0%	77.5%	22.5%
21,225	DELTA	9,639	6,678	2,835	126	3,843 R	69.3%	29.4%	70.2%	29.8%
492,365	DENVER	219,741	105,096	110,200	4,445	5,104 D	47.8%	50.1%	48.8%	51.2%
1,658	DOLORES	850	667	173	10	494 R	78.5%	20.4%	79.4%	20.6%
25,153	DOUGLAS	15,441	12,249	3,011	181	9,238 R	79.3%	19.5%	80.3%	19.7%
13,320	EAGLE	6,633	4,500	2,032	101	2,468 R	67.8%	30.6%	68.9%	31.1%
6,850	ELBERT	3,461	2,605	802	54	1,803 R	75.3%	23.2%	76.5%	23.5%
309,424	EL PASO	117,773	88,377	28,185	1,211	60,192 R	75.0%	23.9%	75.8%	24.2%
28,676	FREMONT	12,256	8,250	3,895	111	4,355 R	67.3%	31.8%	67.9%	32.1%
22,514	GARFIELD	10,285	7,111	3,076	98	4,035 R	69.1%	29.9%	69.8%	30.2%
2,441	GILPIN	1,571	896	634	41	262 R	57.0%	40.4%	58.6%	41.4%
7,475	GRAND	3,940	2,865	1,017	58	1,848 R	72.7%	25.8%	73.8%	26.2%
10,689	GUNNISON	4,606	3,100	1,424	82	1,676 R	67.3%	30.9%	68.5%	31.5%
408	HINSDALE	414	310	98	6	212 R	74.9%	23.7%	76.0%	24.0%
6,440	HUERFANO	3,224	1,581	1,602	41	21 D	49.0%	49.7%	49.7%	50.3%
1,863	JACKSON	923	722	191	10	531 R	78.2%	20.7%	79.1%	20.9%
371,753	JEFFERSON	180,628	124,496	53,700	2,432	70,796 R	68.9%	29.7%	69.9%	30.1%
1,936	KIOWA	1,130	850	265	15	585 R	75.2%	23.5%	76.2%	23.8%
7,599	KIT CARSON	3,584	2,762	778	44	1,984 R	77.1%	21.7%	78.0%	22.0%
8,830	LAKE	2,747	1,364	1,324	59	40 R	49.7%	48.2%	50.7%	49.3%
27,424	LA PLATA	12,918	8,719	4,040	159	4,679 R	67.5%	31.3%	68.3%	31.7%
149,184	LARIMER	74,849	49,883	23,896	1,070	25,987 R	66.6%	31.9%	67.6%	32.4%
14,897	LAS ANIMAS	6,742	2,992	3,670	80	678 D	44.4%	54.4%	44.9%	55.1%
4,663	LINCOLN	2,278	1,661	587	30	1,074 R	72.9%	25.8%	73.9%	26.1%
19,800	LOGAN	8,133	5,883	2,155	95	3,728 R	72.3%	26.5%	73.2%	26.8%
81,530	MESA	34,074	23,736	9,938	400	13,798 R	69.7%	29.2%	70.5%	29.5%
804	MINERAL	459	333	117	9	216 R	72.5%	25.5%	74.0%	26.0%
13,133	MOFFAT	4,981	3,630	1,228	123	2,402 R	72.9%	24.7%	74.7%	25.3%
16,510	MONTEZUMA	6,506	4,753	1,665	88	3,088 R	73.1%	25.6%	74.1%	25.9%
24,352	MONTROSE	10,173	7,162	2,864	147	4,298 R	70.4%	28.2%	71.4%	28.6%
22,513	MORGAN	8,556	6,097	2,331	128	3,766 R	71.3%	27.2%	72.3%	27.7%
22,567	OTERO	8,615	5,373	3,005	237	2,368 R	62.4%	34.9%	64.1%	35.9%
1,925	OURAY	1,290	914	366	10	548 R	70.9%	28.4%	71.4%	28.6%
5,333	PARK	2,902	2,041	782	79	1,259 R	70.3%	26.9%	72.3%	27.7%
4,542	PHILLIPS	2,367	1,689	651	27	1,038 R	71.4%	27.5%	72.2%	27.8%
10,338	PITKIN	5,528	3,117	2,293	118	824 R	56.4%	41.5%	57.6%	42.4%
13,070	PROWERS	5,095	3,501	1,467	127	2,034 R	68.7%	28.8%	70.5%	29.5%
125,972	PUEBLO	52,200	24,634	27,126	440	2,492 D	47.2%	52.0%	47.6%	52.4%
6,255	RIO BLANCO	2,637	2,131	484	22	1,647 R	80.8%	18.4%	81.5%	18.5%
10,511	RIO GRANDE	4,262	3,122	1,104	36	2,018 R	73.3%	25.9%	73.9%	26.1%
13,404	ROUTT	6,408	4,239	2,051	118	2,188 R	66.2%	32.0%	67.4%	32.6%
3,935	SAGUACHE	2,084	1,201	867	16	334 R	57.6%	41.6%	58.1%	41.9%
833	SAN JUAN	519	320	183	16	137 R	61.7%	35.3%	63.6%	36.4%
3,192	SAN MIGUEL	1,521	833	654	34	179 R	54.8%	43.0%	56.0%	44.0%
3,266	SEDGWICK	1,583	1,146	429	8	717 R	72.4%	27.1%	72.8%	27.2%
8,848	SUMMIT	4,918	3,253	1,588	77	1,665 R	66.1%	32.3%	67.2%	32.8%
8,034	TELLER	4,562	3,460	1,043	59	2,417 R	75.8%	22.9%	76.8%	23.2%

COLORADO

PRESIDENT 1984

1980 Census Population	County	Total Vote	Republican	Democratic	Other	Rep.-Dem. Plurality	Percentage Total Vote Rep.	Percentage Total Vote Dem.	Percentage Major Vote Rep.	Percentage Major Vote Dem.
5,304	WASHINGTON	2,684	2,080	568	36	1,512 R	77.5%	21.2%	78.5%	21.5%
123,438	WELD	45,679	31,293	13,863	523	17,430 R	68.5%	30.3%	69.3%	30.7%
9,682	YUMA	4,567	3,394	1,121	52	2,273 R	74.3%	24.5%	75.2%	24.8%
2,889,964	TOTAL	1,295,380	821,817	454,975	18,588	366,842 R	63.4%	35.1%	64.4%	35.6%

COLORADO

PRESIDENT 1980

1980 Census Population	County	Total Vote	Republican	Democratic	Other	Rep.-Dem. Plurality	Percentage Total Vote Rep.	Total Vote Dem.	Major Vote Rep.	Major Vote Dem.
245,944	ADAMS	84,975	42,916	31,357	10,702	11,559 R	50.5%	36.9%	57.8%	42.2%
11,799	ALAMOSA	4,828	2,601	1,821	406	780 R	53.9%	37.7%	58.8%	41.2%
293,621	ARAPAHOE	127,980	79,594	30,148	18,238	49,446 R	62.2%	23.6%	72.5%	27.5%
3,664	ARCHULETA	1,900	1,252	532	116	720 R	65.9%	28.0%	70.2%	29.8%
5,419	BACA	2,692	1,999	551	142	1,448 R	74.3%	20.5%	78.4%	21.6%
5,945	BENT	2,330	1,206	894	230	312 R	51.8%	38.4%	57.4%	42.6%
189,625	BOULDER	87,069	40,698	28,422	17,949	12,276 R	46.7%	32.6%	58.9%	41.1%
13,227	CHAFFEE	5,478	3,327	1,583	568	1,744 R	60.7%	28.9%	67.8%	32.2%
2,153	CHEYENNE	1,239	816	322	101	494 R	65.9%	26.0%	71.7%	28.3%
7,308	CLEAR CREEK	3,173	1,784	837	552	947 R	56.2%	26.4%	68.1%	31.9%
7,794	CONEJOS	3,232	1,597	1,503	132	94 R	49.4%	46.5%	51.5%	48.5%
3,071	COSTILLA	1,583	489	1,036	58	547 D	30.9%	65.4%	32.1%	67.9%
2,988	CROWLEY	1,473	926	472	75	454 R	62.9%	32.0%	66.2%	33.8%
1,528	CUSTER	1,010	674	231	105	443 R	66.7%	22.9%	74.5%	25.5%
21,225	DELTA	9,227	6,179	2,348	700	3,831 R	67.0%	25.4%	72.5%	27.5%
492,365	DENVER	209,508	88,398	85,903	35,207	2,495 R	42.2%	41.0%	50.7%	49.3%
1,658	DOLORES	817	615	157	45	458 R	75.3%	19.2%	79.7%	20.3%
25,153	DOUGLAS	11,596	8,126	2,108	1,362	6,018 R	70.1%	18.2%	79.4%	20.6%
13,320	EAGLE	5,816	3,061	1,608	1,147	1,453 R	52.6%	27.6%	65.6%	34.4%
6,850	ELBERT	3,122	2,107	698	317	1,409 R	67.5%	22.4%	75.1%	24.9%
309,424	EL PASO	103,990	66,199	27,463	10,328	38,736 R	63.7%	26.4%	70.7%	29.3%
28,676	FREMONT	12,113	7,162	3,952	999	3,210 R	59.1%	32.6%	64.4%	35.6%
22,514	GARFIELD	9,325	5,416	2,639	1,270	2,777 R	58.1%	28.3%	67.2%	32.8%
2,441	GILPIN	1,387	694	441	252	253 R	50.0%	31.8%	61.1%	38.9%
7,475	GRAND	3,481	2,133	820	528	1,313 R	61.3%	23.6%	72.2%	27.8%
10,689	GUNNISON	4,970	2,756	1,297	917	1,459 R	55.5%	26.1%	68.0%	32.0%
408	HINSDALE	336	232	76	28	156 R	69.0%	22.6%	75.3%	24.7%
6,440	HUERFANO	3,032	1,258	1,574	200	316 D	41.5%	51.9%	44.4%	55.6%
1,863	JACKSON	1,059	673	283	103	390 R	63.6%	26.7%	70.4%	29.6%
371,753	JEFFERSON	162,611	97,008	41,525	24,078	55,483 R	59.7%	25.5%	70.0%	30.0%
1,936	KIOWA	1,159	754	331	74	423 R	65.1%	28.6%	69.5%	30.5%
7,599	KIT CARSON	3,653	2,622	790	241	1,832 R	71.8%	21.6%	76.8%	23.2%
8,830	LAKE	3,025	1,375	1,213	437	162 R	45.5%	40.1%	53.1%	46.9%
27,424	LA PLATA	12,201	7,291	3,034	1,876	4,257 R	59.8%	24.9%	70.6%	29.4%
149,184	LARIMER	64,129	36,240	17,072	10,817	19,168 R	56.5%	26.6%	68.0%	32.0%
14,897	LAS ANIMAS	7,409	2,917	4,117	375	1,200 D	39.4%	55.6%	41.5%	58.5%
4,663	LINCOLN	2,371	1,535	602	234	933 R	64.7%	25.4%	71.8%	28.2%
19,800	LOGAN	8,293	5,238	2,332	723	2,906 R	63.2%	28.1%	69.2%	30.8%
81,530	MESA	32,916	22,686	7,549	2,681	15,137 R	68.9%	22.9%	75.0%	25.0%
804	MINERAL	450	271	125	54	146 R	60.2%	27.8%	68.4%	31.6%
13,133	MOFFAT	4,925	3,344	1,079	502	2,265 R	67.9%	21.9%	75.6%	24.4%
16,510	MONTEZUMA	6,006	4,120	1,467	419	2,653 R	68.6%	24.4%	73.7%	26.3%
24,352	MONTROSE	9,800	6,685	2,232	883	4,453 R	68.2%	22.8%	75.0%	25.0%
22,513	MORGAN	8,334	5,209	2,246	879	2,963 R	62.5%	26.9%	69.9%	30.1%
22,567	OTERO	8,801	4,801	3,294	706	1,507 R	54.6%	37.4%	59.3%	40.7%
1,925	OURAY	1,201	813	237	151	576 R	67.7%	19.7%	77.4%	22.6%
5,333	PARK	2,735	1,623	674	438	949 R	59.3%	24.6%	70.7%	29.3%
4,542	PHILLIPS	2,354	1,488	640	226	848 R	63.2%	27.2%	69.9%	30.1%
10,338	PITKIN	5,417	2,153	1,760	1,504	393 R	39.7%	32.5%	55.0%	45.0%
13,070	PROWERS	5,212	3,115	1,669	428	1,446 R	59.8%	32.0%	65.1%	34.9%
125,972	PUEBLO	46,441	20,770	21,874	3,797	1,104 D	44.7%	47.1%	48.7%	51.3%
6,255	RIO BLANCO	2,647	1,971	462	214	1,509 R	74.5%	17.5%	81.0%	19.0%
10,511	RIO GRANDE	4,488	2,844	1,370	274	1,474 R	63.4%	30.5%	67.5%	32.5%
13,404	ROUTT	6,702	3,574	1,944	1,184	1,630 R	53.3%	29.0%	64.8%	35.2%
3,935	SAGUACHE	2,135	1,124	893	118	231 R	52.6%	41.8%	55.7%	44.3%
833	SAN JUAN	549	268	146	135	122 R	48.8%	26.6%	64.7%	35.3%
3,192	SAN MIGUEL	1,809	774	651	384	123 R	42.8%	36.0%	54.3%	45.7%
3,266	SEDGWICK	1,708	1,151	438	119	713 R	67.4%	25.6%	72.4%	27.6%
8,848	SUMMIT	4,355	2,027	1,285	1,043	742 R	46.5%	29.5%	61.2%	38.8%
8,034	TELLER	3,707	2,457	802	448	1,655 R	66.3%	21.6%	75.4%	24.6%

COLORADO

PRESIDENT 1980

1980 Census Population	County	Total Vote	Republican	Democratic	Other	Rep.-Dem. Plurality	Percentage Total Vote Rep.	Percentage Total Vote Dem.	Percentage Major Vote Rep.	Percentage Major Vote Dem.
5,304	WASHINGTON	2,811	2,007	568	236	1,439 R	71.4%	20.2%	77.9%	22.1%
123,438	WELD	40,646	23,901	11,433	5,312	12,468 R	58.8%	28.1%	67.6%	32.4%
9,682	YUMA	4,674	3,220	1,043	411	2,177 R	68.9%	22.3%	75.5%	24.5%
2,889,964	TOTAL	1,184,415	652,264	367,973	164,178	284,291 R	55.1%	31.1%	63.9%	36.1%

COLORADO

PRESIDENT 1976

1970 Census Population	County	Total Vote	Republican	Democratic	Other	Rep.-Dem. Plurality	Percentage Total Vote Rep.	Total Vote Dem.	Major Vote Rep.	Major Vote Dem.
185,789	ADAMS	78,127	35,392	40,551	2,184	5,159 D	45.3%	51.9%	46.6%	53.4%
11,422	ALAMOSA	4,862	2,599	2,052	211	547 R	53.5%	42.2%	55.9%	44.1%
162,142	ARAPAHOE	99,526	63,154	33,685	2,687	29,469 R	63.5%	33.8%	65.2%	34.8%
2,733	ARCHULETA	1,432	768	632	32	136 R	53.6%	44.1%	54.9%	45.1%
5,674	BACA	2,507	1,303	1,164	40	139 R	52.0%	46.4%	52.8%	47.2%
6,493	BENT	2,480	1,156	1,268	56	112 D	46.6%	51.1%	47.7%	52.3%
131,889	BOULDER	81,300	42,830	33,284	5,186	9,546 R	52.7%	40.9%	56.3%	43.7%
10,162	CHAFFEE	5,162	2,925	2,064	173	861 R	56.7%	40.0%	58.6%	41.4%
2,396	CHEYENNE	1,271	610	625	36	15 D	48.0%	49.2%	49.4%	50.6%
4,819	CLEAR CREEK	2,669	1,477	1,069	123	408 R	55.3%	40.1%	58.0%	42.0%
7,846	CONEJOS	3,194	1,426	1,698	70	272 D	44.6%	53.2%	45.6%	54.4%
3,091	COSTILLA	1,454	392	1,033	29	641 D	27.0%	71.0%	27.5%	72.5%
3,086	CROWLEY	1,519	834	667	18	167 R	54.9%	43.9%	55.6%	44.4%
1,120	CUSTER	791	491	259	41	232 R	62.1%	32.7%	65.5%	34.5%
15,286	DELTA	8,483	4,980	3,232	271	1,748 R	58.7%	38.1%	60.6%	39.4%
514,678	DENVER	226,773	105,960	112,229	8,584	6,269 D	46.7%	49.5%	48.6%	51.4%
1,641	DOLORES	752	343	374	35	31 D	45.6%	49.7%	47.8%	52.2%
8,407	DOUGLAS	7,757	5,078	2,459	220	2,619 R	65.5%	31.7%	67.4%	32.6%
7,498	EAGLE	4,618	2,963	1,502	153	1,461 R	64.2%	32.5%	66.4%	33.6%
3,903	ELBERT	2,428	1,279	1,068	81	211 R	52.7%	44.0%	54.5%	45.5%
235,972	EL PASO	86,168	50,929	32,911	2,328	18,018 R	59.1%	38.2%	60.7%	39.3%
21,942	FREMONT	10,769	5,647	4,886	236	761 R	52.4%	45.4%	53.6%	46.4%
14,821	GARFIELD	7,871	4,699	2,852	320	1,847 R	59.7%	36.2%	62.2%	37.8%
1,272	GILPIN	1,095	451	563	81	112 D	41.2%	51.4%	44.5%	55.5%
4,107	GRAND	2,760	1,703	910	147	793 R	61.7%	33.0%	65.2%	34.8%
7,578	GUNNISON	4,150	2,568	1,250	332	1,318 R	61.9%	30.1%	67.3%	32.7%
202	HINSDALE	284	189	83	12	106 R	66.5%	29.2%	69.5%	30.5%
6,590	HUERFANO	3,165	1,182	1,932	51	750 D	37.3%	61.0%	38.0%	62.0%
1,811	JACKSON	748	455	279	14	176 R	60.8%	37.3%	62.0%	38.0%
233,031	JEFFERSON	144,102	87,080	52,782	4,240	34,298 R	60.4%	36.6%	62.3%	37.7%
2,029	KIOWA	1,137	598	529	10	69 R	52.6%	46.5%	53.1%	46.9%
7,530	KIT CARSON	3,621	1,888	1,647	86	241 R	52.1%	45.5%	53.4%	46.6%
8,282	LAKE	3,279	1,575	1,549	155	26 R	48.0%	47.2%	50.4%	49.6%
19,199	LA PLATA	10,573	6,228	3,843	502	2,385 R	58.9%	36.3%	61.8%	38.2%
89,900	LARIMER	53,009	32,169	19,005	1,835	13,164 R	60.7%	35.9%	62.9%	37.1%
15,744	LAS ANIMAS	7,175	2,615	4,459	101	1,844 D	36.4%	62.1%	37.0%	63.0%
4,836	LINCOLN	2,387	1,276	1,059	52	217 R	53.5%	44.4%	54.6%	45.4%
18,852	LOGAN	7,988	4,256	3,543	189	713 R	53.3%	44.4%	54.6%	45.4%
54,374	MESA	27,419	17,924	8,807	688	9,117 R	65.4%	32.1%	67.1%	32.9%
786	MINERAL	423	235	167	21	68 R	55.6%	39.5%	58.5%	41.5%
6,525	MOFFAT	3,775	2,099	1,451	225	648 R	55.6%	38.4%	59.1%	40.9%
12,952	MONTEZUMA	5,190	3,002	1,993	195	1,009 R	57.8%	38.4%	60.1%	39.9%
18,366	MONTROSE	8,300	4,838	3,164	298	1,674 R	58.3%	38.1%	60.5%	39.5%
20,105	MORGAN	8,631	4,603	3,798	230	805 R	53.3%	44.0%	54.8%	45.2%
23,523	OTERO	8,920	4,597	4,118	205	479 R	51.5%	46.2%	52.7%	47.3%
1,546	OURAY	1,032	645	333	54	312 R	62.5%	32.3%	66.0%	34.0%
2,185	PARK	1,872	1,034	741	97	293 R	55.2%	39.6%	58.3%	41.7%
4,131	PHILLIPS	2,373	1,142	1,173	58	31 D	48.1%	49.4%	49.3%	50.7%
6,185	PITKIN	5,512	2,955	2,194	363	761 R	53.6%	39.8%	57.4%	42.6%
13,258	PROWERS	5,592	2,578	2,861	153	283 D	46.1%	51.2%	47.4%	52.6%
118,238	PUEBLO	45,157	18,518	25,841	798	7,323 D	41.0%	57.2%	41.7%	58.3%
4,842	RIO BLANCO	2,141	1,439	627	75	812 R	67.2%	29.3%	69.7%	30.3%
10,494	RIO GRANDE	4,212	2,627	1,475	110	1,152 R	62.4%	35.0%	64.0%	36.0%
6,592	ROUTT	5,213	2,822	2,130	261	692 R	54.1%	40.9%	57.0%	43.0%
3,827	SAGUACHE	2,210	1,094	1,059	57	35 R	49.5%	47.9%	50.8%	49.2%
831	SAN JUAN	411	221	167	23	54 R	53.8%	40.6%	57.0%	43.0%
1,949	SAN MIGUEL	1,419	622	674	123	52 D	43.8%	47.5%	48.0%	52.0%
3,405	SEDGWICK	1,700	902	773	25	129 R	53.1%	45.5%	53.9%	46.1%
2,665	SUMMIT	3,142	1,826	1,087	229	739 R	58.1%	34.6%	62.7%	37.3%
3,316	TELLER	2,521	1,410	986	125	424 R	55.9%	39.1%	58.8%	41.2%

COLORADO

PRESIDENT 1976

1970 Census Population	County	Total Vote	Republican	Democratic	Other	Rep.-Dem. Plurality	Percentage Total Vote Rep.	Percentage Total Vote Dem.	Percentage Major Vote Rep.	Percentage Major Vote Dem.
5,550	WASHINGTON	2,767	1,440	1,211	116	229 R	52.0%	43.8%	54.3%	45.7%
89,297	WELD	39,732	21,976	16,501	1,255	5,475 R	55.3%	41.5%	57.1%	42.9%
8,544	YUMA	4,504	2,350	2,025	129	325 R	52.2%	45.0%	53.7%	46.3%
2,207,259	TOTAL	1,081,554	584,367	460,353	36,834	124,014 R	54.0%	42.6%	55.9%	44.1%

COLORADO

PRESIDENT 1972

1970 Census Population	County	Total Vote	Republican	Democratic	Other	Rep.-Dem. Plurality	Percentage Total Vote Rep.	Percentage Total Vote Dem.	Percentage Major Vote Rep.	Percentage Major Vote Dem.
185,789	ADAMS	66,412	40,372	24,170	1,870	16,202 R	60.8%	36.4%	62.6%	37.4%
11,422	ALAMOSA	4,665	2,916	1,540	209	1,376 R	62.5%	33.0%	65.4%	34.6%
162,142	ARAPAHOE	72,376	52,283	18,631	1,462	33,652 R	72.2%	25.7%	73.7%	26.3%
2,733	ARCHULETA	940	606	300	34	306 R	64.5%	31.9%	66.9%	33.1%
5,674	BACA	2,225	1,645	527	53	1,118 R	73.9%	23.7%	75.7%	24.3%
6,493	BENT	2,372	1,525	787	60	738 R	64.3%	33.2%	66.0%	34.0%
131,889	BOULDER	71,770	40,766	29,484	1,520	11,282 R	56.8%	41.1%	58.0%	42.0%
10,162	CHAFFEE	4,291	2,859	1,354	78	1,505 R	66.6%	31.6%	67.9%	32.1%
2,396	CHEYENNE	1,286	815	400	71	415 R	63.4%	31.1%	67.1%	32.9%
4,819	CLEAR CREEK	2,502	1,557	815	130	742 R	62.2%	32.6%	65.6%	34.4%
7,846	CONEJOS	2,987	1,658	1,140	189	518 R	55.5%	38.2%	59.3%	40.7%
3,091	COSTILLA	1,428	602	744	82	142 D	42.2%	52.1%	44.7%	55.3%
3,086	CROWLEY	1,548	1,094	414	40	680 R	70.7%	26.7%	72.5%	27.5%
1,120	CUSTER	693	495	154	44	341 R	71.4%	22.2%	76.3%	23.7%
15,286	DELTA	7,220	4,890	1,903	427	2,987 R	67.7%	26.4%	72.0%	28.0%
514,678	DENVER	225,335	121,995	98,062	5,278	23,933 R	54.1%	43.5%	55.4%	44.6%
1,641	DOLORES	694	498	166	30	332 R	71.8%	23.9%	75.0%	25.0%
8,407	DOUGLAS	4,800	3,625	1,048	127	2,577 R	75.5%	21.8%	77.6%	22.4%
7,498	EAGLE	3,301	1,920	1,306	75	614 R	58.2%	39.6%	59.5%	40.5%
3,903	ELBERT	1,932	1,416	451	65	965 R	73.3%	23.3%	75.8%	24.2%
235,972	EL PASO	77,985	53,892	21,234	2,859	32,658 R	69.1%	27.2%	71.7%	28.3%
21,942	FREMONT	9,795	6,701	2,813	281	3,888 R	68.4%	28.7%	70.4%	29.6%
14,821	GARFIELD	6,718	4,452	2,088	178	2,364 R	66.3%	31.1%	68.1%	31.9%
1,272	GILPIN	905	516	362	27	154 R	57.0%	40.0%	58.8%	41.2%
4,107	GRAND	2,461	1,721	685	55	1,036 R	69.9%	27.8%	71.5%	28.5%
7,578	GUNNISON	3,508	2,231	1,187	90	1,044 R	63.6%	33.8%	65.3%	34.7%
202	HINSDALE	222	172	44	6	128 R	77.5%	19.8%	79.6%	20.4%
6,590	HUERFANO	3,027	1,620	1,341	66	279 R	53.5%	44.3%	54.7%	45.3%
1,811	JACKSON	812	623	178	11	445 R	76.7%	21.9%	77.8%	22.2%
233,031	JEFFERSON	114,597	80,082	31,555	2,960	48,527 R	69.9%	27.5%	71.7%	28.3%
2,029	KIOWA	1,250	849	372	29	477 R	67.9%	29.8%	69.5%	30.5%
7,530	KIT CARSON	3,267	2,316	824	127	1,492 R	70.9%	25.2%	73.8%	26.2%
8,282	LAKE	2,899	1,556	1,263	80	293 R	53.7%	43.6%	55.2%	44.8%
19,199	LA PLATA	9,144	5,691	2,830	623	2,861 R	62.2%	30.9%	66.8%	33.2%
89,900	LARIMER	42,234	27,462	13,731	1,041	13,731 R	65.0%	32.5%	66.7%	33.3%
15,744	LAS ANIMAS	6,957	3,659	3,222	76	437 R	52.6%	46.3%	53.2%	46.8%
4,836	LINCOLN	2,396	1,678	685	33	993 R	70.0%	28.6%	71.0%	29.0%
18,852	LOGAN	7,956	5,352	2,426	178	2,926 R	67.3%	30.5%	68.8%	31.2%
54,374	MESA	22,613	15,527	6,358	728	9,169 R	68.7%	28.1%	70.9%	29.1%
786	MINERAL	348	247	96	5	151 R	71.0%	27.6%	72.0%	28.0%
6,525	MOFFAT	2,848	1,928	591	329	1,337 R	67.7%	20.8%	76.5%	23.5%
12,952	MONTEZUMA	4,614	3,391	1,223		2,168 R	73.5%	26.5%	73.5%	26.5%
18,366	MONTROSE	7,059	4,571	1,870	618	2,701 R	64.8%	26.5%	71.0%	29.0%
20,105	MORGAN	7,621	5,365	2,081	175	3,284 R	70.4%	27.3%	72.1%	27.9%
23,523	OTERO	9,150	6,016	2,929	205	3,087 R	65.7%	32.0%	67.3%	32.7%
1,546	OURAY	897	669	186	42	483 R	74.6%	20.7%	78.2%	21.8%
2,185	PARK	1,424	1,001	386	37	615 R	70.3%	27.1%	72.2%	27.8%
4,131	PHILLIPS	2,266	1,480	687	99	793 R	65.3%	30.3%	68.3%	31.7%
6,185	PITKIN	4,674	2,064	2,531	79	467 D	44.2%	54.2%	44.9%	55.1%
13,258	PROWERS	5,313	3,272	1,860	181	1,412 R	61.6%	35.0%	63.8%	36.2%
118,238	PUEBLO	47,045	25,607	19,620	1,818	5,987 R	54.4%	41.7%	56.6%	43.4%
4,842	RIO BLANCO	2,053	1,586	414	53	1,172 R	77.3%	20.2%	79.3%	20.7%
10,494	RIO GRANDE	3,998	2,787	1,029	182	1,758 R	69.7%	25.7%	73.0%	27.0%
6,592	ROUTT	4,431	2,629	1,613	189	1,016 R	59.3%	36.4%	62.0%	38.0%
3,827	SAGUACHE	1,681	1,062	578	41	484 R	63.2%	34.4%	64.8%	35.2%
831	SAN JUAN	408	238	140	30	98 R	58.3%	34.3%	63.0%	37.0%
1,949	SAN MIGUEL	1,061	583	426	52	157 R	54.9%	40.2%	57.8%	42.2%
3,405	SEDGWICK	1,664	1,129	485	50	644 R	67.8%	29.1%	70.0%	30.0%
2,665	SUMMIT	1,833	1,082	707	44	375 R	59.0%	38.6%	60.5%	39.5%
3,316	TELLER	2,044	1,440	535	69	905 R	70.5%	26.2%	72.9%	27.1%

COLORADO

PRESIDENT 1972

1970 Census Population	County	Total Vote	Republican	Democratic	Other	Rep.-Dem. Plurality	Percentage Total Vote Rep.	Percentage Total Vote Dem.	Percentage Major Vote Rep.	Percentage Major Vote Dem.
5,550	WASHINGTON	2,629	1,837	643	149	1,194 R	69.9%	24.5%	74.1%	25.9%
89,297	WELD	37,255	24,695	11,690	870	13,005 R	66.3%	31.4%	67.9%	32.1%
8,544	YUMA	4,045	2,873	1,066	106	1,807 R	71.0%	26.4%	72.9%	27.1%
2,207,259	TOTAL	953,884	597,189	329,980	26,715	267,209 R	62.6%	34.6%	64.4%	35.6%

COLORADO

PRESIDENT 1968

1960 Census Population	County	Total Vote	Republican	Democratic	AIP	Other	Plurality	Percentage Rep.	Percentage Dem.	Percentage AIP
120,296	ADAMS	55,493	24,343	25,111	5,702	337	768 D	43.9%	45.3%	10.3%
10,000	ALAMOSA	4,140	2,277	1,574	287	2	703 R	55.0%	38.0%	6.9%
113,426	ARAPAHOE	56,603	33,712	18,569	3,953	369	15,143 R	59.6%	32.8%	7.0%
2,629	ARCHULETA	979	486	409	83	1	77 R	49.6%	41.8%	8.5%
6,310	BACA	2,504	1,441	719	340	4	722 R	57.5%	28.7%	13.6%
7,419	BENT	2,591	1,228	1,126	231	6	102 R	47.4%	43.5%	8.9%
74,254	BOULDER	48,079	27,671	17,422	2,497	489	10,249 R	57.6%	36.2%	5.2%
8,298	CHAFFEE	4,155	2,121	1,667	358	9	454 R	51.0%	40.1%	8.6%
2,789	CHEYENNE	1,193	664	392	136	1	272 R	55.7%	32.9%	11.4%
2,793	CLEAR CREEK	1,918	1,011	719	183	5	292 R	52.7%	37.5%	9.5%
8,428	CONEJOS	2,981	1,361	1,492	117	11	131 D	45.7%	50.1%	3.9%
4,219	COSTILLA	1,482	477	933	32	40	456 D	32.2%	63.0%	2.2%
3,978	CROWLEY	1,540	775	565	196	4	210 R	50.3%	36.7%	12.7%
1,305	CUSTER	716	433	204	77	2	229 R	60.5%	28.5%	10.8%
15,602	DELTA	6,652	3,692	2,327	618	15	1,365 R	55.5%	35.0%	9.3%
493,887	DENVER	211,661	92,003	106,081	11,408	2,169	14,078 D	43.5%	50.1%	5.4%
2,196	DOLORES	741	392	217	131	1	175 R	52.9%	29.3%	17.7%
4,816	DOUGLAS	3,106	1,910	857	327	12	1,053 R	61.5%	27.6%	10.5%
4,677	EAGLE	2,136	1,049	927	160		122 R	49.1%	43.4%	7.5%
3,708	ELBERT	1,713	1,043	484	185	1	559 R	60.9%	28.3%	10.8%
143,742	EL PASO	59,714	32,066	21,232	6,199	217	10,834 R	53.7%	35.6%	10.4%
20,196	FREMONT	9,189	4,908	3,292	967	22	1,616 R	53.4%	35.8%	10.5%
12,017	GARFIELD	6,056	3,157	2,273	607	19	884 R	52.1%	37.5%	10.0%
685	GILPIN	684	358	218	99	9	140 R	52.3%	31.9%	14.5%
3,557	GRAND	1,745	1,167	433	127	18	734 R	66.9%	24.8%	7.3%
5,477	GUNNISON	2,435	1,411	866	139	19	545 R	57.9%	35.6%	5.7%
208	HINSDALE	192	127	43	22		84 R	66.1%	22.4%	11.5%
7,867	HUERFANO	3,228	1,133	1,934	150	11	801 D	35.1%	59.9%	4.6%
1,758	JACKSON	702	474	177	51		297 R	67.5%	25.2%	7.3%
127,520	JEFFERSON	89,502	50,847	31,392	6,767	496	19,455 R	56.8%	35.1%	7.6%
2,425	KIOWA	1,224	689	423	112		266 R	56.3%	34.6%	9.2%
6,957	KIT CARSON	3,242	1,977	1,026	232	7	951 R	61.0%	31.6%	7.2%
7,101	LAKE	2,887	1,025	1,550	287	25	525 D	35.5%	53.7%	9.9%
19,225	LA PLATA	7,483	4,269	2,523	673	18	1,746 R	57.0%	33.7%	9.0%
53,343	LARIMER	29,716	18,438	9,152	1,819	307	9,286 R	62.0%	30.8%	6.1%
19,983	LAS ANIMAS	7,510	2,499	4,602	388	21	2,103 D	33.3%	61.3%	5.2%
5,310	LINCOLN	2,465	1,407	809	247	2	598 R	57.1%	32.8%	10.0%
20,302	LOGAN	7,601	4,323	2,521	736	21	1,802 R	56.9%	33.2%	9.7%
50,715	MESA	21,671	10,745	8,775	2,076	75	1,970 R	49.6%	40.5%	9.6%
424	MINERAL	265	116	126	22	1	10 D	43.8%	47.5%	8.3%
7,061	MOFFAT	2,879	1,785	765	322	7	1,020 R	62.0%	26.6%	11.2%
14,024	MONTEZUMA	4,370	2,461	1,349	545	15	1,112 R	56.3%	30.9%	12.5%
18,286	MONTROSE	6,712	3,547	2,394	753	18	1,153 R	52.8%	35.7%	11.2%
21,192	MORGAN	7,512	4,598	2,310	593	11	2,288 R	61.2%	30.8%	7.9%
24,128	OTERO	9,445	4,690	3,891	723	141	799 R	49.7%	41.2%	7.7%
1,601	OURAY	775	401	250	120	4	151 R	51.7%	32.3%	15.5%
1,822	PARK	1,028	601	286	134	7	315 R	58.5%	27.8%	13.0%
4,440	PHILLIPS	2,177	1,237	723	211	6	514 R	56.8%	33.2%	9.7%
2,381	PITKIN	2,021	1,135	728	136	22	407 R	56.2%	36.0%	6.7%
13,296	PROWERS	5,589	2,741	2,329	503	16	412 R	49.0%	41.7%	9.0%
118,707	PUEBLO	48,306	16,646	27,215	3,823	622	10,569 D	34.5%	56.3%	7.9%
5,150	RIO BLANCO	2,003	1,294	502	204	3	792 R	64.6%	25.1%	10.2%
11,160	RIO GRANDE	4,188	2,442	1,562	182	2	880 R	58.3%	37.3%	4.3%
5,900	ROUTT	2,976	1,602	1,076	292	6	526 R	53.8%	36.2%	9.8%
4,473	SAGUACHE	1,571	824	648	97	2	176 R	52.5%	41.2%	6.2%
849	SAN JUAN	368	165	134	59	10	31 R	44.8%	36.4%	16.0%
2,944	SAN MIGUEL	797	422	311	60	4	111 R	52.9%	39.0%	7.5%
4,242	SEDGWICK	1,655	1,007	546	100	2	461 R	60.8%	33.0%	6.0%
2,073	SUMMIT	936	536	301	95	4	235 R	57.3%	32.2%	10.1%
2,495	TELLER	1,379	722	403	249	5	319 R	52.4%	29.2%	18.1%

COLORADO

PRESIDENT 1968

1960 Census Population	County	Total Vote	Republican	Democratic	AIP	Other	Plurality	Percentage Rep.	Percentage Dem.	Percentage AIP
6,625	WASHINGTON	2,694	1,634	694	352	14	940 R	60.7%	25.8%	13.1%
72,344	WELD	29,886	17,101	10,420	2,189	176	6,681 R	57.2%	34.9%	7.3%
8,912	YUMA	4,038	2,529	1,175	330	4	1,354 R	62.6%	29.1%	8.2%
1,753,947	TOTAL	811,199	409,345	335,174	60,813	5,867	74,171 R	50.5%	41.3%	7.5%

COLORADO

ELECTION NOTES

1984 Other vote was 11,257 Bergland (Libertarian); 4,662 LaRouche (Independent); 978 Serrette (Independent Alliance); 810 Mason (Socialist Workers); 858 Dodge (Prohibition); 23 Johnson (write-in).

1980 Other vote was 130,633 Anderson (National Unity Campaign); 25,744 Clark (Libertarian); 5,614 Commoner (Citizens); 1,180 Bubar (Statesman); 520 Pulley (Socialist Workers); 487 Hall (Communist).

1976 Other vote was 26,107 McCarthy (Independent); 5,330 MacBride (Libertarian); 2,882 Bubar (Prohibition); 1,126 Camejo (Socialist Workers); 567 LaRouche (U.S. Labor); 403 Hall (Communist); 397 Anderson (write-in); 14 Levin (write-in); 6 Miller (write-in); 2 scattered write-in. Early unamended canvass gave the state-wide totals as 284,278 Republican; 460,801 Democratic; 26,047 Independent; 5,338 Libertarian; 2,886 Prohibition; 1,122 Socialist Workers; 565 U.S. Labor; 403 Communist. Listed write-in votes are from the original canvass. Amendments were made in the following counties: Boulder, Las Animas, Moffat, Montrose and Saguache.

1972 Other vote was 17,269 Schmitz (American); 4,361 Fisher (Socialist Labor); 2,403 Spock (People's) 1,111 Hospers (Libertarian); 666 Jenness (Socialist Workers); 467 Munn (Prohibition); 432 Hall (Communist); 6 scattered write-in.

1968 Wallace on the ballot as American Independent. Other vote was 3,016 Blomen (Socialist Labor); 1,393 Gregory (New Party); 275 Munn (Prohibition); 235 Halstead (Socialist Workers); 948 scattered write-in.

CONNECTICUT

POPULAR VOTE FOR PRESIDENT 1920 TO 1984

Year	Total Vote	Republican Vote	Republican Candidate	Democratic Vote	Democratic Candidate	Other Vote	Plurality	Percentage Total Vote Rep.	Percentage Total Vote Dem.	Percentage Major Vote Rep.	Percentage Major Vote Dem.
1984	1,466,900	890,877	Reagan, Ronald	569,597	Mondale, Walter F.	6,426	321,280 R	60.7%	38.8%	61.0%	39.0%
1980	1,406,285	677,210	Reagan, Ronald	541,732	Carter, Jimmy	187,343	135,478 R	48.2%	38.5%	55.6%	44.4%
1976	1,381,526	719,261	Ford, Gerald R.	647,895	Carter, Jimmy	14,370	71,366 R	52.1%	46.9%	52.6%	47.4%
1972	1,384,277	810,763	Nixon, Richard M.	555,498	McGovern, George S.	18,016	255,265 R	58.6%	40.1%	59.3%	40.7%
1968	1,256,232	556,721	Nixon, Richard M.	621,561	Humphrey, Hubert H.	77,950	64,840 D	44.3%	49.5%	47.2%	52.8%
1964	1,218,578	390,996	Goldwater, Barry M.	826,269	Johnson, Lyndon B.	1,313	435,273 D	32.1%	67.8%	32.1%	67.9%
1960	1,222,883	565,813	Nixon, Richard M.	657,055	Kennedy, John F.	15	91,242 D	46.3%	53.7%	46.3%	53.7%
1956	1,117,121	711,837	Eisenhower, Dwight D.	405,079	Stevenson, Adlai E.	205	306,758 R	63.7%	36.3%	63.7%	36.3%
1952	1,096,911	611,012	Eisenhower, Dwight D.	481,649	Stevenson, Adlai E.	4,250	129,363 R	55.7%	43.9%	55.9%	44.1%
1948	883,518	437,754	Dewey, Thomas E.	423,297	Truman, Harry S.	22,467	14,457 R	49.5%	47.9%	50.8%	49.2%
1944	831,990	390,527	Dewey, Thomas E.	435,146	Roosevelt, Franklin D.	6,317	44,619 D	46.9%	52.3%	47.3%	52.7%
1940	781,502	361,819	Willkie, Wendell	417,621	Roosevelt, Franklin D.	2,062	55,802 D	46.3%	53.4%	46.4%	53.6%
1936	690,723	278,685	Landon, Alfred M.	382,129	Roosevelt, Franklin D.	29,909	103,444 D	40.3%	55.3%	42.2%	57.8%
1932	594,183	288,420	Hoover, Herbert C.	281,632	Roosevelt, Franklin D.	24,131	6,788 R	48.5%	47.4%	50.6%	49.4%
1928	553,118	296,641	Hoover, Herbert C.	252,085	Smith, Alfred E.	4,392	44,556 R	53.6%	45.6%	54.1%	45.9%
1924	400,396	246,322	Coolidge, Calvin	110,184	Davis, John W.	43,890	136,138 R	61.5%	27.5%	69.1%	30.9%
1920	365,518	229,238	Harding, Warren G.	120,721	Cox, James M.	15,559	108,517 R	62.7%	33.0%	65.5%	34.5%

ELECTORAL COLLEGE VOTE 1920 TO 1984

Year	Total	Republican	Democratic	Other
1984	8	8	—	—
1980	8	8	—	—
1976	8	8	—	—
1972	8	8	—	—
1968	8	—	8	—
1964	8	—	8	—
1960	8	—	8	—
1956	8	8	—	—
1952	8	8	—	—
1948	8	8	—	—
1944	8	—	8	—
1940	8	—	8	—
1936	8	—	8	—
1932	8	8	—	—
1928	7	7	—	—
1924	7	7	—	—
1920	7	7	—	—

CONNECTICUT

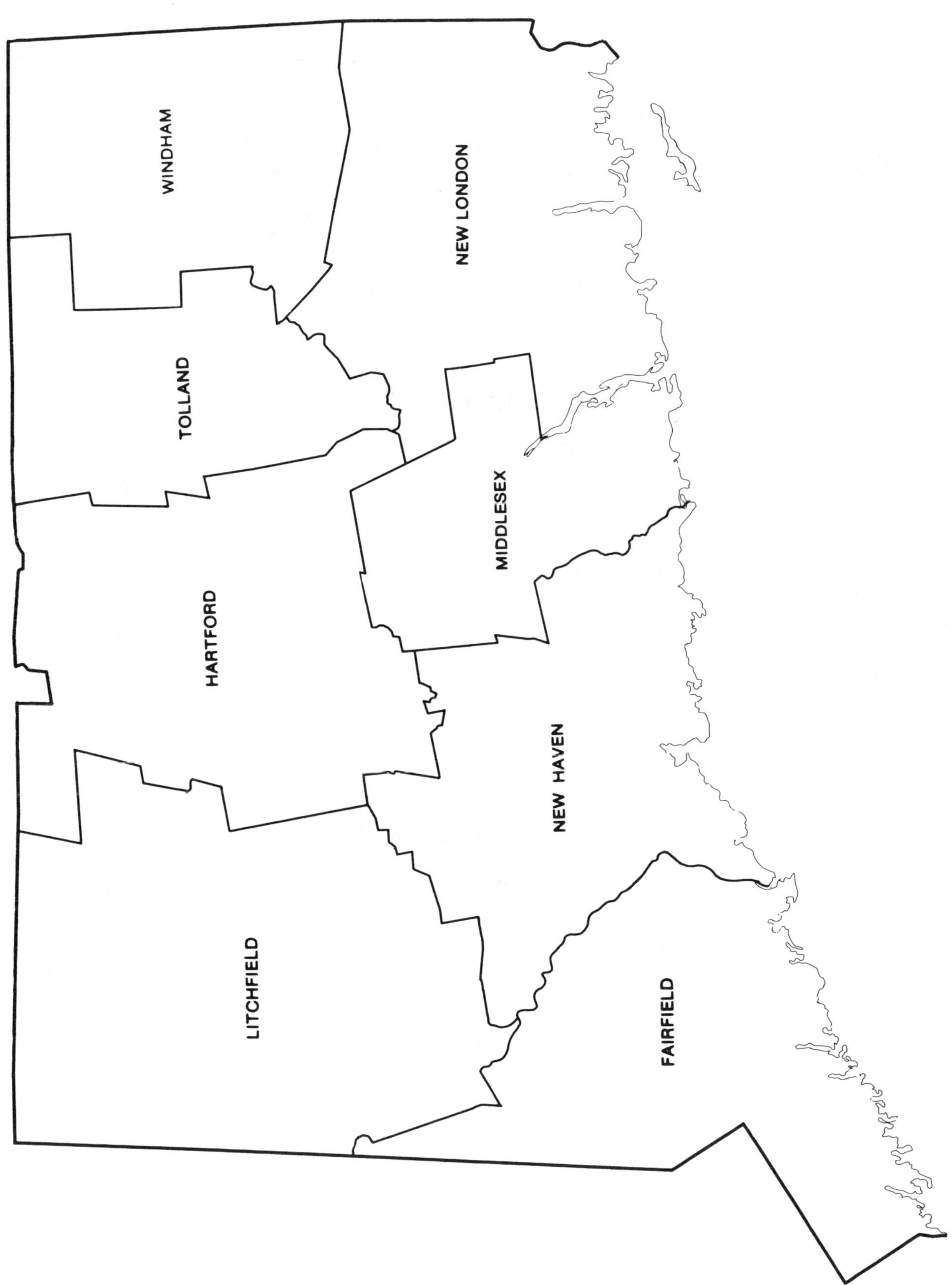

CONNECTICUT

PRESIDENT 1984

1980 Census Population	County	Total Vote	Republican	Democratic	Other	Rep.-Dem. Plurality	Percentage Total Vote Rep.	Total Vote Dem.	Major Vote Rep.	Major Vote Dem.
807,143	FAIRFIELD	391,179	257,319	132,253	1,607	125,066 R	65.8%	33.8%	66.1%	33.9%
807,766	HARTFORD	378,405	208,210	168,609	1,586	39,601 R	55.0%	44.6%	55.3%	44.7%
156,769	LITCHFIELD	79,416	52,583	26,564	269	26,019 R	66.2%	33.4%	66.4%	33.6%
129,017	MIDDLESEX	66,722	39,580	26,915	227	12,665 R	59.3%	40.3%	59.5%	40.5%
761,337	NEW HAVEN	354,712	212,166	140,945	1,601	71,221 R	59.8%	39.7%	60.1%	39.9%
238,409	NEW LONDON	102,487	63,121	38,857	509	24,264 R	61.6%	37.9%	61.9%	38.1%
114,823	TOLLAND	53,298	32,981	20,103	214	12,878 R	61.9%	37.7%	62.1%	37.9%
92,312	WINDHAM	40,455	24,917	15,351	187	9,566 R	61.6%	37.9%	61.9%	38.1%
3,107,576	TOTAL	1,466,900	890,877	569,597	6,426	321,280 R	60.7%	38.8%	61.0%	39.0%

CONNECTICUT

PRESIDENT 1980

1980 Census Population	County	Total Vote	Republican	Democratic	Other	Rep.-Dem. Plurality	Percentage Total Vote Rep.	Total Vote Dem.	Major Vote Rep.	Major Vote Dem.
807,143	FAIRFIELD	368,098	201,997	124,074	42,027	77,923 R	54.9%	33.7%	61.9%	38.1%
807,766	HARTFORD	371,380	150,265	164,643	56,472	14,378 D	40.5%	44.3%	47.7%	52.3%
156,769	LITCHFIELD	76,354	38,725	26,705	10,924	12,020 R	50.7%	35.0%	59.2%	40.8%
129,017	MIDDLESEX	63,672	28,989	24,768	9,915	4,221 R	45.5%	38.9%	53.9%	46.1%
761,337	NEW HAVEN	337,732	169,038	130,913	37,781	38,125 R	50.1%	38.8%	56.4%	43.6%
238,409	NEW LONDON	98,448	47,217	36,628	14,603	10,589 R	48.0%	37.2%	56.3%	43.7%
114,823	TOLLAND	50,346	22,127	18,557	9,662	3,570 R	43.9%	36.9%	54.4%	45.6%
92,312	WINDHAM	39,419	18,852	15,444	5,123	3,408 R	47.8%	39.2%	55.0%	45.0%
3,107,576	TOTAL	1,406,285	677,210	541,732	187,343	135,478 R	48.2%	38.5%	55.6%	44.4%

CONNECTICUT

PRESIDENT 1976

1970 Census Population	County	Total Vote	Republican	Democratic	Other	Rep.-Dem. Plurality	Percentage Total Vote Rep.	Total Vote Dem.	Major Vote Rep.	Major Vote Dem.
792,814	FAIRFIELD	360,224	209,458	148,353	2,413	61,105 R	58.1%	41.2%	58.5%	41.5%
816,737	HARTFORD	368,494	175,064	191,257	2,173	16,193 D	47.5%	51.9%	47.8%	52.2%
144,091	LITCHFIELD	73,583	40,705	32,419	459	8,286 R	55.3%	44.1%	55.7%	44.3%
115,018	MIDDLESEX	60,550	31,115	29,097	338	2,018 R	51.4%	48.1%	51.7%	48.3%
744,948	NEW HAVEN	334,189	174,342	157,402	2,445	16,940 R	52.2%	47.1%	52.6%	47.4%
230,654	NEW LONDON	93,720	47,231	45,908	581	1,323 R	50.4%	49.0%	50.7%	49.3%
103,440	TOLLAND	47,024	23,703	23,079	242	624 R	50.4%	49.1%	50.7%	49.3%
84,515	WINDHAM	38,262	17,643	20,380	239	2,737 D	46.1%	53.3%	46.4%	53.6%
3,032,217	TOTAL	1,381,526	719,261	647,895	14,370	71,366 R	52.1%	46.9%	52.6%	47.4%

CONNECTICUT

PRESIDENT 1972

1970 Census Population	County	Total Vote	Republican	Democratic	Other	Rep.-Dem. Plurality	Percentage Total Vote Rep.	Total Vote Dem.	Major Vote Rep.	Major Vote Dem.
792,814	FAIRFIELD	364,585	233,188	125,128	6,269	108,060 R	64.0%	34.3%	65.1%	34.9%
816,737	HARTFORD	372,786	194,095	174,837	3,854	19,258 R	52.1%	46.9%	52.6%	47.4%
144,091	LITCHFIELD	72,262	43,478	27,929	855	15,549 R	60.2%	38.6%	60.9%	39.1%
115,018	MIDDLESEX	57,453	33,249	23,573	631	9,676 R	57.9%	41.0%	58.5%	41.5%
744,948	NEW HAVEN	340,487	200,818	135,132	4,537	65,686 R	59.0%	39.7%	59.8%	40.2%
230,654	NEW LONDON	92,352	58,516	32,935	901	25,581 R	63.4%	35.7%	64.0%	36.0%
103,440	TOLLAND	45,728	25,798	19,505	425	6,293 R	56.4%	42.7%	56.9%	43.1%
84,515	WINDHAM	38,624	21,621	16,459	544	5,162 R	56.0%	42.6%	56.8%	43.2%
3,032,217	TOTAL	1,384,277	810,763	555,498	18,016	255,265 R	58.6%	40.1%	59.3%	40.7%

CONNECTICUT

PRESIDENT 1968

1960 Census Population	County	Total Vote	Republican	Democratic	AIP	Other	Plurality	Percentage Rep.	Dem.	AIP
653,589	FAIRFIELD	334,292	173,108	139,364	21,477	343	33,744 R	51.8%	41.7%	6.4%
689,555	HARTFORD	339,701	131,740	190,865	16,779	317	59,125 D	38.8%	56.2%	4.9%
119,856	LITCHFIELD	64,380	31,429	29,340	3,526	85	2,089 R	48.8%	45.6%	5.5%
88,865	MIDDLESEX	48,524	21,999	23,727	2,706	92	1,728 D	45.3%	48.9%	5.6%
660,315	NEW HAVEN	314,432	130,501	159,653	23,985	293	29,152 D	41.5%	50.8%	7.6%
185,745	NEW LONDON	83,574	37,116	41,507	4,879	72	4,391 D	44.4%	49.7%	5.8%
68,737	TOLLAND	36,655	16,666	18,007	1,918	64	1,341 D	45.5%	49.1%	5.2%
68,572	WINDHAM	34,674	14,162	19,098	1,380	34	4,936 D	40.8%	55.1%	4.0%
2,535,234	TOTAL	1,256,232	556,721	621,561	76,650	1,300	64,840 D	44.3%	49.5%	6.1%

CONNECTICUT

ELECTION NOTES

1984 Other vote was 4,826 Hall (Communist); 1,374 Serrette (Connecticut Alliance); 204 Bergland (write-in); 14 Johnson (write-in); 8 scattered write-in. The state-wide total for the other vote column includes these 226 write-in votes not reported by county.

1980 Other vote was 171,807 Anderson (Anderson Coalition); 8,570 Clark (Libertarian); 6,130 Commoner (Citizens); 836 scattered write-in. The state-wide total for the other vote column includes the 836 write-in votes not reported by county.

1976 Other vote was 7,101 Maddox (George Wallace Party); 3,759 McCarthy (write-in); 1,789 LaRouche (U.S. Labor); 209 MacBride (write-in); 186 Hall (write-in); 155 Anderson (write-in); 42 Camejo (write-in); 5 Zeidler (write-in); 1 Levin (write-in); 1 Wright (write-in); 1,122 scattered write-in. The state-wide total for the other vote column includes these 5,480 write-in votes not reported by county.

1972 Other vote was 17,239 Schmitz (George Wallace Party); 777 scattered write-in.

1968 Wallace on the ballot as George Wallace party. Other vote was scattered write-in.

DELAWARE

POPULAR VOTE FOR PRESIDENT 1920 TO 1984

Year	Total Vote	Republican Vote	Republican Candidate	Democratic Vote	Democratic Candidate	Other Vote	Plurality	Percentage Total Vote Rep.	Percentage Total Vote Dem.	Percentage Major Vote Rep.	Percentage Major Vote Dem.
1984	254,572	152,190	Reagan, Ronald	101,656	Mondale, Walter F.	726	50,534 R	59.8%	39.9%	60.0%	40.0%
1980	235,900	111,252	Reagan, Ronald	105,754	Carter, Jimmy	18,894	5,498 R	47.2%	44.8%	51.3%	48.7%
1976	235,834	109,831	Ford, Gerald R.	122,596	Carter, Jimmy	3,407	12,765 D	46.6%	52.0%	47.3%	52.7%
1972	235,516	140,357	Nixon, Richard M.	92,283	McGovern, George S.	2,876	48,074 R	59.6%	39.2%	60.3%	39.7%
1968	214,367	96,714	Nixon, Richard M.	89,194	Humphrey, Hubert H.	28,459	7,520 R	45.1%	41.6%	52.0%	48.0%
1964	201,320	78,078	Goldwater, Barry M.	122,704	Johnson, Lyndon B.	538	44,626 D	38.8%	60.9%	38.9%	61.1%
1960	196,683	96,373	Nixon, Richard M.	99,590	Kennedy, John F.	720	3,217 D	49.0%	50.6%	49.2%	50.8%
1956	177,988	98,057	Eisenhower, Dwight D.	79,421	Stevenson, Adlai E.	510	18,636 R	55.1%	44.6%	55.3%	44.7%
1952	174,025	90,059	Eisenhower, Dwight D.	83,315	Stevenson, Adlai E.	651	6,744 R	51.8%	47.9%	51.9%	48.1%
1948	139,073	69,588	Dewey, Thomas E.	67,813	Truman, Harry S.	1,672	1,775 R	50.0%	48.8%	50.6%	49.4%
1944	125,361	56,747	Dewey, Thomas E.	68,166	Roosevelt, Franklin D.	448	11,419 D	45.3%	54.4%	45.4%	54.6%
1940	136,374	61,440	Willkie, Wendell	74,599	Roosevelt, Franklin D.	335	13,159 D	45.1%	54.7%	45.2%	54.8%
1936	127,603	57,236	Landon, Alfred M.	69,702	Roosevelt, Franklin D.	665	12,466 D	44.9%	54.6%	45.1%	54.9%
1932	112,901	57,073	Hoover, Herbert C.	54,319	Roosevelt, Franklin D.	1,509	2,754 R	50.6%	48.1%	51.2%	48.8%
1928	104,602	68,860	Hoover, Herbert C.	35,354	Smith, Alfred E.	388	33,506 R	65.8%	33.8%	66.1%	33.9%
1924	90,885	52,441	Coolidge, Calvin	33,445	Davis, John W.	4,999	18,996 R	57.7%	36.8%	61.1%	38.9%
1920	94,875	52,858	Harding, Warren G.	39,911	Cox, James M.	2,106	12,947 R	55.7%	42.1%	57.0%	43.0%

ELECTORAL COLLEGE VOTE 1920 TO 1984

Year	Total	Republican	Democratic	Other
1984	3	3	—	—
1980	3	3	—	—
1976	3	—	3	—
1972	3	3	—	—
1968	3	3	—	—
1964	3	—	3	—
1960	3	—	3	—
1956	3	3	—	—
1952	3	3	—	—
1948	3	3	—	—
1944	3	—	3	—
1940	3	—	3	—
1936	3	—	3	—
1932	3	3	—	—
1928	3	3	—	—
1924	3	3	—	—
1920	3	3	—	—

DELAWARE

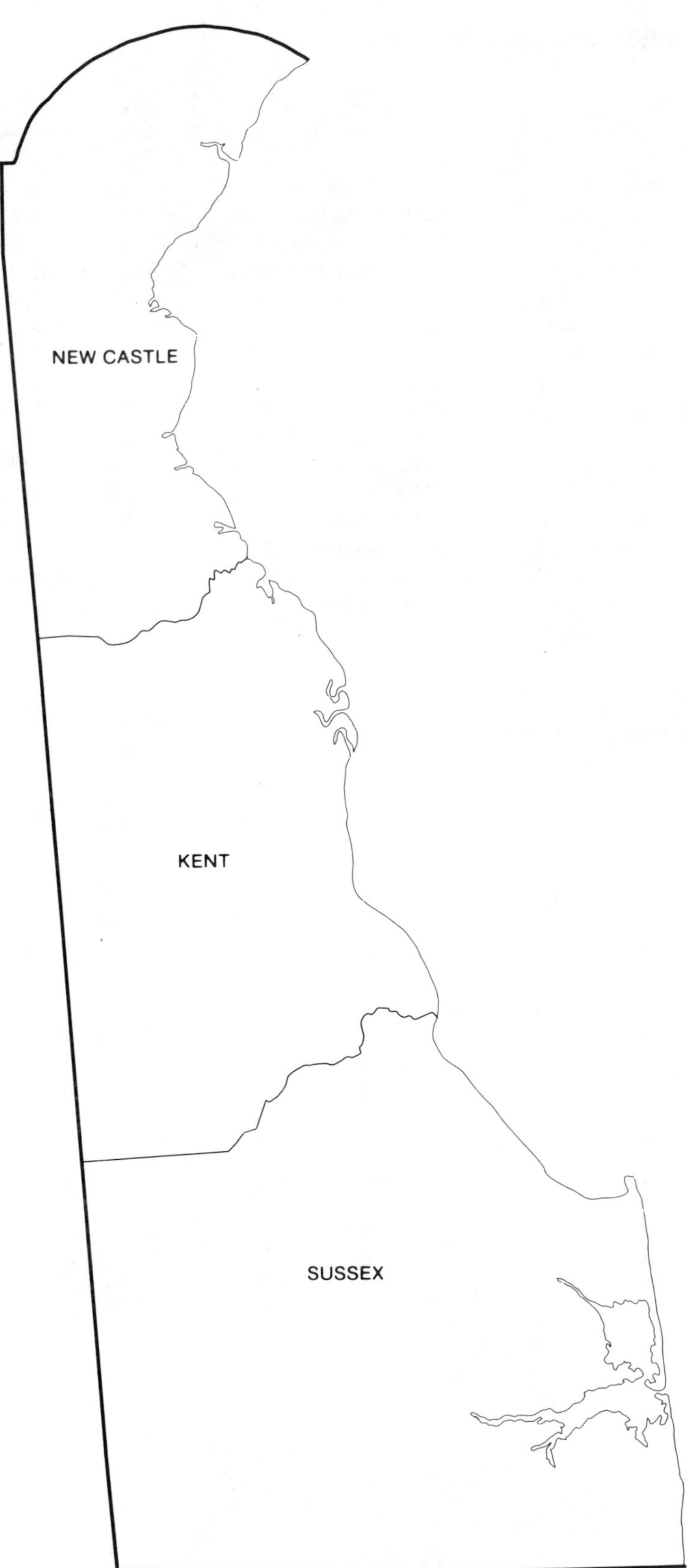

DELAWARE

PRESIDENT 1984

1980 Census Population	County	Total Vote	Republican	Democratic	Other	Rep.-Dem. Plurality	Percentage Total Vote Rep.	Percentage Total Vote Dem.	Percentage Major Vote Rep.	Percentage Major Vote Dem.
98,219	KENT	33,403	21,531	11,789	83	9,742 R	64.5%	35.3%	64.6%	35.4%
398,115	NEW CASTLE	179,077	102,322	76,238	517	26,084 R	57.1%	42.6%	57.3%	42.7%
98,004	SUSSEX	42,092	28,337	13,629	126	14,708 R	67.3%	32.4%	67.5%	32.5%
594,338	TOTAL	254,572	152,190	101,656	726	50,534 R	59.8%	39.9%	60.0%	40.0%

DELAWARE

PRESIDENT 1980

1980 Census Population	County	Total Vote	Republican	Democratic	Other	Rep.-Dem. Plurality	Percentage Total Vote Rep.	Percentage Total Vote Dem.	Percentage Major Vote Rep.	Percentage Major Vote Dem.
98,219	KENT	29,878	14,882	12,884	2,112	1,998 R	49.8%	43.1%	53.6%	46.4%
398,115	NEW CASTLE	168,638	76,898	76,897	14,843	1 R	45.6%	45.6%	50.0%	50.0%
98,004	SUSSEX	37,384	19,472	15,973	1,939	3,499 R	52.1%	42.7%	54.9%	45.1%
594,338	TOTAL	235,900	111,252	105,754	18,894	5,498 R	47.2%	44.8%	51.3%	48.7%

DELAWARE

PRESIDENT 1976

1970 Census Population	County	Total Vote	Republican	Democratic	Other	Rep.-Dem. Plurality	Percentage Total Vote Rep.	Percentage Total Vote Dem.	Percentage Major Vote Rep.	Percentage Major Vote Dem.
81,892	KENT	29,428	12,604	16,523	301	3,919 D	42.8%	56.1%	43.3%	56.7%
385,856	NEW CASTLE	170,338	80,074	87,521	2,743	7,447 D	47.0%	51.4%	47.8%	52.2%
80,356	SUSSEX	36,068	17,153	18,552	363	1,399 D	47.6%	51.4%	48.0%	52.0%
548,104	TOTAL	235,834	109,831	122,596	3,407	12,765 D	46.6%	52.0%	47.3%	52.7%

DELAWARE

PRESIDENT 1972

1970 Census Population	County	Total Vote	Republican	Democratic	Other	Rep.-Dem. Plurality	Percentage Total Vote Rep.	Total Vote Dem.	Major Vote Rep.	Major Vote Dem.
81,892	KENT	28,556	17,712	10,463	381	7,249 R	62.0%	36.6%	62.9%	37.1%
385,856	NEW CASTLE	172,956	100,681	70,190	2,085	30,491 R	58.2%	40.6%	58.9%	41.1%
80,356	SUSSEX	34,004	21,964	11,630	410	10,334 R	64.6%	34.2%	65.4%	34.6%
548,104	TOTAL	235,516	140,357	92,283	2,876	48,074 R	59.6%	39.2%	60.3%	39.7%

DELAWARE

PRESIDENT 1968

1960 Census Population	County	Total Vote	Republican	Democratic	AIP	Other	Plurality	Percentage Rep.	Dem.	AIP
65,651	KENT	24,888	11,082	9,055	4,751		2,027 R	44.5%	36.4%	19.1%
307,446	NEW CASTLE	156,413	70,014	68,468	17,931		1,546 R	44.8%	43.8%	11.5%
73,195	SUSSEX	33,066	15,618	11,671	5,777		3,947 R	47.2%	35.3%	17.5%
446,292	TOTAL	214,367	96,714	89,194	28,459		7,520 R	45.1%	41.6%	13.3%

DELAWARE

ELECTION NOTES

1984 Other vote was 269 Dennis (American); 268 Bergland (Libertarian); 121 Johnson (Citizens); 68 Serrette (Independent).

1980 Other vote was 16,288 Anderson (Anderson Party); 1,974 Clark (Libertarian); 400 Greaves (American); 103 Commoner (write-in); 13 Hall (write-in); 6 Bubar (write-in); 4 Pulley (write-in); 3 Griswold (write-in); 2 McCormack (write-in); 101 scattered write-in.

1976 Other vote was 2,437 McCarthy (Non-Partisan); 645 Anderson (American); 136 LaRouche (U.S. Labor); 103 Bubar (Prohibition); 86 Levin (Socialist Labor). Early unamended canvass gave the vote in New Castle county as 80,023 Republican; 87,484 Democratic; 2,739 Other and the state-wide total vote as 109,780 Republican; 122,454 Democratic; 3,403 Other.

1972 Other vote was 2,638 Schmitz (American); 238 Munn (Prohibition).

1968 Wallace on the ballot as American.

FLORIDA

POPULAR VOTE FOR PRESIDENT 1920 TO 1984

Year	Total Vote	Republican Vote	Republican Candidate	Democratic Vote	Democratic Candidate	Other Vote	Plurality	Percentage Total Vote Rep.	Percentage Total Vote Dem.	Percentage Major Vote Rep.	Percentage Major Vote Dem.
1984	4,180,051	2,730,350	Reagan, Ronald	1,448,816	Mondale, Walter F.	885	1,281,534 R	65.3%	34.7%	65.3%	34.7%
1980	3,686,930	2,046,951	Reagan, Ronald	1,419,475	Carter, Jimmy	220,504	627,476 R	55.5%	38.5%	59.1%	40.9%
1976	3,150,631	1,469,531	Ford, Gerald R.	1,636,000	Carter, Jimmy	45,100	166,469 D	46.6%	51.9%	47.3%	52.7%
1972	2,583,283	1,857,759	Nixon, Richard M.	718,117	McGovern, George S.	7,407	1,139,642 R	71.9%	27.8%	72.1%	27.9%
1968 **	2,187,805	886,804	Nixon, Richard M.	676,794	Humphrey, Hubert H.	624,207	210,010 R	40.5%	30.9%	56.7%	43.3%
1964	1,854,481	905,941	Goldwater, Barry M.	948,540	Johnson, Lyndon B.		42,599 D	48.9%	51.1%	48.9%	51.1%
1960	1,544,176	795,476	Nixon, Richard M.	748,700	Kennedy, John F.		46,776 R	51.5%	48.5%	51.5%	48.5%
1956	1,125,762	643,849	Eisenhower, Dwight D.	480,371	Stevenson, Adlai E.	1,542	163,478 R	57.2%	42.7%	57.3%	42.7%
1952	989,337	544,036	Eisenhower, Dwight D.	444,950	Stevenson, Adlai E.	351	99,086 R	55.0%	45.0%	55.0%	45.0%
1948 **	577,643	194,280	Dewey, Thomas E.	281,988	Truman, Harry S.	101,375	87,708 D	33.6%	48.8%	40.8%	59.2%
1944	482,803	143,215	Dewey, Thomas E.	339,377	Roosevelt, Franklin D.	211	196,162 D	29.7%	70.3%	29.7%	70.3%
1940	485,640	126,158	Willkie, Wendell	359,334	Roosevelt, Franklin D.	148	233,176 D	26.0%	74.0%	26.0%	74.0%
1936	327,436	78,248	Landon, Alfred M.	249,117	Roosevelt, Franklin D.	71	170,869 D	23.9%	76.1%	23.9%	76.1%
1932	276,943	69,170	Hoover, Herbert C.	206,307	Roosevelt, Franklin D.	1,466	137,137 D	25.0%	74.5%	25.1%	74.9%
1928	252,068	145,860	Hoover, Herbert C.	101,764	Smith, Alfred E.	4,444	44,096 R	57.9%	40.4%	58.9%	41.1%
1924	109,158	30,633	Coolidge, Calvin	62,083	Davis, John W.	16,442	31,450 D	28.1%	56.9%	33.0%	67.0%
1920	145,684	44,853	Harding, Warren G.	90,515	Cox, James M.	10,316	45,662 D	30.8%	62.1%	33.1%	66.9%

In 1968 other vote was George Wallace party. In 1948 other vote was 89,755 States Rights and 11,620 Progressive.

ELECTORAL COLLEGE VOTE 1920 TO 1984

Year	Total	Republican	Democratic	Other
1984	21	21	—	—
1980	17	17	—	—
1976	17	—	17	—
1972	17	17	—	—
1968	14	14	—	—
1964	14	—	14	—
1960	10	10	—	—
1956	10	10	—	—
1952	10	10	—	—
1948	8	—	8	—
1944	8	—	8	—
1940	7	—	7	—
1936	7	—	7	—
1932	7	—	7	—
1928	6	6	—	—
1924	6	—	6	—
1920	6	—	6	—

FLORIDA

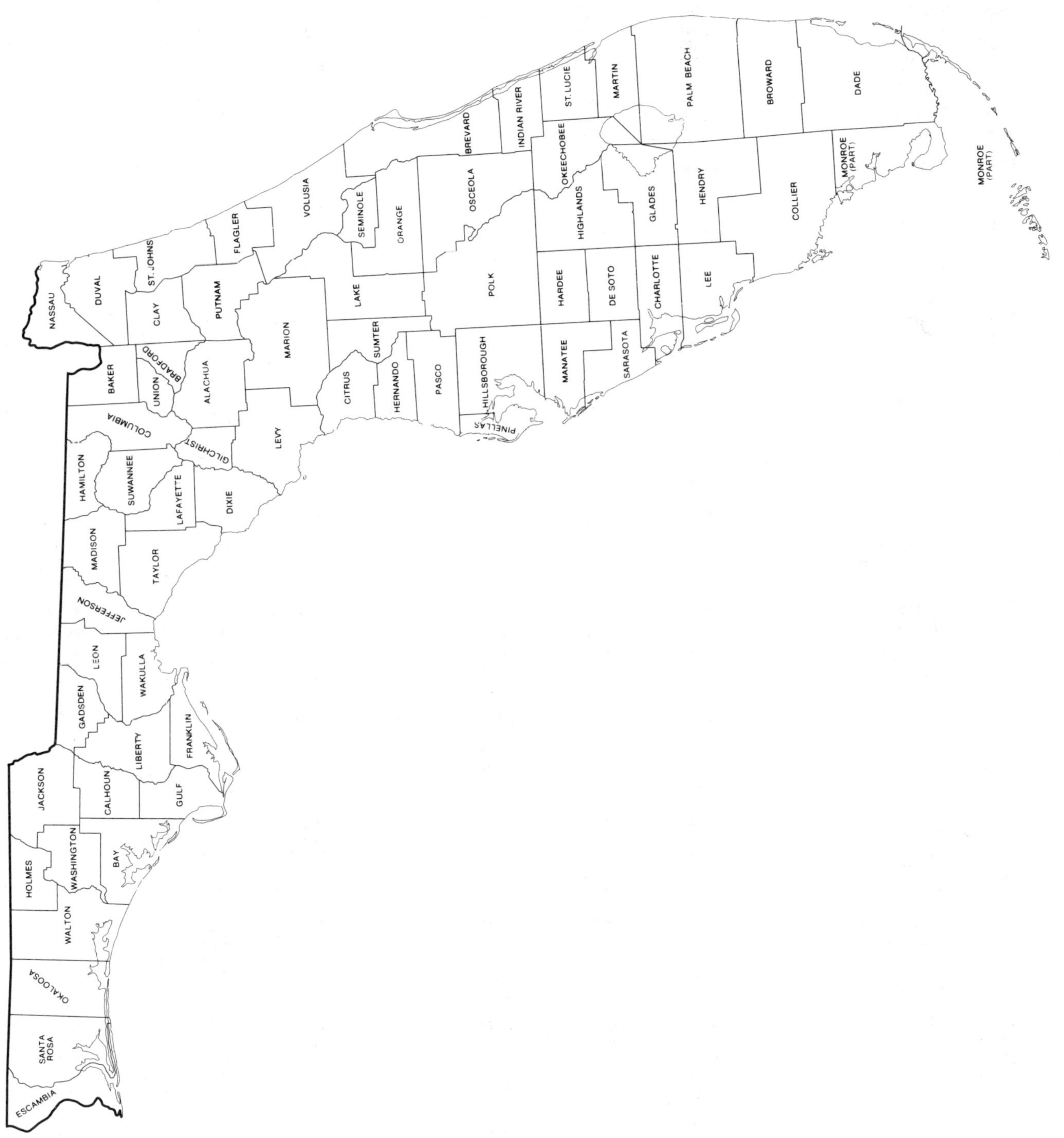
NASSAU
DUVAL
ST. JOHNS
CLAY
PUTNAM
FLAGLER
VOLUSIA
SEMINOLE
ORANGE
BREVARD
INDIAN RIVER
ST. LUCIE
MARTIN
PALM BEACH
BROWARD
DADE
MONROE (PART)
MONROE (PART)
OKEECHOBEE
OSCEOLA
HIGHLANDS
GLADES
HENDRY
COLLIER
LAKE
POLK
HARDEE
DE SOTO
CHARLOTTE
LEE
MARION
SUMTER
CITRUS
HERNANDO
PASCO
HILLSBOROUGH
PINELLAS
MANATEE
SARASOTA
BAKER
BRADFORD
UNION
ALACHUA
COLUMBIA
GILCHRIST
LEVY
HAMILTON
SUWANNEE
LAFAYETTE
DIXIE
MADISON
TAYLOR
JEFFERSON
LEON
WAKULLA
GADSDEN
LIBERTY
FRANKLIN
JACKSON
CALHOUN
GULF
WASHINGTON
BAY
HOLMES
WALTON
OKALOOSA
SANTA ROSA
ESCAMBIA

FLORIDA

PRESIDENT 1984

1980 Census Population	County	Total Vote	Republican	Democratic	Other	Rep.-Dem. Plurality	Percentage Total Vote Rep.	Percentage Total Vote Dem.	Percentage Major Vote Rep.	Percentage Major Vote Dem.
151,348	ALACHUA	57,193	30,582	26,551	60	4,031 R	53.5%	46.4%	53.5%	46.5%
15,289	BAKER	4,866	3,485	1,381		2,104 R	71.6%	28.4%	71.6%	28.4%
97,740	BAY	38,707	29,322	9,381	4	19,941 R	75.8%	24.2%	75.8%	24.2%
20,023	BRADFORD	6,469	4,128	2,341		1,787 R	63.8%	36.2%	63.8%	36.2%
272,959	BREVARD	139,349	102,339	36,963	47	65,376 R	73.4%	26.5%	73.5%	26.5%
1,018,200	BROWARD	449,077	254,501	194,542	34	59,959 R	56.7%	43.3%	56.7%	43.3%
9,294	CALHOUN	3,806	2,493	1,312	1	1,181 R	65.5%	34.5%	65.5%	34.5%
58,460	CHARLOTTE	38,769	27,464	11,303	2	16,161 R	70.8%	29.2%	70.8%	29.2%
54,703	CITRUS	31,221	20,754	10,463	4	10,291 R	66.5%	33.5%	66.5%	33.5%
67,052	CLAY	27,033	21,545	5,488		16,057 R	79.7%	20.3%	79.7%	20.3%
85,971	COLLIER	42,673	33,603	9,065	5	24,538 R	78.7%	21.2%	78.8%	21.2%
35,399	COLUMBIA	13,068	8,807	4,261		4,546 R	67.4%	32.6%	67.4%	32.6%
1,625,781	DADE	548,044	324,216	223,793	35	100,423 R	59.2%	40.8%	59.2%	40.8%
19,039	DESOTO	7,127	4,822	2,302	3	2,520 R	67.7%	32.3%	67.7%	32.3%
7,751	DIXIE	3,428	2,204	1,224		980 R	64.3%	35.7%	64.3%	35.7%
571,003	DUVAL	206,132	128,653	77,459	20	51,194 R	62.4%	37.6%	62.4%	37.6%
233,794	ESCAMBIA	93,458	66,638	26,798	22	39,840 R	71.3%	28.7%	71.3%	28.7%
10,913	FLAGLER	7,907	4,907	2,999	1	1,908 R	62.1%	37.9%	62.1%	37.9%
7,661	FRANKLIN	3,307	2,218	1,089		1,129 R	67.1%	32.9%	67.1%	32.9%
41,565	GADSDEN	13,206	5,805	7,399	2	1,594 D	44.0%	56.0%	44.0%	56.0%
5,767	GILCHRIST	3,108	2,056	1,051	1	1,005 R	66.2%	33.8%	66.2%	33.8%
5,992	GLADES	3,057	1,987	1,070		917 R	65.0%	35.0%	65.0%	35.0%
10,658	GULF	5,356	3,573	1,783		1,790 R	66.7%	33.3%	66.7%	33.3%
8,761	HAMILTON	3,322	1,921	1,401		520 R	57.8%	42.2%	57.8%	42.2%
19,379	HARDEE	5,493	3,957	1,536		2,421 R	72.0%	28.0%	72.0%	28.0%
18,599	HENDRY	6,542	4,524	2,018		2,506 R	69.2%	30.8%	69.2%	30.8%
44,469	HERNANDO	33,481	21,273	12,204	4	9,069 R	63.5%	36.5%	63.5%	36.5%
47,526	HIGHLANDS	23,685	16,465	7,217	3	9,248 R	69.5%	30.5%	69.5%	30.5%
646,960	HILLSBOROUGH	244,068	157,827	86,189	52	71,638 R	64.7%	35.3%	64.7%	35.3%
14,723	HOLMES	5,778	4,547	1,231		3,316 R	78.7%	21.3%	78.7%	21.3%
59,896	INDIAN RIVER	32,425	23,694	8,731		14,963 R	73.1%	26.9%	73.1%	26.9%
39,154	JACKSON	14,042	9,086	4,956		4,130 R	64.7%	35.3%	64.7%	35.3%
10,703	JEFFERSON	4,300	2,244	2,055	1	189 R	52.2%	47.8%	52.2%	47.8%
4,035	LAFAYETTE	2,375	1,513	862		651 R	63.7%	36.3%	63.7%	36.3%
104,870	LAKE	47,526	35,304	12,215	7	23,089 R	74.3%	25.7%	74.3%	25.7%
205,266	LEE	115,047	85,006	30,011	30	54,995 R	73.9%	26.1%	73.9%	26.1%
148,655	LEON	65,993	36,301	29,654	38	6,647 R	55.0%	44.9%	55.0%	45.0%
19,870	LEVY	8,664	5,561	3,103		2,458 R	64.2%	35.8%	64.2%	35.8%
4,260	LIBERTY	2,058	1,409	649		760 R	68.5%	31.5%	68.5%	31.5%
14,894	MADISON	4,917	2,816	2,101		715 R	57.3%	42.7%	57.3%	42.7%
148,442	MANATEE	76,668	55,775	20,887	6	34,888 R	72.7%	27.2%	72.8%	27.2%
122,488	MARION	54,023	37,796	16,221	6	21,575 R	70.0%	30.0%	70.0%	30.0%
64,014	MARTIN	37,882	28,897	8,976	9	19,921 R	76.3%	23.7%	76.3%	23.7%
63,188	MONROE	24,096	16,316	7,771	9	8,545 R	67.7%	32.3%	67.7%	32.3%
32,894	NASSAU	11,517	8,033	3,483	1	4,550 R	69.7%	30.2%	69.8%	30.2%
109,920	OKALOOSA	44,261	36,963	7,289	9	29,674 R	83.5%	16.5%	83.5%	16.5%
20,264	OKEECHOBEE	6,673	4,447	2,226		2,221 R	66.6%	33.4%	66.6%	33.4%
471,016	ORANGE	170,909	122,007	48,737	165	73,270 R	71.4%	28.5%	71.5%	28.5%
49,287	OSCEOLA	24,975	18,344	6,627	4	11,717 R	73.4%	26.5%	73.5%	26.5%
576,863	PALM BEACH	302,855	186,755	116,071	29	70,684 R	61.7%	38.3%	61.7%	38.3%
193,643	PASCO	107,578	66,609	40,961	8	25,648 R	61.9%	38.1%	61.9%	38.1%
728,531	PINELLAS	369,145	240,535	128,547	63	111,988 R	65.2%	34.8%	65.2%	34.8%
321,652	POLK	119,701	84,174	35,505	22	48,669 R	70.3%	29.7%	70.3%	29.7%
50,549	PUTNAM	19,249	11,424	7,821	4	3,603 R	59.3%	40.6%	59.4%	40.6%
51,303	ST. JOHNS	23,147	16,493	6,652	2	9,841 R	71.3%	28.7%	71.3%	28.7%
87,182	ST. LUCIE	41,235	28,189	13,039	7	15,150 R	68.4%	31.6%	68.4%	31.6%
55,988	SANTA ROSA	25,889	21,237	4,646	6	16,591 R	82.0%	17.9%	82.0%	18.0%
202,251	SARASOTA	118,294	87,713	30,512	69	57,201 R	74.1%	25.8%	74.2%	25.8%
179,752	SEMINOLE	74,071	56,229	17,789	53	38,440 R	75.9%	24.0%	76.0%	24.0%
24,272	SUMTER	9,713	6,252	3,460	1	2,792 R	64.4%	35.6%	64.4%	35.6%

FLORIDA

PRESIDENT 1984

1980 Census Population	County	Total Vote	Republican	Democratic	Other	Rep.-Dem. Plurality	Percentage Total Vote Rep.	Total Vote Dem.	Major Vote Rep.	Major Vote Dem.
22,287	SUWANNEE	8,867	6,079	2,788		3,291 R	68.6%	31.4%	68.6%	31.4%
16,532	TAYLOR	5,758	4,030	1,728		2,302 R	70.0%	30.0%	70.0%	30.0%
10,166	UNION	2,567	1,804	761	2	1,043 R	70.3%	29.6%	70.3%	29.7%
258,762	VOLUSIA	112,141	68,317	43,811	13	24,506 R	60.9%	39.1%	60.9%	39.1%
10,887	WAKULLA	4,556	3,087	1,469		1,618 R	67.8%	32.2%	67.8%	32.2%
21,300	WALTON	9,617	7,117	2,500		4,617 R	74.0%	26.0%	74.0%	26.0%
14,509	WASHINGTON	6,520	4,603	1,916	1	2,687 R	70.6%	29.4%	70.6%	29.4%
	SPECIAL ABSENTEE	2,067	1,575	472	20	1,103 R	76.2%	22.8%	76.9%	23.1%
9,746,324	TOTAL	4,180,051	2,730,350	1,448,816	885	1,281,534 R	65.3%	34.7%	65.3%	34.7%

FLORIDA

PRESIDENT 1980

1980 Census Population	County	Total Vote	Republican	Democratic	Other	Rep.-Dem. Plurality	Percentage Total Vote Rep.	Percentage Total Vote Dem.	Percentage Major Vote Rep.	Percentage Major Vote Dem.
151,348	ALACHUA	51,355	19,804	26,849	4,702	7,045 D	38.6%	52.3%	42.4%	57.6%
15,289	BAKER	4,976	2,283	2,611	82	328 D	45.9%	52.5%	46.6%	53.4%
97,740	BAY	34,561	20,948	12,389	1,224	8,559 R	60.6%	35.8%	62.8%	37.2%
20,023	BRADFORD	6,243	2,778	3,347	118	569 D	44.5%	53.6%	45.4%	54.6%
272,959	BREVARD	115,636	69,460	39,007	7,169	30,453 R	60.1%	33.7%	64.0%	36.0%
1,018,200	BROWARD	410,561	229,693	146,323	34,545	83,370 R	55.9%	35.6%	61.1%	38.9%
9,294	CALHOUN	3,884	1,504	2,300	80	796 D	38.7%	59.2%	39.5%	60.5%
58,460	CHARLOTTE	31,700	20,486	9,769	1,445	10,717 R	64.6%	30.8%	67.7%	32.3%
54,703	CITRUS	24,430	14,286	9,162	982	5,124 R	58.5%	37.5%	60.9%	39.1%
67,052	CLAY	24,122	15,643	7,630	849	8,013 R	64.8%	31.6%	67.2%	32.8%
85,971	COLLIER	33,613	23,900	7,739	1,974	16,161 R	71.1%	23.0%	75.5%	24.5%
35,399	COLUMBIA	11,648	5,643	5,680	325	37 D	48.4%	48.8%	49.8%	50.2%
1,625,781	DADE	524,896	265,888	210,868	48,140	55,020 R	50.7%	40.2%	55.8%	44.2%
19,039	DESOTO	6,285	3,356	2,713	216	643 R	53.4%	43.2%	55.3%	44.7%
7,751	DIXIE	3,173	1,101	2,010	62	909 D	34.7%	63.3%	35.4%	64.6%
571,003	DUVAL	195,545	98,664	90,466	6,415	8,198 R	50.5%	46.3%	52.2%	47.8%
233,794	ESCAMBIA	88,559	51,794	33,513	3,252	18,281 R	58.5%	37.8%	60.7%	39.3%
10,913	FLAGLER	5,600	2,895	2,503	202	392 R	51.7%	44.7%	53.6%	46.4%
7,661	FRANKLIN	3,382	1,508	1,775	99	267 D	44.6%	52.5%	45.9%	54.1%
41,565	GADSDEN	12,225	3,718	8,222	285	4,504 D	30.4%	67.3%	31.1%	68.9%
5,767	GILCHRIST	2,793	1,093	1,627	73	534 D	39.1%	58.3%	40.2%	59.8%
5,992	GLADES	2,389	1,098	1,203	88	105 D	46.0%	50.4%	47.7%	52.3%
10,658	GULF	4,926	2,127	2,700	99	573 D	43.2%	54.8%	44.1%	55.9%
8,761	HAMILTON	3,280	1,301	1,923	56	622 D	39.7%	58.6%	40.4%	59.6%
19,379	HARDEE	5,332	2,603	2,599	130	4 R	48.8%	48.7%	50.0%	50.0%
18,599	HENDRY	5,414	2,703	2,543	168	160 R	49.9%	47.0%	51.5%	48.5%
44,469	HERNANDO	22,032	12,115	8,858	1,059	3,257 R	55.0%	40.2%	57.8%	42.2%
47,526	HIGHLANDS	19,249	11,925	6,688	636	5,237 R	62.0%	34.7%	64.1%	35.9%
646,960	HILLSBOROUGH	205,314	106,160	88,271	10,883	17,889 R	51.7%	43.0%	54.6%	45.4%
14,723	HOLMES	6,137	3,221	2,767	149	454 R	52.5%	45.1%	53.8%	46.2%
59,896	INDIAN RIVER	24,717	15,568	7,759	1,390	7,809 R	63.0%	31.4%	66.7%	33.3%
39,154	JACKSON	14,181	6,348	7,567	266	1,219 D	44.8%	53.4%	45.6%	54.4%
10,703	JEFFERSON	4,141	1,623	2,367	151	744 D	39.2%	57.2%	40.7%	59.3%
4,035	LAFAYETTE	1,863	795	1,034	34	239 D	42.7%	55.5%	43.5%	56.5%
104,870	LAKE	41,528	26,798	13,128	1,602	13,670 R	64.5%	31.6%	67.1%	32.9%
205,266	LEE	94,613	61,033	28,125	5,455	32,908 R	64.5%	29.7%	68.5%	31.5%
148,655	LEON	57,308	24,919	28,450	3,939	3,531 D	43.5%	49.6%	46.7%	53.3%
19,870	LEVY	7,596	3,210	4,170	216	960 D	42.3%	54.9%	43.5%	56.5%
4,260	LIBERTY	2,052	899	1,114	39	215 D	43.8%	54.3%	44.7%	55.3%
14,894	MADISON	5,509	2,280	3,134	95	854 D	41.4%	56.9%	42.1%	57.9%
148,442	MANATEE	65,576	40,535	21,679	3,362	18,856 R	61.8%	33.1%	65.2%	34.8%
122,488	MARION	40,592	23,743	15,400	1,449	8,343 R	58.5%	37.9%	60.7%	39.3%
64,014	MARTIN	30,154	20,521	8,087	1,546	12,434 R	68.1%	26.8%	71.7%	28.3%
63,188	MONROE	21,806	11,644	7,920	2,242	3,724 R	53.4%	36.3%	59.5%	40.5%
32,894	NASSAU	10,751	5,440	5,074	237	366 R	50.6%	47.2%	51.7%	48.3%
109,920	OKALOOSA	40,323	28,072	10,845	1,406	17,227 R	69.6%	26.9%	72.1%	27.9%
20,264	OKEECHOBEE	6,210	2,783	3,228	199	445 D	44.8%	52.0%	46.3%	53.7%
471,016	ORANGE	143,201	87,454	48,767	6,980	38,687 R	61.1%	34.1%	64.2%	35.8%
49,287	OSCEOLA	18,205	10,863	6,603	739	4,260 R	59.7%	36.3%	62.2%	37.8%
576,863	PALM BEACH	252,930	143,639	91,991	17,300	51,648 R	56.8%	36.4%	61.0%	39.0%
193,643	PASCO	88,445	50,120	34,054	4,271	16,066 R	56.7%	38.5%	59.5%	40.5%
728,531	PINELLAS	345,003	185,728	138,428	20,847	47,300 R	53.8%	40.1%	57.3%	42.7%
321,652	POLK	106,315	59,651	43,327	3,337	16,324 R	56.1%	40.8%	57.9%	42.1%
50,549	PUTNAM	17,727	8,273	8,906	548	633 D	46.7%	50.2%	48.2%	51.8%
51,303	ST. JOHNS	18,826	11,234	6,898	694	4,336 R	59.7%	36.6%	62.0%	38.0%
87,182	ST. LUCIE	29,830	18,126	10,347	1,357	7,779 R	60.8%	34.7%	63.7%	36.3%
55,988	SANTA ROSA	21,590	13,802	6,964	824	6,838 R	63.9%	32.3%	66.5%	33.5%
202,251	SARASOTA	99,238	68,065	25,621	5,552	42,444 R	68.6%	25.8%	72.7%	27.3%
179,752	SEMINOLE	60,439	39,989	17,443	3,007	22,546 R	66.2%	28.9%	69.6%	30.4%
24,272	SUMTER	8,267	3,671	4,380	216	709 D	44.4%	53.0%	45.6%	54.4%

FLORIDA

PRESIDENT 1980

1980 Census Population	County	Total Vote	Republican	Democratic	Other	Rep.-Dem. Plurality	Percentage Total Vote Rep.	Total Vote Dem.	Major Vote Rep.	Major Vote Dem.
22,287	SUWANNEE	8,436	3,899	4,345	192	446 D	46.2%	51.5%	47.3%	52.7%
16,532	TAYLOR	5,868	2,776	2,963	129	187 D	47.3%	50.5%	48.4%	51.6%
10,166	UNION	2,423	1,123	1,237	63	114 D	46.3%	51.1%	47.6%	52.4%
258,762	VOLUSIA	101,882	52,663	44,513	4,706	8,150 R	51.7%	43.7%	54.2%	45.8%
10,887	WAKULLA	4,276	2,021	2,082	173	61 D	47.3%	48.7%	49.3%	50.7%
21,300	WALTON	9,336	4,694	4,360	282	334 R	50.3%	46.7%	51.8%	48.2%
14,509	WASHINGTON	6,513	3,251	3,110	152	141 R	49.9%	47.8%	51.1%	48.9%
9,746,324	TOTAL	3,686,930	2,046,951	1,419,475	220,504	627,476 R	55.5%	38.5%	59.1%	40.9%

FLORIDA

PRESIDENT 1976

1970 Census Population	County	Total Vote	Republican	Democratic	Other	Rep.-Dem. Plurality	Percentage Total Vote Rep.	Total Vote Dem.	Major Vote Rep.	Major Vote Dem.
104,764	ALACHUA	44,578	15,546	27,895	1,137	12,349 D	34.9%	62.6%	35.8%	64.2%
9,242	BAKER	4,195	1,058	2,985	152	1,927 D	25.2%	71.2%	26.2%	73.8%
75,283	BAY	29,484	14,208	14,858	418	650 D	48.2%	50.4%	48.9%	51.1%
14,625	BRADFORD	5,617	1,680	3,868	69	2,188 D	29.9%	68.9%	30.3%	69.7%
230,006	BREVARD	92,364	44,470	46,421	1,473	1,951 D	48.1%	50.3%	48.9%	51.1%
620,100	BROWARD	342,343	161,411	176,491	4,441	15,080 D	47.1%	51.6%	47.8%	52.2%
7,624	CALHOUN	3,689	1,153	2,487	49	1,334 D	31.3%	67.4%	31.7%	68.3%
27,559	CHARLOTTE	23,333	12,703	10,300	330	2,403 R	54.4%	44.1%	55.2%	44.8%
19,196	CITRUS	17,707	7,973	9,438	296	1,465 D	45.0%	53.3%	45.8%	54.2%
32,059	CLAY	17,148	8,468	8,410	270	58 R	49.4%	49.0%	50.2%	49.8%
38,040	COLLIER	23,710	14,643	8,764	303	5,879 R	61.8%	37.0%	62.6%	37.4%
25,250	COLUMBIA	10,766	3,947	6,683	136	2,736 D	36.7%	62.1%	37.1%	62.9%
1,267,792	DADE	521,942	211,148	303,047	7,747	91,899 D	40.5%	58.1%	41.1%	58.9%
13,060	DESOTO	4,822	2,000	2,715	107	715 D	41.5%	56.3%	42.4%	57.6%
5,480	DIXIE	2,752	558	2,169	25	1,611 D	20.3%	78.8%	20.5%	79.5%
528,865	DUVAL	182,561	74,997	105,912	1,652	30,915 D	41.1%	58.0%	41.5%	58.5%
205,334	ESCAMBIA	80,715	41,471	38,279	965	3,192 R	51.4%	47.4%	52.0%	48.0%
4,454	FLAGLER	3,373	1,262	2,086	25	824 D	37.4%	61.8%	37.7%	62.3%
7,065	FRANKLIN	2,973	1,054	1,859	60	805 D	35.5%	62.5%	36.2%	63.8%
39,184	GADSDEN	10,431	3,531	6,798	102	3,267 D	33.9%	65.2%	34.2%	65.8%
3,551	GILCHRIST	2,354	528	1,807	19	1,279 D	22.4%	76.8%	22.6%	77.4%
3,669	GLADES	1,965	624	1,311	30	687 D	31.8%	66.7%	32.2%	67.8%
10,096	GULF	4,281	1,584	2,641	56	1,057 D	37.0%	61.7%	37.5%	62.5%
7,787	HAMILTON	2,951	794	2,053	104	1,259 D	26.9%	69.6%	27.9%	72.1%
14,889	HARDEE	5,107	2,189	2,670	248	481 D	42.9%	52.3%	45.1%	54.9%
11,859	HENDRY	4,254	1,843	2,337	74	494 D	43.3%	54.9%	44.1%	55.9%
17,004	HERNANDO	13,732	5,793	7,717	222	1,924 D	42.2%	56.2%	42.9%	57.1%
29,507	HIGHLANDS	15,733	8,317	7,218	198	1,099 R	52.9%	45.9%	53.5%	46.5%
490,265	HILLSBOROUGH	175,145	78,504	94,589	2,052	16,085 D	44.8%	54.0%	45.4%	54.6%
10,720	HOLMES	5,180	1,850	3,256	74	1,406 D	35.7%	62.9%	36.2%	63.8%
35,992	INDIAN RIVER	18,654	9,818	8,512	324	1,306 R	52.6%	45.6%	53.6%	46.4%
34,434	JACKSON	12,652	4,795	7,687	170	2,892 D	37.9%	60.8%	38.4%	61.6%
8,778	JEFFERSON	3,749	1,361	2,310	78	949 D	36.3%	61.6%	37.1%	62.9%
2,892	LAFAYETTE	1,665	523	1,126	16	603 D	31.4%	67.6%	31.7%	68.3%
69,305	LAKE	34,787	19,976	14,369	442	5,607 R	57.4%	41.3%	58.2%	41.8%
105,216	LEE	69,789	38,038	30,567	1,184	7,471 R	54.5%	43.8%	55.4%	44.6%
103,047	LEON	53,443	23,739	28,729	975	4,990 D	44.4%	53.8%	45.2%	54.8%
12,756	LEVY	6,166	1,965	4,025	176	2,060 D	31.9%	65.3%	32.8%	67.2%
3,379	LIBERTY	1,776	620	1,137	19	517 D	34.9%	64.0%	35.3%	64.7%
13,481	MADISON	5,040	1,761	3,218	61	1,457 D	34.9%	63.8%	35.4%	64.6%
97,115	MANATEE	54,360	29,300	24,342	718	4,958 R	53.9%	44.8%	54.6%	45.4%
69,030	MARION	33,679	16,163	16,963	553	800 D	48.0%	50.4%	48.8%	51.2%
28,035	MARTIN	20,756	11,682	8,785	289	2,897 R	56.3%	42.3%	57.1%	42.9%
52,586	MONROE	19,757	8,232	11,079	446	2,847 D	41.7%	56.1%	42.6%	57.4%
20,626	NASSAU	9,140	3,136	5,896	108	2,760 D	34.3%	64.5%	34.7%	65.3%
88,187	OKALOOSA	33,295	18,598	14,210	487	4,388 R	55.9%	42.7%	56.7%	43.3%
11,233	OKEECHOBEE	4,825	1,598	3,184	43	1,586 D	33.1%	66.0%	33.4%	66.6%
344,311	ORANGE	130,437	70,451	58,442	1,544	12,009 R	54.0%	44.8%	54.7%	45.3%
25,267	OSCEOLA	14,175	7,062	6,893	220	169 R	49.8%	48.6%	50.6%	49.4%
348,753	PALM BEACH	198,657	98,236	96,705	3,716	1,531 R	49.5%	48.7%	50.4%	49.6%
75,955	PASCO	62,747	28,306	33,710	731	5,404 D	45.1%	53.7%	45.6%	54.4%
522,329	PINELLAS	295,569	150,003	141,879	3,687	8,124 R	50.8%	48.0%	51.4%	48.6%
227,222	POLK	92,706	44,238	47,286	1,182	3,048 D	47.7%	51.0%	48.3%	51.7%
36,290	PUTNAM	14,809	5,040	9,597	172	4,557 D	34.0%	64.8%	34.4%	65.6%
30,727	ST. JOHNS	14,371	6,660	7,412	299	752 D	46.3%	51.6%	47.3%	52.7%
50,836	ST. LUCIE	24,209	11,502	12,386	321	884 D	47.5%	51.2%	48.1%	51.9%
37,741	SANTA ROSA	17,412	9,122	8,020	270	1,102 R	52.4%	46.1%	53.2%	46.8%
120,413	SARASOTA	71,478	44,157	26,293	1,028	17,864 R	61.8%	36.8%	62.7%	37.3%
83,692	SEMINOLE	46,813	26,655	19,609	549	7,046 R	56.9%	41.9%	57.6%	42.4%
14,839	SUMTER	7,090	2,212	4,721	157	2,509 D	31.2%	66.6%	31.9%	68.1%

FLORIDA

PRESIDENT 1976

1970 Census Population	County	Total Vote	Republican	Democratic	Other	Rep.-Dem. Plurality	Percentage Total Vote Rep.	Percentage Total Vote Dem.	Percentage Major Vote Rep.	Percentage Major Vote Dem.
15,559	SUWANNEE	7,402	2,405	4,718	279	2,313 D	32.5%	63.7%	33.8%	66.2%
13,641	TAYLOR	5,406	1,983	3,370	53	1,387 D	36.7%	62.3%	37.0%	63.0%
8,112	UNION	2,040	544	1,480	16	936 D	26.7%	72.5%	26.9%	73.1%
169,487	VOLUSIA	88,225	37,523	49,161	1,541	11,638 D	42.5%	55.7%	43.3%	56.7%
6,308	WAKULLA	4,072	1,580	2,353	139	773 D	38.8%	57.8%	40.2%	59.8%
16,087	WALTON	8,279	2,927	5,196	156	2,269 D	35.4%	62.8%	36.0%	64.0%
11,453	WASHINGTON	5,996	2,313	3,566	117	1,253 D	38.6%	59.5%	39.3%	60.7%
6,789,443	TOTAL	3,150,631	1,469,531	1,636,000	45,100	166,469 D	46.6%	51.9%	47.3%	52.7%

FLORIDA

PRESIDENT 1972

1970 Census Population	County	Total Vote	Republican	Democratic	Other	Rep.-Dem. Plurality	Percentage			
							Total Vote		Major Vote	
							Rep.	Dem.	Rep.	Dem.
104,764	ALACHUA	39,861	22,536	17,245	80	5,291 R	56.5%	43.3%	56.7%	43.3%
9,242	BAKER	2,323	1,943	379	1	1,564 R	83.6%	16.3%	83.7%	16.3%
75,283	BAY	24,159	20,245	3,914		16,331 R	83.8%	16.2%	83.8%	16.2%
14,625	BRADFORD	4,957	3,652	1,217	88	2,435 R	73.7%	24.6%	75.0%	25.0%
230,006	BREVARD	79,733	62,773	16,854	106	45,919 R	78.7%	21.1%	78.8%	21.2%
620,100	BROWARD	271,409	196,528	74,127	754	122,401 R	72.4%	27.3%	72.6%	27.4%
7,624	CALHOUN	2,533	2,069	461	3	1,608 R	81.7%	18.2%	81.8%	18.2%
27,559	CHARLOTTE	16,817	12,888	3,874	55	9,014 R	76.6%	23.0%	76.9%	23.1%
19,196	CITRUS	11,458	8,848	2,607	3	6,241 R	77.2%	22.8%	77.2%	22.8%
32,059	CLAY	12,238	10,467	1,748	23	8,719 R	85.5%	14.3%	85.7%	14.3%
38,040	COLLIER	16,744	13,501	3,201	42	10,300 R	80.6%	19.1%	80.8%	19.2%
25,250	COLUMBIA	8,387	6,723	1,664		5,059 R	80.2%	19.8%	80.2%	19.8%
1,267,792	DADE	435,763	256,529	177,693	1,541	78,836 R	58.9%	40.8%	59.1%	40.9%
13,060	DESOTO	3,813	2,958	852	3	2,106 R	77.6%	22.3%	77.6%	22.4%
5,480	DIXIE	1,997	1,628	367	2	1,261 R	81.5%	18.4%	81.6%	18.4%
528,865	DUVAL	169,204	122,154	46,530	520	75,624 R	72.2%	27.5%	72.4%	27.6%
205,334	ESCAMBIA	70,464	56,071	14,078	315	41,993 R	79.6%	20.0%	79.9%	20.1%
4,454	FLAGLER	1,902	1,409	493		916 R	74.1%	25.9%	74.1%	25.9%
7,065	FRANKLIN	2,772	2,277	490	5	1,787 R	82.1%	17.7%	82.3%	17.7%
39,184	GADSDEN	9,826	5,995	3,829	2	2,166 R	61.0%	39.0%	61.0%	39.0%
3,551	GILCHRIST	1,565	1,306	247	12	1,059 R	83.5%	15.8%	84.1%	15.9%
3,669	GLADES	1,293	1,019	253	21	766 R	78.8%	19.6%	80.1%	19.9%
10,096	GULF	3,346	2,628	713	5	1,915 R	78.5%	21.3%	78.7%	21.3%
7,787	HAMILTON	2,374	1,741	626	7	1,115 R	73.3%	26.4%	73.6%	26.4%
14,889	HARDEE	4,213	3,563	647	3	2,916 R	84.6%	15.4%	84.6%	15.4%
11,859	HENDRY	3,504	2,763	739	2	2,024 R	78.9%	21.1%	78.9%	21.1%
17,004	HERNANDO	8,409	6,296	2,110	3	4,186 R	74.9%	25.1%	74.9%	25.1%
29,507	HIGHLANDS	12,133	9,645	2,458	30	7,187 R	79.5%	20.3%	79.7%	20.3%
490,265	HILLSBOROUGH	152,510	106,956	45,305	249	61,651 R	70.1%	29.7%	70.2%	29.8%
10,720	HOLMES	4,128	3,819	309		3,510 R	92.5%	7.5%	92.5%	7.5%
35,992	INDIAN RIVER	15,082	11,741	3,316	25	8,425 R	77.8%	22.0%	78.0%	22.0%
34,434	JACKSON	11,132	8,904	2,220	8	6,684 R	80.0%	19.9%	80.0%	20.0%
8,778	JEFFERSON	3,192	2,108	1,049	35	1,059 R	66.0%	32.9%	66.8%	33.2%
2,892	LAFAYETTE	1,237	1,060	173	4	887 R	85.7%	14.0%	86.0%	14.0%
69,305	LAKE	27,930	23,079	4,803	48	18,276 R	82.6%	17.2%	82.8%	17.2%
105,216	LEE	46,235	36,738	9,404	93	27,334 R	79.5%	20.3%	79.6%	20.4%
103,047	LEON	43,126	27,479	15,555	92	11,924 R	63.7%	36.1%	63.9%	36.1%
12,756	LEVY	4,137	3,273	862	2	2,411 R	79.1%	20.8%	79.2%	20.8%
3,379	LIBERTY	1,421	1,199	222		977 R	84.4%	15.6%	84.4%	15.6%
13,481	MADISON	4,438	3,236	1,187	15	2,049 R	72.9%	26.7%	73.2%	26.8%
97,115	MANATEE	40,940	32,664	8,058	218	24,606 R	79.8%	19.7%	80.2%	19.8%
69,030	MARION	24,948	19,505	5,397	46	14,108 R	78.2%	21.6%	78.3%	21.7%
28,035	MARTIN	14,330	11,296	2,946	88	8,350 R	78.8%	20.6%	79.3%	20.7%
52,586	MONROE	16,193	11,688	4,469	36	7,219 R	72.2%	27.6%	72.3%	27.7%
20,626	NASSAU	6,392	5,078	1,293	21	3,785 R	79.4%	20.2%	79.7%	20.3%
88,187	OKALOOSA	26,290	23,303	2,843	144	20,460 R	88.6%	10.8%	89.1%	10.9%
11,233	OKEECHOBEE	3,203	2,581	621	1	1,960 R	80.6%	19.4%	80.6%	19.4%
344,311	ORANGE	118,777	94,516	23,840	421	70,676 R	79.6%	20.1%	79.9%	20.1%
25,267	OSCEOLA	11,237	9,320	1,875	42	7,445 R	82.9%	16.7%	83.3%	16.7%
348,753	PALM BEACH	150,203	108,670	40,825	708	67,845 R	72.3%	27.2%	72.7%	27.3%
75,955	PASCO	40,676	29,249	11,330	97	17,919 R	71.9%	27.9%	72.1%	27.9%
522,329	PINELLAS	257,116	179,541	77,197	378	102,344 R	69.8%	30.0%	69.9%	30.1%
227,222	POLK	77,460	60,748	16,419	293	44,329 R	78.4%	21.2%	78.7%	21.3%
36,290	PUTNAM	11,716	8,741	2,901	74	5,840 R	74.6%	24.8%	75.1%	24.9%
30,727	ST. JOHNS	11,511	8,919	2,549	43	6,370 R	77.5%	22.1%	77.8%	22.2%
50,836	ST. LUCIE	18,910	14,258	4,593	59	9,665 R	75.4%	24.3%	75.6%	24.4%
37,741	SANTA ROSA	14,245	12,669	1,491	85	11,178 R	88.9%	10.5%	89.5%	10.5%
120,413	SARASOTA	61,210	48,939	12,235	36	36,704 R	80.0%	20.0%	80.0%	20.0%
83,692	SEMINOLE	34,212	27,658	6,503	51	21,155 R	80.8%	19.0%	81.0%	19.0%
14,839	SUMTER	4,817	3,695	1,107	15	2,588 R	76.7%	23.0%	76.9%	23.1%

FLORIDA

PRESIDENT 1972

1970 Census Population	County	Total Vote	Republican	Democratic	Other	Rep.-Dem. Plurality	Percentage Total Vote Rep.	Percentage Total Vote Dem.	Percentage Major Vote Rep.	Percentage Major Vote Dem.
15,559	SUWANNEE	5,491	4,435	1,027	29	3,408 R	80.8%	18.7%	81.2%	18.8%
13,641	TAYLOR	4,863	4,109	754		3,355 R	84.5%	15.5%	84.5%	15.5%
8,112	UNION	1,567	1,314	253		1,061 R	83.9%	16.1%	83.9%	16.1%
169,487	VOLUSIA	74,583	52,656	21,637	290	31,019 R	70.6%	29.0%	70.9%	29.1%
6,308	WAKULLA	3,007	2,466	539	2	1,927 R	82.0%	17.9%	82.1%	17.9%
16,087	WALTON	7,235	6,217	988	30	5,229 R	85.9%	13.7%	86.3%	13.7%
11,453	WASHINGTON	4,386	3,777	606	3	3,171 R	86.1%	13.8%	86.2%	13.8%
6,789,443	TOTAL	2,583,283	1,857,759	718,117	7,407	1,139,642 R	71.9%	27.8%	72.1%	27.9%

FLORIDA

PRESIDENT 1968

1960 Census Population	County	Total Vote	Republican	Democratic	AIP	Other	Plurality	Percentage		
								Rep.	Dem.	AIP
74,074	ALACHUA	28,426	9,670	10,060	8,696		390 D	34.0%	35.4%	30.6%
7,363	BAKER	2,743	294	487	1,962		1,475 A	10.7%	17.8%	71.5%
67,131	BAY	24,302	5,121	4,020	15,161		10,040 A	21.1%	16.5%	62.4%
12,446	BRADFORD	4,731	718	1,173	2,840		1,667 A	15.2%	24.8%	60.0%
111,435	BREVARD	77,314	37,124	18,281	21,909		15,215 R	48.0%	23.6%	28.3%
333,946	BROWARD	194,727	106,122	56,613	31,992		49,509 R	54.5%	29.1%	16.4%
7,422	CALHOUN	3,129	356	398	2,375		1,977 A	11.4%	12.7%	75.9%
12,594	CHARLOTTE	11,973	6,056	3,647	2,270		2,409 R	50.6%	30.5%	19.0%
9,268	CITRUS	7,148	2,767	1,775	2,606		161 R	38.7%	24.8%	36.5%
19,535	CLAY	9,251	3,251	1,954	4,046		795 A	35.1%	21.1%	43.7%
15,753	COLLIER	10,544	5,362	2,230	2,952		2,410 R	50.9%	21.1%	28.0%
20,077	COLUMBIA	7,349	1,553	1,750	4,046		2,296 A	21.1%	23.8%	55.1%
935,047	DADE	365,302	135,222	176,689	53,391		41,467 D	37.0%	48.4%	14.6%
11,683	DESOTO	4,094	1,103	937	2,054		951 A	26.9%	22.9%	50.2%
4,479	DIXIE	2,088	217	325	1,546		1,221 A	10.4%	15.6%	74.0%
455,411	DUVAL	166,978	51,585	54,834	60,559		5,725 A	30.9%	32.8%	36.3%
173,829	ESCAMBIA	68,370	15,089	16,281	37,000		20,719 A	22.1%	23.8%	54.1%
4,566	FLAGLER	1,778	360	601	817		216 A	20.2%	33.8%	46.0%
6,576	FRANKLIN	3,137	529	699	1,909		1,210 A	16.9%	22.3%	60.9%
41,989	GADSDEN	9,057	1,337	3,274	4,446		1,172 A	14.8%	36.1%	49.1%
2,868	GILCHRIST	1,510	183	208	1,119		911 A	12.1%	13.8%	74.1%
2,950	GLADES	1,091	261	230	600		339 A	23.9%	21.1%	55.0%
9,937	GULF	3,800	364	711	2,725		2,014 A	9.6%	18.7%	71.7%
7,705	HAMILTON	2,731	337	820	1,574		754 A	12.3%	30.0%	57.6%
12,370	HARDEE	4,510	1,278	703	2,529		1,251 A	28.3%	15.6%	56.1%
8,119	HENDRY	3,329	900	791	1,638		738 A	27.0%	23.8%	49.2%
11,205	HERNANDO	5,964	2,053	1,524	2,387		334 A	34.4%	25.6%	40.0%
21,338	HIGHLANDS	10,617	4,560	2,582	3,475		1,085 R	42.9%	24.3%	32.7%
397,788	HILLSBOROUGH	142,202	49,441	45,848	46,913		2,528 R	34.8%	32.2%	33.0%
10,844	HOLMES	5,389	377	312	4,700		4,323 A	7.0%	5.8%	87.2%
25,309	INDIAN RIVER	12,719	6,518	3,179	3,022		3,339 R	51.2%	25.0%	23.8%
36,208	JACKSON	12,330	1,236	2,472	8,622		6,150 A	10.0%	20.0%	69.9%
9,543	JEFFERSON	3,092	459	1,066	1,567		501 A	14.8%	34.5%	50.7%
2,889	LAFAYETTE	1,477	137	215	1,125		910 A	9.3%	14.6%	76.2%
57,383	LAKE	24,804	11,763	4,599	8,442		3,321 R	47.4%	18.5%	34.0%
54,539	LEE	31,095	14,376	7,978	8,741		5,635 R	46.2%	25.7%	28.1%
74,225	LEON	32,606	9,288	10,440	12,878		2,438 A	28.5%	32.0%	39.5%
10,364	LEVY	3,961	745	767	2,449		1,682 A	18.8%	19.4%	61.8%
3,138	LIBERTY	1,718	154	242	1,322		1,080 A	9.0%	14.1%	76.9%
14,154	MADISON	4,735	654	1,378	2,703		1,325 A	13.8%	29.1%	57.1%
69,168	MANATEE	34,747	18,247	8,286	8,214		9,961 R	52.5%	23.8%	23.6%
51,616	MARION	22,866	7,468	5,798	9,600		2,132 A	32.7%	25.4%	42.0%
16,932	MARTIN	10,230	5,179	2,580	2,471		2,599 R	50.6%	25.2%	24.2%
47,921	MONROE	14,899	5,094	5,534	4,271		440 D	34.2%	37.1%	28.7%
17,189	NASSAU	6,533	1,301	1,598	3,634		2,036 A	19.9%	24.5%	55.6%
61,175	OKALOOSA	20,821	5,525	3,059	12,237		6,712 A	26.5%	14.7%	58.8%
6,424	OKEECHOBEE	3,008	862	542	1,604		742 A	28.7%	18.0%	53.3%
263,540	ORANGE	100,669	50,874	22,548	27,247		23,627 R	50.5%	22.4%	27.1%
19,029	OSCEOLA	9,504	4,172	1,870	3,462		710 R	43.9%	19.7%	36.4%
228,106	PALM BEACH	116,922	62,191	32,837	21,894		29,354 R	53.2%	28.1%	18.7%
36,785	PASCO	23,001	9,743	6,292	6,966		2,777 R	42.4%	27.4%	30.3%
374,665	PINELLAS	211,258	109,235	68,209	33,814		41,026 R	51.7%	32.3%	16.0%
195,139	POLK	75,277	27,839	15,898	31,540		3,701 A	37.0%	21.1%	41.9%
32,212	PUTNAM	11,025	2,955	2,920	5,150		2,195 A	26.8%	26.5%	46.7%
30,034	ST. JOHNS	11,310	3,880	2,748	4,682		802 A	34.3%	24.3%	41.4%
39,294	ST. LUCIE	16,923	7,281	5,232	4,410		2,049 R	43.0%	30.9%	26.1%
29,547	SANTA ROSA	12,716	2,567	1,600	8,549		5,982 A	20.2%	12.6%	67.2%
76,895	SARASOTA	47,328	30,160	10,127	7,041		20,033 R	63.7%	21.4%	14.9%
54,947	SEMINOLE	24,216	10,821	6,120	7,275		3,546 R	44.7%	25.3%	30.0%
11,869	SUMTER	5,066	910	1,277	2,879		1,602 A	18.0%	25.2%	56.8%

FLORIDA

PRESIDENT 1968

1960 Census Population	County	Total Vote	Republican	Democratic	AIP	Other	Plurality	Percentage Rep.	Dem.	AIP
14,961	SUWANNEE	5,982	845	1,182	3,955		2,773 A	14.1%	19.8%	66.1%
13,168	TAYLOR	5,053	794	941	3,318		2,377 A	15.7%	18.6%	65.7%
6,043	UNION	1,661	179	290	1,192		902 A	10.8%	17.5%	71.8%
125,319	VOLUSIA	70,220	28,024	24,987	17,209		3,037 R	39.9%	35.6%	24.5%
5,257	WAKULLA	2,355	247	440	1,668		1,228 A	10.5%	18.7%	70.8%
15,576	WALTON	7,162	963	1,064	5,135		4,071 A	13.4%	14.9%	71.7%
11,249	WASHINGTON	4,932	528	722	3,682		2,960 A	10.7%	14.6%	74.7%
4,951,560	TOTAL	2,187,805	886,804	676,794	624,207		210,010 R	40.5%	30.9%	28.5%

FLORIDA

ELECTION NOTES

1984 Other vote was 754 Bergland (write-in); 58 Johnson (write-in); 34 Hall (write-in); 7 Mason (write-in); 32 scattered write-in. Special absentee votes listed in the data table are ballots counted separately by court order.

1980 Other vote was 189,692 Anderson (Independent); 30,524 Clark (Libertarian); 123 Hall (write-in); 116 McReynolds (write-in); 41 DeBerry (write-in); 8 Griswold (write-in). County and state-wide totals include special absentee votes counted separately by court order.

1976 Other vote was 23,643 McCarthy (Independent); 21,325 Anderson (American); 103 MacBride (write-in); 19 Levin (write-in); 8 Zeidler (write-in); 2 Miller (write-in).

1972 Other vote was scattered write-in.

1968 Wallace on the ballot as George Wallace party.

GEORGIA

POPULAR VOTE FOR PRESIDENT 1920 TO 1984

									Percentage			
	Total	Republican		Democratic		Other			Total Vote		Major Vote	
Year	Vote	Vote	Candidate	Vote	Candidate	Vote	Plurality		Rep.	Dem.	Rep.	Dem.
1984	1,776,120	1,068,722	Reagan, Ronald	706,628	Mondale, Walter F.	770	362,094	R	60.2%	39.8%	60.2%	39.8%
1980	1,596,695	654,168	Reagan, Ronald	890,733	Carter, Jimmy	51,794	236,565	D	41.0%	55.8%	42.3%	57.7%
1976	1,467,458	483,743	Ford, Gerald R.	979,409	Carter, Jimmy	4,306	495,666	D	33.0%	66.7%	33.1%	66.9%
1972	1,174,772	881,496	Nixon, Richard M.	289,529	McGovern, George S.	3,747	591,967	R	75.0%	24.6%	75.3%	24.7%
1968 **	1,250,266	380,111	Nixon, Richard M.	334,440	Humphrey, Hubert H.	535,715	155,439	A	30.4%	26.7%	53.2%	46.8%
1964	1,139,335	616,584	Goldwater, Barry M.	522,556	Johnson, Lyndon B.	195	94,028	R	54.1%	45.9%	54.1%	45.9%
1960	733,349	274,472	Nixon, Richard M.	458,638	Kennedy, John F.	239	184,166	D	37.4%	62.5%	37.4%	62.6%
1956	669,655	222,778	Eisenhower, Dwight D.	444,688	Stevenson, Adlai E.	2,189	221,910	D	33.3%	66.4%	33.4%	66.6%
1952	655,785	198,961	Eisenhower, Dwight D.	456,823	Stevenson, Adlai E.	1	257,862	D	30.3%	69.7%	30.3%	69.7%
1948 **	418,844	76,691	Dewey, Thomas E.	254,646	Truman, Harry S.	87,507	169,511	D	18.3%	60.8%	23.1%	76.9%
1944	328,129	59,900	Dewey, Thomas E.	268,187	Roosevelt, Franklin D.	42	208,287	D	18.3%	81.7%	18.3%	81.7%
1940	312,686	46,495	Willkie, Wendell	265,194	Roosevelt, Franklin D.	997	218,699	D	14.9%	84.8%	14.9%	85.1%
1936	293,170	36,943	Landon, Alfred M.	255,363	Roosevelt, Franklin D.	864	218,420	D	12.6%	87.1%	12.6%	87.4%
1932	255,590	19,863	Hoover, Herbert C.	234,118	Roosevelt, Franklin D.	1,609	214,255	D	7.8%	91.6%	7.8%	92.2%
1928	231,592	101,800	Hoover, Herbert C.	129,604	Smith, Alfred E.	188	27,804	D	44.0%	56.0%	44.0%	56.0%
1924	166,635	30,300	Coolidge, Calvin	123,262	Davis, John W.	13,073	92,962	D	18.2%	74.0%	19.7%	80.3%
1920	149,558	42,981	Harding, Warren G.	106,112	Cox, James M.	465	63,131	D	28.7%	71.0%	28.8%	71.2%

In 1968 other vote was 535,550 American (Wallace) and 165 scattered. In 1948 other vote was 85,135 States Rights; 1,636 Progressive; 732 Prohibition; 3 Socialist and 1 scattered.

ELECTORAL COLLEGE VOTE 1920 TO 1984

Year	Total	Republican	Democratic	Other
1984	12	12	—	—
1980	12	—	12	—
1976	12	—	12	—
1972	12	12	—	—
1968	12	—	—	12 AIP
1964	12	12	—	—
1960	12	—	12	—
1956	12	—	12	—
1952	12	—	12	—
1948	12	—	12	—
1944	12	—	12	—
1940	12	—	12	—
1936	12	—	12	—
1932	12	—	12	—
1928	14	—	14	—
1924	14	—	14	—
1920	14	—	14	—

GEORGIA

DADE
CATOOSA
WHITFIELD
MURRAY
FANNIN
TOWNS
UNION
RABUN
WALKER
GILMER
HABERSHAM
WHITE
LUMPKIN
CHATTOOGA
GORDON
PICKENS
DAWSON
STEPHENS
HART
BANKS
FRANKLN
HALL
FLOYD
BARTOW
CHEROKEE
FORSYTH
JACKSON
ELBERT
MADISON
POLK
PAULDING
COBB
GWINNETT
BARROW
CLARKE
OGLETHORPE
OCONEE
WILKES
LINCOLN
HARALSON
WALTON
DOUGLAS
DE KALB
FULTON
ROCK-
DALE
CARROLL
CLAYTON
NEWTON
MORGAN
GREENE
TALIA-
FERRO
McDUFFIE
COLUMBIA
WARREN
FAYETTE
HENRY
COWETA
HEARD
JASPER
PUTNAM
HANCOCK
RICHMOND
BUTTS
SPALDING
GLAS-
COCK
JEFFERSON
BURKE
TROUP
MERIWETHER
PIKE
LAMAR
MONROE
JONES
BALDWIN
WASHINGTON
UPSON
BIBB
WILKINSON
JENKINS
SCREVEN
HARRIS
TALBOT
CRAWFORD
TWIGGS
JOHNSON
EMANUEL
MUSCOGEE
TAYLOR
PEACH
HOUSTON
BLECKLEY
LAURENS
EFFINGHAM
CHATTA-
HOOCHEE
MARION
SCHLEY
MACON
TREUTLEN
CANDLER
BULLOCH
DOOLY
PULASKI
DODGE
MONTGOMERY
TOOMBS
EVANS
STEWART
WEBSTER
SUMTER
WHEELER
TATTNALL
BRYAN
CHATHAM
CRISP
WILCOX
TELFAIR
QUIT-
MAN
LIBERTY
JEFF
DAVIS
TERRELL
LEE
BEN HILL
APPLING
LONG
RANDOLPH
TURNER
IRWIN
CLAY
WORTH
COFFEE
BACON
WAYNE
McINTOSH
CALHOUN
DOUGHERTY
TIFT
PIERCE
EARLY
BAKER
ATKINSON
GLYNN
BERRIEN
MITCHELL
COLQUITT
WARE
BRANTLEY
MILLER
COOK
LANIER
SEMINOLE
CAMDEN
CLINCH
DECATUR
GRADY
THOMAS
BROOKS
CHARLTON
LOWNDES
ECHOLS

GEORGIA

PRESIDENT 1984

1980 Census Population	County	Total Vote	Republican	Democratic	Other	Rep.-Dem. Plurality	Percentage Total Vote Rep.	Percentage Total Vote Dem.	Percentage Major Vote Rep.	Percentage Major Vote Dem.
15,565	APPLING	4,887	2,929	1,958		971 R	59.9%	40.1%	59.9%	40.1%
6,141	ATKINSON	1,845	944	901		43 R	51.2%	48.8%	51.2%	48.8%
9,379	BACON	2,788	1,778	1,010		768 R	63.8%	36.2%	63.8%	36.2%
3,808	BAKER	1,366	675	691		16 D	49.4%	50.6%	49.4%	50.6%
34,686	BALDWIN	9,570	5,717	3,853		1,864 R	59.7%	40.3%	59.7%	40.3%
8,702	BANKS	2,612	1,549	1,063		486 R	59.3%	40.7%	59.3%	40.7%
21,354	BARROW	6,490	4,123	2,367		1,756 R	63.5%	36.5%	63.5%	36.5%
40,760	BARTOW	11,884	7,104	4,780		2,324 R	59.8%	40.2%	59.8%	40.2%
16,000	BEN HILL	4,172	2,313	1,859		454 R	55.4%	44.6%	55.4%	44.6%
13,525	BERRIEN	4,065	2,395	1,670		725 R	58.9%	41.1%	58.9%	41.1%
150,256	BIBB	50,597	24,170	26,427		2,257 D	47.8%	52.2%	47.8%	52.2%
10,767	BLECKLEY	3,377	1,912	1,465		447 R	56.6%	43.4%	56.6%	43.4%
8,701	BRANTLEY	3,196	1,679	1,517		162 R	52.5%	47.5%	52.5%	47.5%
15,255	BROOKS	3,890	2,229	1,661		568 R	57.3%	42.7%	57.3%	42.7%
10,175	BRYAN	3,663	2,265	1,398		867 R	61.8%	38.2%	61.8%	38.2%
35,785	BULLOCH	9,761	6,117	3,644		2,473 R	62.7%	37.3%	62.7%	37.3%
19,349	BURKE	6,264	3,137	3,127		10 R	50.1%	49.9%	50.1%	49.9%
13,665	BUTTS	3,961	2,141	1,820		321 R	54.1%	45.9%	54.1%	45.9%
5,717	CALHOUN	1,853	776	1,077		301 D	41.9%	58.1%	41.9%	58.1%
13,371	CAMDEN	5,005	2,841	2,164		677 R	56.8%	43.2%	56.8%	43.2%
7,518	CANDLER	2,511	1,497	1,014		483 R	59.6%	40.4%	59.6%	40.4%
56,346	CARROLL	17,026	11,436	5,590		5,846 R	67.2%	32.8%	67.2%	32.8%
36,991	CATOOSA	10,997	7,908	3,089		4,819 R	71.9%	28.1%	71.9%	28.1%
7,343	CHARLTON	2,479	1,368	1,111		257 R	55.2%	44.8%	55.2%	44.8%
202,226	CHATHAM	66,753	38,482	28,271		10,211 R	57.6%	42.4%	57.6%	42.4%
21,732	CHATTAHOOCHEE	887	459	428		31 R	51.7%	48.3%	51.7%	48.3%
21,856	CHATTOOGA	5,529	2,953	2,576		377 R	53.4%	46.6%	53.4%	46.6%
51,699	CHEROKEE	14,645	11,146	3,499		7,647 R	76.1%	23.9%	76.1%	23.9%
74,498	CLARKE	21,635	11,503	10,132		1,371 R	53.2%	46.8%	53.2%	46.8%
3,553	CLAY	1,169	419	750		331 D	35.8%	64.2%	35.8%	64.2%
150,357	CLAYTON	43,316	31,553	11,763		19,790 R	72.8%	27.2%	72.8%	27.2%
6,660	CLINCH	1,487	862	625		237 R	58.0%	42.0%	58.0%	42.0%
297,718	COBB	125,843	97,429	28,414		69,015 R	77.4%	22.6%	77.4%	22.6%
26,894	COFFEE	6,833	4,200	2,633		1,567 R	61.5%	38.5%	61.5%	38.5%
35,376	COLQUITT	9,023	5,815	3,208		2,607 R	64.4%	35.6%	64.4%	35.6%
40,118	COLUMBIA	16,021	12,294	3,727		8,567 R	76.7%	23.3%	76.7%	23.3%
13,490	COOK	3,370	1,860	1,510		350 R	55.2%	44.8%	55.2%	44.8%
39,268	COWETA	11,631	7,981	3,650		4,331 R	68.6%	31.4%	68.6%	31.4%
7,684	CRAWFORD	2,721	1,298	1,423		125 D	47.7%	52.3%	47.7%	52.3%
19,489	CRISP	5,023	2,895	2,128		767 R	57.6%	42.4%	57.6%	42.4%
12,318	DADE	3,900	2,750	1,150		1,600 R	70.5%	29.5%	70.5%	29.5%
4,774	DAWSON	1,965	1,322	643		679 R	67.3%	32.7%	67.3%	32.7%
25,495	DECATUR	6,790	4,134	2,656		1,478 R	60.9%	39.1%	60.9%	39.1%
483,024	DE KALB	182,026	104,697	77,329		27,368 R	57.5%	42.5%	57.5%	42.5%
16,955	DODGE	5,278	2,765	2,513		252 R	52.4%	47.6%	52.4%	47.6%
10,826	DOOLY	3,161	1,435	1,726		291 D	45.4%	54.6%	45.4%	54.6%
100,718	DOUGHERTY	29,824	16,920	12,904		4,016 R	56.7%	43.3%	56.7%	43.3%
54,573	DOUGLAS	16,799	12,428	4,371		8,057 R	74.0%	26.0%	74.0%	26.0%
13,158	EARLY	3,733	2,239	1,494		745 R	60.0%	40.0%	60.0%	40.0%
2,297	ECHOLS	680	453	227		226 R	66.6%	33.4%	66.6%	33.4%
18,327	EFFINGHAM	6,321	4,266	2,055		2,211 R	67.5%	32.5%	67.5%	32.5%
18,758	ELBERT	6,036	3,366	2,670		696 R	55.8%	44.2%	55.8%	44.2%
20,795	EMANUEL	6,378	3,920	2,458		1,462 R	61.5%	38.5%	61.5%	38.5%
8,428	EVANS	2,794	1,601	1,193		408 R	57.3%	42.7%	57.3%	42.7%
14,748	FANNIN	6,124	4,159	1,965		2,194 R	67.9%	32.1%	67.9%	32.1%
29043	FAYETTE	15,436	12,575	2,861		9,714 R	81.5%	18.5%	81.5%	18.5%
79,800	FLOYD	24,310	15,437	8,873		6,564 R	63.5%	36.5%	63.5%	36.5%
27,958	FORSYTH	9,116	6,841	2,275		4,566 R	75.0%	25.0%	75.0%	25.0%
15,185	FRANKLIN	4,387	2,549	1,838		711 R	58.1%	41.9%	58.1%	41.9%
589,904	FULTON	220,716	95,149	125,567		30,418 D	43.1%	56.9%	43.1%	56.9%

GEORGIA

PRESIDENT 1984

1980 Census Population	County	Total Vote	Republican	Democratic	Other	Rep.-Dem. Plurality	Percentage Total Vote Rep.	Percentage Total Vote Dem.	Percentage Major Vote Rep.	Percentage Major Vote Dem.
11,110	GILMER	4,206	2,972	1,234		1,738 R	70.7%	29.3%	70.7%	29.3%
2,382	GLASCOCK	1,144	827	317		510 R	72.3%	27.7%	72.3%	27.7%
54,981	GLYNN	18,298	11,724	6,574		5,150 R	64.1%	35.9%	64.1%	35.9%
30,070	GORDON	8,173	5,566	2,607		2,959 R	68.1%	31.9%	68.1%	31.9%
19,845	GRADY	6,147	3,886	2,261		1,625 R	63.2%	36.8%	63.2%	36.8%
11,391	GREENE	3,591	1,599	1,992		393 D	44.5%	55.5%	44.5%	55.5%
166,903	GWINNETT	68,888	54,749	14,139		40,610 R	79.5%	20.5%	79.5%	20.5%
25,020	HABERSHAM	6,772	4,647	2,125		2,522 R	68.6%	31.4%	68.6%	31.4%
75,649	HALL	22,497	15,076	7,421		7,655 R	67.0%	33.0%	67.0%	33.0%
9,466	HANCOCK	2,753	644	2,109		1,465 D	23.4%	76.6%	23.4%	76.6%
18,422	HARALSON	5,883	3,945	1,938		2,007 R	67.1%	32.9%	67.1%	32.9%
15,464	HARRIS	5,234	3,138	2,096		1,042 R	60.0%	40.0%	60.0%	40.0%
18,585	HART	5,338	2,842	2,496		346 R	53.2%	46.8%	53.2%	46.8%
6,520	HEARD	2,302	1,492	810		682 R	64.8%	35.2%	64.8%	35.2%
36,309	HENRY	13,238	9,142	4,096		5,046 R	69.1%	30.9%	69.1%	30.9%
77,605	HOUSTON	23,481	14,255	9,226		5,029 R	60.7%	39.3%	60.7%	39.3%
8,988	IRWIN	2,235	1,330	905		425 R	59.5%	40.5%	59.5%	40.5%
25,343	JACKSON	6,919	4,202	2,717		1,485 R	60.7%	39.3%	60.7%	39.3%
7,553	JASPER	2,553	1,431	1,122		309 R	56.1%	43.9%	56.1%	43.9%
11,473	JEFF DAVIS	3,613	2,233	1,380		853 R	61.8%	38.2%	61.8%	38.2%
18,403	JEFFERSON	5,815	2,999	2,816		183 R	51.6%	48.4%	51.6%	48.4%
8,841	JENKINS	2,507	1,399	1,108		291 R	55.8%	44.2%	55.8%	44.2%
8,660	JOHNSON	2,932	1,733	1,199		534 R	59.1%	40.9%	59.1%	40.9%
16,579	JONES	6,182	3,401	2,781		620 R	55.0%	45.0%	55.0%	45.0%
12,215	LAMAR	3,803	2,198	1,605		593 R	57.8%	42.2%	57.8%	42.2%
5,654	LANIER	1,593	852	741		111 R	53.5%	46.5%	53.5%	46.5%
36,990	LAURENS	12,652	7,181	5,471		1,710 R	56.8%	43.2%	56.8%	43.2%
11,684	LEE	4,256	2,972	1,284		1,688 R	69.8%	30.2%	69.8%	30.2%
37,583	LIBERTY	6,032	3,229	2,803		426 R	53.5%	46.5%	53.5%	46.5%
6,716	LINCOLN	2,472	1,357	1,115		242 R	54.9%	45.1%	54.9%	45.1%
4,524	LONG	1,915	1,099	816		283 R	57.4%	42.6%	57.4%	42.6%
67,972	LOWNDES	16,604	10,437	6,167		4,270 R	62.9%	37.1%	62.9%	37.1%
10,762	LUMPKIN	3,101	1,991	1,110		881 R	64.2%	35.8%	64.2%	35.8%
18,546	MCDUFFIE	5,290	3,284	2,006		1,278 R	62.1%	37.9%	62.1%	37.9%
8,046	MCINTOSH	3,308	1,512	1,796		284 D	45.7%	54.3%	45.7%	54.3%
14,003	MACON	4,036	1,515	2,521		1,006 D	37.5%	62.5%	37.5%	62.5%
17,747	MADISON	5,458	3,768	1,690		2,078 R	69.0%	31.0%	69.0%	31.0%
5,297	MARION	1,797	846	951		105 D	47.1%	52.9%	47.1%	52.9%
21,229	MERIWETHER	6,059	3,195	2,864		331 R	52.7%	47.3%	52.7%	47.3%
7,038	MILLER	1,874	1,348	526		822 R	71.9%	28.1%	71.9%	28.1%
21,114	MITCHELL	5,528	2,737	2,791		54 D	49.5%	50.5%	49.5%	50.5%
14,610	MONROE	4,609	2,420	2,189		231 R	52.5%	47.5%	52.5%	47.5%
7,011	MONTGOMERY	2,315	1,365	950		415 R	59.0%	41.0%	59.0%	41.0%
11,572	MORGAN	4,015	2,301	1,714		587 R	57.3%	42.7%	57.3%	42.7%
19,685	MURRAY	5,170	3,521	1,649		1,872 R	68.1%	31.9%	68.1%	31.9%
170,108	MUSCOGEE	44,651	23,816	20,835		2,981 R	53.3%	46.7%	53.3%	46.7%
34,489	NEWTON	9,199	5,810	3,389		2,421 R	63.2%	36.8%	63.2%	36.8%
12,427	OCONEE	4,938	3,471	1,467		2,004 R	70.3%	29.7%	70.3%	29.7%
8,929	OGLETHORPE	3,360	2,122	1,238		884 R	63.2%	36.8%	63.2%	36.8%
26,110	PAULDING	8,669	6,048	2,621		3,427 R	69.8%	30.2%	69.8%	30.2%
19,151	PEACH	6,021	2,652	3,369		717 D	44.0%	56.0%	44.0%	56.0%
11,652	PICKENS	4,130	2,801	1,329		1,472 R	67.8%	32.2%	67.8%	32.2%
11,897	PIERCE	3,479	1,978	1,501		477 R	56.9%	43.1%	56.9%	43.1%
8,937	PIKE	3,058	1,855	1,203		652 R	60.7%	39.3%	60.7%	39.3%
32,386	POLK	8,697	5,435	3,262		2,173 R	62.5%	37.5%	62.5%	37.5%
8,950	PULASKI	2,949	1,509	1,440		69 R	51.2%	48.8%	51.2%	48.8%
10,295	PUTNAM	3,166	1,830	1,336		494 R	57.8%	42.2%	57.8%	42.2%
2,357	QUITMAN	851	361	490		129 D	42.4%	57.6%	42.4%	57.6%
10,466	RABUN	3,458	2,191	1,267		924 R	63.4%	36.6%	63.4%	36.6%
9,599	RANDOLPH	3,032	1,578	1,454		124 R	52.0%	48.0%	52.0%	48.0%

GEORGIA

PRESIDENT 1984

1980 Census Population	County	Total Vote	Republican	Democratic	Other	Rep.-Dem. Plurality	Percentage Total Vote Rep.	Total Vote Dem.	Major Vote Rep.	Major Vote Dem.
181,629	RICHMOND	51,077	29,869	21,208		8,661 R	58.5%	41.5%	58.5%	41.5%
36,747	ROCKDALE	13,412	10,121	3,291		6,830 R	75.5%	24.5%	75.5%	24.5%
3,433	SCHLEY	1,017	614	403		211 R	60.4%	39.6%	60.4%	39.6%
14,043	SCREVEN	4,330	2,583	1,747		836 R	59.7%	40.3%	59.7%	40.3%
9,057	SEMINOLE	2,986	1,636	1,350		286 R	54.8%	45.2%	54.8%	45.2%
47,899	SPALDING	13,449	8,571	4,878		3,693 R	63.7%	36.3%	63.7%	36.3%
21,763	STEPHENS	6,329	4,057	2,272		1,785 R	64.1%	35.9%	64.1%	35.9%
5,896	STEWART	2,113	805	1,308		503 D	38.1%	61.9%	38.1%	61.9%
29,360	SUMTER	8,332	4,607	3,725		882 R	55.3%	44.7%	55.3%	44.7%
6,536	TALBOT	2,272	778	1,494		716 D	34.2%	65.8%	34.2%	65.8%
2,032	TALIAFERRO	868	318	550		232 D	36.6%	63.4%	36.6%	63.4%
18,134	TATTNALL	5,595	3,641	1,954		1,687 R	65.1%	34.9%	65.1%	34.9%
7,902	TAYLOR	2,632	1,292	1,340		48 D	49.1%	50.9%	49.1%	50.9%
11,445	TELFAIR	4,029	1,980	2,049		69 D	49.1%	50.9%	49.1%	50.9%
12,017	TERRELL	3,342	1,744	1,598		146 R	52.2%	47.8%	52.2%	47.8%
38,098	THOMAS	10,466	6,427	4,039		2,388 R	61.4%	38.6%	61.4%	38.6%
32,862	TIFT	7,165	4,429	2,736		1,693 R	61.8%	38.2%	61.8%	38.2%
22,592	TOOMBS	6,855	4,470	2,385		2,085 R	65.2%	34.8%	65.2%	34.8%
5,638	TOWNS	2,967	1,960	1,007		953 R	66.1%	33.9%	66.1%	33.9%
6,087	TREUTLEN	1,929	1,086	843		243 R	56.3%	43.7%	56.3%	43.7%
50,003	TROUP	14,612	9,340	5,272		4,068 R	63.9%	36.1%	63.9%	36.1%
9,510	TURNER	2,599	1,329	1,270		59 R	51.1%	48.9%	51.1%	48.9%
9,354	TWIGGS	2,898	1,143	1,755		612 D	39.4%	60.6%	39.4%	60.6%
9,390	UNION	3,026	1,914	1,112		802 R	63.3%	36.7%	63.3%	36.7%
25,998	UPSON	7,746	4,803	2,943		1,860 R	62.0%	38.0%	62.0%	38.0%
56,470	WALKER	15,734	10,734	5,000		5,734 R	68.2%	31.8%	68.2%	31.8%
31,211	WALTON	7,476	4,995	2,481		2,514 R	66.8%	33.2%	66.8%	33.2%
37,180	WARE	9,982	5,547	4,435		1,112 R	55.6%	44.4%	55.6%	44.4%
6,583	WARREN	2,345	1,087	1,258		171 D	46.4%	53.6%	46.4%	53.6%
18,842	WASHINGTON	5,921	2,887	3,034		147 D	48.8%	51.2%	48.8%	51.2%
20,750	WAYNE	6,132	3,698	2,434		1,264 R	60.3%	39.7%	60.3%	39.7%
2,341	WEBSTER	936	402	534		132 D	42.9%	57.1%	42.9%	57.1%
5,155	WHEELER	1,607	833	774		59 R	51.8%	48.2%	51.8%	48.2%
10,120	WHITE	3,459	2,369	1,090		1,279 R	68.5%	31.5%	68.5%	31.5%
65,789	WHITFIELD	17,241	11,957	5,284		6,673 R	69.4%	30.6%	69.4%	30.6%
7,682	WILCOX	2,430	1,218	1,212		6 R	50.1%	49.9%	50.1%	49.9%
10,951	WILKES	3,423	1,837	1,586		251 R	53.7%	46.3%	53.7%	46.3%
10,368	WILKINSON	3,858	1,756	2,102		346 D	45.5%	54.5%	45.5%	54.5%
18,064	WORTH	4,595	2,910	1,685		1,225 R	63.3%	36.7%	63.3%	36.7%
5,463,105	TOTAL	1,776,120	1,068,722	706,628	770	362,094 R	60.2%	39.8%	60.2%	39.8%

GEORGIA

PRESIDENT 1980

1980 Census Population	County	Total Vote	Republican	Democratic	Other	Rep.-Dem. Plurality	Percentage			
							Total Vote		Major Vote	
							Rep.	Dem.	Rep.	Dem.
15,565	APPLING	5,007	1,961	2,985	61	1,024 D	39.2%	59.6%	39.6%	60.4%
6,141	ATKINSON	2,222	747	1,449	26	702 D	33.6%	65.2%	34.0%	66.0%
9,379	BACON	3,106	1,427	1,622	57	195 D	45.9%	52.2%	46.8%	53.2%
3,808	BAKER	1,564	510	1,035	19	525 D	32.6%	66.2%	33.0%	67.0%
34,686	BALDWIN	8,326	3,639	4,368	319	729 D	43.7%	52.5%	45.4%	54.6%
8,702	BANKS	2,868	746	2,091	31	1,345 D	26.0%	72.9%	26.3%	73.7%
21,354	BARROW	6,309	2,284	3,876	149	1,592 D	36.2%	61.4%	37.1%	62.9%
40,760	BARTOW	10,853	3,135	7,490	228	4,355 D	28.9%	69.0%	29.5%	70.5%
16,000	BEN HILL	4,067	1,459	2,544	64	1,085 D	35.9%	62.6%	36.4%	63.6%
13,525	BERRIEN	4,404	1,487	2,869	48	1,382 D	33.8%	65.1%	34.1%	65.9%
150,256	BIBB	48,130	15,175	31,770	1,185	16,595 D	31.5%	66.0%	32.3%	67.7%
10,767	BLECKLEY	3,440	1,261	2,014	165	753 D	36.7%	58.5%	38.5%	61.5%
8,701	BRANTLEY	2,977	882	2,066	29	1,184 D	29.6%	69.4%	29.9%	70.1%
15,255	BROOKS	3,827	1,546	2,230	51	684 D	40.4%	58.3%	40.9%	59.1%
10,175	BRYAN	3,235	1,212	1,966	57	754 D	37.5%	60.8%	38.1%	61.9%
35,785	BULLOCH	8,921	3,750	4,921	250	1,171 D	42.0%	55.2%	43.2%	56.8%
19,349	BURKE	4,991	1,871	3,047	73	1,176 D	37.5%	61.0%	38.0%	62.0%
13,665	BUTTS	3,845	1,210	2,574	61	1,364 D	31.5%	66.9%	32.0%	68.0%
5,717	CALHOUN	2,087	652	1,414	21	762 D	31.2%	67.8%	31.6%	68.4%
13,371	CAMDEN	4,443	1,439	2,924	80	1,485 D	32.4%	65.8%	33.0%	67.0%
7,518	CANDLER	2,421	1,030	1,358	33	328 D	42.5%	56.1%	43.1%	56.9%
56,346	CARROLL	14,475	5,815	8,202	458	2,387 D	40.2%	56.7%	41.5%	58.5%
36,991	CATOOSA	11,059	5,962	4,921	176	1,041 R	53.9%	44.5%	54.8%	45.2%
7,343	CHARLTON	2,286	779	1,469	38	690 D	34.1%	64.3%	34.7%	65.3%
202,226	CHATHAM	56,781	26,499	28,413	1,869	1,914 D	46.7%	50.0%	48.3%	51.7%
21,732	CHATTAHOOCHEE	752	256	476	20	220 D	34.0%	63.3%	35.0%	65.0%
21,856	CHATTOOGA	6,330	1,946	4,279	105	2,333 D	30.7%	67.6%	31.3%	68.7%
51,699	CHEROKEE	11,678	5,250	6,020	408	770 D	45.0%	51.5%	46.6%	53.4%
74,498	CLARKE	19,899	8,094	10,519	1,286	2,425 D	40.7%	52.9%	43.5%	56.5%
3,553	CLAY	1,241	316	909	16	593 D	25.5%	73.2%	25.8%	74.2%
150,357	CLAYTON	38,051	19,160	17,540	1,351	1,620 R	50.4%	46.1%	52.2%	47.8%
6,660	CLINCH	1,864	513	1,325	26	812 D	27.5%	71.1%	27.9%	72.1%
297,718	COBB	95,816	51,977	39,157	4,682	12,820 R	54.2%	40.9%	57.0%	43.0%
26,894	COFFEE	6,621	2,499	4,038	84	1,539 D	37.7%	61.0%	38.2%	61.8%
35,376	COLQUITT	9,069	3,593	5,353	123	1,760 D	39.6%	59.0%	40.2%	59.8%
40,118	COLUMBIA	11,938	6,293	5,335	310	958 R	52.7%	44.7%	54.1%	45.9%
13,490	COOK	3,684	1,188	2,461	35	1,273 D	32.2%	66.8%	32.6%	67.4%
39,268	COWETA	10,422	4,480	5,697	245	1,217 D	43.0%	54.7%	44.0%	56.0%
7,684	CRAWFORD	2,375	642	1,673	60	1,031 D	27.0%	70.4%	27.7%	72.3%
19,489	CRISP	5,347	1,861	3,403	83	1,542 D	34.8%	63.6%	35.4%	64.6%
12,318	DADE	3,929	2,114	1,735	80	379 R	53.8%	44.2%	54.9%	45.1%
4,774	DAWSON	1,837	729	1,072	36	343 D	39.7%	58.4%	40.5%	59.5%
25,495	DECATUR	6,243	2,919	3,242	82	323 D	46.8%	51.9%	47.4%	52.6%
483,024	DE KALB	167,405	74,904	82,743	9,758	7,839 D	44.7%	49.4%	47.5%	52.5%
16,955	DODGE	6,453	1,719	4,635	99	2,916 D	26.6%	71.8%	27.1%	72.9%
10,826	DOOLY	3,502	1,083	2,364	55	1,281 D	30.9%	67.5%	31.4%	68.6%
100,718	DOUGHERTY	26,615	12,726	13,430	459	704 D	47.8%	50.5%	48.7%	51.3%
54,573	DOUGLAS	14,238	6,945	6,807	486	138 R	48.8%	47.8%	50.5%	49.5%
13,158	EARLY	3,682	1,538	2,110	34	572 D	41.8%	57.3%	42.2%	57.8%
2,297	ECHOLS	783	259	515	9	256 D	33.1%	65.8%	33.5%	66.5%
18,327	EFFINGHAM	5,377	2,528	2,783	66	255 D	47.0%	51.8%	47.6%	52.4%
18,758	ELBERT	6,061	1,967	4,014	80	2,047 D	32.5%	66.2%	32.9%	67.1%
20,795	EMANUEL	6,251	2,199	3,971	81	1,772 D	35.2%	63.5%	35.6%	64.4%
8,428	EVANS	2,575	1,090	1,456	29	366 D	42.3%	56.5%	42.8%	57.2%
14,748	FANNIN	5,829	3,196	2,526	107	670 R	54.8%	43.3%	55.9%	44.1%
29,043	FAYETTE	10,549	6,351	3,798	400	2,553 R	60.2%	36.0%	62.6%	37.4%
79,800	FLOYD	23,596	9,220	13,710	666	4,490 D	39.1%	58.1%	40.2%	59.8%
27,958	FORSYTH	7,736	3,157	4,325	254	1,168 D	40.8%	55.9%	42.2%	57.8%
15,185	FRANKLIN	4,960	1,387	3,528	45	2,141 D	28.0%	71.1%	28.2%	71.8%
589,904	FULTON	192,723	64,909	118,748	9,066	53,839 D	33.7%	61.6%	35.3%	64.7%

GEORGIA

PRESIDENT 1980

1980 Census Population	County	Total Vote	Republican	Democratic	Other	Rep.-Dem. Plurality	Percentage Total Vote Rep.	Percentage Total Vote Dem.	Percentage Major Vote Rep.	Percentage Major Vote Dem.
11,110	GILMER	4,537	2,170	2,246	121	76 D	47.8%	49.5%	49.1%	50.9%
2,382	GLASCOCK	1,138	510	614	14	104 D	44.8%	54.0%	45.4%	54.6%
54,981	GLYNN	15,173	7,214	7,540	419	326 D	47.5%	49.7%	48.9%	51.1%
30,070	GORDON	8,542	3,107	5,199	236	2,092 D	36.4%	60.9%	37.4%	62.6%
19,845	GRADY	5,117	2,018	3,023	76	1,005 D	39.4%	59.1%	40.0%	60.0%
11,391	GREENE	3,573	961	2,571	41	1,610 D	26.9%	72.0%	27.2%	72.8%
166,903	GWINNETT	51,452	27,185	21,958	2,309	5,227 R	52.8%	42.7%	55.3%	44.7%
25,020	HABERSHAM	6,781	2,224	4,394	163	2,170 D	32.8%	64.8%	33.6%	66.4%
75,649	HALL	20,521	7,760	12,124	637	4,364 D	37.8%	59.1%	39.0%	61.0%
9,466	HANCOCK	2,809	573	2,205	31	1,632 D	20.4%	78.5%	20.6%	79.4%
18,422	HARALSON	5,960	2,229	3,606	125	1,377 D	37.4%	60.5%	38.2%	61.8%
15,464	HARRIS	4,942	2,001	2,807	134	806 D	40.5%	56.8%	41.6%	58.4%
18,585	HART	6,215	1,577	4,539	99	2,962 D	25.4%	73.0%	25.8%	74.2%
6,520	HEARD	2,283	875	1,348	60	473 D	38.3%	59.0%	39.4%	60.6%
36,309	HENRY	11,268	5,326	5,635	307	309 D	47.3%	50.0%	48.6%	51.4%
77,605	HOUSTON	20,695	9,005	10,915	775	1,910 D	43.5%	52.7%	45.2%	54.8%
8,988	IRWIN	2,632	1,056	1,555	21	499 D	40.1%	59.1%	40.4%	59.6%
25,343	JACKSON	6,949	2,209	4,591	149	2,382 D	31.8%	66.1%	32.5%	67.5%
7,553	JASPER	2,484	879	1,546	59	667 D	35.4%	62.2%	36.2%	63.8%
11,473	JEFF DAVIS	3,311	1,191	2,059	61	868 D	36.0%	62.2%	36.6%	63.4%
18,403	JEFFERSON	4,978	1,605	3,305	68	1,700 D	32.2%	66.4%	32.7%	67.3%
8,841	JENKINS	2,493	824	1,632	37	808 D	33.1%	65.5%	33.6%	66.4%
8,660	JOHNSON	3,029	1,123	1,854	52	731 D	37.1%	61.2%	37.7%	62.3%
16,579	JONES	5,220	1,828	3,239	153	1,411 D	35.0%	62.0%	36.1%	63.9%
12,215	LAMAR	3,828	1,298	2,453	77	1,155 D	33.9%	64.1%	34.6%	65.4%
5,654	LANIER	1,604	470	1,116	18	646 D	29.3%	69.6%	29.6%	70.4%
36,990	LAURENS	12,523	4,392	7,860	271	3,468 D	35.1%	62.8%	35.8%	64.2%
11,684	LEE	3,661	1,942	1,670	49	272 R	53.0%	45.6%	53.8%	46.2%
37,583	LIBERTY	4,683	1,507	3,099	77	1,592 D	32.2%	66.2%	32.7%	67.3%
6,716	LINCOLN	2,440	806	1,617	17	811 D	33.0%	66.3%	33.3%	66.7%
4,524	LONG	1,743	514	1,202	27	688 D	29.5%	69.0%	30.0%	70.0%
67,972	LOWNDES	12,912	6,622	5,989	301	633 R	51.3%	46.4%	52.5%	47.5%
10,762	LUMPKIN	3,085	1,024	1,951	110	927 D	33.2%	63.2%	34.4%	65.6%
18,546	MCDUFFIE	4,683	1,928	2,667	88	739 D	41.2%	57.0%	42.0%	58.0%
8,046	MCINTOSH	3,049	876	2,104	69	1,228 D	28.7%	69.0%	29.4%	70.6%
14,003	MACON	3,979	894	3,025	60	2,131 D	22.5%	76.0%	22.8%	77.2%
17,747	MADISON	5,401	2,330	2,980	91	650 D	43.1%	55.2%	43.9%	56.1%
5,297	MARION	1,773	567	1,174	32	607 D	32.0%	66.2%	32.6%	67.4%
21,229	MERIWETHER	5,805	1,838	3,876	91	2,038 D	31.7%	66.8%	32.2%	67.8%
7,038	MILLER	2,053	900	1,127	26	227 D	43.8%	54.9%	44.4%	55.6%
21,114	MITCHELL	5,856	2,231	3,566	59	1,335 D	38.1%	60.9%	38.5%	61.5%
14,610	MONROE	3,860	1,242	2,542	76	1,300 D	32.2%	65.9%	32.8%	67.2%
7,011	MONTGOMERY	2,640	948	1,663	29	715 D	35.9%	63.0%	36.3%	63.7%
11,572	MORGAN	3,671	1,323	2,276	72	953 D	36.0%	62.0%	36.8%	63.2%
19,685	MURRAY	4,701	1,538	3,094	69	1,556 D	32.7%	65.8%	33.2%	66.8%
170,108	MUSCOGEE	39,566	15,203	23,272	1,091	8,069 D	38.4%	58.8%	39.5%	60.5%
34,489	NEWTON	9,056	3,206	5,611	239	2,405 D	35.4%	62.0%	36.4%	63.6%
12,427	OCONEE	4,367	2,065	2,141	161	76 D	47.3%	49.0%	49.1%	50.9%
8,929	OGLETHORPE	2,856	1,187	1,611	58	424 D	41.6%	56.4%	42.4%	57.6%
26,110	PAULDING	7,717	2,845	4,686	186	1,841 D	36.9%	60.7%	37.8%	62.2%
19,151	PEACH	5,170	1,642	3,415	113	1,773 D	31.8%	66.1%	32.5%	67.5%
11,652	PICKENS	4,077	1,612	2,358	107	746 D	39.5%	57.8%	40.6%	59.4%
11,897	PIERCE	2,985	1,027	1,918	40	891 D	34.4%	64.3%	34.9%	65.1%
8,937	PIKE	3,094	1,271	1,755	68	484 D	41.1%	56.7%	42.0%	58.0%
32,386	POLK	8,562	2,949	5,421	192	2,472 D	34.4%	63.3%	35.2%	64.8%
8,950	PULASKI	3,232	1,153	1,997	82	844 D	35.7%	61.8%	36.6%	63.4%
10,295	PUTNAM	3,177	1,166	1,951	60	785 D	36.7%	61.4%	37.4%	62.6%
2,357	QUITMAN	837	240	589	8	349 D	28.7%	70.4%	29.0%	71.0%
10,466	RABUN	3,495	1,070	2,327	98	1,257 D	30.6%	66.6%	31.5%	68.5%
9,599	RANDOLPH	2,743	879	1,861	3	982 D	32.0%	67.8%	32.1%	67.9%

GEORGIA

PRESIDENT 1980

1980 Census Population	County	Total Vote	Republican	Democratic	Other	Rep.-Dem. Plurality	Percentage Total Vote Rep.	Percentage Total Vote Dem.	Percentage Major Vote Rep.	Percentage Major Vote Dem.
181,629	RICHMOND	44,871	19,619	24,104	1,148	4,485 D	43.7%	53.7%	44.9%	55.1%
36,747	ROCKDALE	10,067	5,300	4,395	372	905 R	52.6%	43.7%	54.7%	45.3%
3,433	SCHLEY	1,085	453	613	19	160 D	41.8%	56.5%	42.5%	57.5%
14,043	SCREVEN	3,664	1,490	2,117	57	627 D	40.7%	57.8%	41.3%	58.7%
9,057	SEMINOLE	2,936	1,117	1,794	25	677 D	38.0%	61.1%	38.4%	61.6%
47,899	SPALDING	12,331	4,809	7,176	346	2,367 D	39.0%	58.2%	40.1%	59.9%
21,763	STEPHENS	6,692	2,045	4,529	118	2,484 D	30.6%	67.7%	31.1%	68.9%
5,896	STEWART	2,087	611	1,440	36	829 D	29.3%	69.0%	29.8%	70.2%
29,360	SUMTER	8,060	2,957	4,956	147	1,999 D	36.7%	61.5%	37.4%	62.6%
6,536	TALBOT	2,243	572	1,635	36	1,063 D	25.5%	72.9%	25.9%	74.1%
2,032	TALIAFERRO	954	270	670	14	400 D	28.3%	70.2%	28.7%	71.3%
18,134	TATTNALL	5,002	2,082	2,864	56	782 D	41.6%	57.3%	42.1%	57.9%
7,902	TAYLOR	2,698	815	1,845	38	1,030 D	30.2%	68.4%	30.6%	69.4%
11,445	TELFAIR	3,941	1,173	2,700	68	1,527 D	29.8%	68.5%	30.3%	69.7%
12,017	TERRELL	3,420	1,378	2,010	32	632 D	40.3%	58.8%	40.7%	59.3%
38,098	THOMAS	10,161	4,294	5,695	172	1,401 D	42.3%	56.0%	43.0%	57.0%
32,862	TIFT	8,022	3,280	4,572	170	1,292 D	40.9%	57.0%	41.8%	58.2%
22,592	TOOMBS	6,197	2,835	3,255	107	420 D	45.7%	52.5%	46.6%	53.4%
5,638	TOWNS	3,065	1,475	1,510	80	35 D	48.1%	49.3%	49.4%	50.6%
6,087	TREUTLEN	2,004	668	1,307	29	639 D	33.3%	65.2%	33.8%	66.2%
50,003	TROUP	13,429	5,398	7,716	315	2,318 D	40.2%	57.5%	41.2%	58.8%
9,510	TURNER	2,921	898	1,990	33	1,092 D	30.7%	68.1%	31.1%	68.9%
9,354	TWIGGS	2,980	747	2,213	20	1,466 D	25.1%	74.3%	25.2%	74.8%
9,390	UNION	3,311	1,546	1,700	65	154 D	46.7%	51.3%	47.6%	52.4%
25,998	UPSON	7,635	2,788	4,713	134	1,925 D	36.5%	61.7%	37.2%	62.8%
56,470	WALKER	14,132	7,088	6,809	235	279 R	50.2%	48.2%	51.0%	49.0%
31,211	WALTON	7,303	2,618	4,525	160	1,907 D	35.8%	62.0%	36.7%	63.3%
37,180	WARE	10,137	3,715	6,307	115	2,592 D	36.6%	62.2%	37.1%	62.9%
6,583	WARREN	2,321	779	1,517	25	738 D	33.6%	65.4%	33.9%	66.1%
18,842	WASHINGTON	5,364	1,822	3,452	90	1,630 D	34.0%	64.4%	34.5%	65.5%
20,750	WAYNE	6,157	2,213	3,843	101	1,630 D	35.9%	62.4%	36.5%	63.5%
2,341	WEBSTER	940	312	608	20	296 D	33.2%	64.7%	33.9%	66.1%
5,155	WHEELER	2,186	550	1,599	37	1,049 D	25.2%	73.1%	25.6%	74.4%
10,120	WHITE	3,287	1,175	2,017	95	842 D	35.7%	61.4%	36.8%	63.2%
65,789	WHITFIELD	16,439	6,404	9,691	344	3,287 D	39.0%	59.0%	39.8%	60.2%
7,682	WILCOX	2,630	827	1,780	23	953 D	31.4%	67.7%	31.7%	68.3%
10,951	WILKES	3,623	1,212	2,350	61	1,138 D	33.5%	64.9%	34.0%	66.0%
10,368	WILKINSON	3,532	1,116	2,365	51	1,249 D	31.6%	67.0%	32.1%	67.9%
18,064	WORTH	4,695	2,076	2,567	52	491 D	44.2%	54.7%	44.7%	55.3%
5,463,105	TOTAL	1,596,695	654,168	890,733	51,794	236,565 D	41.0%	55.8%	42.3%	57.7%

GEORGIA

PRESIDENT 1976

1970 Census Population	County	Total Vote	Republican	Democratic	Other	Rep.-Dem. Plurality	Percentage Total Vote Rep.	Percentage Total Vote Dem.	Percentage Major Vote Rep.	Percentage Major Vote Dem.
12,726	APPLING	4,546	961	3,585		2,624 D	21.1%	78.9%	21.1%	78.9%
5,879	ATKINSON	1,907	347	1,560		1,213 D	18.2%	81.8%	18.2%	81.8%
8,233	BACON	2,989	594	2,395		1,801 D	19.9%	80.1%	19.9%	80.1%
3,875	BAKER	1,467	305	1,162		857 D	20.8%	79.2%	20.8%	79.2%
34,240	BALDWIN	8,286	3,612	4,674		1,062 D	43.6%	56.4%	43.6%	56.4%
6,833	BANKS	2,717	330	2,387		2,057 D	12.1%	87.9%	12.1%	87.9%
16,859	BARROW	6,120	1,364	4,756		3,392 D	22.3%	77.7%	22.3%	77.7%
32,663	BARTOW	10,042	1,876	8,166		6,290 D	18.7%	81.3%	18.7%	81.3%
13,171	BEN HILL	3,263	814	2,449		1,635 D	24.9%	75.1%	24.9%	75.1%
11,556	BERRIEN	3,949	555	3,394		2,839 D	14.1%	85.9%	14.1%	85.9%
143,418	BIBB	44,721	12,819	31,902		19,083 D	28.7%	71.3%	28.7%	71.3%
10,291	BLECKLEY	3,577	972	2,605		1,633 D	27.2%	72.8%	27.2%	72.8%
5,940	BRANTLEY	2,652	358	2,294		1,936 D	13.5%	86.5%	13.5%	86.5%
13,739	BROOKS	3,755	1,102	2,653		1,551 D	29.3%	70.7%	29.3%	70.7%
6,539	BRYAN	2,806	761	2,045		1,284 D	27.1%	72.9%	27.1%	72.9%
31,585	BULLOCH	8,355	3,156	5,199		2,043 D	37.8%	62.2%	37.8%	62.2%
18,255	BURKE	4,579	1,565	3,014		1,449 D	34.2%	65.8%	34.2%	65.8%
10,560	BUTTS	3,717	819	2,898		2,079 D	22.0%	78.0%	22.0%	78.0%
6,606	CALHOUN	1,830	436	1,394		958 D	23.8%	76.2%	23.8%	76.2%
11,334	CAMDEN	3,957	995	2,962		1,967 D	25.1%	74.9%	25.1%	74.9%
6,412	CANDLER	2,034	646	1,388		742 D	31.8%	68.2%	31.8%	68.2%
45,404	CARROLL	13,690	3,640	10,050		6,410 D	26.6%	73.4%	26.6%	73.4%
28,271	CATOOSA	9,819	3,799	6,020		2,221 D	38.7%	61.3%	38.7%	61.3%
5,680	CHARLTON	2,202	452	1,750		1,298 D	20.5%	79.5%	20.5%	79.5%
187,767	CHATHAM	56,235	24,160	32,075		7,915 D	43.0%	57.0%	43.0%	57.0%
25,813	CHATTAHOOCHEE	684	178	506		328 D	26.0%	74.0%	26.0%	74.0%
20,541	CHATTOOGA	5,773	1,087	4,686		3,599 D	18.8%	81.2%	18.8%	81.2%
31,059	CHEROKEE	9,148	2,609	6,539		3,930 D	28.5%	71.5%	28.5%	71.5%
65,177	CLARKE	17,952	6,610	11,342		4,732 D	36.8%	63.2%	36.8%	63.2%
3,636	CLAY	1,242	295	947		652 D	23.8%	76.2%	23.8%	76.2%
98,043	CLAYTON	34,337	12,905	21,432		8,527 D	37.6%	62.4%	37.6%	62.4%
6,405	CLINCH	1,797	383	1,414		1,031 D	21.3%	78.7%	21.3%	78.7%
196,793	COBB	79,326	34,324	45,002		10,678 D	43.3%	56.7%	43.3%	56.7%
22,828	COFFEE	6,018	1,417	4,601		3,184 D	23.5%	76.5%	23.5%	76.5%
32,200	COLQUITT	9,109	2,181	6,928		4,747 D	23.9%	76.1%	23.9%	76.1%
22,327	COLUMBIA	8,097	3,423	4,674		1,251 D	42.3%	57.7%	42.3%	57.7%
12,129	COOK	3,552	670	2,882		2,212 D	18.9%	81.1%	18.9%	81.1%
32,310	COWETA	9,239	3,044	6,195		3,151 D	32.9%	67.1%	32.9%	67.1%
5,748	CRAWFORD	2,220	378	1,842		1,464 D	17.0%	83.0%	17.0%	83.0%
18,087	CRISP	5,075	1,328	3,747		2,419 D	26.2%	73.8%	26.2%	73.8%
9,910	DADE	3,651	1,388	2,263		875 D	38.0%	62.0%	38.0%	62.0%
3,639	DAWSON	1,754	370	1,384		1,014 D	21.1%	78.9%	21.1%	78.9%
22,310	DECATUR	6,236	2,500	3,736		1,236 D	40.1%	59.9%	40.1%	59.9%
415,387	DE KALB	154,032	67,160	86,872		19,712 D	43.6%	56.4%	43.6%	56.4%
15,658	DODGE	6,115	848	5,267		4,419 D	13.9%	86.1%	13.9%	86.1%
10,404	DOOLY	3,096	655	2,441		1,786 D	21.2%	78.8%	21.2%	78.8%
89,639	DOUGHERTY	20,798	9,337	11,461		2,124 D	44.9%	55.1%	44.9%	55.1%
28,659	DOUGLAS	11,764	3,959	7,805		3,846 D	33.7%	66.3%	33.7%	66.3%
12,682	EARLY	3,562	1,157	2,405		1,248 D	32.5%	67.5%	32.5%	67.5%
1,924	ECHOLS	696	111	585		474 D	15.9%	84.1%	15.9%	84.1%
13,632	EFFINGHAM	4,560	1,654	2,906		1,252 D	36.3%	63.7%	36.3%	63.7%
17,262	ELBERT	5,691	961	4,730		3,769 D	16.9%	83.1%	16.9%	83.1%
18,189	EMANUEL	6,096	1,493	4,603		3,110 D	24.5%	75.5%	24.5%	75.5%
7,290	EVANS	2,377	746	1,631		885 D	31.4%	68.6%	31.4%	68.6%
13,357	FANNIN	6,048	2,646	3,402		756 D	43.8%	56.3%	43.8%	56.3%
11,364	FAYETTE	6,555	2,837	3,718		881 D	43.3%	56.7%	43.3%	56.7%
73,742	FLOYD	22,864	7,713	15,151		7,438 D	33.7%	66.3%	33.7%	66.3%
16,928	FORSYTH	6,136	1,443	4,693		3,250 D	23.5%	76.5%	23.5%	76.5%
12,784	FRANKLIN	4,879	687	4,192		3,505 D	14.1%	85.9%	14.1%	85.9%
607,592	FULTON	191,401	61,552	129,849		68,297 D	32.2%	67.8%	32.2%	67.8%

GEORGIA

PRESIDENT 1976

1970 Census Population	County	Total Vote	Republican	Democratic	Other	Rep.-Dem. Plurality	Percentage Total Vote Rep.	Total Vote Dem.	Major Vote Rep.	Major Vote Dem.
8,956	GILMER	3,760	1,261	2,499		1,238 D	33.5%	66.5%	33.5%	66.5%
2,280	GLASCOCK	1,075	371	704		333 D	34.5%	65.5%	34.5%	65.5%
50,528	GLYNN	14,862	5,403	9,459		4,056 D	36.4%	63.6%	36.4%	63.6%
23,570	GORDON	7,750	1,698	6,052		4,354 D	21.9%	78.1%	21.9%	78.1%
17,826	GRADY	4,967	1,209	3,758		2,549 D	24.3%	75.7%	24.3%	75.7%
10,212	GREENE	3,186	652	2,534		1,882 D	20.5%	79.5%	20.5%	79.5%
72,349	GWINNETT	34,750	13,912	20,838		6,926 D	40.0%	60.0%	40.0%	60.0%
20,691	HABERSHAM	6,435	1,315	5,120		3,805 D	20.4%	79.6%	20.4%	79.6%
59,405	HALL	17,897	5,093	12,804		7,711 D	28.5%	71.5%	28.5%	71.5%
9,019	HANCOCK	2,768	651	2,117		1,466 D	23.5%	76.5%	23.5%	76.5%
15,927	HARALSON	5,851	1,301	4,550		3,249 D	22.2%	77.8%	22.2%	77.8%
11,520	HARRIS	4,405	1,544	2,861		1,317 D	35.1%	64.9%	35.1%	64.9%
15,814	HART	5,465	860	4,605		3,745 D	15.7%	84.3%	15.7%	84.3%
5,354	HEARD	2,026	433	1,593		1,160 D	21.4%	78.6%	21.4%	78.6%
23,724	HENRY	8,339	2,622	5,717		3,095 D	31.4%	68.6%	31.4%	68.6%
62,924	HOUSTON	18,568	5,404	13,164		7,760 D	29.1%	70.9%	29.1%	70.9%
8,036	IRWIN	2,573	561	2,012		1,451 D	21.8%	78.2%	21.8%	78.2%
21,093	JACKSON	7,170	1,239	5,931		4,692 D	17.3%	82.7%	17.3%	82.7%
5,760	JASPER	2,541	689	1,852		1,163 D	27.1%	72.9%	27.1%	72.9%
9,425	JEFF DAVIS	3,027	622	2,405		1,783 D	20.5%	79.5%	20.5%	79.5%
17,174	JEFFERSON	4,424	1,309	3,115		1,806 D	29.6%	70.4%	29.6%	70.4%
8,332	JENKINS	2,383	563	1,820		1,257 D	23.6%	76.4%	23.6%	76.4%
7,727	JOHNSON	2,908	698	2,210		1,512 D	24.0%	76.0%	24.0%	76.0%
12,218	JONES	4,788	1,317	3,471		2,154 D	27.5%	72.5%	27.5%	72.5%
10,688	LAMAR	3,632	847	2,785		1,938 D	23.3%	76.7%	23.3%	76.7%
5,031	LANIER	1,476	207	1,269		1,062 D	14.0%	86.0%	14.0%	86.0%
32,738	LAURENS	11,898	3,281	8,617		5,336 D	27.6%	72.4%	27.6%	72.4%
7,044	LEE	2,837	1,110	1,727		617 D	39.1%	60.9%	39.1%	60.9%
17,569	LIBERTY	4,307	979	3,328		2,349 D	22.7%	77.3%	22.7%	77.3%
5,895	LINCOLN	2,159	576	1,583		1,007 D	26.7%	73.3%	26.7%	73.3%
3,746	LONG	1,465	222	1,243		1,021 D	15.2%	84.8%	15.2%	84.8%
55,112	LOWNDES	13,342	4,512	8,830		4,318 D	33.8%	66.2%	33.8%	66.2%
8,728	LUMPKIN	2,848	547	2,301		1,754 D	19.2%	80.8%	19.2%	80.8%
15,276	MCDUFFIE	4,718	1,694	3,024		1,330 D	35.9%	64.1%	35.9%	64.1%
7,371	MCINTOSH	2,513	535	1,978		1,443 D	21.3%	78.7%	21.3%	78.7%
12,933	MACON	3,651	638	3,013		2,375 D	17.5%	82.5%	17.5%	82.5%
13,517	MADISON	4,482	1,115	3,367		2,252 D	24.9%	75.1%	24.9%	75.1%
5,099	MARION	1,605	291	1,314		1,023 D	18.1%	81.9%	18.1%	81.9%
19,461	MERIWETHER	6,280	1,450	4,830		3,380 D	23.1%	76.9%	23.1%	76.9%
6,397	MILLER	2,012	476	1,536		1,060 D	23.7%	76.3%	23.7%	76.3%
18,956	MITCHELL	6,067	1,572	4,495		2,923 D	25.9%	74.1%	25.9%	74.1%
10,991	MONROE	4,040	1,078	2,962		1,884 D	26.7%	73.3%	26.7%	73.3%
6,099	MONTGOMERY	2,236	626	1,610		984 D	28.0%	72.0%	28.0%	72.0%
9,904	MORGAN	3,178	904	2,274		1,370 D	28.4%	71.6%	28.4%	71.6%
12,986	MURRAY	4,400	889	3,511		2,622 D	20.2%	79.8%	20.2%	79.8%
167,377	MUSCOGEE	37,588	13,496	24,092		10,596 D	35.9%	64.1%	35.9%	64.1%
26,282	NEWTON	8,431	2,137	6,294		4,157 D	25.3%	74.7%	25.3%	74.7%
7,915	OCONEE	3,412	1,184	2,228		1,044 D	34.7%	65.3%	34.7%	65.3%
7,598	OGLETHORPE	2,665	811	1,854		1,043 D	30.4%	69.6%	30.4%	69.6%
17,520	PAULDING	6,852	1,432	5,420		3,988 D	20.9%	79.1%	20.9%	79.1%
15,990	PEACH	5,152	1,163	3,989		2,826 D	22.6%	77.4%	22.6%	77.4%
9,620	PICKENS	3,544	973	2,571		1,598 D	27.5%	72.5%	27.5%	72.5%
9,281	PIERCE	3,172	544	2,628		2,084 D	17.2%	82.8%	17.2%	82.8%
7,316	PIKE	2,679	776	1,903		1,127 D	29.0%	71.0%	29.0%	71.0%
29,656	POLK	8,059	1,944	6,115		4,171 D	24.1%	75.9%	24.1%	75.9%
8,066	PULASKI	2,803	485	2,318		1,833 D	17.3%	82.7%	17.3%	82.7%
8,394	PUTNAM	2,875	835	2,040		1,205 D	29.0%	71.0%	29.0%	71.0%
2,180	QUITMAN	990	313	677		364 D	31.6%	68.4%	31.6%	68.4%
8,327	RABUN	2,989	591	2,398		1,807 D	19.8%	80.2%	19.8%	80.2%
8,734	RANDOLPH	2,933	747	2,186		1,439 D	25.5%	74.5%	25.5%	74.5%

GEORGIA

PRESIDENT 1976

1970 Census Population	County	Total Vote	Republican	Democratic	Other	Rep.-Dem. Plurality	Percentage Total Vote Rep.	Total Vote Dem.	Major Vote Rep.	Major Vote Dem.
162,437	RICHMOND	41,935	17,893	24,042		6,149 D	42.7%	57.3%	42.7%	57.3%
18,152	ROCKDALE	7,614	2,974	4,640		1,666 D	39.1%	60.9%	39.1%	60.9%
3,097	SCHLEY	1,051	268	783		515 D	25.5%	74.5%	25.5%	74.5%
12,591	SCREVEN	3,344	1,176	2,168		992 D	35.2%	64.8%	35.2%	64.8%
7,059	SEMINOLE	2,755	681	2,074		1,393 D	24.7%	75.3%	24.7%	75.3%
39,514	SPALDING	11,332	3,739	7,593		3,854 D	33.0%	67.0%	33.0%	67.0%
20,331	STEPHENS	6,900	1,340	5,560		4,220 D	19.4%	80.6%	19.4%	80.6%
6,511	STEWART	2,065	433	1,632		1,199 D	21.0%	79.0%	21.0%	79.0%
26,931	SUMTER	7,381	2,053	5,328		3,275 D	27.8%	72.2%	27.8%	72.2%
6,625	TALBOT	2,093	459	1,634		1,175 D	21.9%	78.1%	21.9%	78.1%
2,423	TALIAFERRO	984	236	748		512 D	24.0%	76.0%	24.0%	76.0%
16,557	TATTNALL	4,882	1,326	3,556		2,230 D	27.2%	72.8%	27.2%	72.8%
7,865	TAYLOR	2,466	504	1,962		1,458 D	20.4%	79.6%	20.4%	79.6%
11,381	TELFAIR	4,171	637	3,534		2,897 D	15.3%	84.7%	15.3%	84.7%
11,416	TERRELL	3,516	1,168	2,348		1,180 D	33.2%	66.8%	33.2%	66.8%
34,515	THOMAS	9,410	3,263	6,147		2,884 D	34.7%	65.3%	34.7%	65.3%
27,288	TIFT	7,347	2,162	5,185		3,023 D	29.4%	70.6%	29.4%	70.6%
19,151	TOOMBS	6,173	2,126	4,047		1,921 D	34.4%	65.6%	34.4%	65.6%
4,565	TOWNS	2,961	1,175	1,786		611 D	39.7%	60.3%	39.7%	60.3%
5,647	TREUTLEN	2,032	465	1,567		1,102 D	22.9%	77.1%	22.9%	77.1%
44,466	TROUP	12,121	4,422	7,699		3,277 D	36.5%	63.5%	36.5%	63.5%
8,790	TURNER	2,681	416	2,265		1,849 D	15.5%	84.5%	15.5%	84.5%
8,222	TWIGGS	3,028	513	2,515		2,002 D	16.9%	83.1%	16.9%	83.1%
6,811	UNION	3,949	1,154	2,795		1,641 D	29.2%	70.8%	29.2%	70.8%
23,505	UPSON	7,116	2,897	4,219		1,322 D	40.7%	59.3%	40.7%	59.3%
50,691	WALKER	12,814	4,807	8,007		3,200 D	37.5%	62.5%	37.5%	62.5%
23,404	WALTON	7,089	1,687	5,402		3,715 D	23.8%	76.2%	23.8%	76.2%
33,525	WARE	10,380	2,661	7,719		5,058 D	25.6%	74.4%	25.6%	74.4%
6,669	WARREN	2,055	720	1,335		615 D	35.0%	65.0%	35.0%	65.0%
17,480	WASHINGTON	5,522	1,657	3,865		2,208 D	30.0%	70.0%	30.0%	70.0%
17,858	WAYNE	5,988	1,499	4,489		2,990 D	25.0%	75.0%	25.0%	75.0%
2,362	WEBSTER	787	165	622		457 D	21.0%	79.0%	21.0%	79.0%
4,596	WHEELER	1,722	344	1,378		1,034 D	20.0%	80.0%	20.0%	80.0%
7,742	WHITE	2,750	625	2,125		1,500 D	22.7%	77.3%	22.7%	77.3%
55,108	WHITFIELD	14,973	4,498	10,475		5,977 D	30.0%	70.0%	30.0%	70.0%
6,998	WILCOX	2,499	346	2,153		1,807 D	13.8%	86.2%	13.8%	86.2%
10,184	WILKES	3,528	1,067	2,461		1,394 D	30.2%	69.8%	30.2%	69.8%
9,393	WILKINSON	3,489	837	2,652		1,815 D	24.0%	76.0%	24.0%	76.0%
14,770	WORTH	3,946	1,156	2,790		1,634 D	29.3%	70.7%	29.3%	70.7%
4,589,575	TOTAL	1,467,458	483,743	979,409	4,306	495,666 D	33.0%	66.7%	33.1%	66.9%

GEORGIA

PRESIDENT 1972

1970 Census Population	County	Total Vote	Republican	Democratic	Other	Rep.-Dem. Plurality	Percentage Total Vote Rep.	Total Vote Dem.	Major Vote Rep.	Major Vote Dem.
12,726	APPLING	3,267	2,755	512		2,243 R	84.3%	15.7%	84.3%	15.7%
5,879	ATKINSON	1,235	924	309	2	615 R	74.8%	25.0%	74.9%	25.1%
8,233	BACON	1,963	1,771	192		1,579 R	90.2%	9.8%	90.2%	9.8%
3,875	BAKER	1,314	965	345	4	620 R	73.4%	26.3%	73.7%	26.3%
34,240	BALDWIN	6,265	4,826	1,435	4	3,391 R	77.0%	22.9%	77.1%	22.9%
6,833	BANKS	1,705	1,336	356	13	980 R	78.4%	20.9%	79.0%	21.0%
16,859	BARROW	4,290	3,423	867		2,556 R	79.8%	20.2%	79.8%	20.2%
32,663	BARTOW	6,426	4,836	1,590		3,246 R	75.3%	24.7%	75.3%	24.7%
13,171	BEN HILL	2,828	2,104	703	21	1,401 R	74.4%	24.9%	75.0%	25.0%
11,556	BERRIEN	2,680	2,285	371	24	1,914 R	85.3%	13.8%	86.0%	14.0%
143,418	BIBB	37,838	27,402	10,201	235	17,201 R	72.4%	27.0%	72.9%	27.1%
10,291	BLECKLEY	2,685	2,308	377		1,931 R	86.0%	14.0%	86.0%	14.0%
5,940	BRANTLEY	1,925	1,587	338		1,249 R	82.4%	17.6%	82.4%	17.6%
13,739	BROOKS	3,086	2,430	643	13	1,787 R	78.7%	20.8%	79.1%	20.9%
6,539	BRYAN	1,672	1,409	263		1,146 R	84.3%	15.7%	84.3%	15.7%
31,585	BULLOCH	7,260	5,683	1,524	53	4,159 R	78.3%	21.0%	78.9%	21.1%
18,255	BURKE	3,904	2,846	1,058		1,788 R	72.9%	27.1%	72.9%	27.1%
10,560	BUTTS	2,703	1,968	727	8	1,241 R	72.8%	26.9%	73.0%	27.0%
6,606	CALHOUN	1,391	892	495	4	397 R	64.1%	35.6%	64.3%	35.7%
11,334	CAMDEN	3,133	2,380	753		1,627 R	76.0%	24.0%	76.0%	24.0%
6,412	CANDLER	1,669	1,427	238	4	1,189 R	85.5%	14.3%	85.7%	14.3%
45,404	CARROLL	10,454	8,296	2,158		6,138 R	79.4%	20.6%	79.4%	20.6%
28,271	CATOOSA	7,027	6,008	894	125	5,114 R	85.5%	12.7%	87.0%	13.0%
5,680	CHARLTON	1,554	1,244	310		934 R	80.1%	19.9%	80.1%	19.9%
187,767	CHATHAM	53,674	38,079	15,566	29	22,513 R	70.9%	29.0%	71.0%	29.0%
25,813	CHATTAHOOCHEE	468	345	121	2	224 R	73.7%	25.9%	74.0%	26.0%
20,541	CHATTOOGA	4,145	3,188	923	34	2,265 R	76.9%	22.3%	77.5%	22.5%
31,059	CHEROKEE	6,679	5,509	1,159	11	4,350 R	82.5%	17.4%	82.6%	17.4%
65,177	CLARKE	17,555	11,465	6,090		5,375 R	65.3%	34.7%	65.3%	34.7%
3,636	CLAY	921	632	283	6	349 R	68.6%	30.7%	69.1%	30.9%
98,043	CLAYTON	27,753	23,681	3,740	332	19,941 R	85.3%	13.5%	86.4%	13.6%
6,405	CLINCH	1,366	1,127	239		888 R	82.5%	17.5%	82.5%	17.5%
196,793	COBB	52,002	43,977	7,688	337	36,289 R	84.6%	14.8%	85.1%	14.9%
22,828	COFFEE	4,541	3,934	607		3,327 R	86.6%	13.4%	86.6%	13.4%
32,200	COLQUITT	7,834	6,900	930	4	5,970 R	88.1%	11.9%	88.1%	11.9%
22,327	COLUMBIA	5,785	4,839	946		3,893 R	83.6%	16.4%	83.6%	16.4%
12,129	COOK	2,667	2,135	525	7	1,610 R	80.1%	19.7%	80.3%	19.7%
32,310	COWETA	7,311	5,751	1,560		4,191 R	78.7%	21.3%	78.7%	21.3%
5,748	CRAWFORD	1,686	1,167	512	7	655 R	69.2%	30.4%	69.5%	30.5%
18,087	CRISP	4,307	3,623	682	2	2,941 R	84.1%	15.8%	84.2%	15.8%
9,910	DADE	2,268	2,110	148	10	1,962 R	93.0%	6.5%	93.4%	6.6%
3,639	DAWSON	1,061	828	230	3	598 R	78.0%	21.7%	78.3%	21.7%
22,310	DECATUR	5,504	4,292	1,196	16	3,096 R	78.0%	21.7%	78.2%	21.8%
415,387	DE KALB	135,915	104,750	30,671	494	74,079 R	77.1%	22.6%	77.4%	22.6%
15,658	DODGE	5,237	4,346	884	7	3,462 R	83.0%	16.9%	83.1%	16.9%
10,404	DOOLY	2,494	1,904	590		1,314 R	76.3%	23.7%	76.3%	23.7%
89,639	DOUGHERTY	16,551	12,878	3,625	48	9,253 R	77.8%	21.9%	78.0%	22.0%
28,659	DOUGLAS	7,633	6,610	982	41	5,628 R	86.6%	12.9%	87.1%	12.9%
12,682	EARLY	2,912	2,396	513	3	1,883 R	82.3%	17.6%	82.4%	17.6%
1,924	ECHOLS	472	404	68		336 R	85.6%	14.4%	85.6%	14.4%
13,632	EFFINGHAM	3,672	3,175	497		2,678 R	86.5%	13.5%	86.5%	13.5%
17,262	ELBERT	3,801	2,875	884	42	1,991 R	75.6%	23.3%	76.5%	23.5%
18,189	EMANUEL	4,634	3,684	916	34	2,768 R	79.5%	19.8%	80.1%	19.9%
7,290	EVANS	2,056	1,666	375	15	1,291 R	81.0%	18.2%	81.6%	18.4%
13,357	FANNIN	4,732	3,783	949		2,834 R	79.9%	20.1%	79.9%	20.1%
11,364	FAYETTE	3,861	3,401	450	10	2,951 R	88.1%	11.7%	88.3%	11.7%
73,742	FLOYD	18,922	15,485	3,372	65	12,113 R	81.8%	17.8%	82.1%	17.9%
16,928	FORSYTH	3,536	2,968	549	19	2,419 R	83.9%	15.5%	84.4%	15.6%
12,784	FRANKLIN	2,470	2,022	435	13	1,587 R	81.9%	17.6%	82.3%	17.7%
607,592	FULTON	170,884	96,256	74,329	299	21,927 R	56.3%	43.5%	56.4%	43.6%

GEORGIA

PRESIDENT 1972

1970 Census Population	County	Total Vote	Republican	Democratic	Other	Rep.-Dem. Plurality	Percentage Total Vote Rep.	Total Vote Dem.	Major Vote Rep.	Major Vote Dem.
8,956	GILMER	3,497	2,729	768		1,961 R	78.0%	22.0%	78.0%	22.0%
2,280	GLASCOCK	619	578	41		537 R	93.4%	6.6%	93.4%	6.6%
50,528	GLYNN	12,474	9,443	3,002	29	6,441 R	75.7%	24.1%	75.9%	24.1%
23,570	GORDON	5,228	4,344	870	14	3,474 R	83.1%	16.6%	83.3%	16.7%
17,826	GRADY	4,608	3,732	874	2	2,858 R	81.0%	19.0%	81.0%	19.0%
10,212	GREENE	2,612	1,679	919	14	760 R	64.3%	35.2%	64.6%	35.4%
72,349	GWINNETT	21,177	18,181	2,896	100	15,285 R	85.9%	13.7%	86.3%	13.7%
20,691	HABERSHAM	1,147	971	172	4	799 R	84.7%	15.0%	85.0%	15.0%
59,405	HALL	13,134	10,686	2,440	8	8,246 R	81.4%	18.6%	81.4%	18.6%
9,019	HANCOCK	3,104	1,595	1,502	7	93 R	51.4%	48.4%	51.5%	48.5%
15,927	HARALSON	4,252	3,460	767	25	2,693 R	81.4%	18.0%	81.9%	18.1%
11,520	HARRIS	3,324	2,617	701	6	1,916 R	78.7%	21.1%	78.9%	21.1%
15,814	HART	3,136	2,308	784	44	1,524 R	73.6%	25.0%	74.6%	25.4%
5,354	HEARD	1,530	1,239	276	15	963 R	81.0%	18.0%	81.8%	18.2%
23,724	HENRY	6,622	5,155	1,460	7	3,695 R	77.8%	22.0%	77.9%	22.1%
62,924	HOUSTON	16,170	13,576	2,556	38	11,020 R	84.0%	15.8%	84.2%	15.8%
8,036	IRWIN	2,192	1,851	335	6	1,516 R	84.4%	15.3%	84.7%	15.3%
21,093	JACKSON	5,218	4,124	1,055	39	3,069 R	79.0%	20.2%	79.6%	20.4%
5,760	JASPER	1,752	1,289	463		826 R	73.6%	26.4%	73.6%	26.4%
9,425	JEFF DAVIS	2,159	1,857	302		1,555 R	86.0%	14.0%	86.0%	14.0%
17,174	JEFFERSON	3,987	2,777	1,184	26	1,593 R	69.7%	29.7%	70.1%	29.9%
8,332	JENKINS	2,277	1,769	484	24	1,285 R	77.7%	21.3%	78.5%	21.5%
7,727	JOHNSON	2,637	2,201	417	19	1,784 R	83.5%	15.8%	84.1%	15.9%
12,218	JONES	3,368	2,483	861	24	1,622 R	73.7%	25.6%	74.3%	25.7%
10,688	LAMAR	2,510	1,844	666		1,178 R	73.5%	26.5%	73.5%	26.5%
5,031	LANIER	1,046	850	193	3	657 R	81.3%	18.5%	81.5%	18.5%
32,738	LAURENS	9,513	7,350	2,130	33	5,220 R	77.3%	22.4%	77.5%	22.5%
7,044	LEE	1,853	1,441	390	22	1,051 R	77.8%	21.0%	78.7%	21.3%
17,569	LIBERTY	3,556	2,337	1,217	2	1,120 R	65.7%	34.2%	65.8%	34.2%
5,895	LINCOLN	1,586	1,246	340		906 R	78.6%	21.4%	78.6%	21.4%
3,746	LONG	1,000	764	236		528 R	76.4%	23.6%	76.4%	23.6%
55,112	LOWNDES	9,839	7,812	2,015	12	5,797 R	79.4%	20.5%	79.5%	20.5%
8,728	LUMPKIN	1,869	1,477	385	7	1,092 R	79.0%	20.6%	79.3%	20.7%
15,276	MCDUFFIE	3,988	2,990	996	2	1,994 R	75.0%	25.0%	75.0%	25.0%
7,371	MCINTOSH	2,209	1,367	833	9	534 R	61.9%	37.7%	62.1%	37.9%
12,933	MACON	2,842	2,005	837		1,168 R	70.5%	29.5%	70.5%	29.5%
13,517	MADISON	3,192	2,606	572	14	2,034 R	81.6%	17.9%	82.0%	18.0%
5,099	MARION	1,016	850	164	2	686 R	83.7%	16.1%	83.8%	16.2%
19,461	MERIWETHER	4,643	3,420	1,213	10	2,207 R	73.7%	26.1%	73.8%	26.2%
6,397	MILLER	1,387	1,269	118		1,151 R	91.5%	8.5%	91.5%	8.5%
18,956	MITCHELL	3,537	2,400	1,120	17	1,280 R	67.9%	31.7%	68.2%	31.8%
10,991	MONROE	2,977	2,181	789	7	1,392 R	73.3%	26.5%	73.4%	26.6%
6,099	MONTGOMERY	1,707	1,370	337		1,033 R	80.3%	19.7%	80.3%	19.7%
9,904	MORGAN	2,693	2,007	668	18	1,339 R	74.5%	24.8%	75.0%	25.0%
12,986	MURRAY	3,287	2,643	644		1,999 R	80.4%	19.6%	80.4%	19.6%
167,377	MUSCOGEE	36,739	28,449	8,234	56	20,215 R	77.4%	22.4%	77.6%	22.4%
26,282	NEWTON	6,031	4,647	1,380	4	3,267 R	77.1%	22.9%	77.1%	22.9%
7,915	OCONEE	2,505	2,029	464	12	1,565 R	81.0%	18.5%	81.4%	18.6%
7,598	OGLETHORPE	2,059	1,712	326	21	1,386 R	83.1%	15.8%	84.0%	16.0%
17,520	PAULDING	3,831	2,814	1,004	13	1,810 R	73.5%	26.2%	73.7%	26.3%
15,990	PEACH	6,164	3,747	2,413	4	1,334 R	60.8%	39.1%	60.8%	39.2%
9,620	PICKENS	2,621	2,101	520		1,581 R	80.2%	19.8%	80.2%	19.8%
9,281	PIERCE	2,256	1,982	269	5	1,713 R	87.9%	11.9%	88.0%	12.0%
7,316	PIKE	1,864	1,432	423	9	1,009 R	76.8%	22.7%	77.2%	22.8%
29,656	POLK	6,274	4,929	1,317	28	3,612 R	78.6%	21.0%	78.9%	21.1%
8,066	PULASKI	2,412	1,966	444	2	1,522 R	81.5%	18.4%	81.6%	18.4%
8,394	PUTNAM	2,567	1,963	604		1,359 R	76.5%	23.5%	76.5%	23.5%
2,180	QUITMAN	642	502	140		362 R	78.2%	21.8%	78.2%	21.8%
8,327	RABUN	1,855	1,477	366	12	1,111 R	79.6%	19.7%	80.1%	19.9%
8,734	RANDOLPH	2,401	1,603	798		805 R	66.8%	33.2%	66.8%	33.2%

GEORGIA

PRESIDENT 1972

1970 Census Population	County	Total Vote	Republican	Democratic	Other	Rep.-Dem. Plurality	Percentage: Total Vote Rep.	Percentage: Total Vote Dem.	Percentage: Major Vote Rep.	Percentage: Major Vote Dem.
162,437	RICHMOND	33,607	24,362	9,219	26	15,143 R	72.5%	27.4%	72.5%	27.5%
18,152	ROCKDALE	4,376	3,560	791	25	2,769 R	81.4%	18.1%	81.8%	18.2%
3,097	SCHLEY	858	694	162	2	532 R	80.9%	18.9%	81.1%	18.9%
12,591	SCREVEN	2,977	2,402	575		1,827 R	80.7%	19.3%	80.7%	19.3%
7,059	SEMINOLE	2,227	1,851	376		1,475 R	83.1%	16.9%	83.1%	16.9%
39,514	SPALDING	8,898	7,183	1,702	13	5,481 R	80.7%	19.1%	80.8%	19.2%
20,331	STEPHENS	4,649	3,773	871	5	2,902 R	81.2%	18.7%	81.2%	18.8%
6,511	STEWART	1,375	1,020	353	2	667 R	74.2%	25.7%	74.3%	25.7%
26,931	SUMTER	5,839	4,533	1,268	38	3,265 R	77.6%	21.7%	78.1%	21.9%
6,625	TALBOT	1,500	990	508	2	482 R	66.0%	33.9%	66.1%	33.9%
2,423	TALIAFERRO	957	585	372		213 R	61.1%	38.9%	61.1%	38.9%
16,557	TATTNALL	3,419	2,892	492	35	2,400 R	84.6%	14.4%	85.5%	14.5%
7,865	TAYLOR	2,100	1,580	514	6	1,066 R	75.2%	24.5%	75.5%	24.5%
11,381	TELFAIR	2,932	2,245	687		1,558 R	76.6%	23.4%	76.6%	23.4%
11,416	TERRELL	2,754	2,057	686	11	1,371 R	74.7%	24.9%	75.0%	25.0%
34,515	THOMAS	8,839	6,668	2,171		4,497 R	75.4%	24.6%	75.4%	24.6%
27,288	TIFT	5,408	4,591	816	1	3,775 R	84.9%	15.1%	84.9%	15.1%
19,151	TOOMBS	4,775	4,080	675	20	3,405 R	85.4%	14.1%	85.8%	14.2%
4,565	TOWNS	1,979	1,573	404	2	1,169 R	79.5%	20.4%	79.6%	20.4%
5,647	TREUTLEN	1,556	1,346	210		1,136 R	86.5%	13.5%	86.5%	13.5%
44,466	TROUP	10,429	8,350	2,056	23	6,294 R	80.1%	19.7%	80.2%	19.8%
8,790	TURNER	2,565	2,120	437	8	1,683 R	82.7%	17.0%	82.9%	17.1%
8,222	TWIGGS	2,488	1,363	1,113	12	250 R	54.8%	44.7%	55.0%	45.0%
6,811	UNION	3,068	2,317	742	9	1,575 R	75.5%	24.2%	75.7%	24.3%
23,505	UPSON	5,830	4,892	896	42	3,996 R	83.9%	15.4%	84.5%	15.5%
50,691	WALKER	10,442	8,728	1,574	140	7,154 R	83.6%	15.1%	84.7%	15.3%
23,404	WALTON	5,137	3,994	1,140	3	2,854 R	77.7%	22.2%	77.8%	22.2%
33,525	WARE	8,303	6,578	1,724	1	4,854 R	79.2%	20.8%	79.2%	20.8%
6,669	WARREN	1,654	1,175	475	4	700 R	71.0%	28.7%	71.2%	28.8%
17,480	WASHINGTON	5,234	3,901	1,246	87	2,655 R	74.5%	23.8%	75.8%	24.2%
17,858	WAYNE	4,410	3,677	733		2,944 R	83.4%	16.6%	83.4%	16.6%
2,362	WEBSTER	591	483	108		375 R	81.7%	18.3%	81.7%	18.3%
4,596	WHEELER	1,387	1,093	294		799 R	78.8%	21.2%	78.8%	21.2%
7,742	WHITE	1,893	1,537	343	13	1,194 R	81.2%	18.1%	81.8%	18.2%
55,108	WHITFIELD	10,559	8,591	1,955	13	6,636 R	81.4%	18.5%	81.5%	18.5%
6,998	WILCOX	2,180	1,863	315	2	1,548 R	85.5%	14.4%	85.5%	14.5%
10,184	WILKES	2,841	2,195	646		1,549 R	77.3%	22.7%	77.3%	22.7%
9,393	WILKINSON	2,965	2,196	751	18	1,445 R	74.1%	25.3%	74.5%	25.5%
14,770	WORTH	3,493	2,942	542	9	2,400 R	84.2%	15.5%	84.4%	15.6%
4,589,575	TOTAL	1,174,772	881,496	289,529	3,747	591,967 R	75.0%	24.6%	75.3%	24.7%

GEORGIA

PRESIDENT 1968

1960 Census Population	County	Total Vote	Republican	Democratic	AIP	Other	Plurality	Percentage Rep.	Dem.	AIP
13,246	APPLING	4,233	795	760	2,678		1,883 A	18.8%	18.0%	63.3%
6,188	ATKINSON	2,528	288	686	1,554		868 A	11.4%	27.1%	61.5%
8,359	BACON	2,800	586	279	1,935		1,349 A	20.9%	10.0%	69.1%
4,543	BAKER	1,714	99	548	1,067		519 A	5.8%	32.0%	62.3%
34,064	BALDWIN	7,111	2,318	2,109	2,678	6	360 A	32.6%	29.7%	37.7%
6,497	BANKS	2,128	398	296	1,434		1,036 A	18.7%	13.9%	67.4%
14,485	BARROW	5,173	1,372	1,070	2,731		1,359 A	26.5%	20.7%	52.8%
28,267	BARTOW	8,251	2,045	2,149	4,052	5	1,903 A	24.8%	26.0%	49.1%
13,633	BEN HILL	3,371	661	876	1,833	1	957 A	19.6%	26.0%	54.4%
12,038	BERRIEN	3,828	566	451	2,810	1	2,244 A	14.8%	11.8%	73.4%
141,249	BIBB	41,397	13,490	10,579	17,328		3,838 A	32.6%	25.6%	41.9%
9,642	BLECKLEY	3,611	756	396	2,458	1	1,702 A	20.9%	11.0%	68.1%
5,891	BRANTLEY	2,263	237	317	1,709		1,392 A	10.5%	14.0%	75.5%
15,292	BROOKS	3,780	589	787	2,404		1,617 A	15.6%	20.8%	63.6%
6,226	BRYAN	2,369	381	560	1,428		868 A	16.1%	23.6%	60.3%
24,263	BULLOCH	7,854	2,113	1,788	3,953		1,840 A	26.9%	22.8%	50.3%
20,596	BURKE	4,894	1,416	1,676	1,802		126 A	28.9%	34.2%	36.8%
8,976	BUTTS	3,033	584	959	1,490		531 A	19.3%	31.6%	49.1%
7,341	CALHOUN	1,910	234	697	979		282 A	12.3%	36.5%	51.3%
9,975	CAMDEN	3,885	751	1,146	1,988		842 A	19.3%	29.5%	51.2%
6,672	CANDLER	2,763	552	587	1,624		1,037 A	20.0%	21.2%	58.8%
36,451	CARROLL	11,970	3,135	2,326	6,509		3,374 A	26.2%	19.4%	54.4%
21,101	CATOOSA	9,393	2,043	901	6,449		4,406 A	21.8%	9.6%	68.7%
5,313	CHARLTON	1,944	332	455	1,157		702 A	17.1%	23.4%	59.5%
188,299	CHATHAM	53,545	18,106	18,201	17,238		95 D	33.8%	34.0%	32.2%
13,011	CHATTAHOOCHEE	521	70	148	303		155 A	13.4%	28.4%	58.2%
19,954	CHATTOOGA	5,366	1,087	1,255	3,024		1,769 A	20.3%	23.4%	56.4%
23,001	CHEROKEE	7,462	2,675	1,434	3,351	2	676 A	35.8%	19.2%	44.9%
45,363	CLARKE	14,808	5,800	5,543	3,452	13	257 R	39.2%	37.4%	23.3%
4,551	CLAY	1,258	133	516	608	1	92 A	10.6%	41.0%	48.3%
46,365	CLAYTON	23,438	8,256	3,510	11,665	7	3,409 A	35.2%	15.0%	49.8%
6,545	CLINCH	1,780	304	334	1,142		808 A	17.1%	18.8%	64.2%
114,174	COBB	45,209	18,649	8,755	17,805		844 R	41.3%	19.4%	39.4%
21,953	COFFEE	6,357	1,241	1,331	3,785		2,454 A	19.5%	20.9%	59.5%
34,048	COLQUITT	9,326	1,882	1,119	6,325		4,443 A	20.2%	12.0%	67.8%
13,423	COLUMBIA	4,748	1,636	905	2,207		571 A	34.5%	19.1%	46.5%
11,822	COOK	3,564	521	603	2,438	2	1,835 A	14.6%	16.9%	68.4%
28,893	COWETA	7,437	2,442	1,204	3,791		1,349 A	32.8%	16.2%	51.0%
5,816	CRAWFORD	1,621	246	489	886		397 A	15.2%	30.2%	54.7%
17,768	CRISP	5,223	935	1,017	3,271		2,254 A	17.9%	19.5%	62.6%
8,666	DADE	3,355	613	282	2,460		1,847 A	18.3%	8.4%	73.3%
3,590	DAWSON	1,600	509	246	845		336 A	31.8%	15.4%	52.8%
25,203	DECATUR	7,054	749	1,729	4,576		2,847 A	10.6%	24.5%	64.9%
256,782	DE KALB	104,237	52,485	27,796	23,954	2	24,689 R	50.4%	26.7%	23.0%
16,483	DODGE	5,691	1,055	1,230	3,406		2,176 A	18.5%	21.6%	59.8%
11,474	DOOLY	3,136	454	879	1,803		924 A	14.5%	28.0%	57.5%
75,680	DOUGHERTY	18,762	5,611	3,831	9,317	3	3,706 A	29.9%	20.4%	49.7%
16,741	DOUGLAS	7,249	1,848	1,242	4,159		2,311 A	25.5%	17.1%	57.4%
13,151	EARLY	3,909	327	785	2,797		2,012 A	8.4%	20.1%	71.6%
1,876	ECHOLS	642	53	56	533		477 A	8.3%	8.7%	83.0%
10,144	EFFINGHAM	3,965	769	635	2,561		1,792 A	19.4%	16.0%	64.6%
17,835	ELBERT	5,382	914	1,216	3,252		2,036 A	17.0%	22.6%	60.4%
17,815	EMANUEL	6,112	1,297	1,508	3,307		1,799 A	21.2%	24.7%	54.1%
6,952	EVANS	2,510	543	492	1,475		932 A	21.6%	19.6%	58.8%
13,620	FANNIN	5,892	3,475	1,229	1,188		2,246 R	59.0%	20.9%	20.2%
8,199	FAYETTE	3,307	867	551	1,888	1	1,021 A	26.2%	16.7%	57.1%
69,130	FLOYD	21,512	7,470	4,036	10,001	5	2,531 A	34.7%	18.8%	46.5%
12,170	FORSYTH	4,433	1,389	647	2,397		1,008 A	31.3%	14.6%	54.1%
13,274	FRANKLIN	4,173	716	766	2,691		1,925 A	17.2%	18.4%	64.5%
556,326	FULTON	179,068	64,153	77,847	36,995	73	13,694 D	35.8%	43.5%	20.7%

GEORGIA

PRESIDENT 1968

1960 Census Population	County	Total Vote	Republican	Democratic	AIP	Other	Plurality	Percentage Rep.	Dem.	AIP
8,922	GILMER	4,023	2,074	690	1,259		815 R	51.6%	17.2%	31.3%
2,672	GLASCOCK	965	185	47	733		548 A	19.2%	4.9%	76.0%
41,954	GLYNN	12,317	3,725	3,247	5,341	4	1,616 A	30.2%	26.4%	43.4%
19,228	GORDON	6,053	1,815	1,161	3,077		1,262 A	30.0%	19.2%	50.8%
18,015	GRADY	5,803	561	1,425	3,817		2,392 A	9.7%	24.6%	65.8%
11,193	GREENE	3,510	652	1,635	1,223		412 D	18.6%	46.6%	34.8%
43,541	GWINNETT	17,489	5,350	3,226	8,909	4	3,559 A	30.6%	18.4%	50.9%
18,116	HABERSHAM	5,689	1,611	1,070	3,008		1,397 A	28.3%	18.8%	52.9%
49,739	HALL	13,643	4,923	3,174	5,546		623 A	36.1%	23.3%	40.7%
9,979	HANCOCK	3,650	381	2,165	1,104		1,061 D	10.4%	59.3%	30.2%
14,543	HARALSON	5,473	1,451	771	3,251		1,800 A	26.5%	14.1%	59.4%
11,167	HARRIS	3,944	1,021	1,072	1,851		779 A	25.9%	27.2%	46.9%
15,229	HART	4,774	586	979	3,208	1	2,229 A	12.3%	20.5%	67.2%
5,333	HEARD	1,812	303	356	1,153		797 A	16.7%	19.6%	63.6%
17,619	HENRY	7,938	2,017	2,317	3,604		1,287 A	25.4%	29.2%	45.4%
39,154	HOUSTON	14,457	4,285	2,831	7,339	2	3,054 A	29.6%	19.6%	50.8%
9,211	IRWIN	2,860	430	474	1,955	1	1,481 A	15.0%	16.6%	68.4%
18,499	JACKSON	6,149	1,139	1,537	3,473		1,936 A	18.5%	25.0%	56.5%
6,135	JASPER	2,217	456	835	926		91 A	20.6%	37.7%	41.8%
8,914	JEFF DAVIS	2,911	577	376	1,958		1,381 A	19.8%	12.9%	67.3%
17,468	JEFFERSON	5,218	1,227	1,899	2,090	2	191 A	23.5%	36.4%	40.1%
9,148	JENKINS	2,527	574	704	1,249		545 A	22.7%	27.9%	49.4%
8,048	JOHNSON	2,868	381	446	2,041		1,595 A	13.3%	15.6%	71.2%
8,468	JONES	3,568	693	1,105	1,770		665 A	19.4%	31.0%	49.6%
10,240	LAMAR	2,805	575	790	1,440		650 A	20.5%	28.2%	51.3%
5,097	LANIER	1,542	241	277	1,024		747 A	15.6%	18.0%	66.4%
32,313	LAURENS	12,838	2,738	3,451	6,649		3,198 A	21.3%	26.9%	51.8%
6,204	LEE	2,264	389	673	1,201	1	528 A	17.2%	29.7%	53.0%
14,487	LIBERTY	3,529	592	1,572	1,365		207 D	16.8%	44.5%	38.7%
5,906	LINCOLN	2,189	408	491	1,290		799 A	18.6%	22.4%	58.9%
3,874	LONG	1,767	156	574	1,037		463 A	8.8%	32.5%	58.7%
49,270	LOWNDES	11,154	3,073	2,402	5,679		2,606 A	27.6%	21.5%	50.9%
7,241	LUMPKIN	2,131	687	396	1,048		361 A	32.2%	18.6%	49.2%
12,627	MCDUFFIE	4,025	1,324	991	1,709	1	385 A	32.9%	24.6%	42.5%
6,364	MCINTOSH	2,099	315	943	841		102 D	15.0%	44.9%	40.1%
13,170	MACON	3,111	598	954	1,559		605 A	19.2%	30.7%	50.1%
11,246	MADISON	3,751	600	621	2,529	1	1,908 A	16.0%	16.6%	67.4%
5,477	MARION	1,282	186	247	849		602 A	14.5%	19.3%	66.2%
19,756	MERIWETHER	5,451	1,120	1,760	2,571		811 A	20.5%	32.3%	47.2%
6,908	MILLER	2,282	249	171	1,862		1,613 A	10.9%	7.5%	81.6%
19,652	MITCHELL	5,634	731	1,255	3,647	1	2,392 A	13.0%	22.3%	64.7%
10,495	MONROE	3,220	770	1,028	1,422		394 A	23.9%	31.9%	44.2%
6,284	MONTGOMERY	2,288	352	503	1,433		930 A	15.4%	22.0%	62.6%
10,280	MORGAN	2,980	616	973	1,391		418 A	20.7%	32.7%	46.7%
10,447	MURRAY	3,846	1,278	818	1,750		472 A	33.2%	21.3%	45.5%
158,623	MUSCOGEE	34,590	11,193	7,591	15,804	2	4,611 A	32.4%	21.9%	45.7%
20,999	NEWTON	6,675	1,660	1,996	3,017	2	1,021 A	24.9%	29.9%	45.2%
6,304	OCONEE	2,532	713	414	1,405		692 A	28.2%	16.4%	55.5%
7,926	OGLETHORPE	2,603	383	483	1,737		1,254 A	14.7%	18.6%	66.7%
13,101	PAULDING	5,054	977	1,023	3,054		2,031 A	19.3%	20.2%	60.4%
13,846	PEACH	3,904	904	1,362	1,638		276 A	23.2%	34.9%	42.0%
8,903	PICKENS	3,728	1,659	677	1,392		267 R	44.5%	18.2%	37.3%
9,678	PIERCE	3,230	579	507	2,144		1,565 A	17.9%	15.7%	66.4%
7,138	PIKE	2,419	345	632	1,442		810 A	14.3%	26.1%	59.6%
28,015	POLK	7,976	1,729	2,007	4,240		2,233 A	21.7%	25.2%	53.2%
8,204	PULASKI	2,678	595	514	1,569		974 A	22.2%	19.2%	58.6%
7,798	PUTNAM	2,743	594	972	1,177		205 A	21.7%	35.4%	42.9%
2,432	QUITMAN	747	90	198	459		261 A	12.0%	26.5%	61.4%
7,456	RABUN	2,679	680	590	1,407	2	727 A	25.4%	22.0%	52.5%
11,078	RANDOLPH	2,968	502	1,028	1,438		410 A	16.9%	34.6%	48.5%

GEORGIA

PRESIDENT 1968

1960 Census Population	County	Total Vote	Republican	Democratic	AIP	Other	Plurality	Percentage Rep.	Dem.	AIP
135,601	RICHMOND	36,302	14,993	11,770	9,532	7	3,223 R	41.3%	32.4%	26.3%
10,572	ROCKDALE	4,623	1,195	1,213	2,215		1,002 A	25.8%	26.2%	47.9%
3,256	SCHLEY	1,092	164	309	619		310 A	15.0%	28.3%	56.7%
14,919	SCREVEN	4,157	916	1,411	1,830		419 A	22.0%	33.9%	44.0%
6,802	SEMINOLE	2,493	201	369	1,922	1	1,553 A	8.1%	14.8%	77.1%
35,404	SPALDING	10,979	3,077	2,949	4,953		1,876 A	28.0%	26.9%	45.1%
18,391	STEPHENS	5,132	1,295	1,035	2,802		1,507 A	25.2%	20.2%	54.6%
7,371	STEWART	1,654	233	489	932		443 A	14.1%	29.6%	56.3%
24,652	SUMTER	6,573	1,383	1,701	3,489		1,788 A	21.0%	25.9%	53.1%
7,127	TALBOT	1,515	317	510	688		178 A	20.9%	33.7%	45.4%
3,370	TALIAFERRO	1,418	232	678	508		170 D	16.4%	47.8%	35.8%
15,837	TATTNALL	5,214	852	957	3,405		2,448 A	16.3%	18.4%	65.3%
8,311	TAYLOR	2,710	393	691	1,626		935 A	14.5%	25.5%	60.0%
11,715	TELFAIR	4,260	720	1,038	2,502		1,464 A	16.9%	24.4%	58.7%
12,742	TERRELL	3,619	545	1,275	1,798	1	523 A	15.1%	35.2%	49.7%
34,319	THOMAS	9,885	2,261	2,583	5,039	2	2,456 A	22.9%	26.1%	51.0%
23,487	TIFT	6,821	1,692	1,187	3,942		2,250 A	24.8%	17.4%	57.8%
16,837	TOOMBS	5,698	1,397	896	3,405		2,008 A	24.5%	15.7%	59.8%
4,538	TOWNS	2,851	1,492	770	589		722 R	52.3%	27.0%	20.7%
5,874	TREUTLEN	1,896	474	341	1,081		607 A	25.0%	18.0%	57.0%
47,189	TROUP	12,367	3,239	2,896	6,232		2,993 A	26.2%	23.4%	50.4%
8,439	TURNER	2,676	419	412	1,845		1,426 A	15.7%	15.4%	68.9%
7,935	TWIGGS	2,315	336	812	1,167		355 A	14.5%	35.1%	50.4%
6,510	UNION	3,101	1,221	974	906		247 R	39.4%	31.4%	29.2%
23,800	UPSON	6,573	1,494	1,480	3,599		2,105 A	22.7%	22.5%	54.8%
45,264	WALKER	14,321	3,664	1,930	8,725	2	5,061 A	25.6%	13.5%	60.9%
20,481	WALTON	6,998	1,399	1,552	4,047		2,495 A	20.0%	22.2%	57.8%
34,219	WARE	10,197	2,047	2,255	5,895		3,640 A	20.1%	22.1%	57.8%
7,360	WARREN	1,755	406	582	767		185 A	23.1%	33.2%	43.7%
18,903	WASHINGTON	4,719	1,247	1,443	2,029		586 A	26.4%	30.6%	43.0%
17,921	WAYNE	5,715	1,313	980	3,422		2,109 A	23.0%	17.1%	59.9%
3,247	WEBSTER	713	72	147	494		347 A	10.1%	20.6%	69.3%
5,342	WHEELER	1,673	251	488	934		446 A	15.0%	29.2%	55.8%
6,935	WHITE	2,355	762	435	1,157	1	395 A	32.4%	18.5%	49.1%
42,109	WHITFIELD	11,508	4,828	2,723	3,954	3	874 R	42.0%	23.7%	34.4%
7,905	WILCOX	2,668	381	465	1,822		1,357 A	14.3%	17.4%	68.3%
10,961	WILKES	3,535	873	953	1,709		756 A	24.7%	27.0%	48.3%
9,250	WILKINSON	3,384	685	829	1,870		1,041 A	20.2%	24.5%	55.3%
16,682	WORTH	4,372	603	719	3,049	1	2,330 A	13.8%	16.4%	69.7%
3,943,116	TOTAL	1,250,266	380,111	334,440	535,550	165	155,439 A	30.4%	26.7%	42.8%

GEORGIA

ELECTION NOTES

1984 Other vote was all write-in as follows: 152 Bergland; 95 Richards; 34 LaRouche; 10 Mason; 4 Dennis; 4 Johnson; 3 Anderson; 3 Lowrey; 2 Holmes; 2 Serrette; 1 Hall; 460 scattered write-in. The state-wide total for the other vote column is these 770 write-in votes not reported by county.

1980 Other vote was 36,055 Anderson (Independent); 15,627 Clark (Libertarian); 104 Commoner (write-in); 4 Pulley (write-in); 1 Griswold (write-in); 3 scattered write-in. The state-wide total for the other vote column includes these 112 write-in votes not reported by county. Early unamended canvass gave the Democratic state-wide total vote as 890,955.

1976 Other vote was all write-in as follows: 1,168 Anderson; 1,071 Maddox; 991 McCarthy; 175 MacBride; 43 Camejo; 3 Hall; 3 Miller; 2 Levin; 2 Zeidler; 1 LaRouche; 847 scattered write-in. The state-wide total for the other vote column is these 4,306 write-in votes not reported by county.

1972 Other vote was 812 Schmitz (write-in); 3 Fisher (write-in); 2,932 scattered write-in. Although the data indicate a possible discrepancy in the Republican vote in Mitchell county and in both the Republican and Democratic vote in Habersham county, the official state canvass figures are used here.

1968 Wallace on the ballot as American. Other vote was scattered write-in. The Democratic total vote is carried as certified by the state but the addition of the counties totals 334,438.

HAWAII

POPULAR VOTE FOR PRESIDENT 1960 TO 1984

Year	Total Vote	Republican Vote	Republican Candidate	Democratic Vote	Democratic Candidate	Other Vote	Plurality	Percentage Total Vote Rep.	Percentage Total Vote Dem.	Percentage Major Vote Rep.	Percentage Major Vote Dem.
1984	335,846	185,050	Reagan, Ronald	147,154	Mondale, Walter F.	3,642	37,896 R	55.1%	43.8%	55.7%	44.3%
1980	303,287	130,112	Reagan, Ronald	135,879	Carter, Jimmy	37,296	5,767 D	42.9%	44.8%	48.9%	51.1%
1976	291,301	140,003	Ford, Gerald R.	147,375	Carter, Jimmy	3,923	7,372 D	48.1%	50.6%	48.7%	51.3%
1972	270,274	168,865	Nixon, Richard M.	101,409	McGovern, George S.		67,456 R	62.5%	37.5%	62.5%	37.5%
1968	236,218	91,425	Nixon, Richard M.	141,324	Humphrey, Hubert H.	3,469	49,899 D	38.7%	59.8%	39.3%	60.7%
1964	207,271	44,022	Goldwater, Barry M.	163,249	Johnson, Lyndon B.		119,227 D	21.2%	78.8%	21.2%	78.8%
1960	184,705	92,295	Nixon, Richard M.	92,410	Kennedy, John F.		115 D	50.0%	50.0%	50.0%	50.0%

Hawaii was formally admitted to statehood in August 1959 .

ELECTORAL COLLEGE VOTE 1960 TO 1984

Year	Total	Republican	Democratic	Other
1984	4	4	—	—
1980	4	—	4	—
1976	4	—	4	—
1972	4	4	—	—
1968	4	—	4	—
1964	4	—	4	—
1960	3	—	3	—

HAWAII

PRINCIPAL ISLANDS
HAWAII COUNTY
HAWAII
MAUI
KAHOOLAWE
LANAI
MAUI COUNTY
KALAWAO COUNTY
MOLOKAI
OAHU
HONOLULU COUNTY
KAUAI
KAUAI COUNTY
NIIHAU

HAWAII

PRESIDENT 1984

1980 Census Population	County	Total Vote	Republican	Democratic	Other	Rep.-Dem. Plurality	Percentage Total Vote Rep.	Total Vote Dem.	Major Vote Rep.	Major Vote Dem.
92,053	HAWAII	39,143	20,707	17,866	570	2,841 R	52.9%	45.6%	53.7%	46.3%
762,565	HONOLULU	250,132	140,258	107,404	2,470	32,854 R	56.1%	42.9%	56.6%	43.4%
39,082	KAUAI	18,332	9,249	8,862	221	387 R	50.5%	48.3%	51.1%	48.9%
70,991	MAUI	28,067	14,720	12,966	381	1,754 R	52.4%	46.2%	53.2%	46.8%
	SPECIAL BALLOTS	172	116	56		60 R	67.4%	32.6%	67.4%	32.6%
964,691	TOTAL	335,846	185,050	147,154	3,642	37,896 R	55.1%	43.8%	55.7%	44.3%

HAWAII

PRESIDENT 1980

1980 Census Population	County	Total Vote	Republican	Democratic	Other	Rep.-Dem. Plurality	Percentage Total Vote Rep.	Total Vote Dem.	Major Vote Rep.	Major Vote Dem.
92,053	HAWAII	35,861	14,247	17,630	3,984	3,383 D	39.7%	49.2%	44.7%	55.3%
762,565	HONOLULU	224,995	99,596	96,472	28,927	3,124 R	44.3%	42.9%	50.8%	49.2%
39,082	KAUAI	16,621	5,883	9,081	1,657	3,198 D	35.4%	54.6%	39.3%	60.7%
70,991	MAUI	25,751	10,359	12,674	2,718	2,315 D	40.2%	49.2%	45.0%	55.0%
	SPECIAL BALLOTS	59	27	22	10	5 R	45.8%	37.3%	55.1%	44.9%
964,691	TOTAL	303,287	130,112	135,879	37,296	5,767 D	42.9%	44.8%	48.9%	51.1%

HAWAII

PRESIDENT 1976

1970 Census Population	County	Total Vote	Republican	Democratic	Other	Rep.-Dem. Plurality	Percentage Total Vote Rep.	Total Vote Dem.	Major Vote Rep.	Major Vote Dem.
63,468	HAWAII	31,765	15,366	15,960	439	594 D	48.4%	50.2%	49.1%	50.9%
630,528	HONOLULU	222,416	108,007	111,365	3,044	3,358 D	48.6%	50.1%	49.2%	50.8%
29,761	KAUAI	14,522	6,278	8,105	139	1,827 D	43.2%	55.8%	43.6%	56.4%
46,156	MAUI	22,538	10,318	11,921	299	1,603 D	45.8%	52.9%	46.4%	53.6%
	SPECIAL BALLOTS	60	34	24	2	10 R	56.7%	40.0%	58.6%	41.4%
769,913	TOTAL	291,301	140,003	147,375	3,923	7,372 D	48.1%	50.6%	48.7%	51.3%

HAWAII

PRESIDENT 1972

1970 Census Population	County	Total Vote	Republican	Democratic	Other	Rep.-Dem. Plurality	Percentage Total Vote Rep.	Dem.	Major Vote Rep.	Dem.
63,468	HAWAII	28,484	16,832	11,652		5,180 R	59.1%	40.9%	59.1%	40.9%
630,528	HONOLULU	209,801	132,844	76,957		55,887 R	63.3%	36.7%	63.3%	36.7%
29,761	KAUAI	12,972	7,571	5,401		2,170 R	58.4%	41.6%	58.4%	41.6%
46,156	MAUI	19,017	11,618	7,399		4,219 R	61.1%	38.9%	61.1%	38.9%
769,913	TOTAL	270,274	168,865	101,409		67,456 R	62.5%	37.5%	62.5%	37.5%

HAWAII

PRESIDENT 1968

1960 Census Population	County	Total Vote	Republican	Democratic	AIP	Other	Plurality	Percentage Rep.	Dem.	AIP
61,332	HAWAII	25,727	9,625	15,819	283		6,194 D	37.4%	61.5%	1.1%
500,409	HONOLULU	182,194	71,259	108,141	2,794		36,882 D	39.1%	59.4%	1.5%
28,176	KAUAI	11,346	4,140	7,051	155		2,911 D	36.5%	62.1%	1.4%
42,855	MAUI	16,951	6,401	10,313	237		3,912 D	37.8%	60.8%	1.4%
632,772	TOTAL	236,218	91,425	141,324	3,469		49,899 D	38.7%	59.8%	1.5%

HAWAII

Kalawao county, an area of 14 square miles on Molokai Island, consists entirely of the Kalaupapa Hansen's disease settlement. The population and voting data for this settlement are included in the Maui county statistics.

ELECTION NOTES

1984 Other vote was 2,167 Bergland (Libertarian); 821 Hall (People Before Profits); 654 LaRouche (Hawaiians for LaRouche). Special ballots listed in the table are votes cast by new resident and overseas voters.

1980 Other vote was 32,021 Anderson (Independent); 3,269 Clark (Libertarian); 1,548 Commoner (Citizens); 458 Hall (Hawaii Hall Committee). Special ballots listed in the table are votes cast by new resident and overseas voters.

1976 Other vote was MacBride (Libertarian). Special ballots listed in the table are votes cast by new resident and overseas voters.

1972

1968 Wallace on the ballot as American Independent.

IDAHO

POPULAR VOTE FOR PRESIDENT 1920 TO 1984

Year	Total Vote	Republican Vote	Republican Candidate	Democratic Vote	Democratic Candidate	Other Vote	Plurality	Percentage Total Vote Rep.	Percentage Total Vote Dem.	Percentage Major Vote Rep.	Percentage Major Vote Dem.
1984	411,144	297,523	Reagan, Ronald	108,510	Mondale, Walter F.	5,111	189,013 R	72.4%	26.4%	73.3%	26.7%
1980	437,431	290,699	Reagan, Ronald	110,192	Carter, Jimmy	36,540	180,507 R	66.5%	25.2%	72.5%	27.5%
1976	344,071	204,151	Ford, Gerald R.	126,549	Carter, Jimmy	13,371	77,602 R	59.3%	36.8%	61.7%	38.3%
1972	310,379	199,384	Nixon, Richard M.	80,826	McGovern, George S.	30,169	118,558 R	64.2%	26.0%	71.2%	28.8%
1968	291,183	165,369	Nixon, Richard M.	89,273	Humphrey, Hubert H.	36,541	76,096 R	56.8%	30.7%	64.9%	35.1%
1964	292,477	143,557	Goldwater, Barry M.	148,920	Johnson, Lyndon B.		5,363 D	49.1%	50.9%	49.1%	50.9%
1960	300,450	161,597	Nixon, Richard M.	138,853	Kennedy, John F.		22,744 R	53.8%	46.2%	53.8%	46.2%
1956	272,989	166,979	Eisenhower, Dwight D.	105,868	Stevenson, Adlai E.	142	61,111 R	61.2%	38.8%	61.2%	38.8%
1952	276,254	180,707	Eisenhower, Dwight D.	95,081	Stevenson, Adlai E.	466	85,626 R	65.4%	34.4%	65.5%	34.5%
1948	214,816	101,514	Dewey, Thomas E.	107,370	Truman, Harry S.	5,932	5,856 D	47.3%	50.0%	48.6%	51.4%
1944	208,321	100,137	Dewey, Thomas E.	107,399	Roosevelt, Franklin D.	785	7,262 D	48.1%	51.6%	48.3%	51.7%
1940	235,168	106,553	Willkie, Wendell	127,842	Roosevelt, Franklin D.	773	21,289 D	45.3%	54.4%	45.5%	54.5%
1936	199,617	66,256	Landon, Alfred M.	125,683	Roosevelt, Franklin D.	7,678	59,427 D	33.2%	63.0%	34.5%	65.5%
1932	186,520	71,312	Hoover, Herbert C.	109,479	Roosevelt, Franklin D.	5,729	38,167 D	38.2%	58.7%	39.4%	60.6%
1928	151,541	97,322	Hoover, Herbert C.	52,926	Smith, Alfred E.	1,293	44,396 R	64.2%	34.9%	64.8%	35.2%
1924 **	147,690	69,791	Coolidge, Calvin	23,951	Davis, John W.	53,948	15,843 R	47.3%	16.2%	74.5%	25.5%
1920	138,281	91,351	Harding, Warren G.	46,930	Cox, James M.		44,421 R	66.1%	33.9%	66.1%	33.9%

In 1924 other vote was Progressive.

ELECTORAL COLLEGE VOTE 1920 TO 1984

Year	Total	Republican	Democratic	Other
1984	4	4	—	—
1980	4	4	—	—
1976	4	4	—	—
1972	4	4	—	—
1968	4	4	—	—
1964	4	—	4	—
1960	4	4	—	—
1956	4	4	—	—
1952	4	4	—	—
1948	4	—	4	—
1944	4	—	4	—
1940	4	—	4	—
1936	4	—	4	—
1932	4	—	4	—
1928	4	4	—	—
1924	4	4	—	—
1920	4	4	—	—

IDAHO

BOUNDARY
BONNER
KOOTENAI
SHOSHONE
BENEWAH
LATAH
CLEARWATER
NEZ PERCE
LEWIS
IDAHO
LEMHI
ADAMS
VALLEY
WASHINGTON
CUSTER
CLARK
FREMONT
PAYETTE
GEM
BOISE
JEFFERSON
MADISON
TETON
BUTTE
CANYON
ADA
CAMAS
BLAINE
BONNEVILLE
ELMORE
BINGHAM
GOODING
LINCOLN
MINIDOKA
CARIBOU
JEROME
POWER
BANNOCK
OWYHEE
TWIN FALLS
CASSIA
ONEIDA
BEAR LAKE
FRANKLIN

IDAHO

PRESIDENT 1984

1980 Census Population	County	Total Vote	Republican	Democratic	Other	Rep.-Dem. Plurality	Percentage Total Vote Rep.	Percentage Total Vote Dem.	Percentage Major Vote Rep.	Percentage Major Vote Dem.
173,036	ADA	82,924	60,036	21,760	1,128	38,276 R	72.4%	26.2%	73.4%	26.6%
3,347	ADAMS	1,956	1,381	540	35	841 R	70.6%	27.6%	71.9%	28.1%
65,421	BANNOCK	28,496	18,742	9,399	355	9,343 R	65.8%	33.0%	66.6%	33.4%
6,931	BEAR LAKE	3,267	2,760	481	26	2,279 R	84.5%	14.7%	85.2%	14.8%
8,292	BENEWAH	3,534	2,039	1,447	48	592 R	57.7%	40.9%	58.5%	41.5%
36,489	BINGHAM	15,116	11,900	3,064	152	8,836 R	78.7%	20.3%	79.5%	20.5%
9,841	BLAINE	5,657	3,603	1,971	83	1,632 R	63.7%	34.8%	64.6%	35.4%
2,999	BOISE	1,721	1,249	436	36	813 R	72.6%	25.3%	74.1%	25.9%
24,163	BONNER	11,699	6,889	4,628	182	2,261 R	58.9%	39.6%	59.8%	40.2%
65,980	BONNEVILLE	29,490	24,392	4,877	221	19,515 R	82.7%	16.5%	83.3%	16.7%
7,289	BOUNDARY	3,402	2,159	1,158	85	1,001 R	63.5%	34.0%	65.1%	34.9%
3,342	BUTTE	1,685	1,245	429	11	816 R	73.9%	25.5%	74.4%	25.6%
818	CAMAS	491	364	123	4	241 R	74.1%	25.1%	74.7%	25.3%
83,756	CANYON	32,587	24,613	7,527	447	17,086 R	75.5%	23.1%	76.6%	23.4%
8,695	CARIBOU	3,597	3,032	535	30	2,497 R	84.3%	14.9%	85.0%	15.0%
19,427	CASSIA	7,597	6,503	1,036	58	5,467 R	85.6%	13.6%	86.3%	13.7%
798	CLARK	415	353	59	3	294 R	85.1%	14.2%	85.7%	14.3%
10,390	CLEARWATER	3,848	2,176	1,608	64	568 R	56.5%	41.8%	57.5%	42.5%
3,385	CUSTER	2,144	1,653	461	30	1,192 R	77.1%	21.5%	78.2%	21.8%
21,565	ELMORE	6,105	4,595	1,458	52	3,137 R	75.3%	23.9%	75.9%	24.1%
8,895	FRANKLIN	3,742	3,261	439	42	2,822 R	87.1%	11.7%	88.1%	11.9%
10,813	FREMONT	4,853	4,006	818	29	3,188 R	82.5%	16.9%	83.0%	17.0%
11,972	GEM	5,350	3,644	1,607	99	2,037 R	68.1%	30.0%	69.4%	30.6%
11,874	GOODING	5,119	3,819	1,247	53	2,572 R	74.6%	24.4%	75.4%	24.6%
14,769	IDAHO	6,349	4,219	1,996	134	2,223 R	66.5%	31.4%	67.9%	32.1%
15,304	JEFFERSON	6,563	5,770	743	50	5,027 R	87.9%	11.3%	88.6%	11.4%
14,840	JEROME	6,259	4,913	1,284	62	3,629 R	78.5%	20.5%	79.3%	20.7%
59,770	KOOTENAI	26,689	17,330	9,004	355	8,326 R	64.9%	33.7%	65.8%	34.2%
28,749	LATAH	13,500	7,709	5,571	220	2,138 R	57.1%	41.3%	58.0%	42.0%
7,460	LEMHI	3,708	2,810	852	46	1,958 R	75.8%	23.0%	76.7%	23.3%
4,118	LEWIS	1,666	1,000	648	18	352 R	60.0%	38.9%	60.7%	39.3%
3,436	LINCOLN	1,615	1,211	386	18	825 R	75.0%	23.9%	75.8%	24.2%
19,480	MADISON	7,319	6,798	483	38	6,315 R	92.9%	6.6%	93.4%	6.6%
19,718	MINIDOKA	7,420	5,938	1,398	84	4,540 R	80.0%	18.8%	80.9%	19.1%
33,220	NEZ PERCE	14,330	8,153	5,981	196	2,172 R	56.9%	41.7%	57.7%	42.3%
3,258	ONEIDA	1,898	1,528	360	10	1,168 R	80.5%	19.0%	80.9%	19.1%
8,272	OWYHEE	2,755	2,141	574	40	1,567 R	77.7%	20.8%	78.9%	21.1%
15,722	PAYETTE	6,121	4,605	1,410	106	3,195 R	75.2%	23.0%	76.6%	23.4%
6,844	POWER	3,004	2,298	678	28	1,620 R	76.5%	22.6%	77.2%	22.8%
19,226	SHOSHONE	6,284	3,156	3,033	95	123 R	50.2%	48.3%	51.0%	49.0%
2,897	TETON	1,624	1,242	370	12	872 R	76.5%	22.8%	77.0%	23.0%
52,927	TWIN FALLS	21,771	16,974	4,567	230	12,407 R	78.0%	21.0%	78.8%	21.2%
5,604	VALLEY	3,286	2,299	945	42	1,354 R	70.0%	28.8%	70.9%	29.1%
8,803	WASHINGTON	4,188	3,015	1,119	54	1,896 R	72.0%	26.7%	72.9%	27.1%
943,935	TOTAL	411,144	297,523	108,510	5,111	189,013 R	72.4%	26.4%	73.3%	26.7%

IDAHO

PRESIDENT 1980

1980 Census Population	County	Total Vote	Republican	Democratic	Other	Rep.-Dem. Plurality	Percentage Total Vote Rep.	Percentage Total Vote Dem.	Percentage Major Vote Rep.	Percentage Major Vote Dem.
173,036	ADA	86,544	55,205	21,324	10,015	33,881 R	63.8%	24.6%	72.1%	27.9%
3,347	ADAMS	1,897	1,189	590	118	599 R	62.7%	31.1%	66.8%	33.2%
65,421	BANNOCK	29,859	18,477	8,639	2,743	9,838 R	61.9%	28.9%	68.1%	31.9%
6,931	BEAR LAKE	3,567	2,941	508	118	2,433 R	82.5%	14.2%	85.3%	14.7%
8,292	BENEWAH	3,846	2,111	1,361	374	750 R	54.9%	35.4%	60.8%	39.2%
36,489	BINGHAM	15,487	11,781	2,933	773	8,848 R	76.1%	18.9%	80.1%	19.9%
9,841	BLAINE	5,529	2,716	1,840	973	876 R	49.1%	33.3%	59.6%	40.4%
2,999	BOISE	1,846	1,134	518	194	616 R	61.4%	28.1%	68.6%	31.4%
24,163	BONNER	11,940	6,727	4,060	1,153	2,667 R	56.3%	34.0%	62.4%	37.6%
65,980	BONNEVILLE	31,869	24,715	5,052	2,102	19,663 R	77.6%	15.9%	83.0%	17.0%
7,289	BOUNDARY	3,513	2,088	1,087	338	1,001 R	59.4%	30.9%	65.8%	34.2%
3,342	BUTTE	1,765	1,275	424	66	851 R	72.2%	24.0%	75.0%	25.0%
818	CAMAS	530	360	145	25	215 R	67.9%	27.4%	71.3%	28.7%
83,756	CANYON	36,016	24,375	9,172	2,469	15,203 R	67.7%	25.5%	72.7%	27.3%
8,695	CARIBOU	3,892	3,234	481	177	2,753 R	83.1%	12.4%	87.1%	12.9%
19,427	CASSIA	8,259	6,511	1,369	379	5,142 R	78.8%	16.6%	82.6%	17.4%
798	CLARK	483	379	87	17	292 R	78.5%	18.0%	81.3%	18.7%
10,390	CLEARWATER	4,314	2,178	1,699	437	479 R	50.5%	39.4%	56.2%	43.8%
3,385	CUSTER	1,902	1,398	398	106	1,000 R	73.5%	20.9%	77.8%	22.2%
21,565	ELMORE	6,157	3,994	1,760	403	2,234 R	64.9%	28.6%	69.4%	30.6%
8,895	FRANKLIN	4,301	3,669	511	121	3,158 R	85.3%	11.9%	87.8%	12.2%
10,813	FREMONT	5,253	4,167	926	160	3,241 R	79.3%	17.6%	81.8%	18.2%
11,972	GEM	5,726	3,766	1,613	347	2,153 R	65.8%	28.2%	70.0%	30.0%
11,874	GOODING	5,695	3,897	1,481	317	2,416 R	68.4%	26.0%	72.5%	27.5%
14,769	IDAHO	7,073	4,425	2,078	570	2,347 R	62.6%	29.4%	68.0%	32.0%
15,304	JEFFERSON	6,933	5,860	833	240	5,027 R	84.5%	12.0%	87.6%	12.4%
14,840	JEROME	6,625	4,962	1,368	295	3,594 R	74.9%	20.6%	78.4%	21.6%
59,770	KOOTENAI	26,912	17,022	7,521	2,369	9,501 R	63.3%	27.9%	69.4%	30.6%
28,749	LATAH	14,892	6,967	5,037	2,888	1,930 R	46.8%	33.8%	58.0%	42.0%
7,460	LEMHI	3,699	2,646	794	259	1,852 R	71.5%	21.5%	76.9%	23.1%
4,118	LEWIS	2,053	1,088	774	191	314 R	53.0%	37.7%	58.4%	41.6%
3,436	LINCOLN	1,872	1,294	462	116	832 R	69.1%	24.7%	73.7%	26.3%
19,480	MADISON	7,414	6,555	728	131	5,827 R	88.4%	9.8%	90.0%	10.0%
19,718	MINIDOKA	8,131	6,035	1,689	407	4,346 R	74.2%	20.8%	78.1%	21.9%
33,220	NEZ PERCE	15,744	7,495	6,565	1,684	930 R	47.6%	41.7%	53.3%	46.7%
3,258	ONEIDA	1,970	1,461	434	75	1,027 R	74.2%	22.0%	77.1%	22.9%
8,272	OWYHEE	3,140	2,257	732	151	1,525 R	71.9%	23.3%	75.5%	24.5%
15,722	PAYETTE	6,714	4,508	1,828	378	2,680 R	67.1%	27.2%	71.1%	28.9%
6,844	POWER	3,143	2,235	727	181	1,508 R	71.1%	23.1%	75.5%	24.5%
19,226	SHOSHONE	7,675	3,994	3,102	579	892 R	52.0%	40.4%	56.3%	43.7%
2,897	TETON	1,686	1,227	360	99	867 R	72.8%	21.4%	77.3%	22.7%
52,927	TWIN FALLS	23,708	17,425	4,835	1,448	12,590 R	73.5%	20.4%	78.3%	21.7%
5,604	VALLEY	3,272	2,041	926	305	1,115 R	62.4%	28.3%	68.8%	31.2%
8,803	WASHINGTON	4,585	2,915	1,421	249	1,494 R	63.6%	31.0%	67.2%	32.8%
943,935	TOTAL	437,431	290,699	110,192	36,540	180,507 R	66.5%	25.2%	72.5%	27.5%

IDAHO

PRESIDENT 1976

1970 Census Population	County	Total Vote	Republican	Democratic	Other	Rep.-Dem. Plurality	Percentage Total Vote Rep.	Total Vote Dem.	Major Vote Rep.	Major Vote Dem.
112,230	ADA	64,530	41,135	21,125	2,270	20,010 R	63.7%	32.7%	66.1%	33.9%
2,877	ADAMS	1,492	809	639	44	170 R	54.2%	42.8%	55.9%	44.1%
52,200	BANNOCK	24,706	13,172	10,261	1,273	2,911 R	53.3%	41.5%	56.2%	43.8%
5,801	BEAR LAKE	3,154	2,094	960	100	1,134 R	66.4%	30.4%	68.6%	31.4%
6,230	BENEWAH	3,092	1,458	1,549	85	91 D	47.2%	50.1%	48.5%	51.5%
29,167	BINGHAM	12,121	7,327	4,347	447	2,980 R	60.4%	35.9%	62.8%	37.2%
5,749	BLAINE	3,966	2,176	1,604	186	572 R	54.9%	40.4%	57.6%	42.4%
1,763	BOISE	1,167	684	433	50	251 R	58.6%	37.1%	61.2%	38.8%
15,560	BONNER	8,897	4,549	4,065	283	484 R	51.1%	45.7%	52.8%	47.2%
52,457	BONNEVILLE	24,018	15,793	7,230	995	8,563 R	65.8%	30.1%	68.6%	31.4%
5,484	BOUNDARY	2,837	1,458	1,217	162	241 R	51.4%	42.9%	54.5%	45.5%
2,925	BUTTE	1,491	751	663	77	88 R	50.4%	44.5%	53.1%	46.9%
728	CAMAS	464	288	160	16	128 R	62.1%	34.5%	64.3%	35.7%
61,288	CANYON	27,813	17,263	9,460	1,090	7,803 R	62.1%	34.0%	64.6%	35.4%
6,534	CARIBOU	3,523	2,253	1,110	160	1,143 R	64.0%	31.5%	67.0%	33.0%
17,017	CASSIA	6,909	4,575	1,881	453	2,694 R	66.2%	27.2%	70.9%	29.1%
741	CLARK	524	334	169	21	165 R	63.7%	32.3%	66.4%	33.6%
10,871	CLEARWATER	3,342	1,469	1,752	121	283 D	44.0%	52.4%	45.6%	54.4%
2,967	CUSTER	1,421	850	516	55	334 R	59.8%	36.3%	62.2%	37.8%
17,479	ELMORE	5,122	2,808	2,164	150	644 R	54.8%	42.2%	56.5%	43.5%
7,373	FRANKLIN	4,080	2,720	1,157	203	1,563 R	66.7%	28.4%	70.2%	29.8%
8,710	FREMONT	4,232	2,581	1,445	206	1,136 R	61.0%	34.1%	64.1%	35.9%
9,387	GEM	4,605	2,401	1,978	226	423 R	52.1%	43.0%	54.8%	45.2%
8,645	GOODING	5,035	2,909	1,923	203	986 R	57.8%	38.2%	60.2%	39.8%
12,891	IDAHO	5,750	3,185	2,323	242	862 R	55.4%	40.4%	57.8%	42.2%
11,740	JEFFERSON	5,593	3,599	1,745	249	1,854 R	64.3%	31.2%	67.3%	32.7%
10,253	JEROME	5,192	3,188	1,800	204	1,388 R	61.4%	34.7%	63.9%	36.1%
35,332	KOOTENAI	18,317	10,493	7,225	599	3,268 R	57.3%	39.4%	59.2%	40.8%
24,891	LATAH	12,741	6,846	5,314	581	1,532 R	53.7%	41.7%	56.3%	43.7%
5,566	LEMHI	3,052	1,685	1,159	208	526 R	55.2%	38.0%	59.2%	40.8%
3,867	LEWIS	1,787	824	898	65	74 D	46.1%	50.3%	47.9%	52.1%
3,057	LINCOLN	1,593	909	615	69	294 R	57.1%	38.6%	59.6%	40.4%
13,452	MADISON	5,823	4,190	1,320	313	2,870 R	72.0%	22.7%	76.0%	24.0%
15,731	MINIDOKA	6,378	3,600	2,441	337	1,159 R	56.4%	38.3%	59.6%	40.4%
30,376	NEZ PERCE	12,819	6,151	6,324	344	173 D	48.0%	49.3%	49.3%	50.7%
2,864	ONEIDA	1,755	1,065	637	53	428 R	60.7%	36.3%	62.6%	37.4%
6,422	OWYHEE	2,649	1,519	1,054	76	465 R	57.3%	39.8%	59.0%	41.0%
12,401	PAYETTE	5,463	3,115	2,195	153	920 R	57.0%	40.2%	58.7%	41.3%
4,864	POWER	2,750	1,374	1,286	90	88 R	50.0%	46.8%	51.7%	48.3%
19,718	SHOSHONE	6,909	3,570	3,216	123	354 R	51.7%	46.5%	52.6%	47.4%
2,351	TETON	1,434	904	514	16	390 R	63.0%	35.8%	63.8%	36.2%
41,807	TWIN FALLS	19,298	12,659	6,085	554	6,574 R	65.6%	31.5%	67.5%	32.5%
3,609	VALLEY	2,366	1,374	897	95	477 R	58.1%	37.9%	60.5%	39.5%
7,633	WASHINGTON	3,861	2,044	1,693	124	351 R	52.9%	43.8%	54.7%	45.3%
713,008	TOTAL	344,071	204,151	126,549	13,371	77,602 R	59.3%	36.8%	61.7%	38.3%

IDAHO

PRESIDENT 1972

1970 Census Population	County	Total Vote	Republican	Democratic	Other	Rep.-Dem. Plurality	Percentage Total Vote Rep.	Percentage Total Vote Dem.	Percentage Major Vote Rep.	Percentage Major Vote Dem.
112,230	ADA	54,311	36,665	12,687	4,959	23,978 R	67.5%	23.4%	74.3%	25.7%
2,877	ADAMS	1,421	963	293	165	670 R	67.8%	20.6%	76.7%	23.3%
52,200	BANNOCK	22,191	12,856	7,840	1,495	5,016 R	57.9%	35.3%	62.1%	37.9%
5,801	BEAR LAKE	3,185	2,213	716	256	1,497 R	69.5%	22.5%	75.6%	24.4%
6,230	BENEWAH	2,690	1,494	1,062	134	432 R	55.5%	39.5%	58.5%	41.5%
29,167	BINGHAM	10,705	6,886	2,476	1,343	4,410 R	64.3%	23.1%	73.6%	26.4%
5,749	BLAINE	3,465	2,113	1,240	112	873 R	61.0%	35.8%	63.0%	37.0%
1,763	BOISE	1,020	676	256	88	420 R	66.3%	25.1%	72.5%	27.5%
15,560	BONNER	7,665	4,405	2,599	661	1,806 R	57.5%	33.9%	62.9%	37.1%
52,457	BONNEVILLE	21,466	13,134	4,199	4,133	8,935 R	61.2%	19.6%	75.8%	24.2%
5,484	BOUNDARY	2,678	1,587	860	231	727 R	59.3%	32.1%	64.9%	35.1%
2,925	BUTTE	1,396	788	387	221	401 R	56.4%	27.7%	67.1%	32.9%
728	CAMAS	463	344	95	24	249 R	74.3%	20.5%	78.4%	21.6%
61,288	CANYON	26,857	18,383	5,630	2,844	12,753 R	68.4%	21.0%	76.6%	23.4%
6,534	CARIBOU	2,958	2,069	614	275	1,455 R	69.9%	20.8%	77.1%	22.9%
17,017	CASSIA	6,162	4,576	1,080	506	3,496 R	74.3%	17.5%	80.9%	19.1%
741	CLARK	456	339	64	53	275 R	74.3%	14.0%	84.1%	15.9%
10,871	CLEARWATER	3,138	1,590	1,412	136	178 R	50.7%	45.0%	53.0%	47.0%
2,967	CUSTER	1,432	989	274	169	715 R	69.1%	19.1%	78.3%	21.7%
17,479	ELMORE	4,625	3,078	1,153	394	1,925 R	66.6%	24.9%	72.7%	27.3%
7,373	FRANKLIN	3,893	2,787	611	495	2,176 R	71.6%	15.7%	82.0%	18.0%
8,710	FREMONT	4,270	2,621	819	830	1,802 R	61.4%	19.2%	76.2%	23.8%
9,387	GEM	4,431	2,717	1,069	645	1,648 R	61.3%	24.1%	71.8%	28.2%
8,645	GOODING	4,417	3,124	1,030	263	2,094 R	70.7%	23.3%	75.2%	24.8%
12,891	IDAHO	5,201	3,235	1,622	344	1,613 R	62.2%	31.2%	66.6%	33.4%
11,740	JEFFERSON	5,110	2,983	715	1,412	2,268 R	58.4%	14.0%	80.7%	19.3%
10,253	JEROME	4,874	3,661	888	325	2,773 R	75.1%	18.2%	80.5%	19.5%
35,332	KOOTENAI	16,238	9,958	5,162	1,118	4,796 R	61.3%	31.8%	65.9%	34.1%
24,891	LATAH	10,918	6,043	4,548	327	1,495 R	55.3%	41.7%	57.1%	42.9%
5,566	LEMHI	2,923	1,812	526	585	1,286 R	62.0%	18.0%	77.5%	22.5%
3,867	LEWIS	1,687	961	635	91	326 R	57.0%	37.6%	60.2%	39.8%
3,057	LINCOLN	1,506	1,120	313	73	807 R	74.4%	20.8%	78.2%	21.8%
13,452	MADISON	5,216	3,606	710	900	2,896 R	69.1%	13.6%	83.5%	16.5%
15,731	MINIDOKA	5,967	4,097	1,423	447	2,674 R	68.7%	23.8%	74.2%	25.8%
30,376	NEZ PERCE	11,941	6,232	5,081	628	1,151 R	52.2%	42.6%	55.1%	44.9%
2,864	ONEIDA	1,685	1,204	402	79	802 R	71.5%	23.9%	75.0%	25.0%
6,422	OWYHEE	2,324	1,630	463	231	1,167 R	70.1%	19.9%	77.9%	22.1%
12,401	PAYETTE	5,272	3,577	1,113	582	2,464 R	67.8%	21.1%	76.3%	23.7%
4,864	POWER	2,180	1,405	625	150	780 R	64.4%	28.7%	69.2%	30.8%
19,718	SHOSHONE	7,207	3,868	3,020	319	848 R	53.7%	41.9%	56.2%	43.8%
2,351	TETON	1,359	932	298	129	634 R	68.6%	21.9%	75.8%	24.2%
41,807	TWIN FALLS	17,673	13,075	3,344	1,254	9,731 R	74.0%	18.9%	79.6%	20.4%
3,609	VALLEY	2,151	1,324	537	290	787 R	61.6%	25.0%	71.1%	28.9%
7,633	WASHINGTON	3,652	2,264	935	453	1,329 R	62.0%	25.6%	70.8%	29.2%
713,008	TOTAL	310,379	199,384	80,826	30,169	118,558 R	64.2%	26.0%	71.2%	28.8%

IDAHO

PRESIDENT 1968

1960 Census Population	County	Total Vote	Republican	Democratic	AIP	Other	Plurality	Percentage Rep.	Dem.	AIP
93,460	ADA	47,881	30,185	11,529	6,167		18,656 R	63.0%	24.1%	12.9%
2,978	ADAMS	1,431	844	360	227		484 R	59.0%	25.2%	15.9%
49,342	BANNOCK	21,334	10,234	9,084	2,016		1,150 R	48.0%	42.6%	9.4%
7,148	BEAR LAKE	3,101	1,866	1,058	177		808 R	60.2%	34.1%	5.7%
6,036	BENEWAH	2,533	1,125	1,160	248		35 D	44.4%	45.8%	9.8%
28,218	BINGHAM	10,765	6,484	2,988	1,293		3,496 R	60.2%	27.8%	12.0%
4,598	BLAINE	2,484	1,337	815	332		522 R	53.8%	32.8%	13.4%
1,646	BOISE	809	450	205	154		245 R	55.6%	25.3%	19.0%
15,587	BONNER	7,082	3,240	3,063	779		177 R	45.7%	43.3%	11.0%
46,906	BONNEVILLE	21,050	13,582	5,178	2,290		8,404 R	64.5%	24.6%	10.9%
5,809	BOUNDARY	2,297	1,084	883	330		201 R	47.2%	38.4%	14.4%
3,498	BUTTE	1,356	691	521	144		170 R	51.0%	38.4%	10.6%
917	CAMAS	482	271	118	93		153 R	56.2%	24.5%	19.3%
57,662	CANYON	23,898	14,995	5,717	3,186		9,278 R	62.7%	23.9%	13.3%
5,976	CARIBOU	2,785	1,731	727	327		1,004 R	62.2%	26.1%	11.7%
16,121	CASSIA	6,525	4,187	1,350	988		2,837 R	64.2%	20.7%	15.1%
915	CLARK	407	271	87	49		184 R	66.6%	21.4%	12.0%
8,548	CLEARWATER	3,468	1,287	1,838	343		551 D	37.1%	53.0%	9.9%
2,996	CUSTER	1,423	711	385	327		326 R	50.0%	27.1%	23.0%
16,719	ELMORE	3,769	1,908	1,230	631		678 R	50.6%	32.6%	16.7%
8,457	FRANKLIN	3,795	2,509	831	455		1,678 R	66.1%	21.9%	12.0%
8,679	FREMONT	3,925	2,297	961	667		1,336 R	58.5%	24.5%	17.0%
9,127	GEM	3,997	2,314	1,183	500		1,131 R	57.9%	29.6%	12.5%
9,544	GOODING	4,228	2,349	1,018	861		1,331 R	55.6%	24.1%	20.4%
13,542	IDAHO	4,914	2,317	1,883	714		434 R	47.2%	38.3%	14.5%
11,672	JEFFERSON	4,761	2,927	955	879		1,972 R	61.5%	20.1%	18.5%
11,712	JEROME	4,602	2,785	976	841		1,809 R	60.5%	21.2%	18.3%
29,556	KOOTENAI	14,771	7,092	6,207	1,472		885 R	48.0%	42.0%	10.0%
21,170	LATAH	9,126	4,708	3,782	636		926 R	51.6%	41.4%	7.0%
5,816	LEMHI	2,562	1,476	547	539		929 R	57.6%	21.4%	21.0%
4,423	LEWIS	1,801	697	927	177		230 D	38.7%	51.5%	9.8%
3,686	LINCOLN	1,545	972	350	223		622 R	62.9%	22.7%	14.4%
9,417	MADISON	4,388	2,971	904	513		2,067 R	67.7%	20.6%	11.7%
14,394	MINIDOKA	5,654	3,182	1,332	1,140		1,850 R	56.3%	23.6%	20.2%
27,066	NEZ PERCE	12,579	5,019	6,502	1,058		1,483 D	39.9%	51.7%	8.4%
3,603	ONEIDA	1,684	1,114	465	105		649 R	66.2%	27.6%	6.2%
6,375	OWYHEE	2,323	1,385	562	376		823 R	59.6%	24.2%	16.2%
12,363	PAYETTE	4,956	3,032	1,216	708		1,816 R	61.2%	24.5%	14.3%
4,111	POWER	2,028	1,222	582	224		640 R	60.3%	28.7%	11.0%
20,876	SHOSHONE	7,587	3,080	3,850	657		770 D	40.6%	50.7%	8.7%
2,639	TETON	1,198	694	376	128		318 R	57.9%	31.4%	10.7%
41,842	TWIN FALLS	18,373	11,564	4,001	2,808		7,563 R	62.9%	21.8%	15.3%
3,663	VALLEY	2,002	1,160	534	308		626 R	57.9%	26.7%	15.4%
8,378	WASHINGTON	3,504	2,020	1,033	451		987 R	57.6%	29.5%	12.9%
667,191	TOTAL	291,183	165,369	89,273	36,541		76,096 R	56.8%	30.7%	12.5%

IDAHO

ELECTION NOTES

1984 Other vote was 2,823 Bergland (Libertarian); 2,288 Richards (Populist).

1980 Other vote was 27,058 Anderson (Independent); 8,425 Clark (Libertarian); 1,057 Rarick (American).

1976 Other vote was 5,935 Maddox (American); 3,558 MacBride (Libertarian); 1,194 McCarthy (write-in); 739 LaRouche (U.S. Labor); 493 Anderson (write-in); 14 Camejo (write-in); 5 Hall (write-in); 2 Zeidler (write-in); 1 Wright (write-in); 1,430 scattered write-in. The write-in vote for McCarthy in Bannock county was amended from 82 to 74 which changed his state-wide total from 1,202 to the vote given above.

1972 Other vote was 28,869 Schmitz (American); 903 Spock (Peace and Freedom); 397 Jenness (Socialist Workers). In using the Republican-Democratic plurality figures, it should be noted that the American candidate ran second in Fremont, Jefferson, Lemhi and Madison counties.

1968 Wallace on the ballot as American Independent.

ILLINOIS

POPULAR VOTE FOR PRESIDENT 1920 TO 1984

Year	Total Vote	Republican Vote	Republican Candidate	Democratic Vote	Democratic Candidate	Other Vote	Plurality	Percentage Total Vote Rep.	Percentage Total Vote Dem.	Percentage Major Vote Rep.	Percentage Major Vote Dem.
1984	4,819,088	2,707,103	Reagan, Ronald	2,086,499	Mondale, Walter F.	25,486	620,604 R	56.2%	43.3%	56.5%	43.5%
1980	4,749,721	2,358,049	Reagan, Ronald	1,981,413	Carter, Jimmy	410,259	376,636 R	49.6%	41.7%	54.3%	45.7%
1976	4,718,914	2,364,269	Ford, Gerald R.	2,271,295	Carter, Jimmy	83,350	92,974 R	50.1%	48.1%	51.0%	49.0%
1972	4,723,236	2,788,179	Nixon, Richard M.	1,913,472	McGovern, George S.	21,585	874,707 R	59.0%	40.5%	59.3%	40.7%
1968	4,619,749	2,174,774	Nixon, Richard M.	2,039,814	Humphrey, Hubert H.	405,161	134,960 R	47.1%	44.2%	51.6%	48.4%
1964	4,702,841	1,905,946	Goldwater, Barry M.	2,796,833	Johnson, Lyndon B.	62	890,887 D	40.5%	59.5%	40.5%	59.5%
1960	4,757,409	2,368,988	Nixon, Richard M.	2,377,846	Kennedy, John F.	10,575	8,858 D	49.8%	50.0%	49.9%	50.1%
1956	4,407,407	2,623,327	Eisenhower, Dwight D.	1,775,682	Stevenson, Adlai E.	8,398	847,645 R	59.5%	40.3%	59.6%	40.4%
1952	4,481,058	2,457,327	Eisenhower, Dwight D.	2,013,920	Stevenson, Adlai E.	9,811	443,407 R	54.8%	44.9%	55.0%	45.0%
1948	3,984,046	1,961,103	Dewey, Thomas E.	1,994,715	Truman, Harry S.	28,228	33,612 D	49.2%	50.1%	49.6%	50.4%
1944	4,036,061	1,939,314	Dewey, Thomas E.	2,079,479	Roosevelt, Franklin D.	17,268	140,165 D	48.0%	51.5%	48.3%	51.7%
1940	4,217,935	2,047,240	Willkie, Wendell	2,149,934	Roosevelt, Franklin D.	20,761	102,694 D	48.5%	51.0%	48.8%	51.2%
1936	3,956,522	1,570,393	Landon, Alfred M.	2,282,999	Roosevelt, Franklin D.	103,130	712,606 D	39.7%	57.7%	40.8%	59.2%
1932	3,407,926	1,432,756	Hoover, Herbert C.	1,882,304	Roosevelt, Franklin D.	92,866	449,548 D	42.0%	55.2%	43.2%	56.8%
1928	3,107,489	1,769,141	Hoover, Herbert C.	1,313,817	Smith, Alfred E.	24,531	455,324 R	56.9%	42.3%	57.4%	42.6%
1924 **	2,470,067	1,453,321	Coolidge, Calvin	576,975	Davis, John W.	439,771	876,346 R	58.8%	23.4%	71.6%	28.4%
1920	2,094,714	1,420,480	Harding, Warren G.	534,395	Cox, James M.	139,839	886,085 R	67.8%	25.5%	72.7%	27.3%

In 1924 other vote was 432,027 Progressive; 2,622 Communist; 2,367 Prohibition; 2,334 Socialist Labor and 421 Commonwealth Land.

ELECTORAL COLLEGE VOTE 1920 TO 1984

Year	Total	Republican	Democratic	Other
1984	24	24	—	—
1980	26	26	—	—
1976	26	26	—	—
1972	26	26	—	—
1968	26	26	—	—
1964	26	—	26	—
1960	27	—	27	—
1956	27	27	—	—
1952	27	27	—	—
1948	28	—	28	—
1944	28	—	28	—
1940	29	—	29	—
1936	29	—	29	—
1932	29	—	29	—
1928	29	29	—	—
1924	29	29	—	—
1920	29	29	—	—

ILLINOIS

JO DAVIESS
STEPHENSON
WINNEBAGO
BOONE
McHENRY
LAKE
CARROLL
OGLE
DE KALB
KANE
DU PAGE
COOK
WHITESIDE
LEE
KENDALL
WILL
ROCK ISLAND
HENRY
BUREAU
LA SALLE
GRUNDY
MERCER
PUTNAM
KANKAKEE
STARK
MARSHALL
LIVINGSTON
HENDERSON
WARREN
KNOX
PEORIA
WOODFORD
IROQUOIS
HANCOCK
McDONOUGH
FULTON
TAZEWELL
McLEAN
FORD
MASON
SCHUYLER
DE WITT
CHAMPAIGN
VERMILION
LOGAN
ADAMS
BROWN
CASS
MENARD
PIATT
MACON
DOUGLAS
SANGAMON
MORGAN
MOULTRIE
EDGAR
PIKE
SCOTT
CHRISTIAN
COLES
SHELBY
GREENE
CLARK
MACOUPIN
MONTGOMERY
CUMBER-
LAND
CALHOUN
JERSEY
FAYETTE
EFFINGHAM
JASPER
CRAWFORD
BOND
MADISON
CLAY
RICHLAND
LAWRENCE
MARION
CLINTON
WAYNE
EDWARDS
WABASH
ST. CLAIR
WASHINGTON
JEFFERSON
MONROE
WHITE
RANDOLPH
PERRY
FRANKLIN
HAMILTON
JACKSON
SALINE
GALLATIN
WILLIAMSON
HARDIN
UNION
JOHNSON
POPE
ALEX-
ANDER
PULASKI
MASSAC

ILLINOIS

PRESIDENT 1984

1980 Census Population	County	Total Vote	Republican	Democratic	Other	Rep.-Dem. Plurality	Percentage Total Vote Rep.	Percentage Total Vote Dem.	Percentage Major Vote Rep.	Percentage Major Vote Dem.
71,622	ADAMS	30,649	20,225	10,336	88	9,889 R	66.0%	33.7%	66.2%	33.8%
12,264	ALEXANDER	5,467	2,574	2,872	21	298 D	47.1%	52.5%	47.3%	52.7%
16,224	BOND	7,131	4,240	2,870	21	1,370 R	59.5%	40.2%	59.6%	40.4%
28,630	BOONE	11,306	7,536	3,717	53	3,819 R	66.7%	32.9%	67.0%	33.0%
5,411	BROWN	2,446	1,478	959	9	519 R	60.4%	39.2%	60.6%	39.4%
39,114	BUREAU	18,765	11,741	6,925	99	4,816 R	62.6%	36.9%	62.9%	37.1%
5,867	CALHOUN	3,107	1,648	1,443	16	205 R	53.0%	46.4%	53.3%	46.7%
18779	CARROLL	7,658	5,237	2,398	23	2,839 R	68.4%	31.3%	68.6%	31.4%
15,084	CASS	6,399	3,435	2,937	27	498 R	53.7%	45.9%	53.9%	46.1%
168,392	CHAMPAIGN	66,925	39,224	27,266	435	11,958 R	58.6%	40.7%	59.0%	41.0%
36,446	CHRISTIAN	16,152	8,534	7,541	77	993 R	52.8%	46.7%	53.1%	46.9%
16,913	CLARK	8,382	5,318	3,032	32	2,286 R	63.4%	36.2%	63.7%	36.3%
15,283	CLAY	7,104	4,562	2,524	18	2,038 R	64.2%	35.5%	64.4%	35.6%
32,617	CLINTON	13,899	9,233	4,628	38	4,605 R	66.4%	33.3%	66.6%	33.4%
52,260	COLES	21,295	14,044	7,156	95	6,888 R	65.9%	33.6%	66.2%	33.8%
5,253,655	COOK	2,180,735	1,055,558	1,112,641	12,536	57,083 D	48.4%	51.0%	48.7%	51.3%
20,818	CRAWFORD	9,424	6,261	3,130	33	3,131 R	66.4%	33.2%	66.7%	33.3%
11,062	CUMBERLAND	4,762	3,002	1,733	27	1,269 R	63.0%	36.4%	63.4%	36.6%
74,624	DE KALB	31,465	20,294	10,942	229	9,352 R	64.5%	34.8%	65.0%	35.0%
18,108	DE WITT	6,915	4,534	2,352	29	2,182 R	65.6%	34.0%	65.8%	34.2%
19,774	DOUGLAS	8,604	5,691	2,886	27	2,805 R	66.1%	33.5%	66.4%	33.6%
658,835	DU PAGE	300,215	227,141	71,430	1,644	155,711 R	75.7%	23.8%	76.1%	23.9%
21,725	EDGAR	10,099	6,821	3,241	37	3,580 R	67.5%	32.1%	67.8%	32.2%
7,961	EDWARDS	3,845	2,778	1,057	10	1,721 R	72.2%	27.5%	72.4%	27.6%
30,944	EFFINGHAM	13,504	9,617	3,841	46	5,776 R	71.2%	28.4%	71.5%	28.5%
22,167	FAYETTE	10,473	6,607	3,844	22	2,763 R	63.1%	36.7%	63.2%	36.8%
15,265	FORD	6,663	4,871	1,763	29	3,108 R	73.1%	26.5%	73.4%	26.6%
43,201	FRANKLIN	20,377	9,656	10,667	54	1,011 D	47.4%	52.3%	47.5%	52.5%
43,687	FULTON	18,377	9,147	9,131	99	16 R	49.8%	49.7%	50.0%	50.0%
7,590	GALLATIN	4,112	1,939	2,164	9	225 D	47.2%	52.6%	47.3%	52.7%
16,661	GREENE	6,655	4,057	2,563	35	1,494 R	61.0%	38.5%	61.3%	38.7%
30,582	GRUNDY	14,325	9,595	4,671	59	4,924 R	67.0%	32.6%	67.3%	32.7%
9,172	HAMILTON	5,346	3,074	2,251	21	823 R	57.5%	42.1%	57.7%	42.3%
23,877	HANCOCK	10,001	6,251	3,713	37	2,538 R	62.5%	37.1%	62.7%	37.3%
5,383	HARDIN	2,899	1,689	1,205	5	484 R	58.3%	41.6%	58.4%	41.6%
9,114	HENDERSON	4,278	2,289	1,969	20	320 R	53.5%	46.0%	53.8%	46.2%
57,968	HENRY	25,262	14,504	10,679	79	3,825 R	57.4%	42.3%	57.6%	42.4%
32,976	IROQUOIS	14,685	11,327	3,300	58	8,027 R	77.1%	22.5%	77.4%	22.6%
61,522	JACKSON	25,896	13,609	12,105	182	1,504 R	52.6%	46.7%	52.9%	47.1%
11,318	JASPER	5,454	3,673	1,750	31	1,923 R	67.3%	32.1%	67.7%	32.3%
36,552	JEFFERSON	16,885	9,642	7,200	43	2,442 R	57.1%	42.6%	57.2%	42.8%
20,538	JERSEY	8,934	5,146	3,762	26	1,384 R	57.6%	42.1%	57.8%	42.2%
23,520	JO DAVIESS	9,302	5,877	3,348	77	2,529 R	63.2%	36.0%	63.7%	36.3%
9,624	JOHNSON	5,083	3,424	1,647	12	1,777 R	67.4%	32.4%	67.5%	32.5%
278,405	KANE	105,159	72,655	31,875	629	40,780 R	69.1%	30.3%	69.5%	30.5%
102,926	KANKAKEE	39,665	23,807	15,246	612	8,561 R	60.0%	38.4%	61.0%	39.0%
37,202	KENDALL	14,730	10,872	3,789	69	7,083 R	73.8%	25.7%	74.2%	25.8%
61,607	KNOX	27,122	14,974	12,027	121	2,947 R	55.2%	44.3%	55.5%	44.5%
440,372	LAKE	173,224	118,401	53,947	876	64,454 R	68.4%	31.1%	68.7%	31.3%
112,033	LA SALLE	48,139	27,388	20,532	219	6,856 R	56.9%	42.7%	57.2%	42.8%
17,807	LAWRENCE	7,638	4,686	2,924	28	1,762 R	61.4%	38.3%	61.6%	38.4%
36,328	LEE	15,155	11,178	3,919	58	7,259 R	73.8%	25.9%	74.0%	26.0%
41,381	LIVINGSTON	16,919	12,291	4,567	61	7,724 R	72.6%	27.0%	72.9%	27.1%
31,802	LOGAN	14,046	9,932	4,052	62	5,880 R	70.7%	28.8%	71.0%	29.0%
37,467	MCDONOUGH	14,001	9,383	4,561	57	4,822 R	67.0%	32.6%	67.3%	32.7%
147,897	MCHENRY	62,042	47,282	14,420	340	32,862 R	76.2%	23.2%	76.6%	23.4%
119,149	MCLEAN	48,349	32,221	15,880	248	16,341 R	66.6%	32.8%	67.0%	33.0%
131,375	MACON	56,112	30,457	25,463	192	4,994 R	54.3%	45.4%	54.5%	45.5%
49,384	MACOUPIN	22,953	12,282	10,602	69	1,680 R	53.5%	46.2%	53.7%	46.3%
247,691	MADISON	105,713	57,021	48,352	340	8,669 R	53.9%	45.7%	54.1%	45.9%

ILLINOIS

PRESIDENT 1984

1980 Census Population	County	Total Vote	Republican	Democratic	Other	Rep.-Dem. Plurality	Percentage Total Vote Rep.	Total Vote Dem.	Major Vote Rep.	Major Vote Dem.
43,523	MARION	18,945	11,300	7,599	46	3,701 R	59.6%	40.1%	59.8%	40.2%
14,479	MARSHALL	6,493	4,060	2,386	47	1,674 R	62.5%	36.7%	63.0%	37.0%
19,492	MASON	7,486	4,109	3,354	23	755 R	54.9%	44.8%	55.1%	44.9%
14,990	MASSAC	7,049	3,827	3,194	28	633 R	54.3%	45.3%	54.5%	45.5%
11,700	MENARD	5,766	3,925	1,826	15	2,099 R	68.1%	31.7%	68.2%	31.8%
19,286	MERCER	8,927	4,907	3,982	38	925 R	55.0%	44.6%	55.2%	44.8%
20,117	MONROE	10,217	6,936	3,256	25	3,680 R	67.9%	31.9%	68.1%	31.9%
31,686	MONTGOMERY	14,605	8,191	6,360	54	1,831 R	56.1%	43.5%	56.3%	43.7%
37,502	MORGAN	16,097	10,683	5,361	53	5,322 R	66.4%	33.3%	66.6%	33.4%
14,546	MOULTRIE	6,072	3,593	2,458	21	1,135 R	59.2%	40.5%	59.4%	40.6%
46,338	OGLE	18,396	13,503	4,803	90	8,700 R	73.4%	26.1%	73.8%	26.2%
200,466	PEORIA	82,899	45,607	36,830	462	8,777 R	55.0%	44.4%	55.3%	44.7%
21,714	PERRY	10,472	5,852	4,584	36	1,268 R	55.9%	43.8%	56.1%	43.9%
16,581	PIATT	7,879	5,000	2,840	39	2,160 R	63.5%	36.0%	63.8%	36.2%
18,896	PIKE	9,285	5,295	3,965	25	1,330 R	57.0%	42.7%	57.2%	42.8%
4,404	POPE	2,492	1,545	940	7	605 R	62.0%	37.7%	62.2%	37.8%
8,840	PULASKI	3,664	1,923	1,724	17	199 R	52.5%	47.1%	52.7%	47.3%
6,085	PUTNAM	3,413	1,912	1,487	14	425 R	56.0%	43.6%	56.3%	43.7%
35,652	RANDOLPH	15,829	9,415	6,355	59	3,060 R	59.5%	40.1%	59.7%	40.3%
17,587	RICHLAND	7,874	5,665	2,182	27	3,483 R	71.9%	27.7%	72.2%	27.8%
165,968	ROCK ISLAND	75,672	35,121	40,208	343	5,087 D	46.4%	53.1%	46.6%	53.4%
267,531	ST. CLAIR	104,148	51,046	52,294	808	1,248 D	49.0%	50.2%	49.4%	50.6%
28,448	SALINE	13,251	7,176	6,038	37	1,138 R	54.2%	45.6%	54.3%	45.7%
176,089	SANGAMON	88,523	54,086	34,059	378	20,027 R	61.1%	38.5%	61.4%	38.6%
8,365	SCHUYLER	4,061	2,515	1,533	13	982 R	61.9%	37.7%	62.1%	37.9%
6,142	SCOTT	2,935	1,976	943	16	1,033 R	67.3%	32.1%	67.7%	32.3%
23,923	SHELBY	10,730	6,372	4,317	41	2,055 R	59.4%	40.2%	59.6%	40.4%
7,389	STARK	3,318	2,228	1,072	18	1,156 R	67.1%	32.3%	67.5%	32.5%
49,536	STEPHENSON	21,131	14,237	6,723	171	7,514 R	67.4%	31.8%	67.9%	32.1%
132,078	TAZEWELL	57,115	33,782	23,095	238	10,687 R	59.1%	40.4%	59.4%	40.6%
17,765	UNION	8,564	4,721	3,815	28	906 R	55.1%	44.5%	55.3%	44.7%
95,222	VERMILION	39,611	22,932	16,530	149	6,402 R	57.9%	41.7%	58.1%	41.9%
13,713	WABASH	5,453	3,639	1,795	19	1,844 R	66.7%	32.9%	67.0%	33.0%
21,943	WARREN	9,193	5,846	3,318	29	2,528 R	63.6%	36.1%	63.8%	36.2%
15,472	WASHINGTON	7,516	5,129	2,363	24	2,766 R	68.2%	31.4%	68.5%	31.5%
18,059	WAYNE	8,951	6,298	2,621	32	3,677 R	70.4%	29.3%	70.6%	29.4%
17,864	WHITE	8,983	5,500	3,457	26	2,043 R	61.2%	38.5%	61.4%	38.6%
65,970	WHITESIDE	28,096	16,743	11,226	127	5,517 R	59.6%	40.0%	59.9%	40.1%
324,460	WILL	124,397	78,684	45,193	520	33,491 R	63.3%	36.3%	63.5%	36.5%
56,538	WILLIAMSON	26,630	14,930	11,614	86	3,316 R	56.1%	43.6%	56.2%	43.8%
250,884	WINNEBAGO	109,451	64,203	44,629	619	19,574 R	58.7%	40.8%	59.0%	41.0%
33,320	WOODFORD	15,272	10,758	4,425	89	6,333 R	70.4%	29.0%	70.9%	29.1%
11,426,518	TOTAL	4,819,088	2,707,103	2,086,499	25,486	620,604 R	56.2%	43.3%	56.5%	43.5%

ILLINOIS

PRESIDENT 1980

1980 Census Population	County	Total Vote	Republican	Democratic	Other	Rep.-Dem. Plurality	Percentage Total Vote Rep.	Total Vote Dem.	Major Vote Rep.	Major Vote Dem.
71,622	ADAMS	31,917	19,842	10,606	1,469	9,236 R	62.2%	33.2%	65.2%	34.8%
12,264	ALEXANDER	5,678	2,650	2,925	103	275 D	46.7%	51.5%	47.5%	52.5%
16,224	BOND	7,532	4,398	2,834	300	1,564 R	58.4%	37.6%	60.8%	39.2%
28,630	BOONE	11,614	6,697	3,175	1,742	3,522 R	57.7%	27.3%	67.8%	32.2%
5,411	BROWN	2,692	1,660	950	82	710 R	61.7%	35.3%	63.6%	36.4%
39,114	BUREAU	18,587	11,484	5,753	1,350	5,731 R	61.8%	31.0%	66.6%	33.4%
5,867	CALHOUN	2,895	1,591	1,208	96	383 R	55.0%	41.7%	56.8%	43.2%
18,779	CARROLL	8,023	5,084	2,154	785	2,930 R	63.4%	26.8%	70.2%	29.8%
15,084	CASS	6,770	3,965	2,543	262	1,422 R	58.6%	37.6%	60.9%	39.1%
168,392	CHAMPAIGN	65,360	33,329	21,017	11,014	12,312 R	51.0%	32.2%	61.3%	38.7%
36,446	CHRISTIAN	16,036	8,770	6,625	641	2,145 R	54.7%	41.3%	57.0%	43.0%
16,913	CLARK	8,666	5,476	2,855	335	2,621 R	63.2%	32.9%	65.7%	34.3%
15,283	CLAY	7,266	4,447	2,587	232	1,860 R	61.2%	35.6%	63.2%	36.8%
32,617	CLINTON	13,593	8,500	4,470	623	4,030 R	62.5%	32.9%	65.5%	34.5%
52,260	COLES	20,671	11,994	6,743	1,934	5,251 R	58.0%	32.6%	64.0%	36.0%
5,253,655	COOK	2,163,097	856,574	1,124,584	181,939	268,010 D	39.6%	52.0%	43.2%	56.8%
20,818	CRAWFORD	9,710	5,894	3,372	444	2,522 R	60.7%	34.7%	63.6%	36.4%
11,062	CUMBERLAND	5,289	3,159	1,892	238	1,267 R	59.7%	35.8%	62.5%	37.5%
74,624	DE KALB	30,365	16,370	8,913	5,082	7,457 R	53.9%	29.4%	64.7%	35.3%
18,108	DE WITT	7,344	4,648	2,262	434	2,386 R	63.3%	30.8%	67.3%	32.7%
19,774	DOUGLAS	8,294	5,330	2,564	400	2,766 R	64.3%	30.9%	67.5%	32.5%
658,835	DU PAGE	284,749	182,308	68,991	33,450	113,317 R	64.0%	24.2%	72.5%	27.5%
21,725	EDGAR	10,515	6,639	3,394	482	3,245 R	63.1%	32.3%	66.2%	33.8%
7,961	EDWARDS	3,751	2,556	1,041	154	1,515 R	68.1%	27.8%	71.1%	28.9%
30,944	EFFINGHAM	13,808	9,104	4,229	475	4,875 R	65.9%	30.6%	68.3%	31.7%
22,167	FAYETTE	10,408	6,523	3,614	271	2,909 R	62.7%	34.7%	64.3%	35.7%
15,265	FORD	7,214	5,024	1,803	387	3,221 R	69.6%	25.0%	73.6%	26.4%
43,201	FRANKLIN	19,856	9,731	9,425	700	306 R	49.0%	47.5%	50.8%	49.2%
43,687	FULTON	18,957	10,316	7,481	1,160	2,835 R	54.4%	39.5%	58.0%	42.0%
7,590	GALLATIN	3,466	1,700	1,678	88	22 R	49.0%	48.4%	50.3%	49.7%
16,661	GREENE	7,120	4,224	2,607	289	1,617 R	59.3%	36.6%	61.8%	38.2%
30,582	GRUNDY	13,204	8,397	3,970	837	4,427 R	63.6%	30.1%	67.9%	32.1%
9,172	HAMILTON	5,456	3,254	1,990	212	1,264 R	59.6%	36.5%	62.1%	37.9%
23,877	HANCOCK	10,585	6,597	3,522	466	3,075 R	62.3%	33.3%	65.2%	34.8%
5,383	HARDIN	3,114	1,721	1,314	79	407 R	55.3%	42.2%	56.7%	43.3%
9,114	HENDERSON	4,246	2,443	1,609	194	834 R	57.5%	37.9%	60.3%	39.7%
57,968	HENRY	24,206	14,506	7,977	1,723	6,529 R	59.9%	33.0%	64.5%	35.5%
32,976	IROQUOIS	15,327	11,247	3,362	718	7,885 R	73.4%	21.9%	77.0%	23.0%
61,522	JACKSON	23,829	10,505	10,291	3,033	214 R	44.1%	43.2%	50.5%	49.5%
11,318	JASPER	5,612	3,548	1,846	218	1,702 R	63.2%	32.9%	65.8%	34.2%
36,552	JEFFERSON	16,340	8,972	6,761	607	2,211 R	54.9%	41.4%	57.0%	43.0%
20,538	JERSEY	8,985	5,266	3,324	395	1,942 R	58.6%	37.0%	61.3%	38.7%
23,520	JO DAVIESS	8,971	5,186	2,678	1,107	2,508 R	57.8%	29.9%	65.9%	34.1%
9,624	JOHNSON	4,888	3,201	1,586	101	1,615 R	65.5%	32.4%	66.9%	33.1%
278,405	KANE	103,784	64,106	29,015	10,663	35,091 R	61.8%	28.0%	68.8%	31.2%
102,926	KANKAKEE	40,873	23,810	14,626	2,437	9,184 R	58.3%	35.8%	61.9%	38.1%
37,202	KENDALL	14,327	10,028	3,143	1,156	6,885 R	70.0%	21.9%	76.1%	23.9%
61,607	KNOX	26,198	14,907	8,749	2,542	6,158 R	56.9%	33.4%	63.0%	37.0%
440,372	LAKE	164,853	96,350	48,287	20,216	48,063 R	58.4%	29.3%	66.6%	33.4%
112,033	LA SALLE	47,835	27,323	16,818	3,694	10,505 R	57.1%	35.2%	61.9%	38.1%
17,807	LAWRENCE	7,856	4,453	3,030	373	1,423 R	56.7%	38.6%	59.5%	40.5%
36,328	LEE	15,438	11,373	3,170	895	8,203 R	73.7%	20.5%	78.2%	21.8%
41,381	LIVINGSTON	16,823	11,544	4,111	1,168	7,433 R	68.6%	24.4%	73.7%	26.3%
31,802	LOGAN	14,366	9,681	3,916	769	5,765 R	67.4%	27.3%	71.2%	28.8%
37,467	MCDONOUGH	14,589	8,995	4,093	1,501	4,902 R	61.7%	28.1%	68.7%	31.3%
147,897	MCHENRY	61,655	40,045	14,540	7,070	25,505 R	65.0%	23.6%	73.4%	26.6%
119,149	MCLEAN	49,232	30,096	13,587	5,549	16,509 R	61.1%	27.6%	68.9%	31.1%
131,375	MACON	53,956	28,298	22,325	3,333	5,973 R	52.4%	41.4%	55.9%	44.1%
49,384	MACOUPIN	22,354	12,131	9,116	1,107	3,015 R	54.3%	40.8%	57.1%	42.9%
247,691	MADISON	100,124	51,160	43,860	5,104	7,300 R	51.1%	43.8%	53.8%	46.2%

ILLINOIS

PRESIDENT 1980

1980 Census Population	County	Total Vote	Republican	Democratic	Other	Rep.-Dem. Plurality	Percentage Total Vote Rep.	Total Vote Dem.	Major Vote Rep.	Major Vote Dem.
43,523	MARION	18,678	10,969	6,990	719	3,979 R	58.7%	37.4%	61.1%	38.9%
14,479	MARSHALL	6,711	4,349	1,903	459	2,446 R	64.8%	28.4%	69.6%	30.4%
19,492	MASON	7,693	4,644	2,680	369	1,964 R	60.4%	34.8%	63.4%	36.6%
14,990	MASSAC	7,272	4,284	2,821	167	1,463 R	58.9%	38.8%	60.3%	39.7%
11,700	MENARD	5,534	3,622	1,589	323	2,033 R	65.4%	28.7%	69.5%	30.5%
19,286	MERCER	9,156	5,144	3,361	651	1,783 R	56.2%	36.7%	60.5%	39.5%
20,117	MONROE	9,924	6,315	3,121	488	3,194 R	63.6%	31.4%	66.9%	33.1%
31,686	MONTGOMERY	15,415	8,947	5,721	747	3,226 R	58.0%	37.1%	61.0%	39.0%
37,502	MORGAN	16,997	10,406	5,483	1,108	4,923 R	61.2%	32.3%	65.5%	34.5%
14,546	MOULTRIE	6,161	3,495	2,332	334	1,163 R	56.7%	37.9%	60.0%	40.0%
46,338	OGLE	18,871	12,533	4,067	2,271	8,466 R	66.4%	21.6%	75.5%	24.5%
200,466	PEORIA	83,510	47,815	28,276	7,419	19,539 R	57.3%	33.9%	62.8%	37.2%
21,714	PERRY	10,610	5,888	4,337	385	1,551 R	55.5%	40.9%	57.6%	42.4%
16,581	PIATT	7,818	4,867	2,421	530	2,446 R	62.3%	31.0%	66.8%	33.2%
18,896	PIKE	9,361	5,301	3,695	365	1,606 R	56.6%	39.5%	58.9%	41.1%
4,404	POPE	2,455	1,501	880	74	621 R	61.1%	35.8%	63.0%	37.0%
8,840	PULASKI	4,099	2,083	1,955	61	128 R	50.8%	47.7%	51.6%	48.4%
6,085	PUTNAM	3,414	1,959	1,158	297	801 R	57.4%	33.9%	62.8%	37.2%
35,652	RANDOLPH	15,494	8,810	6,052	632	2,758 R	56.9%	39.1%	59.3%	40.7%
17,587	RICHLAND	8,126	5,241	2,463	422	2,778 R	64.5%	30.3%	68.0%	32.0%
165,968	ROCK ISLAND	71,775	34,788	30,045	6,942	4,743 R	48.5%	41.9%	53.7%	46.3%
267,531	ST. CLAIR	100,673	46,063	50,046	4,564	3,983 D	45.8%	49.7%	47.9%	52.1%
28,448	SALINE	13,265	7,157	5,683	425	1,474 R	54.0%	42.8%	55.7%	44.3%
176,089	SANGAMON	85,200	49,372	29,354	6,474	20,018 R	57.9%	34.5%	62.7%	37.3%
8,365	SCHUYLER	4,460	2,799	1,445	216	1,354 R	62.8%	32.4%	66.0%	34.0%
6,142	SCOTT	3,042	1,990	941	111	1,049 R	65.4%	30.9%	67.9%	32.1%
23,923	SHELBY	10,894	6,441	3,988	465	2,453 R	59.1%	36.6%	61.8%	38.2%
7,389	STARK	3,380	2,358	806	216	1,552 R	69.8%	23.8%	74.5%	25.5%
49,536	STEPHENSON	20,388	10,779	6,195	3,414	4,584 R	52.9%	30.4%	63.5%	36.5%
132,078	TAZEWELL	56,462	35,481	16,924	4,057	18,557 R	62.8%	30.0%	67.7%	32.3%
17,765	UNION	8,441	4,289	3,781	371	508 R	50.8%	44.8%	53.1%	46.9%
95,222	VERMILION	39,567	22,579	14,498	2,490	8,081 R	57.1%	36.6%	60.9%	39.1%
13,713	WABASH	5,837	3,571	1,975	291	1,596 R	61.2%	33.8%	64.4%	35.6%
21,943	WARREN	9,071	5,667	2,756	648	2,911 R	62.5%	30.4%	67.3%	32.7%
15,472	WASHINGTON	7,762	5,354	2,158	250	3,196 R	69.0%	27.8%	71.3%	28.7%
18,059	WAYNE	9,557	6,013	3,258	286	2,755 R	62.9%	34.1%	64.9%	35.1%
17,864	WHITE	9,072	5,279	3,463	330	1,816 R	58.2%	38.2%	60.4%	39.6%
65,970	WHITESIDE	26,064	17,389	7,191	1,484	10,198 R	66.7%	27.6%	70.7%	29.3%
324,460	WILL	120,658	69,310	41,975	9,373	27,335 R	57.4%	34.8%	62.3%	37.7%
56,538	WILLIAMSON	26,228	14,451	10,779	998	3,672 R	55.1%	41.1%	57.3%	42.7%
250,884	WINNEBAGO	105,089	48,825	32,384	23,880	16,441 R	46.5%	30.8%	60.1%	39.9%
33,320	WOODFORD	15,268	10,791	3,552	925	7,239 R	70.7%	23.3%	75.2%	24.8%
11,426,518	TOTAL	4,749,721	2,358,049	1,981,413	410,259	376,636 R	49.6%	41.7%	54.3%	45.7%

ILLINOIS

PRESIDENT 1976

1970 Census Population	County	Total Vote	Republican	Democratic	Other	Rep.-Dem. Plurality	Percentage Total Vote Rep.	Percentage Total Vote Dem.	Percentage Major Vote Rep.	Percentage Major Vote Dem.
70,861	ADAMS	30,485	18,189	11,926	370	6,263 R	59.7%	39.1%	60.4%	39.6%
12,015	ALEXANDER	5,658	2,349	3,246	63	897 D	41.5%	57.4%	42.0%	58.0%
14,012	BOND	7,478	3,716	3,682	80	34 R	49.7%	49.2%	50.2%	49.8%
25,440	BOONE	11,082	6,470	4,458	154	2,012 R	58.4%	40.2%	59.2%	40.8%
5,586	BROWN	3,103	1,519	1,533	51	14 D	49.0%	49.4%	49.8%	50.2%
38,541	BUREAU	18,648	10,854	7,566	228	3,288 R	58.2%	40.6%	58.9%	41.1%
5,675	CALHOUN	2,943	1,364	1,549	30	185 D	46.3%	52.6%	46.8%	53.2%
19,276	CARROLL	8,526	5,059	3,372	95	1,687 R	59.3%	39.5%	60.0%	40.0%
14,219	CASS	7,144	3,524	3,589	31	65 D	49.3%	50.2%	49.5%	50.5%
163,281	CHAMPAIGN	63,107	34,546	26,858	1,703	7,688 R	54.7%	42.6%	56.3%	43.7%
35,948	CHRISTIAN	16,960	7,445	9,306	209	1,861 D	43.9%	54.9%	44.4%	55.6%
16,216	CLARK	8,622	4,506	4,071	45	435 R	52.3%	47.2%	52.5%	47.5%
14,735	CLAY	7,729	3,860	3,837	32	23 R	49.9%	49.6%	50.1%	49.9%
28,315	CLINTON	13,671	7,245	6,275	151	970 R	53.0%	45.9%	53.6%	46.4%
47,815	COLES	20,162	11,021	8,639	502	2,382 R	54.7%	42.8%	56.1%	43.9%
5,492,369	COOK	2,209,581	987,498	1,180,814	41,269	193,316 D	44.7%	53.4%	45.5%	54.5%
19,824	CRAWFORD	10,622	5,522	5,007	93	515 R	52.0%	47.1%	52.4%	47.6%
9,772	CUMBERLAND	5,344	2,518	2,752	74	234 D	47.1%	51.5%	47.8%	52.2%
71,654	DE KALB	30,728	18,193	11,535	1,000	6,658 R	59.2%	37.5%	61.2%	38.8%
16,975	DE WITT	7,666	4,137	3,477	52	660 R	54.0%	45.4%	54.3%	45.7%
18,997	DOUGLAS	8,522	4,635	3,826	61	809 R	54.4%	44.9%	54.8%	45.2%
491,882	DU PAGE	254,547	175,055	72,137	7,355	102,918 R	68.8%	28.3%	70.8%	29.2%
21,591	EDGAR	11,021	5,842	5,058	121	784 R	53.0%	45.9%	53.6%	46.4%
7,090	EDWARDS	4,066	2,379	1,648	39	731 R	58.5%	40.5%	59.1%	40.9%
24,608	EFFINGHAM	13,391	7,194	5,952	245	1,242 R	53.7%	44.4%	54.7%	45.3%
20,752	FAYETTE	10,255	5,059	5,128	68	69 D	49.3%	50.0%	49.7%	50.3%
16,382	FORD	7,553	4,801	2,690	62	2,111 R	63.6%	35.6%	64.1%	35.9%
38,329	FRANKLIN	20,324	7,420	12,818	86	5,398 D	36.5%	63.1%	36.7%	63.3%
41,890	FULTON	19,090	9,588	9,314	188	274 R	50.2%	48.8%	50.7%	49.3%
7,418	GALLATIN	4,123	1,499	2,611	13	1,112 D	36.4%	63.3%	36.5%	63.5%
17,014	GREENE	7,827	3,706	4,057	64	351 D	47.3%	51.8%	47.7%	52.3%
26,535	GRUNDY	13,201	7,581	5,534	86	2,047 R	57.4%	41.9%	57.8%	42.2%
8,665	HAMILTON	5,498	2,433	3,036	29	603 D	44.3%	55.2%	44.5%	55.5%
23,645	HANCOCK	10,881	6,043	4,730	108	1,313 R	55.5%	43.5%	56.1%	43.9%
4,914	HARDIN	3,017	1,393	1,602	22	209 D	46.2%	53.1%	46.5%	53.5%
8,451	HENDERSON	4,407	2,210	2,152	45	58 R	50.1%	48.8%	50.7%	49.3%
53,217	HENRY	22,934	12,849	9,822	263	3,027 R	56.0%	42.8%	56.7%	43.3%
33,532	IROQUOIS	15,481	10,129	5,167	185	4,962 R	65.4%	33.4%	66.2%	33.8%
55,008	JACKSON	24,122	10,152	12,940	1,030	2,788 D	42.1%	53.6%	44.0%	56.0%
10,741	JASPER	5,650	2,794	2,772	84	22 R	49.5%	49.1%	50.2%	49.8%
31,446	JEFFERSON	16,520	7,422	8,989	109	1,567 D	44.9%	54.4%	45.2%	54.8%
18,492	JERSEY	8,983	4,273	4,625	85	352 D	47.6%	51.5%	48.0%	52.0%
21,766	JO DAVIESS	9,628	5,478	3,979	171	1,499 R	56.9%	41.3%	57.9%	42.1%
7,550	JOHNSON	4,628	2,417	2,182	29	235 R	52.2%	47.1%	52.6%	47.4%
251,005	KANE	95,374	59,275	34,057	2,042	25,218 R	62.2%	35.7%	63.5%	36.5%
97,250	KANKAKEE	42,108	23,003	18,394	711	4,609 R	54.6%	43.7%	55.6%	44.4%
26,374	KENDALL	13,349	9,011	4,202	136	4,809 R	67.5%	31.5%	68.2%	31.8%
61,280	KNOX	25,967	14,123	11,525	319	2,598 R	54.4%	44.4%	55.1%	44.9%
382,638	LAKE	153,204	92,231	57,741	3,232	34,490 R	60.2%	37.7%	61.5%	38.5%
111,409	LA SALLE	48,865	25,114	23,105	646	2,009 R	51.4%	47.3%	52.1%	47.9%
17,522	LAWRENCE	8,442	4,345	4,044	53	301 R	51.5%	47.9%	51.8%	48.2%
37,947	LEE	15,076	8,674	6,076	326	2,598 R	57.5%	40.3%	58.8%	41.2%
40,690	LIVINGSTON	15,640	10,097	5,174	369	4,923 R	64.6%	33.1%	66.1%	33.9%
33,538	LOGAN	14,386	8,623	5,686	77	2,937 R	59.9%	39.5%	60.3%	39.7%
36,653	MCDONOUGH	15,534	9,683	5,464	387	4,219 R	62.3%	35.2%	63.9%	36.1%
111,555	MCHENRY	54,989	37,115	16,799	1,075	20,316 R	67.5%	30.5%	68.8%	31.2%
104,389	MCLEAN	45,879	28,493	16,601	785	11,892 R	62.1%	36.2%	63.2%	36.8%
125,010	MACON	53,599	24,893	28,243	463	3,350 D	46.4%	52.7%	46.8%	53.2%
44,557	MACOUPIN	22,486	10,242	11,910	334	1,668 D	45.5%	53.0%	46.2%	53.8%
250,934	MADISON	101,998	44,183	56,457	1,358	12,274 D	43.3%	55.4%	43.9%	56.1%

ILLINOIS

PRESIDENT 1976

1970 Census Population	County	Total Vote	Republican	Democratic	Other	Rep.-Dem. Plurality	Percentage Total Vote Rep.	Total Vote Dem.	Major Vote Rep.	Major Vote Dem.
38,986	MARION	18,720	8,729	9,834	157	1,105 D	46.6%	52.5%	47.0%	53.0%
13,302	MARSHALL	6,662	4,017	2,570	75	1,447 R	60.3%	38.6%	61.0%	39.0%
16,161	MASON	7,849	3,847	3,947	55	100 D	49.0%	50.3%	49.4%	50.6%
13,889	MASSAC	6,937	3,226	3,666	45	440 D	46.5%	52.8%	46.8%	53.2%
9,685	MENARD	5,479	3,137	2,301	41	836 R	57.3%	42.0%	57.7%	42.3%
17,294	MERCER	8,982	4,816	4,090	76	726 R	53.6%	45.5%	54.1%	45.9%
18,831	MONROE	9,716	5,602	3,984	130	1,618 R	57.7%	41.0%	58.4%	41.6%
30,260	MONTGOMERY	15,848	7,379	8,322	147	943 D	46.6%	52.5%	47.0%	53.0%
36,174	MORGAN	16,489	8,885	7,403	201	1,482 R	53.9%	44.9%	54.5%	45.5%
13,263	MOULTRIE	6,169	2,803	3,332	34	529 D	45.4%	54.0%	45.7%	54.3%
42,867	OGLE	17,797	11,073	6,463	261	4,610 R	62.2%	36.3%	63.1%	36.9%
195,318	PEORIA	82,123	46,526	34,606	991	11,920 R	56.7%	42.1%	57.3%	42.7%
19,757	PERRY	11,395	5,286	5,976	133	690 D	46.4%	52.4%	46.9%	53.1%
15,509	PIATT	8,020	4,442	3,509	69	933 R	55.4%	43.8%	55.9%	44.1%
19,185	PIKE	10,110	4,975	5,006	129	31 D	49.2%	49.5%	49.8%	50.2%
3,857	POPE	2,275	1,187	1,070	18	117 R	52.2%	47.0%	52.6%	47.4%
8,741	PULASKI	4,345	1,836	2,489	20	653 D	42.3%	57.3%	42.5%	57.5%
5,007	PUTNAM	2,959	1,572	1,344	43	228 R	53.1%	45.4%	53.9%	46.1%
31,379	RANDOLPH	17,038	8,190	8,693	155	503 D	48.1%	51.0%	48.5%	51.5%
16,829	RICHLAND	8,057	4,434	3,485	138	949 R	55.0%	43.3%	56.0%	44.0%
166,734	ROCK ISLAND	71,261	34,007	35,994	1,260	1,987 D	47.7%	50.5%	48.6%	51.4%
285,176	ST. CLAIR	101,065	40,333	59,177	1,555	18,844 D	39.9%	58.6%	40.5%	59.5%
25,721	SALINE	13,493	5,970	7,472	51	1,502 D	44.2%	55.4%	44.4%	55.6%
161,335	SANGAMON	82,910	43,309	38,017	1,584	5,292 R	52.2%	45.9%	53.3%	46.7%
8,135	SCHUYLER	4,669	2,635	2,014	20	621 R	56.4%	43.1%	56.7%	43.3%
6,096	SCOTT	3,232	1,789	1,424	19	365 R	55.4%	44.1%	55.7%	44.3%
22,589	SHELBY	11,493	5,234	6,172	87	938 D	45.5%	53.7%	45.9%	54.1%
7,510	STARK	3,459	2,191	1,146	122	1,045 R	63.3%	33.1%	65.7%	34.3%
48,861	STEPHENSON	19,137	11,678	7,192	267	4,486 R	61.0%	37.6%	61.9%	38.1%
118,649	TAZEWELL	52,503	28,951	22,821	731	6,130 R	55.1%	43.5%	55.9%	44.1%
16,071	UNION	8,578	3,531	5,003	44	1,472 D	41.2%	58.3%	41.4%	58.6%
97,047	VERMILION	38,546	19,751	18,438	357	1,313 R	51.2%	47.8%	51.7%	48.3%
12,841	WABASH	6,227	3,388	2,781	58	607 R	54.4%	44.7%	54.9%	45.1%
21,595	WARREN	9,826	5,822	3,808	196	2,014 R	59.3%	38.8%	60.5%	39.5%
13,780	WASHINGTON	7,843	4,485	3,222	136	1,263 R	57.2%	41.1%	58.2%	41.8%
17,004	WAYNE	9,581	5,211	4,303	67	908 R	54.4%	44.9%	54.8%	45.2%
17,312	WHITE	9,933	4,600	5,306	27	706 D	46.3%	53.4%	46.4%	53.6%
62,877	WHITESIDE	25,854	14,308	11,255	291	3,053 R	55.3%	43.5%	56.0%	44.0%
249,498	WILL	114,695	61,784	51,103	1,808	10,681 R	53.9%	44.6%	54.7%	45.3%
49,021	WILLIAMSON	24,553	10,703	13,600	250	2,897 D	43.6%	55.4%	44.0%	56.0%
246,623	WINNEBAGO	97,360	52,736	42,399	2,225	10,337 R	54.2%	43.5%	55.4%	44.6%
28,012	WOODFORD	13,902	8,899	4,819	184	4,080 R	64.0%	34.7%	64.9%	35.1%
11,113,976	TOTAL	4,718,914	2,364,269	2,271,295	83,350	92,974 R	50.1%	48.1%	51.0%	49.0%

ILLINOIS

PRESIDENT 1972

1970 Census Population	County	Total Vote	Republican	Democratic	Other	Rep.-Dem. Plurality	Percentage Total Vote Rep.	Percentage Total Vote Dem.	Percentage Major Vote Rep.	Percentage Major Vote Dem.
70,861	ADAMS	29,846	20,731	9,055	60	11,676 R	69.5%	30.3%	69.6%	30.4%
12,015	ALEXANDER	6,209	3,669	2,482	58	1,187 R	59.1%	40.0%	59.6%	40.4%
14,012	BOND	7,183	4,475	2,704	4	1,771 R	62.3%	37.6%	62.3%	37.7%
25,440	BOONE	10,165	7,003	3,131	31	3,872 R	68.9%	30.8%	69.1%	30.9%
5,586	BROWN	3,022	1,780	1,203	39	577 R	58.9%	39.8%	59.7%	40.3%
38,541	BUREAU	18,952	12,786	6,133	33	6,653 R	67.5%	32.4%	67.6%	32.4%
5,675	CALHOUN	3,017	1,705	1,299	13	406 R	56.5%	43.1%	56.8%	43.2%
19,276	CARROLL	8,631	6,041	2,571	19	3,470 R	70.0%	29.8%	70.1%	29.9%
14,219	CASS	7,219	4,414	2,803	2	1,611 R	61.1%	38.8%	61.2%	38.8%
163,281	CHAMPAIGN	58,679	33,700	24,743	236	8,957 R	57.4%	42.2%	57.7%	42.3%
35,948	CHRISTIAN	17,675	10,072	7,556	47	2,516 R	57.0%	42.7%	57.1%	42.9%
16,216	CLARK	8,680	5,706	2,965	9	2,741 R	65.7%	34.2%	65.8%	34.2%
14,735	CLAY	8,138	5,283	2,844	11	2,439 R	64.9%	34.9%	65.0%	35.0%
28,315	CLINTON	12,712	7,931	4,756	25	3,175 R	62.4%	37.4%	62.5%	37.5%
47,815	COLES	21,751	13,681	7,988	82	5,693 R	62.9%	36.7%	63.1%	36.9%
5,492,369	COOK	2,311,037	1,234,307	1,063,268	13,462	171,039 R	53.4%	46.0%	53.7%	46.3%
19,824	CRAWFORD	10,055	6,568	3,477	10	3,091 R	65.3%	34.6%	65.4%	34.6%
9,772	CUMBERLAND	5,358	3,257	2,083	18	1,174 R	60.8%	38.9%	61.0%	39.0%
71,654	DE KALB	31,384	18,910	12,375	99	6,535 R	60.3%	39.4%	60.4%	39.6%
16,975	DE WITT	7,705	5,025	2,672	8	2,353 R	65.2%	34.7%	65.3%	34.7%
18,997	DOUGLAS	8,506	5,840	2,656	10	3,184 R	68.7%	31.2%	68.7%	31.3%
491,882	DU PAGE	229,739	172,341	57,043	355	115,298 R	75.0%	24.8%	75.1%	24.9%
21,591	EDGAR	11,116	7,195	3,889	32	3,306 R	64.7%	35.0%	64.9%	35.1%
7,090	EDWARDS	4,081	3,017	1,055	9	1,962 R	73.9%	25.9%	74.1%	25.9%
24,608	EFFINGHAM	13,193	8,752	4,431	10	4,321 R	66.3%	33.6%	66.4%	33.6%
20,752	FAYETTE	10,768	6,574	4,192	2	2,382 R	61.1%	38.9%	61.1%	38.9%
16,382	FORD	7,591	5,656	1,934	1	3,722 R	74.5%	25.5%	74.5%	25.5%
38,329	FRANKLIN	18,729	10,121	8,545	63	1,576 R	54.0%	45.6%	54.2%	45.8%
41,890	FULTON	19,949	12,328	7,529	92	4,799 R	61.8%	37.7%	62.1%	37.9%
7,418	GALLATIN	4,001	2,148	1,844	9	304 R	53.7%	46.1%	53.8%	46.2%
17,014	GREENE	7,521	4,673	2,824	24	1,849 R	62.1%	37.5%	62.3%	37.7%
26,535	GRUNDY	12,341	8,725	3,584	32	5,141 R	70.7%	29.0%	70.9%	29.1%
8,665	HAMILTON	5,299	3,282	2,006	11	1,276 R	61.9%	37.9%	62.1%	37.9%
23,645	HANCOCK	11,129	7,519	3,592	18	3,927 R	67.6%	32.3%	67.7%	32.3%
4,914	HARDIN	3,062	1,915	1,140	7	775 R	62.5%	37.2%	62.7%	37.3%
8,451	HENDERSON	4,436	2,689	1,744	3	945 R	60.6%	39.3%	60.7%	39.3%
53,217	HENRY	23,185	14,796	8,368	21	6,428 R	63.8%	36.1%	63.9%	36.1%
33,532	IROQUOIS	15,784	11,995	3,723	66	8,272 R	76.0%	23.6%	76.3%	23.7%
55,008	JACKSON	25,594	12,393	13,146	55	753 D	48.4%	51.4%	48.5%	51.5%
10,741	JASPER	5,657	3,461	2,114	82	1,347 R	61.2%	37.4%	62.1%	37.9%
31,446	JEFFERSON	15,905	9,448	6,396	61	3,052 R	59.4%	40.2%	59.6%	40.4%
18,492	JERSEY	8,507	5,164	3,317	26	1,847 R	60.7%	39.0%	60.9%	39.1%
21,766	JO DAVIESS	9,097	5,763	3,318	16	2,445 R	63.4%	36.5%	63.5%	36.5%
7,550	JOHNSON	4,123	2,826	1,293	4	1,533 R	68.5%	31.4%	68.6%	31.4%
251,005	KANE	92,377	64,546	27,525	306	37,021 R	69.9%	29.8%	70.1%	29.9%
97,250	KANKAKEE	40,373	26,866	13,434	73	13,432 R	66.5%	33.3%	66.7%	33.3%
26,374	KENDALL	11,917	9,373	2,525	19	6,848 R	78.7%	21.2%	78.8%	21.2%
61,280	KNOX	26,766	17,315	9,333	118	7,982 R	64.7%	34.9%	65.0%	35.0%
382,638	LAKE	139,812	92,052	47,416	344	44,636 R	65.8%	33.9%	66.0%	34.0%
111,409	LA SALLE	52,687	31,190	21,405	92	9,785 R	59.2%	40.6%	59.3%	40.7%
17,522	LAWRENCE	8,181	5,347	2,818	16	2,529 R	65.4%	34.4%	65.5%	34.5%
37,947	LEE	15,489	10,636	4,788	65	5,848 R	68.7%	30.9%	69.0%	31.0%
40,690	LIVINGSTON	18,339	13,217	5,110	12	8,107 R	72.1%	27.9%	72.1%	27.9%
33,538	LOGAN	14,692	10,277	4,395	20	5,882 R	69.9%	29.9%	70.0%	30.0%
36,653	MCDONOUGH	15,738	10,573	5,143	22	5,430 R	67.2%	32.7%	67.3%	32.7%
111,555	MCHENRY	48,312	36,114	12,090	108	24,024 R	74.8%	25.0%	74.9%	25.1%
104,389	MCLEAN	45,955	31,060	14,824	71	16,236 R	67.6%	32.3%	67.7%	32.3%
125,010	MACON	50,029	29,596	20,296	137	9,300 R	59.2%	40.6%	59.3%	40.7%
44,557	MACOUPIN	23,407	13,583	9,662	162	3,921 R	58.0%	41.3%	58.4%	41.6%
250,934	MADISON	99,116	55,385	43,289	442	12,096 R	55.9%	43.7%	56.1%	43.9%

ILLINOIS

PRESIDENT 1972

1970 Census Population	County	Total Vote	Republican	Democratic	Other	Rep.-Dem. Plurality	Percentage Total Vote Rep.	Total Vote Dem.	Major Vote Rep.	Major Vote Dem.
38,986	MARION	17,754	10,755	6,968	31	3,787 R	60.6%	39.2%	60.7%	39.3%
13,302	MARSHALL	6,602	4,452	2,141	9	2,311 R	67.4%	32.4%	67.5%	32.5%
16,161	MASON	7,810	4,897	2,901	12	1,996 R	62.7%	37.1%	62.8%	37.2%
13,889	MASSAC	6,162	4,313	1,831	18	2,482 R	70.0%	29.7%	70.2%	29.8%
9,685	MENARD	5,263	3,657	1,587	19	2,070 R	69.5%	30.2%	69.7%	30.3%
17,294	MERCER	8,940	5,452	3,477	11	1,975 R	61.0%	38.9%	61.1%	38.9%
18,831	MONROE	9,466	6,479	2,958	29	3,521 R	68.4%	31.2%	68.7%	31.3%
30,260	MONTGOMERY	15,913	9,025	6,858	30	2,167 R	56.7%	43.1%	56.8%	43.2%
36,174	MORGAN	16,789	11,103	5,674	12	5,429 R	66.1%	33.8%	66.2%	33.8%
13,263	MOULTRIE	5,507	3,143	2,350	14	793 R	57.1%	42.7%	57.2%	42.8%
42,867	OGLE	18,290	13,512	4,743	35	8,769 R	73.9%	25.9%	74.0%	26.0%
195,318	PEORIA	78,032	50,324	27,264	444	23,060 R	64.5%	34.9%	64.9%	35.1%
19,757	PERRY	11,064	6,968	4,084	12	2,884 R	63.0%	36.9%	63.0%	37.0%
15,509	PIATT	7,468	5,057	2,394	17	2,663 R	67.7%	32.1%	67.9%	32.1%
19,185	PIKE	9,863	5,940	3,883	40	2,057 R	60.2%	39.4%	60.5%	39.5%
3,857	POPE	2,218	1,440	773	5	667 R	64.9%	34.9%	65.1%	34.9%
8,741	PULASKI	4,193	2,485	1,683	25	802 R	59.3%	40.1%	59.6%	40.4%
5,007	PUTNAM	2,787	1,665	1,112	10	553 R	59.7%	39.9%	60.0%	40.0%
31,379	RANDOLPH	16,215	9,761	6,440	14	3,321 R	60.2%	39.7%	60.2%	39.8%
16,829	RICHLAND	8,125	5,558	2,553	14	3,005 R	68.4%	31.4%	68.5%	31.5%
166,734	ROCK ISLAND	70,330	37,548	32,529	253	5,019 R	53.4%	46.3%	53.6%	46.4%
285,176	ST. CLAIR	98,097	50,519	46,636	942	3,883 R	51.5%	47.5%	52.0%	48.0%
25,721	SALINE	12,918	7,660	5,226	32	2,434 R	59.3%	40.5%	59.4%	40.6%
161,335	SANGAMON	77,075	50,458	25,720	897	24,738 R	65.5%	33.4%	66.2%	33.8%
8,135	SCHUYLER	4,534	2,994	1,534	6	1,460 R	66.0%	33.8%	66.1%	33.9%
6,096	SCOTT	3,376	2,228	1,145	3	1,083 R	66.0%	33.9%	66.1%	33.9%
22,589	SHELBY	11,626	7,217	4,389	20	2,828 R	62.1%	37.8%	62.2%	37.8%
7,510	STARK	3,540	2,529	993	18	1,536 R	71.4%	28.1%	71.8%	28.2%
48,861	STEPHENSON	20,019	13,584	6,404	31	7,180 R	67.9%	32.0%	68.0%	32.0%
118,649	TAZEWELL	47,613	31,937	15,576	100	16,361 R	67.1%	32.7%	67.2%	32.8%
16,071	UNION	8,480	5,034	3,428	18	1,606 R	59.4%	40.4%	59.5%	40.5%
97,047	VERMILION	39,425	24,863	14,413	149	10,450 R	63.1%	36.6%	63.3%	36.7%
12,841	WABASH	6,306	4,310	1,985	11	2,325 R	68.3%	31.5%	68.5%	31.5%
21,595	WARREN	10,008	7,021	2,969	18	4,052 R	70.2%	29.7%	70.3%	29.7%
13,780	WASHINGTON	7,522	5,179	2,327	16	2,852 R	68.9%	30.9%	69.0%	31.0%
17,004	WAYNE	9,175	6,400	2,763	12	3,637 R	69.8%	30.1%	69.8%	30.2%
17,312	WHITE	9,746	6,052	3,678	16	2,374 R	62.1%	37.7%	62.2%	37.8%
62,877	WHITESIDE	25,301	17,305	7,909	87	9,396 R	68.4%	31.3%	68.6%	31.4%
249,498	WILL	99,218	65,155	33,633	430	31,522 R	65.7%	33.9%	66.0%	34.0%
49,021	WILLIAMSON	23,329	14,101	9,202	26	4,899 R	60.4%	39.4%	60.5%	39.5%
246,623	WINNEBAGO	94,013	57,682	35,937	394	21,745 R	61.4%	38.2%	61.6%	38.4%
28,012	WOODFORD	13,203	9,622	3,558	23	6,064 R	72.9%	26.9%	73.0%	27.0%
11,113,976	TOTAL	4,723,236	2,788,179	1,913,472	21,585	874,707 R	59.0%	40.5%	59.3%	40.7%

ILLINOIS

PRESIDENT 1968

1960 Census Population	County	Total Vote	Republican	Democratic	AIP	Other	Plurality	Percentage Rep.	Dem.	AIP
68,467	ADAMS	32,108	17,444	11,521	3,115	28	5,923 R	54.3%	35.9%	9.7%
16,061	ALEXANDER	6,934	2,540	2,929	1,443	22	389 D	36.6%	42.2%	20.8%
14,060	BOND	6,953	3,674	2,516	758	5	1,158 R	52.8%	36.2%	10.9%
20,326	BOONE	9,533	5,936	2,801	783	13	3,135 R	62.3%	29.4%	8.2%
6,210	BROWN	3,163	1,629	1,265	247	22	364 R	51.5%	40.0%	7.8%
37,594	BUREAU	18,703	11,216	6,304	1,171	12	4,912 R	60.0%	33.7%	6.3%
5,933	CALHOUN	3,139	1,542	1,329	266	2	213 R	49.1%	42.3%	8.5%
19,507	CARROLL	8,282	5,275	2,558	440	9	2,717 R	63.7%	30.9%	5.3%
14,539	CASS	7,139	3,411	3,302	424	2	109 R	47.8%	46.3%	5.9%
132,436	CHAMPAIGN	48,648	26,027	18,425	3,857	339	7,602 R	53.5%	37.9%	7.9%
37,207	CHRISTIAN	17,694	7,486	8,465	1,730	13	979 D	42.3%	47.8%	9.8%
16,546	CLARK	8,575	4,809	2,813	949	4	1,996 R	56.1%	32.8%	11.1%
15,815	CLAY	7,986	4,429	2,878	672	7	1,551 R	55.5%	36.0%	8.4%
24,029	CLINTON	12,199	6,561	4,453	1,180	5	2,108 R	53.8%	36.5%	9.7%
42,860	COLES	19,766	10,449	7,337	1,973	7	3,112 R	52.9%	37.1%	10.0%
5,129,725	COOK	2,336,538	960,493	1,181,316	186,921	7,808	220,823 D	41.1%	50.6%	8.0%
20,751	CRAWFORD	10,098	5,870	3,383	840	5	2,487 R	58.1%	33.5%	8.3%
9,936	CUMBERLAND	5,028	2,671	1,828	512	17	843 R	53.1%	36.4%	10.2%
51,714	DE KALB	22,999	14,535	6,974	1,238	252	7,561 R	63.2%	30.3%	5.4%
17,253	DE WITT	7,834	4,247	2,823	759	5	1,424 R	54.2%	36.0%	9.7%
19,243	DOUGLAS	8,537	5,058	2,824	651	4	2,234 R	59.2%	33.1%	7.6%
313,459	DU PAGE	187,496	124,893	48,492	13,814	297	76,401 R	66.6%	25.9%	7.4%
22,550	EDGAR	11,151	6,281	3,565	1,292	13	2,716 R	56.3%	32.0%	11.6%
7,940	EDWARDS	4,135	2,633	1,095	403	4	1,538 R	63.7%	26.5%	9.7%
23,107	EFFINGHAM	11,972	6,698	4,496	777	1	2,202 R	55.9%	37.6%	6.5%
21,946	FAYETTE	10,403	5,449	4,011	939	4	1,438 R	52.4%	38.6%	9.0%
16,606	FORD	8,004	5,233	2,216	550	5	3,017 R	65.4%	27.7%	6.9%
39,281	FRANKLIN	21,074	9,036	10,095	1,930	13	1,059 D	42.9%	47.9%	9.2%
41,954	FULTON	20,509	9,582	9,622	1,234	71	40 D	46.7%	46.9%	6.0%
7,638	GALLATIN	4,190	1,802	1,980	404	4	178 D	43.0%	47.3%	9.6%
17,460	GREENE	7,708	3,944	3,094	660	10	850 R	51.2%	40.1%	8.6%
22,350	GRUNDY	11,105	6,607	3,407	1,085	6	3,200 R	59.5%	30.7%	9.8%
10,010	HAMILTON	5,513	2,912	1,951	643	7	961 R	52.8%	35.4%	11.7%
24,574	HANCOCK	11,397	6,866	3,720	806	5	3,146 R	60.2%	32.6%	7.1%
5,879	HARDIN	2,883	1,492	1,199	187	5	293 R	51.8%	41.6%	6.5%
8,237	HENDERSON	4,148	2,224	1,635	288	1	589 R	53.6%	39.4%	6.9%
49,317	HENRY	22,731	12,524	8,455	1,725	27	4,069 R	55.1%	37.2%	7.6%
33,562	IROQUOIS	16,033	10,885	3,897	1,225	26	6,988 R	67.9%	24.3%	7.6%
42,151	JACKSON	19,657	9,134	8,856	1,645	22	278 R	46.5%	45.1%	8.4%
11,346	JASPER	5,686	2,944	2,012	728	2	932 R	51.8%	35.4%	12.8%
32,315	JEFFERSON	15,467	7,367	6,476	1,612	12	891 R	47.6%	41.9%	10.4%
17,023	JERSEY	8,130	3,806	3,350	971	3	456 R	46.8%	41.2%	11.9%
21,821	JO DAVIESS	9,408	5,563	3,228	607	10	2,335 R	59.1%	34.3%	6.5%
6,928	JOHNSON	3,975	2,406	1,143	421	5	1,263 R	60.5%	28.8%	10.6%
208,246	KANE	87,420	54,144	26,609	6,340	327	27,535 R	61.9%	30.4%	7.3%
92,063	KANKAKEE	38,250	20,025	14,460	3,735	30	5,565 R	52.4%	37.8%	9.8%
17,540	KENDALL	10,198	7,184	2,228	780	6	4,956 R	70.4%	21.8%	7.6%
61,280	KNOX	26,396	14,216	9,707	2,394	79	4,509 R	53.9%	36.8%	9.1%
293,656	LAKE	121,903	68,999	43,409	8,738	757	25,590 R	56.6%	35.6%	7.2%
110,800	LA SALLE	51,610	26,054	22,940	2,590	26	3,114 R	50.5%	44.4%	5.0%
18,540	LAWRENCE	8,946	4,883	3,075	972	16	1,808 R	54.6%	34.4%	10.9%
38,749	LEE	15,255	9,598	4,727	925	5	4,871 R	62.9%	31.0%	6.1%
40,341	LIVINGSTON	18,160	11,963	5,234	950	13	6,729 R	65.9%	28.8%	5.2%
33,656	LOGAN	14,289	8,638	4,552	1,083	16	4,086 R	60.5%	31.9%	7.6%
28,928	MCDONOUGH	12,924	8,496	3,785	628	15	4,711 R	65.7%	29.3%	4.9%
84,210	MCHENRY	41,185	27,245	10,896	2,701	343	16,349 R	66.2%	26.5%	6.6%
83,877	MCLEAN	37,630	22,284	12,779	2,351	216	9,505 R	59.2%	34.0%	6.2%
118,257	MACON	49,741	21,027	23,369	5,163	182	2,342 D	42.3%	47.0%	10.4%
43,524	MACOUPIN	23,368	10,262	10,750	2,325	31	488 D	43.9%	46.0%	9.9%
224,689	MADISON	101,129	39,622	46,384	14,987	136	6,762 D	39.2%	45.9%	14.8%

ILLINOIS

PRESIDENT 1968

1960 Census Population	County	Total Vote	Republican	Democratic	AIP	Other	Plurality	Percentage Rep.	Dem.	AIP
39,349	MARION	17,649	8,134	7,737	1,680	98	397 R	46.1%	43.8%	9.5%
13,334	MARSHALL	6,677	3,897	2,455	313	12	1,442 R	58.4%	36.8%	4.7%
15,193	MASON	7,853	3,899	3,365	572	17	534 R	49.6%	42.8%	7.3%
14,341	MASSAC	6,446	3,578	1,934	926	8	1,644 R	55.5%	30.0%	14.4%
9,248	MENARD	4,995	2,980	1,640	372	3	1,340 R	59.7%	32.8%	7.4%
17,149	MERCER	8,600	4,844	3,143	607	6	1,701 R	56.3%	36.5%	7.1%
15,507	MONROE	9,167	5,086	2,822	1,253	6	2,264 R	55.5%	30.8%	13.7%
31,244	MONTGOMERY	16,339	7,547	7,318	1,468	6	229 R	46.2%	44.8%	9.0%
36,571	MORGAN	16,327	8,902	6,281	1,137	7	2,621 R	54.5%	38.5%	7.0%
13,635	MOULTRIE	6,127	3,094	2,447	571	15	647 R	50.5%	39.9%	9.3%
38,106	OGLE	17,641	12,168	4,399	1,060	14	7,769 R	69.0%	24.9%	6.0%
189,044	PEORIA	74,105	37,021	30,937	5,648	499	6,084 R	50.0%	41.7%	7.6%
19,184	PERRY	10,983	5,384	4,449	1,144	6	935 R	49.0%	40.5%	10.4%
14,960	PIATT	7,059	3,973	2,447	636	3	1,526 R	56.3%	34.7%	9.0%
20,552	PIKE	9,939	5,035	4,191	697	16	844 R	50.7%	42.2%	7.0%
4,061	POPE	2,268	1,307	732	226	3	575 R	57.6%	32.3%	10.0%
10,490	PULASKI	4,632	1,741	2,076	815		335 D	37.6%	44.8%	17.6%
4,570	PUTNAM	2,505	1,351	988	162	4	363 R	53.9%	39.4%	6.5%
29,988	RANDOLPH	15,250	7,681	5,953	1,607	9	1,728 R	50.4%	39.0%	10.5%
16,299	RICHLAND	8,137	4,781	2,495	853	8	2,286 R	58.8%	30.7%	10.5%
150,991	ROCK ISLAND	70,140	30,404	34,506	5,054	176	4,102 D	43.3%	49.2%	7.2%
262,509	ST. CLAIR	100,874	34,442	50,726	15,260	446	16,284 D	34.1%	50.3%	15.1%
26,227	SALINE	13,849	6,913	5,985	939	12	928 R	49.9%	43.2%	6.8%
146,539	SANGAMON	72,996	36,510	29,542	6,586	358	6,968 R	50.0%	40.5%	9.0%
8,746	SCHUYLER	4,600	2,760	1,475	346	19	1,285 R	60.0%	32.1%	7.5%
6,377	SCOTT	3,548	1,971	1,252	325		719 R	55.6%	35.3%	9.2%
23,404	SHELBY	11,137	5,487	4,528	1,115	7	959 R	49.3%	40.7%	10.0%
8,152	STARK	3,665	2,292	1,128	239	6	1,164 R	62.5%	30.8%	6.5%
46,207	STEPHENSON	19,928	11,821	7,040	1,050	17	4,781 R	59.3%	35.3%	5.3%
99,789	TAZEWELL	48,422	22,971	20,712	4,711	28	2,259 R	47.4%	42.8%	9.7%
17,645	UNION	8,372	3,889	3,603	871	9	286 R	46.5%	43.0%	10.4%
96,176	VERMILION	43,424	21,391	16,238	5,726	69	5,153 R	49.3%	37.4%	13.2%
14,047	WABASH	6,392	3,529	2,244	614	5	1,285 R	55.2%	35.1%	9.6%
21,587	WARREN	9,795	5,877	3,085	824	9	2,792 R	60.0%	31.5%	8.4%
13,569	WASHINGTON	7,569	4,793	2,093	671	12	2,700 R	63.3%	27.7%	8.9%
19,008	WAYNE	9,284	5,532	2,993	745	14	2,539 R	59.6%	32.2%	8.0%
19,373	WHITE	9,952	5,351	3,837	761	3	1,514 R	53.8%	38.6%	7.6%
59,887	WHITESIDE	24,534	15,177	8,132	1,179	46	7,045 R	61.9%	33.1%	4.8%
191,617	WILL	88,460	43,630	31,576	12,595	659	12,054 R	49.3%	35.7%	14.2%
46,117	WILLIAMSON	23,588	11,886	9,660	2,031	11	2,226 R	50.4%	41.0%	8.6%
209,765	WINNEBAGO	90,739	47,646	36,702	6,176	215	10,944 R	52.5%	40.4%	6.8%
24,579	WOODFORD	12,747	7,876	4,005	856	10	3,871 R	61.8%	31.4%	6.7%
10,081,158	TOTAL	4,619,749	2,174,774	2,039,814	390,958	14,203	134,960 R	47.1%	44.2%	8.5%

ILLINOIS

ELECTION NOTES

1984 Other vote was 10,086 Bergland (Libertarian); 4,672 Hall (Communist); 2,716 Johnson (Citizens); 2,632 Winn (Independent); 2,386 Serrette (Independent); 2,132 Mason (Socialist Workers); 862 scattered write-in.

1980 Other vote was 346,754 Anderson (Independent); 38,939 Clark (Libertarian); 10,692 Commoner (Citizens); 9,711 Hall (Communist); 2,257 Griswold (Workers World); 1,302 DeBerry (Socialist Workers); 604 scattered write-in.

1976 Other vote was 55,939 McCarthy (Independent); 9,250 Hall (Communist); 8,057 MacBride (Libertarian); 3,615 Camejo (Socialist Workers); 2,422 Levin (Socialist Labor); 2,018 LaRouche (U.S. Labor); 387 Anderson (write-in); 1,662 scattered write-in. In the final printed return - The Official Vote - the Schuyler county Republican vote was carried incorrectly as 22,635 and the Republican total statewide vote as 2,384,269.

1972 Other vote was 12,344 Fisher (Socialist Labor); 4,541 Hall (Communist); 2,471 Schmitz (American); 2,229 scattered write-in.

1968 Wallace on the ballot as Independent. Other vote was 13,878 Blomen (Socialist Labor); 325 scattered write-in.

INDIANA

POPULAR VOTE FOR PRESIDENT 1920 TO 1984

Year	Total Vote	Republican Vote	Republican Candidate	Democratic Vote	Democratic Candidate	Other Vote	Plurality	Percentage Total Vote Rep.	Percentage Total Vote Dem.	Percentage Major Vote Rep.	Percentage Major Vote Dem.
1984	2,233,069	1,377,230	Reagan, Ronald	841,481	Mondale, Walter F.	14,358	535,749 R	61.7%	37.7%	62.1%	37.9%
1980	2,242,033	1,255,656	Reagan, Ronald	844,197	Carter, Jimmy	142,180	411,459 R	56.0%	37.7%	59.8%	40.2%
1976	2,220,362	1,183,958	Ford, Gerald R.	1,014,714	Carter, Jimmy	21,690	169,244 R	53.3%	45.7%	53.8%	46.2%
1972	2,125,529	1,405,154	Nixon, Richard M.	708,568	McGovern, George S.	11,807	696,586 R	66.1%	33.3%	66.5%	33.5%
1968	2,123,597	1,067,885	Nixon, Richard M.	806,659	Humphrey, Hubert H.	249,053	261,226 R	50.3%	38.0%	57.0%	43.0%
1964	2,091,606	911,118	Goldwater, Barry M.	1,170,848	Johnson, Lyndon B.	9,640	259,730 D	43.6%	56.0%	43.8%	56.2%
1960	2,135,360	1,175,120	Nixon, Richard M.	952,358	Kennedy, John F.	7,882	222,762 R	55.0%	44.6%	55.2%	44.8%
1956	1,974,607	1,182,811	Eisenhower, Dwight D.	783,908	Stevenson, Adlai E.	7,888	398,903 R	59.9%	39.7%	60.1%	39.9%
1952	1,955,049	1,136,259	Eisenhower, Dwight D.	801,530	Stevenson, Adlai E.	17,260	334,729 R	58.1%	41.0%	58.6%	41.4%
1948	1,656,212	821,079	Dewey, Thomas E.	807,831	Truman, Harry S.	27,302	13,248 R	49.6%	48.8%	50.4%	49.6%
1944	1,672,091	875,891	Dewey, Thomas E.	781,403	Roosevelt, Franklin D.	14,797	94,488 R	52.4%	46.7%	52.9%	47.1%
1940	1,782,747	899,466	Willkie, Wendell	874,063	Roosevelt, Franklin D.	9,218	25,403 R	50.5%	49.0%	50.7%	49.3%
1936	1,650,897	691,570	Landon, Alfred M.	934,974	Roosevelt, Franklin D.	24,353	243,404 D	41.9%	56.6%	42.5%	57.5%
1932	1,576,927	677,184	Hoover, Herbert C.	862,054	Roosevelt, Franklin D.	37,689	184,870 D	42.9%	54.7%	44.0%	56.0%
1928	1,421,314	848,290	Hoover, Herbert C.	562,691	Smith, Alfred E.	10,333	285,599 R	59.7%	39.6%	60.1%	39.9%
1924	1,272,390	703,042	Coolidge, Calvin	492,245	Davis, John W.	77,103	210,797 R	55.3%	38.7%	58.8%	41.2%
1920	1,262,974	696,370	Harding, Warren G.	511,364	Cox, James M.	55,240	185,006 R	55.1%	40.5%	57.7%	42.3%

ELECTORAL COLLEGE VOTE 1920 TO 1984

Year	Total	Republican	Democratic	Other
1984	12	12	—	—
1980	13	13	—	—
1976	13	13	—	—
1972	13	13	—	—
1968	13	13	—	—
1964	13	—	13	—
1960	13	13	—	—
1956	13	13	—	—
1952	13	13	—	—
1948	13	13	—	—
1944	13	13	—	—
1940	14	14	—	—
1936	14	—	14	—
1932	14	—	14	—
1928	15	15	—	—
1924	15	15	—	—
1920	15	15	—	—

INDIANA

ST. JOSEPH
ELKHART
LAGRANGE
STEUBEN
LA PORTE
LAKE
PORTER
NOBLE
DE KALB
STARKE
MARSHALL
KOSCIUSKO
WHITLEY
ALLEN
NEWTON
JASPER
PULASKI
FULTON
WABASH
HUNTINGTON
MIAMI
WHITE
CASS
WELLS
ADAMS
BENTON
CARROLL
GRANT
BLACK-FORD
JAY
HOWARD
WARREN
TIPPECANOE
CLINTON
TIPTON
MADISON
DELAWARE
RANDOLPH
FOUNTAIN
MONTGOMERY
BOONE
HAMILTON
VERMILLION
HENRY
WAYNE
PARKE
PUTNAM
HENDRICKS
MARION
HANCOCK
RUSH
FAYETTE
UNION
VIGO
CLAY
MORGAN
JOHNSON
SHELBY
FRANKLIN
OWEN
DECATUR
MONROE
BROWN
BARTHOLOMEW
RIPLEY
DEARBORN
SULLIVAN
GREENE
JENNINGS
JACKSON
OHIO
LAWRENCE
SWITZER-LAND
JEFFERSON
KNOX
DAVIESS
MARTIN
SCOTT
ORANGE
WASHINGTON
CLARK
GIBSON
PIKE
DUBOIS
FLOYD
CRAWFORD
HARRISON
PERRY
WARRICK
SPENCER
POSEY
VANDER-BURGH

INDIANA

PRESIDENT 1984

1980 Census Population	County	Total Vote	Republican	Democratic	Other	Rep.-Dem. Plurality	Percentage Total Vote Rep.	Total Vote Dem.	Major Vote Rep.	Major Vote Dem.
29,619	ADAMS	11,952	7,958	3,923	71	4,035 R	66.6%	32.8%	67.0%	33.0%
294,335	ALLEN	114,975	75,505	38,462	1,008	37,043 R	65.7%	33.5%	66.3%	33.7%
65,088	BARTHOLOMEW	26,970	18,704	8,075	191	10,629 R	69.4%	29.9%	69.8%	30.2%
10,218	BENTON	4,662	3,281	1,357	24	1,924 R	70.4%	29.1%	70.7%	29.3%
15,570	BLACKFORD	6,230	3,787	2,395	48	1,392 R	60.8%	38.4%	61.3%	38.7%
36,446	BOONE	15,850	11,790	3,982	78	7,808 R	74.4%	25.1%	74.8%	25.2%
12,377	BROWN	6,198	3,517	2,657	24	860 R	56.7%	42.9%	57.0%	43.0%
19,722	CARROLL	8,364	5,528	2,774	62	2,754 R	66.1%	33.2%	66.6%	33.4%
40,936	CASS	17,971	12,355	5,521	95	6,834 R	68.7%	30.7%	69.1%	30.9%
88,838	CLARK	33,785	19,419	14,138	228	5,281 R	57.5%	41.8%	57.9%	42.1%
24,862	CLAY	10,725	6,957	3,707	61	3,250 R	64.9%	34.6%	65.2%	34.8%
31,545	CLINTON	13,363	8,969	4,329	65	4,640 R	67.1%	32.4%	67.4%	32.6%
9,820	CRAWFORD	4,910	2,633	2,256	21	377 R	53.6%	45.9%	53.9%	46.1%
27,836	DAVIESS	11,311	7,721	3,545	45	4,176 R	68.3%	31.3%	68.5%	31.5%
34,291	DEARBORN	14,132	9,149	4,920	63	4,229 R	64.7%	34.8%	65.0%	35.0%
23,841	DECATUR	9,363	6,551	2,766	46	3,785 R	70.0%	29.5%	70.3%	29.7%
33,606	DE KALB	13,528	8,769	4,617	142	4,152 R	64.8%	34.1%	65.5%	34.5%
128,587	DELAWARE	50,171	30,092	19,791	288	10,301 R	60.0%	39.4%	60.3%	39.7%
34,238	DUBOIS	14,962	9,391	5,423	148	3,968 R	62.8%	36.2%	63.4%	36.6%
137,330	ELKHART	48,097	34,621	13,240	236	21,381 R	72.0%	27.5%	72.3%	27.7%
28,272	FAYETTE	11,346	7,142	4,122	82	3,020 R	62.9%	36.3%	63.4%	36.6%
61,169	FLOYD	26,279	15,466	10,616	197	4,850 R	58.9%	40.4%	59.3%	40.7%
19,033	FOUNTAIN	8,397	5,450	2,897	50	2,553 R	64.9%	34.5%	65.3%	34.7%
19,612	FRANKLIN	7,472	5,202	2,225	45	2,977 R	69.6%	29.8%	70.0%	30.0%
19,335	FULTON	8,635	6,057	2,527	51	3,530 R	70.1%	29.3%	70.6%	29.4%
33,156	GIBSON	15,777	8,618	7,082	77	1,536 R	54.6%	44.9%	54.9%	45.1%
80,934	GRANT	30,673	20,482	9,986	205	10,496 R	66.8%	32.6%	67.2%	32.8%
30,416	GREENE	13,898	8,438	5,267	193	3,171 R	60.7%	37.9%	61.6%	38.4%
82,027	HAMILTON	36,761	30,254	6,364	143	23,890 R	82.3%	17.3%	82.6%	17.4%
43,939	HANCOCK	17,504	12,880	4,550	74	8,330 R	73.6%	26.0%	73.9%	26.1%
27,276	HARRISON	11,969	7,255	4,634	80	2,621 R	60.6%	38.7%	61.0%	39.0%
69,804	HENDRICKS	28,135	21,307	6,659	169	14,648 R	75.7%	23.7%	76.2%	23.8%
53,336	HENRY	19,062	11,926	7,064	72	4,862 R	62.6%	37.1%	62.8%	37.2%
86,896	HOWARD	33,046	22,386	10,458	202	11,928 R	67.7%	31.6%	68.2%	31.8%
35,596	HUNTINGTON	15,487	10,805	4,598	84	6,207 R	69.8%	29.7%	70.1%	29.9%
36,523	JACKSON	15,234	9,879	5,163	192	4,716 R	64.8%	33.9%	65.7%	34.3%
26,138	JASPER	9,444	6,537	2,821	86	3,716 R	69.2%	29.9%	69.9%	30.1%
23,239	JAY	9,207	5,975	3,174	58	2,801 R	64.9%	34.5%	65.3%	34.7%
30,419	JEFFERSON	12,639	7,482	4,952	205	2,530 R	59.2%	39.2%	60.2%	39.8%
22,854	JENNINGS	9,707	6,356	3,264	87	3,092 R	65.5%	33.6%	66.1%	33.9%
77,240	JOHNSON	31,368	23,482	7,715	171	15,767 R	74.9%	24.6%	75.3%	24.7%
41,838	KNOX	17,459	10,872	6,417	170	4,455 R	62.3%	36.8%	62.9%	37.1%
59,555	KOSCIUSKO	22,547	17,560	4,877	110	12,683 R	77.9%	21.6%	78.3%	21.7%
25,550	LAGRANGE	6,692	4,772	1,884	36	2,888 R	71.3%	28.2%	71.7%	28.3%
522,965	LAKE	214,143	94,870	117,984	1,289	23,114 D	44.3%	55.1%	44.6%	55.4%
108,632	LA PORTE	39,567	23,346	15,904	317	7,442 R	59.0%	40.2%	59.5%	40.5%
42,472	LAWRENCE	17,150	11,440	5,608	102	5,832 R	66.7%	32.7%	67.1%	32.9%
139,336	MADISON	59,014	36,510	22,254	250	14,256 R	61.9%	37.7%	62.1%	37.9%
765,233	MARION	317,148	184,880	130,185	2,083	54,695 R	58.3%	41.0%	58.7%	41.3%
39,155	MARSHALL	16,144	11,100	4,931	113	6,169 R	68.8%	30.5%	69.2%	30.8%
11,001	MARTIN	5,332	3,363	1,937	32	1,426 R	63.1%	36.3%	63.5%	36.5%
39,820	MIAMI	13,892	9,551	4,224	117	5,327 R	68.8%	30.4%	69.3%	30.7%
98,785	MONROE	36,826	21,772	14,719	335	7,053 R	59.1%	40.0%	59.7%	40.3%
35,501	MONTGOMERY	14,834	11,119	3,626	89	7,493 R	75.0%	24.4%	75.4%	24.6%
51,999	MORGAN	19,607	14,884	4,627	96	10,257 R	75.9%	23.6%	76.3%	23.7%
14,844	NEWTON	5,194	3,560	1,596	38	1,964 R	68.5%	30.7%	69.0%	31.0%
35,443	NOBLE	12,867	8,459	4,237	171	4,222 R	65.7%	32.9%	66.6%	33.4%
5,114	OHIO	2,577	1,503	1,068	6	435 R	58.3%	41.4%	58.5%	41.5%
18,677	ORANGE	8,515	5,909	2,571	35	3,338 R	69.4%	30.2%	69.7%	30.3%
15,841	OWEN	6,323	4,204	2,082	37	2,122 R	66.5%	32.9%	66.9%	33.1%

INDIANA

PRESIDENT 1984

1980 Census Population	County	Total Vote	Republican	Democratic	Other	Rep.-Dem. Plurality	Percentage Total Vote Rep.	Total Vote Dem.	Major Vote Rep.	Major Vote Dem.
16,372	PARKE	7,294	5,052	2,205	37	2,847 R	69.3%	30.2%	69.6%	30.4%
19,346	PERRY	9,588	4,785	4,760	43	25 R	49.9%	49.6%	50.1%	49.9%
13,465	PIKE	6,963	3,689	3,231	43	458 R	53.0%	46.4%	53.3%	46.7%
119,816	PORTER	50,682	32,505	17,862	315	14,643 R	64.1%	35.2%	64.5%	35.5%
26,414	POSEY	10,957	6,472	4,452	33	2,020 R	59.1%	40.6%	59.2%	40.8%
13,258	PULASKI	6,226	4,167	2,008	51	2,159 R	66.9%	32.3%	67.5%	32.5%
29,163	PUTNAM	11,272	7,820	3,392	60	4,428 R	69.4%	30.1%	69.7%	30.3%
29,997	RANDOLPH	11,671	7,793	3,805	73	3,988 R	66.8%	32.6%	67.2%	32.8%
24,398	RIPLEY	10,506	7,143	3,336	27	3,807 R	68.0%	31.8%	68.2%	31.8%
19,604	RUSH	7,771	5,429	2,307	35	3,122 R	69.9%	29.7%	70.2%	29.8%
241,617	ST. JOSEPH	102,493	54,404	47,513	576	6,891 R	53.1%	46.4%	53.4%	46.6%
20,422	SCOTT	7,588	4,110	3,460	18	650 R	54.2%	45.6%	54.3%	45.7%
39,887	SHELBY	16,522	11,056	5,357	109	5,699 R	66.9%	32.4%	67.4%	32.6%
19,361	SPENCER	9,846	5,816	4,005	25	1,811 R	59.1%	40.7%	59.2%	40.8%
21,997	STARKE	8,889	5,104	3,674	111	1,430 R	57.4%	41.3%	58.1%	41.9%
24,694	STEUBEN	8,921	6,424	2,441	56	3,983 R	72.0%	27.4%	72.5%	27.5%
21,107	SULLIVAN	8,813	4,771	4,006	36	765 R	54.1%	45.5%	54.4%	45.6%
7,153	SWITZERLAND	3,347	1,857	1,484	6	373 R	55.5%	44.3%	55.6%	44.4%
121,702	TIPPECANOE	45,876	29,706	15,789	381	13,917 R	64.8%	34.4%	65.3%	34.7%
16,819	TIPTON	8,069	5,687	2,328	54	3,359 R	70.5%	28.9%	71.0%	29.0%
6,860	UNION	2,800	1,970	816	14	1,154 R	70.4%	29.1%	70.7%	29.3%
167,515	VANDERBURGH	72,330	40,994	31,049	287	9,945 R	56.7%	42.9%	56.9%	43.1%
18,229	VERMILLION	8,154	4,428	3,666	60	762 R	54.3%	45.0%	54.7%	45.3%
112,385	VIGO	44,973	26,259	18,429	285	7,830 R	58.4%	41.0%	58.8%	41.2%
36,640	WABASH	14,028	9,862	4,077	89	5,785 R	70.3%	29.1%	70.8%	29.2%
8,976	WARREN	3,862	2,525	1,309	28	1,216 R	65.4%	33.9%	65.9%	34.1%
41,474	WARRICK	16,637	10,202	6,345	90	3,857 R	61.3%	38.1%	61.7%	38.3%
21,932	WASHINGTON	9,380	5,874	3,334	172	2,540 R	62.6%	35.5%	63.8%	36.2%
76,058	WAYNE	29,251	18,955	10,173	123	8,782 R	64.8%	34.8%	65.1%	34.9%
25,401	WELLS	10,920	7,579	3,274	67	4,305 R	69.4%	30.0%	69.8%	30.2%
23,867	WHITE	10,499	7,279	3,157	63	4,122 R	69.3%	30.1%	69.7%	30.3%
26,215	WHITLEY	11,551	7,763	3,690	98	4,073 R	67.2%	31.9%	67.8%	32.2%
5,490,224	TOTAL	2,233,069	1,377,230	841,481	14,358	535,749 R	61.7%	37.7%	62.1%	37.9%

INDIANA

PRESIDENT 1980

1980 Census Population	County	Total Vote	Republican	Democratic	Other	Rep.-Dem. Plurality	Percentage Total Vote Rep.	Percentage Total Vote Dem.	Percentage Major Vote Rep.	Percentage Major Vote Dem.
29,619	ADAMS	11,978	6,368	4,673	937	1,695 R	53.2%	39.0%	57.7%	42.3%
294,335	ALLEN	118,898	68,524	37,765	12,609	30,759 R	57.6%	31.8%	64.5%	35.5%
65,088	BARTHOLOMEW	26,974	15,801	9,260	1,913	6,541 R	58.6%	34.3%	63.1%	36.9%
10,218	BENTON	4,963	3,189	1,520	254	1,669 R	64.3%	30.6%	67.7%	32.3%
15,570	BLACKFORD	5,962	3,168	2,431	363	737 R	53.1%	40.8%	56.6%	43.4%
36,446	BOONE	15,859	10,484	4,535	840	5,949 R	66.1%	28.6%	69.8%	30.2%
12,377	BROWN	5,291	2,884	2,014	393	870 R	54.5%	38.1%	58.9%	41.1%
19,722	CARROLL	8,699	5,262	2,966	471	2,296 R	60.5%	34.1%	64.0%	36.0%
40,936	CASS	18,274	11,500	5,838	936	5,662 R	62.9%	31.9%	66.3%	33.7%
88,838	CLARK	31,181	15,508	14,137	1,536	1,371 R	49.7%	45.3%	52.3%	47.7%
24,862	CLAY	11,812	6,980	4,363	469	2,617 R	59.1%	36.9%	61.5%	38.5%
31,545	CLINTON	13,962	8,158	5,258	546	2,900 R	58.4%	37.7%	60.8%	39.2%
9,820	CRAWFORD	4,864	2,554	2,130	180	424 R	52.5%	43.8%	54.5%	45.5%
27,836	DAVIESS	11,532	7,022	4,057	453	2,965 R	60.9%	35.2%	63.4%	36.6%
34,291	DEARBORN	13,249	7,467	5,135	647	2,332 R	56.4%	38.8%	59.3%	40.7%
23,841	DECATUR	9,951	5,819	3,646	486	2,173 R	58.5%	36.6%	61.5%	38.5%
33,606	DE KALB	13,950	7,886	4,911	1,153	2,975 R	56.5%	35.2%	61.6%	38.4%
128,587	DELAWARE	52,647	28,342	20,923	3,382	7,419 R	53.8%	39.7%	57.5%	42.5%
34,238	DUBOIS	14,276	6,775	6,700	801	75 R	47.5%	46.9%	50.3%	49.7%
137,330	ELKHART	48,994	30,081	14,883	4,030	15,198 R	61.4%	30.4%	66.9%	33.1%
28,272	FAYETTE	10,732	6,004	4,304	424	1,700 R	55.9%	40.1%	58.2%	41.8%
61,169	FLOYD	25,467	12,456	11,543	1,468	913 R	48.9%	45.3%	51.9%	48.1%
19,033	FOUNTAIN	8,506	5,289	2,845	372	2,444 R	62.2%	33.4%	65.0%	35.0%
19,612	FRANKLIN	7,701	4,551	2,834	316	1,717 R	59.1%	36.8%	61.6%	38.4%
19,335	FULTON	8,728	5,458	2,788	482	2,670 R	62.5%	31.9%	66.2%	33.8%
33,156	GIBSON	15,189	7,643	6,834	712	809 R	50.3%	45.0%	52.8%	47.2%
80,934	GRANT	30,909	19,078	10,390	1,441	8,688 R	61.7%	33.6%	64.7%	35.3%
30,416	GREENE	14,098	7,452	6,027	619	1,425 R	52.9%	42.8%	55.3%	44.7%
82,027	HAMILTON	35,327	26,218	7,036	2,073	19,182 R	74.2%	19.9%	78.8%	21.2%
43,939	HANCOCK	18,138	12,093	5,124	921	6,969 R	66.7%	28.3%	70.2%	29.8%
27,276	HARRISON	11,594	6,287	4,865	442	1,422 R	54.2%	42.0%	56.4%	43.6%
69,804	HENDRICKS	28,117	19,366	7,412	1,339	11,954 R	68.9%	26.4%	72.3%	27.7%
53,336	HENRY	21,196	12,724	7,626	846	5,098 R	60.0%	36.0%	62.5%	37.5%
86,896	HOWARD	35,910	21,272	12,916	1,722	8,356 R	59.2%	36.0%	62.2%	37.8%
35,596	HUNTINGTON	15,937	9,497	5,415	1,025	4,082 R	59.6%	34.0%	63.7%	36.3%
36,523	JACKSON	15,942	8,903	6,425	614	2,478 R	55.8%	40.3%	58.1%	41.9%
26,138	JASPER	9,276	6,316	2,544	416	3,772 R	68.1%	27.4%	71.3%	28.7%
23,239	JAY	9,217	5,351	3,256	610	2,095 R	58.1%	35.3%	62.2%	37.8%
30,419	JEFFERSON	13,087	6,831	5,496	760	1,335 R	52.2%	42.0%	55.4%	44.6%
22,854	JENNINGS	9,822	5,498	3,931	393	1,567 R	56.0%	40.0%	58.3%	41.7%
77,240	JOHNSON	30,174	20,018	8,445	1,711	11,573 R	66.3%	28.0%	70.3%	29.7%
41,838	KNOX	18,822	10,083	7,829	910	2,254 R	53.6%	41.6%	56.3%	43.7%
59,555	KOSCIUSKO	22,730	15,633	5,684	1,413	9,949 R	68.8%	25.0%	73.3%	26.7%
25,550	LAGRANGE	6,815	4,259	2,095	461	2,164 R	62.5%	30.7%	67.0%	33.0%
522,965	LAKE	207,339	95,408	101,145	10,786	5,737 D	46.0%	48.8%	48.5%	51.5%
108,632	LA PORTE	40,538	22,424	15,387	2,727	7,037 R	55.3%	38.0%	59.3%	40.7%
42,472	LAWRENCE	17,296	10,846	5,826	624	5,020 R	62.7%	33.7%	65.1%	34.9%
139,336	MADISON	62,092	35,582	23,554	2,956	12,028 R	57.3%	37.9%	60.2%	39.8%
765,233	MARION	314,269	168,680	126,103	19,486	42,577 R	53.7%	40.1%	57.2%	42.8%
39,155	MARSHALL	16,411	10,209	5,113	1,089	5,096 R	62.2%	31.2%	66.6%	33.4%
11,001	MARTIN	5,779	3,082	2,479	218	603 R	53.3%	42.9%	55.4%	44.6%
39,820	MIAMI	14,304	8,672	4,927	705	3,745 R	60.6%	34.4%	63.8%	36.2%
98,785	MONROE	36,894	18,233	13,316	5,345	4,917 R	49.4%	36.1%	57.8%	42.2%
35,501	MONTGOMERY	14,917	9,936	4,158	823	5,778 R	66.6%	27.9%	70.5%	29.5%
51,999	MORGAN	19,438	13,321	5,439	678	7,882 R	68.5%	28.0%	71.0%	29.0%
14,844	NEWTON	5,763	3,850	1,649	264	2,201 R	66.8%	28.6%	70.0%	30.0%
35,443	NOBLE	13,282	7,624	4,721	937	2,903 R	57.4%	35.5%	61.8%	38.2%
5,114	OHIO	2,420	1,264	1,074	82	190 R	52.2%	44.4%	54.1%	45.9%
18,677	ORANGE	8,558	5,073	3,228	257	1,845 R	59.3%	37.7%	61.1%	38.9%
15,841	OWEN	6,212	3,632	2,325	255	1,307 R	58.5%	37.4%	61.0%	39.0%

INDIANA

PRESIDENT 1980

1980 Census Population	County	Total Vote	Republican	Democratic	Other	Rep.-Dem. Plurality	Percentage Total Vote Rep.	Total Vote Dem.	Major Vote Rep.	Major Vote Dem.
16,372	PARKE	7,315	4,595	2,432	288	2,163 R	62.8%	33.2%	65.4%	34.6%
19,346	PERRY	9,468	4,350	4,540	578	190 D	45.9%	48.0%	48.9%	51.1%
13,465	PIKE	6,952	3,343	3,346	263	3 D	48.1%	48.1%	50.0%	50.0%
119,816	PORTER	46,816	30,055	12,869	3,892	17,186 R	64.2%	27.5%	70.0%	30.0%
26,414	POSEY	11,354	6,096	4,465	793	1,631 R	53.7%	39.3%	57.7%	42.3%
13,258	PULASKI	6,310	3,916	2,092	302	1,824 R	62.1%	33.2%	65.2%	34.8%
29,163	PUTNAM	11,748	7,090	3,996	662	3,094 R	60.4%	34.0%	64.0%	36.0%
29,997	RANDOLPH	12,390	7,762	4,025	603	3,737 R	62.6%	32.5%	65.9%	34.1%
24,398	RIPLEY	10,233	5,770	4,022	441	1,748 R	56.4%	39.3%	58.9%	41.1%
19,604	RUSH	7,511	4,829	2,388	294	2,441 R	64.3%	31.8%	66.9%	33.1%
241,617	ST. JOSEPH	103,114	50,607	44,218	8,289	6,389 R	49.1%	42.9%	53.4%	46.6%
20,422	SCOTT	7,329	3,432	3,694	203	262 D	46.8%	50.4%	48.2%	51.8%
39,887	SHELBY	17,150	10,496	5,861	793	4,635 R	61.2%	34.2%	64.2%	35.8%
19,361	SPENCER	9,705	5,284	4,153	268	1,131 R	54.4%	42.8%	56.0%	44.0%
21,997	STARKE	9,110	5,035	3,615	460	1,420 R	55.3%	39.7%	58.2%	41.8%
24,694	STEUBEN	9,008	5,670	2,606	732	3,064 R	62.9%	28.9%	68.5%	31.5%
21,107	SULLIVAN	9,103	4,465	4,335	303	130 R	49.0%	47.6%	50.7%	49.3%
7,153	SWITZERLAND	3,360	1,584	1,704	72	120 D	47.1%	50.7%	48.2%	51.8%
121,702	TIPPECANOE	48,470	27,589	14,636	6,245	12,953 R	56.9%	30.2%	65.3%	34.7%
16,819	TIPTON	8,071	5,150	2,547	374	2,603 R	63.8%	31.6%	66.9%	33.1%
6,860	UNION	2,780	1,766	898	116	868 R	63.5%	32.3%	66.3%	33.7%
167,515	VANDERBURGH	70,982	36,248	29,930	4,804	6,318 R	51.1%	42.2%	54.8%	45.2%
18,229	VERMILLION	8,400	4,195	3,793	412	402 R	49.9%	45.2%	52.5%	47.5%
112,385	VIGO	46,527	24,133	19,261	3,133	4,872 R	51.9%	41.4%	55.6%	44.4%
36,640	WABASH	14,368	8,738	4,620	1,010	4,118 R	60.8%	32.2%	65.4%	34.6%
8,976	WARREN	4,157	2,665	1,287	205	1,378 R	64.1%	31.0%	67.4%	32.6%
41,474	WARRICK	16,570	8,681	6,845	1,044	1,836 R	52.4%	41.3%	55.9%	44.1%
21,932	WASHINGTON	9,297	5,234	3,663	400	1,571 R	56.3%	39.4%	58.8%	41.2%
76,058	WAYNE	28,052	16,981	9,599	1,472	7,382 R	60.5%	34.2%	63.9%	36.1%
25,401	WELLS	10,445	5,864	3,760	821	2,104 R	56.1%	36.0%	60.9%	39.1%
23,867	WHITE	10,855	6,999	3,247	609	3,752 R	64.5%	29.9%	68.3%	31.7%
26,215	WHITLEY	12,821	7,146	4,497	1,178	2,649 R	55.7%	35.1%	61.4%	38.6%
5,490,224	TOTAL	2,242,033	1,255,656	844,197	142,180	411,459 R	56.0%	37.7%	59.8%	40.2%

INDIANA

PRESIDENT 1976

1970 Census Population	County	Total Vote	Republican	Democratic	Other	Rep.-Dem. Plurality	Percentage Total Vote Rep.	Percentage Total Vote Dem.	Percentage Major Vote Rep.	Percentage Major Vote Dem.
26,871	ADAMS	11,306	6,280	4,908	118	1,372 R	55.5%	43.4%	56.1%	43.9%
280,455	ALLEN	117,769	71,321	44,744	1,704	26,577 R	60.6%	38.0%	61.4%	38.6%
57,022	BARTHOLOMEW	26,187	14,771	11,203	213	3,568 R	56.4%	42.8%	56.9%	43.1%
11,262	BENTON	5,234	3,093	2,071	70	1,022 R	59.1%	39.6%	59.9%	40.1%
15,888	BLACKFORD	6,120	2,886	3,174	60	288 D	47.2%	51.9%	47.6%	52.4%
30,870	BOONE	14,986	9,214	5,686	86	3,528 R	61.5%	37.9%	61.8%	38.2%
9,057	BROWN	4,904	2,466	2,381	57	85 R	50.3%	48.6%	50.9%	49.1%
17,734	CARROLL	8,493	4,797	3,606	90	1,191 R	56.5%	42.5%	57.1%	42.9%
40,456	CASS	18,231	10,342	7,610	279	2,732 R	56.7%	41.7%	57.6%	42.4%
75,876	CLARK	29,731	12,732	16,670	329	3,938 D	42.8%	56.1%	43.3%	56.7%
23,933	CLAY	11,265	5,674	5,433	158	241 R	50.4%	48.2%	51.1%	48.9%
30,547	CLINTON	14,963	8,199	6,662	102	1,537 R	54.8%	44.5%	55.2%	44.8%
8,033	CRAWFORD	4,948	2,181	2,721	46	540 D	44.1%	55.0%	44.5%	55.5%
26,602	DAVIESS	11,838	6,829	4,952	57	1,877 R	57.7%	41.8%	58.0%	42.0%
29,430	DEARBORN	12,595	6,176	6,348	71	172 D	49.0%	50.4%	49.3%	50.7%
22,738	DECATUR	9,985	5,555	4,365	65	1,190 R	55.6%	43.7%	56.0%	44.0%
30,837	DE KALB	14,246	7,860	6,151	235	1,709 R	55.2%	43.2%	56.1%	43.9%
129,219	DELAWARE	52,087	26,417	25,151	519	1,266 R	50.7%	48.3%	51.2%	48.8%
30,934	DUBOIS	13,884	6,383	7,385	116	1,002 D	46.0%	53.2%	46.4%	53.6%
126,529	ELKHART	45,429	27,291	17,581	557	9,710 R	60.1%	38.7%	60.8%	39.2%
26,216	FAYETTE	11,288	5,704	5,519	65	185 R	50.5%	48.9%	50.8%	49.2%
55,622	FLOYD	24,255	11,259	12,744	252	1,485 D	46.4%	52.5%	46.9%	53.1%
18,257	FOUNTAIN	9,052	4,903	4,089	60	814 R	54.2%	45.2%	54.5%	45.5%
16,943	FRANKLIN	6,845	3,557	3,234	54	323 R	52.0%	47.2%	52.4%	47.6%
16,984	FULTON	8,703	5,083	3,488	132	1,595 R	58.4%	40.1%	59.3%	40.7%
30,444	GIBSON	15,599	7,105	8,430	64	1,325 D	45.5%	54.0%	45.7%	54.3%
83,955	GRANT	30,554	16,847	13,468	239	3,379 R	55.1%	44.1%	55.6%	44.4%
26,894	GREENE	13,843	6,442	7,263	138	821 D	46.5%	52.5%	47.0%	53.0%
54,532	HAMILTON	29,958	21,828	7,857	273	13,971 R	72.9%	26.2%	73.5%	26.5%
35,096	HANCOCK	16,427	10,072	6,191	164	3,881 R	61.3%	37.7%	61.9%	38.1%
20,423	HARRISON	10,699	4,911	5,685	103	774 D	45.9%	53.1%	46.3%	53.7%
53,974	HENDRICKS	26,104	16,725	9,066	313	7,659 R	64.1%	34.7%	64.8%	35.2%
52,603	HENRY	21,848	11,620	10,137	91	1,483 R	53.2%	46.4%	53.4%	46.6%
83,198	HOWARD	34,653	19,571	14,815	267	4,756 R	56.5%	42.8%	56.9%	43.1%
34,970	HUNTINGTON	15,890	9,182	6,515	193	2,667 R	57.8%	41.0%	58.5%	41.5%
33,187	JACKSON	15,358	7,615	7,610	133	5 R	49.6%	49.6%	50.0%	50.0%
20,429	JASPER	8,884	5,398	3,286	200	2,112 R	60.8%	37.0%	62.2%	37.8%
23,575	JAY	8,817	4,606	4,124	87	482 R	52.2%	46.8%	52.8%	47.2%
27,006	JEFFERSON	11,873	5,573	6,139	161	566 D	46.9%	51.7%	47.6%	52.4%
19,454	JENNINGS	9,012	4,505	4,430	77	75 R	50.0%	49.2%	50.4%	49.6%
61,138	JOHNSON	26,749	16,414	10,075	260	6,339 R	61.4%	37.7%	62.0%	38.0%
41,546	KNOX	18,860	9,100	9,612	148	512 D	48.3%	51.0%	48.6%	51.4%
48,127	KOSCIUSKO	22,124	14,505	7,328	291	7,177 R	65.6%	33.1%	66.4%	33.6%
20,890	LAGRANGE	6,772	3,876	2,835	61	1,041 R	57.2%	41.9%	57.8%	42.2%
546,253	LAKE	212,741	90,119	120,700	1,922	30,581 D	42.4%	56.7%	42.7%	57.3%
105,342	LA PORTE	40,655	21,989	18,217	449	3,772 R	54.1%	44.8%	54.7%	45.3%
38,038	LAWRENCE	17,440	9,278	7,908	254	1,370 R	53.2%	45.3%	54.0%	46.0%
138,451	MADISON	62,820	32,437	29,811	572	2,626 R	51.6%	47.5%	52.1%	47.9%
792,299	MARION	325,576	177,767	145,274	2,535	32,493 R	54.6%	44.6%	55.0%	45.0%
34,986	MARSHALL	16,408	9,707	6,424	277	3,283 R	59.2%	39.2%	60.2%	39.8%
10,969	MARTIN	5,565	2,702	2,827	36	125 D	48.6%	50.8%	48.9%	51.1%
39,246	MIAMI	14,665	8,263	6,257	145	2,006 R	56.3%	42.7%	56.9%	43.1%
84,849	MONROE	36,182	18,938	16,609	635	2,329 R	52.3%	45.9%	53.3%	46.7%
33,930	MONTGOMERY	14,977	9,509	5,320	148	4,189 R	63.5%	35.5%	64.1%	35.9%
44,176	MORGAN	18,427	10,983	7,181	263	3,802 R	59.6%	39.0%	60.5%	39.5%
11,606	NEWTON	5,483	3,204	2,236	43	968 R	58.4%	40.8%	58.9%	41.1%
31,382	NOBLE	13,013	6,885	5,875	253	1,010 R	52.9%	45.1%	54.0%	46.0%
4,289	OHIO	2,337	1,027	1,300	10	273 D	43.9%	55.6%	44.1%	55.9%
16,968	ORANGE	8,476	4,399	4,031	46	368 R	51.9%	47.6%	52.2%	47.8%
12,163	OWEN	6,055	2,896	3,103	56	207 D	47.8%	51.2%	48.3%	51.7%

INDIANA

PRESIDENT 1976

1970 Census Population	County	Total Vote	Republican	Democratic	Other	Rep.-Dem. Plurality	Percentage Total Vote Rep.	Total Vote Dem.	Major Vote Rep.	Major Vote Dem.
14,600	PARKE	7,144	3,929	3,158	57	771 R	55.0%	44.2%	55.4%	44.6%
19,075	PERRY	9,746	4,088	5,620	38	1,532 D	41.9%	57.7%	42.1%	57.9%
12,281	PIKE	7,101	3,138	3,938	25	800 D	44.2%	55.5%	44.3%	55.7%
87,114	PORTER	42,658	25,489	16,468	701	9,021 R	59.8%	38.6%	60.8%	39.2%
21,740	POSEY	10,488	5,136	5,298	54	162 D	49.0%	50.5%	49.2%	50.8%
12,534	PULASKI	6,615	3,586	2,813	216	773 R	54.2%	42.5%	56.0%	44.0%
26,932	PUTNAM	11,297	6,063	5,116	118	947 R	53.7%	45.3%	54.2%	45.8%
28,915	RANDOLPH	12,320	6,891	5,330	99	1,561 R	55.9%	43.3%	56.4%	43.6%
21,138	RIPLEY	10,157	5,293	4,792	72	501 R	52.1%	47.2%	52.5%	47.5%
20,352	RUSH	7,830	4,723	3,052	55	1,671 R	60.3%	39.0%	60.7%	39.3%
245,045	ST. JOSEPH	100,324	50,358	49,156	810	1,202 R	50.2%	49.0%	50.6%	49.4%
17,144	SCOTT	6,966	2,657	4,229	80	1,572 D	38.1%	60.7%	38.6%	61.4%
37,797	SHELBY	16,150	8,918	7,098	134	1,820 R	55.2%	44.0%	55.7%	44.3%
17,134	SPENCER	8,990	4,166	4,796	28	630 D	46.3%	53.3%	46.5%	53.5%
19,280	STARKE	9,241	4,354	4,753	134	399 D	47.1%	51.4%	47.8%	52.2%
20,159	STEUBEN	8,575	5,079	3,323	173	1,756 R	59.2%	38.8%	60.4%	39.6%
19,889	SULLIVAN	9,006	3,747	5,198	61	1,451 D	41.6%	57.7%	41.9%	58.1%
6,306	SWITZERLAND	3,491	1,329	2,150	12	821 D	38.1%	61.6%	38.2%	61.8%
109,378	TIPPECANOE	47,587	29,186	17,850	551	11,336 R	61.3%	37.5%	62.1%	37.9%
16,650	TIPTON	8,328	4,776	3,428	124	1,348 R	57.3%	41.2%	58.2%	41.8%
6,582	UNION	2,800	1,631	1,160	9	471 R	58.3%	41.4%	58.4%	41.6%
168,772	VANDERBURGH	73,211	37,975	34,911	325	3,064 R	51.9%	47.7%	52.1%	47.9%
16,793	VERMILLION	8,538	3,674	4,791	73	1,117 D	43.0%	56.1%	43.4%	56.6%
114,528	VIGO	48,610	23,555	24,684	371	1,129 D	48.5%	50.8%	48.8%	51.2%
35,553	WABASH	14,340	8,534	5,704	102	2,830 R	59.5%	39.8%	59.9%	40.1%
8,705	WARREN	4,312	2,377	1,906	29	471 R	55.1%	44.2%	55.5%	44.5%
27,972	WARRICK	15,096	7,200	7,804	92	604 D	47.7%	51.7%	48.0%	52.0%
19,278	WASHINGTON	8,318	3,794	4,409	115	615 D	45.6%	53.0%	46.3%	53.7%
79,109	WAYNE	29,191	16,697	12,306	188	4,391 R	57.2%	42.2%	57.6%	42.4%
23,821	WELLS	9,934	5,596	4,250	88	1,346 R	56.3%	42.8%	56.8%	43.2%
20,995	WHITE	10,369	6,287	3,963	119	2,324 R	60.6%	38.2%	61.3%	38.7%
23,395	WHITLEY	12,441	6,761	5,445	235	1,316 R	54.3%	43.8%	55.4%	44.6%
5,193,669	TOTAL	2,220,362	1,183,958	1,014,714	21,690	169,244 R	53.3%	45.7%	53.8%	46.2%

INDIANA

PRESIDENT 1972

1970 Census Population	County	Total Vote	Republican	Democratic	Other	Rep.-Dem. Plurality	Percentage Total Vote Rep.	Percentage Total Vote Dem.	Percentage Major Vote Rep.	Percentage Major Vote Dem.
26,871	ADAMS	11,572	7,549	3,971	52	3,578 R	65.2%	34.3%	65.5%	34.5%
280,455	ALLEN	116,199	76,924	38,621	654	38,303 R	66.2%	33.2%	66.6%	33.4%
57,022	BARTHOLOMEW	24,502	17,365	6,974	163	10,391 R	70.9%	28.5%	71.3%	28.7%
11,262	BENTON	5,289	3,703	1,566	20	2,137 R	70.0%	29.6%	70.3%	29.7%
15,888	BLACKFORD	6,219	3,876	2,311	32	1,565 R	62.3%	37.2%	62.6%	37.4%
30,870	BOONE	13,147	9,874	3,235	38	6,639 R	75.1%	24.6%	75.3%	24.7%
9,057	BROWN	4,207	2,737	1,443	27	1,294 R	65.1%	34.3%	65.5%	34.5%
17,734	CARROLL	8,137	5,885	2,214	38	3,671 R	72.3%	27.2%	72.7%	27.3%
40,456	CASS	18,176	12,681	5,317	178	7,364 R	69.8%	29.3%	70.5%	29.5%
75,876	CLARK	27,113	16,111	10,838	164	5,273 R	59.4%	40.0%	59.8%	40.2%
23,933	CLAY	10,937	7,146	3,742	49	3,404 R	65.3%	34.2%	65.6%	34.4%
30,547	CLINTON	14,187	9,849	4,283	55	5,566 R	69.4%	30.2%	69.7%	30.3%
8,033	CRAWFORD	4,449	2,623	1,801	25	822 R	59.0%	40.5%	59.3%	40.7%
26,602	DAVIESS	12,071	8,490	3,538	43	4,952 R	70.3%	29.3%	70.6%	29.4%
29,430	DEARBORN	11,885	7,689	4,137	59	3,552 R	64.7%	34.8%	65.0%	35.0%
22,738	DECATUR	9,822	6,761	2,994	67	3,767 R	68.8%	30.5%	69.3%	30.7%
30,837	DE KALB	13,297	8,834	4,354	109	4,480 R	66.4%	32.7%	67.0%	33.0%
129,219	DELAWARE	50,567	32,468	17,936	163	14,532 R	64.2%	35.5%	64.4%	35.6%
30,934	DUBOIS	13,179	6,637	6,365	177	272 R	50.4%	48.3%	51.0%	49.0%
126,529	ELKHART	43,941	31,009	12,659	273	18,350 R	70.6%	28.8%	71.0%	29.0%
26,216	FAYETTE	10,829	7,273	3,519	37	3,754 R	67.2%	32.5%	67.4%	32.6%
55,622	FLOYD	22,636	13,198	9,243	195	3,955 R	58.3%	40.8%	58.8%	41.2%
18,257	FOUNTAIN	9,003	5,979	2,977	47	3,002 R	66.4%	33.1%	66.8%	33.2%
16,943	FRANKLIN	6,479	4,324	2,131	24	2,193 R	66.7%	32.9%	67.0%	33.0%
16,984	FULTON	8,358	6,170	2,150	38	4,020 R	73.8%	25.7%	74.2%	25.8%
30,444	GIBSON	14,819	9,115	5,633	71	3,482 R	61.5%	38.0%	61.8%	38.2%
83,955	GRANT	28,958	20,969	7,912	77	13,057 R	72.4%	27.3%	72.6%	27.4%
26,894	GREENE	13,045	8,453	4,450	142	4,003 R	64.8%	34.1%	65.5%	34.5%
54,532	HAMILTON	24,470	20,247	4,151	72	16,096 R	82.7%	17.0%	83.0%	17.0%
35,096	HANCOCK	14,150	11,019	3,069	62	7,950 R	77.9%	21.7%	78.2%	21.8%
20,423	HARRISON	9,888	5,910	3,927	51	1,983 R	59.8%	39.7%	60.1%	39.9%
53,974	HENDRICKS	22,153	17,699	4,384	70	13,315 R	79.9%	19.8%	80.1%	19.9%
52,603	HENRY	20,208	14,538	5,610	60	8,928 R	71.9%	27.8%	72.2%	27.8%
83,198	HOWARD	31,341	23,089	8,083	169	15,006 R	73.7%	25.8%	74.1%	25.9%
34,970	HUNTINGTON	15,855	10,858	4,908	89	5,950 R	68.5%	31.0%	68.9%	31.1%
33,187	JACKSON	14,689	9,546	4,984	159	4,562 R	65.0%	33.9%	65.7%	34.3%
20,429	JASPER	8,357	6,369	1,920	68	4,449 R	76.2%	23.0%	76.8%	23.2%
23,575	JAY	9,484	6,090	3,349	45	2,741 R	64.2%	35.3%	64.5%	35.5%
27,006	JEFFERSON	11,103	6,722	4,267	114	2,455 R	60.5%	38.4%	61.2%	38.8%
19,454	JENNINGS	8,157	5,156	2,903	98	2,253 R	63.2%	35.6%	64.0%	36.0%
61,138	JOHNSON	22,724	17,537	5,067	120	12,470 R	77.2%	22.3%	77.6%	22.4%
41,546	KNOX	18,196	11,940	6,089	167	5,851 R	65.6%	33.5%	66.2%	33.8%
48,127	KOSCIUSKO	20,545	16,216	4,233	96	11,983 R	78.9%	20.6%	79.3%	20.7%
20,890	LAGRANGE	5,839	4,152	1,658	29	2,494 R	71.1%	28.4%	71.5%	28.5%
546,253	LAKE	205,342	115,480	88,510	1,352	26,970 R	56.2%	43.1%	56.6%	43.4%
105,342	LA PORTE	39,776	26,243	13,222	311	13,021 R	66.0%	33.2%	66.5%	33.5%
38,038	LAWRENCE	15,284	10,936	4,278	70	6,658 R	71.6%	28.0%	71.9%	28.1%
138,451	MADISON	60,134	39,036	20,921	177	18,115 R	64.9%	34.8%	65.1%	34.9%
792,299	MARION	309,766	206,065	102,166	1,535	103,899 R	66.5%	33.0%	66.9%	33.1%
34,986	MARSHALL	16,308	11,908	4,349	51	7,559 R	73.0%	26.7%	73.2%	26.8%
10,969	MARTIN	5,509	3,470	2,021	18	1,449 R	63.0%	36.7%	63.2%	36.8%
39,246	MIAMI	13,450	9,477	3,889	84	5,588 R	70.5%	28.9%	70.9%	29.1%
84,849	MONROE	35,596	19,953	15,241	402	4,712 R	56.1%	42.8%	56.7%	43.3%
33,930	MONTGOMERY	14,471	10,997	3,431	43	7,566 R	76.0%	23.7%	76.2%	23.8%
44,176	MORGAN	15,435	11,980	3,390	65	8,590 R	77.6%	22.0%	77.9%	22.1%
11,606	NEWTON	5,028	3,771	1,252	5	2,519 R	75.0%	24.9%	75.1%	24.9%
31,382	NOBLE	12,226	7,916	4,250	60	3,666 R	64.7%	34.8%	65.1%	34.9%
4,289	OHIO	2,299	1,368	922	9	446 R	59.5%	40.1%	59.7%	40.3%
16,968	ORANGE	8,674	5,715	2,932	27	2,783 R	65.9%	33.8%	66.1%	33.9%
12,163	OWEN	5,626	3,896	1,708	22	2,188 R	69.2%	30.4%	69.5%	30.5%

INDIANA

PRESIDENT 1972

1970 Census Population	County	Total Vote	Republican	Democratic	Other	Rep.-Dem. Plurality	Percentage Total Vote Rep.	Total Vote Dem.	Major Vote Rep.	Major Vote Dem.
14,600	PARKE	7,250	5,014	2,207	29	2,807 R	69.2%	30.4%	69.4%	30.6%
19,075	PERRY	9,510	5,204	4,277	29	927 R	54.7%	45.0%	54.9%	45.1%
12,281	PIKE	6,939	4,252	2,648	39	1,604 R	61.3%	38.2%	61.6%	38.4%
87,114	PORTER	36,030	26,877	8,943	210	17,934 R	74.6%	24.8%	75.0%	25.0%
21,740	POSEY	10,378	6,771	3,586	21	3,185 R	65.2%	34.6%	65.4%	34.6%
12,534	PULASKI	6,146	4,243	1,863	40	2,380 R	69.0%	30.3%	69.5%	30.5%
26,932	PUTNAM	11,243	7,879	3,339	25	4,540 R	70.1%	29.7%	70.2%	29.8%
28,915	RANDOLPH	12,232	8,754	3,409	69	5,345 R	71.6%	27.9%	72.0%	28.0%
21,138	RIPLEY	10,231	6,594	3,601	36	2,993 R	64.5%	35.2%	64.7%	35.3%
20,352	RUSH	7,752	5,965	1,764	23	4,201 R	76.9%	22.8%	77.2%	22.8%
245,045	ST. JOSEPH	107,039	64,808	41,629	602	23,179 R	60.5%	38.9%	60.9%	39.1%
17,144	SCOTT	6,391	3,564	2,785	42	779 R	55.8%	43.6%	56.1%	43.9%
37,797	SHELBY	14,900	10,794	4,028	78	6,766 R	72.4%	27.0%	72.8%	27.2%
17,134	SPENCER	9,415	5,518	3,867	30	1,651 R	58.6%	41.1%	58.8%	41.2%
19,280	STARKE	8,567	5,520	2,994	53	2,526 R	64.4%	34.9%	64.8%	35.2%
20,159	STEUBEN	8,075	5,636	2,401	38	3,235 R	69.8%	29.7%	70.1%	29.9%
19,889	SULLIVAN	9,001	5,338	3,624	39	1,714 R	59.3%	40.3%	59.6%	40.4%
6,306	SWITZERLAND	3,497	1,872	1,612	13	260 R	53.5%	46.1%	53.7%	46.3%
109,378	TIPPECANOE	46,366	31,565	14,598	203	16,967 R	68.1%	31.5%	68.4%	31.6%
16,650	TIPTON	7,808	5,674	2,095	39	3,579 R	72.7%	26.8%	73.0%	27.0%
6,582	UNION	2,818	2,043	765	10	1,278 R	72.5%	27.1%	72.8%	27.2%
168,772	VANDERBURGH	71,437	48,806	22,163	468	26,643 R	68.3%	31.0%	68.8%	31.2%
16,793	VERMILLION	8,323	4,764	3,515	44	1,249 R	57.2%	42.2%	57.5%	42.5%
114,528	VIGO	48,957	29,730	18,898	329	10,832 R	60.7%	38.6%	61.1%	38.9%
35,553	WABASH	14,659	10,011	4,601	47	5,410 R	68.3%	31.4%	68.5%	31.5%
8,705	WARREN	3,925	2,746	1,164	15	1,582 R	70.0%	29.7%	70.2%	29.8%
27,972	WARRICK	12,941	8,520	4,296	125	4,224 R	65.8%	33.2%	66.5%	33.5%
19,278	WASHINGTON	7,922	4,758	3,086	78	1,672 R	60.1%	39.0%	60.7%	39.3%
79,109	WAYNE	29,361	21,610	7,655	96	13,955 R	73.6%	26.1%	73.8%	26.2%
23,821	WELLS	9,769	6,425	3,244	100	3,181 R	65.8%	33.2%	66.4%	33.6%
20,995	WHITE	10,137	7,419	2,675	43	4,744 R	73.2%	26.4%	73.5%	26.5%
23,395	WHITLEY	11,404	7,489	3,838	77	3,651 R	65.7%	33.7%	66.1%	33.9%
5,193,669	TOTAL	2,125,529	1,405,154	708,568	11,807	696,586 R	66.1%	33.3%	66.5%	33.5%

INDIANA

PRESIDENT 1968

1960 Census Population	County	Total Vote	Republican	Democratic	AIP	Other	Plurality	Percentage Rep.	Percentage Dem.	Percentage AIP
24,643	ADAMS	11,259	5,774	4,667	762	56	1,107 R	51.3%	41.5%	6.8%
232,196	ALLEN	108,954	59,211	40,411	9,121	211	18,800 R	54.3%	37.1%	8.4%
48,198	BARTHOLOMEW	24,424	13,628	8,268	2,438	90	5,360 R	55.8%	33.9%	10.0%
11,912	BENTON	5,586	3,326	1,854	400	6	1,472 R	59.5%	33.2%	7.2%
14,792	BLACKFORD	6,504	3,052	2,898	534	20	154 R	46.9%	44.6%	8.2%
27,543	BOONE	13,407	7,905	4,118	1,346	38	3,787 R	59.0%	30.7%	10.0%
7,024	BROWN	3,807	1,881	1,327	587	12	554 R	49.4%	34.9%	15.4%
16,934	CARROLL	8,535	4,796	2,816	918	5	1,980 R	56.2%	33.0%	10.8%
40,931	CASS	18,318	9,441	7,142	1,678	57	2,299 R	51.5%	39.0%	9.2%
62,795	CLARK	26,886	10,305	11,493	4,982	106	1,188 D	38.3%	42.7%	18.5%
24,207	CLAY	11,298	5,743	3,956	1,569	30	1,787 R	50.8%	35.0%	13.9%
30,765	CLINTON	14,707	7,929	5,714	1,033	31	2,215 R	53.9%	38.9%	7.0%
8,379	CRAWFORD	4,280	2,132	1,536	589	23	596 R	49.8%	35.9%	13.8%
26,636	DAVIESS	12,393	7,036	4,071	1,274	12	2,965 R	56.8%	32.8%	10.3%
28,674	DEARBORN	12,760	6,208	4,842	1,704	6	1,366 R	48.7%	37.9%	13.4%
20,019	DECATUR	9,833	5,474	3,602	731	26	1,872 R	55.7%	36.6%	7.4%
28,271	DE KALB	13,438	7,650	4,790	931	67	2,860 R	56.9%	35.6%	6.9%
110,938	DELAWARE	49,523	23,554	19,532	6,349	88	4,022 R	47.6%	39.4%	12.8%
27,463	DUBOIS	13,563	5,865	6,725	958	15	860 D	43.2%	49.6%	7.1%
106,790	ELKHART	42,289	24,484	14,222	3,440	143	10,262 R	57.9%	33.6%	8.1%
24,454	FAYETTE	11,266	5,286	4,549	1,413	18	737 R	46.9%	40.4%	12.5%
51,397	FLOYD	23,701	9,714	10,671	3,266	50	957 D	41.0%	45.0%	13.8%
18,706	FOUNTAIN	9,637	5,110	3,237	1,280	10	1,873 R	53.0%	33.6%	13.3%
17,015	FRANKLIN	6,634	3,468	2,386	775	5	1,082 R	52.3%	36.0%	11.7%
16,957	FULTON	8,474	5,145	2,561	757	11	2,584 R	60.7%	30.2%	8.9%
29,949	GIBSON	15,957	7,645	6,777	1,497	38	868 R	47.9%	42.5%	9.4%
75,741	GRANT	30,826	16,170	10,938	3,602	116	5,232 R	52.5%	35.5%	11.7%
26,327	GREENE	13,491	6,525	5,493	1,419	54	1,032 R	48.4%	40.7%	10.5%
40,132	HAMILTON	21,069	14,250	4,586	2,202	31	9,664 R	67.6%	21.8%	10.5%
26,665	HANCOCK	13,366	7,516	3,902	1,896	52	3,614 R	56.2%	29.2%	14.2%
19,207	HARRISON	9,731	4,410	3,725	1,557	39	685 R	45.3%	38.3%	16.0%
40,896	HENDRICKS	21,032	12,597	5,155	3,231	49	7,442 R	59.9%	24.5%	15.4%
48,899	HENRY	22,097	11,626	8,045	2,366	60	3,581 R	52.6%	36.4%	10.7%
69,509	HOWARD	31,566	15,905	11,026	4,507	128	4,879 R	50.4%	34.9%	14.3%
33,814	HUNTINGTON	16,523	9,002	6,238	1,250	33	2,764 R	54.5%	37.8%	7.6%
30,556	JACKSON	14,821	7,710	5,140	1,891	80	2,570 R	52.0%	34.7%	12.8%
18,842	JASPER	8,252	4,996	2,201	1,003	52	2,795 R	60.5%	26.7%	12.2%
22,572	JAY	10,705	5,460	4,290	918	37	1,170 R	51.0%	40.1%	8.6%
24,061	JEFFERSON	11,623	5,731	4,635	1,196	61	1,096 R	49.3%	39.9%	10.3%
17,267	JENNINGS	8,640	4,416	2,996	1,214	14	1,420 R	51.1%	34.7%	14.1%
43,704	JOHNSON	21,111	12,089	5,946	3,021	55	6,143 R	57.3%	28.2%	14.3%
41,561	KNOX	17,818	8,369	7,297	2,053	99	1,072 R	47.0%	41.0%	11.5%
40,373	KOSCIUSKO	19,744	12,633	5,342	1,700	69	7,291 R	64.0%	27.1%	8.6%
17,380	LAGRANGE	5,408	3,328	1,691	380	9	1,637 R	61.5%	31.3%	7.0%
513,269	LAKE	213,574	77,911	99,897	35,099	667	21,986 D	36.5%	46.8%	16.4%
95,111	LA PORTE	40,783	20,295	15,780	4,587	121	4,515 R	49.8%	38.7%	11.2%
36,564	LAWRENCE	16,248	8,830	5,349	1,995	74	3,481 R	54.3%	32.9%	12.3%
125,819	MADISON	59,368	28,726	23,886	6,613	143	4,840 R	48.4%	40.2%	11.1%
697,567	MARION	310,922	162,503	115,715	32,043	661	46,788 R	52.3%	37.2%	10.3%
32,443	MARSHALL	16,394	9,290	5,385	1,685	34	3,905 R	56.7%	32.8%	10.3%
10,608	MARTIN	5,435	2,512	2,315	604	4	197 R	46.2%	42.6%	11.1%
38,000	MIAMI	13,655	7,295	5,019	1,294	47	2,276 R	53.4%	36.8%	9.5%
59,225	MONROE	27,080	13,752	10,789	2,361	178	2,963 R	50.8%	39.8%	8.7%
32,089	MONTGOMERY	15,175	9,085	4,752	1,309	29	4,333 R	59.9%	31.3%	8.6%
33,875	MORGAN	16,130	8,944	4,042	3,122	22	4,902 R	55.4%	25.1%	19.4%
11,502	NEWTON	5,093	3,145	1,453	483	12	1,692 R	61.8%	28.5%	9.5%
28,162	NOBLE	13,046	6,699	5,075	1,253	19	1,624 R	51.3%	38.9%	9.6%
4,165	OHIO	2,287	1,053	991	243		62 R	46.0%	43.3%	10.6%
16,877	ORANGE	8,512	4,666	2,918	915	13	1,748 R	54.8%	34.3%	10.7%
11,400	OWEN	5,618	2,898	1,932	776	12	966 R	51.6%	34.4%	13.8%

INDIANA

PRESIDENT 1968

1960 Census Population	County	Total Vote	Republican	Democratic	AIP	Other	Plurality	Percentage Rep.	Dem.	AIP
14,804	PARKE	7,124	3,738	2,472	907	7	1,266 R	52.5%	34.7%	12.7%
17,232	PERRY	9,108	4,211	4,343	547	7	132 D	46.2%	47.7%	6.0%
12,797	PIKE	6,802	3,087	2,953	745	17	134 R	45.4%	43.4%	11.0%
60,279	PORTER	32,582	17,328	8,914	6,126	214	8,414 R	53.2%	27.4%	18.8%
19,214	POSEY	10,150	5,045	3,889	1,204	12	1,156 R	49.7%	38.3%	11.9%
12,837	PULASKI	6,133	3,361	2,071	681	20	1,290 R	54.8%	33.8%	11.1%
24,927	PUTNAM	11,410	5,873	3,692	1,826	19	2,181 R	51.5%	32.4%	16.0%
28,434	RANDOLPH	12,667	7,238	3,962	1,431	36	3,276 R	57.1%	31.3%	11.3%
20,641	RIPLEY	10,399	5,389	3,787	1,215	8	1,602 R	51.8%	36.4%	11.7%
20,393	RUSH	8,421	5,004	2,636	761	20	2,368 R	59.4%	31.3%	9.0%
238,614	ST. JOSEPH	106,864	47,114	47,414	11,948	388	300 D	44.1%	44.4%	11.2%
14,643	SCOTT	6,267	2,671	2,796	784	16	125 D	42.6%	44.6%	12.5%
34,093	SHELBY	16,226	8,574	5,417	2,205	30	3,157 R	52.8%	33.4%	13.6%
16,074	SPENCER	8,993	4,603	3,767	612	11	836 R	51.2%	41.9%	6.8%
17,911	STARKE	8,365	4,011	3,208	1,097	49	803 R	47.9%	38.4%	13.1%
17,184	STEUBEN	7,618	4,762	2,268	577	11	2,494 R	62.5%	29.8%	7.6%
21,721	SULLIVAN	9,874	4,266	4,453	1,135	20	187 D	43.2%	45.1%	11.5%
7,092	SWITZERLAND	3,438	1,515	1,466	452	5	49 R	44.1%	42.6%	13.1%
89,122	TIPPECANOE	40,968	24,352	14,528	2,000	88	9,824 R	59.4%	35.5%	4.9%
15,856	TIPTON	7,802	4,270	2,646	861	25	1,624 R	54.7%	33.9%	11.0%
6,457	UNION	3,019	1,691	920	404	4	771 R	56.0%	30.5%	13.4%
165,794	VANDERBURGH	77,577	38,231	31,326	7,737	283	6,905 R	49.3%	40.4%	10.0%
17,683	VERMILLION	8,637	3,607	3,845	1,175	10	238 D	41.8%	44.5%	13.6%
108,458	VIGO	46,664	20,814	20,328	5,386	136	486 R	44.6%	43.6%	11.5%
32,605	WABASH	14,101	8,611	4,598	836	56	4,013 R	61.1%	32.6%	5.9%
8,545	WARREN	4,342	2,475	1,375	483	9	1,100 R	57.0%	31.7%	11.1%
23,577	WARRICK	12,081	5,742	4,784	1,503	52	958 R	47.5%	39.6%	12.4%
17,819	WASHINGTON	8,004	3,891	2,936	1,143	34	955 R	48.6%	36.7%	14.3%
74,039	WAYNE	32,308	17,335	10,686	4,240	47	6,649 R	53.7%	33.1%	13.1%
21,220	WELLS	10,101	5,361	3,827	882	31	1,534 R	53.1%	37.9%	8.7%
19,709	WHITE	10,305	5,932	3,395	965	13	2,537 R	57.6%	32.9%	9.4%
20,954	WHITLEY	10,671	5,684	3,848	1,120	19	1,836 R	53.3%	36.1%	10.5%
4,662,498	TOTAL	2,123,597	1,067,885	806,659	243,108	5,945	261,226 R	50.3%	38.0%	11.4%

INDIANA

ELECTION NOTES

1984 Other vote was 7,617 Dennis (American); 6,741 Bergland (Libertarian).

1980 Other vote was 111,639 Anderson (Independent); 19,627 Clark (Libertarian); 4,852 Commoner (Citizens); 4,750 Greaves (American); 702 Hall (Communist); 610 DeBerry (Socialist Workers).

1976 Other vote was 14,048 Anderson (American); 5,695 Camejo (Socialist Workers); 1,947 LaRouche (U.S. Labor). Early unamended canvass gave the total state-wide Republican vote as 1,185,958.

1972 Other vote was 5,575 Reed (Socialist Workers); 4,544 Spock (Peace and Freedom); 1,688 Fisher (Socialist Labor).

1968 Wallace on the ballot as George C. Wallace party. Other vote was 4,616 Munn (Prohibition); 1,293 Halstead (Socialist Workers); 36 Gregory (write-in).

IOWA

POPULAR VOTE FOR PRESIDENT 1920 TO 1984

Year	Total Vote	Republican Vote	Republican Candidate	Democratic Vote	Democratic Candidate	Other Vote	Plurality	Percentage Total Vote Rep.	Percentage Total Vote Dem.	Percentage Major Vote Rep.	Percentage Major Vote Dem.
1984	1,319,805	703,088	Reagan, Ronald	605,620	Mondale, Walter F.	11,097	97,468 R	53.3%	45.9%	53.7%	46.3%
1980	1,317,661	676,026	Reagan, Ronald	508,672	Carter, Jimmy	132,963	167,354 R	51.3%	38.6%	57.1%	42.9%
1976	1,279,306	632,863	Ford, Gerald R.	619,931	Carter, Jimmy	26,512	12,932 R	49.5%	48.5%	50.5%	49.5%
1972	1,225,944	706,207	Nixon, Richard M.	496,206	McGovern, George S.	23,531	210,001 R	57.6%	40.5%	58.7%	41.3%
1968	1,167,931	619,106	Nixon, Richard M.	476,699	Humphrey, Hubert H.	72,126	142,407 R	53.0%	40.8%	56.5%	43.5%
1964	1,184,539	449,148	Goldwater, Barry M.	733,030	Johnson, Lyndon B.	2,361	283,882 D	37.9%	61.9%	38.0%	62.0%
1960	1,273,810	722,381	Nixon, Richard M.	550,565	Kennedy, John F.	864	171,816 R	56.7%	43.2%	56.7%	43.3%
1956	1,234,564	729,187	Eisenhower, Dwight D.	501,858	Stevenson, Adlai E.	3,519	227,329 R	59.1%	40.7%	59.2%	40.8%
1952	1,268,773	808,906	Eisenhower, Dwight D.	451,513	Stevenson, Adlai E.	8,354	357,393 R	63.8%	35.6%	64.2%	35.8%
1948	1,038,264	494,018	Dewey, Thomas E.	522,380	Truman, Harry S.	21,866	28,362 D	47.6%	50.3%	48.6%	51.4%
1944	1,052,599	547,267	Dewey, Thomas E.	499,876	Roosevelt, Franklin D.	5,456	47,391 R	52.0%	47.5%	52.3%	47.7%
1940	1,215,432	632,370	Willkie, Wendell	578,802	Roosevelt, Franklin D.	4,260	53,568 R	52.0%	47.6%	52.2%	47.8%
1936	1,142,737	487,977	Landon, Alfred M.	621,756	Roosevelt, Franklin D.	33,004	133,779 D	42.7%	54.4%	44.0%	56.0%
1932	1,036,687	414,433	Hoover, Herbert C.	598,019	Roosevelt, Franklin D.	24,235	183,586 D	40.0%	57.7%	40.9%	59.1%
1928	1,009,189	623,570	Hoover, Herbert C.	379,011	Smith, Alfred E.	6,608	244,559 R	61.8%	37.6%	62.2%	37.8%
1924 **	976,770	537,458	Coolidge, Calvin	160,382	Davis, John W.	278,930	263,010 R	55.0%	16.4%	77.0%	23.0%
1920	894,959	634,674	Harding, Warren G.	227,804	Cox, James M.	32,481	406,870 R	70.9%	25.5%	73.6%	26.4%

In 1924 other vote was 274,448 Progressive; 4,037 Communist and 445 scattered.

ELECTORAL COLLEGE VOTE 1920 TO 1984

Year	Total	Republican	Democratic	Other
1984	8	8	—	—
1980	8	8	—	—
1976	8	8	—	—
1972	8	8	—	—
1968	9	9	—	—
1964	9	—	9	—
1960	10	10	—	—
1956	10	10	—	—
1952	10	10	—	—
1948	10	—	10	—
1944	10	10	—	—
1940	11	11	—	—
1936	11	—	11	—
1932	11	—	11	—
1928	13	13	—	—
1924	13	13	—	—
1920	13	13	—	—

IOWA

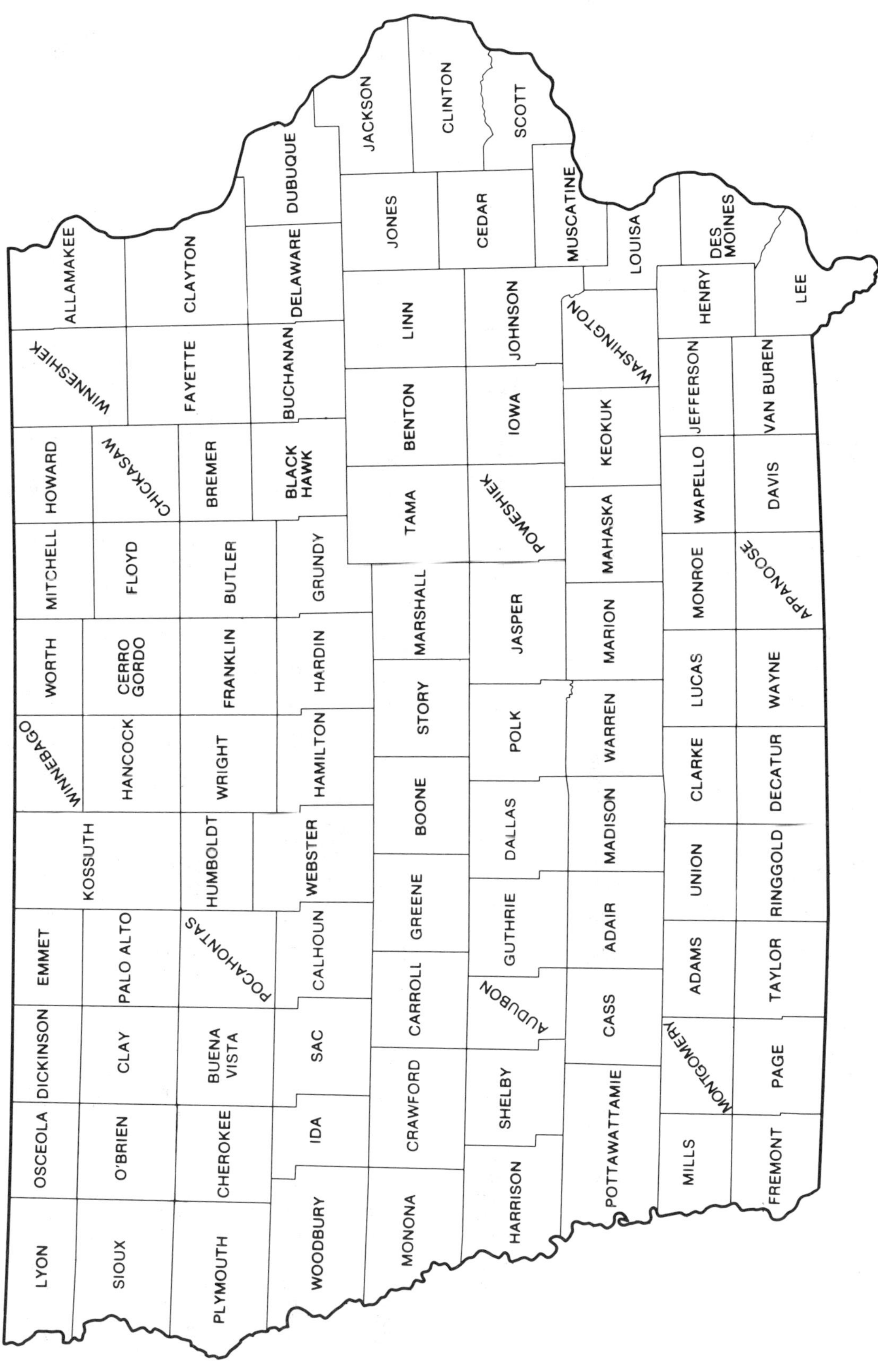
JACKSON
CLINTON
SCOTT
DUBUQUE
JONES
CEDAR
MUSCATINE
LOUISA
DES MOINES
ALLAMAKEE
CLAYTON
DELAWARE
LINN
JOHNSON
WASHINGTON
HENRY
LEE
WINNESHIEK
FAYETTE
BUCHANAN
BENTON
IOWA
KEOKUK
JEFFERSON
VAN BUREN
HOWARD
CHICKASAW
BREMER
BLACK HAWK
TAMA
POWESHIEK
MAHASKA
WAPELLO
DAVIS
MITCHELL
FLOYD
BUTLER
GRUNDY
MARSHALL
JASPER
MARION
MONROE
APPANOOSE
WORTH
CERRO GORDO
FRANKLIN
HARDIN
STORY
POLK
WARREN
LUCAS
WAYNE
WINNEBAGO
HANCOCK
WRIGHT
HAMILTON
BOONE
DALLAS
MADISON
CLARKE
DECATUR
KOSSUTH
HUMBOLDT
WEBSTER
GREENE
GUTHRIE
ADAIR
UNION
RINGGOLD
EMMET
PALO ALTO
POCAHONTAS
CALHOUN
CARROLL
AUDUBON
CASS
ADAMS
TAYLOR
DICKINSON
CLAY
BUENA VISTA
SAC
CRAWFORD
SHELBY
POTTAWATTAMIE
MONTGOMERY
PAGE
OSCEOLA
O'BRIEN
CHEROKEE
IDA
MONONA
HARRISON
MILLS
FREMONT
LYON
SIOUX
PLYMOUTH
WOODBURY

IOWA

PRESIDENT 1984

1980 Census Population	County	Total Vote	Republican	Democratic	Other	Rep.-Dem. Plurality	Percentage Total Vote Rep.	Percentage Total Vote Dem.	Percentage Major Vote Rep.	Percentage Major Vote Dem.
9,509	ADAIR	4,619	2,615	1,979	25	636 R	56.6%	42.8%	56.9%	43.1%
5,731	ADAMS	2,960	1,706	1,221	33	485 R	57.6%	41.3%	58.3%	41.7%
15,108	ALLAMAKEE	6,354	3,997	2,282	75	1,715 R	62.9%	35.9%	63.7%	36.3%
15,511	APPANOOSE	6,759	3,412	3,289	58	123 R	50.5%	48.7%	50.9%	49.1%
8,559	AUDUBON	4,195	2,306	1,854	35	452 R	55.0%	44.2%	55.4%	44.6%
23,649	BENTON	10,678	5,566	4,993	119	573 R	52.1%	46.8%	52.7%	47.3%
137,961	BLACK HAWK	64,233	32,262	31,467	504	795 R	50.2%	49.0%	50.6%	49.4%
26,184	BOONE	12,277	5,746	6,485	46	739 D	46.8%	52.8%	47.0%	53.0%
24,820	BREMER	11,055	6,895	4,084	76	2,811 R	62.4%	36.9%	62.8%	37.2%
22,900	BUCHANAN	9,152	4,965	4,129	58	836 R	54.3%	45.1%	54.6%	45.4%
20,774	BUENA VISTA	9,405	5,193	4,109	103	1,084 R	55.2%	43.7%	55.8%	44.2%
17,668	BUTLER	6,924	4,570	2,323	31	2,247 R	66.0%	33.5%	66.3%	33.7%
13,542	CALHOUN	5,898	3,311	2,541	46	770 R	56.1%	43.1%	56.6%	43.4%
22,951	CARROLL	10,077	5,021	4,960	96	61 R	49.8%	49.2%	50.3%	49.7%
16,932	CASS	7,531	5,053	2,417	61	2,636 R	67.1%	32.1%	67.6%	32.4%
18,635	CEDAR	7,748	4,617	3,086	45	1,531 R	59.6%	39.8%	59.9%	40.1%
48,458	CERRO GORDO	22,950	11,214	11,570	166	356 D	48.9%	50.4%	49.2%	50.8%
16,238	CHEROKEE	7,470	4,046	3,349	75	697 R	54.2%	44.8%	54.7%	45.3%
15,437	CHICKASAW	6,917	3,661	3,186	70	475 R	52.9%	46.1%	53.5%	46.5%
8,612	CLARKE	4,321	2,262	2,030	29	232 R	52.3%	47.0%	52.7%	47.3%
19,576	CLAY	8,316	4,450	3,774	92	676 R	53.5%	45.4%	54.1%	45.9%
21,098	CLAYTON	8,553	5,029	3,446	78	1,583 R	58.8%	40.3%	59.3%	40.7%
57,122	CLINTON	25,404	13,914	11,240	250	2,674 R	54.8%	44.2%	55.3%	44.7%
18,935	CRAWFORD	8,053	4,552	3,396	105	1,156 R	56.5%	42.2%	57.3%	42.7%
29,513	DALLAS	12,707	6,080	6,564	63	484 D	47.8%	51.7%	48.1%	51.9%
9,104	DAVIS	4,182	1,956	2,187	39	231 D	46.8%	52.3%	47.2%	52.8%
9,794	DECATUR	4,242	2,104	2,098	40	6 R	49.6%	49.5%	50.1%	49.9%
18,933	DELAWARE	8,001	4,769	3,158	74	1,611 R	59.6%	39.5%	60.2%	39.8%
46,203	DES MOINES	20,850	9,559	11,173	118	1,614 D	45.8%	53.6%	46.1%	53.9%
15,629	DICKINSON	7,170	4,064	3,025	81	1,039 R	56.7%	42.2%	57.3%	42.7%
93,745	DUBUQUE	41,491	19,239	21,876	376	2,637 D	46.4%	52.7%	46.8%	53.2%
13,336	EMMET	5,725	2,946	2,746	33	200 R	51.5%	48.0%	51.8%	48.2%
25,488	FAYETTE	11,302	6,505	4,677	120	1,828 R	57.6%	41.4%	58.2%	41.8%
19,597	FLOYD	8,553	4,341	4,154	58	187 R	50.8%	48.6%	51.1%	48.9%
13,036	FRANKLIN	5,545	3,129	2,349	67	780 R	56.4%	42.4%	57.1%	42.9%
9,401	FREMONT	4,147	2,686	1,426	35	1,260 R	64.8%	34.4%	65.3%	34.7%
12,119	GREENE	5,554	2,579	2,831	144	252 D	46.4%	51.0%	47.7%	52.3%
14,366	GRUNDY	6,518	4,527	1,915	76	2,612 R	69.5%	29.4%	70.3%	29.7%
11,983	GUTHRIE	5,363	2,783	2,517	63	266 R	51.9%	46.9%	52.5%	47.5%
17,862	HAMILTON	7,695	4,279	3,330	86	949 R	55.6%	43.3%	56.2%	43.8%
13,833	HANCOCK	5,938	3,362	2,539	37	823 R	56.6%	42.8%	57.0%	43.0%
21,776	HARDIN	9,732	5,195	4,477	60	718 R	53.4%	46.0%	53.7%	46.3%
16,348	HARRISON	6,882	4,352	2,495	35	1,857 R	63.2%	36.3%	63.6%	36.4%
18,890	HENRY	7,955	4,516	3,377	62	1,139 R	56.8%	42.5%	57.2%	42.8%
11,114	HOWARD	4,898	2,718	2,135	45	583 R	55.5%	43.6%	56.0%	44.0%
12,246	HUMBOLDT	5,863	3,396	2,406	61	990 R	57.9%	41.0%	58.5%	41.5%
8,908	IDA	4,202	2,618	1,559	25	1,059 R	62.3%	37.1%	62.7%	37.3%
15,429	IOWA	7,251	4,352	2,815	84	1,537 R	60.0%	38.8%	60.7%	39.3%
22,503	JACKSON	9,340	4,811	4,400	129	411 R	51.5%	47.1%	52.2%	47.8%
36,425	JASPER	16,699	8,576	8,023	100	553 R	51.4%	48.0%	51.7%	48.3%
16,316	JEFFERSON	7,725	4,727	2,961	37	1,766 R	61.2%	38.3%	61.5%	38.5%
81,717	JOHNSON	45,044	18,677	26,000	367	7,323 D	41.5%	57.7%	41.8%	58.2%
20,401	JONES	8,791	4,907	3,825	59	1,082 R	55.8%	43.5%	56.2%	43.8%
12,921	KEOKUK	5,656	2,913	2,649	94	264 R	51.5%	46.8%	52.4%	47.6%
21,891	KOSSUTH	9,814	4,872	4,838	104	34 R	49.6%	49.3%	50.2%	49.8%
43,106	LEE	17,809	8,756	8,912	141	156 D	49.2%	50.0%	49.6%	50.4%
169,775	LINN	80,315	41,061	38,528	726	2,533 R	51.1%	48.0%	51.6%	48.4%
12,055	LOUISA	4,573	2,623	1,927	23	696 R	57.4%	42.1%	57.6%	42.4%
10,313	LUCAS	5,085	2,630	2,422	33	208 R	51.7%	47.6%	52.1%	47.9%
12,896	LYON	5,642	4,178	1,401	63	2,777 R	74.1%	24.8%	74.9%	25.1%

IOWA

PRESIDENT 1984

1980 Census Population	County	Total Vote	Republican	Democratic	Other	Rep.-Dem. Plurality	Percentage Total Vote Rep.	Percentage Total Vote Dem.	Percentage Major Vote Rep.	Percentage Major Vote Dem.
12,597	MADISON	6,261	3,168	3,067	26	101 R	50.6%	49.0%	50.8%	49.2%
22,867	MAHASKA	10,293	6,086	4,107	100	1,979 R	59.1%	39.9%	59.7%	40.3%
29,669	MARION	13,634	7,259	6,313	62	946 R	53.2%	46.3%	53.5%	46.5%
41,652	MARSHALL	19,840	10,839	8,809	192	2,030 R	54.6%	44.4%	55.2%	44.8%
13,406	MILLS	5,486	3,994	1,434	58	2,560 R	72.8%	26.1%	73.6%	26.4%
12,329	MITCHELL	5,743	3,144	2,531	68	613 R	54.7%	44.1%	55.4%	44.6%
11,692	MONONA	4,959	2,746	2,159	54	587 R	55.4%	43.5%	56.0%	44.0%
9,209	MONROE	4,291	1,927	2,342	22	415 D	44.9%	54.6%	45.1%	54.9%
13,413	MONTGOMERY	5,930	4,224	1,661	45	2,563 R	71.2%	28.0%	71.8%	28.2%
40,436	MUSCATINE	15,168	9,069	5,986	113	3,083 R	59.8%	39.5%	60.2%	39.8%
16,972	O'BRIEN	7,569	5,008	2,479	82	2,529 R	66.2%	32.8%	66.9%	33.1%
8,371	OSCEOLA	3,463	2,285	1,146	32	1,139 R	66.0%	33.1%	66.6%	33.4%
19,063	PAGE	7,828	5,876	1,914	38	3,962 R	75.1%	24.5%	75.4%	24.6%
12,721	PALO ALTO	5,810	2,715	3,018	77	303 D	46.7%	51.9%	47.4%	52.6%
24,743	PLYMOUTH	10,027	6,482	3,464	81	3,018 R	64.6%	34.5%	65.2%	34.8%
11,369	POCAHONTAS	5,188	2,627	2,481	80	146 R	50.6%	47.8%	51.4%	48.6%
303,170	POLK	147,848	71,413	75,413	1,022	4,000 D	48.3%	51.0%	48.6%	51.4%
86,561	POTTAWATTAMIE	34,112	21,527	12,329	256	9,198 R	63.1%	36.1%	63.6%	36.4%
19,306	POWESHIEK	8,889	4,715	4,103	71	612 R	53.0%	46.2%	53.5%	46.5%
6,112	RINGGOLD	3,117	1,512	1,593	12	81 D	48.5%	51.1%	48.7%	51.3%
14,118	SAC	5,729	3,298	2,363	68	935 R	57.6%	41.2%	58.3%	41.7%
160,022	SCOTT	71,212	38,034	32,550	628	5,484 R	53.4%	45.7%	53.9%	46.1%
15,043	SHELBY	6,537	4,200	2,291	46	1,909 R	64.2%	35.0%	64.7%	35.3%
30,813	SIOUX	14,293	11,665	2,585	43	9,080 R	81.6%	18.1%	81.9%	18.1%
72,326	STORY	38,410	19,804	18,277	329	1,527 R	51.6%	47.6%	52.0%	48.0%
19,533	TAMA	8,990	4,882	4,061	47	821 R	54.3%	45.2%	54.6%	45.4%
8,353	TAYLOR	4,022	2,496	1,499	27	997 R	62.1%	37.3%	62.5%	37.5%
13,858	UNION	6,576	3,583	2,875	118	708 R	54.5%	43.7%	55.5%	44.5%
8,626	VAN BUREN	3,769	2,138	1,606	25	532 R	56.7%	42.6%	57.1%	42.9%
40,241	WAPELLO	17,800	7,098	10,545	157	3,447 D	39.9%	59.2%	40.2%	59.8%
34,878	WARREN	16,570	8,277	8,171	122	106 R	50.0%	49.3%	50.3%	49.7%
20,141	WASHINGTON	7,770	4,613	3,079	78	1,534 R	59.4%	39.6%	60.0%	40.0%
8,199	WAYNE	4,021	2,061	1,927	33	134 R	51.3%	47.9%	51.7%	48.3%
45,953	WEBSTER	19,802	9,619	9,930	253	311 D	48.6%	50.1%	49.2%	50.8%
13,010	WINNEBAGO	6,314	3,616	2,669	29	947 R	57.3%	42.3%	57.5%	42.5%
21,876	WINNESHIEK	9,105	5,277	3,724	104	1,553 R	58.0%	40.9%	58.6%	41.4%
100,004	WOODBURY	42,350	23,002	18,951	397	4,051 R	54.3%	44.7%	54.8%	45.2%
9,075	WORTH	4,266	1,985	2,263	18	278 D	46.5%	53.0%	46.7%	53.3%
16,319	WRIGHT	6,705	3,675	2,980	50	695 R	54.8%	44.4%	55.2%	44.8%
2,913,808	TOTAL	1,319,805	703,088	605,620	11,097	97,468 R	53.3%	45.9%	53.7%	46.3%

IOWA

PRESIDENT 1980

1980 Census Population	County	Total Vote	Republican	Democratic	Other	Rep.-Dem. Plurality	Percentage: Total Vote Rep.	Percentage: Total Vote Dem.	Percentage: Major Vote Rep.	Percentage: Major Vote Dem.
9,509	ADAIR	4,689	2,821	1,454	414	1,367 R	60.2%	31.0%	66.0%	34.0%
5,731	ADAMS	2,984	1,779	940	265	839 R	59.6%	31.5%	65.4%	34.6%
15,108	ALLAMAKEE	6,586	4,000	2,170	416	1,830 R	60.7%	32.9%	64.8%	35.2%
15,511	APPANOOSE	6,728	3,544	2,769	415	775 R	52.7%	41.2%	56.1%	43.9%
8,559	AUDUBON	4,353	2,523	1,546	284	977 R	58.0%	35.5%	62.0%	38.0%
23,649	BENTON	10,635	5,329	4,223	1,083	1,106 R	50.1%	39.7%	55.8%	44.2%
137,961	BLACK HAWK	63,722	29,627	27,443	6,652	2,184 R	46.5%	43.1%	51.9%	48.1%
26,184	BOONE	12,087	5,732	5,126	1,229	606 R	47.4%	42.4%	52.8%	47.2%
24,820	BREMER	11,318	6,706	3,527	1,085	3,179 R	59.3%	31.2%	65.5%	34.5%
22,900	BUCHANAN	9,422	5,041	3,605	776	1,436 R	53.5%	38.3%	58.3%	41.7%
20,774	BUENA VISTA	9,676	5,272	3,468	936	1,804 R	54.5%	35.8%	60.3%	39.7%
17,668	BUTLER	7,177	4,730	1,990	457	2,740 R	65.9%	27.7%	70.4%	29.6%
13,542	CALHOUN	6,328	3,633	2,150	545	1,483 R	57.4%	34.0%	62.8%	37.2%
22,951	CARROLL	9,737	5,017	3,885	835	1,132 R	51.5%	39.9%	56.4%	43.6%
16,932	CASS	8,126	5,391	2,176	559	3,215 R	66.3%	26.8%	71.2%	28.8%
18,635	CEDAR	7,797	4,398	2,589	810	1,809 R	56.4%	33.2%	62.9%	37.1%
48,458	CERRO GORDO	22,828	11,189	9,363	2,276	1,826 R	49.0%	41.0%	54.4%	45.6%
16,238	CHEROKEE	7,500	4,087	2,719	694	1,368 R	54.5%	36.3%	60.0%	40.0%
15,437	CHICKASAW	7,433	3,929	2,935	569	994 R	52.9%	39.5%	57.2%	42.8%
8,612	CLARKE	4,404	2,417	1,614	373	803 R	54.9%	36.6%	60.0%	40.0%
19,576	CLAY	8,764	4,479	3,179	1,106	1,300 R	51.1%	36.3%	58.5%	41.5%
21,098	CLAYTON	9,206	5,115	3,297	794	1,818 R	55.6%	35.8%	60.8%	39.2%
57,122	CLINTON	25,211	13,025	9,698	2,488	3,327 R	51.7%	38.5%	57.3%	42.7%
18,935	CRAWFORD	8,002	4,883	2,500	619	2,383 R	61.0%	31.2%	66.1%	33.9%
29,513	DALLAS	12,964	6,296	5,310	1,358	986 R	48.6%	41.0%	54.2%	45.8%
9,104	DAVIS	3,930	2,003	1,689	238	314 R	51.0%	43.0%	54.3%	45.7%
9,794	DECATUR	4,640	2,212	2,048	380	164 R	47.7%	44.1%	51.9%	48.1%
18,933	DELAWARE	7,794	4,316	2,671	807	1,645 R	55.4%	34.3%	61.8%	38.2%
46,203	DES MOINES	20,417	9,158	9,977	1,282	819 D	44.9%	48.9%	47.9%	52.1%
15,629	DICKINSON	7,442	4,028	2,620	794	1,408 R	54.1%	35.2%	60.6%	39.4%
93,745	DUBUQUE	41,539	18,649	18,689	4,201	40 D	44.9%	45.0%	49.9%	50.1%
13,336	EMMET	5,724	3,062	2,153	509	909 R	53.5%	37.6%	58.7%	41.3%
25,488	FAYETTE	11,523	6,374	4,377	772	1,997 R	55.3%	38.0%	59.3%	40.7%
19,597	FLOYD	9,118	4,665	3,634	819	1,031 R	51.2%	39.9%	56.2%	43.8%
13,036	FRANKLIN	5,682	3,290	1,920	472	1,370 R	57.9%	33.8%	63.1%	36.9%
9,401	FREMONT	4,131	2,693	1,203	235	1,490 R	65.2%	29.1%	69.1%	30.9%
12,119	GREENE	5,939	3,154	2,210	575	944 R	53.1%	37.2%	58.8%	41.2%
14,366	GRUNDY	7,026	4,644	1,869	513	2,775 R	66.1%	26.6%	71.3%	28.7%
11,983	GUTHRIE	5,514	3,214	1,866	434	1,348 R	58.3%	33.8%	63.3%	36.7%
17,862	HAMILTON	8,266	4,745	2,741	780	2,004 R	57.4%	33.2%	63.4%	36.6%
13,833	HANCOCK	6,092	3,681	1,918	493	1,763 R	60.4%	31.5%	65.7%	34.3%
21,776	HARDIN	9,920	5,329	3,757	834	1,572 R	53.7%	37.9%	58.7%	41.3%
16,348	HARRISON	7,053	4,502	2,152	399	2,350 R	63.8%	30.5%	67.7%	32.3%
18,890	HENRY	8,462	4,430	3,317	715	1,113 R	52.4%	39.2%	57.2%	42.8%
11,114	HOWARD	5,576	2,975	2,214	387	761 R	53.4%	39.7%	57.3%	42.7%
12,246	HUMBOLDT	5,899	3,575	1,840	484	1,735 R	60.6%	31.2%	66.0%	34.0%
8,908	IDA	4,354	2,825	1,235	294	1,590 R	64.9%	28.4%	69.6%	30.4%
15,429	IOWA	7,522	4,153	2,606	763	1,547 R	55.2%	34.6%	61.4%	38.6%
22,503	JACKSON	8,754	4,479	3,518	757	961 R	51.2%	40.2%	56.0%	44.0%
36,425	JASPER	16,966	8,286	7,258	1,422	1,028 R	48.8%	42.8%	53.3%	46.7%
16,316	JEFFERSON	7,299	4,099	2,577	623	1,522 R	56.2%	35.3%	61.4%	38.6%
81,717	JOHNSON	42,997	13,642	20,122	9,233	6,480 D	31.7%	46.8%	40.4%	59.6%
20,401	JONES	8,913	4,506	3,521	886	985 R	50.6%	39.5%	56.1%	43.9%
12,921	KEOKUK	5,975	3,145	2,390	440	755 R	52.6%	40.0%	56.8%	43.2%
21,891	KOSSUTH	10,262	5,568	3,810	884	1,758 R	54.3%	37.1%	59.4%	40.6%
43,106	LEE	18,265	8,793	8,204	1,268	589 R	48.1%	44.9%	51.7%	48.3%
169,775	LINN	78,224	36,254	31,950	10,020	4,304 R	46.3%	40.8%	53.2%	46.8%
12,055	LOUISA	4,584	2,530	1,700	354	830 R	55.2%	37.1%	59.8%	40.2%
10,313	LUCAS	4,929	2,593	1,989	347	604 R	52.6%	40.4%	56.6%	43.4%
12,896	LYON	6,208	4,349	1,431	428	2,918 R	70.1%	23.1%	75.2%	24.8%

IOWA

PRESIDENT 1980

1980 Census Population	County	Total Vote	Republican	Democratic	Other	Rep.-Dem. Plurality	Percentage Total Vote Rep.	Total Vote Dem.	Major Vote Rep.	Major Vote Dem.
12,597	MADISON	6,411	3,320	2,496	595	824 R	51.8%	38.9%	57.1%	42.9%
22,867	MAHASKA	10,363	5,650	3,968	745	1,682 R	54.5%	38.3%	58.7%	41.3%
29,669	MARION	13,518	6,665	5,490	1,363	1,175 R	49.3%	40.6%	54.8%	45.2%
41,652	MARSHALL	19,626	10,707	7,114	1,805	3,593 R	54.6%	36.2%	60.1%	39.9%
13,406	MILLS	5,183	3,581	1,244	358	2,337 R	69.1%	24.0%	74.2%	25.8%
12,329	MITCHELL	5,864	3,401	2,040	423	1,361 R	58.0%	34.8%	62.5%	37.5%
11,692	MONONA	5,284	3,268	1,660	356	1,608 R	61.8%	31.4%	66.3%	33.7%
9,209	MONROE	4,117	2,003	1,866	248	137 R	48.7%	45.3%	51.8%	48.2%
13,413	MONTGOMERY	6,054	4,115	1,556	383	2,559 R	68.0%	25.7%	72.6%	27.4%
40,436	MUSCATINE	15,145	7,829	5,597	1,719	2,232 R	51.7%	37.0%	58.3%	41.7%
16,972	O'BRIEN	7,761	4,937	2,210	614	2,727 R	63.6%	28.5%	69.1%	30.9%
8,371	OSCEOLA	3,486	2,177	1,051	258	1,126 R	62.4%	30.1%	67.4%	32.6%
19,063	PAGE	7,810	5,618	1,772	420	3,846 R	71.9%	22.7%	76.0%	24.0%
12,721	PALO ALTO	5,968	3,025	2,463	480	562 R	50.7%	41.3%	55.1%	44.9%
24,743	PLYMOUTH	10,346	6,515	2,965	866	3,550 R	63.0%	28.7%	68.7%	31.3%
11,369	POCAHONTAS	5,686	3,194	1,959	533	1,235 R	56.2%	34.5%	62.0%	38.0%
303,170	POLK	143,758	64,156	61,984	17,618	2,172 R	44.6%	43.1%	50.9%	49.1%
86,561	POTTAWATTAMIE	33,170	20,222	10,709	2,239	9,513 R	61.0%	32.3%	65.4%	34.6%
19,306	POWESHIEK	9,102	4,598	3,529	975	1,069 R	50.5%	38.8%	56.6%	43.4%
6,112	RINGGOLD	3,251	1,884	1,150	217	734 R	58.0%	35.4%	62.1%	37.9%
14,118	SAC	6,264	3,725	1,976	563	1,749 R	59.5%	31.5%	65.3%	34.7%
160,022	SCOTT	67,926	34,701	26,391	6,834	8,310 R	51.1%	38.9%	56.8%	43.2%
15,043	SHELBY	6,477	4,147	1,892	438	2,255 R	64.0%	29.2%	68.7%	31.3%
30,813	SIOUX	14,167	10,768	2,698	701	8,070 R	76.0%	19.0%	80.0%	20.0%
72,326	STORY	37,371	15,829	13,529	8,013	2,300 R	42.4%	36.2%	53.9%	46.1%
19,533	TAMA	8,602	4,840	3,049	713	1,791 R	56.3%	35.4%	61.4%	38.6%
8,353	TAYLOR	4,213	2,715	1,226	272	1,489 R	64.4%	29.1%	68.9%	31.1%
13,858	UNION	5,979	3,372	2,182	425	1,190 R	56.4%	36.5%	60.7%	39.3%
8,626	VAN BUREN	3,680	2,142	1,311	227	831 R	58.2%	35.6%	62.0%	38.0%
40,241	WAPELLO	17,668	7,475	8,923	1,270	1,448 D	42.3%	50.5%	45.6%	54.4%
34,878	WARREN	15,519	7,360	6,610	1,549	750 R	47.4%	42.6%	52.7%	47.3%
20,141	WASHINGTON	7,627	3,967	2,877	783	1,090 R	52.0%	37.7%	58.0%	42.0%
8,199	WAYNE	4,104	2,221	1,627	256	594 R	54.1%	39.6%	57.7%	42.3%
45,953	WEBSTER	21,030	10,438	9,001	1,591	1,437 R	49.6%	42.8%	53.7%	46.3%
13,010	WINNEBAGO	6,479	3,808	2,208	463	1,600 R	58.8%	34.1%	63.3%	36.7%
21,876	WINNESHIEK	9,304	5,033	3,201	1,070	1,832 R	54.1%	34.4%	61.1%	38.9%
100,884	WOODBURY	43,275	23,553	15,930	3,792	7,623 R	54.4%	36.8%	59.7%	40.3%
9,075	WORTH	4,310	2,247	1,721	342	526 R	52.1%	39.9%	56.6%	43.4%
16,319	WRIGHT	7,147	3,936	2,645	566	1,291 R	55.1%	37.0%	59.8%	40.2%
2,913,808	TOTAL	1,317,661	676,026	508,672	132,963	167,354 R	51.3%	38.6%	57.1%	42.9%

IOWA

PRESIDENT 1976

1970 Census Population	County	Total Vote	Republican	Democratic	Other	Rep.-Dem. Plurality	Percentage: Total Vote Rep.	Percentage: Total Vote Dem.	Percentage: Major Vote Rep.	Percentage: Major Vote Dem.
9,487	ADAIR	4,722	2,326	2,294	102	32 R	49.3%	48.6%	50.3%	49.7%
6,322	ADAMS	2,937	1,388	1,507	42	119 D	47.3%	51.3%	47.9%	52.1%
14,968	ALLAMAKEE	6,303	3,648	2,568	87	1,080 R	57.9%	40.7%	58.7%	41.3%
15,007	APPANOOSE	6,558	3,036	3,424	98	388 D	46.3%	52.2%	47.0%	53.0%
9,595	AUDUBON	4,133	1,978	2,104	51	126 D	47.9%	50.9%	48.5%	51.5%
22,885	BENTON	10,703	5,014	5,514	175	500 D	46.8%	51.5%	47.6%	52.4%
132,916	BLACK HAWK	61,715	30,994	29,508	1,213	1,486 R	50.2%	47.8%	51.2%	48.8%
26,470	BOONE	12,263	5,413	6,595	255	1,182 D	44.1%	53.8%	45.1%	54.9%
22,737	BREMER	10,685	6,252	4,203	230	2,049 R	58.5%	39.3%	59.8%	40.2%
21,746	BUCHANAN	9,223	4,794	4,258	171	536 R	52.0%	46.2%	53.0%	47.0%
20,693	BUENA VISTA	9,567	5,126	4,227	214	899 R	53.6%	44.2%	54.8%	45.2%
16,953	BUTLER	6,808	4,207	2,503	98	1,704 R	61.8%	36.8%	62.7%	37.3%
14,287	CALHOUN	6,300	3,215	3,001	84	214 R	51.0%	47.6%	51.7%	48.3%
22,912	CARROLL	9,608	4,094	5,333	181	1,239 D	42.6%	55.5%	43.4%	56.6%
17,007	CASS	7,549	4,589	2,866	94	1,723 R	60.8%	38.0%	61.6%	38.4%
17,655	CEDAR	7,822	4,308	3,354	160	954 R	55.1%	42.9%	56.2%	43.8%
49,335	CERRO GORDO	22,196	10,604	11,189	403	585 D	47.8%	50.4%	48.7%	51.3%
17,269	CHEROKEE	7,478	3,993	3,358	127	635 R	53.4%	44.9%	54.3%	45.7%
14,969	CHICKASAW	6,988	3,432	3,503	53	71 D	49.1%	50.1%	49.5%	50.5%
7,581	CLARKE	4,149	1,737	2,333	79	596 D	41.9%	56.2%	42.7%	57.3%
18,464	CLAY	8,500	4,548	3,776	176	772 R	53.5%	44.4%	54.6%	45.4%
20,606	CLAYTON	8,807	4,826	3,804	177	1,022 R	54.8%	43.2%	55.9%	44.1%
56,749	CLINTON	24,534	12,401	11,746	387	655 R	50.5%	47.9%	51.4%	48.6%
19,116	CRAWFORD	7,948	3,879	3,903	166	24 D	48.8%	49.1%	49.8%	50.2%
26,085	DALLAS	12,247	5,308	6,722	217	1,414 D	43.3%	54.9%	44.1%	55.9%
8,207	DAVIS	4,129	1,631	2,426	72	795 D	39.5%	58.8%	40.2%	59.8%
9,737	DECATUR	4,707	1,932	2,698	77	766 D	41.0%	57.3%	41.7%	58.3%
18,770	DELAWARE	7,481	4,161	3,168	152	993 R	55.6%	42.3%	56.8%	43.2%
46,982	DES MOINES	20,536	9,023	11,268	245	2,245 D	43.9%	54.9%	44.5%	55.5%
12,565	DICKINSON	7,010	3,795	3,074	141	721 R	54.1%	43.9%	55.2%	44.8%
90,609	DUBUQUE	39,049	17,459	20,548	1,042	3,089 D	44.7%	52.6%	45.9%	54.1%
14,009	EMMET	5,687	2,872	2,720	95	152 R	50.5%	47.8%	51.4%	48.6%
26,898	FAYETTE	12,102	6,618	5,220	264	1,398 R	54.7%	43.1%	55.9%	44.1%
19,860	FLOYD	9,178	4,361	4,646	171	285 D	47.5%	50.6%	48.4%	51.6%
13,255	FRANKLIN	5,843	3,056	2,682	105	374 R	52.3%	45.9%	53.3%	46.7%
9,282	FREMONT	4,176	2,163	1,964	49	199 R	51.8%	47.0%	52.4%	47.6%
12,716	GREENE	5,989	2,811	3,094	84	283 D	46.9%	51.7%	47.6%	52.4%
14,119	GRUNDY	6,660	4,173	2,410	77	1,763 R	62.7%	36.2%	63.4%	36.6%
12,243	GUTHRIE	5,641	2,644	2,873	124	229 D	46.9%	50.9%	47.9%	52.1%
18,383	HAMILTON	8,025	3,932	3,953	140	21 D	49.0%	49.3%	49.9%	50.1%
13,330	HANCOCK	6,187	3,127	2,975	85	152 R	50.5%	48.1%	51.2%	48.8%
22,248	HARDIN	9,328	4,682	4,479	167	203 R	50.2%	48.0%	51.1%	48.9%
16,240	HARRISON	6,790	3,489	3,228	73	261 R	51.4%	47.5%	51.9%	48.1%
18,114	HENRY	7,887	3,848	3,882	157	34 D	48.8%	49.2%	49.8%	50.2%
11,442	HOWARD	5,616	2,618	2,917	81	299 D	46.6%	51.9%	47.3%	52.7%
12,519	HUMBOLDT	5,841	3,075	2,677	89	398 R	52.6%	45.8%	53.5%	46.5%
9,190	IDA	4,555	2,590	1,868	97	722 R	56.9%	41.0%	58.1%	41.9%
15,419	IOWA	7,411	3,926	3,367	118	559 R	53.0%	45.4%	53.8%	46.2%
20,839	JACKSON	8,886	4,221	4,467	198	246 D	47.5%	50.3%	48.6%	51.4%
35,425	JASPER	16,786	7,728	8,783	275	1,055 D	46.0%	52.3%	46.8%	53.2%
15,774	JEFFERSON	7,244	3,746	3,377	121	369 R	51.7%	46.6%	52.6%	47.4%
72,127	JOHNSON	38,710	16,090	20,208	2,412	4,118 D	41.6%	52.2%	44.3%	55.7%
19,868	JONES	8,831	4,463	4,245	123	218 R	50.5%	48.1%	51.3%	48.7%
13,943	KEOKUK	6,504	2,920	3,482	102	562 D	44.9%	53.5%	45.6%	54.4%
22,937	KOSSUTH	10,046	4,653	5,190	203	537 D	46.3%	51.7%	47.3%	52.7%
42,996	LEE	17,465	8,195	9,017	253	822 D	46.9%	51.6%	47.6%	52.4%
163,213	LINN	76,397	36,513	38,252	1,632	1,739 D	47.8%	50.1%	48.8%	51.2%
10,682	LOUISA	4,441	2,284	2,089	68	195 R	51.4%	47.0%	52.2%	47.8%
10,163	LUCAS	4,894	2,071	2,733	90	662 D	42.3%	55.8%	43.1%	56.9%
13,340	LYON	5,554	3,558	1,870	126	1,688 R	64.1%	33.7%	65.5%	34.5%

IOWA

PRESIDENT 1976

1970 Census Population	County	Total Vote	Republican	Democratic	Other	Rep.-Dem. Plurality	Percentage Total Vote Rep.	Total Vote Dem.	Major Vote Rep.	Major Vote Dem.
11,558	MADISON	5,910	2,681	3,109	120	428 D	45.4%	52.6%	46.3%	53.7%
22,177	MAHASKA	10,251	5,267	4,838	146	429 R	51.4%	47.2%	52.1%	47.9%
26,352	MARION	11,857	5,429	6,226	202	797 D	45.8%	52.5%	46.6%	53.4%
41,076	MARSHALL	18,630	9,562	8,695	373	867 R	51.3%	46.7%	52.4%	47.6%
11,832	MILLS	4,710	2,722	1,908	80	814 R	57.8%	40.5%	58.8%	41.2%
13,108	MITCHELL	5,892	2,887	2,906	99	19 D	49.0%	49.3%	49.8%	50.2%
12,069	MONONA	5,370	2,636	2,661	73	25 D	49.1%	49.6%	49.8%	50.2%
9,357	MONROE	3,996	1,581	2,360	55	779 D	39.6%	59.1%	40.1%	59.9%
12,781	MONTGOMERY	5,974	3,673	2,229	72	1,444 R	61.5%	37.3%	62.2%	37.8%
37,181	MUSCATINE	14,496	7,697	6,567	232	1,130 R	53.1%	45.3%	54.0%	46.0%
17,522	O'BRIEN	7,506	4,643	2,732	131	1,911 R	61.9%	36.4%	63.0%	37.0%
8,555	OSCEOLA	3,341	1,955	1,309	77	646 R	58.5%	39.2%	59.9%	40.1%
18,507	PAGE	8,335	5,343	2,865	127	2,478 R	64.1%	34.4%	65.1%	34.9%
13,289	PALO ALTO	5,904	2,623	3,182	99	559 D	44.4%	53.9%	45.2%	54.8%
24,312	PLYMOUTH	10,016	5,590	4,284	142	1,306 R	55.8%	42.8%	56.6%	43.4%
12,729	POCAHONTAS	5,889	2,700	3,055	134	355 D	45.8%	51.9%	46.9%	53.1%
286,101	POLK	137,763	62,316	71,917	3,530	9,601 D	45.2%	52.2%	46.4%	53.6%
86,991	POTTAWATTAMIE	32,519	17,264	14,754	501	2,510 R	53.1%	45.4%	53.9%	46.1%
18,803	POWESHIEK	8,735	4,194	4,360	181	166 D	48.0%	49.9%	49.0%	51.0%
6,373	RINGGOLD	3,336	1,543	1,739	54	196 D	46.3%	52.1%	47.0%	53.0%
15,573	SAC	6,493	3,347	2,996	150	351 R	51.5%	46.1%	52.8%	47.2%
142,687	SCOTT	65,940	35,021	29,771	1,148	5,250 R	53.1%	45.1%	54.1%	45.9%
15,528	SHELBY	6,261	3,301	2,851	109	450 R	52.7%	45.5%	53.7%	46.3%
27,996	SIOUX	12,935	9,448	3,322	165	6,126 R	73.0%	25.7%	74.0%	26.0%
62,783	STORY	35,476	18,394	15,717	1,365	2,677 R	51.8%	44.3%	53.9%	46.1%
20,147	TAMA	9,107	4,379	4,580	148	201 D	48.1%	50.3%	48.9%	51.1%
8,790	TAYLOR	4,054	2,059	1,947	48	112 R	50.8%	48.0%	51.4%	48.6%
13,557	UNION	5,948	2,873	2,955	120	82 D	48.3%	49.7%	49.3%	50.7%
8,643	VAN BUREN	3,671	1,804	1,807	60	3 D	49.1%	49.2%	50.0%	50.0%
42,149	WAPELLO	17,268	6,786	10,249	233	3,463 D	39.3%	59.4%	39.8%	60.2%
27,432	WARREN	14,108	6,099	7,653	356	1,554 D	43.2%	54.2%	44.3%	55.7%
18,967	WASHINGTON	7,807	4,218	3,448	141	770 R	54.0%	44.2%	55.0%	45.0%
8,405	WAYNE	3,995	1,781	2,145	69	364 D	44.6%	53.7%	45.4%	54.6%
48,391	WEBSTER	19,995	9,068	10,543	384	1,475 D	45.4%	52.7%	46.2%	53.8%
12,990	WINNEBAGO	6,346	3,315	2,950	81	365 R	52.2%	46.5%	52.9%	47.1%
21,758	WINNESHIEK	9,149	4,765	4,158	226	607 R	52.1%	45.4%	53.4%	46.6%
103,052	WOODBURY	43,287	22,853	19,664	770	3,189 R	52.8%	45.4%	53.8%	46.2%
8,968	WORTH	4,425	1,964	2,399	62	435 D	44.4%	54.2%	45.0%	55.0%
17,294	WRIGHT	7,282	3,544	3,637	101	93 D	48.7%	49.9%	49.4%	50.6%
2,825,041	TOTAL	1,279,306	632,863	619,931	26,512	12,932 R	49.5%	48.5%	50.5%	49.5%

IOWA

PRESIDENT 1972

1970 Census Population	County	Total Vote	Republican	Democratic	Other	Rep.-Dem. Plurality	Percentage Total Vote Rep.	Total Vote Dem.	Major Vote Rep.	Major Vote Dem.
9,487	ADAIR	4,782	3,041	1,642	99	1,399 R	63.6%	34.3%	64.9%	35.1%
6,322	ADAMS	3,045	1,814	1,161	70	653 R	59.6%	38.1%	61.0%	39.0%
14,968	ALLAMAKEE	6,562	4,150	2,271	141	1,879 R	63.2%	34.6%	64.6%	35.4%
15,007	APPANOOSE	6,747	4,321	2,283	143	2,038 R	64.0%	33.8%	65.4%	34.6%
9,595	AUDUBON	4,082	2,515	1,533	34	982 R	61.6%	37.6%	62.1%	37.9%
22,885	BENTON	9,749	5,273	4,282	194	991 R	54.1%	43.9%	55.2%	44.8%
132,916	BLACK HAWK	53,782	30,929	21,721	1,132	9,208 R	57.5%	40.4%	58.7%	41.3%
26,470	BOONE	11,551	6,271	5,057	223	1,214 R	54.3%	43.8%	55.4%	44.6%
22,737	BREMER	9,611	6,333	3,122	156	3,211 R	65.9%	32.5%	67.0%	33.0%
21,746	BUCHANAN	9,048	5,277	3,609	162	1,668 R	58.3%	39.9%	59.4%	40.6%
20,693	BUENA VISTA	9,281	5,685	3,460	136	2,225 R	61.3%	37.3%	62.2%	37.8%
16,953	BUTLER	6,426	4,615	1,682	129	2,933 R	71.8%	26.2%	73.3%	26.7%
14,287	CALHOUN	6,368	3,821	2,446	101	1,375 R	60.0%	38.4%	61.0%	39.0%
22,912	CARROLL	9,285	4,415	4,608	262	193 D	47.5%	49.6%	48.9%	51.1%
17,007	CASS	7,263	5,234	1,923	106	3,311 R	72.1%	26.5%	73.1%	26.9%
17,655	CEDAR	7,023	4,452	2,465	106	1,987 R	63.4%	35.1%	64.4%	35.6%
49,335	CERRO GORDO	21,693	11,856	9,460	377	2,396 R	54.7%	43.6%	55.6%	44.4%
17,269	CHEROKEE	7,594	4,726	2,780	88	1,946 R	62.2%	36.6%	63.0%	37.0%
14,969	CHICKASAW	7,030	3,836	3,134	60	702 R	54.6%	44.6%	55.0%	45.0%
7,581	CLARKE	3,901	2,214	1,590	97	624 R	56.8%	40.8%	58.2%	41.8%
18,464	CLAY	7,696	4,564	2,887	245	1,677 R	59.3%	37.5%	61.3%	38.7%
20,606	CLAYTON	9,048	5,447	3,366	235	2,081 R	60.2%	37.2%	61.8%	38.2%
56,749	CLINTON	22,964	12,768	9,895	301	2,873 R	55.6%	43.1%	56.3%	43.7%
19,116	CRAWFORD	7,667	4,493	3,018	156	1,475 R	58.6%	39.4%	59.8%	40.2%
26,085	DALLAS	11,436	6,143	5,085	208	1,058 R	53.7%	44.5%	54.7%	45.3%
8,207	DAVIS	4,188	2,287	1,806	95	481 R	54.6%	43.1%	55.9%	44.1%
9,737	DECATUR	4,593	2,638	1,880	75	758 R	57.4%	40.9%	58.4%	41.6%
18,770	DELAWARE	7,920	4,848	2,944	128	1,904 R	61.2%	37.2%	62.2%	37.8%
46,982	DES MOINES	19,358	10,216	8,869	273	1,347 R	52.8%	45.8%	53.5%	46.5%
12,565	DICKINSON	6,381	3,739	2,373	269	1,366 R	58.6%	37.2%	61.2%	38.8%
90,609	DUBUQUE	36,521	17,272	18,417	832	1,145 D	47.3%	50.4%	48.4%	51.6%
14,009	EMMET	5,461	3,436	1,970	55	1,466 R	62.9%	36.1%	63.6%	36.4%
26,898	FAYETTE	11,940	7,263	4,413	264	2,850 R	60.8%	37.0%	62.2%	37.8%
19,860	FLOYD	8,192	4,726	3,338	128	1,388 R	57.7%	40.7%	58.6%	41.4%
13,255	FRANKLIN	5,786	3,643	1,986	157	1,657 R	63.0%	34.3%	64.7%	35.3%
9,282	FREMONT	3,907	2,642	1,210	55	1,432 R	67.6%	31.0%	68.6%	31.4%
12,716	GREENE	5,680	3,371	2,152	157	1,219 R	59.3%	37.9%	61.0%	39.0%
14,119	GRUNDY	6,625	4,706	1,844	75	2,862 R	71.0%	27.8%	71.8%	28.2%
12,243	GUTHRIE	6,022	3,655	2,258	109	1,397 R	60.7%	37.5%	61.8%	38.2%
18,383	HAMILTON	7,890	4,803	2,913	174	1,890 R	60.9%	36.9%	62.2%	37.8%
13,330	HANCOCK	6,129	3,706	2,349	74	1,357 R	60.5%	38.3%	61.2%	38.8%
22,248	HARDIN	9,556	5,869	3,516	171	2,353 R	61.4%	36.8%	62.5%	37.5%
16,240	HARRISON	7,171	4,721	2,369	81	2,352 R	65.8%	33.0%	66.6%	33.4%
18,114	HENRY	7,884	5,066	2,721	97	2,345 R	64.3%	34.5%	65.1%	34.9%
11,442	HOWARD	5,481	2,980	2,439	62	541 R	54.4%	44.5%	55.0%	45.0%
12,519	HUMBOLDT	5,792	3,622	2,062	108	1,560 R	62.5%	35.6%	63.7%	36.3%
9,190	IDA	4,359	2,819	1,490	50	1,329 R	64.7%	34.2%	65.4%	34.6%
15,419	IOWA	6,964	4,202	2,578	184	1,624 R	60.3%	37.0%	62.0%	38.0%
20,839	JACKSON	8,924	4,975	3,704	245	1,271 R	55.7%	41.5%	57.3%	42.7%
35,425	JASPER	16,513	9,133	7,007	373	2,126 R	55.3%	42.4%	56.6%	43.4%
15,774	JEFFERSON	7,139	4,628	2,362	149	2,266 R	64.8%	33.1%	66.2%	33.8%
72,127	JOHNSON	36,236	14,823	20,922	491	6,099 D	40.9%	57.7%	41.5%	58.5%
19,868	JONES	8,521	4,962	3,468	91	1,494 R	58.2%	40.7%	58.9%	41.1%
13,943	KEOKUK	6,565	3,831	2,619	115	1,212 R	58.4%	39.9%	59.4%	40.6%
22,937	KOSSUTH	10,358	5,841	4,393	124	1,448 R	56.4%	42.4%	57.1%	42.9%
42,996	LEE	17,618	9,748	7,510	360	2,238 R	55.3%	42.6%	56.5%	43.5%
163,213	LINN	69,160	36,503	31,370	1,287	5,133 R	52.8%	45.4%	53.8%	46.2%
10,682	LOUISA	4,577	2,806	1,707	64	1,099 R	61.3%	37.3%	62.2%	37.8%
10,163	LUCAS	4,690	2,851	1,759	80	1,092 R	60.8%	37.5%	61.8%	38.2%
13,340	LYON	5,252	3,788	1,407	57	2,381 R	72.1%	26.8%	72.9%	27.1%

IOWA

PRESIDENT 1972

1970 Census Population	County	Total Vote	Republican	Democratic	Other	Rep.-Dem. Plurality	Percentage Total Vote Rep.	Percentage Total Vote Dem.	Percentage Major Vote Rep.	Percentage Major Vote Dem.
11,558	MADISON	5,864	3,480	2,234	150	1,246 R	59.3%	38.1%	60.9%	39.1%
22,177	MAHASKA	9,988	6,374	3,382	232	2,992 R	63.8%	33.9%	65.3%	34.7%
26,352	MARION	11,531	6,583	4,643	305	1,940 R	57.1%	40.3%	58.6%	41.4%
41,076	MARSHALL	17,744	10,798	6,618	328	4,180 R	60.9%	37.3%	62.0%	38.0%
11,832	MILLS	4,712	3,531	1,060	121	2,471 R	74.9%	22.5%	76.9%	23.1%
13,108	MITCHELL	5,911	3,395	2,449	67	946 R	57.4%	41.4%	58.1%	41.9%
12,069	MONONA	5,495	3,237	2,189	69	1,048 R	58.9%	39.8%	59.7%	40.3%
9,357	MONROE	4,155	2,357	1,736	62	621 R	56.7%	41.8%	57.6%	42.4%
12,781	MONTGOMERY	6,041	4,391	1,559	91	2,832 R	72.7%	25.8%	73.8%	26.2%
37,181	MUSCATINE	13,642	8,436	4,917	289	3,519 R	61.8%	36.0%	63.2%	36.8%
17,522	O'BRIEN	7,491	5,159	2,224	108	2,935 R	68.9%	29.7%	69.9%	30.1%
8,555	OSCEOLA	3,616	2,262	1,317	37	945 R	62.6%	36.4%	63.2%	36.8%
18,507	PAGE	8,112	6,200	1,790	122	4,410 R	76.4%	22.1%	77.6%	22.4%
13,289	PALO ALTO	6,066	3,141	2,845	80	296 R	51.8%	46.9%	52.5%	47.5%
24,312	PLYMOUTH	10,466	6,339	4,033	94	2,306 R	60.6%	38.5%	61.1%	38.9%
12,729	POCAHONTAS	5,487	3,138	2,241	108	897 R	57.2%	40.8%	58.3%	41.7%
286,101	POLK	132,659	70,245	59,169	3,245	11,076 R	53.0%	44.6%	54.3%	45.7%
86,991	POTTAWATTAMIE	28,450	19,722	8,074	654	11,648 R	69.3%	28.4%	71.0%	29.0%
18,803	POWESHIEK	8,648	4,785	3,718	145	1,067 R	55.3%	43.0%	56.3%	43.7%
6,373	RINGGOLD	3,303	2,264	1,003	36	1,261 R	68.5%	30.4%	69.3%	30.7%
15,573	SAC	6,541	4,017	2,452	72	1,565 R	61.4%	37.5%	62.1%	37.9%
142,687	SCOTT	59,455	34,135	23,810	1,510	10,325 R	57.4%	40.0%	58.9%	41.1%
15,528	SHELBY	6,439	4,052	2,259	128	1,793 R	62.9%	35.1%	64.2%	35.8%
27,996	SIOUX	13,697	10,721	2,867	109	7,854 R	78.3%	20.9%	78.9%	21.1%
62,783	STORY	31,025	16,617	13,972	436	2,645 R	53.6%	45.0%	54.3%	45.7%
20,147	TAMA	8,880	5,058	3,693	129	1,365 R	57.0%	41.6%	57.8%	42.2%
8,790	TAYLOR	4,336	3,042	1,247	47	1,795 R	70.2%	28.8%	70.9%	29.1%
13,557	UNION	5,977	3,734	2,112	131	1,622 R	62.5%	35.3%	63.9%	36.1%
8,643	VAN BUREN	3,596	2,272	1,268	56	1,004 R	63.2%	35.3%	64.2%	35.8%
42,149	WAPELLO	18,171	9,301	8,348	522	953 R	51.2%	45.9%	52.7%	47.3%
27,432	WARREN	12,804	7,332	5,143	329	2,189 R	57.3%	40.2%	58.8%	41.2%
18,967	WASHINGTON	8,089	5,187	2,784	118	2,403 R	64.1%	34.4%	65.1%	34.9%
8,405	WAYNE	4,324	2,681	1,574	69	1,107 R	62.0%	36.4%	63.0%	37.0%
48,391	WEBSTER	19,893	11,133	8,358	402	2,775 R	56.0%	42.0%	57.1%	42.9%
12,990	WINNEBAGO	6,669	4,300	2,324	45	1,976 R	64.5%	34.8%	64.9%	35.1%
21,758	WINNESHIEK	10,452	5,877	4,401	174	1,476 R	56.2%	42.1%	57.2%	42.8%
103,052	WOODBURY	41,430	23,757	16,974	699	6,783 R	57.3%	41.0%	58.3%	41.7%
8,968	WORTH	4,636	2,564	2,034	38	530 R	55.3%	43.9%	55.8%	44.2%
17,294	WRIGHT	7,162	4,278	2,780	104	1,498 R	59.7%	38.8%	60.6%	39.4%
2,825,041	TOTAL	1,225,944	706,207	496,206	23,531	210,001 R	57.6%	40.5%	58.7%	41.3%

IOWA

PRESIDENT 1968

1960 Census Population	County	Total Vote	Republican	Democratic	AIP	Other	Plurality	Percentage Rep.	Dem.	AIP
10,893	ADAIR	4,586	2,789	1,559	234	4	1,230 R	60.8%	34.0%	5.1%
7,468	ADAMS	3,128	1,868	993	260	7	875 R	59.7%	31.7%	8.3%
15,982	ALLAMAKEE	7,110	4,449	2,245	407	9	2,204 R	62.6%	31.6%	5.7%
16,015	APPANOOSE	7,053	3,497	3,005	540	11	492 R	49.6%	42.6%	7.7%
10,919	AUDUBON	4,504	2,592	1,710	198	4	882 R	57.5%	38.0%	4.4%
23,422	BENTON	9,635	5,016	3,944	602	73	1,072 R	52.1%	40.9%	6.2%
122,482	BLACK HAWK	49,554	25,594	21,097	2,621	242	4,497 R	51.6%	42.6%	5.3%
28,037	BOONE	11,096	5,260	5,219	562	55	41 R	47.4%	47.0%	5.1%
21,108	BREMER	8,523	5,604	2,481	423	15	3,123 R	65.8%	29.1%	5.0%
22,293	BUCHANAN	8,674	4,541	3,670	454	9	871 R	52.4%	42.3%	5.2%
21,189	BUENA VISTA	9,050	5,599	3,051	386	14	2,548 R	61.9%	33.7%	4.3%
17,467	BUTLER	6,589	4,651	1,673	252	13	2,978 R	70.6%	25.4%	3.8%
15,923	CALHOUN	6,458	3,715	2,361	335	47	1,354 R	57.5%	36.6%	5.2%
23,431	CARROLL	9,202	3,927	4,809	412	54	882 D	42.7%	52.3%	4.5%
17,919	CASS	7,761	5,223	2,136	369	33	3,087 R	67.3%	27.5%	4.8%
17,791	CEDAR	7,614	4,494	2,675	438	7	1,819 R	59.0%	35.1%	5.8%
49,894	CERRO GORDO	20,310	10,661	8,554	1,036	59	2,107 R	52.5%	42.1%	5.1%
18,598	CHEROKEE	7,496	4,436	2,705	340	15	1,731 R	59.2%	36.1%	4.5%
15,034	CHICKASAW	6,764	3,510	2,966	286	2	544 R	51.9%	43.8%	4.2%
8,222	CLARKE	4,000	2,059	1,655	286		404 R	51.5%	41.4%	7.1%
18,504	CLAY	7,628	4,325	2,840	369	94	1,485 R	56.7%	37.2%	4.8%
21,962	CLAYTON	8,878	5,132	3,168	541	37	1,964 R	57.8%	35.7%	6.1%
55,060	CLINTON	22,175	11,513	9,515	1,059	88	1,998 R	51.9%	42.9%	4.8%
18,569	CRAWFORD	7,744	4,287	2,851	539	67	1,436 R	55.4%	36.8%	7.0%
24,123	DALLAS	11,287	5,549	5,062	640	36	487 R	49.2%	44.8%	5.7%
9,199	DAVIS	4,278	2,016	1,904	355	3	112 R	47.1%	44.5%	8.3%
10,539	DECATUR	4,588	2,261	2,057	262	8	204 R	49.3%	44.8%	5.7%
18,483	DELAWARE	7,829	4,650	2,760	412	7	1,890 R	59.4%	35.3%	5.3%
44,605	DES MOINES	19,979	8,452	10,164	1,318	45	1,712 D	42.3%	50.9%	6.6%
12,574	DICKINSON	6,151	3,472	2,286	281	112	1,186 R	56.4%	37.2%	4.6%
80,048	DUBUQUE	34,863	14,197	18,664	1,701	301	4,467 D	40.7%	53.5%	4.9%
14,871	EMMET	5,847	3,444	2,163	230	10	1,281 R	58.9%	37.0%	3.9%
28,581	FAYETTE	11,687	6,935	4,098	636	18	2,837 R	59.3%	35.1%	5.4%
21,102	FLOYD	8,178	4,792	2,971	390	25	1,821 R	58.6%	36.3%	4.8%
15,472	FRANKLIN	5,677	3,604	1,777	240	56	1,827 R	63.5%	31.3%	4.2%
10,282	FREMONT	4,270	2,385	1,484	396	5	901 R	55.9%	34.8%	9.3%
14,379	GREENE	5,736	3,208	2,208	269	51	1,000 R	55.9%	38.5%	4.7%
14,132	GRUNDY	6,840	4,866	1,675	290	9	3,191 R	71.1%	24.5%	4.2%
13,607	GUTHRIE	5,751	3,346	2,063	335	7	1,283 R	58.2%	35.9%	5.8%
20,032	HAMILTON	8,001	4,607	3,058	301	35	1,549 R	57.6%	38.2%	3.8%
14,604	HANCOCK	5,949	3,544	2,131	249	25	1,413 R	59.6%	35.8%	4.2%
22,533	HARDIN	9,134	5,308	3,227	407	192	2,081 R	58.1%	35.3%	4.5%
17,600	HARRISON	6,825	3,867	2,410	540	8	1,457 R	56.7%	35.3%	7.9%
18,187	HENRY	7,659	4,613	2,532	503	11	2,081 R	60.2%	33.1%	6.6%
12,734	HOWARD	5,827	3,141	2,420	253	13	721 R	53.9%	41.5%	4.3%
13,156	HUMBOLDT	5,410	3,239	1,940	217	14	1,299 R	59.9%	35.9%	4.0%
10,269	IDA	4,425	2,753	1,463	208	1	1,290 R	62.2%	33.1%	4.7%
16,396	IOWA	7,111	4,133	2,586	367	25	1,547 R	58.1%	36.4%	5.2%
20,754	JACKSON	8,553	4,535	3,413	489	116	1,122 R	53.0%	39.9%	5.7%
35,282	JASPER	15,255	7,901	6,556	742	56	1,345 R	51.8%	43.0%	4.9%
15,818	JEFFERSON	6,939	4,130	2,411	377	21	1,719 R	59.5%	34.7%	5.4%
53,663	JOHNSON	25,944	11,384	13,541	736	283	2,157 D	43.9%	52.2%	2.8%
20,693	JONES	8,412	4,513	3,415	475	9	1,098 R	53.6%	40.6%	5.6%
15,492	KEOKUK	6,737	3,588	2,807	332	10	781 R	53.3%	41.7%	4.9%
25,314	KOSSUTH	10,089	5,350	4,392	310	37	958 R	53.0%	43.5%	3.1%
44,207	LEE	18,036	8,883	8,076	1,052	25	807 R	49.3%	44.8%	5.8%
136,899	LINN	64,430	30,918	29,898	3,182	432	1,020 R	48.0%	46.4%	4.9%
10,290	LOUISA	4,484	2,529	1,632	323		897 R	56.4%	36.4%	7.2%
10,923	LUCAS	4,782	2,543	1,942	290	7	601 R	53.2%	40.6%	6.1%
14,468	LYON	5,754	4,195	1,403	151	5	2,792 R	72.9%	24.4%	2.6%

IOWA

PRESIDENT 1968

1960 Census Population	County	Total Vote	Republican	Democratic	AIP	Other	Plurality	Percentage Rep.	Dem.	AIP
12,295	MADISON	5,679	3,151	2,192	327	9	959 R	55.5%	38.6%	5.8%
23,602	MAHASKA	9,970	5,670	3,721	420	159	1,949 R	56.9%	37.3%	4.2%
25,886	MARION	11,062	5,791	4,618	597	56	1,173 R	52.4%	41.7%	5.4%
37,984	MARSHALL	16,686	9,402	6,362	819	103	3,040 R	56.3%	38.1%	4.9%
13,050	MILLS	4,672	2,916	1,216	532	8	1,700 R	62.4%	26.0%	11.4%
14,043	MITCHELL	5,830	3,533	2,103	192	2	1,430 R	60.6%	36.1%	3.3%
13,916	MONONA	5,610	2,980	2,184	437	9	796 R	53.1%	38.9%	7.8%
10,463	MONROE	4,705	2,143	2,240	312	10	97 D	45.5%	47.6%	6.6%
14,467	MONTGOMERY	6,481	4,155	1,892	425	9	2,263 R	64.1%	29.2%	6.6%
33,840	MUSCATINE	12,874	7,361	4,726	643	144	2,635 R	57.2%	36.7%	5.0%
18,840	O'BRIEN	8,068	5,594	2,146	322	6	3,448 R	69.3%	26.6%	4.0%
10,064	OSCEOLA	4,102	2,516	1,420	164	2	1,096 R	61.3%	34.6%	4.0%
21,023	PAGE	8,679	5,907	2,128	634	10	3,779 R	68.1%	24.5%	7.3%
14,736	PALO ALTO	6,223	3,114	2,874	234	1	240 R	50.0%	46.2%	3.8%
23,906	PLYMOUTH	10,037	6,236	3,234	557	10	3,002 R	62.1%	32.2%	5.5%
14,234	POCAHONTAS	5,594	2,940	2,364	254	36	576 R	52.6%	42.3%	4.5%
266,315	POLK	114,784	51,814	52,731	9,524	715	917 D	45.1%	45.9%	8.3%
83,102	POTTAWATTAMIE	28,399	16,038	9,495	2,758	108	6,543 R	56.5%	33.4%	9.7%
19,300	POWESHIEK	8,112	4,470	3,250	367	25	1,220 R	55.1%	40.1%	4.5%
7,910	RINGGOLD	3,481	1,986	1,237	256	2	749 R	57.1%	35.5%	7.4%
17,007	SAC	6,676	4,182	2,207	280	7	1,975 R	62.6%	33.1%	4.2%
119,067	SCOTT	55,018	25,783	24,596	4,133	506	1,187 R	46.9%	44.7%	7.5%
15,825	SHELBY	6,626	3,886	2,365	330	45	1,521 R	58.6%	35.7%	5.0%
26,375	SIOUX	12,507	10,010	2,181	315	1	7,829 R	80.0%	17.4%	2.5%
49,327	STORY	23,675	13,327	9,456	772	120	3,871 R	56.3%	39.9%	3.3%
21,413	TAMA	9,253	4,955	3,767	494	37	1,188 R	53.6%	40.7%	5.3%
10,288	TAYLOR	4,636	2,765	1,501	368	2	1,264 R	59.6%	32.4%	7.9%
13,712	UNION	5,898	3,365	2,137	374	22	1,228 R	57.1%	36.2%	6.3%
9,778	VAN BUREN	3,869	2,294	1,331	237	7	963 R	59.3%	34.4%	6.1%
46,126	WAPELLO	18,647	7,825	9,375	1,355	92	1,550 D	42.0%	50.3%	7.3%
20,829	WARREN	11,171	5,619	4,613	919	20	1,006 R	50.3%	41.3%	8.2%
19,406	WASHINGTON	7,943	4,899	2,679	349	16	2,220 R	61.7%	33.7%	4.4%
9,800	WAYNE	4,573	2,553	1,723	283	14	830 R	55.8%	37.7%	6.2%
47,810	WEBSTER	19,097	9,349	8,572	1,026	150	777 R	49.0%	44.9%	5.4%
13,099	WINNEBAGO	5,954	3,543	2,163	246	2	1,380 R	59.5%	36.3%	4.1%
21,651	WINNESHIEK	9,319	5,600	3,364	344	11	2,236 R	60.1%	36.1%	3.7%
107,849	WOODBURY	41,803	21,159	18,281	2,153	210	2,878 R	50.6%	43.7%	5.2%
10,259	WORTH	4,420	2,383	1,815	214	8	568 R	53.9%	41.1%	4.8%
19,447	WRIGHT	7,549	4,299	2,969	248	33	1,330 R	56.9%	39.3%	3.3%
2,757,537	TOTAL	1,167,931	619,106	476,699	66,422	5,704	142,407 R	53.0%	40.8%	5.7%

IOWA

ELECTION NOTES

1984 Other vote was 6,248 LaRouche (by petition); 1,844 Bergland (Libertarian); 892 Baker (Big Deal); 463 Serrette (by petition); 313 Mason (Socialist Workers); 286 Hall (Communist); 1,051 scattered write-in.

1980 Other vote was 115,633 Anderson (by petition); 13,123 Clark (Libertarian); 2,273 Commoner (Citizens); 534 McReynolds (Socialist); 298 Hall (Communist); 244 DeBerry (Socialist Workers); 189 Greaves (American); 150 Bubar (Statesman); 519 scattered write-in.

1976 Other vote was 20,051 McCarthy (Independent); 3,040 Anderson (American); 1,452 MacBride (Libertarian); 554 Hall (Communist); 267 Camejo (Socialist Workers); 241 LaRouche (U.S. Labor); 234 Zeidler (Socialist); 167 Levin (Socialist Labor); 506 scattered write-in.

1972 Other vote was 22,056 Schmitz (American Independent); 488 Jenness (Socialist Workers); 272 Hall (Communist); 199 Green (Universal); 195 Fisher (Socialist Labor); 321 scattered write-in.

1968 Wallace on the ballot as American Independent. Other vote was 3,377 Halstead (Socialist Workers); 1,332 Cleaver (Peace and Freedom); 362 Munn (Prohibition); 241 Blomen (Socialist Labor); 142 Hensley (Universal); 250 scattered write-in.

KANSAS

POPULAR VOTE FOR PRESIDENT 1920 TO 1984

Year	Total Vote	Republican Vote	Republican Candidate	Democratic Vote	Democratic Candidate	Other Vote	Plurality	Percentage Total Vote Rep.	Percentage Total Vote Dem.	Percentage Major Vote Rep.	Percentage Major Vote Dem.
1984	1,021,991	677,296	Reagan, Ronald	333,149	Mondale, Walter F.	11,546	344,147 R	66.3%	32.6%	67.0%	33.0%
1980	979,795	566,812	Reagan, Ronald	326,150	Carter, Jimmy	86,833	240,662 R	57.9%	33.3%	63.5%	36.5%
1976	957,845	502,752	Ford, Gerald R.	430,421	Carter, Jimmy	24,672	72,331 R	52.5%	44.9%	53.9%	46.1%
1972	916,095	619,812	Nixon, Richard M.	270,287	McGovern, George S.	25,996	349,525 R	67.7%	29.5%	69.6%	30.4%
1968	872,783	478,674	Nixon, Richard M.	302,996	Humphrey, Hubert H.	91,113	175,678 R	54.8%	34.7%	61.2%	38.8%
1964	857,901	386,579	Goldwater, Barry M.	464,028	Johnson, Lyndon B.	7,294	77,449 D	45.1%	54.1%	45.4%	54.6%
1960	928,825	561,474	Nixon, Richard M.	363,213	Kennedy, John F.	4,138	198,261 R	60.4%	39.1%	60.7%	39.3%
1956	866,243	566,878	Eisenhower, Dwight D.	296,317	Stevenson, Adlai E.	3,048	270,561 R	65.4%	34.2%	65.7%	34.3%
1952	896,166	616,302	Eisenhower, Dwight D.	273,296	Stevenson, Adlai E.	6,568	343,006 R	68.8%	30.5%	69.3%	30.7%
1948	788,819	423,039	Dewey, Thomas E.	351,902	Truman, Harry S.	13,878	71,137 R	53.6%	44.6%	54.6%	45.4%
1944	733,776	442,096	Dewey, Thomas E.	287,458	Roosevelt, Franklin D.	4,222	154,638 R	60.2%	39.2%	60.6%	39.4%
1940	860,297	489,169	Willkie, Wendell	364,725	Roosevelt, Franklin D.	6,403	124,444 R	56.9%	42.4%	57.3%	42.7%
1936	865,507	397,727	Landon, Alfred M.	464,520	Roosevelt, Franklin D.	3,260	66,793 D	46.0%	53.7%	46.1%	53.9%
1932	791,978	349,498	Hoover, Herbert C.	424,204	Roosevelt, Franklin D.	18,276	74,706 D	44.1%	53.6%	45.2%	54.8%
1928	713,200	513,672	Hoover, Herbert C.	193,003	Smith, Alfred E.	6,525	320,669 R	72.0%	27.1%	72.7%	27.3%
1924 **	662,456	407,671	Coolidge, Calvin	156,320	Davis, John W.	98,465	251,351 R	61.5%	23.6%	72.3%	27.7%
1920	570,243	369,268	Harding, Warren G.	185,464	Cox, James M.	15,511	183,804 R	64.8%	32.5%	66.6%	33.4%

In 1924 other vote was 98,461 Progressive and 4 scattered.

ELECTORAL COLLEGE VOTE 1920 TO 1984

Year	Total	Republican	Democratic	Other
1984	7	7	—	—
1980	7	7	—	
1976	7	7	—	—
1972	7	7	—	—
1968	7	7	—	—
1964	7	—	7	—
1960	8	8	—	—
1956	8	8	—	—
1952	8	8	—	—
1948	8	8	—	—
1944	8	8	—	—
1940	9	9	—	—
1936	9	—	9	—
1932	9	—	9	—
1928	10	10	—	—
1924	10	10	—	—
1920	10	10	—	—

KANSAS

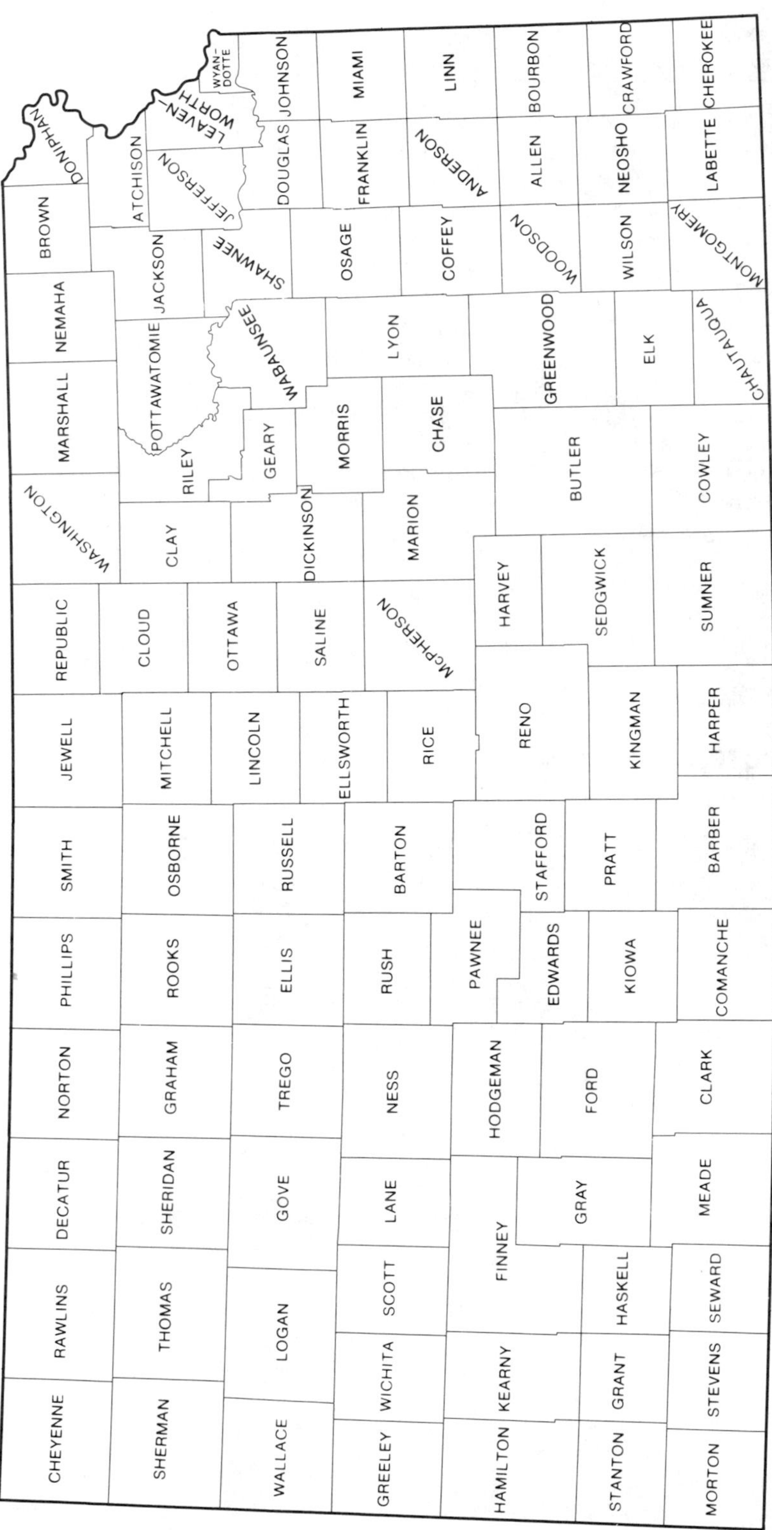
DONIPHAN
BROWN
NEMAHA
MARSHALL
WASHINGTON
REPUBLIC
JEWELL
SMITH
PHILLIPS
NORTON
DECATUR
RAWLINS
CHEYENNE
ATCHISON
JACKSON
POTTAWATOMIE
RILEY
CLAY
CLOUD
MITCHELL
OSBORNE
ROOKS
GRAHAM
SHERIDAN
THOMAS
SHERMAN
WYAN-DOTTE
LEAVEN-WORTH
JEFFERSON
SHAWNEE
WABAUNSEE
GEARY
DICKINSON
OTTAWA
LINCOLN
RUSSELL
ELLIS
TREGO
GOVE
LOGAN
WALLACE
JOHNSON
DOUGLAS
OSAGE
LYON
MORRIS
SALINE
ELLSWORTH
BARTON
RUSH
NESS
LANE
SCOTT
WICHITA
GREELEY
MIAMI
FRANKLIN
COFFEY
CHASE
MARION
McPHERSON
RICE
PAWNEE
HODGEMAN
FINNEY
KEARNY
HAMILTON
LINN
ANDERSON
WOODSON
GREENWOOD
BUTLER
HARVEY
RENO
STAFFORD
EDWARDS
FORD
GRAY
HASKELL
GRANT
STANTON
BOURBON
ALLEN
SEDGWICK
KINGMAN
PRATT
KIOWA
CRAWFORD
NEOSHO
WILSON
ELK
CLARK
MEADE
SEWARD
STEVENS
MORTON
CHEROKEE
LABETTE
MONTGOMERY
CHAUTAUQUA
COWLEY
SUMNER
HARPER
BARBER
COMANCHE

KANSAS

PRESIDENT 1984

1980 Census Population	County	Total Vote	Republican	Democratic	Other	Rep.-Dem. Plurality	Percentage Total Vote Rep.	Percentage Total Vote Dem.	Percentage Major Vote Rep.	Percentage Major Vote Dem.
15,654	ALLEN	6,117	4,267	1,778	72	2,489 R	69.8%	29.1%	70.6%	29.4%
8,749	ANDERSON	3,667	2,462	1,155	50	1,307 R	67.1%	31.5%	68.1%	31.9%
18,397	ATCHISON	7,255	4,537	2,641	77	1,896 R	62.5%	36.4%	63.2%	36.8%
6,548	BARBER	2,940	2,112	806	22	1,306 R	71.8%	27.4%	72.4%	27.6%
31,343	BARTON	13,538	10,232	3,111	195	7,121 R	75.6%	23.0%	76.7%	23.3%
15,969	BOURBON	7,102	4,858	2,175	69	2,683 R	68.4%	30.6%	69.1%	30.9%
11,955	BROWN	5,264	3,894	1,303	67	2,591 R	74.0%	24.8%	74.9%	25.1%
44,782	BUTLER	19,564	12,976	6,371	217	6,605 R	66.3%	32.6%	67.1%	32.9%
3,309	CHASE	1,570	1,162	393	15	769 R	74.0%	25.0%	74.7%	25.3%
5,016	CHAUTAUQUA	2,205	1,688	497	20	1,191 R	76.6%	22.5%	77.3%	22.7%
22,304	CHEROKEE	9,553	5,801	3,663	89	2,138 R	60.7%	38.3%	61.3%	38.7%
3,678	CHEYENNE	1,824	1,442	356	26	1,086 R	79.1%	19.5%	80.2%	19.8%
2,599	CLARK	1,426	1,075	324	27	751 R	75.4%	22.7%	76.8%	23.2%
9,802	CLAY	4,519	3,559	919	41	2,640 R	78.8%	20.3%	79.5%	20.5%
12,494	CLOUD	5,811	3,860	1,880	71	1,980 R	66.4%	32.4%	67.2%	32.8%
9,370	COFFEY	4,139	3,063	1,037	39	2,026 R	74.0%	25.1%	74.7%	25.3%
2,554	COMANCHE	1,293	993	285	15	708 R	76.8%	22.0%	77.7%	22.3%
36,824	COWLEY	15,399	10,008	5,193	198	4,815 R	65.0%	33.7%	65.8%	34.2%
37,916	CRAWFORD	16,381	9,518	6,722	141	2,796 R	58.1%	41.0%	58.6%	41.4%
4,509	DECATUR	2,265	1,770	467	28	1,303 R	78.1%	20.6%	79.1%	20.9%
20,175	DICKINSON	8,771	6,487	2,168	116	4,319 R	74.0%	24.7%	75.0%	25.0%
9,268	DONIPHAN	3,820	2,818	962	40	1,856 R	73.8%	25.2%	74.6%	25.4%
67,640	DOUGLAS	32,233	18,975	12,880	378	6,095 R	58.9%	40.0%	59.6%	40.4%
4,271	EDWARDS	2,002	1,352	606	44	746 R	67.5%	30.3%	69.1%	30.9%
3,918	ELK	1,785	1,301	452	32	849 R	72.9%	25.3%	74.2%	25.8%
26,098	ELLIS	11,099	7,509	3,457	133	4,052 R	67.7%	31.1%	68.5%	31.5%
6,640	ELLSWORTH	3,298	2,353	905	40	1,448 R	71.3%	27.4%	72.2%	27.8%
23,825	FINNEY	9,494	6,938	2,458	98	4,480 R	73.1%	25.9%	73.8%	26.2%
24,315	FORD	9,947	6,935	2,914	98	4,021 R	69.7%	29.3%	70.4%	29.6%
22,062	FRANKLIN	8,899	6,284	2,523	92	3,761 R	70.6%	28.4%	71.4%	28.6%
29,852	GEARY	6,821	4,464	2,296	61	2,168 R	65.4%	33.7%	66.0%	34.0%
3,726	GOVE	1,784	1,310	426	48	884 R	73.4%	23.9%	75.5%	24.5%
3,995	GRAHAM	1,923	1,423	480	20	943 R	74.0%	25.0%	74.8%	25.2%
6,977	GRANT	2,679	2,043	615	21	1,428 R	76.3%	23.0%	76.9%	23.1%
5,138	GRAY	2,126	1,580	514	32	1,066 R	74.3%	24.2%	75.5%	24.5%
1,845	GREELEY	954	699	227	28	472 R	73.3%	23.8%	75.5%	24.5%
8,764	GREENWOOD	4,118	2,901	1,173	44	1,728 R	70.4%	28.5%	71.2%	28.8%
2,514	HAMILTON	1,468	1,037	408	23	629 R	70.6%	27.8%	71.8%	28.2%
7,778	HARPER	3,449	2,521	893	35	1,628 R	73.1%	25.9%	73.8%	26.2%
30,531	HARVEY	13,280	8,507	4,599	174	3,908 R	64.1%	34.6%	64.9%	35.1%
3,814	HASKELL	1,452	1,152	283	17	869 R	79.3%	19.5%	80.3%	19.7%
2,269	HODGEMAN	1,266	939	306	21	633 R	74.2%	24.2%	75.4%	24.6%
11,644	JACKSON	5,179	3,466	1,667	46	1,799 R	66.9%	32.2%	67.5%	32.5%
15,207	JEFFERSON	6,563	4,524	1,990	49	2,534 R	68.9%	30.3%	69.5%	30.5%
5,241	JEWELL	2,604	1,992	583	29	1,409 R	76.5%	22.4%	77.4%	22.6%
270,269	JOHNSON	140,882	101,987	38,019	876	63,968 R	72.4%	27.0%	72.8%	27.2%
3,435	KEARNY	1,548	1,214	321	13	893 R	78.4%	20.7%	79.1%	20.9%
8,960	KINGMAN	3,923	2,826	1,047	50	1,779 R	72.0%	26.7%	73.0%	27.0%
4,046	KIOWA	1,933	1,537	361	35	1,176 R	79.5%	18.7%	81.0%	19.0%
25,682	LABETTE	10,260	6,542	3,631	87	2,911 R	63.8%	35.4%	64.3%	35.7%
2,472	LANE	1,306	1,008	282	16	726 R	77.2%	21.6%	78.1%	21.9%
54,809	LEAVENWORTH	17,970	11,194	6,604	172	4,590 R	62.3%	36.8%	62.9%	37.1%
4,145	LINCOLN	2,293	1,723	551	19	1,172 R	75.1%	24.0%	75.8%	24.2%
8,234	LINN	3,974	2,795	1,152	27	1,643 R	70.3%	29.0%	70.8%	29.2%
3,478	LOGAN	1,603	1,235	331	37	904 R	77.0%	20.6%	78.9%	21.1%
35,108	LYON	14,121	9,796	4,188	137	5,608 R	69.4%	29.7%	70.1%	29.9%
26,855	MCPHERSON	12,004	8,630	3,185	189	5,445 R	71.9%	26.5%	73.0%	27.0%
13,522	MARION	6,116	4,407	1,632	77	2,775 R	72.1%	26.7%	73.0%	27.0%
12,787	MARSHALL	5,983	4,098	1,813	72	2,285 R	68.5%	30.3%	69.3%	30.7%
4,788	MEADE	2,338	1,804	491	43	1,313 R	77.2%	21.0%	78.6%	21.4%

KANSAS

PRESIDENT 1984

1980 Census Population	County	Total Vote	Republican	Democratic	Other	Rep.-Dem. Plurality	Percentage Total Vote Rep.	Total Vote Dem.	Major Vote Rep.	Major Vote Dem.
21,618	MIAMI	9,036	5,877	3,076	83	2,801 R	65.0%	34.0%	65.6%	34.4%
8,117	MITCHELL	3,996	3,036	919	41	2,117 R	76.0%	23.0%	76.8%	23.2%
42,281	MONTGOMERY	17,127	12,023	4,933	171	7,090 R	70.2%	28.8%	70.9%	29.1%
6,419	MORRIS	3,103	2,240	820	43	1,420 R	72.2%	26.4%	73.2%	26.8%
3,454	MORTON	1,874	1,533	322	19	1,211 R	81.8%	17.2%	82.6%	17.4%
11,211	NEMAHA	5,485	3,653	1,761	71	1,892 R	66.6%	32.1%	67.5%	32.5%
18,967	NEOSHO	7,749	4,968	2,679	102	2,289 R	64.1%	34.6%	65.0%	35.0%
4,498	NESS	2,362	1,779	540	43	1,239 R	75.3%	22.9%	76.7%	23.3%
6,689	NORTON	3,176	2,515	611	50	1,904 R	79.2%	19.2%	80.5%	19.5%
15,319	OSAGE	6,443	4,288	2,072	83	2,216 R	66.6%	32.2%	67.4%	32.6%
5,959	OSBORNE	2,909	2,171	686	52	1,485 R	74.6%	23.6%	76.0%	24.0%
5,971	OTTAWA	3,096	2,345	699	52	1,646 R	75.7%	22.6%	77.0%	23.0%
8,065	PAWNEE	3,730	2,570	1,092	68	1,478 R	68.9%	29.3%	70.2%	29.8%
7,406	PHILLIPS	3,477	2,813	626	38	2,187 R	80.9%	18.0%	81.8%	18.2%
14,782	POTTAWATOMIE	6,468	4,598	1,798	72	2,800 R	71.1%	27.8%	71.9%	28.1%
10,275	PRATT	4,549	3,244	1,255	50	1,989 R	71.3%	27.6%	72.1%	27.9%
4,105	RAWLINS	2,082	1,625	412	45	1,213 R	78.0%	19.8%	79.8%	20.2%
64,983	RENO	26,159	16,568	9,229	362	7,339 R	63.3%	35.3%	64.2%	35.8%
7,569	REPUBLIC	3,934	3,009	887	38	2,122 R	76.5%	22.5%	77.2%	22.8%
11,900	RICE	5,239	3,598	1,559	82	2,039 R	68.7%	29.8%	69.8%	30.2%
63,505	RILEY	17,458	11,308	5,975	175	5,333 R	64.8%	34.2%	65.4%	34.6%
7,006	ROOKS	3,349	2,604	699	46	1,905 R	77.8%	20.9%	78.8%	21.2%
4,516	RUSH	2,530	1,758	718	54	1,040 R	69.5%	28.4%	71.0%	29.0%
8,868	RUSSELL	4,771	3,673	1,055	43	2,618 R	77.0%	22.1%	77.7%	22.3%
48,905	SALINE	21,961	15,244	6,526	191	8,718 R	69.4%	29.7%	70.0%	30.0%
5,782	SCOTT	2,486	2,017	427	42	1,590 R	81.1%	17.2%	82.5%	17.5%
366,531	SEDGWICK	153,315	95,874	55,263	2,178	40,611 R	62.5%	36.0%	63.4%	36.6%
17,071	SEWARD	6,484	5,222	1,198	64	4,024 R	80.5%	18.5%	81.3%	18.7%
154,916	SHAWNEE	70,589	43,465	26,338	786	17,127 R	61.6%	37.3%	62.3%	37.7%
3,544	SHERIDAN	1,725	1,274	419	32	855 R	73.9%	24.3%	75.3%	24.7%
7,759	SHERMAN	3,463	2,702	714	47	1,988 R	78.0%	20.6%	79.1%	20.9%
5,947	SMITH	3,079	2,332	684	63	1,648 R	75.7%	22.2%	77.3%	22.7%
5,694	STAFFORD	2,958	2,062	844	52	1,218 R	69.7%	28.5%	71.0%	29.0%
2,339	STANTON	1,022	783	205	34	578 R	76.6%	20.1%	79.3%	20.7%
4,736	STEVENS	2,271	1,863	386	22	1,477 R	82.0%	17.0%	82.8%	17.2%
24,928	SUMNER	10,793	6,942	3,708	143	3,234 R	64.3%	34.4%	65.2%	34.8%
8,451	THOMAS	4,051	3,107	887	57	2,220 R	76.7%	21.9%	77.8%	22.2%
4,165	TREGO	2,118	1,491	598	29	893 R	70.4%	28.2%	71.4%	28.6%
6,867	WABAUNSEE	3,130	2,276	805	49	1,471 R	72.7%	25.7%	73.9%	26.1%
2,045	WALLACE	1,010	838	152	20	686 R	83.0%	15.0%	84.6%	15.4%
8,543	WASHINGTON	3,936	2,979	889	68	2,090 R	75.7%	22.6%	77.0%	23.0%
3,041	WICHITA	1,161	916	232	13	684 R	78.9%	20.0%	79.8%	20.2%
12,128	WILSON	5,071	3,663	1,344	64	2,319 R	72.2%	26.5%	73.2%	26.8%
4,600	WOODSON	2,030	1,408	596	26	812 R	69.4%	29.4%	70.3%	29.7%
172,335	WYANDOTTE	64,136	27,459	36,042	635	8,583 D	42.8%	56.2%	43.2%	56.8%
2,363,679	TOTAL	1,021,991	677,296	333,149	11,546	344,147 R	66.3%	32.6%	67.0%	33.0%

KANSAS

PRESIDENT 1980

1980 Census Population	County	Total Vote	Republican	Democratic	Other	Rep.-Dem. Plurality	Percentage Total Vote Rep.	Total Vote Dem.	Major Vote Rep.	Major Vote Dem.
15,654	ALLEN	6,317	3,811	2,009	497	1,802 R	60.3%	31.8%	65.5%	34.5%
8,749	ANDERSON	3,773	2,363	1,170	240	1,193 R	62.6%	31.0%	66.9%	33.1%
18,397	ATCHISON	7,581	4,084	3,063	434	1,021 R	53.9%	40.4%	57.1%	42.9%
6,548	BARBER	2,994	1,872	914	208	958 R	62.5%	30.5%	67.2%	32.8%
31,343	BARTON	13,852	9,147	3,663	1,042	5,484 R	66.0%	26.4%	71.4%	28.6%
15,969	BOURBON	7,199	4,263	2,605	331	1,658 R	59.2%	36.2%	62.1%	37.9%
11,955	BROWN	5,322	3,598	1,370	354	2,228 R	67.6%	25.7%	72.4%	27.6%
44,782	BUTLER	18,453	10,210	6,875	1,368	3,335 R	55.3%	37.3%	59.8%	40.2%
3,309	CHASE	1,603	1,073	413	117	660 R	66.9%	25.8%	72.2%	27.8%
5,016	CHAUTAUQUA	2,187	1,566	543	78	1,023 R	71.6%	24.8%	74.3%	25.7%
22,304	CHEROKEE	9,662	5,296	3,969	397	1,327 R	54.8%	41.1%	57.2%	42.8%
3,678	CHEYENNE	1,800	1,330	358	112	972 R	73.9%	19.9%	78.8%	21.2%
2,599	CLARK	1,417	901	430	86	471 R	63.6%	30.3%	67.7%	32.3%
9,802	CLAY	4,667	3,449	932	286	2,517 R	73.9%	20.0%	78.7%	21.3%
12,494	CLOUD	5,817	3,581	1,793	443	1,788 R	61.6%	30.8%	66.6%	33.4%
9,370	COFFEY	3,602	2,491	938	173	1,553 R	69.2%	26.0%	72.6%	27.4%
2,554	COMANCHE	1,340	877	393	70	484 R	65.4%	29.3%	69.1%	30.9%
36,824	COWLEY	15,312	8,749	5,474	1,089	3,275 R	57.1%	35.7%	61.5%	38.5%
37,916	CRAWFORD	16,855	8,058	7,658	1,139	400 R	47.8%	45.4%	51.3%	48.7%
4,509	DECATUR	2,250	1,642	443	165	1,199 R	73.0%	19.7%	78.8%	21.2%
20,175	DICKINSON	8,359	5,654	2,108	597	3,546 R	67.6%	25.2%	72.8%	27.2%
9,268	DONIPHAN	3,719	2,523	1,001	195	1,522 R	67.8%	26.9%	71.6%	28.4%
67,640	DOUGLAS	28,784	14,106	9,360	5,318	4,746 R	49.0%	32.5%	60.1%	39.9%
4,271	EDWARDS	2,204	1,409	616	179	793 R	63.9%	27.9%	69.6%	30.4%
3,918	ELK	1,837	1,280	482	75	798 R	69.7%	26.2%	72.6%	27.4%
26,098	ELLIS	10,724	5,634	3,940	1,150	1,694 R	52.5%	36.7%	58.8%	41.2%
6,640	ELLSWORTH	3,270	2,155	886	229	1,269 R	65.9%	27.1%	70.9%	29.1%
23,825	FINNEY	8,246	4,831	2,689	726	2,142 R	58.6%	32.6%	64.2%	35.8%
24,315	FORD	9,661	5,686	3,194	781	2,492 R	58.9%	33.1%	64.0%	36.0%
22,062	FRANKLIN	8,808	5,525	2,726	557	2,799 R	62.7%	30.9%	67.0%	33.0%
29,852	GEARY	6,304	3,534	2,357	413	1,177 R	56.1%	37.4%	60.0%	40.0%
3,726	GOVE	1,776	1,263	396	117	867 R	71.1%	22.3%	76.1%	23.9%
3,995	GRAHAM	2,045	1,450	473	122	977 R	70.9%	23.1%	75.4%	24.6%
6,977	GRANT	2,592	1,711	683	198	1,028 R	66.0%	26.4%	71.5%	28.5%
5,138	GRAY	2,057	1,310	583	164	727 R	63.7%	28.3%	69.2%	30.8%
1,845	GREELEY	947	600	235	112	365 R	63.4%	24.8%	71.9%	28.1%
8,764	GREENWOOD	4,155	2,685	1,241	229	1,444 R	64.6%	29.9%	68.4%	31.6%
2,514	HAMILTON	1,375	889	402	84	487 R	64.7%	29.2%	68.9%	31.1%
7,778	HARPER	3,512	2,254	990	268	1,264 R	64.2%	28.2%	69.5%	30.5%
30,531	HARVEY	12,912	7,045	4,173	1,694	2,872 R	54.6%	32.3%	62.8%	37.2%
3,814	HASKELL	1,499	1,014	374	111	640 R	67.6%	24.9%	73.1%	26.9%
2,269	HODGEMAN	1,256	831	339	86	492 R	66.2%	27.0%	71.0%	29.0%
11,644	JACKSON	5,070	3,211	1,537	322	1,674 R	63.3%	30.3%	67.6%	32.4%
15,207	JEFFERSON	6,263	4,046	1,776	441	2,270 R	64.6%	28.4%	69.5%	30.5%
5,241	JEWELL	2,849	2,074	578	197	1,496 R	72.8%	20.3%	78.2%	21.8%
270,269	JOHNSON	123,983	78,048	33,210	12,725	44,838 R	63.0%	26.8%	70.2%	29.8%
3,435	KEARNY	1,392	924	375	93	549 R	66.4%	26.9%	71.1%	28.9%
8,960	KINGMAN	4,102	2,610	1,133	359	1,477 R	63.6%	27.6%	69.7%	30.3%
4,046	KIOWA	1,986	1,433	438	115	995 R	72.2%	22.1%	76.6%	23.4%
25,682	LABETTE	9,921	5,244	3,947	730	1,297 R	52.9%	39.8%	57.1%	42.9%
2,472	LANE	1,368	924	321	123	603 R	67.5%	23.5%	74.2%	25.8%
54,809	LEAVENWORTH	16,656	9,157	6,354	1,145	2,803 R	55.0%	38.1%	59.0%	41.0%
4,145	LINCOLN	2,335	1,685	528	122	1,157 R	72.2%	22.6%	76.1%	23.9%
8,234	LINN	3,710	2,407	1,157	146	1,250 R	64.9%	31.2%	67.5%	32.5%
3,478	LOGAN	1,730	1,261	358	111	903 R	72.9%	20.7%	77.9%	22.1%
35,108	LYON	14,551	8,431	4,680	1,440	3,751 R	57.9%	32.2%	64.3%	35.7%
26,855	MCPHERSON	11,631	6,843	3,340	1,448	3,503 R	58.8%	28.7%	67.2%	32.8%
13,522	MARION	6,150	3,960	1,569	621	2,391 R	64.4%	25.5%	71.6%	28.4%
12,787	MARSHALL	6,097	4,127	1,555	415	2,572 R	67.7%	25.5%	72.6%	27.4%
4,788	MEADE	2,258	1,618	482	158	1,136 R	71.7%	21.3%	77.0%	23.0%

KANSAS

PRESIDENT 1980

1980 Census Population	County	Total Vote	Republican	Democratic	Other	Rep.-Dem. Plurality	Percentage Total Vote Rep.	Total Vote Dem.	Major Vote Rep.	Major Vote Dem.
21,618	MIAMI	8,301	4,740	3,071	490	1,669 R	57.1%	37.0%	60.7%	39.3%
8,117	MITCHELL	3,953	2,821	876	256	1,945 R	71.4%	22.2%	76.3%	23.7%
42,281	MONTGOMERY	16,915	10,856	5,282	777	5,574 R	64.2%	31.2%	67.3%	32.7%
6,419	MORRIS	2,949	1,933	810	206	1,123 R	65.5%	27.5%	70.5%	29.5%
3,454	MORTON	1,662	1,157	414	91	743 R	69.6%	24.9%	73.6%	26.4%
11,211	NEMAHA	5,456	3,546	1,600	310	1,946 R	65.0%	29.3%	68.9%	31.1%
18,967	NEOSHO	8,077	4,613	2,923	541	1,690 R	57.1%	36.2%	61.2%	38.8%
4,498	NESS	2,455	1,657	616	182	1,041 R	67.5%	25.1%	72.9%	27.1%
6,689	NORTON	3,477	2,625	666	186	1,959 R	75.5%	19.2%	79.8%	20.2%
15,319	OSAGE	6,324	3,817	2,088	419	1,729 R	60.4%	33.0%	64.6%	35.4%
5,959	OSBORNE	2,984	2,188	620	176	1,568 R	73.3%	20.8%	77.9%	22.1%
5,971	OTTAWA	2,947	2,118	630	199	1,488 R	71.9%	21.4%	77.1%	22.9%
8,065	PAWNEE	3,691	2,170	1,184	337	986 R	58.8%	32.1%	64.7%	35.3%
7,406	PHILLIPS	3,667	2,731	748	188	1,983 R	74.5%	20.4%	78.5%	21.5%
14,782	POTTAWATOMIE	6,144	3,895	1,724	525	2,171 R	63.4%	28.1%	69.3%	30.7%
10,275	PRATT	4,683	2,866	1,369	448	1,497 R	61.2%	29.2%	67.7%	32.3%
4,105	RAWLINS	2,076	1,524	427	125	1,097 R	73.4%	20.6%	78.1%	21.9%
64,983	RENO	26,121	13,804	9,615	2,702	4,189 R	52.8%	36.8%	58.9%	41.1%
7,569	REPUBLIC	4,120	3,031	850	239	2,181 R	73.6%	20.6%	78.1%	21.9%
11,900	RICE	5,568	3,211	1,847	510	1,364 R	57.7%	33.2%	63.5%	36.5%
63,505	RILEY	16,818	8,904	5,224	2,690	3,680 R	52.9%	31.1%	63.0%	37.0%
7,006	ROOKS	3,187	2,275	725	187	1,550 R	71.4%	22.7%	75.8%	24.2%
4,516	RUSH	2,572	1,840	557	175	1,283 R	71.5%	21.7%	76.8%	23.2%
8,868	RUSSELL	4,437	3,241	910	286	2,331 R	73.0%	20.5%	78.1%	21.9%
48,905	SALINE	21,169	12,758	6,382	2,029	6,376 R	60.3%	30.1%	66.7%	33.3%
5,782	SCOTT	2,418	1,829	456	133	1,373 R	75.6%	18.9%	80.0%	20.0%
366,531	SEDGWICK	145,431	75,317	55,105	15,009	20,212 R	51.8%	37.9%	57.7%	42.3%
17,071	SEWARD	6,191	4,385	1,460	346	2,925 R	70.8%	23.6%	75.0%	25.0%
154,916	SHAWNEE	67,776	36,290	24,852	6,634	11,438 R	53.5%	36.7%	59.4%	40.6%
3,544	SHERIDAN	1,693	1,202	391	100	811 R	71.0%	23.1%	75.5%	24.5%
7,759	SHERMAN	3,362	2,315	779	268	1,536 R	68.9%	23.2%	74.8%	25.2%
5,947	SMITH	3,368	2,415	719	234	1,696 R	71.7%	21.3%	77.1%	22.9%
5,694	STAFFORD	2,976	1,865	872	239	993 R	62.7%	29.3%	68.1%	31.9%
2,339	STANTON	992	672	231	89	441 R	67.7%	23.3%	74.4%	25.6%
4,736	STEVENS	2,085	1,502	478	105	1,024 R	72.0%	22.9%	75.9%	24.1%
24,928	SUMNER	10,496	6,038	3,761	697	2,277 R	57.5%	35.8%	61.6%	38.4%
8,451	THOMAS	4,202	2,789	1,045	368	1,744 R	66.4%	24.9%	72.7%	27.3%
4,165	TREGO	2,048	1,340	523	185	817 R	65.4%	25.5%	71.9%	28.1%
6,867	WABAUNSEE	3,317	2,255	853	209	1,402 R	68.0%	25.7%	72.6%	27.4%
2,045	WALLACE	1,036	811	167	58	644 R	78.3%	16.1%	82.9%	17.1%
8,543	WASHINGTON	4,083	3,058	784	241	2,274 R	74.9%	19.2%	79.6%	20.4%
3,041	WICHITA	1,258	880	303	75	577 R	70.0%	24.1%	74.4%	25.6%
12,128	WILSON	4,801	3,328	1,205	268	2,123 R	69.3%	25.1%	73.4%	26.6%
4,600	WOODSON	2,189	1,435	646	108	789 R	65.6%	29.5%	69.0%	31.0%
172,335	WYANDOTTE	60,223	23,012	32,763	4,448	9,751 D	38.2%	54.4%	41.3%	58.7%
2,363,679	TOTAL	979,795	566,812	326,150	86,833	240,662 R	57.9%	33.3%	63.5%	36.5%

KANSAS

PRESIDENT 1976

1970 Census Population	County	Total Vote	Republican	Democratic	Other	Rep.-Dem. Plurality	Percentage Total Vote Rep.	Total Vote Dem.	Major Vote Rep.	Major Vote Dem.
15,043	ALLEN	6,141	3,269	2,746	126	523 R	53.2%	44.7%	54.3%	45.7%
8,501	ANDERSON	3,844	1,872	1,886	86	14 D	48.7%	49.1%	49.8%	50.2%
19,165	ATCHISON	8,344	4,030	4,108	206	78 D	48.3%	49.2%	49.5%	50.5%
7,016	BARBER	3,109	1,568	1,494	47	74 R	50.4%	48.1%	51.2%	48.8%
30,663	BARTON	13,142	7,311	5,497	334	1,814 R	55.6%	41.8%	57.1%	42.9%
15,215	BOURBON	6,929	3,589	3,237	103	352 R	51.8%	46.7%	52.6%	47.4%
11,685	BROWN	5,245	3,407	1,745	93	1,662 R	65.0%	33.3%	66.1%	33.9%
38,658	BUTLER	17,316	8,390	8,540	386	150 D	48.5%	49.3%	49.6%	50.4%
3,408	CHASE	1,601	922	643	36	279 R	57.6%	40.2%	58.9%	41.1%
4,642	CHAUTAUQUA	2,078	1,159	866	53	293 R	55.8%	41.7%	57.2%	42.8%
21,549	CHEROKEE	9,218	3,957	5,154	107	1,197 D	42.9%	55.9%	43.4%	56.6%
4,256	CHEYENNE	1,805	1,008	758	39	250 R	55.8%	42.0%	57.1%	42.9%
2,896	CLARK	1,469	761	680	28	81 R	51.8%	46.3%	52.8%	47.2%
9,890	CLAY	4,832	3,085	1,610	137	1,475 R	63.8%	33.3%	65.7%	34.3%
13,466	CLOUD	6,061	2,954	2,976	131	22 D	48.7%	49.1%	49.8%	50.2%
7,397	COFFEY	3,783	2,145	1,549	89	596 R	56.7%	40.9%	58.1%	41.9%
2,702	COMANCHE	1,364	719	630	15	89 R	52.7%	46.2%	53.3%	46.7%
35,012	COWLEY	14,931	7,513	7,095	323	418 R	50.3%	47.5%	51.4%	48.6%
37,850	CRAWFORD	16,504	7,225	9,021	258	1,796 D	43.8%	54.7%	44.5%	55.5%
4,988	DECATUR	2,336	1,232	1,011	93	221 R	52.7%	43.3%	54.9%	45.1%
19,993	DICKINSON	8,617	4,759	3,672	186	1,087 R	55.2%	42.6%	56.4%	43.6%
9,107	DONIPHAN	3,969	2,469	1,428	72	1,041 R	62.2%	36.0%	63.4%	36.6%
57,932	DOUGLAS	27,842	14,277	11,922	1,643	2,355 R	51.3%	42.8%	54.5%	45.5%
4,581	EDWARDS	2,357	1,001	1,304	52	303 D	42.5%	55.3%	43.4%	56.6%
3,858	ELK	1,982	1,087	865	30	222 R	54.8%	43.6%	55.7%	44.3%
24,730	ELLIS	11,240	4,719	6,280	241	1,561 D	42.0%	55.9%	42.9%	57.1%
6,146	ELLSWORTH	3,246	1,618	1,573	55	45 R	49.8%	48.5%	50.7%	49.3%
19,029	FINNEY	7,667	3,711	3,813	143	102 D	48.4%	49.7%	49.3%	50.7%
22,587	FORD	9,827	4,679	4,934	214	255 D	47.6%	50.2%	48.7%	51.3%
20,007	FRANKLIN	8,578	4,760	3,607	211	1,153 R	55.5%	42.0%	56.9%	43.1%
28,111	GEARY	6,196	3,230	2,843	123	387 R	52.1%	45.9%	53.2%	46.8%
3,940	GOVE	1,757	860	848	49	12 R	48.9%	48.3%	50.4%	49.6%
4,751	GRAHAM	2,088	1,112	936	40	176 R	53.3%	44.8%	54.3%	45.7%
5,961	GRANT	2,422	1,226	1,151	45	75 R	50.6%	47.5%	51.6%	48.4%
4,516	GRAY	1,989	837	1,111	41	274 D	42.1%	55.9%	43.0%	57.0%
1,819	GREELEY	896	389	479	28	90 D	43.4%	53.5%	44.8%	55.2%
9,141	GREENWOOD	4,144	2,319	1,737	88	582 R	56.0%	41.9%	57.2%	42.8%
2,747	HAMILTON	1,343	560	746	37	186 D	41.7%	55.5%	42.9%	57.1%
7,871	HARPER	3,554	1,777	1,681	96	96 R	50.0%	47.3%	51.4%	48.6%
27,236	HARVEY	12,987	6,624	6,003	360	621 R	51.0%	46.2%	52.5%	47.5%
3,672	HASKELL	1,464	761	676	27	85 R	52.0%	46.2%	53.0%	47.0%
2,662	HODGEMAN	1,315	576	697	42	121 D	43.8%	53.0%	45.2%	54.8%
10,342	JACKSON	4,968	2,725	2,129	114	596 R	54.9%	42.9%	56.1%	43.9%
11,945	JEFFERSON	5,851	3,225	2,470	156	755 R	55.1%	42.2%	56.6%	43.4%
6,099	JEWELL	2,770	1,592	1,111	67	481 R	57.5%	40.1%	58.9%	41.1%
220,073	JOHNSON	114,142	75,798	35,605	2,739	40,193 R	66.4%	31.2%	68.0%	32.0%
3,047	KEARNY	1,377	674	658	45	16 R	48.9%	47.8%	50.6%	49.4%
8,886	KINGMAN	4,093	1,839	2,142	112	303 D	44.9%	52.3%	46.2%	53.8%
4,088	KIOWA	1,984	1,180	764	40	416 R	59.5%	38.5%	60.7%	39.3%
25,775	LABETTE	10,177	4,640	5,294	243	654 D	45.6%	52.0%	46.7%	53.3%
2,707	LANE	1,331	651	646	34	5 R	48.9%	48.5%	50.2%	49.8%
53,340	LEAVENWORTH	16,778	8,407	8,022	349	385 R	50.1%	47.8%	51.2%	48.8%
4,582	LINCOLN	2,247	1,225	985	37	240 R	54.5%	43.8%	55.4%	44.6%
7,770	LINN	3,602	1,873	1,681	48	192 R	52.0%	46.7%	52.7%	47.3%
3,814	LOGAN	1,697	957	694	46	263 R	56.4%	40.9%	58.0%	42.0%
32,071	LYON	13,428	7,062	5,634	732	1,428 R	52.6%	42.0%	55.6%	44.4%
24,778	MCPHERSON	11,860	6,187	5,366	307	821 R	52.2%	45.2%	53.6%	46.4%
13,935	MARION	6,140	3,519	2,483	138	1,036 R	57.3%	40.4%	58.6%	41.4%
13,139	MARSHALL	6,360	3,226	3,004	130	222 R	50.7%	47.2%	51.8%	48.2%
4,912	MEADE	2,152	1,109	983	60	126 R	51.5%	45.7%	53.0%	47.0%

KANSAS

PRESIDENT 1976

1970 Census Population	County	Total Vote	Republican	Democratic	Other	Rep.-Dem. Plurality	Percentage Total Vote Rep.	Percentage Total Vote Dem.	Percentage Major Vote Rep.	Percentage Major Vote Dem.
19,254	MIAMI	8,216	3,999	4,000	217	1 D	48.7%	48.7%	50.0%	50.0%
8,010	MITCHELL	3,880	2,095	1,700	85	395 R	54.0%	43.8%	55.2%	44.8%
39,949	MONTGOMERY	16,391	8,864	7,157	370	1,707 R	54.1%	43.7%	55.3%	44.7%
6,432	MORRIS	3,102	1,698	1,337	67	361 R	54.7%	43.1%	55.9%	44.1%
3,576	MORTON	1,509	738	735	36	3 R	48.9%	48.7%	50.1%	49.9%
11,825	NEMAHA	5,441	2,759	2,586	96	173 R	50.7%	47.5%	51.6%	48.4%
18,812	NEOSHO	8,024	4,038	3,842	144	196 R	50.3%	47.9%	51.2%	48.8%
4,791	NESS	2,184	1,016	1,106	62	90 D	46.5%	50.6%	47.9%	52.1%
7,279	NORTON	3,635	2,201	1,337	97	864 R	60.6%	36.8%	62.2%	37.8%
13,352	OSAGE	5,828	2,945	2,755	128	190 R	50.5%	47.3%	51.7%	48.3%
6,416	OSBORNE	2,840	1,574	1,190	76	384 R	55.4%	41.9%	56.9%	43.1%
6,183	OTTAWA	3,082	1,629	1,393	60	236 R	52.9%	45.2%	53.9%	46.1%
8,484	PAWNEE	3,751	1,692	1,959	100	267 D	45.1%	52.2%	46.3%	53.7%
7,888	PHILLIPS	3,675	2,317	1,264	94	1,053 R	63.0%	34.4%	64.7%	35.3%
11,755	POTTAWATOMIE	5,897	3,483	2,316	98	1,167 R	59.1%	39.3%	60.1%	39.9%
10,056	PRATT	4,850	2,427	2,307	116	120 R	50.0%	47.6%	51.3%	48.7%
4,393	RAWLINS	2,131	1,148	903	80	245 R	53.9%	42.4%	56.0%	44.0%
60,765	RENO	26,512	11,212	14,620	680	3,408 D	42.3%	55.1%	43.4%	56.6%
8,498	REPUBLIC	3,994	2,294	1,617	83	677 R	57.4%	40.5%	58.7%	41.3%
12,320	RICE	5,765	2,584	3,056	125	472 D	44.8%	53.0%	45.8%	54.2%
56,788	RILEY	16,568	9,518	6,540	510	2,978 R	57.4%	39.5%	59.3%	40.7%
7,628	ROOKS	3,137	1,664	1,412	61	252 R	53.0%	45.0%	54.1%	45.9%
5,117	RUSH	2,581	1,170	1,359	52	189 D	45.3%	52.7%	46.3%	53.7%
9,428	RUSSELL	4,669	3,165	1,453	51	1,712 R	67.8%	31.1%	68.5%	31.5%
46,592	SALINE	20,107	11,218	8,476	413	2,742 R	55.8%	42.2%	57.0%	43.0%
5,606	SCOTT	2,183	1,195	919	69	276 R	54.7%	42.1%	56.5%	43.5%
350,694	SEDGWICK	137,629	69,828	63,989	3,812	5,839 R	50.7%	46.5%	52.2%	47.8%
15,744	SEWARD	5,615	3,604	1,907	104	1,697 R	64.2%	34.0%	65.4%	34.6%
155,322	SHAWNEE	67,370	37,101	28,578	1,691	8,523 R	55.1%	42.4%	56.5%	43.5%
3,859	SHERIDAN	1,705	838	793	74	45 R	49.1%	46.5%	51.4%	48.6%
7,792	SHERMAN	3,332	1,671	1,573	88	98 R	50.2%	47.2%	51.5%	48.5%
6,757	SMITH	3,436	2,009	1,333	94	676 R	58.5%	38.8%	60.1%	39.9%
5,943	STAFFORD	3,162	1,430	1,659	73	229 D	45.2%	52.5%	46.3%	53.7%
2,287	STANTON	1,040	510	489	41	21 R	49.0%	47.0%	51.1%	48.9%
4,198	STEVENS	2,205	1,262	901	42	361 R	57.2%	40.9%	58.3%	41.7%
23,553	SUMNER	10,340	4,645	5,385	310	740 D	44.9%	52.1%	46.3%	53.7%
7,501	THOMAS	4,164	2,246	1,802	116	444 R	53.9%	43.3%	55.5%	44.5%
4,436	TREGO	2,068	1,025	1,003	40	22 R	49.6%	48.5%	50.5%	49.5%
6,397	WABAUNSEE	3,336	1,921	1,354	61	567 R	57.6%	40.6%	58.7%	41.3%
2,215	WALLACE	1,137	600	486	51	114 R	52.8%	42.7%	55.2%	44.8%
9,249	WASHINGTON	4,213	2,543	1,564	106	979 R	60.4%	37.1%	61.9%	38.1%
3,274	WICHITA	1,238	593	614	31	21 D	47.9%	49.6%	49.1%	50.9%
11,317	WILSON	4,818	2,682	2,047	89	635 R	55.7%	42.5%	56.7%	43.3%
4,789	WOODSON	2,041	1,104	904	33	200 R	54.1%	44.3%	55.0%	45.0%
186,845	WYANDOTTE	62,555	23,141	37,478	1,936	14,337 D	37.0%	59.9%	38.2%	61.8%
2,249,071	TOTAL	957,845	502,752	430,421	24,672	72,331 R	52.5%	44.9%	53.9%	46.1%

KANSAS

PRESIDENT 1972

1970 Census Population	County	Total Vote	Republican	Democratic	Other	Rep.-Dem. Plurality	Percentage Total Vote Rep.	Total Vote Dem.	Major Vote Rep.	Major Vote Dem.
15,043	ALLEN	5,669	3,938	1,610	121	2,328 R	69.5%	28.4%	71.0%	29.0%
8,501	ANDERSON	3,836	2,718	1,035	83	1,683 R	70.9%	27.0%	72.4%	27.6%
19,165	ATCHISON	8,066	5,471	2,404	191	3,067 R	67.8%	29.8%	69.5%	30.5%
7,016	BARBER	3,108	2,308	727	73	1,581 R	74.3%	23.4%	76.0%	24.0%
30,663	BARTON	12,312	8,479	3,481	352	4,998 R	68.9%	28.3%	70.9%	29.1%
15,215	BOURBON	6,814	4,776	1,912	126	2,864 R	70.1%	28.1%	71.4%	28.6%
11,685	BROWN	5,466	4,314	1,038	114	3,276 R	78.9%	19.0%	80.6%	19.4%
38,658	BUTLER	16,389	11,045	4,669	675	6,376 R	67.4%	28.5%	70.3%	29.7%
3,408	CHASE	1,557	1,184	315	58	869 R	76.0%	20.2%	79.0%	21.0%
4,642	CHAUTAUQUA	1,982	1,546	378	58	1,168 R	78.0%	19.1%	80.4%	19.6%
21,549	CHEROKEE	8,980	6,019	2,806	155	3,213 R	67.0%	31.2%	68.2%	31.8%
4,256	CHEYENNE	1,907	1,440	399	68	1,041 R	75.5%	20.9%	78.3%	21.7%
2,896	CLARK	1,502	1,142	311	49	831 R	76.0%	20.7%	78.6%	21.4%
9,890	CLAY	4,542	3,562	887	93	2,675 R	78.4%	19.5%	80.1%	19.9%
13,466	CLOUD	5,773	3,832	1,806	135	2,026 R	66.4%	31.3%	68.0%	32.0%
7,397	COFFEY	3,523	2,667	782	74	1,885 R	75.7%	22.2%	77.3%	22.7%
2,702	COMANCHE	1,363	1,052	281	30	771 R	77.2%	20.6%	78.9%	21.1%
35,012	COWLEY	14,653	10,332	3,592	729	6,740 R	70.5%	24.5%	74.2%	25.8%
37,850	CRAWFORD	16,637	9,652	6,683	302	2,969 R	58.0%	40.2%	59.1%	40.9%
4,988	DECATUR	2,431	1,707	616	108	1,091 R	70.2%	25.3%	73.5%	26.5%
19,993	DICKINSON	8,647	6,515	1,957	175	4,558 R	75.3%	22.6%	76.9%	23.1%
9,107	DONIPHAN	3,643	2,856	690	97	2,166 R	78.4%	18.9%	80.5%	19.5%
57,932	DOUGLAS	27,527	15,316	11,646	565	3,670 R	55.6%	42.3%	56.8%	43.2%
4,581	EDWARDS	2,377	1,534	757	86	777 R	64.5%	31.8%	67.0%	33.0%
3,858	ELK	2,002	1,522	428	52	1,094 R	76.0%	21.4%	78.1%	21.9%
24,730	ELLIS	9,813	5,463	4,113	237	1,350 R	55.7%	41.9%	57.0%	43.0%
6,146	ELLSWORTH	3,201	2,087	1,028	86	1,059 R	65.2%	32.1%	67.0%	33.0%
19,029	FINNEY	6,602	4,335	2,062	205	2,273 R	65.7%	31.2%	67.8%	32.2%
22,587	FORD	9,285	6,232	2,804	249	3,428 R	67.1%	30.2%	69.0%	31.0%
20,007	FRANKLIN	8,267	6,011	2,056	200	3,955 R	72.7%	24.9%	74.5%	25.5%
28,111	GEARY	6,140	4,299	1,708	133	2,591 R	70.0%	27.8%	71.6%	28.4%
3,940	GOVE	1,755	1,226	466	63	760 R	69.9%	26.6%	72.5%	27.5%
4,751	GRAHAM	1,964	1,440	488	36	952 R	73.3%	24.8%	74.7%	25.3%
5,961	GRANT	2,007	1,469	476	62	993 R	73.2%	23.7%	75.5%	24.5%
4,516	GRAY	1,786	1,235	511	40	724 R	69.1%	28.6%	70.7%	29.3%
1,819	GREELEY	933	639	212	82	427 R	68.5%	22.7%	75.1%	24.9%
9,141	GREENWOOD	4,238	3,157	951	130	2,206 R	74.5%	22.4%	76.9%	23.1%
2,747	HAMILTON	1,399	941	394	64	547 R	67.3%	28.2%	70.5%	29.5%
7,871	HARPER	3,471	2,628	729	114	1,899 R	75.7%	21.0%	78.3%	21.7%
27,236	HARVEY	12,327	8,287	3,555	485	4,732 R	67.2%	28.8%	70.0%	30.0%
3,672	HASKELL	1,448	1,036	383	29	653 R	71.5%	26.5%	73.0%	27.0%
2,662	HODGEMAN	1,247	853	331	63	522 R	68.4%	26.5%	72.0%	28.0%
10,342	JACKSON	4,672	3,363	1,191	118	2,172 R	72.0%	25.5%	73.8%	26.2%
11,945	JEFFERSON	5,061	3,679	1,237	145	2,442 R	72.7%	24.4%	74.8%	25.2%
6,099	JEWELL	3,028	2,242	716	70	1,526 R	74.0%	23.6%	75.8%	24.2%
220,073	JOHNSON	102,727	76,161	24,324	2,242	51,837 R	74.1%	23.7%	75.8%	24.2%
3,047	KEARNY	1,236	876	325	35	551 R	70.9%	26.3%	72.9%	27.1%
8,886	KINGMAN	4,000	2,756	1,107	137	1,649 R	68.9%	27.7%	71.3%	28.7%
4,088	KIOWA	2,042	1,559	406	77	1,153 R	76.3%	19.9%	79.3%	20.7%
25,775	LABETTE	9,881	6,399	3,210	272	3,189 R	64.8%	32.5%	66.6%	33.4%
2,707	LANE	1,288	943	294	51	649 R	73.2%	22.8%	76.2%	23.8%
53,340	LEAVENWORTH	15,897	10,762	4,727	408	6,035 R	67.7%	29.7%	69.5%	30.5%
4,582	LINCOLN	2,182	1,649	476	57	1,173 R	75.6%	21.8%	77.6%	22.4%
7,770	LINN	3,532	2,593	876	63	1,717 R	73.4%	24.8%	74.7%	25.3%
3,814	LOGAN	1,663	1,164	428	71	736 R	70.0%	25.7%	73.1%	26.9%
32,071	LYON	13,143	9,157	3,720	266	5,437 R	69.7%	28.3%	71.1%	28.9%
24,778	MCPHERSON	10,569	7,457	2,858	254	4,599 R	70.6%	27.0%	72.3%	27.7%
13,935	MARION	6,059	4,373	1,478	208	2,895 R	72.2%	24.4%	74.7%	25.3%
13,139	MARSHALL	6,098	4,127	1,823	148	2,304 R	67.7%	29.9%	69.4%	30.6%
4,912	MEADE	2,296	1,712	526	58	1,186 R	74.6%	22.9%	76.5%	23.5%

KANSAS

PRESIDENT 1972

1970 Census Population	County	Total Vote	Republican	Democratic	Other	Rep.-Dem. Plurality	Percentage Total Vote Rep.	Percentage Total Vote Dem.	Percentage Major Vote Rep.	Percentage Major Vote Dem.
19,254	MIAMI	7,581	5,234	2,140	207	3,094 R	69.0%	28.2%	71.0%	29.0%
8,010	MITCHELL	3,953	2,830	1,030	93	1,800 R	71.6%	26.1%	73.3%	26.7%
39,949	MONTGOMERY	15,907	11,717	3,685	505	8,032 R	73.7%	23.2%	76.1%	23.9%
6,432	MORRIS	3,246	2,471	704	71	1,767 R	76.1%	21.7%	77.8%	22.2%
3,576	MORTON	1,603	1,165	363	75	802 R	72.7%	22.6%	76.2%	23.8%
11,825	NEMAHA	5,342	3,422	1,777	143	1,645 R	64.1%	33.3%	65.8%	34.2%
18,812	NEOSHO	7,738	5,034	2,559	145	2,475 R	65.1%	33.1%	66.3%	33.7%
4,791	NESS	2,251	1,539	652	60	887 R	68.4%	29.0%	70.2%	29.8%
7,279	NORTON	3,546	2,688	776	82	1,912 R	75.8%	21.9%	77.6%	22.4%
13,352	OSAGE	5,728	4,073	1,522	133	2,551 R	71.1%	26.6%	72.8%	27.2%
6,416	OSBORNE	2,972	2,182	724	66	1,458 R	73.4%	24.4%	75.1%	24.9%
6,183	OTTAWA	2,831	2,065	705	61	1,360 R	72.9%	24.9%	74.5%	25.5%
8,484	PAWNEE	3,600	2,370	1,110	120	1,260 R	65.8%	30.8%	68.1%	31.9%
7,888	PHILLIPS	3,833	2,919	827	87	2,092 R	76.2%	21.6%	77.9%	22.1%
11,755	POTTAWATOMIE	5,369	3,947	1,298	124	2,649 R	73.5%	24.2%	75.3%	24.7%
10,056	PRATT	4,569	3,253	1,214	102	2,039 R	71.2%	26.6%	72.8%	27.2%
4,393	RAWLINS	2,204	1,553	560	91	993 R	70.5%	25.4%	73.5%	26.5%
60,765	RENO	24,628	15,714	8,183	731	7,531 R	63.8%	33.2%	65.8%	34.2%
8,498	REPUBLIC	4,068	2,921	1,059	88	1,862 R	71.8%	26.0%	73.4%	26.6%
12,320	RICE	5,803	3,843	1,825	135	2,018 R	66.2%	31.4%	67.8%	32.2%
56,788	RILEY	16,809	11,120	5,333	356	5,787 R	66.2%	31.7%	67.6%	32.4%
7,628	ROOKS	3,425	2,457	904	64	1,553 R	71.7%	26.4%	73.1%	26.9%
5,117	RUSH	2,512	1,639	806	67	833 R	65.2%	32.1%	67.0%	33.0%
9,428	RUSSELL	4,292	3,168	1,011	113	2,157 R	73.8%	23.6%	75.8%	24.2%
46,592	SALINE	18,319	12,592	5,406	321	7,186 R	68.7%	29.5%	70.0%	30.0%
5,606	SCOTT	2,082	1,547	449	86	1,098 R	74.3%	21.6%	77.5%	22.5%
350,694	SEDGWICK	127,701	83,949	39,220	4,532	44,729 R	65.7%	30.7%	68.2%	31.8%
15,744	SEWARD	5,003	3,866	989	148	2,877 R	77.3%	19.8%	79.6%	20.4%
155,322	SHAWNEE	65,506	43,727	20,383	1,396	23,344 R	66.8%	31.1%	68.2%	31.8%
3,859	SHERIDAN	1,761	1,134	552	75	582 R	64.4%	31.3%	67.3%	32.7%
7,792	SHERMAN	3,182	2,225	785	172	1,440 R	69.9%	24.7%	73.9%	26.1%
6,757	SMITH	3,501	2,600	818	83	1,782 R	74.3%	23.4%	76.1%	23.9%
5,943	STAFFORD	3,127	2,200	844	83	1,356 R	70.4%	27.0%	72.3%	27.7%
2,287	STANTON	1,054	754	259	41	495 R	71.5%	24.6%	74.4%	25.6%
4,198	STEVENS	1,869	1,392	408	69	984 R	74.5%	21.8%	77.3%	22.7%
23,553	SUMNER	10,195	6,941	2,685	569	4,256 R	68.1%	26.3%	72.1%	27.9%
7,501	THOMAS	3,396	2,300	943	153	1,357 R	67.7%	27.8%	70.9%	29.1%
4,436	TREGO	2,046	1,369	621	56	748 R	66.9%	30.4%	68.8%	31.2%
6,397	WABAUNSEE	3,203	2,461	662	80	1,799 R	76.8%	20.7%	78.8%	21.2%
2,215	WALLACE	1,068	782	214	72	568 R	73.2%	20.0%	78.5%	21.5%
9,249	WASHINGTON	4,394	3,301	996	97	2,305 R	75.1%	22.7%	76.8%	23.2%
3,274	WICHITA	1,136	794	288	54	506 R	69.9%	25.4%	73.4%	26.6%
11,317	WILSON	4,770	3,568	1,043	159	2,525 R	74.8%	21.9%	77.4%	22.6%
4,789	WOODSON	2,193	1,592	550	51	1,042 R	72.6%	25.1%	74.3%	25.7%
186,845	WYANDOTTE	64,816	34,157	28,206	2,453	5,951 R	52.7%	43.5%	54.8%	45.2%
2,249,071	TOTAL	916,095	619,812	270,287	25,996	349,525 R	67.7%	29.5%	69.6%	30.4%

KANSAS

PRESIDENT 1968

1960 Census Population	County	Total Vote	Republican	Democratic	AIP	Other	Plurality	Percentage Rep.	Dem.	AIP
16,369	ALLEN	5,900	3,520	1,875	492	13	1,645 R	59.7%	31.8%	8.3%
9,035	ANDERSON	3,814	2,168	1,242	397	7	926 R	56.8%	32.6%	10.4%
20,898	ATCHISON	7,922	3,644	3,379	888	11	265 R	46.0%	42.7%	11.2%
8,713	BARBER	3,341	2,023	1,027	283	8	996 R	60.6%	30.7%	8.5%
32,368	BARTON	12,208	6,700	4,464	1,017	27	2,236 R	54.9%	36.6%	8.3%
16,090	BOURBON	7,004	3,983	2,241	769	11	1,742 R	56.9%	32.0%	11.0%
13,229	BROWN	5,420	3,748	1,199	463	10	2,549 R	69.2%	22.1%	8.5%
38,395	BUTLER	15,541	7,893	5,952	1,671	25	1,941 R	50.8%	38.3%	10.8%
3,921	CHASE	1,658	1,038	462	154	4	576 R	62.6%	27.9%	9.3%
5,956	CHAUTAUQUA	2,346	1,537	478	329	2	1,059 R	65.5%	20.4%	14.0%
22,279	CHEROKEE	8,872	4,211	3,597	1,054	10	614 R	47.5%	40.5%	11.9%
4,708	CHEYENNE	2,014	1,423	412	174	5	1,011 R	70.7%	20.5%	8.6%
3,396	CLARK	1,579	920	446	210	3	474 R	58.3%	28.2%	13.3%
10,675	CLAY	4,635	3,335	926	357	17	2,409 R	72.0%	20.0%	7.7%
14,407	CLOUD	5,843	3,282	2,132	412	17	1,150 R	56.2%	36.5%	7.1%
8,403	COFFEY	3,525	2,223	933	367	2	1,290 R	63.1%	26.5%	10.4%
3,271	COMANCHE	1,446	906	451	85	4	455 R	62.7%	31.2%	5.9%
37,861	COWLEY	14,861	8,070	5,014	1,751	26	3,056 R	54.3%	33.7%	11.8%
37,032	CRAWFORD	16,213	7,344	7,191	1,653	25	153 R	45.3%	44.4%	10.2%
5,778	DECATUR	2,516	1,654	652	206	4	1,002 R	65.7%	25.9%	8.2%
21,572	DICKINSON	8,666	5,574	2,399	675	18	3,175 R	64.3%	27.7%	7.8%
9,574	DONIPHAN	3,794	2,402	958	425	9	1,444 R	63.3%	25.3%	11.2%
43,720	DOUGLAS	19,583	10,533	6,936	2,080	34	3,597 R	53.8%	35.4%	10.6%
5,118	EDWARDS	2,264	1,243	832	182	7	411 R	54.9%	36.7%	8.0%
5,048	ELK	2,053	1,327	503	216	7	824 R	64.6%	24.5%	10.5%
21,270	ELLIS	8,441	3,944	3,809	671	17	135 R	46.7%	45.1%	7.9%
7,677	ELLSWORTH	3,087	1,776	1,060	246	5	716 R	57.5%	34.3%	8.0%
16,093	FINNEY	6,323	3,295	2,521	496	11	774 R	52.1%	39.9%	7.8%
20,938	FORD	8,797	4,645	3,191	935	26	1,454 R	52.8%	36.3%	10.6%
19,548	FRANKLIN	8,239	4,875	2,524	825	15	2,351 R	59.2%	30.6%	10.0%
28,779	GEARY	5,827	2,954	2,228	625	20	726 R	50.7%	38.2%	10.7%
4,107	GOVE	1,724	1,018	538	164	4	480 R	59.0%	31.2%	9.5%
5,586	GRAHAM	2,154	1,308	597	243	6	711 R	60.7%	27.7%	11.3%
5,269	GRANT	1,961	1,121	618	217	5	503 R	57.2%	31.5%	11.1%
4,380	GRAY	1,723	952	612	151	8	340 R	55.3%	35.5%	8.8%
2,087	GREELEY	777	465	227	82	3	238 R	59.8%	29.2%	10.6%
11,253	GREENWOOD	4,451	2,937	1,122	381	11	1,815 R	66.0%	25.2%	8.6%
3,144	HAMILTON	1,335	751	410	170	4	341 R	56.3%	30.7%	12.7%
9,541	HARPER	3,674	2,351	1,015	297	11	1,336 R	64.0%	27.6%	8.1%
25,865	HARVEY	10,841	6,682	3,351	780	28	3,331 R	61.6%	30.9%	7.2%
2,990	HASKELL	1,407	762	476	167	2	286 R	54.2%	33.8%	11.9%
3,115	HODGEMAN	1,277	756	387	130	4	369 R	59.2%	30.3%	10.2%
10,309	JACKSON	4,411	2,678	1,225	501	7	1,453 R	60.7%	27.8%	11.4%
11,252	JEFFERSON	4,915	2,781	1,355	774	5	1,426 R	56.6%	27.6%	15.7%
7,217	JEWELL	3,282	2,172	842	252	16	1,330 R	66.2%	25.7%	7.7%
143,792	JOHNSON	87,912	55,060	26,034	6,635	183	29,026 R	62.6%	29.6%	7.5%
3,108	KEARNY	1,243	721	423	95	4	298 R	58.0%	34.0%	7.6%
9,958	KINGMAN	3,845	2,318	1,201	319	7	1,117 R	60.3%	31.2%	8.3%
4,626	KIOWA	2,094	1,484	481	123	6	1,003 R	70.9%	23.0%	5.9%
26,805	LABETTE	10,750	5,503	3,974	1,251	22	1,529 R	51.2%	37.0%	11.6%
3,060	LANE	1,288	781	385	118	4	396 R	60.6%	29.9%	9.2%
48,524	LEAVENWORTH	14,645	7,081	5,546	2,000	18	1,535 R	48.4%	37.9%	13.7%
5,556	LINCOLN	2,525	1,721	583	217	4	1,138 R	68.2%	23.1%	8.6%
8,274	LINN	3,565	2,250	893	419	3	1,357 R	63.1%	25.0%	11.8%
4,036	LOGAN	1,756	1,120	411	221	4	709 R	63.8%	23.4%	12.6%
26,928	LYON	11,446	6,558	4,020	847	21	2,538 R	57.3%	35.1%	7.4%
24,285	MCPHERSON	9,880	6,420	2,893	543	24	3,527 R	65.0%	29.3%	5.5%
15,143	MARION	6,092	4,287	1,494	304	7	2,793 R	70.4%	24.5%	5.0%
15,598	MARSHALL	6,517	3,835	1,949	731	2	1,886 R	58.8%	29.9%	11.2%
5,505	MEADE	2,281	1,511	572	196	2	939 R	66.2%	25.1%	8.6%

KANSAS

PRESIDENT 1968

1960 Census Population	County	Total Vote	Republican	Democratic	AIP	Other	Plurality	Percentage Rep.	Dem.	AIP
19,884	MIAMI	7,386	3,614	2,739	1,023	10	875 R	48.9%	37.1%	13.9%
8,866	MITCHELL	3,861	2,428	1,144	283	6	1,284 R	62.9%	29.6%	7.3%
45,007	MONTGOMERY	17,386	9,697	5,210	2,456	23	4,487 R	55.8%	30.0%	14.1%
7,392	MORRIS	3,230	1,938	976	313	3	962 R	60.0%	30.2%	9.7%
3,354	MORTON	1,509	770	475	262	2	295 R	51.0%	31.5%	17.4%
12,897	NEMAHA	5,560	3,003	1,925	628	4	1,078 R	54.0%	34.6%	11.3%
19,455	NEOSHO	7,464	3,950	2,725	784	5	1,225 R	52.9%	36.5%	10.5%
5,470	NESS	2,322	1,352	767	192	11	585 R	58.2%	33.0%	8.3%
8,035	NORTON	3,586	2,543	841	193	9	1,702 R	70.9%	23.5%	5.4%
12,886	OSAGE	5,622	3,157	1,664	792	9	1,493 R	56.2%	29.6%	14.1%
7,506	OSBORNE	3,170	2,073	793	301	3	1,280 R	65.4%	25.0%	9.5%
6,779	OTTAWA	2,777	1,740	777	253	7	963 R	62.7%	28.0%	9.1%
10,254	PAWNEE	3,759	2,037	1,416	300	6	621 R	54.2%	37.7%	8.0%
8,709	PHILLIPS	3,759	2,567	844	340	8	1,723 R	68.3%	22.5%	9.0%
11,957	POTTAWATOMIE	5,130	3,267	1,368	490	5	1,899 R	63.7%	26.7%	9.6%
12,122	PRATT	4,611	2,670	1,490	435	16	1,180 R	57.9%	32.3%	9.4%
5,279	RAWLINS	2,182	1,438	553	153	38	885 R	65.9%	25.3%	7.0%
59,055	RENO	23,474	11,804	9,872	1,710	88	1,932 R	50.3%	42.1%	7.3%
9,768	REPUBLIC	4,288	2,841	1,187	240	20	1,654 R	66.3%	27.7%	5.6%
13,909	RICE	5,586	3,141	2,049	386	10	1,092 R	56.2%	36.7%	6.9%
41,914	RILEY	13,345	8,296	4,258	772	19	4,038 R	62.2%	31.9%	5.8%
9,734	ROOKS	3,574	2,252	1,012	307	3	1,240 R	63.0%	28.3%	8.6%
6,160	RUSH	2,560	1,471	864	217	8	607 R	57.5%	33.8%	8.5%
11,348	RUSSELL	4,739	3,177	1,261	290	11	1,916 R	67.0%	26.6%	6.1%
54,715	SALINE	16,822	9,324	6,286	1,169	43	3,038 R	55.4%	37.4%	6.9%
5,228	SCOTT	2,074	1,374	500	193	7	874 R	66.2%	24.1%	9.3%
343,231	SEDGWICK	117,469	60,853	44,041	12,255	320	16,812 R	51.8%	37.5%	10.4%
15,930	SEWARD	4,918	3,065	1,291	550	12	1,774 R	62.3%	26.3%	11.2%
141,286	SHAWNEE	59,850	31,140	21,735	6,817	158	9,405 R	52.0%	36.3%	11.4%
4,267	SHERIDAN	1,717	1,002	563	144	8	439 R	58.4%	32.8%	8.4%
6,682	SHERMAN	3,134	1,803	954	368	9	849 R	57.5%	30.4%	11.7%
7,776	SMITH	3,790	2,558	939	279	14	1,619 R	67.5%	24.8%	7.4%
7,451	STAFFORD	3,320	1,851	1,205	253	11	646 R	55.8%	36.3%	7.6%
2,108	STANTON	909	541	288	78	2	253 R	59.5%	31.7%	8.6%
4,400	STEVENS	1,982	1,157	528	296	1	629 R	58.4%	26.6%	14.9%
25,316	SUMNER	10,320	5,622	3,562	1,116	20	2,060 R	54.5%	34.5%	10.8%
7,358	THOMAS	3,295	1,971	1,074	241	9	897 R	59.8%	32.6%	7.3%
5,473	TREGO	2,064	1,211	623	226	4	588 R	58.7%	30.2%	10.9%
6,648	WABAUNSEE	3,084	1,979	695	402	8	1,284 R	64.2%	22.5%	13.0%
2,069	WALLACE	988	608	235	144	1	373 R	61.5%	23.8%	14.6%
10,739	WASHINGTON	4,652	3,177	1,131	332	12	2,046 R	68.3%	24.3%	7.1%
2,765	WICHITA	1,254	757	364	130	3	393 R	60.4%	29.0%	10.4%
13,077	WILSON	5,272	3,340	1,276	640	16	2,064 R	63.4%	24.2%	12.1%
5,423	WOODSON	2,315	1,450	639	222	4	811 R	62.6%	27.6%	9.6%
185,495	WYANDOTTE	69,171	23,091	34,189	11,510	381	11,098 D	33.4%	49.4%	16.6%
2,178,611	TOTAL	872,783	478,674	302,996	88,921	2,192	175,678 R	54.8%	34.7%	10.2%

KANSAS

ELECTION NOTES

1984 Other vote was 3,564 Richards (Conservative); 3,329 Bergland (Libertarian); 2,544 Serrette (Independent); 2,109 Dodge (Prohibition).

1980 Other vote was 68,231 Anderson (Independent); 14,470 Clark (Independent); 1,555 Shelton (American); 967 Hall (Independent); 821 Bubar (Statesman); 789 Rarick (Conservative).

1976 Other vote was 13,185 McCarthy (Independent); 4,724 Anderson (American); 3,242 MacBride (Independent); 2,118 Maddox (Conservative); 1,403 Bubar (Prohibition).

1972 Other vote was 21,808 Schmitz (Conservative); 4,188 Munn (Prohibition).

1968 Wallace on the ballot as Conservative. Other vote was Munn (Prohibition).

KENTUCKY

POPULAR VOTE FOR PRESIDENT 1920 TO 1984

Year	Total Vote	Republican Vote	Republican Candidate	Democratic Vote	Democratic Candidate	Other Vote	Plurality	Percentage Total Vote Rep.	Percentage Total Vote Dem.	Percentage Major Vote Rep.	Percentage Major Vote Dem.
1984	1,369,345	821,702	Reagan, Ronald	539,539	Mondale, Walter F.	8,104	282,163 R	60.0%	39.4%	60.4%	39.6%
1980	1,294,627	635,274	Reagan, Ronald	616,417	Carter, Jimmy	42,936	18,857 R	49.1%	47.6%	50.8%	49.2%
1976	1,167,142	531,852	Ford, Gerald R.	615,717	Carter, Jimmy	19,573	83,865 D	45.6%	52.8%	46.3%	53.7%
1972	1,067,499	676,446	Nixon, Richard M.	371,159	McGovern, George S.	19,894	305,287 R	63.4%	34.8%	64.6%	35.4%
1968	1,055,893	462,411	Nixon, Richard M.	397,541	Humphrey, Hubert H.	195,941	64,870 R	43.8%	37.6%	53.8%	46.2%
1964	1,046,105	372,977	Goldwater, Barry M.	669,659	Johnson, Lyndon B.	3,469	296,682 D	35.7%	64.0%	35.8%	64.2%
1960	1,124,462	602,607	Nixon, Richard M.	521,855	Kennedy, John F.		80,752 R	53.6%	46.4%	53.6%	46.4%
1956	1,053,805	572,192	Eisenhower, Dwight D.	476,453	Stevenson, Adlai E.	5,160	95,739 R	54.3%	45.2%	54.6%	45.4%
1952	993,148	495,029	Eisenhower, Dwight D.	495,729	Stevenson, Adlai E.	2,390	700 D	49.8%	49.9%	50.0%	50.0%
1948	822,658	341,210	Dewey, Thomas E.	466,756	Truman, Harry S.	14,692	125,546 D	41.5%	56.7%	42.2%	57.8%
1944	867,924	392,448	Dewey, Thomas E.	472,589	Roosevelt, Franklin D.	2,887	80,141 D	45.2%	54.5%	45.4%	54.6%
1940	970,163	410,384	Willkie, Wendell	557,322	Roosevelt, Franklin D.	2,457	146,938 D	42.3%	57.4%	42.4%	57.6%
1936	926,214	369,702	Landon, Alfred M.	541,944	Roosevelt, Franklin D.	14,568	172,242 D	39.9%	58.5%	40.6%	59.4%
1932	983,059	394,716	Hoover, Herbert C.	580,574	Roosevelt, Franklin D.	7,769	185,858 D	40.2%	59.1%	40.5%	59.5%
1928	940,521	558,064	Hoover, Herbert C.	381,070	Smith, Alfred E.	1,387	176,994 R	59.3%	40.5%	59.4%	40.6%
1924	813,843	396,758	Coolidge, Calvin	375,593	Davis, John W.	41,492	21,165 R	48.8%	46.2%	51.4%	48.6%
1920	918,636	452,480	Harding, Warren G.	456,497	Cox, James M.	9,659	4,017 D	49.3%	49.7%	49.8%	50.2%

ELECTORAL COLLEGE VOTE 1920 TO 1984

Year	Total	Republican	Democratic	Other
1984	9	9	—	—
1980	9	9	—	—
1976	9	—	9	—
1972	9	9	—	—
1968	9	9	—	—
1964	9	—	9	—
1960	10	10	—	—
1956	10	10	—	—
1952	10	—	10	—
1948	11	—	11	—
1944	11	—	11	—
1940	11	—	11	—
1936	11	—	11	—
1932	11	—	11	—
1928	13	13	—	—
1924	13	13	—	—
1920	13	—	13	—

KENTUCKY

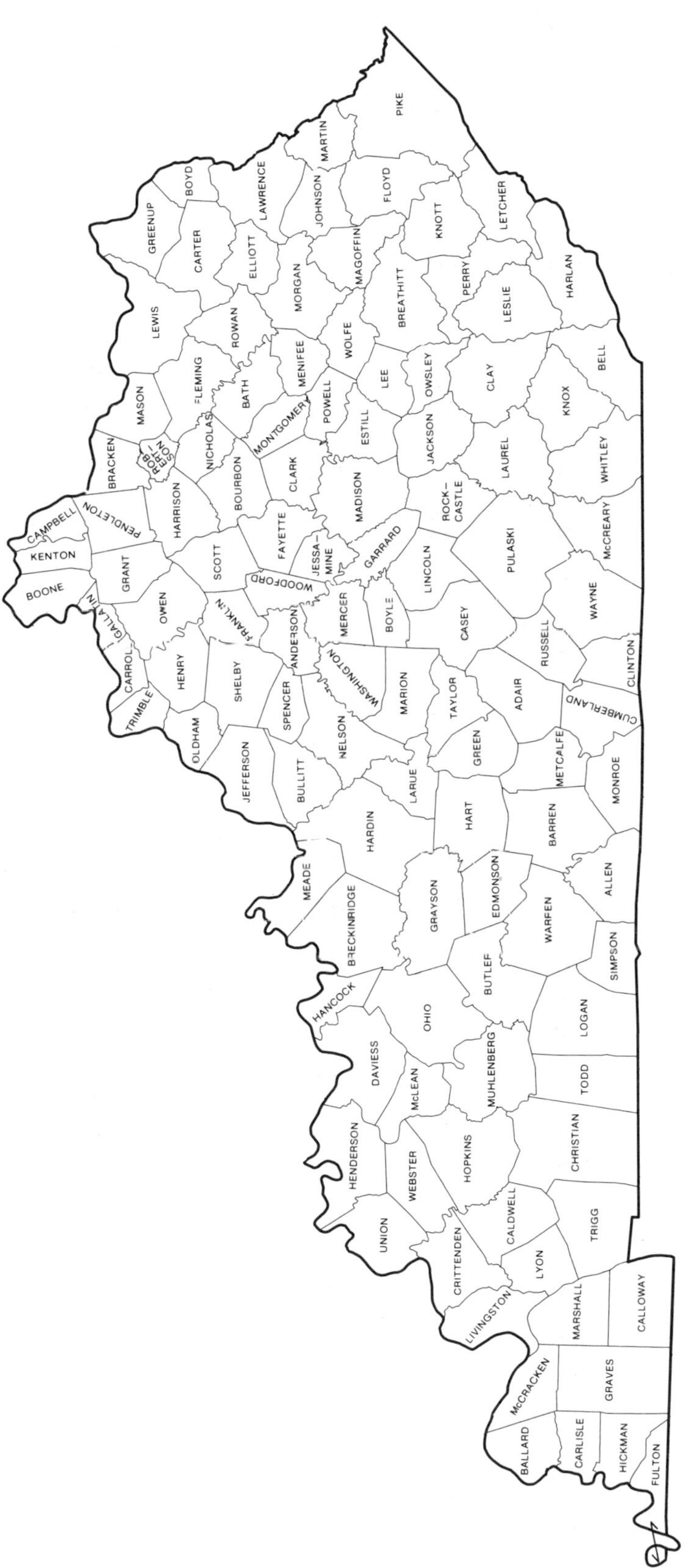
PIKE
MARTIN
JOHNSON
LAWRENCE
BOYD
GREENUP
CARTER
ELLIOTT
FLOYD
KNOTT
LETCHER
MAGOFFIN
MORGAN
HARLAN
PERRY
LESLIE
BREATHITT
WOLFE
ROWAN
LEWIS
FLEMING
MENIFEE
BATH
MASON
LEE
OWSLEY
CLAY
BELL
KNOX
POWELL
ESTILL
JACKSON
MONTGOMERY
NICHOLAS
ROB-ERT-SON
BRACKEN
CLARK
BOURBON
LAUREL
WHITLEY
MADISON
ROCK-CASTLE
HARRISON
PENDLETON
CAMPBELL
KENTON
BOONE
GRANT
SCOTT
FAYETTE
JESSA-MINE
GARRARD
LINCOLN
PULASKI
McCREARY
WOODFORD
GALLATIN
OWEN
FRANKLIN
ANDERSON
MERCER
BOYLE
CASEY
WAYNE
RUSSELL
CLINTON
CARROL
HENRY
SHELBY
SPENCER
WASHINGTON
MARION
TAYLOR
ADAIR
CUMBERLAND
TRIMBLE
OLDHAM
JEFFERSON
BULLITT
NELSON
LARUE
GREEN
METCALFE
MONROE
HARDIN
HART
BARREN
MEADE
BRECKINRIDGE
GRAYSON
EDMONSON
ALLEN
WARFEN
SIMPSON
BUTLEF
HANCOCK
OHIO
LOGAN
DAVIESS
McLEAN
MUHLENBERG
TODD
HENDERSON
WEBSTER
HOPKINS
CHRISTIAN
UNION
CRITTENDEN
CALDWELL
TRIGG
LYON
LIVINGSTON
MARSHALL
CALLOWAY
McCRACKEN
GRAVES
BALLARD
CARLISLE
HICKMAN
FULTON

KENTUCKY

PRESIDENT 1984

1980 Census Population	County	Total Vote	Republican	Democratic	Other	Rep.-Dem. Plurality	Percentage: Total Vote Rep.	Percentage: Total Vote Dem.	Percentage: Major Vote Rep.	Percentage: Major Vote Dem.
15,233	ADAIR	6,344	4,500	1,812	32	2,688 R	70.9%	28.6%	71.3%	28.7%
14,128	ALLEN	4,963	3,427	1,521	15	1,906 R	69.1%	30.6%	69.3%	30.7%
12,567	ANDERSON	5,185	3,425	1,717	43	1,708 R	66.1%	33.1%	66.6%	33.4%
8,798	BALLARD	3,685	1,663	2,002	20	339 D	45.1%	54.3%	45.4%	54.6%
34,009	BARREN	12,277	7,717	4,503	57	3,214 R	62.9%	36.7%	63.2%	36.8%
10,025	BATH	3,820	2,020	1,781	19	239 R	52.9%	46.6%	53.1%	46.9%
34,330	BELL	12,961	7,249	5,490	222	1,759 R	55.9%	42.4%	56.9%	43.1%
45,842	BOONE	17,649	12,690	4,853	106	7,837 R	71.9%	27.5%	72.3%	27.7%
19,405	BOURBON	6,553	3,836	2,649	68	1,187 R	58.5%	40.4%	59.2%	40.8%
55,513	BOYD	20,621	10,925	9,601	95	1,324 R	53.0%	46.6%	53.2%	46.8%
25,066	BOYLE	9,076	5,675	3,378	23	2,297 R	62.5%	37.2%	62.7%	37.3%
7,738	BRACKEN	2,976	1,812	1,136	28	676 R	60.9%	38.2%	61.5%	38.5%
17,004	BREATHITT	6,309	2,855	3,435	19	580 D	45.3%	54.4%	45.4%	54.6%
16,861	BRECKINRIDGE	7,132	4,432	2,669	31	1,763 R	62.1%	37.4%	62.4%	37.6%
43,346	BULLITT	14,676	9,556	5,005	115	4,551 R	65.1%	34.1%	65.6%	34.4%
11,064	BUTLER	4,191	3,121	1,055	15	2,066 R	74.5%	25.2%	74.7%	25.3%
13,473	CALDWELL	5,653	3,162	2,427	64	735 R	55.9%	42.9%	56.6%	43.4%
30,031	CALLOWAY	11,515	6,442	5,028	45	1,414 R	55.9%	43.7%	56.2%	43.8%
83,317	CAMPBELL	30,679	21,473	9,068	138	12,405 R	70.0%	29.6%	70.3%	29.7%
5,487	CARLISLE	2,608	1,308	1,277	23	31 R	50.2%	49.0%	50.6%	49.4%
9,270	CARROLL	3,400	1,824	1,564	12	260 R	53.6%	46.0%	53.8%	46.2%
25,060	CARTER	8,675	4,656	3,985	34	671 R	53.7%	45.9%	53.9%	46.1%
14,818	CASEY	5,513	4,356	1,122	35	3,234 R	79.0%	20.4%	79.5%	20.5%
66,878	CHRISTIAN	16,209	10,708	5,432	69	5,276 R	66.1%	33.5%	66.3%	33.7%
28,322	CLARK	9,757	6,130	3,595	32	2,535 R	62.8%	36.8%	63.0%	37.0%
22,752	CLAY	6,426	4,772	1,634	20	3,138 R	74.3%	25.4%	74.5%	25.5%
9,321	CLINTON	4,322	3,459	838	25	2,621 R	80.0%	19.4%	80.5%	19.5%
9,207	CRITTENDEN	3,663	2,167	1,483	13	684 R	59.2%	40.5%	59.4%	40.6%
7,289	CUMBERLAND	3,509	2,729	766	14	1,963 R	77.8%	21.8%	78.1%	21.9%
85,949	DAVIESS	33,086	19,495	13,347	244	6,148 R	58.9%	40.3%	59.4%	40.6%
9,962	EDMONSON	4,224	3,001	1,200	23	1,801 R	71.0%	28.4%	71.4%	28.6%
6,908	ELLIOTT	2,294	601	1,683	10	1,082 D	26.2%	73.4%	26.3%	73.7%
14,495	ESTILL	5,122	3,512	1,593	17	1,919 R	68.6%	31.1%	68.8%	31.2%
204,165	FAYETTE	81,746	51,993	28,961	792	23,032 R	63.6%	35.4%	64.2%	35.8%
12,323	FLEMING	4,459	2,824	1,616	19	1,208 R	63.3%	36.2%	63.6%	36.4%
48,764	FLOYD	15,543	5,218	10,259	66	5,041 D	33.6%	66.0%	33.7%	66.3%
41,830	FRANKLIN	19,024	11,057	7,790	177	3,267 R	58.1%	40.9%	58.7%	41.3%
8,971	FULTON	3,330	1,780	1,534	16	246 R	53.5%	46.1%	53.7%	46.3%
4,842	GALLATIN	2,093	1,042	1,042	9		49.8%	49.8%	50.0%	50.0%
10,853	GARRARD	4,885	3,284	1,566	35	1,718 R	67.2%	32.1%	67.7%	32.3%
13,308	GRANT	4,620	2,840	1,685	95	1,155 R	61.5%	36.5%	62.8%	37.2%
34,049	GRAVES	14,170	7,287	6,759	124	528 R	51.4%	47.7%	51.9%	48.1%
20,854	GRAYSON	7,777	5,524	2,200	53	3,324 R	71.0%	28.3%	71.5%	28.5%
11,043	GREEN	4,838	3,210	1,611	17	1,599 R	66.3%	33.3%	66.6%	33.4%
39,132	GREENUP	14,462	7,451	6,923	88	528 R	51.5%	47.9%	51.8%	48.2%
7,742	HANCOCK	3,301	1,967	1,287	47	680 R	59.6%	39.0%	60.4%	39.6%
88,917	HARDIN	20,771	14,293	6,329	149	7,964 R	68.8%	30.5%	69.3%	30.7%
41,889	HARLAN	14,762	6,959	7,663	140	704 D	47.1%	51.9%	47.6%	52.4%
15,166	HARRISON	5,890	3,467	2,405	18	1,062 R	58.9%	40.8%	59.0%	41.0%
15,402	HART	5,372	3,065	2,278	29	787 R	57.1%	42.4%	57.4%	42.6%
40,849	HENDERSON	14,242	7,389	6,795	58	594 R	51.9%	47.7%	52.1%	47.9%
12,740	HENRY	5,110	2,802	2,279	29	523 R	54.8%	44.6%	55.1%	44.9%
6,065	HICKMAN	2,437	1,380	1,049	8	331 R	56.6%	43.0%	56.8%	43.2%
46,174	HOPKINS	16,166	9,368	6,743	55	2,625 R	57.9%	41.7%	58.1%	41.9%
11,996	JACKSON	4,413	3,856	542	15	3,314 R	87.4%	12.3%	87.7%	12.3%
685,004	JEFFERSON	290,750	167,640	122,133	977	45,507 R	57.7%	42.0%	57.9%	42.1%
26,146	JESSAMINE	9,556	7,081	2,379	96	4,702 R	74.1%	24.9%	74.9%	25.1%
24,432	JOHNSON	8,349	5,225	3,078	46	2,147 R	62.6%	36.9%	62.9%	37.1%
137,058	KENTON	49,245	34,304	14,642	299	19,662 R	69.7%	29.7%	70.1%	29.9%
17,940	KNOTT	6,248	1,728	4,487	33	2,759 D	27.7%	71.8%	27.8%	72.2%

KENTUCKY

PRESIDENT 1984

1980 Census Population	County	Total Vote	Republican	Democratic	Other	Rep.-Dem. Plurality	Percentage Total Vote Rep.	Percentage Total Vote Dem.	Percentage Major Vote Rep.	Percentage Major Vote Dem.
30,239	KNOX	8,699	5,730	2,932	37	2,798 R	65.9%	33.7%	66.2%	33.8%
11,922	LARUE	4,400	2,873	1,514	13	1,359 R	65.3%	34.4%	65.5%	34.5%
38,982	LAUREL	12,929	9,621	3,267	41	6,354 R	74.4%	25.3%	74.7%	25.3%
14,121	LAWRENCE	4,959	2,713	2,223	23	490 R	54.7%	44.8%	55.0%	45.0%
7,754	LEE	2,640	1,862	768	10	1,094 R	70.5%	29.1%	70.8%	29.2%
14,882	LESLIE	4,475	3,385	1,075	15	2,310 R	75.6%	24.0%	75.9%	24.1%
30,687	LETCHER	8,830	4,073	4,707	50	634 D	46.1%	53.3%	46.4%	53.6%
14,545	LEWIS	4,947	3,445	1,484	18	1,961 R	69.6%	30.0%	69.9%	30.1%
19,053	LINCOLN	6,522	3,996	2,498	28	1,498 R	61.3%	38.3%	61.5%	38.5%
9,219	LIVINGSTON	3,891	1,866	2,007	18	141 D	48.0%	51.6%	48.2%	51.8%
24,138	LOGAN	8,310	4,889	3,347	74	1,542 R	58.8%	40.3%	59.4%	40.6%
6,490	LYON	2,255	969	1,272	14	303 D	43.0%	56.4%	43.2%	56.8%
61,310	MCCRACKEN	25,765	12,903	12,535	327	368 R	50.1%	48.7%	50.7%	49.3%
15,634	MCCREARY	5,707	4,028	1,609	70	2,419 R	70.6%	28.2%	71.5%	28.5%
10,090	MCLEAN	3,882	1,942	1,917	23	25 R	50.0%	49.4%	50.3%	49.7%
53,352	MADISON	17,926	11,309	6,509	108	4,800 R	63.1%	36.3%	63.5%	36.5%
13,515	MAGOFFIN	5,298	2,343	2,942	13	599 D	44.2%	55.5%	44.3%	55.7%
17,910	MARION	6,159	3,305	2,835	19	470 R	53.7%	46.0%	53.8%	46.2%
25,637	MARSHALL	10,917	5,152	5,725	40	573 D	47.2%	52.4%	47.4%	52.6%
13,925	MARTIN	4,770	3,248	1,471	51	1,777 R	68.1%	30.8%	68.8%	31.2%
17,765	MASON	5,446	2,751	2,663	32	88 R	50.5%	48.9%	50.8%	49.2%
22,854	MEADE	6,347	3,820	2,503	24	1,317 R	60.2%	39.4%	60.4%	39.6%
5,117	MENIFEE	1,770	785	956	29	171 D	44.4%	54.0%	45.1%	54.9%
19,011	MERCER	7,189	4,592	2,516	81	2,076 R	63.9%	35.0%	64.6%	35.4%
9,484	METCALFE	3,944	2,349	1,575	20	774 R	59.6%	39.9%	59.9%	40.1%
12,353	MONROE	5,753	4,670	1,052	31	3,618 R	81.2%	18.3%	81.6%	18.4%
20,046	MONTGOMERY	6,377	3,864	2,490	23	1,374 R	60.6%	39.0%	60.8%	39.2%
12,103	MORGAN	4,330	1,834	2,481	15	647 D	42.4%	57.3%	42.5%	57.5%
32,238	MUHLENBERG	12,277	6,094	6,157	26	63 D	49.6%	50.2%	49.7%	50.3%
27,584	NELSON	10,319	6,044	4,199	76	1,845 R	58.6%	40.7%	59.0%	41.0%
7,157	NICHOLAS	2,675	1,535	1,107	33	428 R	57.4%	41.4%	58.1%	41.9%
21,765	OHIO	8,417	5,119	3,253	45	1,866 R	60.8%	38.6%	61.1%	38.9%
27,795	OLDHAM	10,991	8,112	2,857	22	5,255 R	73.8%	26.0%	74.0%	26.0%
8,924	OWEN	3,408	1,778	1,612	18	166 R	52.2%	47.3%	52.4%	47.6%
5,709	OWSLEY	1,851	1,466	375	10	1,091 R	79.2%	20.3%	79.6%	20.4%
10,989	PENDLETON	4,340	2,767	1,529	44	1,238 R	63.8%	35.2%	64.4%	35.6%
33,763	PERRY	10,537	5,218	5,258	61	40 D	49.5%	49.9%	49.8%	50.2%
81,123	PIKE	27,812	11,869	15,817	126	3,948 D	42.7%	56.9%	42.9%	57.1%
11,101	POWELL	3,857	2,269	1,575	13	694 R	58.8%	40.8%	59.0%	41.0%
45,803	PULASKI	18,893	14,434	4,384	75	10,050 R	76.4%	23.2%	76.7%	23.3%
2,265	ROBERTSON	1,043	567	467	9	100 R	54.4%	44.8%	54.8%	45.2%
13,973	ROCKCASTLE	5,428	4,328	1,089	11	3,239 R	79.7%	20.1%	79.9%	20.1%
19,049	ROWAN	6,470	3,698	2,748	24	950 R	57.2%	42.5%	57.4%	42.6%
13,708	RUSSELL	5,954	4,476	1,448	30	3,028 R	75.2%	24.3%	75.6%	24.4%
21,813	SCOTT	7,144	4,461	2,606	77	1,855 R	62.4%	36.5%	63.1%	36.9%
23,328	SHELBY	8,739	5,390	3,326	23	2,064 R	61.7%	38.1%	61.8%	38.2%
14,673	SIMPSON	5,236	3,073	2,140	23	933 R	58.7%	40.9%	58.9%	41.1%
5,929	SPENCER	2,372	1,456	910	6	546 R	61.4%	38.4%	61.5%	38.5%
21,178	TAYLOR	9,245	5,932	3,286	27	2,646 R	64.2%	35.5%	64.4%	35.6%
11,874	TODD	4,280	2,364	1,505	411	859 R	55.2%	35.2%	61.1%	38.9%
9,384	TRIGG	4,436	2,512	1,905	19	607 R	56.6%	42.9%	56.9%	43.1%
6,253	TRIMBLE	2,490	1,389	1,088	13	301 R	55.8%	43.7%	56.1%	43.9%
17,821	UNION	5,637	2,524	3,090	23	566 D	44.8%	54.8%	45.0%	55.0%
71,828	WARREN	24,178	16,167	7,937	74	8,230 R	66.9%	32.8%	67.1%	32.9%
10,764	WASHINGTON	4,655	2,804	1,786	65	1,018 R	60.2%	38.4%	61.1%	38.9%
17,022	WAYNE	6,691	4,449	2,227	15	2,222 R	66.5%	33.3%	66.6%	33.4%
14,832	WEBSTER	5,580	2,504	3,042	34	538 D	44.9%	54.5%	45.1%	54.9%
33,396	WHITLEY	11,516	7,851	3,575	90	4,276 R	68.2%	31.0%	68.7%	31.3%
6,698	WOLFE	2,693	1,257	1,394	42	137 D	46.7%	51.8%	47.4%	52.6%
17,778	WOODFORD	7,112	4,746	2,290	76	2,456 R	66.7%	32.2%	67.5%	32.5%
3,660,777	TOTAL	1,369,345	821,702	539,539	8,104	282,163 R	60.0%	39.4%	60.4%	39.6%

KENTUCKY

PRESIDENT 1980

1980 Census Population	County	Total Vote	Republican	Democratic	Other	Rep.-Dem. Plurality	Percentage Total Vote Rep.	Percentage Total Vote Dem.	Percentage Major Vote Rep.	Percentage Major Vote Dem.
15,233	ADAIR	6,418	4,051	2,285	82	1,766 R	63.1%	35.6%	63.9%	36.1%
14,128	ALLEN	5,278	3,186	2,010	82	1,176 R	60.4%	38.1%	61.3%	38.7%
12,567	ANDERSON	4,764	2,052	2,567	145	515 D	43.1%	53.9%	44.4%	55.6%
8,798	BALLARD	3,826	1,190	2,583	53	1,393 D	31.1%	67.5%	31.5%	68.5%
34,009	BARREN	11,933	6,405	5,285	243	1,120 R	53.7%	44.3%	54.8%	45.2%
10,025	BATH	3,698	1,463	2,174	61	711 D	39.6%	58.8%	40.2%	59.8%
34,330	BELL	12,088	5,433	6,362	293	929 D	44.9%	52.6%	46.1%	53.9%
45,842	BOONE	14,148	8,263	5,374	511	2,889 R	58.4%	38.0%	60.6%	39.4%
19,405	BOURBON	6,346	2,475	3,641	230	1,166 D	39.0%	57.4%	40.5%	59.5%
55,513	BOYD	21,695	10,367	10,702	626	335 D	47.8%	49.3%	49.2%	50.8%
25,066	BOYLE	8,574	3,848	4,429	297	581 D	44.9%	51.7%	46.5%	53.5%
7,738	BRACKEN	2,644	1,154	1,420	70	266 D	43.6%	53.7%	44.8%	55.2%
17,004	BREATHITT	5,532	1,532	3,916	84	2,384 D	27.7%	70.8%	28.1%	71.9%
16,861	BRECKINRIDGE	6,891	3,629	3,163	99	466 R	52.7%	45.9%	53.4%	46.6%
43,346	BULLITT	12,576	6,364	5,884	328	480 R	50.6%	46.8%	52.0%	48.0%
11,064	BUTLER	4,450	3,129	1,274	47	1,855 R	70.3%	28.6%	71.1%	28.9%
13,473	CALDWELL	5,645	2,609	2,924	112	315 D	46.2%	51.8%	47.2%	52.8%
30,031	CALLOWAY	11,964	4,498	6,809	657	2,311 D	37.6%	56.9%	39.8%	60.2%
83,317	CAMPBELL	29,208	16,743	11,059	1,406	5,684 R	57.3%	37.9%	60.2%	39.8%
5,487	CARLISLE	2,545	975	1,542	28	567 D	38.3%	60.6%	38.7%	61.3%
9,270	CARROLL	3,328	1,076	2,127	125	1,051 D	32.3%	63.9%	33.6%	66.4%
25,060	CARTER	7,839	3,934	3,782	123	152 R	50.2%	48.2%	51.0%	49.0%
14,818	CASEY	5,632	4,239	1,298	95	2,941 R	75.3%	23.0%	76.6%	23.4%
66,878	CHRISTIAN	15,512	8,209	7,048	255	1,161 R	52.9%	45.4%	53.8%	46.2%
28,322	CLARK	9,685	4,302	5,071	312	769 D	44.4%	52.4%	45.9%	54.1%
22,752	CLAY	6,778	4,594	2,121	63	2,473 R	67.8%	31.3%	68.4%	31.6%
9,321	CLINTON	4,590	3,539	1,000	51	2,539 R	77.1%	21.8%	78.0%	22.0%
9,207	CRITTENDEN	3,771	2,219	1,508	44	711 R	58.8%	40.0%	59.5%	40.5%
7,289	CUMBERLAND	3,081	2,216	821	44	1,395 R	71.9%	26.6%	73.0%	27.0%
85,949	DAVIESS	30,717	14,643	14,902	1,172	259 D	47.7%	48.5%	49.6%	50.4%
9,962	EDMONSON	4,233	2,913	1,252	68	1,661 R	68.8%	29.6%	69.9%	30.1%
6,908	ELLIOTT	2,241	551	1,668	22	1,117 D	24.6%	74.4%	24.8%	75.2%
14,495	ESTILL	4,861	2,818	1,965	78	853 R	58.0%	40.4%	58.9%	41.1%
204,165	FAYETTE	71,817	35,349	30,511	5,957	4,838 R	49.2%	42.5%	53.7%	46.3%
12,323	FLEMING	4,315	2,189	2,051	75	138 R	50.7%	47.5%	51.6%	48.4%
48,764	FLOYD	15,385	4,179	10,975	231	6,796 D	27.2%	71.3%	27.6%	72.4%
41,830	FRANKLIN	18,530	6,455	11,193	882	4,738 D	34.8%	60.4%	36.6%	63.4%
8,971	FULTON	3,547	1,462	2,016	69	554 D	41.2%	56.8%	42.0%	58.0%
4,842	GALLATIN	1,704	684	988	32	304 D	40.1%	58.0%	40.9%	59.1%
10,853	GARRARD	4,480	2,585	1,774	121	811 R	57.7%	39.6%	59.3%	40.7%
13,308	GRANT	4,183	1,779	2,272	132	493 D	42.5%	54.3%	43.9%	56.1%
34,049	GRAVES	13,816	6,556	6,999	261	443 D	47.5%	50.7%	48.4%	51.6%
20,854	GRAYSON	8,076	5,084	2,788	204	2,296 R	63.0%	34.5%	64.6%	35.4%
11,043	GREEN	4,587	2,775	1,758	54	1,017 R	60.5%	38.3%	61.2%	38.8%
39,132	GREENUP	14,275	6,857	7,126	292	269 D	48.0%	49.9%	49.0%	51.0%
7,742	HANCOCK	3,004	1,367	1,530	107	163 D	45.5%	50.9%	47.2%	52.8%
88,917	HARDIN	18,738	9,779	8,339	620	1,440 R	52.2%	44.5%	54.0%	46.0%
41,889	HARLAN	14,457	5,460	8,798	199	3,338 D	37.8%	60.9%	38.3%	61.7%
15,166	HARRISON	5,645	2,184	3,319	142	1,135 D	38.7%	58.8%	39.7%	60.3%
15,402	HART	6,204	3,129	3,005	70	124 R	50.4%	48.4%	51.0%	49.0%
40,849	HENDERSON	13,659	5,074	8,082	503	3,008 D	37.1%	59.2%	38.6%	61.4%
12,740	HENRY	4,810	1,723	2,999	88	1,276 D	35.8%	62.3%	36.5%	63.5%
6,065	HICKMAN	2,668	1,143	1,456	69	313 D	42.8%	54.6%	44.0%	56.0%
46,174	HOPKINS	15,355	6,238	8,810	307	2,572 D	40.6%	57.4%	41.5%	58.5%
11,996	JACKSON	4,123	3,379	702	42	2,677 R	82.0%	17.0%	82.8%	17.2%
685,004	JEFFERSON	265,286	127,254	125,844	12,188	1,410 R	48.0%	47.4%	50.3%	49.7%
26,146	JESSAMINE	8,530	4,809	3,310	411	1,499 R	56.4%	38.8%	59.2%	40.8%
24,432	JOHNSON	8,329	5,039	3,142	148	1,897 R	60.5%	37.7%	61.6%	38.4%
137,058	KENTON	46,232	25,965	17,907	2,360	8,058 R	56.2%	38.7%	59.2%	40.8%
17,940	KNOTT	7,065	1,602	5,405	58	3,803 D	22.7%	76.5%	22.9%	77.1%

KENTUCKY

PRESIDENT 1980

1980 Census Population	County	Total Vote	Republican	Democratic	Other	Rep.-Dem. Plurality	Percentage Total Vote Rep.	Total Vote Dem.	Major Vote Rep.	Major Vote Dem.
30,239	KNOX	9,240	5,539	3,543	158	1,996 R	59.9%	38.3%	61.0%	39.0%
11,922	LARUE	4,249	2,000	2,183	66	183 D	47.1%	51.4%	47.8%	52.2%
38,982	LAUREL	12,997	8,868	3,969	160	4,899 R	68.2%	30.5%	69.1%	30.9%
14,121	LAWRENCE	4,980	2,564	2,362	54	202 R	51.5%	47.4%	52.1%	47.9%
7,754	LEE	2,726	1,650	1,017	59	633 R	60.5%	37.3%	61.9%	38.1%
14,882	LESLIE	4,921	3,536	1,327	58	2,209 R	71.9%	27.0%	72.7%	27.3%
30,687	LETCHER	7,818	3,426	4,280	112	854 D	43.8%	54.7%	44.5%	55.5%
14,545	LEWIS	4,393	2,802	1,543	48	1,259 R	63.8%	35.1%	64.5%	35.5%
19,053	LINCOLN	6,105	3,034	2,991	80	43 R	49.7%	49.0%	50.4%	49.6%
9,219	LIVINGSTON	4,008	1,670	2,287	51	617 D	41.7%	57.1%	42.2%	57.8%
24,138	LOGAN	7,781	3,366	4,264	151	898 D	43.3%	54.8%	44.1%	55.9%
6,490	LYON	2,527	968	1,496	63	528 D	38.3%	59.2%	39.3%	60.7%
61,310	MCCRACKEN	24,325	10,281	13,365	679	3,084 D	42.3%	54.9%	43.5%	56.5%
15,634	MCCREARY	5,312	3,786	1,377	149	2,409 R	71.3%	25.9%	73.3%	26.7%
10,090	MCLEAN	3,710	1,497	2,147	66	650 D	40.4%	57.9%	41.1%	58.9%
53,352	MADISON	17,671	8,437	8,208	1,026	229 R	47.7%	46.4%	50.7%	49.3%
13,515	MAGOFFIN	5,297	2,265	2,986	46	721 D	42.8%	56.4%	43.1%	56.9%
17,910	MARION	5,816	2,126	3,577	113	1,451 D	36.6%	61.5%	37.3%	62.7%
25,637	MARSHALL	10,779	4,403	6,231	145	1,828 D	40.8%	57.8%	41.4%	58.6%
13,925	MARTIN	4,430	2,793	1,567	70	1,226 R	63.0%	35.4%	64.1%	35.9%
17,765	MASON	6,287	2,926	3,181	180	255 D	46.5%	50.6%	47.9%	52.1%
22,854	MEADE	6,059	2,740	3,205	114	465 D	45.2%	52.9%	46.1%	53.9%
5,117	MENIFEE	1,543	547	966	30	419 D	35.5%	62.6%	36.2%	63.8%
19,011	MERCER	6,970	3,275	3,528	167	253 D	47.0%	50.6%	48.1%	51.9%
9,484	METCALFE	3,707	2,013	1,628	66	385 R	54.3%	43.9%	55.3%	44.7%
12,353	MONROE	5,813	4,592	1,156	65	3,436 R	79.0%	19.9%	79.9%	20.1%
20,046	MONTGOMERY	6,418	2,869	3,391	158	522 D	44.7%	52.8%	45.8%	54.2%
12,103	MORGAN	4,199	1,450	2,698	51	1,248 D	34.5%	64.3%	35.0%	65.0%
32,238	MUHLENBERG	11,706	4,893	6,616	197	1,723 D	41.8%	56.5%	42.5%	57.5%
27,584	NELSON	9,114	3,349	5,514	251	2,165 D	36.7%	60.5%	37.8%	62.2%
7,157	NICHOLAS	2,351	915	1,349	87	434 D	38.9%	57.4%	40.4%	59.6%
21,765	OHIO	8,921	5,272	3,486	163	1,786 R	59.1%	39.1%	60.2%	39.8%
27,795	OLDHAM	9,510	5,586	3,487	437	2,099 R	58.7%	36.7%	61.6%	38.4%
8,924	OWEN	3,344	944	2,323	77	1,379 D	28.2%	69.5%	28.9%	71.1%
5,709	OWSLEY	1,699	1,250	437	12	813 R	73.6%	25.7%	74.1%	25.9%
10,989	PENDLETON	3,866	1,757	1,992	117	235 D	45.4%	51.5%	46.9%	53.1%
33,763	PERRY	10,367	4,226	6,031	110	1,805 D	40.8%	58.2%	41.2%	58.8%
81,123	PIKE	25,720	10,550	14,878	292	4,328 D	41.0%	57.8%	41.5%	58.5%
11,101	POWELL	3,767	1,716	2,006	45	290 D	45.6%	53.3%	46.1%	53.9%
45,803	PULASKI	19,919	12,970	6,570	379	6,400 R	65.1%	33.0%	66.4%	33.6%
2,265	ROBERTSON	999	416	562	21	146 D	41.6%	56.3%	42.5%	57.5%
13,973	ROCKCASTLE	4,947	3,543	1,345	59	2,198 R	71.6%	27.2%	72.5%	27.5%
19,049	ROWAN	5,987	2,758	2,975	254	217 D	46.1%	49.7%	48.1%	51.9%
13,708	RUSSELL	5,540	3,804	1,693	43	2,111 R	68.7%	30.6%	69.2%	30.8%
21,813	SCOTT	6,667	2,868	3,531	268	663 D	43.0%	53.0%	44.8%	55.2%
23,328	SHELBY	8,108	3,423	4,429	256	1,006 D	42.2%	54.6%	43.6%	56.4%
14,673	SIMPSON	4,819	2,020	2,713	86	693 D	41.9%	56.3%	42.7%	57.3%
5,929	SPENCER	2,200	935	1,216	49	281 D	42.5%	55.3%	43.5%	56.5%
21,178	TAYLOR	7,768	4,243	3,400	125	843 R	54.6%	43.8%	55.5%	44.5%
11,874	TODD	3,981	1,945	1,956	80	11 D	48.9%	49.1%	49.9%	50.1%
9,384	TRIGG	4,605	1,913	2,619	73	706 D	41.5%	56.9%	42.2%	57.8%
6,253	TRIMBLE	2,392	824	1,478	90	654 D	34.4%	61.8%	35.8%	64.2%
17,821	UNION	5,437	1,847	3,479	111	1,632 D	34.0%	64.0%	34.7%	65.3%
71,828	WARREN	22,604	12,184	9,643	777	2,541 R	53.9%	42.7%	55.8%	44.2%
10,764	WASHINGTON	4,249	2,008	2,147	94	139 D	47.3%	50.5%	48.3%	51.7%
17,022	WAYNE	6,716	3,972	2,673	71	1,299 R	59.1%	39.8%	59.8%	40.2%
14,832	WEBSTER	5,535	1,939	3,506	90	1,567 D	35.0%	63.3%	35.6%	64.4%
33,396	WHITLEY	11,077	7,007	3,889	181	3,118 R	63.3%	35.1%	64.3%	35.7%
6,698	WOLFE	2,805	951	1,814	40	863 D	33.9%	64.7%	34.4%	65.6%
17,778	WOODFORD	6,515	3,105	3,122	288	17 D	47.7%	47.9%	49.9%	50.1%
3,660,777	TOTAL	1,294,627	635,274	616,417	42,936	18,857 R	49.1%	47.6%	50.8%	49.2%

KENTUCKY

PRESIDENT 1976

1970 Census Population	County	Total Vote	Republican	Democratic	Other	Rep.-Dem. Plurality	Percentage Total Vote Rep.	Percentage Total Vote Dem.	Percentage Major Vote Rep.	Percentage Major Vote Dem.
13,037	ADAIR	5,634	3,201	2,366	67	835 R	56.8%	42.0%	57.5%	42.5%
12,598	ALLEN	4,778	2,508	2,231	39	277 R	52.5%	46.7%	52.9%	47.1%
9,358	ANDERSON	4,132	1,682	2,388	62	706 D	40.7%	57.8%	41.3%	58.7%
8,276	BALLARD	3,693	649	2,794	250	2,145 D	17.6%	75.7%	18.8%	81.2%
28,677	BARREN	9,771	3,797	5,878	96	2,081 D	38.9%	60.2%	39.2%	60.8%
9,235	BATH	3,071	938	2,113	20	1,175 D	30.5%	68.8%	30.7%	69.3%
31,087	BELL	10,483	5,035	5,284	164	249 D	48.0%	50.4%	48.8%	51.2%
32,812	BOONE	11,385	5,602	5,602	181		49.2%	49.2%	50.0%	50.0%
18,476	BOURBON	5,904	2,260	3,504	140	1,244 D	38.3%	59.3%	39.2%	60.8%
52,376	BOYD	20,459	9,106	11,150	203	2,044 D	44.5%	54.5%	45.0%	55.0%
21,090	BOYLE	7,703	3,511	4,095	97	584 D	45.6%	53.2%	46.2%	53.8%
7,227	BRACKEN	2,495	879	1,577	39	698 D	35.2%	63.2%	35.8%	64.2%
14,221	BREATHITT	4,576	1,014	3,544	18	2,530 D	22.2%	77.4%	22.2%	77.8%
14,789	BRECKINRIDGE	6,111	2,698	3,347	66	649 D	44.1%	54.8%	44.6%	55.4%
26,090	BULLITT	9,477	3,639	5,623	215	1,984 D	38.4%	59.3%	39.3%	60.7%
9,723	BUTLER	3,981	2,363	1,588	30	775 R	59.4%	39.9%	59.8%	40.2%
13,179	CALDWELL	4,899	1,808	3,016	75	1,208 D	36.9%	61.6%	37.5%	62.5%
27,692	CALLOWAY	11,507	3,171	8,141	195	4,970 D	27.6%	70.7%	28.0%	72.0%
88,561	CAMPBELL	28,821	15,798	12,423	600	3,375 R	54.8%	43.1%	56.0%	44.0%
5,354	CARLISLE	2,456	435	1,985	36	1,550 D	17.7%	80.8%	18.0%	82.0%
8,523	CARROLL	3,099	815	2,251	33	1,436 D	26.3%	72.6%	26.6%	73.4%
19,850	CARTER	7,133	3,185	3,915	33	730 D	44.7%	54.9%	44.9%	55.1%
12,930	CASEY	5,032	3,379	1,602	51	1,777 R	67.2%	31.8%	67.8%	32.2%
56,224	CHRISTIAN	12,914	4,964	7,845	105	2,881 D	38.4%	60.7%	38.8%	61.2%
24,090	CLARK	7,768	3,114	4,575	79	1,461 D	40.1%	58.9%	40.5%	59.5%
18,481	CLAY	5,336	3,652	1,674	10	1,978 R	68.4%	31.4%	68.6%	31.4%
8,174	CLINTON	3,389	2,354	987	48	1,367 R	69.5%	29.1%	70.5%	29.5%
8,493	CRITTENDEN	3,352	1,596	1,715	41	119 D	47.6%	51.2%	48.2%	51.8%
6,850	CUMBERLAND	2,527	1,653	853	21	800 R	65.4%	33.8%	66.0%	34.0%
79,486	DAVIESS	27,454	12,826	14,114	514	1,288 D	46.7%	51.4%	47.6%	52.4%
8,751	EDMONSON	3,411	1,976	1,418	17	558 R	57.9%	41.6%	58.2%	41.8%
5,933	ELLIOTT	2,461	455	1,987	19	1,532 D	18.5%	80.7%	18.6%	81.4%
12,752	ESTILL	4,314	2,250	2,034	30	216 R	52.2%	47.1%	52.5%	47.5%
174,323	FAYETTE	64,989	35,170	28,012	1,807	7,158 R	54.1%	43.1%	55.7%	44.3%
11,366	FLEMING	3,983	1,647	2,317	19	670 D	41.4%	58.2%	41.5%	58.5%
35,889	FLOYD	13,333	3,108	10,151	74	7,043 D	23.3%	76.1%	23.4%	76.6%
34,481	FRANKLIN	16,441	5,536	10,475	430	4,939 D	33.7%	63.7%	34.6%	65.4%
10,183	FULTON	3,470	1,060	2,370	40	1,310 D	30.5%	68.3%	30.9%	69.1%
4,134	GALLATIN	1,623	436	1,164	23	728 D	26.9%	71.7%	27.3%	72.8%
9,457	GARRARD	3,988	2,045	1,887	56	158 R	51.3%	47.3%	52.0%	48.0%
9,999	GRANT	3,634	1,212	2,336	86	1,124 D	33.4%	64.3%	34.2%	65.8%
30,939	GRAVES	12,420	3,195	8,982	243	5,787 D	25.7%	72.3%	26.2%	73.8%
16,445	GRAYSON	6,790	3,658	3,064	68	594 R	53.9%	45.1%	54.4%	45.6%
10,350	GREEN	4,519	2,397	2,085	37	312 R	53.0%	46.1%	53.5%	46.5%
33,192	GREENUP	12,013	5,062	6,880	71	1,818 D	42.1%	57.3%	42.4%	57.6%
7,080	HANCOCK	2,747	1,124	1,562	61	438 D	40.9%	56.9%	41.8%	58.2%
78,421	HARDIN	15,185	6,965	7,977	243	1,012 D	45.9%	52.5%	46.6%	53.4%
37,370	HARLAN	12,006	4,624	7,300	82	2,676 D	38.5%	60.8%	38.8%	61.2%
14,158	HARRISON	5,551	1,911	3,582	58	1,671 D	34.4%	64.5%	34.8%	65.2%
13,980	HART	5,244	2,013	3,189	42	1,176 D	38.4%	60.8%	38.7%	61.3%
36,031	HENDERSON	12,118	4,053	7,916	149	3,863 D	33.4%	65.3%	33.9%	66.1%
10,910	HENRY	4,220	1,192	2,985	43	1,793 D	28.2%	70.7%	28.5%	71.5%
6,264	HICKMAN	2,716	585	2,035	96	1,450 D	21.5%	74.9%	22.3%	77.7%
38,167	HOPKINS	12,990	5,115	7,749	126	2,634 D	39.4%	59.7%	39.8%	60.2%
10,005	JACKSON	3,466	2,766	680	20	2,086 R	79.8%	19.6%	80.3%	19.7%
695,055	JEFFERSON	259,445	130,262	122,731	6,452	7,531 R	50.2%	47.3%	51.5%	48.5%
17,430	JESSAMINE	6,004	3,081	2,795	128	286 R	51.3%	46.6%	52.4%	47.6%
17,539	JOHNSON	8,635	4,891	3,683	61	1,208 R	56.6%	42.7%	57.0%	43.0%
129,440	KENTON	41,680	22,087	18,833	760	3,254 R	53.0%	45.2%	54.0%	46.0%
14,698	KNOTT	5,779	962	4,762	55	3,800 D	16.6%	82.4%	16.8%	83.2%

KENTUCKY

PRESIDENT 1976

1970 Census Population	County	Total Vote	Republican	Democratic	Other	Rep.-Dem. Plurality	Percentage: Total Vote Rep.	Total Vote Dem.	Major Vote Rep.	Major Vote Dem.
23,689	KNOX	8,661	4,931	3,642	88	1,289 R	56.9%	42.1%	57.5%	42.5%
10,672	LARUE	3,655	1,409	2,207	39	798 D	38.5%	60.4%	39.0%	61.0%
27,386	LAUREL	10,073	6,186	3,813	74	2,373 R	61.4%	37.9%	61.9%	38.1%
10,726	LAWRENCE	4,283	1,838	2,402	43	564 D	42.9%	56.1%	43.3%	56.7%
6,587	LEE	2,563	1,449	1,091	23	358 R	56.5%	42.6%	57.0%	43.0%
11,623	LESLIE	5,271	3,770	1,478	23	2,292 R	71.5%	28.0%	71.8%	28.2%
23,165	LETCHER	7,748	3,122	4,590	36	1,468 D	40.3%	59.2%	40.5%	59.5%
12,355	LEWIS	4,332	2,383	1,929	20	454 R	55.0%	44.5%	55.3%	44.7%
16,663	LINCOLN	5,925	2,694	3,198	33	504 D	45.5%	54.0%	45.7%	54.3%
7,596	LIVINGSTON	3,415	878	2,497	40	1,619 D	25.7%	73.1%	26.0%	74.0%
21,793	LOGAN	7,389	2,430	4,850	109	2,420 D	32.9%	65.6%	33.4%	66.6%
5,562	LYON	2,221	585	1,606	30	1,021 D	26.3%	72.3%	26.7%	73.3%
58,281	MCCRACKEN	22,687	6,997	14,956	734	7,959 D	30.8%	65.9%	31.9%	68.1%
12,548	MCCREARY	5,142	3,272	1,827	43	1,445 R	63.6%	35.5%	64.2%	35.8%
9,062	MCLEAN	3,593	1,212	2,346	35	1,134 D	33.7%	65.3%	34.1%	65.9%
42,730	MADISON	14,114	6,581	7,299	234	718 D	46.6%	51.7%	47.4%	52.6%
10,443	MAGOFFIN	4,263	1,793	2,451	19	658 D	42.1%	57.5%	42.2%	57.8%
16,714	MARION	5,322	1,723	3,520	79	1,797 D	32.4%	66.1%	32.9%	67.1%
20,381	MARSHALL	9,614	2,578	6,906	130	4,328 D	26.8%	71.8%	27.2%	72.8%
9,377	MARTIN	3,413	2,120	1,267	26	853 R	62.1%	37.1%	62.6%	37.4%
17,273	MASON	6,004	2,529	3,397	78	868 D	42.1%	56.6%	42.7%	57.3%
18,796	MEADE	4,868	1,755	3,030	83	1,275 D	36.1%	62.2%	36.7%	63.3%
4,050	MENIFEE	1,356	304	1,041	11	737 D	22.4%	76.8%	22.6%	77.4%
15,960	MERCER	5,991	2,451	3,411	129	960 D	40.9%	56.9%	41.8%	58.2%
8,177	METCALFE	3,266	1,356	1,877	33	521 D	41.5%	57.5%	41.9%	58.1%
11,642	MONROE	4,795	3,352	1,412	31	1,940 R	69.9%	29.4%	70.4%	29.6%
15,364	MONTGOMERY	5,234	2,032	3,141	61	1,109 D	38.8%	60.0%	39.3%	60.7%
10,019	MORGAN	3,897	973	2,897	27	1,924 D	25.0%	74.3%	25.1%	74.9%
27,537	MUHLENBERG	11,449	4,292	7,058	99	2,766 D	37.5%	61.6%	37.8%	62.2%
23,477	NELSON	7,504	2,804	4,454	246	1,650 D	37.4%	59.4%	38.6%	61.4%
6,508	NICHOLAS	2,378	738	1,582	58	844 D	31.0%	66.5%	31.8%	68.2%
18,790	OHIO	7,337	3,764	3,508	65	256 R	51.3%	47.8%	51.8%	48.2%
14,687	OLDHAM	6,631	3,695	2,819	117	876 R	55.7%	42.5%	56.7%	43.3%
7,470	OWEN	3,051	676	2,332	43	1,656 D	22.2%	76.4%	22.5%	77.5%
5,023	OWSLEY	1,367	1,053	305	9	748 R	77.0%	22.3%	77.5%	22.5%
9,949	PENDLETON	3,427	1,230	2,147	50	917 D	35.9%	62.6%	36.4%	63.6%
26,259	PERRY	10,116	4,434	5,633	49	1,199 D	43.8%	55.7%	44.0%	56.0%
61,059	PIKE	23,691	9,178	14,320	193	5,142 D	38.7%	60.4%	39.1%	60.9%
7,704	POWELL	3,029	1,148	1,859	22	711 D	37.9%	61.4%	38.2%	61.8%
35,234	PULASKI	15,083	9,226	5,752	105	3,474 R	61.2%	38.1%	61.6%	38.4%
2,163	ROBERTSON	828	275	546	7	271 D	33.2%	65.9%	33.5%	66.5%
12,305	ROCKCASTLE	4,013	2,583	1,408	22	1,175 R	64.4%	35.1%	64.7%	35.3%
17,010	ROWAN	5,868	2,244	3,541	83	1,297 D	38.2%	60.3%	38.8%	61.2%
10,542	RUSSELL	4,732	2,882	1,803	47	1,079 R	60.9%	38.1%	61.5%	38.5%
17,948	SCOTT	5,638	2,408	3,118	112	710 D	42.7%	55.3%	43.6%	56.4%
18,999	SHELBY	6,847	2,916	3,841	90	925 D	42.6%	56.1%	43.2%	56.8%
13,054	SIMPSON	4,299	1,481	2,782	36	1,301 D	34.4%	64.7%	34.7%	65.3%
5,488	SPENCER	1,983	742	1,209	32	467 D	37.4%	61.0%	38.0%	62.0%
17,138	TAYLOR	6,866	3,337	3,456	73	119 D	48.6%	50.3%	49.1%	50.9%
10,823	TODD	3,597	1,095	2,436	66	1,341 D	30.4%	67.7%	31.0%	69.0%
8,620	TRIGG	3,745	991	2,727	27	1,736 D	26.5%	72.8%	26.7%	73.3%
5,349	TRIMBLE	2,113	517	1,568	28	1,051 D	24.5%	74.2%	24.8%	75.2%
15,882	UNION	5,312	1,716	3,540	56	1,824 D	32.3%	66.6%	32.6%	67.4%
57,432	WARREN	19,291	9,439	9,657	195	218 D	48.9%	50.1%	49.4%	50.6%
10,728	WASHINGTON	4,235	1,765	2,376	94	611 D	41.7%	56.1%	42.6%	57.4%
14,268	WAYNE	5,817	3,243	2,537	37	706 R	55.8%	43.6%	56.1%	43.9%
13,282	WEBSTER	4,970	1,402	3,523	45	2,121 D	28.2%	70.9%	28.5%	71.5%
24,145	WHITLEY	10,392	6,100	4,212	80	1,888 R	58.7%	40.5%	59.2%	40.8%
5,669	WOLFE	2,458	659	1,777	22	1,118 D	26.8%	72.3%	27.1%	72.9%
14,434	WOODFORD	5,465	2,646	2,689	130	43 D	48.4%	49.2%	49.6%	50.4%
3,219,311	TOTAL	1,167,142	531,852	615,717	19,573	83,865 D	45.6%	52.8%	46.3%	53.7%

KENTUCKY

PRESIDENT 1972

1970 Census Population	County	Total Vote	Republican	Democratic	Other	Rep.-Dem. Plurality	Percentage Total Vote Rep.	Percentage Total Vote Dem.	Percentage Major Vote Rep.	Percentage Major Vote Dem.
13,037	ADAIR	5,531	3,859	1,610	62	2,249 R	69.8%	29.1%	70.6%	29.4%
12,598	ALLEN	4,332	3,025	1,259	48	1,766 R	69.8%	29.1%	70.6%	29.4%
9,358	ANDERSON	3,670	2,298	1,302	70	996 R	62.6%	35.5%	63.8%	36.2%
8,276	BALLARD	3,089	1,542	1,411	136	131 R	49.9%	45.7%	52.2%	47.8%
28,677	BARREN	9,696	6,070	3,384	242	2,686 R	62.6%	34.9%	64.2%	35.8%
9,235	BATH	3,282	1,919	1,347	16	572 R	58.5%	41.0%	58.8%	41.2%
31,087	BELL	9,867	6,518	3,219	130	3,299 R	66.1%	32.6%	66.9%	33.1%
32,812	BOONE	10,280	7,355	2,595	330	4,760 R	71.5%	25.2%	73.9%	26.1%
18,476	BOURBON	5,127	3,180	1,860	87	1,320 R	62.0%	36.3%	63.1%	36.9%
52,376	BOYD	19,437	12,812	6,434	191	6,378 R	65.9%	33.1%	66.6%	33.4%
21,090	BOYLE	6,781	4,317	2,395	69	1,922 R	63.7%	35.3%	64.3%	35.7%
7,227	BRACKEN	2,532	1,628	873	31	755 R	64.3%	34.5%	65.1%	34.9%
14,221	BREATHITT	4,541	1,846	2,677	18	831 D	40.7%	59.0%	40.8%	59.2%
14,789	BRECKINRIDGE	5,563	3,574	1,921	68	1,653 R	64.2%	34.5%	65.0%	35.0%
26,090	BULLITT	7,553	4,517	2,827	209	1,690 R	59.8%	37.4%	61.5%	38.5%
9,723	BUTLER	3,818	2,941	835	42	2,106 R	77.0%	21.9%	77.9%	22.1%
13,179	CALDWELL	4,451	2,952	1,345	154	1,607 R	66.3%	30.2%	68.7%	31.3%
27,692	CALLOWAY	8,732	5,167	3,468	97	1,699 R	59.2%	39.7%	59.8%	40.2%
88,561	CAMPBELL	29,445	20,025	8,585	835	11,440 R	68.0%	29.2%	70.0%	30.0%
5,354	CARLISLE	2,097	1,169	872	56	297 R	55.7%	41.6%	57.3%	42.7%
8,523	CARROLL	2,574	1,228	1,308	38	80 D	47.7%	50.8%	48.4%	51.6%
19,850	CARTER	6,727	4,082	2,591	54	1,491 R	60.7%	38.5%	61.2%	38.8%
12,930	CASEY	4,728	3,727	913	88	2,814 R	78.8%	19.3%	80.3%	19.7%
56,224	CHRISTIAN	11,705	7,414	4,063	228	3,351 R	63.3%	34.7%	64.6%	35.4%
24,090	CLARK	6,585	4,506	2,020	59	2,486 R	68.4%	30.7%	69.0%	31.0%
18,481	CLAY	5,781	4,046	1,709	26	2,337 R	70.0%	29.6%	70.3%	29.7%
8,174	CLINTON	3,307	2,632	659	16	1,973 R	79.6%	19.9%	80.0%	20.0%
8,493	CRITTENDEN	3,143	2,248	859	36	1,389 R	71.5%	27.3%	72.4%	27.6%
6,850	CUMBERLAND	3,002	2,294	686	22	1,608 R	76.4%	22.9%	77.0%	23.0%
79,486	DAVIESS	26,256	17,234	8,168	854	9,066 R	65.6%	31.1%	67.8%	32.2%
8,751	EDMONSON	3,074	2,327	722	25	1,605 R	75.7%	23.5%	76.3%	23.7%
5,933	ELLIOTT	2,297	782	1,499	16	717 D	34.0%	65.3%	34.3%	65.7%
12,752	ESTILL	4,399	3,054	1,322	23	1,732 R	69.4%	30.1%	69.8%	30.2%
174,323	FAYETTE	63,666	42,362	19,828	1,476	22,534 R	66.5%	31.1%	68.1%	31.9%
11,366	FLEMING	3,982	2,484	1,455	43	1,029 R	62.4%	36.5%	63.1%	36.9%
35,889	FLOYD	13,800	6,099	7,544	157	1,445 D	44.2%	54.7%	44.7%	55.3%
34,481	FRANKLIN	13,679	7,781	5,601	297	2,180 R	56.9%	40.9%	58.1%	41.9%
10,183	FULTON	2,947	1,807	1,024	116	783 R	61.3%	34.7%	63.8%	36.2%
4,134	GALLATIN	1,347	719	612	16	107 R	53.4%	45.4%	54.0%	46.0%
9,457	GARRARD	4,657	3,143	1,441	73	1,702 R	67.5%	30.9%	68.6%	31.4%
9,999	GRANT	3,258	2,086	1,054	118	1,032 R	64.0%	32.4%	66.4%	33.6%
30,939	GRAVES	10,100	6,098	3,701	301	2,397 R	60.4%	36.6%	62.2%	37.8%
16,445	GRAYSON	6,111	4,155	1,839	117	2,316 R	68.0%	30.1%	69.3%	30.7%
10,350	GREEN	4,003	2,755	1,209	39	1,546 R	68.8%	30.2%	69.5%	30.5%
33,192	GREENUP	11,437	6,828	4,491	118	2,337 R	59.7%	39.3%	60.3%	39.7%
7,080	HANCOCK	2,450	1,583	791	76	792 R	64.6%	32.3%	66.7%	33.3%
78,421	HARDIN	13,256	8,740	4,060	456	4,680 R	65.9%	30.6%	68.3%	31.7%
37,370	HARLAN	10,985	6,527	4,349	109	2,178 R	59.4%	39.6%	60.0%	40.0%
14,158	HARRISON	4,576	2,732	1,780	64	952 R	59.7%	38.9%	60.5%	39.5%
13,980	HART	5,939	3,582	2,307	50	1,275 R	60.3%	38.8%	60.8%	39.2%
36,031	HENDERSON	10,269	6,231	3,889	149	2,342 R	60.7%	37.9%	61.6%	38.4%
10,910	HENRY	3,656	1,919	1,688	49	231 R	52.5%	46.2%	53.2%	46.8%
6,264	HICKMAN	2,524	1,430	976	118	454 R	56.7%	38.7%	59.4%	40.6%
38,167	HOPKINS	10,388	7,133	3,129	126	4,004 R	68.7%	30.1%	69.5%	30.5%
10,005	JACKSON	5,753	5,303	436	14	4,867 R	92.2%	7.6%	92.4%	7.6%
695,055	JEFFERSON	235,764	142,436	88,143	5,185	54,293 R	60.4%	37.4%	61.8%	38.2%
17,430	JESSAMINE	5,238	3,819	1,269	150	2,550 R	72.9%	24.2%	75.1%	24.9%
17,539	JOHNSON	6,792	4,907	1,840	45	3,067 R	72.2%	27.1%	72.7%	27.3%
129,440	KENTON	42,121	28,076	12,872	1,173	15,204 R	66.7%	30.6%	68.6%	31.4%
14,698	KNOTT	4,287	1,479	2,774	34	1,295 D	34.5%	64.7%	34.8%	65.2%

KENTUCKY

PRESIDENT 1972

1970 Census Population	County	Total Vote	Republican	Democratic	Other	Rep.-Dem. Plurality	Percentage Total Vote Rep.	Percentage Total Vote Dem.	Percentage Major Vote Rep.	Percentage Major Vote Dem.
23,689	KNOX	6,879	5,017	1,805	57	3,212 R	72.9%	26.2%	73.5%	26.5%
10,672	LARUE	3,980	2,449	1,483	48	966 R	61.5%	37.3%	62.3%	37.7%
27,386	LAUREL	9,620	7,276	2,274	70	5,002 R	75.6%	23.6%	76.2%	23.8%
10,726	LAWRENCE	3,955	2,392	1,529	34	863 R	60.5%	38.7%	61.0%	39.0%
6,587	LEE	2,388	1,629	744	15	885 R	68.2%	31.2%	68.6%	31.4%
11,623	LESLIE	4,236	3,299	913	24	2,386 R	77.9%	21.6%	78.3%	21.7%
23,165	LETCHER	7,197	4,213	2,908	76	1,305 R	58.5%	40.4%	59.2%	40.8%
12,355	LEWIS	4,365	3,124	1,200	41	1,924 R	71.6%	27.5%	72.2%	27.8%
16,663	LINCOLN	5,571	3,623	1,882	66	1,741 R	65.0%	33.8%	65.8%	34.2%
7,596	LIVINGSTON	2,790	1,673	1,065	52	608 R	60.0%	38.2%	61.1%	38.9%
21,793	LOGAN	6,175	3,573	2,459	143	1,114 R	57.9%	39.8%	59.2%	40.8%
5,562	LYON	1,760	1,030	687	43	343 R	58.5%	39.0%	60.0%	40.0%
58,281	MCCRACKEN	19,518	11,260	7,567	691	3,693 R	57.7%	38.8%	59.8%	40.2%
12,548	MCCREARY	3,976	3,203	684	89	2,519 R	80.6%	17.2%	82.4%	17.6%
9,062	MCLEAN	3,530	2,298	1,191	41	1,107 R	65.1%	33.7%	65.9%	34.1%
42,730	MADISON	13,199	8,659	4,328	212	4,331 R	65.6%	32.8%	66.7%	33.3%
10,443	MAGOFFIN	4,281	2,243	2,024	14	219 R	52.4%	47.3%	52.6%	47.4%
16,714	MARION	4,765	2,370	2,351	44	19 R	49.7%	49.3%	50.2%	49.8%
20,381	MARSHALL	7,252	4,290	2,806	156	1,484 R	59.2%	38.7%	60.5%	39.5%
9,377	MARTIN	3,204	2,495	661	48	1,834 R	77.9%	20.6%	79.1%	20.9%
17,273	MASON	6,037	3,529	2,459	49	1,070 R	58.5%	40.7%	58.9%	41.1%
18,796	MEADE	4,090	2,492	1,541	57	951 R	60.9%	37.7%	61.8%	38.2%
4,050	MENIFEE	1,358	596	732	30	136 D	43.9%	53.9%	44.9%	55.1%
15,960	MERCER	5,410	3,575	1,707	128	1,868 R	66.1%	31.6%	67.7%	32.3%
8,177	METCALFE	3,238	1,896	1,308	34	588 R	58.6%	40.4%	59.2%	40.8%
11,642	MONROE	4,566	3,770	768	28	3,002 R	82.6%	16.8%	83.1%	16.9%
15,364	MONTGOMERY	4,579	2,868	1,657	54	1,211 R	62.6%	36.2%	63.4%	36.6%
10,019	MORGAN	3,369	1,535	1,815	19	280 D	45.6%	53.9%	45.8%	54.2%
27,537	MUHLENBERG	8,978	5,596	3,246	136	2,350 R	62.3%	36.2%	63.3%	36.7%
23,477	NELSON	6,528	3,495	2,828	205	667 R	53.5%	43.3%	55.3%	44.7%
6,508	NICHOLAS	1,914	1,076	804	34	272 R	56.2%	42.0%	57.2%	42.8%
18,790	OHIO	3,334	2,392	906	36	1,486 R	71.7%	27.2%	72.5%	27.5%
14,687	OLDHAM	4,472	3,041	1,311	120	1,730 R	68.0%	29.3%	69.9%	30.1%
7,470	OWEN	2,651	1,456	1,161	34	295 R	54.9%	43.8%	55.6%	44.4%
5,023	OWSLEY	1,587	1,328	251	8	1,077 R	83.7%	15.8%	84.1%	15.9%
9,949	PENDLETON	2,922	1,966	909	47	1,057 R	67.3%	31.1%	68.4%	31.6%
26,259	PERRY	9,050	5,373	3,601	76	1,772 R	59.4%	39.8%	59.9%	40.1%
61,059	PIKE	22,200	12,535	9,513	152	3,022 R	56.5%	42.9%	56.9%	43.1%
7,704	POWELL	3,024	1,766	1,230	28	536 R	58.4%	40.7%	58.9%	41.1%
35,234	PULASKI	13,770	10,602	3,080	88	7,522 R	77.0%	22.4%	77.5%	22.5%
2,163	ROBERTSON	894	456	421	17	35 R	51.0%	47.1%	52.0%	48.0%
12,305	ROCKCASTLE	4,446	3,437	968	41	2,469 R	77.3%	21.8%	78.0%	22.0%
17,010	ROWAN	5,458	3,245	2,169	44	1,076 R	59.5%	39.7%	59.9%	40.1%
10,542	RUSSELL	5,220	3,992	1,169	59	2,823 R	76.5%	22.4%	77.3%	22.7%
17,948	SCOTT	5,026	3,255	1,642	129	1,613 R	64.8%	32.7%	66.5%	33.5%
18,999	SHELBY	6,065	3,893	2,074	98	1,819 R	64.2%	34.2%	65.2%	34.8%
13,054	SIMPSON	3,652	2,285	1,325	42	960 R	62.6%	36.3%	63.3%	36.7%
5,488	SPENCER	1,629	1,120	481	28	639 R	68.8%	29.5%	70.0%	30.0%
17,138	TAYLOR	5,952	4,035	1,859	58	2,176 R	67.8%	31.2%	68.5%	31.5%
10,823	TODD	3,315	1,964	1,222	129	742 R	59.2%	36.9%	61.6%	38.4%
8,620	TRIGG	3,337	1,767	1,514	56	253 R	53.0%	45.4%	53.9%	46.1%
5,349	TRIMBLE	1,712	935	757	20	178 R	54.6%	44.2%	55.3%	44.7%
15,882	UNION	4,604	2,701	1,855	48	846 R	58.7%	40.3%	59.3%	40.7%
57,432	WARREN	18,691	12,481	5,934	276	6,547 R	66.8%	31.7%	67.8%	32.2%
10,728	WASHINGTON	4,051	2,378	1,552	121	826 R	58.7%	38.3%	60.5%	39.5%
14,268	WAYNE	5,420	3,514	1,853	53	1,661 R	64.8%	34.2%	65.5%	34.5%
13,282	WEBSTER	4,162	2,396	1,712	54	684 R	57.6%	41.1%	58.3%	41.7%
24,145	WHITLEY	9,062	6,788	2,199	75	4,589 R	74.9%	24.3%	75.5%	24.5%
5,669	WOLFE	1,917	936	957	24	21 D	48.8%	49.9%	49.4%	50.6%
14,434	WOODFORD	4,781	3,363	1,268	150	2,095 R	70.3%	26.5%	72.6%	27.4%
3,219,311	TOTAL	1,067,499	676,446	371,159	19,894	305,287 R	63.4%	34.8%	64.6%	35.4%

KENTUCKY

PRESIDENT 1968

1960 Census Population	County	Total Vote	Republican	Democratic	AIP	Other	Plurality	Percentage Rep.	Dem.	AIP
14,699	ADAIR	5,450	3,239	1,362	844	5	1,877 R	59.4%	25.0%	15.5%
12,269	ALLEN	4,790	2,952	927	905	6	2,025 R	61.6%	19.4%	18.9%
8,618	ANDERSON	3,596	1,594	1,334	657	11	260 R	44.3%	37.1%	18.3%
8,291	BALLARD	3,444	564	1,632	1,197	51	435 D	16.4%	47.4%	34.8%
28,303	BARREN	9,826	4,209	3,464	2,140	13	745 R	42.8%	35.3%	21.8%
9,114	BATH	3,331	1,277	1,394	658	2	117 D	38.3%	41.8%	19.8%
35,336	BELL	10,275	4,905	4,138	1,204	28	767 R	47.7%	40.3%	11.7%
21,940	BOONE	9,051	4,081	2,725	2,240	5	1,356 R	45.1%	30.1%	24.7%
18,178	BOURBON	5,460	1,848	2,566	1,023	23	718 D	33.8%	47.0%	18.7%
52,163	BOYD	19,001	8,632	7,914	2,443	12	718 R	45.4%	41.7%	12.9%
21,257	BOYLE	6,738	2,715	2,663	1,356	4	52 R	40.3%	39.5%	20.1%
7,422	BRACKEN	2,732	1,115	1,067	548	2	48 R	40.8%	39.1%	20.1%
15,490	BREATHITT	4,678	1,361	2,954	361	2	1,593 D	29.1%	63.1%	7.7%
14,734	BRECKINRIDGE	5,873	2,779	2,024	1,067	3	755 R	47.3%	34.5%	18.2%
15,726	BULLITT	6,310	1,965	2,135	2,180	30	45 A	31.1%	33.8%	34.5%
9,586	BUTLER	3,967	2,637	691	634	5	1,946 R	66.5%	17.4%	16.0%
13,073	CALDWELL	5,065	2,139	1,439	1,426	61	700 R	42.2%	28.4%	28.2%
20,972	CALLOWAY	8,682	2,672	3,854	2,150	6	1,182 D	30.8%	44.4%	24.8%
86,803	CAMPBELL	28,203	13,681	9,747	4,750	25	3,934 R	48.5%	34.6%	16.8%
5,608	CARLISLE	2,438	479	1,144	807	8	337 D	19.6%	46.9%	33.1%
7,978	CARROLL	3,152	868	1,765	514	5	897 D	27.5%	56.0%	16.3%
20,817	CARTER	6,511	3,234	2,344	926	7	890 R	49.7%	36.0%	14.2%
14,327	CASEY	5,235	3,698	879	649	9	2,819 R	70.6%	16.8%	12.4%
56,904	CHRISTIAN	12,614	3,788	4,281	4,527	18	246 A	30.0%	33.9%	35.9%
21,075	CLARK	6,808	2,698	2,385	1,722	3	313 R	39.6%	35.0%	25.3%
20,748	CLAY	6,204	4,663	1,213	327	1	3,450 R	75.2%	19.6%	5.3%
8,886	CLINTON	3,425	2,572	568	280	5	2,004 R	75.1%	16.6%	8.2%
8,648	CRITTENDEN	3,533	1,942	838	748	5	1,104 R	55.0%	23.7%	21.2%
7,835	CUMBERLAND	3,120	2,116	646	355	3	1,470 R	67.8%	20.7%	11.4%
70,588	DAVIESS	25,142	10,111	9,947	5,015	69	164 R	40.2%	39.6%	19.9%
8,085	EDMONSON	3,484	2,280	679	516	9	1,601 R	65.4%	19.5%	14.8%
6,330	ELLIOTT	2,186	515	1,387	280	4	872 D	23.6%	63.4%	12.8%
12,466	ESTILL	4,174	2,236	1,261	675	2	975 R	53.6%	30.2%	16.2%
131,906	FAYETTE	50,373	24,948	16,902	8,354	169	8,046 R	49.5%	33.6%	16.6%
10,890	FLEMING	4,167	2,220	1,406	535	6	814 R	53.3%	33.7%	12.8%
41,642	FLOYD	13,043	3,550	8,333	1,150	10	4,783 D	27.2%	63.9%	8.8%
29,421	FRANKLIN	13,165	4,057	6,396	2,655	57	2,339 D	30.8%	48.6%	20.2%
11,256	FULTON	3,818	1,079	1,204	1,526	9	322 A	28.3%	31.5%	40.0%
3,867	GALLATIN	1,407	413	685	304	5	272 D	29.4%	48.7%	21.6%
9,747	GARRARD	3,927	2,205	1,000	675	47	1,205 R	56.1%	25.5%	17.2%
9,489	GRANT	3,522	1,386	1,169	941	26	217 R	39.4%	33.2%	26.7%
30,021	GRAVES	12,213	3,239	5,103	3,829	42	1,274 D	26.5%	41.8%	31.4%
15,834	GRAYSON	5,885	3,598	1,595	657	35	2,003 R	61.1%	27.1%	11.2%
11,249	GREEN	4,170	2,448	1,003	712	7	1,445 R	58.7%	24.1%	17.1%
29,238	GREENUP	10,755	4,698	4,689	1,365	3	9 R	43.7%	43.6%	12.7%
5,330	HANCOCK	2,347	1,049	867	419	12	182 R	44.7%	36.9%	17.9%
67,789	HARDIN	12,737	5,329	4,470	2,845	93	859 R	41.8%	35.1%	22.3%
51,107	HARLAN	13,077	4,572	6,389	2,099	17	1,817 D	35.0%	48.9%	16.1%
13,704	HARRISON	4,850	1,637	2,373	839	1	736 D	33.8%	48.9%	17.3%
14,119	HART	5,484	2,817	1,658	1,002	7	1,159 R	51.4%	30.2%	18.3%
33,519	HENDERSON	10,726	3,512	5,062	2,132	20	1,550 D	32.7%	47.2%	19.9%
10,987	HENRY	3,967	1,271	1,978	711	7	707 D	32.0%	49.9%	17.9%
6,747	HICKMAN	2,686	623	880	1,154	29	274 A	23.2%	32.8%	43.0%
38,458	HOPKINS	11,869	3,791	4,391	3,668	19	600 D	31.9%	37.0%	30.9%
10,677	JACKSON	3,684	3,098	304	279	3	2,794 R	84.1%	8.3%	7.6%
610,947	JEFFERSON	222,657	95,942	90,242	35,561	912	5,700 R	43.1%	40.5%	16.0%
13,625	JESSAMINE	5,143	2,338	1,334	1,440	31	898 R	45.5%	25.9%	28.0%
19,748	JOHNSON	6,536	4,046	2,142	344	4	1,904 R	61.9%	32.8%	5.3%
120,700	KENTON	39,557	17,263	14,656	7,612	26	2,607 R	43.6%	37.1%	19.2%
17,362	KNOTT	4,867	1,098	3,335	428	6	2,237 D	22.6%	68.5%	8.8%

KENTUCKY

PRESIDENT 1968

1960 Census Population	County	Total Vote	Republican	Democratic	AIP	Other	Plurality	Percentage Rep.	Dem.	AIP
25,258	KNOX	7,595	4,388	2,244	944	19	2,144 R	57.8%	29.5%	12.4%
10,346	LARUE	3,897	1,862	1,251	776	8	611 R	47.8%	32.1%	19.9%
24,901	LAUREL	9,251	6,251	1,756	1,236	8	4,495 R	67.6%	19.0%	13.4%
12,134	LAWRENCE	4,249	1,946	1,825	476	2	121 R	45.8%	43.0%	11.2%
7,420	LEE	2,298	1,339	674	285		665 R	58.3%	29.3%	12.4%
10,941	LESLIE	3,679	2,615	828	236		1,787 R	71.1%	22.5%	6.4%
30,102	LETCHER	7,667	3,243	3,499	920	5	256 D	42.3%	45.6%	12.0%
13,115	LEWIS	4,257	2,760	1,017	472	8	1,743 R	64.8%	23.9%	11.1%
16,503	LINCOLN	5,461	2,591	1,736	1,129	5	855 R	47.4%	31.8%	20.7%
7,029	LIVINGSTON	3,307	1,079	1,272	953	3	193 D	32.6%	38.5%	28.8%
20,896	LOGAN	8,687	3,402	3,339	1,881	65	63 R	39.2%	38.4%	21.7%
5,924	LYON	1,938	579	719	619	21	100 D	29.9%	37.1%	31.9%
57,306	MCCRACKEN	21,544	5,887	9,741	5,810	106	3,854 D	27.3%	45.2%	27.0%
12,463	MCCREARY	3,949	2,670	759	479	41	1,911 R	67.6%	19.2%	12.1%
9,355	MCLEAN	3,840	1,372	1,373	1,084	11	1 D	35.7%	35.8%	28.2%
33,482	MADISON	11,878	5,325	3,884	2,558	111	1,441 R	44.8%	32.7%	21.5%
11,156	MAGOFFIN	4,123	1,967	1,927	229		40 R	47.7%	46.7%	5.6%
16,887	MARION	4,906	1,620	2,436	849	1	816 D	33.0%	49.7%	17.3%
16,736	MARSHALL	7,921	2,432	3,301	2,183	5	869 D	30.7%	41.7%	27.6%
10,201	MARTIN	2,840	1,943	759	136	2	1,184 R	68.4%	26.7%	4.8%
18,454	MASON	6,570	2,661	2,772	1,131	6	111 D	40.5%	42.2%	17.2%
18,938	MEADE	4,200	1,385	1,926	886	3	541 D	33.0%	45.9%	21.1%
4,276	MENIFEE	1,317	509	554	247	7	45 D	38.6%	42.1%	18.8%
14,596	MERCER	5,646	2,432	1,950	1,227	37	482 R	43.1%	34.5%	21.7%
8,367	METCALFE	3,046	1,566	1,001	469	10	565 R	51.4%	32.9%	15.4%
11,799	MONROE	5,372	4,086	693	590	3	3,393 R	76.1%	12.9%	11.0%
13,461	MONTGOMERY	4,508	2,113	1,408	980	7	705 R	46.9%	31.2%	21.7%
11,056	MORGAN	3,961	1,341	2,222	398		881 D	33.9%	56.1%	10.0%
27,791	MUHLENBERG	9,750	3,853	3,688	2,198	11	165 R	39.5%	37.8%	22.5%
22,168	NELSON	6,916	2,373	3,420	1,104	19	1,047 D	34.3%	49.5%	16.0%
6,677	NICHOLAS	2,062	725	911	413	13	186 D	35.2%	44.2%	20.0%
17,725	OHIO	6,470	3,504	1,695	1,263	8	1,809 R	54.2%	26.2%	19.5%
13,388	OLDHAM	3,993	1,655	1,399	937	2	256 R	41.4%	35.0%	23.5%
8,237	OWEN	3,134	827	1,608	697	2	781 D	26.4%	51.3%	22.2%
5,369	OWSLEY	1,877	1,417	303	157		1,114 R	75.5%	16.1%	8.4%
9,968	PENDLETON	3,533	1,614	1,156	760	3	458 R	45.7%	32.7%	21.5%
34,961	PERRY	9,541	3,993	4,562	983	3	569 D	41.9%	47.8%	10.3%
68,264	PIKE	22,526	8,911	11,663	1,933	19	2,752 D	39.6%	51.8%	8.6%
6,674	POWELL	2,718	1,157	934	625	2	223 R	42.6%	34.4%	23.0%
34,403	PULASKI	12,901	8,290	2,823	1,780	8	5,467 R	64.3%	21.9%	13.8%
2,443	ROBERTSON	1,011	416	406	186	3	10 R	41.1%	40.2%	18.4%
12,334	ROCKCASTLE	4,588	3,072	868	644	4	2,204 R	67.0%	18.9%	14.0%
12,808	ROWAN	4,459	2,017	1,898	541	3	119 R	45.2%	42.6%	12.1%
11,076	RUSSELL	4,721	3,035	961	718	7	2,074 R	64.3%	20.4%	15.2%
15,376	SCOTT	4,984	1,748	1,961	1,242	33	213 D	35.1%	39.3%	24.9%
18,493	SHELBY	6,054	2,287	2,579	1,185	3	292 D	37.8%	42.6%	19.6%
11,548	SIMPSON	4,339	1,435	1,505	1,390	9	70 D	33.1%	34.7%	32.0%
5,680	SPENCER	1,750	733	564	448	5	169 R	41.9%	32.2%	25.6%
16,285	TAYLOR	5,959	3,032	1,367	1,554	6	1,478 R	50.9%	22.9%	26.1%
11,364	TODD	4,479	1,433	1,082	1,932	32	499 A	32.0%	24.2%	43.1%
8,870	TRIGG	3,621	1,100	1,330	1,180	11	150 D	30.4%	36.7%	32.6%
5,102	TRIMBLE	1,967	511	1,045	406	5	534 D	26.0%	53.1%	20.6%
14,537	UNION	5,794	1,371	2,616	1,804	3	812 D	23.7%	45.2%	31.1%
45,491	WARREN	17,665	8,084	5,200	4,365	16	2,884 R	45.8%	29.4%	24.7%
11,168	WASHINGTON	4,019	1,863	1,675	472	9	188 R	46.4%	41.7%	11.7%
14,700	WAYNE	5,002	3,055	1,467	475	5	1,588 R	61.1%	29.3%	9.5%
14,244	WEBSTER	4,905	1,446	2,114	1,337	8	668 D	29.5%	43.1%	27.3%
25,815	WHITLEY	9,439	5,639	2,134	1,650	16	3,505 R	59.7%	22.6%	17.5%
6,534	WOLFE	2,207	758	1,162	282	5	404 D	34.3%	52.7%	12.8%
11,913	WOODFORD	4,472	1,901	1,646	894	31	255 R	42.5%	36.8%	20.0%
3,038,156	TOTAL	1,055,893	462,411	397,541	193,098	2,843	64,870 R	43.8%	37.6%	18.3%

KENTUCKY

ELECTION NOTES

1984 Other vote was 3,129 Mason (Socialist Workers); 1,776 LaRouche (Independent); 1,479 Anderson (National Unity); 599 Johnson (Citizens); 428 Dennis (American); 365 Serrette (Independent Alliance); 328 Hall (Communist).

1980 Other vote was 31,127 Anderson (Anderson Coalition); 5,531 Clark (Libertarian); 4,233 McCormack (Respect for Life); 1,304 Commoner (Citizens); 393 Pulley (Socialist Workers); 348 Hall (Communist). Early unamended canvass gave the Democratic state-wide total vote as 617,417.

1976 Other vote was 8,308 Anderson (American); 6,837 McCarthy (Independent); 2,328 Maddox (American Independent); 814 MacBride (Libertarian); 510 LaRouche (U.S. Labor); 426 Hall (Communist); 350 Camejo (Socialist Workers).

1972 Other vote was 17,627 Schmitz (American); 1,118 Spock (People's); 685 Jenness (Socialist Workers); 464 Hall (Communist). Although the data indicate a possible discrepancy in the Republican vote in Jackson county, the official state canvass figures are used here. Although the data indicate a possible undercount in the vote in Ohio county, the official state canvass figures are used here.

1968 Wallace on the ballot as American. Other vote was Halstead (Socialist Workers). Early unamended canvass gave the Hart county Democratic vote as 1,657.

LOUISIANA

POPULAR VOTE FOR PRESIDENT 1920 TO 1984

Year	Total Vote	Republican Vote	Republican Candidate	Democratic Vote	Democratic Candidate	Other Vote	Plurality	Percentage Total Vote Rep.	Percentage Total Vote Dem.	Percentage Major Vote Rep.	Percentage Major Vote Dem.
1984	1,706,822	1,037,299	Reagan, Ronald	651,586	Mondale, Walter F.	17,937	385,713 R	60.8%	38.2%	61.4%	38.6%
1980	1,548,591	792,853	Reagan, Ronald	708,453	Carter, Jimmy	47,285	84,400 R	51.2%	45.7%	52.8%	47.2%
1976	1,278,439	587,446	Ford, Gerald R.	661,365	Carter, Jimmy	29,628	73,919 D	46.0%	51.7%	47.0%	53.0%
1972	1,051,491	686,852	Nixon, Richard M.	298,142	McGovern, George S.	66,497	388,710 R	65.3%	28.4%	69.7%	30.3%
1968 **	1,097,450	257,535	Nixon, Richard M.	309,615	Humphrey, Hubert H.	530,300	220,685 A	23.5%	28.2%	45.4%	54.6%
1964	896,293	509,225	Goldwater, Barry M.	387,068	Johnson, Lyndon B.		122,157 R	56.8%	43.2%	56.8%	43.2%
1960	807,891	230,980	Nixon, Richard M.	407,339	Kennedy, John F.	169,572	176,359 D	28.6%	50.4%	36.2%	63.8%
1956	617,544	329,047	Eisenhower, Dwight D.	243,977	Stevenson, Adlai E.	44,520	85,070 R	53.3%	39.5%	57.4%	42.6%
1952	651,952	306,925	Eisenhower, Dwight D.	345,027	Stevenson, Adlai E.		38,102 D	47.1%	52.9%	47.1%	52.9%
1948 **	416,336	72,657	Dewey, Thomas E.	136,344	Truman, Harry S.	207,335	67,946 SR	17.5%	32.7%	34.8%	65.2%
1944	349,383	67,750	Dewey, Thomas E.	281,564	Roosevelt, Franklin D.	69	213,814 D	19.4%	80.6%	19.4%	80.6%
1940	372,305	52,446	Willkie, Wendell	319,751	Roosevelt, Franklin D.	108	267,305 D	14.1%	85.9%	14.1%	85.9%
1936	329,778	36,791	Landon, Alfred M.	292,894	Roosevelt, Franklin D.	93	256,103 D	11.2%	88.8%	11.2%	88.8%
1932	268,804	18,853	Hoover, Herbert C.	249,418	Roosevelt, Franklin D.	533	230,565 D	7.0%	92.8%	7.0%	93.0%
1928	215,833	51,160	Hoover, Herbert C.	164,655	Smith, Alfred E.	18	113,495 D	23.7%	76.3%	23.7%	76.3%
1924	121,951	24,670	Coolidge, Calvin	93,218	Davis, John W.	4,063	68,548 D	20.2%	76.4%	20.9%	79.1%
1920	126,397	38,539	Harding, Warren G.	87,519	Cox, James M.	339	48,980 D	30.5%	69.2%	30.6%	69.4%

In 1968 other vote was American (Wallace). In 1948 other vote was 204,290 States Rights; 3,035 Progressive and 10 scattered.

ELECTORAL COLLEGE VOTE 1920 TO 1984

Year	Total	Republican	Democratic	Other
1984	10	10	—	—
1980	10	10	—	—
1976	10	—	10	—
1972	10	10	—	—
1968	10	—	—	10 AIP
1964	10	10	—	—
1960	10	—	10	—
1956	10	10	—	—
1952	10	—	10	—
1948	10	—	—	10 SR
1944	10	—	10	—
1940	10	—	10	—
1936	10	—	10	—
1932	10	—	10	—
1928	10	—	10	—
1924	10	—	10	—
1920	10	—	10	—

LOUISIANA

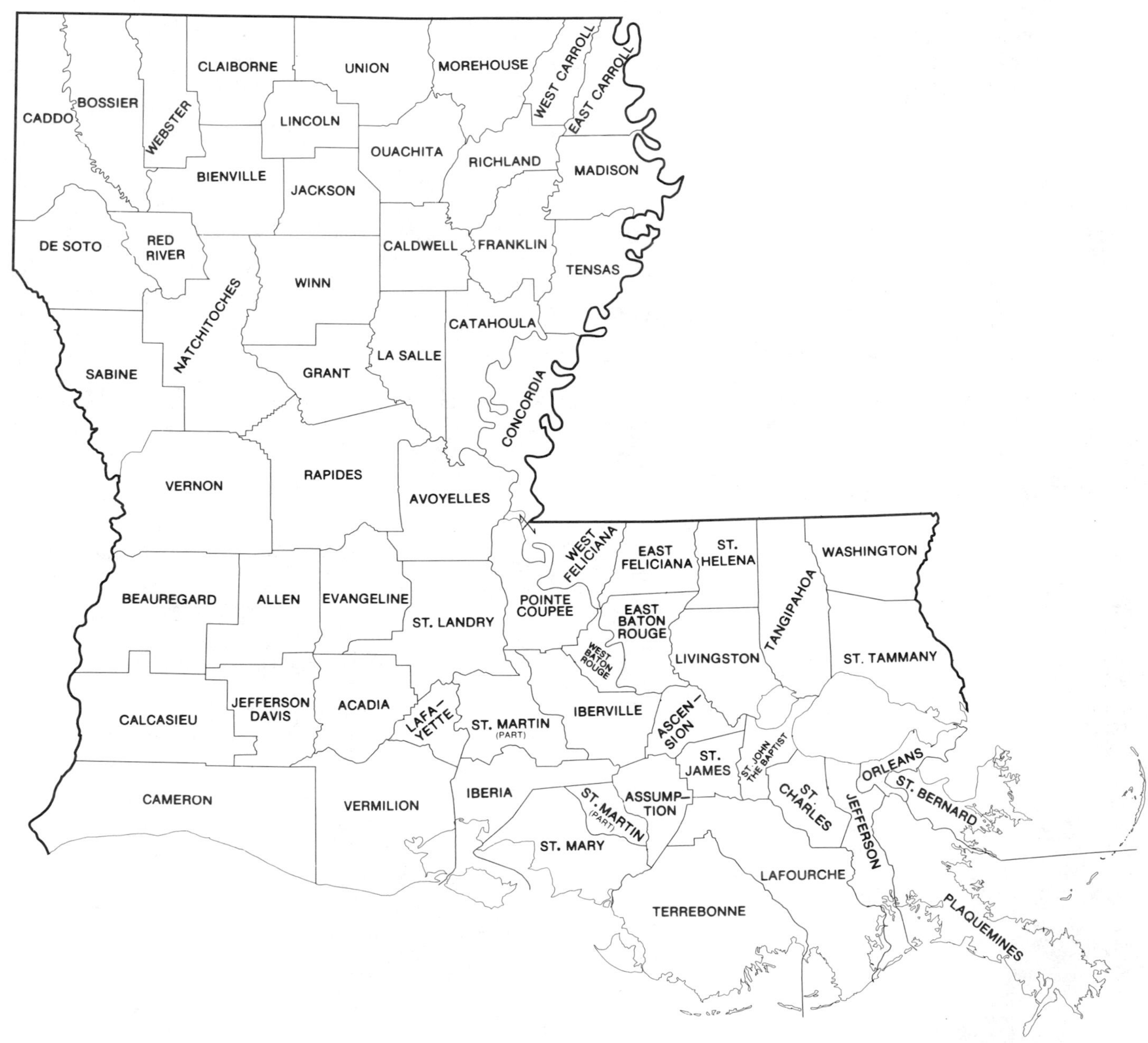

CADDO
BOSSIER
WEBSTER
CLAIBORNE
UNION
MOREHOUSE
WEST CARROLL
EAST CARROLL
LINCOLN
OUACHITA
RICHLAND
MADISON
BIENVILLE
JACKSON
DE SOTO
RED RIVER
CALDWELL
FRANKLIN
TENSAS
WINN
NATCHITOCHES
CATAHOULA
LA SALLE
GRANT
SABINE
CONCORDIA
RAPIDES
VERNON
AVOYELLES
WEST FELICIANA
EAST FELICIANA
ST. HELENA
WASHINGTON
BEAUREGARD
ALLEN
EVANGELINE
POINTE COUPEE
ST. LANDRY
EAST BATON ROUGE
TANGIPAHOA
WEST BATON ROUGE
LIVINGSTON
ST. TAMMANY
CALCASIEU
JEFFERSON DAVIS
ACADIA
LAFAYETTE
ST. MARTIN (PART)
IBERVILLE
ASCENSION
ST. JAMES
ST. JOHN THE BAPTIST
ORLEANS
ST. BERNARD
ST. CHARLES
CAMERON
VERMILION
IBERIA
ST. MARTIN (PART)
ASSUMPTION
JEFFERSON
ST. MARY
LAFOURCHE
TERREBONNE
PLAQUEMINES

LOUISIANA

PRESIDENT 1984

1980 Census Population	Parish	Total Vote	Republican	Democratic	Other	Rep.-Dem. Plurality	Percentage Total Vote Rep.	Percentage Total Vote Dem.	Percentage Major Vote Rep.	Percentage Major Vote Dem.
56,427	ACADIA	24,602	14,906	9,262	434	5,644 R	60.6%	37.6%	61.7%	38.3%
21,390	ALLEN	9,382	4,474	4,842	66	368 D	47.7%	51.6%	48.0%	52.0%
50,068	ASCENSION	23,170	11,945	11,048	177	897 R	51.6%	47.7%	52.0%	48.0%
22,084	ASSUMPTION	10,363	5,433	4,660	270	773 R	52.4%	45.0%	53.8%	46.2%
41,393	AVOYELLES	16,673	9,402	6,808	463	2,594 R	56.4%	40.8%	58.0%	42.0%
29,692	BEAUREGARD	11,648	7,353	4,199	96	3,154 R	63.1%	36.0%	63.7%	36.3%
16,387	BIENVILLE	8,226	4,587	3,530	109	1,057 R	55.8%	42.9%	56.5%	43.5%
80,721	BOSSIER	29,782	22,638	7,006	138	15,632 R	76.0%	23.5%	76.4%	23.6%
252,358	CADDO	99,601	63,429	35,727	445	27,702 R	63.7%	35.9%	64.0%	36.0%
167,223	CALCASIEU	69,210	35,566	33,214	430	2,352 R	51.4%	48.0%	51.7%	48.3%
10,761	CALDWELL	4,819	3,341	1,348	130	1,993 R	69.3%	28.0%	71.3%	28.7%
9,336	CAMERON	3,906	2,265	1,608	33	657 R	58.0%	41.2%	58.5%	41.5%
12,287	CATAHOULA	5,391	3,640	1,649	102	1,991 R	67.5%	30.6%	68.8%	31.2%
17,095	CLAIBORNE	7,214	4,349	2,788	77	1,561 R	60.3%	38.6%	60.9%	39.1%
22,981	CONCORDIA	9,692	6,177	3,332	183	2,845 R	63.7%	34.4%	65.0%	35.0%
25,727	DE SOTO	10,739	5,989	4,642	108	1,347 R	55.8%	43.2%	56.3%	43.7%
366,191	EAST BATON ROUGE	153,268	95,704	56,673	891	39,031 R	62.4%	37.0%	62.8%	37.2%
11,772	EAST CARROLL	4,132	1,974	2,089	69	115 D	47.8%	50.6%	48.6%	51.4%
19,015	EAST FELICIANA	8,401	4,166	4,122	113	44 R	49.6%	49.1%	50.3%	49.7%
33,343	EVANGELINE	15,844	8,680	6,981	183	1,699 R	54.8%	44.1%	55.4%	44.6%
24,141	FRANKLIN	9,894	6,708	2,937	249	3,771 R	67.8%	29.7%	69.5%	30.5%
16,703	GRANT	8,097	5,334	2,588	175	2,746 R	65.9%	32.0%	67.3%	32.7%
63,752	IBERIA	28,526	17,727	10,170	629	7,557 R	62.1%	35.7%	63.5%	36.5%
32,159	IBERVILLE	15,159	6,455	8,587	117	2,132 D	42.6%	56.6%	42.9%	57.1%
17,321	JACKSON	7,761	5,034	2,568	159	2,466 R	64.9%	33.1%	66.2%	33.8%
454,592	JEFFERSON	166,023	123,997	41,183	843	82,814 R	74.7%	24.8%	75.1%	24.9%
32,168	JEFFERSON DAVIS	14,464	8,296	5,962	206	2,334 R	57.4%	41.2%	58.2%	41.8%
150,017	LAFAYETTE	64,458	44,344	19,265	849	25,079 R	68.8%	29.9%	69.7%	30.3%
82,483	LAFOURCHE	32,005	20,930	10,186	889	10,744 R	65.4%	31.8%	67.3%	32.7%
17,004	LA SALLE	6,875	5,404	1,318	153	4,086 R	78.6%	19.2%	80.4%	19.6%
39,763	LINCOLN	14,701	9,087	5,432	182	3,655 R	61.8%	36.9%	62.6%	37.4%
58,806	LIVINGSTON	26,576	17,465	8,913	198	8,552 R	65.7%	33.5%	66.2%	33.8%
15,975	MADISON	5,864	2,849	2,906	109	57 D	48.6%	49.6%	49.5%	50.5%
34,803	MOREHOUSE	13,685	8,585	4,829	271	3,756 R	62.7%	35.3%	64.0%	36.0%
39,863	NATCHITOCHES	14,978	8,836	5,806	336	3,030 R	59.0%	38.8%	60.3%	39.7%
557,515	ORLEANS	206,956	86,316	119,478	1,162	33,162 D	41.7%	57.7%	41.9%	58.1%
139,241	OUACHITA	53,574	37,270	15,525	779	21,745 R	69.6%	29.0%	70.6%	29.4%
26,049	PLAQUEMINES	10,977	7,655	3,261	61	4,394 R	69.7%	29.7%	70.1%	29.9%
24,045	POINTE COUPEE	12,287	5,477	6,732	78	1,255 D	44.6%	54.8%	44.9%	55.1%
135,282	RAPIDES	49,963	32,879	16,121	963	16,758 R	65.8%	32.3%	67.1%	32.9%
10,433	RED RIVER	5,067	3,060	1,958	49	1,102 R	60.4%	38.6%	61.0%	39.0%
22,187	RICHLAND	9,083	5,980	2,918	185	3,062 R	65.8%	32.1%	67.2%	32.8%
25,280	SABINE	9,500	6,295	2,980	225	3,315 R	66.3%	31.4%	67.9%	32.1%
64,097	ST. BERNARD	32,657	24,428	8,076	153	16,352 R	74.8%	24.7%	75.2%	24.8%
37,259	ST. CHARLES	17,082	10,185	6,784	113	3,401 R	59.6%	39.7%	60.0%	40.0%
9,827	ST. HELENA	5,435	2,366	2,956	113	590 D	43.5%	54.4%	44.5%	55.5%
21,495	ST. JAMES	10,735	4,627	5,989	119	1,362 D	43.1%	55.8%	43.6%	56.4%
31,924	ST. JOHN THE BAPTIST	16,851	9,093	7,646	112	1,447 R	54.0%	45.4%	54.3%	45.7%
84,128	ST. LANDRY	37,223	19,055	17,950	218	1,105 R	51.2%	48.2%	51.5%	48.5%
40,214	ST. MARTIN	18,591	9,698	8,589	304	1,109 R	52.2%	46.2%	53.0%	47.0%
64,253	ST. MARY	24,974	15,275	9,411	288	5,864 R	61.2%	37.7%	61.9%	38.1%
110,869	ST. TAMMANY	50,775	38,664	11,719	392	26,945 R	76.1%	23.1%	76.7%	23.3%
80,698	TANGIPAHOA	32,579	19,580	12,799	200	6,781 R	60.1%	39.3%	60.5%	39.5%
8,525	TENSAS	3,655	1,956	1,628	71	328 R	53.5%	44.5%	54.6%	45.4%
94,393	TERREBONNE	34,089	23,696	9,640	753	14,056 R	69.5%	28.3%	71.1%	28.9%
21,167	UNION	9,723	6,585	2,916	222	3,669 R	67.7%	30.0%	69.3%	30.7%
48,458	VERMILION	22,378	12,721	9,033	624	3,688 R	56.8%	40.4%	58.5%	41.5%
53,475	VERNON	13,369	9,035	4,076	258	4,959 R	67.6%	30.5%	68.9%	31.1%
44,207	WASHINGTON	18,988	11,185	7,680	123	3,505 R	58.9%	40.4%	59.3%	40.7%
43,631	WEBSTER	18,677	12,055	6,509	113	5,546 R	64.5%	34.9%	64.9%	35.1%

LOUISIANA

PRESIDENT 1984

1980 Census Population	Parish	Total Vote	Republican	Democratic	Other	Rep.-Dem. Plurality	Percentage Total Vote Rep.	Percentage Total Vote Dem.	Percentage Major Vote Rep.	Percentage Major Vote Dem.
19,086	WEST BATON ROUGE	8,883	4,189	4,631	63	442 D	47.2%	52.1%	47.5%	52.5%
12,922	WEST CARROLL	5,469	3,874	1,474	121	2,400 R	70.8%	27.0%	72.4%	27.6%
12,186	WEST FELICIANA	4,426	2,097	2,296	33	199 D	47.4%	51.9%	47.7%	52.3%
17,253	WINN	7,727	4,934	2,633	160	2,301 R	63.9%	34.1%	65.2%	34.8%
4,205,900	TOTAL	1,706,822	1,037,299	651,586	17,937	385,713 R	60.8%	38.2%	61.4%	38.6%

LOUISIANA

PRESIDENT 1980

1980 Census Population	Parish	Total Vote	Republican	Democratic	Other	Rep.-Dem. Plurality	Percentage Total Vote Rep.	Percentage Total Vote Dem.	Percentage Major Vote Rep.	Percentage Major Vote Dem.
56,427	ACADIA	22,100	11,533	9,948	619	1,585 R	52.2%	45.0%	53.7%	46.3%
21,390	ALLEN	9,564	3,328	6,057	179	2,729 D	34.8%	63.3%	35.5%	64.5%
50,068	ASCENSION	20,200	7,238	12,381	581	5,143 D	35.8%	61.3%	36.9%	63.1%
22,084	ASSUMPTION	9,073	4,001	4,679	393	678 D	44.1%	51.6%	46.1%	53.9%
41,393	AVOYELLES	16,071	8,216	7,174	681	1,042 R	51.1%	44.6%	53.4%	46.6%
29,692	BEAUREGARD	11,059	5,250	5,556	253	306 D	47.5%	50.2%	48.6%	51.4%
16,387	BIENVILLE	7,770	3,508	4,123	139	615 D	45.1%	53.1%	46.0%	54.0%
80,721	BOSSIER	26,339	16,515	9,377	447	7,138 R	62.7%	35.6%	63.8%	36.2%
252,358	CADDO	89,184	51,202	36,422	1,560	14,780 R	57.4%	40.8%	58.4%	41.6%
167,223	CALCASIEU	64,859	27,600	35,446	1,813	7,846 D	42.6%	54.7%	43.8%	56.2%
10,761	CALDWELL	4,581	2,653	1,786	142	867 R	57.9%	39.0%	59.8%	40.2%
9,336	CAMERON	3,798	1,449	2,221	128	772 D	38.2%	58.5%	39.5%	60.5%
12,287	CATAHOULA	5,531	2,942	2,414	175	528 R	53.2%	43.6%	54.9%	45.1%
17,095	CLAIBORNE	7,074	3,538	3,443	93	95 R	50.0%	48.7%	50.7%	49.3%
22,981	CONCORDIA	9,102	4,933	3,956	213	977 R	54.2%	43.5%	55.5%	44.5%
25,727	DE SOTO	10,327	4,349	5,861	117	1,512 D	42.1%	56.8%	42.6%	57.4%
366,191	EAST BATON ROUGE	133,168	71,063	57,442	4,663	13,621 R	53.4%	43.1%	55.3%	44.7%
11,772	EAST CARROLL	4,231	1,867	2,283	81	416 D	44.1%	54.0%	45.0%	55.0%
19,015	EAST FELICIANA	6,873	2,650	4,033	190	1,383 D	38.6%	58.7%	39.7%	60.3%
33,343	EVANGELINE	14,461	7,412	6,722	327	690 R	51.3%	46.5%	52.4%	47.6%
24,141	FRANKLIN	9,748	5,301	4,177	270	1,124 R	54.4%	42.8%	55.9%	44.1%
16,703	GRANT	7,148	3,611	3,290	247	321 R	50.5%	46.0%	52.3%	47.7%
63,752	IBERIA	25,028	14,273	9,681	1,074	4,592 R	57.0%	38.7%	59.6%	40.4%
32,159	IBERVILLE	14,135	4,463	9,361	311	4,898 D	31.6%	66.2%	32.3%	67.7%
17,321	JACKSON	7,730	3,923	3,609	198	314 R	50.8%	46.7%	52.1%	47.9%
454,592	JEFFERSON	155,111	99,403	50,870	4,838	48,533 R	64.1%	32.8%	66.1%	33.9%
32,168	JEFFERSON DAVIS	12,127	5,667	6,140	320	473 D	46.7%	50.6%	48.0%	52.0%
150,017	LAFAYETTE	53,526	31,429	19,694	2,403	11,735 R	58.7%	36.8%	61.5%	38.5%
82,483	LAFOURCHE	30,818	14,951	14,222	1,645	729 R	48.5%	46.1%	51.2%	48.8%
17,004	LA SALLE	6,634	3,792	2,665	177	1,127 R	57.2%	40.2%	58.7%	41.3%
39,763	LINCOLN	13,470	7,515	5,598	357	1,917 R	55.8%	41.6%	57.3%	42.7%
58,806	LIVINGSTON	22,609	10,666	11,319	624	653 D	47.2%	50.1%	48.5%	51.5%
15,975	MADISON	5,928	2,531	3,264	133	733 D	42.7%	55.1%	43.7%	56.3%
34,803	MOREHOUSE	12,397	7,254	4,856	287	2,398 R	58.5%	39.2%	59.9%	40.1%
39,863	NATCHITOCHES	14,189	6,668	7,102	419	434 D	47.0%	50.1%	48.4%	51.6%
557,515	ORLEANS	187,904	74,302	106,858	6,744	32,556 D	39.5%	56.9%	41.0%	59.0%
139,241	OUACHITA	47,314	29,799	16,306	1,209	13,493 R	63.0%	34.5%	64.6%	35.4%
26,049	PLAQUEMINES	10,079	5,489	4,318	272	1,171 R	54.5%	42.8%	56.0%	44.0%
24,045	POINTE COUPEE	10,263	3,667	6,395	201	2,728 D	35.7%	62.3%	36.4%	63.6%
135,282	RAPIDES	46,302	25,576	19,436	1,290	6,140 R	55.2%	42.0%	56.8%	43.2%
10,433	RED RIVER	4,986	2,147	2,776	63	629 D	43.1%	55.7%	43.6%	56.4%
22,187	RICHLAND	8,744	4,772	3,745	227	1,027 R	54.6%	42.8%	56.0%	44.0%
25,280	SABINE	9,585	4,265	5,100	220	835 D	44.5%	53.2%	45.5%	54.5%
64,097	ST. BERNARD	32,065	19,410	11,367	1,288	8,043 R	60.5%	35.4%	63.1%	36.9%
37,259	ST. CHARLES	15,123	6,779	7,898	446	1,119 D	44.8%	52.2%	46.2%	53.8%
9,827	ST. HELENA	4,852	1,531	3,183	138	1,652 D	31.6%	65.6%	32.5%	67.5%
21,495	ST. JAMES	9,824	3,429	6,206	189	2,777 D	34.9%	63.2%	35.6%	64.4%
31,924	ST. JOHN THE BAPTIST	13,861	5,819	7,647	395	1,828 D	42.0%	55.2%	43.2%	56.8%
84,128	ST. LANDRY	32,678	14,940	17,125	613	2,185 D	45.7%	52.4%	46.6%	53.4%
40,214	ST. MARTIN	15,040	6,701	7,760	579	1,059 D	44.6%	51.6%	46.3%	53.7%
64,253	ST. MARY	21,606	10,378	10,506	722	128 D	48.0%	48.6%	49.7%	50.3%
110,869	ST. TAMMANY	42,698	27,214	14,161	1,323	13,053 R	63.7%	33.2%	65.8%	34.2%
80,698	TANGIPAHOA	31,342	15,187	15,272	883	85 D	48.5%	48.7%	49.9%	50.1%
8,525	TENSAS	3,785	1,645	2,046	94	401 D	43.5%	54.1%	44.6%	55.4%
94,393	TERREBONNE	28,681	16,644	10,804	1,233	5,840 R	58.0%	37.7%	60.6%	39.4%
21,167	UNION	9,198	5,130	3,841	227	1,289 R	55.8%	41.8%	57.2%	42.8%
48,458	VERMILION	21,409	10,481	9,743	1,185	738 R	49.0%	45.5%	51.8%	48.2%
53,475	VERNON	13,436	5,869	7,198	369	1,329 D	43.7%	53.6%	44.9%	55.1%
44,207	WASHINGTON	19,472	8,681	10,413	378	1,732 D	44.6%	53.5%	45.5%	54.5%
43,631	WEBSTER	17,647	8,865	8,568	214	297 R	50.2%	48.6%	50.9%	49.1%

LOUISIANA

PRESIDENT 1980

1980 Census Population	Parish	Total Vote	Republican	Democratic	Other	Rep.-Dem. Plurality	Percentage Total Vote Rep.	Percentage Total Vote Dem.	Percentage Major Vote Rep.	Percentage Major Vote Dem.
19,086	WEST BATON ROUGE	7,753	2,828	4,739	186	1,911 D	36.5%	61.1%	37.4%	62.6%
12,922	WEST CARROLL	5,712	3,430	2,118	164	1,312 R	60.0%	37.1%	61.8%	38.2%
12,186	WEST FELICIANA	3,722	1,237	2,341	144	1,104 D	33.2%	62.9%	34.6%	65.4%
17,253	WINN	7,547	3,944	3,411	192	533 R	52.3%	45.2%	53.6%	46.4%
4,205,900	TOTAL	1,548,591	792,853	708,453	47,285	84,400 R	51.2%	45.7%	52.8%	47.2%

LOUISIANA

PRESIDENT 1976

1970 Census Population	Parish	Total Vote	Republican	Democratic	Other	Rep.-Dem. Plurality	Percentage Total Vote Rep.	Percentage Total Vote Dem.	Percentage Major Vote Rep.	Percentage Major Vote Dem.
52,109	ACADIA	17,648	6,296	10,814	538	4,518 D	35.7%	61.3%	36.8%	63.2%
20,794	ALLEN	7,673	2,080	5,373	220	3,293 D	27.1%	70.0%	27.9%	72.1%
37,086	ASCENSION	13,978	4,435	9,100	443	4,665 D	31.7%	65.1%	32.8%	67.2%
19,654	ASSUMPTION	7,711	3,117	4,401	193	1,284 D	40.4%	57.1%	41.5%	58.5%
37,751	AVOYELLES	13,315	4,574	8,104	637	3,530 D	34.4%	60.9%	36.1%	63.9%
22,888	BEAUREGARD	8,786	3,196	5,322	268	2,126 D	36.4%	60.6%	37.5%	62.5%
16,024	BIENVILLE	6,011	2,499	3,402	110	903 D	41.6%	56.6%	42.3%	57.7%
63,703	BOSSIER	20,487	12,132	8,062	293	4,070 R	59.2%	39.4%	60.1%	39.9%
230,184	CADDO	74,340	42,627	30,593	1,120	12,034 R	57.3%	41.2%	58.2%	41.8%
145,415	CALCASIEU	52,595	17,485	33,980	1,130	16,495 D	33.2%	64.6%	34.0%	66.0%
9,354	CALDWELL	3,806	1,890	1,830	86	60 R	49.7%	48.1%	50.8%	49.2%
8,194	CAMERON	3,338	819	2,432	87	1,613 D	24.5%	72.9%	25.2%	74.8%
11,769	CATAHOULA	4,767	2,086	2,547	134	461 D	43.8%	53.4%	45.0%	55.0%
17,024	CLAIBORNE	6,207	3,216	2,891	100	325 R	51.8%	46.6%	52.7%	47.3%
22,578	CONCORDIA	7,912	3,849	3,892	171	43 D	48.6%	49.2%	49.7%	50.3%
22,764	DE SOTO	8,348	3,601	4,630	117	1,029 D	43.1%	55.5%	43.7%	56.3%
285,167	EAST BATON ROUGE	103,807	51,655	49,956	2,196	1,699 R	49.8%	48.1%	50.8%	49.2%
12,884	EAST CARROLL	4,158	1,681	2,367	110	686 D	40.4%	56.9%	41.5%	58.5%
17,657	EAST FELICIANA	5,323	1,668	3,485	170	1,817 D	31.3%	65.5%	32.4%	67.6%
31,932	EVANGELINE	11,558	3,715	7,578	265	3,863 D	32.1%	65.6%	32.9%	67.1%
23,946	FRANKLIN	7,991	3,947	3,824	220	123 R	49.4%	47.9%	50.8%	49.2%
13,671	GRANT	6,136	2,280	3,670	186	1,390 D	37.2%	59.8%	38.3%	61.7%
57,397	IBERIA	20,753	10,392	9,984	377	408 R	50.1%	48.1%	51.0%	49.0%
30,746	IBERVILLE	11,389	3,822	7,254	313	3,432 D	33.6%	63.7%	34.5%	65.5%
15,963	JACKSON	7,060	3,310	3,605	145	295 D	46.9%	51.1%	47.9%	52.1%
338,229	JEFFERSON	127,560	71,787	53,257	2,516	18,530 R	56.3%	41.8%	57.4%	42.6%
29,554	JEFFERSON DAVIS	10,278	3,603	6,376	299	2,773 D	35.1%	62.0%	36.1%	63.9%
111,745	LAFAYETTE	43,699	22,805	19,918	976	2,887 R	52.2%	45.6%	53.4%	46.6%
68,941	LAFOURCHE	26,266	11,434	14,131	701	2,697 D	43.5%	53.8%	44.7%	55.3%
13,295	LA SALLE	6,310	3,161	2,961	188	200 R	50.1%	46.9%	51.6%	48.4%
33,800	LINCOLN	11,969	6,828	4,971	170	1,857 R	57.0%	41.5%	57.9%	42.1%
36,511	LIVINGSTON	15,895	5,555	9,875	465	4,320 D	34.9%	62.1%	36.0%	64.0%
15,065	MADISON	7,128	2,096	4,933	99	2,837 D	29.4%	69.2%	29.8%	70.2%
32,463	MOREHOUSE	9,692	5,418	4,017	257	1,401 R	55.9%	41.4%	57.4%	42.6%
35,219	NATCHITOCHES	12,417	5,248	6,692	477	1,444 D	42.3%	53.9%	44.0%	56.0%
593,471	ORLEANS	168,304	70,925	93,130	4,249	22,205 D	42.1%	55.3%	43.2%	56.8%
115,387	OUACHITA	40,451	24,082	15,738	631	8,344 R	59.5%	38.9%	60.5%	39.5%
25,225	PLAQUEMINES	8,855	6,052	2,614	189	3,438 R	68.3%	29.5%	69.8%	30.2%
22,002	POINTE COUPEE	7,876	2,567	5,147	162	2,580 D	32.6%	65.4%	33.3%	66.7%
118,078	RAPIDES	39,264	17,766	20,851	647	3,085 D	45.2%	53.1%	46.0%	54.0%
9,226	RED RIVER	3,707	1,728	1,906	73	178 D	46.6%	51.4%	47.6%	52.4%
21,774	RICHLAND	7,270	3,630	3,495	145	135 R	49.9%	48.1%	50.9%	49.1%
18,638	SABINE	8,351	3,531	4,555	265	1,024 D	42.3%	54.5%	43.7%	56.3%
51,185	ST. BERNARD	26,508	12,707	12,969	832	262 D	47.9%	48.9%	49.5%	50.5%
29,550	ST. CHARLES	11,505	4,270	6,872	363	2,602 D	37.1%	59.7%	38.3%	61.7%
9,937	ST. HELENA	3,788	1,046	2,622	120	1,576 D	27.6%	69.2%	28.5%	71.5%
19,733	ST. JAMES	7,466	2,751	4,531	184	1,780 D	36.8%	60.7%	37.8%	62.2%
23,813	ST. JOHN THE BAPTIST	9,609	3,597	5,700	312	2,103 D	37.4%	59.3%	38.7%	61.3%
80,364	ST. LANDRY	26,243	9,956	15,613	674	5,657 D	37.9%	59.5%	38.9%	61.1%
32,453	ST. MARTIN	12,433	4,112	7,992	329	3,880 D	33.1%	64.3%	34.0%	66.0%
60,752	ST. MARY	18,708	8,919	9,401	388	482 D	47.7%	50.3%	48.7%	51.3%
63,585	ST. TAMMANY	31,399	15,822	14,691	886	1,131 R	50.4%	46.8%	51.9%	48.1%
65,875	TANGIPAHOA	24,311	9,242	14,432	637	5,190 D	38.0%	59.4%	39.0%	61.0%
9,732	TENSAS	3,677	1,553	2,081	43	528 D	42.2%	56.6%	42.7%	57.3%
76,049	TERREBONNE	24,282	12,895	10,627	760	2,268 R	53.1%	43.8%	54.8%	45.2%
18,447	UNION	7,905	4,139	3,600	166	539 R	52.4%	45.5%	53.5%	46.5%
43,071	VERMILION	17,850	6,133	11,246	471	5,113 D	34.4%	63.0%	35.3%	64.7%
53,794	VERNON	10,465	3,970	6,202	293	2,232 D	37.9%	59.3%	39.0%	61.0%
41,987	WASHINGTON	16,073	5,677	10,000	396	4,323 D	35.3%	62.2%	36.2%	63.8%
39,939	WEBSTER	15,017	7,550	7,286	181	264 R	50.3%	48.5%	50.9%	49.1%

LOUISIANA

PRESIDENT 1976

1970 Census Population	Parish	Total Vote	Republican	Democratic	Other	Rep.-Dem. Plurality	Percentage Total Vote Rep.	Percentage Total Vote Dem.	Percentage Major Vote Rep.	Percentage Major Vote Dem.
16,864	WEST BATON ROUGE	5,884	1,913	3,809	162	1,896 D	32.5%	64.7%	33.4%	66.6%
13,028	WEST CARROLL	5,112	2,407	2,595	110	188 D	47.1%	50.8%	48.1%	51.9%
11,376	WEST FELICIANA	2,926	990	1,890	46	900 D	33.8%	64.6%	34.4%	65.6%
16,369	WINN	6,889	3,209	3,543	137	334 D	46.6%	51.4%	47.5%	52.5%
3,643,180	TOTAL	1,278,439	587,446	661,365	29,628	73,919 D	46.0%	51.7%	47.0%	53.0%

LOUISIANA

PRESIDENT 1972

1970 Census Population	Parish	Total Vote	Republican	Democratic	Other	Rep.-Dem. Plurality	Percentage Total Vote Rep.	Total Vote Dem.	Major Vote Rep.	Major Vote Dem.
52,109	ACADIA	15,194	9,698	4,406	1,090	5,292 R	63.8%	29.0%	68.8%	31.2%
20,794	ALLEN	6,028	3,581	2,029	418	1,552 R	59.4%	33.7%	63.8%	36.2%
37,086	ASCENSION	9,521	5,187	3,324	1,010	1,863 R	54.5%	34.9%	60.9%	39.1%
19,654	ASSUMPTION	6,365	3,751	2,065	549	1,686 R	58.9%	32.4%	64.5%	35.5%
37,751	AVOYELLES	10,778	6,225	3,395	1,158	2,830 R	57.8%	31.5%	64.7%	35.3%
22,888	BEAUREGARD	7,139	4,955	1,728	456	3,227 R	69.4%	24.2%	74.1%	25.9%
16,024	BIENVILLE	5,737	3,384	1,890	463	1,494 R	59.0%	32.9%	64.2%	35.8%
63,703	BOSSIER	16,350	12,856	2,914	580	9,942 R	78.6%	17.8%	81.5%	18.5%
230,184	CADDO	65,867	47,215	15,649	3,003	31,566 R	71.7%	23.8%	75.1%	24.9%
145,415	CALCASIEU	42,925	24,778	15,330	2,817	9,448 R	57.7%	35.7%	61.8%	38.2%
9,354	CALDWELL	2,995	2,306	508	181	1,798 R	77.0%	17.0%	81.9%	18.1%
8,194	CAMERON	2,284	1,391	739	154	652 R	60.9%	32.4%	65.3%	34.7%
11,769	CATAHOULA	3,668	2,683	823	162	1,860 R	73.1%	22.4%	76.5%	23.5%
17,024	CLAIBORNE	5,356	3,432	1,551	373	1,881 R	64.1%	29.0%	68.9%	31.1%
22,578	CONCORDIA	7,023	4,521	2,142	360	2,379 R	64.4%	30.5%	67.9%	32.1%
22,764	DE SOTO	7,153	4,017	2,596	540	1,421 R	56.2%	36.3%	60.7%	39.3%
285,167	EAST BATON ROUGE	80,542	52,648	23,617	4,277	29,031 R	65.4%	29.3%	69.0%	31.0%
12,884	EAST CARROLL	3,587	1,736	1,661	190	75 R	48.4%	46.3%	51.1%	48.9%
17,657	EAST FELICIANA	4,067	1,992	1,603	472	389 R	49.0%	39.4%	55.4%	44.6%
31,932	EVANGELINE	9,201	5,523	2,919	759	2,604 R	60.0%	31.7%	65.4%	34.6%
23,946	FRANKLIN	6,734	4,967	1,272	495	3,695 R	73.8%	18.9%	79.6%	20.4%
13,671	GRANT	4,739	3,626	859	254	2,767 R	76.5%	18.1%	80.8%	19.2%
57,397	IBERIA	17,940	11,812	5,143	985	6,669 R	65.8%	28.7%	69.7%	30.3%
30,746	IBERVILLE	8,466	3,972	3,650	844	322 R	46.9%	43.1%	52.1%	47.9%
15,963	JACKSON	5,935	4,152	1,477	306	2,675 R	70.0%	24.9%	73.8%	26.2%
338,229	JEFFERSON	101,841	75,348	20,981	5,512	54,367 R	74.0%	20.6%	78.2%	21.8%
29,554	JEFFERSON DAVIS	8,949	5,903	2,551	495	3,352 R	66.0%	28.5%	69.8%	30.2%
111,745	LAFAYETTE	33,198	22,939	8,740	1,519	14,199 R	69.1%	26.3%	72.4%	27.6%
68,941	LAFOURCHE	20,737	13,936	5,713	1,088	8,223 R	67.2%	27.5%	70.9%	29.1%
13,295	LA SALLE	4,733	3,858	651	224	3,207 R	81.5%	13.8%	85.6%	14.4%
33,800	LINCOLN	9,741	6,736	2,589	416	4,147 R	69.2%	26.6%	72.2%	27.8%
36,511	LIVINGSTON	10,253	7,481	1,898	874	5,583 R	73.0%	18.5%	79.8%	20.2%
15,065	MADISON	4,917	2,420	2,249	248	171 R	49.2%	45.7%	51.8%	48.2%
32,463	MOREHOUSE	8,620	5,770	2,355	495	3,415 R	66.9%	27.3%	71.0%	29.0%
35,219	NATCHITOCHES	10,803	6,994	3,180	629	3,814 R	64.7%	29.4%	68.7%	31.3%
593,471	ORLEANS	161,446	88,075	60,790	12,581	27,285 R	54.6%	37.7%	59.2%	40.8%
115,387	OUACHITA	33,263	24,860	6,920	1,483	17,940 R	74.7%	20.8%	78.2%	21.8%
25,225	PLAQUEMINES	7,941	6,595	990	356	5,605 R	83.0%	12.5%	86.9%	13.1%
22,002	POINTE COUPEE	6,853	3,192	3,133	528	59 R	46.6%	45.7%	50.5%	49.5%
118,078	RAPIDES	32,011	22,306	8,422	1,283	13,884 R	69.7%	26.3%	72.6%	27.4%
9,226	RED RIVER	3,404	2,245	957	202	1,288 R	66.0%	28.1%	70.1%	29.9%
21,774	RICHLAND	6,079	4,304	1,335	440	2,969 R	70.8%	22.0%	76.3%	23.7%
18,638	SABINE	6,680	4,935	1,332	413	3,603 R	73.9%	19.9%	78.7%	21.3%
51,185	ST. BERNARD	19,563	15,198	3,189	1,176	12,009 R	77.7%	16.3%	82.7%	17.3%
29,550	ST. CHARLES	9,052	5,469	2,788	795	2,681 R	60.4%	30.8%	66.2%	33.8%
9,937	ST. HELENA	2,781	1,446	943	392	503 R	52.0%	33.9%	60.5%	39.5%
19,733	ST. JAMES	6,291	3,112	2,633	546	479 R	49.5%	41.9%	54.2%	45.8%
23,813	ST. JOHN THE BAPTIST	7,086	3,525	2,815	746	710 R	49.7%	39.7%	55.6%	44.4%
80,364	ST. LANDRY	21,945	12,510	7,421	2,014	5,089 R	57.0%	33.8%	62.8%	37.2%
32,453	ST. MARTIN	10,221	6,337	3,202	682	3,135 R	62.0%	31.3%	66.4%	33.6%
60,752	ST. MARY	16,243	11,117	4,435	691	6,682 R	68.4%	27.3%	71.5%	28.5%
63,585	ST. TAMMANY	20,825	15,438	3,949	1,438	11,489 R	74.1%	19.0%	79.6%	20.4%
65,875	TANGIPAHOA	18,457	11,607	5,227	1,623	6,380 R	62.9%	28.3%	68.9%	31.1%
9,732	TENSAS	3,426	1,729	1,568	129	161 R	50.5%	45.8%	52.4%	47.6%
76,049	TERREBONNE	19,182	13,753	4,415	1,014	9,338 R	71.7%	23.0%	75.7%	24.3%
18,447	UNION	6,157	4,322	1,465	370	2,857 R	70.2%	23.8%	74.7%	25.3%
43,071	VERMILION	13,420	8,909	3,876	635	5,033 R	66.4%	28.9%	69.7%	30.3%
53,794	VERNON	8,020	6,225	1,345	450	4,880 R	77.6%	16.8%	82.2%	17.8%
41,987	WASHINGTON	12,196	8,162	2,947	1,087	5,215 R	66.9%	24.2%	73.5%	26.5%
39,939	WEBSTER	12,349	8,829	2,859	661	5,970 R	71.5%	23.2%	75.5%	24.5%

LOUISIANA

PRESIDENT 1972

1970 Census Population	Parish	Total Vote	Republican	Democratic	Other	Rep.-Dem. Plurality	Percentage Total Vote Rep.	Total Vote Dem.	Major Vote Rep.	Major Vote Dem.
16,864	WEST BATON ROUGE	4,942	2,626	1,849	467	777 R	53.1%	37.4%	58.7%	41.3%
13,028	WEST CARROLL	3,880	2,997	571	312	2,426 R	77.2%	14.7%	84.0%	16.0%
11,376	WEST FELICIANA	2,376	1,001	1,079	296	78 D	42.1%	45.4%	48.1%	51.9%
16,369	WINN	6,016	4,235	1,490	291	2,745 R	70.4%	24.8%	74.0%	26.0%
3,643,180	TOTAL	1,051,491	686,852	298,142	66,497	388,710 R	65.3%	28.4%	69.7%	30.3%

LOUISIANA

PRESIDENT 1968

1960 Census Population	Parish	Total Vote	Republican	Democratic	AIP	Other	Plurality	Percentage Rep.	Dem.	AIP
49,931	ACADIA	16,991	3,178	4,098	9,715		5,617 A	18.7%	24.1%	57.2%
19,867	ALLEN	7,259	1,004	2,026	4,229		2,203 A	13.8%	27.9%	58.3%
27,927	ASCENSION	10,545	1,338	3,203	6,004		2,801 A	12.7%	30.4%	56.9%
17,991	ASSUMPTION	6,205	1,222	2,085	2,898		813 A	19.7%	33.6%	46.7%
37,606	AVOYELLES	12,192	2,459	2,973	6,760		3,787 A	20.2%	24.4%	55.4%
19,191	BEAUREGARD	7,232	1,615	1,569	4,048		2,433 A	22.3%	21.7%	56.0%
16,726	BIENVILLE	6,175	941	1,768	3,466		1,698 A	15.2%	28.6%	56.1%
57,622	BOSSIER	15,776	3,745	2,782	9,249		5,504 A	23.7%	17.6%	58.6%
223,859	CADDO	67,362	21,224	17,675	28,463		7,239 A	31.5%	26.2%	42.3%
145,475	CALCASIEU	44,363	9,520	14,593	20,250		5,657 A	21.5%	32.9%	45.6%
9,004	CALDWELL	3,715	490	973	2,252		1,279 A	13.2%	26.2%	60.6%
6,909	CAMERON	2,593	405	533	1,655		1,122 A	15.6%	20.6%	63.8%
11,421	CATAHOULA	4,201	755	769	2,677		1,908 A	18.0%	18.3%	63.7%
19,407	CLAIBORNE	5,973	1,117	1,545	3,311		1,766 A	18.7%	25.9%	55.4%
20,467	CONCORDIA	7,499	974	1,983	4,542		2,559 A	13.0%	26.4%	60.6%
24,248	DE SOTO	8,564	974	3,400	4,190		790 A	11.4%	39.7%	48.9%
230,058	EAST BATON ROUGE	78,681	21,661	21,770	35,250		13,480 A	27.5%	27.7%	44.8%
14,433	EAST CARROLL	4,218	586	1,926	1,706		220 D	13.9%	45.7%	40.4%
20,198	EAST FELICIANA	4,091	457	1,409	2,225		816 A	11.2%	34.4%	54.4%
31,639	EVANGELINE	11,558	1,549	2,647	7,362		4,715 A	13.4%	22.9%	63.7%
26,088	FRANKLIN	7,127	1,052	681	5,394		4,342 A	14.8%	9.6%	75.7%
13,330	GRANT	5,515	1,113	932	3,470		2,357 A	20.2%	16.9%	62.9%
51,657	IBERIA	19,029	5,448	5,510	8,071		2,561 A	28.6%	29.0%	42.4%
29,939	IBERVILLE	9,787	1,413	4,084	4,290		206 A	14.4%	41.7%	43.8%
15,828	JACKSON	6,570	1,104	1,525	3,941		2,416 A	16.8%	23.2%	60.0%
208,769	JEFFERSON	91,573	29,478	20,193	41,902		12,424 A	32.2%	22.1%	45.8%
29,825	JEFFERSON DAVIS	9,751	2,213	2,641	4,897		2,256 A	22.7%	27.1%	50.2%
84,656	LAFAYETTE	30,375	10,669	7,983	11,723		1,054 A	35.1%	26.3%	38.6%
55,381	LAFOURCHE	21,223	4,797	5,516	10,910		5,394 A	22.6%	26.0%	51.4%
13,011	LA SALLE	5,846	1,258	710	3,878		2,620 A	21.5%	12.1%	66.3%
28,535	LINCOLN	8,877	2,643	2,009	4,225		1,582 A	29.8%	22.6%	47.6%
26,974	LIVINGSTON	12,254	947	1,400	9,907		8,507 A	7.7%	11.4%	80.8%
16,444	MADISON	5,688	649	2,659	2,380		279 D	11.4%	46.7%	41.8%
33,709	MOREHOUSE	8,942	1,772	1,793	5,377		3,584 A	19.8%	20.1%	60.1%
35,653	NATCHITOCHES	11,802	2,352	3,945	5,505		1,560 A	19.9%	33.4%	46.6%
627,525	ORLEANS	178,668	47,728	72,451	58,489		13,962 D	26.7%	40.6%	32.7%
101,663	OUACHITA	31,704	10,089	6,470	15,145		5,056 A	31.8%	20.4%	47.8%
22,545	PLAQUEMINES	8,542	968	1,144	6,430		5,286 A	11.3%	13.4%	75.3%
22,488	POINTE COUPEE	7,497	850	3,139	3,508		369 A	11.3%	41.9%	46.8%
111,351	RAPIDES	35,231	10,199	8,793	16,239		6,040 A	28.9%	25.0%	46.1%
9,978	RED RIVER	3,771	380	914	2,477		1,563 A	10.1%	24.2%	65.7%
23,824	RICHLAND	6,463	1,031	1,017	4,415		3,384 A	16.0%	15.7%	68.3%
18,564	SABINE	6,810	1,125	1,159	4,526		3,367 A	16.5%	17.0%	66.5%
32,186	ST. BERNARD	19,027	3,486	2,485	13,056		9,570 A	18.3%	13.1%	68.6%
21,219	ST. CHARLES	9,128	1,675	3,070	4,383		1,313 A	18.4%	33.6%	48.0%
9,162	ST. HELENA	3,370	219	1,351	1,800		449 A	6.5%	40.1%	53.4%
18,369	ST. JAMES	6,530	778	2,987	2,765		222 D	11.9%	45.7%	42.3%
18,439	ST. JOHN THE BAPTIST	7,431	940	3,245	3,246		1 A	12.6%	43.7%	43.7%
81,493	ST. LANDRY	25,242	3,508	9,075	12,659		3,584 A	13.9%	36.0%	50.2%
29,063	ST. MARTIN	9,705	1,625	3,321	4,759		1,438 A	16.7%	34.2%	49.0%
48,833	ST. MARY	16,659	4,586	5,312	6,761		1,449 A	27.5%	31.9%	40.6%
38,643	ST. TAMMANY	20,761	4,846	4,445	11,470		6,624 A	23.3%	21.4%	55.2%
59,434	TANGIPAHOA	20,978	2,907	4,983	13,088		8,105 A	13.9%	23.8%	62.4%
11,796	TENSAS	2,638	503	845	1,290		445 A	19.1%	32.0%	48.9%
60,771	TERREBONNE	18,677	5,214	4,627	8,836		3,622 A	27.9%	24.8%	47.3%
17,624	UNION	6,746	1,113	1,336	4,297		2,961 A	16.5%	19.8%	63.7%
38,855	VERMILION	15,208	3,278	3,806	8,124		4,318 A	21.6%	25.0%	53.4%
18,301	VERNON	8,606	1,574	1,496	5,536		3,962 A	18.3%	17.4%	64.3%
44,015	WASHINGTON	15,718	1,695	3,021	11,002		7,981 A	10.8%	19.2%	70.0%
39,701	WEBSTER	14,013	2,496	2,871	8,646		5,775 A	17.8%	20.5%	61.7%

LOUISIANA

PRESIDENT 1968

1960 Census Population	Parish	Total Vote	Republican	Democratic	AIP	Other	Plurality	Percentage Rep.	Dem.	AIP
14,796	WEST BATON ROUGE	5,254	669	2,016	2,569		553 A	12.7%	38.4%	48.9%
14,177	WEST CARROLL	4,554	585	395	3,574		2,989 A	12.8%	8.7%	78.5%
12,395	WEST FELICIANA	2,672	296	1,303	1,073		230 D	11.1%	48.8%	40.2%
16,034	WINN	6,295	1,050	1,230	4,015		2,785 A	16.7%	19.5%	63.8%
3,257,022	TOTAL	1,097,450	257,535	309,615	530,300		220,685 A	23.5%	28.2%	48.3%

LOUISIANA

ELECTION NOTES

1984 Other vote was 9,502 Johnson (Citizens); 3,552 LaRouche (Independent); 1,876 Bergland (Libertarian); 1,310 Richards (Populist); 1,164 Mason (Socialist Workers); 533 Serrette (New Alliance).

1980 Other vote was 26,345 Anderson (Independent); 10,333 Rarick (American Independent); 8,240 Clark (Libertarian); 1,584 Commoner (Citizens); 783 DeBerry (Socialist Workers).

1976 Other vote was 10,058 Maddox (American); 7,417 Hall (Communist); 6,588 McCarthy (Independent); 3,325 MacBride (Libertarian); 2,240 Camejo (Socialist Workers). Although the data indicate a possible discrepancy in the Democratic vote in Madison county, the official state canvass figures are used here.

1972 Other vote was 52,099 Schmitz (American); 14,398 no Presidential candidate indicated (Socialist Workers).

1968 Wallace on the ballot as American.

MAINE

POPULAR VOTE FOR PRESIDENT 1920 TO 1984

Year	Total Vote	Republican Vote	Republican Candidate	Democratic Vote	Democratic Candidate	Other Vote	Plurality	Percentage Total Vote Rep.	Percentage Total Vote Dem.	Percentage Major Vote Rep.	Percentage Major Vote Dem.
1984	553,144	336,500	Reagan, Ronald	214,515	Mondale, Walter F.	2,129	121,985 R	60.8%	38.8%	61.1%	38.9%
1980	523,011	238,522	Reagan, Ronald	220,974	Carter, Jimmy	63,515	17,548 R	45.6%	42.3%	51.9%	48.1%
1976	483,216	236,320	Ford, Gerald R.	232,279	Carter, Jimmy	14,617	4,041 R	48.9%	48.1%	50.4%	49.6%
1972	417,042	256,458	Nixon, Richard M.	160,584	McGovern, George S.		95,874 R	61.5%	38.5%	61.5%	38.5%
1968	392,936	169,254	Nixon, Richard M.	217,312	Humphrey, Hubert H.	6,370	48,058 D	43.1%	55.3%	43.8%	56.2%
1964	380,965	118,701	Goldwater, Barry M.	262,264	Johnson, Lyndon B.		143,563 D	31.2%	68.8%	31.2%	68.8%
1960	421,767	240,608	Nixon, Richard M.	181,159	Kennedy, John F.		59,449 R	57.0%	43.0%	57.0%	43.0%
1956	351,706	249,238	Eisenhower, Dwight D.	102,468	Stevenson, Adlai E.		146,770 R	70.9%	29.1%	70.9%	29.1%
1952	351,786	232,353	Eisenhower, Dwight D.	118,806	Stevenson, Adlai E.	627	113,547 R	66.0%	33.8%	66.2%	33.8%
1948	264,787	150,234	Dewey, Thomas E.	111,916	Truman, Harry S.	2,637	38,318 R	56.7%	42.3%	57.3%	42.7%
1944	296,400	155,434	Dewey, Thomas E.	140,631	Roosevelt, Franklin D.	335	14,803 R	52.4%	47.4%	52.5%	47.5%
1940	320,840	163,951	Willkie, Wendell	156,478	Roosevelt, Franklin D.	411	7,473 R	51.1%	48.8%	51.2%	48.8%
1936	304,240	168,823	Landon, Alfred M.	126,333	Roosevelt, Franklin D.	9,084	42,490 R	55.5%	41.5%	57.2%	42.8%
1932	298,444	166,631	Hoover, Herbert C.	128,907	Roosevelt, Franklin D.	2,906	37,724 R	55.8%	43.2%	56.4%	43.6%
1928	262,170	179,923	Hoover, Herbert C.	81,179	Smith, Alfred E.	1,068	98,744 R	68.6%	31.0%	68.9%	31.1%
1924	192,192	138,440	Coolidge, Calvin	41,964	Davis, John W.	11,788	96,476 R	72.0%	21.8%	76.7%	23.3%
1920	197,840	136,355	Harding, Warren G.	58,961	Cox, James M.	2,524	77,394 R	68.9%	29.8%	69.8%	30.2%

ELECTORAL COLLEGE VOTE 1920 TO 1984

Year	Total	Republican	Democratic	Other
1984	4	4	—	—
1980	4	4	—	—
1976	4	4	—	—
1972	4	4	—	—
1968	4	—	4	—
1964	4	—	4	—
1960	5	5	—	—
1956	5	5	—	—
1952	5	5	—	—
1948	5	5	—	—
1944	5	5	—	—
1940	5	5	—	—
1936	5	5	—	—
1932	5	5	—	—
1928	6	6	—	—
1924	6	6	—	—
1920	6	6	—	—

MAINE

AROOSTOOK
PISCATAQUIS
SOMERSET
PENOBSCOT
WASHINGTON
FRANKLIN
HANCOCK
WALDO
OXFORD
KENNEBEC
ANDROSCOGGIN
KNOX
SAGADAHOC
LINCOLN
CUMBERLAND
YORK

MAINE

PRESIDENT 1984

1980 Census Population	County	Total Vote	Republican	Democratic	Other	Rep.-Dem. Plurality	Percentage Total Vote Rep.	Total Vote Dem.	Major Vote Rep.	Major Vote Dem.
99,657	ANDROSCOGGIN	47,000	26,904	19,885	211	7,019 R	57.2%	42.3%	57.5%	42.5%
91,331	AROOSTOOK	34,338	21,837	12,348	153	9,489 R	63.6%	36.0%	63.9%	36.1%
215,789	CUMBERLAND	116,026	65,842	49,894	290	15,948 R	56.7%	43.0%	56.9%	43.1%
27,098	FRANKLIN	13,349	8,330	4,954	65	3,376 R	62.4%	37.1%	62.7%	37.3%
41,781	HANCOCK	22,511	14,660	7,764	87	6,896 R	65.1%	34.5%	65.4%	34.6%
109,889	KENNEBEC	53,191	31,753	21,183	255	10,570 R	59.7%	39.8%	60.0%	40.0%
32,941	KNOX	17,401	11,311	6,024	66	5,287 R	65.0%	34.6%	65.2%	34.8%
25,691	LINCOLN	15,236	10,312	4,869	55	5,443 R	67.7%	32.0%	67.9%	32.1%
48,968	OXFORD	23,948	15,408	8,430	110	6,978 R	64.3%	35.2%	64.6%	35.4%
137,015	PENOBSCOT	65,054	40,403	24,445	206	15,958 R	62.1%	37.6%	62.3%	37.7%
17,634	PISCATAQUIS	8,482	5,427	3,016	39	2,411 R	64.0%	35.6%	64.3%	35.7%
28,795	SAGADAHOC	14,520	9,222	5,208	90	4,014 R	63.5%	35.9%	63.9%	36.1%
45,028	SOMERSET	20,771	13,010	7,657	104	5,353 R	62.6%	36.9%	63.0%	37.0%
28,414	WALDO	14,166	8,814	5,289	63	3,525 R	62.2%	37.3%	62.5%	37.5%
34,963	WASHINGTON	15,081	9,713	5,308	60	4,405 R	64.4%	35.2%	64.7%	35.3%
139,666	YORK	72,070	43,554	28,241	275	15,313 R	60.4%	39.2%	60.7%	39.3%
1,124,660	TOTAL	553,144	336,500	214,515	2,129	121,985 R	60.8%	38.8%	61.1%	38.9%

MAINE

PRESIDENT 1980

1980 Census Population	County	Total Vote	Republican	Democratic	Other	Rep.-Dem. Plurality	Percentage Total Vote Rep.	Total Vote Dem.	Major Vote Rep.	Major Vote Dem.
99,657	ANDROSCOGGIN	46,080	18,399	22,715	4,966	4,316 D	39.9%	49.3%	44.8%	55.2%
91,331	AROOSTOOK	33,846	16,343	14,492	3,011	1,851 R	48.3%	42.8%	53.0%	47.0%
215,789	CUMBERLAND	107,461	45,820	47,337	14,304	1,517 D	42.6%	44.1%	49.2%	50.8%
27,098	FRANKLIN	12,128	5,680	4,979	1,469	701 R	46.8%	41.1%	53.3%	46.7%
41,781	HANCOCK	21,334	11,435	7,027	2,872	4,408 R	53.6%	32.9%	61.9%	38.1%
109,889	KENNEBEC	49,077	21,517	20,943	6,617	574 R	43.8%	42.7%	50.7%	49.3%
32,941	KNOX	15,581	7,631	5,732	2,218	1,899 R	49.0%	36.8%	57.1%	42.9%
25,691	LINCOLN	14,259	7,434	4,776	2,049	2,658 R	52.1%	33.5%	60.9%	39.1%
48,968	OXFORD	23,474	11,041	9,914	2,519	1,127 R	47.0%	42.2%	52.7%	47.3%
137,015	PENOBSCOT	62,793	28,869	26,519	7,405	2,350 R	46.0%	42.2%	52.1%	47.9%
17,634	PISCATAQUIS	8,555	4,015	3,550	990	465 R	46.9%	41.5%	53.1%	46.9%
28,795	SAGADAHOC	13,145	5,946	5,663	1,536	283 R	45.2%	43.1%	51.2%	48.8%
45,028	SOMERSET	19,513	9,286	8,115	2,112	1,171 R	47.6%	41.6%	53.4%	46.6%
28,414	WALDO	13,140	6,514	4,883	1,743	1,631 R	49.6%	37.2%	57.2%	42.8%
34,963	WASHINGTON	14,788	7,180	6,050	1,558	1,130 R	48.6%	40.9%	54.3%	45.7%
139,666	YORK	67,837	31,412	28,279	8,146	3,133 R	46.3%	41.7%	52.6%	47.4%
1,124,660	TOTAL	523,011	238,522	220,974	63,515	17,548 R	45.6%	42.3%	51.9%	48.1%

MAINE

PRESIDENT 1976

1970 Census Population	County	Total Vote	Republican	Democratic	Other	Rep.-Dem. Plurality	Percentage Total Vote Rep.	Percentage Total Vote Dem.	Percentage Major Vote Rep.	Percentage Major Vote Dem.
91,279	ANDROSCOGGIN	43,665	16,330	26,484	851	10,154 D	37.4%	60.7%	38.1%	61.9%
94,078	AROOSTOOK	32,051	15,550	15,484	1,017	66 R	48.5%	48.3%	50.1%	49.9%
192,528	CUMBERLAND	98,626	48,959	47,007	2,660	1,952 R	49.6%	47.7%	51.0%	49.0%
22,444	FRANKLIN	11,384	5,799	5,140	445	659 R	50.9%	45.2%	53.0%	47.0%
34,590	HANCOCK	19,647	12,064	6,725	858	5,339 R	61.4%	34.2%	64.2%	35.8%
95,247	KENNEBEC	47,412	22,534	23,473	1,405	939 D	47.5%	49.5%	49.0%	51.0%
29,013	KNOX	14,786	8,315	5,922	549	2,393 R	56.2%	40.1%	58.4%	41.6%
20,537	LINCOLN	12,797	7,554	4,818	425	2,736 R	59.0%	37.6%	61.1%	38.9%
43,457	OXFORD	21,516	10,551	10,340	625	211 R	49.0%	48.1%	50.5%	49.5%
125,393	PENOBSCOT	55,613	29,016	24,672	1,925	4,344 R	52.2%	44.4%	54.0%	46.0%
16,285	PISCATAQUIS	8,090	4,084	3,727	279	357 R	50.5%	46.1%	52.3%	47.7%
23,452	SAGADAHOC	11,876	5,988	5,529	359	459 R	50.4%	46.6%	52.0%	48.0%
40,597	SOMERSET	18,966	8,868	9,465	633	597 D	46.8%	49.9%	48.4%	51.6%
23,328	WALDO	11,633	6,289	4,853	491	1,436 R	54.1%	41.7%	56.4%	43.6%
29,859	WASHINGTON	14,235	7,039	6,644	552	395 R	49.4%	46.7%	51.4%	48.6%
111,576	YORK	60,919	27,380	31,996	1,543	4,616 D	44.9%	52.5%	46.1%	53.9%
993,663	TOTAL	483,216	236,320	232,279	14,617	4,041 R	48.9%	48.1%	50.4%	49.6%

MAINE

PRESIDENT 1972

1970 Census Population	County	Total Vote	Republican	Democratic	Other	Rep.-Dem. Plurality	Percentage Total Vote Rep.	Percentage Total Vote Dem.	Percentage Major Vote Rep.	Percentage Major Vote Dem.
91,279	ANDROSCOGGIN	38,915	19,406	19,509		103 D	49.9%	50.1%	49.9%	50.1%
94,078	AROOSTOOK	30,525	19,051	11,474		7,577 R	62.4%	37.6%	62.4%	37.6%
192,528	CUMBERLAND	84,594	51,268	33,326		17,942 R	60.6%	39.4%	60.6%	39.4%
22,444	FRANKLIN	8,946	5,958	2,988		2,970 R	66.6%	33.4%	66.6%	33.4%
34,590	HANCOCK	16,080	11,889	4,191		7,698 R	73.9%	26.1%	73.9%	26.1%
95,247	KENNEBEC	40,996	24,617	16,379		8,238 R	60.0%	40.0%	60.0%	40.0%
29,013	KNOX	12,079	8,478	3,601		4,877 R	70.2%	29.8%	70.2%	29.8%
20,537	LINCOLN	10,483	7,580	2,903		4,677 R	72.3%	27.7%	72.3%	27.7%
43,457	OXFORD	18,775	12,114	6,661		5,453 R	64.5%	35.5%	64.5%	35.5%
125,393	PENOBSCOT	48,738	30,186	18,552		11,634 R	61.9%	38.1%	61.9%	38.1%
16,285	PISCATAQUIS	7,135	4,617	2,518		2,099 R	64.7%	35.3%	64.7%	35.3%
23,452	SAGADAHOC	9,877	6,463	3,414		3,049 R	65.4%	34.6%	65.4%	34.6%
40,597	SOMERSET	16,000	10,079	5,921		4,158 R	63.0%	37.0%	63.0%	37.0%
23,328	WALDO	9,421	6,480	2,941		3,539 R	68.8%	31.2%	68.8%	31.2%
29,859	WASHINGTON	11,562	7,820	3,742		4,078 R	67.6%	32.4%	67.6%	32.4%
111,576	YORK	52,916	30,452	22,464		7,988 R	57.5%	42.5%	57.5%	42.5%
993,663	TOTAL	417,042	256,458	160,584		95,874 R	61.5%	38.5%	61.5%	38.5%

MAINE

PRESIDENT 1968

1960 Census Population	County	Total Vote	Republican	Democratic	AIP	Other	Plurality	Percentage Rep.	Dem.	AIP
86,312	ANDROSCOGGIN	37,752	10,390	26,820	542		16,430 D	27.5%	71.0%	1.4%
106,064	AROOSTOOK	29,236	13,919	15,044	273		1,125 D	47.6%	51.5%	0.9%
182,751	CUMBERLAND	78,048	32,275	44,697	1,076		12,422 D	41.4%	57.3%	1.4%
20,069	FRANKLIN	8,596	4,127	4,307	162		180 D	48.0%	50.1%	1.9%
32,293	HANCOCK	14,185	8,929	4,979	277		3,950 R	62.9%	35.1%	2.0%
89,150	KENNEBEC	38,292	16,009	21,752	531		5,743 D	41.8%	56.8%	1.4%
28,575	KNOX	11,918	6,585	5,119	214		1,466 R	55.3%	43.0%	1.8%
18,497	LINCOLN	9,261	5,659	3,380	222		2,279 R	61.1%	36.5%	2.4%
44,345	OXFORD	19,275	8,030	10,870	375		2,840 D	41.7%	56.4%	1.9%
126,346	PENOBSCOT	44,999	20,011	24,327	661		4,316 D	44.5%	54.1%	1.5%
17,379	PISCATAQUIS	6,918	3,199	3,561	158		362 D	46.2%	51.5%	2.3%
22,793	SAGADAHOC	9,888	4,126	5,553	209		1,427 D	41.7%	56.2%	2.1%
39,749	SOMERSET	15,356	6,720	8,312	324		1,592 D	43.8%	54.1%	2.1%
22,632	WALDO	8,580	4,821	3,525	234		1,296 R	56.2%	41.1%	2.7%
32,908	WASHINGTON	11,980	5,523	6,249	208		726 D	46.1%	52.2%	1.7%
99,402	YORK	48,652	18,931	28,817	904		9,886 D	38.9%	59.2%	1.9%
969,265	TOTAL	392,936	169,254	217,312	6,370		48,058 D	43.1%	55.3%	1.6%

MAINE

ELECTION NOTES

1984 Other vote was 1,292 Hall (Independent); 755 Serrette (Independent); 82 scattered write-in.

1980 Other vote was 53,327 Anderson (Independent); 5,119 Clark (Libertarian); 4,394 Commoner (Citizens); 591 Hall (Communist); 84 scattered write-in.

1976 Other vote was 10,874 McCarthy (Independent); 3,495 Bubar (Prohibition); 28 Anderson (write-in); 14 Hall (write-in); 11 MacBride (write-in); 8 Maddox (write-in); 1 Camejo (write-in); 1 Levin (write-in); 185 scattered write-in.

1972

1968 Wallace on the ballot as George C. Wallace party.

MARYLAND

POPULAR VOTE FOR PRESIDENT 1920 TO 1984

Year	Total Vote	Republican Vote	Republican Candidate	Democratic Vote	Democratic Candidate	Other Vote	Plurality	Percentage Total Vote Rep.	Percentage Total Vote Dem.	Percentage Major Vote Rep.	Percentage Major Vote Dem.
1984	1,675,873	879,918	Reagan, Ronald	787,935	Mondale, Walter F.	8,020	91,983 R	52.5%	47.0%	52.8%	47.2%
1980	1,540,496	680,606	Reagan, Ronald	726,161	Carter, Jimmy	133,729	45,555 D	44.2%	47.1%	48.4%	51.6%
1976	1,439,897	672,661	Ford, Gerald R.	759,612	Carter, Jimmy	7,624	86,951 D	46.7%	52.8%	47.0%	53.0%
1972	1,353,812	829,305	Nixon, Richard M.	505,781	McGovern, George S.	18,726	323,524 R	61.3%	37.4%	62.1%	37.9%
1968	1,235,039	517,995	Nixon, Richard M.	538,310	Humphrey, Hubert H.	178,734	20,315 D	41.9%	43.6%	49.0%	51.0%
1964	1,116,457	385,495	Goldwater, Barry M.	730,912	Johnson, Lyndon B.	50	345,417 D	34.5%	65.5%	34.5%	65.5%
1960	1,055,349	489,538	Nixon, Richard M.	565,808	Kennedy, John F.	3	76,270 D	46.4%	53.6%	46.4%	53.6%
1956	932,827	559,738	Eisenhower, Dwight D.	372,613	Stevenson, Adlai E.	476	187,125 R	60.0%	39.9%	60.0%	40.0%
1952	902,074	499,424	Eisenhower, Dwight D.	395,337	Stevenson, Adlai E.	7,313	104,087 R	55.4%	43.8%	55.8%	44.2%
1948	596,748	294,814	Dewey, Thomas E.	286,521	Truman, Harry S.	15,413	8,293 R	49.4%	48.0%	50.7%	49.3%
1944	608,439	292,949	Dewey, Thomas E.	315,490	Roosevelt, Franklin D.		22,541 D	48.1%	51.9%	48.1%	51.9%
1940	660,104	269,534	Willkie, Wendell	384,546	Roosevelt, Franklin D.	6,024	115,012 D	40.8%	58.3%	41.2%	58.8%
1936	624,896	231,435	Landon, Alfred M.	389,612	Roosevelt, Franklin D.	3,849	158,177 D	37.0%	62.3%	37.3%	62.7%
1932	511,054	184,184	Hoover, Herbert C.	314,314	Roosevelt, Franklin D.	12,556	130,130 D	36.0%	61.5%	36.9%	63.1%
1928	528,348	301,479	Hoover, Herbert C.	223,626	Smith, Alfred E.	3,243	77,853 R	57.1%	42.3%	57.4%	42.6%
1924	358,630	162,414	Coolidge, Calvin	148,072	Davis, John W.	48,144	14,342 R	45.3%	41.3%	52.3%	47.7%
1920	428,443	236,117	Harding, Warren G.	180,626	Cox, James M.	11,700	55,491 R	55.1%	42.2%	56.7%	43.3%

ELECTORAL COLLEGE VOTE 1920 TO 1984

Year	Total	Republican	Democratic	Other
1984	10	10	—	—
1980	10	—	10	—
1976	10	—	10	—
1972	10	10	—	—
1968	10	—	10	—
1964	10	—	10	—
1960	9	—	9	—
1956	9	9	—	—
1952	9	9	—	—
1948	8	8	—	—
1944	8	—	8	—
1940	8	—	8	—
1936	8	—	8	—
1932	8	—	8	—
1928	8	8	—	—
1924	8	8	—	—
1920	8	8	—	—

MARYLAND

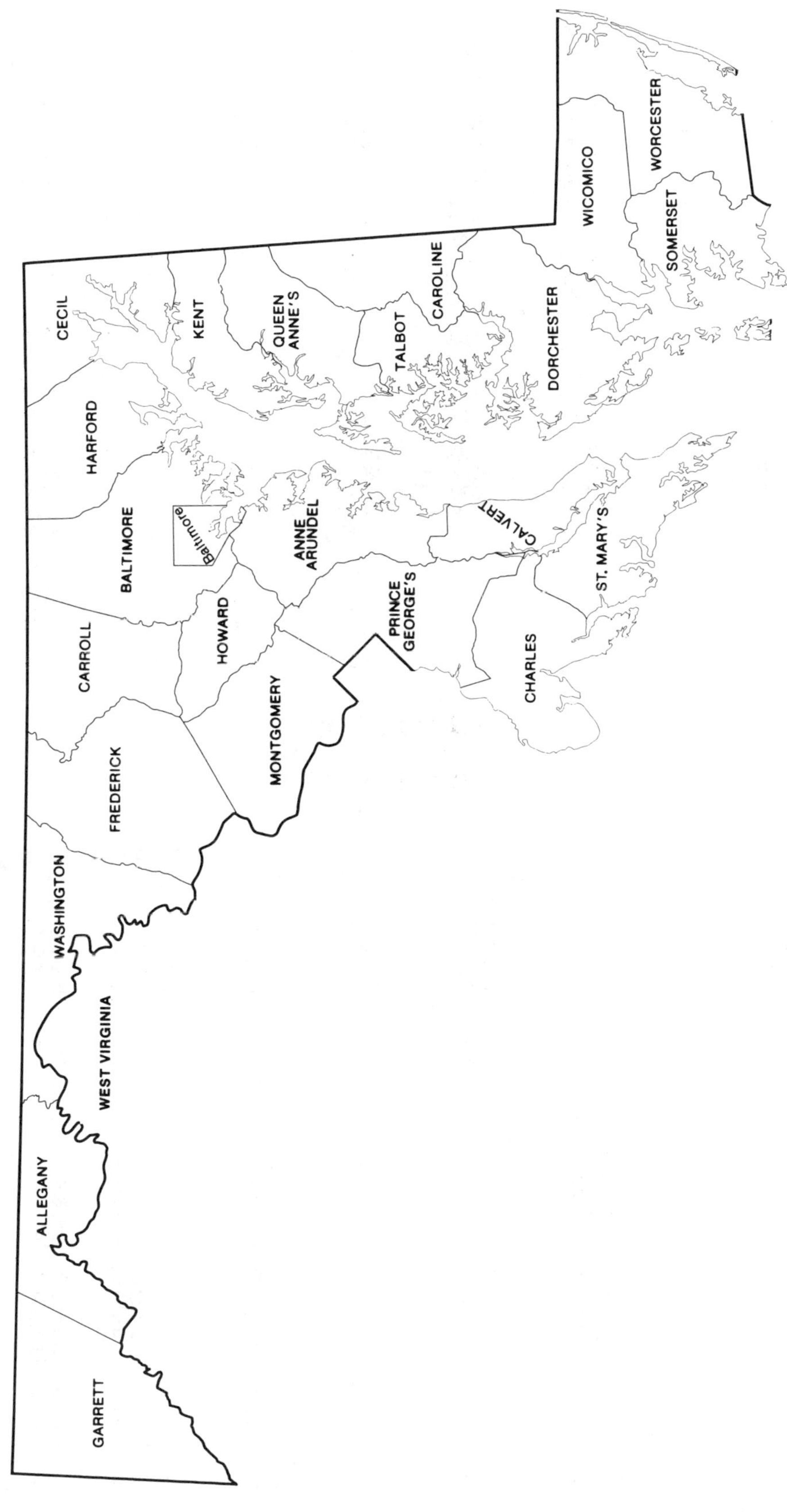
CECIL
KENT
QUEEN ANNE'S
TALBOT
CAROLINE
DORCHESTER
WICOMICO
WORCESTER
SOMERSET
HARFORD
BALTIMORE
Baltimore
ANNE ARUNDEL
CALVERT
ST. MARY'S
CARROLL
HOWARD
PRINCE GEORGE'S
CHARLES
MONTGOMERY
FREDERICK
WASHINGTON
WEST VIRGINIA
ALLEGANY
GARRETT

MARYLAND

PRESIDENT 1984

1980 Census Population	County	Total Vote	Republican	Democratic	Other	Rep.-Dem. Plurality	Percentage Total Vote Rep.	Total Vote Dem.	Major Vote Rep.	Major Vote Dem.
80,548	ALLEGANY	31,223	19,763	11,143	317	8,620 R	63.3%	35.7%	63.9%	36.1%
370,775	ANNE ARUNDEL	142,591	94,171	47,565	855	46,606 R	66.0%	33.4%	66.4%	33.6%
786,775	BALTIMORE CITY	284,163	80,120	202,277	1,766	122,157 D	28.2%	71.2%	28.4%	71.6%
655,615	BALTIMORE COUNTY	280,428	171,929	106,908	1,591	65,021 R	61.3%	38.1%	61.7%	38.3%
34,638	CALVERT	13,840	8,303	5,455	82	2,848 R	60.0%	39.4%	60.4%	39.6%
23,143	CAROLINE	7,099	4,876	2,198	25	2,678 R	68.7%	31.0%	68.9%	31.1%
96,356	CARROLL	36,199	27,230	8,898	71	18,332 R	75.2%	24.6%	75.4%	24.6%
60,430	CECIL	19,885	13,111	6,681	93	6,430 R	65.9%	33.6%	66.2%	33.8%
72,751	CHARLES	26,460	16,132	10,264	64	5,868 R	61.0%	38.8%	61.1%	38.9%
30,623	DORCHESTER	9,981	6,699	3,160	122	3,539 R	67.1%	31.7%	67.9%	32.1%
114,792	FREDERICK	43,113	29,606	13,411	96	16,195 R	68.7%	31.1%	68.8%	31.2%
26,498	GARRETT	9,477	7,042	2,386	49	4,656 R	74.3%	25.2%	74.7%	25.3%
145,930	HARFORD	54,642	37,382	17,133	127	20,249 R	68.4%	31.4%	68.6%	31.4%
118,572	HOWARD	61,688	35,641	25,713	334	9,928 R	57.8%	41.7%	58.1%	41.9%
16,695	KENT	6,323	3,897	2,390	36	1,507 R	61.6%	37.8%	62.0%	38.0%
579,053	MONTGOMERY	293,870	146,924	146,036	910	888 R	50.0%	49.7%	50.2%	49.8%
665,071	PRINCE GEORGES	232,220	95,121	136,063	1,036	40,942 D	41.0%	58.6%	41.1%	58.9%
25,508	QUEEN ANNES	9,763	6,784	2,938	41	3,846 R	69.5%	30.1%	69.8%	30.2%
59,895	ST. MARYS	17,670	11,201	6,420	49	4,781 R	63.4%	36.3%	63.6%	36.4%
19,188	SOMERSET	6,970	4,508	2,439	23	2,069 R	64.7%	35.0%	64.9%	35.1%
25,604	TALBOT	11,256	8,028	3,198	30	4,830 R	71.3%	28.4%	71.5%	28.5%
113,086	WASHINGTON	40,666	27,118	13,329	219	13,789 R	66.7%	32.8%	67.0%	33.0%
64,540	WICOMICO	24,332	16,124	8,160	48	7,964 R	66.3%	33.5%	66.4%	33.6%
30,889	WORCESTER	12,014	8,208	3,770	36	4,438 R	68.3%	31.4%	68.5%	31.5%
4,216,975	TOTAL	1,675,873	879,918	787,935	8,020	91,983 R	52.5%	47.0%	52.8%	47.2%

MARYLAND

PRESIDENT 1980

1980 Census Population	County	Total Vote	Republican	Democratic	Other	Rep.-Dem. Plurality	Percentage Total Vote Rep.	Total Vote Dem.	Major Vote Rep.	Major Vote Dem.
80,548	ALLEGANY	31,484	17,512	12,167	1,805	5,345 R	55.6%	38.6%	59.0%	41.0%
370,775	ANNE ARUNDEL	131,632	69,443	50,780	11,409	18,663 R	52.8%	38.6%	57.8%	42.2%
786,775	BALTIMORE CITY	264,775	57,902	191,911	14,962	134,009 D	21.9%	72.5%	23.2%	76.8%
655,615	BALTIMORE COUNTY	279,917	132,490	121,280	26,147	11,210 R	47.3%	43.3%	52.2%	47.8%
34,638	CALVERT	10,870	5,440	4,745	685	695 R	50.0%	43.7%	53.4%	46.6%
23,143	CAROLINE	6,765	3,582	2,833	350	749 R	52.9%	41.9%	55.8%	44.2%
96,356	CARROLL	32,940	19,859	10,393	2,688	9,466 R	60.3%	31.6%	65.6%	34.4%
60,430	CECIL	18,846	9,673	7,937	1,236	1,736 R	51.3%	42.1%	54.9%	45.1%
72,751	CHARLES	22,020	11,807	8,887	1,326	2,920 R	53.6%	40.4%	57.1%	42.9%
30,623	DORCHESTER	10,550	5,160	4,908	482	252 R	48.9%	46.5%	51.3%	48.7%
114,792	FREDERICK	39,130	22,033	13,629	3,468	8,404 R	56.3%	34.8%	61.8%	38.2%
26,498	GARRETT	8,545	5,475	2,708	362	2,767 R	64.1%	31.7%	66.9%	33.1%
145,930	HARFORD	50,941	26,713	20,042	4,186	6,671 R	52.4%	39.3%	57.1%	42.9%
118,572	HOWARD	51,599	24,272	20,702	6,625	3,570 R	47.0%	40.1%	54.0%	46.0%
16,695	KENT	6,304	2,889	2,986	429	97 D	45.8%	47.4%	49.2%	50.8%
579,053	MONTGOMERY	266,151	125,515	105,822	34,814	19,693 R	47.2%	39.8%	54.3%	45.7%
665,071	PRINCE GEORGES	193,987	78,977	98,757	16,253	19,780 D	40.7%	50.9%	44.4%	55.6%
25,508	QUEEN ANNES	9,112	4,749	3,820	543	929 R	52.1%	41.9%	55.4%	44.6%
59,895	ST. MARYS	16,056	8,267	6,773	1,016	1,494 R	51.5%	42.2%	55.0%	45.0%
19,188	SOMERSET	6,937	3,312	3,342	283	30 D	47.7%	48.2%	49.8%	50.2%
25,604	TALBOT	10,711	6,044	3,995	672	2,049 R	56.4%	37.3%	60.2%	39.8%
113,086	WASHINGTON	39,083	22,901	14,118	2,064	8,783 R	58.6%	36.1%	61.9%	38.1%
64,540	WICOMICO	21,905	11,229	9,431	1,245	1,798 R	51.3%	43.1%	54.4%	45.6%
30,889	WORCESTER	10,236	5,362	4,195	679	1,167 R	52.4%	41.0%	56.1%	43.9%
4,216,975	TOTAL	1,540,496	680,606	726,161	133,729	45,555 D	44.2%	47.1%	48.4%	51.6%

MARYLAND

PRESIDENT 1976

1970 Census Population	County	Total Vote	Republican	Democratic	Other	Rep.-Dem. Plurality	Percentage Total Vote Rep.	Percentage Total Vote Dem.	Percentage Major Vote Rep.	Percentage Major Vote Dem.
84,044	ALLEGANY	31,496	15,435	15,967	94	532 D	49.0%	50.7%	49.2%	50.8%
297,539	ANNE ARUNDEL	116,100	61,353	54,351	396	7,002 R	52.8%	46.8%	53.0%	47.0%
905,759	BALTIMORE CITY	261,832	81,762	178,593	1,477	96,831 D	31.2%	68.2%	31.4%	68.6%
621,077	BALTIMORE COUNTY	262,866	143,293	118,505	1,068	24,788 R	54.5%	45.1%	54.7%	45.3%
20,682	CALVERT	8,074	3,439	4,626	9	1,187 D	42.6%	57.3%	42.6%	57.4%
19,781	CAROLINE	6,140	3,114	3,017	9	97 R	50.7%	49.1%	50.8%	49.2%
69,006	CARROLL	25,684	15,661	9,940	83	5,721 R	61.0%	38.7%	61.2%	38.8%
53,291	CECIL	16,811	7,833	8,950	28	1,117 D	46.6%	53.2%	46.7%	53.3%
47,678	CHARLES	17,343	7,792	9,525	26	1,733 D	44.9%	54.9%	45.0%	55.0%
29,405	DORCHESTER	9,301	4,768	4,528	5	240 R	51.3%	48.7%	51.3%	48.7%
84,927	FREDERICK	32,704	17,941	14,542	221	3,399 R	54.9%	44.5%	55.2%	44.8%
21,476	GARRETT	8,000	4,640	3,332	28	1,308 R	58.0%	41.7%	58.2%	41.8%
115,378	HARFORD	44,227	24,309	19,890	28	4,419 R	55.0%	45.0%	55.0%	45.0%
61,911	HOWARD	42,007	21,200	20,533	274	667 R	50.5%	48.9%	50.8%	49.2%
16,146	KENT	6,041	2,821	3,211	9	390 D	46.7%	53.2%	46.8%	53.2%
522,809	MONTGOMERY	256,177	122,674	131,098	2,405	8,424 D	47.9%	51.2%	48.3%	51.7%
660,567	PRINCE GEORGES	193,966	81,027	111,743	1,196	30,716 D	41.8%	57.6%	42.0%	58.0%
18,422	QUEEN ANNES	6,966	3,479	3,457	30	22 R	49.9%	49.6%	50.2%	49.8%
47,388	ST. MARYS	12,905	5,640	7,227	38	1,587 D	43.7%	56.0%	43.8%	56.2%
18,924	SOMERSET	6,727	3,254	3,472	1	218 D	48.4%	51.6%	48.4%	51.6%
23,682	TALBOT	9,590	5,848	3,715	27	2,133 R	61.0%	38.7%	61.2%	38.8%
103,829	WASHINGTON	36,233	20,194	15,902	137	4,292 R	55.7%	43.9%	55.9%	44.1%
54,236	WICOMICO	19,977	10,537	9,412	28	1,125 R	52.7%	47.1%	52.8%	47.2%
24,442	WORCESTER	8,730	4,647	4,076	7	571 R	53.2%	46.7%	53.3%	46.7%
3,922,399	TOTAL	1,439,897	672,661	759,612	7,624	86,951 D	46.7%	52.8%	47.0%	53.0%

MARYLAND

PRESIDENT 1972

1970 Census Population	County	Total Vote	Republican	Democratic	Other	Rep.-Dem. Plurality	Percentage Total Vote Rep.	Percentage Total Vote Dem.	Percentage Major Vote Rep.	Percentage Major Vote Dem.
84,044	ALLEGANY	32,048	20,687	10,808	553	9,879 R	64.6%	33.7%	65.7%	34.3%
297,539	ANNE ARUNDEL	99,239	71,707	26,082	1,450	45,625 R	72.3%	26.3%	73.3%	26.7%
905,759	BALTIMORE CITY	264,652	119,486	141,323	3,843	21,837 D	45.1%	53.4%	45.8%	54.2%
621,077	BALTIMORE COUNTY	250,224	175,897	70,309	4,018	105,588 R	70.3%	28.1%	71.4%	28.6%
20,682	CALVERT	6,344	4,024	2,232	88	1,792 R	63.4%	35.2%	64.3%	35.7%
19,781	CAROLINE	5,948	4,325	1,567	56	2,758 R	72.7%	26.3%	73.4%	26.6%
69,006	CARROLL	21,808	16,847	4,408	553	12,439 R	77.3%	20.2%	79.3%	20.7%
53,291	CECIL	15,191	10,759	4,113	319	6,646 R	70.8%	27.1%	72.3%	27.7%
47,678	CHARLES	14,353	9,665	4,502	186	5,163 R	67.3%	31.4%	68.2%	31.8%
29,405	DORCHESTER	9,149	6,859	2,136	154	4,723 R	75.0%	23.3%	76.3%	23.7%
84,927	FREDERICK	28,651	19,907	8,235	509	11,672 R	69.5%	28.7%	70.7%	29.3%
21,476	GARRETT	7,154	5,480	1,510	164	3,970 R	76.6%	21.1%	78.4%	21.6%
115,378	HARFORD	34,366	25,141	8,737	488	16,404 R	73.2%	25.4%	74.2%	25.8%
61,911	HOWARD	30,316	19,265	10,668	383	8,597 R	63.5%	35.2%	64.4%	35.6%
16,146	KENT	6,271	4,036	2,168	67	1,868 R	64.4%	34.6%	65.1%	34.9%
522,809	MONTGOMERY	235,557	133,090	100,228	2,239	32,862 R	56.5%	42.5%	57.0%	43.0%
660,567	PRINCE GEORGES	198,410	116,166	79,914	2,330	36,252 R	58.5%	40.3%	59.2%	40.8%
18,422	QUEEN ANNES	6,217	4,380	1,712	125	2,668 R	70.5%	27.5%	71.9%	28.1%
47,388	ST. MARYS	11,382	7,689	3,571	122	4,118 R	67.6%	31.4%	68.3%	31.7%
18,924	SOMERSET	6,449	4,342	2,036	71	2,306 R	67.3%	31.6%	68.1%	31.9%
23,682	TALBOT	8,859	6,620	2,181	58	4,439 R	74.7%	24.6%	75.2%	24.8%
103,829	WASHINGTON	34,985	24,234	10,039	712	14,195 R	69.3%	28.7%	70.7%	29.3%
54,236	WICOMICO	18,815	13,115	5,510	190	7,605 R	69.7%	29.3%	70.4%	29.6%
24,442	WORCESTER	7,424	5,584	1,792	48	3,792 R	75.2%	24.1%	75.7%	24.3%
3,922,399	TOTAL	1,353,812	829,305	505,781	18,726	323,524 R	61.3%	37.4%	62.1%	37.9%

MARYLAND

PRESIDENT 1968

1960 Census Population	County	Total Vote	Republican	Democratic	AIP	Other	Plurality	Percentage Rep.	Dem.	AIP
84,169	ALLEGANY	31,910	13,561	13,227	5,122		334 R	42.5%	41.5%	16.1%
206,634	ANNE ARUNDEL	77,625	36,557	25,381	15,687		11,176 R	47.1%	32.7%	20.2%
939,024	BALTIMORE CITY	289,884	80,146	178,450	31,288		98,304 D	27.6%	61.6%	10.8%
492,428	BALTIMORE COUNTY	219,011	108,930	80,798	29,283		28,132 R	49.7%	36.9%	13.4%
15,826	CALVERT	5,449	1,946	2,032	1,471		86 D	35.7%	37.3%	27.0%
19,462	CAROLINE	6,231	3,120	1,697	1,414		1,423 R	50.1%	27.2%	22.7%
52,785	CARROLL	19,631	11,888	4,658	3,085		7,230 R	60.6%	23.7%	15.7%
48,408	CECIL	14,214	6,462	4,517	3,235		1,945 R	45.5%	31.8%	22.8%
32,572	CHARLES	12,065	4,645	4,247	3,173		398 R	38.5%	35.2%	26.3%
29,666	DORCHESTER	10,114	4,183	2,714	3,217		966 R	41.4%	26.8%	31.8%
71,930	FREDERICK	26,313	13,649	8,316	4,348		5,333 R	51.9%	31.6%	16.5%
20,420	GARRETT	6,772	4,021	1,933	818		2,088 R	59.4%	28.5%	12.1%
76,722	HARFORD	30,691	15,799	9,914	4,978		5,885 R	51.5%	32.3%	16.2%
36,152	HOWARD	18,505	9,957	5,752	2,796		4,205 R	53.8%	31.1%	15.1%
15,481	KENT	6,335	2,946	2,243	1,146		703 R	46.5%	35.4%	18.1%
340,928	MONTGOMERY	191,403	84,651	92,026	14,726		7,375 D	44.2%	48.1%	7.7%
357,395	PRINCE GEORGES	177,660	73,269	71,524	32,867		1,745 R	41.2%	40.3%	18.5%
16,569	QUEEN ANNES	6,155	2,888	1,969	1,298		919 R	46.9%	32.0%	21.1%
38,915	ST. MARYS	9,175	3,348	3,280	2,547		68 R	36.5%	35.7%	27.8%
19,623	SOMERSET	7,047	2,829	2,319	1,899		510 R	40.1%	32.9%	26.9%
21,578	TALBOT	8,883	4,902	2,609	1,372		2,293 R	55.2%	29.4%	15.4%
91,219	WASHINGTON	34,053	16,050	11,266	6,737		4,784 R	47.1%	33.1%	19.8%
49,050	WICOMICO	18,455	8,707	5,392	4,356		3,315 R	47.2%	29.2%	23.6%
23,733	WORCESTER	7,458	3,541	2,046	1,871		1,495 R	47.5%	27.4%	25.1%
3,100,689	TOTAL	1,235,039	517,995	538,310	178,734		20,315 D	41.9%	43.6%	14.5%

MARYLAND

ELECTION NOTES

1984 Other vote was 5,721 Bergland (Libertarian); 898 Hall (Communist); 745 Holmes (Workers); 656 Serrette (Alliance).

1980 Other vote was 119,537 Anderson (Independent); 14,192 Clark (Libertarian).

1976 Other vote was 4,541 McCarthy (write-in); 321 Anderson (write-in); 261 Camejo (write-in); 255 MacBride (write-in); 171 Maddox (write-in); 68 Hall (write-in); 21 LaRouche (write-in); 16 Zeidler (write-in); 8 Miller (write-in); 8 Wright (write-in); 7 Levin (write-in); 2 Bubar (write-in); 1,945 scattered write-in.

1972 Other vote was Schmitz (American).

1968 Wallace on the ballot as American.

MASSACHUSETTS

POPULAR VOTE FOR PRESIDENT 1920 TO 1984

Year	Total Vote	Republican Vote	Republican Candidate	Democratic Vote	Democratic Candidate	Other Vote	Plurality	Percentage Total Vote Rep.	Percentage Total Vote Dem.	Percentage Major Vote Rep.	Percentage Major Vote Dem.
1984	2,559,453	1,310,936	Reagan, Ronald	1,239,606	Mondale, Walter F.	8,911	71,330 R	51.2%	48.4%	51.4%	48.6%
1980	2,524,298	1,057,631	Reagan, Ronald	1,053,802	Carter, Jimmy	412,865	3,829 R	41.9%	41.7%	50.1%	49.9%
1976	2,547,558	1,030,276	Ford, Gerald R.	1,429,475	Carter, Jimmy	87,807	399,199 D	40.4%	56.1%	41.9%	58.1%
1972	2,458,756	1,112,078	Nixon, Richard M.	1,332,540	McGovern, George S.	14,138	220,462 D	45.2%	54.2%	45.5%	54.5%
1968	2,331,752	766,844	Nixon, Richard M.	1,469,218	Humphrey, Hubert H.	95,690	702,374 D	32.9%	63.0%	34.3%	65.7%
1964	2,344,798	549,727	Goldwater, Barry M.	1,786,422	Johnson, Lyndon B.	8,649	1,236,695 D	23.4%	76.2%	23.5%	76.5%
1960	2,469,480	976,750	Nixon, Richard M.	1,487,174	Kennedy, John F.	5,556	510,424 D	39.6%	60.2%	39.6%	60.4%
1956	2,348,506	1,393,197	Eisenhower, Dwight D.	948,190	Stevenson, Adlai E.	7,119	445,007 R	59.3%	40.4%	59.5%	40.5%
1952	2,383,398	1,292,325	Eisenhower, Dwight D.	1,083,525	Stevenson, Adlai E.	7,548	208,800 R	54.2%	45.5%	54.4%	45.6%
1948	2,107,146	909,370	Dewey, Thomas E.	1,151,788	Truman, Harry S.	45,988	242,418 D	43.2%	54.7%	44.1%	55.9%
1944	1,960,665	921,350	Dewey, Thomas E.	1,035,296	Roosevelt, Franklin D.	4,019	113,946 D	47.0%	52.8%	47.1%	52.9%
1940	2,026,993	939,700	Willkie, Wendell	1,076,522	Roosevelt, Franklin D.	10,771	136,822 D	46.4%	53.1%	46.6%	53.4%
1936	1,840,357	768,613	Landon, Alfred M.	942,716	Roosevelt, Franklin D.	129,028	174,103 D	41.8%	51.2%	44.9%	55.1%
1932	1,580,114	736,959	Hoover, Herbert C.	800,148	Roosevelt, Franklin D.	43,007	63,189 D	46.6%	50.6%	47.9%	52.1%
1928	1,577,823	775,566	Hoover, Herbert C.	792,758	Smith, Alfred E.	9,499	17,192 D	49.2%	50.2%	49.5%	50.5%
1924	1,129,837	703,476	Coolidge, Calvin	280,831	Davis, John W.	145,530	422,645 R	62.3%	24.9%	71.5%	28.5%
1920	993,718	681,153	Harding, Warren G.	276,691	Cox, James M.	35,874	404,462 R	68.5%	27.8%	71.1%	28.9%

ELECTORAL COLLEGE VOTE 1920 TO 1984

Year	Total	Republican	Democratic	Other
1984	13	13	—	—
1980	14	14	—	—
1976	14	—	14	—
1972	14	—	14	—
1968	14	—	14	—
1964	14	—	14	—
1960	16	—	16	—
1956	16	16	—	—
1952	16	16	—	—
1948	16	—	16	—
1944	16	—	16	—
1940	17	—	17	—
1936	17	—	17	—
1932	17	—	17	—
1928	18	—	18	—
1924	18	18	—	—
1920	18	18	—	—

MASSACHUSETTS

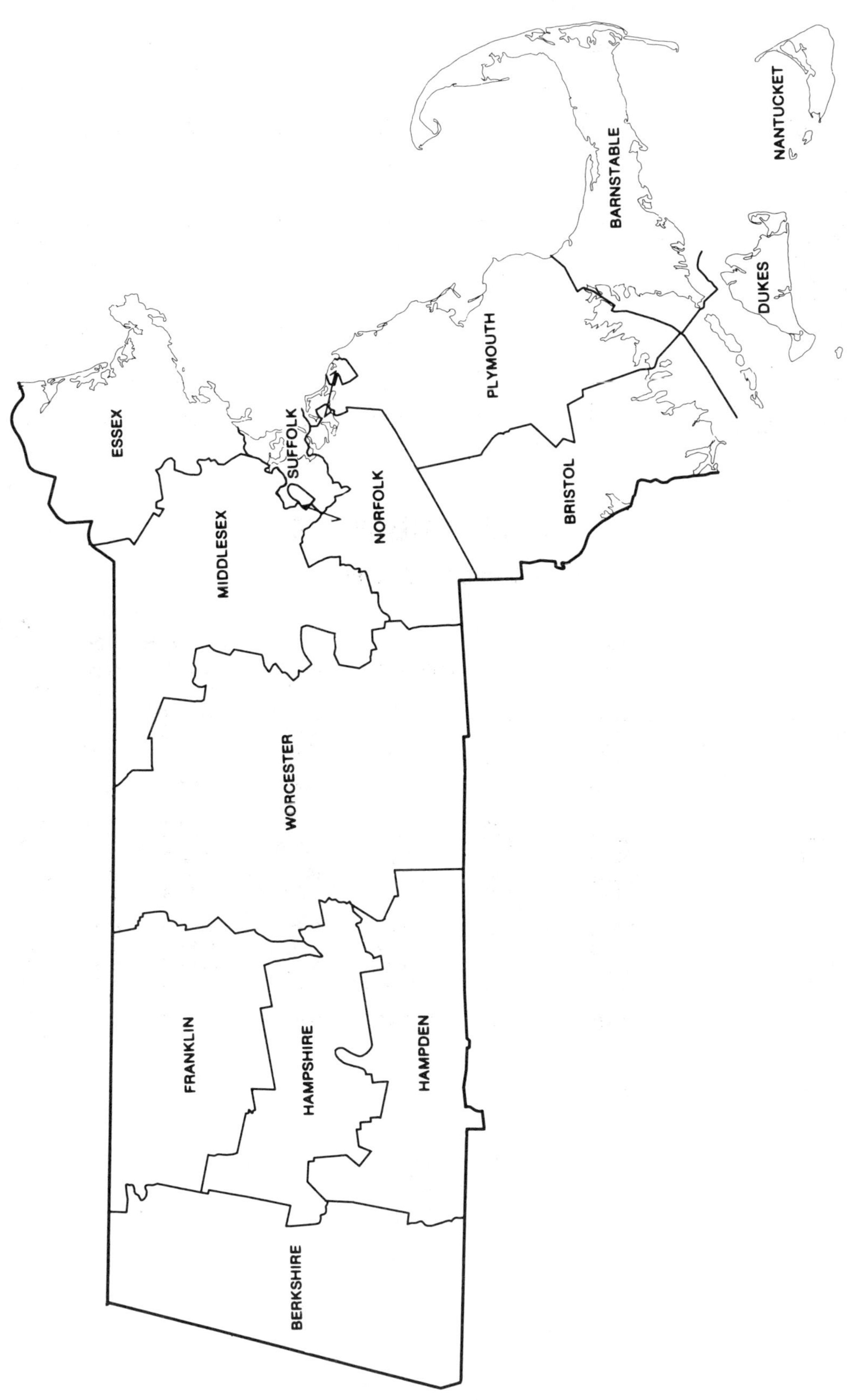

MASSACHUSETTS

PRESIDENT 1984

1980 Census Population	County	Total Vote	Republican	Democratic	Other	Rep.-Dem. Plurality	Percentage Total Vote Rep.	Percentage Total Vote Dem.	Percentage Major Vote Rep.	Percentage Major Vote Dem.
147,925	BARNSTABLE	89,951	51,261	38,369	321	12,892 R	57.0%	42.7%	57.2%	42.8%
145,110	BERKSHIRE	63,785	33,712	29,745	328	3,967 R	52.9%	46.6%	53.1%	46.9%
474,641	BRISTOL	188,039	93,232	94,010	797	778 D	49.6%	50.0%	49.8%	50.2%
8,942	DUKES	6,125	2,788	3,313	24	525 D	45.5%	54.1%	45.7%	54.3%
633,632	ESSEX	295,656	162,152	132,353	1,151	29,799 R	54.8%	44.8%	55.1%	44.9%
64,317	FRANKLIN	31,533	15,883	15,502	148	381 R	50.4%	49.2%	50.6%	49.4%
443,018	HAMPDEN	174,971	89,330	84,985	656	4,345 R	51.1%	48.6%	51.2%	48.8%
138,813	HAMPSHIRE	63,942	28,111	35,597	234	7,486 D	44.0%	55.7%	44.1%	55.9%
1,367,034	MIDDLESEX	646,754	319,604	325,065	2,085	5,461 D	49.4%	50.3%	49.6%	50.4%
5,087	NANTUCKET	3,170	1,697	1,456	17	241 R	53.5%	45.9%	53.8%	46.2%
606,587	NORFOLK	299,319	160,313	138,222	784	22,091 R	53.6%	46.2%	53.7%	46.3%
405,437	PLYMOUTH	174,771	105,230	68,923	618	36,307 R	60.2%	39.4%	60.4%	39.6%
650,142	SUFFOLK	244,997	91,563	152,568	866	61,005 D	37.4%	62.3%	37.5%	62.5%
646,352	WORCESTER	276,440	156,060	119,498	882	36,562 R	56.5%	43.2%	56.6%	43.4%
5,737,037	TOTAL	2,559,453	1,310,936	1,239,606	8,911	71,330 R	51.2%	48.4%	51.4%	48.6%

MASSACHUSETTS

PRESIDENT 1980

1980 Census Population	County	Total Vote	Republican	Democratic	Other	Rep.-Dem. Plurality	Percentage Total Vote Rep.	Percentage Total Vote Dem.	Percentage Major Vote Rep.	Percentage Major Vote Dem.
147,925	BARNSTABLE	82,273	41,493	23,952	16,828	17,541 R	50.4%	29.1%	63.4%	36.6%
145,110	BERKSHIRE	68,031	27,063	29,458	11,510	2,395 D	39.8%	43.3%	47.9%	52.1%
474,641	BRISTOL	188,605	77,545	83,460	27,600	5,915 D	41.1%	44.3%	48.2%	51.8%
8,942	DUKES	5,397	1,809	2,370	1,218	561 D	33.5%	43.9%	43.3%	56.7%
633,632	ESSEX	297,533	130,252	116,173	51,108	14,079 R	43.8%	39.0%	52.9%	47.1%
64,317	FRANKLIN	30,122	12,528	11,830	5,764	698 R	41.6%	39.3%	51.4%	48.6%
443,018	HAMPDEN	179,720	72,528	80,369	26,823	7,841 D	40.4%	44.7%	47.4%	52.6%
138,813	HAMPSHIRE	60,355	21,117	27,611	11,627	6,494 D	35.0%	45.7%	43.3%	56.7%
1,367,034	MIDDLESEX	637,679	256,999	270,751	109,929	13,752 D	40.3%	42.5%	48.7%	51.3%
5,087	NANTUCKET	2,838	1,149	1,040	649	109 R	40.5%	36.6%	52.5%	47.5%
606,587	NORFOLK	303,729	136,184	117,274	50,271	18,910 R	44.8%	38.6%	53.7%	46.3%
405,437	PLYMOUTH	173,248	85,593	58,772	28,883	26,821 R	49.4%	33.9%	59.3%	40.7%
650,142	SUFFOLK	216,207	73,271	113,416	29,520	40,145 D	33.9%	52.5%	39.2%	60.8%
646,352	WORCESTER	278,561	120,100	117,326	41,135	2,774 R	43.1%	42.1%	50.6%	49.4%
5,737,037	TOTAL	2,524,298	1,057,631	1,053,802	412,865	3,829 R	41.9%	41.7%	50.1%	49.9%

MASSACHUSETTS

PRESIDENT 1976

1970 Census Population	County	Total Vote	Republican	Democratic	Other	Rep.-Dem. Plurality	Percentage Total Vote Rep.	Total Vote Dem.	Major Vote Rep.	Major Vote Dem.
96,656	BARNSTABLE	73,117	39,295	31,268	2,554	8,027 R	53.7%	42.8%	55.7%	44.3%
149,402	BERKSHIRE	68,871	27,462	39,337	2,072	11,875 D	39.9%	57.1%	41.1%	58.9%
444,301	BRISTOL	191,771	69,957	116,318	5,496	46,361 D	36.5%	60.7%	37.6%	62.4%
6,117	DUKES	5,135	2,365	2,513	257	148 D	46.1%	48.9%	48.5%	51.5%
637,887	ESSEX	301,444	125,538	165,710	10,196	40,172 D	41.6%	55.0%	43.1%	56.9%
59,210	FRANKLIN	31,181	14,837	14,985	1,359	148 D	47.6%	48.1%	49.8%	50.2%
459,050	HAMPDEN	185,290	70,008	110,028	5,254	40,020 D	37.8%	59.4%	38.9%	61.1%
123,981	HAMPSHIRE	60,075	22,219	34,947	2,909	12,728 D	37.0%	58.2%	38.9%	61.1%
1,397,268	MIDDLESEX	643,382	260,044	359,919	23,419	99,875 D	40.4%	55.9%	41.9%	58.1%
3,774	NANTUCKET	2,626	1,399	1,115	112	284 R	53.3%	42.5%	55.6%	44.4%
605,051	NORFOLK	302,616	136,628	155,342	10,646	18,714 D	45.1%	51.3%	46.8%	53.2%
333,314	PLYMOUTH	164,433	74,684	83,663	6,086	8,979 D	45.4%	50.9%	47.2%	52.8%
735,190	SUFFOLK	232,372	80,623	142,010	9,739	61,387 D	34.7%	61.1%	36.2%	63.8%
637,969	WORCESTER	285,245	105,217	172,320	7,708	67,103 D	36.9%	60.4%	37.9%	62.1%
5,689,170	TOTAL	2,547,558	1,030,276	1,429,475	87,807	399,199 D	40.4%	56.1%	41.9%	58.1%

MASSACHUSETTS

PRESIDENT 1972

1970 Census Population	County	Total Vote	Republican	Democratic	Other	Rep.-Dem. Plurality	Percentage Total Vote Rep.	Total Vote Dem.	Major Vote Rep.	Major Vote Dem.
96,656	BARNSTABLE	59,442	36,340	22,636	466	13,704 R	61.1%	38.1%	61.6%	38.4%
149,402	BERKSHIRE	66,284	30,380	35,391	513	5,011 D	45.8%	53.4%	46.2%	53.8%
444,301	BRISTOL	188,768	84,390	103,163	1,215	18,773 D	44.7%	54.7%	45.0%	55.0%
6,117	DUKES	4,336	2,312	2,001	23	311 R	53.3%	46.1%	53.6%	46.4%
637,887	ESSEX	297,084	138,040	157,324	1,720	19,284 D	46.5%	53.0%	46.7%	53.3%
59,210	FRANKLIN	28,263	16,088	11,968	207	4,120 R	56.9%	42.3%	57.3%	42.7%
459,050	HAMPDEN	182,133	86,164	94,945	1,024	8,781 D	47.3%	52.1%	47.6%	52.4%
123,981	HAMPSHIRE	53,654	24,529	28,572	553	4,043 D	45.7%	53.3%	46.2%	53.8%
1,397,268	MIDDLESEX	617,651	269,064	345,343	3,244	76,279 D	43.6%	55.9%	43.8%	56.2%
3,774	NANTUCKET	2,380	1,418	952	10	466 R	59.6%	40.0%	59.8%	40.2%
605,051	NORFOLK	286,749	134,459	150,732	1,558	16,273 D	46.9%	52.6%	47.1%	52.9%
333,314	PLYMOUTH	146,064	76,062	69,124	878	6,938 R	52.1%	47.3%	52.4%	47.6%
735,190	SUFFOLK	252,821	85,272	166,250	1,299	80,978 D	33.7%	65.8%	33.9%	66.1%
637,969	WORCESTER	273,127	127,560	144,139	1,428	16,579 D	46.7%	52.8%	46.9%	53.1%
5,689,170	TOTAL	2,458,756	1,112,078	1,332,540	14,138	220,462 D	45.2%	54.2%	45.5%	54.5%

MASSACHUSETTS

PRESIDENT 1968

1960 Census Population	County	Total Vote	Republican	Democratic	AIP	Other	Plurality	Percentage Rep.	Dem.	AIP
70,286	BARNSTABLE	42,162	24,296	16,546	1,242	78	7,750 R	57.6%	39.2%	2.9%
142,135	BERKSHIRE	64,465	23,078	38,497	2,593	297	15,419 D	35.8%	59.7%	4.0%
398,488	BRISTOL	183,569	56,672	119,439	6,999	459	62,767 D	30.9%	65.1%	3.8%
5,829	DUKES	3,196	1,576	1,540	75	5	36 R	49.3%	48.2%	2.3%
568,831	ESSEX	281,685	99,721	171,901	9,236	827	72,180 D	35.4%	61.0%	3.3%
54,864	FRANKLIN	25,386	12,345	12,072	893	76	273 R	48.6%	47.6%	3.5%
429,353	HAMPDEN	178,150	55,783	111,376	9,846	1,145	55,593 D	31.3%	62.5%	5.5%
103,229	HAMPSHIRE	45,412	16,270	26,666	2,314	162	10,396 D	35.8%	58.7%	5.1%
1,238,742	MIDDLESEX	577,596	188,304	370,310	16,561	2,421	182,006 D	32.6%	64.1%	2.9%
3,559	NANTUCKET	1,792	991	744	52	5	247 R	55.3%	41.5%	2.9%
510,256	NORFOLK	266,206	95,858	160,513	9,080	755	64,655 D	36.0%	60.3%	3.4%
248,449	PLYMOUTH	127,977	54,644	67,771	5,342	220	13,127 D	42.7%	53.0%	4.2%
791,329	SUFFOLK	268,977	48,952	203,406	15,121	1,498	154,454 D	18.2%	75.6%	5.6%
583,228	WORCESTER	265,179	88,354	168,437	7,734	654	80,083 D	33.3%	63.5%	2.9%
5,148,578	TOTAL	2,331,752	766,844	1,469,218	87,088	8,602	702,374 D	32.9%	63.0%	3.7%

MASSACHUSETTS

ELECTION NOTES

1984 Other vote was 7,998 Serrette (Independent Alliance); 18 Johnson (write-in); 3 Dodge (write-in); 892 scattered write-in.

1980 Other vote was 382,539 Anderson (Anderson Coalition); 22,038 Clark (Libertarian); 3,735 DeBerry (Socialist Workers); 2,056 Commoner (write-in); 62 McReynolds (write-in); 34 Bubar (write-in); 19 Griswold (write-in); 2,382 scattered write-in. Early unamended canvass gave the Republican state-wide total vote as 1,056,223 and the Socialist Workers state-wide total vote as 5,143.

1976 Other vote was 65,637 McCarthy (Independent); 8,138 Camejo (Socialist Workers); 7,555 Anderson (American); 4,922 LaRouche (U.S. Labor); 135 MacBride (write-in); 33 Wright (write-in); 19 Levin (write-in); 14 Bubar (write-in); 1,354 scattered write-in.

1972 Other vote was 10,600 Jenness (Socialist Workers); 2,877 Schmitz (write-in); 129 Fisher (write-in); 101 Spock (write-in); 46 Hall (write-in); 43 Hospers (write-in); 342 scattered write-in.

1968 Wallace on the ballot as Independent. Other vote was 6,180 Blomen (Socialist Labor); 2,369 Munn (Prohibition); 53 scattered write-in.

MICHIGAN

POPULAR VOTE FOR PRESIDENT 1920 TO 1984

Year	Total Vote	Republican Vote	Republican Candidate	Democratic Vote	Democratic Candidate	Other Vote	Plurality	Percentage Total Vote Rep.	Percentage Total Vote Dem.	Percentage Major Vote Rep.	Percentage Major Vote Dem.
1984	3,801,658	2,251,571	Reagan, Ronald	1,529,638	Mondale, Walter F.	20,449	721,933 R	59.2%	40.2%	59.5%	40.5%
1980	3,909,725	1,915,225	Reagan, Ronald	1,661,532	Carter, Jimmy	332,968	253,693 R	49.0%	42.5%	53.5%	46.5%
1976	3,653,749	1,893,742	Ford, Gerald R.	1,696,714	Carter, Jimmy	63,293	197,028 R	51.8%	46.4%	52.7%	47.3%
1972	3,489,727	1,961,721	Nixon, Richard M.	1,459,435	McGovern, George S.	68,571	502,286 R	56.2%	41.8%	57.3%	42.7%
1968	3,306,250	1,370,665	Nixon, Richard M.	1,593,082	Humphrey, Hubert H.	342,503	222,417 D	41.5%	48.2%	46.2%	53.8%
1964	3,203,102	1,060,152	Goldwater, Barry M.	2,136,615	Johnson, Lyndon B.	6,335	1,076,463 D	33.1%	66.7%	33.2%	66.8%
1960	3,318,097	1,620,428	Nixon, Richard M.	1,687,269	Kennedy, John F.	10,400	66,841 D	48.8%	50.9%	49.0%	51.0%
1956	3,080,468	1,713,647	Eisenhower, Dwight D.	1,359,898	Stevenson, Adlai E.	6,923	353,749 R	55.6%	44.1%	55.8%	44.2%
1952	2,798,592	1,551,529	Eisenhower, Dwight D.	1,230,657	Stevenson, Adlai E.	16,406	320,872 R	55.4%	44.0%	55.8%	44.2%
1948	2,109,609	1,038,595	Dewey, Thomas E.	1,003,448	Truman, Harry S.	67,566	35,147 R	49.2%	47.6%	50.9%	49.1%
1944	2,205,223	1,084,423	Dewey, Thomas E.	1,106,899	Roosevelt, Franklin D.	13,901	22,476 D	49.2%	50.2%	49.5%	50.5%
1940	2,085,929	1,039,917	Willkie, Wendell	1,032,991	Roosevelt, Franklin D.	13,021	6,926 R	49.9%	49.5%	50.2%	49.8%
1936	1,805,098	699,733	Landon, Alfred M.	1,016,794	Roosevelt, Franklin D.	88,571	317,061 D	38.8%	56.3%	40.8%	59.2%
1932	1,664,765	739,894	Hoover, Herbert C.	871,700	Roosevelt, Franklin D.	53,171	131,806 D	44.4%	52.4%	45.9%	54.1%
1928	1,372,082	965,396	Hoover, Herbert C.	396,762	Smith, Alfred E.	9,924	568,634 R	70.4%	28.9%	70.9%	29.1%
1924 **	1,160,419	874,631	Coolidge, Calvin	152,359	Davis, John W.	133,429	722,272 R	75.4%	13.1%	85.2%	14.8%
1920	1,048,411	762,865	Harding, Warren G.	233,450	Cox, James M.	52,096	529,415 R	72.8%	22.3%	76.6%	23.4%

In 1924 other vote was 122,014 Progressive; 6,085 Prohibition and 5,330 Socialist Labor.

ELECTORAL COLLEGE VOTE 1920 TO 1984

Year	Total	Republican	Democratic	Other
1984	20	20	—	—
1980	21	21	—	—
1976	21	21	—	—
1972	21	21	—	—
1968	21	—	21	—
1964	21	—	21	—
1960	20	—	20	—
1956	20	20	—	—
1952	20	20	—	—
1948	19	19	—	—
1944	19	—	19	—
1940	19	19	—	—
1936	19	—	19	—
1932	19	—	19	—
1928	15	15	—	—
1924	15	15	—	—
1920	15	15	—	—

MICHIGAN

KEWEENAW (PART)
KEWEENAW (PART)
HOUGHTON
ONTONAGON
BARAGA
GOGEBIC
IRON
MARQUETTE
ALGER
LUCE
CHIPPEWA
SCHOOLCRAFT
MACKINAC
DICKINSON
DELTA
MENOMINEE
EMMET
CHEBOYGAN
PRESQUE ISLE
CHARLEVOIX
MONTMORENCY
ANTRIM
OTSEGO
ALPENA
LEELANAU
BENZIE
GRAND TRAVERSE
KALKASKA
CRAWFORD
OSCODA
ALCONA
MANISTEE
WEXFORD
MISSAUKEE
ROSCOMMON
OGEMAW
IOSCO
ARENAC
MAGON
LAKE
OSCEOLA
CLARE
GLADWIN
HURON
OCEANA
NEWAYGO
MECOSTA
ISABELLA
MIDLAND
BAY
TUSCOLA
SANILAC
MUSKEGON
MONTCALM
GRATIOT
SAGINAW
LAPEER
GENESEE
ST. CLAIR
OTTAWA
KENT
IONIA
CLINTON
SHIAWASSEE
MACOMB
OAKLAND
ALLEGAN
BARRY
EATON
INGHAM
LIVINGSTON
VAN BUREN
KALAMAZOO
CALHOUN
JACKSON
WASHTENAW
WAYNE
BERRIEN
CASS
ST. JOSEPH
BRANCH
HILLSDALE
LENAWEE
MONROE

MICHIGAN

PRESIDENT 1984

1980 Census Population	County	Total Vote	Republican	Democratic	Other	Rep.-Dem. Plurality	Percentage Total Vote Rep.	Total Vote Dem.	Major Vote Rep.	Major Vote Dem.
9,740	ALCONA	4,853	3,223	1,616	14	1,607 R	66.4%	33.3%	66.6%	33.4%
9,225	ALGER	4,208	2,175	2,018	15	157 R	51.7%	48.0%	51.9%	48.1%
81,555	ALLEGAN	32,338	23,762	8,389	187	15,373 R	73.5%	25.9%	73.9%	26.1%
32,315	ALPENA	13,397	8,212	5,136	49	3,076 R	61.3%	38.3%	61.5%	38.5%
16,194	ANTRIM	8,277	5,726	2,507	44	3,219 R	69.2%	30.3%	69.5%	30.5%
14,706	ARENAC	5,941	3,483	2,436	22	1,047 R	58.6%	41.0%	58.8%	41.2%
8,484	BARAGA	3,792	1,965	1,818	9	147 R	51.8%	47.9%	51.9%	48.1%
45,781	BARRY	20,265	14,245	5,898	122	8,347 R	70.3%	29.1%	70.7%	29.3%
119,881	BAY	49,030	26,198	22,597	235	3,601 R	53.4%	46.1%	53.7%	46.3%
11,205	BENZIE	5,502	3,590	1,866	46	1,724 R	65.2%	33.9%	65.8%	34.2%
171,276	BERRIEN	64,824	43,160	21,228	436	21,932 R	66.6%	32.7%	67.0%	33.0%
40,188	BRANCH	14,945	11,004	3,860	81	7,144 R	73.6%	25.8%	74.0%	26.0%
141,557	CALHOUN	55,067	34,470	20,313	284	14,157 R	62.6%	36.9%	62.9%	37.1%
49,499	CASS	18,394	11,647	6,634	113	5,013 R	63.3%	36.1%	63.7%	36.3%
19,907	CHARLEVOIX	9,595	6,355	3,175	65	3,180 R	66.2%	33.1%	66.7%	33.3%
20,649	CHEBOYGAN	9,452	6,053	3,358	41	2,695 R	64.0%	35.5%	64.3%	35.7%
29,029	CHIPPEWA	12,757	8,135	4,575	47	3,560 R	63.8%	35.9%	64.0%	36.0%
23,822	CLARE	10,412	6,587	3,764	61	2,823 R	63.3%	36.2%	63.6%	36.4%
55,893	CLINTON	23,726	17,387	6,226	113	11,161 R	73.3%	26.2%	73.6%	26.4%
9,465	CRAWFORD	4,896	3,303	1,558	35	1,745 R	67.5%	31.8%	67.9%	32.1%
38,947	DELTA	16,942	8,952	7,934	56	1,018 R	52.8%	46.8%	53.0%	47.0%
25,341	DICKINSON	12,530	6,880	5,614	36	1,266 R	54.9%	44.8%	55.1%	44.9%
88,337	EATON	38,199	27,720	10,290	189	17,430 R	72.6%	26.9%	72.9%	27.1%
22,992	EMMET	11,080	7,760	3,254	66	4,506 R	70.0%	29.4%	70.5%	29.5%
450,449	GENESEE	183,387	92,943	89,491	953	3,452 R	50.7%	48.8%	50.9%	49.1%
19,957	GLADWIN	8,844	5,401	3,368	75	2,033 R	61.1%	38.1%	61.6%	38.4%
19,686	GOGEBIC	9,581	4,006	5,554	21	1,548 D	41.8%	58.0%	41.9%	58.1%
54,899	GRAND TRAVERSE	25,464	18,036	7,271	157	10,765 R	70.8%	28.6%	71.3%	28.7%
40,448	GRATIOT	14,506	10,456	4,000	50	6,456 R	72.1%	27.6%	72.3%	27.7%
42,071	HILLSDALE	15,768	12,063	3,616	89	8,447 R	76.5%	22.9%	76.9%	23.1%
37,872	HOUGHTON	15,141	8,652	6,434	55	2,218 R	57.1%	42.5%	57.4%	42.6%
36,459	HURON	15,091	11,073	3,966	52	7,107 R	73.4%	26.3%	73.6%	26.4%
275,520	INGHAM	116,083	68,753	46,411	919	22,342 R	59.2%	40.0%	59.7%	40.3%
51,815	IONIA	20,035	14,162	5,735	138	8,427 R	70.7%	28.6%	71.2%	28.8%
28,349	IOSCO	11,804	7,907	3,850	47	4,057 R	67.0%	32.6%	67.3%	32.7%
13,635	IRON	7,056	3,468	3,559	29	91 D	49.1%	50.4%	49.4%	50.6%
54,110	ISABELLA	18,793	12,215	6,435	143	5,780 R	65.0%	34.2%	65.5%	34.5%
151,495	JACKSON	58,785	40,133	18,340	312	21,793 R	68.3%	31.2%	68.6%	31.4%
212,378	KALAMAZOO	91,388	58,327	32,460	601	25,867 R	63.8%	35.5%	64.2%	35.8%
10,952	KALKASKA	5,239	3,623	1,595	21	2,028 R	69.2%	30.4%	69.4%	30.6%
444,506	KENT	205,020	137,417	66,238	1,365	71,179 R	67.0%	32.3%	67.5%	32.5%
1,963	KEWEENAW	1,227	599	628		29 D	48.8%	51.2%	48.8%	51.2%
7,711	LAKE	4,003	2,125	1,845	33	280 R	53.1%	46.1%	53.5%	46.5%
70,038	LAPEER	27,200	19,222	7,800	178	11,422 R	70.7%	28.7%	71.1%	28.9%
14,007	LEELANAU	7,921	5,356	2,498	67	2,858 R	67.6%	31.5%	68.2%	31.8%
89,948	LENAWEE	33,597	22,409	11,012	176	11,397 R	66.7%	32.8%	67.1%	32.9%
100,289	LIVINGSTON	42,812	31,846	10,720	246	21,126 R	74.4%	25.0%	74.8%	25.2%
6,659	LUCE	2,561	1,715	833	13	882 R	67.0%	32.5%	67.3%	32.7%
10,178	MACKINAC	5,593	3,627	1,949	17	1,678 R	64.8%	34.8%	65.0%	35.0%
694,600	MACOMB	293,525	194,300	97,816	1,409	96,484 R	66.2%	33.3%	66.5%	33.5%
23,019	MANISTEE	10,298	6,328	3,917	53	2,411 R	61.4%	38.0%	61.8%	38.2%
74,101	MARQUETTE	28,402	14,196	14,074	132	122 R	50.0%	49.6%	50.2%	49.8%
26,365	MASON	12,092	8,202	3,803	87	4,399 R	67.8%	31.5%	68.3%	31.7%
36,961	MECOSTA	13,142	9,023	4,048	71	4,975 R	68.7%	30.8%	69.0%	31.0%
26,201	MENOMINEE	11,089	6,618	4,425	46	2,193 R	59.7%	39.9%	59.9%	40.1%
73,578	MIDLAND	32,552	21,521	10,769	262	10,752 R	66.1%	33.1%	66.6%	33.4%
10,009	MISSAUKEE	5,256	3,970	1,256	30	2,714 R	75.5%	23.9%	76.0%	24.0%
134,659	MONROE	49,287	29,419	19,617	251	9,802 R	59.7%	39.8%	60.0%	40.0%
47,555	MONTCALM	18,689	13,109	5,491	89	7,618 R	70.1%	29.4%	70.5%	29.5%
7,492	MONTMORENCY	4,313	2,913	1,387	13	1,526 R	67.5%	32.2%	67.7%	32.3%

MICHIGAN

PRESIDENT 1984

1980 Census Population	County	Total Vote	Republican	Democratic	Other	Rep.-Dem. Plurality	Percentage Total Vote Rep.	Percentage Total Vote Dem.	Percentage Major Vote Rep.	Percentage Major Vote Dem.
157,589	MUSKEGON	64,863	39,355	25,247	261	14,108 R	60.7%	38.9%	60.9%	39.1%
34,917	NEWAYGO	15,205	10,636	4,496	73	6,140 R	70.0%	29.6%	70.3%	29.7%
1,011,793	OAKLAND	458,800	306,050	150,286	2,464	155,764 R	66.7%	32.8%	67.1%	32.9%
22,002	OCEANA	9,325	6,405	2,865	55	3,540 R	68.7%	30.7%	69.1%	30.9%
16,436	OGEMAW	8,060	4,901	3,132	27	1,769 R	60.8%	38.9%	61.0%	39.0%
9,861	ONTONAGON	4,836	2,464	2,350	22	114 R	51.0%	48.6%	51.2%	48.8%
18,928	OSCEOLA	8,090	5,923	2,127	40	3,796 R	73.2%	26.3%	73.6%	26.4%
6,858	OSCODA	3,209	2,239	951	19	1,288 R	69.8%	29.6%	70.2%	29.8%
14,993	OTSEGO	6,795	4,639	2,117	39	2,522 R	68.3%	31.2%	68.7%	31.3%
157,174	OTTAWA	75,468	60,142	15,000	326	45,142 R	79.7%	19.9%	80.0%	20.0%
14,267	PRESQUE ISLE	6,724	4,207	2,481	36	1,726 R	62.6%	36.9%	62.9%	37.1%
16,374	ROSCOMMON	9,823	6,419	3,359	45	3,060 R	65.3%	34.2%	65.6%	34.4%
228,059	SAGINAW	90,416	51,495	38,420	501	13,075 R	57.0%	42.5%	57.3%	42.7%
138,802	ST. CLAIR	53,399	36,114	16,998	287	19,116 R	67.6%	31.8%	68.0%	32.0%
56,083	ST. JOSEPH	21,296	15,405	5,795	96	9,610 R	72.3%	27.2%	72.7%	27.3%
40,789	SANILAC	16,810	12,627	4,126	57	8,501 R	75.1%	24.5%	75.4%	24.6%
8,575	SCHOOLCRAFT	4,077	2,139	1,920	18	219 R	52.5%	47.1%	52.7%	47.3%
71,140	SHIAWASSEE	28,431	18,756	9,514	161	9,242 R	66.0%	33.5%	66.3%	33.7%
56,961	TUSCOLA	20,993	14,698	6,212	83	8,486 R	70.0%	29.6%	70.3%	29.7%
66,814	VAN BUREN	25,445	16,426	8,853	166	7,573 R	64.6%	34.8%	65.0%	35.0%
264,748	WASHTENAW	114,569	58,736	55,084	749	3,652 R	51.3%	48.1%	51.6%	48.4%
2,337,891	WAYNE	868,343	367,391	496,632	4,320	129,241 D	42.3%	57.2%	42.5%	57.5%
25,102	WEXFORD	10,715	7,279	3,398	38	3,881 R	67.9%	31.7%	68.2%	31.8%
9,262,078	TOTAL	3,801,658	2,251,571	1,529,638	20,449	721,933 R	59.2%	40.2%	59.5%	40.5%

MICHIGAN

PRESIDENT 1980

1980 Census Population	County	Total Vote	Republican	Democratic	Other	Rep.-Dem. Plurality	Percentage: Total Vote Rep.	Percentage: Total Vote Dem.	Percentage: Major Vote Rep.	Percentage: Major Vote Dem.
9,740	ALCONA	5,062	2,905	1,857	300	1,048 R	57.4%	36.7%	61.0%	39.0%
9,225	ALGER	4,647	2,059	2,242	346	183 D	44.3%	48.2%	47.9%	52.1%
81,555	ALLEGAN	33,031	20,560	9,877	2,594	10,683 R	62.2%	29.9%	67.5%	32.5%
32,315	ALPENA	13,832	6,901	5,834	1,097	1,067 R	49.9%	42.2%	54.2%	45.8%
16,194	ANTRIM	8,364	4,706	2,909	749	1,797 R	56.3%	34.8%	61.8%	38.2%
14,706	ARENAC	6,431	3,436	2,547	448	889 R	53.4%	39.6%	57.4%	42.6%
8,484	BARAGA	3,921	2,046	1,609	266	437 R	52.2%	41.0%	56.0%	44.0%
45,781	BARRY	20,654	12,006	6,857	1,791	5,149 R	58.1%	33.2%	63.6%	36.4%
119,881	BAY	54,592	25,331	24,517	4,744	814 R	46.4%	44.9%	50.8%	49.2%
11,205	BENZIE	5,498	3,054	1,842	602	1,212 R	55.5%	33.5%	62.4%	37.6%
171,276	BERRIEN	67,978	41,458	22,152	4,368	19,306 R	61.0%	32.6%	65.2%	34.8%
40,188	BRANCH	16,230	10,224	4,635	1,371	5,589 R	63.0%	28.6%	68.8%	31.2%
141,557	CALHOUN	59,176	30,912	23,022	5,242	7,890 R	52.2%	38.9%	57.3%	42.7%
49,499	CASS	19,735	11,206	7,058	1,471	4,148 R	56.8%	35.8%	61.4%	38.6%
19,907	CHARLEVOIX	9,796	5,053	3,741	1,002	1,312 R	51.6%	38.2%	57.5%	42.5%
20,649	CHEBOYGAN	9,954	5,221	3,938	795	1,283 R	52.5%	39.6%	57.0%	43.0%
29,029	CHIPPEWA	13,494	7,059	5,268	1,167	1,791 R	52.3%	39.0%	57.3%	42.7%
23,822	CLARE	10,718	5,719	4,164	835	1,555 R	53.4%	38.9%	57.9%	42.1%
55,893	CLINTON	24,691	14,968	7,539	2,184	7,429 R	60.6%	30.5%	66.5%	33.5%
9,465	CRAWFORD	4,964	2,652	1,826	486	826 R	53.4%	36.8%	59.2%	40.8%
38,947	DELTA	17,692	8,146	8,475	1,071	329 D	46.0%	47.9%	49.0%	51.0%
25,341	DICKINSON	13,077	6,614	5,694	769	920 R	50.6%	43.5%	53.7%	46.3%
88,337	EATON	39,977	22,927	12,742	4,308	10,185 R	57.4%	31.9%	64.3%	35.7%
22,992	EMMET	11,006	5,930	3,724	1,352	2,206 R	53.9%	33.8%	61.4%	38.6%
450,449	GENESEE	183,900	78,572	90,393	14,935	11,821 D	42.7%	49.2%	46.5%	53.5%
19,957	GLADWIN	8,825	4,509	3,733	583	776 R	51.1%	42.3%	54.7%	45.3%
19,686	GOGEBIC	10,252	4,388	5,254	610	866 D	42.8%	51.2%	45.5%	54.5%
54,899	GRAND TRAVERSE	24,706	14,484	7,150	3,072	7,334 R	58.6%	28.9%	67.0%	33.0%
40,448	GRATIOT	15,670	9,294	4,916	1,460	4,378 R	59.3%	31.4%	65.4%	34.6%
42,071	HILLSDALE	16,501	10,951	4,375	1,175	6,576 R	66.4%	26.5%	71.5%	28.5%
37,872	HOUGHTON	16,534	7,926	6,858	1,750	1,068 R	47.9%	41.5%	53.6%	46.4%
36,459	HURON	16,167	10,553	4,434	1,180	6,119 R	65.3%	27.4%	70.4%	29.6%
275,520	INGHAM	125,631	56,777	48,278	20,576	8,499 R	45.2%	38.4%	54.0%	46.0%
51,815	IONIA	20,982	12,040	7,039	1,903	5,001 R	57.4%	33.5%	63.1%	36.9%
28,349	IOSCO	11,815	6,680	4,255	880	2,425 R	56.5%	36.0%	61.1%	38.9%
13,635	IRON	7,732	3,507	3,742	483	235 D	45.4%	48.4%	48.4%	51.6%
54,110	ISABELLA	20,715	10,407	7,293	3,015	3,114 R	50.2%	35.2%	58.8%	41.2%
151,495	JACKSON	62,580	33,749	23,685	5,146	10,064 R	53.9%	37.8%	58.8%	41.2%
212,378	KALAMAZOO	95,617	48,669	34,528	12,420	14,141 R	50.9%	36.1%	58.5%	41.5%
10,952	KALKASKA	4,966	2,802	1,807	357	995 R	56.4%	36.4%	60.8%	39.2%
444,506	KENT	206,290	112,604	72,790	20,896	39,814 R	54.6%	35.3%	60.7%	39.3%
1,963	KEWEENAW	1,260	583	570	107	13 R	46.3%	45.2%	50.6%	49.4%
7,711	LAKE	4,003	1,730	2,041	232	311 D	43.2%	51.0%	45.9%	54.1%
70,038	LAPEER	28,069	15,996	9,671	2,402	6,325 R	57.0%	34.5%	62.3%	37.7%
14,007	LEELANAU	7,935	4,585	2,348	1,002	2,237 R	57.8%	29.6%	66.1%	33.9%
89,948	LENAWEE	36,085	20,366	12,935	2,784	7,431 R	56.4%	35.8%	61.2%	38.8%
100,289	LIVINGSTON	41,570	25,012	12,626	3,932	12,386 R	60.2%	30.4%	66.5%	33.5%
6,659	LUCE	2,882	1,659	992	231	667 R	57.6%	34.4%	62.6%	37.4%
10,178	MACKINAC	5,784	3,021	2,262	501	759 R	52.2%	39.1%	57.2%	42.8%
694,600	MACOMB	297,119	154,155	120,125	22,839	34,030 R	51.9%	40.4%	56.2%	43.8%
23,019	MANISTEE	10,702	5,662	4,164	876	1,498 R	52.9%	38.9%	57.6%	42.4%
74,101	MARQUETTE	29,479	13,181	13,312	2,986	131 D	44.7%	45.2%	49.8%	50.2%
26,365	MASON	12,276	7,137	4,134	1,005	3,003 R	58.1%	33.7%	63.3%	36.7%
36,961	MECOSTA	14,528	7,754	5,228	1,546	2,526 R	53.4%	36.0%	59.7%	40.3%
26,201	MENOMINEE	11,749	6,170	4,962	617	1,208 R	52.5%	42.2%	55.4%	44.6%
73,578	MIDLAND	33,610	17,828	12,019	3,763	5,809 R	53.0%	35.8%	59.7%	40.3%
10,009	MISSAUKEE	5,075	3,221	1,563	291	1,658 R	63.5%	30.8%	67.3%	32.7%
134,659	MONROE	49,964	25,612	20,578	3,774	5,034 R	51.3%	41.2%	55.4%	44.6%
47,555	MONTCALM	19,150	10,822	6,706	1,622	4,116 R	56.5%	35.0%	61.7%	38.3%
7,492	MONTMORENCY	4,308	2,400	1,654	254	746 R	55.7%	38.4%	59.2%	40.8%

MICHIGAN

PRESIDENT 1980

1980 Census Population	County	Total Vote	Republican	Democratic	Other	Rep.-Dem. Plurality	Percentage Total Vote Rep.	Percentage Total Vote Dem.	Percentage Major Vote Rep.	Percentage Major Vote Dem.
157,589	MUSKEGON	67,954	36,512	26,645	4,797	9,867 R	53.7%	39.2%	57.8%	42.2%
34,917	NEWAYGO	15,223	8,918	5,236	1,069	3,682 R	58.6%	34.4%	63.0%	37.0%
1,011,793	OAKLAND	463,328	253,211	164,869	45,248	88,342 R	54.7%	35.6%	60.6%	39.4%
22,002	OCEANA	9,564	5,465	3,386	713	2,079 R	57.1%	35.4%	61.7%	38.3%
16,436	OGEMAW	8,128	4,169	3,426	533	743 R	51.3%	42.2%	54.9%	45.1%
9,861	ONTONAGON	5,248	2,569	2,375	304	194 R	49.0%	45.3%	52.0%	48.0%
18,928	OSCEOLA	8,164	4,902	2,650	612	2,252 R	60.0%	32.5%	64.9%	35.1%
6,858	OSCODA	3,466	1,915	1,325	226	590 R	55.3%	38.2%	59.1%	40.9%
14,993	OTSEGO	7,023	3,771	2,666	586	1,105 R	53.7%	38.0%	58.6%	41.4%
157,174	OTTAWA	75,484	51,217	18,435	5,832	32,782 R	67.9%	24.4%	73.5%	26.5%
14,267	PRESQUE ISLE	6,912	3,486	2,952	474	534 R	50.4%	42.7%	54.1%	45.9%
16,374	ROSCOMMON	9,659	5,280	3,763	616	1,517 R	54.7%	39.0%	58.4%	41.6%
228,059	SAGINAW	93,800	45,233	41,650	6,917	3,583 R	48.2%	44.4%	52.1%	47.9%
138,802	ST. CLAIR	55,778	31,021	20,410	4,347	10,611 R	55.6%	36.6%	60.3%	39.7%
56,083	ST. JOSEPH	21,570	13,631	6,318	1,621	7,313 R	63.2%	29.3%	68.3%	31.7%
40,789	SANILAC	18,117	12,158	4,898	1,061	7,260 R	67.1%	27.0%	71.3%	28.7%
8,575	SCHOOLCRAFT	4,374	2,097	1,964	313	133 R	47.9%	44.9%	51.6%	48.4%
71,140	SHIAWASSEE	30,470	15,756	11,985	2,729	3,771 R	51.7%	39.3%	56.8%	43.2%
56,961	TUSCOLA	22,505	13,306	7,632	1,567	5,674 R	59.1%	33.9%	63.5%	36.5%
66,814	VAN BUREN	25,824	14,451	9,248	2,125	5,203 R	56.0%	35.8%	61.0%	39.0%
264,748	WASHTENAW	116,179	48,699	51,013	16,467	2,314 D	41.9%	43.9%	48.8%	51.2%
2,337,891	WAYNE	890,844	315,532	522,024	53,288	206,492 D	35.4%	58.6%	37.7%	62.3%
25,102	WEXFORD	11,160	6,027	4,173	960	1,854 R	54.0%	37.4%	59.1%	40.9%
9,262,078	TOTAL	3,909,725	1,915,225	1,661,532	332,968	253,693 R	49.0%	42.5%	53.5%	46.5%

MICHIGAN

PRESIDENT 1976

1970 Census Population	County	Total Vote	Republican	Democratic	Other	Rep.-Dem. Plurality	Percentage Total Vote Rep.	Percentage Total Vote Dem.	Percentage Major Vote Rep.	Percentage Major Vote Dem.
7,113	ALCONA	4,403	2,328	2,038	37	290 R	52.9%	46.3%	53.3%	46.7%
8,568	ALGER	4,161	1,722	2,379	60	657 D	41.4%	57.2%	42.0%	58.0%
66,575	ALLEGAN	29,471	19,330	9,794	347	9,536 R	65.6%	33.2%	66.4%	33.6%
30,708	ALPENA	12,866	6,380	6,310	176	70 R	49.6%	49.0%	50.3%	49.7%
12,612	ANTRIM	7,518	4,369	3,032	117	1,337 R	58.1%	40.3%	59.0%	41.0%
11,149	ARENAC	5,423	2,687	2,695	41	8 D	49.5%	49.7%	49.9%	50.1%
7,789	BARAGA	3,614	1,788	1,778	48	10 R	49.5%	49.2%	50.1%	49.9%
38,166	BARRY	18,388	11,178	6,967	243	4,211 R	60.8%	37.9%	61.6%	38.4%
117,339	BAY	49,689	23,174	25,958	557	2,784 D	46.6%	52.2%	47.2%	52.8%
8,593	BENZIE	5,038	3,085	1,891	62	1,194 R	61.2%	37.5%	62.0%	38.0%
163,875	BERRIEN	66,798	40,835	25,163	800	15,672 R	61.1%	37.7%	61.9%	38.1%
37,906	BRANCH	14,802	8,251	6,301	250	1,950 R	55.7%	42.6%	56.7%	43.3%
141,963	CALHOUN	56,520	30,390	25,229	901	5,161 R	53.8%	44.6%	54.6%	45.4%
43,312	CASS	17,939	9,893	7,843	203	2,050 R	55.1%	43.7%	55.8%	44.2%
16,541	CHARLEVOIX	9,258	5,145	3,953	160	1,192 R	55.6%	42.7%	56.6%	43.4%
16,573	CHEBOYGAN	8,878	4,894	3,880	104	1,014 R	55.1%	43.7%	55.8%	44.2%
32,412	CHIPPEWA	13,175	7,025	6,022	128	1,003 R	53.3%	45.7%	53.8%	46.2%
16,695	CLARE	9,126	4,879	4,153	94	726 R	53.5%	45.5%	54.0%	46.0%
48,492	CLINTON	21,353	13,475	7,549	329	5,926 R	63.1%	35.4%	64.1%	35.9%
6,482	CRAWFORD	4,303	2,359	1,889	55	470 R	54.8%	43.9%	55.5%	44.5%
35,924	DELTA	17,033	7,809	9,027	197	1,218 D	45.8%	53.0%	46.4%	53.6%
23,753	DICKINSON	12,177	5,922	6,134	121	212 D	48.6%	50.4%	49.1%	50.9%
68,892	EATON	34,750	22,120	12,083	547	10,037 R	63.7%	34.8%	64.7%	35.3%
18,331	EMMET	10,104	5,910	4,013	181	1,897 R	58.5%	39.7%	59.6%	40.4%
444,341	GENESEE	171,438	80,004	88,967	2,467	8,963 D	46.7%	51.9%	47.3%	52.7%
13,471	GLADWIN	7,567	3,794	3,719	54	75 R	50.1%	49.1%	50.5%	49.5%
20,676	GOGEBIC	10,392	3,953	6,341	98	2,388 D	38.0%	61.0%	38.4%	61.6%
39,175	GRAND TRAVERSE	21,150	13,505	7,263	382	6,242 R	63.9%	34.3%	65.0%	35.0%
39,246	GRATIOT	15,118	9,526	5,429	163	4,097 R	63.0%	35.9%	63.7%	36.3%
37,171	HILLSDALE	14,955	9,307	5,427	221	3,880 R	62.2%	36.3%	63.2%	36.8%
34,652	HOUGHTON	15,600	8,049	7,352	199	697 R	51.6%	47.1%	52.3%	47.7%
34,083	HURON	15,176	9,297	5,721	158	3,576 R	61.3%	37.7%	61.9%	38.1%
261,039	INGHAM	119,327	66,729	47,890	4,708	18,839 R	55.9%	40.1%	58.2%	41.8%
45,848	IONIA	18,791	11,737	6,820	234	4,917 R	62.5%	36.3%	63.2%	36.8%
24,905	IOSCO	10,498	5,500	4,875	123	625 R	52.4%	46.4%	53.0%	47.0%
13,813	IRON	7,718	3,224	4,401	93	1,177 D	41.8%	57.0%	42.3%	57.7%
44,594	ISABELLA	18,345	10,577	7,281	487	3,296 R	57.7%	39.7%	59.2%	40.8%
143,274	JACKSON	58,457	32,873	24,726	858	8,147 R	56.2%	42.3%	57.1%	42.9%
201,550	KALAMAZOO	87,085	51,462	33,411	2,212	18,051 R	59.1%	38.4%	60.6%	39.4%
5,272	KALKASKA	4,291	2,280	1,957	54	323 R	53.1%	45.6%	53.8%	46.2%
411,044	KENT	188,633	126,805	59,000	2,828	67,805 R	67.2%	31.3%	68.2%	31.8%
2,264	KEWEENAW	1,271	606	658	7	52 D	47.7%	51.8%	47.9%	52.1%
5,661	LAKE	3,808	1,598	2,179	31	581 D	42.0%	57.2%	42.3%	57.7%
52,317	LAPEER	22,215	12,349	9,503	363	2,846 R	55.6%	42.8%	56.5%	43.5%
10,872	LEELANAU	6,803	4,240	2,437	126	1,803 R	62.3%	35.8%	63.5%	36.5%
81,609	LENAWEE	33,435	18,397	14,610	428	3,787 R	55.0%	43.7%	55.7%	44.3%
58,967	LIVINGSTON	32,486	19,437	12,415	634	7,022 R	59.8%	38.2%	61.0%	39.0%
6,789	LUCE	2,495	1,379	1,099	17	280 R	55.3%	44.0%	55.6%	44.4%
9,660	MACKINAC	5,627	3,107	2,452	68	655 R	55.2%	43.6%	55.9%	44.1%
625,309	MACOMB	258,603	132,499	121,176	4,928	11,323 R	51.2%	46.9%	52.2%	47.8%
20,094	MANISTEE	10,134	5,532	4,479	123	1,053 R	54.6%	44.2%	55.3%	44.7%
64,686	MARQUETTE	26,315	12,984	12,837	494	147 R	49.3%	48.8%	50.3%	49.7%
22,612	MASON	11,516	6,812	4,541	163	2,271 R	59.2%	39.4%	60.0%	40.0%
27,992	MECOSTA	12,221	7,287	4,725	209	2,562 R	59.6%	38.7%	60.7%	39.3%
24,587	MENOMINEE	11,357	5,633	5,596	128	37 R	49.6%	49.3%	50.2%	49.8%
63,769	MIDLAND	30,101	17,631	11,959	511	5,672 R	58.6%	39.7%	59.6%	40.4%
7,126	MISSAUKEE	4,681	2,943	1,688	50	1,255 R	62.9%	36.1%	63.5%	36.5%
118,479	MONROE	44,597	20,676	23,290	631	2,614 D	46.4%	52.2%	47.0%	53.0%
39,660	MONTCALM	17,294	10,439	6,684	171	3,755 R	60.4%	38.6%	61.0%	39.0%
5,247	MONTMORENCY	3,617	1,882	1,684	51	198 R	52.0%	46.6%	52.8%	47.2%

MICHIGAN

PRESIDENT 1976

1970 Census Population	County	Total Vote	Republican	Democratic	Other	Rep.-Dem. Plurality	Percentage Total Vote Rep.	Total Vote Dem.	Major Vote Rep.	Major Vote Dem.
157,426	MUSKEGON	63,407	35,548	27,013	846	8,535 R	56.1%	42.6%	56.8%	43.2%
27,992	NEWAYGO	14,050	8,258	5,622	170	2,636 R	58.8%	40.0%	59.5%	40.5%
907,871	OAKLAND	416,205	244,271	164,266	7,668	80,005 R	58.7%	39.5%	59.8%	40.2%
17,984	OCEANA	8,798	5,236	3,427	135	1,809 R	59.5%	39.0%	60.4%	39.6%
11,903	OGEMAW	6,824	3,212	3,545	67	333 D	47.1%	51.9%	47.5%	52.5%
10,548	ONTONAGON	5,607	2,462	3,104	41	642 D	43.9%	55.4%	44.2%	55.8%
14,838	OSCEOLA	7,178	4,467	2,603	108	1,864 R	62.2%	36.3%	63.2%	36.8%
4,726	OSCODA	2,677	1,541	1,108	28	433 R	57.6%	41.4%	58.2%	41.8%
10,422	OTSEGO	5,952	3,155	2,724	73	431 R	53.0%	45.8%	53.7%	46.3%
128,181	OTTAWA	66,370	49,196	16,381	793	32,815 R	74.1%	24.7%	75.0%	25.0%
12,836	PRESQUE ISLE	6,948	3,545	3,334	69	211 R	51.0%	48.0%	51.5%	48.5%
9,892	ROSCOMMON	8,401	4,608	3,691	102	917 R	54.9%	43.9%	55.5%	44.5%
219,743	SAGINAW	84,071	46,765	36,280	1,026	10,485 R	55.6%	43.2%	56.3%	43.7%
120,175	ST. CLAIR	49,889	26,311	22,734	844	3,577 R	52.7%	45.6%	53.6%	46.4%
47,392	ST. JOSEPH	19,295	11,784	7,306	205	4,478 R	61.1%	37.9%	61.7%	38.3%
34,889	SANILAC	16,856	10,597	6,042	217	4,555 R	62.9%	35.8%	63.7%	36.3%
8,226	SCHOOLCRAFT	4,154	1,933	2,158	63	225 D	46.5%	51.9%	47.3%	52.7%
63,075	SHIAWASSEE	27,721	15,113	12,202	406	2,911 R	54.5%	44.0%	55.3%	44.7%
48,603	TUSCOLA	20,144	12,059	7,932	153	4,127 R	59.9%	39.4%	60.3%	39.7%
56,173	VAN BUREN	24,302	13,615	10,366	321	3,249 R	56.0%	42.7%	56.8%	43.2%
234,103	WASHTENAW	111,689	56,807	50,917	3,965	5,890 R	50.9%	45.6%	52.7%	47.3%
2,666,751	WAYNE	912,990	348,588	548,767	15,635	200,179 D	38.2%	60.1%	38.8%	61.2%
19,717	WEXFORD	10,317	5,670	4,519	128	1,151 R	55.0%	43.8%	55.6%	44.4%
8,875,083	TOTAL	3,653,749	1,893,742	1,696,714	63,293	197,028 R	51.8%	46.4%	52.7%	47.3%

MICHIGAN

PRESIDENT 1972

1970 Census Population	County	Total Vote	Republican	Democratic	Other	Rep.-Dem. Plurality	Percentage Total Vote Rep.	Total Vote Dem.	Major Vote Rep.	Major Vote Dem.
7,113	ALCONA	3,693	2,434	1,195	64	1,239 R	65.9%	32.4%	67.1%	32.9%
8,568	ALGER	3,878	2,035	1,803	40	232 R	52.5%	46.5%	53.0%	47.0%
66,575	ALLEGAN	26,873	18,407	7,883	583	10,524 R	68.5%	29.3%	70.0%	30.0%
30,708	ALPENA	11,831	6,513	5,104	214	1,409 R	55.1%	43.1%	56.1%	43.9%
12,612	ANTRIM	6,280	4,068	2,000	212	2,068 R	64.8%	31.8%	67.0%	33.0%
11,149	ARENAC	4,506	2,588	1,829	89	759 R	57.4%	40.6%	58.6%	41.4%
7,789	BARAGA	3,468	1,905	1,517	46	388 R	54.9%	43.7%	55.7%	44.3%
38,166	BARRY	16,229	10,393	5,484	352	4,909 R	64.0%	33.8%	65.5%	34.5%
117,339	BAY	46,118	23,094	21,712	1,312	1,382 R	50.1%	47.1%	51.5%	48.5%
8,593	BENZIE	4,054	2,686	1,310	58	1,376 R	66.3%	32.3%	67.2%	32.8%
163,875	BERRIEN	63,051	43,047	18,597	1,407	24,450 R	68.3%	29.5%	69.8%	30.2%
37,906	BRANCH	13,521	8,388	4,887	246	3,501 R	62.0%	36.1%	63.2%	36.8%
141,963	CALHOUN	55,828	32,531	22,154	1,143	10,377 R	58.3%	39.7%	59.5%	40.5%
43,312	CASS	15,679	10,398	4,982	299	5,416 R	66.3%	31.8%	67.6%	32.4%
16,541	CHARLEVOIX	7,658	4,522	2,831	305	1,691 R	59.0%	37.0%	61.5%	38.5%
16,573	CHEBOYGAN	7,662	4,529	2,985	148	1,544 R	59.1%	39.0%	60.3%	39.7%
32,412	CHIPPEWA	11,906	7,028	4,744	134	2,284 R	59.0%	39.8%	59.7%	40.3%
16,695	CLARE	6,986	4,402	2,434	150	1,968 R	63.0%	34.8%	64.4%	35.6%
48,492	CLINTON	19,648	13,438	5,870	340	7,568 R	68.4%	29.9%	69.6%	30.4%
6,482	CRAWFORD	3,151	1,953	1,143	55	810 R	62.0%	36.3%	63.1%	36.9%
35,924	DELTA	15,886	7,647	8,003	236	356 D	48.1%	50.4%	48.9%	51.1%
23,753	DICKINSON	11,715	5,989	5,339	387	650 R	51.1%	45.6%	52.9%	47.1%
68,892	EATON	29,811	20,413	8,986	412	11,427 R	68.5%	30.1%	69.4%	30.6%
18,331	EMMET	8,541	5,288	3,081	172	2,207 R	61.9%	36.1%	63.2%	36.8%
444,341	GENESEE	162,449	85,747	73,896	2,806	11,851 R	52.8%	45.5%	53.7%	46.3%
13,471	GLADWIN	5,625	3,484	2,016	125	1,468 R	61.9%	35.8%	63.3%	36.7%
20,676	GOGEBIC	10,776	5,631	4,984	161	647 R	52.3%	46.3%	53.0%	47.0%
39,175	GRAND TRAVERSE	17,621	11,421	5,810	390	5,611 R	64.8%	33.0%	66.3%	33.7%
39,246	GRATIOT	14,478	9,904	4,370	204	5,534 R	68.4%	30.2%	69.4%	30.6%
37,171	HILLSDALE	13,484	9,261	3,942	281	5,319 R	68.7%	29.2%	70.1%	29.9%
34,652	HOUGHTON	15,590	9,053	6,402	135	2,651 R	58.1%	41.1%	58.6%	41.4%
34,083	HURON	14,595	9,832	4,456	307	5,376 R	67.4%	30.5%	68.8%	31.2%
261,039	INGHAM	118,182	63,376	53,458	1,348	9,918 R	53.6%	45.2%	54.2%	45.8%
45,848	IONIA	17,412	10,898	6,240	274	4,658 R	62.6%	35.8%	63.6%	36.4%
24,905	IOSCO	8,971	5,750	3,065	156	2,685 R	64.1%	34.2%	65.2%	34.8%
13,813	IRON	7,376	3,630	3,512	234	118 R	49.2%	47.6%	50.8%	49.2%
44,594	ISABELLA	17,443	9,682	7,446	315	2,236 R	55.5%	42.7%	56.5%	43.5%
143,274	JACKSON	54,891	34,220	19,350	1,321	14,870 R	62.3%	35.3%	63.9%	36.1%
201,550	KALAMAZOO	85,710	50,405	33,324	1,981	17,081 R	58.8%	38.9%	60.2%	39.8%
5,272	KALKASKA	2,881	1,855	924	102	931 R	64.4%	32.1%	66.8%	33.2%
411,044	KENT	175,441	104,041	67,587	3,813	36,454 R	59.3%	38.5%	60.6%	39.4%
2,264	KEWEENAW	1,182	715	456	11	259 R	60.5%	38.6%	61.1%	38.9%
5,661	LAKE	3,129	1,532	1,548	49	16 D	49.0%	49.5%	49.7%	50.3%
52,317	LAPEER	17,585	11,615	5,531	439	6,084 R	66.1%	31.5%	67.7%	32.3%
10,872	LEELANAU	5,786	3,809	1,855	122	1,954 R	65.8%	32.1%	67.2%	32.8%
81,609	LENAWEE	30,647	19,125	11,018	504	8,107 R	62.4%	36.0%	63.4%	36.6%
58,967	LIVINGSTON	25,210	16,856	7,634	720	9,222 R	66.9%	30.3%	68.8%	31.2%
6,789	LUCE	2,487	1,579	862	46	717 R	63.5%	34.7%	64.7%	35.3%
9,660	MACKINAC	5,102	3,096	1,937	69	1,159 R	60.7%	38.0%	61.5%	38.5%
625,309	MACOMB	235,746	147,777	82,346	5,623	65,431 R	62.7%	34.9%	64.2%	35.8%
20,094	MANISTEE	8,863	5,070	3,625	168	1,445 R	57.2%	40.9%	58.3%	41.7%
64,686	MARQUETTE	25,157	13,249	11,555	353	1,694 R	52.7%	45.9%	53.4%	46.6%
22,612	MASON	10,703	6,811	3,697	195	3,114 R	63.6%	34.5%	64.8%	35.2%
27,992	MECOSTA	11,134	7,158	3,799	177	3,359 R	64.3%	34.1%	65.3%	34.7%
24,587	MENOMINEE	10,980	6,060	4,657	263	1,403 R	55.2%	42.4%	56.5%	43.5%
63,769	MIDLAND	26,825	16,473	9,504	848	6,969 R	61.4%	35.4%	63.4%	36.6%
7,126	MISSAUKEE	3,685	2,647	924	114	1,723 R	71.8%	25.1%	74.1%	25.9%
118,479	MONROE	42,465	23,263	17,726	1,476	5,537 R	54.8%	41.7%	56.8%	43.2%
39,660	MONTCALM	15,477	9,591	5,602	284	3,989 R	62.0%	36.2%	63.1%	36.9%
5,247	MONTMORENCY	2,788	1,798	914	76	884 R	64.5%	32.8%	66.3%	33.7%

MICHIGAN

PRESIDENT 1972

1970 Census Population	County	Total Vote	Republican	Democratic	Other	Rep.-Dem. Plurality	Percentage Total Vote Rep.	Percentage Total Vote Dem.	Percentage Major Vote Rep.	Percentage Major Vote Dem.
157,426	MUSKEGON	61,109	36,428	22,804	1,877	13,624 R	59.6%	37.3%	61.5%	38.5%
27,992	NEWAYGO	12,565	8,245	3,978	342	4,267 R	65.6%	31.7%	67.5%	32.5%
907,871	OAKLAND	378,640	241,613	129,400	7,627	112,213 R	63.8%	34.2%	65.1%	34.9%
17,984	OCEANA	7,775	4,992	2,525	258	2,467 R	64.2%	32.5%	66.4%	33.6%
11,903	OGEMAW	5,541	3,367	2,056	118	1,311 R	60.8%	37.1%	62.1%	37.9%
10,548	ONTONAGON	5,286	3,040	2,140	106	900 R	57.5%	40.5%	58.7%	41.3%
14,838	OSCEOLA	6,345	4,441	1,706	198	2,735 R	70.0%	26.9%	72.2%	27.8%
4,726	OSCODA	2,309	1,561	678	70	883 R	67.6%	29.4%	69.7%	30.3%
10,422	OTSEGO	4,838	2,854	1,912	72	942 R	59.0%	39.5%	59.9%	40.1%
128,181	OTTAWA	58,559	42,169	15,119	1,271	27,050 R	72.0%	25.8%	73.6%	26.4%
12,836	PRESQUE ISLE	5,997	3,372	2,440	185	932 R	56.2%	40.7%	58.0%	42.0%
9,892	ROSCOMMON	6,445	4,136	2,187	122	1,949 R	64.2%	33.9%	65.4%	34.6%
219,743	SAGINAW	78,521	47,920	29,424	1,177	18,496 R	61.0%	37.5%	62.0%	38.0%
120,175	ST. CLAIR	45,159	28,471	15,712	976	12,759 R	63.0%	34.8%	64.4%	35.6%
47,392	ST. JOSEPH	17,988	12,438	5,119	431	7,319 R	69.1%	28.5%	70.8%	29.2%
34,889	SANILAC	15,124	11,031	3,780	313	7,251 R	72.9%	25.0%	74.5%	25.5%
8,226	SCHOOLCRAFT	4,123	2,310	1,759	54	551 R	56.0%	42.7%	56.8%	43.2%
63,075	SHIAWASSEE	25,136	15,489	8,932	715	6,557 R	61.6%	35.5%	63.4%	36.6%
48,603	TUSCOLA	17,947	12,198	5,449	300	6,749 R	68.0%	30.4%	69.1%	30.9%
56,173	VAN BUREN	21,520	13,903	7,159	458	6,744 R	64.6%	33.3%	66.0%	34.0%
234,103	WASHTENAW	107,575	50,535	55,350	1,690	4,815 D	47.0%	51.5%	47.7%	52.3%
2,666,751	WAYNE	966,877	435,877	514,913	16,087	79,036 D	45.1%	53.3%	45.8%	54.2%
19,717	WEXFORD	8,499	5,221	3,048	230	2,173 R	61.4%	35.9%	63.1%	36.9%
8,875,083	TOTAL	3,489,727	1,961,721	1,459,435	68,571	502,286 R	56.2%	41.8%	57.3%	42.7%

MICHIGAN

PRESIDENT 1968

1960 Census Population	County	Total Vote	Republican	Democratic	AIP	Other	Plurality	Percentage Rep.	Dem.	AIP
6,352	ALCONA	3,152	1,852	958	338	4	894 R	58.8%	30.4%	10.7%
9,250	ALGER	3,512	1,406	1,927	173	6	521 D	40.0%	54.9%	4.9%
57,729	ALLEGAN	24,483	14,769	7,276	2,389	49	7,493 R	60.3%	29.7%	9.8%
28,556	ALPENA	11,261	5,717	4,788	747	9	929 R	50.8%	42.5%	6.6%
10,373	ANTRIM	5,068	3,002	1,690	374	2	1,312 R	59.2%	33.3%	7.4%
9,860	ARENAC	3,989	2,089	1,573	324	3	516 R	52.4%	39.4%	8.1%
7,151	BARAGA	3,318	1,508	1,680	116	14	172 D	45.4%	50.6%	3.5%
31,738	BARRY	15,400	8,492	5,206	1,674	28	3,286 R	55.1%	33.8%	10.9%
107,042	BAY	42,567	18,779	21,410	2,291	87	2,631 D	44.1%	50.3%	5.4%
7,834	BENZIE	3,510	2,138	1,147	219	6	991 R	60.9%	32.7%	6.2%
149,865	BERRIEN	62,916	32,136	21,266	9,333	181	10,870 R	51.1%	33.8%	14.8%
34,903	BRANCH	12,654	7,071	4,518	1,037	28	2,553 R	55.9%	35.7%	8.2%
138,858	CALHOUN	54,960	26,181	22,633	5,944	202	3,548 R	47.6%	41.2%	10.8%
36,932	CASS	14,906	6,996	5,616	2,257	37	1,380 R	46.9%	37.7%	15.1%
13,421	CHARLEVOIX	6,703	3,696	2,446	556	5	1,250 R	55.1%	36.5%	8.3%
14,550	CHEBOYGAN	6,899	3,422	2,840	634	3	582 R	49.6%	41.2%	9.2%
32,655	CHIPPEWA	10,297	5,359	4,132	793	13	1,227 R	52.0%	40.1%	7.7%
11,647	CLARE	5,831	3,315	1,909	602	5	1,406 R	56.9%	32.7%	10.3%
37,969	CLINTON	16,585	9,416	5,548	1,591	30	3,868 R	56.8%	33.5%	9.6%
4,971	CRAWFORD	2,300	1,266	845	187	2	421 R	55.0%	36.7%	8.1%
34,298	DELTA	14,364	5,829	7,821	700	14	1,992 D	40.6%	54.4%	4.9%
23,917	DICKINSON	11,194	4,920	5,726	533	15	806 D	44.0%	51.2%	4.8%
49,684	EATON	24,826	14,184	8,347	2,252	43	5,837 R	57.1%	33.6%	9.1%
15,904	EMMET	7,488	4,405	2,624	446	13	1,781 R	58.8%	35.0%	6.0%
374,313	GENESEE	164,013	63,948	75,174	24,539	352	11,226 D	39.0%	45.8%	15.0%
10,769	GLADWIN	5,022	2,840	1,668	511	3	1,172 R	56.6%	33.2%	10.2%
24,370	GOGEBIC	10,426	4,140	5,839	434	13	1,699 D	39.7%	56.0%	4.2%
33,490	GRAND TRAVERSE	14,567	8,960	4,741	843	23	4,219 R	61.5%	32.5%	5.8%
37,012	GRATIOT	13,408	8,404	4,040	949	15	4,364 R	62.7%	30.1%	7.1%
34,742	HILLSDALE	13,444	8,506	3,803	1,107	28	4,703 R	63.3%	28.3%	8.2%
35,654	HOUGHTON	14,143	6,639	6,988	473	43	349 D	46.9%	49.4%	3.3%
34,006	HURON	13,552	8,743	3,607	1,178	24	5,136 R	64.5%	26.6%	8.7%
211,296	INGHAM	90,953	46,805	37,362	6,432	354	9,443 R	51.5%	41.1%	7.1%
43,132	IONIA	15,968	8,625	6,055	1,261	27	2,570 R	54.0%	37.9%	7.9%
16,505	IOSCO	7,340	4,068	2,533	736	3	1,535 R	55.4%	34.5%	10.0%
17,184	IRON	7,772	3,292	4,130	340	10	838 D	42.4%	53.1%	4.4%
35,348	ISABELLA	12,396	7,111	4,450	808	27	2,661 R	57.4%	35.9%	6.5%
131,994	JACKSON	51,857	27,828	18,205	5,689	135	9,623 R	53.7%	35.1%	11.0%
169,712	KALAMAZOO	73,832	39,796	26,437	7,398	201	13,359 R	53.9%	35.8%	10.0%
4,382	KALKASKA	2,233	1,190	753	288	2	437 R	53.3%	33.7%	12.9%
363,187	KENT	159,850	85,810	61,891	11,584	565	23,919 R	53.7%	38.7%	7.2%
2,417	KEWEENAW	1,194	525	602	65	2	77 D	44.0%	50.4%	5.4%
5,338	LAKE	2,798	1,094	1,482	220	2	388 D	39.1%	53.0%	7.9%
41,926	LAPEER	16,163	8,866	5,199	2,081	17	3,667 R	54.9%	32.2%	12.9%
9,321	LEELANAU	4,659	2,798	1,562	292	7	1,236 R	60.1%	33.5%	6.3%
77,789	LENAWEE	29,147	16,280	10,552	2,197	118	5,728 R	55.9%	36.2%	7.5%
38,233	LIVINGSTON	19,670	10,034	7,052	2,543	41	2,982 R	51.0%	35.9%	12.9%
7,827	LUCE	2,316	1,351	855	109	1	496 R	58.3%	36.9%	4.7%
10,853	MACKINAC	4,577	2,507	1,751	317	2	756 R	54.8%	38.3%	6.9%
405,804	MACOMB	207,577	63,139	114,552	29,239	647	51,413 D	30.4%	55.2%	14.1%
19,042	MANISTEE	8,306	4,007	3,671	614	14	336 R	48.2%	44.2%	7.4%
56,154	MARQUETTE	20,995	8,960	11,199	802	34	2,239 D	42.7%	53.3%	3.8%
21,929	MASON	9,831	5,311	3,660	854	6	1,651 R	54.0%	37.2%	8.7%
21,051	MECOSTA	8,426	5,053	2,738	625	10	2,315 R	60.0%	32.5%	7.4%
24,685	MENOMINEE	10,108	4,599	4,877	620	12	278 D	45.5%	48.2%	6.1%
51,450	MIDLAND	23,658	14,329	7,428	1,849	52	6,901 R	60.6%	31.4%	7.8%
6,784	MISSAUKEE	3,191	2,161	736	292	2	1,425 R	67.7%	23.1%	9.2%
101,120	MONROE	39,572	15,685	18,921	4,873	93	3,236 D	39.6%	47.8%	12.3%
35,795	MONTCALM	14,902	8,329	5,303	1,244	26	3,026 R	55.9%	35.6%	8.3%
4,424	MONTMORENCY	2,351	1,279	810	260	2	469 R	54.4%	34.5%	11.1%

MICHIGAN

PRESIDENT 1968

1960 Census Population	County	Total Vote	Republican	Democratic	AIP	Other	Plurality	Percentage Rep.	Dem.	AIP
149,943	MUSKEGON	58,683	28,233	24,492	5,808	150	3,741 R	48.1%	41.7%	9.9%
24,160	NEWAYGO	11,048	6,626	3,369	1,042	11	3,257 R	60.0%	30.5%	9.4%
690,259	OAKLAND	345,458	156,538	154,630	33,024	1,266	1,908 R	45.3%	44.8%	9.6%
16,547	OCEANA	6,957	3,911	2,152	876	18	1,759 R	56.2%	30.9%	12.6%
9,680	OGEMAW	4,630	2,526	1,647	454	3	879 R	54.6%	35.6%	9.8%
10,584	ONTONAGON	5,009	2,290	2,462	252	5	172 D	45.7%	49.2%	5.0%
13,595	OSCEOLA	5,810	3,705	1,509	583	13	2,196 R	63.8%	26.0%	10.0%
3,447	OSCODA	1,844	1,124	563	157		561 R	61.0%	30.5%	8.5%
7,545	OTSEGO	3,793	1,871	1,661	259	2	210 R	49.3%	43.8%	6.8%
98,719	OTTAWA	49,342	33,356	12,431	3,460	95	20,925 R	67.6%	25.2%	7.0%
13,117	PRESQUE ISLE	5,251	2,565	2,300	385	1	265 R	48.8%	43.8%	7.3%
7,200	ROSCOMMON	4,713	2,635	1,639	431	8	996 R	55.9%	34.8%	9.1%
190,752	SAGINAW	77,423	38,070	32,266	6,906	181	5,804 R	49.2%	41.7%	8.9%
107,201	ST. CLAIR	42,669	21,084	16,251	5,261	73	4,833 R	49.4%	38.1%	12.3%
42,332	ST. JOSEPH	17,645	10,445	5,413	1,759	28	5,032 R	59.2%	30.7%	10.0%
32,314	SANILAC	14,168	9,273	3,193	1,692	10	6,080 R	65.5%	22.5%	11.9%
8,953	SCHOOLCRAFT	3,844	1,745	1,869	227	3	124 D	45.4%	48.6%	5.9%
53,446	SHIAWASSEE	22,532	11,465	8,619	2,377	71	2,846 R	50.9%	38.3%	10.5%
43,305	TUSCOLA	16,610	10,205	4,698	1,682	25	5,507 R	61.4%	28.3%	10.1%
48,395	VAN BUREN	20,607	10,676	7,304	2,560	67	3,372 R	51.8%	35.4%	12.4%
172,440	WASHTENAW	77,814	36,432	33,073	7,456	853	3,359 R	46.8%	42.5%	9.6%
2,666,297	WAYNE	1,034,260	270,566	654,157	105,606	3,931	383,591 D	26.2%	63.2%	10.2%
18,466	WEXFORD	7,740	4,364	2,832	535	9	1,532 R	56.4%	36.6%	6.9%
7,823,194	TOTAL	3,306,250	1,370,665	1,593,082	331,968	10,535	222,417 D	41.5%	48.2%	10.0%

MICHIGAN

ELECTION NOTES

1984 Other vote was 10,055 Bergland (Libertarian); 3,862 LaRouche (Independent); 1,416 Holmes (Workers World); 1,191 Johnson (Independent); 1,049 Mason (Socialist Workers); 1,048 Hall (Communist); 665 Serrette (Independent); 561 Winn (Workers League); 602 scattered write-in.

1980 Other vote was 275,223 Anderson (Anderson Coalition); 41,597 Clark (Libertarian); 11,930 Commoner (Citizens); 3,262 Hall (Independent); 30 Griswold (write-in); 21 Greaves (write-in); 9 Bubar (write-in); 5 Rarick (write-in); 891 scattered write-in.

1976 Other vote was 47,905 McCarthy (Independent); 5,406 MacBride (Libertarian); 3,504 Wright (Human Rights); 1,804 Camejo (Socialist Workers); 1,366 LaRouche (U.S. Labor); 1,148 Levin (Socialist Labor); 2,160 scattered write-in.

1972 Other vote was 63,321 Schmitz (American Independent); 2,437 Fisher (Socialist Labor); 1,603 Jenness (Socialist Workers); 1,210 Hall (Communist).

1968 Wallace on the ballot as American Independent. Other vote was 4,585 Cleaver (New Politics); 4,099 Halstead (Socialist Workers); 1,762 Blomen (Socialist Labor); 60 Munn (write-in); 29 scattered write-in.

MINNESOTA

POPULAR VOTE FOR PRESIDENT 1920 TO 1984

Year	Total Vote	Republican Vote	Republican Candidate	Democratic Vote	Democratic Candidate	Other Vote	Plurality	Percentage Total Vote Rep.	Percentage Total Vote Dem.	Percentage Major Vote Rep.	Percentage Major Vote Dem.
1984	2,084,449	1,032,603	Reagan, Ronald	1,036,364	Mondale, Walter F.	15,482	3,761 D	49.5%	49.7%	49.9%	50.1%
1980	2,051,980	873,268	Reagan, Ronald	954,174	Carter, Jimmy	224,538	80,906 D	42.6%	46.5%	47.8%	52.2%
1976	1,949,931	819,395	Ford, Gerald R.	1,070,440	Carter, Jimmy	60,096	251,045 D	42.0%	54.9%	43.4%	56.6%
1972	1,741,652	898,269	Nixon, Richard M.	802,346	McGovern, George S.	41,037	95,923 R	51.6%	46.1%	52.8%	47.2%
1968	1,588,506	658,643	Nixon, Richard M.	857,738	Humphrey, Hubert H.	72,125	199,095 D	41.5%	54.0%	43.4%	56.6%
1964	1,554,462	559,624	Goldwater, Barry M.	991,117	Johnson, Lyndon B.	3,721	431,493 D	36.0%	63.8%	36.1%	63.9%
1960	1,541,887	757,915	Nixon, Richard M.	779,933	Kennedy, John F.	4,039	22,018 D	49.2%	50.6%	49.3%	50.7%
1956	1,340,005	719,302	Eisenhower, Dwight D.	617,525	Stevenson, Adlai E.	3,178	101,777 R	53.7%	46.1%	53.8%	46.2%
1952	1,379,483	763,211	Eisenhower, Dwight D.	608,458	Stevenson, Adlai E.	7,814	154,753 R	55.3%	44.1%	55.6%	44.4%
1948	1,212,226	483,617	Dewey, Thomas E.	692,966	Truman, Harry S.	35,643	209,349 D	39.9%	57.2%	41.1%	58.9%
1944	1,125,504	527,416	Dewey, Thomas E.	589,864	Roosevelt, Franklin D.	8,224	62,448 D	46.9%	52.4%	47.2%	52.8%
1940	1,251,188	596,274	Willkie, Wendell	644,196	Roosevelt, Franklin D.	10,718	47,922 D	47.7%	51.5%	48.1%	51.9%
1936	1,129,975	350,461	Landon, Alfred M.	698,811	Roosevelt, Franklin D.	80,703	348,350 D	31.0%	61.8%	33.4%	66.6%
1932	1,002,843	363,959	Hoover, Herbert C.	600,806	Roosevelt, Franklin D.	38,078	236,847 D	36.3%	59.9%	37.7%	62.3%
1928	970,976	560,977	Hoover, Herbert C.	396,451	Smith, Alfred E.	13,548	164,526 R	57.8%	40.8%	58.6%	41.4%
1924 **	822,146	420,759	Coolidge, Calvin	55,913	Davis, John W.	345,474	81,567 R	51.2%	6.8%	88.3%	11.7%
1920	735,838	519,421	Harding, Warren G.	142,994	Cox, James M.	73,423	376,427 R	70.6%	19.4%	78.4%	21.6%

In 1924 other vote was 339,192 Progressive; 4,427 Communist and 1,855 Socialist Labor.

ELECTORAL COLLEGE VOTE 1920 TO 1984

Year	Total	Republican	Democratic	Other
1984	10	—	10	—
1980	10	—	10	—
1976	10	—	10	—
1972	10	10	—	—
1968	10	—	10	—
1964	10	—	10	—
1960	11	—	11	—
1956	11	11	—	—
1952	11	11	—	—
1948	11	—	11	—
1944	11	—	11	—
1940	11	—	11	—
1936	11	—	11	—
1932	11	—	11	—
1928	12	12	—	—
1924	12	12	—	—
1920	12	12	—	—

MINNESOTA

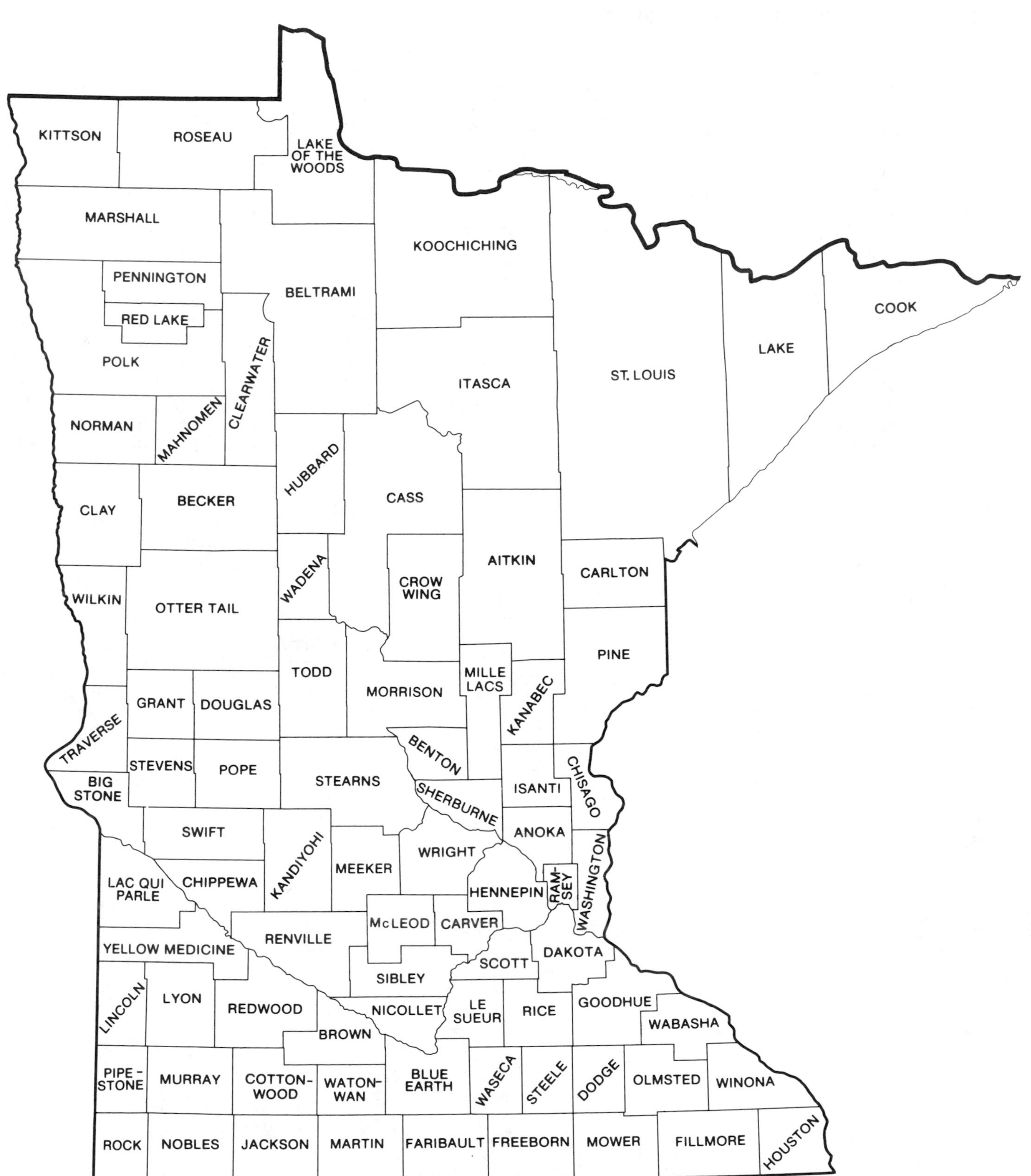
KITTSON
ROSEAU
LAKE OF THE WOODS
MARSHALL
KOOCHICHING
PENNINGTON
BELTRAMI
RED LAKE
COOK
LAKE
POLK
CLEARWATER
ITASCA
ST. LOUIS
NORMAN
MAHNOMEN
HUBBARD
CLAY
BECKER
CASS
AITKIN
CARLTON
WADENA
CROW WING
WILKIN
OTTER TAIL
PINE
TODD
MILLE LACS
MORRISON
GRANT
DOUGLAS
KANABEC
TRAVERSE
BENTON
STEVENS
POPE
STEARNS
ISANTI
BIG STONE
SHERBURNE
CHISAGO
SWIFT
ANOKA
WASHINGTON
KANDIYOHI
WRIGHT
MEEKER
LAC QUI PARLE
CHIPPEWA
HENNEPIN
RAM-SEY
McLEOD
CARVER
RENVILLE
YELLOW MEDICINE
DAKOTA
SCOTT
SIBLEY
LINCOLN
LYON
GOODHUE
REDWOOD
NICOLLET
LE SUEUR
RICE
WABASHA
BROWN
PIPE-STONE
MURRAY
COTTON-WOOD
WATON-WAN
BLUE EARTH
WASECA
STEELE
DODGE
OLMSTED
WINONA
ROCK
NOBLES
JACKSON
MARTIN
FARIBAULT
FREEBORN
MOWER
FILLMORE
HOUSTON

MINNESOTA

PRESIDENT 1984

1980 Census Population	County	Total Vote	Republican	Democratic	Other	Rep.-Dem. Plurality	Percentage Total Vote Rep.	Total Vote Dem.	Major Vote Rep.	Major Vote Dem.
13,404	AITKIN	7,419	3,422	3,943	54	521 D	46.1%	53.1%	46.5%	53.5%
195,998	ANOKA	97,486	46,578	50,305	603	3,727 D	47.8%	51.6%	48.1%	51.9%
29,336	BECKER	13,107	7,553	5,456	98	2,097 R	57.6%	41.6%	58.1%	41.9%
30,982	BELTRAMI	15,002	7,414	7,481	107	67 D	49.4%	49.9%	49.8%	50.2%
25,187	BENTON	11,886	6,830	4,922	134	1,908 R	57.5%	41.4%	58.1%	41.9%
7,716	BIG STONE	3,847	1,821	1,994	32	173 D	47.3%	51.8%	47.7%	52.3%
52,314	BLUE EARTH	26,353	14,298	11,877	178	2,421 R	54.3%	45.1%	54.6%	45.4%
28,645	BROWN	12,977	8,399	4,469	109	3,930 R	64.7%	34.4%	65.3%	34.7%
29,936	CARLTON	14,206	4,877	9,189	140	4,312 D	34.3%	64.7%	34.7%	65.3%
37,046	CARVER	18,816	11,963	6,725	128	5,238 R	63.6%	35.7%	64.0%	36.0%
21,050	CASS	11,482	6,619	4,773	90	1,846 R	57.6%	41.6%	58.1%	41.9%
14,941	CHIPPEWA	7,085	3,964	3,047	74	917 R	55.9%	43.0%	56.5%	43.5%
25,717	CHISAGO	13,063	6,279	6,683	101	404 D	48.1%	51.2%	48.4%	51.6%
49,327	CLAY	21,978	11,565	10,294	119	1,271 R	52.6%	46.8%	52.9%	47.1%
8,761	CLEARWATER	4,027	2,066	1,917	44	149 R	51.3%	47.6%	51.9%	48.1%
4,092	COOK	2,362	1,219	1,129	14	90 R	51.6%	47.8%	51.9%	48.1%
14,854	COTTONWOOD	7,385	4,275	3,073	37	1,202 R	57.9%	41.6%	58.2%	41.8%
41,722	CROW WING	20,236	11,362	8,719	155	2,643 R	56.1%	43.1%	56.6%	43.4%
194,279	DAKOTA	104,946	55,119	49,125	702	5,994 R	52.5%	46.8%	52.9%	47.1%
14,773	DODGE	7,267	4,428	2,786	53	1,642 R	60.9%	38.3%	61.4%	38.6%
27,839	DOUGLAS	14,546	9,005	5,444	97	3,561 R	61.9%	37.4%	62.3%	37.7%
19,714	FARIBAULT	9,739	5,690	3,993	56	1,697 R	58.4%	41.0%	58.8%	41.2%
21,930	FILLMORE	10,762	6,342	4,351	69	1,991 R	58.9%	40.4%	59.3%	40.7%
36,329	FREEBORN	17,873	8,413	9,338	122	925 D	47.1%	52.2%	47.4%	52.6%
38,749	GOODHUE	19,988	11,171	8,679	138	2,492 R	55.9%	43.4%	56.3%	43.7%
7,171	GRANT	3,999	2,111	1,867	21	244 R	52.8%	46.7%	53.1%	46.9%
941,411	HENNEPIN	529,485	253,921	272,401	3,163	18,480 D	48.0%	51.4%	48.2%	51.8%
18,382	HOUSTON	9,249	5,645	3,512	92	2,133 R	61.0%	38.0%	61.6%	38.4%
14,098	HUBBARD	7,483	4,621	2,806	56	1,815 R	61.8%	37.5%	62.2%	37.8%
23,600	ISANTI	11,120	5,660	5,378	82	282 R	50.9%	48.4%	51.3%	48.7%
43,069	ITASCA	20,958	9,306	11,455	197	2,149 D	44.4%	54.7%	44.8%	55.2%
13,690	JACKSON	6,626	3,131	3,437	58	306 D	47.3%	51.9%	47.7%	52.3%
12,161	KANABEC	5,725	3,027	2,660	38	367 R	52.9%	46.5%	53.2%	46.8%
36,763	KANDIYOHI	18,108	9,539	8,402	167	1,137 R	52.7%	46.4%	53.2%	46.8%
6,672	KITTSON	3,351	1,716	1,610	25	106 R	51.2%	48.0%	51.6%	48.4%
17,571	KOOCHICHING	7,746	3,466	4,238	42	772 D	44.7%	54.7%	45.0%	55.0%
10,592	LAC QUI PARLE	5,497	2,731	2,685	81	46 R	49.7%	48.8%	50.4%	49.6%
13,043	LAKE	6,534	2,003	4,468	63	2,465 D	30.7%	68.4%	31.0%	69.0%
3,764	LAKE OF THE WOODS	1,940	1,094	824	22	270 R	56.4%	42.5%	57.0%	43.0%
23,434	LE SUEUR	11,154	6,033	5,070	51	963 R	54.1%	45.5%	54.3%	45.7%
8,207	LINCOLN	3,815	1,905	1,827	83	78 R	49.9%	47.9%	51.0%	49.0%
25,207	LYON	12,664	7,170	5,389	105	1,781 R	56.6%	42.6%	57.1%	42.9%
29,657	MCLEOD	13,731	8,728	4,864	139	3,864 R	63.6%	35.4%	64.2%	35.8%
5,535	MAHNOMEN	2,597	1,328	1,241	28	87 R	51.1%	47.8%	51.7%	48.3%
13,027	MARSHALL	6,209	3,433	2,705	71	728 R	55.3%	43.6%	55.9%	44.1%
24,687	MARTIN	12,046	7,308	4,673	65	2,635 R	60.7%	38.8%	61.0%	39.0%
20,594	MEEKER	9,726	5,511	4,156	59	1,355 R	56.7%	42.7%	57.0%	43.0%
18,430	MILLE LACS	8,371	4,307	4,011	53	296 R	51.5%	47.9%	51.8%	48.2%
29,311	MORRISON	13,885	7,556	6,225	104	1,331 R	54.4%	44.8%	54.8%	45.2%
40,390	MOWER	20,648	8,054	12,498	96	4,444 D	39.0%	60.5%	39.2%	60.8%
11,507	MURRAY	5,578	2,780	2,741	57	39 R	49.8%	49.1%	50.4%	49.6%
26,929	NICOLLET	13,359	7,472	5,789	98	1,683 R	55.9%	43.3%	56.3%	43.7%
21,840	NOBLES	9,605	4,876	4,619	110	257 R	50.8%	48.1%	51.4%	48.6%
9,379	NORMAN	4,377	2,152	2,202	23	50 D	49.2%	50.3%	49.4%	50.6%
92,006	OLMSTED	44,831	28,129	16,335	367	11,794 R	62.7%	36.4%	63.3%	36.7%
51,937	OTTER TAIL	25,554	15,664	9,714	176	5,950 R	61.3%	38.0%	61.7%	38.3%
15,258	PENNINGTON	6,489	3,536	2,913	40	623 R	54.5%	44.9%	54.8%	45.2%
19,871	PINE	9,780	4,493	5,223	64	730 D	45.9%	53.4%	46.2%	53.8%
11,690	PIPESTONE	5,501	3,043	2,391	67	652 R	55.3%	43.5%	56.0%	44.0%
34,844	POLK	15,789	8,617	7,033	139	1,584 R	54.6%	44.5%	55.1%	44.9%

MINNESOTA

PRESIDENT 1984

1980 Census Population	County	Total Vote	Republican	Democratic	Other	Rep.-Dem. Plurality	Percentage Total Vote Rep.	Total Vote Dem.	Major Vote Rep.	Major Vote Dem.
11,657	POPE	5,863	3,064	2,757	42	307 R	52.3%	47.0%	52.6%	47.4%
459,784	RAMSEY	239,511	95,667	141,623	2,221	45,956 D	39.9%	59.1%	40.3%	59.7%
5,471	RED LAKE	2,495	1,184	1,294	17	110 D	47.5%	51.9%	47.8%	52.2%
19,341	REDWOOD	9,061	6,020	2,957	84	3,063 R	66.4%	32.6%	67.1%	32.9%
20,401	RENVILLE	9,632	5,571	3,972	89	1,599 R	57.8%	41.2%	58.4%	41.6%
46,087	RICE	21,537	10,456	10,880	201	424 D	48.5%	50.5%	49.0%	51.0%
10,703	ROCK	5,196	2,971	2,188	37	783 R	57.2%	42.1%	57.6%	42.4%
12,574	ROSEAU	5,811	3,445	2,319	47	1,126 R	59.3%	39.9%	59.8%	40.2%
222,229	ST. LOUIS	112,879	34,162	77,683	1,034	43,521 D	30.3%	68.8%	30.5%	69.5%
43,784	SCOTT	22,133	12,573	9,452	108	3,121 R	56.8%	42.7%	57.1%	42.9%
29,908	SHERBURNE	13,962	7,738	6,140	84	1,598 R	55.4%	44.0%	55.8%	44.2%
15,448	SIBLEY	7,471	4,638	2,761	72	1,877 R	62.1%	37.0%	62.7%	37.3%
108,161	STEARNS	51,663	30,216	20,944	503	9,272 R	58.5%	40.5%	59.1%	40.9%
30,328	STEELE	13,910	8,780	5,060	70	3,720 R	63.1%	36.4%	63.4%	36.6%
11,322	STEVENS	5,752	3,251	2,451	50	800 R	56.5%	42.6%	57.0%	43.0%
12,920	SWIFT	6,488	2,893	3,531	64	638 D	44.6%	54.4%	45.0%	55.0%
24,991	TODD	11,310	6,585	4,657	68	1,928 R	58.2%	41.2%	58.6%	41.4%
5,542	TRAVERSE	2,744	1,399	1,325	20	74 R	51.0%	48.3%	51.4%	48.6%
19,335	WABASHA	9,247	5,299	3,872	76	1,427 R	57.3%	41.9%	57.8%	42.2%
14,192	WADENA	6,794	4,306	2,454	34	1,852 R	63.4%	36.1%	63.7%	36.3%
18,448	WASECA	9,092	5,509	3,527	56	1,982 R	60.6%	38.8%	61.0%	39.0%
113,571	WASHINGTON	57,961	29,046	28,527	388	519 R	50.1%	49.2%	50.5%	49.5%
12,361	WATONWAN	5,978	3,526	2,425	27	1,101 R	59.0%	40.6%	59.3%	40.7%
8,454	WILKIN	3,796	2,367	1,410	19	957 R	62.4%	37.1%	62.7%	37.3%
46,256	WINONA	21,770	11,981	9,577	212	2,404 R	55.0%	44.0%	55.6%	44.4%
58,681	WRIGHT	28,108	15,399	12,486	223	2,913 R	54.8%	44.4%	55.2%	44.8%
13,653	YELLOW MEDICINE	6,917	3,819	3,018	80	801 R	55.2%	43.6%	55.9%	44.1%
4,075,970	TOTAL	2,084,449	1,032,603	1,036,364	15,482	3,761 D	49.5%	49.7%	49.9%	50.1%

MINNESOTA

PRESIDENT 1980

1980 Census Population	County	Total Vote	Republican	Democratic	Other	Rep.-Dem. Plurality	Percentage Total Vote Rep.	Total Vote Dem.	Major Vote Rep.	Major Vote Dem.
13,404	AITKIN	7,670	3,396	3,677	597	281 D	44.3%	47.9%	48.0%	52.0%
195,998	ANOKA	87,843	33,100	45,532	9,211	12,432 D	37.7%	51.8%	42.1%	57.9%
29,336	BECKER	13,134	6,848	5,221	1,065	1,627 R	52.1%	39.8%	56.7%	43.3%
30,982	BELTRAMI	15,537	6,481	7,432	1,624	951 D	41.7%	47.8%	46.6%	53.4%
25,187	BENTON	11,782	5,513	5,272	997	241 R	46.8%	44.7%	51.1%	48.9%
7,716	BIG STONE	4,091	1,950	1,814	327	136 R	47.7%	44.3%	51.8%	48.2%
52,314	BLUE EARTH	26,138	11,966	10,930	3,242	1,036 R	45.8%	41.8%	52.3%	47.7%
28,645	BROWN	14,122	8,051	4,915	1,156	3,136 R	57.0%	34.8%	62.1%	37.9%
29,936	CARLTON	14,850	4,760	8,822	1,268	4,062 D	32.1%	59.4%	35.0%	65.0%
37,046	CARVER	18,481	9,909	6,621	1,951	3,288 R	53.6%	35.8%	59.9%	40.1%
21,050	CASS	11,504	6,119	4,717	668	1,402 R	53.2%	41.0%	56.5%	43.5%
14,941	CHIPPEWA	8,101	4,252	3,164	685	1,088 R	52.5%	39.1%	57.3%	42.7%
25,717	CHISAGO	12,535	5,017	6,240	1,278	1,223 D	40.0%	49.8%	44.6%	55.4%
49,327	CLAY	22,508	10,447	8,940	3,121	1,507 R	46.4%	39.7%	53.9%	46.1%
8,761	CLEARWATER	4,138	1,919	1,955	264	36 D	46.4%	47.2%	49.5%	50.5%
4,092	COOK	2,293	1,174	871	248	303 R	51.2%	38.0%	57.4%	42.6%
14,854	COTTONWOOD	7,847	4,258	2,958	631	1,300 R	54.3%	37.7%	59.0%	41.0%
41,722	CROW WING	21,677	10,844	9,323	1,510	1,521 R	50.0%	43.0%	53.8%	46.2%
194,279	DAKOTA	94,755	40,708	43,433	10,614	2,725 D	43.0%	45.8%	48.4%	51.6%
14,773	DODGE	7,100	3,900	2,698	502	1,202 R	54.9%	38.0%	59.1%	40.9%
27,839	DOUGLAS	14,445	7,778	5,530	1,137	2,248 R	53.8%	38.3%	58.4%	41.6%
19,714	FARIBAULT	10,481	6,206	3,620	655	2,586 R	59.2%	34.5%	63.2%	36.8%
21,930	FILLMORE	11,312	6,452	4,010	850	2,442 R	57.0%	35.4%	61.7%	38.3%
36,329	FREEBORN	17,785	8,475	8,212	1,098	263 R	47.7%	46.2%	50.8%	49.2%
38,749	GOODHUE	20,262	9,329	8,566	2,367	763 R	46.0%	42.3%	52.1%	47.9%
7,171	GRANT	4,272	2,054	1,822	396	232 R	48.1%	42.6%	53.0%	47.0%
941,411	HENNEPIN	505,372	194,898	239,592	70,882	44,694 D	38.6%	47.4%	44.9%	55.1%
18,382	HOUSTON	9,483	5,582	3,218	683	2,364 R	58.9%	33.9%	63.4%	36.6%
14,098	HUBBARD	7,524	4,172	2,840	512	1,332 R	55.4%	37.7%	59.5%	40.5%
23,600	ISANTI	10,809	4,480	5,457	872	977 D	41.4%	50.5%	45.1%	54.9%
43,069	ITASCA	22,256	8,368	12,134	1,754	3,766 D	37.6%	54.5%	40.8%	59.2%
13,690	JACKSON	7,064	3,391	3,062	611	329 R	48.0%	43.3%	52.5%	47.5%
12,161	KANABEC	5,508	2,500	2,654	354	154 D	45.4%	48.2%	48.5%	51.5%
36,763	KANDIYOHI	18,095	8,480	8,038	1,577	442 R	46.9%	44.4%	51.3%	48.7%
6,672	KITTSON	3,577	1,875	1,407	295	468 R	52.4%	39.3%	57.1%	42.9%
17,571	KOOCHICHING	8,250	3,433	4,181	636	748 D	41.6%	50.7%	45.1%	54.9%
10,592	LAC QUI PARLE	5,903	2,981	2,457	465	524 R	50.5%	41.6%	54.8%	45.2%
13,043	LAKE	6,931	2,414	3,864	653	1,450 D	34.8%	55.7%	38.5%	61.5%
3,764	LAKE OF THE WOODS	2,000	1,052	763	185	289 R	52.6%	38.2%	58.0%	42.0%
23,434	LE SUEUR	11,631	5,478	5,161	992	317 R	47.1%	44.4%	51.5%	48.5%
8,207	LINCOLN	4,130	2,122	1,640	368	482 R	51.4%	39.7%	56.4%	43.6%
25,207	LYON	12,911	5,852	5,626	1,433	226 R	45.3%	43.6%	51.0%	49.0%
29,657	MCLEOD	14,040	7,819	4,987	1,234	2,832 R	55.7%	35.5%	61.1%	38.9%
5,535	MAHNOMEN	2,637	1,275	1,175	187	100 R	48.4%	44.6%	52.0%	48.0%
13,027	MARSHALL	6,775	3,638	2,636	501	1,002 R	53.7%	38.9%	58.0%	42.0%
24,687	MARTIN	12,294	7,057	4,301	936	2,756 R	57.4%	35.0%	62.1%	37.9%
20,594	MEEKER	10,095	5,032	4,238	825	794 R	49.8%	42.0%	54.3%	45.7%
18,430	MILLE LACS	9,013	3,860	4,443	710	583 D	42.8%	49.3%	46.5%	53.5%
29,311	MORRISON	14,024	6,296	6,930	798	634 D	44.9%	49.4%	47.6%	52.4%
40,390	MOWER	20,335	7,908	10,538	1,889	2,630 D	38.9%	51.8%	42.9%	57.1%
11,507	MURRAY	6,186	3,004	2,714	468	290 R	48.6%	43.9%	52.5%	47.5%
26,929	NICOLLET	13,643	6,436	5,400	1,807	1,036 R	47.2%	39.6%	54.4%	45.6%
21,840	NOBLES	10,365	4,706	4,703	956	3 R	45.4%	45.4%	50.0%	50.0%
9,379	NORMAN	4,880	2,192	2,253	435	61 D	44.9%	46.2%	49.3%	50.7%
92,006	OLMSTED	40,911	22,704	13,983	4,224	8,721 R	55.5%	34.2%	61.9%	38.1%
51,937	OTTER TAIL	26,138	15,091	9,108	1,939	5,983 R	57.7%	34.8%	62.4%	37.6%
15,258	PENNINGTON	7,416	3,715	3,101	600	614 R	50.1%	41.8%	54.5%	45.5%
19,871	PINE	9,687	3,899	5,121	667	1,222 D	40.2%	52.9%	43.2%	56.8%
11,690	PIPESTONE	6,243	3,207	2,392	644	815 R	51.4%	38.3%	57.3%	42.7%
34,844	POLK	17,644	9,036	7,151	1,457	1,885 R	51.2%	40.5%	55.8%	44.2%

MINNESOTA

PRESIDENT 1980

1980 Census Population	County	Total Vote	Republican	Democratic	Other	Rep.-Dem. Plurality	Percentage Total Vote Rep.	Percentage Total Vote Dem.	Percentage Major Vote Rep.	Percentage Major Vote Dem.
11,657	POPE	6,153	3,159	2,527	467	632 R	51.3%	41.1%	55.6%	44.4%
459,784	RAMSEY	232,744	78,860	124,774	29,110	45,914 D	33.9%	53.6%	38.7%	61.3%
5,471	RED LAKE	2,707	1,223	1,318	166	95 D	45.2%	48.7%	48.1%	51.9%
19,341	REDWOOD	9,699	5,993	2,952	754	3,041 R	61.8%	30.4%	67.0%	33.0%
20,401	RENVILLE	10,444	5,544	4,058	842	1,486 R	53.1%	38.9%	57.7%	42.3%
46,087	RICE	20,677	8,168	9,531	2,978	1,363 D	39.5%	46.1%	46.1%	53.9%
10,703	ROCK	5,713	3,164	2,089	460	1,075 R	55.4%	36.6%	60.2%	39.8%
12,574	ROSEAU	6,317	3,358	2,616	343	742 R	53.2%	41.4%	56.2%	43.8%
222,229	ST. LOUIS	114,757	33,407	69,403	11,947	35,996 D	29.1%	60.5%	32.5%	67.5%
43,784	SCOTT	20,038	9,018	9,115	1,905	97 D	45.0%	45.5%	49.7%	50.3%
29,908	SHERBURNE	13,620	6,035	6,229	1,356	194 D	44.3%	45.7%	49.2%	50.8%
15,448	SIBLEY	7,642	4,460	2,521	661	1,939 R	58.4%	33.0%	63.9%	36.1%
108,161	STEARNS	51,522	24,888	21,862	4,772	3,026 R	48.3%	42.4%	53.2%	46.8%
30,328	STEELE	14,279	7,805	5,095	1,379	2,710 R	54.7%	35.7%	60.5%	39.5%
11,322	STEVENS	6,487	3,283	2,559	645	724 R	50.6%	39.4%	56.2%	43.8%
12,920	SWIFT	6,823	2,943	3,245	635	302 D	43.1%	47.6%	47.6%	52.4%
24,991	TODD	12,111	6,451	4,975	685	1,476 R	53.3%	41.1%	56.5%	43.5%
5,542	TRAVERSE	3,032	1,574	1,258	200	316 R	51.9%	41.5%	55.6%	44.4%
19,335	WABASHA	9,453	4,986	3,712	755	1,274 R	52.7%	39.3%	57.3%	42.7%
14,192	WADENA	7,103	4,089	2,635	379	1,454 R	57.6%	37.1%	60.8%	39.2%
18,448	WASECA	9,303	4,801	3,535	967	1,266 R	51.6%	38.0%	57.6%	42.4%
113,571	WASHINGTON	54,902	22,718	25,634	6,550	2,916 D	41.4%	46.7%	47.0%	53.0%
12,361	WATONWAN	6,587	3,629	2,442	516	1,187 R	55.1%	37.1%	59.8%	40.2%
8,454	WILKIN	4,113	2,224	1,496	393	728 R	54.1%	36.4%	59.8%	40.2%
46,256	WINONA	22,903	10,332	9,814	2,757	518 R	45.1%	42.9%	51.3%	48.7%
58,681	WRIGHT	26,991	12,293	12,383	2,315	90 D	45.5%	45.9%	49.8%	50.2%
13,653	YELLOW MEDICINE	7,427	4,004	2,833	590	1,171 R	53.9%	38.1%	58.6%	41.4%
4,075,970	TOTAL	2,051,980	873,268	954,174	224,538	80,906 D	42.6%	46.5%	47.8%	52.2%

MINNESOTA

PRESIDENT 1976

1970 Census Population	County	Total Vote	Republican	Democratic	Other	Rep.-Dem. Plurality	Percentage Total Vote Rep.	Total Vote Dem.	Major Vote Rep.	Major Vote Dem.
11,403	AITKIN	6,949	2,476	4,308	165	1,832 D	35.6%	62.0%	36.5%	63.5%
154,556	ANOKA	78,315	27,863	48,173	2,279	20,310 D	35.6%	61.5%	36.6%	63.4%
24,372	BECKER	12,575	5,611	6,597	367	986 D	44.6%	52.5%	46.0%	54.0%
26,373	BELTRAMI	13,285	5,214	7,540	531	2,326 D	39.2%	56.8%	40.9%	59.1%
20,841	BENTON	10,965	4,099	6,235	631	2,136 D	37.4%	56.9%	39.7%	60.3%
7,941	BIG STONE	4,011	1,332	2,581	98	1,249 D	33.2%	64.3%	34.0%	66.0%
52,322	BLUE EARTH	25,688	11,998	12,930	760	932 D	46.7%	50.3%	48.1%	51.9%
28,887	BROWN	14,039	7,479	5,792	768	1,687 R	53.3%	41.3%	56.4%	43.6%
28,072	CARLTON	13,952	4,371	9,247	334	4,876 D	31.3%	66.3%	32.1%	67.9%
28,310	CARVER	16,363	8,199	7,574	590	625 R	50.1%	46.3%	52.0%	48.0%
17,323	CASS	10,234	4,443	5,424	367	981 D	43.4%	53.0%	45.0%	55.0%
15,109	CHIPPEWA	8,051	3,254	4,648	149	1,394 D	40.4%	57.7%	41.2%	58.8%
17,492	CHISAGO	10,867	3,874	6,625	368	2,751 D	35.6%	61.0%	36.9%	63.1%
46,585	CLAY	21,711	10,317	10,876	518	559 D	47.5%	50.1%	48.7%	51.3%
8,013	CLEARWATER	4,016	1,374	2,437	205	1,063 D	34.2%	60.7%	36.1%	63.9%
3,423	COOK	2,130	1,034	1,018	78	16 R	48.5%	47.8%	50.4%	49.6%
14,887	COTTONWOOD	7,859	3,906	3,813	140	93 R	49.7%	48.5%	50.6%	49.4%
34,826	CROW WING	19,608	8,072	10,653	883	2,581 D	41.2%	54.3%	43.1%	56.9%
139,808	DAKOTA	84,080	37,542	44,253	2,285	6,711 D	44.7%	52.6%	45.9%	54.1%
13,037	DODGE	6,598	3,446	3,009	143	437 R	52.2%	45.6%	53.4%	46.6%
22,892	DOUGLAS	13,321	5,910	7,097	314	1,187 D	44.4%	53.3%	45.4%	54.6%
20,896	FARIBAULT	10,848	5,577	5,049	222	528 R	51.4%	46.5%	52.5%	47.5%
21,916	FILLMORE	10,957	5,984	4,758	215	1,226 R	54.6%	43.4%	55.7%	44.3%
38,064	FREEBORN	18,018	8,220	9,470	328	1,250 D	45.6%	52.6%	46.5%	53.5%
34,763	GOODHUE	19,352	9,967	8,926	459	1,041 R	51.5%	46.1%	52.8%	47.2%
7,462	GRANT	4,338	1,635	2,624	79	989 D	37.7%	60.5%	38.4%	61.6%
960,080	HENNEPIN	483,378	211,892	257,380	14,106	45,488 D	43.8%	53.2%	45.2%	54.8%
17,556	HOUSTON	8,926	4,853	3,861	212	992 R	54.4%	43.3%	55.7%	44.3%
10,583	HUBBARD	6,502	2,985	3,196	321	211 D	45.9%	49.2%	48.3%	51.7%
16,560	ISANTI	9,428	3,159	6,013	256	2,854 D	33.5%	63.8%	34.4%	65.6%
35,530	ITASCA	20,281	6,646	12,979	656	6,333 D	32.8%	64.0%	33.9%	66.1%
14,352	JACKSON	7,298	2,870	4,311	117	1,441 D	39.3%	59.1%	40.0%	60.0%
9,775	KANABEC	5,311	1,943	3,188	180	1,245 D	36.6%	60.0%	37.9%	62.1%
30,548	KANDIYOHI	17,145	6,664	9,992	489	3,328 D	38.9%	58.3%	40.0%	60.0%
6,853	KITTSON	3,629	1,555	2,008	66	453 D	42.8%	55.3%	43.6%	56.4%
17,131	KOOCHICHING	8,010	2,893	4,846	271	1,953 D	36.1%	60.5%	37.4%	62.6%
11,164	LAC QUI PARLE	6,065	2,292	3,647	126	1,355 D	37.8%	60.1%	38.6%	61.4%
13,351	LAKE	6,619	2,313	3,973	333	1,660 D	34.9%	60.0%	36.8%	63.2%
3,987	LAKE OF THE WOODS	1,968	757	1,105	106	348 D	38.5%	56.1%	40.7%	59.3%
21,332	LE SUEUR	11,396	4,565	6,556	275	1,991 D	40.1%	57.5%	41.0%	59.0%
8,143	LINCOLN	4,272	1,599	2,594	79	995 D	37.4%	60.7%	38.1%	61.9%
24,273	LYON	12,470	5,036	7,122	312	2,086 D	40.4%	57.1%	41.4%	58.6%
27,662	MCLEOD	13,245	6,519	6,249	477	270 R	49.2%	47.2%	51.1%	48.9%
5,638	MAHNOMEN	2,621	905	1,590	126	685 D	34.5%	60.7%	36.3%	63.7%
13,060	MARSHALL	6,490	2,605	3,744	141	1,139 D	40.1%	57.7%	41.0%	59.0%
24,316	MARTIN	12,488	6,484	5,672	332	812 R	51.9%	45.4%	53.3%	46.7%
18,810	MEEKER	9,765	4,097	5,295	373	1,198 D	42.0%	54.2%	43.6%	56.4%
15,703	MILLE LACS	8,670	3,212	5,172	286	1,960 D	37.0%	59.7%	38.3%	61.7%
26,949	MORRISON	13,294	4,590	8,176	528	3,586 D	34.5%	61.5%	36.0%	64.0%
43,783	MOWER	21,487	8,163	12,837	487	4,674 D	38.0%	59.7%	38.9%	61.1%
12,508	MURRAY	6,399	2,605	3,685	109	1,080 D	40.7%	57.6%	41.4%	58.6%
24,518	NICOLLET	12,245	6,071	5,777	397	294 R	49.6%	47.2%	51.2%	48.8%
23,208	NOBLES	10,735	4,503	6,034	198	1,531 D	41.9%	56.2%	42.7%	57.3%
10,008	NORMAN	5,012	1,983	2,946	83	963 D	39.6%	58.8%	40.2%	59.8%
84,104	OLMSTED	39,617	24,030	14,676	911	9,354 R	60.7%	37.0%	62.1%	37.9%
46,097	OTTER TAIL	24,510	12,113	11,881	516	232 R	49.4%	48.5%	50.5%	49.5%
13,266	PENNINGTON	6,948	3,023	3,787	138	764 D	43.5%	54.5%	44.4%	55.6%
16,821	PINE	8,887	3,057	5,442	388	2,385 D	34.4%	61.2%	36.0%	64.0%
12,791	PIPESTONE	6,402	3,018	3,272	112	254 D	47.1%	51.1%	48.0%	52.0%
34,435	POLK	16,052	6,552	9,078	422	2,526 D	40.8%	56.6%	41.9%	58.1%

MINNESOTA

PRESIDENT 1976

1970 Census Population	County	Total Vote	Republican	Democratic	Other	Rep.-Dem. Plurality	Percentage Total Vote Rep.	Total Vote Dem.	Major Vote Rep.	Major Vote Dem.
11,107	POPE	6,127	2,251	3,746	130	1,495 D	36.7%	61.1%	37.5%	62.5%
476,255	RAMSEY	228,067	86,480	133,682	7,905	47,202 D	37.9%	58.6%	39.3%	60.7%
5,388	RED LAKE	2,613	737	1,748	128	1,011 D	28.2%	66.9%	29.7%	70.3%
20,024	REDWOOD	9,822	4,926	4,525	371	401 R	50.2%	46.1%	52.1%	47.9%
21,139	RENVILLE	10,545	4,482	5,762	301	1,280 D	42.5%	54.6%	43.8%	56.2%
41,582	RICE	19,607	8,311	10,590	706	2,279 D	42.4%	54.0%	44.0%	56.0%
11,346	ROCK	5,739	2,892	2,769	78	123 R	50.4%	48.2%	51.1%	48.9%
11,569	ROSEAU	5,755	2,382	3,215	158	833 D	41.4%	55.9%	42.6%	57.4%
220,693	ST. LOUIS	114,075	35,331	75,040	3,704	39,709 D	31.0%	65.8%	32.0%	68.0%
32,423	SCOTT	17,622	7,154	9,912	556	2,758 D	40.6%	56.2%	41.9%	58.1%
18,344	SHERBURNE	11,442	4,361	6,678	403	2,317 D	38.1%	58.4%	39.5%	60.5%
15,845	SIBLEY	7,860	3,871	3,752	237	119 R	49.2%	47.7%	50.8%	49.2%
95,400	STEARNS	47,821	19,574	25,027	3,220	5,453 D	40.9%	52.3%	43.9%	56.1%
26,931	STEELE	13,648	7,053	6,263	332	790 R	51.7%	45.9%	53.0%	47.0%
11,218	STEVENS	5,793	2,484	3,171	138	687 D	42.9%	54.7%	43.9%	56.1%
13,177	SWIFT	6,762	2,190	4,428	144	2,238 D	32.4%	65.5%	33.1%	66.9%
22,114	TODD	11,248	4,278	6,530	440	2,252 D	38.0%	58.1%	39.6%	60.4%
6,254	TRAVERSE	3,207	1,130	2,020	57	890 D	35.2%	63.0%	35.9%	64.1%
17,224	WABASHA	9,049	4,484	4,286	279	198 R	49.6%	47.4%	51.1%	48.9%
12,412	WADENA	6,424	3,048	3,164	212	116 D	47.4%	49.3%	49.1%	50.9%
16,663	WASECA	8,805	4,582	4,002	221	580 R	52.0%	45.5%	53.4%	46.6%
82,948	WASHINGTON	48,583	20,716	26,454	1,413	5,738 D	42.6%	54.5%	43.9%	56.1%
13,298	WATONWAN	6,662	3,351	3,177	134	174 R	50.3%	47.7%	51.3%	48.7%
9,389	WILKIN	4,112	1,882	2,103	127	221 D	45.8%	51.1%	47.2%	52.8%
44,409	WINONA	21,914	10,436	10,939	539	503 D	47.6%	49.9%	48.8%	51.2%
38,933	WRIGHT	23,464	9,314	13,379	771	4,065 D	39.7%	57.0%	41.0%	59.0%
14,516	YELLOW MEDICINE	7,470	2,946	4,337	187	1,391 D	39.4%	58.1%	40.5%	59.5%
3,805,069	TOTAL	1,949,931	819,395	1,070,440	60,096	251,045 D	42.0%	54.9%	43.4%	56.6%

MINNESOTA

PRESIDENT 1972

1970 Census Population	County	Total Vote	Republican	Democratic	Other	Rep.-Dem. Plurality	Percentage Total Vote Rep.	Percentage Total Vote Dem.	Percentage Major Vote Rep.	Percentage Major Vote Dem.
11,403	AITKIN	6,032	3,241	2,687	104	554 R	53.7%	44.5%	54.7%	45.3%
154,556	ANOKA	59,360	29,546	28,031	1,783	1,515 R	49.8%	47.2%	51.3%	48.7%
24,372	BECKER	10,884	6,033	4,695	156	1,338 R	55.4%	43.1%	56.2%	43.8%
26,373	BELTRAMI	11,393	5,947	5,194	252	753 R	52.2%	45.6%	53.4%	46.6%
20,841	BENTON	9,426	4,652	4,282	492	370 R	49.4%	45.4%	52.1%	47.9%
7,941	BIG STONE	4,017	1,748	2,185	84	437 D	43.5%	54.4%	44.4%	55.6%
52,322	BLUE EARTH	23,662	12,702	10,638	322	2,064 R	53.7%	45.0%	54.4%	45.6%
28,887	BROWN	12,729	7,791	4,347	591	3,444 R	61.2%	34.2%	64.2%	35.8%
28,072	CARLTON	12,730	5,445	7,116	169	1,671 D	42.8%	55.9%	43.3%	56.7%
28,310	CARVER	13,905	8,546	4,852	507	3,694 R	61.5%	34.9%	63.8%	36.2%
17,323	CASS	8,503	4,906	3,347	250	1,559 R	57.7%	39.4%	59.4%	40.6%
15,109	CHIPPEWA	7,547	3,787	3,630	130	157 R	50.2%	48.1%	51.1%	48.9%
17,492	CHISAGO	9,241	4,718	4,174	349	544 R	51.1%	45.2%	53.1%	46.9%
46,585	CLAY	20,400	11,089	9,076	235	2,013 R	54.4%	44.5%	55.0%	45.0%
8,013	CLEARWATER	3,683	1,819	1,751	113	68 R	49.4%	47.5%	51.0%	49.0%
3,423	COOK	1,817	1,047	742	28	305 R	57.6%	40.8%	58.5%	41.5%
14,887	COTTONWOOD	7,303	4,396	2,802	105	1,594 R	60.2%	38.4%	61.1%	38.9%
34,826	CROW WING	16,551	8,774	7,328	449	1,446 R	53.0%	44.3%	54.5%	45.5%
139,808	DAKOTA	64,796	34,967	28,479	1,350	6,488 R	54.0%	44.0%	55.1%	44.9%
13,037	DODGE	5,936	3,863	1,921	152	1,942 R	65.1%	32.4%	66.8%	33.2%
22,892	DOUGLAS	12,606	6,678	5,501	427	1,177 R	53.0%	43.6%	54.8%	45.2%
20,896	FARIBAULT	10,153	6,503	3,519	131	2,984 R	64.1%	34.7%	64.9%	35.1%
21,916	FILLMORE	10,460	7,107	3,155	198	3,952 R	67.9%	30.2%	69.3%	30.7%
38,064	FREEBORN	17,130	9,747	7,163	220	2,584 R	56.9%	41.8%	57.6%	42.4%
34,763	GOODHUE	17,631	11,107	6,147	377	4,960 R	63.0%	34.9%	64.4%	35.6%
7,462	GRANT	4,054	1,899	2,085	70	186 D	46.8%	51.4%	47.7%	52.3%
960,080	HENNEPIN	443,358	228,951	205,943	8,464	23,008 R	51.6%	46.5%	52.6%	47.4%
17,556	HOUSTON	7,790	5,186	2,467	137	2,719 R	66.6%	31.7%	67.8%	32.2%
10,583	HUBBARD	5,554	3,294	2,136	124	1,158 R	59.3%	38.5%	60.7%	39.3%
16,560	ISANTI	7,634	3,715	3,660	259	55 R	48.7%	47.9%	50.4%	49.6%
35,530	ITASCA	16,583	7,558	8,683	342	1,125 D	45.6%	52.4%	46.5%	53.5%
14,352	JACKSON	6,989	3,599	3,304	86	295 R	51.5%	47.3%	52.1%	47.9%
9,775	KANABEC	4,632	2,395	1,969	268	426 R	51.7%	42.5%	54.9%	45.1%
30,548	KANDIYOHI	14,481	6,624	7,241	616	617 D	45.7%	50.0%	47.8%	52.2%
6,853	KITTSON	3,479	1,832	1,584	63	248 R	52.7%	45.5%	53.6%	46.4%
17,131	KOOCHICHING	7,230	3,681	3,396	153	285 R	50.9%	47.0%	52.0%	48.0%
11,164	LAC QUI PARLE	5,726	2,773	2,845	108	72 D	48.4%	49.7%	49.4%	50.6%
13,351	LAKE	6,327	2,575	3,640	112	1,065 D	40.7%	57.5%	41.4%	58.6%
3,987	LAKE OF THE WOODS	1,582	877	672	33	205 R	55.4%	42.5%	56.6%	43.4%
21,332	LE SUEUR	10,262	5,388	4,725	149	663 R	52.5%	46.0%	53.3%	46.7%
8,143	LINCOLN	4,095	1,881	2,148	66	267 D	45.9%	52.5%	46.7%	53.3%
24,273	LYON	11,630	5,820	5,614	196	206 R	50.0%	48.3%	50.9%	49.1%
27,662	MCLEOD	12,733	7,820	4,538	375	3,282 R	61.4%	35.6%	63.3%	36.7%
5,638	MAHNOMEN	2,691	1,246	1,397	48	151 D	46.3%	51.9%	47.1%	52.9%
13,060	MARSHALL	6,190	3,264	2,790	136	474 R	52.7%	45.1%	53.9%	46.1%
24,316	MARTIN	11,718	7,569	3,816	333	3,753 R	64.6%	32.6%	66.5%	33.5%
18,810	MEEKER	8,933	5,097	3,601	235	1,496 R	57.1%	40.3%	58.6%	41.4%
15,703	MILLE LACS	7,686	4,291	3,221	174	1,070 R	55.8%	41.9%	57.1%	42.9%
26,949	MORRISON	12,329	5,714	5,993	622	279 D	46.3%	48.6%	48.8%	51.2%
43,783	MOWER	20,530	9,929	10,286	315	357 D	48.4%	50.1%	49.1%	50.9%
12,508	MURRAY	5,927	2,959	2,893	75	66 R	49.9%	48.8%	50.6%	49.4%
24,518	NICOLLET	11,069	6,230	4,680	159	1,550 R	56.3%	42.3%	57.1%	42.9%
23,208	NOBLES	10,525	4,951	5,464	110	513 D	47.0%	51.9%	47.5%	52.5%
10,008	NORMAN	5,021	2,536	2,444	41	92 R	50.5%	48.7%	50.9%	49.1%
84,104	OLMSTED	34,521	23,806	9,817	898	13,989 R	69.0%	28.4%	70.8%	29.2%
46,097	OTTER TAIL	21,731	13,519	7,881	331	5,638 R	62.2%	36.3%	63.2%	36.8%
13,266	PENNINGTON	6,600	3,548	2,892	160	656 R	53.8%	43.8%	55.1%	44.9%
16,821	PINE	8,017	3,881	3,794	342	87 R	48.4%	47.3%	50.6%	49.4%
12,791	PIPESTONE	6,376	3,543	2,758	75	785 R	55.6%	43.3%	56.2%	43.8%
34,435	POLK	15,885	8,139	7,366	380	773 R	51.2%	46.4%	52.5%	47.5%

MINNESOTA

PRESIDENT 1972

1970 Census Population	County	Total Vote	Republican	Democratic	Other	Rep.-Dem. Plurality	Percentage Total Vote Rep.	Total Vote Dem.	Major Vote Rep.	Major Vote Dem.
11,107	POPE	5,681	2,610	2,910	161	300 D	45.9%	51.2%	47.3%	52.7%
476,255	RAMSEY	209,951	95,716	108,392	5,843	12,676 D	45.6%	51.6%	46.9%	53.1%
5,388	RED LAKE	2,541	1,052	1,409	80	357 D	41.4%	55.5%	42.7%	57.3%
20,024	REDWOOD	9,252	5,776	3,177	299	2,599 R	62.4%	34.3%	64.5%	35.5%
21,139	RENVILLE	10,044	5,329	4,499	216	830 R	53.1%	44.8%	54.2%	45.8%
41,582	RICE	17,475	9,195	8,065	215	1,130 R	52.6%	46.2%	53.3%	46.7%
11,346	ROCK	5,612	3,470	2,089	53	1,381 R	61.8%	37.2%	62.4%	37.6%
11,569	ROSEAU	5,344	2,844	2,396	104	448 R	53.2%	44.8%	54.3%	45.7%
220,693	ST. LOUIS	104,180	41,435	61,103	1,642	19,668 D	39.8%	58.7%	40.4%	59.6%
32,423	SCOTT	14,376	7,310	6,745	321	565 R	50.8%	46.9%	52.0%	48.0%
18,344	SHERBURNE	8,658	4,332	4,070	256	262 R	50.0%	47.0%	51.6%	48.4%
15,845	SIBLEY	7,080	4,543	2,433	104	2,110 R	64.2%	34.4%	65.1%	34.9%
95,400	STEARNS	41,400	18,951	19,315	3,134	364 D	45.8%	46.7%	49.5%	50.5%
26,931	STEELE	11,868	7,678	4,010	180	3,668 R	64.7%	33.8%	65.7%	34.3%
11,218	STEVENS	5,811	2,830	2,870	111	40 D	48.7%	49.4%	49.6%	50.4%
13,177	SWIFT	6,617	2,673	3,823	121	1,150 D	40.4%	57.8%	41.1%	58.9%
22,114	TODD	10,137	5,387	4,270	480	1,117 R	53.1%	42.1%	55.8%	44.2%
6,254	TRAVERSE	3,055	1,276	1,744	35	468 D	41.8%	57.1%	42.3%	57.7%
17,224	WABASHA	8,413	5,158	3,017	238	2,141 R	61.3%	35.9%	63.1%	36.9%
12,412	WADENA	5,974	3,408	2,430	136	978 R	57.0%	40.7%	58.4%	41.6%
16,663	WASECA	7,926	5,064	2,767	95	2,297 R	63.9%	34.9%	64.7%	35.3%
82,948	WASHINGTON	36,098	19,142	16,102	854	3,040 R	53.0%	44.6%	54.3%	45.7%
13,298	WATONWAN	6,251	3,960	2,229	62	1,731 R	63.3%	35.7%	64.0%	36.0%
9,389	WILKIN	4,093	2,292	1,739	62	553 R	56.0%	42.5%	56.9%	43.1%
44,409	WINONA	19,327	10,910	8,080	337	2,830 R	56.4%	41.8%	57.5%	42.5%
38,933	WRIGHT	19,386	9,996	8,695	695	1,301 R	51.6%	44.9%	53.5%	46.5%
14,516	YELLOW MEDICINE	7,319	3,683	3,462	174	221 R	50.3%	47.3%	51.5%	48.5%
3,805,069	TOTAL	1,741,652	898,269	802,346	41,037	95,923 R	51.6%	46.1%	52.8%	47.2%

MINNESOTA

PRESIDENT 1968

1960 Census Population	County	Total Vote	Republican	Democratic	AIP	Other	Plurality	Percentage		
								Rep.	Dem.	AIP
12,162	AITKIN	5,657	2,254	3,094	286	23	840 D	39.8%	54.7%	5.1%
85,916	ANOKA	50,134	16,358	30,656	3,073	47	14,298 D	32.6%	61.1%	6.1%
23,959	BECKER	10,196	4,728	4,875	568	25	147 D	46.4%	47.8%	5.6%
23,425	BELTRAMI	9,565	3,912	5,034	599	20	1,122 D	40.9%	52.6%	6.3%
17,287	BENTON	8,016	3,470	4,022	514	10	552 D	43.3%	50.2%	6.4%
8,954	BIG STONE	3,946	1,645	2,119	176	6	474 D	41.7%	53.7%	4.5%
44,385	BLUE EARTH	19,537	9,571	9,254	686	26	317 R	49.0%	47.4%	3.5%
27,676	BROWN	12,350	7,039	4,585	703	23	2,454 R	57.0%	37.1%	5.7%
27,932	CARLTON	12,018	3,016	8,538	444	20	5,522 D	25.1%	71.0%	3.7%
21,358	CARVER	11,780	6,649	4,590	528	13	2,059 R	56.4%	39.0%	4.5%
16,720	CASS	7,950	3,888	3,569	486	7	319 R	48.9%	44.9%	6.1%
16,320	CHIPPEWA	7,147	3,195	3,701	243	8	506 D	44.7%	51.8%	3.4%
13,419	CHISAGO	7,651	3,053	4,102	492	4	1,049 D	39.9%	53.6%	6.4%
39,080	CLAY	16,560	7,910	7,987	640	23	77 D	47.8%	48.2%	3.9%
8,864	CLEARWATER	3,561	1,284	2,046	217	14	762 D	36.1%	57.5%	6.1%
3,377	COOK	1,729	853	777	96	3	76 R	49.3%	44.9%	5.6%
16,166	COTTONWOOD	7,391	4,050	3,046	293	2	1,004 R	54.8%	41.2%	4.0%
32,134	CROW WING	14,795	6,687	7,411	672	25	724 D	45.2%	50.1%	4.5%
78,303	DAKOTA	49,908	19,290	28,416	2,142	60	9,126 D	38.7%	56.9%	4.3%
13,259	DODGE	5,709	3,064	2,437	201	7	627 R	53.7%	42.7%	3.5%
21,313	DOUGLAS	10,839	5,464	4,826	536	13	638 R	50.4%	44.5%	4.9%
23,685	FARIBAULT	10,384	5,662	4,335	379	8	1,327 R	54.5%	41.7%	3.6%
23,768	FILLMORE	10,607	6,257	3,918	426	6	2,339 R	59.0%	36.9%	4.0%
37,891	FREEBORN	16,563	7,315	8,671	558	19	1,356 D	44.2%	52.4%	3.4%
33,035	GOODHUE	15,964	8,283	7,220	451	10	1,063 R	51.9%	45.2%	2.8%
8,870	GRANT	4,095	1,929	1,982	179	5	53 D	47.1%	48.4%	4.4%
842,854	HENNEPIN	407,024	170,002	220,078	15,659	1,285	50,076 D	41.8%	54.1%	3.8%
16,588	HOUSTON	7,681	4,450	2,703	521	7	1,747 R	57.9%	35.2%	6.8%
9,962	HUBBARD	4,950	2,720	1,920	304	6	800 R	54.9%	38.8%	6.1%
13,530	ISANTI	6,337	2,429	3,439	451	18	1,010 D	38.3%	54.3%	7.1%
38,006	ITASCA	16,206	4,898	10,512	780	16	5,614 D	30.2%	64.9%	4.8%
15,501	JACKSON	6,766	2,886	3,515	359	6	629 D	42.7%	52.0%	5.3%
9,007	KANABEC	4,248	1,847	2,154	240	7	307 D	43.5%	50.7%	5.6%
29,987	KANDIYOHI	13,400	5,086	7,639	658	17	2,553 D	38.0%	57.0%	4.9%
8,343	KITTSON	3,513	1,436	1,894	179	4	458 D	40.9%	53.9%	5.1%
18,190	KOOCHICHING	7,116	2,104	4,697	299	16	2,593 D	29.6%	66.0%	4.2%
13,330	LAC QUI PARLE	5,828	2,672	2,937	212	7	265 D	45.8%	50.4%	3.6%
13,702	LAKE	5,891	1,351	4,266	263	11	2,915 D	22.9%	72.4%	4.5%
4,304	LAKE OF THE WOODS	1,558	607	875	69	7	268 D	39.0%	56.2%	4.4%
19,906	LE SUEUR	9,581	4,189	5,094	292	6	905 D	43.7%	53.2%	3.0%
9,651	LINCOLN	4,030	1,732	2,109	187	2	377 D	43.0%	52.3%	4.6%
22,655	LYON	9,966	4,331	5,317	306	12	986 D	43.5%	53.4%	3.1%
24,401	MCLEOD	12,064	6,619	4,861	576	8	1,758 R	54.9%	40.3%	4.8%
6,341	MAHNOMEN	2,605	893	1,508	201	3	615 D	34.3%	57.9%	7.7%
14,262	MARSHALL	5,956	2,367	3,161	418	10	794 D	39.7%	53.1%	7.0%
26,986	MARTIN	11,973	7,115	4,271	580	7	2,844 R	59.4%	35.7%	4.8%
18,887	MEEKER	8,704	4,044	4,213	438	9	169 D	46.5%	48.4%	5.0%
14,560	MILLE LACS	6,890	2,990	3,494	399	7	504 D	43.4%	50.7%	5.8%
26,641	MORRISON	11,256	4,511	6,111	612	22	1,600 D	40.1%	54.3%	5.4%
48,498	MOWER	19,486	7,736	11,022	692	36	3,286 D	39.7%	56.6%	3.6%
14,743	MURRAY	5,888	2,906	2,662	316	4	244 R	49.4%	45.2%	5.4%
23,196	NICOLLET	9,234	4,671	4,244	312	7	427 R	50.6%	46.0%	3.4%
23,365	NOBLES	10,107	4,451	5,171	477	8	720 D	44.0%	51.2%	4.7%
11,253	NORMAN	5,012	1,981	2,828	200	3	847 D	39.5%	56.4%	4.0%
65,532	OLMSTED	31,840	17,292	13,417	1,103	28	3,875 R	54.3%	42.1%	3.5%
48,960	OTTER TAIL	20,701	12,483	7,400	802	16	5,083 R	60.3%	35.7%	3.9%
12,468	PENNINGTON	5,465	2,247	2,998	212	8	751 D	41.1%	54.9%	3.9%
17,004	PINE	7,117	2,591	4,044	463	19	1,453 D	36.4%	56.8%	6.5%
13,605	PIPESTONE	5,738	3,241	2,234	260	3	1,007 R	56.5%	38.9%	4.5%
36,182	POLK	15,169	6,074	8,380	700	15	2,306 D	40.0%	55.2%	4.6%

MINNESOTA

PRESIDENT 1968

1960 Census Population	County	Total Vote	Republican	Democratic	AIP	Other	Plurality	Percentage Rep.	Percentage Dem.	Percentage AIP
11,914	POPE	5,368	2,504	2,592	265	7	88 D	46.6%	48.3%	4.9%
422,525	RAMSEY	195,656	64,068	122,568	8,543	477	58,500 D	32.7%	62.6%	4.4%
5,830	RED LAKE	2,318	718	1,467	130	3	749 D	31.0%	63.3%	5.6%
21,718	REDWOOD	9,285	5,134	3,680	462	9	1,454 R	55.3%	39.6%	5.0%
23,249	RENVILLE	9,906	4,821	4,535	543	7	286 R	48.7%	45.8%	5.5%
38,988	RICE	15,319	7,037	7,785	477	20	748 D	45.9%	50.8%	3.1%
11,864	ROCK	5,374	3,056	2,084	232	2	972 R	56.9%	38.8%	4.3%
12,154	ROSEAU	5,035	2,048	2,649	326	12	601 D	40.7%	52.6%	6.5%
231,588	ST. LOUIS	101,797	25,981	72,267	3,255	294	46,286 D	25.5%	71.0%	3.2%
21,909	SCOTT	11,837	4,632	6,656	540	9	2,024 D	39.1%	56.2%	4.6%
12,861	SHERBURNE	6,593	2,737	3,481	369	6	744 D	41.5%	52.8%	5.6%
16,228	SIBLEY	7,154	4,250	2,540	361	3	1,710 R	59.4%	35.5%	5.0%
80,345	STEARNS	33,580	15,422	15,990	2,081	87	568 D	45.9%	47.6%	6.2%
25,029	STEELE	11,190	6,193	4,631	358	8	1,562 R	55.3%	41.4%	3.2%
11,262	STEVENS	5,062	2,560	2,247	246	9	313 R	50.6%	44.4%	4.9%
14,936	SWIFT	6,451	2,476	3,716	247	12	1,240 D	38.4%	57.6%	3.8%
23,119	TODD	9,460	4,883	3,992	572	13	891 R	51.6%	42.2%	6.0%
7,503	TRAVERSE	3,084	1,277	1,669	137	1	392 D	41.4%	54.1%	4.4%
17,007	WABASHA	7,886	4,081	3,452	346	7	629 R	51.7%	43.8%	4.4%
12,199	WADENA	5,386	2,912	2,198	269	7	714 R	54.1%	40.8%	5.0%
16,041	WASECA	7,605	4,292	3,057	244	12	1,235 R	56.4%	40.2%	3.2%
52,432	WASHINGTON	28,954	10,921	16,449	1,527	57	5,528 D	37.7%	56.8%	5.3%
14,460	WATONWAN	6,433	3,446	2,701	278	8	745 R	53.6%	42.0%	4.3%
10,650	WILKIN	4,165	2,037	1,946	181	1	91 R	48.9%	46.7%	4.3%
40,937	WINONA	17,443	7,998	8,627	781	37	629 D	45.9%	49.5%	4.5%
29,935	WRIGHT	15,753	6,321	8,793	627	12	2,472 D	40.1%	55.8%	4.0%
15,523	YELLOW MEDICINE	7,060	3,060	3,587	406	7	527 D	43.3%	50.8%	5.8%
3,413,864	TOTAL	1,588,506	658,643	857,738	68,931	3,194	199,095 D	41.5%	54.0%	4.3%

MINNESOTA

In Minnesota the Democratic party is known as the Democratic-Farmer-Labor party and the Republican party as the Independent-Republican party; candidates appear on the ballot with these designations.

ELECTION NOTES

1984 Other vote was 3,865 LaRouche (Independent); 3,180 Mason (Socialist Workers); 2,996 Bergland (Libertarian); 2,377 Richards (American Populist); 1,219 Johnson (Citizens); 630 Hall (Communist); 260 Winn (Workers League); 232 Serrette (National Alliance); 723 scattered write-in.

1980 Other vote was 174,990 Anderson (Anderson Coalition); 31,592 Clark (Libertarian); 8,407 Commoner (Citizens); 6,139 no Presidential candidate indicated (American); 1,184 Hall (Communist); 711 DeBerry (Socialist Workers); 698 Griswold (Workers World); 536 McReynolds (Socialist); 281 scattered write-in. Early unamended canvass gave the state-wide total votes as 954,173 Democratic; 174,997 Anderson Coalition; 31,593 Libertarian; 8,406 Citizens; 6,136 American; 1,117 Communist.

1976 Other vote was 35,490 McCarthy (McCarthy '76 Principle); 13,592 Anderson (American); 4,149 Camejo (Socialist Workers); 3,529 MacBride (Libertarian); 1,092 Hall (Communist); 635 Wright (People's); 543 LaRouche (International Development Bank); 370 Levin (Industrial Government); 354 Zeidler (Socialist); 342 scattered write-in.

1972 Other vote was 31,407 Schmitz (American); 4,261 Fisher (Industrial Government); 2,805 Spock (People's); 940 Jenness (Socialist Workers); 662 Hall (Communist); 962 scattered write-in.

1968 Wallace on the ballot as American. Other vote was 933 Cleaver (Peace and Freedom); 807 Halstead (Socialist Workers); 415 Mitchell (Communist); 285 Blomen (Industrial Government); 584 McCarthy (write-in); 170 scattered write-in.

MISSISSIPPI

POPULAR VOTE FOR PRESIDENT 1920 TO 1984

	Total	Republican		Democratic		Other		Percentage			
								Total Vote		Major Vote	
Year	Vote	Vote	Candidate	Vote	Candidate	Vote	Plurality	Rep.	Dem.	Rep.	Dem.
1984	941,104	582,377	Reagan, Ronald	352,192	Mondale, Walter F.	6,535	230,185 R	61.9%	37.4%	62.3%	37.7%
1980	892,620	441,089	Reagan, Ronald	429,281	Carter, Jimmy	22,250	11,808 R	49.4%	48.1%	50.7%	49.3%
1976	769,361	366,846	Ford, Gerald R.	381,309	Carter, Jimmy	21,206	14,463 D	47.7%	49.6%	49.0%	51.0%
1972	645,963	505,125	Nixon, Richard M.	126,782	McGovern, George S.	14,056	378,343 R	78.2%	19.6%	79.9%	20.1%
1968 **	654,509	88,516	Nixon, Richard M.	150,644	Humphrey, Hubert H.	415,349	264,705 A	13.5%	23.0%	37.0%	63.0%
1964	409,146	356,528	Goldwater, Barry M.	52,618	Johnson, Lyndon B.		303,910 R	87.1%	12.9%	87.1%	12.9%
1960 **	298,171	73,561	Nixon, Richard M.	108,362	Kennedy, John F.	116,248	7,886 U	24.7%	36.3%	40.4%	59.6%
1956	248,104	60,685	Eisenhower, Dwight D.	144,453	Stevenson, Adlai E.	42,966	83,768 D	24.5%	58.2%	29.6%	70.4%
1952	285,532	112,966	Eisenhower, Dwight D.	172,566	Stevenson, Adlai E.		59,600 D	39.6%	60.4%	39.6%	60.4%
1948 **	192,190	5,043	Dewey, Thomas E.	19,384	Truman, Harry S.	167,763	148,154 SR	2.6%	10.1%	20.6%	79.4%
1944	180,234	11,613	Dewey, Thomas E.	168,621	Roosevelt, Franklin D.		157,008 D	6.4%	93.6%	6.4%	93.6%
1940	175,824	7,364	Willkie, Wendell	168,267	Roosevelt, Franklin D.	193	160,903 D	4.2%	95.7%	4.2%	95.8%
1936	162,142	4,467	Landon, Alfred M.	157,333	Roosevelt, Franklin D.	342	152,866 D	2.8%	97.0%	2.8%	97.2%
1932	146,034	5,180	Hoover, Herbert C.	140,168	Roosevelt, Franklin D.	686	134,988 D	3.5%	96.0%	3.6%	96.4%
1928	151,568	27,030	Hoover, Herbert C.	124,538	Smith, Alfred E.		97,508 D	17.8%	82.2%	17.8%	82.2%
1924	112,442	8,494	Coolidge, Calvin	100,474	Davis, John W.	3,474	91,980 D	7.6%	89.4%	7.8%	92.2%
1920	82,351	11,576	Harding, Warren G.	69,136	Cox, James M.	1,639	57,560 D	14.1%	84.0%	14.3%	85.7%

In 1968 other vote was Independent (Wallace). In 1960 other vote was Unpledged Independent Democratic. In 1948 other vote was 167,538 States Rights and 225 Progressive.

ELECTORAL COLLEGE VOTE 1920 TO 1984

Year	Total	Republican	Democratic	Other
1984	7	7	—	—
1980	7	7	—	—
1976	7	—	7	—
1972	7	7	—	—
1968	7	—	—	7 AIP
1964	7	7	—	—
1960 **	8	—	—	8 BYRD
1956	8	—	8	—
1952	8	—	8	—
1948	9	—	—	9 SR
1944	9	—	9	—
1940	9	—	9	—
1936	9	—	9	—
1932	9	—	9	—
1928	10	—	10	—
1924	10	—	10	—
1920	10	—	10	—

In 1960 the Unpledged Independent Democratic electors voted in the Electoral College for Harry Flood Byrd and Strom Thurmond.

MISSISSIPPI

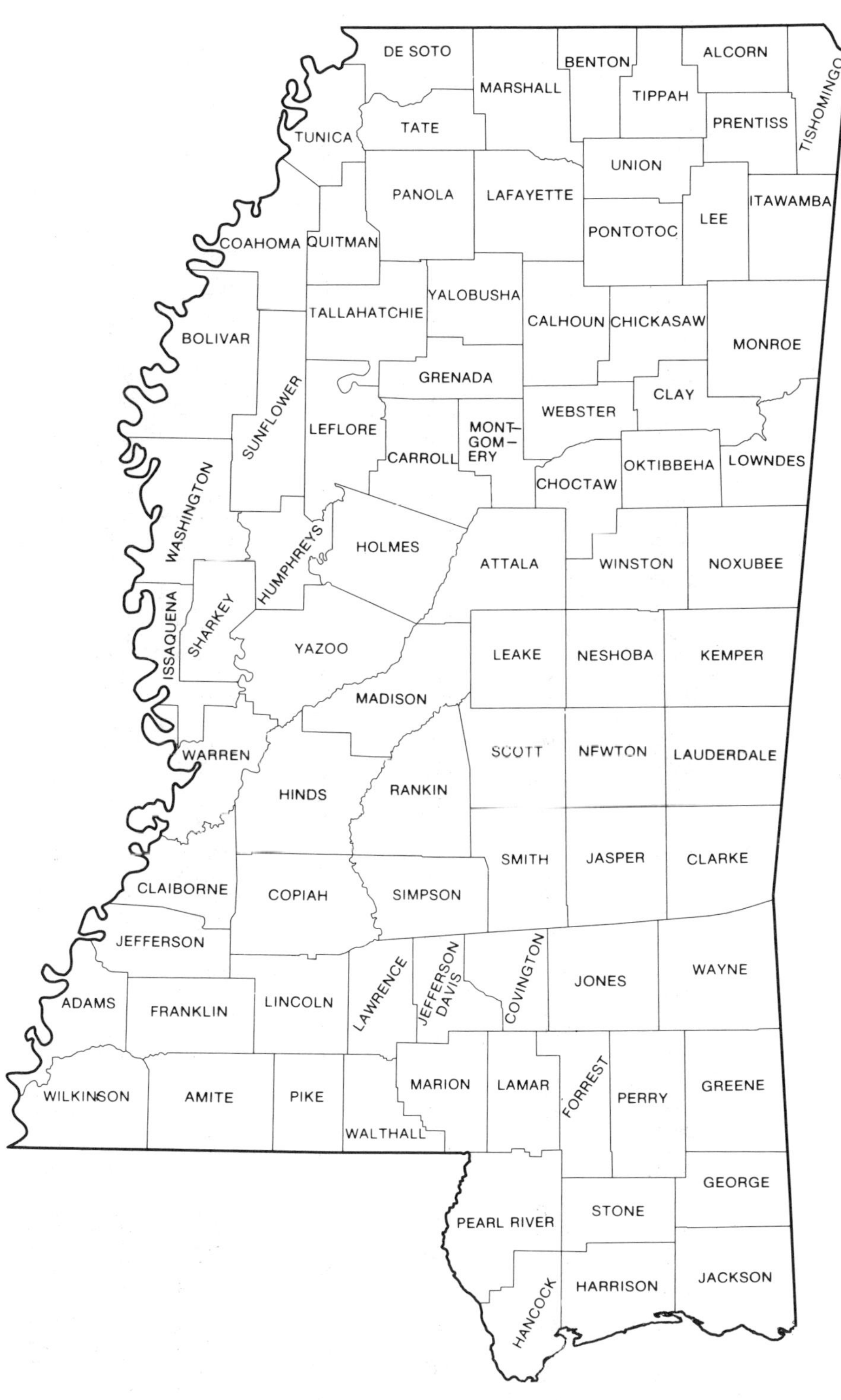

MISSISSIPPI

PRESIDENT 1984

1980 Census Population	County	Total Vote	Republican	Democratic	Other	Rep.-Dem. Plurality	Percentage Total Vote Rep.	Total Vote Dem.	Major Vote Rep.	Major Vote Dem.
38,035	ADAMS	17,378	9,440	7,849	89	1,591 R	54.3%	45.2%	54.6%	45.4%
33,036	ALCORN	12,279	7,203	4,862	214	2,341 R	58.7%	39.6%	59.7%	40.3%
13,369	AMITE	6,050	3,463	2,569	18	894 R	57.2%	42.5%	57.4%	42.6%
19,865	ATTALA	8,215	4,870	3,327	18	1,543 R	59.3%	40.5%	59.4%	40.6%
8,153	BENTON	3,466	1,737	1,715	14	22 R	50.1%	49.5%	50.3%	49.7%
45,965	BOLIVAR	15,824	6,939	8,769	116	1,830 D	43.9%	55.4%	44.2%	55.8%
15,664	CALHOUN	5,337	3,579	1,749	9	1,830 R	67.1%	32.8%	67.2%	32.8%
9,776	CARROLL	4,297	2,823	1,462	12	1,361 R	65.7%	34.0%	65.9%	34.1%
17,853	CHICKASAW	5,957	3,605	2,329	23	1,276 R	60.5%	39.1%	60.8%	39.2%
8,996	CHOCTAW	3,663	2,491	1,166	6	1,325 R	68.0%	31.8%	68.1%	31.9%
12,279	CLAIBORNE	4,484	1,294	3,179	11	1,885 D	28.9%	70.9%	28.9%	71.1%
16,945	CLARKE	6,832	4,551	2,262	19	2,289 R	66.6%	33.1%	66.8%	33.2%
21,082	CLAY	8,187	4,112	4,046	29	66 R	50.2%	49.4%	50.4%	49.6%
36,918	COAHOMA	12,810	5,759	6,839	212	1,080 D	45.0%	53.4%	45.7%	54.3%
26,503	COPIAH	10,416	5,806	4,591	19	1,215 R	55.7%	44.1%	55.8%	44.2%
15,927	COVINGTON	6,413	4,165	2,219	29	1,946 R	64.9%	34.6%	65.2%	34.8%
53,930	DE SOTO	17,022	12,576	4,369	77	8,207 R	73.9%	25.7%	74.2%	25.8%
66,018	FORREST	22,576	15,719	6,786	71	8,933 R	69.6%	30.1%	69.8%	30.2%
8,208	FRANKLIN	4,079	2,564	1,494	21	1,070 R	62.9%	36.6%	63.2%	36.8%
15,297	GEORGE	6,028	4,346	1,655	27	2,691 R	72.1%	27.5%	72.4%	27.6%
9,827	GREENE	4,062	2,744	1,297	21	1,447 R	67.6%	31.9%	67.9%	32.1%
21,043	GRENADA	8,521	5,181	3,325	15	1,856 R	60.8%	39.0%	60.9%	39.1%
24,537	HANCOCK	10,344	7,662	2,630	52	5,032 R	74.1%	25.4%	74.4%	25.6%
157,665	HARRISON	46,677	33,995	12,495	187	21,500 R	72.8%	26.8%	73.1%	26.9%
250,998	HINDS	100,468	56,953	42,373	1,142	14,580 R	56.7%	42.2%	57.3%	42.7%
22,970	HOLMES	8,753	3,102	5,641	10	2,539 D	35.4%	64.4%	35.5%	64.5%
13,931	HUMPHREYS	4,914	2,309	2,596	9	287 D	47.0%	52.8%	47.1%	52.9%
2,513	ISSAQUENA	1,034	512	501	21	11 R	49.5%	48.5%	50.5%	49.5%
20,518	ITAWAMBA	7,285	4,587	2,674	24	1,913 R	63.0%	36.7%	63.2%	36.8%
118,015	JACKSON	38,529	29,585	8,821	123	20,764 R	76.8%	22.9%	77.0%	23.0%
17,265	JASPER	6,902	3,727	3,104	71	623 R	54.0%	45.0%	54.6%	45.4%
9,181	JEFFERSON	3,912	856	3,049	7	2,193 D	21.9%	77.9%	21.9%	78.1%
13,846	JEFFERSON DAVIS	5,566	2,884	2,644	38	240 R	51.8%	47.5%	52.2%	47.8%
61,912	JONES	24,954	17,586	7,298	70	10,288 R	70.5%	29.2%	70.7%	29.3%
10,148	KEMPER	4,456	2,354	2,089	13	265 R	52.8%	46.9%	53.0%	47.0%
31,030	LAFAYETTE	9,680	6,006	3,646	28	2,360 R	62.0%	37.7%	62.2%	37.8%
23,821	LAMAR	9,930	7,929	1,964	37	5,965 R	79.8%	19.8%	80.1%	19.9%
77,285	LAUDERDALE	27,267	18,807	7,534	926	11,273 R	69.0%	27.6%	71.4%	28.6%
12,518	LAWRENCE	6,253	3,970	2,274	9	1,696 R	63.5%	36.4%	63.6%	36.4%
18,790	LEAKE	7,516	4,663	2,845	8	1,818 R	62.0%	37.9%	62.1%	37.9%
57,061	LEE	19,730	13,312	6,208	210	7,104 R	67.5%	31.5%	68.2%	31.8%
41,525	LEFLORE	15,212	7,550	7,443	219	107 R	49.6%	48.9%	50.4%	49.6%
30,174	LINCOLN	13,381	8,898	4,458	25	4,440 R	66.5%	33.3%	66.6%	33.4%
57,304	LOWNDES	18,177	12,049	6,078	50	5,971 R	66.3%	33.4%	66.5%	33.5%
41,613	MADISON	17,463	9,298	8,002	163	1,296 R	53.2%	45.8%	53.7%	46.3%
25,708	MARION	11,125	7,355	3,757	13	3,598 R	66.1%	33.8%	66.2%	33.8%
29,296	MARSHALL	10,278	4,389	5,845	44	1,456 D	42.7%	56.9%	42.9%	57.1%
36,404	MONROE	11,860	7,387	4,437	36	2,950 R	62.3%	37.4%	62.5%	37.5%
13,366	MONTGOMERY	4,983	3,093	1,881	9	1,212 R	62.1%	37.7%	62.2%	37.8%
23,789	NESHOBA	9,364	6,715	2,630	19	4,085 R	71.7%	28.1%	71.9%	28.1%
19,944	NEWTON	8,072	5,911	2,127	34	3,784 R	73.2%	26.4%	73.5%	26.5%
13,212	NOXUBEE	5,149	2,123	2,928	98	805 D	41.2%	56.9%	42.0%	58.0%
36,018	OKTIBBEHA	12,697	7,574	5,097	26	2,477 R	59.7%	40.1%	59.8%	40.2%
28,164	PANOLA	11,375	5,850	5,465	60	385 R	51.4%	48.0%	51.7%	48.3%
33,795	PEARL RIVER	13,112	9,978	3,085	49	6,893 R	76.1%	23.5%	76.4%	23.6%
9,864	PERRY	4,744	3,098	1,415	231	1,683 R	65.3%	29.8%	68.6%	31.4%
36,173	PIKE	14,411	8,254	6,137	20	2,117 R	57.3%	42.6%	57.4%	42.6%
20,918	PONTOTOC	7,643	5,182	2,434	27	2,748 R	67.8%	31.8%	68.0%	32.0%
24,025	PRENTISS	7,732	4,821	2,897	14	1,924 R	62.4%	37.5%	62.5%	37.5%
12,636	QUITMAN	4,548	2,198	2,343	7	145 D	48.3%	51.5%	48.4%	51.6%

MISSISSIPPI

PRESIDENT 1984

1980 Census Population	County	Total Vote	Republican	Democratic	Other	Rep.-Dem. Plurality	Percentage Total Vote Rep.	Percentage Total Vote Dem.	Percentage Major Vote Rep.	Percentage Major Vote Dem.
69,427	RANKIN	28,308	22,393	5,874	41	16,519 R	79.1%	20.8%	79.2%	20.8%
24,556	SCOTT	9,053	5,763	3,274	16	2,489 R	63.7%	36.2%	63.8%	36.2%
7,964	SHARKEY	3,398	1,487	1,723	188	236 D	43.8%	50.7%	46.3%	53.7%
23,441	SIMPSON	8,924	5,983	2,894	47	3,089 R	67.0%	32.4%	67.4%	32.6%
15,077	SMITH	6,710	5,116	1,573	21	3,543 R	76.2%	23.4%	76.5%	23.5%
9,716	STONE	4,193	2,980	1,185	28	1,795 R	71.1%	28.3%	71.5%	28.5%
34,844	SUNFLOWER	10,111	5,178	4,913	20	265 R	51.2%	48.6%	51.3%	48.7%
17,157	TALLAHATCHIE	5,646	2,901	2,725	20	176 R	51.4%	48.3%	51.6%	48.4%
20,119	TATE	7,557	4,677	2,846	34	1,831 R	61.9%	37.7%	62.2%	37.8%
18,739	TIPPAH	7,301	4,706	2,566	29	2,140 R	64.5%	35.1%	64.7%	35.3%
18,434	TISHOMINGO	6,428	3,527	2,879	22	648 R	54.9%	44.8%	55.1%	44.9%
9,652	TUNICA	2,804	1,109	1,621	74	512 D	39.6%	57.8%	40.6%	59.4%
21,741	UNION	8,617	5,837	2,766	14	3,071 R	67.7%	32.1%	67.8%	32.2%
13,761	WALTHALL	5,541	3,305	2,219	17	1,086 R	59.6%	40.0%	59.8%	40.2%
51,627	WARREN	21,248	12,959	8,054	235	4,905 R	61.0%	37.9%	61.7%	38.3%
72,344	WASHINGTON	23,414	12,454	10,617	343	1,837 R	53.2%	45.3%	54.0%	46.0%
19,135	WAYNE	7,836	5,000	2,818	18	2,182 R	63.8%	36.0%	64.0%	36.0%
10,300	WEBSTER	4,794	3,390	1,397	7	1,993 R	70.7%	29.1%	70.8%	29.2%
10,021	WILKINSON	4,386	1,722	2,627	37	905 D	39.3%	59.9%	39.6%	60.4%
19,474	WINSTON	8,746	5,192	3,543	11	1,649 R	59.4%	40.5%	59.4%	40.6%
13,139	YALOBUSHA	5,285	2,934	2,337	14	597 R	55.5%	44.2%	55.7%	44.3%
27,349	YAZOO	11,412	6,275	5,037	100	1,238 R	55.0%	44.1%	55.5%	44.5%
2,520,638	TOTAL	941,104	582,377	352,192	6,535	230,185 R	61.9%	37.4%	62.3%	37.7%

MISSISSIPPI

PRESIDENT 1980

1980 Census Population	County	Total Vote	Republican	Democratic	Other	Rep.-Dem. Plurality	Percentage Total Vote Rep.	Total Vote Dem.	Major Vote Rep.	Major Vote Dem.
38,035	ADAMS	15,363	7,523	7,228	612	295 R	49.0%	47.0%	51.0%	49.0%
33,036	ALCORN	12,595	5,196	6,242	1,157	1,046 D	41.3%	49.6%	45.4%	54.6%
13,369	AMITE	5,971	2,653	3,229	89	576 D	44.4%	54.1%	45.1%	54.9%
19,865	ATTALA	8,214	3,975	4,117	122	142 D	48.4%	50.1%	49.1%	50.9%
8,153	BENTON	3,427	1,254	2,094	79	840 D	36.6%	61.1%	37.5%	62.5%
45,965	BOLIVAR	14,491	5,148	8,839	504	3,691 D	35.5%	61.0%	36.8%	63.2%
15,664	CALHOUN	6,019	2,579	3,295	145	716 D	42.8%	54.7%	43.9%	56.1%
9,776	CARROLL	4,228	2,153	2,037	38	116 R	50.9%	48.2%	51.4%	48.6%
17,853	CHICKASAW	6,329	2,540	3,622	167	1,082 D	40.1%	57.2%	41.2%	58.8%
8,996	CHOCTAW	3,695	1,927	1,729	39	198 R	52.2%	46.8%	52.7%	47.3%
12,279	CLAIBORNE	4,228	1,129	3,032	67	1,903 D	26.7%	71.7%	27.1%	72.9%
16,945	CLARKE	6,721	3,303	3,303	115		49.1%	49.1%	50.0%	50.0%
21,082	CLAY	7,964	3,439	4,275	250	836 D	43.2%	53.7%	44.6%	55.4%
36,918	COAHOMA	12,015	4,592	7,030	393	2,438 D	38.2%	58.5%	39.5%	60.5%
26,503	COPIAH	10,140	4,461	5,517	162	1,056 D	44.0%	54.4%	44.7%	55.3%
15,927	COVINGTON	6,531	3,471	2,956	104	515 R	53.1%	45.3%	54.0%	46.0%
53,930	DE SOTO	16,419	9,655	6,344	420	3,311 R	58.8%	38.6%	60.3%	39.7%
66,018	FORREST	21,327	12,656	8,274	397	4,382 R	59.3%	38.8%	60.5%	39.5%
8,208	FRANKLIN	4,109	2,026	2,040	43	14 D	49.3%	49.6%	49.8%	50.2%
15,297	GEORGE	5,932	3,052	2,757	123	295 R	51.4%	46.5%	52.5%	47.5%
9,827	GREENE	3,541	1,772	1,740	29	32 R	50.0%	49.1%	50.5%	49.5%
21,043	GRENADA	8,300	3,993	4,182	125	189 D	48.1%	50.4%	48.8%	51.2%
24,537	HANCOCK	8,915	5,088	3,544	283	1,544 R	57.1%	39.8%	58.9%	41.1%
157,665	HARRISON	42,888	25,175	16,318	1,395	8,857 R	58.7%	38.0%	60.7%	39.3%
250,998	HINDS	90,074	48,135	39,369	2,570	8,766 R	53.4%	43.7%	55.0%	45.0%
22,970	HOLMES	8,336	2,693	5,463	180	2,770 D	32.3%	65.5%	33.0%	67.0%
13,931	HUMPHREYS	5,020	1,841	2,970	209	1,129 D	36.7%	59.2%	38.3%	61.7%
2,513	ISSAQUENA	968	349	598	21	249 D	36.1%	61.8%	36.9%	63.1%
20,518	ITAWAMBA	7,853	2,906	4,852	95	1,946 D	37.0%	61.8%	37.5%	62.5%
118,015	JACKSON	35,958	22,498	12,226	1,234	10,272 R	62.6%	34.0%	64.8%	35.2%
17,265	JASPER	6,673	2,781	3,813	79	1,032 D	41.7%	57.1%	42.2%	57.8%
9,181	JEFFERSON	3,724	751	2,871	102	2,120 D	20.2%	77.1%	20.7%	79.3%
13,846	JEFFERSON DAVIS	6,187	2,280	3,831	76	1,551 D	36.9%	61.9%	37.3%	62.7%
61,912	JONES	24,289	12,900	11,117	272	1,783 R	53.1%	45.8%	53.7%	46.3%
10,148	KEMPER	4,439	1,822	2,601	16	779 D	41.0%	58.6%	41.2%	58.8%
31,030	LAFAYETTE	9,571	4,366	4,887	318	521 D	45.6%	51.1%	47.2%	52.8%
23,821	LAMAR	8,546	5,395	3,005	146	2,390 R	63.1%	35.2%	64.2%	35.8%
77,285	LAUDERDALE	26,119	14,727	9,918	1,474	4,809 R	56.4%	38.0%	59.8%	40.2%
12,518	LAWRENCE	5,560	2,781	2,692	87	89 R	50.0%	48.4%	50.8%	49.2%
18,790	LEAKE	7,738	3,624	4,033	81	409 D	46.8%	52.1%	47.3%	52.7%
57,061	LEE	18,889	8,326	10,047	516	1,721 D	44.1%	53.2%	45.3%	54.7%
41,525	LEFLORE	13,675	5,798	7,498	379	1,700 D	42.4%	54.8%	43.6%	56.4%
30,174	LINCOLN	12,610	7,286	5,213	111	2,073 R	57.8%	41.3%	58.3%	41.7%
57,304	LOWNDES	16,355	9,973	6,187	195	3,786 R	61.0%	37.8%	61.7%	38.3%
41,613	MADISON	14,039	6,024	7,621	394	1,597 D	42.9%	54.3%	44.1%	55.9%
25,708	MARION	10,707	5,218	5,366	123	148 D	48.7%	50.1%	49.3%	50.7%
29,296	MARSHALL	10,848	3,455	7,153	240	3,698 D	31.8%	65.9%	32.6%	67.4%
36,404	MONROE	12,239	4,793	6,998	448	2,205 D	39.2%	57.2%	40.6%	59.4%
13,366	MONTGOMERY	5,326	2,479	2,730	117	251 D	46.5%	51.3%	47.6%	52.4%
23,789	NESHOBA	9,149	5,165	3,872	112	1,293 R	56.5%	42.3%	57.2%	42.8%
19,944	NEWTON	7,941	4,317	3,455	169	862 R	54.4%	43.5%	55.5%	44.5%
13,212	NOXUBEE	5,555	1,970	3,434	151	1,464 D	35.5%	61.8%	36.5%	63.5%
36,018	OKTIBBEHA	12,675	6,300	6,039	336	261 R	49.7%	47.6%	51.1%	48.9%
28,164	PANOLA	10,728	4,219	6,179	330	1,960 D	39.3%	57.6%	40.6%	59.4%
33,795	PEARL RIVER	12,141	6,822	5,028	291	1,794 R	56.2%	41.4%	57.6%	42.4%
9,864	PERRY	4,263	2,255	1,957	51	298 R	52.9%	45.9%	53.5%	46.5%
36,173	PIKE	13,716	6,661	6,694	361	33 D	48.6%	48.8%	49.9%	50.1%
20,918	PONTOTOC	7,802	3,198	4,499	105	1,301 D	41.0%	57.7%	41.5%	58.5%
24,025	PRENTISS	8,178	3,264	4,832	82	1,568 D	39.9%	59.1%	40.3%	59.7%
12,636	QUITMAN	4,810	1,691	2,926	193	1,235 D	35.2%	60.8%	36.6%	63.4%

MISSISSIPPI

PRESIDENT 1980

1980 Census Population	County	Total Vote	Republican	Democratic	Other	Rep.-Dem. Plurality	Percentage Total Vote Rep.	Percentage Total Vote Dem.	Percentage Major Vote Rep.	Percentage Major Vote Dem.
69,427	RANKIN	25,132	16,650	8,047	435	8,603 R	66.3%	32.0%	67.4%	32.6%
24,556	SCOTT	8,832	4,645	4,043	144	602 R	52.6%	45.8%	53.5%	46.5%
7,964	SHARKEY	3,021	996	1,957	68	961 D	33.0%	64.8%	33.7%	66.3%
23,441	SIMPSON	9,334	5,190	4,015	129	1,175 R	55.6%	43.0%	56.4%	43.6%
15,077	SMITH	6,340	3,772	2,474	94	1,298 R	59.5%	39.0%	60.4%	39.6%
9,716	STONE	3,837	1,888	1,821	128	67 R	49.2%	47.5%	50.9%	49.1%
34,844	SUNFLOWER	8,927	3,728	5,035	164	1,307 D	41.8%	56.4%	42.5%	57.5%
17,157	TALLAHATCHIE	5,776	2,183	3,467	126	1,284 D	37.8%	60.0%	38.6%	61.4%
20,119	TATE	7,366	3,343	3,892	131	549 D	45.4%	52.8%	46.2%	53.8%
18,739	TIPPAH	7,423	3,338	3,878	207	540 D	45.0%	52.2%	46.3%	53.7%
18,434	TISHOMINGO	7,221	2,489	4,595	137	2,106 D	34.5%	63.6%	35.1%	64.9%
9,652	TUNICA	3,205	954	2,198	53	1,244 D	29.8%	68.6%	30.3%	69.7%
21,741	UNION	8,715	3,545	5,001	169	1,456 D	40.7%	57.4%	41.5%	58.5%
13,761	WALTHALL	5,762	2,703	2,960	99	257 D	46.9%	51.4%	47.7%	52.3%
51,627	WARREN	18,128	10,151	7,489	488	2,662 R	56.0%	41.3%	57.5%	42.5%
72,344	WASHINGTON	20,117	8,978	10,722	417	1,744 D	44.6%	53.3%	45.6%	54.4%
19,135	WAYNE	7,383	3,844	3,494	45	350 R	52.1%	47.3%	52.4%	47.6%
10,300	WEBSTER	4,712	2,386	2,178	148	208 R	50.6%	46.2%	52.3%	47.7%
10,021	WILKINSON	4,500	1,442	2,981	77	1,539 D	32.0%	66.2%	32.6%	67.4%
19,474	WINSTON	8,545	3,998	4,416	131	418 D	46.8%	51.7%	47.5%	52.5%
13,139	YALOBUSHA	5,783	2,224	3,432	127	1,208 D	38.5%	59.3%	39.3%	60.7%
27,349	YAZOO	10,498	4,819	5,468	211	649 D	45.9%	52.1%	46.8%	53.2%
2,520,638	TOTAL	892,620	441,089	429,281	22,250	11,808 R	49.4%	48.1%	50.7%	49.3%

MISSISSIPPI

PRESIDENT 1976

1970 Census Population	County	Total Vote	Republican	Democratic	Other	Rep.-Dem. Plurality	Percentage Total Vote Rep.	Total Vote Dem.	Major Vote Rep.	Major Vote Dem.
37,293	ADAMS	13,861	6,431	6,619	811	188 D	46.4%	47.8%	49.3%	50.7%
27,179	ALCORN	10,770	3,430	6,995	345	3,565 D	31.8%	64.9%	32.9%	67.1%
13,763	AMITE	4,999	2,256	2,574	169	318 D	45.1%	51.5%	46.7%	53.3%
19,570	ATTALA	7,423	3,146	4,068	209	922 D	42.4%	54.8%	43.6%	56.4%
7,505	BENTON	3,209	790	2,375	44	1,585 D	24.6%	74.0%	25.0%	75.0%
49,409	BOLIVAR	12,875	5,136	7,561	178	2,425 D	39.9%	58.7%	40.5%	59.5%
14,623	CALHOUN	4,788	1,892	2,724	172	832 D	39.5%	56.9%	41.0%	59.0%
9,397	CARROLL	3,167	1,561	1,566	40	5 D	49.3%	49.4%	49.9%	50.1%
16,805	CHICKASAW	5,723	2,581	2,891	251	310 D	45.1%	50.5%	47.2%	52.8%
8,440	CHOCTAW	3,172	1,562	1,520	90	42 R	49.2%	47.9%	50.7%	49.3%
10,086	CLAIBORNE	3,852	1,078	2,657	117	1,579 D	28.0%	69.0%	28.9%	71.1%
15,049	CLARKE	5,995	2,935	2,816	244	119 R	49.0%	47.0%	51.0%	49.0%
18,840	CLAY	6,837	3,017	3,514	306	497 D	44.1%	51.4%	46.2%	53.8%
40,447	COAHOMA	11,113	4,269	6,412	432	2,143 D	38.4%	57.7%	40.0%	60.0%
24,749	COPIAH	8,646	4,108	4,267	271	159 D	47.5%	49.4%	49.1%	50.9%
14,002	COVINGTON	5,568	2,591	2,862	115	271 D	46.5%	51.4%	47.5%	52.5%
35,885	DE SOTO	14,312	6,240	7,756	316	1,516 D	43.6%	54.2%	44.6%	55.4%
57,849	FORREST	19,120	10,770	7,914	436	2,856 R	56.3%	41.4%	57.6%	42.4%
8,011	FRANKLIN	3,395	1,719	1,578	98	141 R	50.6%	46.5%	52.1%	47.9%
12,459	GEORGE	5,229	1,957	3,072	200	1,115 D	37.4%	58.7%	38.9%	61.1%
8,545	GREENE	3,770	1,538	2,127	105	589 D	40.8%	56.4%	42.0%	58.0%
19,854	GRENADA	7,020	3,569	3,263	188	306 R	50.8%	46.5%	52.2%	47.8%
17,387	HANCOCK	7,842	3,765	3,855	222	90 D	48.0%	49.2%	49.4%	50.6%
134,582	HARRISON	37,139	19,207	16,569	1,363	2,638 R	51.7%	44.6%	53.7%	46.3%
214,973	HINDS	75,756	45,803	28,748	1,205	17,055 R	60.5%	37.9%	61.4%	38.6%
23,120	HOLMES	7,203	2,438	4,616	149	2,178 D	33.8%	64.1%	34.6%	65.4%
14,601	HUMPHREYS	3,774	1,445	2,172	157	727 D	38.3%	57.6%	40.0%	60.0%
2,737	ISSAQUENA	954	325	567	62	242 D	34.1%	59.4%	36.4%	63.6%
16,847	ITAWAMBA	6,705	2,153	4,480	72	2,327 D	32.1%	66.8%	32.5%	67.5%
87,975	JACKSON	31,082	17,177	12,533	1,372	4,644 R	55.3%	40.3%	57.8%	42.2%
15,994	JASPER	5,513	2,356	3,109	48	753 D	42.7%	56.4%	43.1%	56.9%
9,295	JEFFERSON	3,426	782	2,562	82	1,780 D	22.8%	74.8%	23.4%	76.6%
12,936	JEFFERSON DAVIS	4,698	1,868	2,747	83	879 D	39.8%	58.5%	40.5%	59.5%
56,357	JONES	21,552	11,098	10,139	315	959 R	51.5%	47.0%	52.3%	47.7%
10,233	KEMPER	4,160	1,680	2,436	44	756 D	40.4%	58.6%	40.8%	59.2%
24,181	LAFAYETTE	8,351	3,735	4,375	241	640 D	44.7%	52.4%	46.1%	53.9%
15,209	LAMAR	7,414	4,056	3,109	249	947 R	54.7%	41.9%	56.6%	43.4%
67,087	LAUDERDALE	24,446	14,273	9,813	360	4,460 R	58.4%	40.1%	59.3%	40.7%
11,137	LAWRENCE	4,436	2,109	2,242	85	133 D	47.5%	50.5%	48.5%	51.5%
17,085	LEAKE	6,508	2,952	3,415	141	463 D	45.4%	52.5%	46.4%	53.6%
46,148	LEE	16,333	7,366	8,504	463	1,138 D	45.1%	52.1%	46.4%	53.6%
42,111	LEFLORE	12,589	5,872	6,135	582	263 D	46.6%	48.7%	48.9%	51.1%
26,198	LINCOLN	10,392	6,084	4,043	265	2,041 R	58.5%	38.9%	60.1%	39.9%
49,700	LOWNDES	14,700	8,003	6,181	516	1,822 R	54.4%	42.0%	56.4%	43.6%
29,737	MADISON	11,316	4,838	6,240	238	1,402 D	42.8%	55.1%	43.7%	56.3%
22,871	MARION	10,737	5,300	5,283	154	17 R	49.4%	49.2%	50.1%	49.9%
24,027	MARSHALL	9,226	2,242	6,769	215	4,527 D	24.3%	73.4%	24.9%	75.1%
34,043	MONROE	11,234	4,737	6,097	400	1,360 D	42.2%	54.3%	43.7%	56.3%
12,918	MONTGOMERY	4,827	2,278	2,410	139	132 D	47.2%	49.9%	48.6%	51.4%
20,802	NESHOBA	7,819	3,859	3,891	69	32 D	49.4%	49.8%	49.8%	50.2%
18,983	NEWTON	6,690	3,813	2,741	136	1,072 R	57.0%	41.0%	58.2%	41.8%
14,288	NOXUBEE	4,136	1,860	2,121	155	261 D	45.0%	51.3%	46.7%	53.3%
28,752	OKTIBBEHA	9,725	5,194	4,339	192	855 R	53.4%	44.6%	54.5%	45.5%
26,829	PANOLA	9,067	3,341	5,517	209	2,176 D	36.8%	60.8%	37.7%	62.3%
27,802	PEARL RIVER	9,665	4,332	5,024	309	692 D	44.8%	52.0%	46.3%	53.7%
9,065	PERRY	3,725	1,527	1,965	233	438 D	41.0%	52.8%	43.7%	56.3%
31,756	PIKE	11,751	5,659	5,749	343	90 D	48.2%	48.9%	49.6%	50.4%
17,363	PONTOTOC	6,491	2,245	4,066	180	1,821 D	34.6%	62.6%	35.6%	64.4%
20,133	PRENTISS	6,977	2,362	4,431	184	2,069 D	33.9%	63.5%	34.8%	65.2%
15,888	QUITMAN	4,045	1,287	2,621	137	1,334 D	31.8%	64.8%	32.9%	67.1%

MISSISSIPPI

PRESIDENT 1976

1970 Census Population	County	Total Vote	Republican	Democratic	Other	Rep.-Dem. Plurality	Percentage Total Vote Rep.	Total Vote Dem.	Major Vote Rep.	Major Vote Dem.
43,933	RANKIN	18,878	11,507	6,937	434	4,570 R	61.0%	36.7%	62.4%	37.6%
21,369	SCOTT	7,468	3,649	3,643	176	6 R	48.9%	48.8%	50.0%	50.0%
8,937	SHARKEY	2,449	1,024	1,283	142	259 D	41.8%	52.4%	44.4%	55.6%
19,947	SIMPSON	7,960	4,291	3,600	69	691 R	53.9%	45.2%	54.4%	45.6%
13,561	SMITH	5,748	3,147	2,434	167	713 R	54.7%	42.3%	56.4%	43.6%
8,101	STONE	3,278	1,575	1,648	55	73 D	48.0%	50.3%	48.9%	51.1%
37,047	SUNFLOWER	8,024	3,456	4,322	246	866 D	43.1%	53.9%	44.4%	55.6%
19,338	TALLAHATCHIE	5,252	2,146	2,991	115	845 D	40.9%	56.9%	41.8%	58.2%
18,544	TATE	6,436	2,497	3,747	192	1,250 D	38.8%	58.2%	40.0%	60.0%
15,852	TIPPAH	6,274	1,887	4,260	127	2,373 D	30.1%	67.9%	30.7%	69.3%
14,940	TISHOMINGO	5,839	1,969	3,734	136	1,765 D	33.7%	63.9%	34.5%	65.5%
11,854	TUNICA	2,756	951	1,695	110	744 D	34.5%	61.5%	35.9%	64.1%
19,096	UNION	7,659	2,507	5,021	131	2,514 D	32.7%	65.6%	33.3%	66.7%
12,500	WALTHALL	4,927	2,110	2,650	167	540 D	42.8%	53.8%	44.3%	55.7%
44,981	WARREN	15,705	8,699	6,299	707	2,400 R	55.4%	40.1%	58.0%	42.0%
70,581	WASHINGTON	18,146	7,474	9,650	1,022	2,176 D	41.2%	53.2%	43.6%	56.4%
16,650	WAYNE	6,422	3,022	3,306	94	284 D	47.1%	51.5%	47.8%	52.2%
10,047	WEBSTER	4,281	1,943	2,218	120	275 D	45.4%	51.8%	46.7%	53.3%
11,099	WILKINSON	3,845	1,273	2,514	58	1,241 D	33.1%	65.4%	33.6%	66.4%
18,406	WINSTON	7,792	3,659	3,956	177	297 D	47.0%	50.8%	48.0%	52.0%
11,915	YALOBUSHA	4,503	1,808	2,603	92	795 D	40.2%	57.8%	41.0%	59.0%
27,304	YAZOO	8,471	4,255	4,053	163	202 R	50.2%	47.8%	51.2%	48.8%
2,216,912	TOTAL	769,361	366,846	381,309	21,206	14,463 D	47.7%	49.6%	49.0%	51.0%

MISSISSIPPI

PRESIDENT 1972

1970 Census Population	County	Total Vote	Republican	Democratic	Other	Rep.-Dem. Plurality	Percentage: Total Vote Rep.	Percentage: Total Vote Dem.	Percentage: Major Vote Rep.	Percentage: Major Vote Dem.
37,293	ADAMS	12,657	8,500	3,697	460	4,803 R	67.2%	29.2%	69.7%	30.3%
27,179	ALCORN	6,883	5,732	982	169	4,750 R	83.3%	14.3%	85.4%	14.6%
13,763	AMITE	4,128	2,846	1,185	97	1,661 R	68.9%	28.7%	70.6%	29.4%
19,570	ATTALA	5,960	4,738	1,103	119	3,635 R	79.5%	18.5%	81.1%	18.9%
7,505	BENTON	2,235	1,483	701	51	782 R	66.4%	31.4%	67.9%	32.1%
49,409	BOLIVAR	11,187	7,397	3,616	174	3,781 R	66.1%	32.3%	67.2%	32.8%
14,623	CALHOUN	3,345	3,023	245	77	2,778 R	90.4%	7.3%	92.5%	7.5%
9,397	CARROLL	2,424	1,777	580	67	1,197 R	73.3%	23.9%	75.4%	24.6%
16,805	CHICKASAW	4,433	3,753	579	101	3,174 R	84.7%	13.1%	86.6%	13.4%
8,440	CHOCTAW	2,658	2,301	326	31	1,975 R	86.6%	12.3%	87.6%	12.4%
10,086	CLAIBORNE	3,642	1,521	2,076	45	555 D	41.8%	57.0%	42.3%	57.7%
15,049	CLARKE	5,592	4,561	954	77	3,607 R	81.6%	17.1%	82.7%	17.3%
18,840	CLAY	5,652	4,035	1,410	207	2,625 R	71.4%	24.9%	74.1%	25.9%
40,447	COAHOMA	10,725	6,602	3,708	415	2,894 R	61.6%	34.6%	64.0%	36.0%
24,749	COPIAH	7,520	5,498	1,803	219	3,695 R	73.1%	24.0%	75.3%	24.7%
14,002	COVINGTON	4,569	3,842	642	85	3,200 R	84.1%	14.1%	85.7%	14.3%
35,885	DE SOTO	9,789	7,917	1,557	315	6,360 R	80.9%	15.9%	83.6%	16.4%
57,849	FORREST	17,898	14,418	2,933	547	11,485 R	80.6%	16.4%	83.1%	16.9%
8,011	FRANKLIN	2,999	2,361	561	77	1,800 R	78.7%	18.7%	80.8%	19.2%
12,459	GEORGE	4,283	3,979	270	34	3,709 R	92.9%	6.3%	93.6%	6.4%
8,545	GREENE	3,453	2,884	513	56	2,371 R	83.5%	14.9%	84.9%	15.1%
19,854	GRENADA	6,392	4,800	1,471	121	3,329 R	75.1%	23.0%	76.5%	23.5%
17,387	HANCOCK	5,949	5,133	745	71	4,388 R	86.3%	12.5%	87.3%	12.7%
134,582	HARRISON	34,470	28,962	4,761	747	24,201 R	84.0%	13.8%	85.9%	14.1%
214,973	HINDS	64,096	49,877	12,679	1,540	37,198 R	77.8%	19.8%	79.7%	20.3%
23,120	HOLMES	6,686	3,158	3,459	69	301 D	47.2%	51.7%	47.7%	52.3%
14,601	HUMPHREYS	3,382	2,334	892	156	1,442 R	69.0%	26.4%	72.3%	27.7%
2,737	ISSAQUENA	1,153	701	395	57	306 R	60.8%	34.3%	64.0%	36.0%
16,847	ITAWAMBA	4,954	4,419	509	26	3,910 R	89.2%	10.3%	89.7%	10.3%
87,975	JACKSON	25,038	22,204	2,534	300	19,670 R	88.7%	10.1%	89.8%	10.2%
15,994	JASPER	4,584	3,597	935	52	2,662 R	78.5%	20.4%	79.4%	20.6%
9,295	JEFFERSON	2,608	1,131	1,457	20	326 D	43.4%	55.9%	43.7%	56.3%
12,936	JEFFERSON DAVIS	3,886	2,830	1,005	51	1,825 R	72.8%	25.9%	73.8%	26.2%
56,357	JONES	19,679	16,489	2,790	400	13,699 R	83.8%	14.2%	85.5%	14.5%
10,233	KEMPER	3,652	2,748	837	67	1,911 R	75.2%	22.9%	76.7%	23.3%
24,181	LAFAYETTE	7,011	5,391	1,545	75	3,846 R	76.9%	22.0%	77.7%	22.3%
15,209	LAMAR	5,682	5,022	493	167	4,529 R	88.4%	8.7%	91.1%	8.9%
67,087	LAUDERDALE	22,420	18,337	3,453	630	14,884 R	81.8%	15.4%	84.2%	15.8%
11,137	LAWRENCE	4,154	3,394	709	51	2,685 R	81.7%	17.1%	82.7%	17.3%
17,085	LEAKE	5,329	4,217	1,053	59	3,164 R	79.1%	19.8%	80.0%	20.0%
46,148	LEE	12,991	10,730	1,632	629	9,098 R	82.6%	12.6%	86.8%	13.2%
42,111	LEFLORE	8,969	6,779	2,038	152	4,741 R	75.6%	22.7%	76.9%	23.1%
26,198	LINCOLN	8,828	7,593	1,070	165	6,523 R	86.0%	12.1%	87.6%	12.4%
49,700	LOWNDES	12,831	10,098	2,398	335	7,700 R	78.7%	18.7%	80.8%	19.2%
29,737	MADISON	8,824	5,047	3,464	313	1,583 R	57.2%	39.3%	59.3%	40.7%
22,871	MARION	8,570	6,805	1,693	72	5,112 R	79.4%	19.8%	80.1%	19.9%
24,027	MARSHALL	5,356	3,326	1,875	155	1,451 R	62.1%	35.0%	63.9%	36.1%
34,043	MONROE	8,648	7,273	1,279	96	5,994 R	84.1%	14.8%	85.0%	15.0%
12,918	MONTGOMERY	4,206	3,210	925	71	2,285 R	76.3%	22.0%	77.6%	22.4%
20,802	NESHOBA	7,725	6,815	812	98	6,003 R	88.2%	10.5%	89.4%	10.6%
18,983	NEWTON	6,343	5,585	597	161	4,988 R	88.0%	9.4%	90.3%	9.7%
14,288	NOXUBEE	3,378	2,239	1,052	87	1,187 R	66.3%	31.1%	68.0%	32.0%
28,752	OKTIBBEHA	8,153	6,160	1,880	113	4,280 R	75.6%	23.1%	76.6%	23.4%
26,829	PANOLA	7,483	5,284	2,091	108	3,193 R	70.6%	27.9%	71.6%	28.4%
27,802	PEARL RIVER	8,504	7,487	901	116	6,586 R	88.0%	10.6%	89.3%	10.7%
9,065	PERRY	3,196	2,689	446	61	2,243 R	84.1%	14.0%	85.8%	14.2%
31,756	PIKE	9,076	6,542	2,332	202	4,210 R	72.1%	25.7%	73.7%	26.3%
17,363	PONTOTOC	5,004	4,476	488	40	3,988 R	89.4%	9.8%	90.2%	9.8%
20,133	PRENTISS	5,056	4,607	398	51	4,209 R	91.1%	7.9%	92.0%	8.0%
15,888	QUITMAN	3,392	2,524	790	78	1,734 R	74.4%	23.3%	76.2%	23.8%

MISSISSIPPI

PRESIDENT 1972

1970 Census Population	County	Total Vote	Republican	Democratic	Other	Rep.-Dem. Plurality	Percentage Total Vote Rep.	Percentage Total Vote Dem.	Percentage Major Vote Rep.	Percentage Major Vote Dem.
43,933	RANKIN	14,305	12,187	1,913	205	10,274 R	85.2%	13.4%	86.4%	13.6%
21,369	SCOTT	6,559	5,244	1,213	102	4,031 R	80.0%	18.5%	81.2%	18.8%
8,937	SHARKEY	2,099	1,426	655	18	771 R	67.9%	31.2%	68.5%	31.5%
19,947	SIMPSON	6,602	5,669	871	62	4,798 R	85.9%	13.2%	86.7%	13.3%
13,561	SMITH	4,785	4,419	329	37	4,090 R	92.4%	6.9%	93.1%	6.9%
8,101	STONE	2,788	2,467	293	28	2,174 R	88.5%	10.5%	89.4%	10.6%
37,047	SUNFLOWER	7,355	5,389	1,874	92	3,515 R	73.3%	25.5%	74.2%	25.8%
19,338	TALLAHATCHIE	4,449	3,442	835	172	2,607 R	77.4%	18.8%	80.5%	19.5%
18,544	TATE	5,236	3,966	1,151	119	2,815 R	75.7%	22.0%	77.5%	22.5%
15,852	TIPPAH	4,585	3,937	569	79	3,368 R	85.9%	12.4%	87.4%	12.6%
14,940	TISHOMINGO	4,681	4,177	443	61	3,734 R	89.2%	9.5%	90.4%	9.6%
11,854	TUNICA	2,325	1,446	858	21	588 R	62.2%	36.9%	62.8%	37.2%
19,096	UNION	6,230	5,477	658	95	4,819 R	87.9%	10.6%	89.3%	10.7%
12,500	WALTHALL	3,904	3,110	747	47	2,363 R	79.7%	19.1%	80.6%	19.4%
44,981	WARREN	14,478	10,420	3,480	578	6,940 R	72.0%	24.0%	75.0%	25.0%
70,581	WASHINGTON	15,104	9,634	4,623	847	5,011 R	63.8%	30.6%	67.6%	32.4%
16,650	WAYNE	5,663	4,648	975	40	3,673 R	82.1%	17.2%	82.7%	17.3%
10,047	WEBSTER	4,065	3,624	403	38	3,221 R	89.2%	9.9%	90.0%	10.0%
11,099	WILKINSON	3,054	1,608	1,409	37	199 R	52.7%	46.1%	53.3%	46.7%
18,406	WINSTON	6,555	5,155	1,354	46	3,801 R	78.6%	20.7%	79.2%	20.8%
11,915	YALOBUSHA	3,797	2,944	797	56	2,147 R	77.5%	21.0%	78.7%	21.3%
27,304	YAZOO	7,654	5,555	2,008	91	3,547 R	72.6%	26.2%	73.4%	26.6%
2,216,912	TOTAL	645,963	505,125	126,782	14,056	378,343 R	78.2%	19.6%	79.9%	20.1%

MISSISSIPPI

PRESIDENT 1968

1960 Census Population	County	Total Vote	Republican	Democratic	AIP	Other	Plurality	Percentage Rep.	Dem.	AIP
37,730	ADAMS	13,501	1,475	5,214	6,812		1,598 A	10.9%	38.6%	50.5%
25,282	ALCORN	9,186	1,760	1,122	6,304		4,544 A	19.2%	12.2%	68.6%
15,573	AMITE	5,132	393	1,533	3,206		1,673 A	7.7%	29.9%	62.5%
21,335	ATTALA	6,963	599	1,588	4,776		3,188 A	8.6%	22.8%	68.6%
7,723	BENTON	2,665	185	850	1,630		780 A	6.9%	31.9%	61.2%
54,464	BOLIVAR	11,504	1,790	4,696	5,018		322 A	15.6%	40.8%	43.6%
15,941	CALHOUN	5,493	394	276	4,823		4,429 A	7.2%	5.0%	87.8%
11,177	CARROLL	3,194	138	925	2,131		1,206 A	4.3%	29.0%	66.7%
16,891	CHICKASAW	5,163	381	720	4,062		3,342 A	7.4%	13.9%	78.7%
8,423	CHOCTAW	3,171	211	417	2,543		2,126 A	6.7%	13.2%	80.2%
10,845	CLAIBORNE	3,502	230	2,129	1,143		986 D	6.6%	60.8%	32.6%
16,493	CLARKE	5,390	298	878	4,214		3,336 A	5.5%	16.3%	78.2%
18,933	CLAY	5,509	494	1,510	3,505		1,995 A	9.0%	27.4%	63.6%
46,212	COAHOMA	10,898	1,875	5,352	3,671		1,681 D	17.2%	49.1%	33.7%
27,051	COPIAH	8,379	704	2,724	4,951		2,227 A	8.4%	32.5%	59.1%
13,637	COVINGTON	4,804	445	691	3,668		2,977 A	9.3%	14.4%	76.4%
23,891	DE SOTO	8,336	1,092	1,898	5,346		3,448 A	13.1%	22.8%	64.1%
52,722	FORREST	16,226	3,294	2,957	9,975		6,681 A	20.3%	18.2%	61.5%
9,286	FRANKLIN	3,442	231	782	2,429		1,647 A	6.7%	22.7%	70.6%
11,098	GEORGE	4,377	171	214	3,992		3,778 A	3.9%	4.9%	91.2%
8,366	GREENE	3,325	132	449	2,744		2,295 A	4.0%	13.5%	82.5%
18,409	GRENADA	7,103	718	2,050	4,335		2,285 A	10.1%	28.9%	61.0%
14,039	HANCOCK	6,041	1,065	904	4,072		3,007 A	17.6%	15.0%	67.4%
119,489	HARRISON	29,248	6,542	4,549	18,157		11,615 A	22.4%	15.6%	62.1%
187,045	HINDS	60,734	13,488	14,880	32,366		17,486 A	22.2%	24.5%	53.3%
27,096	HOLMES	7,409	520	3,881	3,008		873 D	7.0%	52.4%	40.6%
19,093	HUMPHREYS	3,628	258	1,219	2,151		932 A	7.1%	33.6%	59.3%
3,576	ISSAQUENA	1,105	44	527	534		7 A	4.0%	47.7%	48.3%
15,080	ITAWAMBA	6,190	569	417	5,204		4,635 A	9.2%	6.7%	84.1%
55,522	JACKSON	20,439	2,942	2,236	15,261		12,319 A	14.4%	10.9%	74.7%
16,909	JASPER	4,460	373	987	3,100		2,113 A	8.4%	22.1%	69.5%
10,142	JEFFERSON	3,380	147	2,121	1,112		1,009 D	4.3%	62.8%	32.9%
13,540	JEFFERSON DAVIS	4,376	297	1,465	2,614		1,149 A	6.8%	33.5%	59.7%
59,542	JONES	17,994	3,242	2,476	12,276		9,034 A	18.0%	13.8%	68.2%
12,277	KEMPER	3,352	167	655	2,530		1,875 A	5.0%	19.5%	75.5%
21,355	LAFAYETTE	6,142	1,235	1,578	3,329		1,751 A	20.1%	25.7%	54.2%
13,675	LAMAR	5,319	546	351	4,422		3,876 A	10.3%	6.6%	83.1%
67,119	LAUDERDALE	20,365	2,328	3,195	14,842		11,647 A	11.4%	15.7%	72.9%
10,215	LAWRENCE	3,894	329	740	2,825		2,085 A	8.4%	19.0%	72.5%
18,660	LEAKE	6,316	453	1,295	4,568		3,273 A	7.2%	20.5%	72.3%
40,589	LEE	13,666	2,522	1,912	9,232		6,710 A	18.5%	14.0%	67.6%
47,142	LEFLORE	11,632	1,514	4,386	5,732		1,346 A	13.0%	37.7%	49.3%
26,759	LINCOLN	9,918	1,057	1,585	7,276		5,691 A	10.7%	16.0%	73.4%
46,639	LOWNDES	11,026	1,968	2,229	6,829		4,600 A	17.8%	20.2%	61.9%
32,904	MADISON	9,462	876	4,515	4,071		444 D	9.3%	47.7%	43.0%
23,293	MARION	8,333	763	1,722	5,848		4,126 A	9.2%	20.7%	70.2%
24,503	MARSHALL	6,278	577	2,907	2,794		113 D	9.2%	46.3%	44.5%
33,953	MONROE	10,529	1,167	1,506	7,856		6,350 A	11.1%	14.3%	74.6%
13,320	MONTGOMERY	4,359	475	896	2,988		2,092 A	10.9%	20.6%	68.5%
20,927	NESHOBA	7,815	531	867	6,417		5,550 A	6.8%	11.1%	82.1%
19,517	NEWTON	6,902	542	799	5,561		4,762 A	7.9%	11.6%	80.6%
16,826	NOXUBEE	3,659	232	1,387	2,040		653 A	6.3%	37.9%	55.8%
26,175	OKTIBBEHA	7,229	1,276	1,826	4,127		2,301 A	17.7%	25.3%	57.1%
28,791	PANOLA	7,974	1,098	2,743	4,133		1,390 A	13.8%	34.4%	51.8%
22,411	PEARL RIVER	8,274	1,298	926	6,050		4,752 A	15.7%	11.2%	73.1%
8,745	PERRY	3,207	227	439	2,541		2,102 A	7.1%	13.7%	79.2%
35,063	PIKE	10,154	1,460	2,848	5,846		2,998 A	14.4%	28.0%	57.6%
17,232	PONTOTOC	6,130	733	599	4,798		4,065 A	12.0%	9.8%	78.3%
17,949	PRENTISS	6,218	723	440	5,055		4,332 A	11.6%	7.1%	81.3%
21,019	QUITMAN	4,379	434	1,502	2,443		941 A	9.9%	34.3%	55.8%

MISSISSIPPI

PRESIDENT 1968

1960 Census Population	County	Total Vote	Republican	Democratic	AIP	Other	Plurality	Percentage Rep.	Dem.	AIP
34,322	RANKIN	12,323	1,124	1,975	9,224		7,249 A	9.1%	16.0%	74.9%
21,187	SCOTT	6,764	604	1,067	5,093		4,026 A	8.9%	15.8%	75.3%
10,738	SHARKEY	2,409	249	972	1,188		216 A	10.3%	40.3%	49.3%
20,454	SIMPSON	7,018	875	1,079	5,064		3,985 A	12.5%	15.4%	72.2%
14,303	SMITH	5,156	437	352	4,367		3,930 A	8.5%	6.8%	84.7%
7,013	STONE	2,712	258	314	2,140		1,826 A	9.5%	11.6%	78.9%
45,750	SUNFLOWER	7,570	1,036	2,602	3,932		1,330 A	13.7%	34.4%	51.9%
24,081	TALLAHATCHIE	5,130	577	1,477	3,076		1,599 A	11.2%	28.8%	60.0%
18,138	TATE	4,577	605	1,162	2,810		1,648 A	13.2%	25.4%	61.4%
15,093	TIPPAH	5,879	589	663	4,627		3,964 A	10.0%	11.3%	78.7%
13,889	TISHOMINGO	5,544	617	358	4,569		3,952 A	11.1%	6.5%	82.4%
16,826	TUNICA	2,329	413	1,133	783		350 D	17.7%	48.6%	33.6%
18,904	UNION	6,770	948	624	5,198		4,250 A	14.0%	9.2%	76.8%
13,512	WALTHALL	4,806	387	1,233	3,186		1,953 A	8.1%	25.7%	66.3%
42,206	WARREN	14,112	2,392	4,503	7,217		2,714 A	17.0%	31.9%	51.1%
78,638	WASHINGTON	15,320	3,500	5,520	6,300		780 A	22.8%	36.0%	41.1%
16,258	WAYNE	5,075	247	739	4,089		3,350 A	4.9%	14.6%	80.6%
10,580	WEBSTER	4,023	330	295	3,398		3,068 A	8.2%	7.3%	84.5%
13,235	WILKINSON	3,919	272	2,144	1,503		641 D	6.9%	54.7%	38.4%
19,246	WINSTON	6,054	508	911	4,635		3,724 A	8.4%	15.0%	76.6%
12,502	YALOBUSHA	4,160	562	873	2,725		1,852 A	13.5%	21.0%	65.5%
31,653	YAZOO	8,060	958	2,163	4,939		2,776 A	11.9%	26.8%	61.3%
2,178,141	TOTAL	654,509	88,516	150,644	415,349		264,705 A	13.5%	23.0%	63.5%

MISSISSIPPI

ELECTION NOTES

1984 Other vote was 2,336 Bergland (Libertarian); 1,169 Holmes (Independent); 1,032 Mason (Independent); 1,001 LaRouche (Independent); 641 Richards (Independent); 356 Serrette (Independent).

1980 Other vote was 12,036 Anderson (Independent); 5,465 Clark (Independent); 2,402 Griswold (Independent); 2,347 Pulley (Independent).

1976 Other vote was 6,678 Anderson (American); 4,861 Maddox (Independent); 4,074 McCarthy (Independent); 2,805 Camejo (Independent); 2,788 MacBride (Independent). Early unamended canvass gave the state-wide total votes as 381,329 Republican; 2,787 MacBride (Independent); and the Republican vote in Jefferson Davis county as 1,808; the Democratic vote in Noxubee county as 3,121.

1972 Other vote was 11,598 Schmitz (Independent); 2,458 Jenness (Independent).

1968 Wallace on the ballot as Independent.

MISSOURI

POPULAR VOTE FOR PRESIDENT 1920 TO 1984

Year	Total Vote	Republican Vote	Republican Candidate	Democratic Vote	Democratic Candidate	Other Vote	Plurality	Percentage Total Vote Rep.	Percentage Total Vote Dem.	Percentage Major Vote Rep.	Percentage Major Vote Dem.
1984	2,122,783	1,274,188	Reagan, Ronald	848,583	Mondale, Walter F.	12	425,605 R	60.0%	40.0%	60.0%	40.0%
1980	2,099,824	1,074,181	Reagan, Ronald	931,182	Carter, Jimmy	94,461	142,999 R	51.2%	44.3%	53.6%	46.4%
1976	1,953,600	927,443	Ford, Gerald R.	998,387	Carter, Jimmy	27,770	70,944 D	47.5%	51.1%	48.2%	51.8%
1972	1,855,803	1,153,852	Nixon, Richard M.	697,147	McGovern, George S.	4,804	456,705 R	62.2%	37.6%	62.3%	37.7%
1968	1,809,502	811,932	Nixon, Richard M.	791,444	Humphrey, Hubert H.	206,126	20,488 R	44.9%	43.7%	50.6%	49.4%
1964	1,817,879	653,535	Goldwater, Barry M.	1,164,344	Johnson, Lyndon B.		510,809 D	36.0%	64.0%	36.0%	64.0%
1960	1,934,422	962,221	Nixon, Richard M.	972,201	Kennedy, John F.		9,980 D	49.7%	50.3%	49.7%	50.3%
1956	1,832,562	914,289	Eisenhower, Dwight D.	918,273	Stevenson, Adlai E.		3,984 D	49.9%	50.1%	49.9%	50.1%
1952	1,892,062	959,429	Eisenhower, Dwight D.	929,830	Stevenson, Adlai E.	2,803	29,599 R	50.7%	49.1%	50.8%	49.2%
1948	1,578,628	655,039	Dewey, Thomas E.	917,315	Truman, Harry S.	6,274	262,276 D	41.5%	58.1%	41.7%	58.3%
1944	1,571,697	761,175	Dewey, Thomas E.	807,356	Roosevelt, Franklin D.	3,166	46,181 D	48.4%	51.4%	48.5%	51.5%
1940	1,833,729	871,009	Willkie, Wendell	958,476	Roosevelt, Franklin D.	4,244	87,467 D	47.5%	52.3%	47.6%	52.4%
1936	1,828,635	697,891	Landon, Alfred M.	1,111,043	Roosevelt, Franklin D.	19,701	413,152 D	38.2%	60.8%	38.6%	61.4%
1932	1,609,894	564,713	Hoover, Herbert C.	1,025,406	Roosevelt, Franklin D.	19,775	460,693 D	35.1%	63.7%	35.5%	64.5%
1928	1,500,845	834,080	Hoover, Herbert C.	662,684	Smith, Alfred E.	4,081	171,396 R	55.6%	44.2%	55.7%	44.3%
1924	1,310,095	648,488	Coolidge, Calvin	574,962	Davis, John W.	86,645	73,526 R	49.5%	43.9%	53.0%	47.0%
1920	1,332,140	727,252	Harding, Warren G.	574,699	Cox, James M.	30,189	152,553 R	54.6%	43.1%	55.9%	44.1%

ELECTORAL COLLEGE VOTE 1920 TO 1984

Year	Total	Republican	Democratic	Other
1984	11	11	—	—
1980	12	12	—	—
1976	12	—	12	—
1972	12	12	—	—
1968	12	12	—	—
1964	12	—	12	—
1960	13	—	13	—
1956	13	—	13	—
1952	13	13	—	—
1948	15	—	15	—
1944	15	—	15	—
1940	15	—	15	—
1936	15	—	15	—
1932	15	—	15	—
1928	18	18	—	—
1924	18	18	—	—
1920	18	18	—	—

MISSOURI

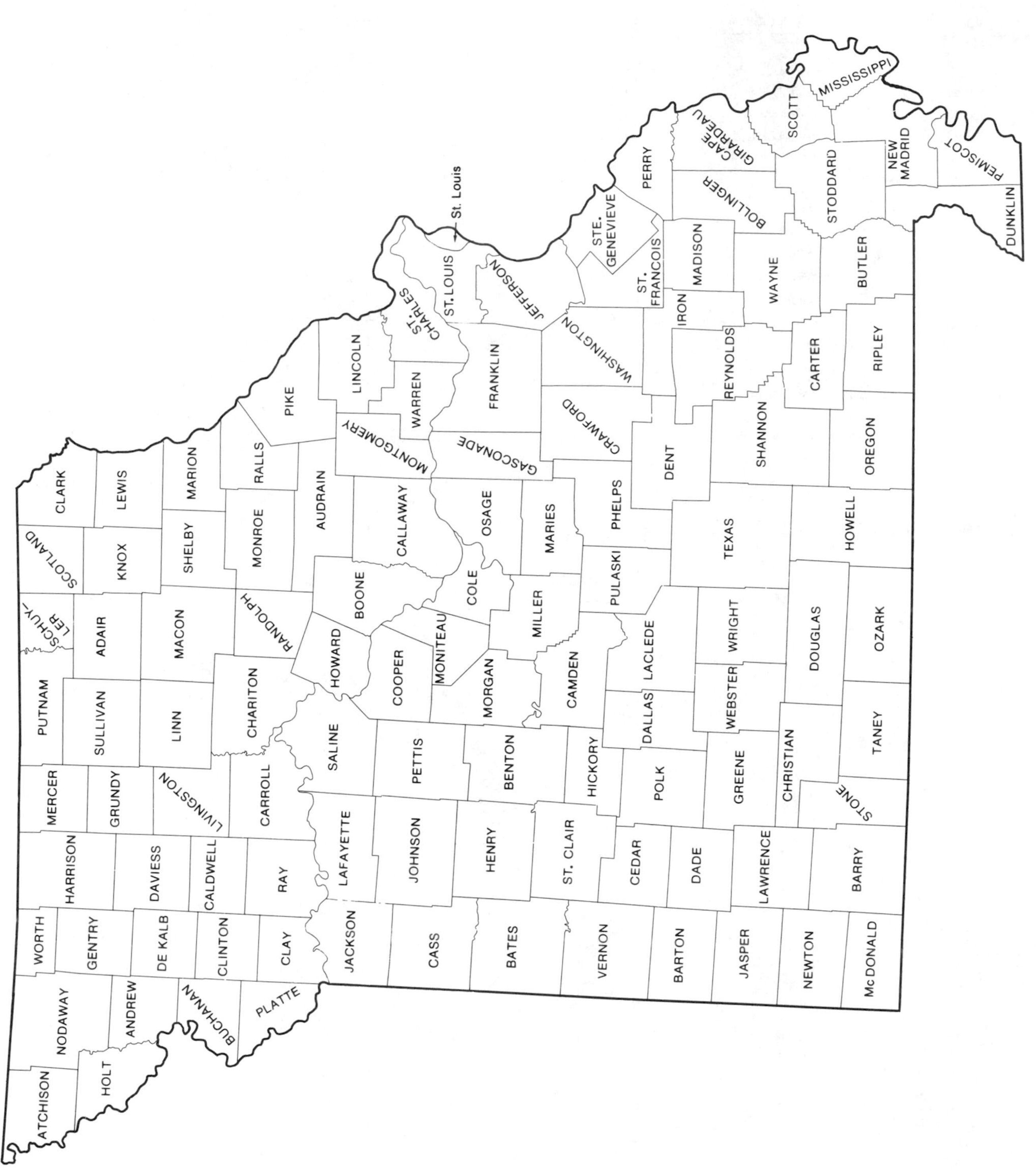
St. Louis
MISSISSIPPI
SCOTT
CAPE GIRARDEAU
PERRY
NEW MADRID
PEMISCOT
STODDARD
BOLLINGER
DUNKLIN
STE. GENEVIEVE
ST. FRANCOIS
MADISON
WAYNE
BUTLER
ST. LOUIS
JEFFERSON
ST. CHARLES
IRON
WASHINGTON
REYNOLDS
CARTER
RIPLEY
LINCOLN
WARREN
FRANKLIN
PIKE
CRAWFORD
DENT
SHANNON
OREGON
MONTGOMERY
GASCONADE
CLARK
LEWIS
MARION
RALLS
AUDRAIN
CALLAWAY
OSAGE
MARIES
PHELPS
TEXAS
HOWELL
SCOTLAND
KNOX
SHELBY
MONROE
BOONE
COLE
PULASKI
MILLER
SCHUY-LER
ADAIR
MACON
RANDOLPH
HOWARD
MONITEAU
COOPER
MORGAN
CAMDEN
LACLEDE
WRIGHT
DOUGLAS
OZARK
PUTNAM
SULLIVAN
LINN
CHARITON
SALINE
PETTIS
BENTON
HICKORY
DALLAS
WEBSTER
CHRISTIAN
TANEY
MERCER
GRUNDY
LIVINGSTON
CARROLL
POLK
GREENE
STONE
HARRISON
DAVIESS
CALDWELL
RAY
LAFAYETTE
JOHNSON
HENRY
ST. CLAIR
CEDAR
DADE
LAWRENCE
BARRY
WORTH
GENTRY
DE KALB
CLINTON
CLAY
JACKSON
CASS
BATES
VERNON
BARTON
JASPER
NEWTON
McDONALD
NODAWAY
ANDREW
BUCHANAN
PLATTE
ATCHISON
HOLT

MISSOURI

PRESIDENT 1984

1980 Census Population	County	Total Vote	Republican	Democratic	Other	Rep.-Dem. Plurality	Percentage Total Vote Rep.	Total Vote Dem.	Major Vote Rep.	Major Vote Dem.
24,870	ADAIR	9,549	6,430	3,119		3,311 R	67.3%	32.7%	67.3%	32.7%
13,980	ANDREW	6,709	4,252	2,457		1,795 R	63.4%	36.6%	63.4%	36.6%
8,605	ATCHISON	3,496	2,277	1,219		1,058 R	65.1%	34.9%	65.1%	34.9%
26,458	AUDRAIN	11,923	7,261	4,662		2,599 R	60.9%	39.1%	60.9%	39.1%
24,408	BARRY	11,166	7,683	3,483		4,200 R	68.8%	31.2%	68.8%	31.2%
11,292	BARTON	5,344	3,996	1,348		2,648 R	74.8%	25.2%	74.8%	25.2%
15,873	BATES	7,112	4,223	2,889		1,334 R	59.4%	40.6%	59.4%	40.6%
12,183	BENTON	6,056	3,805	2,251		1,554 R	62.8%	37.2%	62.8%	37.2%
10,301	BOLLINGER	4,701	2,778	1,923		855 R	59.1%	40.9%	59.1%	40.9%
100,376	BOONE	45,964	26,600	19,364		7,236 R	57.9%	42.1%	57.9%	42.1%
87,888	BUCHANAN	35,104	19,735	15,369		4,366 R	56.2%	43.8%	56.2%	43.8%
37,693	BUTLER	13,411	8,712	4,699		4,013 R	65.0%	35.0%	65.0%	35.0%
8,660	CALDWELL	4,060	2,678	1,382		1,296 R	66.0%	34.0%	66.0%	34.0%
32,252	CALLAWAY	12,589	8,262	4,327		3,935 R	65.6%	34.4%	65.6%	34.4%
20,017	CAMDEN	11,145	8,057	3,088		4,969 R	72.3%	27.7%	72.3%	27.7%
58,837	CAPE GIRARDEAU	24,750	17,404	7,346		10,058 R	70.3%	29.7%	70.3%	29.7%
12,131	CARROLL	5,475	3,495	1,980		1,515 R	63.8%	36.2%	63.8%	36.2%
5,428	CARTER	2,318	1,402	916		486 R	60.5%	39.5%	60.5%	39.5%
51,029	CASS	21,973	14,456	7,517		6,939 R	65.8%	34.2%	65.8%	34.2%
11,894	CEDAR	4,979	3,539	1,440		2,099 R	71.1%	28.9%	71.1%	28.9%
10,489	CHARITON	4,988	2,744	2,244		500 R	55.0%	45.0%	55.0%	45.0%
22,402	CHRISTIAN	10,857	7,634	3,223		4,411 R	70.3%	29.7%	70.3%	29.7%
8,493	CLARK	3,695	2,068	1,627		441 R	56.0%	44.0%	56.0%	44.0%
136,488	CLAY	59,116	36,529	22,586	1	13,943 R	61.8%	38.2%	61.8%	38.2%
15,916	CLINTON	7,004	4,226	2,778		1,448 R	60.3%	39.7%	60.3%	39.7%
56,663	COLE	27,068	20,366	6,702		13,664 R	75.2%	24.8%	75.2%	24.8%
14,643	COOPER	6,822	4,603	2,219		2,384 R	67.5%	32.5%	67.5%	32.5%
18,300	CRAWFORD	7,326	4,716	2,610		2,106 R	64.4%	35.6%	64.4%	35.6%
7,383	DADE	3,700	2,600	1,100		1,500 R	70.3%	29.7%	70.3%	29.7%
12,096	DALLAS	5,479	3,577	1,902		1,675 R	65.3%	34.7%	65.3%	34.7%
8,905	DAVIESS	3,940	2,414	1,526		888 R	61.3%	38.7%	61.3%	38.7%
8,222	DE KALB	3,652	2,188	1,464		724 R	59.9%	40.1%	59.9%	40.1%
14,517	DENT	6,034	3,490	2,544		946 R	57.8%	42.2%	57.8%	42.2%
11,594	DOUGLAS	5,199	3,662	1,536	1	2,126 R	70.4%	29.5%	70.5%	29.5%
36,324	DUNKLIN	11,059	6,092	4,967		1,125 R	55.1%	44.9%	55.1%	44.9%
71,233	FRANKLIN	26,988	18,669	8,319		10,350 R	69.2%	30.8%	69.2%	30.8%
13,181	GASCONADE	5,808	4,678	1,130		3,548 R	80.5%	19.5%	80.5%	19.5%
7,887	GENTRY	3,647	2,047	1,600		447 R	56.1%	43.9%	56.1%	43.9%
185,302	GREENE	85,215	57,250	27,965		29,285 R	67.2%	32.8%	67.2%	32.8%
11,959	GRUNDY	5,017	3,156	1,861		1,295 R	62.9%	37.1%	62.9%	37.1%
9,890	HARRISON	4,493	2,844	1,649		1,195 R	63.3%	36.7%	63.3%	36.7%
19,672	HENRY	9,160	5,419	3,741		1,678 R	59.2%	40.8%	59.2%	40.8%
6,367	HICKORY	3,402	2,190	1,212		978 R	64.4%	35.6%	64.4%	35.6%
6,882	HOLT	3,113	2,087	1,026		1,061 R	67.0%	33.0%	67.0%	33.0%
10,008	HOWARD	4,374	2,360	2,014		346 R	54.0%	46.0%	54.0%	46.0%
28,807	HOWELL	11,971	8,204	3,767		4,437 R	68.5%	31.5%	68.5%	31.5%
11,084	IRON	4,339	2,316	2,023		293 R	53.4%	46.6%	53.4%	46.6%
629,266	JACKSON	267,347	132,271	135,067	9	2,796 D	49.5%	50.5%	49.5%	50.5%
86,958	JASPER	32,325	23,066	9,259		13,807 R	71.4%	28.6%	71.4%	28.6%
146,183	JEFFERSON	54,551	34,525	20,026		14,499 R	63.3%	36.7%	63.3%	36.7%
39,059	JOHNSON	12,651	8,413	4,238		4,175 R	66.5%	33.5%	66.5%	33.5%
5,508	KNOX	2,610	1,513	1,097		416 R	58.0%	42.0%	58.0%	42.0%
24,323	LACLEDE	9,071	6,406	2,665		3,741 R	70.6%	29.4%	70.6%	29.4%
29,925	LAFAYETTE	13,429	8,581	4,848		3,733 R	63.9%	36.1%	63.9%	36.1%
28,973	LAWRENCE	12,090	8,370	3,720		4,650 R	69.2%	30.8%	69.2%	30.8%
10,901	LEWIS	4,415	2,438	1,977		461 R	55.2%	44.8%	55.2%	44.8%
22,193	LINCOLN	9,427	6,137	3,290		2,847 R	65.1%	34.9%	65.1%	34.9%
15,495	LINN	6,934	3,822	3,112		710 R	55.1%	44.9%	55.1%	44.9%
15,739	LIVINGSTON	6,789	4,090	2,699		1,391 R	60.2%	39.8%	60.2%	39.8%
14,917	MCDONALD	6,630	4,521	2,109		2,412 R	68.2%	31.8%	68.2%	31.8%

MISSOURI

PRESIDENT 1984

1980 Census Population	County	Total Vote	Republican	Democratic	Other	Rep.-Dem. Plurality	Percentage Total Vote Rep.	Percentage Total Vote Dem.	Percentage Major Vote Rep.	Percentage Major Vote Dem.
16,313	MACON	7,579	4,542	3,037		1,505 R	59.9%	40.1%	59.9%	40.1%
10,725	MADISON	4,670	2,808	1,862		946 R	60.1%	39.9%	60.1%	39.9%
7,551	MARIES	3,655	2,267	1,388		879 R	62.0%	38.0%	62.0%	38.0%
28,638	MARION	11,497	6,831	4,666		2,165 R	59.4%	40.6%	59.4%	40.6%
4,685	MERCER	2,104	1,229	875		354 R	58.4%	41.6%	58.4%	41.6%
18,532	MILLER	8,760	6,706	2,054		4,652 R	76.6%	23.4%	76.6%	23.4%
15,726	MISSISSIPPI	5,026	2,502	2,524		22 D	49.8%	50.2%	49.8%	50.2%
12,068	MONITEAU	5,811	4,197	1,614		2,583 R	72.2%	27.8%	72.2%	27.8%
9,716	MONROE	4,155	2,163	1,992		171 R	52.1%	47.9%	52.1%	47.9%
11,537	MONTGOMERY	4,929	3,261	1,668		1,593 R	66.2%	33.8%	66.2%	33.8%
13,807	MORGAN	6,561	4,392	2,169		2,223 R	66.9%	33.1%	66.9%	33.1%
22,945	NEW MADRID	8,099	4,323	3,776		547 R	53.4%	46.6%	53.4%	46.6%
40,555	NEWTON	16,332	11,709	4,623		7,086 R	71.7%	28.3%	71.7%	28.3%
21,996	NODAWAY	9,086	5,471	3,615		1,856 R	60.2%	39.8%	60.2%	39.8%
10,238	OREGON	4,005	1,979	2,026		47 D	49.4%	50.6%	49.4%	50.6%
12,014	OSAGE	5,724	4,381	1,343		3,038 R	76.5%	23.5%	76.5%	23.5%
7,961	OZARK	3,724	2,614	1,110		1,504 R	70.2%	29.8%	70.2%	29.8%
24,987	PEMISCOT	7,026	3,733	3,293		440 R	53.1%	46.9%	53.1%	46.9%
16,784	PERRY	6,330	4,493	1,837		2,656 R	71.0%	29.0%	71.0%	29.0%
36,378	PETTIS	16,404	10,991	5,413		5,578 R	67.0%	33.0%	67.0%	33.0%
33,633	PHELPS	14,086	9,012	5,074		3,938 R	64.0%	36.0%	64.0%	36.0%
17,568	PIKE	7,246	3,933	3,313		620 R	54.3%	45.7%	54.3%	45.7%
46,341	PLATTE	20,527	12,859	7,668		5,191 R	62.6%	37.4%	62.6%	37.4%
18,822	POLK	8,286	5,467	2,819		2,648 R	66.0%	34.0%	66.0%	34.0%
42,011	PULASKI	8,195	5,330	2,865		2,465 R	65.0%	35.0%	65.0%	35.0%
6,092	PUTNAM	2,337	1,540	797		743 R	65.9%	34.1%	65.9%	34.1%
8,911	RALLS	4,078	2,067	2,011		56 R	50.7%	49.3%	50.7%	49.3%
25,460	RANDOLPH	10,206	5,735	4,471		1,264 R	56.2%	43.8%	56.2%	43.8%
21,378	RAY	8,854	4,875	3,979		896 R	55.1%	44.9%	55.1%	44.9%
7,230	REYNOLDS	3,356	1,330	2,026		696 D	39.6%	60.4%	39.6%	60.4%
12,458	RIPLEY	4,810	2,927	1,883		1,044 R	60.9%	39.1%	60.9%	39.1%
144,107	ST. CHARLES	65,401	47,784	17,617		30,167 R	73.1%	26.9%	73.1%	26.9%
8,622	ST. CLAIR	4,322	2,667	1,655		1,012 R	61.7%	38.3%	61.7%	38.3%
42,600	ST. FRANCOIS	16,929	9,792	7,137		2,655 R	57.8%	42.2%	57.8%	42.2%
453,085	ST. LOUIS CITY	173,338	61,020	112,318		51,298 D	35.2%	64.8%	35.2%	64.8%
973,896	ST. LOUIS COUNTY	480,828	307,684	173,144		134,540 R	64.0%	36.0%	64.0%	36.0%
15,180	STE. GENEVIEVE	5,968	3,245	2,723		522 R	54.4%	45.6%	54.4%	45.6%
24,919	SALINE	10,323	6,042	4,281		1,761 R	58.5%	41.5%	58.5%	41.5%
4,979	SCHUYLER	2,391	1,250	1,141		109 R	52.3%	47.7%	52.3%	47.7%
5,415	SCOTLAND	2,560	1,485	1,075		410 R	58.0%	42.0%	58.0%	42.0%
39,647	SCOTT	14,297	8,727	5,569	1	3,158 R	61.0%	39.0%	61.0%	39.0%
7,885	SHANNON	3,359	1,779	1,580		199 R	53.0%	47.0%	53.0%	47.0%
7,826	SHELBY	3,816	2,243	1,573		670 R	58.8%	41.2%	58.8%	41.2%
29,009	STODDARD	10,995	6,701	4,294		2,407 R	60.9%	39.1%	60.9%	39.1%
15,587	STONE	7,825	5,706	2,119		3,587 R	72.9%	27.1%	72.9%	27.1%
7,434	SULLIVAN	4,090	2,306	1,784		522 R	56.4%	43.6%	56.4%	43.6%
20,467	TANEY	9,994	7,082	2,912		4,170 R	70.9%	29.1%	70.9%	29.1%
21,070	TEXAS	9,253	5,591	3,662		1,929 R	60.4%	39.6%	60.4%	39.6%
19,806	VERNON	8,165	5,181	2,984		2,197 R	63.5%	36.5%	63.5%	36.5%
14,900	WARREN	7,114	5,150	1,964		3,186 R	72.4%	27.6%	72.4%	27.6%
17,983	WASHINGTON	6,742	3,755	2,987		768 R	55.7%	44.3%	55.7%	44.3%
11,277	WAYNE	5,230	2,867	2,363		504 R	54.8%	45.2%	54.8%	45.2%
20,414	WEBSTER	8,511	5,529	2,982		2,547 R	65.0%	35.0%	65.0%	35.0%
3,008	WORTH	1,655	921	734		187 R	55.6%	44.4%	55.6%	44.4%
16,188	WRIGHT	6,660	4,687	1,973		2,714 R	70.4%	29.6%	70.4%	29.6%
4,916,686	TOTAL	2,122,783	1,274,188	848,583	12	425,605 R	60.0%	40.0%	60.0%	40.0%

MISSOURI

PRESIDENT 1980

1980 Census Population	County	Total Vote	Republican	Democratic	Other	Rep.-Dem. Plurality	Percentage Total Vote Rep.	Percentage Total Vote Dem.	Percentage Major Vote Rep.	Percentage Major Vote Dem.
24,870	ADAIR	9,522	5,513	3,507	502	2,006 R	57.9%	36.8%	61.1%	38.9%
13,980	ANDREW	6,573	3,690	2,575	308	1,115 R	56.1%	39.2%	58.9%	41.1%
8,605	ATCHISON	3,556	2,096	1,273	187	823 R	58.9%	35.8%	62.2%	37.8%
26,458	AUDRAIN	11,834	6,347	5,168	319	1,179 R	53.6%	43.7%	55.1%	44.9%
24,408	BARRY	11,458	7,038	4,193	227	2,845 R	61.4%	36.6%	62.7%	37.3%
11,292	BARTON	5,398	3,337	1,901	160	1,436 R	61.8%	35.2%	63.7%	36.3%
15,873	BATES	7,521	4,061	3,297	163	764 R	54.0%	43.8%	55.2%	44.8%
12,183	BENTON	5,852	3,451	2,241	160	1,210 R	59.0%	38.3%	60.6%	39.4%
10,301	BOLLINGER	5,105	2,863	2,160	82	703 R	56.1%	42.3%	57.0%	43.0%
100,376	BOONE	38,837	16,313	18,527	3,997	2,214 D	42.0%	47.7%	46.8%	53.2%
87,888	BUCHANAN	35,150	16,551	16,967	1,632	416 D	47.1%	48.3%	49.4%	50.6%
37,693	BUTLER	14,181	8,342	5,605	234	2,737 R	58.8%	39.5%	59.8%	40.2%
8,660	CALDWELL	4,226	2,551	1,541	134	1,010 R	60.4%	36.5%	62.3%	37.7%
32,252	CALLAWAY	12,835	6,755	5,560	520	1,195 R	52.6%	43.3%	54.9%	45.1%
20,017	CAMDEN	10,246	6,541	3,416	289	3,125 R	63.8%	33.3%	65.7%	34.3%
58,837	CAPE GIRARDEAU	24,549	14,861	8,625	1,063	6,236 R	60.5%	35.1%	63.3%	36.7%
12,131	CARROLL	5,583	3,291	2,130	162	1,161 R	58.9%	38.2%	60.7%	39.3%
5,428	CARTER	2,368	1,218	1,087	63	131 R	51.4%	45.9%	52.8%	47.2%
51,029	CASS	19,134	10,105	8,198	831	1,907 R	52.8%	42.8%	55.2%	44.8%
11,894	CEDAR	5,283	3,469	1,703	111	1,766 R	65.7%	32.2%	67.1%	32.9%
10,489	CHARITON	4,973	2,641	2,250	82	391 R	53.1%	45.2%	54.0%	46.0%
22,402	CHRISTIAN	10,251	6,487	3,502	262	2,985 R	63.3%	34.2%	64.9%	35.1%
8,493	CLARK	3,614	2,042	1,494	78	548 R	56.5%	41.3%	57.7%	42.3%
136,488	CLAY	56,314	28,521	24,250	3,543	4,271 R	50.6%	43.1%	54.0%	46.0%
15,916	CLINTON	6,852	3,599	3,001	252	598 R	52.5%	43.8%	54.5%	45.5%
56,663	COLE	26,423	16,373	9,210	840	7,163 R	62.0%	34.9%	64.0%	36.0%
14,643	COOPER	6,849	3,996	2,687	166	1,309 R	58.3%	39.2%	59.8%	40.2%
18,300	CRAWFORD	7,011	4,081	2,710	220	1,371 R	58.2%	38.7%	60.1%	39.9%
7,383	DADE	3,778	2,410	1,283	85	1,127 R	63.8%	34.0%	65.3%	34.7%
12,096	DALLAS	5,438	3,297	2,011	130	1,286 R	60.6%	37.0%	62.1%	37.9%
8,905	DAVIESS	3,984	2,125	1,770	89	355 R	53.3%	44.4%	54.6%	45.4%
8,222	DE KALB	3,885	2,062	1,677	146	385 R	53.1%	43.2%	55.1%	44.9%
14,517	DENT	6,131	3,477	2,528	126	949 R	56.7%	41.2%	57.9%	42.1%
11,594	DOUGLAS	5,252	3,440	1,677	135	1,763 R	65.5%	31.9%	67.2%	32.8%
36,324	DUNKLIN	11,530	5,253	6,120	157	867 D	45.6%	53.1%	46.2%	53.8%
71,233	FRANKLIN	26,832	15,210	10,480	1,142	4,730 R	56.7%	39.1%	59.2%	40.8%
13,181	GASCONADE	6,203	4,481	1,550	172	2,931 R	72.2%	25.0%	74.3%	25.7%
7,887	GENTRY	3,869	2,005	1,720	144	285 R	51.8%	44.5%	53.8%	46.2%
185,302	GREENE	77,425	43,116	30,498	3,811	12,618 R	55.7%	39.4%	58.6%	41.4%
11,959	GRUNDY	5,106	2,890	2,064	152	826 R	56.6%	40.4%	58.3%	41.7%
9,890	HARRISON	4,655	2,734	1,732	189	1,002 R	58.7%	37.2%	61.2%	38.8%
19,672	HENRY	9,772	4,807	4,648	317	159 R	49.2%	47.6%	50.8%	49.2%
6,367	HICKORY	3,213	1,893	1,248	72	645 R	58.9%	38.8%	60.3%	39.7%
6,882	HOLT	3,190	1,993	1,119	78	874 R	62.5%	35.1%	64.0%	36.0%
10,008	HOWARD	4,554	2,179	2,243	132	64 D	47.8%	49.3%	49.3%	50.7%
28,807	HOWELL	11,903	7,149	4,472	282	2,677 R	60.1%	37.6%	61.5%	38.5%
11,084	IRON	4,551	2,205	2,226	120	21 D	48.5%	48.9%	49.8%	50.2%
629,266	JACKSON	256,687	106,156	135,805	14,726	29,649 D	41.4%	52.9%	43.9%	56.1%
86,958	JASPER	34,666	21,664	11,953	1,049	9,711 R	62.5%	34.5%	64.4%	35.6%
146,183	JEFFERSON	54,882	28,546	24,042	2,294	4,504 R	52.0%	43.8%	54.3%	45.7%
39,059	JOHNSON	12,585	6,449	5,441	695	1,008 R	51.2%	43.2%	54.2%	45.8%
5,508	KNOX	2,710	1,475	1,187	48	288 R	54.4%	43.8%	55.4%	44.6%
24,323	LACLEDE	9,282	5,642	3,443	197	2,199 R	60.8%	37.1%	62.1%	37.9%
29,925	LAFAYETTE	13,468	7,271	5,792	405	1,479 R	54.0%	43.0%	55.7%	44.3%
28,973	LAWRENCE	12,843	7,921	4,670	252	3,251 R	61.7%	36.4%	62.9%	37.1%
10,901	LEWIS	4,789	2,350	2,314	125	36 R	49.1%	48.3%	50.4%	49.6%
22,193	LINCOLN	9,335	4,963	4,110	262	853 R	53.2%	44.0%	54.7%	45.3%
15,495	LINN	7,224	3,585	3,467	172	118 R	49.6%	48.0%	50.8%	49.2%
15,739	LIVINGSTON	7,270	3,654	3,368	248	286 R	50.3%	46.3%	52.0%	48.0%
14,917	MCDONALD	6,783	4,114	2,485	184	1,629 R	60.7%	36.6%	62.3%	37.7%

MISSOURI

PRESIDENT 1980

1980 Census Population	County	Total Vote	Republican	Democratic	Other	Rep.-Dem. Plurality	Percentage Total Vote Rep.	Total Vote Dem.	Major Vote Rep.	Major Vote Dem.
16,313	MACON	8,187	4,430	3,578	179	852 R	54.1%	43.7%	55.3%	44.7%
10,725	MADISON	4,938	2,618	2,231	89	387 R	53.0%	45.2%	54.0%	46.0%
7,551	MARIES	3,789	1,985	1,732	72	253 R	52.4%	45.7%	53.4%	46.6%
28,638	MARION	12,186	6,036	5,890	260	146 R	49.5%	48.3%	50.6%	49.4%
4,685	MERCER	2,158	1,266	821	71	445 R	58.7%	38.0%	60.7%	39.3%
18,532	MILLER	8,185	5,560	2,469	156	3,091 R	67.9%	30.2%	69.2%	30.8%
15,726	MISSISSIPPI	5,579	2,459	3,040	80	581 D	44.1%	54.5%	44.7%	55.3%
12,068	MONITEAU	5,834	3,430	2,284	120	1,146 R	58.8%	39.1%	60.0%	40.0%
9,716	MONROE	4,555	2,026	2,445	84	419 D	44.5%	53.7%	45.3%	54.7%
11,537	MONTGOMERY	5,225	3,061	2,007	157	1,054 R	58.6%	38.4%	60.4%	39.6%
13,807	MORGAN	6,182	3,577	2,460	145	1,117 R	57.9%	39.8%	59.3%	40.7%
22,945	NEW MADRID	8,298	4,041	4,171	86	130 D	48.7%	50.3%	49.2%	50.8%
40,555	NEWTON	16,662	10,515	5,621	526	4,894 R	63.1%	33.7%	65.2%	34.8%
21,996	NODAWAY	9,290	4,544	4,257	489	287 R	48.9%	45.8%	51.6%	48.4%
10,238	OREGON	3,898	1,523	2,326	49	803 D	39.1%	59.7%	39.6%	60.4%
12,014	OSAGE	5,822	3,679	2,045	98	1,634 R	63.2%	35.1%	64.3%	35.7%
7,961	OZARK	3,770	2,434	1,242	94	1,192 R	64.6%	32.9%	66.2%	33.8%
24,987	PEMISCOT	7,732	3,519	4,140	73	621 D	45.5%	53.5%	45.9%	54.1%
16,784	PERRY	7,689	5,053	2,416	220	2,637 R	65.7%	31.4%	67.7%	32.3%
36,378	PETTIS	15,841	8,833	6,475	533	2,358 R	55.8%	40.9%	57.7%	42.3%
33,633	PHELPS	13,566	7,366	5,470	730	1,896 R	54.3%	40.3%	57.4%	42.6%
17,568	PIKE	7,591	3,932	3,454	205	478 R	51.8%	45.5%	53.2%	46.8%
46,341	PLATTE	18,756	10,092	7,342	1,322	2,750 R	53.8%	39.1%	57.9%	42.1%
18,822	POLK	8,368	4,842	3,336	190	1,506 R	57.9%	39.9%	59.2%	40.8%
42,011	PULASKI	7,871	3,998	3,707	166	291 R	50.8%	47.1%	51.9%	48.1%
6,092	PUTNAM	2,655	1,722	871	62	851 R	64.9%	32.8%	66.4%	33.6%
8,911	RALLS	4,142	1,968	2,069	105	101 D	47.5%	50.0%	48.7%	51.3%
25,460	RANDOLPH	10,276	5,141	4,884	251	257 R	50.0%	47.5%	51.3%	48.7%
21,378	RAY	8,871	4,064	4,518	289	454 D	45.8%	50.9%	47.4%	52.6%
7,230	REYNOLDS	3,250	1,271	1,919	60	648 D	39.1%	59.0%	39.8%	60.2%
12,458	RIPLEY	4,765	2,524	2,156	85	368 R	53.0%	45.2%	53.9%	46.1%
144,107	ST. CHARLES	59,768	36,050	20,668	3,050	15,382 R	60.3%	34.6%	63.6%	36.4%
8,622	ST. CLAIR	4,210	2,419	1,706	85	713 R	57.5%	40.5%	58.6%	41.4%
42,600	ST. FRANCOIS	16,916	8,914	7,495	507	1,419 R	52.7%	44.3%	54.3%	45.7%
453,085	ST. LOUIS CITY	170,751	50,333	113,697	6,721	63,364 D	29.5%	66.6%	30.7%	69.3%
973,896	ST. LOUIS COUNTY	484,831	263,518	192,796	28,517	70,722 R	54.4%	39.8%	57.7%	42.3%
15,180	STE. GENEVIEVE	6,291	2,768	3,324	199	556 D	44.0%	52.8%	45.4%	54.6%
24,919	SALINE	10,576	5,218	4,943	415	275 R	49.3%	46.7%	51.4%	48.6%
4,979	SCHUYLER	2,559	1,386	1,114	59	272 R	54.2%	43.5%	55.4%	44.6%
5,415	SCOTLAND	2,869	1,592	1,200	77	392 R	55.5%	41.8%	57.0%	43.0%
39,647	SCOTT	15,336	8,227	6,854	255	1,373 R	53.6%	44.7%	54.6%	45.4%
7,885	SHANNON	3,401	1,523	1,818	60	295 D	44.8%	53.5%	45.6%	54.4%
7,826	SHELBY	4,079	2,151	1,849	79	302 R	52.7%	45.3%	53.8%	46.2%
29,009	STODDARD	11,512	6,199	5,128	185	1,071 R	53.8%	44.5%	54.7%	45.3%
15,587	STONE	7,209	4,780	2,210	219	2,570 R	66.3%	30.7%	68.4%	31.6%
7,434	SULLIVAN	4,325	2,412	1,824	89	588 R	55.8%	42.2%	56.9%	43.1%
20,467	TANEY	9,854	6,230	3,389	235	2,841 R	63.2%	34.4%	64.8%	35.2%
21,070	TEXAS	9,309	4,879	4,261	169	618 R	52.4%	45.8%	53.4%	46.6%
19,806	VERNON	8,456	4,391	3,704	361	687 R	51.9%	43.8%	54.2%	45.8%
14,900	WARREN	6,743	4,366	2,132	245	2,234 R	64.7%	31.6%	67.2%	32.8%
17,983	WASHINGTON	6,465	3,439	2,873	153	566 R	53.2%	44.4%	54.5%	45.5%
11,277	WAYNE	5,444	2,823	2,549	72	274 R	51.9%	46.8%	52.6%	47.4%
20,414	WEBSTER	8,719	5,121	3,409	189	1,712 R	58.7%	39.1%	60.0%	40.0%
3,008	WORTH	1,657	833	760	64	73 R	50.3%	45.9%	52.3%	47.7%
16,188	WRIGHT	6,716	4,451	2,182	83	2,269 R	66.3%	32.5%	67.1%	32.9%
4,916,686	TOTAL	2,099,824	1,074,181	931,182	94,461	142,999 R	51.2%	44.3%	53.6%	46.4%

MISSOURI

PRESIDENT 1976

1970 Census Population	County	Total Vote	Republican	Democratic	Other	Rep.-Dem. Plurality	Percentage Total Vote Rep.	Percentage Total Vote Dem.	Percentage Major Vote Rep.	Percentage Major Vote Dem.
22,472	ADAIR	9,133	5,249	3,684	200	1,565 R	57.5%	40.3%	58.8%	41.2%
11,913	ANDREW	6,213	3,130	3,042	41	88 R	50.4%	49.0%	50.7%	49.3%
9,240	ATCHISON	3,930	1,960	1,926	44	34 R	49.9%	49.0%	50.4%	49.6%
25,362	AUDRAIN	11,032	5,378	5,600	54	222 D	48.7%	50.8%	49.0%	51.0%
19,597	BARRY	10,148	5,053	5,046	49	7 R	49.8%	49.7%	50.0%	50.0%
10,431	BARTON	5,077	2,708	2,326	43	382 R	53.3%	45.8%	53.8%	46.2%
15,468	BATES	7,684	3,350	4,288	46	938 D	43.6%	55.8%	43.9%	56.1%
9,695	BENTON	5,587	2,875	2,684	28	191 R	51.5%	48.0%	51.7%	48.3%
8,820	BOLLINGER	4,862	2,113	2,740	9	627 D	43.5%	56.4%	43.5%	56.5%
80,911	BOONE	34,893	16,373	17,674	846	1,301 D	46.9%	50.7%	48.1%	51.9%
86,915	BUCHANAN	34,124	16,446	17,427	251	981 D	48.2%	51.1%	48.6%	51.4%
33,529	BUTLER	12,485	5,669	6,759	57	1,090 D	45.4%	54.1%	45.6%	54.4%
8,351	CALDWELL	4,233	2,094	2,113	26	19 D	49.5%	49.9%	49.8%	50.2%
25,950	CALLAWAY	10,059	5,115	4,843	101	272 R	50.8%	48.1%	51.4%	48.6%
13,315	CAMDEN	8,510	4,469	3,975	66	494 R	52.5%	46.7%	52.9%	47.1%
49,350	CAPE GIRARDEAU	23,164	12,607	10,440	117	2,167 R	54.4%	45.1%	54.7%	45.3%
12,565	CARROLL	6,077	2,936	3,114	27	178 D	48.3%	51.2%	48.5%	51.5%
3,878	CARTER	2,007	842	1,154	11	312 D	42.0%	57.5%	42.2%	57.8%
39,448	CASS	16,330	7,182	9,008	140	1,826 D	44.0%	55.2%	44.4%	55.6%
9,424	CEDAR	4,965	2,752	2,192	21	560 R	55.4%	44.1%	55.7%	44.3%
11,084	CHARITON	5,204	2,128	3,055	21	927 D	40.9%	58.7%	41.1%	58.9%
15,124	CHRISTIAN	8,442	4,553	3,830	59	723 R	53.9%	45.4%	54.3%	45.7%
8,260	CLARK	3,274	1,582	1,679	13	97 D	48.3%	51.3%	48.5%	51.5%
123,644	CLAY	52,315	24,962	26,609	744	1,647 D	47.7%	50.9%	48.4%	51.6%
12,462	CLINTON	6,272	2,807	3,424	41	617 D	44.8%	54.6%	45.0%	55.0%
46,228	COLE	22,503	14,370	7,949	184	6,421 R	63.9%	35.3%	64.4%	35.6%
14,732	COOPER	6,809	3,694	3,087	28	607 R	54.3%	45.3%	54.5%	45.5%
14,828	CRAWFORD	6,833	3,224	3,565	44	341 D	47.2%	52.2%	47.5%	52.5%
6,850	DADE	3,710	2,015	1,681	14	334 R	54.3%	45.3%	54.5%	45.5%
10,054	DALLAS	4,910	2,430	2,453	27	23 D	49.5%	50.0%	49.8%	50.2%
8,420	DAVIESS	4,191	1,919	2,250	22	331 D	45.8%	53.7%	46.0%	54.0%
7,305	DE KALB	3,779	1,739	2,023	17	284 D	46.0%	53.5%	46.2%	53.8%
11,457	DENT	5,401	2,433	2,931	37	498 D	45.0%	54.3%	45.4%	54.6%
9,268	DOUGLAS	4,667	2,652	1,981	34	671 R	56.8%	42.4%	57.2%	42.8%
33,742	DUNKLIN	10,443	3,314	7,107	22	3,793 D	31.7%	68.1%	31.8%	68.2%
55,116	FRANKLIN	24,342	12,242	11,695	405	547 R	50.3%	48.0%	51.1%	48.9%
11,878	GASCONADE	5,682	3,925	1,702	55	2,223 R	69.1%	30.0%	69.8%	30.2%
8,060	GENTRY	4,035	1,772	2,249	14	477 D	43.9%	55.7%	44.1%	55.9%
152,929	GREENE	72,205	37,691	33,824	690	3,867 R	52.2%	46.8%	52.7%	47.3%
11,819	GRUNDY	5,273	2,646	2,597	30	49 R	50.2%	49.3%	50.5%	49.5%
10,257	HARRISON	4,813	2,478	2,304	31	174 R	51.5%	47.9%	51.8%	48.2%
18,451	HENRY	9,497	4,168	5,282	47	1,114 D	43.9%	55.6%	44.1%	55.9%
4,481	HICKORY	2,822	1,403	1,398	21	5 R	49.7%	49.5%	50.1%	49.9%
6,654	HOLT	3,318	1,777	1,529	12	248 R	53.6%	46.1%	53.8%	46.2%
10,561	HOWARD	4,494	1,690	2,769	35	1,079 D	37.6%	61.6%	37.9%	62.1%
23,521	HOWELL	10,035	4,692	5,265	78	573 D	46.8%	52.5%	47.1%	52.9%
9,529	IRON	4,434	1,765	2,646	23	881 D	39.8%	59.7%	40.0%	60.0%
654,558	JACKSON	235,441	101,401	130,120	3,920	28,719 D	43.1%	55.3%	43.8%	56.2%
79,852	JASPER	32,149	17,086	14,910	153	2,176 R	53.1%	46.4%	53.4%	46.6%
105,248	JEFFERSON	43,915	18,261	25,159	495	6,898 D	41.6%	57.3%	42.1%	57.9%
34,172	JOHNSON	11,220	5,513	5,551	156	38 D	49.1%	49.5%	49.8%	50.2%
5,692	KNOX	2,556	1,216	1,319	21	103 D	47.6%	51.6%	48.0%	52.0%
19,944	LACLEDE	8,475	4,067	4,381	27	314 D	48.0%	51.7%	48.1%	51.9%
26,626	LAFAYETTE	13,305	6,823	6,410	72	413 R	51.3%	48.2%	51.6%	48.4%
24,585	LAWRENCE	11,137	5,784	5,315	38	469 R	51.9%	47.7%	52.1%	47.9%
10,993	LEWIS	4,497	1,983	2,486	28	503 D	44.1%	55.3%	44.4%	55.6%
18,041	LINCOLN	8,140	3,581	4,473	86	892 D	44.0%	55.0%	44.5%	55.5%
15,125	LINN	7,236	3,114	4,092	30	978 D	43.0%	56.6%	43.2%	56.8%
15,368	LIVINGSTON	6,857	3,010	3,819	28	809 D	43.9%	55.7%	44.1%	55.9%
12,357	MCDONALD	6,108	2,949	3,111	48	162 D	48.3%	50.9%	48.7%	51.3%

MISSOURI

PRESIDENT 1976

1970 Census Population	County	Total Vote	Republican	Democratic	Other	Rep.-Dem. Plurality	Percentage Total Vote Rep.	Total Vote Dem.	Major Vote Rep.	Major Vote Dem.
15,432	MACON	7,688	3,360	4,296	32	936 D	43.7%	55.9%	43.9%	56.1%
8,641	MADISON	3,989	1,739	2,229	21	490 D	43.6%	55.9%	43.8%	56.2%
6,851	MARIES	3,294	1,485	1,796	13	311 D	45.1%	54.5%	45.3%	54.7%
28,121	MARION	11,663	5,501	6,124	38	623 D	47.2%	52.5%	47.3%	52.7%
4,910	MERCER	2,207	1,025	1,177	5	152 D	46.4%	53.3%	46.5%	53.5%
15,026	MILLER	6,866	4,095	2,739	32	1,356 R	59.6%	39.9%	59.9%	40.1%
16,647	MISSISSIPPI	5,116	1,733	3,366	17	1,633 D	33.9%	65.8%	34.0%	66.0%
10,742	MONITEAU	5,555	3,077	2,462	16	615 R	55.4%	44.3%	55.6%	44.4%
9,542	MONROE	4,650	1,585	3,039	26	1,454 D	34.1%	65.4%	34.3%	65.7%
11,000	MONTGOMERY	5,243	2,665	2,535	43	130 R	50.8%	48.4%	51.2%	48.8%
10,068	MORGAN	5,595	2,831	2,738	26	93 R	50.6%	48.9%	50.8%	49.2%
23,420	NEW MADRID	8,136	2,798	5,319	19	2,521 D	34.4%	65.4%	34.5%	65.5%
32,901	NEWTON	14,301	7,142	7,045	114	97 R	49.9%	49.3%	50.3%	49.7%
22,467	NODAWAY	9,534	4,558	4,875	101	317 D	47.8%	51.1%	48.3%	51.7%
9,180	OREGON	3,712	1,122	2,564	26	1,442 D	30.2%	69.1%	30.4%	69.6%
10,994	OSAGE	5,269	3,224	2,015	30	1,209 R	61.2%	38.2%	61.5%	38.5%
6,226	OZARK	3,105	1,754	1,341	10	413 R	56.5%	43.2%	56.7%	43.3%
26,373	PEMISCOT	7,236	2,541	4,681	14	2,140 D	35.1%	64.7%	35.2%	64.8%
14,393	PERRY	6,918	4,086	2,801	31	1,285 R	59.1%	40.5%	59.3%	40.7%
34,137	PETTIS	15,296	7,344	7,887	65	543 D	48.0%	51.6%	48.2%	51.8%
29,567	PHELPS	12,512	6,153	6,261	98	108 D	49.2%	50.0%	49.6%	50.4%
16,928	PIKE	7,162	3,355	3,770	37	415 D	46.8%	52.6%	47.1%	52.9%
32,081	PLATTE	17,054	8,103	8,651	300	548 D	47.5%	50.7%	48.4%	51.6%
15,415	POLK	7,590	3,893	3,663	34	230 R	51.3%	48.3%	51.5%	48.5%
53,967	PULASKI	7,267	2,865	4,370	32	1,505 D	39.4%	60.1%	39.6%	60.4%
5,916	PUTNAM	2,550	1,444	1,097	9	347 R	56.6%	43.0%	56.8%	43.2%
7,764	RALLS	3,682	1,334	2,318	30	984 D	36.2%	63.0%	36.5%	63.5%
22,434	RANDOLPH	9,481	3,594	5,839	48	2,245 D	37.9%	61.6%	38.1%	61.9%
17,599	RAY	8,461	2,853	5,535	73	2,682 D	33.7%	65.4%	34.0%	66.0%
6,106	REYNOLDS	3,030	879	2,143	8	1,264 D	29.0%	70.7%	29.1%	70.9%
9,803	RIPLEY	4,245	1,640	2,577	28	937 D	38.6%	60.7%	38.9%	61.1%
92,954	ST. CHARLES	48,704	26,105	22,063	536	4,042 R	53.6%	45.3%	54.2%	45.8%
7,667	ST. CLAIR	4,103	1,808	2,271	24	463 D	44.1%	55.3%	44.3%	55.7%
36,818	ST. FRANCOIS	15,911	7,002	8,852	57	1,850 D	44.0%	55.6%	44.2%	55.8%
622,236	ST. LOUIS CITY	179,784	58,367	118,703	2,714	60,336 D	32.5%	66.0%	33.0%	67.0%
951,353	ST. LOUIS COUNTY	452,626	246,988	196,915	8,723	50,073 R	54.6%	43.5%	55.6%	44.4%
12,867	STE. GENEVIEVE	5,372	2,241	3,091	40	850 D	41.7%	57.5%	42.0%	58.0%
24,837	SALINE	10,845	4,883	5,890	72	1,007 D	45.0%	54.3%	45.3%	54.7%
4,665	SCHUYLER	2,620	1,193	1,417	10	224 D	45.5%	54.1%	45.7%	54.3%
5,499	SCOTLAND	2,752	1,286	1,449	17	163 D	46.7%	52.7%	47.0%	53.0%
33,250	SCOTT	13,576	5,473	8,075	28	2,602 D	40.3%	59.5%	40.4%	59.6%
7,196	SHANNON	2,971	989	1,960	22	971 D	33.3%	66.0%	33.5%	66.5%
7,906	SHELBY	3,702	1,453	2,227	22	774 D	39.2%	60.2%	39.5%	60.5%
25,771	STODDARD	10,111	3,989	6,097	25	2,108 D	39.5%	60.3%	39.5%	60.5%
9,921	STONE	5,842	3,457	2,358	27	1,099 R	59.2%	40.4%	59.4%	40.6%
7,572	SULLIVAN	4,484	2,141	2,313	30	172 D	47.7%	51.6%	48.1%	51.9%
13,023	TANEY	8,344	4,696	3,626	22	1,070 R	56.3%	43.5%	56.4%	43.6%
18,320	TEXAS	8,018	3,338	4,638	42	1,300 D	41.6%	57.8%	41.9%	58.1%
19,065	VERNON	8,684	3,715	4,921	48	1,206 D	42.8%	56.7%	43.0%	57.0%
9,699	WARREN	5,430	3,214	2,164	52	1,050 R	59.2%	39.9%	59.8%	40.2%
15,086	WASHINGTON	6,108	2,526	3,543	39	1,017 D	41.4%	58.0%	41.6%	58.4%
8,546	WAYNE	4,958	1,963	2,987	8	1,024 D	39.6%	60.2%	39.7%	60.3%
15,562	WEBSTER	7,315	3,510	3,759	46	249 D	48.0%	51.4%	48.3%	51.7%
3,359	WORTH	1,749	771	969	9	198 D	44.1%	55.4%	44.3%	55.7%
13,667	WRIGHT	6,191	3,397	2,781	13	616 R	54.9%	44.9%	55.0%	45.0%
4,677,399	TOTAL	1,953,600	927,443	998,387	27,770	70,944 D	47.5%	51.1%	48.2%	51.8%

MISSOURI

PRESIDENT 1972

1970 Census Population	County	Total Vote	Republican	Democratic	Other	Rep.-Dem. Plurality	Percentage Total Vote Rep.	Total Vote Dem.	Major Vote Rep.	Major Vote Dem.
22,472	ADAIR	8,449	6,157	2,286	6	3,871 R	72.9%	27.1%	72.9%	27.1%
11,913	ANDREW	5,869	4,180	1,686	3	2,494 R	71.2%	28.7%	71.3%	28.7%
9,240	ATCHISON	4,447	2,927	1,509	11	1,418 R	65.8%	33.9%	66.0%	34.0%
25,362	AUDRAIN	10,969	7,197	3,706	66	3,491 R	65.6%	33.8%	66.0%	34.0%
19,597	BARRY	10,512	7,295	3,167	50	4,128 R	69.4%	30.1%	69.7%	30.3%
10,431	BARTON	5,183	4,026	1,140	17	2,886 R	77.7%	22.0%	77.9%	22.1%
15,468	BATES	8,346	5,314	3,020	12	2,294 R	63.7%	36.2%	63.8%	36.2%
9,695	BENTON	4,990	3,537	1,423	30	2,114 R	70.9%	28.5%	71.3%	28.7%
8,820	BOLLINGER	4,890	3,069	1,818	3	1,251 R	62.8%	37.2%	62.8%	37.2%
80,911	BOONE	31,154	17,488	13,666		3,822 R	56.1%	43.9%	56.1%	43.9%
86,915	BUCHANAN	33,582	21,850	11,395	337	10,455 R	65.1%	33.9%	65.7%	34.3%
33,529	BUTLER	12,702	9,198	3,466	38	5,732 R	72.4%	27.3%	72.6%	27.4%
8,351	CALDWELL	4,408	3,167	1,231	10	1,936 R	71.8%	27.9%	72.0%	28.0%
25,950	CALLAWAY	9,380	6,313	3,036	31	3,277 R	67.3%	32.4%	67.5%	32.5%
13,315	CAMDEN	6,782	4,996	1,761	25	3,235 R	73.7%	26.0%	73.9%	26.1%
49,350	CAPE GIRARDEAU	22,080	15,693	6,280	107	9,413 R	71.1%	28.4%	71.4%	28.6%
12,565	CARROLL	6,042	4,100	1,927	15	2,173 R	67.9%	31.9%	68.0%	32.0%
3,878	CARTER	1,822	1,257	565		692 R	69.0%	31.0%	69.0%	31.0%
39,448	CASS	12,973	9,242	3,731		5,511 R	71.2%	28.8%	71.2%	28.8%
9,424	CEDAR	4,685	3,520	1,152	13	2,368 R	75.1%	24.6%	75.3%	24.7%
11,084	CHARITON	4,819	2,812	1,999	8	813 R	58.4%	41.5%	58.4%	41.6%
15,124	CHRISTIAN	8,266	6,305	1,945	16	4,360 R	76.3%	23.5%	76.4%	23.6%
8,260	CLARK	3,935	2,499	1,403	33	1,096 R	63.5%	35.7%	64.0%	36.0%
123,644	CLAY	47,794	33,017	14,538	239	18,479 R	69.1%	30.4%	69.4%	30.6%
12,462	CLINTON	5,868	3,924	1,944		1,980 R	66.9%	33.1%	66.9%	33.1%
46,228	COLE	21,539	16,685	4,754	100	11,931 R	77.5%	22.1%	77.8%	22.2%
14,732	COOPER	7,521	5,172	2,332	17	2,840 R	68.8%	31.0%	68.9%	31.1%
14,828	CRAWFORD	6,857	4,595	2,248	14	2,347 R	67.0%	32.8%	67.1%	32.9%
6,850	DADE	3,375	2,624	747	4	1,877 R	77.7%	22.1%	77.8%	22.2%
10,054	DALLAS	4,218	3,120	1,085	13	2,035 R	74.0%	25.7%	74.2%	25.8%
8,420	DAVIESS	4,289	2,840	1,430	19	1,410 R	66.2%	33.3%	66.5%	33.5%
7,305	DE KALB	4,113	2,766	1,339	8	1,427 R	67.3%	32.6%	67.4%	32.6%
11,457	DENT	4,743	3,024	1,710	9	1,314 R	63.8%	36.1%	63.9%	36.1%
9,268	DOUGLAS	4,995	3,773	1,209	13	2,564 R	75.5%	24.2%	75.7%	24.3%
33,742	DUNKLIN	8,732	5,926	2,776	30	3,150 R	67.9%	31.8%	68.1%	31.9%
55,116	FRANKLIN	21,343	13,785	7,464	94	6,321 R	64.6%	35.0%	64.9%	35.1%
11,878	GASCONADE	6,175	4,944	1,226	5	3,718 R	80.1%	19.9%	80.1%	19.9%
8,060	GENTRY	4,626	2,984	1,642		1,342 R	64.5%	35.5%	64.5%	35.5%
152,929	GREENE	68,674	48,348	20,155	171	28,193 R	70.4%	29.3%	70.6%	29.4%
11,819	GRUNDY	5,439	3,969	1,428	42	2,541 R	73.0%	26.3%	73.5%	26.5%
10,257	HARRISON	4,970	3,574	1,383	13	2,191 R	71.9%	27.8%	72.1%	27.9%
18,451	HENRY	8,948	5,802	3,125	21	2,677 R	64.8%	34.9%	65.0%	35.0%
4,481	HICKORY	2,473	1,851	622		1,229 R	74.8%	25.2%	74.8%	25.2%
6,654	HOLT	3,620	2,578	1,011	31	1,567 R	71.2%	27.9%	71.8%	28.2%
10,561	HOWARD	4,666	2,613	2,041	12	572 R	56.0%	43.7%	56.1%	43.9%
23,521	HOWELL	10,078	7,253	2,795	30	4,458 R	72.0%	27.7%	72.2%	27.8%
9,529	IRON	3,559	2,203	1,346	10	857 R	61.9%	37.8%	62.1%	37.9%
654,558	JACKSON	223,626	129,989	92,830	807	37,159 R	58.1%	41.5%	58.3%	41.7%
79,852	JASPER	30,241	22,482	7,652	107	14,830 R	74.3%	25.3%	74.6%	25.4%
105,248	JEFFERSON	35,922	21,947	13,787	188	8,160 R	61.1%	38.4%	61.4%	38.6%
34,172	JOHNSON	10,288	7,228	3,044	16	4,184 R	70.3%	29.6%	70.4%	29.6%
5,692	KNOX	2,929	1,896	1,031	2	865 R	64.7%	35.2%	64.8%	35.2%
19,944	LACLEDE	8,370	6,152	2,186	32	3,966 R	73.5%	26.1%	73.8%	26.2%
26,626	LAFAYETTE	13,250	9,187	4,063		5,124 R	69.3%	30.7%	69.3%	30.7%
24,585	LAWRENCE	11,594	8,445	3,130	19	5,315 R	72.8%	27.0%	73.0%	27.0%
10,993	LEWIS	4,434	2,738	1,695	1	1,043 R	61.8%	38.2%	61.8%	38.2%
18,041	LINCOLN	7,956	5,127	2,784	45	2,343 R	64.4%	35.0%	64.8%	35.2%
15,125	LINN	7,702	4,595	3,073	34	1,522 R	59.7%	39.9%	59.9%	40.1%
15,368	LIVINGSTON	7,971	5,253	2,662	56	2,591 R	65.9%	33.4%	66.4%	33.6%
12,357	MCDONALD	6,137	4,339	1,787	11	2,552 R	70.7%	29.1%	70.8%	29.2%

MISSOURI

PRESIDENT 1972

1970 Census Population	County	Total Vote	Republican	Democratic	Other	Rep.-Dem. Plurality	Percentage Total Vote Rep.	Total Vote Dem.	Major Vote Rep.	Major Vote Dem.
15,432	MACON	7,393	4,538	2,844	11	1,694 R	61.4%	38.5%	61.5%	38.5%
8,641	MADISON	4,298	2,837	1,451	10	1,386 R	66.0%	33.8%	66.2%	33.8%
6,851	MARIES	3,312	2,082	1,219	11	863 R	62.9%	36.8%	63.1%	36.9%
28,121	MARION	11,392	7,197	4,171	24	3,026 R	63.2%	36.6%	63.3%	36.7%
4,910	MERCER	2,208	1,592	607	9	985 R	72.1%	27.5%	72.4%	27.6%
15,026	MILLER	7,280	5,682	1,598		4,084 R	78.0%	22.0%	78.0%	22.0%
16,647	MISSISSIPPI	4,204	2,727	1,470	7	1,257 R	64.9%	35.0%	65.0%	35.0%
10,742	MONITEAU	5,358	3,963	1,395		2,568 R	74.0%	26.0%	74.0%	26.0%
9,542	MONROE	4,441	2,141	2,299	1	158 D	48.2%	51.8%	48.2%	51.8%
11,000	MONTGOMERY	5,419	3,707	1,691	21	2,016 R	68.4%	31.2%	68.7%	31.3%
10,068	MORGAN	5,723	4,021	1,685	17	2,336 R	70.3%	29.4%	70.5%	29.5%
23,420	NEW MADRID	8,288	4,735	3,500	53	1,235 R	57.1%	42.2%	57.5%	42.5%
32,901	NEWTON	15,023	10,701	4,291	31	6,410 R	71.2%	28.6%	71.4%	28.6%
22,467	NODAWAY	9,264	5,942	3,322		2,620 R	64.1%	35.9%	64.1%	35.9%
9,180	OREGON	3,479	2,118	1,352	9	766 R	60.9%	38.9%	61.0%	39.0%
10,994	OSAGE	5,751	4,266	1,485		2,781 R	74.2%	25.8%	74.2%	25.8%
6,226	OZARK	2,748	2,119	625	4	1,494 R	77.1%	22.7%	77.2%	22.8%
26,373	PEMISCOT	6,747	4,697	2,017	33	2,680 R	69.6%	29.9%	70.0%	30.0%
14,393	PERRY	6,696	4,736	1,953	7	2,783 R	70.7%	29.2%	70.8%	29.2%
34,137	PETTIS	15,120	10,065	5,016	39	5,049 R	66.6%	33.2%	66.7%	33.3%
29,567	PHELPS	11,192	7,598	3,567	27	4,031 R	67.9%	31.9%	68.1%	31.9%
16,928	PIKE	7,146	4,452	2,659	35	1,793 R	62.3%	37.2%	62.6%	37.4%
32,081	PLATTE	12,973	8,764	4,183	26	4,581 R	67.6%	32.2%	67.7%	32.3%
15,415	POLK	7,676	5,409	2,245	22	3,164 R	70.5%	29.2%	70.7%	29.3%
53,967	PULASKI	6,164	4,243	1,903	18	2,340 R	68.8%	30.9%	69.0%	31.0%
5,916	PUTNAM	2,684	2,112	571	1	1,541 R	78.7%	21.3%	78.7%	21.3%
7,764	RALLS	3,213	1,827	1,371	15	456 R	56.9%	42.7%	57.1%	42.9%
22,434	RANDOLPH	9,009	5,195	3,814		1,381 R	57.7%	42.3%	57.7%	42.3%
17,599	RAY	7,075	4,205	2,844	26	1,361 R	59.4%	40.2%	59.7%	40.3%
6,106	REYNOLDS	2,579	1,541	1,031	7	510 R	59.8%	40.0%	59.9%	40.1%
9,803	RIPLEY	4,179	2,810	1,361	8	1,449 R	67.2%	32.6%	67.4%	32.6%
92,954	ST. CHARLES	36,868	25,677	11,034	157	14,643 R	69.6%	29.9%	69.9%	30.1%
7,667	ST. CLAIR	4,257	2,847	1,410		1,437 R	66.9%	33.1%	66.9%	33.1%
36,818	ST. FRANCOIS	13,518	8,812	4,658	48	4,154 R	65.2%	34.5%	65.4%	34.6%
622,236	ST. LOUIS CITY	192,867	72,402	119,817	648	47,415 D	37.5%	62.1%	37.7%	62.3%
951,353	ST. LOUIS COUNTY	425,056	264,147	160,801	108	103,346 R	62.1%	37.8%	62.2%	37.8%
12,867	STE. GENEVIEVE	5,153	2,900	2,247	6	653 R	56.3%	43.6%	56.3%	43.7%
24,837	SALINE	10,148	6,641	3,460	47	3,181 R	65.4%	34.1%	65.7%	34.3%
4,665	SCHUYLER	2,491	1,495	991	5	504 R	60.0%	39.8%	60.1%	39.9%
5,499	SCOTLAND	3,190	1,918	1,269	3	649 R	60.1%	39.8%	60.2%	39.8%
33,250	SCOTT	10,998	7,316	3,646	36	3,670 R	66.5%	33.2%	66.7%	33.3%
7,196	SHANNON	2,758	1,623	1,134	1	489 R	58.8%	41.1%	58.9%	41.1%
7,906	SHELBY	3,639	2,057	1,569	13	488 R	56.5%	43.1%	56.7%	43.3%
25,771	STODDARD	8,933	6,282	2,636	15	3,646 R	70.3%	29.5%	70.4%	29.6%
9,921	STONE	5,297	4,180	1,094	23	3,086 R	78.9%	20.7%	79.3%	20.7%
7,572	SULLIVAN	4,211	2,611	1,588	12	1,023 R	62.0%	37.7%	62.2%	37.8%
13,023	TANEY	6,450	4,982	1,435	33	3,547 R	77.2%	22.2%	77.6%	22.4%
18,320	TEXAS	7,870	5,104	2,737	29	2,367 R	64.9%	34.8%	65.1%	34.9%
19,065	VERNON	7,974	4,892	3,057	25	1,835 R	61.3%	38.3%	61.5%	38.5%
9,699	WARREN	4,775	3,530	1,225	20	2,305 R	73.9%	25.7%	74.2%	25.8%
15,086	WASHINGTON	6,085	3,818	2,229	38	1,589 R	62.7%	36.6%	63.1%	36.9%
8,546	WAYNE	4,839	3,091	1,746	2	1,345 R	63.9%	36.1%	63.9%	36.1%
15,562	WEBSTER	7,447	5,095	2,343	9	2,752 R	68.4%	31.5%	68.5%	31.5%
3,359	WORTH	1,900	1,170	727	3	443 R	61.6%	38.3%	61.7%	38.3%
13,667	WRIGHT	5,725	4,350	1,368	7	2,982 R	76.0%	23.9%	76.1%	23.9%
4,677,399	TOTAL	1,855,803	1,153,852	697,147	4,804	456,705 R	62.2%	37.6%	62.3%	37.7%

MISSOURI

PRESIDENT 1968

1960 Census Population	County	Total Vote	Republican	Democratic	AIP	Other	Plurality	Percentage Rep.	Dem.	AIP
20,105	ADAIR	7,861	4,624	2,645	592		1,979 R	58.8%	33.6%	7.5%
11,062	ANDREW	5,762	3,398	2,005	359		1,393 R	59.0%	34.8%	6.2%
9,213	ATCHISON	4,295	2,206	1,752	337		454 R	51.4%	40.8%	7.8%
26,079	AUDRAIN	10,823	5,005	4,806	1,012		199 R	46.2%	44.4%	9.4%
18,921	BARRY	9,693	5,537	3,398	758		2,139 R	57.1%	35.1%	7.8%
11,113	BARTON	5,259	2,928	1,832	499		1,096 R	55.7%	34.8%	9.5%
15,905	BATES	8,258	4,087	3,370	801		717 R	49.5%	40.8%	9.7%
8,737	BENTON	4,742	2,899	1,345	498		1,554 R	61.1%	28.4%	10.5%
9,167	BOLLINGER	4,559	2,283	1,693	583		590 R	50.1%	37.1%	12.8%
55,202	BOONE	25,703	11,917	11,771	2,015		146 R	46.4%	45.8%	7.8%
90,581	BUCHANAN	34,713	16,101	15,860	2,752		241 R	46.4%	45.7%	7.9%
34,656	BUTLER	13,464	6,326	4,379	2,759		1,947 R	47.0%	32.5%	20.5%
8,830	CALDWELL	4,551	2,631	1,490	430		1,141 R	57.8%	32.7%	9.4%
23,858	CALLAWAY	9,291	4,277	3,738	1,276		539 R	46.0%	40.2%	13.7%
9,116	CAMDEN	5,738	3,500	1,605	633		1,895 R	61.0%	28.0%	11.0%
42,020	CAPE GIRARDEAU	19,305	10,298	6,656	2,351		3,642 R	53.3%	34.5%	12.2%
13,847	CARROLL	6,798	3,680	2,473	645		1,207 R	54.1%	36.4%	9.5%
3,973	CARTER	1,888	861	738	289		123 R	45.6%	39.1%	15.3%
29,702	CASS	11,677	5,271	4,468	1,938		803 R	45.1%	38.3%	16.6%
9,185	CEDAR	4,588	2,940	1,218	430		1,722 R	64.1%	26.5%	9.4%
12,720	CHARITON	5,284	2,404	2,371	509		33 R	45.5%	44.9%	9.6%
12,359	CHRISTIAN	6,238	4,019	1,586	633		2,433 R	64.4%	25.4%	10.1%
8,725	CLARK	3,942	2,111	1,489	342		622 R	53.6%	37.8%	8.7%
87,474	CLAY	44,162	19,643	17,547	6,972		2,096 R	44.5%	39.7%	15.8%
11,588	CLINTON	5,803	2,659	2,525	619		134 R	45.8%	43.5%	10.7%
40,761	COLE	19,116	11,575	5,916	1,625		5,659 R	60.6%	30.9%	8.5%
15,448	COOPER	7,443	4,115	2,798	530		1,317 R	55.3%	37.6%	7.1%
12,647	CRAWFORD	6,319	3,525	2,123	671		1,402 R	55.8%	33.6%	10.6%
7,577	DADE	3,497	2,250	917	330		1,333 R	64.3%	26.2%	9.4%
9,314	DALLAS	4,537	2,835	1,237	465		1,598 R	62.5%	27.3%	10.2%
9,502	DAVIESS	4,298	2,288	1,676	334		612 R	53.2%	39.0%	7.8%
7,226	DE KALB	3,849	2,112	1,452	285		660 R	54.9%	37.7%	7.4%
10,445	DENT	4,648	2,369	1,810	469		559 R	51.0%	38.9%	10.1%
9,653	DOUGLAS	4,226	2,836	978	412		1,858 R	67.1%	23.1%	9.7%
39,139	DUNKLIN	12,332	4,366	5,063	2,903		697 D	35.4%	41.1%	23.5%
44,566	FRANKLIN	19,349	9,823	7,566	1,960		2,257 R	50.8%	39.1%	10.1%
12,195	GASCONADE	5,895	4,400	1,131	364		3,269 R	74.6%	19.2%	6.2%
8,793	GENTRY	4,691	2,286	2,189	216		97 R	48.7%	46.7%	4.6%
126,276	GREENE	59,048	32,638	19,659	6,751		12,979 R	55.3%	33.3%	11.4%
12,220	GRUNDY	5,608	3,213	1,976	419		1,237 R	57.3%	35.2%	7.5%
11,603	HARRISON	5,192	3,092	1,688	412		1,404 R	59.6%	32.5%	7.9%
19,226	HENRY	8,020	3,824	3,514	682		310 R	47.7%	43.8%	8.5%
4,516	HICKORY	2,230	1,484	537	209		947 R	66.5%	24.1%	9.4%
7,885	HOLT	3,621	2,031	1,211	379		820 R	56.1%	33.4%	10.5%
10,859	HOWARD	4,665	1,825	2,333	507		508 D	39.1%	50.0%	10.9%
22,027	HOWELL	9,838	5,631	2,763	1,444		2,868 R	57.2%	28.1%	14.7%
8,041	IRON	3,846	1,600	1,755	491		155 D	41.6%	45.6%	12.8%
622,732	JACKSON	232,220	91,086	112,154	28,980		21,068 D	39.2%	48.3%	12.5%
78,863	JASPER	30,962	16,794	10,987	3,181		5,807 R	54.2%	35.5%	10.3%
66,377	JEFFERSON	31,053	11,708	13,230	6,115		1,522 D	37.7%	42.6%	19.7%
28,981	JOHNSON	9,336	4,834	3,484	1,018		1,350 R	51.8%	37.3%	10.9%
6,558	KNOX	3,169	1,562	1,257	350		305 R	49.3%	39.7%	11.0%
18,991	LACLEDE	8,670	4,860	2,958	852		1,902 R	56.1%	34.1%	9.8%
25,274	LAFAYETTE	12,804	6,840	4,859	1,105		1,981 R	53.4%	37.9%	8.6%
23,260	LAWRENCE	11,442	6,834	3,710	898		3,124 R	59.7%	32.4%	7.8%
10,984	LEWIS	4,642	2,038	2,067	537		29 D	43.9%	44.5%	11.6%
14,783	LINCOLN	7,624	3,185	3,142	1,297		43 R	41.8%	41.2%	17.0%
16,815	LINN	8,241	3,795	3,933	513		138 D	46.1%	47.7%	6.2%
15,771	LIVINGSTON	7,812	3,827	3,467	518		360 R	49.0%	44.4%	6.6%
11,798	MCDONALD	5,894	3,025	2,188	681		837 R	51.3%	37.1%	11.6%

MISSOURI

PRESIDENT 1968

1960 Census Population	County	Total Vote	Republican	Democratic	AIP	Other	Plurality	Percentage Rep.	Dem.	AIP
16,473	MACON	8,087	3,804	3,462	821		342 R	47.0%	42.8%	10.2%
9,366	MADISON	4,300	2,164	1,521	615		643 R	50.3%	35.4%	14.3%
7,282	MARIES	3,026	1,438	1,185	403		253 R	47.5%	39.2%	13.3%
29,522	MARION	11,369	4,732	5,416	1,221		684 D	41.6%	47.6%	10.7%
5,750	MERCER	2,314	1,406	783	125		623 R	60.8%	33.8%	5.4%
13,800	MILLER	6,820	4,425	1,727	668		2,698 R	64.9%	25.3%	9.8%
20,695	MISSISSIPPI	5,299	1,421	2,303	1,575		728 D	26.8%	43.5%	29.7%
10,500	MONITEAU	5,483	3,210	1,687	586		1,523 R	58.5%	30.8%	10.7%
10,688	MONROE	4,641	1,349	2,776	516		1,427 D	29.1%	59.8%	11.1%
11,097	MONTGOMERY	5,417	2,903	1,891	623		1,012 R	53.6%	34.9%	11.5%
9,476	MORGAN	5,059	2,906	1,649	504		1,257 R	57.4%	32.6%	10.0%
31,350	NEW MADRID	9,496	2,317	4,195	2,984		1,211 D	24.4%	44.2%	31.4%
30,093	NEWTON	13,888	7,343	5,064	1,481		2,279 R	52.9%	36.5%	10.7%
22,215	NODAWAY	9,845	4,736	4,494	615		242 R	48.1%	45.6%	6.2%
9,845	OREGON	3,564	1,213	1,726	625		513 D	34.0%	48.4%	17.5%
10,867	OSAGE	5,041	3,107	1,540	394		1,567 R	61.6%	30.5%	7.8%
6,744	OZARK	2,877	1,967	606	304		1,361 R	68.4%	21.1%	10.6%
38,095	PEMISCOT	7,822	2,191	2,681	2,950		269 A	28.0%	34.3%	37.7%
14,642	PERRY	6,278	3,858	1,958	462		1,900 R	61.5%	31.2%	7.4%
35,120	PETTIS	14,621	6,738	6,334	1,549		404 R	46.1%	43.3%	10.6%
25,396	PHELPS	11,783	5,577	4,211	1,995		1,366 R	47.3%	35.7%	16.9%
16,706	PIKE	7,067	3,072	3,192	803		120 D	43.5%	45.2%	11.4%
23,350	PLATTE	11,316	4,836	4,665	1,815		171 R	42.7%	41.2%	16.0%
13,753	POLK	6,929	4,145	2,170	614		1,975 R	59.8%	31.3%	8.9%
46,567	PULASKI	5,576	2,555	2,303	718		252 R	45.8%	41.3%	12.9%
6,999	PUTNAM	3,092	1,971	952	169		1,019 R	63.7%	30.8%	5.5%
8,078	RALLS	3,553	1,175	1,900	478		725 D	33.1%	53.5%	13.5%
22,014	RANDOLPH	9,285	3,582	4,810	893		1,228 D	38.6%	51.8%	9.6%
16,075	RAY	7,206	2,587	3,541	1,078		954 D	35.9%	49.1%	15.0%
5,161	REYNOLDS	2,581	898	1,245	438		347 D	34.8%	48.2%	17.0%
9,096	RIPLEY	4,090	1,973	1,440	677		533 R	48.2%	35.2%	16.6%
52,970	ST. CHARLES	29,659	13,533	10,374	5,752		3,159 R	45.6%	35.0%	19.4%
8,421	ST. CLAIR	4,178	2,271	1,496	411		775 R	54.4%	35.8%	9.8%
36,516	ST. FRANCOIS	15,738	7,492	6,379	1,867		1,113 R	47.6%	40.5%	11.9%
750,026	ST. LOUIS CITY	220,914	58,252	143,010	19,652		84,758 D	26.4%	64.7%	8.9%
703,532	ST. LOUIS COUNTY	385,375	180,355	165,786	39,234		14,569 R	46.8%	43.0%	10.2%
12,116	STE. GENEVIEVE	4,602	1,937	2,225	440		288 D	42.1%	48.3%	9.6%
25,148	SALINE	10,048	4,698	4,646	704		52 R	46.8%	46.2%	7.0%
5,052	SCHUYLER	2,428	1,291	969	168		322 R	53.2%	39.9%	6.9%
6,484	SCOTLAND	3,104	1,554	1,340	210		214 R	50.1%	43.2%	6.8%
32,748	SCOTT	10,643	3,856	4,313	2,474		457 D	36.2%	40.5%	23.2%
7,087	SHANNON	2,710	1,048	1,216	446		168 D	38.7%	44.9%	16.5%
9,063	SHELBY	4,096	1,693	2,045	358		352 D	41.3%	49.9%	8.7%
29,490	STODDARD	8,820	3,919	3,150	1,751		769 R	44.4%	35.7%	19.9%
8,176	STONE	4,465	3,006	1,004	455		2,002 R	67.3%	22.5%	10.2%
8,783	SULLIVAN	4,464	2,332	1,907	225		425 R	52.2%	42.7%	5.0%
10,238	TANEY	4,922	3,289	1,219	414		2,070 R	66.8%	24.8%	8.4%
17,758	TEXAS	8,120	4,022	3,117	981		905 R	49.5%	38.4%	12.1%
20,540	VERNON	7,930	3,590	3,557	783		33 R	45.3%	44.9%	9.9%
8,750	WARREN	4,267	2,669	1,033	565		1,636 R	62.5%	24.2%	13.2%
14,346	WASHINGTON	5,709	2,641	2,292	776		349 R	46.3%	40.1%	13.6%
8,638	WAYNE	4,511	2,156	1,714	641		442 R	47.8%	38.0%	14.2%
13,753	WEBSTER	7,237	4,118	2,547	572		1,571 R	56.9%	35.2%	7.9%
3,936	WORTH	1,903	924	853	126		71 R	48.6%	44.8%	6.6%
14,183	WRIGHT	5,400	3,576	1,337	487		2,239 R	66.2%	24.8%	9.0%
4,319,813	TOTAL	1,809,502	811,932	791,444	206,126		20,488 R	44.9%	43.7%	11.4%

MISSOURI

ELECTION NOTES

1984 Other vote was 8 Mason (write-in); 2 Johnson (write-in); 1 Dennis (write-in); 1 scattered write-in.

1980 Other vote was 77,920 Anderson (Independent); 14,422 Clark (Libertarian); 1,515 DeBerry (Socialist Workers); 573 Commoner (write-in); 26 Hall (write-in); 5 McCormack (write-in). The state-wide total for the other vote column includes these 604 write-in votes not reported by county.

1976 Other vote was 24,029 McCarthy (Independent); 3,741 scattered write-in. Early unamended canvass gave the state-wide totals as 928,808 Republican; 999,163 Democratic; 24,329 McCarthy (Independent). The state-wide total for the other vote column includes the 3,741 write-in votes not reported by county.

1972 Other vote was scattered write-in. Unidentified write-in votes cast in the Republican (206) and Democratic (1,384) columns on the ballot are included in the other vote column.

1968 Wallace on the ballot as American.

MONTANA

POPULAR VOTE FOR PRESIDENT 1920 TO 1984

Year	Total Vote	Republican Vote	Republican Candidate	Democratic Vote	Democratic Candidate	Other Vote	Plurality	Percentage Total Vote Rep.	Percentage Total Vote Dem.	Percentage Major Vote Rep.	Percentage Major Vote Dem.
1984	384,377	232,450	Reagan, Ronald	146,742	Mondale, Walter F.	5,185	85,708 R	60.5%	38.2%	61.3%	38.7%
1980	363,952	206,814	Reagan, Ronald	118,032	Carter, Jimmy	39,106	88,782 R	56.8%	32.4%	63.7%	36.3%
1976	328,734	173,703	Ford, Gerald R.	149,259	Carter, Jimmy	5,772	24,444 R	52.8%	45.4%	53.8%	46.2%
1972	317,603	183,976	Nixon, Richard M.	120,197	McGovern, George S.	13,430	63,779 R	57.9%	37.8%	60.5%	39.5%
1968	274,404	138,835	Nixon, Richard M.	114,117	Humphrey, Hubert H.	21,452	24,718 R	50.6%	41.6%	54.9%	45.1%
1964	278,628	113,032	Goldwater, Barry M.	164,246	Johnson, Lyndon B.	1,350	51,214 D	40.6%	58.9%	40.8%	59.2%
1960	277,579	141,841	Nixon, Richard M.	134,891	Kennedy, John F.	847	6,950 R	51.1%	48.6%	51.3%	48.7%
1956	271,171	154,933	Eisenhower, Dwight D.	116,238	Stevenson, Adlai E.		38,695 R	57.1%	42.9%	57.1%	42.9%
1952	265,037	157,394	Eisenhower, Dwight D.	106,213	Stevenson, Adlai E.	1,430	51,181 R	59.4%	40.1%	59.7%	40.3%
1948	224,278	96,770	Dewey, Thomas E.	119,071	Truman, Harry S.	8,437	22,301 D	43.1%	53.1%	44.8%	55.2%
1944	207,355	93,163	Dewey, Thomas E.	112,556	Roosevelt, Franklin D.	1,636	19,393 D	44.9%	54.3%	45.3%	54.7%
1940	247,873	99,579	Willkie, Wendell	145,698	Roosevelt, Franklin D.	2,596	46,119 D	40.2%	58.8%	40.6%	59.4%
1936	230,502	63,598	Landon, Alfred M.	159,690	Roosevelt, Franklin D.	7,214	96,092 D	27.6%	69.3%	28.5%	71.5%
1932	216,479	78,078	Hoover, Herbert C.	127,286	Roosevelt, Franklin D.	11,115	49,208 D	36.1%	58.8%	38.0%	62.0%
1928	194,108	113,300	Hoover, Herbert C.	78,578	Smith, Alfred E.	2,230	34,722 R	58.4%	40.5%	59.0%	41.0%
1924 **	174,425	74,138	Coolidge, Calvin	33,805	Davis, John W.	66,482	8,014 R	42.5%	19.4%	68.7%	31.3%
1920	179,006	109,430	Harding, Warren G.	57,372	Cox, James M.	12,204	52,058 R	61.1%	32.1%	65.6%	34.4%

In 1924 other vote was 66,124 Progressive and 358 Communist.

ELECTORAL COLLEGE VOTE 1920 TO 1984

Year	Total	Republican	Democratic	Other
1984	4	4	—	—
1980	4	4	—	—
1976	4	4	—	—
1972	4	4	—	—
1968	4	4	—	—
1964	4	—	4	—
1960	4	4	—	—
1956	4	4	—	—
1952	4	4	—	—
1948	4	—	4	—
1944	4	—	4	—
1940	4	—	4	—
1936	4	—	4	—
1932	4	—	4	—
1928	4	4	—	—
1924	4	4	—	—
1920	4	4	—	—

MONTANA

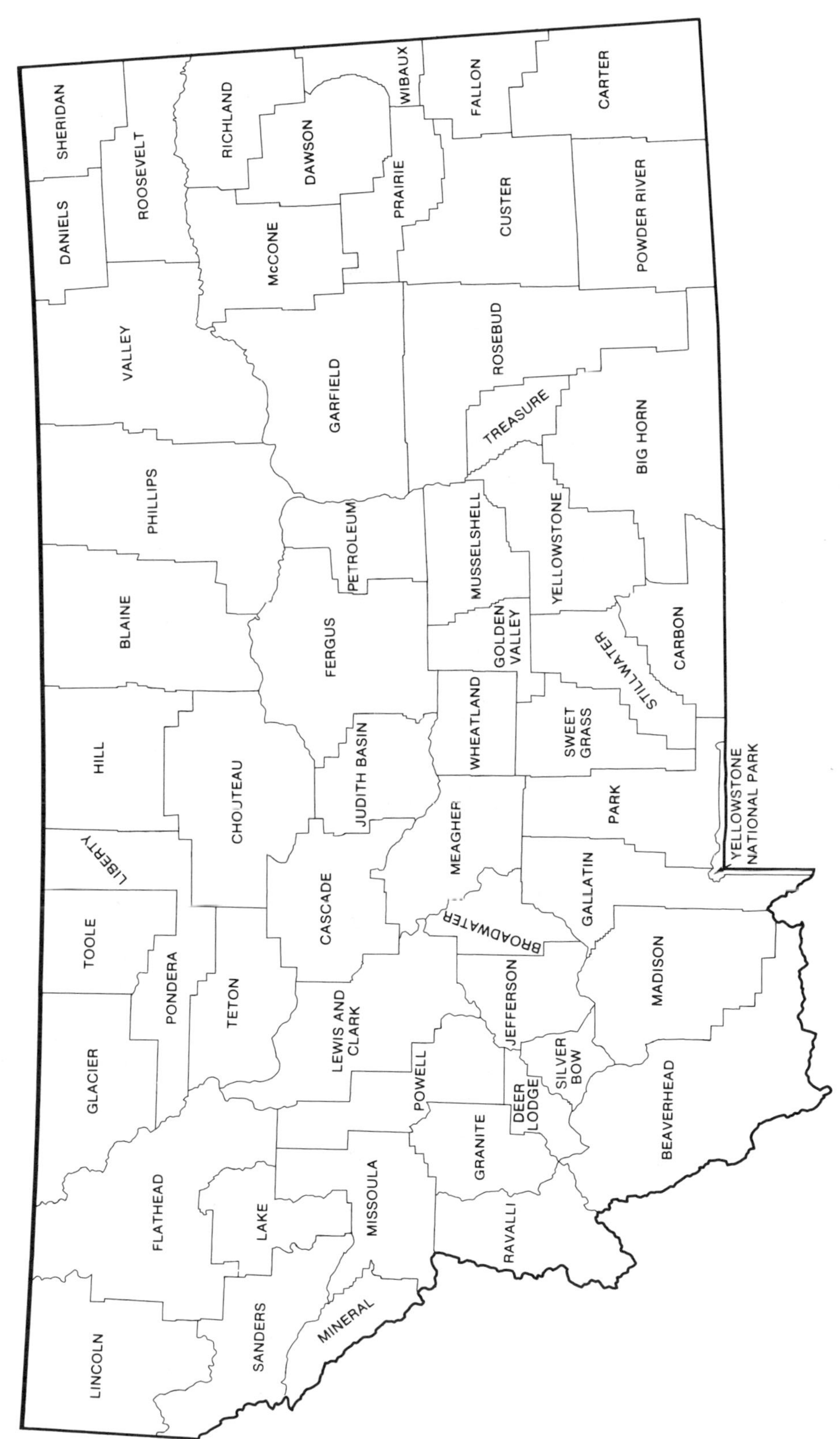
SHERIDAN
DANIELS
ROOSEVELT
RICHLAND
DAWSON
WIBAUX
PRAIRIE
McCONE
FALLON
CARTER
CUSTER
POWDER RIVER
VALLEY
GARFIELD
ROSEBUD
TREASURE
BIG HORN
PHILLIPS
PETROLEUM
MUSSELSHELL
YELLOWSTONE
BLAINE
FERGUS
GOLDEN VALLEY
STILLWATER
CARBON
HILL
CHOUTEAU
JUDITH BASIN
WHEATLAND
SWEET GRASS
YELLOWSTONE NATIONAL PARK
LIBERTY
PARK
MEAGHER
CASCADE
GALLATIN
TOOLE
BROADWATER
PONDERA
TETON
MADISON
JEFFERSON
LEWIS AND CLARK
GLACIER
SILVER BOW
POWELL
DEER LODGE
BEAVERHEAD
GRANITE
FLATHEAD
LAKE
MISSOULA
RAVALLI
MINERAL
SANDERS
LINCOLN

MONTANA

PRESIDENT 1984

1980 Census Population	County	Total Vote	Republican	Democratic	Other	Rep.-Dem. Plurality	Percentage Total Vote Rep.	Total Vote Dem.	Major Vote Rep.	Major Vote Dem.
8,186	BEAVERHEAD	4,035	3,044	942	49	2,102 R	75.4%	23.3%	76.4%	23.6%
11,096	BIG HORN	5,110	2,390	2,681	39	291 D	46.8%	52.5%	47.1%	52.9%
6,999	BLAINE	2,997	1,736	1,229	32	507 R	57.9%	41.0%	58.5%	41.5%
3,267	BROADWATER	1,830	1,345	458	27	887 R	73.5%	25.0%	74.6%	25.4%
8,099	CARBON	4,587	2,877	1,657	53	1,220 R	62.7%	36.1%	63.5%	36.5%
1,799	CARTER	1,028	823	194	11	629 R	80.1%	18.9%	80.9%	19.1%
80,696	CASCADE	34,505	19,846	14,252	407	5,594 R	57.5%	41.3%	58.2%	41.8%
6,092	CHOUTEAU	3,360	2,425	896	39	1,529 R	72.2%	26.7%	73.0%	27.0%
13,109	CUSTER	5,919	3,879	1,982	58	1,897 R	65.5%	33.5%	66.2%	33.8%
2,835	DANIELS	1,477	984	473	20	511 R	66.6%	32.0%	67.5%	32.5%
11,805	DAWSON	5,314	3,468	1,776	70	1,692 R	65.3%	33.4%	66.1%	33.9%
12,518	DEER LODGE	5,505	1,901	3,539	65	1,638 D	34.5%	64.3%	34.9%	65.1%
3,763	FALLON	1,829	1,237	569	23	668 R	67.6%	31.1%	68.5%	31.5%
13,076	FERGUS	6,459	4,585	1,804	70	2,781 R	71.0%	27.9%	71.8%	28.2%
51,966	FLATHEAD	25,803	17,012	8,310	481	8,702 R	65.9%	32.2%	67.2%	32.8%
42,865	GALLATIN	24,140	15,643	8,163	334	7,480 R	64.8%	33.8%	65.7%	34.3%
1,656	GARFIELD	911	770	134	7	636 R	84.5%	14.7%	85.2%	14.8%
10,628	GLACIER	4,435	2,228	2,167	40	61 R	50.2%	48.9%	50.7%	49.3%
1,026	GOLDEN VALLEY	600	384	211	5	173 R	64.0%	35.2%	64.5%	35.5%
2,700	GRANITE	1,322	880	417	25	463 R	66.6%	31.5%	67.8%	32.2%
17,985	HILL	8,390	4,635	3,657	98	978 R	55.2%	43.6%	55.9%	44.1%
7,029	JEFFERSON	3,618	2,226	1,324	68	902 R	61.5%	36.6%	62.7%	37.3%
2,646	JUDITH BASIN	1,550	1,050	483	17	567 R	67.7%	31.2%	68.5%	31.5%
19,056	LAKE	9,348	5,754	3,473	121	2,281 R	61.6%	37.2%	62.4%	37.6%
43,039	LEWIS AND CLARK	22,626	13,569	8,768	289	4,801 R	60.0%	38.8%	60.7%	39.3%
2,329	LIBERTY	1,229	895	323	11	572 R	72.8%	26.3%	73.5%	26.5%
17,752	LINCOLN	7,184	4,080	2,959	145	1,121 R	56.8%	41.2%	58.0%	42.0%
2,702	MCCONE	1,497	1,015	459	23	556 R	67.8%	30.7%	68.9%	31.1%
5,448	MADISON	3,069	2,308	708	53	1,600 R	75.2%	23.1%	76.5%	23.5%
2,154	MEAGHER	1,069	771	283	15	488 R	72.1%	26.5%	73.1%	26.9%
3,675	MINERAL	1,704	943	718	43	225 R	55.3%	42.1%	56.8%	43.2%
76,016	MISSOULA	36,937	19,777	16,540	620	3,237 R	53.5%	44.8%	54.5%	45.5%
4,428	MUSSELSHELL	2,359	1,541	781	37	760 R	65.3%	33.1%	66.4%	33.6%
12,660	PARK	6,581	4,115	2,387	79	1,728 R	62.5%	36.3%	63.3%	36.7%
655	PETROLEUM	347	258	86	3	172 R	74.4%	24.8%	75.0%	25.0%
5,367	PHILLIPS	2,749	1,934	787	28	1,147 R	70.4%	28.6%	71.1%	28.9%
6,731	PONDERA	3,316	2,239	1,039	38	1,200 R	67.5%	31.3%	68.3%	31.7%
2,520	POWDER RIVER	1,429	1,066	346	17	720 R	74.6%	24.2%	75.5%	24.5%
6,958	POWELL	3,012	1,877	1,066	69	811 R	62.3%	35.4%	63.8%	36.2%
1,836	PRAIRIE	991	693	289	9	404 R	69.9%	29.2%	70.6%	29.4%
22,493	RAVALLI	12,154	8,161	3,825	168	4,336 R	67.1%	31.5%	68.1%	31.9%
12,243	RICHLAND	5,281	3,847	1,382	52	2,465 R	72.8%	26.2%	73.6%	26.4%
10,467	ROOSEVELT	4,464	2,431	1,962	71	469 R	54.5%	44.0%	55.3%	44.7%
9,899	ROSEBUD	4,402	2,413	1,920	69	493 R	54.8%	43.6%	55.7%	44.3%
8,675	SANDERS	4,204	2,467	1,654	83	813 R	58.7%	39.3%	59.9%	40.1%
5,414	SHERIDAN	2,879	1,774	1,087	18	687 R	61.6%	37.8%	62.0%	38.0%
38,092	SILVER BOW	18,010	6,637	11,095	278	4,458 D	36.9%	61.6%	37.4%	62.6%
5,598	STILLWATER	3,258	2,118	1,100	40	1,018 R	65.0%	33.8%	65.8%	34.2%
3,216	SWEET GRASS	1,803	1,417	378	8	1,039 R	78.6%	21.0%	78.9%	21.1%
6,491	TETON	3,384	2,257	1,102	25	1,155 R	66.7%	32.6%	67.2%	32.8%
5,559	TOOLE	2,768	1,949	789	30	1,160 R	70.4%	28.5%	71.2%	28.8%
981	TREASURE	576	353	209	14	144 R	61.3%	36.3%	62.8%	37.2%
10,250	VALLEY	5,046	3,123	1,849	74	1,274 R	61.9%	36.6%	62.8%	37.2%
2,359	WHEATLAND	1,173	753	407	13	346 R	64.2%	34.7%	64.9%	35.1%
1,476	WIBAUX	651	423	216	12	207 R	65.0%	33.2%	66.2%	33.8%
108,035	YELLOWSTONE	54,153	34,124	19,437	592	14,687 R	63.0%	35.9%	63.7%	36.3%
786,690	TOTAL	384,377	232,450	146,742	5,185	85,708 R	60.5%	38.2%	61.3%	38.7%

MONTANA

PRESIDENT 1980

1980 Census Population	County	Total Vote	Republican	Democratic	Other	Rep.-Dem. Plurality	Percentage: Total Vote Rep.	Percentage: Total Vote Dem.	Percentage: Major Vote Rep.	Percentage: Major Vote Dem.
8,186	BEAVERHEAD	4,103	2,955	842	306	2,113 R	72.0%	20.5%	77.8%	22.2%
11,096	BIG HORN	3,735	1,730	1,644	361	86 R	46.3%	44.0%	51.3%	48.7%
6,999	BLAINE	2,995	1,686	1,107	202	579 R	56.3%	37.0%	60.4%	39.6%
3,267	BROADWATER	1,564	1,052	401	111	651 R	67.3%	25.6%	72.4%	27.6%
8,099	CARBON	4,363	2,471	1,468	424	1,003 R	56.6%	33.6%	62.7%	37.3%
1,799	CARTER	1,058	766	237	55	529 R	72.4%	22.4%	76.4%	23.6%
80,696	CASCADE	32,234	17,664	11,105	3,465	6,559 R	54.8%	34.5%	61.4%	38.6%
6,092	CHOUTEAU	3,583	2,448	853	282	1,595 R	68.3%	23.8%	74.2%	25.8%
13,109	CUSTER	5,816	3,533	1,822	461	1,711 R	60.7%	31.3%	66.0%	34.0%
2,835	DANIELS	1,666	1,086	483	97	603 R	65.2%	29.0%	69.2%	30.8%
11,805	DAWSON	5,118	3,045	1,543	530	1,502 R	59.5%	30.1%	66.4%	33.6%
12,518	DEER LODGE	5,638	1,905	3,077	656	1,172 D	33.8%	54.6%	38.2%	61.8%
3,763	FALLON	1,920	1,286	512	122	774 R	67.0%	26.7%	71.5%	28.5%
13,076	FERGUS	6,852	4,455	1,840	557	2,615 R	65.0%	26.9%	70.8%	29.2%
51,966	FLATHEAD	23,767	15,102	6,349	2,316	8,753 R	63.5%	26.7%	70.4%	29.6%
42,865	GALLATIN	21,726	12,738	5,747	3,241	6,991 R	58.6%	26.5%	68.9%	31.1%
1,656	GARFIELD	974	760	169	45	591 R	78.0%	17.4%	81.8%	18.2%
10,628	GLACIER	4,093	2,283	1,394	416	889 R	55.8%	34.1%	62.1%	37.9%
1,026	GOLDEN VALLEY	556	362	155	39	207 R	65.1%	27.9%	70.0%	30.0%
2,700	GRANITE	1,371	811	439	121	372 R	59.2%	32.0%	64.9%	35.1%
17,985	HILL	8,089	4,448	2,875	766	1,573 R	55.0%	35.5%	60.7%	39.3%
7,029	JEFFERSON	3,223	1,841	1,055	327	786 R	57.1%	32.7%	63.6%	36.4%
2,646	JUDITH BASIN	1,627	1,030	480	117	550 R	63.3%	29.5%	68.2%	31.8%
19,056	LAKE	8,532	5,083	2,615	834	2,468 R	59.6%	30.6%	66.0%	34.0%
43,039	LEWIS AND CLARK	21,212	12,128	6,815	2,269	5,313 R	57.2%	32.1%	64.0%	36.0%
2,329	LIBERTY	1,256	872	283	101	589 R	69.4%	22.5%	75.5%	24.5%
17,752	LINCOLN	7,348	4,202	2,422	724	1,780 R	57.2%	33.0%	63.4%	36.6%
2,702	MCCONE	1,471	1,000	349	122	651 R	68.0%	23.7%	74.1%	25.9%
5,448	MADISON	3,145	2,220	676	249	1,544 R	70.6%	21.5%	76.7%	23.3%
2,154	MEAGHER	990	689	247	54	442 R	69.6%	24.9%	73.6%	26.4%
3,675	MINERAL	1,657	800	660	197	140 R	48.3%	39.8%	54.8%	45.2%
76,016	MISSOULA	34,594	16,161	13,115	5,318	3,046 R	46.7%	37.9%	55.2%	44.8%
4,428	MUSSELSHELL	2,204	1,279	784	141	495 R	58.0%	35.6%	62.0%	38.0%
12,660	PARK	6,195	3,929	1,663	603	2,266 R	63.4%	26.8%	70.3%	29.7%
655	PETROLEUM	341	225	90	26	135 R	66.0%	26.4%	71.4%	28.6%
5,367	PHILLIPS	2,653	1,723	745	185	978 R	64.9%	28.1%	69.8%	30.2%
6,731	PONDERA	3,432	2,270	897	265	1,373 R	66.1%	26.1%	71.7%	28.3%
2,520	POWDER RIVER	1,443	985	336	122	649 R	68.3%	23.3%	74.6%	25.4%
6,958	POWELL	2,993	1,770	883	340	887 R	59.1%	29.5%	66.7%	33.3%
1,836	PRAIRIE	927	580	283	64	297 R	62.6%	30.5%	67.2%	32.8%
22,493	RAVALLI	11,404	7,268	3,063	1,073	4,205 R	63.7%	26.9%	70.4%	29.6%
12,243	RICHLAND	5,038	3,348	1,252	438	2,096 R	66.5%	24.9%	72.8%	27.2%
10,467	ROOSEVELT	4,160	2,298	1,504	358	794 R	55.2%	36.2%	60.4%	39.6%
9,899	ROSEBUD	3,443	1,875	1,167	401	708 R	54.5%	33.9%	61.6%	38.4%
8,675	SANDERS	3,999	2,194	1,395	410	799 R	54.9%	34.9%	61.1%	38.9%
5,414	SHERIDAN	2,912	1,658	955	299	703 R	56.9%	32.8%	63.5%	36.5%
38,092	SILVER BOW	19,377	7,301	9,721	2,355	2,420 D	37.7%	50.2%	42.9%	57.1%
5,598	STILLWATER	2,984	1,828	919	237	909 R	61.3%	30.8%	66.5%	33.5%
3,216	SWEET GRASS	1,739	1,169	440	130	729 R	67.2%	25.3%	72.7%	27.3%
6,491	TETON	3,564	2,415	902	247	1,513 R	67.8%	25.3%	72.8%	27.2%
5,559	TOOLE	2,850	2,000	634	216	1,366 R	70.2%	22.2%	75.9%	24.1%
981	TREASURE	554	321	181	52	140 R	57.9%	32.7%	63.9%	36.1%
10,250	VALLEY	5,190	3,242	1,567	381	1,675 R	62.5%	30.2%	67.4%	32.6%
2,359	WHEATLAND	1,230	742	381	107	361 R	60.3%	31.0%	66.1%	33.9%
1,476	WIBAUX	731	450	219	62	231 R	61.6%	30.0%	67.3%	32.7%
108,035	YELLOWSTONE	48,313	27,332	15,272	5,709	12,060 R	56.6%	31.6%	64.2%	35.8%
786,690	TOTAL	363,952	206,814	118,032	39,106	88,782 R	56.8%	32.4%	63.7%	36.3%

MONTANA

PRESIDENT 1976

1970 Census Population	County	Total Vote	Republican	Democratic	Other	Rep.-Dem. Plurality	Percentage Total Vote Rep.	Total Vote Dem.	Major Vote Rep.	Major Vote Dem.
8,187	BEAVERHEAD	3,543	2,461	1,013	69	1,448 R	69.5%	28.6%	70.8%	29.2%
10,057	BIG HORN	3,630	1,615	1,962	53	347 D	44.5%	54.0%	45.1%	54.9%
6,727	BLAINE	2,739	1,349	1,356	34	7 D	49.3%	49.5%	49.9%	50.1%
2,526	BROADWATER	1,389	820	557	12	263 R	59.0%	40.1%	59.5%	40.5%
7,080	CARBON	4,045	2,121	1,853	71	268 R	52.4%	45.8%	53.4%	46.6%
1,956	CARTER	972	558	344	70	214 R	57.4%	35.4%	61.9%	38.1%
81,804	CASCADE	30,511	15,289	14,678	544	611 R	50.1%	48.1%	51.0%	49.0%
6,473	CHOUTEAU	3,465	1,814	1,568	83	246 R	52.4%	45.3%	53.6%	46.4%
12,174	CUSTER	5,647	3,120	2,425	102	695 R	55.3%	42.9%	56.3%	43.7%
3,083	DANIELS	1,639	816	797	26	19 R	49.8%	48.6%	50.6%	49.4%
11,269	DAWSON	4,960	2,639	2,201	120	438 R	53.2%	44.4%	54.5%	45.5%
15,652	DEER LODGE	6,176	2,197	3,859	120	1,662 D	35.6%	62.5%	36.3%	63.7%
4,050	FALLON	1,797	934	847	16	87 R	52.0%	47.1%	52.4%	47.6%
12,611	FERGUS	6,160	3,556	2,470	134	1,086 R	57.7%	40.1%	59.0%	41.0%
39,460	FLATHEAD	18,845	10,494	7,827	524	2,667 R	55.7%	41.5%	57.3%	42.7%
32,505	GALLATIN	17,460	11,062	6,215	183	4,847 R	63.4%	35.6%	64.0%	36.0%
1,796	GARFIELD	922	625	273	24	352 R	67.8%	29.6%	69.6%	30.4%
10,783	GLACIER	3,724	1,892	1,755	77	137 R	50.8%	47.1%	51.9%	48.1%
931	GOLDEN VALLEY	569	302	255	12	47 R	53.1%	44.8%	54.2%	45.8%
2,737	GRANITE	1,272	746	509	17	237 R	58.6%	40.0%	59.4%	40.6%
17,358	HILL	7,260	3,274	3,878	108	604 D	45.1%	53.4%	45.8%	54.2%
5,238	JEFFERSON	2,654	1,387	1,210	57	177 R	52.3%	45.6%	53.4%	46.6%
2,667	JUDITH BASIN	1,614	809	772	33	37 R	50.1%	47.8%	51.2%	48.8%
14,445	LAKE	7,210	3,809	3,253	148	556 R	52.8%	45.1%	53.9%	46.1%
33,281	LEWIS AND CLARK	18,517	10,155	8,118	244	2,037 R	54.8%	43.8%	55.6%	44.4%
2,359	LIBERTY	1,163	638	506	19	132 R	54.9%	43.5%	55.8%	44.2%
18,063	LINCOLN	6,283	3,017	3,146	120	129 D	48.0%	50.1%	49.0%	51.0%
2,875	MCCONE	1,499	730	749	20	19 D	48.7%	50.0%	49.4%	50.6%
5,014	MADISON	2,610	1,688	870	52	818 R	64.7%	33.3%	66.0%	34.0%
2,122	MEAGHER	939	565	364	10	201 R	60.2%	38.8%	60.8%	39.2%
2,958	MINERAL	1,514	679	819	16	140 D	44.8%	54.1%	45.3%	54.7%
58,263	MISSOULA	31,837	16,350	15,099	388	1,251 R	51.4%	47.4%	52.0%	48.0%
3,734	MUSSELSHELL	2,065	1,117	922	26	195 R	54.1%	44.6%	54.8%	45.2%
11,197	PARK	5,740	3,281	2,364	95	917 R	57.2%	41.2%	58.1%	41.9%
675	PETROLEUM	331	211	110	10	101 R	63.7%	33.2%	65.7%	34.3%
5,386	PHILLIPS	2,486	1,347	1,117	22	230 R	54.2%	44.9%	54.7%	45.3%
6,611	PONDERA	3,150	1,666	1,413	71	253 R	52.9%	44.9%	54.1%	45.9%
2,862	POWDER RIVER	1,235	683	429	123	254 R	55.3%	34.7%	61.4%	38.6%
6,660	POWELL	2,951	1,610	1,302	39	308 R	54.6%	44.1%	55.3%	44.7%
1,752	PRAIRIE	1,019	597	415	7	182 R	58.6%	40.7%	59.0%	41.0%
14,409	RAVALLI	8,694	4,894	3,504	296	1,390 R	56.3%	40.3%	58.3%	41.7%
9,837	RICHLAND	4,263	2,189	1,961	113	228 R	51.3%	46.0%	52.7%	47.3%
10,365	ROOSEVELT	3,928	1,822	2,061	45	239 D	46.4%	52.5%	46.9%	53.1%
6,032	ROSEBUD	3,006	1,538	1,413	55	125 R	51.2%	47.0%	52.1%	47.9%
7,093	SANDERS	3,576	1,738	1,725	113	13 R	48.6%	48.2%	50.2%	49.8%
5,779	SHERIDAN	2,714	1,114	1,560	40	446 D	41.0%	57.5%	41.7%	58.3%
41,981	SILVER BOW	19,110	7,506	11,377	227	3,871 D	39.3%	59.5%	39.8%	60.2%
4,632	STILLWATER	2,635	1,446	1,143	46	303 R	54.9%	43.4%	55.9%	44.1%
2,980	SWEET GRASS	1,659	1,135	502	22	633 R	68.4%	30.3%	69.3%	30.7%
6,116	TETON	3,345	1,730	1,506	109	224 R	51.7%	45.0%	53.5%	46.5%
5,839	TOOLE	2,603	1,469	1,080	54	389 R	56.4%	41.5%	57.6%	42.4%
1,069	TREASURE	564	315	239	10	76 R	55.9%	42.4%	56.9%	43.1%
11,471	VALLEY	4,959	2,520	2,352	87	168 R	50.8%	47.4%	51.7%	48.3%
2,529	WHEATLAND	1,320	755	535	30	220 R	57.2%	40.5%	58.5%	41.5%
1,465	WIBAUX	691	308	352	31	44 D	44.6%	50.9%	46.7%	53.3%
87,367	YELLOWSTONE	44,125	25,201	18,329	595	6,872 R	57.1%	41.5%	57.9%	42.1%
694,409	TOTAL	328,734	173,703	149,259	5,772	24,444 R	52.8%	45.4%	53.8%	46.2%

MONTANA

PRESIDENT 1972

1970 Census Population	County	Total Vote	Republican	Democratic	Other	Rep.-Dem. Plurality	Percentage			
							Total Vote		Major Vote	
							Rep.	Dem.	Rep.	Dem.
8,187	BEAVERHEAD	3,417	2,460	775	182	1,685 R	72.0%	22.7%	76.0%	24.0%
10,057	BIG HORN	3,824	2,148	1,552	124	596 R	56.2%	40.6%	58.1%	41.9%
6,727	BLAINE	2,779	1,513	1,151	115	362 R	54.4%	41.4%	56.8%	43.2%
2,526	BROADWATER	1,376	916	411	49	505 R	66.6%	29.9%	69.0%	31.0%
7,080	CARBON	3,841	2,378	1,292	171	1,086 R	61.9%	33.6%	64.8%	35.2%
1,956	CARTER	983	726	218	39	508 R	73.9%	22.2%	76.9%	23.1%
81,804	CASCADE	30,836	16,159	12,899	1,778	3,260 R	52.4%	41.8%	55.6%	44.4%
6,473	CHOUTEAU	3,399	2,027	1,149	223	878 R	59.6%	33.8%	63.8%	36.2%
12,174	CUSTER	5,506	3,486	1,875	145	1,611 R	63.3%	34.1%	65.0%	35.0%
3,083	DANIELS	1,574	973	570	31	403 R	61.8%	36.2%	63.1%	36.9%
11,269	DAWSON	5,014	3,207	1,685	122	1,522 R	64.0%	33.6%	65.6%	34.4%
15,652	DEER LODGE	6,604	2,373	3,979	252	1,606 D	35.9%	60.3%	37.4%	62.6%
4,050	FALLON	1,604	1,034	531	39	503 R	64.5%	33.1%	66.1%	33.9%
12,611	FERGUS	6,049	4,082	1,652	315	2,430 R	67.5%	27.3%	71.2%	28.8%
39,460	FLATHEAD	17,156	10,417	5,412	1,327	5,005 R	60.7%	31.5%	65.8%	34.2%
32,505	GALLATIN	16,088	10,663	5,096	329	5,567 R	66.3%	31.7%	67.7%	32.3%
1,796	GARFIELD	893	695	173	25	522 R	77.8%	19.4%	80.1%	19.9%
10,783	GLACIER	3,819	2,143	1,469	207	674 R	56.1%	38.5%	59.3%	40.7%
931	GOLDEN VALLEY	553	359	170	24	189 R	64.9%	30.7%	67.9%	32.1%
2,737	GRANITE	1,291	804	422	65	382 R	62.3%	32.7%	65.6%	34.4%
17,358	HILL	7,085	3,759	3,061	265	698 R	53.1%	43.2%	55.1%	44.9%
5,238	JEFFERSON	2,285	1,281	904	100	377 R	56.1%	39.6%	58.6%	41.4%
2,667	JUDITH BASIN	1,614	961	557	96	404 R	59.5%	34.5%	63.3%	36.7%
14,445	LAKE	6,719	4,172	2,260	287	1,912 R	62.1%	33.6%	64.9%	35.1%
33,281	LEWIS AND CLARK	17,316	10,719	6,081	516	4,638 R	61.9%	35.1%	63.8%	36.2%
2,359	LIBERTY	1,235	808	365	62	443 R	65.4%	29.6%	68.9%	31.1%
18,063	LINCOLN	6,208	3,276	2,402	530	874 R	52.8%	38.7%	57.7%	42.3%
2,875	MCCONE	1,465	854	562	49	292 R	58.3%	38.4%	60.3%	39.7%
5,014	MADISON	2,588	1,780	669	139	1,111 R	68.8%	25.9%	72.7%	27.3%
2,122	MEAGHER	942	674	230	38	444 R	71.5%	24.4%	74.6%	25.4%
2,958	MINERAL	1,419	706	659	54	47 R	49.8%	46.4%	51.7%	48.3%
58,263	MISSOULA	30,049	15,557	13,784	708	1,773 R	51.8%	45.9%	53.0%	47.0%
3,734	MUSSELSHELL	1,967	1,202	689	76	513 R	61.1%	35.0%	63.6%	36.4%
11,197	PARK	5,902	3,771	1,923	208	1,848 R	63.9%	32.6%	66.2%	33.8%
675	PETROLEUM	325	232	87	6	145 R	71.4%	26.8%	72.7%	27.3%
5,386	PHILLIPS	2,557	1,659	828	70	831 R	64.9%	32.4%	66.7%	33.3%
6,611	PONDERA	3,292	1,890	1,215	187	675 R	57.4%	36.9%	60.9%	39.1%
2,862	POWDER RIVER	1,217	844	267	106	577 R	69.4%	21.9%	76.0%	24.0%
6,660	POWELL	2,882	1,720	1,050	112	670 R	59.7%	36.4%	62.1%	37.9%
1,752	PRAIRIE	999	685	303	11	382 R	68.6%	30.3%	69.3%	30.7%
14,409	RAVALLI	7,458	4,611	2,480	367	2,131 R	61.8%	33.3%	65.0%	35.0%
9,837	RICHLAND	4,300	2,645	1,438	217	1,207 R	61.5%	33.4%	64.8%	35.2%
10,365	ROOSEVELT	3,907	2,304	1,464	139	840 R	59.0%	37.5%	61.1%	38.9%
6,032	ROSEBUD	2,350	1,486	777	87	709 R	63.2%	33.1%	65.7%	34.3%
7,093	SANDERS	3,251	1,779	1,197	275	582 R	54.7%	36.8%	59.8%	40.2%
5,779	SHERIDAN	2,780	1,500	1,197	83	303 R	54.0%	43.1%	55.6%	44.4%
41,981	SILVER BOW	20,404	7,967	11,704	733	3,737 D	39.0%	57.4%	40.5%	59.5%
4,632	STILLWATER	2,499	1,698	716	85	982 R	67.9%	28.7%	70.3%	29.7%
2,980	SWEET GRASS	1,658	1,260	350	48	910 R	76.0%	21.1%	78.3%	21.7%
6,116	TETON	3,321	1,991	1,121	209	870 R	60.0%	33.8%	64.0%	36.0%
5,839	TOOLE	2,815	1,679	897	239	782 R	59.6%	31.9%	65.2%	34.8%
1,069	TREASURE	574	377	176	21	201 R	65.7%	30.7%	68.2%	31.8%
11,471	VALLEY	5,348	3,210	1,973	165	1,237 R	60.0%	36.9%	61.9%	38.1%
2,529	WHEATLAND	1,326	761	445	120	316 R	57.4%	33.6%	63.1%	36.9%
1,465	WIBAUX	703	390	283	30	107 R	55.5%	40.3%	57.9%	42.1%
87,367	YELLOWSTONE	40,237	25,205	13,602	1,430	11,603 R	62.6%	33.8%	64.9%	35.1%
694,409	TOTAL	317,603	183,976	120,197	13,430	63,779 R	57.9%	37.8%	60.5%	39.5%

MONTANA

PRESIDENT 1968

1960 Census Population	County	Total Vote	Republican	Democratic	AIP	Other	Plurality	Percentage Rep.	Dem.	AIP
7,194	BEAVERHEAD	3,106	1,896	853	357		1,043 R	61.0%	27.5%	11.5%
10,007	BIG HORN	3,321	1,789	1,319	209	4	470 R	53.9%	39.7%	6.3%
8,091	BLAINE	2,655	1,291	1,198	165	1	93 R	48.6%	45.1%	6.2%
2,804	BROADWATER	1,236	671	439	125	1	232 R	54.3%	35.5%	10.1%
8,317	CARBON	3,587	1,972	1,353	258	4	619 R	55.0%	37.7%	7.2%
2,493	CARTER	1,003	624	269	110		355 R	62.2%	26.8%	11.0%
73,418	CASCADE	26,803	11,588	13,507	1,539	169	1,919 D	43.2%	50.4%	5.7%
7,348	CHOUTEAU	3,159	1,695	1,216	247	1	479 R	53.7%	38.5%	7.8%
13,227	CUSTER	4,876	2,831	1,760	275	10	1,071 R	58.1%	36.1%	5.6%
3,755	DANIELS	1,584	826	688	69	1	138 R	52.1%	43.4%	4.4%
12,314	DAWSON	4,568	2,650	1,695	220	3	955 R	58.0%	37.1%	4.8%
18,640	DEER LODGE	6,074	1,554	4,208	308	4	2,654 D	25.6%	69.3%	5.1%
3,997	FALLON	1,565	990	477	97	1	513 R	63.3%	30.5%	6.2%
14,018	FERGUS	6,057	3,367	2,070	616	4	1,297 R	55.6%	34.2%	10.2%
32,965	FLATHEAD	14,000	7,215	5,253	1,524	8	1,962 R	51.5%	37.5%	10.9%
26,045	GALLATIN	11,978	7,433	3,818	706	21	3,615 R	62.1%	31.9%	5.9%
1,981	GARFIELD	844	542	190	112		352 R	64.2%	22.5%	13.3%
11,565	GLACIER	3,671	1,643	1,723	295	10	80 D	44.8%	46.9%	8.0%
1,203	GOLDEN VALLEY	553	332	194	26	1	138 R	60.0%	35.1%	4.7%
3,014	GRANITE	1,263	626	502	135		124 R	49.6%	39.7%	10.7%
18,653	HILL	6,669	2,970	3,386	305	8	416 D	44.5%	50.8%	4.6%
4,297	JEFFERSON	1,771	798	820	152	1	22 D	45.1%	46.3%	8.6%
3,085	JUDITH BASIN	1,516	804	606	106		198 R	53.0%	40.0%	7.0%
13,104	LAKE	5,999	3,358	1,956	679	6	1,402 R	56.0%	32.6%	11.3%
28,006	LEWIS AND CLARK	14,115	7,979	5,379	723	34	2,600 R	56.5%	38.1%	5.1%
2,624	LIBERTY	1,144	670	390	83	1	280 R	58.6%	34.1%	7.3%
12,537	LINCOLN	5,807	2,355	2,677	765	10	322 D	40.6%	46.1%	13.2%
3,321	MCCONE	1,405	733	589	82	1	144 R	52.2%	41.9%	5.8%
5,211	MADISON	2,286	1,289	734	261	2	555 R	56.4%	32.1%	11.4%
2,616	MEAGHER	863	543	218	102		325 R	62.9%	25.3%	11.8%
3,037	MINERAL	1,169	483	576	108	2	93 D	41.3%	49.3%	9.2%
44,663	MISSOULA	20,292	9,745	8,398	1,638	511	1,347 R	48.0%	41.4%	8.1%
4,888	MUSSELSHELL	1,863	953	795	111	4	158 R	51.2%	42.7%	6.0%
13,168	PARK	5,340	3,063	1,815	460	2	1,248 R	57.4%	34.0%	8.6%
894	PETROLEUM	335	211	98	26		113 R	63.0%	29.3%	7.8%
6,027	PHILLIPS	2,632	1,353	1,100	177	2	253 R	51.4%	41.8%	6.7%
7,653	PONDERA	2,888	1,530	1,149	205	4	381 R	53.0%	39.8%	7.1%
2,485	POWDER RIVER	1,076	699	258	118	1	441 R	65.0%	24.0%	11.0%
7,002	POWELL	2,739	1,301	1,206	231	1	95 R	47.5%	44.0%	8.4%
2,318	PRAIRIE	937	635	270	30	2	365 R	67.8%	28.8%	3.2%
12,341	RAVALLI	5,977	3,183	2,080	709	5	1,103 R	53.3%	34.8%	11.9%
10,504	RICHLAND	4,016	2,381	1,399	228	8	982 R	59.3%	34.8%	5.7%
11,731	ROOSEVELT	3,885	1,947	1,771	162	5	176 R	50.1%	45.6%	4.2%
6,187	ROSEBUD	2,109	1,190	711	204	4	479 R	56.4%	33.7%	9.7%
6,880	SANDERS	2,996	1,459	1,242	292	3	217 R	48.7%	41.5%	9.7%
6,458	SHERIDAN	2,576	1,180	1,275	115	6	95 D	45.8%	49.5%	4.5%
46,454	SILVER BOW	19,617	5,488	12,626	1,120	383	7,138 D	28.0%	64.4%	5.7%
5,526	STILLWATER	2,201	1,347	676	177	1	671 R	61.2%	30.7%	8.0%
3,290	SWEET GRASS	1,490	1,043	336	110	1	707 R	70.0%	22.6%	7.4%
7,295	TETON	3,109	1,697	1,228	179	5	469 R	54.6%	39.5%	5.8%
7,904	TOOLE	2,708	1,407	1,048	249	4	359 R	52.0%	38.7%	9.2%
1,345	TREASURE	527	298	188	41		110 R	56.5%	35.7%	7.8%
17,080	VALLEY	4,632	2,290	1,926	393	23	364 R	49.4%	41.6%	8.5%
3,026	WHEATLAND	1,300	673	525	101	1	148 R	51.8%	40.4%	7.8%
1,698	WIBAUX	655	347	252	56		95 R	53.0%	38.5%	8.5%
79,016	YELLOWSTONE	33,857	19,898	11,682	2,124	153	8,216 R	58.8%	34.5%	6.3%
674,767	TOTAL	274,404	138,835	114,117	20,015	1,437	24,718 R	50.6%	41.6%	7.3%

MONTANA

Population total includes persons living in Yellowstone National Park and not under any county jurisdiction (275 in the 1980 Census, 64 in the 1970 Census, 47 in the 1960 Census).

ELECTION NOTES

1984 Other vote was Bergland (Libertarian).

1980 Other vote was 29,281 Anderson (Independent); 9,825 Clark (Libertarian).

1976 Other vote was Anderson (Americanist for President).

1972 Other vote was Schmitz (American).

1968 Wallace on the ballot as American. Other vote was 510 Munn (Prohibition); 470 no Presidential candidate indicated (New Reformist); 457 Halstead (Socialist Workers).

NEBRASKA

POPULAR VOTE FOR PRESIDENT 1920 TO 1984

Year	Total Vote	Republican Vote	Republican Candidate	Democratic Vote	Democratic Candidate	Other Vote	Plurality	Percentage Total Vote Rep.	Percentage Total Vote Dem.	Percentage Major Vote Rep.	Percentage Major Vote Dem.
1984	652,090	460,054	Reagan, Ronald	187,866	Mondale, Walter F.	4,170	272,188 R	70.6%	28.8%	71.0%	29.0%
1980	640,854	419,937	Reagan, Ronald	166,851	Carter, Jimmy	54,066	253,086 R	65.5%	26.0%	71.6%	28.4%
1976	607,668	359,705	Ford, Gerald R.	233,692	Carter, Jimmy	14,271	126,013 R	59.2%	38.5%	60.6%	39.4%
1972	576,289	406,298	Nixon, Richard M.	169,991	McGovern, George S.		236,307 R	70.5%	29.5%	70.5%	29.5%
1968	536,851	321,163	Nixon, Richard M.	170,784	Humphrey, Hubert H.	44,904	150,379 R	59.8%	31.8%	65.3%	34.7%
1964	584,154	276,847	Goldwater, Barry M.	307,307	Johnson, Lyndon B.		30,460 D	47.4%	52.6%	47.4%	52.6%
1960	613,095	380,553	Nixon, Richard M.	232,542	Kennedy, John F.		148,011 R	62.1%	37.9%	62.1%	37.9%
1956	577,137	378,108	Eisenhower, Dwight D.	199,029	Stevenson, Adlai E.		179,079 R	65.5%	34.5%	65.5%	34.5%
1952	609,660	421,603	Eisenhower, Dwight D.	188,057	Stevenson, Adlai E.		233,546 R	69.2%	30.8%	69.2%	30.8%
1948	488,940	264,774	Dewey, Thomas E.	224,165	Truman, Harry S.	1	40,609 R	54.2%	45.8%	54.2%	45.8%
1944	563,126	329,880	Dewey, Thomas E.	233,246	Roosevelt, Franklin D.		96,634 R	58.6%	41.4%	58.6%	41.4%
1940	615,878	352,201	Willkie, Wendell	263,677	Roosevelt, Franklin D.		88,524 R	57.2%	42.8%	57.2%	42.8%
1936	608,023	247,731	Landon, Alfred M.	347,445	Roosevelt, Franklin D.	12,847	99,714 D	40.7%	57.1%	41.6%	58.4%
1932	570,135	201,177	Hoover, Herbert C.	359,082	Roosevelt, Franklin D.	9,876	157,905 D	35.3%	63.0%	35.9%	64.1%
1928	547,128	345,745	Hoover, Herbert C.	197,950	Smith, Alfred E.	3,433	147,795 R	63.2%	36.2%	63.6%	36.4%
1924 **	463,559	218,985	Coolidge, Calvin	137,299	Davis, John W.	107,275	81,686 R	47.2%	29.6%	61.5%	38.5%
1920	382,743	247,498	Harding, Warren G.	119,608	Cox, James M.	15,637	127,890 R	64.7%	31.3%	67.4%	32.6%

In 1924 other vote was 105,681 Progressive and 1,594 Prohibition.

ELECTORAL COLLEGE VOTE 1920 TO 1984

Year	Total	Republican	Democratic	Other
1984	5	5	—	—
1980	5	5	—	—
1976	5	5	—	—
1972	5	5	—	—
1968	5	5	—	—
1964	5	—	5	—
1960	6	6	—	—
1956	6	6	—	—
1952	6	6	—	—
1948	6	6	—	—
1944	6	6	—	—
1940	7	7	—	—
1936	7	—	7	—
1932	7	—	7	—
1928	8	8	—	—
1924	8	8	—	—
1920	8	8	—	—

NEBRASKA

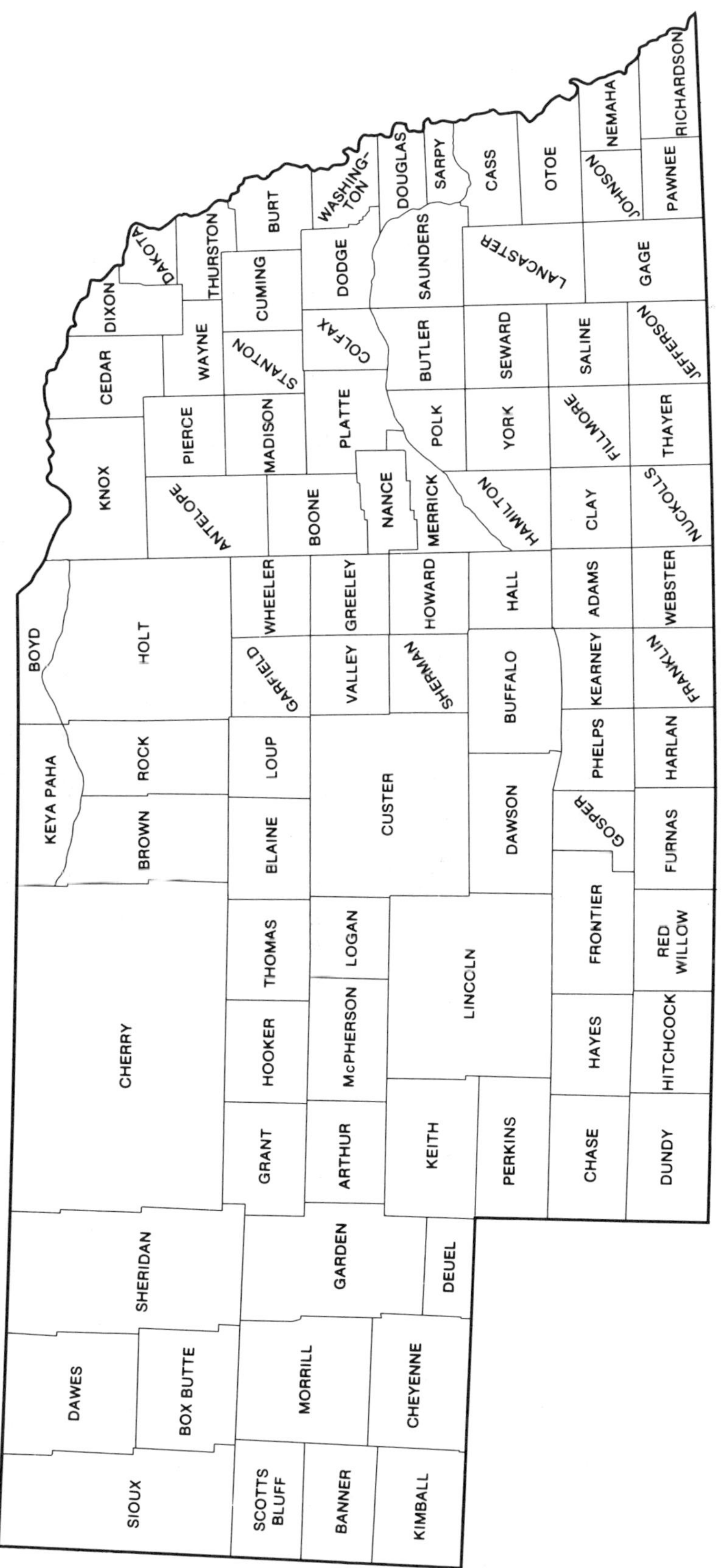
RICHARDSON
NEMAHA
PAWNEE
JOHNSON
OTOE
CASS
SARPY
DOUGLAS
WASHING-
TON
BURT
THURSTON
DAKOTA
DIXON
CEDAR
KNOX
WAYNE
CUMING
DODGE
SAUNDERS
LANCASTER
GAGE
JEFFERSON
SALINE
SEWARD
BUTLER
COLFAX
STANTON
PIERCE
MADISON
PLATTE
POLK
YORK
FILLMORE
THAYER
NUCKOLLS
CLAY
HAMILTON
MERRICK
NANCE
BOONE
ANTELOPE
BOYD
HOLT
WHEELER
GREELEY
HOWARD
HALL
ADAMS
WEBSTER
FRANKLIN
KEARNEY
BUFFALO
SHERMAN
VALLEY
GARFIELD
KEYA PAHA
ROCK
LOUP
CUSTER
PHELPS
HARLAN
BROWN
BLAINE
DAWSON
GOSPER
FURNAS
CHERRY
THOMAS
LOGAN
LINCOLN
FRONTIER
RED
WILLOW
HOOKER
McPHERSON
HAYES
HITCHCOCK
GRANT
ARTHUR
KEITH
PERKINS
CHASE
DUNDY
SHERIDAN
GARDEN
DEUEL
DAWES
BOX BUTTE
MORRILL
CHEYENNE
SIOUX
SCOTTS
BLUFF
BANNER
KIMBALL

NEBRASKA

PRESIDENT 1984

1980 Census Population	County	Total Vote	Republican	Democratic	Other	Rep.-Dem. Plurality	Percentage Total Vote Rep.	Percentage Total Vote Dem.	Percentage Major Vote Rep.	Percentage Major Vote Dem.
30,656	ADAMS	12,155	9,127	2,945	83	6,182 R	75.1%	24.2%	75.6%	24.4%
8,675	ANTELOPE	3,939	3,222	697	20	2,525 R	81.8%	17.7%	82.2%	17.8%
513	ARTHUR	281	248	33		215 R	88.3%	11.7%	88.3%	11.7%
918	BANNER	522	457	58	7	399 R	87.5%	11.1%	88.7%	11.3%
867	BLAINE	411	363	48		315 R	88.3%	11.7%	88.3%	11.7%
7,391	BOONE	3,215	2,508	690	17	1,818 R	78.0%	21.5%	78.4%	21.6%
13,696	BOX BUTTE	5,525	4,011	1,471	43	2,540 R	72.6%	26.6%	73.2%	26.8%
3,331	BOYD	1,496	1,175	308	13	867 R	78.5%	20.6%	79.2%	20.8%
4,377	BROWN	1,833	1,514	312	7	1,202 R	82.6%	17.0%	82.9%	17.1%
34,797	BUFFALO	14,550	11,365	3,086	99	8,279 R	78.1%	21.2%	78.6%	21.4%
8,813	BURT	3,721	2,645	1,054	22	1,591 R	71.1%	28.3%	71.5%	28.5%
9,330	BUTLER	3,785	2,557	1,193	35	1,364 R	67.6%	31.5%	68.2%	31.8%
20,297	CASS	8,026	5,461	2,499	66	2,962 R	68.0%	31.1%	68.6%	31.4%
11,375	CEDAR	4,536	3,298	1,201	37	2,097 R	72.7%	26.5%	73.3%	26.7%
4,758	CHASE	2,097	1,697	368	32	1,329 R	80.9%	17.5%	82.2%	17.8%
6,758	CHERRY	3,198	2,720	463	15	2,257 R	85.1%	14.5%	85.5%	14.5%
10,057	CHEYENNE	4,064	3,159	857	48	2,302 R	77.7%	21.1%	78.7%	21.3%
8,106	CLAY	3,756	2,920	811	25	2,109 R	77.7%	21.6%	78.3%	21.7%
9,890	COLFAX	4,016	2,999	981	36	2,018 R	74.7%	24.4%	75.4%	24.6%
11,664	CUMING	4,740	3,931	779	30	3,152 R	82.9%	16.4%	83.5%	16.5%
13,877	CUSTER	5,867	4,749	1,090	28	3,659 R	80.9%	18.6%	81.3%	18.7%
16,573	DAKOTA	6,002	3,467	2,510	25	957 R	57.8%	41.8%	58.0%	42.0%
9,609	DAWES	4,232	3,326	865	41	2,461 R	78.6%	20.4%	79.4%	20.6%
22,304	DAWSON	8,407	6,887	1,487	33	5,400 R	81.9%	17.7%	82.2%	17.8%
2,462	DEUEL	1,167	962	198	7	764 R	82.4%	17.0%	82.9%	17.1%
7,137	DIXON	3,164	2,155	986	23	1,169 R	68.1%	31.2%	68.6%	31.4%
35,847	DODGE	14,541	10,201	4,266	74	5,935 R	70.2%	29.3%	70.5%	29.5%
397,038	DOUGLAS	172,658	112,676	58,979	1,003	53,697 R	65.3%	34.2%	65.6%	34.4%
2,861	DUNDY	1,225	992	225	8	767 R	81.0%	18.4%	81.5%	18.5%
7,920	FILLMORE	3,511	2,474	1,009	28	1,465 R	70.5%	28.7%	71.0%	29.0%
4,377	FRANKLIN	2,127	1,597	522	8	1,075 R	75.1%	24.5%	75.4%	24.6%
3,647	FRONTIER	1,617	1,351	258	8	1,093 R	83.5%	16.0%	84.0%	16.0%
6,486	FURNAS	2,966	2,363	579	24	1,784 R	79.7%	19.5%	80.3%	19.7%
24,456	GAGE	8,892	6,116	2,709	67	3,407 R	68.8%	30.5%	69.3%	30.7%
2,802	GARDEN	1,351	1,158	180	13	978 R	85.7%	13.3%	86.5%	13.5%
2,363	GARFIELD	1,104	899	196	9	703 R	81.4%	17.8%	82.1%	17.9%
2,140	GOSPER	1,011	802	201	8	601 R	79.3%	19.9%	80.0%	20.0%
877	GRANT	459	406	51	2	355 R	88.5%	11.1%	88.8%	11.2%
3,462	GREELEY	1,442	948	485	9	463 R	65.7%	33.6%	66.2%	33.8%
47,690	HALL	17,956	13,193	4,655	108	8,538 R	73.5%	25.9%	73.9%	26.1%
9,301	HAMILTON	4,285	3,418	842	25	2,576 R	79.8%	19.6%	80.2%	19.8%
4,292	HARLAN	2,203	1,692	493	18	1,199 R	76.8%	22.4%	77.4%	22.6%
1,356	HAYES	694	593	101		492 R	85.4%	14.6%	85.4%	14.6%
4,079	HITCHCOCK	1,739	1,391	341	7	1,050 R	80.0%	19.6%	80.3%	19.7%
13,552	HOLT	5,545	4,613	893	39	3,720 R	83.2%	16.1%	83.8%	16.2%
990	HOOKER	493	433	55	5	378 R	87.8%	11.2%	88.7%	11.3%
6,773	HOWARD	2,806	1,899	887	20	1,012 R	67.7%	31.6%	68.2%	31.8%
9,817	JEFFERSON	4,523	3,116	1,367	40	1,749 R	68.9%	30.2%	69.5%	30.5%
5,285	JOHNSON	2,396	1,542	821	33	721 R	64.4%	34.3%	65.3%	34.7%
7,053	KEARNEY	3,262	2,508	726	28	1,782 R	76.9%	22.3%	77.6%	22.4%
9,364	KEITH	4,082	3,433	631	18	2,802 R	84.1%	15.5%	84.5%	15.5%
1,301	KEYA PAHA	635	507	128		379 R	79.8%	20.2%	79.8%	20.2%
4,882	KIMBALL	2,087	1,734	339	14	1,395 R	83.1%	16.2%	83.6%	16.4%
11,457	KNOX	4,560	3,364	1,149	47	2,215 R	73.8%	25.2%	74.5%	25.5%
192,884	LANCASTER	82,245	48,778	32,898	569	15,880 R	59.3%	40.0%	59.7%	40.3%
36,455	LINCOLN	15,307	10,717	4,509	81	6,208 R	70.0%	29.5%	70.4%	29.6%
983	LOGAN	514	446	67	1	379 R	86.8%	13.0%	86.9%	13.1%
859	LOUP	404	323	79	2	244 R	80.0%	19.6%	80.3%	19.7%
593	MCPHERSON	356	295	57	4	238 R	82.9%	16.0%	83.8%	16.2%
31,382	MADISON	11,589	9,790	1,757	42	8,033 R	84.5%	15.2%	84.8%	15.2%

NEBRASKA

PRESIDENT 1984

1980 Census Population	County	Total Vote	Republican	Democratic	Other	Rep.-Dem. Plurality	Percentage Total Vote Rep.	Total Vote Dem.	Major Vote Rep.	Major Vote Dem.
8,945	MERRICK	3,546	2,700	818	28	1,882 R	76.1%	23.1%	76.7%	23.3%
6,085	MORRILL	2,366	1,888	464	14	1,424 R	79.8%	19.6%	80.3%	19.7%
4,740	NANCE	1,931	1,393	525	13	868 R	72.1%	27.2%	72.6%	27.4%
8,367	NEMAHA	3,793	2,752	1,004	37	1,748 R	72.6%	26.5%	73.3%	26.7%
6,726	NUCKOLLS	3,098	2,132	947	19	1,185 R	68.8%	30.6%	69.2%	30.8%
15,183	OTOE	6,596	4,679	1,869	48	2,810 R	70.9%	28.3%	71.5%	28.5%
3,937	PAWNEE	1,884	1,306	552	26	754 R	69.3%	29.3%	70.3%	29.7%
3,637	PERKINS	1,736	1,420	307	9	1,113 R	81.8%	17.7%	82.2%	17.8%
9,769	PHELPS	4,501	3,741	740	20	3,001 R	83.1%	16.4%	83.5%	16.5%
8,481	PIERCE	3,589	3,017	545	27	2,472 R	84.1%	15.2%	84.7%	15.3%
28,852	PLATTE	12,222	10,069	2,061	92	8,008 R	82.4%	16.9%	83.0%	17.0%
6,320	POLK	2,776	2,149	610	17	1,539 R	77.4%	22.0%	77.9%	22.1%
12,615	RED WILLOW	5,184	4,131	1,026	27	3,105 R	79.7%	19.8%	80.1%	19.9%
11,315	RICHARDSON	5,098	3,634	1,422	42	2,212 R	71.3%	27.9%	71.9%	28.1%
2,383	ROCK	1,023	873	147	3	726 R	85.3%	14.4%	85.6%	14.4%
13,131	SALINE	5,394	2,942	2,385	67	557 R	54.5%	44.2%	55.2%	44.8%
86,015	SARPY	27,160	20,192	6,838	130	13,354 R	74.3%	25.2%	74.7%	25.3%
18,716	SAUNDERS	7,747	5,217	2,467	63	2,750 R	67.3%	31.8%	67.9%	32.1%
38,344	SCOTTS BLUFF	13,878	10,711	3,074	93	7,637 R	77.2%	22.2%	77.7%	22.3%
15,789	SEWARD	5,937	3,983	1,911	43	2,072 R	67.1%	32.2%	67.6%	32.4%
7,544	SHERIDAN	3,061	2,661	377	23	2,284 R	86.9%	12.3%	87.6%	12.4%
4,226	SHERMAN	1,862	1,144	701	17	443 R	61.4%	37.6%	62.0%	38.0%
1,845	SIOUX	860	732	121	7	611 R	85.1%	14.1%	85.8%	14.2%
6,549	STANTON	2,508	2,082	411	15	1,671 R	83.0%	16.4%	83.5%	16.5%
7,582	THAYER	3,551	2,580	946	25	1,634 R	72.7%	26.6%	73.2%	26.8%
973	THOMAS	374	298	73	3	225 R	79.7%	19.5%	80.3%	19.7%
7,186	THURSTON	2,500	1,410	1,077	13	333 R	56.4%	43.1%	56.7%	43.3%
5,633	VALLEY	2,807	2,055	739	13	1,316 R	73.2%	26.3%	73.6%	26.4%
15,508	WASHINGTON	6,791	5,191	1,565	35	3,626 R	76.4%	23.0%	76.8%	23.2%
9,858	WAYNE	3,936	3,075	833	28	2,242 R	78.1%	21.2%	78.7%	21.3%
4,858	WEBSTER	2,355	1,694	645	16	1,049 R	71.9%	27.4%	72.4%	27.6%
1,060	WHEELER	465	365	97	3	268 R	78.5%	20.9%	79.0%	21.0%
14,798	YORK	6,271	5,147	1,124		4,023 R	82.1%	17.9%	82.1%	17.9%
1,569,825	TOTAL	652,090	460,054	187,866	4,170	272,188 R	70.6%	28.8%	71.0%	29.0%

NEBRASKA

PRESIDENT 1980

1980 Census Population	County	Total Vote	Republican	Democratic	Other	Rep.-Dem. Plurality	Percentage Total Vote Rep.	Total Vote Dem.	Major Vote Rep.	Major Vote Dem.
30,656	ADAMS	12,973	8,500	3,372	1,101	5,128 R	65.5%	26.0%	71.6%	28.4%
8,675	ANTELOPE	4,057	3,192	659	206	2,533 R	78.7%	16.2%	82.9%	17.1%
513	ARTHUR	319	245	57	17	188 R	76.8%	17.9%	81.1%	18.9%
918	BANNER	532	481	33	18	448 R	90.4%	6.2%	93.6%	6.4%
867	BLAINE	442	361	63	18	298 R	81.7%	14.3%	85.1%	14.9%
7,391	BOONE	3,603	2,598	769	236	1,829 R	72.1%	21.3%	77.2%	22.8%
13,696	BOX BUTTE	5,532	3,912	1,208	412	2,704 R	70.7%	21.8%	76.4%	23.6%
3,331	BOYD	1,733	1,261	376	96	885 R	72.8%	21.7%	77.0%	23.0%
4,377	BROWN	2,087	1,615	341	131	1,274 R	77.4%	16.3%	82.6%	17.4%
34,797	BUFFALO	14,243	9,769	3,167	1,307	6,602 R	68.6%	22.2%	75.5%	24.5%
8,813	BURT	3,893	2,806	814	273	1,992 R	72.1%	20.9%	77.5%	22.5%
9,330	BUTLER	3,929	2,596	1,112	221	1,484 R	66.1%	28.3%	70.0%	30.0%
20,297	CASS	7,818	5,193	2,007	618	3,186 R	66.4%	25.7%	72.1%	27.9%
11,375	CEDAR	4,858	3,259	1,265	334	1,994 R	67.1%	26.0%	72.0%	28.0%
4,758	CHASE	2,103	1,593	324	186	1,269 R	75.7%	15.4%	83.1%	16.9%
6,758	CHERRY	3,155	2,517	489	149	2,028 R	79.8%	15.5%	83.7%	16.3%
10,057	CHEYENNE	4,108	3,073	776	259	2,297 R	74.8%	18.9%	79.8%	20.2%
8,106	CLAY	3,824	2,739	840	245	1,899 R	71.6%	22.0%	76.5%	23.5%
9,890	COLFAX	4,454	3,259	893	302	2,366 R	73.2%	20.0%	78.5%	21.5%
11,664	CUMING	5,131	4,006	803	322	3,203 R	78.1%	15.6%	83.3%	16.7%
13,877	CUSTER	5,934	4,563	1,011	360	3,552 R	76.9%	17.0%	81.9%	18.1%
16,573	DAKOTA	5,488	3,165	1,930	393	1,235 R	57.7%	35.2%	62.1%	37.9%
9,609	DAWES	4,306	3,283	705	318	2,578 R	76.2%	16.4%	82.3%	17.7%
22,304	DAWSON	8,609	6,689	1,463	457	5,226 R	77.7%	17.0%	82.1%	17.9%
2,462	DEUEL	1,220	946	192	82	754 R	77.5%	15.7%	83.1%	16.9%
7,137	DIXON	3,385	2,328	822	235	1,506 R	68.8%	24.3%	73.9%	26.1%
35,847	DODGE	14,250	9,522	3,564	1,164	5,958 R	66.8%	25.0%	72.8%	27.2%
397,038	DOUGLAS	163,930	96,908	51,668	15,354	45,240 R	59.1%	31.5%	65.2%	34.8%
2,861	DUNDY	1,411	1,138	192	81	946 R	80.7%	13.6%	85.6%	14.4%
7,920	FILLMORE	3,746	2,435	1,025	286	1,410 R	65.0%	27.4%	70.4%	29.6%
4,377	FRANKLIN	2,265	1,675	441	149	1,234 R	74.0%	19.5%	79.2%	20.8%
3,647	FRONTIER	1,698	1,346	259	93	1,087 R	79.3%	15.3%	83.9%	16.1%
6,486	FURNAS	3,172	2,483	536	153	1,947 R	78.3%	16.9%	82.2%	17.8%
24,456	GAGE	9,201	6,089	2,259	853	3,830 R	66.2%	24.6%	72.9%	27.1%
2,802	GARDEN	1,580	1,297	202	81	1,095 R	82.1%	12.8%	86.5%	13.5%
2,363	GARFIELD	1,108	811	238	59	573 R	73.2%	21.5%	77.3%	22.7%
2,140	GOSPER	1,029	783	181	65	602 R	76.1%	17.6%	81.2%	18.8%
877	GRANT	465	373	76	16	297 R	80.2%	16.3%	83.1%	16.9%
3,462	GREELEY	1,625	1,028	495	102	533 R	63.3%	30.5%	67.5%	32.5%
47,690	HALL	17,857	12,166	4,422	1,269	7,744 R	68.1%	24.8%	73.3%	26.7%
9,301	HAMILTON	4,271	3,200	778	293	2,422 R	74.9%	18.2%	80.4%	19.6%
4,292	HARLAN	2,317	1,690	486	141	1,204 R	72.9%	21.0%	77.7%	22.3%
1,356	HAYES	730	617	82	31	535 R	84.5%	11.2%	88.3%	11.7%
4,079	HITCHCOCK	1,963	1,474	329	160	1,145 R	75.1%	16.8%	81.8%	18.2%
13,552	HOLT	5,838	4,495	1,016	327	3,479 R	77.0%	17.4%	81.6%	18.4%
990	HOOKER	472	386	63	23	323 R	81.8%	13.3%	86.0%	14.0%
6,773	HOWARD	2,970	1,971	789	210	1,182 R	66.4%	26.6%	71.4%	28.6%
9,817	JEFFERSON	4,572	3,090	1,125	357	1,965 R	67.6%	24.6%	73.3%	26.7%
5,285	JOHNSON	2,565	1,719	626	220	1,093 R	67.0%	24.4%	73.3%	26.7%
7,053	KEARNEY	3,530	2,512	726	292	1,786 R	71.2%	20.6%	77.6%	22.4%
9,364	KEITH	4,354	3,381	710	263	2,671 R	77.7%	16.3%	82.6%	17.4%
1,301	KEYA PAHA	688	526	130	32	396 R	76.5%	18.9%	80.2%	19.8%
4,882	KIMBALL	2,136	1,615	385	136	1,230 R	75.6%	18.0%	80.8%	19.3%
11,457	KNOX	4,789	3,404	1,057	328	2,347 R	71.1%	22.1%	76.3%	23.7%
192,884	LANCASTER	76,233	38,780	27,162	10,291	11,618 R	50.9%	35.6%	58.8%	41.2%
36,455	LINCOLN	14,479	9,643	3,768	1,068	5,875 R	66.6%	26.0%	71.9%	28.1%
983	LOGAN	536	442	71	23	371 R	82.5%	13.2%	86.2%	13.8%
859	LOUP	470	368	74	28	294 R	78.3%	15.7%	83.3%	16.7%
593	MCPHERSON	343	285	49	9	236 R	83.1%	14.3%	85.3%	14.7%
31,382	MADISON	12,329	9,718	1,926	685	7,792 R	78.8%	15.6%	83.5%	16.5%

NEBRASKA

PRESIDENT 1980

1980 Census Population	County	Total Vote	Republican	Democratic	Other	Rep.-Dem. Plurality	Percentage Total Vote Rep.	Total Vote Dem.	Major Vote Rep.	Major Vote Dem.
8,945	MERRICK	3,694	2,710	712	272	1,998 R	73.4%	19.3%	79.2%	20.8%
6,085	MORRILL	2,540	1,893	512	135	1,381 R	74.5%	20.2%	78.7%	21.3%
4,740	NANCE	2,143	1,442	561	140	881 R	67.3%	26.2%	72.0%	28.0%
8,367	NEMAHA	3,911	2,695	930	286	1,765 R	68.9%	23.8%	74.3%	25.7%
6,726	NUCKOLLS	3,282	2,180	899	203	1,281 R	66.4%	27.4%	70.8%	29.2%
15,183	OTOE	6,559	4,611	1,471	477	3,140 R	70.3%	22.4%	75.8%	24.2%
3,937	PAWNEE	1,993	1,418	431	144	987 R	71.1%	21.6%	76.7%	23.3%
3,637	PERKINS	1,762	1,342	313	107	1,029 R	76.2%	17.8%	81.1%	18.9%
9,769	PHELPS	4,445	3,465	734	246	2,731 R	78.0%	16.5%	82.5%	17.5%
8,481	PIERCE	3,639	2,938	517	184	2,421 R	80.7%	14.2%	85.0%	15.0%
28,852	PLATTE	11,975	8,803	2,389	783	6,414 R	73.5%	19.9%	78.7%	21.3%
6,320	POLK	2,936	2,206	538	192	1,668 R	75.1%	18.3%	80.4%	19.6%
12,615	RED WILLOW	5,278	4,050	899	329	3,151 R	76.7%	17.0%	81.8%	18.2%
11,315	RICHARDSON	5,344	3,634	1,350	360	2,284 R	68.0%	25.3%	72.9%	27.1%
2,383	ROCK	1,059	855	146	58	709 R	80.7%	13.8%	85.4%	14.6%
13,131	SALINE	5,416	2,934	1,908	574	1,026 R	54.2%	35.2%	60.6%	39.4%
86,015	SARPY	23,202	15,552	5,689	1,961	9,863 R	67.0%	24.5%	73.2%	26.8%
18,716	SAUNDERS	7,906	5,223	2,034	649	3,189 R	66.1%	25.7%	72.0%	28.0%
38,344	SCOTTS BLUFF	13,249	9,504	2,854	891	6,650 R	71.7%	21.5%	76.9%	23.1%
15,789	SEWARD	5,965	3,527	1,803	635	1,724 R	59.1%	30.2%	66.2%	33.8%
7,544	SHERIDAN	3,271	2,749	370	152	2,379 R	84.0%	11.3%	88.1%	11.9%
4,226	SHERMAN	1,970	1,254	578	138	676 R	63.7%	29.3%	68.4%	31.6%
1,845	SIOUX	932	760	120	52	640 R	81.5%	12.9%	86.4%	13.6%
6,549	STANTON	2,466	1,945	362	159	1,583 R	78.9%	14.7%	84.3%	15.7%
7,582	THAYER	3,650	2,514	926	210	1,588 R	68.9%	25.4%	73.1%	26.9%
973	THOMAS	402	306	65	31	241 R	76.1%	16.2%	82.5%	17.5%
7,186	THURSTON	2,356	1,454	726	176	728 R	61.7%	30.8%	66.7%	33.3%
5,633	VALLEY	2,929	2,101	655	173	1,446 R	71.7%	22.4%	76.2%	23.8%
15,508	WASHINGTON	6,463	4,570	1,454	439	3,116 R	70.7%	22.5%	75.9%	24.1%
9,858	WAYNE	3,921	2,844	733	344	2,111 R	72.5%	18.7%	79.5%	20.5%
4,858	WEBSTER	2,403	1,676	547	180	1,129 R	69.7%	22.8%	75.4%	24.6%
1,060	WHEELER	501	374	93	34	281 R	74.7%	18.6%	80.1%	19.9%
14,798	YORK	6,634	5,089	1,131	414	3,958 R	76.7%	17.0%	81.8%	18.2%
1,569,825	TOTAL	640,854	419,937	166,851	54,066	253,086 R	65.5%	26.0%	71.6%	28.4%

NEBRASKA

PRESIDENT 1976

1970 Census Population	County	Total Vote	Republican	Democratic	Other	Rep.-Dem. Plurality	Percentage Total Vote Rep.	Percentage Total Vote Dem.	Percentage Major Vote Rep.	Percentage Major Vote Dem.
30,553	ADAMS	12,839	7,623	4,959	257	2,664 R	59.4%	38.6%	60.6%	39.4%
9,047	ANTELOPE	3,887	2,488	1,325	74	1,163 R	64.0%	34.1%	65.3%	34.7%
606	ARTHUR	262	193	64	5	129 R	73.7%	24.4%	75.1%	24.9%
1,034	BANNER	513	281	210	22	71 R	54.8%	40.9%	57.2%	42.8%
847	BLAINE	422	281	133	8	148 R	66.6%	31.5%	67.9%	32.1%
8,190	BOONE	3,437	2,035	1,329	73	706 R	59.2%	38.7%	60.5%	39.5%
10,094	BOX BUTTE	4,579	2,956	1,516	107	1,440 R	64.6%	33.1%	66.1%	33.9%
3,752	BOYD	1,821	1,004	792	25	212 R	55.1%	43.5%	55.9%	44.1%
4,021	BROWN	1,836	1,241	557	38	684 R	67.6%	30.3%	69.0%	31.0%
31,222	BUFFALO	12,777	8,095	4,308	374	3,787 R	63.4%	33.7%	65.3%	34.7%
9,247	BURT	3,967	2,510	1,375	82	1,135 R	63.3%	34.7%	64.6%	35.4%
9,461	BUTLER	4,271	1,809	2,337	125	528 D	42.4%	54.7%	43.6%	56.4%
18,076	CASS	7,141	3,807	3,205	129	602 R	53.3%	44.9%	54.3%	45.7%
12,192	CEDAR	4,760	2,415	2,225	120	190 R	50.7%	46.7%	52.0%	48.0%
4,129	CHASE	1,937	1,146	725	66	421 R	59.2%	37.4%	61.3%	38.7%
6,846	CHERRY	3,192	2,197	906	89	1,291 R	68.8%	28.4%	70.8%	29.2%
10,778	CHEYENNE	4,052	2,285	1,665	102	620 R	56.4%	41.1%	57.8%	42.2%
8,266	CLAY	3,703	2,254	1,369	80	885 R	60.9%	37.0%	62.2%	37.8%
9,498	COLFAX	4,123	2,364	1,666	93	698 R	57.3%	40.4%	58.7%	41.3%
12,034	CUMING	4,774	3,303	1,374	97	1,929 R	69.2%	28.8%	70.6%	29.4%
14,092	CUSTER	6,175	3,935	1,985	255	1,950 R	63.7%	32.1%	66.5%	33.5%
13,137	DAKOTA	4,995	2,631	2,292	72	339 R	52.7%	45.9%	53.4%	46.6%
9,761	DAWES	3,910	2,446	1,286	178	1,160 R	62.6%	32.9%	65.5%	34.5%
19,467	DAWSON	7,985	5,413	2,395	177	3,018 R	67.8%	30.0%	69.3%	30.7%
2,717	DEUEL	1,191	776	398	17	378 R	65.2%	33.4%	66.1%	33.9%
7,453	DIXON	3,338	1,981	1,286	71	695 R	59.3%	38.5%	60.6%	39.4%
34,782	DODGE	14,481	8,982	5,283	216	3,699 R	62.0%	36.5%	63.0%	37.0%
389,455	DOUGLAS	158,707	93,204	61,877	3,626	31,327 R	58.7%	39.0%	60.1%	39.9%
2,926	DUNDY	1,263	774	457	32	317 R	61.3%	36.2%	62.9%	37.1%
8,137	FILLMORE	3,671	2,098	1,489	84	609 R	57.2%	40.6%	58.5%	41.5%
4,566	FRANKLIN	2,163	1,170	941	52	229 R	54.1%	43.5%	55.4%	44.6%
3,982	FRONTIER	1,635	994	588	53	406 R	60.8%	36.0%	62.8%	37.2%
6,897	FURNAS	3,061	1,844	1,126	91	718 R	60.2%	36.8%	62.1%	37.9%
25,719	GAGE	9,908	5,206	4,512	190	694 R	52.5%	45.5%	53.6%	46.4%
2,929	GARDEN	1,442	928	445	69	483 R	64.4%	30.9%	67.6%	32.4%
2,411	GARFIELD	1,121	726	343	52	383 R	64.8%	30.6%	67.9%	32.1%
2,178	GOSPER	1,009	654	332	23	322 R	64.8%	32.9%	66.3%	33.7%
1,019	GRANT	446	314	116	16	198 R	70.4%	26.0%	73.0%	27.0%
4,000	GREELEY	1,709	787	877	45	90 D	46.1%	51.3%	47.3%	52.7%
42,851	HALL	17,386	10,935	6,079	372	4,856 R	62.9%	35.0%	64.3%	35.7%
8,867	HAMILTON	4,181	2,737	1,337	107	1,400 R	65.5%	32.0%	67.2%	32.8%
4,357	HARLAN	2,255	1,325	879	51	446 R	58.8%	39.0%	60.1%	39.9%
1,530	HAYES	695	411	267	17	144 R	59.1%	38.4%	60.6%	39.4%
4,051	HITCHCOCK	1,732	898	786	48	112 R	51.8%	45.4%	53.3%	46.7%
12,933	HOLT	5,278	3,389	1,751	138	1,638 R	64.2%	33.2%	65.9%	34.1%
939	HOOKER	427	326	98	3	228 R	76.3%	23.0%	76.9%	23.1%
6,807	HOWARD	2,736	1,362	1,316	58	46 R	49.8%	48.1%	50.9%	49.1%
10,436	JEFFERSON	4,789	2,628	2,068	93	560 R	54.9%	43.2%	56.0%	44.0%
5,743	JOHNSON	2,455	1,298	1,115	42	183 R	52.9%	45.4%	53.8%	46.2%
6,707	KEARNEY	3,124	1,830	1,219	75	611 R	58.6%	39.0%	60.0%	40.0%
8,487	KEITH	3,760	2,485	1,139	136	1,346 R	66.1%	30.3%	68.6%	31.4%
1,340	KEYA PAHA	667	405	245	17	160 R	60.7%	36.7%	62.3%	37.7%
6,009	KIMBALL	2,001	1,257	696	48	561 R	62.8%	34.8%	64.4%	35.6%
11,723	KNOX	4,654	2,610	1,922	122	688 R	56.1%	41.3%	57.6%	42.4%
167,972	LANCASTER	69,131	39,041	28,301	1,789	10,740 R	56.5%	40.9%	58.0%	42.0%
29,538	LINCOLN	12,739	7,076	5,355	308	1,721 R	55.5%	42.0%	56.9%	43.1%
991	LOGAN	494	283	196	15	87 R	57.3%	39.7%	59.1%	40.9%
854	LOUP	456	299	140	17	159 R	65.6%	30.7%	68.1%	31.9%
623	MCPHERSON	333	221	104	8	117 R	66.4%	31.2%	68.0%	32.0%
27,402	MADISON	11,455	7,846	3,433	176	4,413 R	68.5%	30.0%	69.6%	30.4%

NEBRASKA

PRESIDENT 1976

1970 Census Population	County	Total Vote	Republican	Democratic	Other	Rep.-Dem. Plurality	Percentage Total Vote Rep.	Total Vote Dem.	Major Vote Rep.	Major Vote Dem.
8,751	MERRICK	3,702	2,229	1,360	113	869 R	60.2%	36.7%	62.1%	37.9%
5,813	MORRILL	2,379	1,351	971	57	380 R	56.8%	40.8%	58.2%	41.8%
5,142	NANCE	2,113	1,121	936	56	185 R	53.1%	44.3%	54.5%	45.5%
8,976	NEMAHA	3,544	2,093	1,406	45	687 R	59.1%	39.7%	59.8%	40.2%
7,404	NUCKOLLS	3,224	1,753	1,424	47	329 R	54.4%	44.2%	55.2%	44.8%
15,576	OTOE	6,237	3,715	2,436	86	1,279 R	59.6%	39.1%	60.4%	39.6%
4,473	PAWNEE	1,873	990	845	38	145 R	52.9%	45.1%	54.0%	46.0%
3,423	PERKINS	1,649	981	622	46	359 R	59.5%	37.7%	61.2%	38.8%
9,553	PHELPS	4,509	3,210	1,168	131	2,042 R	71.2%	25.9%	73.3%	26.7%
8,493	PIERCE	3,244	2,172	1,004	68	1,168 R	67.0%	30.9%	68.4%	31.6%
26,508	PLATTE	11,179	7,217	3,693	269	3,524 R	64.6%	33.0%	66.2%	33.8%
6,468	POLK	3,053	1,797	1,190	66	607 R	58.9%	39.0%	60.2%	39.8%
12,191	RED WILLOW	4,810	2,978	1,722	110	1,256 R	61.9%	35.8%	63.4%	36.6%
12,277	RICHARDSON	5,627	3,119	2,416	92	703 R	55.4%	42.9%	56.4%	43.6%
2,231	ROCK	1,009	732	255	22	477 R	72.5%	25.3%	74.2%	25.8%
12,809	SALINE	5,662	2,330	3,205	127	875 D	41.2%	56.6%	42.1%	57.9%
65,007	SARPY	19,716	11,917	7,385	414	4,532 R	60.4%	37.5%	61.7%	38.3%
17,018	SAUNDERS	7,502	3,844	3,507	151	337 R	51.2%	46.7%	52.3%	47.7%
36,432	SCOTTS BLUFF	11,468	6,887	4,298	283	2,589 R	60.1%	37.5%	61.6%	38.4%
14,460	SEWARD	5,950	3,220	2,610	120	610 R	54.1%	43.9%	55.2%	44.8%
7,285	SHERIDAN	2,953	2,003	810	140	1,193 R	67.8%	27.4%	71.2%	28.8%
4,725	SHERMAN	2,093	935	1,078	80	143 D	44.7%	51.5%	46.4%	53.6%
2,034	SIOUX	883	532	329	22	203 R	60.2%	37.3%	61.8%	38.2%
5,758	STANTON	2,286	1,469	764	53	705 R	64.3%	33.4%	65.8%	34.2%
7,779	THAYER	3,360	1,994	1,315	51	679 R	59.3%	39.1%	60.3%	39.7%
954	THOMAS	468	343	103	22	240 R	73.3%	22.0%	76.9%	23.1%
6,942	THURSTON	2,393	1,290	1,021	82	269 R	53.9%	42.7%	55.8%	44.2%
5,783	VALLEY	2,769	1,587	1,042	140	545 R	57.3%	37.6%	60.4%	39.6%
13,310	WASHINGTON	6,111	3,799	2,233	79	1,566 R	62.2%	36.5%	63.0%	37.0%
10,400	WAYNE	3,708	2,521	1,089	98	1,432 R	68.0%	29.4%	69.8%	30.2%
5,396	WEBSTER	2,441	1,267	1,130	44	137 R	51.9%	46.3%	52.9%	47.1%
1,054	WHEELER	436	274	146	16	128 R	62.8%	33.5%	65.2%	34.8%
13,685	YORK	6,066	4,223	1,665	178	2,558 R	69.6%	27.4%	71.7%	28.3%
1,483,791	TOTAL	607,668	359,705	233,692	14,271	126,013 R	59.2%	38.5%	60.6%	39.4%

NEBRASKA

PRESIDENT 1972

1970 Census Population	County	Total Vote	Republican	Democratic	Other	Rep.-Dem. Plurality	Percentage Total Vote Rep.	Total Vote Dem.	Major Vote Rep.	Major Vote Dem.
30,553	ADAMS	12,200	8,841	3,359		5,482 R	72.5%	27.5%	72.5%	27.5%
9,047	ANTELOPE	4,079	3,228	851		2,377 R	79.1%	20.9%	79.1%	20.9%
606	ARTHUR	281	236	45		191 R	84.0%	16.0%	84.0%	16.0%
1,034	BANNER	500	404	96		308 R	80.8%	19.2%	80.8%	19.2%
847	BLAINE	399	343	56		287 R	86.0%	14.0%	86.0%	14.0%
8,190	BOONE	3,289	2,406	883		1,523 R	73.2%	26.8%	73.2%	26.8%
10,094	BOX BUTTE	4,391	3,431	960		2,471 R	78.1%	21.9%	78.1%	21.9%
3,752	BOYD	1,925	1,419	506		913 R	73.7%	26.3%	73.7%	26.3%
4,021	BROWN	1,792	1,462	330		1,132 R	81.6%	18.4%	81.6%	18.4%
31,222	BUFFALO	11,575	8,587	2,988		5,599 R	74.2%	25.8%	74.2%	25.8%
9,247	BURT	3,837	2,937	900		2,037 R	76.5%	23.5%	76.5%	23.5%
9,461	BUTLER	4,113	2,301	1,812		489 R	55.9%	44.1%	55.9%	44.1%
18,076	CASS	6,308	4,503	1,805		2,698 R	71.4%	28.6%	71.4%	28.6%
12,192	CEDAR	4,802	2,995	1,807		1,188 R	62.4%	37.6%	62.4%	37.6%
4,129	CHASE	1,625	1,318	307		1,011 R	81.1%	18.9%	81.1%	18.9%
6,846	CHERRY	3,073	2,610	463		2,147 R	84.9%	15.1%	84.9%	15.1%
10,778	CHEYENNE	4,070	3,120	950		2,170 R	76.7%	23.3%	76.7%	23.3%
8,266	CLAY	3,403	2,542	861		1,681 R	74.7%	25.3%	74.7%	25.3%
9,498	COLFAX	3,906	2,799	1,107		1,692 R	71.7%	28.3%	71.7%	28.3%
12,034	CUMING	4,829	3,810	1,019		2,791 R	78.9%	21.1%	78.9%	21.1%
14,092	CUSTER	5,983	4,836	1,147		3,689 R	80.8%	19.2%	80.8%	19.2%
13,137	DAKOTA	4,627	2,879	1,748		1,131 R	62.2%	37.8%	62.2%	37.8%
9,761	DAWES	3,698	2,987	711		2,276 R	80.8%	19.2%	80.8%	19.2%
19,467	DAWSON	7,635	6,211	1,424		4,787 R	81.3%	18.7%	81.3%	18.7%
2,717	DEUEL	1,225	1,001	224		777 R	81.7%	18.3%	81.7%	18.3%
7,453	DIXON	3,240	2,299	941		1,358 R	71.0%	29.0%	71.0%	29.0%
34,782	DODGE	13,663	9,837	3,826		6,011 R	72.0%	28.0%	72.0%	28.0%
389,455	DOUGLAS	149,780	101,579	48,201		53,378 R	67.8%	32.2%	67.8%	32.2%
2,926	DUNDY	1,224	1,003	221		782 R	81.9%	18.1%	81.9%	18.1%
8,137	FILLMORE	3,781	2,511	1,270		1,241 R	66.4%	33.6%	66.4%	33.6%
4,566	FRANKLIN	2,109	1,510	599		911 R	71.6%	28.4%	71.6%	28.4%
3,982	FRONTIER	1,639	1,315	324		991 R	80.2%	19.8%	80.2%	19.8%
6,897	FURNAS	2,958	2,282	676		1,606 R	77.1%	22.9%	77.1%	22.9%
25,719	GAGE	9,886	6,298	3,588		2,710 R	63.7%	36.3%	63.7%	36.3%
2,929	GARDEN	1,365	1,161	204		957 R	85.1%	14.9%	85.1%	14.9%
2,411	GARFIELD	1,112	903	209		694 R	81.2%	18.8%	81.2%	18.8%
2,178	GOSPER	1,071	829	242		587 R	77.4%	22.6%	77.4%	22.6%
1,019	GRANT	445	376	69		307 R	84.5%	15.5%	84.5%	15.5%
4,000	GREELEY	1,765	1,005	760		245 R	56.9%	43.1%	56.9%	43.1%
42,851	HALL	15,205	10,987	4,218		6,769 R	72.3%	27.7%	72.3%	27.7%
8,867	HAMILTON	3,867	2,960	907		2,053 R	76.5%	23.5%	76.5%	23.5%
4,357	HARLAN	2,088	1,549	539		1,010 R	74.2%	25.8%	74.2%	25.8%
1,530	HAYES	609	486	123		363 R	79.8%	20.2%	79.8%	20.2%
4,051	HITCHCOCK	1,703	1,339	364		975 R	78.6%	21.4%	78.6%	21.4%
12,933	HOLT	5,200	4,147	1,053		3,094 R	79.8%	20.3%	79.8%	20.3%
939	HOOKER	446	394	52		342 R	88.3%	11.7%	88.3%	11.7%
6,807	HOWARD	2,636	1,691	945		746 R	64.2%	35.8%	64.2%	35.8%
10,436	JEFFERSON	4,484	3,008	1,476		1,532 R	67.1%	32.9%	67.1%	32.9%
5,743	JOHNSON	2,554	1,637	917		720 R	64.1%	35.9%	64.1%	35.9%
6,707	KEARNEY	2,962	2,203	759		1,444 R	74.4%	25.6%	74.4%	25.6%
8,487	KEITH	3,178	2,513	665		1,848 R	79.1%	20.9%	79.1%	20.9%
1,340	KEYA PAHA	709	563	146		417 R	79.4%	20.6%	79.4%	20.6%
6,009	KIMBALL	2,087	1,650	437		1,213 R	79.1%	20.9%	79.1%	20.9%
11,723	KNOX	4,607	3,318	1,289		2,029 R	72.0%	28.0%	72.0%	28.0%
167,972	LANCASTER	68,497	42,573	25,924		16,649 R	62.2%	37.8%	62.2%	37.8%
29,538	LINCOLN	10,722	7,502	3,220		4,282 R	70.0%	30.0%	70.0%	30.0%
991	LOGAN	393	320	73		247 R	81.4%	18.6%	81.4%	18.6%
854	LOUP	403	345	58		287 R	85.6%	14.4%	85.6%	14.4%
623	MCPHERSON	289	247	42		205 R	85.5%	14.5%	85.5%	14.5%
27,402	MADISON	10,804	8,580	2,224		6,356 R	79.4%	20.6%	79.4%	20.6%

NEBRASKA

PRESIDENT 1972

1970 Census Population	County	Total Vote	Republican	Democratic	Other	Rep.-Dem. Plurality	Percentage Total Vote Rep.	Total Vote Dem.	Major Vote Rep.	Major Vote Dem.
8,751	MERRICK	3,305	2,418	887		1,531 R	73.2%	26.8%	73.2%	26.8%
5,813	MORRILL	2,260	1,740	520		1,220 R	77.0%	23.0%	77.0%	23.0%
5,142	NANCE	2,054	1,413	641		772 R	68.8%	31.2%	68.8%	31.2%
8,976	NEMAHA	3,509	2,600	909		1,691 R	74.1%	25.9%	74.1%	25.9%
7,404	NUCKOLLS	3,088	2,089	999		1,090 R	67.6%	32.4%	67.6%	32.4%
15,576	OTOE	6,533	4,815	1,718		3,097 R	73.7%	26.3%	73.7%	26.3%
4,473	PAWNEE	1,823	1,299	524		775 R	71.3%	28.7%	71.3%	28.7%
3,423	PERKINS	1,519	1,165	354		811 R	76.7%	23.3%	76.7%	23.3%
9,553	PHELPS	4,091	3,356	735		2,621 R	82.0%	18.0%	82.0%	18.0%
8,493	PIERCE	3,104	2,451	653		1,798 R	79.0%	21.0%	79.0%	21.0%
26,508	PLATTE	10,726	7,871	2,855		5,016 R	73.4%	26.6%	73.4%	26.6%
6,468	POLK	2,877	2,050	827		1,223 R	71.3%	28.7%	71.3%	28.7%
12,191	RED WILLOW	4,632	3,701	931		2,770 R	79.9%	20.1%	79.9%	20.1%
12,277	RICHARDSON	5,170	3,662	1,508		2,154 R	70.8%	29.2%	70.8%	29.2%
2,231	ROCK	1,075	937	138		799 R	87.2%	12.8%	87.2%	12.8%
12,809	SALINE	5,482	2,828	2,654		174 R	51.6%	48.4%	51.6%	48.4%
65,007	SARPY	15,418	11,514	3,904		7,610 R	74.7%	25.3%	74.7%	25.3%
17,018	SAUNDERS	6,783	4,282	2,501		1,781 R	63.1%	36.9%	63.1%	36.9%
36,432	SCOTTS BLUFF	11,413	8,649	2,764		5,885 R	75.8%	24.2%	75.8%	24.2%
14,460	SEWARD	5,794	3,707	2,087		1,620 R	64.0%	36.0%	64.0%	36.0%
7,285	SHERIDAN	2,867	2,386	481		1,905 R	83.2%	16.8%	83.2%	16.8%
4,725	SHERMAN	1,910	1,099	811		288 R	57.5%	42.5%	57.5%	42.5%
2,034	SIOUX	768	639	129		510 R	83.2%	16.8%	83.2%	16.8%
5,758	STANTON	2,140	1,662	478		1,184 R	77.7%	22.3%	77.7%	22.3%
7,779	THAYER	3,252	2,274	978		1,296 R	69.9%	30.1%	69.9%	30.1%
954	THOMAS	470	397	73		324 R	84.5%	15.5%	84.5%	15.5%
6,942	THURSTON	2,405	1,565	840		725 R	65.1%	34.9%	65.1%	34.9%
5,783	VALLEY	2,782	2,011	771		1,240 R	72.3%	27.7%	72.3%	27.7%
13,310	WASHINGTON	5,691	4,290	1,401		2,889 R	75.4%	24.6%	75.4%	24.6%
10,400	WAYNE	3,561	2,659	902		1,757 R	74.7%	25.3%	74.7%	25.3%
5,396	WEBSTER	2,327	1,631	696		935 R	70.1%	29.9%	70.1%	29.9%
1,054	WHEELER	445	361	84		277 R	81.1%	18.9%	81.1%	18.9%
13,685	YORK	5,969	4,651	1,318		3,333 R	77.9%	22.1%	77.9%	22.1%
1,483,791	TOTAL	576,289	406,298	169,991		236,307 R	70.5%	29.5%	70.5%	29.5%

NEBRASKA

PRESIDENT 1968

1960 Census Population	County	Total Vote	Republican	Democratic	AIP	Other	Plurality	Percentage Rep.	Dem.	AIP
28,944	ADAMS	11,362	7,191	3,524	647		3,667 R	63.3%	31.0%	5.7%
10,176	ANTELOPE	4,117	2,805	952	360		1,853 R	68.1%	23.1%	8.7%
680	ARTHUR	280	218	47	15		171 R	77.9%	16.8%	5.4%
1,269	BANNER	491	350	72	69		278 R	71.3%	14.7%	14.1%
1,016	BLAINE	433	344	64	25		280 R	79.4%	14.8%	5.8%
9,134	BOONE	3,404	2,179	934	291		1,245 R	64.0%	27.4%	8.5%
11,688	BOX BUTTE	4,043	2,728	1,052	263		1,676 R	67.5%	26.0%	6.5%
4,513	BOYD	1,934	1,250	437	247		813 R	64.6%	22.6%	12.8%
4,436	BROWN	1,871	1,340	369	162		971 R	71.6%	19.7%	8.7%
26,236	BUFFALO	10,394	6,786	2,875	733		3,911 R	65.3%	27.7%	7.1%
10,192	BURT	3,815	2,615	937	263		1,678 R	68.5%	24.6%	6.9%
10,312	BUTLER	3,514	1,646	1,544	324		102 R	46.8%	43.9%	9.2%
17,821	CASS	5,529	3,185	1,739	605		1,446 R	57.6%	31.5%	10.9%
13,368	CEDAR	4,637	2,853	1,444	340		1,409 R	61.5%	31.1%	7.3%
4,317	CHASE	1,727	1,171	363	193		808 R	67.8%	21.0%	11.2%
8,218	CHERRY	3,003	2,199	582	222		1,617 R	73.2%	19.4%	7.4%
14,828	CHEYENNE	4,132	2,725	993	414		1,732 R	65.9%	24.0%	10.0%
8,717	CLAY	3,414	2,273	935	206		1,338 R	66.6%	27.4%	6.0%
9,595	COLFAX	3,511	2,264	932	315		1,332 R	64.5%	26.5%	9.0%
12,435	CUMING	4,485	3,254	935	296		2,319 R	72.6%	20.8%	6.6%
16,517	CUSTER	6,133	4,325	1,407	401		2,918 R	70.5%	22.9%	6.5%
12,168	DAKOTA	4,210	2,383	1,541	286		842 R	56.6%	36.6%	6.8%
9,536	DAWES	3,614	2,600	741	273		1,859 R	71.9%	20.5%	7.6%
19,405	DAWSON	7,254	5,221	1,614	419		3,607 R	72.0%	22.2%	5.8%
3,125	DEUEL	1,325	997	250	78		747 R	75.2%	18.9%	5.9%
8,106	DIXON	3,124	2,051	890	183		1,161 R	65.7%	28.5%	5.9%
32,471	DODGE	12,636	8,059	3,755	822		4,304 R	63.8%	29.7%	6.5%
343,490	DOUGLAS	137,164	69,808	51,617	15,739		18,191 R	50.9%	37.6%	11.5%
3,570	DUNDY	1,390	1,001	261	128		740 R	72.0%	18.8%	9.2%
9,425	FILLMORE	3,713	2,213	1,297	203		916 R	59.6%	34.9%	5.5%
5,449	FRANKLIN	2,225	1,447	626	152		821 R	65.0%	28.1%	6.8%
4,311	FRONTIER	1,685	1,183	345	157		838 R	70.2%	20.5%	9.3%
7,711	FURNAS	3,061	2,137	701	223		1,436 R	69.8%	22.9%	7.3%
26,818	GAGE	9,806	5,465	3,704	637		1,761 R	55.7%	37.8%	6.5%
3,472	GARDEN	1,425	1,120	206	99		914 R	78.6%	14.5%	6.9%
2,699	GARFIELD	1,043	797	183	63		614 R	76.4%	17.5%	6.0%
2,489	GOSPER	987	701	229	57		472 R	71.0%	23.2%	5.8%
1,009	GRANT	415	311	84	20		227 R	74.9%	20.2%	4.8%
4,595	GREELEY	1,763	882	739	142		143 R	50.0%	41.9%	8.1%
35,757	HALL	13,861	8,457	4,571	833		3,886 R	61.0%	33.0%	6.0%
8,714	HAMILTON	3,654	2,592	918	144		1,674 R	70.9%	25.1%	3.9%
5,081	HARLAN	2,174	1,392	579	203		813 R	64.0%	26.6%	9.3%
1,919	HAYES	696	496	127	73		369 R	71.3%	18.2%	10.5%
4,829	HITCHCOCK	1,753	1,173	387	193		786 R	66.9%	22.1%	11.0%
13,722	HOLT	5,027	3,319	1,278	430		2,041 R	66.0%	25.4%	8.6%
1,130	HOOKER	398	350	36	12		314 R	87.9%	9.0%	3.0%
6,541	HOWARD	2,445	1,256	1,003	186		253 R	51.4%	41.0%	7.6%
11,620	JEFFERSON	4,637	2,793	1,572	272		1,221 R	60.2%	33.9%	5.9%
6,281	JOHNSON	2,482	1,508	759	215		749 R	60.8%	30.6%	8.7%
6,580	KEARNEY	2,822	1,806	825	191		981 R	64.0%	29.2%	6.8%
7,958	KEITH	2,998	2,126	694	178		1,432 R	70.9%	23.1%	5.9%
1,672	KEYA PAHA	690	531	109	50		422 R	77.0%	15.8%	7.2%
7,975	KIMBALL	2,074	1,423	414	237		1,009 R	68.6%	20.0%	11.4%
13,300	KNOX	4,588	3,129	1,131	328		1,998 R	68.2%	24.7%	7.1%
155,272	LANCASTER	59,530	33,051	23,539	2,940		9,512 R	55.5%	39.5%	4.9%
28,491	LINCOLN	10,269	5,996	3,491	782		2,505 R	58.4%	34.0%	7.6%
1,108	LOGAN	547	363	130	54		233 R	66.4%	23.8%	9.9%
1,097	LOUP	433	331	64	38		267 R	76.4%	14.8%	8.8%
735	MCPHERSON	310	236	40	34		196 R	76.1%	12.9%	11.0%
25,145	MADISON	10,044	7,066	2,364	614		4,702 R	70.4%	23.5%	6.1%

NEBRASKA

PRESIDENT 1968

1960 Census Population	County	Total Vote	Republican	Democratic	AIP	Other	Plurality	Percentage Rep.	Dem.	AIP
8,363	MERRICK	3,083	2,031	840	212		1,191 R	65.9%	27.2%	6.9%
7,057	MORRILL	2,281	1,516	480	285		1,036 R	66.5%	21.0%	12.5%
5,635	NANCE	2,165	1,316	677	172		639 R	60.8%	31.3%	7.9%
9,099	NEMAHA	3,608	2,290	1,023	295		1,267 R	63.5%	28.4%	8.2%
8,217	NUCKOLLS	3,193	1,894	1,127	172		767 R	59.3%	35.3%	5.4%
16,503	OTOE	5,822	3,840	1,508	474		2,332 R	66.0%	25.9%	8.1%
5,356	PAWNEE	2,005	1,209	583	213		626 R	60.3%	29.1%	10.6%
4,189	PERKINS	1,652	1,165	360	127		805 R	70.5%	21.8%	7.7%
9,800	PHELPS	4,055	2,976	825	254		2,151 R	73.4%	20.3%	6.3%
8,722	PIERCE	3,279	2,408	674	197		1,734 R	73.4%	20.6%	6.0%
23,992	PLATTE	9,584	5,817	2,999	768		2,818 R	60.7%	31.3%	8.0%
7,210	POLK	2,686	1,795	690	201		1,105 R	66.8%	25.7%	7.5%
12,940	RED WILLOW	4,575	3,066	1,145	364		1,921 R	67.0%	25.0%	8.0%
13,903	RICHARDSON	5,251	3,133	1,591	527		1,542 R	59.7%	30.3%	10.0%
2,554	ROCK	1,031	791	146	94		645 R	76.7%	14.2%	9.1%
12,542	SALINE	5,234	2,341	2,543	350		202 D	44.7%	48.6%	6.7%
31,281	SARPY	11,470	6,019	3,506	1,945		2,513 R	52.5%	30.6%	17.0%
17,270	SAUNDERS	5,975	3,429	1,990	556		1,439 R	57.4%	33.3%	9.3%
33,809	SCOTTS BLUFF	10,951	7,356	2,649	946		4,707 R	67.2%	24.2%	8.6%
13,581	SEWARD	4,851	2,939	1,658	254		1,281 R	60.6%	34.2%	5.2%
9,049	SHERIDAN	2,931	2,236	454	241		1,782 R	76.3%	15.5%	8.2%
5,382	SHERMAN	1,986	955	851	180		104 R	48.1%	42.8%	9.1%
2,575	SIOUX	791	565	157	69		408 R	71.4%	19.8%	8.7%
5,783	STANTON	1,973	1,408	411	154		997 R	71.4%	20.8%	7.8%
9,118	THAYER	3,569	2,331	1,061	177		1,270 R	65.3%	29.7%	5.0%
1,078	THOMAS	461	354	76	31		278 R	76.8%	16.5%	6.7%
7,237	THURSTON	2,353	1,341	802	210		539 R	57.0%	34.1%	8.9%
6,590	VALLEY	2,731	1,759	793	179		966 R	64.4%	29.0%	6.6%
12,103	WASHINGTON	4,834	3,063	1,279	492		1,784 R	63.4%	26.5%	10.2%
9,959	WAYNE	3,560	2,582	786	192		1,796 R	72.5%	22.1%	5.4%
6,224	WEBSTER	2,488	1,521	781	186		740 R	61.1%	31.4%	7.5%
1,297	WHEELER	503	323	131	49		192 R	64.2%	26.0%	9.7%
13,724	YORK	5,419	3,923	1,237	259		2,686 R	72.4%	22.8%	4.8%
1,411,330	TOTAL	536,851	321,163	170,784	44,904		150,379 R	59.8%	31.8%	8.4%

NEBRASKA

ELECTION NOTES

1984 Other vote was 2,079 Bergland (Libertarian); 1,066 Mason (Independent); 1,025 Serrette (Independent). State and county data include new resident votes reported separately.

1980 Other vote was 44,993 Anderson (Independent); 9,073 Clark (Libertarian). State and county data include new resident votes reported separately.

1976 Other vote was 9,409 McCarthy (Independent); 3,380 Maddox (American); 1,482 MacBride (Libertarian). State and county data include new resident votes reported separately. Due to a printers error in the Official Report, the Democratic state-wide total vote is given as 233,287.

1972

1968 Wallace on the ballot as American.

NEVADA

POPULAR VOTE FOR PRESIDENT 1920 TO 1984

								Percentage			
	Total	Republican		Democratic		Other		Total Vote		Major Vote	
Year	Vote	Vote	Candidate	Vote	Candidate	Vote	Plurality	Rep.	Dem.	Rep.	Dem.
1984	286,667	188,770	Reagan, Ronald	91,655	Mondale, Walter F.	6,242	97,115 R	65.8%	32.0%	67.3%	32.7%
1980	247,885	155,017	Reagan, Ronald	66,666	Carter, Jimmy	26,202	88,351 R	62.5%	26.9%	69.9%	30.1%
1976	201,876	101,273	Ford, Gerald R.	92,479	Carter, Jimmy	8,124	8,794 R	50.2%	45.8%	52.3%	47.7%
1972	181,766	115,750	Nixon, Richard M.	66,016	McGovern, George S.		49,734 R	63.7%	36.3%	63.7%	36.3%
1968	154,218	73,188	Nixon, Richard M.	60,598	Humphrey, Hubert H.	20,432	12,590 R	47.5%	39.3%	54.7%	45.3%
1964	135,433	56,094	Goldwater, Barry M.	79,339	Johnson, Lyndon B.		23,245 D	41.4%	58.6%	41.4%	58.6%
1960	107,267	52,387	Nixon, Richard M.	54,880	Kennedy, John F.		2,493 D	48.8%	51.2%	48.8%	51.2%
1956	96,689	56,049	Eisenhower, Dwight D.	40,640	Stevenson, Adlai E.		15,409 R	58.0%	42.0%	58.0%	42.0%
1952	82,190	50,502	Eisenhower, Dwight D.	31,688	Stevenson, Adlai E.		18,814 R	61.4%	38.6%	61.4%	38.6%
1948	62,117	29,357	Dewey, Thomas E.	31,291	Truman, Harry S.	1,469	1,934 D	47.3%	50.4%	48.4%	51.6%
1944	54,234	24,611	Dewey, Thomas E.	29,623	Roosevelt, Franklin D.		5,012 D	45.4%	54.6%	45.4%	54.6%
1940	53,174	21,229	Willkie, Wendell	31,945	Roosevelt, Franklin D.		10,716 D	39.9%	60.1%	39.9%	60.1%
1936	43,848	11,923	Landon, Alfred M.	31,925	Roosevelt, Franklin D.		20,002 D	27.2%	72.8%	27.2%	72.8%
1932	41,430	12,674	Hoover, Herbert C.	28,756	Roosevelt, Franklin D.		16,082 D	30.6%	69.4%	30.6%	69.4%
1928	32,417	18,327	Hoover, Herbert C.	14,090	Smith, Alfred E.		4,237 R	56.5%	43.5%	56.5%	43.5%
1924 **	26,921	11,243	Coolidge, Calvin	5,909	Davis, John W.	9,769	1,474 R	41.8%	21.9%	65.5%	34.5%
1920	27,194	15,479	Harding, Warren G.	9,851	Cox, James M.	1,864	5,628 R	56.9%	36.2%	61.1%	38.9%

In 1924 other vote was Progressive.

ELECTORAL COLLEGE VOTE 1920 TO 1984

Year	Total	Republican	Democratic	Other
1984	4	4	—	—
1980	3	3	—	—
1976	3	3	—	—
1972	3	3	—	—
1968	3	3	—	—
1964	3	—	3	—
1960	3	—	3	—
1956	3	3	—	—
1952	3	3	—	—
1948	3	—	3	—
1944	3	—	3	—
1940	3	—	3	—
1936	3	—	3	—
1932	3	—	3	—
1928	3	3	—	—
1924	3	3	—	—
1920	3	3	—	—

NEVADA

HUMBOLDT
ELKO
WASHOE
PERSHING
LANDER
EUREKA
CHURCHILL
WHITE PINE
STOREY
Carson City
DOUGLAS
LYON
MINERAL
NYE
ESMERALDA
LINCOLN
CLARK

NEVADA

PRESIDENT 1984

1980 Census Population	County	Total Vote	Republican	Democratic	Other	Rep.-Dem. Plurality	Percentage Total Vote Rep.	Percentage Total Vote Dem.	Percentage Major Vote Rep.	Percentage Major Vote Dem.
32,022	CARSON CITY	13,536	9,477	3,790	269	5,687 R	70.0%	28.0%	71.4%	28.6%
13,917	CHURCHILL	5,930	4,479	1,304	147	3,175 R	75.5%	22.0%	77.5%	22.5%
463,087	CLARK	150,363	94,133	53,386	2,844	40,747 R	62.6%	35.5%	63.8%	36.2%
19,421	DOUGLAS	8,449	6,385	1,877	187	4,508 R	75.6%	22.2%	77.3%	22.7%
17,269	ELKO	6,861	5,110	1,566	185	3,544 R	74.5%	22.8%	76.5%	23.5%
777	ESMERALDA	647	453	158	36	295 R	70.0%	24.4%	74.1%	25.9%
1,198	EUREKA	578	439	124	15	315 R	76.0%	21.5%	78.0%	22.0%
9,434	HUMBOLDT	3,450	2,498	862	90	1,636 R	72.4%	25.0%	74.3%	25.7%
4,076	LANDER	1,561	1,222	301	38	921 R	78.3%	19.3%	80.2%	19.8%
3,732	LINCOLN	1,616	1,175	397	44	778 R	72.7%	24.6%	74.7%	25.3%
13,594	LYON	6,177	4,320	1,673	184	2,647 R	69.9%	27.1%	72.1%	27.9%
6,217	MINERAL	2,504	1,645	766	93	879 R	65.7%	30.6%	68.2%	31.8%
9,048	NYE	4,989	3,573	1,269	147	2,304 R	71.6%	25.4%	73.8%	26.2%
	ORMSBY									
3,408	PERSHING	1,330	956	333	41	623 R	71.9%	25.0%	74.2%	25.8%
1,503	STOREY	854	570	252	32	318 R	66.7%	29.5%	69.3%	30.7%
193,623	WASHOE	74,511	50,418	22,321	1,772	28,097 R	67.7%	30.0%	69.3%	30.7%
8,167	WHITE PINE	3,311	1,917	1,276	118	641 R	57.9%	38.5%	60.0%	40.0%
800,493	TOTAL	286,667	188,770	91,655	6,242	97,115 R	65.8%	32.0%	67.3%	32.7%

NEVADA

PRESIDENT 1980

1980 Census Population	County	Total Vote	Republican	Democratic	Other	Rep.-Dem. Plurality	Percentage Total Vote Rep.	Percentage Total Vote Dem.	Percentage Major Vote Rep.	Percentage Major Vote Dem.
32,022	CARSON CITY	12,556	8,389	2,769	1,398	5,620 R	66.8%	22.1%	75.2%	24.8%
13,917	CHURCHILL	5,273	3,841	1,055	377	2,786 R	72.8%	20.0%	78.5%	21.5%
463,087	CLARK	127,424	76,194	38,313	12,917	37,881 R	59.8%	30.1%	66.5%	33.5%
19,421	DOUGLAS	7,343	5,254	1,352	737	3,902 R	71.6%	18.4%	79.5%	20.5%
17,269	ELKO	6,197	4,393	1,296	508	3,097 R	70.9%	20.9%	77.2%	22.8%
777	ESMERALDA	469	311	110	48	201 R	66.3%	23.5%	73.9%	26.1%
1,198	EUREKA	564	430	103	31	327 R	76.2%	18.3%	80.7%	19.3%
9,434	HUMBOLDT	2,843	1,950	684	209	1,266 R	68.6%	24.1%	74.0%	26.0%
4,076	LANDER	1,425	935	361	129	574 R	65.6%	25.3%	72.1%	27.9%
3,732	LINCOLN	1,586	1,087	396	103	691 R	68.5%	25.0%	73.3%	26.7%
13,594	LYON	5,456	3,709	1,288	459	2,421 R	68.0%	23.6%	74.2%	25.8%
6,217	MINERAL	2,546	1,628	631	287	997 R	63.9%	24.8%	72.1%	27.9%
9,048	NYE	3,720	2,387	973	360	1,414 R	64.2%	26.2%	71.0%	29.0%
	ORMSBY									
3,408	PERSHING	1,282	877	311	94	566 R	68.4%	24.3%	73.8%	26.2%
1,503	STOREY	783	460	222	101	238 R	58.7%	28.4%	67.4%	32.6%
193,623	WASHOE	64,956	41,276	15,621	8,059	25,655 R	63.5%	24.0%	72.5%	27.5%
8,167	WHITE PINE	3,462	1,896	1,181	385	715 R	54.8%	34.1%	61.6%	38.4%
800,493	TOTAL	247,885	155,017	66,666	26,202	88,351 R	62.5%	26.9%	69.9%	30.1%

NEVADA

PRESIDENT 1976

1970 Census Population	County	Total Vote	Republican	Democratic	Other	Rep.-Dem. Plurality	Percentage Total Vote Rep.	Total Vote Dem.	Major Vote Rep.	Major Vote Dem.
15,468	CARSON CITY	9,761	5,282	3,874	605	1,408 R	54.1%	39.7%	57.7%	42.3%
10,513	CHURCHILL	4,446	2,358	1,800	288	558 R	53.0%	40.5%	56.7%	43.3%
273,288	CLARK	102,812	48,236	51,178	3,398	2,942 D	46.9%	49.8%	48.5%	51.5%
6,882	DOUGLAS	5,282	3,095	1,934	253	1,161 R	58.6%	36.6%	61.5%	38.5%
13,958	ELKO	5,459	3,293	1,955	211	1,338 R	60.3%	35.8%	62.7%	37.3%
629	ESMERALDA	416	181	214	21	33 D	43.5%	51.4%	45.8%	54.2%
948	EUREKA	467	272	163	32	109 R	58.2%	34.9%	62.5%	37.5%
6,375	HUMBOLDT	2,585	1,380	1,074	131	306 R	53.4%	41.5%	56.2%	43.8%
2,666	LANDER	1,123	561	518	44	43 R	50.0%	46.1%	52.0%	48.0%
2,557	LINCOLN	1,399	700	642	57	58 R	50.0%	45.9%	52.2%	47.8%
8,221	LYON	4,162	2,068	1,866	228	202 R	49.7%	44.8%	52.6%	47.4%
7,051	MINERAL	2,594	1,104	1,361	129	257 D	42.6%	52.5%	44.8%	55.2%
5,599	NYE	2,415	1,027	1,261	127	234 D	42.5%	52.2%	44.9%	55.1%
	ORMSBY									
2,670	PERSHING	1,353	635	633	85	2 R	46.9%	46.8%	50.1%	49.9%
695	STOREY	636	274	310	52	36 D	43.1%	48.7%	46.9%	53.1%
121,068	WASHOE	53,227	29,264	21,687	2,276	7,577 R	55.0%	40.7%	57.4%	42.6%
10,150	WHITE PINE	3,739	1,543	2,009	187	466 D	41.3%	53.7%	43.4%	56.6%
488,738	TOTAL	201,876	101,273	92,479	8,124	8,794 R	50.2%	45.8%	52.3%	47.7%

NEVADA

PRESIDENT 1972

1970 Census Population	County	Total Vote	Republican	Democratic	Other	Rep.-Dem. Plurality	Percentage Total Vote Rep.	Total Vote Dem.	Major Vote Rep.	Major Vote Dem.
15,468	CARSON CITY	7,516	5,396	2,120		3,276 R	71.8%	28.2%	71.8%	28.2%
10,513	CHURCHILL	4,008	2,970	1,038		1,932 R	74.1%	25.9%	74.1%	25.9%
273,288	CLARK	89,908	53,101	36,807		16,294 R	59.1%	40.9%	59.1%	40.9%
6,882	DOUGLAS	3,881	2,898	983		1,915 R	74.7%	25.3%	74.7%	25.3%
13,958	ELKO	5,353	3,886	1,467		2,419 R	72.6%	27.4%	72.6%	27.4%
629	ESMERALDA	400	273	127		146 R	68.3%	31.8%	68.3%	31.8%
948	EUREKA	510	371	139		232 R	72.7%	27.3%	72.7%	27.3%
6,375	HUMBOLDT	2,372	1,659	713		946 R	69.9%	30.1%	69.9%	30.1%
2,666	LANDER	1,266	798	468		330 R	63.0%	37.0%	63.0%	37.0%
2,557	LINCOLN	1,223	841	382		459 R	68.8%	31.2%	68.8%	31.2%
8,221	LYON	3,772	2,813	959		1,854 R	74.6%	25.4%	74.6%	25.4%
7,051	MINERAL	2,879	2,111	768		1,343 R	73.3%	26.7%	73.3%	26.7%
5,599	NYE	2,089	1,287	802		485 R	61.6%	38.4%	61.6%	38.4%
	ORMSBY									
2,670	PERSHING	1,218	853	365		488 R	70.0%	30.0%	70.0%	30.0%
695	STOREY	734	508	226		282 R	69.2%	30.8%	69.2%	30.8%
121,068	WASHOE	50,645	33,539	17,106		16,433 R	66.2%	33.8%	66.2%	33.8%
10,150	WHITE PINE	3,992	2,446	1,546		900 R	61.3%	38.7%	61.3%	38.7%
488,738	TOTAL	181,766	115,750	66,016		49,734 R	63.7%	36.3%	63.7%	36.3%

NEVADA

PRESIDENT 1968

1960 Census Population	County	Total Vote	Republican	Democratic	AIP	Other	Plurality	Percentage Rep.	Dem.	AIP
	CARSON CITY									
8,452	CHURCHILL	3,740	1,954	1,211	575		743 R	52.2%	32.4%	15.4%
127,016	CLARK	75,065	31,522	33,225	10,318		1,703 D	42.0%	44.3%	13.7%
3,481	DOUGLAS	2,798	1,801	670	327		1,131 R	64.4%	23.9%	11.7%
12,011	ELKO	4,932	2,687	1,686	559		1,001 R	54.5%	34.2%	11.3%
619	ESMERALDA	353	138	118	97		20 R	39.1%	33.4%	27.5%
767	EUREKA	490	277	149	64		128 R	56.5%	30.4%	13.1%
5,708	HUMBOLDT	2,525	1,287	885	353		402 R	51.0%	35.0%	14.0%
1,566	LANDER	909	461	301	147		160 R	50.7%	33.1%	16.2%
2,431	LINCOLN	1,113	555	414	144		141 R	49.9%	37.2%	12.9%
6,143	LYON	2,999	1,616	939	444		677 R	53.9%	31.3%	14.8%
6,329	MINERAL	2,869	927	1,242	700		315 D	32.3%	43.3%	24.4%
4,374	NYE	2,071	843	728	500		115 R	40.7%	35.2%	24.1%
8,063	ORMSBY	5,601	3,169	1,770	662		1,399 R	56.6%	31.6%	11.8%
3,199	PERSHING	1,213	567	466	180		101 R	46.7%	38.4%	14.8%
568	STOREY	444	222	172	50		50 R	50.0%	38.7%	11.3%
84,743	WASHOE	42,988	23,492	14,560	4,936		8,932 R	54.6%	33.9%	11.5%
9,808	WHITE PINE	4,108	1,670	2,062	376		392 D	40.7%	50.2%	9.2%
285,278	TOTAL	154,218	73,188	60,598	20,432		12,590 R	47.5%	39.3%	13.2%

NEVADA

After a state-wide vote in the General Election of November 1968, Carson City, the state capital, and Ormsby county were combined under the name Carson City.

ELECTION NOTES

1984 Other vote was 2,292 Bergland (Libertarian); 3,950 "None of these Candidates".

1980 Other vote was 17,651 Anderson (Independent); 4,358 Clark (Libertarian); 4,193 "None of these Candidates".

1976 Other vote was 1,519 MacBride (Libertarian); 1,497 Maddox (Independent American); 5,108 "None of these Candidates".

1972

1968 Wallace on the ballot as Independent American.

NEW HAMPSHIRE

POPULAR VOTE FOR PRESIDENT 1920 TO 1984

Year	Total Vote	Republican Vote	Republican Candidate	Democratic Vote	Democratic Candidate	Other Vote	Plurality	Percentage Total Vote Rep.	Percentage Total Vote Dem.	Percentage Major Vote Rep.	Percentage Major Vote Dem.
1984	389,066	267,051	Reagan, Ronald	120,395	Mondale, Walter F.	1,620	146,656 R	68.6%	30.9%	68.9%	31.1%
1980	383,990	221,705	Reagan, Ronald	108,864	Carter, Jimmy	53,421	112,841 R	57.7%	28.4%	67.1%	32.9%
1976	339,618	185,935	Ford, Gerald R.	147,635	Carter, Jimmy	6,048	38,300 R	54.7%	43.5%	55.7%	44.3%
1972	334,055	213,724	Nixon, Richard M.	116,435	McGovern, George S.	3,896	97,289 R	64.0%	34.9%	64.7%	35.3%
1968	297,298	154,903	Nixon, Richard M.	130,589	Humphrey, Hubert H.	11,806	24,314 R	52.1%	43.9%	54.3%	45.7%
1964	288,093	104,029	Goldwater, Barry M.	184,064	Johnson, Lyndon B.		80,035 D	36.1%	63.9%	36.1%	63.9%
1960	295,761	157,989	Nixon, Richard M.	137,772	Kennedy, John F.		20,217 R	53.4%	46.6%	53.4%	46.6%
1956	266,994	176,519	Eisenhower, Dwight D.	90,364	Stevenson, Adlai E.	111	86,155 R	66.1%	33.8%	66.1%	33.9%
1952	272,950	166,287	Eisenhower, Dwight D.	106,663	Stevenson, Adlai E.		59,624 R	60.9%	39.1%	60.9%	39.1%
1948	231,440	121,299	Dewey, Thomas E.	107,995	Truman, Harry S.	2,146	13,304 R	52.4%	46.7%	52.9%	47.1%
1944	229,625	109,916	Dewey, Thomas E.	119,663	Roosevelt, Franklin D.	46	9,747 D	47.9%	52.1%	47.9%	52.1%
1940	235,419	110,127	Willkie, Wendell	125,292	Roosevelt, Franklin D.		15,165 D	46.8%	53.2%	46.8%	53.2%
1936	218,114	104,642	Landon, Alfred M.	108,460	Roosevelt, Franklin D.	5,012	3,818 D	48.0%	49.7%	49.1%	50.9%
1932	205,520	103,629	Hoover, Herbert C.	100,680	Roosevelt, Franklin D.	1,211	2,949 R	50.4%	49.0%	50.7%	49.3%
1928	196,757	115,404	Hoover, Herbert C.	80,715	Smith, Alfred E.	638	34,689 R	58.7%	41.0%	58.8%	41.2%
1924	164,769	98,575	Coolidge, Calvin	57,201	Davis, John W.	8,993	41,374 R	59.8%	34.7%	63.3%	36.7%
1920	159,092	95,196	Harding, Warren G.	62,662	Cox, James M.	1,234	32,534 R	59.8%	39.4%	60.3%	39.7%

ELECTORAL COLLEGE VOTE 1920 TO 1984

Year	Total	Republican	Democratic	Other
1984	4	4	—	—
1980	4	4	—	—
1976	4	4	—	—
1972	4	4	—	—
1968	4	4	—	—
1964	4	—	4	—
1960	4	4	—	—
1956	4	4	—	—
1952	4	4	—	—
1948	4	4	—	—
1944	4	—	4	—
1940	4	—	4	—
1936	4	—	4	—
1932	4	4	—	—
1928	4	4	—	—
1924	4	4	—	—
1920	4	4	—	—

NEW HAMPSHIRE

NEW HAMPSHIRE

PRESIDENT 1984

1980 Census Population	County	Total Vote	Republican	Democratic	Other	Rep.-Dem. Plurality	Percentage Total Vote Rep.	Total Vote Dem.	Major Vote Rep.	Major Vote Dem.
42,884	BELKNAP	19,065	14,200	4,743	122	9,457 R	74.5%	24.9%	75.0%	25.0%
27,931	CARROLL	15,764	11,891	3,806	67	8,085 R	75.4%	24.1%	75.8%	24.2%
62,116	CHESHIRE	24,943	15,851	8,990	102	6,861 R	63.5%	36.0%	63.8%	36.2%
35,147	COOS	14,059	10,013	4,004	42	6,009 R	71.2%	28.5%	71.4%	28.6%
65,806	GRAFTON	27,300	18,451	8,757	92	9,694 R	67.6%	32.1%	67.8%	32.2%
276,608	HILLSBOROUGH	115,278	81,462	33,314	502	48,148 R	70.7%	28.9%	71.0%	29.0%
98,302	MERRIMACK	41,591	27,925	13,510	156	14,415 R	67.1%	32.5%	67.4%	32.6%
190,345	ROCKINGHAM	83,439	57,586	25,557	296	32,029 R	69.0%	30.6%	69.3%	30.7%
85,408	STRAFFORD	33,388	20,452	12,752	184	7,700 R	61.3%	38.2%	61.6%	38.4%
36,063	SULLIVAN	14,239	9,220	4,962	57	4,258 R	64.8%	34.8%	65.0%	35.0%
920,610	TOTAL	389,066	267,051	120,395	1,620	146,656 R	68.6%	30.9%	68.9%	31.1%

NEW HAMPSHIRE

PRESIDENT 1980

1980 Census Population	County	Total Vote	Republican	Democratic	Other	Rep.-Dem. Plurality	Percentage Total Vote Rep.	Total Vote Dem.	Major Vote Rep.	Major Vote Dem.
42,884	BELKNAP	18,558	12,077	4,365	2,116	7,712 R	65.1%	23.5%	73.5%	26.5%
27,931	CARROLL	14,853	9,980	3,119	1,754	6,861 R	67.2%	21.0%	76.2%	23.8%
62,116	CHESHIRE	25,467	13,242	7,835	4,390	5,407 R	52.0%	30.8%	62.8%	37.2%
35,147	COOS	14,520	8,724	4,749	1,047	3,975 R	60.1%	32.7%	64.8%	35.2%
65,806	GRAFTON	27,142	15,273	7,282	4,587	7,991 R	56.3%	26.8%	67.7%	32.3%
276,608	HILLSBOROUGH	115,343	68,994	31,789	14,560	37,205 R	59.8%	27.6%	68.5%	31.5%
98,302	MERRIMACK	41,963	23,584	12,083	6,296	11,501 R	56.2%	28.8%	66.1%	33.9%
190,345	ROCKINGHAM	79,474	45,960	21,712	11,802	24,248 R	57.8%	27.3%	67.9%	32.1%
85,408	STRAFFORD	32,533	16,399	11,041	5,093	5,358 R	50.4%	33.9%	59.8%	40.2%
36,063	SULLIVAN	14,137	7,472	4,889	1,776	2,583 R	52.9%	34.6%	60.4%	39.6%
920,610	TOTAL	383,990	221,705	108,864	53,421	112,841 R	57.7%	28.4%	67.1%	32.9%

NEW HAMPSHIRE

PRESIDENT 1976

1970 Census Population	County	Total Vote	Republican	Democratic	Other	Rep.-Dem. Plurality	Percentage Total Vote Rep.	Total Vote Dem.	Major Vote Rep.	Major Vote Dem.
32,367	BELKNAP	16,249	9,876	6,143	230	3,733 R	60.8%	37.8%	61.7%	38.3%
18,548	CARROLL	12,198	8,561	3,374	263	5,187 R	70.2%	27.7%	71.7%	28.3%
52,364	CHESHIRE	23,305	12,554	10,388	363	2,166 R	53.9%	44.6%	54.7%	45.3%
34,291	COOS	14,638	7,094	7,385	159	291 D	48.5%	50.5%	49.0%	51.0%
54,914	GRAFTON	23,914	14,430	8,996	488	5,434 R	60.3%	37.6%	61.6%	38.4%
223,941	HILLSBOROUGH	100,880	53,581	45,544	1,755	8,037 R	53.1%	45.1%	54.1%	45.9%
80,925	MERRIMACK	37,282	21,853	14,865	564	6,988 R	58.6%	39.9%	59.5%	40.5%
138,951	ROCKINGHAM	68,130	36,738	30,051	1,341	6,687 R	53.9%	44.1%	55.0%	45.0%
70,431	STRAFFORD	29,815	14,569	14,566	680	3 R	48.9%	48.9%	50.0%	50.0%
30,949	SULLIVAN	13,207	6,679	6,323	205	356 R	50.6%	47.9%	51.4%	48.6%
737,681	TOTAL	339,618	185,935	147,635	6,048	38,300 R	54.7%	43.5%	55.7%	44.3%

NEW HAMPSHIRE

PRESIDENT 1972

1970 Census Population	County	Total Vote	Republican	Democratic	Other	Rep.-Dem. Plurality	Percentage Total Vote Rep.	Total Vote Dem.	Major Vote Rep.	Major Vote Dem.
32,367	BELKNAP	16,312	11,536	4,610	166	6,926 R	70.7%	28.3%	71.4%	28.6%
18,548	CARROLL	11,070	8,525	2,395	150	6,130 R	77.0%	21.6%	78.1%	21.9%
52,364	CHESHIRE	22,703	13,390	9,157	156	4,233 R	59.0%	40.3%	59.4%	40.6%
34,291	COOS	15,563	9,468	5,829	266	3,639 R	60.8%	37.5%	61.9%	38.1%
54,914	GRAFTON	25,319	16,605	8,388	326	8,217 R	65.6%	33.1%	66.4%	33.6%
223,941	HILLSBOROUGH	101,377	65,274	34,739	1,364	30,535 R	64.4%	34.3%	65.3%	34.7%
80,925	MERRIMACK	37,449	25,354	11,737	358	13,617 R	67.7%	31.3%	68.4%	31.6%
138,951	ROCKINGHAM	61,541	38,825	21,998	718	16,827 R	63.1%	35.7%	63.8%	36.2%
70,431	STRAFFORD	29,129	16,846	12,028	255	4,818 R	57.8%	41.3%	58.3%	41.7%
30,949	SULLIVAN	13,592	7,901	5,554	137	2,347 R	58.1%	40.9%	58.7%	41.3%
737,681	TOTAL	334,055	213,724	116,435	3,896	97,289 R	64.0%	34.9%	64.7%	35.3%

NEW HAMPSHIRE

PRESIDENT 1968

1960 Census Population	County	Total Vote	Republican	Democratic	AIP	Other	Plurality	Percentage Rep.	Percentage Dem.	Percentage AIP
28,912	BELKNAP	14,071	8,642	4,942	454	33	3,700 R	61.4%	35.1%	3.2%
15,829	CARROLL	9,317	6,795	2,163	348	11	4,632 R	72.9%	23.2%	3.7%
43,342	CHESHIRE	20,332	10,702	9,135	441	54	1,567 R	52.6%	44.9%	2.2%
37,140	COOS	15,497	6,822	8,261	399	15	1,439 D	44.0%	53.3%	2.6%
48,857	GRAFTON	21,554	12,881	7,813	727	133	5,068 R	59.8%	36.2%	3.4%
178,161	HILLSBOROUGH	92,169	42,409	45,423	4,231	106	3,014 D	46.0%	49.3%	4.6%
67,785	MERRIMACK	33,291	19,289	12,711	1,201	90	6,578 R	57.9%	38.2%	3.6%
99,029	ROCKINGHAM	52,456	28,842	21,195	2,333	86	7,647 R	55.0%	40.4%	4.4%
59,799	STRAFFORD	26,283	12,427	13,129	650	77	702 D	47.3%	50.0%	2.5%
28,067	SULLIVAN	12,328	6,094	5,817	389	28	277 R	49.4%	47.2%	3.2%
606,921	TOTAL	297,298	154,903	130,589	11,173	633	24,314 R	52.1%	43.9%	3.8%

NEW HAMPSHIRE

ELECTION NOTES

1984 Other vote was 735 Bergland (Libertarian); 467 LaRouche (Independent); 305 Serrette (Alliance); 113 scattered write-in. Early unamended canvass gave the Republican state-wide total vote as 267,050 and the Democratic state-wide total vote as 120,347; vote totals in Hillsborough and Grafton counties were amended.

1980 Other vote was 49,693 Anderson (Independent); 2,064 Clark (Libertarian); 1,320 Commoner (Citizens); 129 Hall (Communist); 76 Griswold (Workers World); 71 DeBerry (Socialist Workers); 68 scattered write-in. Data published in the "Manual for the General Court" amended the minor party vote slightly to read 2,067 Libertarian; 1,325 Citizens; the original canvass is used here in the data table.

1976 Other vote was 4,095 McCarthy (McCarthy '76); 936 MacBride (Libertarian); 186 LaRouche (U.S. Labor); 161 Camejo (Socialist Workers); 66 Levin (Socialist Labor); 604 scattered write-in. Early unamended canvass gave the Democratic state-wide total vote as 147,645 and the state-wide total vote for other as 6,047; the vote in Hillsborough county was amended from 45,554 Democratic and 1,754 other.

1972 Other vote was 3,386 Schmitz (American); 368 Jenness (Socialist Workers); 142 scattered write-in.

1968 Wallace on the ballot as George Wallace party. Other vote was 421 no Presidential candidate indicated (New Party); 104 Halstead (Socialist Workers); 108 scattered write-in.

NEW JERSEY

POPULAR VOTE FOR PRESIDENT 1920 TO 1984

Year	Total Vote	Republican Vote	Republican Candidate	Democratic Vote	Democratic Candidate	Other Vote	Plurality	Percentage Total Vote Rep.	Percentage Total Vote Dem.	Percentage Major Vote Rep.	Percentage Major Vote Dem.
1984	3,217,862	1,933,630	Reagan, Ronald	1,261,323	Mondale, Walter F.	22,909	672,307 R	60.1%	39.2%	60.5%	39.5%
1980	2,975,684	1,546,557	Reagan, Ronald	1,147,364	Carter, Jimmy	281,763	399,193 R	52.0%	38.6%	57.4%	42.6%
1976	3,014,472	1,509,688	Ford, Gerald R.	1,444,653	Carter, Jimmy	60,131	65,035 R	50.1%	47.9%	51.1%	48.9%
1972	2,997,229	1,845,502	Nixon, Richard M.	1,102,211	McGovern, George S.	49,516	743,291 R	61.6%	36.8%	62.6%	37.4%
1968	2,875,395	1,325,467	Nixon, Richard M.	1,264,206	Humphrey, Hubert H.	285,722	61,261 R	46.1%	44.0%	51.2%	48.8%
1964	2,847,663	964,174	Goldwater, Barry M.	1,868,231	Johnson, Lyndon B.	15,258	904,057 D	33.9%	65.6%	34.0%	66.0%
1960	2,773,111	1,363,324	Nixon, Richard M.	1,385,415	Kennedy, John F.	24,372	22,091 D	49.2%	50.0%	49.6%	50.4%
1956	2,484,312	1,606,942	Eisenhower, Dwight D.	850,337	Stevenson, Adlai E.	27,033	756,605 R	64.7%	34.2%	65.4%	34.6%
1952	2,418,554	1,373,613	Eisenhower, Dwight D.	1,015,902	Stevenson, Adlai E.	29,039	357,711 R	56.8%	42.0%	57.5%	42.5%
1948	1,949,555	981,124	Dewey, Thomas E.	895,455	Truman, Harry S.	72,976	85,669 R	50.3%	45.9%	52.3%	47.7%
1944	1,963,761	961,335	Dewey, Thomas E.	987,874	Roosevelt, Franklin D.	14,552	26,539 D	49.0%	50.3%	49.3%	50.7%
1940	1,972,552	945,475	Willkie, Wendell	1,016,808	Roosevelt, Franklin D.	10,269	71,333 D	47.9%	51.5%	48.2%	51.8%
1936	1,820,437	720,322	Landon, Alfred M.	1,083,850	Roosevelt, Franklin D.	16,265	363,528 D	39.6%	59.5%	39.9%	60.1%
1932	1,630,063	775,684	Hoover, Herbert C.	806,630	Roosevelt, Franklin D.	47,749	30,946 D	47.6%	49.5%	49.0%	51.0%
1928	1,549,381	926,050	Hoover, Herbert C.	616,517	Smith, Alfred E.	6,814	309,533 R	59.8%	39.8%	60.0%	40.0%
1924	1,088,054	676,277	Coolidge, Calvin	298,043	Davis, John W.	113,734	378,234 R	62.2%	27.4%	69.4%	30.6%
1920	910,251	615,333	Harding, Warren G.	258,761	Cox, James M.	36,157	356,572 R	67.6%	28.4%	70.4%	29.6%

ELECTORAL COLLEGE VOTE 1920 TO 1984

Year	Total	Republican	Democratic	Other
1984	16	16	—	—
1980	17	17	—	—
1976	17	17	—	—
1972	17	17	—	—
1968	17	17	—	—
1964	17	—	17	—
1960	16	—	16	—
1956	16	16	—	—
1952	16	16	—	—
1948	16	16	—	—
1944	16	—	16	—
1940	16	—	16	—
1936	16	—	16	—
1932	16	—	16	—
1928	14	14	—	—
1924	14	14	—	—
1920	14	14	—	—

NEW JERSEY

SUSSEX
PASSAIC
BERGEN
WARREN
MORRIS
ESSEX
HUDSON
UNION
SOMERSET
HUNTERDON
MIDDLESEX
MERCER
MONMOUTH
BURLINGTON
OCEAN
CAMDEN
GLOUCESTER
SALEM
ATLANTIC
CUMBERLAND
CAPE MAY

NEW JERSEY

PRESIDENT 1984

1980 Census Population	County	Total Vote	Republican	Democratic	Other	Rep.-Dem. Plurality	Percentage Total Vote Rep.	Total Vote Dem.	Major Vote Rep.	Major Vote Dem.
194,119	ATLANTIC	82,851	49,158	33,240	453	15,918 R	59.3%	40.1%	59.7%	40.3%
845,385	BERGEN	424,718	268,507	155,039	1,172	113,468 R	63.2%	36.5%	63.4%	36.6%
362,542	BURLINGTON	147,659	89,815	57,467	377	32,348 R	60.8%	38.9%	61.0%	39.0%
471,650	CAMDEN	200,886	109,749	90,233	904	19,516 R	54.6%	44.9%	54.9%	45.1%
82,266	CAPE MAY	42,297	28,786	13,378	133	15,408 R	68.1%	31.6%	68.3%	31.7%
132,866	CUMBERLAND	51,155	29,398	21,141	616	8,257 R	57.5%	41.3%	58.2%	41.8%
851,116	ESSEX	314,543	136,798	173,295	4,450	36,497 D	43.5%	55.1%	44.1%	55.9%
199,917	GLOUCESTER	87,050	54,041	32,702	307	21,339 R	62.1%	37.6%	62.3%	37.7%
556,972	HUDSON	208,244	112,834	94,304	1,106	18,530 R	54.2%	45.3%	54.5%	45.5%
87,361	HUNTERDON	41,079	29,737	10,972	370	18,765 R	72.4%	26.7%	73.0%	27.0%
307,863	MERCER	138,121	71,195	66,398	528	4,797 R	51.5%	48.1%	51.7%	48.3%
595,893	MIDDLESEX	267,853	160,221	104,905	2,727	55,316 R	59.8%	39.2%	60.4%	39.6%
503,173	MONMOUTH	232,909	152,595	79,382	932	73,213 R	65.5%	34.1%	65.8%	34.2%
407,630	MORRIS	191,504	137,719	53,201	584	84,518 R	71.9%	27.8%	72.1%	27.9%
346,038	OCEAN	177,113	124,391	51,012	1,710	73,379 R	70.2%	28.8%	70.9%	29.1%
447,585	PASSAIC	174,940	101,951	69,590	3,399	32,361 R	58.3%	39.8%	59.4%	40.6%
64,676	SALEM	26,452	17,368	8,935	149	8,433 R	65.7%	33.8%	66.0%	34.0%
203,129	SOMERSET	99,296	66,303	31,924	1,069	34,379 R	66.8%	32.2%	67.5%	32.5%
116,119	SUSSEX	47,345	35,680	11,502	163	24,178 R	75.4%	24.3%	75.6%	24.4%
504,094	UNION	229,140	135,446	92,056	1,638	43,390 R	59.1%	40.2%	59.5%	40.5%
84,429	WARREN	32,707	21,938	10,647	122	11,291 R	67.1%	32.6%	67.3%	32.7%
7,364,823	TOTAL	3,217,862	1,933,630	1,261,323	22,909	672,307 R	60.1%	39.2%	60.5%	39.5%

NEW JERSEY

PRESIDENT 1980

1980 Census Population	County	Total Vote	Republican	Democratic	Other	Rep.-Dem. Plurality	Percentage Total Vote Rep.	Total Vote Dem.	Major Vote Rep.	Major Vote Dem.
194,119	ATLANTIC	76,202	37,973	31,286	6,943	6,687 R	49.8%	41.1%	54.8%	45.2%
845,385	BERGEN	415,157	232,043	139,474	43,640	92,569 R	55.9%	33.6%	62.5%	37.5%
362,542	BURLINGTON	131,709	68,415	50,083	13,211	18,332 R	51.9%	38.0%	57.7%	42.3%
471,650	CAMDEN	186,808	87,939	80,033	18,836	7,906 R	47.1%	42.8%	52.4%	47.6%
82,266	CAPE MAY	38,471	22,729	12,708	3,034	10,021 R	59.1%	33.0%	64.1%	35.9%
132,866	CUMBERLAND	46,403	23,242	19,356	3,805	3,886 R	50.1%	41.7%	54.6%	45.4%
851,116	ESSEX	287,166	117,222	145,281	24,663	28,059 D	40.8%	50.6%	44.7%	55.3%
199,917	GLOUCESTER	78,903	40,306	29,804	8,793	10,502 R	51.1%	37.8%	57.5%	42.5%
556,972	HUDSON	198,688	91,207	95,622	11,859	4,415 D	45.9%	48.1%	48.8%	51.2%
87,361	HUNTERDON	36,430	21,403	10,029	4,998	11,374 R	58.8%	27.5%	68.1%	31.9%
307,863	MERCER	128,582	53,450	60,888	14,244	7,438 D	41.6%	47.4%	46.7%	53.3%
595,893	MIDDLESEX	241,206	122,354	97,304	21,548	25,050 R	50.7%	40.3%	55.7%	44.3%
503,173	MONMOUTH	211,971	120,173	71,328	20,470	48,845 R	56.7%	33.6%	62.8%	37.2%
407,630	MORRIS	173,604	105,260	48,965	19,379	56,295 R	60.6%	28.2%	68.3%	31.7%
346,038	OCEAN	157,568	98,433	46,923	12,212	51,510 R	62.5%	29.8%	67.7%	32.3%
447,585	PASSAIC	158,951	82,531	61,486	14,934	21,045 R	51.9%	38.7%	57.3%	42.7%
64,676	SALEM	25,474	13,000	10,209	2,265	2,791 R	51.0%	40.1%	56.0%	44.0%
203,129	SOMERSET	91,928	52,591	29,470	9,867	23,121 R	57.2%	32.1%	64.1%	35.9%
116,119	SUSSEX	42,327	27,063	10,531	4,733	16,532 R	63.9%	24.9%	72.0%	28.0%
504,094	UNION	217,339	112,288	86,074	18,977	26,214 R	51.7%	39.6%	56.6%	43.4%
84,429	WARREN	30,797	16,935	10,510	3,352	6,425 R	55.0%	34.1%	61.7%	38.3%
7,364,823	TOTAL	2,975,684	1,546,557	1,147,364	281,763	399,193 R	52.0%	38.6%	57.4%	42.6%

NEW JERSEY

PRESIDENT 1976

1970 Census Population	County	Total Vote	Republican	Democratic	Other	Rep.-Dem. Plurality	Percentage Total Vote Rep.	Percentage Total Vote Dem.	Percentage Major Vote Rep.	Percentage Major Vote Dem.
175,043	ATLANTIC	80,630	36,733	41,965	1,932	5,232 D	45.6%	52.0%	46.7%	53.3%
898,012	BERGEN	424,853	237,331	180,738	6,784	56,593 R	55.9%	42.5%	56.8%	43.2%
323,132	BURLINGTON	126,820	60,960	63,309	2,551	2,349 D	48.1%	49.9%	49.1%	50.9%
456,291	CAMDEN	195,611	82,801	108,854	3,956	26,053 D	42.3%	55.6%	43.2%	56.8%
59,554	CAPE MAY	36,667	19,498	16,489	680	3,009 R	53.2%	45.0%	54.2%	45.8%
121,374	CUMBERLAND	50,287	20,535	29,165	587	8,630 D	40.8%	58.0%	41.3%	58.7%
929,986	ESSEX	315,812	133,911	174,434	7,467	40,523 D	42.4%	55.2%	43.4%	56.6%
172,681	GLOUCESTER	75,302	34,888	38,726	1,688	3,838 D	46.3%	51.4%	47.4%	52.6%
609,266	HUDSON	212,730	92,636	116,241	3,853	23,605 D	43.5%	54.6%	44.3%	55.7%
69,718	HUNTERDON	32,966	19,616	12,592	758	7,024 R	59.5%	38.2%	60.9%	39.1%
303,968	MERCER	130,856	58,453	69,621	2,782	11,168 D	44.7%	53.2%	45.6%	54.4%
583,813	MIDDLESEX	240,864	113,539	122,859	4,466	9,320 D	47.1%	51.0%	48.0%	52.0%
459,379	MONMOUTH	202,790	110,104	88,956	3,730	21,148 R	54.3%	43.9%	55.3%	44.7%
383,454	MORRIS	172,373	105,921	63,749	2,703	42,172 R	61.4%	37.0%	62.4%	37.6%
208,470	OCEAN	136,781	77,875	56,413	2,493	21,462 R	56.9%	41.2%	58.0%	42.0%
460,782	PASSAIC	166,226	85,102	76,194	4,930	8,908 R	51.2%	45.8%	52.8%	47.2%
60,346	SALEM	24,977	11,639	12,826	512	1,187 D	46.6%	51.4%	47.6%	52.4%
198,372	SOMERSET	89,691	51,260	36,258	2,173	15,002 R	57.2%	40.4%	58.6%	41.4%
77,528	SUSSEX	39,229	23,613	14,759	857	8,854 R	60.2%	37.6%	61.5%	38.5%
543,116	UNION	228,902	118,019	106,267	4,616	11,752 R	51.6%	46.4%	52.6%	47.4%
73,879	WARREN	30,105	15,254	14,238	613	1,016 R	50.7%	47.3%	51.7%	48.3%
7,168,164	TOTAL	3,014,472	1,509,688	1,444,653	60,131	65,035 R	50.1%	47.9%	51.1%	48.9%

NEW JERSEY

PRESIDENT 1972

1970 Census Population	County	Total Vote	Republican	Democratic	Other	Rep.-Dem. Plurality	Percentage Total Vote Rep.	Percentage Total Vote Dem.	Percentage Major Vote Rep.	Percentage Major Vote Dem.
175,043	ATLANTIC	76,700	45,667	28,203	2,830	17,464 R	59.5%	36.8%	61.8%	38.2%
898,012	BERGEN	436,894	285,458	147,155	4,281	138,303 R	65.3%	33.7%	66.0%	34.0%
323,132	BURLINGTON	114,260	70,805	41,520	1,935	29,285 R	62.0%	36.3%	63.0%	37.0%
456,291	CAMDEN	190,207	111,935	75,202	3,070	36,733 R	58.8%	39.5%	59.8%	40.2%
59,554	CAPE MAY	32,069	22,621	8,729	719	13,892 R	70.5%	27.2%	72.2%	27.8%
121,374	CUMBERLAND	45,392	26,409	18,692	291	7,717 R	58.2%	41.2%	58.6%	41.4%
929,986	ESSEX	338,888	170,036	161,270	7,582	8,766 R	50.2%	47.6%	51.3%	48.7%
172,681	GLOUCESTER	71,209	44,806	25,509	894	19,297 R	62.9%	35.8%	63.7%	36.3%
609,266	HUDSON	227,600	136,895	87,977	2,728	48,918 R	60.1%	38.7%	60.9%	39.1%
69,718	HUNTERDON	30,856	21,282	9,031	543	12,251 R	69.0%	29.3%	70.2%	29.8%
303,968	MERCER	133,191	69,303	62,180	1,708	7,123 R	52.0%	46.7%	52.7%	47.3%
583,813	MIDDLESEX	242,694	149,033	88,397	5,264	60,636 R	61.4%	36.4%	62.8%	37.2%
459,379	MONMOUTH	189,977	124,830	63,176	1,971	61,654 R	65.7%	33.3%	66.4%	33.6%
383,454	MORRIS	166,434	113,469	50,937	2,028	62,532 R	68.2%	30.6%	69.0%	31.0%
208,470	OCEAN	107,667	77,979	27,710	1,978	50,269 R	72.4%	25.7%	73.8%	26.2%
460,782	PASSAIC	174,923	108,511	62,302	4,110	46,209 R	62.0%	35.6%	63.5%	36.5%
60,346	SALEM	25,249	16,371	8,609	269	7,762 R	64.8%	34.1%	65.5%	34.5%
198,372	SOMERSET	85,605	56,524	26,537	2,544	29,987 R	66.0%	31.0%	68.1%	31.9%
77,528	SUSSEX	34,898	25,977	8,585	336	17,392 R	74.4%	24.6%	75.2%	24.8%
543,116	UNION	242,973	148,290	90,482	4,201	57,808 R	61.0%	37.2%	62.1%	37.9%
73,879	WARREN	29,543	19,301	10,008	234	9,293 R	65.3%	33.9%	65.9%	34.1%
7,168,164	TOTAL	2,997,229	1,845,502	1,102,211	49,516	743,291 R	61.6%	36.8%	62.6%	37.4%

NEW JERSEY

PRESIDENT 1968

1960 Census Population	County	Total Vote	Republican	Democratic	AIP	Other	Plurality	Percentage Rep.	Dem.	AIP
160,880	ATLANTIC	77,834	32,807	35,581	7,528	1,918	2,774 D	42.1%	45.7%	9.7%
780,255	BERGEN	413,037	224,911	162,182	23,663	2,281	62,729 R	54.5%	39.3%	5.7%
224,499	BURLINGTON	99,747	46,177	41,651	11,635	284	4,526 R	46.3%	41.8%	11.7%
392,035	CAMDEN	188,887	77,642	87,347	23,111	787	9,705 D	41.1%	46.2%	12.2%
48,555	CAPE MAY	28,172	14,970	9,664	3,498	40	5,306 R	53.1%	34.3%	12.4%
106,850	CUMBERLAND	45,488	18,388	21,661	5,356	83	3,273 D	40.4%	47.6%	11.8%
923,545	ESSEX	357,095	140,084	185,440	26,823	4,748	45,356 D	39.2%	51.9%	7.5%
134,840	GLOUCESTER	68,731	30,596	27,438	10,626	71	3,158 R	44.5%	39.9%	15.5%
610,734	HUDSON	244,560	91,324	124,939	23,138	5,159	33,615 D	37.3%	51.1%	9.5%
54,107	HUNTERDON	27,439	15,851	8,755	2,749	84	7,096 R	57.8%	31.9%	10.0%
266,392	MERCER	125,529	45,354	63,218	16,104	853	17,864 D	36.1%	50.4%	12.8%
433,856	MIDDLESEX	225,530	96,515	103,339	24,138	1,538	6,824 D	42.8%	45.8%	10.7%
334,401	MONMOUTH	170,456	87,311	69,669	13,047	429	17,642 R	51.2%	40.9%	7.7%
261,620	MORRIS	148,062	85,512	52,398	9,659	493	33,114 R	57.8%	35.4%	6.5%
108,241	OCEAN	77,963	41,995	26,909	8,520	539	15,086 R	53.9%	34.5%	10.9%
406,618	PASSAIC	172,657	79,862	74,442	16,617	1,736	5,420 R	46.3%	43.1%	9.6%
58,711	SALEM	26,251	11,407	11,172	3,647	25	235 R	43.5%	42.6%	13.9%
143,913	SOMERSET	78,475	42,459	27,580	7,331	1,105	14,879 R	54.1%	35.1%	9.3%
49,255	SUSSEX	29,240	18,043	8,325	2,843	29	9,718 R	61.7%	28.5%	9.7%
504,255	UNION	241,256	110,309	109,674	19,963	1,310	635 R	45.7%	45.5%	8.3%
63,220	WARREN	28,986	13,950	12,822	2,191	23	1,128 R	48.1%	44.2%	7.6%
6,066,782	TOTAL	2,875,395	1,325,467	1,264,206	262,187	23,535	61,261 R	46.1%	44.0%	9.1%

NEW JERSEY

ELECTION NOTES

1984 Other vote was 8,404 Holmes (Workers World); 6,416 Bergland (Libertarian); 2,293 Serrette (New Alliance); 1,721 Winn (Workers League); 1,564 Hall (Communist); 1,264 Mason (Socialist Workers); 1,247 Johnson (Citizens).

1980 Other vote was 234,632 Anderson (The Anderson Alternative); 20,652 Clark (Libertarian); 8,203 Commoner (Citizens); 3,927 McCormack (Right to Life); 3,694 Lynen (Middle Class Candidate); 2,555 Hall (Communist); 2,198 Pulley (Socialist Workers); 1,973 McReynolds (Socialist); 1,718 Gahres (Down with Lawyers); 1,288 Griswold (Workers World); 923 Wendelken (Independent).

1976 Other vote was 32,717 McCarthy (Independent); 9,449 MacBride (Libertarian); 7,716 Maddox (American); 3,686 Levin (Socialist Labor); 1,662 Hall (Communist); 1,650 LaRouche (Labor); 1,184 Camejo (Socialist Workers); 1,044 Wright (People's); 554 Bubar (Prohibition); 469 Zeidler (Socialist).

1972 Other vote was 34,378 Schmitz (American); 5,355 Spock (People's); 4,544 Fisher (Socialist Labor); 2,233 Jenness (Socialist Workers); 1,743 Mahalchik (America First); 1,263 Hall (Communist).

1968 Wallace on the ballot as George Wallace party. Other vote was 8,667 Halstead (Socialist Workers); 8,084 Gregory (Peace and Freedom Alternative); 6,784 Blomen (Socialist Labor).

NEW MEXICO

POPULAR VOTE FOR PRESIDENT 1920 TO 1984

Year	Total Vote	Republican Vote	Republican Candidate	Democratic Vote	Democratic Candidate	Other Vote	Plurality	Percentage Total Vote Rep.	Percentage Total Vote Dem.	Percentage Major Vote Rep.	Percentage Major Vote Dem.
1984	514,370	307,101	Reagan, Ronald	201,769	Mondale, Walter F.	5,500	105,332 R	59.7%	39.2%	60.3%	39.7%
1980	456,971	250,779	Reagan, Ronald	167,826	Carter, Jimmy	38,366	82,953 R	54.9%	36.7%	59.9%	40.1%
1976	418,409	211,419	Ford, Gerald R.	201,148	Carter, Jimmy	5,842	10,271 R	50.5%	48.1%	51.2%	48.8%
1972	386,241	235,606	Nixon, Richard M.	141,084	McGovern, George S.	9,551	94,522 R	61.0%	36.5%	62.5%	37.5%
1968	327,350	169,692	Nixon, Richard M.	130,081	Humphrey, Hubert H.	27,577	39,611 R	51.8%	39.7%	56.6%	43.4%
1964	328,645	132,838	Goldwater, Barry M.	194,015	Johnson, Lyndon B.	1,792	61,177 D	40.4%	59.0%	40.6%	59.4%
1960	311,107	153,733	Nixon, Richard M.	156,027	Kennedy, John F.	1,347	2,294 D	49.4%	50.2%	49.6%	50.4%
1956	253,926	146,788	Eisenhower, Dwight D.	106,098	Stevenson, Adlai E.	1,040	40,690 R	57.8%	41.8%	58.0%	42.0%
1952	238,608	132,170	Eisenhower, Dwight D.	105,661	Stevenson, Adlai E.	777	26,509 R	55.4%	44.3%	55.6%	44.4%
1948	187,063	80,303	Dewey, Thomas E.	105,464	Truman, Harry S.	1,296	25,161 D	42.9%	56.4%	43.2%	56.8%
1944	152,225	70,688	Dewey, Thomas E.	81,389	Roosevelt, Franklin D.	148	10,701 D	46.4%	53.5%	46.5%	53.5%
1940	183,258	79,315	Willkie, Wendell	103,699	Roosevelt, Franklin D.	244	24,384 D	43.3%	56.6%	43.3%	56.7%
1936	169,135	61,727	Landon, Alfred M.	106,037	Roosevelt, Franklin D.	1,371	44,310 D	36.5%	62.7%	36.8%	63.2%
1932	151,606	54,217	Hoover, Herbert C.	95,089	Roosevelt, Franklin D.	2,300	40,872 D	35.8%	62.7%	36.3%	63.7%
1928	118,077	69,708	Hoover, Herbert C.	48,211	Smith, Alfred E.	158	21,497 R	59.0%	40.8%	59.1%	40.9%
1924	112,830	54,745	Coolidge, Calvin	48,542	Davis, John W.	9,543	6,203 R	48.5%	43.0%	53.0%	47.0%
1920	105,412	57,634	Harding, Warren G.	46,668	Cox, James M.	1,110	10,966 R	54.7%	44.3%	55.3%	44.7%

ELECTORAL COLLEGE VOTE 1920 TO 1984

Year	Total	Republican	Democratic	Other
1984	5	5	—	—
1980	4	4	—	—
1976	4	4	—	—
1972	4	4	—	—
1968	4	4	—	—
1964	4	—	4	—
1960	4	—	4	—
1956	4	4	—	—
1952	4	4	—	—
1948	4	—	4	—
1944	4	—	4	—
1940	3	—	3	—
1936	3	—	3	—
1932	3	—	3	—
1928	3	3	—	—
1924	3	3	—	—
1920	3	3	—	—

NEW MEXICO

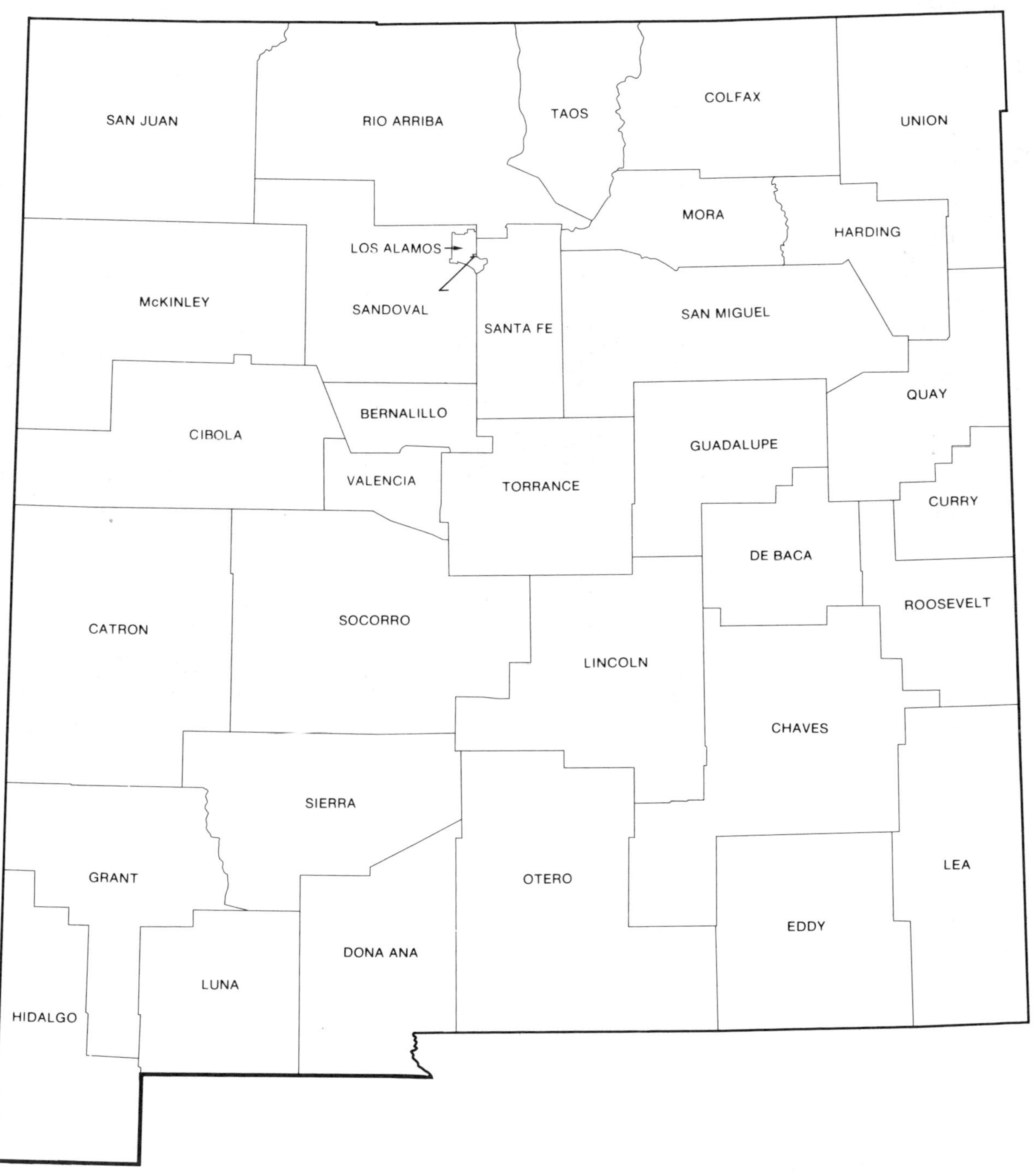
SAN JUAN
RIO ARRIBA
TAOS
COLFAX
UNION
MORA
HARDING
LOS ALAMOS
McKINLEY
SANDOVAL
SANTA FE
SAN MIGUEL
QUAY
BERNALILLO
CIBOLA
GUADALUPE
VALENCIA
TORRANCE
CURRY
DE BACA
ROOSEVELT
CATRON
SOCORRO
LINCOLN
CHAVES
SIERRA
LEA
GRANT
OTERO
EDDY
DONA ANA
LUNA
HIDALGO

NEW MEXICO

PRESIDENT 1984

1980 Census Population	County	Total Vote	Republican	Democratic	Other	Rep.-Dem. Plurality	Percentage Total Vote Rep.	Total Vote Dem.	Major Vote Rep.	Major Vote Dem.
419,700	BERNALILLO	174,262	104,694	67,789	1,779	36,905 R	60.1%	38.9%	60.7%	39.3%
2,720	CATRON	1,415	970	418	27	552 R	68.6%	29.5%	69.9%	30.1%
51,103	CHAVES	20,782	15,248	5,332	202	9,916 R	73.4%	25.7%	74.1%	25.9%
30,364	CIBOLA	6,740	3,578	3,140	22	438 R	53.1%	46.6%	53.3%	46.7%
13,667	COLFAX	5,485	2,994	2,435	56	559 R	54.6%	44.4%	55.1%	44.9%
42,019	CURRY	12,415	9,188	3,108	119	6,080 R	74.0%	25.0%	74.7%	25.3%
2,454	DE BACA	1,159	756	386	17	370 R	65.2%	33.3%	66.2%	33.8%
96,340	DONA ANA	36,393	22,153	13,878	362	8,275 R	60.9%	38.1%	61.5%	38.5%
47,855	EDDY	19,365	11,810	7,364	191	4,446 R	61.0%	38.0%	61.6%	38.4%
26,204	GRANT	10,840	4,979	5,755	106	776 D	45.9%	53.1%	46.4%	53.6%
4,496	GUADALUPE	1,966	990	946	30	44 R	50.4%	48.1%	51.1%	48.9%
1,090	HARDING	631	401	224	6	177 R	63.5%	35.5%	64.2%	35.8%
6,049	HIDALGO	2,161	1,282	860	19	422 R	59.3%	39.8%	59.9%	40.1%
55,993	LEA	19,357	14,569	4,558	230	10,011 R	75.3%	23.5%	76.2%	23.8%
10,997	LINCOLN	5,182	3,992	1,134	56	2,858 R	77.0%	21.9%	77.9%	22.1%
17,599	LOS ALAMOS	9,888	6,882	2,859	147	4,023 R	69.6%	28.9%	70.6%	29.4%
15,585	LUNA	6,776	4,145	2,557	74	1,588 R	61.2%	37.7%	61.8%	38.2%
56,449	MCKINLEY	14,643	6,557	7,915	171	1,358 D	44.8%	54.1%	45.3%	54.7%
4,205	MORA	2,287	1,017	1,235	35	218 D	44.5%	54.0%	45.2%	54.8%
44,665	OTERO	14,087	9,751	4,167	169	5,584 R	69.2%	29.6%	70.1%	29.9%
10,577	QUAY	4,253	2,842	1,368	43	1,474 R	66.8%	32.2%	67.5%	32.5%
29,282	RIO ARRIBA	11,146	4,116	6,938	92	2,822 D	36.9%	62.2%	37.2%	62.8%
15,695	ROOSEVELT	6,363	4,598	1,696	69	2,902 R	72.3%	26.7%	73.1%	26.9%
34,799	SANDOVAL	16,246	9,005	7,080	161	1,925 R	55.4%	43.6%	56.0%	44.0%
81,433	SAN JUAN	27,910	18,690	8,963	257	9,727 R	67.0%	32.1%	67.6%	32.4%
22,751	SAN MIGUEL	8,850	3,485	5,227	138	1,742 D	39.4%	59.1%	40.0%	60.0%
75,360	SANTA FE	34,552	15,886	18,262	404	2,376 D	46.0%	52.9%	46.5%	53.5%
8,454	SIERRA	4,035	2,663	1,335	37	1,328 R	66.0%	33.1%	66.6%	33.4%
12,566	SOCORRO	6,048	3,403	2,541	104	862 R	56.3%	42.0%	57.3%	42.7%
19,456	TAOS	9,432	4,154	5,144	134	990 D	44.0%	54.5%	44.7%	55.3%
7,491	TORRANCE	3,633	2,326	1,274	33	1,052 R	64.0%	35.1%	64.6%	35.4%
4,725	UNION	2,019	1,503	488	28	1,015 R	74.4%	24.2%	75.5%	24.5%
30,751	VALENCIA	14,049	8,474	5,393	182	3,081 R	60.3%	38.4%	61.1%	38.9%
1,302,894	TOTAL	514,370	307,101	201,769	5,500	105,332 R	59.7%	39.2%	60.3%	39.7%

NEW MEXICO

PRESIDENT 1980

1980 Census Population	County	Total Vote	Republican	Democratic	Other	Rep.-Dem. Plurality	Percentage: Total Vote Rep.	Total Vote Dem.	Major Vote Rep.	Major Vote Dem.
419,700	BERNALILLO	157,284	83,956	54,841	18,487	29,115 R	53.4%	34.9%	60.5%	39.5%
2,720	CATRON	1,448	906	466	76	440 R	62.6%	32.2%	66.0%	34.0%
51,103	CHAVES	18,657	12,502	5,350	805	7,152 R	67.0%	28.7%	70.0%	30.0%
	CIBOLA									
13,667	COLFAX	5,094	2,537	2,266	291	271 R	49.8%	44.5%	52.8%	47.2%
42,019	CURRY	12,070	8,132	3,622	316	4,510 R	67.4%	30.0%	69.2%	30.8%
2,454	DE BACA	1,167	655	484	28	171 R	56.1%	41.5%	57.5%	42.5%
96,340	DONA ANA	28,852	15,539	10,839	2,474	4,700 R	53.9%	37.6%	58.9%	41.1%
47,855	EDDY	17,417	9,817	7,028	572	2,789 R	56.4%	40.4%	58.3%	41.7%
26,204	GRANT	9,778	4,628	4,600	550	28 R	47.3%	47.0%	50.2%	49.8%
4,496	GUADALUPE	2,145	1,065	980	100	85 R	49.7%	45.7%	52.1%	47.9%
1,090	HARDING	601	356	225	20	131 R	59.2%	37.4%	61.3%	38.7%
6,049	HIDALGO	1,993	1,059	840	94	219 R	53.1%	42.1%	55.8%	44.2%
55,993	LEA	16,261	10,727	5,006	528	5,721 R	66.0%	30.8%	68.2%	31.8%
10,997	LINCOLN	4,393	3,009	1,127	257	1,882 R	68.5%	25.7%	72.8%	27.2%
17,599	LOS ALAMOS	9,383	5,460	2,368	1,555	3,092 R	58.2%	25.2%	69.7%	30.3%
15,585	LUNA	6,373	3,636	2,443	294	1,193 R	57.1%	38.3%	59.8%	40.2%
56,449	MCKINLEY	12,934	7,329	4,869	736	2,460 R	56.7%	37.6%	60.1%	39.9%
4,205	MORA	2,385	1,037	1,274	74	237 D	43.5%	53.4%	44.9%	55.1%
44,665	OTERO	11,995	7,210	4,111	674	3,099 R	60.1%	34.3%	63.7%	36.3%
10,577	QUAY	4,026	2,499	1,422	105	1,077 R	62.1%	35.3%	63.7%	36.3%
29,282	RIO ARRIBA	10,594	3,794	6,245	555	2,451 D	35.8%	58.9%	37.8%	62.2%
15,695	ROOSEVELT	6,497	3,950	2,240	307	1,710 R	60.8%	34.5%	63.8%	36.2%
34,799	SANDOVAL	12,597	6,762	4,740	1,095	2,022 R	53.7%	37.6%	58.8%	41.2%
81,433	SAN JUAN	23,556	15,579	6,705	1,272	8,874 R	66.1%	28.5%	69.9%	30.1%
22,751	SAN MIGUEL	8,369	3,292	4,514	563	1,222 D	39.3%	53.9%	42.2%	57.8%
75,360	SANTA FE	28,871	12,361	12,658	3,852	297 D	42.8%	43.8%	49.4%	50.6%
8,454	SIERRA	3,567	2,222	1,169	176	1,053 R	62.3%	32.8%	65.5%	34.5%
12,566	SOCORRO	5,427	2,685	2,226	516	459 R	49.5%	41.0%	54.7%	45.3%
19,456	TAOS	8,603	3,584	4,346	673	762 D	41.7%	50.5%	45.2%	54.8%
7,491	TORRANCE	3,322	1,907	1,261	154	646 R	57.4%	38.0%	60.2%	39.8%
4,725	UNION	2,140	1,407	675	58	732 R	65.7%	31.5%	67.6%	32.4%
61,115	VALENCIA	19,172	11,177	6,886	1,109	4,291 R	58.3%	35.9%	61.9%	38.1%
1,302,894	TOTAL	456,971	250,779	167,826	38,366	82,953 R	54.9%	36.7%	59.9%	40.1%

NEW MEXICO

PRESIDENT 1976

1970 Census Population	County	Total Vote	Republican	Democratic	Other	Rep.-Dem. Plurality	Percentage: Total Vote Rep.	Total Vote Dem.	Major Vote Rep.	Major Vote Dem.
315,774	BERNALILLO	142,921	76,614	63,949	2,358	12,665 R	53.6%	44.7%	54.5%	45.5%
2,198	CATRON	1,135	602	517	16	85 R	53.0%	45.6%	53.8%	46.2%
43,335	CHAVES	17,985	10,631	7,139	215	3,492 R	59.1%	39.7%	59.8%	40.2%
	CIBOLA									
12,170	COLFAX	5,018	2,259	2,718	41	459 D	45.0%	54.2%	45.4%	54.6%
39,517	CURRY	11,374	6,232	5,004	138	1,228 R	54.8%	44.0%	55.5%	44.5%
2,547	DE BACA	1,160	556	597	7	41 D	47.9%	51.5%	48.2%	51.8%
69,773	DONA ANA	26,261	13,888	12,036	337	1,852 R	52.9%	45.8%	53.6%	46.4%
41,119	EDDY	16,905	7,698	9,073	134	1,375 D	45.5%	53.7%	45.9%	54.1%
22,030	GRANT	9,349	4,095	5,176	78	1,081 D	43.8%	55.4%	44.2%	55.8%
4,969	GUADALUPE	2,456	1,047	1,379	30	332 D	42.6%	56.1%	43.2%	56.8%
1,348	HARDING	678	387	285	6	102 R	57.1%	42.0%	57.6%	42.4%
4,734	HIDALGO	1,837	891	938	8	47 D	48.5%	51.1%	48.7%	51.3%
49,554	LEA	15,457	8,773	6,533	151	2,240 R	56.8%	42.3%	57.3%	42.7%
7,560	LINCOLN	3,772	2,320	1,415	37	905 R	61.5%	37.5%	62.1%	37.9%
15,198	LOS ALAMOS	8,429	5,383	2,890	156	2,493 R	63.9%	34.3%	65.1%	34.9%
11,706	LUNA	5,914	2,966	2,872	76	94 R	50.2%	48.6%	50.8%	49.2%
43,208	MCKINLEY	11,624	4,617	6,856	151	2,239 D	39.7%	59.0%	40.2%	59.8%
4,673	MORA	2,361	904	1,438	19	534 D	38.3%	60.9%	38.6%	61.4%
41,097	OTERO	11,380	5,914	5,333	133	581 R	52.0%	46.9%	52.6%	47.4%
10,903	QUAY	4,197	2,059	2,095	43	36 D	49.1%	49.9%	49.6%	50.4%
25,170	RIO ARRIBA	10,455	3,213	7,125	117	3,912 D	30.7%	68.1%	31.1%	68.9%
16,479	ROOSEVELT	6,445	3,269	3,111	65	158 R	50.7%	48.3%	51.2%	48.8%
17,492	SANDOVAL	9,319	4,110	5,072	137	962 D	44.1%	54.4%	44.8%	55.2%
52,517	SAN JUAN	19,742	10,852	8,615	275	2,237 R	55.0%	43.6%	55.7%	44.3%
21,951	SAN MIGUEL	8,523	3,162	5,204	157	2,042 D	37.1%	61.1%	37.8%	62.2%
53,756	SANTA FE	26,165	11,576	14,127	462	2,551 D	44.2%	54.0%	45.0%	55.0%
7,189	SIERRA	3,264	1,665	1,564	35	101 R	51.0%	47.9%	51.6%	48.4%
9,763	SOCORRO	4,980	2,265	2,606	109	341 D	45.5%	52.3%	46.5%	53.5%
17,516	TAOS	7,532	3,012	4,414	106	1,402 D	40.0%	58.6%	40.6%	59.4%
5,290	TORRANCE	3,015	1,462	1,526	27	64 D	48.5%	50.6%	48.9%	51.1%
4,925	UNION	2,152	1,146	975	31	171 R	53.3%	45.3%	54.0%	46.0%
40,539	VALENCIA	16,604	7,851	8,566	187	715 D	47.3%	51.6%	47.8%	52.2%
1,016,000	TOTAL	418,409	211,419	201,148	5,842	10,271 R	50.5%	48.1%	51.2%	48.8%

NEW MEXICO

PRESIDENT 1972

1970 Census Population	County	Total Vote	Republican	Democratic	Other	Rep.-Dem. Plurality	Percentage Total Vote Rep.	Percentage Total Vote Dem.	Percentage Major Vote Rep.	Percentage Major Vote Dem.
315,774	BERNALILLO	131,703	79,993	48,753	2,957	31,240 R	60.7%	37.0%	62.1%	37.9%
2,198	CATRON	1,132	829	271	32	558 R	73.2%	23.9%	75.4%	24.6%
43,335	CHAVES	16,227	11,493	4,296	438	7,197 R	70.8%	26.5%	72.8%	27.2%
	CIBOLA									
12,170	COLFAX	4,603	2,663	1,855	85	808 R	57.9%	40.3%	58.9%	41.1%
39,517	CURRY	11,068	8,392	2,416	260	5,976 R	75.8%	21.8%	77.6%	22.4%
2,547	DE BACA	1,047	752	270	25	482 R	71.8%	25.8%	73.6%	26.4%
69,773	DONA ANA	24,397	14,562	9,416	419	5,146 R	59.7%	38.6%	60.7%	39.3%
41,119	EDDY	15,357	9,921	5,040	396	4,881 R	64.6%	32.8%	66.3%	33.7%
22,030	GRANT	8,784	4,431	4,081	272	350 R	50.4%	46.5%	52.1%	47.9%
4,969	GUADALUPE	2,525	1,297	1,202	26	95 R	51.4%	47.6%	51.9%	48.1%
1,348	HARDING	760	522	220	18	302 R	68.7%	28.9%	70.4%	29.6%
4,734	HIDALGO	1,657	1,051	562	44	489 R	63.4%	33.9%	65.2%	34.8%
49,554	LEA	16,343	12,478	3,429	436	9,049 R	76.4%	21.0%	78.4%	21.6%
7,560	LINCOLN	3,285	2,528	696	61	1,832 R	77.0%	21.2%	78.4%	21.6%
15,198	LOS ALAMOS	7,647	5,039	2,435	173	2,604 R	65.9%	31.8%	67.4%	32.6%
11,706	LUNA	4,680	2,958	1,560	162	1,398 R	63.2%	33.3%	65.5%	34.5%
43,208	MCKINLEY	10,798	5,366	5,124	308	242 R	49.7%	47.5%	51.2%	48.8%
4,673	MORA	2,318	1,165	1,135	18	30 R	50.3%	49.0%	50.7%	49.3%
41,097	OTERO	10,677	7,033	2,981	663	4,052 R	65.9%	27.9%	70.2%	29.8%
10,903	QUAY	4,522	3,224	1,161	137	2,063 R	71.3%	25.7%	73.5%	26.5%
25,170	RIO ARRIBA	10,195	4,351	5,642	202	1,291 D	42.7%	55.3%	43.5%	56.5%
16,479	ROOSEVELT	6,478	4,727	1,612	139	3,115 R	73.0%	24.9%	74.6%	25.4%
17,492	SANDOVAL	6,979	3,507	3,293	179	214 R	50.3%	47.2%	51.6%	48.4%
52,517	SAN JUAN	15,983	10,788	4,296	899	6,492 R	67.5%	26.9%	71.5%	28.5%
21,951	SAN MIGUEL	9,302	4,434	4,663	205	229 D	47.7%	50.1%	48.7%	51.3%
53,756	SANTA FE	23,258	12,211	10,761	286	1,450 R	52.5%	46.3%	53.2%	46.8%
7,189	SIERRA	3,075	2,074	934	67	1,140 R	67.4%	30.4%	68.9%	31.1%
9,763	SOCORRO	4,732	2,658	1,994	80	664 R	56.2%	42.1%	57.1%	42.9%
17,516	TAOS	7,164	3,617	3,472	75	145 R	50.5%	48.5%	51.0%	49.0%
5,290	TORRANCE	2,726	1,758	908	60	850 R	64.5%	33.3%	65.9%	34.1%
4,925	UNION	2,131	1,545	496	90	1,049 R	72.5%	23.3%	75.7%	24.3%
40,539	VALENCIA	14,688	8,239	6,110	339	2,129 R	56.1%	41.6%	57.4%	42.6%
1,016,000	TOTAL	386,241	235,606	141,084	9,551	94,522 R	61.0%	36.5%	62.5%	37.5%

NEW MEXICO

PRESIDENT 1968

1960 Census Population	County	Total Vote	Republican	Democratic	AIP	Other	Plurality	Percentage Rep.	Percentage Dem.	Percentage AIP
262,199	BERNALILLO	102,321	56,234	40,835	4,920	332	15,399 R	55.0%	39.9%	4.8%
2,773	CATRON	1,082	674	278	128	2	396 R	62.3%	25.7%	11.8%
57,649	CHAVES	13,938	8,866	3,612	1,425	35	5,254 R	63.6%	25.9%	10.2%
	CIBOLA									
13,806	COLFAX	4,983	2,212	2,477	263	31	265 D	44.4%	49.7%	5.3%
32,691	CURRY	10,304	5,562	2,915	1,754	73	2,647 R	54.0%	28.3%	17.0%
2,991	DE BACA	1,141	658	345	130	8	313 R	57.7%	30.2%	11.4%
59,948	DONA ANA	19,990	10,824	7,658	1,453	55	3,166 R	54.1%	38.3%	7.3%
50,783	EDDY	15,071	7,193	6,093	1,671	114	1,100 R	47.7%	40.4%	11.1%
18,700	GRANT	7,549	2,908	3,817	793	31	909 D	38.5%	50.6%	10.5%
5,610	GUADALUPE	2,288	1,176	1,027	77	8	149 R	51.4%	44.9%	3.4%
1,874	HARDING	780	450	284	44	2	166 R	57.7%	36.4%	5.6%
4,961	HIDALGO	1,544	606	678	257	3	72 D	39.2%	43.9%	16.6%
53,429	LEA	15,382	7,415	4,751	3,025	191	2,664 R	48.2%	30.9%	19.7%
7,744	LINCOLN	3,107	2,004	802	287	14	1,202 R	64.5%	25.8%	9.2%
13,037	LOS ALAMOS	6,288	3,447	2,552	268	21	895 R	54.8%	40.6%	4.3%
9,839	LUNA	3,896	1,952	1,438	490	16	514 R	50.1%	36.9%	12.6%
37,209	MCKINLEY	9,573	4,376	4,491	547	159	115 D	45.7%	46.9%	5.7%
6,028	MORA	2,266	1,155	1,069	35	7	86 R	51.0%	47.2%	1.5%
36,976	OTERO	10,229	4,475	3,978	1,688	88	497 R	43.7%	38.9%	16.5%
12,279	QUAY	4,132	2,123	1,399	567	43	724 R	51.4%	33.9%	13.7%
24,193	RIO ARRIBA	9,102	3,935	4,799	269	99	864 D	43.2%	52.7%	3.0%
16,198	ROOSEVELT	5,607	3,256	1,547	773	31	1,709 R	58.1%	27.6%	13.8%
14,201	SANDOVAL	4,731	1,959	2,609	129	34	650 D	41.4%	55.1%	2.7%
53,306	SAN JUAN	14,192	7,664	4,036	2,304	188	3,628 R	54.0%	28.4%	16.2%
23,468	SAN MIGUEL	8,368	4,027	4,088	195	58	61 D	48.1%	48.9%	2.3%
44,970	SANTA FE	19,475	9,359	9,544	492	80	185 D	48.1%	49.0%	2.5%
6,409	SIERRA	2,846	1,624	930	282	10	694 R	57.1%	32.7%	9.9%
10,168	SOCORRO	4,283	2,230	1,871	173	9	359 R	52.1%	43.7%	4.0%
15,934	TAOS	6,252	3,119	2,993	124	16	126 R	49.9%	47.9%	2.0%
6,497	TORRANCE	2,486	1,316	974	188	8	342 R	52.9%	39.2%	7.6%
6,068	UNION	2,197	1,217	678	279	23	539 R	55.4%	30.9%	12.7%
39,085	VALENCIA	11,947	5,676	5,513	707	51	163 R	47.5%	46.1%	5.9%
951,023	TOTAL	327,350	169,692	130,081	25,737	1,840	39,611 R	51.8%	39.7%	7.9%

NEW MEXICO

The new county of Cibola was created by the state legislature in 1981 from the western part of Valencia county.

ELECTION NOTES

1984 Other vote was 4,459 Bergland (Libertarian); 455 Johnson (Citizens); 224 Mason (Socialist Workers); 206 Dodge (Prohibition); 155 Serrette (Alliance); 1 scattered write-in.

1980 Other vote was 29,459 Anderson (Independent); 4,365 Clark (Libertarian); 2,202 Commoner (Citizens); 1,281 Bubar (Statesman); 325 Pulley (Socialist Workers); 734 scattered write-in.

1976 Other vote was 2,462 Camejo (Socialist Workers); 1,161 McCarthy (write-in); 1,110 MacBride (Libertarian); 240 Zeidler (Socialist); 211 Bubar (Prohibition); 106 Anderson (write-in); 31 Maddox (write-in); 19 Hall (write-in); 1 LaRouche (write-in); 501 scattered write-in.

1972 Other vote was 8,767 Schmitz (American Independent); 474 Jenness (Socialist Workers); 310 scattered write-in.

1968 Wallace on the ballot as American Independent. Other vote was 1,519 Chavez (People's Constitutional party); 252 Halstead (Socialist Workers); 69 scattered write-in.

NEW YORK

POPULAR VOTE FOR PRESIDENT 1920 TO 1984

Year	Total Vote	Republican Vote	Republican Candidate	Democratic Vote	Democratic Candidate	Other Vote	Plurality	Percentage Total Vote Rep.	Percentage Total Vote Dem.	Percentage Major Vote Rep.	Percentage Major Vote Dem.
1984	6,806,810	3,664,763	Reagan, Ronald	3,119,609	Mondale, Walter F.	22,438	545,154 R	53.8%	45.8%	54.0%	46.0%
1980	6,201,959	2,893,831	Reagan, Ronald	2,728,372	Carter, Jimmy	579,756	165,459 R	46.7%	44.0%	51.5%	48.5%
1976	6,534,170	3,100,791	Ford, Gerald R.	3,389,558	Carter, Jimmy	43,821	288,767 D	47.5%	51.9%	47.8%	52.2%
1972	7,165,919	4,192,778	Nixon, Richard M.	2,951,084	McGovern, George S.	22,057	1,241,694 R	58.5%	41.2%	58.7%	41.3%
1968	6,791,688	3,007,932	Nixon, Richard M.	3,378,470	Humphrey, Hubert H.	405,286	370,538 D	44.3%	49.7%	47.1%	52.9%
1964	7,166,275	2,243,559	Goldwater, Barry M.	4,913,102	Johnson, Lyndon B.	9,614	2,669,543 D	31.3%	68.6%	31.3%	68.7%
1960	7,291,079	3,446,419	Nixon, Richard M.	3,830,085	Kennedy, John F.	14,575	383,666 D	47.3%	52.5%	47.4%	52.6%
1956	7,095,971	4,345,506	Eisenhower, Dwight D.	2,747,944	Stevenson, Adlai E.	2,521	1,597,562 R	61.2%	38.7%	61.3%	38.7%
1952	7,128,239	3,952,813	Eisenhower, Dwight D.	3,104,601	Stevenson, Adlai E.	70,825	848,212 R	55.5%	43.6%	56.0%	44.0%
1948	6,177,337	2,841,163	Dewey, Thomas E.	2,780,204	Truman, Harry S.	555,970	60,959 R	46.0%	45.0%	50.5%	49.5%
1944	6,316,790	2,987,647	Dewey, Thomas E.	3,304,238	Roosevelt, Franklin D.	24,905	316,591 D	47.3%	52.3%	47.5%	52.5%
1940	6,301,596	3,027,478	Willkie, Wendell	3,251,918	Roosevelt, Franklin D.	22,200	224,440 D	48.0%	51.6%	48.2%	51.8%
1936	5,596,398	2,180,670	Landon, Alfred M.	3,293,222	Roosevelt, Franklin D.	122,506	1,112,552 D	39.0%	58.8%	39.8%	60.2%
1932	4,688,614	1,937,963	Hoover, Herbert C.	2,534,959	Roosevelt, Franklin D.	215,692	596,996 D	41.3%	54.1%	43.3%	56.7%
1928	4,405,626	2,193,344	Hoover, Herbert C.	2,089,863	Smith, Alfred E.	122,419	103,481 R	49.8%	47.4%	51.2%	48.8%
1924 **	3,263,939	1,820,058	Coolidge, Calvin	950,796	Davis, John W.	493,085	869,262 R	55.8%	29.1%	65.7%	34.3%
1920	2,898,513	1,871,167	Harding, Warren G.	781,238	Cox, James M.	246,108	1,089,929 R	64.6%	27.0%	70.5%	29.5%

In 1924 other vote was 474,913 Progressive; 9,928 Socialist Labor and 8,244 Communist.

ELECTORAL COLLEGE VOTE 1920 TO 1984

Year	Total	Republican	Democratic	Other
1984	36	36	—	—
1980	41	41	—	—
1976	41	—	41	—
1972	41	41	—	—
1968	43	—	43	—
1964	43	—	43	—
1960	45	—	45	—
1956	45	45	—	—
1952	45	45	—	—
1948	47	47	—	—
1944	47	—	47	—
1940	47	—	47	—
1936	47	—	47	—
1932	47	—	47	—
1928	45	45	—	—
1924	45	45	—	—
1920	45	45	—	—

NEW YORK

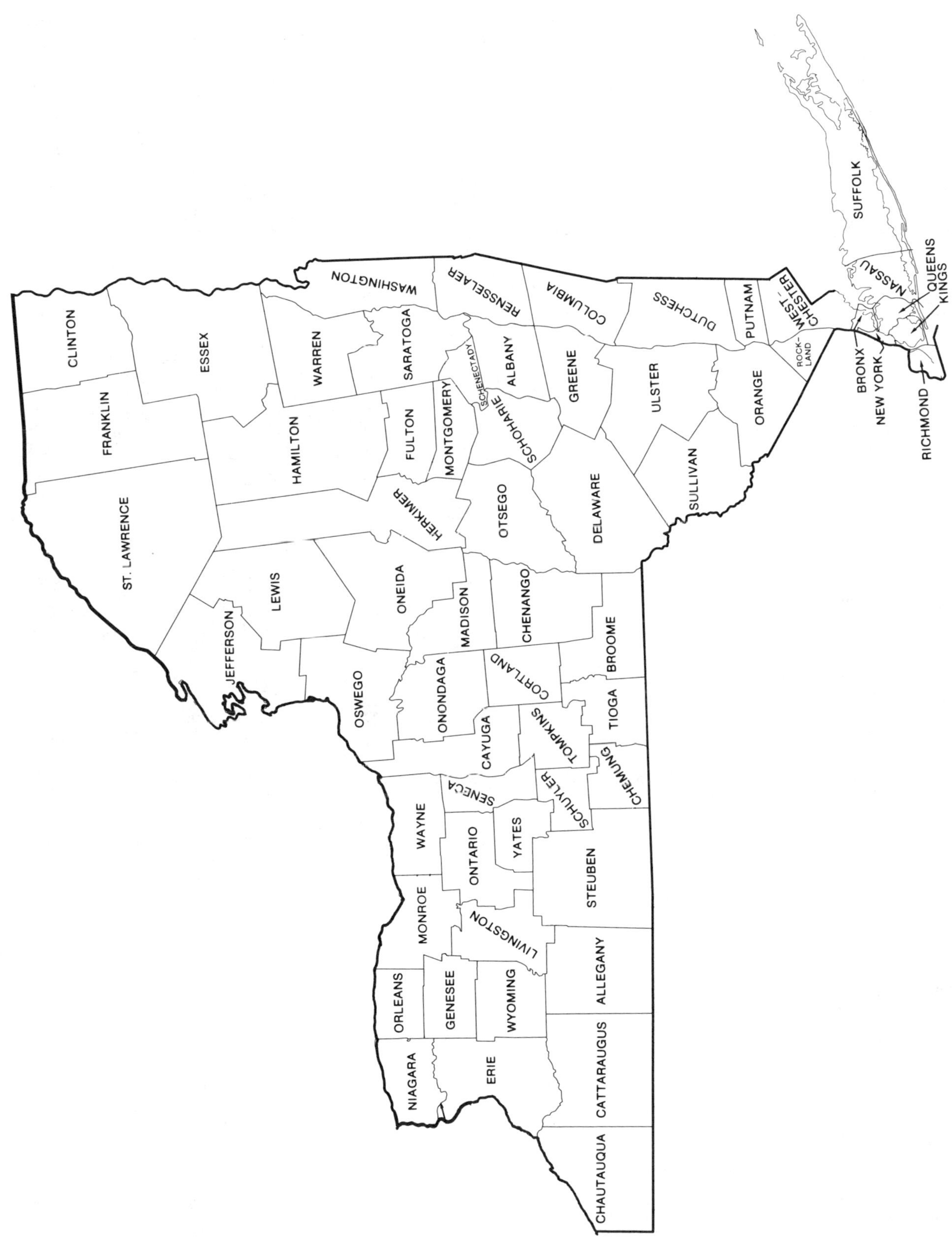
SUFFOLK
NASSAU
QUEENS
KINGS
BRONX
NEW YORK
RICHMOND
WESTCHESTER
ROCKLAND
PUTNAM
DUTCHESS
COLUMBIA
RENSSELAER
WASHINGTON
CLINTON
ESSEX
WARREN
SARATOGA
SCHENECTADY
ALBANY
GREENE
ULSTER
ORANGE
FRANKLIN
HAMILTON
FULTON
MONTGOMERY
SCHOHARIE
SULLIVAN
DELAWARE
ST. LAWRENCE
HERKIMER
OTSEGO
LEWIS
ONEIDA
MADISON
CHENANGO
JEFFERSON
BROOME
OSWEGO
ONONDAGA
CORTLAND
TIOGA
TOMPKINS
CAYUGA
CHEMUNG
SCHUYLER
SENECA
WAYNE
ONTARIO
YATES
STEUBEN
MONROE
LIVINGSTON
ORLEANS
GENESEE
WYOMING
ALLEGANY
NIAGARA
ERIE
CATTARAUGUS
CHAUTAUQUA

NEW YORK

PRESIDENT 1984

1980 Census Population	County	Total Vote	Republican	Democratic	Other	Rep.-Dem. Plurality	Percentage Total Vote Rep.	Total Vote Dem.	Major Vote Rep.	Major Vote Dem.
285,909	ALBANY	150,592	74,542	75,447	603	905 D	49.5%	50.1%	49.7%	50.3%
51,742	ALLEGANY	19,304	14,527	4,720	57	9,807 R	75.3%	24.5%	75.5%	24.5%
1,168,972	BRONX	333,683	109,308	223,112	1,263	113,804 D	32.8%	66.9%	32.9%	67.1%
213,648	BROOME	96,089	58,109	37,658	322	20,451 R	60.5%	39.2%	60.7%	39.3%
85,697	CATTARAUGUS	34,468	24,162	10,194	112	13,968 R	70.1%	29.6%	70.3%	29.7%
79,894	CAYUGA	33,779	21,451	12,207	121	9,244 R	63.5%	36.1%	63.7%	36.3%
146,925	CHAUTAUQUA	62,724	39,597	22,986	141	16,611 R	63.1%	36.6%	63.3%	36.7%
97,656	CHEMUNG	39,647	24,909	14,638	100	10,271 R	62.8%	36.9%	63.0%	37.0%
49,344	CHENANGO	20,648	14,254	6,343	51	7,911 R	69.0%	30.7%	69.2%	30.8%
80,750	CLINTON	30,443	19,549	10,804	90	8,745 R	64.2%	35.5%	64.4%	35.6%
59,487	COLUMBIA	27,891	18,814	8,960	117	9,854 R	67.5%	32.1%	67.7%	32.3%
48,820	CORTLAND	20,224	13,691	6,438	95	7,253 R	67.7%	31.8%	68.0%	32.0%
46,824	DELAWARE	19,830	14,002	5,745	83	8,257 R	70.6%	29.0%	70.9%	29.1%
245,055	DUTCHESS	103,580	70,324	32,867	389	37,457 R	67.9%	31.7%	68.1%	31.9%
1,015,472	ERIE	461,671	222,882	237,631	1,158	14,749 D	48.3%	51.5%	48.4%	51.6%
36,176	ESSEX	17,320	12,114	5,119	87	6,995 R	69.9%	29.6%	70.3%	29.7%
44,929	FRANKLIN	17,064	10,617	6,400	47	4,217 R	62.2%	37.5%	62.4%	37.6%
55,153	FULTON	22,618	14,887	7,644	87	7,243 R	65.8%	33.8%	66.1%	33.9%
59,400	GENESEE	25,210	16,582	8,549	79	8,033 R	65.8%	33.9%	66.0%	34.0%
40,861	GREENE	20,070	14,150	5,858	62	8,292 R	70.5%	29.2%	70.7%	29.3%
5,034	HAMILTON	3,382	2,637	737	8	1,900 R	78.0%	21.8%	78.2%	21.8%
66,714	HERKIMER	29,258	18,827	10,346	85	8,481 R	64.3%	35.4%	64.5%	35.5%
88,151	JEFFERSON	34,496	23,445	10,960	91	12,485 R	68.0%	31.8%	68.1%	31.9%
2,230,936	KINGS	600,771	230,064	368,518	2,189	138,454 D	38.3%	61.3%	38.4%	61.6%
25,035	LEWIS	9,860	7,069	2,757	34	4,312 R	71.7%	28.0%	71.9%	28.1%
57,006	LIVINGSTON	23,892	16,389	7,399	104	8,990 R	68.6%	31.0%	68.9%	31.1%
65,150	MADISON	25,963	17,568	8,291	104	9,277 R	67.7%	31.9%	67.9%	32.1%
702,238	MONROE	316,277	182,696	132,109	1,472	50,587 R	57.8%	41.8%	58.0%	42.0%
53,439	MONTGOMERY	23,520	14,398	9,044	78	5,354 R	61.2%	38.5%	61.4%	38.6%
1,321,582	NASSAU	634,063	392,017	240,697	1,349	151,320 R	61.8%	38.0%	62.0%	38.0%
1,428,285	NEW YORK	526,671	144,281	379,521	2,869	235,240 D	27.4%	72.1%	27.5%	72.5%
227,354	NIAGARA	92,858	51,289	41,368	201	9,921 R	55.2%	44.5%	55.4%	44.6%
253,466	ONEIDA	108,269	65,377	42,603	289	22,774 R	60.4%	39.3%	60.5%	39.5%
463,920	ONONDAGA	204,314	121,857	81,777	680	40,080 R	59.6%	40.0%	59.8%	40.2%
88,909	ONTARIO	37,494	24,507	12,844	143	11,663 R	65.4%	34.3%	65.6%	34.4%
259,603	ORANGE	102,413	69,413	32,663	337	36,750 R	67.8%	31.9%	68.0%	32.0%
38,496	ORLEANS	15,024	10,543	4,429	52	6,114 R	70.2%	29.5%	70.4%	29.6%
113,901	OSWEGO	46,034	31,481	14,347	206	17,134 R	68.4%	31.2%	68.7%	31.3%
59,075	OTSEGO	26,511	16,777	9,582	152	7,195 R	63.3%	36.1%	63.6%	36.4%
77,193	PUTNAM	35,277	25,707	9,473	97	16,234 R	72.9%	26.9%	73.1%	26.9%
1,891,325	QUEENS	615,578	285,477	328,379	1,722	42,902 D	46.4%	53.3%	46.5%	53.5%
151,966	RENSSELAER	70,864	43,892	26,755	217	17,137 R	61.9%	37.8%	62.1%	37.9%
352,121	RICHMOND	127,826	83,187	44,345	294	38,842 R	65.1%	34.7%	65.2%	34.8%
259,530	ROCKLAND	115,018	70,020	44,687	311	25,333 R	60.9%	38.9%	61.0%	39.0%
114,254	ST. LAWRENCE	42,149	26,062	15,963	124	10,099 R	61.8%	37.9%	62.0%	38.0%
153,759	SARATOGA	69,788	47,394	22,166	228	25,228 R	67.9%	31.8%	68.1%	31.9%
149,946	SCHENECTADY	73,697	42,808	30,612	277	12,196 R	58.1%	41.5%	58.3%	41.7%
29,710	SCHOHARIE	12,788	8,692	3,996	100	4,696 R	68.0%	31.2%	68.5%	31.5%
17,686	SCHUYLER	7,660	5,207	2,422	31	2,785 R	68.0%	31.6%	68.3%	31.7%
33,733	SENECA	14,307	9,420	4,825	62	4,595 R	65.8%	33.7%	66.1%	33.9%
99,217	STEUBEN	39,417	28,848	10,471	98	18,377 R	73.2%	26.6%	73.4%	26.6%
1,284,231	SUFFOLK	508,056	335,485	171,295	1,276	164,190 R	66.0%	33.7%	66.2%	33.8%
65,155	SULLIVAN	28,590	18,037	10,475	78	7,562 R	63.1%	36.6%	63.3%	36.7%
49,812	TIOGA	20,817	14,856	5,860	101	8,996 R	71.4%	28.2%	71.7%	28.3%
87,085	TOMPKINS	37,777	18,255	19,357	165	1,102 D	48.3%	51.2%	48.5%	51.5%
158,158	ULSTER	74,102	47,372	26,445	285	20,927 R	63.9%	35.7%	64.2%	35.8%
54,854	WARREN	23,568	17,616	5,886	66	11,730 R	74.7%	25.0%	75.0%	25.0%
54,795	WASHINGTON	22,563	16,580	5,909	74	10,671 R	73.5%	26.2%	73.7%	26.3%
84,581	WAYNE	34,051	24,171	9,700	180	14,471 R	71.0%	28.5%	71.4%	28.6%
866,599	WESTCHESTER	390,308	229,005	160,225	1,078	68,780 R	58.7%	41.1%	58.8%	41.2%
39,895	WYOMING	15,622	11,199	4,381	42	6,818 R	71.7%	28.0%	71.9%	28.1%
21,459	YATES	9,062	6,367	2,670	25	3,697 R	70.3%	29.5%	70.5%	29.5%
17,558,072	TOTAL	6,806,810	3,664,763	3,119,609	22,438	545,154 R	53.8%	45.8%	54.0%	46.0%

NEW YORK

PRESIDENT 1980

1980 Census Population	County	Total Vote	Republican	Democratic	Other	Rep.-Dem. Plurality	Percentage Total Vote Rep.	Total Vote Dem.	Major Vote Rep.	Major Vote Dem.
285,909	ALBANY	144,364	52,354	74,429	17,581	22,075 D	36.3%	51.6%	41.3%	58.7%
51,742	ALLEGANY	17,640	10,423	5,879	1,338	4,544 R	59.1%	33.3%	63.9%	36.1%
1,168,972	BRONX	282,847	86,843	181,090	14,914	94,247 D	30.7%	64.0%	32.4%	67.6%
213,648	BROOME	89,280	39,275	37,013	12,992	2,262 R	44.0%	41.5%	51.5%	48.5%
85,697	CATTARAUGUS	32,709	17,222	12,917	2,570	4,305 R	52.7%	39.5%	57.1%	42.9%
79,894	CAYUGA	32,756	17,945	11,708	3,103	6,237 R	54.8%	35.7%	60.5%	39.5%
146,925	CHAUTAUQUA	58,756	30,081	22,871	5,804	7,210 R	51.2%	38.9%	56.8%	43.2%
97,656	CHEMUNG	37,209	19,674	14,565	2,970	5,109 R	52.9%	39.1%	57.5%	42.5%
49,344	CHENANGO	19,592	10,400	6,917	2,275	3,483 R	53.1%	35.3%	60.1%	39.9%
80,750	CLINTON	26,890	13,120	11,498	2,272	1,622 R	48.8%	42.8%	53.3%	46.7%
59,487	COLUMBIA	26,274	13,946	9,500	2,828	4,446 R	53.1%	36.2%	59.5%	40.5%
48,820	CORTLAND	18,048	9,885	6,176	1,987	3,709 R	54.8%	34.2%	61.5%	38.5%
46,824	DELAWARE	19,164	10,609	6,333	2,222	4,276 R	55.4%	33.0%	62.6%	37.4%
245,055	DUTCHESS	93,007	53,616	28,616	10,775	25,000 R	57.6%	30.8%	65.2%	34.8%
1,015,472	ERIE	420,473	169,209	215,283	35,981	46,074 D	40.2%	51.2%	44.0%	56.0%
36,176	ESSEX	16,978	9,025	6,443	1,510	2,582 R	53.2%	37.9%	58.3%	41.7%
44,929	FRANKLIN	16,292	7,620	7,281	1,391	339 R	46.8%	44.7%	51.1%	48.9%
55,153	FULTON	21,522	11,448	8,105	1,969	3,343 R	53.2%	37.7%	58.5%	41.5%
59,400	GENESEE	24,489	11,650	10,677	2,162	973 R	47.6%	43.6%	52.2%	47.8%
40,861	GREENE	19,498	11,286	6,488	1,724	4,798 R	57.9%	33.3%	63.5%	36.5%
5,034	HAMILTON	3,230	2,038	925	267	1,113 R	63.1%	28.6%	68.8%	31.2%
66,714	HERKIMER	27,888	14,105	11,497	2,286	2,608 R	50.6%	41.2%	55.1%	44.9%
88,151	JEFFERSON	33,128	16,455	13,271	3,402	3,184 R	49.7%	40.1%	55.4%	44.6%
2,230,936	KINGS	521,109	200,306	288,893	31,910	88,587 D	38.4%	55.4%	40.9%	59.1%
25,035	LEWIS	9,822	4,937	3,973	912	964 R	50.3%	40.5%	55.4%	44.6%
57,006	LIVINGSTON	22,454	11,193	9,030	2,231	2,163 R	49.8%	40.2%	55.3%	44.7%
65,150	MADISON	23,937	13,369	7,843	2,725	5,526 R	55.9%	32.8%	63.0%	37.0%
702,238	MONROE	306,733	128,615	142,423	35,695	13,808 D	41.9%	46.4%	47.5%	52.5%
53,439	MONTGOMERY	24,088	11,917	9,645	2,526	2,272 R	49.5%	40.0%	55.3%	44.7%
1,321,582	NASSAU	596,154	333,567	207,602	54,985	125,965 R	56.0%	34.8%	61.6%	38.4%
1,428,285	NEW YORK	441,901	115,911	275,742	50,248	159,831 D	26.2%	62.4%	29.6%	70.4%
227,354	NIAGARA	86,409	38,760	40,405	7,244	1,645 D	44.9%	46.8%	49.0%	51.0%
253,466	ONEIDA	104,799	51,968	44,292	8,539	7,676 R	49.6%	42.3%	54.0%	46.0%
463,920	ONONDAGA	193,372	97,887	73,453	22,032	24,434 R	50.6%	38.0%	57.1%	42.9%
88,909	ONTARIO	35,506	17,036	14,477	3,993	2,559 R	48.0%	40.8%	54.1%	45.9%
259,603	ORANGE	90,470	51,268	30,022	9,180	21,246 R	56.7%	33.2%	63.1%	36.9%
38,496	ORLEANS	14,611	7,536	5,767	1,308	1,769 R	51.6%	39.5%	56.6%	43.4%
113,901	OSWEGO	42,541	22,816	15,343	4,382	7,473 R	53.6%	36.1%	59.8%	40.2%
59,075	OTSEGO	23,907	11,814	8,795	3,298	3,019 R	49.4%	36.8%	57.3%	42.7%
77,193	PUTNAM	31,819	20,193	8,691	2,935	11,502 R	63.5%	27.3%	69.9%	30.1%
1,891,325	QUEENS	560,923	251,333	269,147	40,443	17,814 D	44.8%	48.0%	48.3%	51.7%
151,966	RENSSELAER	69,747	32,005	29,880	7,862	2,125 R	45.9%	42.8%	51.7%	48.3%
352,121	RICHMOND	110,651	64,885	37,306	8,460	27,579 R	58.6%	33.7%	63.5%	36.5%
259,530	ROCKLAND	104,995	59,068	35,277	10,650	23,791 R	56.3%	33.6%	62.6%	37.4%
114,254	ST. LAWRENCE	39,624	18,437	17,006	4,181	1,431 R	46.5%	42.9%	52.0%	48.0%
153,759	SARATOGA	65,362	34,184	23,641	7,537	10,543 R	52.3%	36.2%	59.1%	40.9%
149,946	SCHENECTADY	70,534	32,003	29,932	8,599	2,071 R	45.4%	42.4%	51.7%	48.3%
29,710	SCHOHARIE	12,262	6,382	4,715	1,165	1,667 R	52.0%	38.5%	57.5%	42.5%
17,686	SCHUYLER	6,957	3,838	2,514	605	1,324 R	55.2%	36.1%	60.4%	39.6%
33,733	SENECA	13,690	7,174	5,010	1,506	2,164 R	52.4%	36.6%	58.9%	41.1%
99,217	STEUBEN	38,170	22,418	12,826	2,926	9,592 R	58.7%	33.6%	63.6%	36.4%
1,284,231	SUFFOLK	449,655	256,294	149,945	43,416	106,349 R	57.0%	33.3%	63.1%	36.9%
65,155	SULLIVAN	27,218	15,089	9,553	2,576	5,536 R	55.4%	35.1%	61.2%	38.8%
49,812	TIOGA	19,214	10,291	6,690	2,233	3,601 R	53.6%	34.8%	60.6%	39.4%
87,085	TOMPKINS	29,668	12,448	11,970	5,250	478 R	42.0%	40.3%	51.0%	49.0%
158,158	ULSTER	66,726	36,709	22,179	7,838	14,530 R	55.0%	33.2%	62.3%	37.7%
54,854	WARREN	22,377	13,264	6,971	2,142	6,293 R	59.3%	31.2%	65.5%	34.5%
54,795	WASHINGTON	21,906	12,835	7,144	1,927	5,691 R	58.6%	32.6%	64.2%	35.8%
84,581	WAYNE	32,512	16,498	12,590	3,424	3,908 R	50.7%	38.7%	56.7%	43.3%
866,599	WESTCHESTER	365,166	198,552	130,136	36,478	68,416 R	54.4%	35.6%	60.4%	39.6%
39,895	WYOMING	14,552	8,108	5,234	1,210	2,874 R	55.7%	36.0%	60.8%	39.2%
21,459	YATES	8,384	4,694	2,828	862	1,866 R	56.0%	33.7%	62.4%	37.6%
17,558,072	TOTAL	6,201,959	2,893,831	2,728,372	579,756	165,459 R	46.7%	44.0%	51.5%	48.5%

NEW YORK

PRESIDENT 1976

1970 Census Population	County	Total Vote	Republican	Democratic	Other	Rep.-Dem. Plurality	Percentage Total Vote Rep.	Total Vote Dem.	Major Vote Rep.	Major Vote Dem.
285,618	ALBANY	142,409	69,592	71,616	1,201	2,024 D	48.9%	50.3%	49.3%	50.7%
46,458	ALLEGANY	18,010	11,769	6,134	107	5,635 R	65.3%	34.1%	65.7%	34.3%
1,472,216	BRONX	337,391	96,842	238,786	1,763	141,944 D	28.7%	70.8%	28.9%	71.1%
221,815	BROOME	90,658	50,340	39,827	491	10,513 R	55.5%	43.9%	55.8%	44.2%
81,666	CATTARAUGUS	33,422	19,469	13,768	185	5,701 R	58.3%	41.2%	58.6%	41.4%
77,439	CAYUGA	33,343	19,775	13,348	220	6,427 R	59.3%	40.0%	59.7%	40.3%
147,305	CHAUTAUQUA	61,436	33,730	27,447	259	6,283 R	54.9%	44.7%	55.1%	44.9%
101,537	CHEMUNG	38,026	20,640	17,207	179	3,433 R	54.3%	45.3%	54.5%	45.5%
46,368	CHENANGO	19,837	12,384	7,356	97	5,028 R	62.4%	37.1%	62.7%	37.3%
72,934	CLINTON	27,103	15,433	11,555	115	3,878 R	56.9%	42.6%	57.2%	42.8%
51,519	COLUMBIA	26,574	15,871	10,514	189	5,357 R	59.7%	39.6%	60.2%	39.8%
45,894	CORTLAND	18,300	11,222	6,947	131	4,275 R	61.3%	38.0%	61.8%	38.2%
44,718	DELAWARE	19,827	12,443	7,254	130	5,189 R	62.8%	36.6%	63.2%	36.8%
222,295	DUTCHESS	89,505	51,312	37,531	662	13,781 R	57.3%	41.9%	57.8%	42.2%
1,113,491	ERIE	452,843	220,310	229,397	3,136	9,087 D	48.7%	50.7%	49.0%	51.0%
34,631	ESSEX	16,824	10,194	6,556	74	3,638 R	60.6%	39.0%	60.9%	39.1%
43,931	FRANKLIN	16,152	8,846	7,248	58	1,598 R	54.8%	44.9%	55.0%	45.0%
52,637	FULTON	21,629	12,161	9,323	145	2,838 R	56.2%	43.1%	56.6%	43.4%
58,722	GENESEE	25,536	14,567	10,803	166	3,764 R	57.0%	42.3%	57.4%	42.6%
33,136	GREENE	19,264	11,370	7,740	154	3,630 R	59.0%	40.2%	59.5%	40.5%
4,714	HAMILTON	3,370	2,306	1,052	12	1,254 R	68.4%	31.2%	68.7%	31.3%
67,440	HERKIMER	28,377	15,362	12,875	140	2,487 R	54.1%	45.4%	54.4%	45.6%
88,508	JEFFERSON	34,028	20,401	13,503	124	6,898 R	60.0%	39.7%	60.2%	39.8%
2,601,852	KINGS	613,643	190,728	419,382	3,533	228,654 D	31.1%	68.3%	31.3%	68.7%
23,644	LEWIS	9,633	5,840	3,764	29	2,076 R	60.6%	39.1%	60.8%	39.2%
54,041	LIVINGSTON	23,819	14,044	9,629	146	4,415 R	59.0%	40.4%	59.3%	40.7%
62,864	MADISON	24,591	15,674	8,822	95	6,852 R	63.7%	35.9%	64.0%	36.0%
711,917	MONROE	303,434	167,303	134,739	1,392	32,564 R	55.1%	44.4%	55.4%	44.6%
55,883	MONTGOMERY	24,730	13,281	11,271	178	2,010 R	53.7%	45.6%	54.1%	45.9%
1,422,905	NASSAU	637,438	329,176	302,869	5,393	26,307 R	51.6%	47.5%	52.1%	47.9%
1,524,541	NEW YORK	460,838	117,702	337,438	5,698	219,736 D	25.5%	73.2%	25.9%	74.1%
235,720	NIAGARA	90,239	46,101	43,667	471	2,434 R	51.1%	48.4%	51.4%	48.6%
273,037	ONEIDA	105,988	57,655	47,779	554	9,876 R	54.4%	45.1%	54.7%	45.3%
472,185	ONONDAGA	192,578	115,474	76,097	1,007	39,377 R	60.0%	39.5%	60.3%	39.7%
78,849	ONTARIO	35,441	21,118	14,044	279	7,074 R	59.6%	39.6%	60.1%	39.9%
220,558	ORANGE	90,677	49,685	40,362	630	9,323 R	54.8%	44.5%	55.2%	44.8%
37,305	ORLEANS	15,023	8,994	5,927	102	3,067 R	59.9%	39.5%	60.3%	39.7%
100,897	OSWEGO	40,463	23,949	16,332	182	7,617 R	59.2%	40.4%	59.5%	40.5%
56,181	OTSEGO	24,754	14,796	9,787	171	5,009 R	59.8%	39.5%	60.2%	39.8%
56,696	PUTNAM	30,711	18,523	11,963	225	6,560 R	60.3%	39.0%	60.8%	39.2%
1,973,708	QUEENS	627,352	244,396	379,907	3,049	135,511 D	39.0%	60.6%	39.1%	60.9%
152,510	RENSSELAER	69,653	40,229	28,979	445	11,250 R	57.8%	41.6%	58.1%	41.9%
295,443	RICHMOND	105,477	56,995	47,867	615	9,128 R	54.0%	45.4%	54.4%	45.6%
229,903	ROCKLAND	101,489	52,087	48,673	729	3,414 R	51.3%	48.0%	51.7%	48.3%
111,991	ST. LAWRENCE	39,934	22,249	17,503	182	4,746 R	55.7%	43.8%	56.0%	44.0%
121,679	SARATOGA	62,486	38,296	23,768	422	14,528 R	61.3%	38.0%	61.7%	38.3%
160,979	SCHENECTADY	73,450	40,789	31,838	823	8,951 R	55.5%	43.3%	56.2%	43.8%
24,750	SCHOHARIE	12,515	7,154	5,250	111	1,904 R	57.2%	41.9%	57.7%	42.3%
16,737	SCHUYLER	7,189	4,267	2,885	37	1,382 R	59.4%	40.1%	59.7%	40.3%
35,083	SENECA	13,508	7,659	5,745	104	1,914 R	56.7%	42.5%	57.1%	42.9%
99,546	STEUBEN	38,015	23,164	14,685	166	8,479 R	60.9%	38.6%	61.2%	38.8%
1,116,672	SUFFOLK	460,048	248,908	208,263	2,877	40,645 R	54.1%	45.3%	54.4%	45.6%
52,580	SULLIVAN	28,096	13,709	14,189	198	480 D	48.8%	50.5%	49.1%	50.9%
46,513	TIOGA	18,893	11,824	6,969	100	4,855 R	62.6%	36.9%	62.9%	37.1%
76,879	TOMPKINS	28,671	15,463	12,808	400	2,655 R	53.9%	44.7%	54.7%	45.3%
141,241	ULSTER	66,155	35,353	30,190	612	5,163 R	53.4%	45.6%	53.9%	46.1%
49,402	WARREN	21,912	14,548	7,264	100	7,284 R	66.4%	33.2%	66.7%	33.3%
52,725	WASHINGTON	21,324	13,946	7,262	116	6,684 R	65.4%	34.1%	65.8%	34.2%
79,404	WAYNE	31,562	19,324	12,061	177	7,263 R	61.2%	38.2%	61.6%	38.4%
891,409	WESTCHESTER	384,296	208,527	173,153	2,616	35,374 R	54.3%	45.1%	54.6%	45.4%
37,688	WYOMING	15,539	9,726	5,737	76	3,989 R	62.6%	36.9%	62.9%	37.1%
19,831	YATES	8,742	5,796	2,903	43	2,893 R	66.3%	33.2%	66.6%	33.4%
18,190,740	TOTAL	6,534,170	3,100,791	3,389,558	43,821	288,767 D	47.5%	51.9%	47.8%	52.2%

NEW YORK

PRESIDENT 1972

1970 Census Population	County	Total Vote	Republican	Democratic	Other	Rep.-Dem. Plurality	Percentage			
							Total Vote		Major Vote	
							Rep.	Dem.	Rep.	Dem.
285,618	ALBANY	149,562	81,848	67,297	417	14,551 R	54.7%	45.0%	54.9%	45.1%
46,458	ALLEGANY	18,320	13,426	4,812	82	8,614 R	73.3%	26.3%	73.6%	26.4%
1,472,216	BRONX	441,199	196,754	243,345	1,100	46,591 D	44.6%	55.2%	44.7%	55.3%
221,815	BROOME	93,135	55,736	37,154	245	18,582 R	59.8%	39.9%	60.0%	40.0%
81,666	CATTARAUGUS	32,950	21,906	10,909	135	10,997 R	66.5%	33.1%	66.8%	33.2%
77,439	CAYUGA	34,030	22,774	11,097	159	11,677 R	66.9%	32.6%	67.2%	32.8%
147,305	CHAUTAUQUA	63,583	37,158	26,253	172	10,905 R	58.4%	41.3%	58.6%	41.4%
101,537	CHEMUNG	38,944	26,200	12,650	94	13,550 R	67.3%	32.5%	67.4%	32.6%
46,368	CHENANGO	19,509	13,770	5,695	44	8,075 R	70.6%	29.2%	70.7%	29.3%
72,934	CLINTON	26,844	17,048	9,703	93	7,345 R	63.5%	36.1%	63.7%	36.3%
51,519	COLUMBIA	25,643	17,995	7,558	90	10,437 R	70.2%	29.5%	70.4%	29.6%
45,894	CORTLAND	18,180	12,885	5,234	61	7,651 R	70.9%	28.8%	71.1%	28.9%
44,718	DELAWARE	20,449	15,136	5,243	70	9,893 R	74.0%	25.6%	74.3%	25.7%
222,295	DUTCHESS	92,987	64,864	27,872	251	36,992 R	69.8%	30.0%	69.9%	30.1%
1,113,491	ERIE	476,424	256,462	218,105	1,857	38,357 R	53.8%	45.8%	54.0%	46.0%
34,631	ESSEX	16,759	11,763	4,955	41	6,808 R	70.2%	29.6%	70.4%	29.6%
43,931	FRANKLIN	16,282	10,959	5,266	57	5,693 R	67.3%	32.3%	67.5%	32.5%
52,637	FULTON	22,599	15,200	7,303	96	7,897 R	67.3%	32.3%	67.5%	32.5%
58,722	GENESEE	25,843	17,107	8,631	105	8,476 R	66.2%	33.4%	66.5%	33.5%
33,136	GREENE	19,675	14,313	5,260	102	9,053 R	72.7%	26.7%	73.1%	26.9%
4,714	HAMILTON	3,334	2,597	731	6	1,866 R	77.9%	21.9%	78.0%	22.0%
67,440	HERKIMER	29,775	20,194	9,487	94	10,707 R	67.8%	31.9%	68.0%	32.0%
88,508	JEFFERSON	34,827	23,123	11,629	75	11,494 R	66.4%	33.4%	66.5%	33.5%
2,601,852	KINGS	763,742	373,903	387,768	2,071	13,865 D	49.0%	50.8%	49.1%	50.9%
23,644	LEWIS	9,608	6,591	2,987	30	3,604 R	68.6%	31.1%	68.8%	31.2%
54,041	LIVINGSTON	22,999	15,886	7,031	82	8,855 R	69.1%	30.6%	69.3%	30.7%
62,864	MADISON	24,697	18,392	6,241	64	12,151 R	74.5%	25.3%	74.7%	25.3%
711,917	MONROE	317,905	196,579	120,031	1,295	76,548 R	61.8%	37.8%	62.1%	37.9%
55,883	MONTGOMERY	26,210	16,640	9,460	110	7,180 R	63.5%	36.1%	63.8%	36.2%
1,422,905	NASSAU	693,429	438,723	252,831	1,875	185,892 R	63.3%	36.5%	63.4%	36.6%
1,524,541	NEW YORK	534,972	178,515	354,326	2,131	175,811 D	33.4%	66.2%	33.5%	66.5%
235,720	NIAGARA	94,096	54,777	38,991	328	15,786 R	58.2%	41.4%	58.4%	41.6%
273,037	ONEIDA	112,444	78,549	33,642	253	44,907 R	69.9%	29.9%	70.0%	30.0%
472,185	ONONDAGA	202,421	140,039	61,895	487	78,144 R	69.2%	30.6%	69.3%	30.7%
78,849	ONTARIO	34,968	23,828	11,012	128	12,816 R	68.1%	31.5%	68.4%	31.6%
220,558	ORANGE	89,533	63,556	25,778	199	37,778 R	71.0%	28.8%	71.1%	28.9%
37,305	ORLEANS	15,347	10,938	4,371	38	6,567 R	71.3%	28.5%	71.4%	28.6%
100,897	OSWEGO	40,528	29,109	11,317	102	17,792 R	71.8%	27.9%	72.0%	28.0%
56,181	OTSEGO	25,337	17,364	7,898	75	9,466 R	68.5%	31.2%	68.7%	31.3%
56,696	PUTNAM	29,557	21,673	7,747	137	13,926 R	73.3%	26.2%	73.7%	26.3%
1,973,708	QUEENS	756,369	426,015	328,316	2,038	97,699 R	56.3%	43.4%	56.5%	43.5%
152,510	RENSSELAER	73,166	48,864	24,019	283	24,845 R	66.8%	32.8%	67.0%	33.0%
295,443	RICHMOND	114,181	84,686	29,241	254	55,445 R	74.2%	25.6%	74.3%	25.7%
229,903	ROCKLAND	100,806	64,753	35,771	282	28,982 R	64.2%	35.5%	64.4%	35.6%
111,991	ST. LAWRENCE	41,503	26,145	15,286	72	10,859 R	63.0%	36.8%	63.1%	36.9%
121,679	SARATOGA	58,685	40,582	17,899	204	22,683 R	69.2%	30.5%	69.4%	30.6%
160,979	SCHENECTADY	77,503	47,529	29,619	355	17,910 R	61.3%	38.2%	61.6%	38.4%
24,750	SCHOHARIE	12,408	8,644	3,730	34	4,914 R	69.7%	30.1%	69.9%	30.1%
16,737	SCHUYLER	6,927	4,945	1,937	45	3,008 R	71.4%	28.0%	71.9%	28.1%
35,083	SENECA	13,842	9,368	4,441	33	4,927 R	67.7%	32.1%	67.8%	32.2%
99,546	STEUBEN	38,253	28,708	9,462	83	19,246 R	75.0%	24.7%	75.2%	24.8%
1,116,672	SUFFOLK	450,186	316,452	132,441	1,293	184,011 R	70.3%	29.4%	70.5%	29.5%
52,580	SULLIVAN	26,938	17,035	9,847	56	7,188 R	63.2%	36.6%	63.4%	36.6%
46,513	TIOGA	18,927	13,396	5,470	61	7,926 R	70.8%	28.9%	71.0%	29.0%
76,879	TOMPKINS	30,038	17,605	12,344	89	5,261 R	58.6%	41.1%	58.8%	41.2%
141,241	ULSTER	68,467	46,883	21,371	213	25,512 R	68.5%	31.2%	68.7%	31.3%
49,402	WARREN	22,480	16,649	5,760	71	10,889 R	74.1%	25.6%	74.3%	25.7%
52,725	WASHINGTON	21,895	16,136	5,677	82	10,459 R	73.7%	25.9%	74.0%	26.0%
79,404	WAYNE	31,679	23,379	8,203	97	15,176 R	73.8%	25.9%	74.0%	26.0%
891,409	WESTCHESTER	418,814	262,901	154,412	1,501	108,489 R	62.8%	36.9%	63.0%	37.0%
37,688	WYOMING	15,588	11,184	4,365	39	6,819 R	71.7%	28.0%	71.9%	28.1%
19,831	YATES	8,618	6,639	1,958	21	4,681 R	77.0%	22.7%	77.2%	22.8%
18,190,740	TOTAL	7,165,919	4,192,778	2,951,084	22,057	1,241,694 R	58.5%	41.2%	58.7%	41.3%

NEW YORK

PRESIDENT 1968

1960 Census Population	County	Total Vote	Republican	Democratic	AIP	Other	Plurality	Percentage		
								Rep.	Dem.	AIP
272,926	ALBANY	139,394	52,948	80,724	5,025	697	27,776 D	38.0%	57.9%	3.6%
43,978	ALLEGANY	17,156	11,222	4,986	851	97	6,236 R	65.4%	29.1%	5.0%
1,424,815	BRONX	444,532	142,314	277,385	21,950	2,883	135,071 D	32.0%	62.4%	4.9%
212,661	BROOME	89,372	46,872	37,451	4,618	431	9,421 R	52.4%	41.9%	5.2%
80,187	CATTARAUGUS	31,157	16,594	12,733	1,674	156	3,861 R	53.3%	40.9%	5.4%
73,942	CAYUGA	32,670	16,167	14,604	1,826	73	1,563 R	49.5%	44.7%	5.6%
145,377	CHAUTAUQUA	58,507	28,561	26,431	3,273	242	2,130 R	48.8%	45.2%	5.6%
98,706	CHEMUNG	39,553	20,693	15,820	2,807	233	4,873 R	52.3%	40.0%	7.1%
43,243	CHENANGO	18,455	11,785	5,706	887	77	6,079 R	63.9%	30.9%	4.8%
72,722	CLINTON	23,176	11,951	10,153	931	141	1,798 R	51.6%	43.8%	4.0%
47,322	COLUMBIA	23,086	13,857	7,762	1,372	95	6,095 R	60.0%	33.6%	5.9%
41,113	CORTLAND	16,818	10,209	5,791	720	98	4,418 R	60.7%	34.4%	4.3%
43,540	DELAWARE	18,898	12,366	5,360	1,121	51	7,006 R	65.4%	28.4%	5.9%
176,008	DUTCHESS	82,122	45,032	31,025	5,662	403	14,007 R	54.8%	37.8%	6.9%
1,064,688	ERIE	453,271	167,853	250,054	33,402	1,962	82,201 D	37.0%	55.2%	7.4%
35,300	ESSEX	15,361	9,377	5,218	701	65	4,159 R	61.0%	34.0%	4.6%
44,742	FRANKLIN	15,604	8,314	6,678	544	68	1,636 R	53.3%	42.8%	3.5%
51,304	FULTON	21,818	11,895	8,871	989	63	3,024 R	54.5%	40.7%	4.5%
53,994	GENESEE	23,150	12,418	9,533	1,141	58	2,885 R	53.6%	41.2%	4.9%
31,372	GREENE	18,021	10,954	5,499	1,421	147	5,455 R	60.8%	30.5%	7.9%
4,267	HAMILTON	3,053	2,123	762	163	5	1,361 R	69.5%	25.0%	5.3%
66,370	HERKIMER	27,677	15,192	10,940	1,455	90	4,252 R	54.9%	39.5%	5.3%
87,835	JEFFERSON	33,123	18,552	13,438	1,016	117	5,114 R	56.0%	40.6%	3.1%
2,627,319	KINGS	775,067	247,936	489,174	33,563	4,394	241,238 D	32.0%	63.1%	4.3%
23,249	LEWIS	9,180	5,524	3,205	430	21	2,319 R	60.2%	34.9%	4.7%
44,053	LIVINGSTON	19,516	11,659	6,989	775	93	4,670 R	59.7%	35.8%	4.0%
54,635	MADISON	22,010	13,819	7,056	1,053	82	6,763 R	62.8%	32.1%	4.8%
586,387	MONROE	296,755	143,233	141,437	10,875	1,210	1,796 R	48.3%	47.7%	3.7%
57,240	MONTGOMERY	25,257	12,566	11,449	1,147	95	1,117 R	49.8%	45.3%	4.5%
1,300,171	NASSAU	643,582	329,792	278,599	30,860	4,331	51,193 R	51.2%	43.3%	4.8%
1,698,281	NEW YORK	529,464	135,458	370,806	12,958	10,242	235,348 D	25.6%	70.0%	2.4%
242,269	NIAGARA	87,925	38,796	41,999	6,617	513	3,203 D	44.1%	47.8%	7.5%
264,401	ONEIDA	103,761	52,875	44,685	5,666	535	8,190 R	51.0%	43.1%	5.5%
423,028	ONONDAGA	189,880	95,806	83,576	9,459	1,039	12,230 R	50.5%	44.0%	5.0%
68,070	ONTARIO	30,098	17,114	11,719	1,180	85	5,395 R	56.9%	38.9%	3.9%
183,734	ORANGE	80,181	44,955	28,122	6,473	631	16,833 R	56.1%	35.1%	8.1%
34,159	ORLEANS	14,032	8,509	4,786	696	41	3,723 R	60.6%	34.1%	5.0%
86,118	OSWEGO	36,845	20,041	14,636	1,962	206	5,405 R	54.4%	39.7%	5.3%
51,942	OTSEGO	22,708	13,543	7,981	1,091	93	5,562 R	59.6%	35.1%	4.8%
31,722	PUTNAM	24,327	13,293	8,472	2,388	174	4,821 R	54.6%	34.8%	9.8%
1,809,578	QUEENS	766,012	306,620	410,546	44,198	4,648	103,926 D	40.0%	53.6%	5.8%
142,585	RENSSELAER	68,681	34,674	30,232	3,461	314	4,442 R	50.5%	44.0%	5.0%
221,991	RICHMOND	98,838	54,631	34,770	9,112	325	19,861 R	55.3%	35.2%	9.2%
136,803	ROCKLAND	83,337	40,880	36,948	5,028	481	3,932 R	49.1%	44.3%	6.0%
111,239	ST. LAWRENCE	37,937	20,982	15,662	1,178	115	5,320 R	55.3%	41.3%	3.1%
89,096	SARATOGA	45,935	25,658	17,766	2,220	291	7,892 R	55.9%	38.7%	4.8%
152,896	SCHENECTADY	72,052	33,687	34,786	3,246	333	1,099 D	46.8%	48.3%	4.5%
22,616	SCHOHARIE	10,777	6,166	3,883	689	39	2,283 R	57.2%	36.0%	6.4%
15,044	SCHUYLER	6,696	4,105	2,034	522	35	2,071 R	61.3%	30.4%	7.8%
31,984	SENECA	13,008	7,083	5,222	635	68	1,861 R	54.5%	40.1%	4.9%
97,691	STEUBEN	38,690	24,189	12,229	2,194	78	11,960 R	62.5%	31.6%	5.7%
666,784	SUFFOLK	374,875	218,027	122,590	31,304	2,954	95,437 R	58.2%	32.7%	8.4%
45,272	SULLIVAN	24,198	11,657	10,860	1,487	194	797 R	48.2%	44.9%	6.1%
37,802	TIOGA	16,956	10,441	5,336	1,127	52	5,105 R	61.6%	31.5%	6.6%
66,164	TOMPKINS	25,310	13,446	10,343	1,236	285	3,103 R	53.1%	40.9%	4.9%
118,804	ULSTER	60,452	34,798	20,886	4,183	585	13,912 R	57.6%	34.5%	6.9%
44,002	WARREN	20,280	12,963	6,460	807	50	6,503 R	63.9%	31.9%	4.0%
48,476	WASHINGTON	20,570	12,694	6,806	930	140	5,888 R	61.7%	33.1%	4.5%
67,989	WAYNE	27,695	17,470	8,907	1,211	107	8,563 R	63.1%	32.2%	4.4%
808,891	WESTCHESTER	400,945	201,652	173,954	22,115	3,224	27,698 R	50.3%	43.4%	5.5%
34,793	WYOMING	13,765	8,459	4,477	799	30	3,982 R	61.5%	32.5%	5.8%
18,614	YATES	8,117	5,482	2,158	440	37	3,324 R	67.5%	26.6%	5.4%
16,782,304	TOTAL	6,791,688	3,007,932	3,378,470	358,864	46,422	370,538 D	44.3%	49.7%	5.3%

NEW YORK

ELECTION NOTES

1984 Other vote was 11,949 Bergland (Free Libertarian); 4,226 Hall (Communist); 3,200 Serrette (New Alliance); 2,226 Holmes (Workers World); 837 scattered write-in. The Republican candidate was also the Conservative nominee and 288,244 of his votes were received as the Conservative candidate. The Democratic candidate was also the Liberal nominee and 118,324 of his votes were received as the Liberal candidate.

1980 Other vote was 467,801 Anderson (Liberal); 52,648 Clark (Free Libertarian); 24,159 McCormack (Right to Life); 23,186 Commoner (Citizens); 7,414 Hall (Communist); 2,068 DeBerry (Socialist Workers); 1,416 Griswold (Workers World); 1,064 scattered write-in. The Republican candidate was also the Conservative nominee and 256,131 of his votes were received as the Conservative candidate. Early unamended canvass gave the Republican vote in Oswego county as 31,151.

1976 Other vote was 12,197 MacBride (Free Libertarian); 10,270 Hall (Communist); 6,996 Camejo (Socialist Workers); 5,413 LaRouche (Labor); 4,303 McCarthy (write-in); 451 Anderson (write-in); 97 Maddox (write-in); 28 Levin (write-in); 14 Zeidler (write-in); 4,052 scattered write-in. The Republican candidate was also the Conservative nominee and 274,878 of his votes were received as the Conservative candidate. The Democratic candidate was also the Liberal nominee and 145,393 of his votes were received as the Liberal candidate. Early unamended canvass gave the total write-in votes as 8,975.

1972 Other vote was 7,797 Reed (Socialist Workers); 4,530 Fisher (Socialist Labor); 5,641 Hall (Communist); 4,089 scattered write-in. The Republican candidate was also the Conservative nominee and 368,136 of his votes were received as the Conservative candidate. The Democratic candidate was also the Liberal nominee and 183,128 of his votes were received as the Liberal candidate.

1968 Wallace on the ballot as Courage. Other vote was 24,517 Gregory (Freedom and Peace); 11,851 Halstead (Socialist Workers); 8,432 Blomen (Socialist Labor); 1,622 scattered write-in. The Democratic candidate was also the Liberal nominee and 311,622 of his votes were received as the Liberal candidate.

NORTH CAROLINA

POPULAR VOTE FOR PRESIDENT 1920 TO 1984

Year	Total Vote	Republican Vote	Republican Candidate	Democratic Vote	Democratic Candidate	Other Vote	Plurality	Percentage Total Vote Rep.	Percentage Total Vote Dem.	Percentage Major Vote Rep.	Percentage Major Vote Dem.
1984	2,175,361	1,346,481	Reagan, Ronald	824,287	Mondale, Walter F.	4,593	522,194 R	61.9%	37.9%	62.0%	38.0%
1980	1,855,833	915,018	Reagan, Ronald	875,635	Carter, Jimmy	65,180	39,383 R	49.3%	47.2%	51.1%	48.9%
1976	1,678,914	741,960	Ford, Gerald R.	927,365	Carter, Jimmy	9,589	185,405 D	44.2%	55.2%	44.4%	55.6%
1972	1,518,612	1,054,889	Nixon, Richard M.	438,705	McGovern, George S.	25,018	616,184 R	69.5%	28.9%	70.6%	29.4%
1968 **	1,587,493	627,192	Nixon, Richard M.	464,113	Humphrey, Hubert H.	496,188	131,004 R	39.5%	29.2%	57.5%	42.5%
1964	1,424,983	624,844	Goldwater, Barry M.	800,139	Johnson, Lyndon B.		175,295 D	43.8%	56.2%	43.8%	56.2%
1960	1,368,556	655,420	Nixon, Richard M.	713,136	Kennedy, John F.		57,716 D	47.9%	52.1%	47.9%	52.1%
1956	1,165,592	575,062	Eisenhower, Dwight D.	590,530	Stevenson, Adlai E.		15,468 D	49.3%	50.7%	49.3%	50.7%
1952	1,210,910	558,107	Eisenhower, Dwight D.	652,803	Stevenson, Adlai E.		94,696 D	46.1%	53.9%	46.1%	53.9%
1948	791,209	258,572	Dewey, Thomas E.	459,070	Truman, Harry S.	73,567	200,498 D	32.7%	58.0%	36.0%	64.0%
1944	790,554	263,155	Dewey, Thomas E.	527,399	Roosevelt, Franklin D.		264,244 D	33.3%	66.7%	33.3%	66.7%
1940	822,648	213,633	Willkie, Wendell	609,015	Roosevelt, Franklin D.		395,382 D	26.0%	74.0%	26.0%	74.0%
1936	839,475	223,294	Landon, Alfred M.	616,141	Roosevelt, Franklin D.	40	392,847 D	26.6%	73.4%	26.6%	73.4%
1932	711,498	208,344	Hoover, Herbert C.	497,566	Roosevelt, Franklin D.	5,588	289,222 D	29.3%	69.9%	29.5%	70.5%
1928	635,150	348,923	Hoover, Herbert C.	286,227	Smith, Alfred E.		62,696 R	54.9%	45.1%	54.9%	45.1%
1924	481,608	190,754	Coolidge, Calvin	284,190	Davis, John W.	6,664	93,436 D	39.6%	59.0%	40.2%	59.8%
1920	538,649	232,819	Harding, Warren G.	305,367	Cox, James M.	463	72,548 D	43.2%	56.7%	43.3%	56.7%

In 1968 other vote was American (Wallace).

ELECTORAL COLLEGE VOTE 1920 TO 1984

Year	Total	Republican	Democratic	Other
1984	13	13	—	—
1980	13	13	—	—
1976	13	—	13	—
1972	13	13	—	—
1968 **	13	12	—	1 AIP
1964	13	—	13	—
1960	14	—	14	—
1956	14	—	14	—
1952	14	—	14	—
1948	14	—	14	—
1944	14	—	14	—
1940	13	—	13	—
1936	13	—	13	—
1932	13	—	13	—
1928	12	12	—	—
1924	12	—	12	—
1920	12	—	12	—

In 1968 one of the thirteen Republican electors voted in the Electoral College for the American Independent candidates rather than for the national Republican candidates.

NORTH CAROLINA

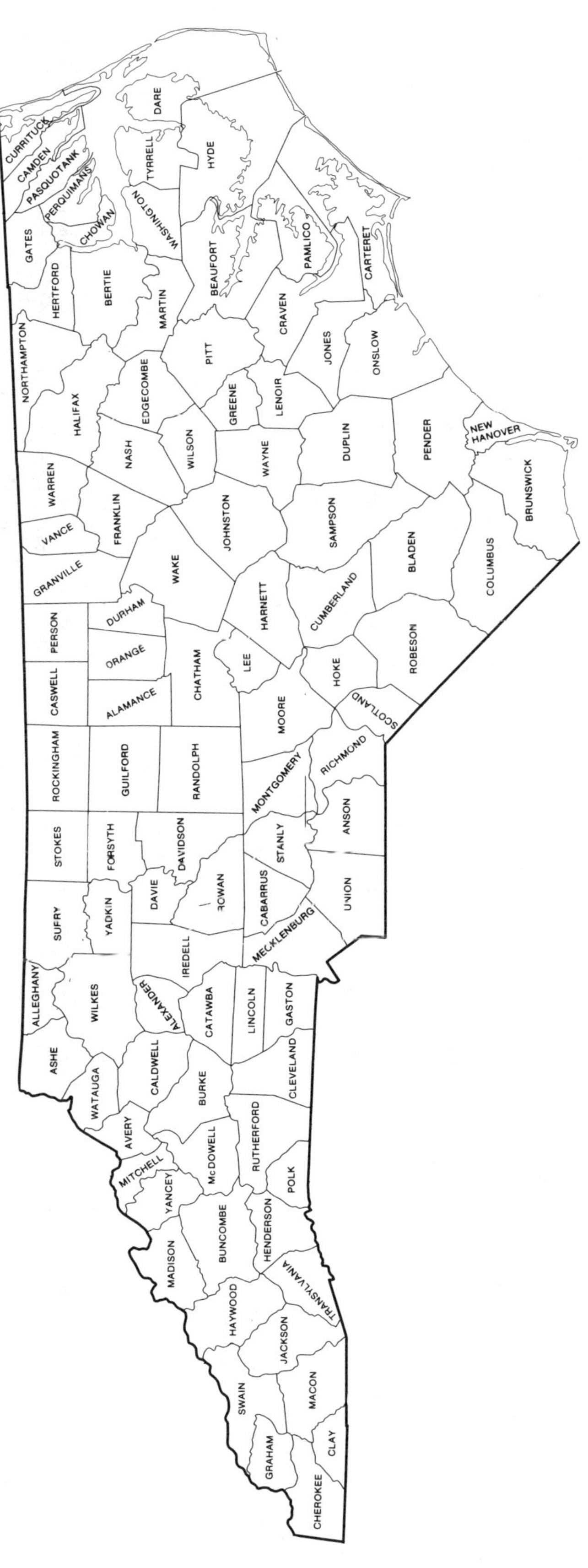

NORTH CAROLINA

PRESIDENT 1984

1980 Census Population	County	Total Vote	Republican	Democratic	Other	Rep.-Dem. Plurality	Percentage: Total Vote Rep.	Percentage: Total Vote Dem.	Percentage: Major Vote Rep.	Percentage: Major Vote Dem.
99,319	ALAMANCE	37,370	26,063	11,230	77	14,833 R	69.7%	30.1%	69.9%	30.1%
24,999	ALEXANDER	12,107	8,502	3,581	24	4,921 R	70.2%	29.6%	70.4%	29.6%
9,587	ALLEGHANY	4,617	2,589	2,013	15	576 R	56.1%	43.6%	56.3%	43.7%
25,649	ANSON	8,760	3,719	5,015	26	1,296 D	42.5%	57.2%	42.6%	57.4%
22,325	ASHE	10,645	6,611	4,009	25	2,602 R	62.1%	37.7%	62.3%	37.7%
14,409	AVERY	5,886	4,702	1,159	25	3,543 R	79.9%	19.7%	80.2%	19.8%
40,355	BEAUFORT	15,304	9,284	5,987	33	3,297 R	60.7%	39.1%	60.8%	39.2%
21,024	BERTIE	6,870	2,879	3,953	38	1,074 D	41.9%	57.5%	42.1%	57.9%
30,491	BLADEN	9,779	4,701	5,064	14	363 D	48.1%	51.8%	48.1%	51.9%
35,777	BRUNSWICK	16,488	9,673	6,774	41	2,899 R	58.7%	41.1%	58.8%	41.2%
160,934	BUNCOMBE	61,183	37,698	23,337	148	14,361 R	61.6%	38.1%	61.8%	38.2%
72,504	BURKE	29,178	18,766	10,353	59	8,413 R	64.3%	35.5%	64.4%	35.6%
85,895	CABARRUS	31,058	22,528	8,477	53	14,051 R	72.5%	27.3%	72.7%	27.3%
67,746	CALDWELL	24,394	17,024	7,311	59	9,713 R	69.8%	30.0%	70.0%	30.0%
5,829	CAMDEN	2,363	1,282	1,075	6	207 R	54.3%	45.5%	54.4%	45.6%
41,092	CARTERET	17,557	11,637	5,882	38	5,755 R	66.3%	33.5%	66.4%	33.6%
20,705	CASWELL	8,174	3,992	4,157	25	165 D	48.8%	50.9%	49.0%	51.0%
105,208	CATAWBA	43,250	31,476	11,700	74	19,776 R	72.8%	27.1%	72.9%	27.1%
33,415	CHATHAM	16,099	8,595	7,458	46	1,137 R	53.4%	46.3%	53.5%	46.5%
18,933	CHEROKEE	7,679	4,894	2,776	9	2,118 R	63.7%	36.2%	63.8%	36.2%
12,558	CHOWAN	3,918	2,171	1,736	11	435 R	55.4%	44.3%	55.6%	44.4%
6,619	CLAY	3,619	2,259	1,340	20	919 R	62.4%	37.0%	62.8%	37.2%
83,435	CLEVELAND	27,472	17,095	10,288	89	6,807 R	62.2%	37.4%	62.4%	37.6%
51,037	COLUMBUS	17,904	9,150	8,728	26	422 R	51.1%	48.7%	51.2%	48.8%
71,043	CRAVEN	20,134	12,893	7,186	55	5,707 R	64.0%	35.7%	64.2%	35.8%
247,160	CUMBERLAND	54,319	31,602	22,614	103	8,988 R	58.2%	41.6%	58.3%	41.7%
11,089	CURRITUCK	4,562	2,885	1,668	9	1,217 R	63.2%	36.6%	63.4%	36.6%
13,377	DARE	6,596	4,738	1,839	19	2,899 R	71.8%	27.9%	72.0%	28.0%
113,162	DAVIDSON	42,001	30,471	11,469	61	19,002 R	72.5%	27.3%	72.7%	27.3%
24,599	DAVIE	11,125	8,201	2,911	13	5,290 R	73.7%	26.2%	73.8%	26.2%
40,952	DUPLIN	14,555	7,708	6,830	17	878 R	53.0%	46.9%	53.0%	47.0%
152,785	DURHAM	61,584	29,185	32,244	155	3,059 D	47.4%	52.4%	47.5%	52.5%
55,988	EDGECOMBE	20,216	9,635	10,545	36	910 D	47.7%	52.2%	47.7%	52.3%
243,683	FORSYTH	96,211	59,208	36,814	189	22,394 R	61.5%	38.3%	61.7%	38.3%
30,055	FRANKLIN	10,768	5,984	4,766	18	1,218 R	55.6%	44.3%	55.7%	44.3%
162,568	GASTON	53,392	39,167	14,142	83	25,025 R	73.4%	26.5%	73.5%	26.5%
8,875	GATES	3,930	1,694	2,225	11	531 D	43.1%	56.6%	43.2%	56.8%
7,217	GRAHAM	4,014	2,514	1,494	6	1,020 R	62.6%	37.2%	62.7%	37.3%
34,043	GRANVILLE	11,580	6,302	5,217	61	1,085 R	54.4%	45.1%	54.7%	45.3%
16,117	GREENE	5,975	3,195	2,772	8	423 R	53.5%	46.4%	53.5%	46.5%
317,154	GUILFORD	119,336	73,096	46,027	213	27,069 R	61.3%	38.6%	61.4%	38.6%
55,286	HALIFAX	18,153	8,832	9,278	43	446 D	48.7%	51.1%	48.8%	51.2%
59,570	HARNETT	18,323	11,198	7,106	19	4,092 R	61.1%	38.8%	61.2%	38.8%
46,495	HAYWOOD	18,131	10,146	7,958	27	2,188 R	56.0%	43.9%	56.0%	44.0%
58,580	HENDERSON	26,697	19,369	7,222	106	12,147 R	72.6%	27.1%	72.8%	27.2%
23,368	HERTFORD	7,695	3,176	4,498	21	1,322 D	41.3%	58.5%	41.4%	58.6%
20,383	HOKE	5,677	2,449	3,214	14	765 D	43.1%	56.6%	43.2%	56.8%
5,873	HYDE	2,202	1,195	1,004	3	191 R	54.3%	45.6%	54.3%	45.7%
82,538	IREDELL	33,704	23,641	9,999	64	13,642 R	70.1%	29.7%	70.3%	29.7%
25,811	JACKSON	9,974	5,582	4,367	25	1,215 R	56.0%	43.8%	56.1%	43.9%
70,599	JOHNSTON	24,080	16,210	7,833	37	8,377 R	67.3%	32.5%	67.4%	32.6%
9,705	JONES	4,099	2,062	2,025	12	37 R	50.3%	49.4%	50.5%	49.5%
36,718	LEE	12,151	8,198	3,925	28	4,273 R	67.5%	32.3%	67.6%	32.4%
59,819	LENOIR	21,914	13,321	8,556	37	4,765 R	60.8%	39.0%	60.9%	39.1%
42,372	LINCOLN	18,659	12,621	5,996	42	6,625 R	67.6%	32.1%	67.8%	32.2%
35,135	MCDOWELL	11,736	7,639	4,076	21	3,563 R	65.1%	34.7%	65.2%	34.8%
20,178	MACON	10,256	6,661	3,570	25	3,091 R	64.9%	34.8%	65.1%	34.9%
16,827	MADISON	6,689	3,666	2,988	35	678 R	54.8%	44.7%	55.1%	44.9%
25,948	MARTIN	8,153	4,266	3,870	17	396 R	52.3%	47.5%	52.4%	47.6%
404,270	MECKLENBURG	170,337	106,754	63,190	393	43,564 R	62.7%	37.1%	62.8%	37.2%

NORTH CAROLINA

PRESIDENT 1984

1980 Census Population	County	Total Vote	Republican	Democratic	Other	Rep.-Dem. Plurality	Percentage Total Vote Rep.	Total Vote Dem.	Major Vote Rep.	Major Vote Dem.
14,428	MITCHELL	6,034	4,737	1,286	11	3,451 R	78.5%	21.3%	78.6%	21.4%
22,469	MONTGOMERY	8,952	5,109	3,831	12	1,278 R	57.1%	42.8%	57.1%	42.9%
50,505	MOORE	21,782	14,681	7,063	38	7,618 R	67.4%	32.4%	67.5%	32.5%
67,153	NASH	25,917	17,295	8,588	34	8,707 R	66.7%	33.1%	66.8%	33.2%
103,471	NEW HANOVER	36,452	23,771	12,591	90	11,180 R	65.2%	34.5%	65.4%	34.6%
22,584	NORTHAMPTON	8,330	3,198	5,094	38	1,896 D	38.4%	61.2%	38.6%	61.4%
112,784	ONSLOW	19,687	13,928	5,713	46	8,215 R	70.7%	29.0%	70.9%	29.1%
77,055	ORANGE	36,277	15,585	20,564	128	4,979 D	43.0%	56.7%	43.1%	56.9%
10,398	PAMLICO	4,717	2,554	2,152	11	402 R	54.1%	45.6%	54.3%	45.7%
28,462	PASQUOTANK	8,513	4,646	3,854	13	792 R	54.6%	45.3%	54.7%	45.3%
22,215	PENDER	9,453	5,079	4,354	20	725 R	53.7%	46.1%	53.8%	46.2%
9,486	PERQUIMANS	3,385	1,939	1,441	5	498 R	57.3%	42.6%	57.4%	42.6%
29,164	PERSON	9,397	5,854	3,528	15	2,326 R	62.3%	37.5%	62.4%	37.6%
90,146	PITT	32,526	18,983	13,481	62	5,502 R	58.4%	41.4%	58.5%	41.5%
12,984	POLK	6,251	4,046	2,169	36	1,877 R	64.7%	34.7%	65.1%	34.9%
91,728	RANDOLPH	33,299	25,759	7,511	29	18,248 R	77.4%	22.6%	77.4%	22.6%
45,481	RICHMOND	14,330	6,807	7,494	29	687 D	47.5%	52.3%	47.6%	52.4%
101,610	ROBESON	28,291	12,947	15,257	87	2,310 D	45.8%	53.9%	45.9%	54.1%
83,426	ROCKINGHAM	28,539	17,895	10,605	39	7,290 R	62.7%	37.2%	62.8%	37.2%
99,186	ROWAN	35,907	25,207	10,643	57	14,564 R	70.2%	29.6%	70.3%	29.7%
53,787	RUTHERFORD	18,268	11,369	6,862	37	4,507 R	62.2%	37.6%	62.4%	37.6%
49,687	SAMPSON	19,796	10,665	9,115	16	1,550 R	53.9%	46.0%	53.9%	46.1%
32,273	SCOTLAND	8,117	4,077	4,028	12	49 R	50.2%	49.6%	50.3%	49.7%
48,517	STANLY	19,289	13,116	6,138	35	6,978 R	68.0%	31.8%	68.1%	31.9%
33,086	STOKES	14,498	9,515	4,950	33	4,565 R	65.6%	34.1%	65.8%	34.2%
59,449	SURRY	20,562	13,340	7,188	34	6,152 R	64.9%	35.0%	65.0%	35.0%
10,283	SWAIN	4,022	2,012	2,000	10	12 R	50.0%	49.7%	50.1%	49.9%
23,417	TRANSYLVANIA	10,717	6,956	3,733	28	3,223 R	64.9%	34.8%	65.1%	34.9%
3,975	TYRRELL	1,583	774	807	2	33 D	48.9%	51.0%	49.0%	51.0%
70,380	UNION	23,968	16,885	7,048	35	9,837 R	70.4%	29.4%	70.6%	29.4%
36,748	VANCE	12,734	6,836	5,880	18	956 R	53.7%	46.2%	53.8%	46.2%
301,327	WAKE	131,871	81,251	50,323	297	30,928 R	61.6%	38.2%	61.8%	38.2%
16,232	WARREN	6,618	2,664	3,946	8	1,282 D	40.3%	59.6%	40.3%	59.7%
14,801	WASHINGTON	5,852	2,731	3,114	7	383 D	46.7%	53.2%	46.7%	53.3%
31,666	WATAUGA	14,579	9,370	5,163	46	4,207 R	64.3%	35.4%	64.5%	35.5%
97,054	WAYNE	28,008	17,961	10,011	36	7,950 R	64.1%	35.7%	64.2%	35.8%
58,657	WILKES	25,564	18,670	6,852	42	11,818 R	73.0%	26.8%	73.2%	26.8%
63,132	WILSON	20,643	12,243	8,343	57	3,900 R	59.3%	40.4%	59.5%	40.5%
28,439	YADKIN	12,070	8,976	3,075	19	5,901 R	74.4%	25.5%	74.5%	25.5%
14,934	YANCEY	7,961	4,296	3,651	14	645 R	54.0%	45.9%	54.1%	45.9%
5,881,766	TOTAL	2,175,361	1,346,481	824,287	4,593	522,194 R	61.9%	37.9%	62.0%	38.0%

NORTH CAROLINA

PRESIDENT 1980

1980 Census Population	County	Total Vote	Republican	Democratic	Other	Rep.-Dem. Plurality	Percentage: Total Vote Rep.	Total Vote Dem.	Major Vote Rep.	Major Vote Dem.
99,319	ALAMANCE	34,066	18,077	15,042	947	3,035 R	53.1%	44.2%	54.6%	45.4%
24,999	ALEXANDER	11,109	6,376	4,546	187	1,830 R	57.4%	40.9%	58.4%	41.6%
9,587	ALLEGHANY	4,310	1,995	2,198	117	203 D	46.3%	51.0%	47.6%	52.4%
25,649	ANSON	7,087	1,968	4,973	146	3,005 D	27.8%	70.2%	28.4%	71.6%
22,325	ASHE	10,312	5,643	4,461	208	1,182 R	54.7%	43.3%	55.8%	44.2%
14,409	AVERY	5,182	3,480	1,527	175	1,953 R	67.2%	29.5%	69.5%	30.5%
40,355	BEAUFORT	13,037	6,773	6,024	240	749 R	52.0%	46.2%	52.9%	47.1%
21,024	BERTIE	5,632	1,695	3,863	74	2,168 D	30.1%	68.6%	30.5%	69.5%
30,491	BLADEN	8,941	2,745	6,104	92	3,359 D	30.7%	68.3%	31.0%	69.0%
35,777	BRUNSWICK	13,003	5,897	6,761	345	864 D	45.4%	52.0%	46.6%	53.4%
160,934	BUNCOMBE	53,530	26,124	24,837	2,569	1,287 R	48.8%	46.4%	51.3%	48.7%
72,504	BURKE	25,417	12,956	11,680	781	1,276 R	51.0%	46.0%	52.6%	47.4%
85,895	CABARRUS	25,585	15,143	9,768	674	5,375 R	59.2%	38.2%	60.8%	39.2%
67,746	CALDWELL	22,310	12,965	8,738	607	4,227 R	58.1%	39.2%	59.7%	40.3%
5,829	CAMDEN	2,088	813	1,212	63	399 D	38.9%	58.0%	40.1%	59.9%
41,092	CARTERET	14,767	7,733	6,485	549	1,248 R	52.4%	43.9%	54.4%	45.6%
20,705	CASWELL	5,777	2,156	3,529	92	1,373 D	37.3%	61.1%	37.9%	62.1%
105,208	CATAWBA	37,878	22,873	13,873	1,132	9,000 R	60.4%	36.6%	62.2%	37.8%
33,415	CHATHAM	13,205	5,414	7,144	647	1,730 D	41.0%	54.1%	43.1%	56.9%
18,933	CHEROKEE	7,079	3,849	3,114	116	735 R	54.4%	44.0%	55.3%	44.7%
12,558	CHOWAN	3,660	1,424	2,146	90	722 D	38.9%	58.6%	39.9%	60.1%
6,619	CLAY	3,547	2,136	1,324	87	812 R	60.2%	37.3%	61.7%	38.3%
83,435	CLEVELAND	23,498	10,828	12,219	451	1,391 D	46.1%	52.0%	47.0%	53.0%
51,037	COLUMBUS	15,940	5,522	10,212	206	4,690 D	34.6%	64.1%	35.1%	64.9%
71,043	CRAVEN	16,783	8,554	7,781	448	773 R	51.0%	46.4%	52.4%	47.6%
247,160	CUMBERLAND	45,228	21,540	22,073	1,615	533 D	47.6%	48.8%	49.4%	50.6%
11,089	CURRITUCK	3,786	1,668	1,980	138	312 D	44.1%	52.3%	45.7%	54.3%
13,377	DARE	5,615	2,794	2,497	324	297 R	49.8%	44.5%	52.8%	47.2%
113,162	DAVIDSON	38,269	22,794	14,579	896	8,215 R	59.6%	38.1%	61.0%	39.0%
24,599	DAVIE	9,880	6,302	3,289	289	3,013 R	63.8%	33.3%	65.7%	34.3%
40,952	DUPLIN	13,069	5,403	7,524	142	2,121 D	41.3%	57.6%	41.8%	58.2%
152,785	DURHAM	47,901	19,276	24,969	3,656	5,693 D	40.2%	52.1%	43.6%	56.4%
55,988	EDGECOMBE	14,056	5,916	7,945	195	2,029 D	42.1%	56.5%	42.7%	57.3%
243,683	FORSYTH	84,798	42,389	38,870	3,539	3,519 R	50.0%	45.8%	52.2%	47.8%
30,055	FRANKLIN	9,081	3,508	5,427	146	1,919 D	38.6%	59.8%	39.3%	60.7%
162,568	GASTON	45,204	25,139	19,016	1,049	6,123 R	55.6%	42.1%	56.9%	43.1%
8,875	GATES	3,467	957	2,435	75	1,478 D	27.6%	70.2%	28.2%	71.8%
7,217	GRAHAM	3,615	1,961	1,608	46	353 R	54.2%	44.5%	54.9%	45.1%
34,043	GRANVILLE	9,246	3,513	5,556	177	2,043 D	38.0%	60.1%	38.7%	61.3%
16,117	GREENE	5,113	2,221	2,835	57	614 D	43.4%	55.4%	43.9%	56.1%
317,154	GUILFORD	102,622	53,291	44,516	4,815	8,775 R	51.9%	43.4%	54.5%	45.5%
55,286	HALIFAX	14,648	6,033	8,364	251	2,331 D	41.2%	57.1%	41.9%	58.1%
59,570	HARNETT	16,295	7,284	8,791	220	1,507 D	44.7%	53.9%	45.3%	54.7%
46,495	HAYWOOD	17,462	7,217	9,814	431	2,597 D	41.3%	56.2%	42.4%	57.6%
58,580	HENDERSON	22,181	13,573	7,578	1,030	5,995 R	61.2%	34.2%	64.2%	35.8%
23,368	HERTFORD	6,060	1,854	4,102	104	2,248 D	30.6%	67.7%	31.1%	68.9%
20,383	HOKE	4,628	1,168	3,376	84	2,208 D	25.2%	72.9%	25.7%	74.3%
5,873	HYDE	2,072	807	1,221	44	414 D	38.9%	58.9%	39.8%	60.2%
82,538	IREDELL	27,794	14,926	12,067	801	2,859 R	53.7%	43.4%	55.3%	44.7%
25,811	JACKSON	9,310	4,140	4,857	313	717 D	44.5%	52.2%	46.0%	54.0%
70,599	JOHNSTON	20,376	10,444	9,601	331	843 R	51.3%	47.1%	52.1%	47.9%
9,705	JONES	3,630	1,401	2,198	31	797 D	38.6%	60.6%	38.9%	61.1%
36,718	LEE	10,574	4,847	5,426	301	579 D	45.8%	51.3%	47.2%	52.8%
59,819	LENOIR	17,714	9,832	7,546	336	2,286 R	55.5%	42.6%	56.6%	43.4%
42,372	LINCOLN	17,196	9,009	7,796	391	1,213 R	52.4%	45.3%	53.6%	46.4%
35,135	MCDOWELL	10,606	5,680	4,703	223	977 R	53.6%	44.3%	54.7%	45.3%
20,178	MACON	9,031	4,727	4,105	199	622 R	52.3%	45.5%	53.5%	46.5%
16,827	MADISON	5,972	2,629	3,202	141	573 D	44.0%	53.6%	45.1%	54.9%
25,948	MARTIN	7,412	2,564	4,750	98	2,186 D	34.6%	64.1%	35.1%	64.9%
404,270	MECKLENBURG	143,058	68,384	66,995	7,679	1,389 R	47.8%	46.8%	50.5%	49.5%

NORTH CAROLINA

PRESIDENT 1980

1980 Census Population	County	Total Vote	Republican	Democratic	Other	Rep.-Dem. Plurality	Percentage Total Vote Rep.	Total Vote Dem.	Major Vote Rep.	Major Vote Dem.
14,428	MITCHELL	6,270	4,322	1,765	183	2,557 R	68.9%	28.1%	71.0%	29.0%
22,469	MONTGOMERY	7,842	3,587	4,129	126	542 D	45.7%	52.7%	46.5%	53.5%
50,505	MOORE	18,911	10,158	8,084	669	2,074 R	53.7%	42.7%	55.7%	44.3%
67,153	NASH	19,601	11,043	8,184	374	2,859 R	56.3%	41.8%	57.4%	42.6%
103,471	NEW HANOVER	32,244	17,243	13,670	1,331	3,573 R	53.5%	42.4%	55.8%	44.2%
22,584	NORTHAMPTON	6,861	1,847	4,933	81	3,086 D	26.9%	71.9%	27.2%	72.8%
112,784	ONSLOW	16,736	8,861	7,371	504	1,490 R	52.9%	44.0%	54.6%	45.4%
77,055	ORANGE	28,589	9,261	15,226	4,102	5,965 D	32.4%	53.3%	37.8%	62.2%
10,398	PAMLICO	3,803	1,504	2,224	75	720 D	39.5%	58.5%	40.3%	59.7%
28,462	PASQUOTANK	7,698	3,340	4,128	230	788 D	43.4%	53.6%	44.7%	55.3%
22,215	PENDER	7,536	3,018	4,382	136	1,364 D	40.0%	58.1%	40.8%	59.2%
9,486	PERQUIMANS	2,854	1,210	1,560	84	350 D	42.4%	54.7%	43.7%	56.3%
29,164	PERSON	7,534	3,281	4,111	142	830 D	43.5%	54.6%	44.4%	55.6%
90,146	PITT	26,371	12,816	12,590	965	226 R	48.6%	47.7%	50.4%	49.6%
12,984	POLK	5,609	3,021	2,375	213	646 R	53.9%	42.3%	56.0%	44.0%
91,728	RANDOLPH	30,717	19,881	10,107	729	9,774 R	64.7%	32.9%	66.3%	33.7%
45,481	RICHMOND	11,609	3,911	7,416	282	3,505 D	33.7%	63.9%	34.5%	65.5%
101,610	ROBESON	25,030	6,982	17,618	430	10,636 D	27.9%	70.4%	28.4%	71.6%
83,426	ROCKINGHAM	23,522	11,205	11,708	609	503 D	47.6%	49.8%	48.9%	51.1%
99,186	ROWAN	31,109	18,566	11,671	872	6,895 R	59.7%	37.5%	61.4%	38.6%
53,787	RUTHERFORD	16,966	8,363	8,315	288	48 R	49.3%	49.0%	50.1%	49.9%
49,687	SAMPSON	17,578	8,097	9,090	391	993 D	46.1%	51.7%	47.1%	52.9%
32,273	SCOTLAND	6,782	2,133	4,446	203	2,313 D	31.5%	65.6%	32.4%	67.6%
48,517	STANLY	17,846	9,734	7,784	328	1,950 R	54.5%	43.6%	55.6%	44.4%
33,086	STOKES	13,245	7,275	5,764	206	1,511 R	54.9%	43.5%	55.8%	44.2%
59,449	SURRY	19,408	10,065	8,987	356	1,078 R	51.9%	46.3%	52.8%	47.2%
10,283	SWAIN	3,520	1,457	1,987	76	530 D	41.4%	56.4%	42.3%	57.7%
23,417	TRANSYLVANIA	9,175	4,826	4,008	341	818 R	52.6%	43.7%	54.6%	45.4%
3,975	TYRRELL	1,370	466	887	17	421 D	34.0%	64.7%	34.4%	65.6%
70,380	UNION	19,688	9,012	10,073	603	1,061 D	45.8%	51.2%	47.2%	52.8%
36,748	VANCE	9,774	4,217	5,415	142	1,198 D	43.1%	55.4%	43.8%	56.2%
301,327	WAKE	105,193	49,768	49,003	6,422	765 R	47.3%	46.6%	50.4%	49.6%
16,232	WARREN	5,430	1,582	3,750	98	2,168 D	29.1%	69.1%	29.7%	70.3%
14,801	WASHINGTON	5,037	1,943	3,008	86	1,065 D	38.6%	59.7%	39.2%	60.8%
31,666	WATAUGA	11,958	6,149	5,022	787	1,127 R	51.4%	42.0%	55.0%	45.0%
97,054	WAYNE	22,836	12,860	9,586	390	3,274 R	56.3%	42.0%	57.3%	42.7%
58,657	WILKES	23,049	14,462	8,184	403	6,278 R	62.7%	35.5%	63.9%	36.1%
63,132	WILSON	16,704	8,329	8,042	333	287 R	49.9%	48.1%	50.9%	49.1%
28,439	YADKIN	11,570	7,530	3,850	190	3,680 R	65.1%	33.3%	66.2%	33.8%
14,934	YANCEY	7,546	3,363	4,010	173	647 D	44.6%	53.1%	45.6%	54.4%
5,881,766	TOTAL	1,855,833	915,018	875,635	65,180	39,383 R	49.3%	47.2%	51.1%	48.9%

NORTH CAROLINA

PRESIDENT 1976

1970 Census Population	County	Total Vote	Republican	Democratic	Other	Rep.-Dem. Plurality	Percentage Total Vote Rep.	Total Vote Dem.	Major Vote Rep.	Major Vote Dem.
96,362	ALAMANCE	30,247	12,680	17,371	196	4,691 D	41.9%	57.4%	42.2%	57.8%
19,466	ALEXANDER	9,975	4,661	5,287	27	626 D	46.7%	53.0%	46.9%	53.1%
8,134	ALLEGHANY	4,099	1,532	2,550	17	1,018 D	37.4%	62.2%	37.5%	62.5%
23,488	ANSON	6,425	1,608	4,796	21	3,188 D	25.0%	74.6%	25.1%	74.9%
19,571	ASHE	10,155	4,937	5,193	25	256 D	48.6%	51.1%	48.7%	51.3%
12,655	AVERY	4,995	3,085	1,869	41	1,216 R	61.8%	37.4%	62.3%	37.7%
35,980	BEAUFORT	10,467	4,677	5,728	62	1,051 D	44.7%	54.7%	44.9%	55.1%
20,528	BERTIE	5,470	1,332	4,117	21	2,785 D	24.4%	75.3%	24.4%	75.6%
26,477	BLADEN	7,589	1,546	6,009	34	4,463 D	20.4%	79.2%	20.5%	79.5%
24,223	BRUNSWICK	11,066	3,636	7,377	53	3,741 D	32.9%	66.7%	33.0%	67.0%
145,056	BUNCOMBE	49,426	22,461	26,633	332	4,172 D	45.4%	53.9%	45.8%	54.2%
60,364	BURKE	24,440	10,070	14,254	116	4,184 D	41.2%	58.3%	41.4%	58.6%
74,629	CABARRUS	24,644	12,455	12,049	140	406 R	50.5%	48.9%	50.8%	49.2%
56,699	CALDWELL	21,875	9,872	11,894	109	2,022 D	45.1%	54.4%	45.4%	54.6%
5,453	CAMDEN	1,809	562	1,231	16	669 D	31.1%	68.0%	31.3%	68.7%
31,603	CARTERET	12,939	5,786	7,080	73	1,294 D	44.7%	54.7%	45.0%	55.0%
19,055	CASWELL	5,489	1,761	3,707	21	1,946 D	32.1%	67.5%	32.2%	67.8%
90,873	CATAWBA	35,718	18,696	16,862	160	1,834 R	52.3%	47.2%	52.6%	47.4%
29,554	CHATHAM	10,730	4,279	6,397	54	2,118 D	39.9%	59.6%	40.1%	59.9%
16,330	CHEROKEE	6,849	3,210	3,571	68	361 D	46.9%	52.1%	47.3%	52.7%
10,764	CHOWAN	2,890	1,019	1,862	9	843 D	35.3%	64.4%	35.4%	64.6%
5,180	CLAY	3,012	1,428	1,569	15	141 D	47.4%	52.1%	47.6%	52.4%
72,556	CLEVELAND	22,605	8,106	14,406	93	6,300 D	35.9%	63.7%	36.0%	64.0%
46,937	COLUMBUS	14,401	3,184	11,148	69	7,964 D	22.1%	77.4%	22.2%	77.8%
62,554	CRAVEN	13,549	5,881	7,553	115	1,672 D	43.4%	55.7%	43.8%	56.2%
212,042	CUMBERLAND	38,694	14,226	24,297	171	10,071 D	36.8%	62.8%	36.9%	63.1%
6,976	CURRITUCK	2,972	954	1,999	19	1,045 D	32.1%	67.3%	32.3%	67.7%
6,995	DARE	3,891	1,680	2,191	20	511 D	43.2%	56.3%	43.4%	56.6%
95,627	DAVIDSON	36,863	18,813	17,859	191	954 R	51.0%	48.4%	51.3%	48.7%
18,855	DAVIE	8,463	4,772	3,635	56	1,137 R	56.4%	43.0%	56.8%	43.2%
38,015	DUPLIN	11,694	3,912	7,696	86	3,784 D	33.5%	65.8%	33.7%	66.3%
132,681	DURHAM	41,575	18,945	22,425	205	3,480 D	45.6%	53.9%	45.8%	54.2%
52,341	EDGECOMBE	12,970	4,850	8,001	119	3,151 D	37.4%	61.7%	37.7%	62.3%
214,348	FORSYTH	78,934	38,886	39,561	487	675 D	49.3%	50.1%	49.6%	50.4%
26,820	FRANKLIN	8,097	2,630	5,405	62	2,775 D	32.5%	66.8%	32.7%	67.3%
148,415	GASTON	42,776	19,727	22,878	171	3,151 D	46.1%	53.5%	46.3%	53.7%
8,524	GATES	3,028	722	2,291	15	1,569 D	23.8%	75.7%	24.0%	76.0%
6,562	GRAHAM	3,424	1,621	1,791	12	170 D	47.3%	52.3%	47.5%	52.5%
32,762	GRANVILLE	8,251	2,955	5,244	52	2,289 D	35.8%	63.6%	36.0%	64.0%
14,967	GREENE	4,126	1,356	2,740	30	1,384 D	32.9%	66.4%	33.1%	66.9%
288,590	GUILFORD	92,740	45,441	46,826	473	1,385 D	49.0%	50.5%	49.2%	50.8%
53,884	HALIFAX	13,254	5,257	7,892	105	2,635 D	39.7%	59.5%	40.0%	60.0%
49,667	HARNETT	14,988	5,935	8,992	61	3,057 D	39.6%	60.0%	39.8%	60.2%
41,710	HAYWOOD	16,655	5,885	10,692	78	4,807 D	35.3%	64.2%	35.5%	64.5%
42,804	HENDERSON	19,156	10,830	8,155	171	2,675 R	56.5%	42.6%	57.0%	43.0%
23,529	HERTFORD	5,511	1,517	3,986	8	2,469 D	27.5%	72.3%	27.6%	72.4%
16,436	HOKE	4,123	920	3,186	17	2,266 D	22.3%	77.3%	22.4%	77.6%
5,571	HYDE	1,718	623	1,084	11	461 D	36.3%	63.1%	36.5%	63.5%
72,197	IREDELL	25,142	11,573	13,295	274	1,722 D	46.0%	52.9%	46.5%	53.5%
21,593	JACKSON	8,798	3,536	5,223	39	1,687 D	40.2%	59.4%	40.4%	59.6%
61,737	JOHNSTON	18,881	8,511	10,301	69	1,790 D	45.1%	54.6%	45.2%	54.8%
9,779	JONES	3,011	948	2,016	47	1,068 D	31.5%	67.0%	32.0%	68.0%
30,467	LEE	8,834	3,691	5,104	39	1,413 D	41.8%	57.8%	42.0%	58.0%
55,204	LENOIR	15,484	7,715	7,650	119	65 R	49.8%	49.4%	50.2%	49.8%
32,682	LINCOLN	16,214	6,682	9,462	70	2,780 D	41.2%	58.4%	41.4%	58.6%
30,648	MCDOWELL	10,750	4,450	6,246	54	1,796 D	41.4%	58.1%	41.6%	58.4%
15,788	MACON	8,123	3,673	4,406	44	733 D	45.2%	54.2%	45.5%	54.5%
16,003	MADISON	5,896	2,446	3,433	17	987 D	41.5%	58.2%	41.6%	58.4%
24,730	MARTIN	6,478	1,931	4,518	29	2,587 D	29.8%	69.7%	29.9%	70.1%
354,656	MECKLENBURG	125,549	61,715	63,198	636	1,483 D	49.2%	50.3%	49.4%	50.6%

NORTH CAROLINA

PRESIDENT 1976

1970 Census Population	County	Total Vote	Republican	Democratic	Other	Rep.-Dem. Plurality	Percentage Total Vote Rep.	Total Vote Dem.	Major Vote Rep.	Major Vote Dem.
13,447	MITCHELL	5,781	3,728	2,031	22	1,697 R	64.5%	35.1%	64.7%	35.3%
19,267	MONTGOMERY	7,214	2,872	4,308	34	1,436 D	39.8%	59.7%	40.0%	60.0%
39,048	MOORE	15,030	7,577	7,373	80	204 R	50.4%	49.1%	50.7%	49.3%
59,122	NASH	17,617	8,477	8,937	203	460 D	48.1%	50.7%	48.7%	51.3%
82,996	NEW HANOVER	28,502	13,687	14,504	311	817 D	48.0%	50.9%	48.6%	51.4%
24,009	NORTHAMPTON	6,380	1,238	5,118	24	3,880 D	19.4%	80.2%	19.5%	80.5%
103,126	ONSLOW	13,978	5,953	7,954	71	2,001 D	42.6%	56.9%	42.8%	57.2%
57,707	ORANGE	25,297	9,302	15,755	240	6,453 D	36.8%	62.3%	37.1%	62.9%
9,467	PAMLICO	3,209	1,068	2,113	28	1,045 D	33.3%	65.8%	33.6%	66.4%
26,824	PASQUOTANK	6,996	2,651	4,302	43	1,651 D	37.9%	61.5%	38.1%	61.9%
18,149	PENDER	6,538	2,063	4,422	53	2,359 D	31.6%	67.6%	31.8%	68.2%
8,351	PERQUIMANS	2,581	909	1,666	6	757 D	35.2%	64.5%	35.3%	64.7%
25,914	PERSON	7,038	3,038	3,977	23	939 D	43.2%	56.5%	43.3%	56.7%
73,900	PITT	21,309	9,532	11,636	141	2,104 D	44.7%	54.6%	45.0%	55.0%
11,735	POLK	5,812	2,605	3,155	52	550 D	44.8%	54.3%	45.2%	54.8%
76,358	RANDOLPH	27,212	14,337	12,714	161	1,623 R	52.7%	46.7%	53.0%	47.0%
39,889	RICHMOND	11,665	2,848	8,793	24	5,945 D	24.4%	75.4%	24.5%	75.5%
84,842	ROBESON	25,699	4,907	20,695	97	15,788 D	19.1%	80.5%	19.2%	80.8%
72,402	ROCKINGHAM	22,872	9,362	13,413	97	4,051 D	40.9%	58.6%	41.1%	58.9%
90,035	ROWAN	30,248	14,644	15,363	241	719 D	48.4%	50.8%	48.8%	51.2%
47,337	RUTHERFORD	17,124	6,718	10,361	45	3,643 D	39.2%	60.5%	39.3%	60.7%
44,954	SAMPSON	15,902	6,968	8,869	65	1,901 D	43.8%	55.8%	44.0%	56.0%
26,929	SCOTLAND	6,391	1,932	4,430	29	2,498 D	30.2%	69.3%	30.4%	69.6%
42,822	STANLY	18,190	8,845	9,262	83	417 D	48.6%	50.9%	48.8%	51.2%
23,782	STOKES	12,711	6,029	6,647	35	618 D	47.4%	52.3%	47.6%	52.4%
51,415	SURRY	17,490	7,403	10,024	63	2,621 D	42.3%	57.3%	42.5%	57.5%
7,861	SWAIN	3,771	1,608	2,151	12	543 D	42.6%	57.0%	42.8%	57.2%
19,713	TRANSYLVANIA	8,795	4,089	4,636	70	547 D	46.5%	52.7%	46.9%	53.1%
3,806	TYRRELL	1,305	403	900	2	497 D	30.9%	69.0%	30.9%	69.1%
54,714	UNION	16,847	6,184	10,578	85	4,394 D	36.7%	62.8%	36.9%	63.1%
32,691	VANCE	9,461	3,813	5,620	28	1,807 D	40.3%	59.4%	40.4%	59.6%
228,453	WAKE	88,947	44,291	44,005	651	286 R	49.8%	49.5%	50.2%	49.8%
15,810	WARREN	4,635	1,427	3,185	23	1,758 D	30.8%	68.7%	30.9%	69.1%
14,038	WASHINGTON	4,364	1,486	2,840	38	1,354 D	34.1%	65.1%	34.4%	65.6%
23,404	WATAUGA	10,834	5,400	5,358	76	42 R	49.8%	49.5%	50.2%	49.8%
85,408	WAYNE	19,002	9,607	9,265	130	342 R	50.6%	48.8%	50.9%	49.1%
49,524	WILKES	22,032	11,768	10,176	88	1,592 R	53.4%	46.2%	53.6%	46.4%
57,486	WILSON	15,087	6,795	8,209	83	1,414 D	45.0%	54.4%	45.3%	54.7%
24,599	YADKIN	10,471	5,916	4,497	58	1,419 R	56.5%	42.9%	56.8%	43.2%
12,629	YANCEY	6,650	2,688	3,932	30	1,244 D	40.4%	59.1%	40.6%	59.4%
5,082,059	TOTAL	1,678,914	741,960	927,365	9,589	185,405 D	44.2%	55.2%	44.4%	55.6%

NORTH CAROLINA

PRESIDENT 1972

1970 Census Population	County	Total Vote	Republican	Democratic	Other	Rep.-Dem. Plurality	Percentage Total Vote Rep.	Percentage Total Vote Dem.	Percentage Major Vote Rep.	Percentage Major Vote Dem.
96,362	ALAMANCE	29,549	22,046	6,833	670	15,213 R	74.6%	23.1%	76.3%	23.7%
19,466	ALEXANDER	8,506	5,865	2,468	173	3,397 R	69.0%	29.0%	70.4%	29.6%
8,134	ALLEGHANY	3,521	2,158	1,304	59	854 R	61.3%	37.0%	62.3%	37.7%
23,488	ANSON	5,833	3,551	2,188	94	1,363 R	60.9%	37.5%	61.9%	38.1%
19,571	ASHE	9,188	5,784	3,313	91	2,471 R	63.0%	36.1%	63.6%	36.4%
12,655	AVERY	4,179	3,510	627	42	2,883 R	84.0%	15.0%	84.8%	15.2%
35,980	BEAUFORT	9,928	6,915	2,901	112	4,014 R	69.7%	29.2%	70.4%	29.6%
20,528	BERTIE	4,747	2,874	1,819	54	1,055 R	60.5%	38.3%	61.2%	38.8%
26,477	BLADEN	6,497	4,205	2,201	91	2,004 R	64.7%	33.9%	65.6%	34.4%
24,223	BRUNSWICK	8,909	6,153	2,500	256	3,653 R	69.1%	28.1%	71.1%	28.9%
145,056	BUNCOMBE	45,594	32,091	12,626	877	19,465 R	70.4%	27.7%	71.8%	28.2%
60,364	BURKE	20,950	14,447	6,197	306	8,250 R	69.0%	29.6%	70.0%	30.0%
74,629	CABARRUS	24,048	18,384	5,336	328	13,048 R	76.4%	22.2%	77.5%	22.5%
56,699	CALDWELL	18,171	12,976	4,886	309	8,090 R	71.4%	26.9%	72.6%	27.4%
5,453	CAMDEN	1,510	909	556	45	353 R	60.2%	36.8%	62.0%	38.0%
31,603	CARTERET	11,415	8,463	2,805	147	5,658 R	74.1%	24.6%	75.1%	24.9%
19,055	CASWELL	5,001	2,983	1,922	96	1,061 R	59.6%	38.4%	60.8%	39.2%
90,873	CATAWBA	32,375	24,106	7,744	525	16,362 R	74.5%	23.9%	75.7%	24.3%
29,554	CHATHAM	9,941	6,175	3,624	142	2,551 R	62.1%	36.5%	63.0%	37.0%
16,330	CHEROKEE	6,604	4,113	2,411	80	1,702 R	62.3%	36.5%	63.0%	37.0%
10,764	CHOWAN	2,871	1,906	936	29	970 R	66.4%	32.6%	67.1%	32.9%
5,180	CLAY	2,370	1,545	797	28	748 R	65.2%	33.6%	66.0%	34.0%
72,556	CLEVELAND	19,048	13,726	4,994	328	8,732 R	72.1%	26.2%	73.3%	26.7%
46,937	COLUMBUS	11,987	8,468	3,305	214	5,163 R	70.6%	27.6%	71.9%	28.1%
62,554	CRAVEN	11,903	9,372	2,384	147	6,988 R	78.7%	20.0%	79.7%	20.3%
212,042	CUMBERLAND	34,595	24,376	9,853	366	14,523 R	70.5%	28.5%	71.2%	28.8%
6,976	CURRITUCK	2,367	1,578	718	71	860 R	66.7%	30.3%	68.7%	31.3%
6,995	DARE	2,641	1,986	634	21	1,352 R	75.2%	24.0%	75.8%	24.2%
95,627	DAVIDSON	33,262	24,875	7,691	696	17,184 R	74.8%	23.1%	76.4%	23.6%
18,855	DAVIE	7,416	5,613	1,578	225	4,035 R	75.7%	21.3%	78.1%	21.9%
38,015	DUPLIN	10,130	7,153	2,857	120	4,296 R	70.6%	28.2%	71.5%	28.5%
132,681	DURHAM	41,667	25,576	15,566	525	10,010 R	61.4%	37.4%	62.2%	37.8%
52,341	EDGECOMBE	13,184	8,244	4,635	305	3,609 R	62.5%	35.2%	64.0%	36.0%
214,348	FORSYTH	68,569	46,415	20,928	1,226	25,487 R	67.7%	30.5%	68.9%	31.1%
26,820	FRANKLIN	7,944	5,431	2,341	172	3,090 R	68.4%	29.5%	69.9%	30.1%
148,415	GASTON	36,901	27,956	8,462	483	19,494 R	75.8%	22.9%	76.8%	23.2%
8,524	GATES	2,478	1,264	1,177	37	87 R	51.0%	47.5%	51.8%	48.2%
6,562	GRAHAM	2,783	1,699	1,057	27	642 R	61.0%	38.0%	61.6%	38.4%
32,762	GRANVILLE	9,035	6,037	2,918	80	3,119 R	66.8%	32.3%	67.4%	32.6%
14,967	GREENE	3,684	2,788	847	49	1,941 R	75.7%	23.0%	76.7%	23.3%
288,590	GUILFORD	88,366	61,381	25,800	1,185	35,581 R	69.5%	29.2%	70.4%	29.6%
53,884	HALIFAX	13,375	8,908	4,241	226	4,667 R	66.6%	31.7%	67.7%	32.3%
49,667	HARNETT	13,744	10,259	3,347	138	6,912 R	74.6%	24.4%	75.4%	24.6%
41,710	HAYWOOD	13,731	8,903	4,515	313	4,388 R	64.8%	32.9%	66.4%	33.6%
42,804	HENDERSON	15,135	12,134	2,701	300	9,433 R	80.2%	17.8%	81.8%	18.2%
23,529	HERTFORD	4,789	2,794	1,928	67	866 R	58.3%	40.3%	59.2%	40.8%
16,436	HOKE	3,426	1,927	1,466	33	461 R	56.2%	42.8%	56.8%	43.2%
5,571	HYDE	1,545	1,112	403	30	709 R	72.0%	26.1%	73.4%	26.6%
72,197	IREDELL	22,682	16,736	5,088	858	11,648 R	73.8%	22.4%	76.7%	23.3%
21,593	JACKSON	7,967	4,709	3,169	89	1,540 R	59.1%	39.8%	59.8%	40.2%
61,737	JOHNSTON	18,011	14,272	3,488	251	10,784 R	79.2%	19.4%	80.4%	19.6%
9,779	JONES	2,800	1,650	1,093	57	557 R	58.9%	39.0%	60.2%	39.8%
30,467	LEE	8,026	5,836	2,024	166	3,812 R	72.7%	25.2%	74.2%	25.8%
55,204	LENOIR	14,975	11,065	3,672	238	7,393 R	73.9%	24.5%	75.1%	24.9%
32,682	LINCOLN	13,892	8,597	5,100	195	3,497 R	61.9%	36.7%	62.8%	37.2%
30,648	MCDOWELL	9,114	6,570	2,348	196	4,222 R	72.1%	25.8%	73.7%	26.3%
15,788	MACON	5,974	4,134	1,749	91	2,385 R	69.2%	29.3%	70.3%	29.7%
16,003	MADISON	5,350	3,273	2,039	38	1,234 R	61.2%	38.1%	61.6%	38.4%
24,730	MARTIN	6,091	4,188	1,840	63	2,348 R	68.8%	30.2%	69.5%	30.5%
354,656	MECKLENBURG	113,176	77,546	33,730	1,900	43,816 R	68.5%	29.8%	69.7%	30.3%

NORTH CAROLINA

PRESIDENT 1972

1970 Census Population	County	Total Vote	Republican	Democratic	Other	Rep.-Dem. Plurality	Percentage Total Vote Rep.	Percentage Total Vote Dem.	Percentage Major Vote Rep.	Percentage Major Vote Dem.
13,447	MITCHELL	5,081	4,240	800	41	3,440 R	83.4%	15.7%	84.1%	15.9%
19,267	MONTGOMERY	6,726	4,417	2,175	134	2,242 R	65.7%	32.3%	67.0%	33.0%
39,048	MOORE	13,308	9,406	3,627	275	5,779 R	70.7%	27.3%	72.2%	27.8%
59,122	NASH	17,761	12,679	4,503	579	8,176 R	71.4%	25.4%	73.8%	26.2%
82,996	NEW HANOVER	25,615	19,060	5,894	661	13,166 R	74.4%	23.0%	76.4%	23.6%
24,009	NORTHAMPTON	6,282	2,997	3,233	52	236 D	47.7%	51.5%	48.1%	51.9%
103,126	ONSLOW	12,921	10,343	2,424	154	7,919 R	80.0%	18.8%	81.0%	19.0%
57,707	ORANGE	24,408	11,632	12,634	142	1,002 D	47.7%	51.8%	47.9%	52.1%
9,467	PAMLICO	2,794	1,847	919	28	928 R	66.1%	32.9%	66.8%	33.2%
26,824	PASQUOTANK	6,193	3,906	2,115	172	1,791 R	63.1%	34.2%	64.9%	35.1%
18,149	PENDER	4,829	3,327	1,415	87	1,912 R	68.9%	29.3%	70.2%	29.8%
8,351	PERQUIMANS	2,076	1,299	723	54	576 R	62.6%	34.8%	64.2%	35.8%
25,914	PERSON	8,264	5,941	2,246	77	3,695 R	71.9%	27.2%	72.6%	27.4%
73,900	PITT	20,459	14,406	5,858	195	8,548 R	70.4%	28.6%	71.1%	28.9%
11,735	POLK	4,637	3,121	1,416	100	1,705 R	67.3%	30.5%	68.8%	31.2%
76,358	RANDOLPH	24,629	18,724	5,346	559	13,378 R	76.0%	21.7%	77.8%	22.2%
39,889	RICHMOND	9,356	5,692	3,508	156	2,184 R	60.8%	37.5%	61.9%	38.1%
84,842	ROBESON	18,941	11,362	7,391	188	3,971 R	60.0%	39.0%	60.6%	39.4%
72,402	ROCKINGHAM	20,407	14,519	5,530	358	8,989 R	71.1%	27.1%	72.4%	27.6%
90,035	ROWAN	28,274	20,735	6,834	705	13,901 R	73.3%	24.2%	75.2%	24.8%
47,337	RUTHERFORD	13,816	9,506	4,140	170	5,366 R	68.8%	30.0%	69.7%	30.3%
44,954	SAMPSON	14,726	9,684	4,888	154	4,796 R	65.8%	33.2%	66.5%	33.5%
26,929	SCOTLAND	5,472	3,485	1,938	49	1,547 R	63.7%	35.4%	64.3%	35.7%
42,822	STANLY	17,972	12,459	5,218	295	7,241 R	69.3%	29.0%	70.5%	29.5%
23,782	STOKES	10,646	7,118	3,254	274	3,864 R	66.9%	30.6%	68.6%	31.4%
51,415	SURRY	15,487	10,497	4,706	284	5,791 R	67.8%	30.4%	69.0%	31.0%
7,861	SWAIN	3,184	2,052	1,101	31	951 R	64.4%	34.6%	65.1%	34.9%
19,713	TRANSYLVANIA	8,404	5,860	2,321	223	3,539 R	69.7%	27.6%	71.6%	28.4%
3,806	TYRRELL	1,140	676	459	5	217 R	59.3%	40.3%	59.6%	40.4%
54,714	UNION	14,336	10,264	3,886	186	6,378 R	71.6%	27.1%	72.5%	27.5%
32,691	VANCE	9,710	6,491	3,117	102	3,374 R	66.8%	32.1%	67.6%	32.4%
228,453	WAKE	80,789	56,808	22,807	1,174	34,001 R	70.3%	28.2%	71.4%	28.6%
15,810	WARREN	4,366	2,603	1,698	65	905 R	59.6%	38.9%	60.5%	39.5%
14,038	WASHINGTON	4,151	2,559	1,546	46	1,013 R	61.6%	37.2%	62.3%	37.7%
23,404	WATAUGA	9,573	6,017	3,451	105	2,566 R	62.9%	36.0%	63.6%	36.4%
85,408	WAYNE	19,842	14,352	5,234	256	9,118 R	72.3%	26.4%	73.3%	26.7%
49,524	WILKES	17,994	13,105	4,634	255	8,471 R	72.8%	25.8%	73.9%	26.1%
57,486	WILSON	16,512	12,060	4,166	286	7,894 R	73.0%	25.2%	74.3%	25.7%
24,599	YADKIN	8,621	6,824	1,592	205	5,232 R	79.2%	18.5%	81.1%	18.9%
12,629	YANCEY	5,440	3,106	2,278	56	828 R	57.1%	41.9%	57.7%	42.3%
5,082,059	TOTAL	1,518,612	1,054,889	438,705	25,018	616,184 R	69.5%	28.9%	70.6%	29.4%

NORTH CAROLINA

PRESIDENT 1968

1960 Census Population	County	Total Vote	Republican	Democratic	AIP	Other	Plurality	Rep.	Dem.	AIP
								Percentage		
85,674	ALAMANCE	33,690	12,310	8,241	13,139		829 A	36.5%	24.5%	39.0%
15,625	ALEXANDER	8,416	4,379	1,834	2,203		2,176 R	52.0%	21.8%	26.2%
7,734	ALLEGHANY	3,701	1,695	1,102	904		593 R	45.8%	29.8%	24.4%
24,962	ANSON	8,014	1,474	2,969	3,571		602 A	18.4%	37.0%	44.6%
19,768	ASHE	9,208	4,894	3,426	888		1,468 R	53.1%	37.2%	9.6%
12,009	AVERY	4,518	3,197	631	690		2,507 R	70.8%	14.0%	15.3%
36,014	BEAUFORT	11,587	2,669	3,232	5,686		2,454 A	23.0%	27.9%	49.1%
24,350	BERTIE	7,126	811	3,207	3,108		99 D	11.4%	45.0%	43.6%
28,881	BLADEN	8,397	1,746	2,754	3,897		1,143 A	20.8%	32.8%	46.4%
20,278	BRUNSWICK	8,734	2,404	2,972	3,358		386 A	27.5%	34.0%	38.4%
130,074	BUNCOMBE	47,544	21,031	14,624	11,889		6,407 R	44.2%	30.8%	25.0%
52,701	BURKE	22,664	11,068	5,704	5,892		5,176 R	48.8%	25.2%	26.0%
68,137	CABARRUS	25,265	13,226	5,501	6,538		6,688 R	52.3%	21.8%	25.9%
49,552	CALDWELL	20,274	10,433	4,746	5,095		5,338 R	51.5%	23.4%	25.1%
5,598	CAMDEN	1,987	180	707	1,100		393 A	9.1%	35.6%	55.4%
30,940	CARTERET	11,416	4,593	3,762	3,061		831 R	40.2%	33.0%	26.8%
19,912	CASWELL	6,024	1,036	2,137	2,851		714 A	17.2%	35.5%	47.3%
73,191	CATAWBA	32,652	18,393	6,974	7,285		11,108 R	56.3%	21.4%	22.3%
26,785	CHATHAM	10,616	3,845	3,532	3,239		313 R	36.2%	33.3%	30.5%
16,335	CHEROKEE	7,085	3,768	2,402	915		1,366 R	53.2%	33.9%	12.9%
11,729	CHOWAN	3,695	798	1,201	1,696		495 A	21.6%	32.5%	45.9%
5,526	CLAY	2,530	1,390	847	293		543 R	54.9%	33.5%	11.6%
66,048	CLEVELAND	22,608	7,298	5,661	9,649		2,351 A	32.3%	25.0%	42.7%
48,973	COLUMBUS	14,817	3,881	4,243	6,693		2,450 A	26.2%	28.6%	45.2%
58,773	CRAVEN	13,740	2,991	4,240	6,509		2,269 A	21.8%	30.9%	47.4%
148,418	CUMBERLAND	28,620	9,143	9,938	9,539		399 D	31.9%	34.7%	33.3%
6,601	CURRITUCK	2,572	363	738	1,471		733 A	14.1%	28.7%	57.2%
5,935	DARE	2,579	1,035	700	844		191 R	40.1%	27.1%	32.7%
79,493	DAVIDSON	35,816	16,678	7,594	11,544		5,134 R	46.6%	21.2%	32.2%
16,728	DAVIE	7,883	3,866	1,502	2,515		1,351 R	49.0%	19.1%	31.9%
40,270	DUPLIN	12,257	2,724	3,451	6,082		2,631 A	22.2%	28.2%	49.6%
111,995	DURHAM	42,810	12,705	16,563	13,542		3,021 D	29.7%	38.7%	31.6%
54,228	EDGECOMBE	14,302	3,198	5,243	5,861		618 A	22.4%	36.7%	41.0%
189,426	FORSYTH	67,585	31,623	20,281	15,681		11,342 R	46.8%	30.0%	23.2%
28,755	FRANKLIN	9,755	1,375	2,855	5,525		2,670 A	14.1%	29.3%	56.6%
127,074	GASTON	42,814	18,741	10,100	13,973		4,768 R	43.8%	23.6%	32.6%
9,254	GATES	2,784	406	1,151	1,227		76 A	14.6%	41.3%	44.1%
6,432	GRAHAM	2,994	1,570	1,061	363		509 R	52.4%	35.4%	12.1%
33,110	GRANVILLE	8,546	1,837	2,638	4,071		1,433 A	21.5%	30.9%	47.6%
16,741	GREENE	5,116	650	1,560	2,906		1,346 A	12.7%	30.5%	56.8%
246,520	GUILFORD	84,351	38,996	25,604	19,751		13,392 R	46.2%	30.4%	23.4%
58,956	HALIFAX	15,191	3,148	4,927	7,116		2,189 A	20.7%	32.4%	46.8%
48,236	HARNETT	15,722	5,184	4,007	6,531		1,347 A	33.0%	25.5%	41.5%
39,711	HAYWOOD	15,806	6,205	5,703	3,898		502 R	39.3%	36.1%	24.7%
36,163	HENDERSON	16,248	9,334	3,053	3,861		5,473 R	57.4%	18.8%	23.8%
22,718	HERTFORD	6,603	1,125	3,275	2,203		1,072 D	17.0%	49.6%	33.4%
16,356	HOKE	4,542	812	2,185	1,545		640 D	17.9%	48.1%	34.0%
5,765	HYDE	2,003	401	769	833		64 A	20.0%	38.4%	41.6%
62,526	IREDELL	24,456	10,557	4,878	9,021		1,536 R	43.2%	19.9%	36.9%
17,780	JACKSON	7,783	3,747	2,956	1,080		791 R	48.1%	38.0%	13.9%
62,936	JOHNSTON	20,468	6,764	4,492	9,212		2,448 A	33.0%	21.9%	45.0%
11,005	JONES	3,366	361	1,225	1,780		555 A	10.7%	36.4%	52.9%
26,561	LEE	8,821	2,586	2,524	3,711		1,125 A	29.3%	28.6%	42.1%
55,276	LENOIR	15,733	3,844	3,853	8,036		4,183 A	24.4%	24.5%	51.1%
28,814	LINCOLN	13,393	6,188	4,044	3,161		2,144 R	46.2%	30.2%	23.6%
26,742	MCDOWELL	10,301	4,740	2,543	3,018		1,722 R	46.0%	24.7%	29.3%
14,935	MACON	6,527	3,295	2,070	1,162		1,225 R	50.5%	31.7%	17.8%
17,217	MADISON	6,365	3,130	2,201	1,034		929 R	49.2%	34.6%	16.2%
27,139	MARTIN	8,157	1,221	3,118	3,818		700 A	15.0%	38.2%	46.8%
272,111	MECKLENBURG	107,497	56,325	31,102	20,070		25,223 R	52.4%	28.9%	18.7%

NORTH CAROLINA

PRESIDENT 1968

1960 Census Population	County	Total Vote	Republican	Democratic	AIP	Other	Plurality	Percentage Rep.	Percentage Dem.	Percentage AIP
13,906	MITCHELL	5,200	3,778	819	603		2,959 R	72.7%	15.8%	11.6%
18,408	MONTGOMERY	7,739	3,070	2,410	2,259		660 R	39.7%	31.1%	29.2%
36,733	MOORE	12,168	5,322	3,583	3,263		1,739 R	43.7%	29.4%	26.8%
61,002	NASH	19,115	4,602	5,283	9,230		3,947 A	24.1%	27.6%	48.3%
71,742	NEW HANOVER	27,061	10,020	7,750	9,291		729 R	37.0%	28.6%	34.3%
26,811	NORTHAMPTON	7,918	860	4,072	2,986		1,086 D	10.9%	51.4%	37.7%
82,706	ONSLOW	12,267	3,444	3,281	5,542		2,098 A	28.1%	26.7%	45.2%
42,970	ORANGE	18,308	6,097	8,366	3,845		2,269 D	33.3%	45.7%	21.0%
9,850	PAMLICO	3,472	745	1,280	1,447		167 A	21.5%	36.9%	41.7%
25,630	PASQUOTANK	7,591	1,430	2,564	3,597		1,033 A	18.8%	33.8%	47.4%
18,508	PENDER	5,669	1,007	1,942	2,720		778 A	17.8%	34.3%	48.0%
9,178	PERQUIMANS	3,045	468	1,023	1,554		531 A	15.4%	33.6%	51.0%
26,394	PERSON	8,847	2,138	2,644	4,065		1,421 A	24.2%	29.9%	45.9%
69,942	PITT	22,608	5,745	7,696	9,167		1,471 A	25.4%	34.0%	40.5%
11,395	POLK	5,557	2,550	1,523	1,484		1,027 R	45.9%	27.4%	26.7%
61,497	RANDOLPH	25,693	13,450	5,351	6,892		6,558 R	52.3%	20.8%	26.8%
39,202	RICHMOND	12,579	2,865	4,257	5,457		1,200 A	22.8%	33.8%	43.4%
89,102	ROBESON	19,215	4,526	8,248	6,441		1,807 D	23.6%	42.9%	33.5%
69,629	ROCKINGHAM	24,193	8,095	6,774	9,324		1,229 A	33.5%	28.0%	38.5%
82,817	ROWAN	32,501	15,207	8,074	9,220		5,987 R	46.8%	24.8%	28.4%
45,091	RUTHERFORD	16,883	7,785	4,622	4,476		3,163 R	46.1%	27.4%	26.5%
48,013	SAMPSON	15,921	6,597	4,797	4,527		1,800 R	41.4%	30.1%	28.4%
25,183	SCOTLAND	5,985	1,717	2,252	2,016		236 D	28.7%	37.6%	33.7%
40,873	STANLY	18,333	9,428	4,199	4,706		4,722 R	51.4%	22.9%	25.7%
22,314	STOKES	10,565	4,781	2,374	3,410		1,371 R	45.3%	22.5%	32.3%
48,205	SURRY	18,829	9,638	5,088	4,103		4,550 R	51.2%	27.0%	21.8%
8,387	SWAIN	3,258	1,494	1,227	537		267 R	45.9%	37.7%	16.5%
16,372	TRANSYLVANIA	8,608	4,033	2,210	2,365		1,668 R	46.9%	25.7%	27.5%
4,520	TYRRELL	1,287	291	581	415		166 D	22.6%	45.1%	32.2%
44,670	UNION	13,681	5,290	3,630	4,761		529 R	38.7%	26.5%	34.8%
32,002	VANCE	11,348	2,252	3,852	5,244		1,392 A	19.8%	33.9%	46.2%
169,082	WAKE	67,157	28,928	20,979	17,250		7,949 R	43.1%	31.2%	25.7%
19,652	WARREN	5,383	796	2,293	2,294		1 A	14.8%	42.6%	42.6%
13,488	WASHINGTON	4,780	1,016	1,898	1,866		32 D	21.3%	39.7%	39.0%
17,529	WATAUGA	9,093	5,081	2,952	1,060		2,129 R	55.9%	32.5%	11.7%
82,059	WAYNE	19,725	5,678	5,338	8,709		3,031 A	28.8%	27.1%	44.2%
45,269	WILKES	18,568	11,195	4,497	2,876		6,698 R	60.3%	24.2%	15.5%
57,716	WILSON	16,129	4,053	4,173	7,903		3,730 A	25.1%	25.9%	49.0%
22,804	YADKIN	9,725	5,885	1,443	2,397		3,488 R	60.5%	14.8%	24.6%
14,008	YANCEY	5,415	2,448	2,215	752		233 R	45.2%	40.9%	13.9%
4,556,155	TOTAL	1,587,493	627,192	464,113	496,188		131,004 R	39.5%	29.2%	31.3%

NORTH CAROLINA

ELECTION NOTES

1984 Other vote was 3,794 Bergland (Libertarian); 799 Mason (Socialist Workers).

1980 Other vote was 52,800 Anderson (Independent); 9,677 Clark (Libertarian); 2,287 Commoner (Citizens); 416 DeBerry (Socialist Workers).

1976 Other vote was 5,607 Anderson (American); 2,219 MacBride (Libertarian); 755 LaRouche (Labor); 780 McCarthy (write-in); 228 scattered write-in.

1972 Other vote was Schmitz (American).

1968 Wallace on the ballot as American.

NORTH DAKOTA

POPULAR VOTE FOR PRESIDENT 1920 TO 1984

		Republican		Democratic				Percentage			
	Total					Other		Total Vote		Major Vote	
Year	Vote	Vote	Candidate	Vote	Candidate	Vote	Plurality	Rep.	Dem.	Rep.	Dem.
1984	308,971	200,336	Reagan, Ronald	104,429	Mondale, Walter F.	4,206	95,907 R	64.8%	33.8%	65.7%	34.3%
1980	301,545	193,695	Reagan, Ronald	79,189	Carter, Jimmy	28,661	114,506 R	64.2%	26.3%	71.0%	29.0%
1976	297,188	153,470	Ford, Gerald R.	136,078	Carter, Jimmy	7,640	17,392 R	51.6%	45.8%	53.0%	47.0%
1972	280,514	174,109	Nixon, Richard M.	100,384	McGovern, George S.	6,021	73,725 R	62.1%	35.8%	63.4%	36.6%
1968	247,882	138,669	Nixon, Richard M.	94,769	Humphrey, Hubert H.	14,444	43,900 R	55.9%	38.2%	59.4%	40.6%
1964	258,389	108,207	Goldwater, Barry M.	149,784	Johnson, Lyndon B.	398	41,577 D	41.9%	58.0%	41.9%	58.1%
1960	278,431	154,310	Nixon, Richard M.	123,963	Kennedy, John F.	158	30,347 R	55.4%	44.5%	55.5%	44.5%
1956	253,991	156,766	Eisenhower, Dwight D.	96,742	Stevenson, Adlai E.	483	60,024 R	61.7%	38.1%	61.8%	38.2%
1952	270,127	191,712	Eisenhower, Dwight D.	76,694	Stevenson, Adlai E.	1,721	115,018 R	71.0%	28.4%	71.4%	28.6%
1948	220,716	115,139	Dewey, Thomas E.	95,812	Truman, Harry S.	9,765	19,327 R	52.2%	43.4%	54.6%	45.4%
1944	220,182	118,535	Dewey, Thomas E.	100,144	Roosevelt, Franklin D.	1,503	18,391 R	53.8%	45.5%	54.2%	45.8%
1940	280,775	154,590	Willkie, Wendell	124,036	Roosevelt, Franklin D.	2,149	30,554 R	55.1%	44.2%	55.5%	44.5%
1936	273,716	72,751	Landon, Alfred M.	163,148	Roosevelt, Franklin D.	37,817	90,397 D	26.6%	59.6%	30.8%	69.2%
1932	256,290	71,772	Hoover, Herbert C.	178,350	Roosevelt, Franklin D.	6,168	106,578 D	28.0%	69.6%	28.7%	71.3%
1928	239,845	131,419	Hoover, Herbert C.	106,648	Smith, Alfred E.	1,778	24,771 R	54.8%	44.5%	55.2%	44.8%
1924 **	199,081	94,931	Coolidge, Calvin	13,858	Davis, John W.	90,292	5,009 R	47.7%	7.0%	87.3%	12.7%
1920	205,786	160,082	Harding, Warren G.	37,422	Cox, James M.	8,282	122,660 R	77.8%	18.2%	81.1%	18.9%

In 1924 other vote was 89,922 Progressive and 370 Communist.

ELECTORAL COLLEGE VOTE 1920 TO 1984

Year	Total	Republican	Democratic	Other
1984	3	3	—	—
1980	3	3	—	—
1976	3	3	—	—
1972	3	3	—	—
1968	4	4	—	—
1964	4	—	4	—
1960	4	4	—	—
1956	4	4	—	—
1952	4	4	—	—
1948	4	4	—	—
1944	4	4	—	—
1940	4	4	—	—
1936	4	—	4	—
1932	4	—	4	—
1928	5	5	—	—
1924	5	5	—	—
1920	5	5	—	—

NORTH DAKOTA

NORTH DAKOTA

PRESIDENT 1984

1980 Census Population	County	Total Vote	Republican	Democratic	Other	Rep.-Dem. Plurality	Percentage Total Vote Rep.	Total Vote Dem.	Major Vote Rep.	Major Vote Dem.
3,584	ADAMS	1,900	1,343	530	27	813 R	70.7%	27.9%	71.7%	28.3%
13,960	BARNES	6,925	4,348	2,507	70	1,841 R	62.8%	36.2%	63.4%	36.6%
7,944	BENSON	3,363	1,729	1,599	35	130 R	51.4%	47.5%	52.0%	48.0%
1,138	BILLINGS	653	505	133	15	372 R	77.3%	20.4%	79.2%	20.8%
9,239	BOTTINEAU	4,688	3,356	1,279	53	2,077 R	71.6%	27.3%	72.4%	27.6%
4,229	BOWMAN	2,149	1,559	562	28	997 R	72.5%	26.2%	73.5%	26.5%
3,822	BURKE	1,869	1,298	543	28	755 R	69.4%	29.1%	70.5%	29.5%
54,811	BURLEIGH	29,176	19,913	8,781	482	11,132 R	68.3%	30.1%	69.4%	30.6%
88,247	CASS	47,629	29,221	18,054	354	11,167 R	61.4%	37.9%	61.8%	38.2%
7,636	CAVALIER	3,804	2,661	1,110	33	1,551 R	70.0%	29.2%	70.6%	29.4%
7,207	DICKEY	3,546	2,460	1,051	35	1,409 R	69.4%	29.6%	70.1%	29.9%
3,494	DIVIDE	1,840	1,165	626	49	539 R	63.3%	34.0%	65.0%	35.0%
4,627	DUNN	2,324	1,583	716	25	867 R	68.1%	30.8%	68.9%	31.1%
3,554	EDDY	1,860	1,049	796	15	253 R	56.4%	42.8%	56.9%	43.1%
5,877	EMMONS	2,566	1,885	620	61	1,265 R	73.5%	24.2%	75.2%	24.8%
4,611	FOSTER	2,214	1,422	765	27	657 R	64.2%	34.6%	65.0%	35.0%
2,391	GOLDEN VALLEY	1,319	964	325	30	639 R	73.1%	24.6%	74.8%	25.2%
66,100	GRAND FORKS	26,191	15,898	10,050	243	5,848 R	60.7%	38.4%	61.3%	38.7%
4,274	GRANT	2,145	1,607	507	31	1,100 R	74.9%	23.6%	76.0%	24.0%
3,714	GRIGGS	2,094	1,254	828	12	426 R	59.9%	39.5%	60.2%	39.8%
4,275	HETTINGER	2,202	1,646	524	32	1,122 R	74.8%	23.8%	75.9%	24.1%
3,833	KIDDER	1,807	1,240	506	61	734 R	68.6%	28.0%	71.0%	29.0%
6,473	LA MOURE	3,108	1,978	1,086	44	892 R	63.6%	34.9%	64.6%	35.4%
3,493	LOGAN	1,676	1,222	401	53	821 R	72.9%	23.9%	75.3%	24.7%
7,858	MCHENRY	3,801	2,485	1,283	33	1,202 R	65.4%	33.8%	66.0%	34.0%
4,800	MCINTOSH	2,513	2,047	427	39	1,620 R	81.5%	17.0%	82.7%	17.3%
7,132	MCKENZIE	3,627	2,610	974	43	1,636 R	72.0%	26.9%	72.8%	27.2%
12,383	MCLEAN	5,847	3,673	2,062	112	1,611 R	62.8%	35.3%	64.0%	36.0%
9,404	MERCER	5,510	3,705	1,729	76	1,976 R	67.2%	31.4%	68.2%	31.8%
25,177	MORTON	11,356	7,146	3,996	214	3,150 R	62.9%	35.2%	64.1%	35.9%
7,679	MOUNTRAIL	3,555	1,959	1,565	31	394 R	55.1%	44.0%	55.6%	44.4%
5,233	NELSON	2,513	1,445	1,026	42	419 R	57.5%	40.8%	58.5%	41.5%
2,495	OLIVER	1,357	915	419	23	496 R	67.4%	30.9%	68.6%	31.4%
10,399	PEMBINA	4,387	2,895	1,367	125	1,528 R	66.0%	31.2%	67.9%	32.1%
6,166	PIERCE	2,626	1,883	691	52	1,192 R	71.7%	26.3%	73.2%	26.8%
13,048	RAMSEY	6,553	4,150	2,304	99	1,846 R	63.3%	35.2%	64.3%	35.7%
6,698	RANSOM	2,973	1,706	1,222	45	484 R	57.4%	41.1%	58.3%	41.7%
3,608	RENVILLE	1,774	1,163	592	19	571 R	65.6%	33.4%	66.3%	33.7%
19,207	RICHLAND	9,133	5,980	3,047	106	2,933 R	65.5%	33.4%	66.2%	33.8%
12,177	ROLETTE	3,751	1,479	2,179	93	700 D	39.4%	58.1%	40.4%	59.6%
5,512	SARGENT	2,725	1,385	1,295	45	90 R	50.8%	47.5%	51.7%	48.3%
2,819	SHERIDAN	1,396	1,075	306	15	769 R	77.0%	21.9%	77.8%	22.2%
3,620	SIOUX	1,118	442	655	21	213 D	39.5%	58.6%	40.3%	59.7%
1,157	SLOPE	605	419	174	12	245 R	69.3%	28.8%	70.7%	29.3%
23,697	STARK	10,740	7,641	2,759	340	4,882 R	71.1%	25.7%	73.5%	26.5%
3,106	STEELE	1,740	941	781	18	160 R	54.1%	44.9%	54.6%	45.4%
24,154	STUTSMAN	10,208	6,591	3,495	122	3,096 R	64.6%	34.2%	65.3%	34.7%
4,052	TOWNER	2,065	1,242	789	34	453 R	60.1%	38.2%	61.2%	38.8%
9,624	TRAILL	4,694	3,037	1,580	77	1,457 R	64.7%	33.7%	65.8%	34.2%
15,371	WALSH	6,704	4,347	2,264	93	2,083 R	64.8%	33.8%	65.8%	34.2%
58,392	WARD	23,623	16,077	7,336	210	8,741 R	68.1%	31.1%	68.7%	31.3%
6,979	WELLS	3,506	2,426	1,036	44	1,390 R	69.2%	29.5%	70.1%	29.9%
22,237	WILLIAMS	11,523	8,166	3,177	180	4,989 R	70.9%	27.6%	72.0%	28.0%
652,717	TOTAL	308,971	200,336	104,429	4,206	95,907 R	64.8%	33.8%	65.7%	34.3%

NORTH DAKOTA

PRESIDENT 1980

1980 Census Population	County	Total Vote	Republican	Democratic	Other	Rep.-Dem. Plurality	Percentage: Total Vote Rep.	Total Vote Dem.	Major Vote Rep.	Major Vote Dem.
3,584	ADAMS	1,941	1,334	470	137	864 R	68.7%	24.2%	73.9%	26.1%
13,960	BARNES	7,346	4,392	2,128	826	2,264 R	59.8%	29.0%	67.4%	32.6%
7,944	BENSON	3,587	2,149	1,119	319	1,030 R	59.9%	31.2%	65.8%	34.2%
1,138	BILLINGS	689	524	122	43	402 R	76.1%	17.7%	81.1%	18.9%
9,239	BOTTINEAU	4,828	3,394	1,090	344	2,304 R	70.3%	22.6%	75.7%	24.3%
4,229	BOWMAN	2,138	1,507	454	177	1,053 R	70.5%	21.2%	76.8%	23.2%
3,822	BURKE	1,968	1,442	418	108	1,024 R	73.3%	21.2%	77.5%	22.5%
54,811	BURLEIGH	27,137	18,437	6,129	2,571	12,308 R	67.9%	22.6%	75.1%	24.9%
88,247	CASS	43,620	23,886	13,562	6,172	10,324 R	54.8%	31.1%	63.8%	36.2%
7,636	CAVALIER	3,977	2,582	1,105	290	1,477 R	64.9%	27.8%	70.0%	30.0%
7,207	DICKEY	3,574	2,455	917	202	1,538 R	68.7%	25.7%	72.8%	27.2%
3,494	DIVIDE	1,918	1,267	509	142	758 R	66.1%	26.5%	71.3%	28.7%
4,627	DUNN	2,386	1,706	532	148	1,174 R	71.5%	22.3%	76.2%	23.8%
3,554	EDDY	1,883	1,153	539	191	614 R	61.2%	28.6%	68.1%	31.9%
5,877	EMMONS	3,054	2,369	502	183	1,867 R	77.6%	16.4%	82.5%	17.5%
4,611	FOSTER	2,303	1,534	586	183	948 R	66.6%	25.4%	72.4%	27.6%
2,391	GOLDEN VALLEY	1,349	1,006	259	84	747 R	74.6%	19.2%	79.5%	20.5%
66,100	GRAND FORKS	24,731	14,257	6,997	3,477	7,260 R	57.6%	28.3%	67.1%	32.9%
4,274	GRANT	2,339	1,891	317	131	1,574 R	80.8%	13.6%	85.6%	14.4%
3,714	GRIGGS	2,170	1,342	636	192	706 R	61.8%	29.3%	67.8%	32.2%
4,275	HETTINGER	2,257	1,699	434	124	1,265 R	75.3%	19.2%	79.7%	20.3%
3,833	KIDDER	1,913	1,474	326	113	1,148 R	77.1%	17.0%	81.9%	18.1%
6,473	LA MOURE	3,292	2,136	850	306	1,286 R	64.9%	25.8%	71.5%	28.5%
3,493	LOGAN	1,865	1,474	283	108	1,191 R	79.0%	15.2%	83.9%	16.1%
7,858	MCHENRY	4,104	2,922	939	243	1,983 R	71.2%	22.9%	75.7%	24.3%
4,800	MCINTOSH	2,873	2,471	308	94	2,163 R	86.0%	10.7%	88.9%	11.1%
7,132	MCKENZIE	3,368	2,265	867	236	1,398 R	67.3%	25.7%	72.3%	27.7%
12,383	MCLEAN	6,246	4,234	1,613	399	2,621 R	67.8%	25.8%	72.4%	27.6%
9,404	MERCER	4,741	3,224	1,209	308	2,015 R	68.0%	25.5%	72.7%	27.3%
25,177	MORTON	11,458	7,659	2,861	938	4,798 R	66.8%	25.0%	72.8%	27.2%
7,679	MOUNTRAIL	3,587	2,165	1,183	239	982 R	60.4%	33.0%	64.7%	35.3%
5,233	NELSON	2,595	1,611	726	258	885 R	62.1%	28.0%	68.9%	31.1%
2,495	OLIVER	1,316	966	270	80	696 R	73.4%	20.5%	78.2%	21.8%
10,399	PEMBINA	4,718	3,101	1,239	378	1,862 R	65.7%	26.3%	71.5%	28.5%
6,166	PIERCE	2,988	2,273	517	198	1,756 R	76.1%	17.3%	81.5%	18.5%
13,048	RAMSEY	6,285	4,078	1,607	600	2,471 R	64.9%	25.6%	71.7%	28.3%
6,698	RANSOM	3,142	1,883	974	285	909 R	59.9%	31.0%	65.9%	34.1%
3,608	RENVILLE	1,842	1,154	570	118	584 R	62.6%	30.9%	66.9%	33.1%
19,207	RICHLAND	9,337	5,711	2,698	928	3,013 R	61.2%	28.9%	67.9%	32.1%
12,177	ROLETTE	3,566	1,599	1,660	307	61 D	44.8%	46.6%	49.1%	50.9%
5,512	SARGENT	2,823	1,565	1,048	210	517 R	55.4%	37.1%	59.9%	40.1%
2,819	SHERIDAN	1,607	1,326	208	73	1,118 R	82.5%	12.9%	86.4%	13.6%
3,620	SIOUX	1,090	620	383	87	237 R	56.9%	35.1%	61.8%	38.2%
1,157	SLOPE	647	462	128	57	334 R	71.4%	19.8%	78.3%	21.7%
23,697	STARK	9,003	6,312	2,016	675	4,296 R	70.1%	22.4%	75.8%	24.2%
3,106	STEELE	1,870	997	617	256	380 R	53.3%	33.0%	61.8%	38.2%
24,154	STUTSMAN	10,249	6,545	2,573	1,131	3,972 R	63.9%	25.1%	71.8%	28.2%
4,052	TOWNER	2,119	1,375	568	176	807 R	64.9%	26.8%	70.8%	29.2%
9,624	TRAILL	5,076	3,092	1,428	556	1,664 R	60.9%	28.1%	68.4%	31.6%
15,371	WALSH	6,938	4,488	1,850	600	2,638 R	64.7%	26.7%	70.8%	29.2%
58,392	WARD	22,189	14,997	5,554	1,638	9,443 R	67.6%	25.0%	73.0%	27.0%
6,979	WELLS	3,599	2,660	746	193	1,914 R	73.9%	20.7%	78.1%	21.9%
22,237	WILLIAMS	9,904	6,530	2,545	829	3,985 R	65.9%	25.7%	72.0%	28.0%
652,717	TOTAL	301,545	193,695	79,189	28,661	114,506 R	64.2%	26.3%	71.0%	29.0%

NORTH DAKOTA

PRESIDENT 1976

1970 Census Population	County	Total Vote	Republican	Democratic	Other	Rep.-Dem. Plurality	Percentage Total Vote Rep.	Percentage Total Vote Dem.	Percentage Major Vote Rep.	Percentage Major Vote Dem.
3,832	ADAMS	1,937	940	959	38	19 D	48.5%	49.5%	49.5%	50.5%
14,669	BARNES	7,462	4,011	3,321	130	690 R	53.8%	44.5%	54.7%	45.3%
8,245	BENSON	3,725	1,689	1,973	63	284 D	45.3%	53.0%	46.1%	53.9%
1,198	BILLINGS	684	351	285	48	66 R	51.3%	41.7%	55.2%	44.8%
9,496	BOTTINEAU	4,700	2,638	1,987	75	651 R	56.1%	42.3%	57.0%	43.0%
3,901	BOWMAN	1,998	1,033	911	54	122 R	51.7%	45.6%	53.1%	46.9%
4,739	BURKE	2,089	1,087	899	103	188 R	52.0%	43.0%	54.7%	45.3%
40,714	BURLEIGH	23,549	13,680	9,188	681	4,492 R	58.1%	39.0%	59.8%	40.2%
73,653	CASS	41,411	22,583	17,879	949	4,704 R	54.5%	43.2%	55.8%	44.2%
8,213	CAVALIER	4,300	2,046	2,178	76	132 D	47.6%	50.7%	48.4%	51.6%
6,976	DICKEY	3,709	2,027	1,612	70	415 R	54.7%	43.5%	55.7%	44.3%
4,564	DIVIDE	1,978	881	1,057	40	176 D	44.5%	53.4%	45.5%	54.5%
4,895	DUNN	2,157	1,041	1,051	65	10 D	48.3%	48.7%	49.8%	50.2%
4,103	EDDY	2,054	890	1,123	41	233 D	43.3%	54.7%	44.2%	55.8%
7,200	EMMONS	2,984	1,370	1,459	155	89 D	45.9%	48.9%	48.4%	51.6%
4,832	FOSTER	2,305	1,120	1,147	38	27 D	48.6%	49.8%	49.4%	50.6%
2,611	GOLDEN VALLEY	1,208	633	479	96	154 R	52.4%	39.7%	56.9%	43.1%
61,102	GRAND FORKS	26,218	13,820	11,545	853	2,275 R	52.7%	44.0%	54.5%	45.5%
5,009	GRANT	2,258	1,205	952	101	253 R	53.4%	42.2%	55.9%	44.1%
4,184	GRIGGS	2,262	1,086	1,122	54	36 D	48.0%	49.6%	49.2%	50.8%
5,075	HETTINGER	2,302	1,135	1,095	72	40 R	49.3%	47.6%	50.9%	49.1%
4,362	KIDDER	2,023	954	936	133	18 R	47.2%	46.3%	50.5%	49.5%
7,117	LA MOURE	3,538	1,735	1,718	85	17 R	49.0%	48.6%	50.2%	49.8%
4,245	LOGAN	1,876	944	809	123	135 R	50.3%	43.1%	53.9%	46.1%
8,977	MCHENRY	4,111	2,043	1,994	74	49 R	49.7%	48.5%	50.6%	49.4%
5,545	MCINTOSH	2,776	1,785	912	79	873 R	64.3%	32.9%	66.2%	33.8%
6,127	MCKENZIE	2,978	1,595	1,335	48	260 R	53.6%	44.8%	54.4%	45.6%
11,251	MCLEAN	5,665	2,729	2,815	121	86 D	48.2%	49.7%	49.2%	50.8%
6,175	MERCER	3,414	1,982	1,298	134	684 R	58.1%	38.0%	60.4%	39.6%
20,310	MORTON	10,462	4,921	5,241	300	320 D	47.0%	50.1%	48.4%	51.6%
8,437	MOUNTRAIL	3,708	1,430	2,189	89	759 D	38.6%	59.0%	39.5%	60.5%
5,776	NELSON	3,015	1,336	1,610	69	274 D	44.3%	53.4%	45.3%	54.7%
2,322	OLIVER	1,140	575	529	36	46 R	50.4%	46.4%	52.1%	47.9%
10,728	PEMBINA	5,209	2,810	2,274	125	536 R	53.9%	43.7%	55.3%	44.7%
6,323	PIERCE	2,887	1,396	1,434	57	38 D	48.4%	49.7%	49.3%	50.7%
12,915	RAMSEY	6,502	3,293	3,096	113	197 R	50.6%	47.6%	51.5%	48.5%
7,102	RANSOM	3,456	1,696	1,715	45	19 D	49.1%	49.6%	49.7%	50.3%
3,828	RENVILLE	1,846	812	1,008	26	196 D	44.0%	54.6%	44.6%	55.4%
18,089	RICHLAND	9,785	4,991	4,592	202	399 R	51.0%	46.9%	52.1%	47.9%
11,549	ROLETTE	3,693	1,094	2,531	68	1,437 D	29.6%	68.5%	30.2%	69.8%
5,937	SARGENT	3,031	1,344	1,644	43	300 D	44.3%	54.2%	45.0%	55.0%
3,232	SHERIDAN	1,536	935	569	32	366 R	60.9%	37.0%	62.2%	37.8%
3,632	SIOUX	1,081	354	697	30	343 D	32.7%	64.5%	33.7%	66.3%
1,484	SLOPE	726	355	347	24	8 R	48.9%	47.8%	50.6%	49.4%
19,613	STARK	8,760	4,374	4,076	310	298 R	49.9%	46.5%	51.8%	48.2%
3,749	STEELE	1,926	835	1,066	25	231 D	43.4%	55.3%	43.9%	56.1%
23,550	STUTSMAN	10,780	5,653	4,883	244	770 R	52.4%	45.3%	53.7%	46.3%
4,645	TOWNER	2,234	993	1,216	25	223 D	44.4%	54.4%	45.0%	55.0%
9,571	TRAILL	5,251	2,800	2,352	99	448 R	53.3%	44.8%	54.3%	45.7%
16,251	WALSH	7,309	3,518	3,555	236	37 D	48.1%	48.6%	49.7%	50.3%
58,560	WARD	22,721	12,751	9,484	486	3,267 R	56.1%	41.7%	57.3%	42.7%
7,847	WELLS	3,767	1,941	1,742	84	199 R	51.5%	46.2%	52.7%	47.3%
19,301	WILLIAMS	8,692	4,230	4,189	273	41 R	48.7%	48.2%	50.2%	49.8%
617,761	TOTAL	297,188	153,470	136,078	7,640	17,392 R	51.6%	45.8%	53.0%	47.0%

NORTH DAKOTA

PRESIDENT 1972

1970 Census Population	County	Total Vote	Republican	Democratic	Other	Rep.-Dem. Plurality	Percentage Total Vote Rep.	Total Vote Dem.	Major Vote Rep.	Major Vote Dem.
3,832	ADAMS	1,875	1,177	665	33	512 R	62.8%	35.5%	63.9%	36.1%
14,669	BARNES	7,389	4,518	2,804	67	1,714 R	61.1%	37.9%	61.7%	38.3%
8,245	BENSON	3,721	2,050	1,635	36	415 R	55.1%	43.9%	55.6%	44.4%
1,198	BILLINGS	729	509	192	28	317 R	69.8%	26.3%	72.6%	27.4%
9,496	BOTTINEAU	4,688	3,263	1,369	56	1,894 R	69.6%	29.2%	70.4%	29.6%
3,901	BOWMAN	1,801	1,111	643	47	468 R	61.7%	35.7%	63.3%	36.7%
4,739	BURKE	2,179	1,446	651	82	795 R	66.4%	29.9%	69.0%	31.0%
40,714	BURLEIGH	20,644	13,909	5,841	894	8,068 R	67.4%	28.3%	70.4%	29.6%
73,653	CASS	36,306	21,770	14,073	463	7,697 R	60.0%	38.8%	60.7%	39.3%
8,213	CAVALIER	4,824	2,898	1,867	59	1,031 R	60.1%	38.7%	60.8%	39.2%
6,976	DICKEY	3,581	2,277	1,266	38	1,011 R	63.6%	35.4%	64.3%	35.7%
4,564	DIVIDE	2,040	1,230	774	36	456 R	60.3%	37.9%	61.4%	38.6%
4,895	DUNN	2,197	1,438	644	115	794 R	65.5%	29.3%	69.1%	30.9%
4,103	EDDY	1,964	1,022	911	31	111 R	52.0%	46.4%	52.9%	47.1%
7,200	EMMONS	3,400	2,194	1,115	91	1,079 R	64.5%	32.8%	66.3%	33.7%
4,832	FOSTER	2,243	1,352	861	30	491 R	60.3%	38.4%	61.1%	38.9%
2,611	GOLDEN VALLEY	1,229	774	362	93	412 R	63.0%	29.5%	68.1%	31.9%
61,102	GRAND FORKS	23,475	13,361	9,416	698	3,945 R	56.9%	40.1%	58.7%	41.3%
5,009	GRANT	2,236	1,569	596	71	973 R	70.2%	26.7%	72.5%	27.5%
4,184	GRIGGS	2,258	1,312	901	45	411 R	58.1%	39.9%	59.3%	40.7%
5,075	HETTINGER	2,327	1,511	726	90	785 R	64.9%	31.2%	67.5%	32.5%
4,362	KIDDER	1,961	1,315	557	89	758 R	67.1%	28.4%	70.2%	29.8%
7,117	LA MOURE	3,539	2,110	1,399	30	711 R	59.6%	39.5%	60.1%	39.9%
4,245	LOGAN	2,031	1,408	554	69	854 R	69.3%	27.3%	71.8%	28.2%
8,977	MCHENRY	4,346	2,765	1,554	27	1,211 R	63.6%	35.8%	64.0%	36.0%
5,545	MCINTOSH	2,990	2,440	521	29	1,919 R	81.6%	17.4%	82.4%	17.6%
6,127	MCKENZIE	2,904	1,913	937	54	976 R	65.9%	32.3%	67.1%	32.9%
11,251	MCLEAN	5,398	3,575	1,703	120	1,872 R	66.2%	31.5%	67.7%	32.3%
6,175	MERCER	3,456	2,567	784	105	1,783 R	74.3%	22.7%	76.6%	23.4%
20,310	MORTON	9,177	5,494	3,312	371	2,182 R	59.9%	36.1%	62.4%	37.6%
8,437	MOUNTRAIL	3,496	2,038	1,391	67	647 R	58.3%	39.8%	59.4%	40.6%
5,776	NELSON	3,028	1,625	1,358	45	267 R	53.7%	44.8%	54.5%	45.5%
2,322	OLIVER	1,027	669	293	65	376 R	65.1%	28.5%	69.5%	30.5%
10,728	PEMBINA	5,203	3,317	1,801	85	1,516 R	63.8%	34.6%	64.8%	35.2%
6,323	PIERCE	2,978	1,970	973	35	997 R	66.2%	32.7%	66.9%	33.1%
12,915	RAMSEY	6,400	3,954	2,384	62	1,570 R	61.8%	37.3%	62.4%	37.6%
7,102	RANSOM	3,435	2,056	1,355	24	701 R	59.9%	39.4%	60.3%	39.7%
3,828	RENVILLE	1,835	1,121	702	12	419 R	61.1%	38.3%	61.5%	38.5%
18,089	RICHLAND	8,624	5,194	3,367	63	1,827 R	60.2%	39.0%	60.7%	39.3%
11,549	ROLETTE	3,559	1,713	1,803	43	90 D	48.1%	50.7%	48.7%	51.3%
5,937	SARGENT	2,966	1,616	1,331	19	285 R	54.5%	44.9%	54.8%	45.2%
3,232	SHERIDAN	1,809	1,460	334	15	1,126 R	80.7%	18.5%	81.4%	18.6%
3,632	SIOUX	1,142	561	557	24	4 R	49.1%	48.8%	50.2%	49.8%
1,484	SLOPE	690	413	249	28	164 R	59.9%	36.1%	62.4%	37.6%
19,613	STARK	8,131	5,115	2,636	380	2,479 R	62.9%	32.4%	66.0%	34.0%
3,749	STEELE	1,970	1,063	892	15	171 R	54.0%	45.3%	54.4%	45.6%
23,550	STUTSMAN	10,028	6,269	3,589	170	2,680 R	62.5%	35.8%	63.6%	36.4%
4,645	TOWNER	2,325	1,349	944	32	405 R	58.0%	40.6%	58.8%	41.2%
9,571	TRAILL	5,078	3,118	1,892	68	1,226 R	61.4%	37.3%	62.2%	37.8%
16,251	WALSH	7,090	3,991	2,908	191	1,083 R	56.3%	41.0%	57.8%	42.2%
58,560	WARD	20,868	13,900	6,706	262	7,194 R	66.6%	32.1%	67.5%	32.5%
7,847	WELLS	3,910	2,519	1,297	94	1,222 R	64.4%	33.2%	66.0%	34.0%
19,301	WILLIAMS	8,014	4,800	2,989	225	1,811 R	59.9%	37.3%	61.6%	38.4%
617,761	TOTAL	280,514	174,109	100,384	6,021	73,725 R	62.1%	35.8%	63.4%	36.6%

NORTH DAKOTA

PRESIDENT 1968

1960 Census Population	County	Total Vote	Republican	Democratic	AIP	Other	Plurality	Percentage		
								Rep.	Dem.	AIP
4,449	ADAMS	1,781	1,020	641	116	4	379 R	57.3%	36.0%	6.5%
16,719	BARNES	6,805	3,831	2,623	348	3	1,208 R	56.3%	38.5%	5.1%
9,435	BENSON	3,643	1,707	1,772	164		65 D	46.9%	48.6%	4.5%
1,513	BILLINGS	638	395	174	69		221 R	61.9%	27.3%	10.8%
11,315	BOTTINEAU	4,384	2,633	1,520	230	1	1,113 R	60.1%	34.7%	5.2%
4,154	BOWMAN	1,642	927	559	156		368 R	56.5%	34.0%	9.5%
5,886	BURKE	2,180	1,239	808	132	1	431 R	56.8%	37.1%	6.1%
34,016	BURLEIGH	16,649	10,661	5,139	818	31	5,522 R	64.0%	30.9%	4.9%
66,947	CASS	27,271	15,240	10,819	1,167	45	4,421 R	55.9%	39.7%	4.3%
10,064	CAVALIER	3,841	1,953	1,631	257		322 R	50.8%	42.5%	6.7%
8,147	DICKEY	3,348	2,087	1,098	161	2	989 R	62.3%	32.8%	4.8%
5,566	DIVIDE	2,048	1,032	914	102		118 R	50.4%	44.6%	5.0%
6,350	DUNN	2,149	1,207	772	169	1	435 R	56.2%	35.9%	7.9%
4,936	EDDY	1,992	1,018	893	76	5	125 R	51.1%	44.8%	3.8%
8,462	EMMONS	3,061	1,991	756	311	3	1,235 R	65.0%	24.7%	10.2%
5,361	FOSTER	2,139	1,119	897	123		222 R	52.3%	41.9%	5.8%
3,100	GOLDEN VALLEY	1,199	735	348	115	1	387 R	61.3%	29.0%	9.6%
48,677	GRAND FORKS	18,849	9,802	7,695	1,332	20	2,107 R	52.0%	40.8%	7.1%
6,248	GRANT	2,296	1,648	488	157	3	1,160 R	71.8%	21.3%	6.8%
5,023	GRIGGS	2,227	1,110	1,008	109		102 R	49.8%	45.3%	4.9%
6,317	HETTINGER	2,226	1,424	638	163	1	786 R	64.0%	28.7%	7.3%
5,386	KIDDER	1,947	1,204	548	192	3	656 R	61.8%	28.1%	9.9%
8,705	LA MOURE	3,468	2,008	1,269	189	2	739 R	57.9%	36.6%	5.4%
5,369	LOGAN	2,010	1,416	459	135		957 R	70.4%	22.8%	6.7%
11,099	MCHENRY	4,106	2,226	1,595	281	4	631 R	54.2%	38.8%	6.8%
6,702	MCINTOSH	2,732	2,258	342	129	3	1,916 R	82.7%	12.5%	4.7%
7,296	MCKENZIE	2,725	1,625	935	164	1	690 R	59.6%	34.3%	6.0%
14,030	MCLEAN	5,030	2,764	2,050	216		714 R	55.0%	40.8%	4.3%
6,805	MERCER	2,939	2,039	730	169	1	1,309 R	69.4%	24.8%	5.8%
20,992	MORTON	8,115	4,465	3,156	489	5	1,309 R	55.0%	38.9%	6.0%
10,077	MOUNTRAIL	3,370	1,494	1,662	212	2	168 D	44.3%	49.3%	6.3%
7,034	NELSON	3,162	1,526	1,477	157	2	49 R	48.3%	46.7%	5.0%
2,610	OLIVER	971	616	269	85	1	347 R	63.4%	27.7%	8.8%
12,946	PEMBINA	4,596	2,574	1,686	335	1	888 R	56.0%	36.7%	7.3%
7,394	PIERCE	2,979	1,700	1,048	229	2	652 R	57.1%	35.2%	7.7%
13,443	RAMSEY	5,845	3,189	2,384	269	3	805 R	54.6%	40.8%	4.6%
8,078	RANSOM	3,383	1,943	1,286	153	1	657 R	57.4%	38.0%	4.5%
4,698	RENVILLE	1,816	851	880	84	1	29 D	46.9%	48.5%	4.6%
18,824	RICHLAND	7,767	4,224	3,098	443	2	1,126 R	54.4%	39.9%	5.7%
10,641	ROLETTE	3,253	1,211	1,870	172		659 D	37.2%	57.5%	5.3%
6,856	SARGENT	2,849	1,386	1,308	154	1	78 R	48.6%	45.9%	5.4%
4,350	SHERIDAN	1,727	1,295	350	79	3	945 R	75.0%	20.3%	4.6%
3,662	SIOUX	1,065	482	525	58		43 D	45.3%	49.3%	5.4%
1,893	SLOPE	682	379	238	64	1	141 R	55.6%	34.9%	9.4%
18,451	STARK	7,444	4,365	2,577	500	2	1,788 R	58.6%	34.6%	6.7%
4,719	STEELE	2,031	952	991	88		39 D	46.9%	48.8%	4.3%
25,137	STUTSMAN	9,184	5,162	3,532	477	13	1,630 R	56.2%	38.5%	5.2%
5,624	TOWNER	2,225	1,109	990	124	2	119 R	49.8%	44.5%	5.6%
10,583	TRAILL	4,678	2,692	1,740	243	3	952 R	57.5%	37.2%	5.2%
17,997	WALSH	6,812	3,410	2,948	453	1	462 R	50.1%	43.3%	6.7%
47,072	WARD	17,095	9,079	7,105	896	15	1,974 R	53.1%	41.6%	5.2%
9,237	WELLS	3,782	2,266	1,265	247	4	1,001 R	59.9%	33.4%	6.5%
22,051	WILLIAMS	7,726	3,980	3,263	483		717 R	51.5%	42.2%	6.3%
632,446	TOTAL	247,882	138,669	94,769	14,244	200	43,900 R	55.9%	38.2%	5.7%

NORTH DAKOTA

ELECTION NOTES

1984 Other vote was 1,278 LaRouche (Independent); 1,077 Richards (Populist); 703 Bergland (Libertarian); 368 Johnson (Citizens); 239 Mason (Socialist Workers); 220 Dodge (Prohibition); 169 Hall (Communist); 152 Serrette (New Alliance).

1980 Other vote was 23,640 Anderson (Independent); 3,743 Clark (Libertarian); 429 Commoner (Citizens); 296 McLain (Natural Peoples League); 235 Greaves (American); 93 Hall (Communist); 89 DeBerry (Socialist Workers); 82 McReynolds (Socialist); 54 Bubar (Statesman).

1976 Other vote was 3,796 Anderson (American); 2,952 McCarthy (Independent); 269 Maddox (American Independent); 253 MacBride (Libertarian); 142 LaRouche (U.S. Labor); 84 Hall (Communist); 63 Bubar (Prohibition); 43 Camejo (Socialist Workers); 38 Zeidler (Socialist). Early unamended canvass gave the Communist vote as 85; the Libertarian vote as 256 and the American vote as 3,698 (98 votes had been omitted in Mercer county).

1972 Other vote was 5,646 Schmitz (American); 288 Jenness (Socialist Workers); 87 Hall (Communist).

1968 Wallace on the ballot as American. Other vote was 128 Halstead (Socialist Workers); 38 Munn (Prohibition); 34 Troxell (Constitution).

OHIO

POPULAR VOTE FOR PRESIDENT 1920 TO 1984

Year	Total Vote	Republican Vote	Republican Candidate	Democratic Vote	Democratic Candidate	Other Vote	Plurality	Percentage Total Vote Rep.	Percentage Total Vote Dem.	Percentage Major Vote Rep.	Percentage Major Vote Dem.
1984	4,547,619	2,678,560	Reagan, Ronald	1,825,440	Mondale, Walter F.	43,619	853,120 R	58.9%	40.1%	59.5%	40.5%
1980	4,283,603	2,206,545	Reagan, Ronald	1,752,414	Carter, Jimmy	324,644	454,131 R	51.5%	40.9%	55.7%	44.3%
1976	4,111,873	2,000,505	Ford, Gerald R.	2,011,621	Carter, Jimmy	99,747	11,116 D	48.7%	48.9%	49.9%	50.1%
1972	4,094,787	2,441,827	Nixon, Richard M.	1,558,889	McGovern, George S.	94,071	882,938 R	59.6%	38.1%	61.0%	39.0%
1968	3,959,698	1,791,014	Nixon, Richard M.	1,700,586	Humphrey, Hubert H.	468,098	90,428 R	45.2%	42.9%	51.3%	48.7%
1964	3,969,196	1,470,865	Goldwater, Barry M.	2,498,331	Johnson, Lyndon B.		1,027,466 D	37.1%	62.9%	37.1%	62.9%
1960	4,161,859	2,217,611	Nixon, Richard M.	1,944,248	Kennedy, John F.		273,363 R	53.3%	46.7%	53.3%	46.7%
1956	3,702,265	2,262,610	Eisenhower, Dwight D.	1,439,655	Stevenson, Adlai E.		822,955 R	61.1%	38.9%	61.1%	38.9%
1952	3,700,758	2,100,391	Eisenhower, Dwight D.	1,600,367	Stevenson, Adlai E.		500,024 R	56.8%	43.2%	56.8%	43.2%
1948	2,936,071	1,445,684	Dewey, Thomas E.	1,452,791	Truman, Harry S.	37,596	7,107 D	49.2%	49.5%	49.9%	50.1%
1944	3,153,056	1,582,293	Dewey, Thomas E.	1,570,763	Roosevelt, Franklin D.		11,530 R	50.2%	49.8%	50.2%	49.8%
1940	3,319,912	1,586,773	Willkie, Wendell	1,733,139	Roosevelt, Franklin D.		146,366 D	47.8%	52.2%	47.8%	52.2%
1936	3,012,660	1,127,855	Landon, Alfred M.	1,747,140	Roosevelt, Franklin D.	137,665	619,285 D	37.4%	58.0%	39.2%	60.8%
1932	2,609,728	1,227,319	Hoover, Herbert C.	1,301,695	Roosevelt, Franklin D.	80,714	74,376 D	47.0%	49.9%	48.5%	51.5%
1928	2,508,346	1,627,546	Hoover, Herbert C.	864,210	Smith, Alfred E.	16,590	763,336 R	64.9%	34.5%	65.3%	34.7%
1924 **	2,016,296	1,176,130	Coolidge, Calvin	477,887	Davis, John W.	362,279	698,243 R	58.3%	23.7%	71.1%	28.9%
1920	2,021,653	1,182,022	Harding, Warren G.	780,037	Cox, James M.	59,594	401,985 R	58.5%	38.6%	60.2%	39.8%

In 1924 other vote was 358,008 Progressive; 3,025 Socialist Labor and 1,246 Commonwealth Land.

ELECTORAL COLLEGE VOTE 1920 TO 1984

Year	Total	Republican	Democratic	Other
1984	23	23	—	—
1980	25	25	—	—
1976	25	—	25	—
1972	25	25	—	—
1968	26	26	—	—
1964	26	—	26	—
1960	25	25	—	—
1956	25	25	—	—
1952	25	25	—	—
1948	25	—	25	—
1944	25	25	—	—
1940	26	—	26	—
1936	26	—	26	—
1932	26	—	26	—
1928	24	24	—	—
1924	24	24	—	—
1920	24	24	—	—

OHIO

WILLIAMS
FULTON
LUCAS
OTTAWA
LAKE
ASHTABULA
GEAUGA
DEFIANCE
HENRY
WOOD
SANDUSKY
ERIE
LORAIN
CUYAHOGA
TRUMBULL
PAULDING
PUTNAM
HANCOCK
SENECA
HURON
MEDINA
SUMMIT
PORTAGE
MAHONING
VAN WERT
ALLEN
WYANDOT
CRAWFORD
RICHLAND
ASHLAND
WAYNE
STARK
COLUMBIANA
HARDIN
CARROLL
MERCER
AUGLAIZE
MARION
MORROW
HOLMES
KNOX
TUSCARAWAS
JEFFERSON
LOGAN
SHELBY
UNION
DELAWARE
COSHOCTON
HARRISON
DARKE
CHAMPAIGN
MIAMI
LICKING
GUERNSEY
BELMONT
FRANKLIN
MUSKINGUM
CLARK
MADISON
NOBLE
PREBLE
MONTGOMERY
GREENE
FAIRFIELD
PERRY
MONROE
PICKAWAY
MORGAN
FAYETTE
HOCKING
WASHINGTON
BUTLER
WARREN
CLINTON
ROSS
ATHENS
VINTON
HAMILTON
HIGHLAND
MEIGS
CLERMONT
PIKE
JACKSON
BROWN
ADAMS
SCIOTO
GALLIA
LAWRENCE

OHIO

PRESIDENT 1984

1980 Census Population	County	Total Vote	Republican	Democratic	Other	Rep.-Dem. Plurality	Percentage Total Vote Rep.	Percentage Total Vote Dem.	Percentage Major Vote Rep.	Percentage Major Vote Dem.
24,328	ADAMS	9,729	6,113	3,534	82	2,579 R	62.8%	36.3%	63.4%	36.6%
112,241	ALLEN	45,911	33,506	12,176	229	21,330 R	73.0%	26.5%	73.3%	26.7%
46,178	ASHLAND	19,272	14,339	4,786	147	9,553 R	74.4%	24.8%	75.0%	25.0%
104,215	ASHTABULA	41,397	21,669	19,344	384	2,325 R	52.3%	46.7%	52.8%	47.2%
56,399	ATHENS	21,958	11,548	10,201	209	1,347 R	52.6%	46.5%	53.1%	46.9%
42,554	AUGLAIZE	19,000	14,766	4,102	132	10,664 R	77.7%	21.6%	78.3%	21.7%
82,569	BELMONT	34,856	15,170	19,458	228	4,288 D	43.5%	55.8%	43.8%	56.2%
31,920	BROWN	12,404	8,221	4,067	116	4,154 R	66.3%	32.8%	66.9%	33.1%
258,787	BUTLER	104,514	76,216	27,700	598	48,516 R	72.9%	26.5%	73.3%	26.7%
25,598	CARROLL	10,584	6,703	3,771	110	2,932 R	63.3%	35.6%	64.0%	36.0%
33,649	CHAMPAIGN	13,600	9,935	3,544	121	6,391 R	73.1%	26.1%	73.7%	26.3%
150,236	CLARK	57,744	35,831	21,154	759	14,677 R	62.1%	36.6%	62.9%	37.1%
128,483	CLERMONT	47,319	35,316	11,713	290	23,603 R	74.6%	24.8%	75.1%	24.9%
34,603	CLINTON	13,018	9,603	3,332	83	6,271 R	73.8%	25.6%	74.2%	25.8%
113,572	COLUMBIANA	45,110	24,552	20,155	403	4,397 R	54.4%	44.7%	54.9%	45.1%
36,024	COSHOCTON	14,323	9,842	4,392	89	5,450 R	68.7%	30.7%	69.1%	30.9%
50,075	CRAWFORD	19,820	14,682	4,932	206	9,750 R	74.1%	24.9%	74.9%	25.1%
1,498,400	CUYAHOGA	651,633	284,094	362,626	4,913	78,532 D	43.6%	55.6%	43.9%	56.1%
55,096	DARKE	22,494	16,379	5,904	211	10,475 R	72.8%	26.2%	73.5%	26.5%
39,987	DEFIANCE	16,130	10,951	5,004	175	5,947 R	67.9%	31.0%	68.6%	31.4%
53,840	DELAWARE	24,989	19,050	5,773	166	13,277 R	76.2%	23.1%	76.7%	23.3%
79,655	ERIE	33,154	19,174	13,508	472	5,666 R	57.8%	40.7%	58.7%	41.3%
93,678	FAIRFIELD	41,033	30,843	9,817	373	21,026 R	75.2%	23.9%	75.9%	24.1%
27,467	FAYETTE	9,021	6,838	2,126	57	4,712 R	75.8%	23.6%	76.3%	23.7%
869,132	FRANKLIN	390,474	250,360	131,530	8,584	118,830 R	64.1%	33.7%	65.6%	34.4%
37,751	FULTON	15,730	11,412	4,217	101	7,195 R	72.5%	26.8%	73.0%	27.0%
30,098	GALLIA	12,554	8,194	4,251	109	3,943 R	65.3%	33.9%	65.8%	34.2%
74,474	GEAUGA	32,754	22,369	9,954	431	12,415 R	68.3%	30.4%	69.2%	30.8%
129,769	GREENE	51,711	34,267	17,129	315	17,138 R	66.3%	33.1%	66.7%	33.3%
42,024	GUERNSEY	15,344	10,252	4,967	125	5,285 R	66.8%	32.4%	67.4%	32.6%
873,224	HAMILTON	388,817	246,288	140,350	2,179	105,938 R	63.3%	36.1%	63.7%	36.3%
64,581	HANCOCK	28,295	22,169	5,758	368	16,411 R	78.3%	20.3%	79.4%	20.6%
32,719	HARDIN	12,620	8,722	3,813	85	4,909 R	69.1%	30.2%	69.6%	30.4%
18,152	HARRISON	7,712	4,276	3,370	66	906 R	55.4%	43.7%	55.9%	44.1%
28,383	HENRY	12,173	9,317	2,779	77	6,538 R	76.5%	22.8%	77.0%	23.0%
33,477	HIGHLAND	12,875	9,000	3,784	91	5,216 R	69.9%	29.4%	70.4%	29.6%
24,304	HOCKING	9,463	6,071	3,280	112	2,791 R	64.2%	34.7%	64.9%	35.1%
29,416	HOLMES	6,944	5,146	1,737	61	3,409 R	74.1%	25.0%	74.8%	25.2%
54,608	HURON	21,171	14,388	6,609	174	7,779 R	68.0%	31.2%	68.5%	31.5%
30,592	JACKSON	11,908	7,411	4,369	128	3,042 R	62.2%	36.7%	62.9%	37.1%
91,564	JEFFERSON	40,277	17,105	22,832	340	5,727 D	42.5%	56.7%	42.8%	57.2%
46,304	KNOX	19,901	14,062	5,730	109	8,332 R	70.7%	28.8%	71.0%	29.0%
212,801	LAKE	92,325	54,587	36,711	1,027	17,876 R	59.1%	39.8%	59.8%	40.2%
63,849	LAWRENCE	26,437	14,793	11,431	213	3,362 R	56.0%	43.2%	56.4%	43.6%
120,981	LICKING	51,976	37,560	13,995	421	23,565 R	72.3%	26.9%	72.9%	27.1%
39,155	LOGAN	15,979	12,230	3,645	104	8,585 R	76.5%	22.8%	77.0%	23.0%
274,909	LORAIN	113,021	57,379	52,970	2,672	4,409 R	50.8%	46.9%	52.0%	48.0%
471,741	LUCAS	199,554	100,285	97,293	1,976	2,992 R	50.3%	48.8%	50.8%	49.2%
33,004	MADISON	11,987	8,979	2,928	80	6,051 R	74.9%	24.4%	75.4%	24.6%
289,487	MAHONING	131,438	53,424	76,514	1,500	23,090 D	40.6%	58.2%	41.1%	58.9%
67,974	MARION	26,443	17,392	8,827	224	8,565 R	65.8%	33.4%	66.3%	33.7%
113,150	MEDINA	46,944	30,690	15,897	357	14,793 R	65.4%	33.9%	65.9%	34.1%
23,641	MEIGS	9,929	6,307	3,549	73	2,758 R	63.5%	35.7%	64.0%	36.0%
38,334	MERCER	16,144	11,542	4,422	180	7,120 R	71.5%	27.4%	72.3%	27.7%
90,381	MIAMI	36,315	26,300	9,695	320	16,605 R	72.4%	26.7%	73.1%	26.9%
17,382	MONROE	6,978	3,302	3,611	65	309 D	47.3%	51.7%	47.8%	52.2%
571,697	MONTGOMERY	232,402	137,053	94,016	1,333	43,037 R	59.0%	40.5%	59.3%	40.7%
14,241	MORGAN	5,903	3,994	1,868	41	2,126 R	67.7%	31.6%	68.1%	31.9%
26,480	MORROW	11,042	8,116	2,839	87	5,277 R	73.5%	25.7%	74.1%	25.9%
83,340	MUSKINGUM	32,101	21,821	10,037	243	11,784 R	68.0%	31.3%	68.5%	31.5%

OHIO

PRESIDENT 1984

1980 Census Population	County	Total Vote	Republican	Democratic	Other	Rep.-Dem. Plurality	Percentage Total Vote Rep.	Percentage Total Vote Dem.	Percentage Major Vote Rep.	Percentage Major Vote Dem.
11,310	NOBLE	5,691	3,853	1,777	61	2,076 R	67.7%	31.2%	68.4%	31.6%
40,076	OTTAWA	18,075	10,920	7,053	102	3,867 R	60.4%	39.0%	60.8%	39.2%
21,302	PAULDING	8,439	5,545	2,811	83	2,734 R	65.7%	33.3%	66.4%	33.6%
31,032	PERRY	11,597	7,548	3,961	88	3,587 R	65.1%	34.2%	65.6%	34.4%
43,662	PICKAWAY	16,160	11,942	4,110	108	7,832 R	73.9%	25.4%	74.4%	25.6%
22,802	PIKE	11,302	6,318	4,895	89	1,423 R	55.9%	43.3%	56.3%	43.7%
135,856	PORTAGE	51,687	29,536	21,719	432	7,817 R	57.1%	42.0%	57.6%	42.4%
38,223	PREBLE	15,403	11,065	4,198	140	6,867 R	71.8%	27.3%	72.5%	27.5%
32,991	PUTNAM	15,252	11,937	3,194	121	8,743 R	78.3%	20.9%	78.9%	21.1%
131,205	RICHLAND	51,836	35,299	16,141	396	19,158 R	68.1%	31.1%	68.6%	31.4%
65,004	ROSS	25,548	17,015	8,020	513	8,995 R	66.6%	31.4%	68.0%	32.0%
63,267	SANDUSKY	26,020	17,214	8,564	242	8,650 R	66.2%	32.9%	66.8%	33.2%
84,545	SCIOTO	33,219	18,818	14,120	281	4,698 R	56.6%	42.5%	57.1%	42.9%
61,901	SENECA	24,642	16,520	7,905	217	8,615 R	67.0%	32.1%	67.6%	32.4%
43,089	SHELBY	17,983	13,509	4,315	159	9,194 R	75.1%	24.0%	75.8%	24.2%
378,823	STARK	164,916	98,434	65,157	1,325	33,277 R	59.7%	39.5%	60.2%	39.8%
524,472	SUMMIT	226,780	115,637	109,569	1,574	6,068 R	51.0%	48.3%	51.3%	48.7%
241,863	TRUMBULL	103,259	45,623	56,902	734	11,279 D	44.2%	55.1%	44.5%	55.5%
84,614	TUSCARAWAS	32,754	19,366	13,149	239	6,217 R	59.1%	40.1%	59.6%	40.4%
29,536	UNION	12,001	9,336	2,579	86	6,757 R	77.8%	21.5%	78.4%	21.6%
30,458	VAN WERT	12,988	9,570	3,338	80	6,232 R	73.7%	25.7%	74.1%	25.9%
11,584	VINTON	5,085	3,041	1,990	54	1,051 R	59.8%	39.1%	60.4%	39.6%
99,276	WARREN	39,070	29,848	9,031	191	20,817 R	76.4%	23.1%	76.8%	23.2%
64,266	WASHINGTON	24,993	16,529	7,920	544	8,609 R	66.1%	31.7%	67.6%	32.4%
97,408	WAYNE	36,104	24,475	11,323	306	13,152 R	67.8%	31.4%	68.4%	31.6%
36,369	WILLIAMS	14,577	10,804	3,624	149	7,180 R	74.1%	24.9%	74.9%	25.1%
107,372	WOOD	45,954	29,750	15,907	297	13,843 R	64.7%	34.6%	65.2%	34.8%
22,651	WYANDOT	9,630	7,204	2,342	84	4,862 R	74.8%	24.3%	75.5%	24.5%
10,797,630	TOTAL	4,547,619	2,678,560	1,825,440	43,619	853,120 R	58.9%	40.1%	59.5%	40.5%

OHIO

PRESIDENT 1980

1980 Census Population	County	Total Vote	Republican	Democratic	Other	Rep.-Dem. Plurality	Percentage Total Vote Rep.	Total Vote Dem.	Major Vote Rep.	Major Vote Dem.
24,328	ADAMS	9,928	5,336	4,161	431	1,175 R	53.7%	41.9%	56.2%	43.8%
112,241	ALLEN	44,154	29,070	13,140	1,944	15,930 R	65.8%	29.8%	68.9%	31.1%
46,178	ASHLAND	18,689	11,691	5,142	1,856	6,549 R	62.6%	27.5%	69.5%	30.5%
104,215	ASHTABULA	40,467	19,847	17,363	3,257	2,484 R	49.0%	42.9%	53.3%	46.7%
56,399	ATHENS	19,801	8,170	9,514	2,117	1,344 D	41.3%	48.0%	46.2%	53.8%
42,554	AUGLAIZE	17,657	11,537	5,022	1,098	6,515 R	65.3%	28.4%	69.7%	30.3%
82,569	BELMONT	32,024	13,601	16,653	1,770	3,052 D	42.5%	52.0%	45.0%	55.0%
31,920	BROWN	11,337	6,065	4,706	566	1,359 R	53.5%	41.5%	56.3%	43.7%
258,787	BUTLER	98,901	61,231	31,796	5,874	29,435 R	61.9%	32.1%	65.8%	34.2%
25,598	CARROLL	9,851	5,806	3,476	569	2,330 R	58.9%	35.3%	62.6%	37.4%
33,649	CHAMPAIGN	12,225	7,356	4,109	760	3,247 R	60.2%	33.6%	64.2%	35.8%
150,236	CLARK	54,015	27,237	22,630	4,148	4,607 R	50.4%	41.9%	54.6%	45.4%
128,483	CLERMONT	42,091	26,674	13,199	2,218	13,475 R	63.4%	31.4%	66.9%	33.1%
34,603	CLINTON	12,400	7,675	3,967	758	3,708 R	61.9%	32.0%	65.9%	34.1%
113,572	COLUMBIANA	41,143	20,798	17,459	2,886	3,339 R	50.6%	42.4%	54.4%	45.6%
36,024	COSHOCTON	13,856	8,359	4,725	772	3,634 R	60.3%	34.1%	63.9%	36.1%
50,075	CRAWFORD	19,755	12,424	6,058	1,273	6,366 R	62.9%	30.7%	67.2%	32.8%
1,498,400	CUYAHOGA	614,682	254,883	307,448	52,351	52,565 D	41.5%	50.0%	45.3%	54.7%
55,096	DARKE	21,958	12,773	7,635	1,550	5,138 R	58.2%	34.8%	62.6%	37.4%
39,987	DEFIANCE	15,639	9,358	5,096	1,185	4,262 R	59.8%	32.6%	64.7%	35.3%
53,840	DELAWARE	22,861	14,740	6,417	1,704	8,323 R	64.5%	28.1%	69.7%	30.3%
79,655	ERIE	30,470	15,628	12,343	2,499	3,285 R	51.3%	40.5%	55.9%	44.1%
93,678	FAIRFIELD	39,515	24,096	13,144	2,275	10,952 R	61.0%	33.3%	64.7%	35.3%
27,467	FAYETTE	9,068	5,827	2,810	431	3,017 R	64.3%	31.0%	67.5%	32.5%
869,132	FRANKLIN	373,045	200,948	143,932	28,165	57,016 R	53.9%	38.6%	58.3%	41.7%
37,751	FULTON	14,707	9,519	3,972	1,216	5,547 R	64.7%	27.0%	70.6%	29.4%
30,098	GALLIA	11,404	6,469	4,406	529	2,063 R	56.7%	38.6%	59.5%	40.5%
74,474	GEAUGA	30,204	17,762	9,542	2,900	8,220 R	58.8%	31.6%	65.1%	34.9%
129,769	GREENE	48,842	24,922	20,068	3,852	4,854 R	51.0%	41.1%	55.4%	44.6%
42,024	GUERNSEY	14,084	8,180	5,121	783	3,059 R	58.1%	36.4%	61.5%	38.5%
873,224	HAMILTON	358,541	206,979	129,114	22,448	77,865 R	57.7%	36.0%	61.6%	38.4%
64,581	HANCOCK	27,010	18,264	6,843	1,903	11,421 R	67.6%	25.3%	72.7%	27.3%
32,719	HARDIN	12,123	7,457	3,863	803	3,594 R	61.5%	31.9%	65.9%	34.1%
18,152	HARRISON	6,916	3,639	2,848	429	791 R	52.6%	41.2%	56.1%	43.9%
28,383	HENRY	11,489	7,584	3,059	846	4,525 R	66.0%	26.6%	71.3%	28.7%
33,477	HIGHLAND	12,400	7,359	4,363	678	2,996 R	59.3%	35.2%	62.8%	37.2%
24,304	HOCKING	8,819	4,588	3,765	466	823 R	52.0%	42.7%	54.9%	45.1%
29,416	HOLMES	6,394	3,860	2,094	440	1,766 R	60.4%	32.7%	64.8%	35.2%
54,608	HURON	19,159	11,173	6,537	1,449	4,636 R	58.3%	34.1%	63.1%	36.9%
30,592	JACKSON	10,719	5,902	4,409	408	1,493 R	55.1%	41.1%	57.2%	42.8%
91,564	JEFFERSON	38,491	15,777	20,382	2,332	4,605 D	41.0%	53.0%	43.6%	56.4%
46,304	KNOX	18,195	10,384	6,586	1,225	3,798 R	57.1%	36.2%	61.2%	38.8%
212,801	LAKE	86,428	43,485	35,246	7,697	8,239 R	50.3%	40.8%	55.2%	44.8%
63,849	LAWRENCE	26,194	13,799	11,366	1,029	2,433 R	52.7%	43.4%	54.8%	45.2%
120,981	LICKING	48,769	28,425	17,208	3,136	11,217 R	58.3%	35.3%	62.3%	37.7%
39,155	LOGAN	14,994	9,727	4,319	948	5,408 R	64.9%	28.8%	69.3%	30.7%
274,909	LORAIN	103,084	51,034	40,919	11,131	10,115 R	49.5%	39.7%	55.5%	44.5%
471,741	LUCAS	191,298	86,653	85,341	19,304	1,312 R	45.3%	44.6%	50.4%	49.6%
33,004	MADISON	11,350	7,166	3,565	619	3,601 R	63.1%	31.4%	66.8%	33.2%
289,487	MAHONING	125,161	50,153	63,677	11,331	13,524 D	40.1%	50.9%	44.1%	55.9%
67,974	MARION	25,631	14,605	9,419	1,607	5,186 R	57.0%	36.7%	60.8%	39.2%
113,150	MEDINA	42,050	24,723	13,573	3,754	11,150 R	58.8%	32.3%	64.6%	35.4%
23,641	MEIGS	9,170	4,911	3,827	432	1,084 R	53.6%	41.7%	56.2%	43.8%
38,334	MERCER	15,339	8,673	5,506	1,160	3,167 R	56.5%	35.9%	61.2%	38.8%
90,381	MIAMI	35,808	19,928	12,893	2,987	7,035 R	55.7%	36.0%	60.7%	39.3%
17,382	MONROE	6,373	2,870	3,166	337	296 D	45.0%	49.7%	47.5%	52.5%
571,697	MONTGOMERY	223,009	101,443	105,110	16,456	3,667 D	45.5%	47.1%	49.1%	50.9%
14,241	MORGAN	5,366	3,236	1,875	255	1,361 R	60.3%	34.9%	63.3%	36.7%
26,480	MORROW	9,972	6,179	3,239	554	2,940 R	62.0%	32.5%	65.6%	34.4%
83,340	MUSKINGUM	32,688	17,921	12,584	2,183	5,337 R	54.8%	38.5%	58.7%	41.3%

OHIO

PRESIDENT 1980

1980 Census Population	County	Total Vote	Republican	Democratic	Other	Rep.-Dem. Plurality	Percentage Total Vote Rep.	Percentage Total Vote Dem.	Percentage Major Vote Rep.	Percentage Major Vote Dem.
11,310	NOBLE	5,272	3,025	1,944	303	1,081 R	57.4%	36.9%	60.9%	39.1%
40,076	OTTAWA	16,883	8,641	6,753	1,489	1,888 R	51.2%	40.0%	56.1%	43.9%
21,302	PAULDING	8,494	4,971	2,778	745	2,193 R	58.5%	32.7%	64.2%	35.8%
31,032	PERRY	10,648	5,725	4,383	540	1,342 R	53.8%	41.2%	56.6%	43.4%
43,662	PICKAWAY	15,170	9,289	5,052	829	4,237 R	61.2%	33.3%	64.8%	35.2%
22,802	PIKE	9,818	4,426	4,938	454	512 D	45.1%	50.3%	47.3%	52.7%
135,856	PORTAGE	48,190	22,829	20,570	4,791	2,259 R	47.4%	42.7%	52.6%	47.4%
38,223	PREBLE	14,723	8,376	5,416	931	2,960 R	56.9%	36.8%	60.7%	39.3%
32,991	PUTNAM	14,193	9,752	3,742	699	6,010 R	68.7%	26.4%	72.3%	27.7%
131,205	RICHLAND	50,824	29,213	18,253	3,358	10,960 R	57.5%	35.9%	61.5%	38.5%
65,004	ROSS	23,859	13,251	9,355	1,253	3,896 R	55.5%	39.2%	58.6%	41.4%
63,267	SANDUSKY	24,166	13,420	8,482	2,264	4,938 R	55.5%	35.1%	61.3%	38.7%
84,545	SCIOTO	32,568	15,881	15,552	1,135	329 R	48.8%	47.8%	50.5%	49.5%
61,901	SENECA	23,259	14,172	7,303	1,784	6,869 R	60.9%	31.4%	66.0%	34.0%
43,089	SHELBY	16,544	8,988	6,425	1,131	2,563 R	54.3%	38.8%	58.3%	41.7%
378,823	STARK	157,106	87,769	59,005	10,332	28,764 R	55.9%	37.6%	59.8%	40.2%
524,472	SUMMIT	212,919	92,299	102,459	18,161	10,160 D	43.3%	48.1%	47.4%	52.6%
241,863	TRUMBULL	93,002	41,056	44,366	7,580	3,310 D	44.1%	47.7%	48.1%	51.9%
84,614	TUSCARAWAS	30,086	15,708	12,117	2,261	3,591 R	52.2%	40.3%	56.5%	43.5%
29,536	UNION	11,186	7,576	3,038	572	4,538 R	67.7%	27.2%	71.4%	28.6%
30,458	VAN WERT	12,872	7,866	4,070	936	3,796 R	61.1%	31.6%	65.9%	34.1%
11,584	VINTON	5,064	2,484	2,381	199	103 R	49.1%	47.0%	51.1%	48.9%
99,276	WARREN	35,522	22,430	11,306	1,786	11,124 R	63.1%	31.8%	66.5%	33.5%
64,266	WASHINGTON	23,971	14,310	7,936	1,725	6,374 R	59.7%	33.1%	64.3%	35.7%
97,408	WAYNE	33,942	18,962	12,129	2,851	6,833 R	55.9%	35.7%	61.0%	39.0%
36,369	WILLIAMS	14,221	9,146	4,015	1,060	5,131 R	64.3%	28.2%	69.5%	30.5%
107,372	WOOD	42,213	23,315	14,139	4,759	9,176 R	55.2%	33.5%	62.2%	37.8%
22,651	WYANDOT	9,175	5,786	2,757	632	3,029 R	63.1%	30.0%	67.7%	32.3%
10,797,630	TOTAL	4,283,603	2,206,545	1,752,414	324,644	454,131 R	51.5%	40.9%	55.7%	44.3%

OHIO

PRESIDENT 1976

1970 Census Population	County	Total Vote	Republican	Democratic	Other	Rep.-Dem. Plurality	Percentage Total Vote Rep.	Percentage Total Vote Dem.	Percentage Major Vote Rep.	Percentage Major Vote Dem.
18,957	ADAMS	8,780	4,197	4,450	133	253 D	47.8%	50.7%	48.5%	51.5%
111,144	ALLEN	39,167	23,721	14,627	819	9,094 R	60.6%	37.3%	61.9%	38.1%
43,303	ASHLAND	17,354	9,761	7,205	388	2,556 R	56.2%	41.5%	57.5%	42.5%
98,237	ASHTABULA	38,625	16,885	20,883	857	3,998 D	43.7%	54.1%	44.7%	55.3%
54,889	ATHENS	19,016	8,387	9,896	733	1,509 D	44.1%	52.0%	45.9%	54.1%
38,602	AUGLAIZE	15,965	9,772	5,840	353	3,932 R	61.2%	36.6%	62.6%	37.4%
80,917	BELMONT	35,219	13,550	21,162	507	7,612 D	38.5%	60.1%	39.0%	61.0%
26,635	BROWN	10,126	4,549	5,432	145	883 D	44.9%	53.6%	45.6%	54.4%
226,207	BUTLER	86,217	49,625	35,123	1,469	14,502 R	57.6%	40.7%	58.6%	41.4%
21,579	CARROLL	10,325	5,091	5,006	228	85 R	49.3%	48.5%	50.4%	49.6%
30,491	CHAMPAIGN	11,502	6,526	4,748	228	1,778 R	56.7%	41.3%	57.9%	42.1%
157,115	CLARK	54,660	26,745	26,135	1,780	610 R	48.9%	47.8%	50.6%	49.4%
95,725	CLERMONT	35,037	19,616	14,850	571	4,766 R	56.0%	42.4%	56.9%	43.1%
31,464	CLINTON	11,737	6,597	4,959	181	1,638 R	56.2%	42.3%	57.1%	42.9%
108,310	COLUMBIANA	46,367	22,318	23,096	953	778 D	48.1%	49.8%	49.1%	50.9%
33,486	COSHOCTON	12,496	6,361	5,827	308	534 R	50.9%	46.6%	52.2%	47.8%
50,364	CRAWFORD	18,870	10,801	7,553	516	3,248 R	57.2%	40.0%	58.8%	41.2%
1,721,300	CUYAHOGA	623,222	255,594	349,186	18,442	93,592 D	41.0%	56.0%	42.3%	57.7%
49,141	DARKE	21,953	11,580	9,901	472	1,679 R	52.7%	45.1%	53.9%	46.1%
36,949	DEFIANCE	13,679	7,526	5,850	303	1,676 R	55.0%	42.8%	56.3%	43.7%
42,908	DELAWARE	19,853	12,285	7,058	510	5,227 R	61.9%	35.6%	63.5%	36.5%
75,909	ERIE	29,478	14,742	13,843	893	899 R	50.0%	47.0%	51.6%	48.4%
73,301	FAIRFIELD	33,079	19,098	13,361	620	5,737 R	57.7%	40.4%	58.8%	41.2%
25,461	FAYETTE	10,364	5,719	4,477	168	1,242 R	55.2%	43.2%	56.1%	43.9%
833,249	FRANKLIN	340,712	189,645	141,624	9,443	48,021 R	55.7%	41.6%	57.2%	42.8%
33,071	FULTON	12,949	7,891	4,850	208	3,041 R	60.9%	37.5%	61.9%	38.1%
25,239	GALLIA	10,317	5,198	4,971	148	227 R	50.4%	48.2%	51.1%	48.9%
62,977	GEAUGA	26,269	15,004	10,449	816	4,555 R	57.1%	39.8%	58.9%	41.1%
125,057	GREENE	44,077	22,598	20,245	1,234	2,353 R	51.3%	45.9%	52.7%	47.3%
37,665	GUERNSEY	15,524	7,746	7,573	205	173 R	49.9%	48.8%	50.6%	49.4%
924,018	HAMILTON	353,079	211,267	135,605	6,207	75,662 R	59.8%	38.4%	60.9%	39.1%
61,217	HANCOCK	25,333	15,983	8,548	802	7,435 R	63.1%	33.7%	65.2%	34.8%
30,813	HARDIN	11,075	6,076	4,650	349	1,426 R	54.9%	42.0%	56.6%	43.4%
17,013	HARRISON	7,681	3,509	4,070	102	561 D	45.7%	53.0%	46.3%	53.7%
27,058	HENRY	12,470	7,656	4,592	222	3,064 R	61.4%	36.8%	62.5%	37.5%
28,996	HIGHLAND	13,331	6,853	6,327	151	526 R	51.4%	47.5%	52.0%	48.0%
20,322	HOCKING	9,396	4,114	5,126	156	1,012 D	43.8%	54.6%	44.5%	55.5%
23,024	HOLMES	5,299	2,870	2,242	187	628 R	54.2%	42.3%	56.1%	43.9%
49,587	HURON	18,066	9,386	7,742	938	1,644 R	52.0%	42.9%	54.8%	45.2%
27,174	JACKSON	12,822	5,987	6,699	136	712 D	46.7%	52.2%	47.2%	52.8%
96,193	JEFFERSON	37,825	14,839	22,318	668	7,479 D	39.2%	59.0%	39.9%	60.1%
41,795	KNOX	17,081	9,290	7,361	430	1,929 R	54.4%	43.1%	55.8%	44.2%
197,200	LAKE	79,408	36,390	40,734	2,284	4,344 D	45.8%	51.3%	47.2%	52.8%
56,868	LAWRENCE	22,995	10,668	12,072	255	1,404 D	46.4%	52.5%	46.9%	53.1%
107,799	LICKING	43,733	23,518	19,247	968	4,271 R	53.8%	44.0%	55.0%	45.0%
35,072	LOGAN	15,402	9,092	5,949	361	3,143 R	59.0%	38.6%	60.4%	39.6%
256,843	LORAIN	94,711	39,459	52,387	2,865	12,928 D	41.7%	55.3%	43.0%	57.0%
484,370	LUCAS	183,907	76,069	103,658	4,180	27,589 D	41.4%	56.4%	42.3%	57.7%
28,318	MADISON	12,161	7,074	4,885	202	2,189 R	58.2%	40.2%	59.2%	40.8%
303,424	MAHONING	125,294	46,314	75,837	3,143	29,523 D	37.0%	60.5%	37.9%	62.1%
64,724	MARION	24,620	13,141	10,962	517	2,179 R	53.4%	44.5%	54.5%	45.5%
82,717	MEDINA	36,249	19,066	16,251	932	2,815 R	52.6%	44.8%	54.0%	46.0%
19,799	MEIGS	10,348	4,942	5,262	144	320 D	47.8%	50.9%	48.4%	51.6%
35,265	MERCER	14,849	7,678	6,724	447	954 R	51.7%	45.3%	53.3%	46.7%
84,342	MIAMI	32,413	18,686	13,074	653	5,612 R	57.6%	40.3%	58.8%	41.2%
15,739	MONROE	7,132	2,728	4,296	108	1,568 D	38.3%	60.2%	38.8%	61.2%
606,148	MONTGOMERY	211,436	100,223	106,468	4,745	6,245 D	47.4%	50.4%	48.5%	51.5%
12,375	MORGAN	5,809	2,971	2,727	111	244 R	51.1%	46.9%	52.1%	47.9%
21,348	MORROW	10,912	5,814	4,870	228	944 R	53.3%	44.6%	54.4%	45.6%
77,826	MUSKINGUM	30,070	15,358	14,178	534	1,180 R	51.1%	47.1%	52.0%	48.0%

OHIO

PRESIDENT 1976

1970 Census Population	County	Total Vote	Republican	Democratic	Other	Rep.-Dem. Plurality	Percentage Total Vote Rep.	Total Vote Dem.	Major Vote Rep.	Major Vote Dem.
10,428	NOBLE	5,730	3,007	2,612	111	395 R	52.5%	45.6%	53.5%	46.5%
37,099	OTTAWA	18,299	8,241	9,646	412	1,405 D	45.0%	52.7%	46.1%	53.9%
19,329	PAULDING	6,987	3,593	3,229	165	364 R	51.4%	46.2%	52.7%	47.3%
27,434	PERRY	12,138	5,637	6,268	233	631 D	46.4%	51.6%	47.3%	52.7%
40,071	PICKAWAY	14,045	7,695	5,907	443	1,788 R	54.8%	42.1%	56.6%	43.4%
19,114	PIKE	9,574	3,729	5,734	111	2,005 D	38.9%	59.9%	39.4%	60.6%
125,868	PORTAGE	43,824	17,927	24,417	1,480	6,490 D	40.9%	55.7%	42.3%	57.7%
34,719	PREBLE	12,747	6,654	5,850	243	804 R	52.2%	45.9%	53.2%	46.8%
31,134	PUTNAM	12,710	7,332	5,035	343	2,297 R	57.7%	39.6%	59.3%	40.7%
129,997	RICHLAND	49,251	24,310	23,065	1,876	1,245 R	49.4%	46.8%	51.3%	48.7%
61,211	ROSS	22,751	11,477	10,743	531	734 R	50.4%	47.2%	51.7%	48.3%
60,983	SANDUSKY	24,867	13,074	11,202	591	1,872 R	52.6%	45.0%	53.9%	46.1%
76,951	SCIOTO	31,488	13,021	18,019	448	4,998 D	41.4%	57.2%	41.9%	58.1%
60,696	SENECA	22,516	11,730	10,074	712	1,656 R	52.1%	44.7%	53.8%	46.2%
37,748	SHELBY	14,859	8,011	6,414	434	1,597 R	53.9%	43.2%	55.5%	44.5%
372,210	STARK	145,709	72,607	70,012	3,090	2,595 R	49.8%	48.0%	50.9%	49.1%
553,371	SUMMIT	209,350	80,415	123,711	5,224	43,296 D	38.4%	59.1%	39.4%	60.6%
232,579	TRUMBULL	92,544	36,469	53,828	2,247	17,359 D	39.4%	58.2%	40.4%	59.6%
77,211	TUSCARAWAS	31,841	14,279	16,880	682	2,601 D	44.8%	53.0%	45.8%	54.2%
23,786	UNION	12,043	7,464	4,377	202	3,087 R	62.0%	36.3%	63.0%	37.0%
29,194	VAN WERT	14,284	8,344	5,689	251	2,655 R	58.4%	39.8%	59.5%	40.5%
9,420	VINTON	4,846	2,148	2,629	69	481 D	44.3%	54.3%	45.0%	55.0%
84,925	WARREN	29,935	16,115	13,349	471	2,766 R	53.8%	44.6%	54.7%	45.3%
57,160	WASHINGTON	21,096	11,513	8,914	669	2,599 R	54.6%	42.3%	56.4%	43.6%
87,123	WAYNE	30,754	16,976	13,087	691	3,889 R	55.2%	42.6%	56.5%	43.5%
33,669	WILLIAMS	12,762	7,596	4,920	246	2,676 R	59.5%	38.6%	60.7%	39.3%
89,722	WOOD	37,131	19,331	16,926	874	2,405 R	52.1%	45.6%	53.3%	46.7%
21,826	WYANDOT	9,946	5,661	4,043	242	1,618 R	56.9%	40.6%	58.3%	41.7%
10,652,017	TOTAL	4,111,873	2,000,505	2,011,621	99,747	11,116 D	48.7%	48.9%	49.9%	50.1%

OHIO

PRESIDENT 1972

1970 Census Population	County	Total Vote	Republican	Democratic	Other	Rep.-Dem. Plurality	Percentage Total Vote Rep.	Percentage Total Vote Dem.	Percentage Major Vote Rep.	Percentage Major Vote Dem.
18,957	ADAMS	7,882	4,980	2,709	193	2,271 R	63.2%	34.4%	64.8%	35.2%
111,144	ALLEN	38,543	26,966	10,184	1,393	16,782 R	70.0%	26.4%	72.6%	27.4%
43,303	ASHLAND	17,074	12,470	4,302	302	8,168 R	73.0%	25.2%	74.4%	25.6%
98,237	ASHTABULA	38,608	22,762	15,052	794	7,710 R	59.0%	39.0%	60.2%	39.8%
54,889	ATHENS	19,915	9,735	9,977	203	242 D	48.9%	50.1%	49.4%	50.6%
38,602	AUGLAIZE	17,047	11,900	4,617	530	7,283 R	69.8%	27.1%	72.0%	28.0%
80,917	BELMONT	32,878	17,628	14,800	450	2,828 R	53.6%	45.0%	54.4%	45.6%
26,635	BROWN	10,804	6,772	3,770	262	3,002 R	62.7%	34.9%	64.2%	35.8%
226,207	BUTLER	73,635	50,380	21,194	2,061	29,186 R	68.4%	28.8%	70.4%	29.6%
21,579	CARROLL	9,014	5,984	2,755	275	3,229 R	66.4%	30.6%	68.5%	31.5%
30,491	CHAMPAIGN	12,603	8,756	3,626	221	5,130 R	69.5%	28.8%	70.7%	29.3%
157,115	CLARK	55,750	34,447	19,725	1,578	14,722 R	61.8%	35.4%	63.6%	36.4%
95,725	CLERMONT	31,989	22,936	8,276	777	14,660 R	71.7%	25.9%	73.5%	26.5%
31,464	CLINTON	10,988	8,140	2,709	139	5,431 R	74.1%	24.7%	75.0%	25.0%
108,310	COLUMBIANA	43,602	27,308	15,683	611	11,625 R	62.6%	36.0%	63.5%	36.5%
33,486	COSHOCTON	12,206	8,082	3,790	334	4,292 R	66.2%	31.1%	68.1%	31.9%
50,364	CRAWFORD	21,053	14,632	5,518	903	9,114 R	69.5%	26.2%	72.6%	27.4%
1,721,300	CUYAHOGA	659,751	329,493	317,670	12,588	11,823 R	49.9%	48.1%	50.9%	49.1%
49,141	DARKE	21,096	13,862	6,534	700	7,328 R	65.7%	31.0%	68.0%	32.0%
36,949	DEFIANCE	13,630	8,914	4,377	339	4,537 R	65.4%	32.1%	67.1%	32.9%
42,908	DELAWARE	17,886	12,950	4,452	484	8,498 R	72.4%	24.9%	74.4%	25.6%
75,909	ERIE	28,591	16,714	10,889	988	5,825 R	58.5%	38.1%	60.6%	39.4%
73,301	FAIRFIELD	30,568	21,909	7,746	913	14,163 R	71.7%	25.3%	73.9%	26.1%
25,461	FAYETTE	9,515	6,970	2,344	201	4,626 R	73.3%	24.6%	74.8%	25.2%
833,249	FRANKLIN	344,808	219,771	117,562	7,475	102,209 R	63.7%	34.1%	65.1%	34.9%
33,071	FULTON	12,234	8,387	3,615	232	4,772 R	68.6%	29.5%	69.9%	30.1%
25,239	GALLIA	8,986	6,506	2,341	139	4,165 R	72.4%	26.1%	73.5%	26.5%
62,977	GEAUGA	23,577	15,624	7,329	624	8,295 R	66.3%	31.1%	68.1%	31.9%
125,057	GREENE	38,909	25,349	12,736	824	12,613 R	65.1%	32.7%	66.6%	33.4%
37,665	GUERNSEY	14,619	9,648	4,757	214	4,891 R	66.0%	32.5%	67.0%	33.0%
924,018	HAMILTON	364,385	239,212	119,054	6,119	120,158 R	65.6%	32.7%	66.8%	33.2%
61,217	HANCOCK	25,624	18,111	6,084	1,429	12,027 R	70.7%	23.7%	74.9%	25.1%
30,813	HARDIN	12,602	8,713	3,535	354	5,178 R	69.1%	28.1%	71.1%	28.9%
17,013	HARRISON	7,010	4,554	2,388	68	2,166 R	65.0%	34.1%	65.6%	34.4%
27,058	HENRY	11,475	8,099	3,145	231	4,954 R	70.6%	27.4%	72.0%	28.0%
28,996	HIGHLAND	12,226	8,524	3,464	238	5,060 R	69.7%	28.3%	71.1%	28.9%
20,322	HOCKING	8,492	5,407	2,874	211	2,533 R	63.7%	33.8%	65.3%	34.7%
23,024	HOLMES	5,362	3,752	1,507	103	2,245 R	70.0%	28.1%	71.3%	28.7%
49,587	HURON	17,340	10,942	5,491	907	5,451 R	63.1%	31.7%	66.6%	33.4%
27,174	JACKSON	10,923	7,351	3,410	162	3,941 R	67.3%	31.2%	68.3%	31.7%
96,193	JEFFERSON	38,274	21,531	16,198	545	5,333 R	56.3%	42.3%	57.1%	42.9%
41,795	KNOX	16,739	10,705	5,370	664	5,335 R	64.0%	32.1%	66.6%	33.4%
197,200	LAKE	72,141	42,488	27,523	2,130	14,965 R	58.9%	38.2%	60.7%	39.3%
56,868	LAWRENCE	22,567	15,125	7,112	330	8,013 R	67.0%	31.5%	68.0%	32.0%
107,799	LICKING	42,232	28,070	12,460	1,702	15,610 R	66.5%	29.5%	69.3%	30.7%
35,072	LOGAN	15,380	10,938	3,786	656	7,152 R	71.1%	24.6%	74.3%	25.7%
256,843	LORAIN	91,016	51,102	36,634	3,280	14,468 R	56.1%	40.3%	58.2%	41.8%
484,370	LUCAS	182,709	88,401	90,142	4,166	1,741 D	48.4%	49.3%	49.5%	50.5%
28,318	MADISON	11,064	8,372	2,484	208	5,888 R	75.7%	22.5%	77.1%	22.9%
303,424	MAHONING	129,088	64,144	62,428	2,516	1,716 R	49.7%	48.4%	50.7%	49.3%
64,724	MARION	25,659	17,197	7,970	492	9,227 R	67.0%	31.1%	68.3%	31.7%
82,717	MEDINA	32,411	21,010	10,643	758	10,367 R	64.8%	32.8%	66.4%	33.6%
19,799	MEIGS	8,433	5,961	2,335	137	3,626 R	70.7%	27.7%	71.9%	28.1%
35,265	MERCER	14,907	8,587	5,798	522	2,789 R	57.6%	38.9%	59.7%	40.3%
84,342	MIAMI	31,012	21,226	9,121	665	12,105 R	68.4%	29.4%	69.9%	30.1%
15,739	MONROE	6,292	3,721	2,483	88	1,238 R	59.1%	39.5%	60.0%	40.0%
606,148	MONTGOMERY	208,552	120,998	82,231	5,323	38,767 R	58.0%	39.4%	59.5%	40.5%
12,375	MORGAN	5,371	3,679	1,554	138	2,125 R	68.5%	28.9%	70.3%	29.7%
21,348	MORROW	9,759	6,886	2,527	346	4,359 R	70.6%	25.9%	73.2%	26.8%
77,826	MUSKINGUM	31,094	19,897	10,313	884	9,584 R	64.0%	33.2%	65.9%	34.1%

OHIO

PRESIDENT 1972

1970 Census Population	County	Total Vote	Republican	Democratic	Other	Rep.-Dem. Plurality	Percentage Total Vote Rep.	Total Vote Dem.	Major Vote Rep.	Major Vote Dem.
10,428	NOBLE	4,799	3,274	1,449	76	1,825 R	68.2%	30.2%	69.3%	30.7%
37,099	OTTAWA	16,889	9,772	6,465	652	3,307 R	57.9%	38.3%	60.2%	39.8%
19,329	PAULDING	7,025	4,553	2,283	189	2,270 R	64.8%	32.5%	66.6%	33.4%
27,434	PERRY	10,809	6,716	3,728	365	2,988 R	62.1%	34.5%	64.3%	35.7%
40,071	PICKAWAY	13,002	9,661	2,978	363	6,683 R	74.3%	22.9%	76.4%	23.6%
19,114	PIKE	8,761	5,037	3,531	193	1,506 R	57.5%	40.3%	58.8%	41.2%
125,868	PORTAGE	45,002	23,294	20,769	939	2,525 R	51.8%	46.2%	52.9%	47.1%
34,719	PREBLE	12,795	8,993	3,472	330	5,521 R	70.3%	27.1%	72.1%	27.9%
31,134	PUTNAM	12,342	8,185	3,729	428	4,456 R	66.3%	30.2%	68.7%	31.3%
129,997	RICHLAND	45,641	31,117	13,468	1,056	17,649 R	68.2%	29.5%	69.8%	30.2%
61,211	ROSS	21,888	15,573	5,879	436	9,694 R	71.1%	26.9%	72.6%	27.4%
60,983	SANDUSKY	24,343	15,489	8,308	546	7,181 R	63.6%	34.1%	65.1%	34.9%
76,951	SCIOTO	31,679	19,998	11,008	673	8,990 R	63.1%	34.7%	64.5%	35.5%
60,696	SENECA	22,918	13,939	8,180	799	5,759 R	60.8%	35.7%	63.0%	37.0%
37,748	SHELBY	14,703	9,089	4,721	893	4,368 R	61.8%	32.1%	65.8%	34.2%
372,210	STARK	146,810	92,110	51,565	3,135	40,545 R	62.7%	35.1%	64.1%	35.9%
553,371	SUMMIT	225,216	112,419	108,534	4,263	3,885 R	49.9%	48.2%	50.9%	49.1%
232,579	TRUMBULL	85,266	47,680	35,278	2,308	12,402 R	55.9%	41.4%	57.5%	42.5%
77,211	TUSCARAWAS	31,169	18,413	12,255	501	6,158 R	59.1%	39.3%	60.0%	40.0%
23,786	UNION	11,054	8,389	2,447	218	5,942 R	75.9%	22.1%	77.4%	22.6%
29,194	VAN WERT	13,391	9,545	3,644	202	5,901 R	71.3%	27.2%	72.4%	27.6%
9,420	VINTON	4,336	2,725	1,537	74	1,188 R	62.8%	35.4%	63.9%	36.1%
84,925	WARREN	27,897	20,210	6,941	746	13,269 R	72.4%	24.9%	74.4%	25.6%
57,160	WASHINGTON	20,434	14,023	5,814	597	8,209 R	68.6%	28.5%	70.7%	29.3%
87,123	WAYNE	30,076	20,368	9,260	448	11,108 R	67.7%	30.8%	68.7%	31.3%
33,669	WILLIAMS	13,605	9,083	4,278	244	4,805 R	66.8%	31.4%	68.0%	32.0%
89,722	WOOD	35,625	21,080	13,494	1,051	7,586 R	59.2%	37.9%	61.0%	39.0%
21,826	WYANDOT	9,412	6,414	2,771	227	3,643 R	68.1%	29.4%	69.8%	30.2%
10,652,017	TOTAL	4,094,787	2,441,827	1,558,889	94,071	882,938 R	59.6%	38.1%	61.0%	39.0%

OHIO

PRESIDENT 1968

1960 Census Population	County	Total Vote	Republican	Democratic	AIP	Other	Plurality	Percentage Rep.	Percentage Dem.	AIP
19,982	ADAMS	7,708	3,973	2,685	1,049	1	1,288 R	51.5%	34.8%	13.6%
103,691	ALLEN	38,349	23,124	10,994	4,231		12,130 R	60.3%	28.7%	11.0%
38,771	ASHLAND	15,594	9,745	4,526	1,323		5,219 R	62.5%	29.0%	8.5%
93,067	ASHTABULA	36,555	17,058	16,738	2,753	6	320 R	46.7%	45.8%	7.5%
46,998	ATHENS	16,400	7,837	7,351	1,207	5	486 R	47.8%	44.8%	7.4%
36,147	AUGLAIZE	16,447	9,368	5,550	1,528	1	3,818 R	57.0%	33.7%	9.3%
83,864	BELMONT	36,046	11,512	22,056	2,478		10,544 D	31.9%	61.2%	6.9%
25,178	BROWN	10,617	4,700	3,610	2,307		1,090 R	44.3%	34.0%	21.7%
199,076	BUTLER	73,802	35,962	23,649	14,188	3	12,313 R	48.7%	32.0%	19.2%
20,857	CARROLL	8,846	4,634	3,119	1,092	1	1,515 R	52.4%	35.3%	12.3%
29,714	CHAMPAIGN	12,750	6,863	4,264	1,621	2	2,599 R	53.8%	33.4%	12.7%
131,440	CLARK	54,491	23,748	24,029	6,710	4	281 D	43.6%	44.1%	12.3%
80,530	CLERMONT	31,849	15,299	8,859	7,690	1	6,440 R	48.0%	27.8%	24.1%
30,004	CLINTON	11,077	6,265	2,982	1,830		3,283 R	56.6%	26.9%	16.5%
107,004	COLUMBIANA	43,170	19,947	19,382	3,832	9	565 R	46.2%	44.9%	8.9%
32,224	COSHOCTON	13,539	7,256	5,013	1,270		2,243 R	53.6%	37.0%	9.4%
46,775	CRAWFORD	21,008	11,898	6,737	2,373		5,161 R	56.6%	32.1%	11.3%
1,647,895	CUYAHOGA	673,839	238,791	363,540	71,360	148	124,749 D	35.4%	54.0%	10.6%
45,612	DARKE	20,315	10,926	7,371	2,015	3	3,555 R	53.8%	36.3%	9.9%
31,508	DEFIANCE	13,959	7,348	5,686	925		1,662 R	52.6%	40.7%	6.6%
36,107	DELAWARE	15,644	9,029	4,056	2,557	2	4,973 R	57.7%	25.9%	16.3%
68,000	ERIE	26,849	13,023	11,388	2,437	1	1,635 R	48.5%	42.4%	9.1%
63,912	FAIRFIELD	28,467	14,810	9,533	4,124		5,277 R	52.0%	33.5%	14.5%
24,775	FAYETTE	10,269	5,339	2,966	1,962	2	2,373 R	52.0%	28.9%	19.1%
682,962	FRANKLIN	287,624	148,933	101,240	37,390	61	47,693 R	51.8%	35.2%	13.0%
29,301	FULTON	12,188	7,817	3,338	1,033		4,479 R	64.1%	27.4%	8.5%
26,120	GALLIA	8,836	5,134	2,660	1,039	3	2,474 R	58.1%	30.1%	11.8%
47,573	GEAUGA	22,908	11,857	7,825	3,226		4,032 R	51.8%	34.2%	14.1%
94,642	GREENE	38,775	17,589	15,178	5,999	9	2,411 R	45.4%	39.1%	15.5%
38,579	GUERNSEY	14,837	7,336	5,815	1,685	1	1,521 R	49.4%	39.2%	11.4%
864,121	HAMILTON	365,483	183,611	135,057	46,742	73	48,554 R	50.2%	37.0%	12.8%
53,686	HANCOCK	24,609	15,032	6,918	2,659		8,114 R	61.1%	28.1%	10.8%
29,633	HARDIN	12,937	6,963	4,180	1,794		2,783 R	53.8%	32.3%	13.9%
17,995	HARRISON	7,700	3,532	3,594	574		62 D	45.9%	46.7%	7.5%
25,392	HENRY	11,026	6,970	3,256	799	1	3,714 R	63.2%	29.5%	7.2%
29,716	HIGHLAND	12,525	6,489	3,828	2,208		2,661 R	51.8%	30.6%	17.6%
20,168	HOCKING	8,702	3,998	3,701	1,003		297 R	45.9%	42.5%	11.5%
21,591	HOLMES	5,729	3,350	1,898	479	2	1,452 R	58.5%	33.1%	8.4%
47,326	HURON	17,714	9,456	6,515	1,741	2	2,941 R	53.4%	36.8%	9.8%
29,372	JACKSON	10,968	5,870	4,021	1,077		1,849 R	53.5%	36.7%	9.8%
99,201	JEFFERSON	38,615	12,949	21,917	3,740	9	8,968 D	33.5%	56.8%	9.7%
38,808	KNOX	16,492	9,072	5,725	1,695		3,347 R	55.0%	34.7%	10.3%
148,700	LAKE	65,559	28,450	27,932	9,160	17	518 R	43.4%	42.6%	14.0%
55,438	LAWRENCE	20,923	9,782	8,671	2,470		1,111 R	46.8%	41.4%	11.8%
90,242	LICKING	39,970	19,542	15,021	5,405	2	4,521 R	48.9%	37.6%	13.5%
34,803	LOGAN	14,899	8,362	4,889	1,647	1	3,473 R	56.1%	32.8%	11.1%
217,500	LORAIN	85,727	34,252	42,642	8,825	8	8,390 D	40.0%	49.7%	10.3%
456,931	LUCAS	178,037	69,403	91,346	17,260	28	21,943 D	39.0%	51.3%	9.7%
26,454	MADISON	10,293	5,882	2,780	1,631		3,102 R	57.1%	27.0%	15.8%
300,480	MAHONING	123,578	42,948	68,433	12,189	8	25,485 D	34.8%	55.4%	9.9%
60,221	MARION	24,271	12,887	8,611	2,772	1	4,276 R	53.1%	35.5%	11.4%
65,315	MEDINA	26,933	14,089	9,194	3,632	18	4,895 R	52.3%	34.1%	13.5%
22,159	MEIGS	8,455	4,759	2,921	774	1	1,838 R	56.3%	34.5%	9.2%
32,559	MERCER	14,209	6,313	6,801	1,095		488 D	44.4%	47.9%	7.7%
72,901	MIAMI	33,577	16,997	13,228	3,348	4	3,769 R	50.6%	39.4%	10.0%
15,268	MONROE	6,354	2,686	3,105	562	1	419 D	42.3%	48.9%	8.8%
527,080	MONTGOMERY	207,120	84,766	96,082	26,232	40	11,316 D	40.9%	46.4%	12.7%
12,747	MORGAN	5,269	3,030	1,789	450		1,241 R	57.5%	34.0%	8.5%
19,405	MORROW	8,812	4,898	2,405	1,509		2,493 R	55.6%	27.3%	17.1%
79,159	MUSKINGUM	31,705	15,260	13,089	3,356		2,171 R	48.1%	41.3%	10.6%

OHIO

PRESIDENT 1968

1960 Census Population	County	Total Vote	Republican	Democratic	AIP	Other	Plurality	Percentage Rep.	Dem.	AIP
10,982	NOBLE	4,928	2,615	1,726	587		889 R	53.1%	35.0%	11.9%
35,323	OTTAWA	15,115	7,149	6,319	1,647		830 R	47.3%	41.8%	10.9%
16,792	PAULDING	7,685	4,074	2,703	908		1,371 R	53.0%	35.2%	11.8%
27,864	PERRY	10,710	4,815	4,811	1,084		4 R	45.0%	44.9%	10.1%
35,855	PICKAWAY	12,564	6,690	3,536	2,335	3	3,154 R	53.2%	28.1%	18.6%
19,380	PIKE	8,115	3,247	3,445	1,423		198 D	40.0%	42.5%	17.5%
91,798	PORTAGE	36,505	15,064	16,348	5,093		1,284 D	41.3%	44.8%	14.0%
32,498	PREBLE	12,434	6,544	3,817	2,073		2,727 R	52.6%	30.7%	16.7%
28,331	PUTNAM	12,105	7,188	3,530	1,387		3,658 R	59.4%	29.2%	11.5%
117,761	RICHLAND	43,787	23,484	14,988	5,311	4	8,496 R	53.6%	34.2%	12.1%
61,215	ROSS	22,246	11,284	6,873	4,087	2	4,411 R	50.7%	30.9%	18.4%
56,486	SANDUSKY	22,025	11,696	8,581	1,745	3	3,115 R	53.1%	39.0%	7.9%
84,216	SCIOTO	32,317	15,310	13,836	3,171		1,474 R	47.4%	42.8%	9.8%
59,326	SENECA	23,020	12,040	8,970	2,010		3,070 R	52.3%	39.0%	8.7%
33,586	SHELBY	15,226	7,248	6,479	1,499		769 R	47.6%	42.6%	9.8%
340,345	STARK	142,888	68,414	57,675	16,775	24	10,739 R	47.9%	40.4%	11.7%
513,569	SUMMIT	208,941	82,649	100,068	26,157	67	17,419 D	39.6%	47.9%	12.5%
208,526	TRUMBULL	82,760	33,076	40,365	9,314	5	7,289 D	40.0%	48.8%	11.3%
76,789	TUSCARAWAS	32,461	14,102	15,617	2,741	1	1,515 D	43.4%	48.1%	8.4%
22,853	UNION	10,238	6,415	2,431	1,392		3,984 R	62.7%	23.7%	13.6%
28,840	VAN WERT	13,527	7,835	4,360	1,332		3,475 R	57.9%	32.2%	9.8%
10,274	VINTON	4,242	2,219	1,608	414	1	611 R	52.3%	37.9%	9.8%
65,711	WARREN	26,014	12,663	6,756	6,595		5,907 R	48.7%	26.0%	25.4%
51,689	WASHINGTON	20,408	11,888	6,922	1,597	1	4,966 R	58.3%	33.9%	7.8%
75,497	WAYNE	25,970	15,151	8,891	1,924	4	6,260 R	58.3%	34.2%	7.4%
29,968	WILLIAMS	13,485	8,059	4,456	970		3,603 R	59.8%	33.0%	7.2%
72,596	WOOD	29,939	16,111	10,867	2,952	9	5,244 R	53.8%	36.3%	9.9%
21,648	WYANDOT	9,094	5,265	2,919	910		2,346 R	57.9%	32.1%	10.0%
9,706,397	TOTAL	3,959,698	1,791,014	1,700,586	467,495	603	90,428 R	45.2%	42.9%	11.8%

OHIO

ELECTION NOTES

1984 Other vote was 12,090 Serrette (Independent); 10,693 LaRouche (Independent); 5,886 Bergland (Independent); 4,438 Hall (Independent); 4,344 Mason (Independent); 3,565 Winn (Independent); 2,565 Holmes (Independent); 4 Dodge (write-in); 34 scattered write-in. Early unamended canvass gave the Serrette (Independent) vote as 24,180 and the Winn (Independent) vote as 7,130.

1980 Other vote was 254,472 Anderson (Independent); 49,033 Clark (Independent); 8,564 Commoner (Independent); 4,729 Hall (Independent); 4,029 Congress (Independent); 3,790 Griswold (Independent); 27 Bubar (write-in). The vote for Congress (Independent) was with Zimmermann for Vice President who was the Socialist Workers candidate in other states.

1976 Other vote was 58,258 McCarthy (Independent); 15,529 Maddox (American); 8,961 MacBride (Independent); 7,817 Hall (Independent); 4,717 Camejo (Independent); 4,335 LaRouche (Independent); 68 Levin (write-in); 62 Bubar (write-in). Vote detailed in the table is for the recount.

1972 Other vote was 80,067 Schmitz (American Independent); 7,107 Fisher (Socialist Labor); 6,437 Hall (no party label on the ballot); 460 Edward Wallace (write-in).

1968 Wallace on the ballot as American Independent. Other vote was 372 Gregory (write-in); 120 Blomen (write-in); 69 Halstead (write-in); 23 Mitchell (write-in); 19 Munn (write-in).

OKLAHOMA

POPULAR VOTE FOR PRESIDENT 1920 TO 1984

Year	Total Vote	Republican Vote	Republican Candidate	Democratic Vote	Democratic Candidate	Other Vote	Plurality	Percentage Total Vote Rep.	Percentage Total Vote Dem.	Percentage Major Vote Rep.	Percentage Major Vote Dem.
1984	1,255,676	861,530	Reagan, Ronald	385,080	Mondale, Walter F.	9,066	476,450 R	68.6%	30.7%	69.1%	30.9%
1980	1,149,708	695,570	Reagan, Ronald	402,026	Carter, Jimmy	52,112	293,544 R	60.5%	35.0%	63.4%	36.6%
1976	1,092,251	545,708	Ford, Gerald R.	532,442	Carter, Jimmy	14,101	13,266 R	50.0%	48.7%	50.6%	49.4%
1972	1,029,900	759,025	Nixon, Richard M.	247,147	McGovern, George S.	23,728	511,878 R	73.7%	24.0%	75.4%	24.6%
1968	943,086	449,697	Nixon, Richard M.	301,658	Humphrey, Hubert H.	191,731	148,039 R	47.7%	32.0%	59.9%	40.1%
1964	932,499	412,665	Goldwater, Barry M.	519,834	Johnson, Lyndon B.		107,169 D	44.3%	55.7%	44.3%	55.7%
1960	903,150	533,039	Nixon, Richard M.	370,111	Kennedy, John F.		162,928 R	59.0%	41.0%	59.0%	41.0%
1956	859,350	473,769	Eisenhower, Dwight D.	385,581	Stevenson, Adlai E.		88,188 R	55.1%	44.9%	55.1%	44.9%
1952	948,984	518,045	Eisenhower, Dwight D.	430,939	Stevenson, Adlai E.		87,106 R	54.6%	45.4%	54.6%	45.4%
1948	721,599	268,817	Dewey, Thomas E.	452,782	Truman, Harry S.		183,965 D	37.3%	62.7%	37.3%	62.7%
1944	722,636	319,424	Dewey, Thomas E.	401,549	Roosevelt, Franklin D.	1,663	82,125 D	44.2%	55.6%	44.3%	55.7%
1940	826,212	348,872	Willkie, Wendell	474,313	Roosevelt, Franklin D.	3,027	125,441 D	42.2%	57.4%	42.4%	57.6%
1936	749,740	245,122	Landon, Alfred M.	501,069	Roosevelt, Franklin D.	3,549	255,947 D	32.7%	66.8%	32.8%	67.2%
1932	704,633	188,165	Hoover, Herbert C.	516,468	Roosevelt, Franklin D.		328,303 D	26.7%	73.3%	26.7%	73.3%
1928	618,427	394,046	Hoover, Herbert C.	219,174	Smith, Alfred E.	5,207	174,872 R	63.7%	35.4%	64.3%	35.7%
1924	527,828	225,756	Coolidge, Calvin	255,798	Davis, John W.	46,274	30,042 D	42.8%	48.5%	46.9%	53.1%
1920	485,678	243,840	Harding, Warren G.	216,122	Cox, James M.	25,716	27,718 R	50.2%	44.5%	53.0%	47.0%

ELECTORAL COLLEGE VOTE 1920 TO 1984

Year	Total	Republican	Democratic	Other
1984	8	8	—	—
1980	8	8	—	—
1976	8	8	—	—
1972	8	8	—	—
1968	8	8	—	—
1964	8	—	8	—
1960 **	8	7	—	1 BYRD
1956	8	8	—	—
1952	8	8	—	—
1948	10	—	10	—
1944	10	—	10	—
1940	11	—	11	—
1936	11	—	11	—
1932	11	—	11	—
1928	10	10	—	—
1924	10	—	10	—
1920	10	10	—	—

In 1960 one of the eight Republican electors voted in the Electoral College for Harry Flood Byrd and Barry M. Goldwater rather than for the national Republican candidates.

OKLAHOMA

OTTAWA
DELAWARE
ADAIR
SEQUOYAH
CHEROKEE
CRAIG
MAYES
NOWATA
ROGERS
WAGONER
MUSKOGEE
HASKELL
LE FLORE
LATIMER
McCURTAIN
PUSHMATAHA
CHOCTAW
McINTOSH
PITTSBURG
WASHINGTON
TULSA
OKMULGEE
OSAGE
PAWNEE
CREEK
OKFUSKEE
HUGHES
COAL
ATOKA
BRYAN
SEMINOLE
PONTOTOC
JOHNSTON
MAR-
SHALL
KAY
NOBLE
PAYNE
LINCOLN
POTTA-
WATOMIE
MURRAY
CARTER
LOVE
GARVIN
CLEVELAND
McCLAIN
OKLAHOMA
LOGAN
GRANT
GARFIELD
KINGFISHER
CANADIAN
GRADY
STEPHENS
JEFFERSON
ALFALFA
MAJOR
BLAINE
CADDO
COMANCHE
COTTON
WOODS
WOODWARD
DEWEY
CUSTER
WASHITA
KIOWA
TILLMAN
JACKSON
HARPER
ELLIS
ROGER
MILLS
BECKHAM
GREER
HARMON
BEAVER
TEXAS
CIMARRON

OKLAHOMA

PRESIDENT 1984

1980 Census Population	County	Total Vote	Republican	Democratic	Other	Rep.-Dem. Plurality	Percentage Total Vote Rep.	Total Vote Dem.	Major Vote Rep.	Major Vote Dem.
18,575	ADAIR	6,745	4,423	2,266	56	2,157 R	65.6%	33.6%	66.1%	33.9%
7,077	ALFALFA	3,608	2,715	866	27	1,849 R	75.2%	24.0%	75.8%	24.2%
12,748	ATOKA	4,444	2,361	2,047	36	314 R	53.1%	46.1%	53.6%	46.4%
6,806	BEAVER	3,252	2,689	536	27	2,153 R	82.7%	16.5%	83.4%	16.6%
19,243	BECKHAM	7,654	5,005	2,601	48	2,404 R	65.4%	34.0%	65.8%	34.2%
13,443	BLAINE	5,554	4,037	1,484	33	2,553 R	72.7%	26.7%	73.1%	26.9%
30,535	BRYAN	11,769	6,246	5,475	48	771 R	53.1%	46.5%	53.3%	46.7%
30,905	CADDO	11,341	6,811	4,463	67	2,348 R	60.1%	39.4%	60.4%	39.6%
56,452	CANADIAN	26,320	20,929	5,245	146	15,684 R	79.5%	19.9%	80.0%	20.0%
43,610	CARTER	17,822	11,578	6,161	83	5,417 R	65.0%	34.6%	65.3%	34.7%
30,684	CHEROKEE	13,015	7,614	5,307	94	2,307 R	58.5%	40.8%	58.9%	41.1%
17,203	CHOCTAW	5,987	3,155	2,801	31	354 R	52.7%	46.8%	53.0%	47.0%
3,648	CIMARRON	1,794	1,420	359	15	1,061 R	79.2%	20.0%	79.8%	20.2%
133,173	CLEVELAND	59,705	42,806	16,512	387	26,294 R	71.7%	27.7%	72.2%	27.8%
6,041	COAL	2,564	1,259	1,284	21	25 D	49.1%	50.1%	49.5%	50.5%
112,456	COMANCHE	30,394	21,382	8,890	122	12,492 R	70.3%	29.2%	70.6%	29.4%
7,338	COTTON	3,080	1,796	1,264	20	532 R	58.3%	41.0%	58.7%	41.3%
15,014	CRAIG	6,190	3,629	2,515	46	1,114 R	58.6%	40.6%	59.1%	40.9%
59,016	CREEK	22,628	15,011	7,465	152	7,546 R	66.3%	33.0%	66.8%	33.2%
25,995	CUSTER	10,940	8,191	2,700	49	5,491 R	74.9%	24.7%	75.2%	24.8%
23,946	DELAWARE	10,542	6,690	3,789	63	2,901 R	63.5%	35.9%	63.8%	36.2%
5,922	DEWEY	2,777	2,098	664	15	1,434 R	75.5%	23.9%	76.0%	24.0%
5,596	ELLIS	2,460	1,881	562	17	1,319 R	76.5%	22.8%	77.0%	23.0%
62,820	GARFIELD	25,534	19,642	5,730	162	13,912 R	76.9%	22.4%	77.4%	22.6%
27,856	GARVIN	11,811	7,505	4,215	91	3,290 R	63.5%	35.7%	64.0%	36.0%
39,490	GRADY	15,960	11,042	4,846	72	6,196 R	69.2%	30.4%	69.5%	30.5%
6,518	GRANT	3,324	2,470	825	29	1,645 R	74.3%	24.8%	75.0%	25.0%
7,028	GREEN	2,901	1,664	1,220	17	444 R	57.4%	42.1%	57.7%	42.3%
4,519	HARMON	1,805	1,009	785	11	224 R	55.9%	43.5%	56.2%	43.8%
4,715	HARPER	2,146	1,748	373	25	1,375 R	81.5%	17.4%	82.4%	17.6%
11,010	HASKELL	4,981	2,417	2,535	29	118 D	48.5%	50.9%	48.8%	51.2%
14,338	HUGHES	5,598	2,663	2,901	34	238 D	47.6%	51.8%	47.9%	52.1%
30,356	JACKSON	8,795	5,773	2,996	26	2,777 R	65.6%	34.1%	65.8%	34.2%
8,183	JEFFERSON	3,179	1,656	1,496	27	160 R	52.1%	47.1%	52.5%	47.5%
10,356	JOHNSTON	4,038	2,195	1,820	23	375 R	54.4%	45.1%	54.7%	45.3%
49,852	KAY	22,911	16,731	6,044	136	10,687 R	73.0%	26.4%	73.5%	26.5%
14,187	KINGFISHER	6,686	5,528	1,125	33	4,403 R	82.7%	16.8%	83.1%	16.9%
12,711	KIOWA	4,995	2,951	2,016	28	935 R	59.1%	40.4%	59.4%	40.6%
9,840	LATIMER	4,100	2,210	1,858	32	352 R	53.9%	45.3%	54.3%	45.7%
40,698	LE FLORE	14,698	8,604	5,990	104	2,614 R	58.5%	40.8%	59.0%	41.0%
26,601	LINCOLN	11,189	8,088	3,020	81	5,068 R	72.3%	27.0%	72.8%	27.2%
26,881	LOGAN	11,978	8,356	3,551	71	4,805 R	69.8%	29.6%	70.2%	29.8%
7,469	LOVE	3,209	1,833	1,359	17	474 R	57.1%	42.3%	57.4%	42.6%
20,291	MCCLAIN	8,672	6,056	2,549	67	3,507 R	69.8%	29.4%	70.4%	29.6%
36,151	MCCURTAIN	10,416	6,381	3,994	41	2,387 R	61.3%	38.3%	61.5%	38.5%
15,562	MCINTOSH	7,165	3,646	3,479	40	167 R	50.9%	48.6%	51.2%	48.8%
8,772	MAJOR	4,035	3,385	619	31	2,766 R	83.9%	15.3%	84.5%	15.5%
10,550	MARSHALL	4,560	2,488	2,039	33	449 R	54.6%	44.7%	55.0%	45.0%
32,261	MAYES	13,838	8,585	5,154	99	3,431 R	62.0%	37.2%	62.5%	37.5%
12,147	MURRAY	5,347	3,073	2,229	45	844 R	57.5%	41.7%	58.0%	42.0%
66,939	MUSKOGEE	27,183	14,652	12,343	188	2,309 R	53.9%	45.4%	54.3%	45.7%
11,573	NOBLE	5,279	4,018	1,238	23	2,780 R	76.1%	23.5%	76.4%	23.6%
11,486	NOWATA	4,761	3,030	1,687	44	1,343 R	63.6%	35.4%	64.2%	35.8%
11,125	OKFUSKEE	4,145	2,443	1,684	18	759 R	58.9%	40.6%	59.2%	40.8%
568,933	OKLAHOMA	223,261	159,974	60,235	3,052	99,739 R	71.7%	27.0%	72.6%	27.4%
39,169	OKMULGEE	16,189	8,704	7,380	105	1,324 R	53.8%	45.6%	54.1%	45.9%
39,327	OSAGE	16,257	10,083	6,095	79	3,988 R	62.0%	37.5%	62.3%	37.7%
32,870	OTTAWA	13,505	7,666	5,781	58	1,885 R	56.8%	42.8%	57.0%	43.0%
15,310	PAWNEE	6,928	4,699	2,165	64	2,534 R	67.8%	31.3%	68.5%	31.5%
62,435	PAYNE	28,648	20,811	7,653	184	13,158 R	72.6%	26.7%	73.1%	26.9%

OKLAHOMA

PRESIDENT 1984

1980 Census Population	County	Total Vote	Republican	Democratic	Other	Rep.-Dem. Plurality	Percentage Total Vote Rep.	Percentage Total Vote Dem.	Percentage Major Vote Rep.	Percentage Major Vote Dem.
40,524	PITTSBURG	16,760	9,778	6,860	122	2,918 R	58.3%	40.9%	58.8%	41.2%
32,598	PONTOTOC	13,907	8,301	5,526	80	2,775 R	59.7%	39.7%	60.0%	40.0%
55,239	POTTAWATOMIE	23,261	16,143	6,966	152	9,177 R	69.4%	29.9%	69.9%	30.1%
11,773	PUSHMATAHA	4,614	2,499	2,079	36	420 R	54.2%	45.1%	54.6%	45.4%
4,799	ROGER MILLS	2,243	1,550	680	13	870 R	69.1%	30.3%	69.5%	30.5%
46,436	ROGERS	22,288	16,137	6,013	138	10,124 R	72.4%	27.0%	72.9%	27.1%
27,473	SEMINOLE	10,030	6,009	3,957	64	2,052 R	59.9%	39.5%	60.3%	39.7%
30,749	SEQUOYAH	11,300	7,042	4,202	56	2,840 R	62.3%	37.2%	62.6%	37.4%
43,419	STEPHENS	19,333	12,871	6,359	103	6,512 R	66.6%	32.9%	66.9%	33.1%
17,727	TEXAS	7,039	5,968	1,033	38	4,935 R	84.8%	14.7%	85.2%	14.8%
12,398	TILLMAN	4,326	2,637	1,674	15	963 R	61.0%	38.7%	61.2%	38.8%
470,593	TULSA	218,872	159,549	58,274	1,049	101,275 R	72.9%	26.6%	73.2%	26.8%
41,801	WAGONER	17,913	12,534	5,271	108	7,263 R	70.0%	29.4%	70.4%	29.6%
48,113	WASHINGTON	24,667	19,043	5,476	148	13,567 R	77.2%	22.2%	77.7%	22.3%
13,798	WASHITA	5,430	3,847	1,547	36	2,300 R	70.8%	28.5%	71.3%	28.7%
10,923	WOODS	5,018	3,741	1,231	46	2,510 R	74.6%	24.5%	75.2%	24.8%
21,172	WOODWARD	8,063	6,376	1,647	40	4,729 R	79.1%	20.4%	79.5%	20.5%
3,025,290	TOTAL	1,255,676	861,530	385,080	9,066	476,450 R	68.6%	30.7%	69.1%	30.9%

OKLAHOMA

PRESIDENT 1980

1980 Census Population	County	Total Vote	Republican	Democratic	Other	Rep.-Dem. Plurality	Percentage Total Vote Rep.	Percentage Total Vote Dem.	Percentage Major Vote Rep.	Percentage Major Vote Dem.
18,575	ADAIR	6,341	3,429	2,761	151	668 R	54.1%	43.5%	55.4%	44.6%
7,077	ALFALFA	3,642	2,628	899	115	1,729 R	72.2%	24.7%	74.5%	25.5%
12,748	ATOKA	4,216	1,613	2,505	98	892 D	38.3%	59.4%	39.2%	60.8%
6,806	BEAVER	3,218	2,430	696	92	1,734 R	75.5%	21.6%	77.7%	22.3%
19,243	BECKHAM	7,113	3,637	3,298	178	339 R	51.1%	46.4%	52.4%	47.6%
13,443	BLAINE	5,264	3,708	1,399	157	2,309 R	70.4%	26.6%	72.6%	27.4%
30,535	BRYAN	10,582	3,980	6,410	192	2,430 D	37.6%	60.6%	38.3%	61.7%
30,905	CADDO	10,995	5,945	4,695	355	1,250 R	54.1%	42.7%	55.9%	44.1%
56,452	CANADIAN	21,041	15,272	4,889	880	10,383 R	72.6%	23.2%	75.8%	24.2%
43,610	CARTER	16,154	9,262	6,509	383	2,753 R	57.3%	40.3%	58.7%	41.3%
30,684	CHEROKEE	11,308	5,594	5,215	499	379 R	49.5%	46.1%	51.8%	48.2%
17,203	CHOCTAW	6,009	2,394	3,507	108	1,113 D	39.8%	58.4%	40.6%	59.4%
3,648	CIMARRON	1,821	1,404	373	44	1,031 R	77.1%	20.5%	79.0%	21.0%
133,173	CLEVELAND	50,401	31,178	14,536	4,687	16,642 R	61.9%	28.8%	68.2%	31.8%
6,041	COAL	2,431	926	1,442	63	516 D	38.1%	59.3%	39.1%	60.9%
112,456	COMANCHE	27,910	16,609	9,972	1,329	6,637 R	59.5%	35.7%	62.5%	37.5%
7,338	COTTON	3,206	1,702	1,410	94	292 R	53.1%	44.0%	54.7%	45.3%
15,014	CRAIG	5,952	2,956	2,801	195	155 R	49.7%	47.1%	51.3%	48.7%
59,016	CREEK	19,729	11,749	7,339	641	4,410 R	59.6%	37.2%	61.6%	38.4%
25,995	CUSTER	9,854	6,469	3,008	377	3,461 R	65.6%	30.5%	68.3%	31.7%
23,946	DELAWARE	9,819	5,302	4,244	273	1,058 R	54.0%	43.2%	55.5%	44.5%
5,922	DEWEY	2,876	1,943	826	107	1,117 R	67.6%	28.7%	70.2%	29.8%
5,596	ELLIS	2,550	1,908	561	81	1,347 R	74.8%	22.0%	77.3%	22.7%
62,820	GARFIELD	24,828	17,989	5,718	1,121	12,271 R	72.5%	23.0%	75.9%	24.1%
27,856	GARVIN	10,860	5,520	5,033	307	487 R	50.8%	46.3%	52.3%	47.7%
39,490	GRADY	13,971	8,131	5,330	510	2,801 R	58.2%	38.2%	60.4%	39.6%
6,518	GRANT	3,472	2,411	927	134	1,484 R	69.4%	26.7%	72.2%	27.8%
7,028	GREEN	3,099	1,535	1,492	72	43 R	49.5%	48.1%	50.7%	49.3%
4,519	HARMON	1,670	676	961	33	285 D	40.5%	57.5%	41.3%	58.7%
4,715	HARPER	2,230	1,652	517	61	1,135 R	74.1%	23.2%	76.2%	23.8%
11,010	HASKELL	5,011	2,024	2,874	113	850 D	40.4%	57.4%	41.3%	58.7%
14,338	HUGHES	5,515	2,170	3,211	134	1,041 D	39.3%	58.2%	40.3%	59.7%
30,356	JACKSON	8,554	4,327	4,031	196	296 R	50.6%	47.1%	51.8%	48.2%
8,183	JEFFERSON	3,332	1,440	1,812	80	372 D	43.2%	54.4%	44.3%	55.7%
10,356	JOHNSTON	3,857	1,701	2,066	90	365 D	44.1%	53.6%	45.2%	54.8%
49,852	KAY	22,337	15,004	6,449	884	8,555 R	67.2%	28.9%	69.9%	30.1%
14,187	KINGFISHER	6,418	4,962	1,282	174	3,680 R	77.3%	20.0%	79.5%	20.5%
12,711	KIOWA	5,124	2,636	2,372	116	264 R	51.4%	46.3%	52.6%	47.4%
9,840	LATIMER	3,966	1,737	2,105	124	368 D	43.8%	53.1%	45.2%	54.8%
40,698	LE FLORE	13,759	6,807	6,668	284	139 R	49.5%	48.5%	50.5%	49.5%
26,601	LINCOLN	9,585	6,064	3,231	290	2,833 R	63.3%	33.7%	65.2%	34.8%
26,881	LOGAN	9,992	6,311	3,246	435	3,065 R	63.2%	32.5%	66.0%	34.0%
7,469	LOVE	3,075	1,449	1,578	48	129 D	47.1%	51.3%	47.9%	52.1%
20,291	MCCLAIN	7,533	4,284	2,990	259	1,294 R	56.9%	39.7%	58.9%	41.1%
36,151	MCCURTAIN	11,372	5,189	5,953	230	764 D	45.6%	52.3%	46.6%	53.4%
15,562	MCINTOSH	6,763	2,925	3,654	184	729 D	43.3%	54.0%	44.5%	55.5%
8,772	MAJOR	3,739	3,059	584	96	2,475 R	81.8%	15.6%	84.0%	16.0%
10,550	MARSHALL	4,195	1,961	2,157	77	196 D	46.7%	51.4%	47.6%	52.4%
32,261	MAYES	12,358	6,633	5,344	381	1,289 R	53.7%	43.2%	55.4%	44.6%
12,147	MURRAY	5,067	2,494	2,384	189	110 R	49.2%	47.0%	51.1%	48.9%
66,939	MUSKOGEE	25,715	11,511	13,341	863	1,830 D	44.8%	51.9%	46.3%	53.7%
11,573	NOBLE	5,240	3,663	1,398	179	2,265 R	69.9%	26.7%	72.4%	27.6%
11,486	NOWATA	4,470	2,640	1,694	136	946 R	59.1%	37.9%	60.9%	39.1%
11,125	OKFUSKEE	4,401	2,126	2,177	98	51 D	48.3%	49.5%	49.4%	50.6%
568,933	OKLAHOMA	211,273	139,538	58,765	12,970	80,773 R	66.0%	27.8%	70.4%	29.6%
39,169	OKMULGEE	14,285	6,652	7,236	397	584 D	46.6%	50.7%	47.9%	52.1%
39,327	OSAGE	14,246	8,044	5,687	515	2,357 R	56.5%	39.9%	58.6%	41.4%
32,870	OTTAWA	12,919	6,362	6,143	414	219 R	49.2%	47.6%	50.9%	49.1%
15,310	PAWNEE	6,151	3,902	2,020	229	1,882 R	63.4%	32.8%	65.9%	34.1%
62,435	PAYNE	25,691	15,955	7,466	2,270	8,489 R	62.1%	29.1%	68.1%	31.9%

OKLAHOMA

PRESIDENT 1980

1980 Census Population	County	Total Vote	Republican	Democratic	Other	Rep.-Dem. Plurality	Percentage Total Vote Rep.	Percentage Total Vote Dem.	Percentage Major Vote Rep.	Percentage Major Vote Dem.
40,524	PITTSBURG	15,857	7,062	8,292	503	1,230 D	44.5%	52.3%	46.0%	54.0%
32,598	PONTOTOC	12,631	6,232	5,942	457	290 R	49.3%	47.0%	51.2%	48.8%
55,239	POTTAWATOMIE	21,850	12,466	8,526	858	3,940 R	57.1%	39.0%	59.4%	40.6%
11,773	PUSHMATAHA	4,775	1,989	2,666	120	677 D	41.7%	55.8%	42.7%	57.3%
4,799	ROGER MILLS	2,171	1,221	877	73	344 R	56.2%	40.4%	58.2%	41.8%
46,436	ROGERS	18,642	11,581	6,399	662	5,182 R	62.1%	34.3%	64.4%	35.6%
27,473	SEMINOLE	10,145	5,067	4,726	352	341 R	49.9%	46.6%	51.7%	48.3%
30,749	SEQUOYAH	11,246	5,987	4,983	276	1,004 R	53.2%	44.3%	54.6%	45.4%
43,419	STEPHENS	17,852	10,199	7,191	462	3,008 R	57.1%	40.3%	58.6%	41.4%
17,727	TEXAS	7,099	5,503	1,451	145	4,052 R	77.5%	20.4%	79.1%	20.9%
12,398	TILLMAN	4,687	2,450	2,144	93	306 R	52.3%	45.7%	53.3%	46.7%
470,593	TULSA	188,148	124,643	53,438	10,067	71,205 R	66.2%	28.4%	70.0%	30.0%
41,801	WAGONER	14,727	8,969	5,235	523	3,734 R	60.9%	35.5%	63.1%	36.9%
48,113	WASHINGTON	23,503	16,563	5,854	1,086	10,709 R	70.5%	24.9%	73.9%	26.1%
13,798	WASHITA	5,373	3,206	2,044	123	1,162 R	59.7%	38.0%	61.1%	38.9%
10,923	WOODS	5,208	3,592	1,364	252	2,228 R	69.0%	26.2%	72.5%	27.5%
21,172	WOODWARD	7,289	5,318	1,703	268	3,615 R	73.0%	23.4%	75.7%	24.3%
3,025,290	TOTAL	1,149,708	695,570	402,026	52,112	293,544 R	60.5%	35.0%	63.4%	36.6%

OKLAHOMA

PRESIDENT 1976

1970 Census Population	County	Total Vote	Republican	Democratic	Other	Rep.-Dem. Plurality	Percentage Total Vote Rep.	Percentage Total Vote Dem.	Percentage Major Vote Rep.	Percentage Major Vote Dem.
15,141	ADAIR	6,259	3,013	3,183	63	170 D	48.1%	50.9%	48.6%	51.4%
7,224	ALFALFA	3,897	2,113	1,725	59	388 R	54.2%	44.3%	55.1%	44.9%
10,972	ATOKA	4,402	1,098	3,276	28	2,178 D	24.9%	74.4%	25.1%	74.9%
6,282	BEAVER	3,061	1,801	1,213	47	588 R	58.8%	39.6%	59.8%	40.2%
15,754	BECKHAM	6,935	2,351	4,530	54	2,179 D	33.9%	65.3%	34.2%	65.8%
11,794	BLAINE	5,056	2,682	2,297	77	385 R	53.0%	45.4%	53.9%	46.1%
25,552	BRYAN	10,293	2,848	7,410	35	4,562 D	27.7%	72.0%	27.8%	72.2%
28,931	CADDO	11,327	3,854	7,382	91	3,528 D	34.0%	65.2%	34.3%	65.7%
32,245	CANADIAN	17,339	9,766	7,288	285	2,478 R	56.3%	42.0%	57.3%	42.7%
37,349	CARTER	15,070	6,668	8,319	83	1,651 D	44.2%	55.2%	44.5%	55.5%
23,174	CHEROKEE	10,564	4,443	6,006	115	1,563 D	42.1%	56.9%	42.5%	57.5%
15,141	CHOCTAW	6,140	1,821	4,269	50	2,448 D	29.7%	69.5%	29.9%	70.1%
4,145	CIMARRON	1,879	872	962	45	90 D	46.4%	51.2%	47.5%	52.5%
81,839	CLEVELAND	43,281	22,098	20,054	1,129	2,044 R	51.1%	46.3%	52.4%	47.6%
5,525	COAL	2,566	769	1,774	23	1,005 D	30.0%	69.1%	30.2%	69.8%
108,144	COMANCHE	26,303	13,163	12,910	230	253 R	50.0%	49.1%	50.5%	49.5%
6,832	COTTON	3,064	1,127	1,911	26	784 D	36.8%	62.4%	37.1%	62.9%
14,722	CRAIG	6,178	2,540	3,577	61	1,037 D	41.1%	57.9%	41.5%	58.5%
45,532	CREEK	17,591	8,458	8,964	169	506 D	48.1%	51.0%	48.5%	51.5%
22,665	CUSTER	9,546	4,847	4,597	102	250 R	50.8%	48.2%	51.3%	48.7%
17,767	DELAWARE	8,657	3,642	4,924	91	1,282 D	42.1%	56.9%	42.5%	57.5%
5,656	DEWEY	2,825	1,230	1,540	55	310 D	43.5%	54.5%	44.4%	55.6%
5,129	ELLIS	2,746	1,429	1,256	61	173 R	52.0%	45.7%	53.2%	46.8%
56,343	GARFIELD	23,474	14,202	8,969	303	5,233 R	60.5%	38.2%	61.3%	38.7%
24,874	GARVIN	10,785	3,905	6,797	83	2,892 D	36.2%	63.0%	36.5%	63.5%
29,354	GRADY	11,955	4,686	7,155	114	2,469 D	39.2%	59.8%	39.6%	60.4%
7,117	GRANT	3,588	1,685	1,853	50	168 D	47.0%	51.6%	47.6%	52.4%
7,979	GREEN	3,308	1,164	2,113	31	949 D	35.2%	63.9%	35.5%	64.5%
5,136	HARMON	2,045	666	1,371	8	705 D	32.6%	67.0%	32.7%	67.3%
5,151	HARPER	2,320	1,303	978	39	325 R	56.2%	42.2%	57.1%	42.9%
9,578	HASKELL	4,818	1,401	3,388	29	1,987 D	29.1%	70.3%	29.3%	70.7%
13,228	HUGHES	5,956	1,715	4,185	56	2,470 D	28.8%	70.3%	29.1%	70.9%
30,902	JACKSON	8,163	3,189	4,914	60	1,725 D	39.1%	60.2%	39.4%	60.6%
7,125	JEFFERSON	3,285	956	2,303	26	1,347 D	29.1%	70.1%	29.3%	70.7%
7,870	JOHNSTON	3,934	1,127	2,765	42	1,638 D	28.6%	70.3%	29.0%	71.0%
48,791	KAY	22,086	12,441	9,371	274	3,070 R	56.3%	42.4%	57.0%	43.0%
12,857	KINGFISHER	5,897	3,443	2,372	82	1,071 R	58.4%	40.2%	59.2%	40.8%
12,532	KIOWA	5,420	1,971	3,403	46	1,432 D	36.4%	62.8%	36.7%	63.3%
8,601	LATIMER	4,028	1,312	2,661	55	1,349 D	32.6%	66.1%	33.0%	67.0%
32,137	LE FLORE	13,085	4,907	8,033	145	3,126 D	37.5%	61.4%	37.9%	62.1%
19,482	LINCOLN	9,550	4,429	4,988	133	559 D	46.4%	52.2%	47.0%	53.0%
19,645	LOGAN	9,136	4,382	4,594	160	212 D	48.0%	50.3%	48.8%	51.2%
5,637	LOVE	2,778	846	1,923	9	1,077 D	30.5%	69.2%	30.6%	69.4%
14,157	MCCLAIN	6,572	2,444	4,048	80	1,604 D	37.2%	61.6%	37.6%	62.4%
28,642	MCCURTAIN	11,080	3,423	7,560	97	4,137 D	30.9%	68.2%	31.2%	68.8%
12,472	MCINTOSH	6,015	1,822	4,145	48	2,323 D	30.3%	68.9%	30.5%	69.5%
7,529	MAJOR	3,697	2,282	1,357	58	925 R	61.7%	36.7%	62.7%	37.3%
7,682	MARSHALL	4,324	1,358	2,939	27	1,581 D	31.4%	68.0%	31.6%	68.4%
23,302	MAYES	11,419	5,040	6,298	81	1,258 D	44.1%	55.2%	44.5%	55.5%
10,669	MURRAY	4,536	1,563	2,932	41	1,369 D	34.5%	64.6%	34.8%	65.2%
59,542	MUSKOGEE	25,155	10,287	14,678	190	4,391 D	40.9%	58.4%	41.2%	58.8%
10,043	NOBLE	4,965	2,634	2,278	53	356 R	53.1%	45.9%	53.6%	46.4%
9,773	NOWATA	4,311	2,077	2,195	39	118 D	48.2%	50.9%	48.6%	51.4%
10,683	OKFUSKEE	4,325	1,630	2,663	32	1,033 D	37.7%	61.6%	38.0%	62.0%
526,805	OKLAHOMA	210,113	119,120	87,185	3,808	31,935 R	56.7%	41.5%	57.7%	42.3%
35,358	OKMULGEE	13,963	5,333	8,499	131	3,166 D	38.2%	60.9%	38.6%	61.4%
29,750	OSAGE	13,348	6,398	6,832	118	434 D	47.9%	51.2%	48.4%	51.6%
29,800	OTTAWA	12,515	4,985	7,446	84	2,461 D	39.8%	59.5%	40.1%	59.9%
11,338	PAWNEE	6,201	3,111	3,031	59	80 R	50.2%	48.9%	50.7%	49.3%
50,654	PAYNE	23,888	13,481	9,987	420	3,494 R	56.4%	41.8%	57.4%	42.6%

OKLAHOMA

PRESIDENT 1976

1970 Census Population	County	Total Vote	Republican	Democratic	Other	Rep.-Dem. Plurality	Percentage Total Vote Rep.	Percentage Total Vote Dem.	Percentage Major Vote Rep.	Percentage Major Vote Dem.
37,521	PITTSBURG	15,692	4,807	10,743	142	5,936 D	30.6%	68.5%	30.9%	69.1%
27,867	PONTOTOC	12,486	4,895	7,466	125	2,571 D	39.2%	59.8%	39.6%	60.4%
43,134	POTTAWATOMIE	20,571	9,090	11,255	226	2,165 D	44.2%	54.7%	44.7%	55.3%
9,385	PUSHMATAHA	4,376	1,360	2,987	29	1,627 D	31.1%	68.3%	31.3%	68.7%
4,452	ROGER MILLS	2,243	873	1,346	24	473 D	38.9%	60.0%	39.3%	60.7%
28,425	ROGERS	14,815	7,318	7,368	129	50 D	49.4%	49.7%	49.8%	50.2%
25,144	SEMINOLE	10,202	4,237	5,874	91	1,637 D	41.5%	57.6%	41.9%	58.1%
23,370	SEQUOYAH	9,884	3,938	5,873	73	1,935 D	39.8%	59.4%	40.1%	59.9%
35,902	STEPHENS	17,020	7,099	9,795	126	2,696 D	41.7%	57.5%	42.0%	58.0%
16,352	TEXAS	6,580	3,919	2,591	70	1,328 R	59.6%	39.4%	60.2%	39.8%
12,901	TILLMAN	4,695	1,802	2,852	41	1,050 D	38.4%	60.7%	38.7%	61.3%
400,709	TULSA	176,300	108,653	65,298	2,349	43,355 R	61.6%	37.0%	62.5%	37.5%
22,163	WAGONER	11,057	5,071	5,879	107	808 D	45.9%	53.2%	46.3%	53.7%
42,277	WASHINGTON	21,670	14,560	6,898	212	7,662 R	67.2%	31.8%	67.9%	32.1%
12,141	WASHITA	5,531	2,165	3,304	62	1,139 D	39.1%	59.7%	39.6%	60.4%
11,920	WOODS	5,421	2,788	2,530	103	258 R	51.4%	46.7%	52.4%	47.6%
15,537	WOODWARD	6,691	3,782	2,807	102	975 R	56.5%	42.0%	57.4%	42.6%
2,559,253	TOTAL	1,092,251	545,708	532,442	14,101	13,266 R	50.0%	48.7%	50.6%	49.4%

OKLAHOMA

PRESIDENT 1972

1970 Census Population	County	Total Vote	Republican	Democratic	Other	Rep.-Dem. Plurality	Percentage Total Vote Rep.	Percentage Total Vote Dem.	Percentage Major Vote Rep.	Percentage Major Vote Dem.
15,141	ADAIR	6,455	4,720	1,601	134	3,119 R	73.1%	24.8%	74.7%	25.3%
7,224	ALFALFA	3,937	3,208	641	88	2,567 R	81.5%	16.3%	83.3%	16.7%
10,972	ATOKA	3,987	2,905	993	89	1,912 R	72.9%	24.9%	74.5%	25.5%
6,282	BEAVER	3,186	2,562	522	102	2,040 R	80.4%	16.4%	83.1%	16.9%
15,754	BECKHAM	6,235	4,472	1,608	155	2,864 R	71.7%	25.8%	73.6%	26.4%
11,794	BLAINE	5,092	3,958	963	171	2,995 R	77.7%	18.9%	80.4%	19.6%
25,552	BRYAN	8,718	5,397	3,144	177	2,253 R	61.9%	36.1%	63.2%	36.8%
28,931	CADDO	10,912	7,683	2,921	308	4,762 R	70.4%	26.8%	72.5%	27.5%
32,245	CANADIAN	14,564	11,400	2,751	413	8,649 R	78.3%	18.9%	80.6%	19.4%
37,349	CARTER	14,106	9,368	4,577	161	4,791 R	66.4%	32.4%	67.2%	32.8%
23,174	CHEROKEE	10,206	7,080	2,899	227	4,181 R	69.4%	28.4%	70.9%	29.1%
15,141	CHOCTAW	5,278	3,399	1,798	81	1,601 R	64.4%	34.1%	65.4%	34.6%
4,145	CIMARRON	1,885	1,350	323	212	1,027 R	71.6%	17.1%	80.7%	19.3%
81,839	CLEVELAND	37,518	25,777	11,126	615	14,651 R	68.7%	29.7%	69.9%	30.1%
5,525	COAL	2,179	1,461	680	38	781 R	67.0%	31.2%	68.2%	31.8%
108,144	COMANCHE	24,745	19,759	4,559	427	15,200 R	79.9%	18.4%	81.3%	18.7%
6,832	COTTON	2,919	2,050	798	71	1,252 R	70.2%	27.3%	72.0%	28.0%
14,722	CRAIG	5,917	4,163	1,642	112	2,521 R	70.4%	27.8%	71.7%	28.3%
45,532	CREEK	16,503	12,396	3,705	402	8,691 R	75.1%	22.5%	77.0%	23.0%
22,665	CUSTER	9,780	7,267	2,298	215	4,969 R	74.3%	23.5%	76.0%	24.0%
17,767	DELAWARE	7,789	5,476	2,135	178	3,341 R	70.3%	27.4%	71.9%	28.1%
5,656	DEWEY	2,816	2,106	626	84	1,480 R	74.8%	22.2%	77.1%	22.9%
5,129	ELLIS	2,648	2,059	473	116	1,586 R	77.8%	17.9%	81.3%	18.7%
56,343	GARFIELD	24,469	19,348	4,557	564	14,791 R	79.1%	18.6%	80.9%	19.1%
24,874	GARVIN	10,245	7,245	2,685	315	4,560 R	70.7%	26.2%	73.0%	27.0%
29,354	GRADY	11,499	7,762	3,440	297	4,322 R	67.5%	29.9%	69.3%	30.7%
7,117	GRANT	3,755	2,829	805	121	2,024 R	75.3%	21.4%	77.8%	22.2%
7,979	GREEN	3,244	2,154	1,004	86	1,150 R	66.4%	30.9%	68.2%	31.8%
5,136	HARMON	1,929	1,319	568	42	751 R	68.4%	29.4%	69.9%	30.1%
5,151	HARPER	2,475	1,976	385	114	1,591 R	79.8%	15.6%	83.7%	16.3%
9,578	HASKELL	4,460	2,815	1,408	237	1,407 R	63.1%	31.6%	66.7%	33.3%
13,228	HUGHES	5,392	3,497	1,787	108	1,710 R	64.9%	33.1%	66.2%	33.8%
30,902	JACKSON	7,707	5,519	2,054	134	3,465 R	71.6%	26.7%	72.9%	27.1%
7,125	JEFFERSON	2,751	1,709	969	73	740 R	62.1%	35.2%	63.8%	36.2%
7,870	JOHNSTON	3,256	2,205	983	68	1,222 R	67.7%	30.2%	69.2%	30.8%
48,791	KAY	21,984	17,244	4,246	494	12,998 R	78.4%	19.3%	80.2%	19.8%
12,857	KINGFISHER	5,935	4,861	912	162	3,949 R	81.9%	15.4%	84.2%	15.8%
12,532	KIOWA	5,316	3,711	1,495	110	2,216 R	69.8%	28.1%	71.3%	28.7%
8,601	LATIMER	3,889	2,520	1,239	130	1,281 R	64.8%	31.9%	67.0%	33.0%
32,137	LE FLORE	11,759	7,932	3,433	394	4,499 R	67.5%	29.2%	69.8%	30.2%
19,482	LINCOLN	8,685	6,512	1,919	254	4,593 R	75.0%	22.1%	77.2%	22.8%
19,645	LOGAN	9,503	6,543	2,760	200	3,783 R	68.9%	29.0%	70.3%	29.7%
5,637	LOVE	2,108	1,407	671	30	736 R	66.7%	31.8%	67.7%	32.3%
14,157	MCCLAIN	5,797	4,241	1,350	206	2,891 R	73.2%	23.3%	75.9%	24.1%
28,642	MCCURTAIN	9,175	6,441	2,568	166	3,873 R	70.2%	28.0%	71.5%	28.5%
12,472	MCINTOSH	5,034	3,216	1,686	132	1,530 R	63.9%	33.5%	65.6%	34.4%
7,529	MAJOR	3,818	3,203	512	103	2,691 R	83.9%	13.4%	86.2%	13.8%
7,682	MARSHALL	3,477	2,273	1,113	91	1,160 R	65.4%	32.0%	67.1%	32.9%
23,302	MAYES	10,454	7,535	2,656	263	4,879 R	72.1%	25.4%	73.9%	26.1%
10,669	MURRAY	4,372	2,983	1,294	95	1,689 R	68.2%	29.6%	69.7%	30.3%
59,542	MUSKOGEE	23,092	15,161	7,380	551	7,781 R	65.7%	32.0%	67.3%	32.7%
10,043	NOBLE	5,212	4,085	999	128	3,086 R	78.4%	19.2%	80.4%	19.6%
9,773	NOWATA	4,535	3,293	1,096	146	2,197 R	72.6%	24.2%	75.0%	25.0%
10,683	OKFUSKEE	4,289	2,862	1,328	99	1,534 R	66.7%	31.0%	68.3%	31.7%
526,805	OKLAHOMA	207,925	156,437	46,986	4,502	109,451 R	75.2%	22.6%	76.9%	23.1%
35,358	OKMULGEE	13,642	8,706	4,494	442	4,212 R	63.8%	32.9%	66.0%	34.0%
29,750	OSAGE	12,591	9,288	2,968	335	6,320 R	73.8%	23.6%	75.8%	24.2%
29,800	OTTAWA	12,163	8,348	3,657	158	4,691 R	68.6%	30.1%	69.5%	30.5%
11,338	PAWNEE	5,537	4,280	1,135	122	3,145 R	77.3%	20.5%	79.0%	21.0%
50,654	PAYNE	23,070	17,019	5,644	407	11,375 R	73.8%	24.5%	75.1%	24.9%

OKLAHOMA

PRESIDENT 1972

1970 Census Population	County	Total Vote	Republican	Democratic	Other	Rep.-Dem. Plurality	Percentage Total Vote Rep.	Total Vote Dem.	Major Vote Rep.	Major Vote Dem.
37,521	PITTSBURG	15,040	9,989	4,748	303	5,241 R	66.4%	31.6%	67.8%	32.2%
27,867	PONTOTOC	12,162	8,762	3,160	240	5,602 R	72.0%	26.0%	73.5%	26.5%
43,134	POTTAWATOMIE	18,664	13,308	4,822	534	8,486 R	71.3%	25.8%	73.4%	26.6%
9,385	PUSHMATAHA	3,599	2,456	1,016	127	1,440 R	68.2%	28.2%	70.7%	29.3%
4,452	ROGER MILLS	2,170	1,696	420	54	1,276 R	78.2%	19.4%	80.2%	19.8%
28,425	ROGERS	12,728	9,697	2,607	424	7,090 R	76.2%	20.5%	78.8%	21.2%
25,144	SEMINOLE	9,824	6,879	2,746	199	4,133 R	70.0%	28.0%	71.5%	28.5%
23,370	SEQUOYAH	9,551	6,842	2,519	190	4,323 R	71.6%	26.4%	73.1%	26.9%
35,902	STEPHENS	14,396	10,309	3,623	464	6,686 R	71.6%	25.2%	74.0%	26.0%
16,352	TEXAS	6,937	5,726	924	287	4,802 R	82.5%	13.3%	86.1%	13.9%
12,901	TILLMAN	4,697	3,331	1,256	110	2,075 R	70.9%	26.7%	72.6%	27.4%
400,709	TULSA	161,126	125,278	32,779	3,069	92,499 R	77.8%	20.3%	79.3%	20.7%
22,163	WAGONER	9,107	6,569	2,257	281	4,312 R	72.1%	24.8%	74.4%	25.6%
42,277	WASHINGTON	20,500	16,347	3,658	495	12,689 R	79.7%	17.8%	81.7%	18.3%
12,141	WASHITA	5,008	3,578	1,305	125	2,273 R	71.4%	26.1%	73.3%	26.7%
11,920	WOODS	5,789	4,413	1,234	142	3,179 R	76.2%	21.3%	78.1%	21.9%
15,537	WOODWARD	6,683	5,350	1,104	229	4,246 R	80.1%	16.5%	82.9%	17.1%
2,559,253	TOTAL	1,029,900	759,025	247,147	23,728	511,878 R	73.7%	24.0%	75.4%	24.6%

OKLAHOMA

PRESIDENT 1968

1960 Census Population	County	Total Vote	Republican	Democratic	AIP	Other	Plurality	Percentage Rep.	Percentage Dem.	Percentage AIP
13,112	ADAIR	5,426	2,877	1,549	1,000		1,328 R	53.0%	28.5%	18.4%
8,445	ALFALFA	3,847	2,672	865	310		1,807 R	69.5%	22.5%	8.1%
10,352	ATOKA	4,144	1,131	1,400	1,613		213 A	27.3%	33.8%	38.9%
6,965	BEAVER	3,077	2,114	624	339		1,490 R	68.7%	20.3%	11.0%
17,782	BECKHAM	6,839	2,935	2,354	1,550		581 R	42.9%	34.4%	22.7%
12,077	BLAINE	5,053	3,036	1,285	732		1,751 R	60.1%	25.4%	14.5%
24,252	BRYAN	8,205	2,727	3,214	2,264		487 D	33.2%	39.2%	27.6%
28,621	CADDO	10,782	4,712	4,212	1,858		500 R	43.7%	39.1%	17.2%
24,727	CANADIAN	11,993	5,891	3,577	2,525		2,314 R	49.1%	29.8%	21.1%
39,044	CARTER	14,348	5,127	5,807	3,414		680 D	35.7%	40.5%	23.8%
17,762	CHEROKEE	8,391	3,971	2,554	1,866		1,417 R	47.3%	30.4%	22.2%
15,637	CHOCTAW	5,433	1,414	2,268	1,751		517 D	26.0%	41.7%	32.2%
4,496	CIMARRON	2,085	1,122	436	527		595 R	53.8%	20.9%	25.3%
47,600	CLEVELAND	25,774	12,446	8,617	4,711		3,829 R	48.3%	33.4%	18.3%
5,546	COAL	2,257	669	963	625		294 D	29.6%	42.7%	27.7%
90,803	COMANCHE	23,165	9,225	8,061	5,879		1,164 R	39.8%	34.8%	25.4%
8,031	COTTON	3,113	1,016	1,192	905		176 D	32.6%	38.3%	29.1%
16,303	CRAIG	6,013	2,686	2,098	1,229		588 R	44.7%	34.9%	20.4%
40,495	CREEK	15,998	6,934	5,151	3,913		1,783 R	43.3%	32.2%	24.5%
21,040	CUSTER	8,362	4,709	2,717	936		1,992 R	56.3%	32.5%	11.2%
13,198	DELAWARE	6,699	3,168	2,129	1,402		1,039 R	47.3%	31.8%	20.9%
6,051	DEWEY	2,821	1,508	773	540		735 R	53.5%	27.4%	19.1%
5,457	ELLIS	2,560	1,601	533	426		1,068 R	62.5%	20.8%	16.6%
52,975	GARFIELD	23,183	14,370	5,802	3,011		8,568 R	62.0%	25.0%	13.0%
28,290	GARVIN	10,301	3,786	3,845	2,670		59 D	36.8%	37.3%	25.9%
29,590	GRADY	11,119	4,242	4,760	2,117		518 D	38.2%	42.8%	19.0%
8,140	GRANT	3,887	2,403	1,047	437		1,356 R	61.8%	26.9%	11.2%
8,877	GREEN	3,474	1,225	1,419	830		194 D	35.3%	40.8%	23.9%
5,852	HARMON	2,144	644	1,097	403		453 D	30.0%	51.2%	18.8%
5,956	HARPER	2,354	1,483	518	353		965 R	63.0%	22.0%	15.0%
9,121	HASKELL	4,092	1,516	1,563	1,013		47 D	37.0%	38.2%	24.8%
15,144	HUGHES	5,645	1,897	2,578	1,170		681 D	33.6%	45.7%	20.7%
29,736	JACKSON	7,405	2,248	3,371	1,786		1,123 D	30.4%	45.5%	24.1%
8,192	JEFFERSON	3,109	780	1,628	701		848 D	25.1%	52.4%	22.5%
8,517	JOHNSTON	3,238	1,048	1,216	974		168 D	32.4%	37.6%	30.1%
51,042	KAY	21,591	12,751	6,031	2,809		6,720 R	59.1%	27.9%	13.0%
10,635	KINGFISHER	5,504	3,558	1,226	720		2,332 R	64.6%	22.3%	13.1%
14,825	KIOWA	5,594	2,418	2,219	957		199 R	43.2%	39.7%	17.1%
7,738	LATIMER	3,333	1,091	1,350	892		259 D	32.7%	40.5%	26.8%
29,106	LE FLORE	10,965	3,600	4,020	3,345		420 D	32.8%	36.7%	30.5%
18,783	LINCOLN	8,128	3,855	2,304	1,969		1,551 R	47.4%	28.3%	24.2%
18,662	LOGAN	8,157	3,960	2,508	1,689		1,452 R	48.5%	30.7%	20.7%
5,862	LOVE	2,374	677	931	766		165 D	28.5%	39.2%	32.3%
12,740	MCCLAIN	5,536	2,047	1,842	1,647		205 R	37.0%	33.3%	29.8%
25,851	MCCURTAIN	8,619	2,795	2,944	2,880		64 D	32.4%	34.2%	33.4%
12,371	MCINTOSH	4,545	1,532	1,759	1,254		227 D	33.7%	38.7%	27.6%
7,808	MAJOR	3,501	2,550	594	357		1,956 R	72.8%	17.0%	10.2%
7,263	MARSHALL	3,386	1,209	1,191	986		18 R	35.7%	35.2%	29.1%
20,073	MAYES	9,546	4,260	2,855	2,431		1,405 R	44.6%	29.9%	25.5%
10,622	MURRAY	4,254	1,454	1,773	1,027		319 D	34.2%	41.7%	24.1%
61,866	MUSKOGEE	22,680	8,707	9,377	4,596		670 D	38.4%	41.3%	20.3%
10,376	NOBLE	4,941	2,911	1,412	618		1,499 R	58.9%	28.6%	12.5%
10,848	NOWATA	4,510	2,116	1,314	1,080		802 R	46.9%	29.1%	23.9%
11,706	OKFUSKEE	4,444	1,686	1,777	981		91 D	37.9%	40.0%	22.1%
439,506	OKLAHOMA	187,441	93,212	60,395	33,834		32,817 R	49.7%	32.2%	18.1%
36,945	OKMULGEE	13,526	4,709	6,089	2,728		1,380 D	34.8%	45.0%	20.2%
32,441	OSAGE	11,825	5,499	3,919	2,407		1,580 R	46.5%	33.1%	20.4%
28,301	OTTAWA	11,241	5,000	4,820	1,421		180 R	44.5%	42.9%	12.6%
10,884	PAWNEE	4,770	2,437	1,343	990		1,094 R	51.1%	28.2%	20.8%
44,231	PAYNE	17,824	9,577	5,772	2,475		3,805 R	53.7%	32.4%	13.9%

OKLAHOMA

PRESIDENT 1968

1960 Census Population	County	Total Vote	Republican	Democratic	AIP	Other	Plurality	Percentage Rep.	Dem.	AIP
34,360	PITTSBURG	13,816	3,978	6,112	3,726		2,134 D	28.8%	44.2%	27.0%
28,089	PONTOTOC	10,877	4,161	4,291	2,425		130 D	38.3%	39.5%	22.3%
41,486	POTTAWATOMIE	17,493	6,899	6,721	3,873		178 R	39.4%	38.4%	22.1%
9,088	PUSHMATAHA	3,744	1,225	1,232	1,287		55 A	32.7%	32.9%	34.4%
5,090	ROGER MILLS	2,432	1,102	720	610		382 R	45.3%	29.6%	25.1%
20,614	ROGERS	10,437	4,631	2,665	3,141		1,490 R	44.4%	25.5%	30.1%
28,066	SEMINOLE	9,742	3,711	3,889	2,142		178 D	38.1%	39.9%	22.0%
18,001	SEQUOYAH	7,573	2,797	2,618	2,158		179 R	36.9%	34.6%	28.5%
37,990	STEPHENS	14,323	5,508	5,249	3,566		259 R	38.5%	36.6%	24.9%
14,162	TEXAS	5,859	3,729	1,176	954		2,553 R	63.6%	20.1%	16.3%
14,654	TILLMAN	4,895	1,748	1,771	1,376		23 D	35.7%	36.2%	28.1%
346,038	TULSA	142,667	81,476	32,748	28,443		48,728 R	57.1%	23.0%	19.9%
15,673	WAGONER	7,632	3,187	2,183	2,262		925 R	41.8%	28.6%	29.6%
42,347	WASHINGTON	20,544	12,812	4,641	3,091		8,171 R	62.4%	22.6%	15.0%
18,121	WASHITA	5,221	2,592	1,771	858		821 R	49.6%	33.9%	16.4%
11,932	WOODS	5,405	3,449	1,439	517		2,010 R	63.8%	26.6%	9.6%
13,902	WOODWARD	5,855	3,748	1,444	663		2,304 R	64.0%	24.7%	11.3%
2,328,284	TOTAL	943,086	449,697	301,658	191,731		148,039 R	47.7%	32.0%	20.3%

OKLAHOMA

ELECTION NOTES

1984 Other vote was Bergland (Libertarian).

1980 Other vote was 38,284 Anderson (Independent); 13,828 Clark (Libertarian).

1976 Other vote was McCarthy (Independent).

1972 Other vote was Schmitz (American).

1968 Wallace on the ballot as American.

OREGON

POPULAR VOTE FOR PRESIDENT 1920 TO 1984

		Republican		Democratic				Percentage			
								Total Vote		Major Vote	
Year	Total Vote	Vote	Candidate	Vote	Candidate	Other Vote	Plurality	Rep.	Dem.	Rep.	Dem.
1984	1,226,527	685,700	Reagan, Ronald	536,479	Mondale, Walter F.	4,348	149,221 R	55.9%	43.7%	56.1%	43.9%
1980	1,181,516	571,044	Reagan, Ronald	456,890	Carter, Jimmy	153,582	114,154 R	48.3%	38.7%	55.6%	44.4%
1976	1,029,876	492,120	Ford, Gerald R.	490,407	Carter, Jimmy	47,349	1,713 R	47.8%	47.6%	50.1%	49.9%
1972	927,946	486,686	Nixon, Richard M.	392,760	McGovern, George S.	48,500	93,926 R	52.4%	42.3%	55.3%	44.7%
1968	819,622	408,433	Nixon, Richard M.	358,866	Humphrey, Hubert H.	52,323	49,567 R	49.8%	43.8%	53.2%	46.8%
1964	786,305	282,779	Goldwater, Barry M.	501,017	Johnson, Lyndon B.	2,509	218,238 D	36.0%	63.7%	36.1%	63.9%
1960	776,421	408,060	Nixon, Richard M.	367,402	Kennedy, John F.	959	40,658 R	52.6%	47.3%	52.6%	47.4%
1956	736,132	406,393	Eisenhower, Dwight D.	329,204	Stevenson, Adlai E.	535	77,189 R	55.2%	44.7%	55.2%	44.8%
1952	695,059	420,815	Eisenhower, Dwight D.	270,579	Stevenson, Adlai E.	3,665	150,236 R	60.5%	38.9%	60.9%	39.1%
1948	524,080	260,904	Dewey, Thomas E.	243,147	Truman, Harry S.	20,029	17,757 R	49.8%	46.4%	51.8%	48.2%
1944	480,147	225,365	Dewey, Thomas E.	248,635	Roosevelt, Franklin D.	6,147	23,270 D	46.9%	51.8%	47.5%	52.5%
1940	481,240	219,555	Willkie, Wendell	258,415	Roosevelt, Franklin D.	3,270	38,860 D	45.6%	53.7%	45.9%	54.1%
1936	414,021	122,706	Landon, Alfred M.	266,733	Roosevelt, Franklin D.	24,582	144,027 D	29.6%	64.4%	31.5%	68.5%
1932	368,751	136,019	Hoover, Herbert C.	213,871	Roosevelt, Franklin D.	18,861	77,852 D	36.9%	58.0%	38.9%	61.1%
1928	319,942	205,341	Hoover, Herbert C.	109,223	Smith, Alfred E.	5,378	96,118 R	64.2%	34.1%	65.3%	34.7%
1924 **	279,488	142,579	Coolidge, Calvin	67,589	Davis, John W.	69,320	74,176 R	51.0%	24.2%	67.8%	32.2%
1920	238,522	143,592	Harding, Warren G.	80,019	Cox, James M.	14,911	63,573 R	60.2%	33.5%	64.2%	35.8%

In 1924 other vote was 68,403 Progressive and 917 Socialist Labor.

ELECTORAL COLLEGE VOTE 1920 TO 1984

Year	Total	Republican	Democratic	Other
1984	7	7	—	—
1980	6	6	—	—
1976	6	6	—	—
1972	6	6	—	—
1968	6	6	—	—
1964	6	—	6	—
1960	6	6	—	—
1956	6	6	—	—
1952	6	6	—	—
1948	6	6	—	—
1944	6	—	6	—
1940	5	—	5	—
1936	5	—	5	—
1932	5	—	5	—
1928	5	5	—	—
1924	5	5	—	—
1920	5	5	—	—

OREGON

WALLOWA
UNION
BAKER
MALHEUR
UMATILLA
GRANT
HARNEY
MORROW
WHEELER
GILLIAM
CROOK
LAKE
SHERMAN
WASCO
JEFFERSON
DESCHUTES
HOOD RIVER
KLAMATH
MULTNOMAH
CLACKAMAS
LINN
LANE
MARION
COLUMBIA
WASHINGTON
DOUGLAS
JACKSON
CLATSOP
TILLAMOOK
YAMHILL
POLK
BENTON
LINCOLN
JOSEPHINE
COOS
CURRY

OREGON

PRESIDENT 1984

1980 Census Population	County	Total Vote	Republican	Democratic	Other	Rep.-Dem. Plurality	Percentage Total Vote Rep.	Percentage Total Vote Dem.	Percentage Major Vote Rep.	Percentage Major Vote Dem.
16,134	BAKER	7,812	5,204	2,591	17	2,613 R	66.6%	33.2%	66.8%	33.2%
68,211	BENTON	34,062	17,836	16,073	153	1,763 R	52.4%	47.2%	52.6%	47.4%
241,919	CLACKAMAS	116,173	68,630	47,254	289	21,376 R	59.1%	40.7%	59.2%	40.8%
32,489	CLATSOP	15,085	7,522	7,525	38	3 D	49.9%	49.9%	50.0%	50.0%
35,646	COLUMBIA	16,105	7,811	8,219	75	408 D	48.5%	51.0%	48.7%	51.3%
64,047	COOS	27,339	13,637	13,582	120	55 R	49.9%	49.7%	50.1%	49.9%
13,091	CROOK	6,064	3,773	2,268	23	1,505 R	62.2%	37.4%	62.5%	37.5%
16,992	CURRY	8,815	5,363	3,423	29	1,940 R	60.8%	38.8%	61.0%	39.0%
62,142	DESCHUTES	31,066	19,323	11,671	72	7,652 R	62.2%	37.6%	62.3%	37.7%
93,748	DOUGLAS	39,996	25,243	14,609	144	10,634 R	63.1%	36.5%	63.3%	36.7%
2,057	GILLIAM	1,073	700	369	4	331 R	65.2%	34.4%	65.5%	34.5%
8,210	GRANT	4,041	2,695	1,344	2	1,351 R	66.7%	33.3%	66.7%	33.3%
8,314	HARNEY	3,512	2,197	1,290	25	907 R	62.6%	36.7%	63.0%	37.0%
15,835	HOOD RIVER	7,571	4,531	3,022	18	1,509 R	59.8%	39.9%	60.0%	40.0%
132,456	JACKSON	61,359	37,895	23,230	234	14,665 R	61.8%	37.9%	62.0%	38.0%
11,599	JEFFERSON	5,216	3,283	1,920	13	1,363 R	62.9%	36.8%	63.1%	36.9%
58,855	JOSEPHINE	28,062	19,470	8,539	53	10,931 R	69.4%	30.4%	69.5%	30.5%
59,117	KLAMATH	25,335	17,686	7,575	74	10,111 R	69.8%	29.9%	70.0%	30.0%
7,532	LAKE	3,653	2,466	1,184	3	1,282 R	67.5%	32.4%	67.6%	32.4%
275,226	LANE	125,852	61,493	63,999	360	2,506 D	48.9%	50.9%	49.0%	51.0%
35,264	LINCOLN	17,804	9,110	8,637	57	473 R	51.2%	48.5%	51.3%	48.7%
89,495	LINN	39,699	23,463	16,161	75	7,302 R	59.1%	40.7%	59.2%	40.8%
26,896	MALHEUR	11,071	8,441	2,611	19	5,830 R	76.2%	23.6%	76.4%	23.6%
204,692	MARION	91,209	54,535	36,440	234	18,095 R	59.8%	40.0%	59.9%	40.1%
7,519	MORROW	3,397	2,130	1,254	13	876 R	62.7%	36.9%	62.9%	37.1%
562,640	MULTNOMAH	265,539	119,932	144,179	1,428	24,247 D	45.2%	54.3%	45.4%	54.6%
45,203	POLK	21,432	12,678	8,709	45	3,969 R	59.2%	40.6%	59.3%	40.7%
2,172	SHERMAN	1,227	828	398	1	430 R	67.5%	32.4%	67.5%	32.5%
21,164	TILLAMOOK	10,308	5,267	4,988	53	279 R	51.1%	48.4%	51.4%	48.6%
58,861	UMATILLA	22,514	14,211	8,246	57	5,965 R	63.1%	36.6%	63.3%	36.7%
23,921	UNION	10,829	6,645	4,134	50	2,511 R	61.4%	38.2%	61.6%	38.4%
7,273	WALLOWA	3,831	2,619	1,204	8	1,415 R	68.4%	31.4%	68.5%	31.5%
21,732	WASCO	12,472	6,905	5,526	41	1,379 R	55.4%	44.3%	55.5%	44.5%
245,808	WASHINGTON	120,896	75,877	44,602	417	31,275 R	62.8%	36.9%	63.0%	37.0%
1,513	WHEELER	757	504	253		251 R	66.6%	33.4%	66.6%	33.4%
55,332	YAMHILL	25,351	15,797	9,450	104	6,347 R	62.3%	37.3%	62.6%	37.4%
2,633,105	TOTAL	1,226,527	685,700	536,479	4,348	149,221 R	55.9%	43.7%	56.1%	43.9%

OREGON

PRESIDENT 1980

1980 Census Population	County	Total Vote	Republican	Democratic	Other	Rep.-Dem. Plurality	Percentage Total Vote Rep.	Total Vote Dem.	Major Vote Rep.	Major Vote Dem.
16,134	BAKER	8,013	4,747	2,515	751	2,232 R	59.2%	31.4%	65.4%	34.6%
68,211	BENTON	34,507	14,982	13,150	6,375	1,832 R	43.4%	38.1%	53.3%	46.7%
241,919	CLACKAMAS	109,483	54,111	40,462	14,910	13,649 R	49.4%	37.0%	57.2%	42.8%
32,489	CLATSOP	14,959	6,124	6,482	2,353	358 D	40.9%	43.3%	48.6%	51.4%
35,646	COLUMBIA	15,505	6,623	7,124	1,758	501 D	42.7%	45.9%	48.2%	51.8%
64,047	COOS	28,176	13,041	11,817	3,318	1,224 R	46.3%	41.9%	52.5%	47.5%
13,091	CROOK	5,862	3,113	2,162	587	951 R	53.1%	36.9%	59.0%	41.0%
16,992	CURRY	8,488	4,910	2,656	922	2,254 R	57.8%	31.3%	64.9%	35.1%
62,142	DESCHUTES	28,715	15,186	9,641	3,888	5,545 R	52.9%	33.6%	61.2%	38.8%
93,748	DOUGLAS	39,516	23,101	12,564	3,851	10,537 R	58.5%	31.8%	64.8%	35.2%
2,057	GILLIAM	1,140	622	394	124	228 R	54.6%	34.6%	61.2%	38.8%
8,210	GRANT	4,187	2,519	1,274	394	1,245 R	60.2%	30.4%	66.4%	33.6%
8,314	HARNEY	3,785	2,313	1,110	362	1,203 R	61.1%	29.3%	67.6%	32.4%
15,835	HOOD RIVER	7,092	3,450	2,924	718	526 R	48.6%	41.2%	54.1%	45.9%
132,456	JACKSON	58,740	32,879	19,903	5,958	12,976 R	56.0%	33.9%	62.3%	37.7%
11,599	JEFFERSON	4,737	2,523	1,654	560	869 R	53.3%	34.9%	60.4%	39.6%
58,855	JOSEPHINE	26,336	16,827	7,116	2,393	9,711 R	63.9%	27.0%	70.3%	29.7%
59,117	KLAMATH	25,592	16,060	7,371	2,161	8,689 R	62.8%	28.8%	68.5%	31.5%
7,532	LAKE	3,689	2,234	1,147	308	1,087 R	60.6%	31.1%	66.1%	33.9%
275,226	LANE	125,604	54,750	52,240	18,614	2,510 R	43.6%	41.6%	51.2%	48.8%
35,264	LINCOLN	17,127	7,637	7,009	2,481	628 R	44.6%	40.9%	52.1%	47.9%
89,495	LINN	36,293	18,943	13,516	3,834	5,427 R	52.2%	37.2%	58.4%	41.6%
26,896	MALHEUR	11,364	7,705	2,937	722	4,768 R	67.8%	25.8%	72.4%	27.6%
204,692	MARION	85,449	42,191	32,134	11,124	10,057 R	49.4%	37.6%	56.8%	43.2%
7,519	MORROW	3,141	1,728	1,077	336	651 R	55.0%	34.3%	61.6%	38.4%
562,640	MULTNOMAH	258,968	101,606	120,487	36,875	18,881 D	39.2%	46.5%	45.7%	54.3%
45,203	POLK	20,531	10,006	7,833	2,692	2,173 R	48.7%	38.2%	56.1%	43.9%
2,172	SHERMAN	1,170	677	389	104	288 R	57.9%	33.2%	63.5%	36.5%
21,164	TILLAMOOK	9,903	4,123	4,521	1,259	398 D	41.6%	45.7%	47.7%	52.3%
58,861	UMATILLA	22,414	12,950	7,382	2,082	5,568 R	57.8%	32.9%	63.7%	36.3%
23,921	UNION	11,272	6,514	3,677	1,081	2,837 R	57.8%	32.6%	63.9%	36.1%
7,273	WALLOWA	3,792	2,485	995	312	1,490 R	65.5%	26.2%	71.4%	28.6%
21,732	WASCO	10,235	4,703	4,336	1,196	367 R	46.0%	42.4%	52.0%	48.0%
245,808	WASHINGTON	111,355	57,165	37,915	16,275	19,250 R	51.3%	34.0%	60.1%	39.9%
1,513	WHEELER	808	442	282	84	160 R	54.7%	34.9%	61.0%	39.0%
55,332	YAMHILL	23,568	12,054	8,694	2,820	3,360 R	51.1%	36.9%	58.1%	41.9%
2,633,105	TOTAL	1,181,516	571,044	456,890	153,582	114,154 R	48.3%	38.7%	55.6%	44.4%

OREGON

PRESIDENT 1976

1970 Census Population	County	Total Vote	Republican	Democratic	Other	Rep.-Dem. Plurality	Percentage Total Vote Rep.	Percentage Total Vote Dem.	Percentage Major Vote Rep.	Percentage Major Vote Dem.
14,919	BAKER	6,919	3,340	3,306	273	34 R	48.3%	47.8%	50.3%	49.7%
53,776	BENTON	29,307	15,555	11,887	1,865	3,668 R	53.1%	40.6%	56.7%	43.3%
166,088	CLACKAMAS	93,959	47,671	42,504	3,784	5,167 R	50.7%	45.2%	52.9%	47.1%
28,473	CLATSOP	13,616	6,178	6,690	748	512 D	45.4%	49.1%	48.0%	52.0%
28,790	COLUMBIA	13,859	5,226	8,005	628	2,779 D	37.7%	57.8%	39.5%	60.5%
56,515	COOS	24,725	9,481	14,168	1,076	4,687 D	38.3%	57.3%	40.1%	59.9%
9,985	CROOK	4,777	2,093	2,536	148	443 D	43.8%	53.1%	45.2%	54.8%
13,006	CURRY	6,507	2,962	3,227	318	265 D	45.5%	49.6%	47.9%	52.1%
30,442	DESCHUTES	19,382	9,054	9,480	848	426 D	46.7%	48.9%	48.9%	51.1%
71,743	DOUGLAS	32,973	16,500	14,965	1,508	1,535 R	50.0%	45.4%	52.4%	47.6%
2,342	GILLIAM	1,166	612	508	46	104 R	52.5%	43.6%	54.6%	45.4%
6,996	GRANT	3,206	1,640	1,393	173	247 R	51.2%	43.4%	54.1%	45.9%
7,215	HARNEY	3,407	1,652	1,567	188	85 R	48.5%	46.0%	51.3%	48.7%
13,187	HOOD RIVER	6,636	3,210	3,114	312	96 R	48.4%	46.9%	50.8%	49.2%
94,533	JACKSON	50,236	24,237	23,384	2,615	853 R	48.2%	46.5%	50.9%	49.1%
8,548	JEFFERSON	3,777	1,810	1,769	198	41 R	47.9%	46.8%	50.6%	49.4%
35,746	JOSEPHINE	21,110	10,726	9,061	1,323	1,665 R	50.8%	42.9%	54.2%	45.8%
50,021	KLAMATH	22,187	11,649	9,659	879	1,990 R	52.5%	43.5%	54.7%	45.3%
6,343	LAKE	3,088	1,575	1,381	132	194 R	51.0%	44.7%	53.3%	46.7%
213,358	LANE	108,367	46,245	56,479	5,643	10,234 D	42.7%	52.1%	45.0%	55.0%
25,755	LINCOLN	13,199	5,755	6,685	759	930 D	43.6%	50.6%	46.3%	53.7%
71,914	LINN	31,241	14,128	15,776	1,337	1,648 D	45.2%	50.5%	47.2%	52.8%
23,169	MALHEUR	9,610	5,682	3,507	421	2,175 R	59.1%	36.5%	61.8%	38.2%
151,309	MARION	72,331	35,497	33,781	3,053	1,716 R	49.1%	46.7%	51.2%	48.8%
4,465	MORROW	2,367	1,091	1,162	114	71 D	46.1%	49.1%	48.4%	51.6%
556,667	MULTNOMAH	253,159	112,400	129,060	11,699	16,660 D	44.4%	51.0%	46.6%	53.4%
35,349	POLK	17,530	8,528	8,141	861	387 R	48.6%	46.4%	51.2%	48.8%
2,139	SHERMAN	1,109	567	491	51	76 R	51.1%	44.3%	53.6%	46.4%
17,930	TILLAMOOK	8,867	4,033	4,456	378	423 D	45.5%	50.3%	47.5%	52.5%
44,923	UMATILLA	18,031	9,345	7,985	701	1,360 R	51.8%	44.3%	53.9%	46.1%
19,377	UNION	9,829	5,111	4,280	438	831 R	52.0%	43.5%	54.4%	45.6%
6,247	WALLOWA	3,149	1,693	1,310	146	383 R	53.8%	41.6%	56.4%	43.6%
20,133	WASCO	9,240	4,258	4,560	422	302 D	46.1%	49.4%	48.3%	51.7%
157,920	WASHINGTON	90,611	52,376	34,847	3,388	17,529 R	57.8%	38.5%	60.0%	40.0%
1,849	WHEELER	779	355	402	22	47 D	45.6%	51.6%	46.9%	53.1%
40,213	YAMHILL	19,620	9,885	8,881	854	1,004 R	50.4%	45.3%	52.7%	47.3%
2,091,385	TOTAL	1,029,876	492,120	490,407	47,349	1,713 R	47.8%	47.6%	50.1%	49.9%

OREGON

PRESIDENT 1972

1970 Census Population	County	Total Vote	Republican	Democratic	Other	Rep.-Dem. Plurality	Percentage Total Vote Rep.	Total Vote Dem.	Major Vote Rep.	Major Vote Dem.
14,919	BAKER	6,220	3,441	2,047	732	1,394 R	55.3%	32.9%	62.7%	37.3%
53,776	BENTON	26,456	14,906	10,842	708	4,064 R	56.3%	41.0%	57.9%	42.1%
166,088	CLACKAMAS	78,089	41,767	32,540	3,782	9,227 R	53.5%	41.7%	56.2%	43.8%
28,473	CLATSOP	12,647	5,998	6,017	632	19 D	47.4%	47.6%	49.9%	50.1%
28,790	COLUMBIA	12,284	5,348	5,997	939	649 D	43.5%	48.8%	47.1%	52.9%
56,515	COOS	23,213	10,370	11,778	1,065	1,408 D	44.7%	50.7%	46.8%	53.2%
9,985	CROOK	4,123	2,167	1,743	213	424 R	52.6%	42.3%	55.4%	44.6%
13,006	CURRY	5,470	2,832	2,108	530	724 R	51.8%	38.5%	57.3%	42.7%
30,442	DESCHUTES	14,819	7,747	6,319	753	1,428 R	52.3%	42.6%	55.1%	44.9%
71,743	DOUGLAS	27,508	15,881	9,009	2,618	6,872 R	57.7%	32.8%	63.8%	36.2%
2,342	GILLIAM	1,069	665	355	49	310 R	62.2%	33.2%	65.2%	34.8%
6,996	GRANT	2,951	1,781	932	238	849 R	60.4%	31.6%	65.6%	34.4%
7,215	HARNEY	2,863	1,693	1,004	166	689 R	59.1%	35.1%	62.8%	37.2%
13,187	HOOD RIVER	5,841	3,152	2,330	359	822 R	54.0%	39.9%	57.5%	42.5%
94,533	JACKSON	41,561	24,003	14,529	3,029	9,474 R	57.8%	35.0%	62.3%	37.7%
8,548	JEFFERSON	3,221	1,816	1,229	176	587 R	56.4%	38.2%	59.6%	40.4%
35,746	JOSEPHINE	16,927	9,911	5,090	1,926	4,821 R	58.6%	30.1%	66.1%	33.9%
50,021	KLAMATH	18,954	11,169	5,719	2,066	5,450 R	58.9%	30.2%	66.1%	33.9%
6,343	LAKE	2,653	1,619	777	257	842 R	61.0%	29.3%	67.6%	32.4%
213,358	LANE	98,187	47,739	46,177	4,271	1,562 R	48.6%	47.0%	50.8%	49.2%
25,755	LINCOLN	11,854	6,112	5,117	625	995 R	51.6%	43.2%	54.4%	45.6%
71,914	LINN	27,814	15,079	11,178	1,557	3,901 R	54.2%	40.2%	57.4%	42.6%
23,169	MALHEUR	8,771	5,908	1,870	993	4,038 R	67.4%	21.3%	76.0%	24.0%
151,309	MARION	63,361	36,441	23,908	3,012	12,533 R	57.5%	37.7%	60.4%	39.6%
4,465	MORROW	2,007	1,059	718	230	341 R	52.8%	35.8%	59.6%	40.4%
556,667	MULTNOMAH	252,958	118,219	125,470	9,269	7,251 D	46.7%	49.6%	48.5%	51.5%
35,349	POLK	15,609	8,985	5,908	716	3,077 R	57.6%	37.8%	60.3%	39.7%
2,139	SHERMAN	1,043	677	330	36	347 R	64.9%	31.6%	67.2%	32.8%
17,930	TILLAMOOK	8,044	4,120	3,544	380	576 R	51.2%	44.1%	53.8%	46.2%
44,923	UMATILLA	18,071	10,470	6,090	1,511	4,380 R	57.9%	33.7%	63.2%	36.8%
19,377	UNION	8,985	5,073	3,272	640	1,801 R	56.5%	36.4%	60.8%	39.2%
6,247	WALLOWA	3,065	1,909	899	257	1,010 R	62.3%	29.3%	68.0%	32.0%
20,133	WASCO	8,775	4,537	3,749	489	788 R	51.7%	42.7%	54.8%	45.2%
157,920	WASHINGTON	75,238	43,958	27,890	3,390	16,068 R	58.4%	37.1%	61.2%	38.8%
1,849	WHEELER	786	474	267	45	207 R	60.3%	34.0%	64.0%	36.0%
40,213	YAMHILL	16,509	9,660	6,008	841	3,652 R	58.5%	36.4%	61.7%	38.3%
2,091,385	TOTAL	927,946	486,686	392,760	48,500	93,926 R	52.4%	42.3%	55.3%	44.7%

OREGON

PRESIDENT 1968

1960 Census Population	County	Total Vote	Republican	Democratic	AIP	Other	Plurality	Percentage Rep.	Dem.	AIP
17,295	BAKER	6,255	3,311	2,464	480		847 R	52.9%	39.4%	7.7%
39,165	BENTON	19,016	11,654	6,538	749	75	5,116 R	61.3%	34.4%	3.9%
113,038	CLACKAMAS	63,961	32,363	27,939	3,659		4,424 R	50.6%	43.7%	5.7%
27,380	CLATSOP	12,738	5,810	6,243	651	34	433 D	45.6%	49.0%	5.1%
22,379	COLUMBIA	11,047	4,208	6,064	728	47	1,856 D	38.1%	54.9%	6.6%
54,955	COOS	20,890	8,230	10,884	1,767	9	2,654 D	39.4%	52.1%	8.5%
9,430	CROOK	3,607	1,727	1,611	256	13	116 R	47.9%	44.7%	7.1%
13,983	CURRY	4,729	2,323	1,934	436	36	389 R	49.1%	40.9%	9.2%
23,100	DESCHUTES	11,230	5,599	4,859	738	34	740 R	49.9%	43.3%	6.6%
68,458	DOUGLAS	26,092	13,410	9,186	3,433	63	4,224 R	51.4%	35.2%	13.2%
3,069	GILLIAM	1,120	619	436	65		183 R	55.3%	38.9%	5.8%
7,726	GRANT	2,814	1,632	934	239	9	698 R	58.0%	33.2%	8.5%
6,744	HARNEY	2,858	1,617	1,036	197	8	581 R	56.6%	36.2%	6.9%
13,395	HOOD RIVER	5,317	2,597	2,385	323	12	212 R	48.8%	44.9%	6.1%
73,962	JACKSON	34,842	19,577	12,714	2,446	105	6,863 R	56.2%	36.5%	7.0%
7,130	JEFFERSON	3,020	1,669	1,160	180	11	509 R	55.3%	38.4%	6.0%
29,917	JOSEPHINE	14,671	8,456	4,351	1,800	64	4,105 R	57.6%	29.7%	12.3%
47,475	KLAMATH	17,017	9,604	5,629	1,735	49	3,975 R	56.4%	33.1%	10.2%
7,158	LAKE	2,505	1,538	730	229	8	808 R	61.4%	29.1%	9.1%
162,890	LANE	80,549	39,563	34,521	5,830	635	5,042 R	49.1%	42.9%	7.2%
24,635	LINCOLN	10,699	5,031	5,009	659		22 R	47.0%	46.8%	6.2%
58,867	LINN	24,284	12,604	10,032	1,648		2,572 R	51.9%	41.3%	6.8%
22,764	MALHEUR	8,360	5,447	2,021	892		3,426 R	65.2%	24.2%	10.7%
120,888	MARION	55,502	30,417	22,327	2,756	2	8,090 R	54.8%	40.2%	5.0%
4,871	MORROW	1,967	1,068	797	102		271 R	54.3%	40.5%	5.2%
522,813	MULTNOMAH	243,518	106,831	124,651	11,054	982	17,820 D	43.9%	51.2%	4.5%
26,523	POLK	12,571	6,997	4,961	581	32	2,036 R	55.7%	39.5%	4.6%
2,446	SHERMAN	1,089	646	384	59		262 R	59.3%	35.3%	5.4%
18,955	TILLAMOOK	7,291	3,261	3,609	394	27	348 D	44.7%	49.5%	5.4%
44,352	UMATILLA	16,379	8,975	6,402	956	46	2,573 R	54.8%	39.1%	5.8%
18,180	UNION	7,747	3,796	3,409	521	21	387 R	49.0%	44.0%	6.7%
7,102	WALLOWA	2,742	1,527	1,006	194	15	521 R	55.7%	36.7%	7.1%
20,205	WASCO	8,306	3,842	3,918	514	32	76 D	46.3%	47.2%	6.2%
92,237	WASHINGTON	59,842	34,105	22,943	2,566	228	11,162 R	57.0%	38.3%	4.3%
2,722	WHEELER	762	443	292	27		151 R	58.1%	38.3%	3.5%
32,478	YAMHILL	14,285	7,936	5,487	819	43	2,449 R	55.6%	38.4%	5.7%
1,768,687	TOTAL	819,622	408,433	358,866	49,683	2,640	49,567 R	49.8%	43.8%	6.1%

OREGON

ELECTION NOTES

1984 Other vote was scattered write-in.

1980 Other vote was 112,389 Anderson (Independent); 25,838 Clark (Libertarian); 13,642 Commoner (Independent); 1,713 scattered write-in.

1976 Other vote was 40,207 McCarthy (Independent); 1,035 Anderson (write-in); 6,107 scattered write-in. Early unamended canvass gave the McCarthy (Independent) vote as 40,192. Vote detailed in the table is for the recount.

1972 Other vote was 46,211 Schmitz (Independent); 2,289 scattered write-in.

1968 Wallace on the ballot as Independent. Other vote was 1,496 McCarthy (write-in); 1,144 scattered write-in.

PENNSYLVANIA

POPULAR VOTE FOR PRESIDENT 1920 TO 1984

		Republican		Democratic				Percentage			
	Total					Other		Total Vote		Major Vote	
Year	Vote	Vote	Candidate	Vote	Candidate	Vote	Plurality	Rep.	Dem.	Rep.	Dem.
1984	4,844,903	2,584,323	Reagan, Ronald	2,228,131	Mondale, Walter F.	32,449	356,192 R	53.3%	46.0%	53.7%	46.3%
1980	4,561,501	2,261,872	Reagan, Ronald	1,937,540	Carter, Jimmy	362,089	324,332 R	49.6%	42.5%	53.9%	46.1%
1976	4,620,787	2,205,604	Ford, Gerald R.	2,328,677	Carter, Jimmy	86,506	123,073 D	47.7%	50.4%	48.6%	51.4%
1972	4,592,106	2,714,521	Nixon, Richard M.	1,796,951	McGovern, George S.	80,634	917,570 R	59.1%	39.1%	60.2%	39.8%
1968	4,747,928	2,090,017	Nixon, Richard M.	2,259,405	Humphrey, Hubert H.	398,506	169,388 D	44.0%	47.6%	48.1%	51.9%
1964	4,822,690	1,673,657	Goldwater, Barry M.	3,130,954	Johnson, Lyndon B.	18,079	1,457,297 D	34.7%	64.9%	34.8%	65.2%
1960	5,006,541	2,439,956	Nixon, Richard M.	2,556,282	Kennedy, John F.	10,303	116,326 D	48.7%	51.1%	48.8%	51.2%
1956	4,576,503	2,585,252	Eisenhower, Dwight D.	1,981,769	Stevenson, Adlai E.	9,482	603,483 R	56.5%	43.3%	56.6%	43.4%
1952	4,580,969	2,415,789	Eisenhower, Dwight D.	2,146,269	Stevenson, Adlai E.	18,911	269,520 R	52.7%	46.9%	53.0%	47.0%
1948	3,735,348	1,902,197	Dewey, Thomas E.	1,752,426	Truman, Harry S.	80,725	149,771 R	50.9%	46.9%	52.0%	48.0%
1944	3,794,793	1,835,054	Dewey, Thomas E.	1,940,479	Roosevelt, Franklin D.	19,260	105,425 D	48.4%	51.1%	48.6%	51.4%
1940	4,078,714	1,889,848	Willkie, Wendell	2,171,035	Roosevelt, Franklin D.	17,831	281,187 D	46.3%	53.2%	46.5%	53.5%
1936	4,138,105	1,690,300	Landon, Alfred M.	2,353,788	Roosevelt, Franklin D.	94,017	663,488 D	40.8%	56.9%	41.8%	58.2%
1932	2,859,021	1,453,540	Hoover, Herbert C.	1,295,948	Roosevelt, Franklin D.	109,533	157,592 R	50.8%	45.3%	52.9%	47.1%
1928	3,150,612	2,055,382	Hoover, Herbert C.	1,067,586	Smith, Alfred E.	27,644	987,796 R	65.2%	33.9%	65.8%	34.2%
1924 **	2,144,850	1,401,481	Coolidge, Calvin	409,192	Davis, John W.	334,177	992,289 R	65.3%	19.1%	77.4%	22.6%
1920	1,851,248	1,218,215	Harding, Warren G.	503,202	Cox, James M.	129,831	715,013 R	65.8%	27.2%	70.8%	29.2%

In 1924 other vote was 307,567 Progressive; 13,035 American; 9,779 Prohibition; 2,735 Communist; 634 Socialist Labor; 296 Commonwealth Land and 131 scattered.

ELECTORAL COLLEGE VOTE 1920 TO 1984

Year	Total	Republican	Democratic	Other
1984	25	25	—	—
1980	27	27	—	—
1976	27	—	27	—
1972	27	27	—	—
1968	29	—	29	—
1964	29	—	29	—
1960	32	—	32	—
1956	32	32	—	—
1952	32	32	—	—
1948	35	35	—	—
1944	35	—	35	—
1940	36	—	36	—
1936	36	—	36	—
1932	36	36	—	—
1928	38	38	—	—
1924	38	38	—	—
1920	38	38	—	—

PENNSYLVANIA

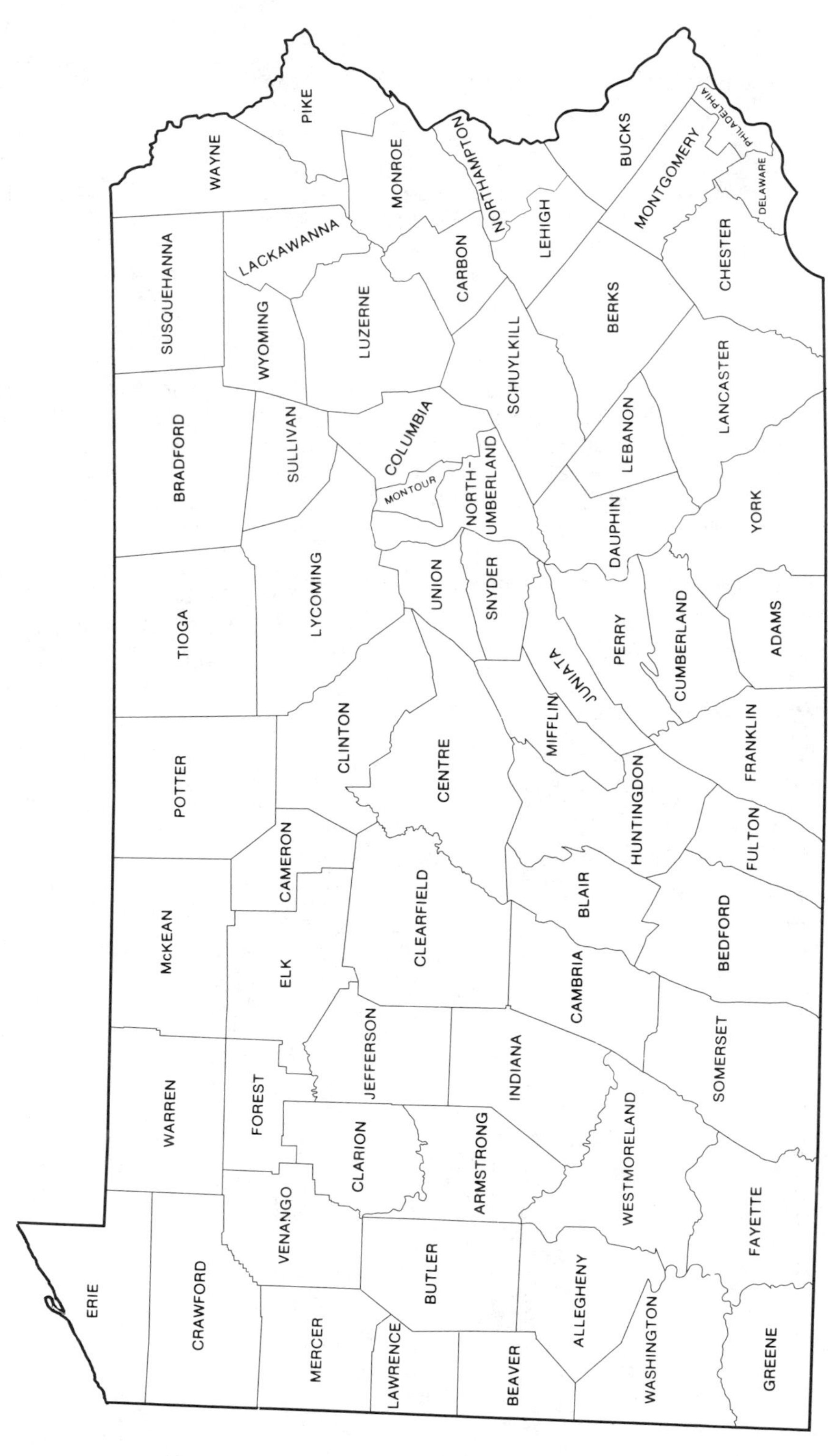

PENNSYLVANIA

PRESIDENT 1984

1980 Census Population	County	Total Vote	Republican	Democratic	Other	Rep.-Dem. Plurality	Percentage Total Vote Rep.	Total Vote Dem.	Major Vote Rep.	Major Vote Dem.
68,292	ADAMS	24,174	16,786	7,289	99	9,497 R	69.4%	30.2%	69.7%	30.3%
1,450,085	ALLEGHENY	665,748	284,692	372,576	8,480	87,884 D	42.8%	56.0%	43.3%	56.7%
77,768	ARMSTRONG	28,344	13,709	14,525	110	816 D	48.4%	51.2%	48.6%	51.4%
204,441	BEAVER	87,117	32,052	54,765	300	22,713 D	36.8%	62.9%	36.9%	63.1%
46,784	BEDFORD	18,543	13,085	5,424	34	7,661 R	70.6%	29.3%	70.7%	29.3%
312,509	BERKS	113,145	74,605	37,849	691	36,756 R	65.9%	33.5%	66.3%	33.7%
136,621	BLAIR	45,945	30,104	15,651	190	14,453 R	65.5%	34.1%	65.8%	34.2%
62,919	BRADFORD	20,367	14,808	5,474	85	9,334 R	72.7%	26.9%	73.0%	27.0%
479,211	BUCKS	205,719	130,119	74,568	1,032	55,551 R	63.3%	36.2%	63.6%	36.4%
147,912	BUTLER	56,626	31,676	24,735	215	6,941 R	55.9%	43.7%	56.2%	43.8%
183,263	CAMBRIA	72,296	32,173	39,865	258	7,692 D	44.5%	55.1%	44.7%	55.3%
6,674	CAMERON	3,029	2,031	990	8	1,041 R	67.1%	32.7%	67.2%	32.8%
53,285	CARBON	19,668	10,701	8,836	131	1,865 R	54.4%	44.9%	54.8%	45.2%
112,760	CENTRE	44,236	27,802	16,194	240	11,608 R	62.8%	36.6%	63.2%	36.8%
316,660	CHESTER	131,531	92,221	38,870	440	53,351 R	70.1%	29.6%	70.3%	29.7%
43,362	CLARION	15,304	9,836	5,407	61	4,429 R	64.3%	35.3%	64.5%	35.5%
83,578	CLEARFIELD	30,769	18,653	11,963	153	6,690 R	60.6%	38.9%	60.9%	39.1%
38,971	CLINTON	11,273	6,678	4,525	70	2,153 R	59.2%	40.1%	59.6%	40.4%
61,967	COLUMBIA	22,718	14,402	8,254	62	6,148 R	63.4%	36.3%	63.6%	36.4%
88,869	CRAWFORD	33,195	20,181	12,792	222	7,389 R	60.8%	38.5%	61.2%	38.8%
178,541	CUMBERLAND	71,123	49,282	21,374	467	27,908 R	69.3%	30.1%	69.7%	30.3%
232,317	DAUPHIN	88,658	54,330	33,576	752	20,754 R	61.3%	37.9%	61.8%	38.2%
555,007	DELAWARE	261,782	161,754	98,207	1,821	63,547 R	61.8%	37.5%	62.2%	37.8%
38,338	ELK	14,007	8,470	5,486	51	2,984 R	60.5%	39.2%	60.7%	39.3%
279,780	ERIE	109,266	55,860	52,471	935	3,389 R	51.1%	48.0%	51.6%	48.4%
159,417	FAYETTE	56,547	21,314	35,098	135	13,784 D	37.7%	62.1%	37.8%	62.2%
5,072	FOREST	2,317	1,468	839	10	629 R	63.4%	36.2%	63.6%	36.4%
113,629	FRANKLIN	38,845	27,243	11,480	122	15,763 R	70.1%	29.6%	70.4%	29.6%
12,842	FULTON	4,574	3,254	1,309	11	1,945 R	71.1%	28.6%	71.3%	28.7%
40,476	GREENE	15,784	6,376	9,365	43	2,989 D	40.4%	59.3%	40.5%	59.5%
42,253	HUNTINGDON	14,691	10,220	4,430	41	5,790 R	69.6%	30.2%	69.8%	30.2%
92,281	INDIANA	34,759	18,845	15,791	123	3,054 R	54.2%	45.4%	54.4%	45.6%
48,303	JEFFERSON	17,355	11,334	5,950	71	5,384 R	65.3%	34.3%	65.6%	34.4%
19,188	JUNIATA	7,705	5,059	2,624	22	2,435 R	65.7%	34.1%	65.8%	34.2%
227,908	LACKAWANNA	95,185	48,132	45,851	1,202	2,281 R	50.6%	48.2%	51.2%	48.8%
362,346	LANCASTER	131,016	99,090	31,308	618	67,782 R	75.6%	23.9%	76.0%	24.0%
107,150	LAWRENCE	43,386	19,277	23,981	128	4,704 D	44.4%	55.3%	44.6%	55.4%
108,582	LEBANON	37,716	27,008	10,520	188	16,488 R	71.6%	27.9%	72.0%	28.0%
272,349	LEHIGH	103,537	61,799	41,089	649	20,710 R	59.7%	39.7%	60.1%	39.9%
343,079	LUZERNE	129,291	69,169	58,482	1,640	10,687 R	53.5%	45.2%	54.2%	45.8%
118,416	LYCOMING	41,895	28,498	13,147	250	15,351 R	68.0%	31.4%	68.4%	31.6%
50,635	MCKEAN	15,839	10,963	4,818	58	6,145 R	69.2%	30.4%	69.5%	30.5%
128,299	MERCER	49,303	24,211	24,658	434	447 D	49.1%	50.0%	49.5%	50.5%
46,908	MIFFLIN	14,373	9,106	5,178	89	3,928 R	63.4%	36.0%	63.7%	36.3%
69,409	MONROE	24,474	16,109	8,193	172	7,916 R	65.8%	33.5%	66.3%	33.7%
643,621	MONTGOMERY	282,666	181,426	99,741	1,499	81,685 R	64.2%	35.3%	64.5%	35.5%
16,675	MONTOUR	6,248	4,174	2,055	19	2,119 R	66.8%	32.9%	67.0%	33.0%
225,418	NORTHAMPTON	83,467	44,648	37,979	840	6,669 R	53.5%	45.5%	54.0%	46.0%
100,381	NORTHUMBERLAND	36,165	22,109	13,748	308	8,361 R	61.1%	38.0%	61.7%	38.3%
35,718	PERRY	13,113	9,365	3,692	56	5,673 R	71.4%	28.2%	71.7%	28.3%
1,688,210	PHILADELPHIA	772,102	267,178	501,369	3,555	234,191 D	34.6%	64.9%	34.8%	65.2%
18,271	PIKE	8,913	6,343	2,503	67	3,840 R	71.2%	28.1%	71.7%	28.3%
17,726	POTTER	6,984	5,164	1,789	31	3,375 R	73.9%	25.6%	74.3%	25.7%
160,630	SCHUYLKILL	63,312	37,330	25,758	224	11,572 R	59.0%	40.7%	59.2%	40.8%
33,584	SNYDER	11,391	8,968	2,383	40	6,585 R	78.7%	20.9%	79.0%	21.0%
81,243	SOMERSET	33,491	19,502	13,900	89	5,602 R	58.2%	41.5%	58.4%	41.6%
6,349	SULLIVAN	2,889	1,926	952	11	974 R	66.7%	33.0%	66.9%	33.1%
37,876	SUSQUEHANNA	15,104	10,566	4,471	67	6,095 R	70.0%	29.6%	70.3%	29.7%
40,973	TIOGA	14,644	10,532	4,060	52	6,472 R	71.9%	27.7%	72.2%	27.8%
32,870	UNION	10,579	7,792	2,747	40	5,045 R	73.7%	26.0%	73.9%	26.1%

PENNSYLVANIA

PRESIDENT 1984

1980 Census Population	County	Total Vote	Republican	Democratic	Other	Rep.-Dem. Plurality	Percentage Total Vote Rep.	Percentage Total Vote Dem.	Percentage Major Vote Rep.	Percentage Major Vote Dem.
64,444	VENANGO	22,725	13,507	9,114	104	4,393 R	59.4%	40.1%	59.7%	40.3%
47,449	WARREN	17,221	10,838	6,244	139	4,594 R	62.9%	36.3%	63.4%	36.6%
217,074	WASHINGTON	85,937	34,782	50,911	244	16,129 D	40.5%	59.2%	40.6%	59.4%
35,237	WAYNE	13,297	10,061	3,155	81	6,906 R	75.7%	23.7%	76.1%	23.9%
392,294	WESTMORELAND	152,464	71,377	79,906	1,181	8,529 D	46.8%	52.4%	47.2%	52.8%
26,433	WYOMING	9,769	7,230	2,518	21	4,712 R	74.0%	25.8%	74.2%	25.8%
312,963	YORK	109,247	75,020	33,359	868	41,661 R	68.7%	30.5%	69.2%	30.8%
11,863,895	TOTAL	4,844,903	2,584,323	2,228,131	32,449	356,192 R	53.3%	46.0%	53.7%	46.3%

PENNSYLVANIA

PRESIDENT 1980

1980 Census Population	County	Total Vote	Republican	Democratic	Other	Rep.-Dem. Plurality	Percentage Total Vote Rep.	Total Vote Dem.	Major Vote Rep.	Major Vote Dem.
68,292	ADAMS	22,404	13,760	7,266	1,378	6,494 R	61.4%	32.4%	65.4%	34.6%
1,450,085	ALLEGHENY	621,418	271,850	297,464	52,104	25,614 D	43.7%	47.9%	47.8%	52.2%
77,768	ARMSTRONG	27,104	12,955	12,718	1,431	237 R	47.8%	46.9%	50.5%	49.5%
204,441	BEAVER	79,765	30,496	43,955	5,314	13,459 D	38.2%	55.1%	41.0%	59.0%
46,784	BEDFORD	16,419	10,930	4,950	539	5,980 R	66.6%	30.1%	68.8%	31.2%
312,509	BERKS	107,385	60,576	36,449	10,360	24,127 R	56.4%	33.9%	62.4%	37.6%
136,621	BLAIR	46,359	28,931	15,014	2,414	13,917 R	62.4%	32.4%	65.8%	34.2%
62,919	BRADFORD	20,865	13,139	6,439	1,287	6,700 R	63.0%	30.9%	67.1%	32.9%
479,211	BUCKS	181,164	100,536	59,120	21,508	41,416 R	55.5%	32.6%	63.0%	37.0%
147,912	BUTLER	52,689	28,821	19,711	4,157	9,110 R	54.7%	37.4%	59.4%	40.6%
183,263	CAMBRIA	72,131	33,072	36,121	2,938	3,049 D	45.8%	50.1%	47.8%	52.2%
6,674	CAMERON	3,030	1,795	1,112	123	683 R	59.2%	36.7%	61.7%	38.3%
53,285	CARBON	19,329	10,042	8,009	1,278	2,033 R	52.0%	41.4%	55.6%	44.4%
112,760	CENTRE	42,631	20,605	15,987	6,039	4,618 R	48.3%	37.5%	56.3%	43.7%
316,660	CHESTER	119,896	73,046	34,307	12,543	38,739 R	60.9%	28.6%	68.0%	32.0%
43,362	CLARION	15,101	8,812	5,472	817	3,340 R	58.4%	36.2%	61.7%	38.3%
83,578	CLEARFIELD	28,192	15,299	11,647	1,246	3,652 R	54.3%	41.3%	56.8%	43.2%
38,971	CLINTON	12,010	6,288	4,842	880	1,446 R	52.4%	40.3%	56.5%	43.5%
61,967	COLUMBIA	23,313	12,426	9,449	1,438	2,977 R	53.3%	40.5%	56.8%	43.2%
88,869	CRAWFORD	30,909	16,552	11,778	2,579	4,774 R	53.6%	38.1%	58.4%	41.6%
178,541	CUMBERLAND	67,260	41,152	19,789	6,319	21,363 R	61.2%	29.4%	67.5%	32.5%
232,317	DAUPHIN	78,387	44,039	27,252	7,096	16,787 R	56.2%	34.8%	61.8%	38.2%
555,007	DELAWARE	256,859	143,282	88,314	25,263	54,968 R	55.8%	34.4%	61.9%	38.1%
38,338	ELK	13,669	7,175	5,898	596	1,277 R	52.5%	43.1%	54.9%	45.1%
279,780	ERIE	103,162	48,918	45,946	8,298	2,972 R	47.4%	44.5%	51.6%	48.4%
159,417	FAYETTE	49,383	19,252	27,963	2,168	8,711 D	39.0%	56.6%	40.8%	59.2%
5,072	FOREST	2,149	1,206	819	124	387 R	56.1%	38.1%	59.6%	40.4%
113,629	FRANKLIN	36,741	22,716	12,061	1,964	10,655 R	61.8%	32.8%	65.3%	34.7%
12,842	FULTON	4,222	2,740	1,342	140	1,398 R	64.9%	31.8%	67.1%	32.9%
40,476	GREENE	14,121	5,336	8,193	592	2,857 D	37.8%	58.0%	39.4%	60.6%
42,253	HUNTINGDON	13,928	8,140	5,094	694	3,046 R	58.4%	36.6%	61.5%	38.5%
92,281	INDIANA	31,451	15,607	13,828	2,016	1,779 R	49.6%	44.0%	53.0%	47.0%
48,303	JEFFERSON	16,778	9,628	6,296	854	3,332 R	57.4%	37.5%	60.5%	39.5%
19,188	JUNIATA	7,161	4,139	2,696	326	1,443 R	57.8%	37.6%	60.6%	39.4%
227,908	LACKAWANNA	95,447	44,242	45,257	5,948	1,015 D	46.4%	47.4%	49.4%	50.6%
362,346	LANCASTER	118,897	79,963	30,026	8,908	49,937 H	67.3%	25.3%	72.7%	27.3%
107,150	LAWRENCE	40,213	18,404	19,506	2,303	1,102 D	45.8%	48.5%	48.5%	51.5%
108,582	LEBANON	35,507	24,495	8,281	2,731	16,214 R	69.0%	23.3%	74.7%	25.3%
272,349	LEHIGH	95,985	50,782	34,827	10,376	15,955 R	52.9%	36.3%	59.3%	40.7%
343,079	LUZERNE	135,080	67,822	59,976	7,282	7,846 R	50.2%	44.4%	53.1%	46.9%
118,416	LYCOMING	40,553	23,415	14,609	2,529	8,806 R	57.7%	36.0%	61.6%	38.4%
50,635	MCKEAN	15,166	9,229	5,064	873	4,165 R	60.9%	33.4%	64.6%	35.4%
128,299	MERCER	46,090	22,372	19,716	4,002	2,656 R	48.5%	42.8%	53.2%	46.8%
46,908	MIFFLIN	13,520	7,541	5,226	753	2,315 R	55.8%	38.7%	59.1%	40.9%
69,409	MONROE	22,289	12,357	7,551	2,381	4,806 R	55.4%	33.9%	62.1%	37.9%
643,621	MONTGOMERY	271,553	156,996	84,289	30,268	72,707 R	57.8%	31.0%	65.1%	34.9%
16,675	MONTOUR	6,096	3,399	2,272	425	1,127 R	55.8%	37.3%	59.9%	40.1%
225,418	NORTHAMPTON	76,037	35,787	31,920	8,330	3,867 R	47.1%	42.0%	52.9%	47.1%
100,381	NORTHUMBERLAND	36,290	20,608	13,750	1,932	6,858 R	56.8%	37.9%	60.0%	40.0%
35,718	PERRY	12,599	8,026	3,681	892	4,345 R	63.7%	29.2%	68.6%	31.4%
1,688,210	PHILADELPHIA	718,100	244,108	421,253	52,739	177,145 D	34.0%	58.7%	36.7%	63.3%
18,271	PIKE	7,973	5,249	2,132	592	3,117 R	65.8%	26.7%	71.1%	28.9%
17,726	POTTER	6,669	4,073	2,299	297	1,774 R	61.1%	34.5%	63.9%	36.1%
160,630	SCHUYLKILL	64,969	36,273	24,968	3,728	11,305 R	55.8%	38.4%	59.2%	40.8%
33,584	SNYDER	10,591	7,634	2,418	539	5,216 R	72.1%	22.8%	75.9%	24.1%
81,243	SOMERSET	30,455	17,729	11,695	1,031	6,034 R	58.2%	38.4%	60.3%	39.7%
6,349	SULLIVAN	2,902	1,676	1,074	152	602 R	57.8%	37.0%	60.9%	39.1%
37,876	SUSQUEHANNA	14,689	8,994	4,660	1,035	4,334 R	61.2%	31.7%	65.9%	34.1%
40,973	TIOGA	13,849	8,770	4,273	806	4,497 R	63.3%	30.9%	67.2%	32.8%
32,870	UNION	10,256	6,798	2,687	771	4,111 R	66.3%	26.2%	71.7%	28.3%

PENNSYLVANIA

PRESIDENT 1980

1980 Census Population	County	Total Vote	Republican	Democratic	Other	Rep.-Dem. Plurality	Percentage Total Vote Rep.	Percentage Total Vote Dem.	Percentage Major Vote Rep.	Percentage Major Vote Dem.
64,444	VENANGO	20,604	11,547	7,800	1,257	3,747 R	56.0%	37.9%	59.7%	40.3%
47,449	WARREN	15,974	9,165	5,560	1,249	3,605 R	57.4%	34.8%	62.2%	37.8%
217,074	WASHINGTON	82,018	32,532	45,295	4,191	12,763 D	39.7%	55.2%	41.8%	58.2%
35,237	WAYNE	12,548	8,468	3,375	705	5,093 R	67.5%	26.9%	71.5%	28.5%
392,294	WESTMORELAND	140,139	63,140	68,627	8,372	5,487 D	45.1%	49.0%	47.9%	52.1%
26,433	WYOMING	9,167	5,919	2,766	482	3,153 R	64.6%	30.2%	68.2%	31.8%
312,963	YORK	101,891	61,098	33,406	7,387	27,692 R	60.0%	32.8%	64.7%	35.3%
11,863,895	TOTAL	4,561,501	2,261,872	1,937,540	362,089	324,332 R	49.6%	42.5%	53.9%	46.1%

PENNSYLVANIA

PRESIDENT 1976

1970 Census Population	County	Total Vote	Republican	Democratic	Other	Rep.-Dem. Plurality	Percentage Total Vote Rep.	Percentage Total Vote Dem.	Percentage Major Vote Rep.	Percentage Major Vote Dem.
56,937	ADAMS	21,322	12,133	8,771	418	3,362 R	56.9%	41.1%	58.0%	42.0%
1,605,016	ALLEGHENY	647,857	303,127	328,343	16,387	25,216 D	46.8%	50.7%	48.0%	52.0%
75,590	ARMSTRONG	29,050	13,378	15,179	493	1,801 D	46.1%	52.3%	46.8%	53.2%
208,418	BEAVER	81,150	33,593	46,117	1,440	12,524 D	41.4%	56.8%	42.1%	57.9%
42,353	BEDFORD	16,138	9,355	6,652	131	2,703 R	58.0%	41.2%	58.4%	41.6%
296,382	BERKS	107,553	54,452	50,994	2,107	3,458 R	50.6%	47.4%	51.6%	48.4%
135,356	BLAIR	47,366	28,290	18,397	679	9,893 R	59.7%	38.8%	60.6%	39.4%
57,962	BRADFORD	21,034	12,851	7,913	270	4,938 R	61.1%	37.6%	61.9%	38.1%
415,056	BUCKS	168,923	85,628	79,838	3,457	5,790 R	50.7%	47.3%	51.7%	48.3%
127,941	BUTLER	50,198	26,366	22,611	1,221	3,755 R	52.5%	45.0%	53.8%	46.2%
186,785	CAMBRIA	72,128	32,469	38,797	862	6,328 D	45.0%	53.8%	45.6%	54.4%
7,096	CAMERON	2,977	1,616	1,319	42	297 R	54.3%	44.3%	55.1%	44.9%
50,573	CARBON	19,973	8,883	10,791	299	1,908 D	44.5%	54.0%	45.2%	54.8%
99,267	CENTRE	40,437	21,177	17,867	1,393	3,310 R	52.4%	44.2%	54.2%	45.8%
278,311	CHESTER	112,026	67,686	42,712	1,628	24,974 R	60.4%	38.1%	61.3%	38.7%
38,414	CLARION	15,210	8,360	6,585	265	1,775 R	55.0%	43.3%	55.9%	44.1%
74,619	CLEARFIELD	27,685	13,626	13,714	345	88 D	49.2%	49.5%	49.8%	50.2%
37,721	CLINTON	12,564	5,858	6,532	174	674 D	46.6%	52.0%	47.3%	52.7%
55,114	COLUMBIA	23,925	11,508	12,051	366	543 D	48.1%	50.4%	48.8%	51.2%
81,342	CRAWFORD	30,610	15,301	14,712	597	589 R	50.0%	48.1%	51.0%	49.0%
158,177	CUMBERLAND	64,270	39,950	23,008	1,312	16,942 R	62.2%	35.8%	63.5%	36.5%
223,834	DAUPHIN	83,122	46,819	34,342	1,961	12,477 R	56.3%	41.3%	57.7%	42.3%
600,035	DELAWARE	270,894	148,679	117,252	4,963	31,427 R	54.9%	43.3%	55.9%	44.1%
37,770	ELK	13,109	6,159	6,713	237	554 D	47.0%	51.2%	47.8%	52.2%
263,654	ERIE	107,439	49,641	55,385	2,413	5,744 D	46.2%	51.6%	47.3%	52.7%
154,667	FAYETTE	53,244	20,021	32,232	991	12,211 D	37.6%	60.5%	38.3%	61.7%
4,926	FOREST	2,187	1,135	1,017	35	118 R	51.9%	46.5%	52.7%	47.3%
100,833	FRANKLIN	35,389	20,009	14,643	737	5,366 R	56.5%	41.4%	57.7%	42.3%
10,776	FULTON	4,052	2,219	1,737	96	482 R	54.8%	42.9%	56.1%	43.9%
36,090	GREENE	14,219	5,293	8,769	157	3,476 D	37.2%	61.7%	37.6%	62.4%
39,108	HUNTINGDON	13,462	7,843	5,410	209	2,433 R	58.3%	40.2%	59.2%	40.8%
79,451	INDIANA	30,949	15,786	14,650	513	1,136 R	51.0%	47.3%	51.9%	48.1%
43,695	JEFFERSON	17,130	9,437	7,456	237	1,981 R	55.1%	43.5%	55.9%	44.1%
16,712	JUNIATA	7,206	3,991	3,105	110	886 R	55.4%	43.1%	56.2%	43.8%
234,107	LACKAWANNA	102,797	43,354	57,685	1,758	14,331 D	42.2%	56.1%	42.9%	57.1%
319,693	LANCASTER	109,676	72,106	35,533	2,037	36,573 R	65.7%	32.4%	67.0%	33.0%
107,374	LAWRENCE	42,640	18,546	23,337	757	4,791 D	43.5%	54.7%	44.3%	55.7%
99,665	LEBANON	33,330	20,880	11,785	665	9,095 R	62.6%	35.4%	63.9%	36.1%
255,304	LEHIGH	95,308	46,895	46,620	1,793	275 R	49.2%	48.9%	50.1%	49.9%
342,301	LUZERNE	136,009	60,058	74,655	1,296	14,597 D	44.2%	54.9%	44.6%	55.4%
113,296	LYCOMING	42,082	22,648	18,635	799	4,013 R	53.8%	44.3%	54.9%	45.1%
51,915	MCKEAN	16,926	10,305	6,424	197	3,881 R	60.9%	38.0%	61.6%	38.4%
127,175	MERCER	48,235	22,469	25,041	725	2,572 D	46.6%	51.9%	47.3%	52.7%
45,268	MIFFLIN	14,109	7,698	6,210	201	1,488 R	54.6%	44.0%	55.3%	44.7%
45,422	MONROE	20,165	10,228	9,544	393	684 R	50.7%	47.3%	51.7%	48.3%
623,799	MONTGOMERY	273,169	155,480	112,644	5,045	42,836 R	56.9%	41.2%	58.0%	42.0%
16,508	MONTOUR	6,075	3,259	2,727	89	532 R	53.6%	44.9%	54.4%	45.6%
214,368	NORTHAMPTON	76,961	32,926	42,514	1,521	9,588 D	42.8%	55.2%	43.6%	56.4%
99,190	NORTHUMBERLAND	38,876	19,283	18,939	654	344 R	49.6%	48.7%	50.5%	49.5%
28,615	PERRY	12,320	7,454	4,605	261	2,849 R	60.5%	37.4%	61.8%	38.2%
1,948,609	PHILADELPHIA	746,197	239,000	494,579	12,618	255,579 D	32.0%	66.3%	32.6%	67.4%
11,818	PIKE	7,146	4,241	2,775	130	1,466 R	59.3%	38.8%	60.4%	39.6%
16,395	POTTER	6,891	3,828	2,983	80	845 R	55.6%	43.3%	56.2%	43.8%
160,089	SCHUYLKILL	66,948	31,944	33,905	1,099	1,961 D	47.7%	50.6%	48.5%	51.5%
29,269	SNYDER	9,929	6,557	3,097	275	3,460 R	66.0%	31.2%	67.9%	32.1%
76,037	SOMERSET	29,685	15,960	13,452	273	2,508 R	53.8%	45.3%	54.3%	45.7%
5,961	SULLIVAN	2,951	1,584	1,347	20	237 R	53.7%	45.6%	54.0%	46.0%
34,344	SUSQUEHANNA	14,682	8,331	6,075	276	2,256 R	56.7%	41.4%	57.8%	42.2%
39,691	TIOGA	14,405	8,417	5,795	193	2,622 R	58.4%	40.2%	59.2%	40.8%
28,603	UNION	9,902	6,309	3,405	188	2,904 R	63.7%	34.4%	64.9%	35.1%

PENNSYLVANIA

PRESIDENT 1976

1970 Census Population	County	Total Vote	Republican	Democratic	Other	Rep.-Dem. Plurality	Percentage Total Vote Rep.	Percentage Total Vote Dem.	Percentage Major Vote Rep.	Percentage Major Vote Dem.
62,353	VENANGO	21,311	12,270	8,653	388	3,617 R	57.6%	40.6%	58.6%	41.4%
47,682	WARREN	16,170	8,508	7,412	250	1,096 R	52.6%	45.8%	53.4%	46.6%
210,876	WASHINGTON	83,251	32,827	49,317	1,107	16,490 D	39.4%	59.2%	40.0%	60.0%
29,581	WAYNE	12,310	7,811	4,244	255	3,567 R	63.5%	34.5%	64.8%	35.2%
376,935	WESTMORELAND	136,134	59,172	74,217	2,745	15,045 D	43.5%	54.5%	44.4%	55.6%
19,082	WYOMING	9,455	5,705	3,628	122	2,077 R	60.3%	38.4%	61.1%	38.9%
272,603	YORK	99,944	56,912	41,281	1,751	15,631 R	56.9%	41.3%	58.0%	42.0%
11,793,909	TOTAL	4,620,787	2,205,604	2,328,677	86,506	123,073 D	47.7%	50.4%	48.6%	51.4%

PENNSYLVANIA

PRESIDENT 1972

1970 Census Population	County	Total Vote	Republican	Democratic	Other	Rep.-Dem. Plurality	Percentage Total Vote Rep.	Total Vote Dem.	Major Vote Rep.	Major Vote Dem.
56,937	ADAMS	19,365	13,593	5,529	243	8,064 R	70.2%	28.6%	71.1%	28.9%
1,605,016	ALLEGHENY	668,535	371,737	282,496	14,302	89,241 R	55.6%	42.3%	56.8%	43.2%
75,590	ARMSTRONG	28,498	17,557	10,490	451	7,067 R	61.6%	36.8%	62.6%	37.4%
208,418	BEAVER	77,337	43,637	31,570	2,130	12,067 R	56.4%	40.8%	58.0%	42.0%
42,353	BEDFORD	15,338	11,243	3,836	259	7,407 R	73.3%	25.0%	74.6%	25.4%
296,382	BERKS	106,127	66,172	36,563	3,392	29,609 R	62.4%	34.5%	64.4%	35.6%
135,356	BLAIR	44,110	33,126	10,023	961	23,103 R	75.1%	22.7%	76.8%	23.2%
57,962	BRADFORD	20,458	15,050	5,204	204	9,846 R	73.6%	25.4%	74.3%	25.7%
415,056	BUCKS	160,059	99,684	56,784	3,591	42,900 R	62.3%	35.5%	63.7%	36.3%
127,941	BUTLER	45,574	29,665	14,695	1,214	14,970 R	65.1%	32.2%	66.9%	33.1%
186,785	CAMBRIA	72,975	43,825	27,950	1,200	15,875 R	60.1%	38.3%	61.1%	38.9%
7,096	CAMERON	2,827	1,935	828	64	1,107 R	68.4%	29.3%	70.0%	30.0%
50,573	CARBON	19,712	11,639	7,774	299	3,865 R	59.0%	39.4%	60.0%	40.0%
99,267	CENTRE	34,197	20,683	13,194	320	7,489 R	60.5%	38.6%	61.1%	38.9%
278,311	CHESTER	106,259	72,726	31,118	2,415	41,608 R	68.4%	29.3%	70.0%	30.0%
38,414	CLARION	14,821	10,073	4,509	239	5,564 R	68.0%	30.4%	69.1%	30.9%
74,619	CLEARFIELD	26,409	16,780	9,246	383	7,534 R	63.5%	35.0%	64.5%	35.5%
37,721	CLINTON	13,119	8,205	4,772	142	3,433 R	62.5%	36.4%	63.2%	36.8%
55,114	COLUMBIA	22,309	14,187	7,222	900	6,965 R	63.6%	32.4%	66.3%	33.7%
81,342	CRAWFORD	28,569	18,393	9,371	805	9,022 R	64.4%	32.8%	66.2%	33.8%
158,177	CUMBERLAND	57,775	42,099	14,562	1,114	27,537 R	72.9%	25.2%	74.3%	25.7%
223,834	DAUPHIN	78,270	54,307	22,587	1,376	31,720 R	69.4%	28.9%	70.6%	29.4%
600,035	DELAWARE	274,451	175,414	94,144	4,893	81,270 R	63.9%	34.3%	65.1%	34.9%
37,770	ELK	12,908	7,900	4,710	298	3,190 R	61.2%	36.5%	62.6%	37.4%
263,654	ERIE	105,713	61,542	42,022	2,149	19,520 R	58.2%	39.8%	59.4%	40.6%
154,667	FAYETTE	50,479	27,288	22,475	716	4,813 R	54.1%	44.5%	54.8%	45.2%
4,926	FOREST	1,915	1,374	509	32	865 R	71.7%	26.6%	73.0%	27.0%
100,833	FRANKLIN	34,415	24,093	9,456	866	14,637 R	70.0%	27.5%	71.8%	28.2%
10,776	FULTON	3,797	2,515	1,192	90	1,323 R	66.2%	31.4%	67.8%	32.2%
36,090	GREENE	13,543	7,790	5,562	191	2,228 R	57.5%	41.1%	58.3%	41.7%
39,108	HUNTINGDON	13,216	9,606	3,394	216	6,212 R	72.7%	25.7%	73.9%	26.1%
79,451	INDIANA	29,274	18,122	10,833	319	7,289 R	61.9%	37.0%	62.6%	37.4%
43,695	JEFFERSON	16,876	11,631	5,024	221	6,607 R	68.9%	29.8%	69.8%	30.2%
16,712	JUNIATA	6,653	4,412	2,156	85	2,256 R	66.3%	32.4%	67.2%	32.8%
234,107	LACKAWANNA	104,869	58,838	45,465	566	13,373 R	56.1%	43.4%	56.4%	43.6%
319,693	LANCASTER	107,138	81,036	24,223	1,879	56,813 R	75.6%	22.6%	77.0%	23.0%
107,374	LAWRENCE	42,297	23,712	17,595	990	6,117 R	56.1%	41.6%	57.4%	42.6%
99,665	LEBANON	32,320	25,008	6,683	629	18,325 R	77.4%	20.7%	78.9%	21.1%
255,304	LEHIGH	93,002	58,023	33,325	1,654	24,698 R	62.4%	35.8%	63.5%	36.5%
342,301	LUZERNE	133,606	81,358	51,128	1,120	30,230 R	60.9%	38.3%	61.4%	38.6%
113,296	LYCOMING	42,087	28,913	11,999	1,175	16,914 R	68.7%	28.5%	70.7%	29.3%
51,915	MCKEAN	16,673	11,958	4,513	202	7,445 R	71.7%	27.1%	72.6%	27.4%
127,175	MERCER	47,100	27,961	18,087	1,052	9,874 R	59.4%	38.4%	60.7%	39.3%
45,268	MIFFLIN	13,855	9,989	3,667	199	6,322 R	72.1%	26.5%	73.1%	26.9%
45,422	MONROE	18,814	12,701	5,619	494	7,082 R	67.5%	29.9%	69.3%	30.7%
623,799	MONTGOMERY	270,018	173,662	91,959	4,397	81,703 R	64.3%	34.1%	65.4%	34.6%
16,508	MONTOUR	6,298	4,386	1,755	157	2,631 R	69.6%	27.9%	71.4%	28.6%
214,368	NORTHAMPTON	74,281	41,822	32,335	124	9,487 R	56.3%	43.5%	56.4%	43.6%
99,190	NORTHUMBERLAND	40,385	25,912	13,885	588	12,027 R	64.2%	34.4%	65.1%	34.9%
28,615	PERRY	11,025	8,082	2,731	212	5,351 R	73.3%	24.8%	74.7%	25.3%
1,948,609	PHILADELPHIA	783,970	344,096	431,736	8,138	87,640 D	43.9%	55.1%	44.4%	55.6%
11,818	PIKE	6,108	4,568	1,385	155	3,183 R	74.8%	22.7%	76.7%	23.3%
16,395	POTTER	6,236	4,422	1,710	104	2,712 R	70.9%	27.4%	72.1%	27.9%
160,089	SCHUYLKILL	71,595	44,071	26,077	1,447	17,994 R	61.6%	36.4%	62.8%	37.2%
29,269	SNYDER	9,345	7,308	1,834	203	5,474 R	78.2%	19.6%	79.9%	20.1%
76,037	SOMERSET	28,841	19,739	8,743	359	10,996 R	68.4%	30.3%	69.3%	30.7%
5,961	SULLIVAN	2,808	1,886	885	37	1,001 R	67.2%	31.5%	68.1%	31.9%
34,344	SUSQUEHANNA	13,979	9,476	4,154	349	5,322 R	67.8%	29.7%	69.5%	30.5%
39,691	TIOGA	13,918	10,028	3,733	157	6,295 R	72.1%	26.8%	72.9%	27.1%
28,603	UNION	9,385	6,905	2,278	202	4,627 R	73.6%	24.3%	75.2%	24.8%

PENNSYLVANIA

PRESIDENT 1972

1970 Census Population	County	Total Vote	Republican	Democratic	Other	Rep.-Dem. Plurality	Percentage Total Vote Rep.	Total Vote Dem.	Major Vote Rep.	Major Vote Dem.
62,353	VENANGO	20,794	13,991	6,302	501	7,689 R	67.3%	30.3%	68.9%	31.1%
47,682	WARREN	15,167	10,018	4,877	272	5,141 R	66.1%	32.2%	67.3%	32.7%
210,876	WASHINGTON	78,862	42,587	34,781	1,494	7,806 R	54.0%	44.1%	55.0%	45.0%
29,581	WAYNE	12,009	8,948	2,733	328	6,215 R	74.5%	22.8%	76.6%	23.4%
376,935	WESTMORELAND	137,527	75,085	59,322	3,120	15,763 R	54.6%	43.1%	55.9%	44.1%
19,082	WYOMING	8,631	6,423	2,112	96	4,311 R	74.4%	24.5%	75.3%	24.7%
272,603	YORK	93,280	63,606	27,520	2,154	36,086 R	68.2%	29.5%	69.8%	30.2%
11,793,909	TOTAL	4,592,106	2,714,521	1,796,951	80,634	917,570 R	59.1%	39.1%	60.2%	39.8%

PENNSYLVANIA

PRESIDENT 1968

1960 Census Population	County	Total Vote	Republican	Democratic	AIP	Other	Plurality	Percentage		
								Rep.	Dem.	AIP
51,906	ADAMS	18,907	11,303	5,993	1,579	32	5,310 R	59.8%	31.7%	8.4%
1,628,587	ALLEGHENY	713,817	264,790	364,906	79,776	4,345	100,116 D	37.1%	51.1%	11.2%
79,524	ARMSTRONG	30,353	14,132	13,921	2,256	44	211 R	46.6%	45.9%	7.4%
206,948	BEAVER	82,028	28,264	45,396	7,974	394	17,132 D	34.5%	55.3%	9.7%
42,451	BEDFORD	16,518	10,482	4,725	1,301	10	5,757 R	63.5%	28.6%	7.9%
275,414	BERKS	108,924	50,623	49,877	8,093	331	746 R	46.5%	45.8%	7.4%
137,270	BLAIR	48,296	28,780	15,803	3,644	69	12,977 R	59.6%	32.7%	7.5%
54,925	BRADFORD	21,058	13,308	6,373	1,347	30	6,935 R	63.2%	30.3%	6.4%
308,567	BUCKS	143,211	69,646	57,634	15,211	720	12,012 R	48.6%	40.2%	10.6%
114,639	BUTLER	45,291	21,618	19,415	4,139	119	2,203 R	47.7%	42.9%	9.1%
203,283	CAMBRIA	79,150	33,280	41,225	4,485	160	7,945 D	42.0%	52.1%	5.7%
7,586	CAMERON	3,090	1,822	1,104	159	5	718 R	59.0%	35.7%	5.1%
52,889	CARBON	21,579	9,954	10,634	952	39	680 D	46.1%	49.3%	4.4%
78,580	CENTRE	28,527	15,865	11,163	1,389	110	4,702 R	55.6%	39.1%	4.9%
210,608	CHESTER	98,051	56,073	32,606	9,142	230	23,467 R	57.2%	33.3%	9.3%
37,408	CLARION	14,423	8,077	5,341	981	24	2,736 R	56.0%	37.0%	6.8%
81,534	CLEARFIELD	29,163	14,471	12,369	2,252	71	2,102 R	49.6%	42.4%	7.7%
37,619	CLINTON	13,508	6,563	6,301	625	19	262 R	48.6%	46.6%	4.6%
53,489	COLUMBIA	22,229	12,202	8,187	1,797	43	4,015 R	54.9%	36.8%	8.1%
77,956	CRAWFORD	28,226	14,991	11,345	1,832	58	3,646 R	53.1%	40.2%	6.5%
124,816	CUMBERLAND	53,472	32,908	15,467	4,893	204	17,441 R	61.5%	28.9%	9.2%
220,255	DAUPHIN	81,788	48,394	25,480	7,534	380	22,914 R	59.2%	31.2%	9.2%
553,154	DELAWARE	266,436	133,777	106,695	25,051	913	27,082 R	50.2%	40.0%	9.4%
37,328	ELK	14,046	6,193	6,886	945	22	693 D	44.1%	49.0%	6.7%
250,682	ERIE	99,847	43,134	51,604	4,868	241	8,470 D	43.2%	51.7%	4.9%
169,340	FAYETTE	59,450	18,921	34,340	5,984	205	15,419 D	31.8%	57.8%	10.1%
4,485	FOREST	1,973	1,172	669	129	3	503 R	59.4%	33.9%	6.5%
88,172	FRANKLIN	35,195	19,146	11,451	4,557	41	7,695 R	54.4%	32.5%	12.9%
10,597	FULTON	3,973	2,200	1,174	592	7	1,026 R	55.4%	29.5%	14.9%
39,424	GREENE	14,401	5,099	8,198	1,094	10	3,099 D	35.4%	56.9%	7.6%
39,457	HUNTINGDON	13,388	8,276	4,128	962	22	4,148 R	61.8%	30.8%	7.2%
75,366	INDIANA	29,196	14,899	12,175	2,078	44	2,724 R	51.0%	41.7%	7.1%
46,792	JEFFERSON	18,347	10,214	6,839	1,278	16	3,375 R	55.7%	37.3%	7.0%
15,874	JUNIATA	6,874	4,039	2,321	507	7	1,718 R	58.8%	33.8%	7.4%
234,531	LACKAWANNA	114,391	44,388	66,297	3,538	168	21,909 D	38.8%	58.0%	3.1%
278,359	LANCASTER	108,307	69,953	29,870	8,194	290	40,083 R	64.6%	27.6%	7.6%
112,965	LAWRENCE	43,103	18,360	21,027	3,635	81	2,667 D	42.6%	48.8%	8.4%
90,853	LEBANON	34,025	21,832	9,529	2,584	80	12,303 R	64.2%	28.0%	7.6%
227,536	LEHIGH	95,408	47,255	44,033	3,900	220	3,222 R	49.5%	46.2%	4.1%
346,972	LUZERNE	143,380	57,044	79,040	6,857	439	21,996 D	39.8%	55.1%	4.8%
109,367	LYCOMING	43,566	23,830	16,888	2,761	87	6,942 R	54.7%	38.8%	6.3%
54,517	MCKEAN	17,607	10,506	6,326	745	30	4,180 R	59.7%	35.9%	4.2%
127,519	MERCER	49,105	23,131	22,814	3,033	127	317 R	47.1%	46.5%	6.2%
44,348	MIFFLIN	14,698	8,133	5,681	859	25	2,452 R	55.3%	38.7%	5.8%
39,567	MONROE	17,747	9,465	6,946	1,267	69	2,519 R	53.3%	39.1%	7.1%
516,682	MONTGOMERY	260,732	141,621	102,464	15,599	1,048	39,157 R	54.3%	39.3%	6.0%
16,730	MONTOUR	5,976	3,289	2,239	438	10	1,050 R	55.0%	37.5%	7.3%
201,412	NORTHAMPTON	78,130	32,033	42,554	3,276	267	10,521 D	41.0%	54.5%	4.2%
104,138	NORTHUMBERLAND	41,899	22,366	17,013	2,456	64	5,353 R	53.4%	40.6%	5.9%
26,582	PERRY	10,849	6,655	2,944	1,222	28	3,711 R	61.3%	27.1%	11.3%
2,002,512	PHILADELPHIA	850,117	254,153	525,768	63,506	6,690	271,615 D	29.9%	61.8%	7.5%
9,158	PIKE	5,790	3,719	1,617	441	13	2,102 R	64.2%	27.9%	7.6%
16,483	POTTER	6,339	4,019	1,860	451	9	2,159 R	63.4%	29.3%	7.1%
173,027	SCHUYLKILL	76,645	37,194	34,982	4,381	88	2,212 R	48.5%	45.6%	5.7%
25,922	SNYDER	9,469	6,784	1,993	676	16	4,791 R	71.6%	21.0%	7.1%
77,450	SOMERSET	30,921	17,511	11,515	1,845	50	5,996 R	56.6%	37.2%	6.0%
6,251	SULLIVAN	2,870	1,629	1,035	200	6	594 R	56.8%	36.1%	7.0%
33,137	SUSQUEHANNA	14,032	8,705	4,364	929	34	4,341 R	62.0%	31.1%	6.6%
36,614	TIOGA	13,863	9,298	3,488	1,065	12	5,810 R	67.1%	25.2%	7.7%
25,646	UNION	9,215	6,422	2,178	581	34	4,244 R	69.7%	23.6%	6.3%

PENNSYLVANIA

PRESIDENT 1968

1960 Census Population	County	Total Vote	Republican	Democratic	AIP	Other	Plurality	Percentage Rep.	Dem.	AIP
65,295	VENANGO	21,949	12,323	8,319	1,262	45	4,004 R	56.1%	37.9%	5.7%
45,582	WARREN	15,968	8,889	6,368	676	35	2,521 R	55.7%	39.9%	4.2%
217,271	WASHINGTON	84,968	28,023	47,805	9,016	124	19,782 D	33.0%	56.3%	10.6%
28,237	WAYNE	11,790	7,827	3,176	754	33	4,651 R	66.4%	26.9%	6.4%
352,629	WESTMORELAND	148,839	52,206	81,833	14,436	364	29,627 D	35.1%	55.0%	9.7%
16,813	WYOMING	8,124	5,207	2,366	539	12	2,841 R	64.1%	29.1%	6.6%
238,336	YORK	93,371	51,631	33,328	8,054	358	18,303 R	55.3%	35.7%	8.6%
11,319,366	TOTAL	4,747,928	2,090,017	2,259,405	378,582	19,924	169,388 D	44.0%	47.6%	8.0%

PENNSYLVANIA

ELECTION NOTES

1984 Other vote was 21,628 Johnson (Consumer); 6,982 Bergland (Libertarian); 2,059 Winn (Workers League); 1,780 Hall (Communist).

1980 Other vote was 292,921 Anderson (Anderson Coalition); 33,263 Clark (Libertarian); 20,291 DeBerry (Socialist Workers); 10,430 Commoner (Consumer); 5,184 Hall (Communist).

1976 Other vote was 50,584 McCarthy (McCarthy '76); 25,344 Maddox (Constitutional); 3,009 Camejo (Socialist Workers); 2,744 LaRouche (Labor); 1,891 Hall (Communist); 2,934 scattered write-in.

1972 Other vote was 70,593 Schmitz (Constitutional); 4,639 Jenness (Socialist Workers); 2,686 Hall (Communist); 2,716 scattered write-in. Early unamended canvass gave the scattered write-in vote as 2,715.

1968 Wallace on the ballot as American Independent. Other vote was 7,821 Gregory (Peace and Freedom); 4,977 Blomen (Socialist Labor); 4,862 Halstead (Militant Workers); 2,264 scattered write-in.

RHODE ISLAND

POPULAR VOTE FOR PRESIDENT 1920 TO 1984

		Republican		Democratic				Percentage			
	Total					Other		Total Vote		Major Vote	
Year	Vote	Vote	Candidate	Vote	Candidate	Vote	Plurality	Rep.	Dem.	Rep.	Dem.
1984	410,492	212,080	Reagan, Ronald	197,106	Mondale, Walter F.	1,306	14,974 R	51.7%	48.0%	51.8%	48.2%
1980	416,072	154,793	Reagan, Ronald	198,342	Carter, Jimmy	62,937	43,549 D	37.2%	47.7%	43.8%	56.2%
1976	411,170	181,249	Ford, Gerald R.	227,636	Carter, Jimmy	2,285	46,387 D	44.1%	55.4%	44.3%	55.7%
1972	415,808	220,383	Nixon, Richard M.	194,645	McGovern, George S.	780	25,738 R	53.0%	46.8%	53.1%	46.9%
1968	385,000	122,359	Nixon, Richard M.	246,518	Humphrey, Hubert H.	16,123	124,159 D	31.8%	64.0%	33.2%	66.8%
1964	390,091	74,615	Goldwater, Barry M.	315,463	Johnson, Lyndon B.	13	240,848 D	19.1%	80.9%	19.1%	80.9%
1960	405,535	147,502	Nixon, Richard M.	258,032	Kennedy, John F.	1	110,530 D	36.4%	63.6%	36.4%	63.6%
1956	387,609	225,819	Eisenhower, Dwight D.	161,790	Stevenson, Adlai E.		64,029 R	58.3%	41.7%	58.3%	41.7%
1952	414,498	210,935	Eisenhower, Dwight D.	203,293	Stevenson, Adlai E.	270	7,642 R	50.9%	49.0%	50.9%	49.1%
1948	327,702	135,787	Dewey, Thomas E.	188,736	Truman, Harry S.	3,179	52,949 D	41.4%	57.6%	41.8%	58.2%
1944	299,276	123,487	Dewey, Thomas E.	175,356	Roosevelt, Franklin D.	433	51,869 D	41.3%	58.6%	41.3%	58.7%
1940	321,152	138,654	Willkie, Wendell	182,181	Roosevelt, Franklin D.	317	43,527 D	43.2%	56.7%	43.2%	56.8%
1936	310,278	125,031	Landon, Alfred M.	164,338	Roosevelt, Franklin D.	20,909	39,307 D	40.3%	53.0%	43.2%	56.8%
1932	266,170	115,266	Hoover, Herbert C.	146,604	Roosevelt, Franklin D.	4,300	31,338 D	43.3%	55.1%	44.0%	56.0%
1928	237,194	117,522	Hoover, Herbert C.	118,973	Smith, Alfred E.	699	1,451 D	49.5%	50.2%	49.7%	50.3%
1924	210,115	125,286	Coolidge, Calvin	76,606	Davis, John W.	8,223	48,680 R	59.6%	36.5%	62.1%	37.9%
1920	167,981	107,463	Harding, Warren G.	55,062	Cox, James M.	5,456	52,401 R	64.0%	32.8%	66.1%	33.9%

ELECTORAL COLLEGE VOTE 1920 TO 1984

Year	Total	Republican	Democratic	Other
1984	4	4	—	—
1980	4	—	4	—
1976	4	—	4	—
1972	4	4	—	—
1968	4	—	4	—
1964	4	—	4	—
1960	4	—	4	—
1956	4	4	—	—
1952	4	4	—	—
1948	4	—	4	—
1944	4	—	4	—
1940	4	—	4	—
1936	4	—	4	—
1932	4	—	4	—
1928	5	—	5	—
1924	5	5	—	—
1920	5	5	—	—

RHODE ISLAND

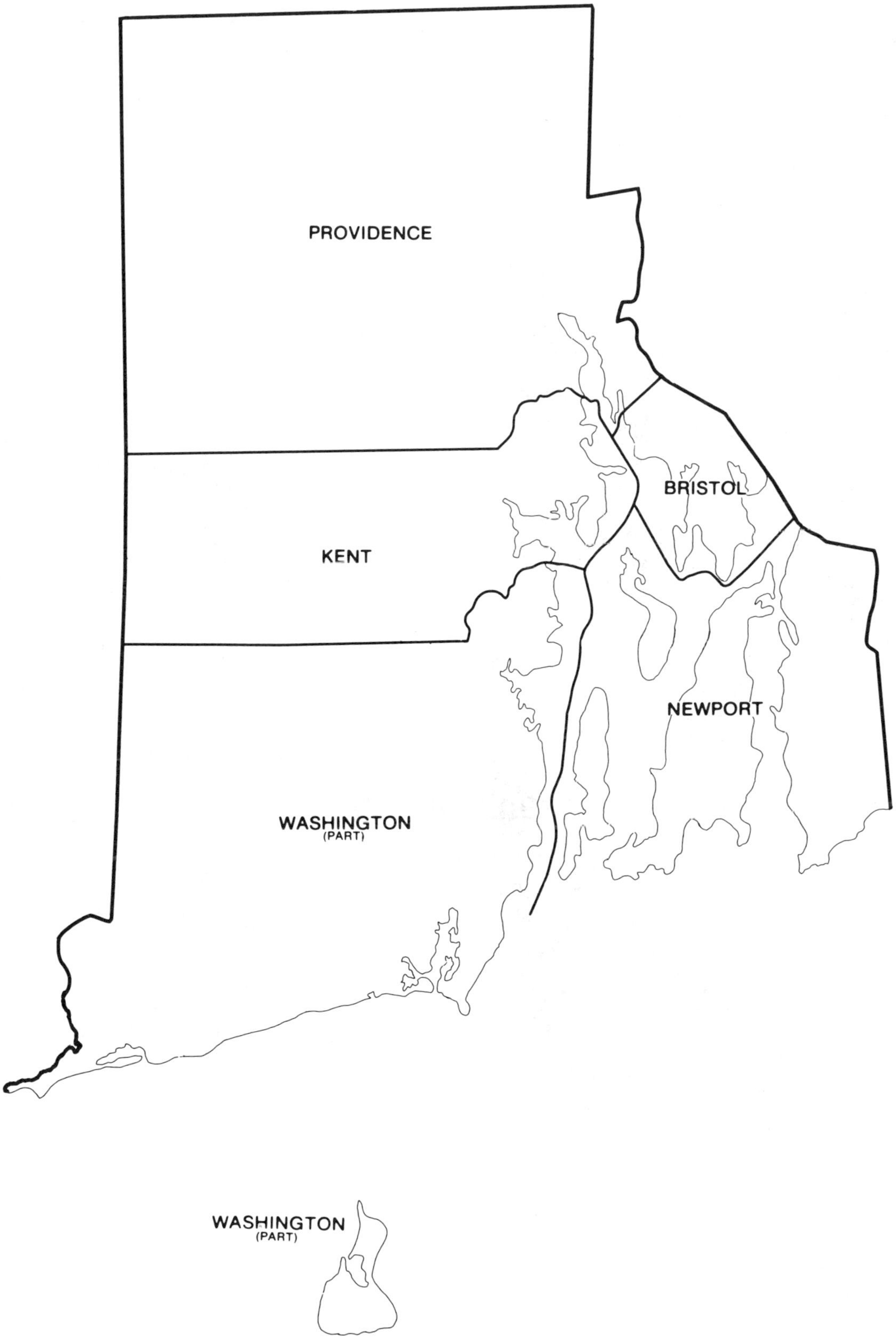
PROVIDENCE
KENT
BRISTOL
NEWPORT
WASHINGTON
(PART)
WASHINGTON
(PART)

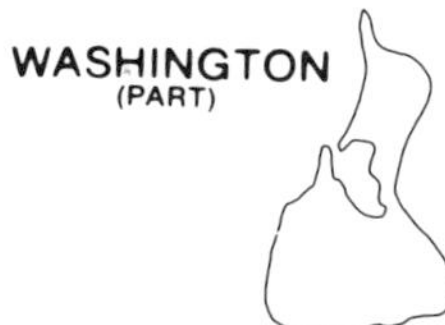

RHODE ISLAND

PRESIDENT 1984

1980 Census Population	County	Total Vote	Republican	Democratic	Other	Rep.-Dem. Plurality	Percentage Total Vote Rep.	Total Vote Dem.	Major Vote Rep.	Major Vote Dem.
46,942	BRISTOL	21,084	11,635	9,386	63	2,249 R	55.2%	44.5%	55.3%	44.7%
154,163	KENT	71,993	40,427	31,352	214	9,075 R	56.2%	43.5%	56.3%	43.7%
81,383	NEWPORT	34,209	19,629	14,466	114	5,163 R	57.4%	42.3%	57.6%	42.4%
571,349	PROVIDENCE	240,898	116,024	124,109	765	8,085 D	48.2%	51.5%	48.3%	51.7%
93,317	WASHINGTON	42,305	24,365	17,793	147	6,572 R	57.6%	42.1%	57.8%	42.2%
947,154	TOTAL	410,492	212,080	197,106	1,306	14,974 R	51.7%	48.0%	51.8%	48.2%

RHODE ISLAND

PRESIDENT 1980

1980 Census Population	County	Total Vote	Republican	Democratic	Other	Rep.-Dem. Plurality	Percentage Total Vote Rep.	Total Vote Dem.	Major Vote Rep.	Major Vote Dem.
46,942	BRISTOL	21,852	8,508	9,851	3,493	1,343 D	38.9%	45.1%	46.3%	53.7%
154,163	KENT	71,005	28,331	31,350	11,324	3,019 D	39.9%	44.2%	47.5%	52.5%
81,383	NEWPORT	34,356	14,555	13,904	5,897	651 R	42.4%	40.5%	51.1%	48.9%
571,349	PROVIDENCE	247,927	86,467	126,808	34,652	40,341 D	34.9%	51.1%	40.5%	59.5%
93,317	WASHINGTON	40,827	16,932	16,429	7,466	503 R	41.5%	40.2%	50.8%	49.2%
947,154	TOTAL	416,072	154,793	198,342	62,937	43,549 D	37.2%	47.7%	43.8%	56.2%

RHODE ISLAND

PRESIDENT 1976

1970 Census Population	County	Total Vote	Republican	Democratic	Other	Rep.-Dem. Plurality	Percentage Total Vote Rep.	Total Vote Dem.	Major Vote Rep.	Major Vote Dem.
45,937	BRISTOL	21,425	10,131	11,228	66	1,097 D	47.3%	52.4%	47.4%	52.6%
142,382	KENT	70,213	34,131	35,855	227	1,724 D	48.6%	51.1%	48.8%	51.2%
94,228	NEWPORT	33,107	15,155	17,768	184	2,613 D	45.8%	53.7%	46.0%	54.0%
581,470	PROVIDENCE	249,817	103,976	144,805	1,036	40,829 D	41.6%	58.0%	41.8%	58.2%
85,706	WASHINGTON	36,022	17,856	17,980	186	124 D	49.6%	49.9%	49.8%	50.2%
949,723	TOTAL	411,170	181,249	227,636	2,285	46,387 D	44.1%	55.4%	44.3%	55.7%

RHODE ISLAND

PRESIDENT 1972

1970 Census Population	County	Total Vote	Republican	Democratic	Other	Rep.-Dem. Plurality	Percentage Total Vote Rep.	Percentage Total Vote Dem.	Percentage Major Vote Rep.	Percentage Major Vote Dem.
45,937	BRISTOL	21,985	12,009	9,928	48	2,081 R	54.6%	45.2%	54.7%	45.3%
142,382	KENT	69,653	40,534	29,004	115	11,530 R	58.2%	41.6%	58.3%	41.7%
94,228	NEWPORT	32,035	19,142	12,844	49	6,298 R	59.8%	40.1%	59.8%	40.2%
581,470	PROVIDENCE	259,156	129,418	129,232	506	186 R	49.9%	49.9%	50.0%	50.0%
85,706	WASHINGTON	32,979	19,280	13,637	62	5,643 R	58.5%	41.4%	58.6%	41.4%
949,723	TOTAL	415,808	220,383	194,645	780	25,738 R	53.0%	46.8%	53.1%	46.9%

RHODE ISLAND

PRESIDENT 1968

1960 Census Population	County	Total Vote	Republican	Democratic	AIP	Other	Plurality	Percentage Rep.	Percentage Dem.	Percentage AIP
37,146	BRISTOL	19,475	7,403	11,561	483	28	4,158 D	38.0%	59.4%	2.5%
112,619	KENT	60,678	22,493	35,609	2,519	57	13,116 D	37.1%	58.7%	4.2%
81,891	NEWPORT	27,830	10,504	16,251	1,043	32	5,747 D	37.7%	58.4%	3.7%
568,778	PROVIDENCE	250,199	70,320	169,246	10,347	286	98,926 D	28.1%	67.6%	4.1%
59,054	WASHINGTON	26,818	11,639	13,851	1,286	42	2,212 D	43.4%	51.6%	4.8%
859,488	TOTAL	385,000	122,359	246,518	15,678	445	124,159 D	31.8%	64.0%	4.1%

RHODE ISLAND

ELECTION NOTES

1984 Other vote was 510 Richards (American Independent); 277 Bergland (Libertarian); 240 Johnson (Citizens); 91 Holmes (Workers World); 75 Hall (Communist); 61 Mason (Socialist Workers); 49 Serrette (Alliance); 3 scattered write-in. The state-wide total for the other vote column includes the 3 scattered write-in votes not reported by county.

1980 Other vote was 59,819 Anderson (Independent); 2,458 Clark (Libertarian); 218 Hall (Communist); 170 McReynolds (Socialist); 90 DeBerry (Socialist Workers); 77 Griswold (Workers World); 67 Commoner (write-in); 1 McCormack (write-in); 37 scattered write-in. The state-wide total for the other vote column includes the 105 write-in votes not reported by county.

1976 Other vote was 715 MacBride (Libertarian); 479 McCarthy (write-in); 462 Camejo (Socialist Workers); 334 Hall (Communist); 188 Levin (Socialist Labor); 24 Anderson (write-in); 1 Maddox (write-in); 82 scattered write-in. The state-wide total for the other vote column includes the 586 write-in votes not available by county.

1972 Other vote was 729 Jenness (Socialist Workers); 25 Schmitz (write-in); 5 Spock (write-in); 2 Hospers (write-in); 19 scattered write-in.

1968 Wallace on the ballot as George Wallace Independent. Other vote was 383 Halstead (Socialist Workers); 62 scattered write-in.

SOUTH CAROLINA

POPULAR VOTE FOR PRESIDENT 1920 TO 1984

								Percentage			
	Total	Republican		Democratic		Other		Total Vote		Major Vote	
Year	Vote	Vote	Candidate	Vote	Candidate	Vote	Plurality	Rep.	Dem.	Rep.	Dem.
1984	968,529	615,539	Reagan, Ronald	344,459	Mondale, Walter F.	8,531	271,080 R	63.6%	35.6%	64.1%	35.9%
1980	894,071	441,841	Reagan, Ronald	430,385	Carter, Jimmy	21,845	11,456 R	49.4%	48.1%	50.7%	49.3%
1976	802,583	346,149	Ford, Gerald R.	450,807	Carter, Jimmy	5,627	104,658 D	43.1%	56.2%	43.4%	56.6%
1972	673,960	477,044	Nixon, Richard M.	186,824	McGovern, George S.	10,092	290,220 R	70.8%	27.7%	71.9%	28.1%
1968 **	666,978	254,062	Nixon, Richard M.	197,486	Humphrey, Hubert H.	215,430	38,632 R	38.1%	29.6%	56.3%	43.7%
1964	524,779	309,048	Goldwater, Barry M.	215,723	Johnson, Lyndon B.	8	93,325 R	58.9%	41.1%	58.9%	41.1%
1960	386,688	188,558	Nixon, Richard M.	198,129	Kennedy, John F.	1	9,571 D	48.8%	51.2%	48.8%	51.2%
1956 **	300,583	75,700	Eisenhower, Dwight D.	136,372	Stevenson, Adlai E.	88,511	47,863 D	25.2%	45.4%	35.7%	64.3%
1952	341,087	168,082	Eisenhower, Dwight D.	173,004	Stevenson, Adlai E.	1	4,922 D	49.3%	50.7%	49.3%	50.7%
1948 **	142,571	5,386	Dewey, Thomas E.	34,423	Truman, Harry S.	102,762	68,184 SR	3.8%	24.1%	13.5%	86.5%
1944 **	103,382	4,617	Dewey, Thomas E.	90,601	Roosevelt, Franklin D.	8,164	82,802 D	4.5%	87.6%	4.8%	95.2%
1940	99,830	4,360	Willkie, Wendell	95,470	Roosevelt, Franklin D.		91,110 D	4.4%	95.6%	4.4%	95.6%
1936	115,437	1,646	Landon, Alfred M.	113,791	Roosevelt, Franklin D.		112,145 D	1.4%	98.6%	1.4%	98.6%
1932	104,407	1,978	Hoover, Herbert C.	102,347	Roosevelt, Franklin D.	82	100,369 D	1.9%	98.0%	1.9%	98.1%
1928	68,605	5,858	Hoover, Herbert C.	62,700	Smith, Alfred E.	47	56,842 D	8.5%	91.4%	8.5%	91.5%
1924	50,755	1,123	Coolidge, Calvin	49,008	Davis, John W.	624	47,885 D	2.2%	96.6%	2.2%	97.8%
1920	66,808	2,610	Harding, Warren G.	64,170	Cox, James M.	28	61,560 D	3.9%	96.1%	3.9%	96.1%

In 1968 other vote was Independent (Wallace). In 1956 other vote was 88,509 Independent (Uncommitted States Rights) and 2 scattered. In 1948 other vote was 102,607 States Rights; 154 Progressive and 1 Socialist. In 1944 other vote was 7,799 Southern Democratic and 365 Prohibition.

ELECTORAL COLLEGE VOTE 1920 TO 1984

Year	Total	Republican	Democratic	Other
1984	8	8	—	—
1980	8	8	—	—
1976	8	—	8	—
1972	8	8	—	—
1968	8	8	—	—
1964	8	8	—	—
1960	8	—	8	—
1956	8	—	8	—
1952	8	—	8	—
1948	8	—	—	8 SR
1944	8	—	8	—
1940	8	—	8	—
1936	8	—	8	—
1932	8	—	8	—
1928	9	—	9	—
1924	9	—	9	—
1920	9	—	9	—

SOUTH CAROLINA

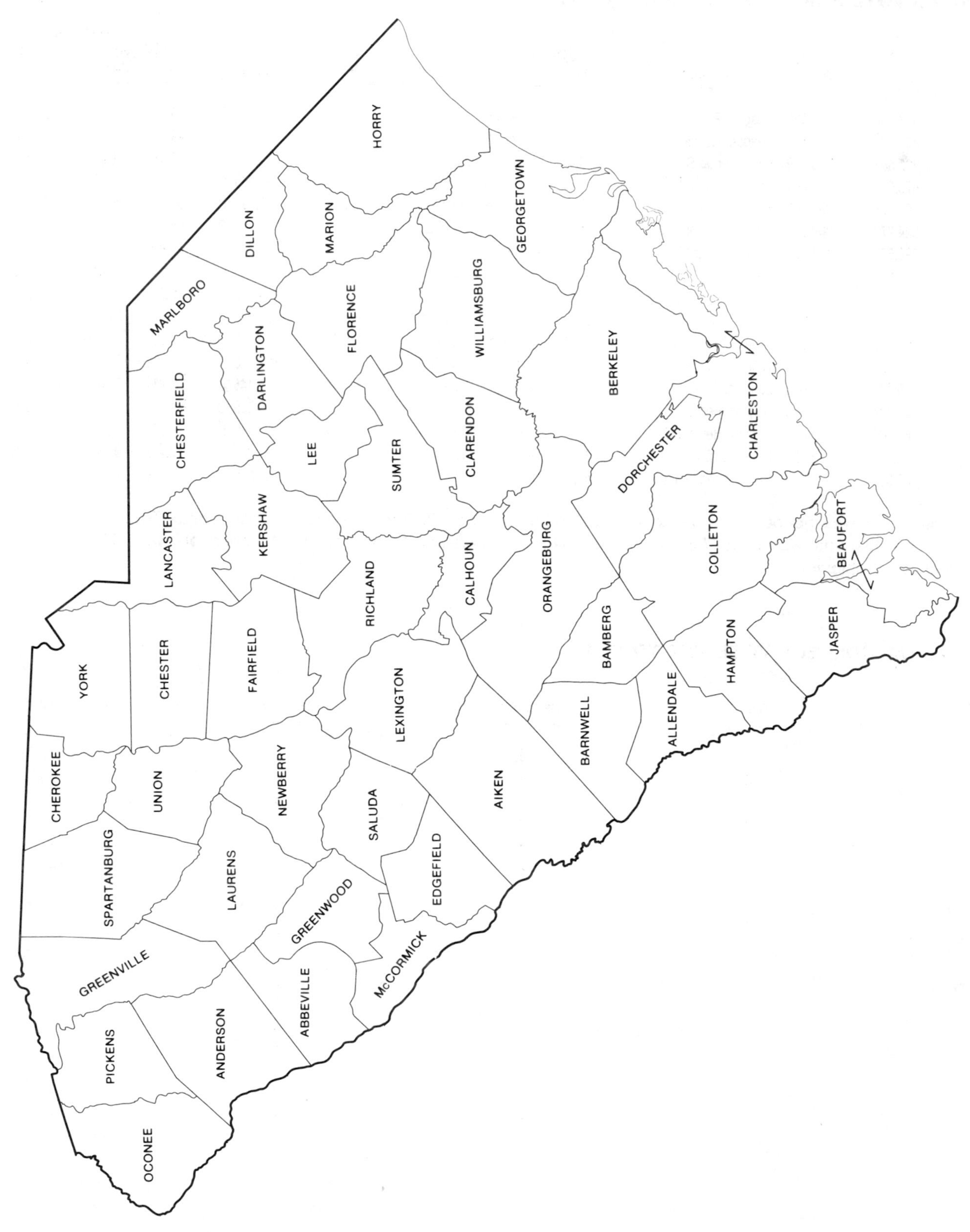

SOUTH CAROLINA

PRESIDENT 1984

1980 Census Population	County	Total Vote	Republican	Democratic	Other	Rep.-Dem. Plurality	Percentage Total Vote Rep.	Total Vote Dem.	Major Vote Rep.	Major Vote Dem.
22,627	ABBEVILLE	6,875	3,798	3,051	26	747 R	55.2%	44.4%	55.5%	44.5%
105,625	AIKEN	36,133	25,872	9,892	369	15,980 R	71.6%	27.4%	72.3%	27.7%
10,700	ALLENDALE	3,769	1,570	2,170	29	600 D	41.7%	57.6%	42.0%	58.0%
133,235	ANDERSON	34,691	24,123	10,324	244	13,799 R	69.5%	29.8%	70.0%	30.0%
18,118	BAMBERG	5,831	2,908	2,892	31	16 R	49.9%	49.6%	50.1%	49.9%
19,868	BARNWELL	7,189	4,346	2,811	32	1,535 R	60.5%	39.1%	60.7%	39.3%
65,364	BEAUFORT	21,118	13,668	7,347	103	6,321 R	64.7%	34.8%	65.0%	35.0%
94,727	BERKELEY	24,511	16,972	7,380	159	9,592 R	69.2%	30.1%	69.7%	30.3%
12,206	CALHOUN	5,094	2,742	2,315	37	427 R	53.8%	45.4%	54.2%	45.8%
276,974	CHARLESTON	84,249	53,779	29,470	1,000	24,309 R	63.8%	35.0%	64.6%	35.4%
40,983	CHEROKEE	12,809	8,655	4,101	53	4,554 R	67.6%	32.0%	67.9%	32.1%
30,148	CHESTER	8,045	4,441	3,559	45	882 R	55.2%	44.2%	55.5%	44.5%
38,161	CHESTERFIELD	10,067	5,451	4,593	23	858 R	54.1%	45.6%	54.3%	45.7%
27,464	CLARENDON	10,746	5,102	5,591	53	489 D	47.5%	52.0%	47.7%	52.3%
31,776	COLLETON	11,145	6,200	4,910	35	1,290 R	55.6%	44.1%	55.8%	44.2%
62,717	DARLINGTON	18,910	11,100	7,456	354	3,644 R	58.7%	39.4%	59.8%	40.2%
31,083	DILLON	8,050	4,646	3,360	44	1,286 R	57.7%	41.7%	58.0%	42.0%
58,761	DORCHESTER	22,399	15,289	7,037	73	8,252 R	68.3%	31.4%	68.5%	31.5%
17,528	EDGEFIELD	6,478	3,224	3,227	27	3 D	49.8%	49.8%	50.0%	50.0%
20,700	FAIRFIELD	7,287	3,147	4,117	23	970 D	43.2%	56.5%	43.3%	56.7%
110,163	FLORENCE	37,600	22,753	14,639	208	8,114 R	60.5%	38.9%	60.8%	39.2%
42,461	GEORGETOWN	13,830	7,370	6,392	68	978 R	53.3%	46.2%	53.6%	46.4%
287,913	GREENVILLE	91,369	66,766	24,137	466	42,629 R	73.1%	26.4%	73.4%	26.6%
57,847	GREENWOOD	17,307	10,887	6,339	81	4,548 R	62.9%	36.6%	63.2%	36.8%
18,159	HAMPTON	7,228	3,464	3,736	28	272 D	47.9%	51.7%	48.1%	51.9%
101,419	HORRY	29,463	20,396	8,940	127	11,456 R	69.2%	30.3%	69.5%	30.5%
14,504	JASPER	6,879	3,102	3,753	24	651 D	45.1%	54.6%	45.3%	54.7%
39,015	KERSHAW	13,226	8,822	4,323	81	4,499 R	66.7%	32.7%	67.1%	32.9%
53,361	LANCASTER	16,244	10,383	5,804	57	4,579 R	63.9%	35.7%	64.1%	35.9%
52,214	LAURENS	15,086	9,729	5,312	45	4,417 R	64.5%	35.2%	64.7%	35.3%
18,929	LEE	7,500	3,548	3,912	40	364 D	47.3%	52.2%	47.6%	52.4%
140,353	LEXINGTON	47,721	38,628	8,828	265	29,800 R	80.9%	18.5%	81.4%	18.6%
7,797	MCCORMICK	2,726	1,186	1,526	14	340 D	43.5%	56.0%	43.7%	56.3%
34,179	MARION	9,773	4,698	5,043	32	345 D	48.1%	51.6%	48.2%	51.8%
31,634	MARLBORO	8,283	3,951	4,294	38	343 D	47.7%	51.8%	47.9%	52.1%
31,242	NEWBERRY	11,008	7,176	3,790	42	3,386 R	65.2%	34.4%	65.4%	34.6%
48,611	OCONEE	12,044	8,625	3,333	86	5,292 R	71.6%	27.7%	72.1%	27.9%
82,276	ORANGEBURG	29,635	14,286	15,121	228	835 D	48.2%	51.0%	48.6%	51.4%
79,292	PICKENS	19,764	15,155	4,481	128	10,674 R	76.7%	22.7%	77.2%	22.8%
269,735	RICHLAND	81,429	46,773	32,212	2,444	14,561 R	57.4%	39.6%	59.2%	40.8%
16,150	SALUDA	5,501	3,515	1,962	24	1,553 R	63.9%	35.7%	64.2%	35.8%
201,861	SPARTANBURG	62,575	41,553	20,130	892	21,423 R	66.4%	32.2%	67.4%	32.6%
88,243	SUMTER	22,591	12,909	9,566	116	3,343 R	57.1%	42.3%	57.4%	42.6%
30,751	UNION	10,796	6,331	4,424	41	1,907 R	58.6%	41.0%	58.9%	41.1%
38,226	WILLIAMSBURG	14,128	6,492	7,586	50	1,094 D	46.0%	53.7%	46.1%	53.9%
106,720	YORK	29,427	20,008	9,273	146	10,735 R	68.0%	31.5%	68.3%	31.7%
3,121,820	TOTAL	968,529	615,539	344,459	8,531	271,080 R	63.6%	35.6%	64.1%	35.9%

SOUTH CAROLINA

PRESIDENT 1980

1980 Census Population	County	Total Vote	Republican	Democratic	Other	Rep.-Dem. Plurality	Percentage Total Vote Rep.	Percentage Total Vote Dem.	Percentage Major Vote Rep.	Percentage Major Vote Dem.
22,627	ABBEVILLE	6,530	2,261	4,049	220	1,788 D	34.6%	62.0%	35.8%	64.2%
105,625	AIKEN	32,369	18,570	13,014	785	5,556 R	57.4%	40.2%	58.8%	41.2%
10,700	ALLENDALE	3,991	1,184	2,775	32	1,591 D	29.7%	69.5%	29.9%	70.1%
133,235	ANDERSON	35,300	15,667	18,801	832	3,134 D	44.4%	53.3%	45.5%	54.5%
18,118	BAMBERG	5,422	2,099	3,294	29	1,195 D	38.7%	60.8%	38.9%	61.1%
19,868	BARNWELL	6,705	3,228	3,399	78	171 D	48.1%	50.7%	48.7%	51.3%
65,364	BEAUFORT	16,684	8,620	7,415	649	1,205 R	51.7%	44.4%	53.8%	46.2%
94,727	BERKELEY	23,024	12,790	9,850	384	2,940 R	55.6%	42.8%	56.5%	43.5%
12,206	CALHOUN	3,850	1,767	2,044	39	277 D	45.9%	53.1%	46.4%	53.6%
276,974	CHARLESTON	81,260	44,833	33,057	3,370	11,776 R	55.2%	40.7%	57.6%	42.4%
40,983	CHEROKEE	12,437	5,392	6,894	151	1,502 D	43.4%	55.4%	43.9%	56.1%
30,148	CHESTER	8,363	3,104	5,145	114	2,041 D	37.1%	61.5%	37.6%	62.4%
38,161	CHESTERFIELD	9,973	3,479	6,393	101	2,914 D	34.9%	64.1%	35.2%	64.8%
27,464	CLARENDON	10,203	4,162	5,983	58	1,821 D	40.8%	58.6%	41.0%	59.0%
31,776	COLLETON	10,543	4,719	5,745	79	1,026 D	44.8%	54.5%	45.1%	54.9%
62,717	DARLINGTON	17,650	8,290	9,011	349	721 D	47.0%	51.1%	47.9%	52.1%
31,083	DILLON	7,998	3,385	4,520	93	1,135 D	42.3%	56.5%	42.8%	57.2%
58,761	DORCHESTER	18,298	10,893	7,237	168	3,656 R	59.5%	39.6%	60.1%	39.9%
17,528	EDGEFIELD	5,945	2,422	3,464	59	1,042 D	40.7%	58.3%	41.1%	58.9%
20,700	FAIRFIELD	6,323	2,098	4,153	72	2,055 D	33.2%	65.7%	33.6%	66.4%
110,163	FLORENCE	33,992	17,069	16,391	532	678 R	50.2%	48.2%	51.0%	49.0%
42,461	GEORGETOWN	12,041	5,151	6,701	189	1,550 D	42.8%	55.7%	43.5%	56.5%
287,913	GREENVILLE	80,415	46,168	32,135	2,112	14,033 R	57.4%	40.0%	59.0%	41.0%
57,847	GREENWOOD	16,886	7,291	9,285	310	1,994 D	43.2%	55.0%	44.0%	56.0%
18,159	HAMPTON	6,612	2,220	4,332	60	2,112 D	33.6%	65.5%	33.9%	66.1%
101,419	HORRY	28,871	14,331	13,897	643	434 R	49.6%	48.1%	50.8%	49.2%
14,504	JASPER	4,977	1,618	3,316	43	1,698 D	32.5%	66.6%	32.8%	67.2%
39,015	KERSHAW	11,970	6,652	5,103	215	1,549 R	55.6%	42.6%	56.6%	43.4%
53,361	LANCASTER	15,166	6,410	8,283	473	1,873 D	42.3%	54.6%	43.6%	56.4%
52,214	LAURENS	14,100	6,041	7,862	197	1,821 D	42.8%	55.8%	43.5%	56.5%
18,929	LEE	7,795	2,952	4,816	27	1,864 D	37.9%	61.8%	38.0%	62.0%
140,353	LEXINGTON	41,711	28,313	12,334	1,064	15,979 R	67.9%	29.6%	69.7%	30.3%
7,797	MCCORMICK	2,610	800	1,775	35	975 D	30.7%	68.0%	31.1%	68.9%
34,179	MARION	8,816	3,323	5,389	104	2,066 D	37.7%	61.1%	38.1%	61.9%
31,634	MARLBORO	8,040	2,585	5,378	77	2,793 D	32.2%	66.9%	32.5%	67.5%
31,242	NEWBERRY	10,508	5,568	4,825	115	743 R	53.0%	45.9%	53.6%	46.4%
48,611	OCONEE	13,588	5,652	7,678	258	2,026 D	41.6%	56.5%	42.4%	57.6%
82,276	ORANGEBURG	27,733	11,313	16,178	242	4,865 D	40.8%	58.3%	41.2%	58.8%
79,292	PICKENS	17,919	9,575	7,789	555	1,786 R	53.4%	43.5%	55.1%	44.9%
269,735	RICHLAND	73,911	36,450	33,916	3,545	2,534 R	49.3%	45.9%	51.8%	48.2%
16,150	SALUDA	5,173	2,450	2,653	70	203 D	47.4%	51.3%	48.0%	52.0%
201,861	SPARTANBURG	60,027	29,979	28,414	1,634	1,565 R	49.9%	47.3%	51.3%	48.7%
88,243	SUMTER	20,126	10,557	9,205	364	1,352 R	52.5%	45.7%	53.4%	46.6%
30,751	UNION	10,450	4,035	6,274	141	2,239 D	38.6%	60.0%	39.1%	60.9%
38,226	WILLIAMSBURG	13,347	5,110	8,138	99	3,028 D	38.3%	61.0%	38.6%	61.4%
106,720	YORK	24,043	11,265	12,075	703	810 D	46.9%	50.2%	48.3%	51.7%
3,121,820	TOTAL	894,071	441,841	430,385	21,845	11,456 R	49.4%	48.1%	50.7%	49.3%

SOUTH CAROLINA

PRESIDENT 1976

1970 Census Population	County	Total Vote	Republican	Democratic	Other	Rep.-Dem. Plurality	Percentage Total Vote Rep.	Dem.	Major Vote Rep.	Dem.
21,112	ABBEVILLE	6,527	1,791	4,700	36	2,909 D	27.4%	72.0%	27.6%	72.4%
91,023	AIKEN	31,173	16,011	14,927	235	1,084 R	51.4%	47.9%	51.8%	48.2%
9,692	ALLENDALE	3,709	1,064	2,634	11	1,570 D	28.7%	71.0%	28.8%	71.2%
105,474	ANDERSON	28,654	9,496	19,002	156	9,506 D	33.1%	66.3%	33.3%	66.7%
15,950	BAMBERG	5,218	1,849	3,330	39	1,481 D	35.4%	63.8%	35.7%	64.3%
17,176	BARNWELL	6,652	2,569	4,083		1,514 D	38.6%	61.4%	38.6%	61.4%
51,136	BEAUFORT	12,052	5,935	6,049	68	114 D	49.2%	50.2%	49.5%	50.5%
56,199	BERKELEY	16,795	6,981	9,741	73	2,760 D	41.6%	58.0%	41.7%	58.3%
10,780	CALHOUN	3,468	1,382	2,055	31	673 D	39.9%	59.3%	40.2%	59.8%
247,650	CHARLESTON	69,265	34,010	34,328	927	318 D	49.1%	49.6%	49.8%	50.2%
36,791	CHEROKEE	11,732	3,931	7,765	36	3,834 D	33.5%	66.2%	33.6%	66.4%
29,811	CHESTER	8,212	2,982	5,200	30	2,218 D	36.3%	63.3%	36.4%	63.6%
33,667	CHESTERFIELD	10,250	2,537	7,687	26	5,150 D	24.8%	75.0%	24.8%	75.2%
25,604	CLARENDON	8,561	3,040	5,489	32	2,449 D	35.5%	64.1%	35.6%	64.4%
27,622	COLLETON	8,522	3,324	5,134	64	1,810 D	39.0%	60.2%	39.3%	60.7%
53,442	DARLINGTON	16,899	6,678	10,165	56	3,487 D	39.5%	60.2%	39.6%	60.4%
28,838	DILLON	7,639	2,527	5,089	23	2,562 D	33.1%	66.6%	33.2%	66.8%
32,421	DORCHESTER	14,779	6,695	8,046	38	1,351 D	45.3%	54.4%	45.4%	54.6%
15,692	EDGEFIELD	5,144	1,878	3,216	50	1,338 D	36.5%	62.5%	36.9%	63.1%
19,999	FAIRFIELD	5,990	1,817	4,155	18	2,338 D	30.3%	69.4%	30.4%	69.6%
89,636	FLORENCE	29,938	13,539	16,294	105	2,755 D	45.2%	54.4%	45.4%	54.6%
33,500	GEORGETOWN	11,293	4,068	7,169	56	3,101 D	36.0%	63.5%	36.2%	63.8%
240,546	GREENVILLE	75,961	39,099	35,923	939	3,176 R	51.5%	47.3%	52.1%	47.9%
49,686	GREENWOOD	15,991	5,974	9,976	41	4,002 D	37.4%	62.4%	37.5%	62.5%
15,878	HAMPTON	5,725	1,773	3,923	29	2,150 D	31.0%	68.5%	31.1%	68.9%
69,992	HORRY	25,117	9,339	15,720	58	6,381 D	37.2%	62.6%	37.3%	62.7%
11,885	JASPER	4,140	1,221	2,903	16	1,682 D	29.5%	70.1%	29.6%	70.4%
34,727	KERSHAW	12,402	6,126	6,211	65	85 D	49.4%	50.1%	49.7%	50.3%
43,328	LANCASTER	13,394	4,997	8,324	73	3,327 D	37.3%	62.1%	37.5%	62.5%
49,713	LAURENS	12,831	5,300	7,440	91	2,140 D	41.3%	58.0%	41.6%	58.4%
18,323	LEE	6,257	2,357	3,869	31	1,512 D	37.7%	61.8%	37.9%	62.1%
89,012	LEXINGTON	36,143	21,442	14,339	362	7,103 R	59.3%	39.7%	59.9%	40.1%
7,955	MCCORMICK	2,431	640	1,774	17	1,134 D	26.3%	73.0%	26.5%	73.5%
30,270	MARION	9,024	3,076	5,927	21	2,851 D	34.1%	65.7%	34.2%	65.8%
27,151	MARLBORO	7,377	1,961	5,409	7	3,448 D	26.6%	73.3%	26.6%	73.4%
29,273	NEWBERRY	10,024	4,931	5,034	59	103 D	49.2%	50.2%	49.5%	50.5%
40,728	OCONEE	12,333	3,805	8,447	81	4,642 D	30.9%	68.5%	31.1%	68.9%
69,789	ORANGEBURG	22,604	8,794	13,652	158	4,858 D	38.9%	60.4%	39.2%	60.8%
58,956	PICKENS	16,655	8,029	8,505	121	476 D	48.2%	51.1%	48.6%	51.4%
233,868	RICHLAND	70,153	32,727	36,855	571	4,128 D	46.7%	52.5%	47.0%	53.0%
14,528	SALUDA	4,853	2,085	2,715	53	630 D	43.0%	55.9%	43.4%	56.6%
173,631	SPARTANBURG	48,820	20,456	27,925	439	7,469 D	41.9%	57.2%	42.3%	57.7%
78,885	SUMTER	19,949	9,332	10,471	146	1,139 D	46.8%	52.5%	47.1%	52.9%
29,133	UNION	9,867	3,463	6,363	41	2,900 D	35.1%	64.5%	35.2%	64.8%
34,203	WILLIAMSBURG	14,055	5,275	8,745	35	3,470 D	37.5%	62.2%	37.6%	62.4%
85,216	YORK	24,005	9,843	14,099	63	4,256 D	41.0%	58.7%	41.1%	58.9%
2,589,891	TOTAL	802,583	346,149	450,807	5,627	104,658 D	43.1%	56.2%	43.4%	56.6%

SOUTH CAROLINA

PRESIDENT 1972

1970 Census Population	County	Total Vote	Republican	Democratic	Other	Rep.-Dem. Plurality	Percentage Total Vote Rep.	Percentage Total Vote Dem.	Percentage Major Vote Rep.	Percentage Major Vote Dem.
21,112	ABBEVILLE	4,733	3,265	1,347	121	1,918 R	69.0%	28.5%	70.8%	29.2%
91,023	AIKEN	27,407	21,117	5,745	545	15,372 R	77.0%	21.0%	78.6%	21.4%
9,692	ALLENDALE	3,141	1,740	1,383	18	357 R	55.4%	44.0%	55.7%	44.3%
105,474	ANDERSON	23,292	17,514	5,241	537	12,273 R	75.2%	22.5%	77.0%	23.0%
15,950	BAMBERG	4,253	2,537	1,680	36	857 R	59.7%	39.5%	60.2%	39.8%
17,176	BARNWELL	5,515	3,955	1,560		2,395 R	71.7%	28.3%	71.7%	28.3%
51,136	BEAUFORT	9,247	5,929	3,237	81	2,692 R	64.1%	35.0%	64.7%	35.3%
56,199	BERKELEY	14,019	9,345	4,497	177	4,848 R	66.7%	32.1%	67.5%	32.5%
10,780	CALHOUN	3,069	1,867	1,148	54	719 R	60.8%	37.4%	61.9%	38.1%
247,650	CHARLESTON	57,912	39,832	16,856	1,224	22,976 R	68.8%	29.1%	70.3%	29.7%
36,791	CHEROKEE	9,800	7,570	2,107	123	5,463 R	77.2%	21.5%	78.2%	21.8%
29,811	CHESTER	7,136	4,724	2,352	60	2,372 R	66.2%	33.0%	66.8%	33.2%
33,667	CHESTERFIELD	8,229	5,230	2,938	61	2,292 R	63.6%	35.7%	64.0%	36.0%
25,604	CLARENDON	7,284	3,958	3,276	50	682 R	54.3%	45.0%	54.7%	45.3%
27,622	COLLETON	8,248	5,738	2,376	134	3,362 R	69.6%	28.8%	70.7%	29.3%
53,442	DARLINGTON	16,319	11,756	4,414	149	7,342 R	72.0%	27.0%	72.7%	27.3%
28,838	DILLON	6,034	4,364	1,604	66	2,760 R	72.3%	26.6%	73.1%	26.9%
32,421	DORCHESTER	11,886	8,095	3,606	185	4,489 R	68.1%	30.3%	69.2%	30.8%
15,692	EDGEFIELD	4,218	2,812	1,326	80	1,486 R	66.7%	31.4%	68.0%	32.0%
19,999	FAIRFIELD	5,146	2,608	2,491	47	117 R	50.7%	48.4%	51.1%	48.9%
89,636	FLORENCE	25,723	18,107	7,451	165	10,656 R	70.4%	29.0%	70.8%	29.2%
33,500	GEORGETOWN	10,676	6,114	4,446	116	1,668 R	57.3%	41.6%	57.9%	42.1%
240,546	GREENVILLE	58,249	46,360	10,163	1,726	36,197 R	79.6%	17.4%	82.0%	18.0%
49,686	GREENWOOD	12,975	9,370	3,400	205	5,970 R	72.2%	26.2%	73.4%	26.6%
15,878	HAMPTON	5,036	2,891	2,086	59	805 R	57.4%	41.4%	58.1%	41.9%
69,992	HORRY	19,944	15,324	4,437	183	10,887 R	76.8%	22.2%	77.5%	22.5%
11,885	JASPER	2,884	1,650	1,203	31	447 R	57.2%	41.7%	57.8%	42.2%
34,727	KERSHAW	10,744	8,035	2,531	178	5,504 R	74.8%	23.6%	76.0%	24.0%
43,328	LANCASTER	11,580	9,016	2,461	103	6,555 R	77.9%	21.3%	78.6%	21.4%
49,713	LAURENS	10,933	8,141	2,650	142	5,491 R	74.5%	24.2%	75.4%	24.6%
18,323	LEE	5,100	3,076	1,996	28	1,080 R	60.3%	39.1%	60.6%	39.4%
89,012	LEXINGTON	29,886	25,327	4,069	490	21,258 R	84.7%	13.6%	86.2%	13.8%
7,955	MCCORMICK	2,162	1,302	844	16	458 R	60.2%	39.0%	60.7%	39.3%
30,270	MARION	7,310	4,719	2,545	46	2,174 R	64.6%	34.8%	65.0%	35.0%
27,151	MARLBORO	5,852	3,838	1,999	15	1,839 R	65.6%	34.2%	65.8%	34.2%
29,273	NEWBERRY	9,521	7,325	2,035	161	5,290 R	76.9%	21.4%	78.3%	21.7%
40,728	OCONEE	8,728	6,825	1,739	164	5,086 R	78.2%	19.9%	79.7%	20.3%
69,789	ORANGEBURG	19,745	11,711	7,652	382	4,059 R	59.3%	38.8%	60.5%	39.5%
58,956	PICKENS	14,296	11,776	2,255	265	9,521 R	82.4%	15.8%	83.9%	16.1%
233,868	RICHLAND	60,065	38,500	20,875	690	17,625 R	64.1%	34.8%	64.8%	35.2%
14,528	SALUDA	4,191	3,095	1,022	74	2,073 R	73.8%	24.4%	75.2%	24.8%
173,631	SPARTANBURG	41,572	31,187	9,723	662	21,464 R	75.0%	23.4%	76.2%	23.8%
78,885	SUMTER	16,794	10,892	5,795	107	5,097 R	64.9%	34.5%	65.3%	34.7%
29,133	UNION	11,065	8,337	2,676	52	5,661 R	75.3%	24.2%	75.7%	24.3%
34,203	WILLIAMSBURG	11,015	5,729	5,213	73	516 R	52.0%	47.3%	52.4%	47.6%
85,216	YORK	21,026	14,441	6,374	211	8,067 R	68.7%	30.3%	69.4%	30.6%
2,589,891	TOTAL	673,960	477,044	186,824	10,092	290,220 R	70.8%	27.7%	71.9%	28.1%

SOUTH CAROLINA

PRESIDENT 1968

1960 Census Population	County	Total Vote	Republican	Democratic	AIP	Other	Plurality	Percentage Rep.	Dem.	AIP
21,417	ABBEVILLE	5,839	1,213	1,425	3,201		1,776 A	20.8%	24.4%	54.8%
81,038	AIKEN	27,398	12,264	6,319	8,815		3,449 R	44.8%	23.1%	32.2%
11,362	ALLENDALE	3,355	997	1,538	820		541 D	29.7%	45.8%	24.4%
98,478	ANDERSON	23,263	5,661	5,218	12,384		6,723 A	24.3%	22.4%	53.2%
16,274	BAMBERG	4,790	1,327	1,845	1,618		227 D	27.7%	38.5%	33.8%
17,659	BARNWELL	5,916	1,849	1,716	2,351		502 A	31.3%	29.0%	39.7%
44,187	BEAUFORT	8,221	2,983	3,740	1,498		757 D	36.3%	45.5%	18.2%
38,196	BERKELEY	13,918	4,021	5,089	4,808		281 D	28.9%	36.6%	34.5%
12,256	CALHOUN	3,079	885	1,216	978		238 D	28.7%	39.5%	31.8%
216,382	CHARLESTON	55,880	24,282	18,343	13,255		5,939 R	43.5%	32.8%	23.7%
35,205	CHEROKEE	10,493	2,853	1,998	5,642		2,789 A	27.2%	19.0%	53.8%
30,888	CHESTER	8,489	2,862	2,865	2,762		3 D	33.7%	33.7%	32.5%
33,717	CHESTERFIELD	10,068	2,564	3,180	4,324		1,144 A	25.5%	31.6%	42.9%
29,490	CLARENDON	7,904	2,201	3,606	2,097		1,405 D	27.8%	45.6%	26.5%
27,816	COLLETON	8,145	2,824	2,651	2,670		154 R	34.7%	32.5%	32.8%
52,928	DARLINGTON	13,981	4,947	3,803	5,231		284 A	35.4%	27.2%	37.4%
30,584	DILLON	6,706	2,396	2,178	2,132		218 R	35.7%	32.5%	31.8%
24,383	DORCHESTER	10,748	3,354	3,855	3,539		316 D	31.2%	35.9%	32.9%
15,735	EDGEFIELD	3,919	1,688	1,225	1,006		463 R	43.1%	31.3%	25.7%
20,713	FAIRFIELD	5,966	1,619	3,011	1,336		1,392 D	27.1%	50.5%	22.4%
84,438	FLORENCE	24,638	8,917	8,079	7,642		838 R	36.2%	32.8%	31.0%
34,798	GEORGETOWN	10,021	3,269	4,110	2,642		841 D	32.6%	41.0%	26.4%
209,776	GREENVILLE	59,821	31,652	12,928	15,241		16,411 R	52.9%	21.6%	25.5%
44,346	GREENWOOD	14,656	4,891	3,741	6,024		1,133 A	33.4%	25.5%	41.1%
17,425	HAMPTON	5,230	1,671	2,107	1,452		436 D	32.0%	40.3%	27.8%
68,247	HORRY	14,549	3,924	3,924	6,701		2,777 A	27.0%	27.0%	46.1%
12,237	JASPER	3,116	633	1,402	1,081		321 D	20.3%	45.0%	34.7%
33,585	KERSHAW	10,578	4,079	2,539	3,960		119 R	38.6%	24.0%	37.4%
39,352	LANCASTER	12,911	4,874	3,151	4,886		12 A	37.8%	24.4%	37.8%
47,609	LAURENS	12,108	4,813	3,016	4,279		534 R	39.8%	24.9%	35.3%
21,832	LEE	5,483	1,219	2,151	2,113		38 D	22.2%	39.2%	38.5%
60,726	LEXINGTON	25,169	12,204	4,058	8,907		3,297 R	48.5%	16.1%	35.4%
8,629	MCCORMICK	2,211	466	988	757		231 D	21.1%	44.7%	34.2%
32,014	MARION	6,817	2,512	2,821	1,484		309 D	36.8%	41.4%	21.8%
28,529	MARLBORO	6,458	2,024	2,294	2,140		154 D	31.3%	35.5%	33.1%
29,416	NEWBERRY	10,716	4,538	2,444	3,734		804 R	42.3%	22.8%	34.8%
40,204	OCONEE	9,369	2,618	2,009	4,742		2,124 A	27.9%	21.4%	50.6%
68,559	ORANGEBURG	21,259	5,144	8,971	7,144		1,827 D	24.2%	42.2%	33.6%
46,030	PICKENS	13,313	6,873	2,016	4,424		2,449 R	51.6%	15.1%	33.2%
200,102	RICHLAND	51,443	26,215	18,198	7,030		8,017 R	51.0%	35.4%	13.7%
14,554	SALUDA	4,802	1,466	1,200	2,136		670 A	30.5%	25.0%	44.5%
156,830	SPARTANBURG	46,996	18,183	11,467	17,346		837 R	38.7%	24.4%	36.9%
74,941	SUMTER	16,308	5,451	6,103	4,754		652 D	33.4%	37.4%	29.2%
30,015	UNION	9,872	3,011	2,271	4,590		1,579 A	30.5%	23.0%	46.5%
40,932	WILLIAMSBURG	10,787	3,029	5,106	2,652		2,077 D	28.1%	47.3%	24.6%
78,760	YORK	20,269	7,596	5,571	7,102		494 R	37.5%	27.5%	35.0%
2,382,594	TOTAL	666,978	254,062	197,486	215,430		38,632 R	38.1%	29.6%	32.3%

SOUTH CAROLINA

ELECTION NOTES

1984 Other vote was 4,359 Bergland (Libertarian); 3,490 Dennis (American); 682 Serrette (United Citizens). Small adjustments were made in the canvass printed in the "Annual Report of the South Carolina Election Commission". The Democratic vote in Charleston county was amended to read 29,481 which changed the Democratic state-wide total vote to 344,459; the Libertarian vote in Orangeburg county was increased by one to 55; the United Citizens vote in Sumter county was decreased by one to 16. The data used in the detailed table are for the original canvass.

1980 Other vote was 14,153 Anderson (Independent); 5,139 Clark (Libertarian); 2,177 Rarick (Independent); 376 scattered write-in. The state-wide total for the other vote column includes these 376 scattered write-in votes not reported by county.

1976 Other vote was 2,996 Anderson (American); 1,950 Maddox (Independent); 289 McCarthy (write-in); 53 MacBride (write-in); 8 Camejo (write-in); 2 LaRouche (write-in); 1 Hall (write-in); 328 scattered write-in.

1972 Other vote was 10,075 Schmitz (Independent); 17 scattered write-in. The Democratic candidate was also the United Citizens nominee and 2,265 of his votes were received as the United Citizens candidate. Early unamended canvass gave the Democratic vote in Marlboro county as 2,990.

1968 Wallace on the ballot as Independent.

SOUTH DAKOTA

POPULAR VOTE FOR PRESIDENT 1920 TO 1984

		Republican		Democratic				Percentage			
	Total					Other		Total Vote		Major Vote	
Year	Vote	Vote	Candidate	Vote	Candidate	Vote	Plurality	Rep.	Dem.	Rep.	Dem.
1984	317,867	200,267	Reagan, Ronald	116,113	Mondale, Walter F.	1,487	84,154 R	63.0%	36.5%	63.3%	36.7%
1980	327,703	198,343	Reagan, Ronald	103,855	Carter, Jimmy	25,505	94,488 R	60.5%	31.7%	65.6%	34.4%
1976	300,678	151,505	Ford, Gerald R.	147,068	Carter, Jimmy	2,105	4,437 R	50.4%	48.9%	50.7%	49.3%
1972	307,415	166,476	Nixon, Richard M.	139,945	McGovern, George S.	994	26,531 R	54.2%	45.5%	54.3%	45.7%
1968	281,264	149,841	Nixon, Richard M.	118,023	Humphrey, Hubert H.	13,400	31,818 R	53.3%	42.0%	55.9%	44.1%
1964	293,118	130,108	Goldwater, Barry M.	163,010	Johnson, Lyndon B.		32,902 D	44.4%	55.6%	44.4%	55.6%
1960	306,487	178,417	Nixon, Richard M.	128,070	Kennedy, John F.		50,347 R	58.2%	41.8%	58.2%	41.8%
1956	293,857	171,569	Eisenhower, Dwight D.	122,288	Stevenson, Adlai E.		49,281 R	58.4%	41.6%	58.4%	41.6%
1952	294,283	203,857	Eisenhower, Dwight D.	90,426	Stevenson, Adlai E.		113,431 R	69.3%	30.7%	69.3%	30.7%
1948	250,105	129,651	Dewey, Thomas E.	117,653	Truman, Harry S.	2,801	11,998 R	51.8%	47.0%	52.4%	47.6%
1944	232,076	135,365	Dewey, Thomas E.	96,711	Roosevelt, Franklin D.		38,654 R	58.3%	41.7%	58.3%	41.7%
1940	308,427	177,065	Willkie, Wendell	131,362	Roosevelt, Franklin D.		45,703 R	57.4%	42.6%	57.4%	42.6%
1936	296,452	125,977	Landon, Alfred M.	160,137	Roosevelt, Franklin D.	10,338	34,160 D	42.5%	54.0%	44.0%	56.0%
1932	288,438	99,212	Hoover, Herbert C.	183,515	Roosevelt, Franklin D.	5,711	84,303 D	34.4%	63.6%	35.1%	64.9%
1928	261,857	157,603	Hoover, Herbert C.	102,660	Smith, Alfred E.	1,594	54,943 R	60.2%	39.2%	60.6%	39.4%
1924 **	203,868	101,299	Coolidge, Calvin	27,214	Davis, John W.	75,355	25,944 R	49.7%	13.3%	78.8%	21.2%
1920 **	182,237	110,692	Harding, Warren G.	35,938	Cox, James M.	35,607	74,754 R	60.7%	19.7%	75.5%	24.5%

In 1924 other vote was Progressive. In 1920 other vote was 34,707 Farmer-Labor and 900 Prohibition.

ELECTORAL COLLEGE VOTE 1920 TO 1984

Year	Total	Republican	Democratic	Other
1984	3	3	—	—
1980	4	4	—	—
1976	4	4	—	—
1972	4	4	—	—
1968	4	4	—	—
1964	4	—	4	—
1960	4	4	—	—
1956	4	4	—	—
1952	4	4	—	—
1948	4	4	—	—
1944	4	4	—	—
1940	4	4	—	—
1936	4	—	4	—
1932	4	—	4	—
1928	5	5	—	—
1924	5	5	—	—
1920	5	5	—	—

SOUTH DAKOTA

SOUTH DAKOTA

PRESIDENT 1984

1980 Census Population	County	Total Vote	Republican	Democratic	Other	Rep.-Dem. Plurality	Percentage Total Vote Rep.	Percentage Total Vote Dem.	Percentage Major Vote Rep.	Percentage Major Vote Dem.
3,628	AURORA	1,883	1,029	840	14	189 R	54.6%	44.6%	55.1%	44.9%
19,195	BEADLE	9,422	5,876	3,523	23	2,353 R	62.4%	37.4%	62.5%	37.5%
3,044	BENNETT	1,316	856	453	7	403 R	65.0%	34.4%	65.4%	34.6%
8,059	BONHOMME	3,906	2,478	1,408	20	1,070 R	63.4%	36.0%	63.8%	36.2%
24,332	BROOKINGS	10,814	6,679	4,089	46	2,590 R	61.8%	37.8%	62.0%	38.0%
36,962	BROWN	17,465	10,541	6,852	72	3,689 R	60.4%	39.2%	60.6%	39.4%
5,245	BRULE	2,556	1,578	961	17	617 R	61.7%	37.6%	62.2%	37.8%
1,795	BUFFALO	494	253	236	5	17 R	51.2%	47.8%	51.7%	48.3%
8,372	BUTTE	3,667	2,865	784	18	2,081 R	78.1%	21.4%	78.5%	21.5%
2,243	CAMPBELL	1,255	1,035	214	6	821 R	82.5%	17.1%	82.9%	17.1%
9,680	CHARLES MIX	4,563	2,660	1,879	24	781 R	58.3%	41.2%	58.6%	41.4%
4,894	CLARK	2,718	1,748	960	10	788 R	64.3%	35.3%	64.5%	35.5%
13,689	CLAY	5,808	3,057	2,711	40	346 R	52.6%	46.7%	53.0%	47.0%
20,885	CODINGTON	9,678	6,108	3,528	42	2,580 R	63.1%	36.5%	63.4%	36.6%
5,196	CORSON	1,753	955	792	6	163 R	54.5%	45.2%	54.7%	45.3%
6,000	CUSTER	3,063	2,183	858	22	1,325 R	71.3%	28.0%	71.8%	28.2%
17,820	DAVISON	8,048	4,783	3,248	17	1,535 R	59.4%	40.4%	59.6%	40.4%
8,133	DAY	4,101	2,150	1,932	19	218 R	52.4%	47.1%	52.7%	47.3%
5,289	DEUEL	2,490	1,537	941	12	596 R	61.7%	37.8%	62.0%	38.0%
5,366	DEWEY	1,727	941	772	14	169 R	54.5%	44.7%	54.9%	45.1%
4,181	DOUGLAS	2,254	1,713	536	5	1,177 R	76.0%	23.8%	76.2%	23.8%
5,159	EDMUNDS	2,570	1,553	1,007	10	546 R	60.4%	39.2%	60.7%	39.3%
8,439	FALL RIVER	3,905	2,748	1,135	22	1,613 R	70.4%	29.1%	70.8%	29.2%
3,327	FAULK	1,706	1,124	579	3	545 R	65.9%	33.9%	66.0%	34.0%
9,013	GRANT	4,360	2,738	1,606	16	1,132 R	62.8%	36.8%	63.0%	37.0%
6,015	GREGORY	2,569	1,777	780	12	997 R	69.2%	30.4%	69.5%	30.5%
2,794	HAAKON	1,410	1,168	237	5	931 R	82.8%	16.8%	83.1%	16.9%
5,261	HAMLIN	2,761	1,782	963	16	819 R	64.5%	34.9%	64.9%	35.1%
4,948	HAND	2,886	2,030	846	10	1,184 R	70.3%	29.3%	70.6%	29.4%
3,415	HANSON	1,530	898	625	7	273 R	58.7%	40.8%	59.0%	41.0%
1,700	HARDING	912	723	186	3	537 R	79.3%	20.4%	79.5%	20.5%
14,220	HUGHES	7,089	4,985	2,072	32	2,913 R	70.3%	29.2%	70.6%	29.4%
9,350	HUTCHINSON	4,624	3,372	1,237	15	2,135 R	72.9%	26.8%	73.2%	26.8%
2,069	HYDE	1,148	797	350	1	447 R	69.4%	30.5%	69.5%	30.5%
3,437	JACKSON	1,275	903	365	7	538 R	70.8%	28.6%	71.2%	28.8%
2,929	JERAULD	1,562	1,012	542	8	470 R	64.8%	34.7%	65.1%	34.9%
1,463	JONES	899	689	206	4	483 R	76.6%	22.9%	77.0%	23.0%
6,679	KINGSBURY	3,383	2,121	1,249	13	872 R	62.7%	36.9%	62.9%	37.1%
10,724	LAKE	5,413	3,027	2,367	19	660 R	55.9%	43.7%	56.1%	43.9%
18,339	LAWRENCE	8,569	5,949	2,565	55	3,384 R	69.4%	29.9%	69.9%	30.1%
13,942	LINCOLN	6,636	3,988	2,626	22	1,362 R	60.1%	39.6%	60.3%	39.7%
3,864	LYMAN	1,605	1,120	478	7	642 R	69.8%	29.8%	70.1%	29.9%
6,444	MCCOOK	3,362	1,902	1,448	12	454 R	56.6%	43.1%	56.8%	43.2%
4,027	MCPHERSON	2,236	1,813	418	5	1,395 R	81.1%	18.7%	81.3%	18.7%
5,404	MARSHALL	2,649	1,529	1,111	9	418 R	57.7%	41.9%	57.9%	42.1%
20,717	MEADE	8,041	5,908	2,093	40	3,815 R	73.5%	26.0%	73.8%	26.2%
2,249	MELLETTE	927	616	303	8	313 R	66.5%	32.7%	67.0%	33.0%
3,739	MINER	1,977	1,004	960	13	44 R	50.8%	48.6%	51.1%	48.9%
109,435	MINNEHAHA	53,171	29,908	23,042	221	6,866 R	56.2%	43.3%	56.5%	43.5%
6,692	MOODY	3,228	1,633	1,586	9	47 R	50.6%	49.1%	50.7%	49.3%
70,361	PENNINGTON	30,389	21,947	8,224	218	13,723 R	72.2%	27.1%	72.7%	27.3%
4,700	PERKINS	2,411	1,686	714	11	972 R	69.9%	29.6%	70.3%	29.8%
3,674	POTTER	2,035	1,551	482	2	1,069 R	76.2%	23.7%	76.3%	23.7%
10,911	ROBERTS	4,840	2,767	2,063	10	704 R	57.2%	42.6%	57.3%	42.7%
3,213	SANBORN	1,695	1,080	611	4	469 R	63.7%	36.0%	63.9%	36.1%
11,323	SHANNON	1,829	324	1,489	16	1,165 D	17.7%	81.4%	17.9%	82.1%
9,201	SPINK	4,324	2,627	1,680	17	947 R	60.8%	38.9%	61.0%	39.0%
2,533	STANLEY	1,299	942	351	6	591 R	72.5%	27.0%	72.9%	27.1%
1,990	SULLY	1,107	836	266	5	570 R	75.5%	24.0%	75.9%	24.1%
7,328	TODD	1,714	679	1,022	13	343 D	39.6%	59.6%	39.9%	60.1%

SOUTH DAKOTA

PRESIDENT 1984

1980 Census Population	County	Total Vote	Republican	Democratic	Other	Rep.-Dem. Plurality	Percentage Total Vote Rep.	Total Vote Dem.	Major Vote Rep.	Major Vote Dem.
7,268	TRIPP	3,440	2,483	935	22	1,548 R	72.2%	27.2%	72.6%	27.4%
9,255	TURNER	4,592	3,086	1,486	20	1,600 R	67.2%	32.4%	67.5%	32.5%
10,938	UNION	4,677	2,431	2,221	25	210 R	52.0%	47.5%	52.3%	47.7%
7,011	WALWORTH	3,194	2,396	779	19	1,617 R	75.0%	24.4%	75.5%	24.5%
	WASHABAUGH									
18,952	YANKTON	8,145	5,161	2,932	52	2,229 R	63.4%	36.0%	63.8%	36.2%
2,308	ZIEBACH	792	429	359	4	70 R	54.2%	45.3%	54.4%	45.6%
690,768	TOTAL	317,867	200,267	116,113	1,487	84,154 R	63.0%	36.5%	63.3%	36.7%

SOUTH DAKOTA

PRESIDENT 1980

1980 Census Population	County	Total Vote	Republican	Democratic	Other	Rep.-Dem. Plurality	Percentage: Total Vote Rep.	Total Vote Dem.	Major Vote Rep.	Major Vote Dem.
3,628	AURORA	2,123	1,251	709	163	542 R	58.9%	33.4%	63.8%	36.2%
19,195	BEADLE	10,104	5,921	3,521	662	2,400 R	58.6%	34.8%	62.7%	37.3%
3,044	BENNETT	1,324	919	350	55	569 R	69.4%	26.4%	72.4%	27.6%
8,059	BONHOMME	4,239	2,794	1,191	254	1,603 R	65.9%	28.1%	70.1%	29.9%
24,332	BROOKINGS	10,981	5,727	3,934	1,320	1,793 R	52.2%	35.8%	59.3%	40.7%
36,962	BROWN	17,999	10,550	6,050	1,399	4,500 R	58.6%	33.6%	63.6%	36.4%
5,245	BRULE	2,800	1,674	925	201	749 R	59.8%	33.0%	64.4%	35.6%
1,795	BUFFALO	456	272	147	37	125 R	59.6%	32.2%	64.9%	35.1%
8,372	BUTTE	3,898	2,850	843	205	2,007 R	73.1%	21.6%	77.2%	22.8%
2,243	CAMPBELL	1,498	1,271	182	45	1,089 R	84.8%	12.1%	87.5%	12.5%
9,680	CHARLES MIX	4,599	2,608	1,741	250	867 R	56.7%	37.9%	60.0%	40.0%
4,894	CLARK	2,911	1,963	774	174	1,189 R	67.4%	26.6%	71.7%	28.3%
13,689	CLAY	6,316	3,004	2,271	1,041	733 R	47.6%	36.0%	56.9%	43.1%
20,885	CODINGTON	9,990	5,903	3,353	734	2,550 R	59.1%	33.6%	63.8%	36.2%
5,196	CORSON	1,855	1,233	522	100	711 R	66.5%	28.1%	70.3%	29.7%
6,000	CUSTER	2,955	2,057	708	190	1,349 R	69.6%	24.0%	74.4%	25.6%
17,820	DAVISON	8,512	4,743	3,107	662	1,636 R	55.7%	36.5%	60.4%	39.6%
8,133	DAY	4,543	2,507	1,720	316	787 R	55.2%	37.9%	59.3%	40.7%
5,289	DEUEL	2,744	1,657	891	196	766 R	60.4%	32.5%	65.0%	35.0%
5,366	DEWEY	1,767	1,045	600	122	445 R	59.1%	34.0%	63.5%	36.5%
4,181	DOUGLAS	2,463	1,855	508	100	1,347 R	75.3%	20.6%	78.5%	21.5%
5,159	EDMUNDS	2,914	1,881	883	150	998 R	64.6%	30.3%	68.1%	31.9%
8,439	FALL RIVER	4,067	2,831	982	254	1,849 R	69.6%	24.1%	74.2%	25.8%
3,327	FAULK	1,945	1,300	520	125	780 R	66.8%	26.7%	71.4%	28.6%
9,013	GRANT	4,594	2,691	1,602	301	1,089 R	58.6%	34.9%	62.7%	37.3%
6,015	GREGORY	3,340	2,283	883	174	1,400 R	68.4%	26.4%	72.1%	27.9%
2,794	HAAKON	1,465	1,162	255	48	907 R	79.3%	17.4%	82.0%	18.0%
5,261	HAMLIN	3,007	1,885	903	219	982 R	62.7%	30.0%	67.6%	32.4%
4,948	HAND	3,066	2,066	803	197	1,263 R	67.4%	26.2%	72.0%	28.0%
3,415	HANSON	1,725	1,015	598	112	417 R	58.8%	34.7%	62.9%	37.1%
1,700	HARDING	974	727	205	42	522 R	74.6%	21.0%	78.0%	22.0%
14,220	HUGHES	7,048	4,652	1,751	645	2,901 R	66.0%	24.8%	72.7%	27.3%
9,350	HUTCHINSON	5,180	3,789	1,145	246	2,644 R	73.1%	22.1%	76.8%	23.2%
2,069	HYDE	1,221	864	273	84	591 R	70.8%	22.4%	76.0%	24.0%
3,437	JACKSON	1,352	929	354	69	575 R	68.7%	26.2%	72.4%	27.6%
2,929	JERAULD	1,729	1,018	595	116	423 R	58.9%	34.4%	63.1%	36.9%
1,463	JONES	919	689	189	41	500 R	75.0%	20.6%	78.5%	21.5%
6,679	KINGSBURY	3,807	2,376	1,132	299	1,244 R	62.4%	29.7%	67.7%	32.3%
10,724	LAKE	5,852	3,093	2,207	552	886 R	52.9%	37.7%	58.4%	41.6%
18,339	LAWRENCE	8,403	5,306	2,259	838	3,047 R	63.1%	26.9%	70.1%	29.9%
13,942	LINCOLN	6,698	3,848	2,261	589	1,587 R	57.4%	33.8%	63.0%	37.0%
3,864	LYMAN	1,878	1,256	486	136	770 R	66.9%	25.9%	72.1%	27.9%
6,444	MCCOOK	3,544	2,014	1,223	307	791 R	56.8%	34.5%	62.2%	37.8%
4,027	MCPHERSON	2,402	2,056	287	59	1,769 R	85.6%	11.9%	87.8%	12.2%
5,404	MARSHALL	3,001	1,710	1,120	171	590 R	57.0%	37.3%	60.4%	39.6%
20,717	MEADE	7,541	5,349	1,721	471	3,628 R	70.9%	22.8%	75.7%	24.3%
2,249	MELLETTE	963	624	279	60	345 R	64.8%	29.0%	69.1%	30.9%
3,739	MINER	2,171	1,172	833	166	339 R	54.0%	38.4%	58.5%	41.5%
109,435	MINNEHAHA	51,478	26,256	20,008	5,214	6,248 R	51.0%	38.9%	56.8%	43.2%
6,692	MOODY	3,480	1,807	1,364	309	443 R	51.9%	39.2%	57.0%	43.0%
70,361	PENNINGTON	28,204	18,991	7,121	2,092	11,870 R	67.3%	25.2%	72.7%	27.3%
4,700	PERKINS	2,655	1,931	595	129	1,336 R	72.7%	22.4%	76.4%	23.6%
3,674	POTTER	2,169	1,633	436	100	1,197 R	75.3%	20.1%	78.9%	21.1%
10,911	ROBERTS	5,009	2,904	1,829	276	1,075 R	58.0%	36.5%	61.4%	38.6%
3,213	SANBORN	1,932	1,178	628	126	550 R	61.0%	32.5%	65.2%	34.8%
11,323	SHANNON	1,687	438	1,132	117	694 D	26.0%	67.1%	27.9%	72.1%
9,201	SPINK	4,834	2,915	1,572	347	1,343 R	60.3%	32.5%	65.0%	35.0%
2,533	STANLEY	1,299	892	339	68	553 R	68.7%	26.1%	72.5%	27.5%
1,990	SULLY	1,149	852	220	77	632 R	74.2%	19.1%	79.5%	20.5%
7,328	TODD	1,923	803	972	148	169 D	41.8%	50.5%	45.2%	54.8%

SOUTH DAKOTA

PRESIDENT 1980

1980 Census Population	County	Total Vote	Republican	Democratic	Other	Rep.-Dem. Plurality	Percentage Total Vote Rep.	Percentage Total Vote Dem.	Percentage Major Vote Rep.	Percentage Major Vote Dem.
7,268	TRIPP	3,776	2,669	947	160	1,722 R	70.7%	25.1%	73.8%	26.2%
9,255	TURNER	5,032	3,343	1,369	320	1,974 R	66.4%	27.2%	70.9%	29.1%
10,938	UNION	5,054	2,788	1,830	436	958 R	55.2%	36.2%	60.4%	39.6%
7,011	WALWORTH	3,588	2,675	753	160	1,922 R	74.6%	21.0%	78.0%	22.0%
	WASHABAUGH									
18,952	YANKTON	8,747	5,355	2,698	694	2,657 R	61.2%	30.8%	66.5%	33.5%
2,308	ZIEBACH	804	523	246	35	277 R	65.0%	30.6%	68.0%	32.0%
690,768	TOTAL	327,703	198,343	103,855	25,505	94,488 R	60.5%	31.7%	65.6%	34.4%

SOUTH DAKOTA

PRESIDENT 1976

1970 Census Population	County	Total Vote	Republican	Democratic	Other	Rep.-Dem. Plurality	Percentage Total Vote Rep.	Percentage Total Vote Dem.	Percentage Major Vote Rep.	Percentage Major Vote Dem.
4,183	AURORA	2,109	831	1,269	9	438 D	39.4%	60.2%	39.6%	60.4%
20,877	BEADLE	9,666	4,758	4,846	62	88 D	49.2%	50.1%	49.5%	50.5%
3,088	BENNETT	1,111	610	481	20	129 R	54.9%	43.3%	55.9%	44.1%
8,577	BONHOMME	4,073	1,897	2,154	22	257 D	46.6%	52.9%	46.8%	53.2%
22,158	BROOKINGS	10,026	5,278	4,685	63	593 R	52.6%	46.7%	53.0%	47.0%
36,920	BROWN	16,633	7,609	8,888	136	1,279 D	45.7%	53.4%	46.1%	53.9%
5,870	BRULE	2,723	1,175	1,534	14	359 D	43.2%	56.3%	43.4%	56.6%
1,739	BUFFALO	434	194	240		46 D	44.7%	55.3%	44.7%	55.3%
7,825	BUTTE	3,472	2,055	1,366	51	689 R	59.2%	39.3%	60.1%	39.9%
2,866	CAMPBELL	1,391	897	489	5	408 R	64.5%	35.2%	64.7%	35.3%
9,994	CHARLES MIX	4,394	1,779	2,593	22	814 D	40.5%	59.0%	40.7%	59.3%
5,515	CLARK	2,838	1,449	1,376	13	73 R	51.1%	48.5%	51.3%	48.7%
12,923	CLAY	5,301	2,647	2,593	61	54 R	49.9%	48.9%	50.5%	49.5%
19,140	CODINGTON	9,213	4,504	4,680	29	176 D	48.9%	50.8%	49.0%	51.0%
4,994	CORSON	1,823	846	967	10	121 D	46.4%	53.0%	46.7%	53.3%
4,698	CUSTER	2,405	1,373	995	37	378 R	57.1%	41.4%	58.0%	42.0%
17,319	DAVISON	8,248	3,688	4,510	50	822 D	44.7%	54.7%	45.0%	55.0%
8,713	DAY	4,257	1,617	2,610	30	993 D	38.0%	61.3%	38.3%	61.7%
5,686	DEUEL	2,652	1,177	1,465	10	288 D	44.4%	55.2%	44.5%	55.5%
5,170	DEWEY	1,534	820	706	8	114 R	53.5%	46.0%	53.7%	46.3%
4,569	DOUGLAS	2,295	1,315	975	5	340 R	57.3%	42.5%	57.4%	42.6%
5,548	EDMUNDS	2,932	1,294	1,629	9	335 D	44.1%	55.6%	44.3%	55.7%
7,505	FALL RIVER	3,615	2,046	1,537	32	509 R	56.6%	42.5%	57.1%	42.9%
3,893	FAULK	1,937	868	1,063	6	195 D	44.8%	54.9%	45.0%	55.0%
9,005	GRANT	4,464	2,051	2,398	15	347 D	45.9%	53.7%	46.1%	53.9%
6,710	GREGORY	3,145	1,475	1,658	12	183 D	46.9%	52.7%	47.1%	52.9%
2,802	HAAKON	1,312	812	477	23	335 R	61.9%	36.4%	63.0%	37.0%
5,520	HAMLIN	2,866	1,452	1,402	12	50 R	50.7%	48.9%	50.9%	49.1%
5,883	HAND	2,994	1,510	1,477	7	33 R	50.4%	49.3%	50.6%	49.4%
3,781	HANSON	1,707	693	1,005	9	312 D	40.6%	58.9%	40.8%	59.2%
1,855	HARDING	945	470	459	16	11 R	49.7%	48.6%	50.6%	49.4%
11,632	HUGHES	6,536	3,997	2,506	33	1,491 R	61.2%	38.3%	61.5%	38.5%
10,379	HUTCHINSON	4,906	2,822	2,062	22	760 R	57.5%	42.0%	57.8%	42.2%
2,515	HYDE	1,263	687	572	4	115 R	54.4%	45.3%	54.6%	45.4%
1,531	JACKSON	865	532	313	20	219 R	61.5%	36.2%	63.0%	37.0%
3,310	JERAULD	1,669	821	845	3	24 D	49.2%	50.6%	49.3%	50.7%
1,882	JONES	890	515	374	1	141 R	57.9%	42.0%	57.9%	42.1%
7,657	KINGSBURY	3,617	1,844	1,762	11	82 R	51.0%	48.7%	51.1%	48.9%
11,456	LAKE	5,476	2,530	2,930	16	400 D	46.2%	53.5%	46.3%	53.7%
17,453	LAWRENCE	7,449	4,206	3,102	141	1,104 R	56.5%	41.6%	57.6%	42.4%
11,761	LINCOLN	6,084	3,105	2,957	22	148 R	51.0%	48.6%	51.2%	48.8%
4,060	LYMAN	1,739	892	831	16	61 R	51.3%	47.8%	51.8%	48.2%
7,246	MCCOOK	3,578	1,744	1,822	12	78 D	48.7%	50.9%	48.9%	51.1%
5,022	MCPHERSON	2,367	1,662	693	12	969 R	70.2%	29.3%	70.6%	29.4%
5,965	MARSHALL	2,967	1,233	1,721	13	488 D	41.6%	58.0%	41.7%	58.3%
17,020	MEADE	5,690	3,096	2,478	116	618 R	54.4%	43.6%	55.5%	44.5%
2,420	MELLETTE	949	508	429	12	79 R	53.5%	45.2%	54.2%	45.8%
4,454	MINER	2,140	839	1,289	12	450 D	39.2%	60.2%	39.4%	60.6%
95,209	MINNEHAHA	45,556	23,286	22,068	202	1,218 R	51.1%	48.4%	51.3%	48.7%
7,622	MOODY	3,428	1,475	1,942	11	467 D	43.0%	56.7%	43.2%	56.8%
59,349	PENNINGTON	23,699	13,352	10,058	289	3,294 R	56.3%	42.4%	57.0%	43.0%
4,769	PERKINS	2,592	1,298	1,262	32	36 R	50.1%	48.7%	50.7%	49.3%
4,449	POTTER	2,052	1,136	908	8	228 R	55.4%	44.2%	55.6%	44.4%
11,678	ROBERTS	4,820	1,915	2,890	15	975 D	39.7%	60.0%	39.9%	60.1%
3,697	SANBORN	1,912	881	1,025	6	144 D	46.1%	53.6%	46.2%	53.8%
8,198	SHANNON	1,081	301	756	24	455 D	27.8%	69.9%	28.5%	71.5%
10,595	SPINK	4,679	2,003	2,650	26	647 D	42.8%	56.6%	43.0%	57.0%
2,457	STANLEY	1,189	637	548	4	89 R	53.6%	46.1%	53.8%	46.2%
2,362	SULLY	1,139	630	505	4	125 R	55.3%	44.3%	55.5%	44.5%
6,606	TODD	1,434	583	826	25	243 D	40.7%	57.6%	41.4%	58.6%

SOUTH DAKOTA

PRESIDENT 1976

1970 Census Population	County	Total Vote	Republican	Democratic	Other	Rep.-Dem. Plurality	Percentage Total Vote Rep.	Percentage Total Vote Dem.	Percentage Major Vote Rep.	Percentage Major Vote Dem.
8,171	TRIPP	3,817	1,980	1,822	15	158 R	51.9%	47.7%	52.1%	47.9%
9,872	TURNER	4,618	2,694	1,906	18	788 R	58.3%	41.3%	58.6%	41.4%
9,643	UNION	4,860	2,297	2,540	23	243 D	47.3%	52.3%	47.5%	52.5%
7,842	WALWORTH	3,728	2,187	1,516	25	671 R	58.7%	40.7%	59.1%	40.9%
1,389	WASHABAUGH	526	229	276	21	47 D	43.5%	52.5%	45.3%	54.7%
19,039	YANKTON	8,087	4,029	3,987	71	42 R	49.8%	49.3%	50.3%	49.7%
2,221	ZIEBACH	761	369	370	22	1 D	48.5%	48.6%	49.9%	50.1%
666,257	TOTAL	300,678	151,505	147,068	2,105	4,437 R	50.4%	48.9%	50.7%	49.3%

SOUTH DAKOTA

PRESIDENT 1972

1970 Census Population	County	Total Vote	Republican	Democratic	Other	Rep.-Dem. Plurality	Percentage Total Vote Rep.	Percentage Total Vote Dem.	Percentage Major Vote Rep.	Percentage Major Vote Dem.
4,183	AURORA	2,339	1,075	1,257	7	182 D	46.0%	53.7%	46.1%	53.9%
20,877	BEADLE	10,244	5,922	4,297	25	1,625 R	57.8%	41.9%	58.0%	42.0%
3,088	BENNETT	1,286	808	476	2	332 R	62.8%	37.0%	62.9%	37.1%
8,577	BONHOMME	4,493	2,116	2,368	9	252 D	47.1%	52.7%	47.2%	52.8%
22,158	BROOKINGS	9,916	5,182	4,701	33	481 R	52.3%	47.4%	52.4%	47.6%
36,920	BROWN	16,451	8,134	8,216	101	82 D	49.4%	49.9%	49.7%	50.3%
5,870	BRULE	3,097	1,421	1,665	11	244 D	45.9%	53.8%	46.0%	54.0%
1,739	BUFFALO	497	221	275	1	54 D	44.5%	55.3%	44.6%	55.4%
7,825	BUTTE	3,563	2,452	1,085	26	1,367 R	68.8%	30.5%	69.3%	30.7%
2,866	CAMPBELL	1,537	1,169	361	7	808 R	76.1%	23.5%	76.4%	23.6%
9,994	CHARLES MIX	4,721	2,020	2,691	10	671 D	42.8%	57.0%	42.9%	57.1%
5,515	CLARK	2,962	1,617	1,336	9	281 R	54.6%	45.1%	54.8%	45.2%
12,923	CLAY	5,352	2,518	2,821	13	303 D	47.0%	52.7%	47.2%	52.8%
19,140	CODINGTON	9,564	4,936	4,601	27	335 R	51.6%	48.1%	51.8%	48.2%
4,994	CORSON	1,673	975	689	9	286 R	58.3%	41.2%	58.6%	41.4%
4,698	CUSTER	2,289	1,476	798	15	678 R	64.5%	34.9%	64.9%	35.1%
17,319	DAVISON	8,531	3,796	4,710	25	914 D	44.5%	55.2%	44.6%	55.4%
8,713	DAY	4,699	1,971	2,719	9	748 D	41.9%	57.9%	42.0%	58.0%
5,686	DEUEL	2,736	1,357	1,370	9	13 D	49.6%	50.1%	49.8%	50.2%
5,170	DEWEY	1,712	1,008	699	5	309 R	58.9%	40.8%	59.1%	40.9%
4,569	DOUGLAS	2,325	1,434	887	4	547 R	61.7%	38.2%	61.8%	38.2%
5,548	EDMUNDS	3,216	1,567	1,646	3	79 D	48.7%	51.2%	48.8%	51.2%
7,505	FALL RIVER	3,497	2,374	1,107	16	1,267 R	67.9%	31.7%	68.2%	31.8%
3,893	FAULK	2,005	1,004	986	15	18 R	50.1%	49.2%	50.5%	49.5%
9,005	GRANT	4,490	2,247	2,231	12	16 R	50.0%	49.7%	50.2%	49.8%
6,710	GREGORY	3,237	1,670	1,555	12	115 R	51.6%	48.0%	51.8%	48.2%
2,802	HAAKON	1,396	1,021	366	9	655 R	73.1%	26.2%	73.6%	26.4%
5,520	HAMLIN	2,978	1,693	1,276	9	417 R	56.9%	42.8%	57.0%	43.0%
5,883	HAND	3,119	1,806	1,307	6	499 R	57.9%	41.9%	58.0%	42.0%
3,781	HANSON	1,906	876	1,022	8	146 D	46.0%	53.6%	46.2%	53.8%
1,855	HARDING	890	637	253		384 R	71.6%	28.4%	71.6%	28.4%
11,632	HUGHES	6,282	4,231	2,037	14	2,194 R	67.4%	32.4%	67.5%	32.5%
10,379	HUTCHINSON	5,348	3,092	2,248	8	844 R	57.8%	42.0%	57.9%	42.1%
2,515	HYDE	1,326	789	533	4	256 R	59.5%	40.2%	59.7%	40.3%
1,531	JACKSON	846	581	261	4	320 R	68.7%	30.9%	69.0%	31.0%
3,310	JERAULD	1,820	988	829	3	159 R	54.3%	45.5%	54.4%	45.6%
1,882	JONES	997	642	346	9	296 R	64.4%	34.7%	65.0%	35.0%
7,657	KINGSBURY	3,958	2,320	1,632	6	688 R	58.6%	41.2%	58.7%	41.3%
11,456	LAKE	5,822	2,919	2,886	17	33 R	50.1%	49.6%	50.3%	49.7%
17,453	LAWRENCE	7,352	4,795	2,533	24	2,262 R	65.2%	34.5%	65.4%	34.6%
11,761	LINCOLN	5,828	3,201	2,617	10	584 R	54.9%	44.9%	55.0%	45.0%
4,060	LYMAN	1,944	1,166	774	4	392 R	60.0%	39.8%	60.1%	39.9%
7,246	MCCOOK	3,963	1,963	1,993	7	30 D	49.5%	50.3%	49.6%	50.4%
5,022	MCPHERSON	2,535	1,950	579	6	1,371 R	76.9%	22.8%	77.1%	22.9%
5,965	MARSHALL	3,147	1,500	1,646	1	146 D	47.7%	52.3%	47.7%	52.3%
17,020	MEADE	5,080	3,416	1,633	31	1,783 R	67.2%	32.1%	67.7%	32.3%
2,420	MELLETTE	1,076	637	433	6	204 R	59.2%	40.2%	59.5%	40.5%
4,454	MINER	2,405	1,059	1,337	9	278 D	44.0%	55.6%	44.2%	55.8%
95,209	MINNEHAHA	44,988	22,447	22,386	155	61 R	49.9%	49.8%	50.1%	49.9%
7,622	MOODY	3,554	1,648	1,895	11	247 D	46.4%	53.3%	46.5%	53.5%
59,349	PENNINGTON	22,326	13,654	8,592	80	5,062 R	61.2%	38.5%	61.4%	38.6%
4,769	PERKINS	2,598	1,691	900	7	791 R	65.1%	34.6%	65.3%	34.7%
4,449	POTTER	2,253	1,389	858	6	531 R	61.7%	38.1%	61.8%	38.2%
11,678	ROBERTS	5,172	2,187	2,976	9	789 D	42.3%	57.5%	42.4%	57.6%
3,697	SANBORN	2,145	1,064	1,074	7	10 D	49.6%	50.1%	49.8%	50.2%
8,198	SHANNON	1,611	356	1,246	9	890 D	22.1%	77.3%	22.2%	77.8%
10,595	SPINK	4,880	2,547	2,321	12	226 R	52.2%	47.6%	52.3%	47.7%
2,457	STANLEY	1,278	779	492	7	287 R	61.0%	38.5%	61.3%	38.7%
2,362	SULLY	1,191	773	414	4	359 R	64.9%	34.8%	65.1%	34.9%
6,606	TODD	1,723	806	907	10	101 D	46.8%	52.6%	47.1%	52.9%

SOUTH DAKOTA

PRESIDENT 1972

1970 Census Population	County	Total Vote	Republican	Democratic	Other	Rep.-Dem. Plurality	Percentage Total Vote Rep.	Percentage Total Vote Dem.	Percentage Major Vote Rep.	Percentage Major Vote Dem.
8,171	TRIPP	4,132	2,592	1,538	2	1,054 R	62.7%	37.2%	62.8%	37.2%
9,872	TURNER	5,010	3,007	1,993	10	1,014 R	60.0%	39.8%	60.1%	39.9%
9,643	UNION	4,842	2,271	2,554	17	283 D	46.9%	52.7%	47.1%	52.9%
7,842	WALWORTH	3,711	2,416	1,287	8	1,129 R	65.1%	34.7%	65.2%	34.8%
1,389	WASHABAUGH	456	245	211		34 R	53.7%	46.3%	53.7%	46.3%
19,039	YANKTON	8,225	4,366	3,835	24	531 R	53.1%	46.6%	53.2%	46.8%
2,221	ZIEBACH	870	486	378	6	108 R	55.9%	43.4%	56.3%	43.8%
666,257	TOTAL	307,415	166,476	139,945	994	26,531 R	54.2%	45.5%	54.3%	45.7%

SOUTH DAKOTA

PRESIDENT 1968

1960 Census Population	County	Total Vote	Republican	Democratic	AIP	Other	Plurality	Percentage Rep.	Percentage Dem.	Percentage AIP
4,749	AURORA	2,233	1,043	1,060	130		17 D	46.7%	47.5%	5.8%
21,682	BEADLE	9,878	4,214	5,357	307		1,143 D	42.7%	54.2%	3.1%
3,053	BENNETT	1,233	665	457	111		208 R	53.9%	37.1%	9.0%
9,229	BONHOMME	4,383	2,411	1,773	199		638 R	55.0%	40.5%	4.5%
20,046	BROOKINGS	8,081	4,674	3,202	205		1,472 R	57.8%	39.6%	2.5%
34,106	BROWN	14,547	6,685	7,302	560		617 D	46.0%	50.2%	3.8%
6,319	BRULE	2,815	1,237	1,425	153		188 D	43.9%	50.6%	5.4%
1,547	BUFFALO	554	261	265	28		4 D	47.1%	47.8%	5.1%
8,592	BUTTE	3,303	2,090	1,017	196		1,073 R	63.3%	30.8%	5.9%
3,531	CAMPBELL	1,534	1,216	245	73		971 R	79.3%	16.0%	4.8%
11,785	CHARLES MIX	4,675	2,093	2,369	213		276 D	44.8%	50.7%	4.6%
7,134	CLARK	3,040	1,596	1,325	119		271 R	52.5%	43.6%	3.9%
10,810	CLAY	4,386	2,249	2,006	131		243 R	51.3%	45.7%	3.0%
20,220	CODINGTON	8,452	3,929	4,235	288		306 D	46.5%	50.1%	3.4%
5,798	CORSON	2,009	1,108	821	80		287 R	55.2%	40.9%	4.0%
4,906	CUSTER	2,064	1,143	727	194		416 R	55.4%	35.2%	9.4%
16,681	DAVISON	7,719	3,869	3,585	265		284 R	50.1%	46.4%	3.4%
10,516	DAY	4,707	2,062	2,463	182		401 D	43.8%	52.3%	3.9%
6,782	DEUEL	2,625	1,398	1,076	151		322 R	53.3%	41.0%	5.8%
5,257	DEWEY	1,785	941	721	123		220 R	52.7%	40.4%	6.9%
5,113	DOUGLAS	2,282	1,613	592	77		1,021 R	70.7%	25.9%	3.4%
6,079	EDMUNDS	2,940	1,534	1,225	181		309 R	52.2%	41.7%	6.2%
10,688	FALL RIVER	3,094	1,843	965	286		878 R	59.6%	31.2%	9.2%
4,397	FAULK	2,015	997	819	199		178 R	49.5%	40.6%	9.9%
9,913	GRANT	4,360	2,259	1,890	211		369 R	51.8%	43.3%	4.8%
7,399	GREGORY	3,327	1,810	1,266	251		544 R	54.4%	38.1%	7.5%
3,303	HAAKON	1,245	759	377	109		382 R	61.0%	30.3%	8.8%
6,303	HAMLIN	2,926	1,649	1,149	128		500 R	56.4%	39.3%	4.4%
6,712	HAND	3,012	1,650	1,136	226		514 R	54.8%	37.7%	7.5%
4,584	HANSON	1,799	901	826	72		75 R	50.1%	45.9%	4.0%
2,371	HARDING	895	564	266	65		298 R	63.0%	29.7%	7.3%
12,725	HUGHES	5,213	3,204	1,666	343		1,538 R	61.5%	32.0%	6.6%
11,085	HUTCHINSON	5,131	3,544	1,412	175		2,132 R	69.1%	27.5%	3.4%
2,602	HYDE	1,325	713	499	113		214 R	53.8%	37.7%	8.5%
1,985	JACKSON	845	480	267	98		213 R	56.8%	31.6%	11.6%
4,048	JERAULD	1,803	1,002	745	56		257 R	55.6%	41.3%	3.1%
2,066	JONES	1,008	562	358	88		204 R	55.8%	35.5%	8.7%
9,227	KINGSBURY	3,937	2,300	1,491	146		809 R	58.4%	37.9%	3.7%
11,764	LAKE	5,358	2,876	2,294	188		582 R	53.7%	42.8%	3.5%
17,075	LAWRENCE	6,948	4,185	2,425	338		1,760 R	60.2%	34.9%	4.9%
12,371	LINCOLN	5,442	3,259	1,961	222		1,298 R	59.9%	36.0%	4.1%
4,428	LYMAN	1,837	1,063	643	131		420 R	57.9%	35.0%	7.1%
8,268	MCCOOK	3,800	1,959	1,653	188		306 R	51.6%	43.5%	4.9%
5,821	MCPHERSON	2,620	2,105	389	126		1,716 R	80.3%	14.8%	4.8%
6,663	MARSHALL	3,129	1,471	1,518	140		47 D	47.0%	48.5%	4.5%
12,044	MEADE	4,257	2,392	1,522	343		870 R	56.2%	35.8%	8.1%
2,664	MELLETTE	1,097	611	407	79		204 R	55.7%	37.1%	7.2%
5,398	MINER	2,392	1,045	1,255	92		210 D	43.7%	52.5%	3.8%
86,575	MINNEHAHA	37,780	20,141	16,462	1,177		3,679 R	53.3%	43.6%	3.1%
8,810	MOODY	3,456	1,689	1,614	153		75 R	48.9%	46.7%	4.4%
58,195	PENNINGTON	18,148	9,671	7,303	1,174		2,368 R	53.3%	40.2%	6.5%
5,977	PERKINS	2,481	1,498	869	114		629 R	60.4%	35.0%	4.6%
4,926	POTTER	2,202	1,273	780	149		493 R	57.8%	35.4%	6.8%
13,190	ROBERTS	5,213	2,225	2,651	337		426 D	42.7%	50.9%	6.5%
4,641	SANBORN	2,060	1,024	956	80		68 R	49.7%	46.4%	3.9%
6,000	SHANNON	1,796	533	1,202	61		669 D	29.7%	66.9%	3.4%
11,706	SPINK	4,915	2,068	2,669	178		601 D	42.1%	54.3%	3.6%
4,085	STANLEY	1,109	572	439	98		133 R	51.6%	39.6%	8.8%
2,607	SULLY	1,125	676	356	93		320 R	60.1%	31.6%	8.3%
4,661	TODD	1,761	683	987	91		304 D	38.8%	56.0%	5.2%

SOUTH DAKOTA

PRESIDENT 1968

1960 Census Population	County	Total Vote	Republican	Democratic	AIP	Other	Plurality	Percentage Rep.	Percentage Dem.	Percentage AIP
8,761	TRIPP	3,849	2,242	1,362	245		880 R	58.2%	35.4%	6.4%
11,159	TURNER	4,801	3,246	1,350	205		1,896 R	67.6%	28.1%	4.3%
10,197	UNION	4,451	2,212	2,014	225		198 R	49.7%	45.2%	5.1%
8,097	WALWORTH	3,662	2,204	1,276	182		928 R	60.2%	34.8%	5.0%
1,042	WASHABAUGH	449	224	203	22		21 R	49.9%	45.2%	4.9%
17,551	YANKTON	7,092	3,977	2,733	382		1,244 R	56.1%	38.5%	5.4%
2,495	ZIEBACH	854	449	350	55		99 R	52.6%	41.0%	6.4%
680,514	TOTAL	281,264	149,841	118,023	13,400		31,818 R	53.3%	42.0%	4.8%

SOUTH DAKOTA

Jackson and Washabaugh counties were consolidated in 1978 under the name Jackson county.

ELECTION NOTES

1984 Other vote was 1,150 Serrette (Independent); 337 Mason (Independent).

1980 Other vote was 21,431 Anderson (Independent); 3,824 Clark (Independent); 250 Pulley (Independent).

1976 Other vote was 1,619 MacBride (Independent); 318 Hall (Independent); 168 Camejo (Independent). Early unamended canvass gave the Democratic vote in Clay county as 2,589.

1972 Other vote was Jenness (Independent).

1968 Wallace on the ballot as Independent.

TENNESSEE

POPULAR VOTE FOR PRESIDENT 1920 TO 1984

Year	Total Vote	Republican Vote	Republican Candidate	Democratic Vote	Democratic Candidate	Other Vote	Plurality	Percentage Total Vote Rep.	Percentage Total Vote Dem.	Percentage Major Vote Rep.	Percentage Major Vote Dem.
1984	1,711,994	990,212	Reagan, Ronald	711,714	Mondale, Walter F.	10,068	278,498 R	57.8%	41.6%	58.2%	41.8%
1980	1,617,616	787,761	Reagan, Ronald	783,051	Carter, Jimmy	46,804	4,710 R	48.7%	48.4%	50.1%	49.9%
1976	1,476,345	633,969	Ford, Gerald R.	825,879	Carter, Jimmy	16,497	191,910 D	42.9%	55.9%	43.4%	56.6%
1972	1,201,182	813,147	Nixon, Richard M.	357,293	McGovern, George S.	30,742	455,854 R	67.7%	29.7%	69.5%	30.5%
1968 **	1,248,617	472,592	Nixon, Richard M.	351,233	Humphrey, Hubert H.	424,792	47,800 R	37.8%	28.1%	57.4%	42.6%
1964	1,143,946	508,965	Goldwater, Barry M.	634,947	Johnson, Lyndon B.	34	125,982 D	44.5%	55.5%	44.5%	55.5%
1960	1,051,792	556,577	Nixon, Richard M.	481,453	Kennedy, John F.	13,762	75,124 R	52.9%	45.8%	53.6%	46.4%
1956	939,404	462,288	Eisenhower, Dwight D.	456,507	Stevenson, Adlai E.	20,609	5,781 R	49.2%	48.6%	50.3%	49.7%
1952	892,553	446,147	Eisenhower, Dwight D.	443,710	Stevenson, Adlai E.	2,696	2,437 R	50.0%	49.7%	50.1%	49.9%
1948	550,283	202,914	Dewey, Thomas E.	270,402	Truman, Harry S.	76,967	67,488 D	36.9%	49.1%	42.9%	57.1%
1944	510,692	200,311	Dewey, Thomas E.	308,707	Roosevelt, Franklin D.	1,674	108,396 D	39.2%	60.4%	39.4%	60.6%
1940	522,823	169,153	Willkie, Wendell	351,601	Roosevelt, Franklin D.	2,069	182,448 D	32.4%	67.3%	32.5%	67.5%
1936	477,086	147,055	Landon, Alfred M.	328,083	Roosevelt, Franklin D.	1,948	181,028 D	30.8%	68.8%	30.9%	69.1%
1932	390,273	126,752	Hoover, Herbert C.	259,473	Roosevelt, Franklin D.	4,048	132,721 D	32.5%	66.5%	32.8%	67.2%
1928	353,192	195,388	Hoover, Herbert C.	157,143	Smith, Alfred E.	661	38,245 R	55.3%	44.5%	55.4%	44.6%
1924	301,030	130,831	Coolidge, Calvin	159,339	Davis, John W.	10,860	28,508 D	43.5%	52.9%	45.1%	54.9%
1920	428,036	219,229	Harding, Warren G.	206,558	Cox, James M.	2,249	12,671 R	51.2%	48.3%	51.5%	48.5%

In 1968 other vote was American (Wallace).

ELECTORAL COLLEGE VOTE 1920 TO 1984

Year	Total	Republican	Democratic	Other
1984	11	11	—	—
1980	10	10	—	—
1976	10	—	10	—
1972	10	10	—	—
1968	11	11	—	—
1964	11	—	11	—
1960	11	11	—	—
1956	11	11	—	—
1952	11	11	—	—
1948 **	12	—	11	1 SR
1944	12	—	12	—
1940	11	—	11	—
1936	11	—	11	—
1932	11	—	11	—
1928	12	12	—	—
1924	12	—	12	—
1920	12	12	—	—

In 1948 one of the twelve Democratic electors voted in the Electoral College for the States Rights candidates rather than for the national Democratic candidates.

TENNESSEE

JOHNSON
SULLIVAN
CARTER
WASH-INGTON
UNICOI
HAWKINS
GREENE
HANCOCK
HAMBLEN
COCKE
GRAINGER
JEFFERSON
SEVIER
CLAIBORNE
UNION
KNOX
BLOUNT
CAMPBELL
ANDERSON
MONROE
LOUDON
SCOTT
POLK
ROANE
McMINN
MORGAN
MEIGS
BRADLEY
FENTRESS
CUMBERLAND
RHEA
HAMILTON
PICKETT
OVERTON
BLEDSOE
WHITE
VAN BUREN
SEQUATCHIE
CLAY
PUTNAM
MARION
JACKSON
GRUNDY
DE KALB
WARREN
MACON
SMITH
CANNON
COFFEE
FRANKLIN
TROUSDALE
WILSON
RUTHERFORD
MOORE
SUMNER
BEDFORD
ROBERTSON
DAVIDSON
MARSHALL
LINCOLN
WILLIAMSON
CHEATHAM
MAURY
GILES
MONTGOMERY
DICKSON
HICKMAN
LEWIS
LAWRENCE
HOUSTON
HUMPHREYS
STEWART
PERRY
WAYNE
BENTON
DECATUR
HARDIN
HENRY
CARROLL
HENDERSON
CHESTER
McNAIRY
WEAKLEY
GIBSON
MADISON
HARDEMAN
OBION
CROCKETT
HAYWOOD
DYER
FAYETTE
LAKE
LAUDERDALE
TIPTON
SHELBY

TENNESSEE

PRESIDENT 1984

1980 Census Population	County	Total Vote	Republican	Democratic	Other	Rep.-Dem. Plurality	Percentage Total Vote Rep.	Total Vote Dem.	Major Vote Rep.	Major Vote Dem.
67,346	ANDERSON	27,374	16,783	10,415	176	6,368 R	61.3%	38.0%	61.7%	38.3%
27,916	BEDFORD	9,296	4,699	4,499	98	200 R	50.5%	48.4%	51.1%	48.9%
14,901	BENTON	5,897	2,481	3,398	18	917 D	42.1%	57.6%	42.2%	57.8%
9,478	BLEDSOE	3,286	1,950	1,316	20	634 R	59.3%	40.0%	59.7%	40.3%
77,770	BLOUNT	29,859	20,525	9,188	146	11,337 R	68.7%	30.8%	69.1%	30.9%
67,547	BRADLEY	22,502	16,322	6,085	95	10,237 R	72.5%	27.0%	72.8%	27.2%
34,923	CAMPBELL	10,444	5,685	4,692	67	993 R	54.4%	44.9%	54.8%	45.2%
10,234	CANNON	3,560	1,669	1,846	45	177 D	46.9%	51.9%	47.5%	52.5%
28,285	CARROLL	10,662	6,017	4,568	77	1,449 R	56.4%	42.8%	56.8%	43.2%
50,205	CARTER	17,933	13,153	4,642	138	8,511 R	73.3%	25.9%	73.9%	26.1%
21,616	CHEATHAM	7,169	4,109	3,007	53	1,102 R	57.3%	41.9%	57.7%	42.3%
12,727	CHESTER	4,680	2,793	1,854	33	939 R	59.7%	39.6%	60.1%	39.9%
24,595	CLAIBORNE	7,371	4,474	2,870	27	1,604 R	60.7%	38.9%	60.9%	39.1%
7,676	CLAY	2,634	1,338	1,281	15	57 R	50.8%	48.6%	51.1%	48.9%
28,792	COCKE	8,828	6,665	2,068	95	4,597 R	75.5%	23.4%	76.3%	23.7%
38,311	COFFEE	13,468	7,695	5,691	82	2,004 R	57.1%	42.3%	57.5%	42.5%
14,941	CROCKETT	4,429	2,479	1,937	13	542 R	56.0%	43.7%	56.1%	43.9%
28,676	CUMBERLAND	10,756	7,083	3,605	68	3,478 R	65.9%	33.5%	66.3%	33.7%
477,811	DAVIDSON	188,814	98,155	89,498	1,161	8,657 R	52.0%	47.4%	52.3%	47.7%
10,857	DECATUR	4,441	2,390	2,031	20	359 R	53.8%	45.7%	54.1%	45.9%
13,589	DE KALB	5,010	2,337	2,645	28	308 D	46.6%	52.8%	46.9%	53.1%
30,037	DICKSON	11,805	5,846	5,809	150	37 R	49.5%	49.2%	50.2%	49.8%
34,663	DYER	10,642	6,610	3,991	41	2,619 R	62.1%	37.5%	62.4%	37.6%
25,305	FAYETTE	7,401	3,733	3,634	34	99 R	50.4%	49.1%	50.7%	49.3%
14,826	FENTRESS	4,699	2,922	1,755	22	1,167 R	62.2%	37.3%	62.5%	37.5%
31,983	FRANKLIN	11,621	5,705	5,846	70	141 D	49.1%	50.3%	49.4%	50.6%
49,467	GIBSON	17,992	9,484	8,334	174	1,150 R	52.7%	46.3%	53.2%	46.8%
24,625	GILES	7,739	3,875	3,812	52	63 R	50.1%	49.3%	50.4%	49.6%
16,751	GRAINGER	4,814	3,212	1,565	37	1,647 R	66.7%	32.5%	67.2%	32.8%
54,422	GREENE	18,065	13,215	4,763	87	8,452 R	73.2%	26.4%	73.5%	26.5%
13,787	GRUNDY	4,015	1,396	2,596	23	1,200 D	34.8%	64.7%	35.0%	65.0%
49,300	HAMBLEN	16,158	11,144	4,922	92	6,222 R	69.0%	30.5%	69.4%	30.6%
287,740	HAMILTON	111,622	69,626	41,449	547	28,177 R	62.4%	37.1%	62.7%	37.3%
6,887	HANCOCK	2,134	1,491	619	24	872 R	69.9%	29.0%	70.7%	29.3%
23,873	HARDEMAN	7,626	3,712	3,797	117	85 D	48.7%	49.8%	49.4%	50.6%
22,280	HARDIN	7,773	4,632	3,051	90	1,581 R	59.6%	39.3%	60.3%	39.7%
43,751	HAWKINS	14,793	9,863	4,802	128	5,061 R	66.7%	32.5%	67.3%	32.7%
20,318	HAYWOOD	6,166	2,839	3,308	19	469 D	46.0%	53.6%	46.2%	53.8%
21,390	HENDERSON	7,821	5,362	2,426	33	2,936 R	68.6%	31.0%	68.8%	31.2%
28,656	HENRY	10,837	5,376	5,407	54	31 D	49.6%	49.9%	49.9%	50.1%
15,151	HICKMAN	5,334	2,370	2,941	23	571 D	44.4%	55.1%	44.6%	55.4%
6,871	HOUSTON	2,619	882	1,716	21	834 D	33.7%	65.5%	33.9%	66.1%
15,957	HUMPHREYS	5,933	2,249	3,668	16	1,419 D	37.9%	61.8%	38.0%	62.0%
9,398	JACKSON	4,486	1,544	2,894	48	1,350 D	34.4%	64.5%	34.8%	65.2%
31,284	JEFFERSON	10,975	7,721	3,185	69	4,536 R	70.4%	29.0%	70.8%	29.2%
13,745	JOHNSON	4,871	3,853	999	19	2,854 R	79.1%	20.5%	79.4%	20.6%
319,694	KNOX	120,987	76,965	43,448	574	33,517 R	63.6%	35.9%	63.9%	36.1%
7,455	LAKE	2,092	878	1,191	23	313 D	42.0%	56.9%	42.4%	57.6%
24,555	LAUDERDALE	7,099	3,566	3,506	27	60 R	50.2%	49.4%	50.4%	49.6%
34,110	LAWRENCE	11,563	6,034	5,458	71	576 R	52.2%	47.2%	52.5%	47.5%
9,700	LEWIS	3,306	1,733	1,556	17	177 R	52.4%	47.1%	52.7%	47.3%
26,483	LINCOLN	8,114	3,982	4,103	29	121 D	49.1%	50.6%	49.3%	50.7%
28,553	LOUDON	10,405	7,113	3,227	65	3,886 R	68.4%	31.0%	68.8%	31.2%
41,878	MCMINN	14,813	9,604	5,141	68	4,463 R	64.8%	34.7%	65.1%	34.9%
22,525	MCNAIRY	8,631	4,776	3,825	30	951 R	55.3%	44.3%	55.5%	44.5%
15,700	MACON	5,105	3,330	1,747	28	1,583 R	65.2%	34.2%	65.6%	34.4%
74,546	MADISON	29,880	17,819	12,006	55	5,813 R	59.6%	40.2%	59.7%	40.3%
24,416	MARION	8,331	4,337	3,942	52	395 R	52.1%	47.3%	52.4%	47.6%
19,698	MARSHALL	6,393	3,416	2,935	42	481 R	53.4%	45.9%	53.8%	46.2%
51,095	MAURY	16,033	9,008	6,950	75	2,058 R	56.2%	43.3%	56.4%	43.6%

TENNESSEE

PRESIDENT 1984

1980 Census Population	County	Total Vote	Republican	Democratic	Other	Rep.-Dem. Plurality	Percentage Total Vote Rep.	Percentage Total Vote Dem.	Percentage Major Vote Rep.	Percentage Major Vote Dem.
7,431	MEIGS	2,602	1,575	1,012	15	563 R	60.5%	38.9%	60.9%	39.1%
28,700	MONROE	10,947	6,665	4,223	59	2,442 R	60.9%	38.6%	61.2%	38.8%
83,342	MONTGOMERY	23,365	13,228	9,939	198	3,289 R	56.6%	42.5%	57.1%	42.9%
4,510	MOORE	1,680	863	808	9	55 R	51.4%	48.1%	51.6%	48.4%
16,604	MORGAN	5,076	2,903	2,121	52	782 R	57.2%	41.8%	57.8%	42.2%
32,781	OBION	11,252	6,384	4,769	99	1,615 R	56.7%	42.4%	57.2%	42.8%
17,575	OVERTON	4,830	2,054	2,749	27	695 D	42.5%	56.9%	42.8%	57.2%
6,111	PERRY	2,267	948	1,316	3	368 D	41.8%	58.1%	41.9%	58.1%
4,358	PICKETT	1,957	1,246	706	5	540 R	63.7%	36.1%	63.8%	36.2%
13,602	POLK	4,960	2,785	2,112	63	673 R	56.1%	42.6%	56.9%	43.1%
47,690	PUTNAM	16,541	8,999	7,443	99	1,556 R	54.4%	45.0%	54.7%	45.3%
24,235	RHEA	8,587	5,692	2,804	91	2,888 R	66.3%	32.7%	67.0%	33.0%
48,425	ROANE	18,614	11,882	6,623	109	5,259 R	63.8%	35.6%	64.2%	35.8%
37,021	ROBERTSON	11,263	5,445	5,756	62	311 D	48.3%	51.1%	48.6%	51.4%
84,058	RUTHERFORD	31,469	19,503	11,618	348	7,885 R	62.0%	36.9%	62.7%	37.3%
19,259	SCOTT	4,961	3,107	1,810	44	1,297 R	62.6%	36.5%	63.2%	36.8%
8,605	SEQUATCHIE	3,042	1,785	1,238	19	547 R	58.7%	40.7%	59.0%	41.0%
41,418	SEVIER	16,041	12,517	3,384	140	9,133 R	78.0%	21.1%	78.7%	21.3%
777,113	SHELBY	337,302	169,717	165,947	1,638	3,770 R	50.3%	49.2%	50.6%	49.4%
14,935	SMITH	5,691	2,393	3,258	40	865 D	42.0%	57.2%	42.3%	57.7%
8,665	STEWART	3,490	1,285	2,174	31	889 D	36.8%	62.3%	37.1%	62.9%
143,968	SULLIVAN	53,835	36,516	16,925	394	19,591 R	67.8%	31.4%	68.3%	31.7%
85,790	SUMNER	30,186	18,442	11,535	209	6,907 R	61.1%	38.2%	61.5%	38.5%
32,930	TIPTON	9,874	5,945	3,895	34	2,050 R	60.2%	39.4%	60.4%	39.6%
6,137	TROUSDALE	1,935	781	1,142	12	361 D	40.4%	59.0%	40.6%	59.4%
16,362	UNICOI	5,979	4,249	1,696	34	2,553 R	71.1%	28.4%	71.5%	28.5%
11,707	UNION	3,978	2,447	1,495	36	952 R	61.5%	37.6%	62.1%	37.9%
4,728	VAN BUREN	1,535	718	810	7	92 D	46.8%	52.8%	47.0%	53.0%
32,653	WARREN	9,691	4,811	4,813	67	2 D	49.6%	49.7%	50.0%	50.0%
88,755	WASHINGTON	31,368	21,762	9,452	154	12,310 R	69.4%	30.1%	69.7%	30.3%
13,946	WAYNE	4,879	3,332	1,534	13	1,798 R	68.3%	31.4%	68.5%	31.5%
32,896	WEAKLEY	11,287	6,480	4,752	55	1,728 R	57.4%	42.1%	57.7%	42.3%
19,567	WHITE	5,958	2,895	3,033	30	138 D	48.6%	50.9%	48.8%	51.2%
58,108	WILLIAMSON	24,997	17,975	6,929	93	11,046 R	71.9%	27.7%	72.2%	27.8%
56,064	WILSON	21,449	12,858	8,433	158	4,425 R	59.9%	39.3%	60.4%	39.6%
4,591,120	TOTAL	1,711,994	990,212	711,714	10,068	278,498 R	57.8%	41.6%	58.2%	41.8%

TENNESSEE

PRESIDENT 1980

1980 Census Population	County	Total Vote	Republican	Democratic	Other	Rep.-Dem. Plurality	Percentage Total Vote Rep.	Total Vote Dem.	Major Vote Rep.	Major Vote Dem.
67,346	ANDERSON	25,736	14,235	10,194	1,307	4,041 R	55.3%	39.6%	58.3%	41.7%
27,916	BEDFORD	9,583	3,377	5,987	219	2,610 D	35.2%	62.5%	36.1%	63.9%
14,901	BENTON	6,193	2,281	3,811	101	1,530 D	36.8%	61.5%	37.4%	62.6%
9,478	BLEDSOE	3,586	1,970	1,585	31	385 R	54.9%	44.2%	55.4%	44.6%
77,770	BLOUNT	28,144	17,959	9,412	773	8,547 R	63.8%	33.4%	65.6%	34.4%
67,547	BRADLEY	19,905	11,869	7,638	398	4,231 R	59.6%	38.4%	60.8%	39.2%
34,923	CAMPBELL	10,450	5,537	4,752	161	785 R	53.0%	45.5%	53.8%	46.2%
10,234	CANNON	3,817	1,403	2,351	63	948 D	36.8%	61.6%	37.4%	62.6%
28,285	CARROLL	11,143	5,681	5,277	185	404 R	51.0%	47.4%	51.8%	48.2%
50,205	CARTER	18,077	11,648	6,006	423	5,642 R	64.4%	33.2%	66.0%	34.0%
21,616	CHEATHAM	6,201	2,296	3,771	134	1,475 D	37.0%	60.8%	37.8%	62.2%
12,727	CHESTER	4,940	2,751	2,123	66	628 R	55.7%	43.0%	56.4%	43.6%
24,595	CLAIBORNE	7,263	4,289	2,844	130	1,445 R	59.1%	39.2%	60.1%	39.9%
7,676	CLAY	2,765	1,344	1,376	45	32 D	48.6%	49.8%	49.4%	50.6%
28,792	COCKE	9,144	6,802	2,139	203	4,663 R	74.4%	23.4%	76.1%	23.9%
38,311	COFFEE	13,393	5,454	7,612	327	2,158 D	40.7%	56.8%	41.7%	58.3%
14,941	CROCKETT	4,588	2,117	2,422	49	305 D	46.1%	52.8%	46.6%	53.4%
28,676	CUMBERLAND	10,436	6,354	3,775	307	2,579 R	60.9%	36.2%	62.7%	37.3%
477,811	DAVIDSON	175,606	65,772	103,741	6,093	37,969 D	37.5%	59.1%	38.8%	61.2%
10,857	DECATUR	4,280	2,095	2,139	46	44 D	48.9%	50.0%	49.5%	50.5%
13,589	DE KALB	4,868	1,841	2,948	79	1,107 D	37.8%	60.6%	38.4%	61.6%
30,037	DICKSON	10,467	3,636	6,622	209	2,986 D	34.7%	63.3%	35.4%	64.6%
34,663	DYER	11,407	5,475	5,713	219	238 D	48.0%	50.1%	48.9%	51.1%
25,305	FAYETTE	7,195	2,944	4,141	110	1,197 D	40.9%	57.6%	41.6%	58.4%
14,826	FENTRESS	4,103	2,493	1,543	67	950 R	60.8%	37.6%	61.8%	38.2%
31,983	FRANKLIN	11,090	3,995	6,760	335	2,765 D	36.0%	61.0%	37.1%	62.9%
49,467	GIBSON	16,923	6,792	9,829	302	3,037 D	40.1%	58.1%	40.9%	59.1%
24,625	GILES	7,537	2,757	4,653	127	1,896 D	36.6%	61.7%	37.2%	62.8%
16,751	GRAINGER	4,848	3,254	1,495	99	1,759 R	67.1%	30.8%	68.5%	31.5%
54,422	GREENE	16,956	10,704	5,822	430	4,882 R	63.1%	34.3%	64.8%	35.2%
13,787	GRUNDY	4,019	1,139	2,837	43	1,698 D	28.3%	70.6%	28.6%	71.4%
49,300	HAMBLEN	16,073	9,741	5,890	442	3,851 R	60.6%	36.6%	62.3%	37.7%
287,740	HAMILTON	102,092	57,575	41,913	2,604	15,662 R	56.4%	41.1%	57.9%	42.1%
6,887	HANCOCK	2,487	1,734	704	49	1,030 R	69.7%	28.3%	71.1%	28.9%
23,873	HARDEMAN	7,205	2,931	4,153	121	1,222 D	40.7%	57.6%	41.4%	58.6%
22,280	HARDIN	7,435	4,152	3,164	119	988 R	55.8%	42.6%	56.8%	43.2%
43,751	HAWKINS	13,529	7,836	5,283	410	2,553 R	57.9%	39.0%	59.7%	40.3%
20,318	HAYWOOD	5,943	2,435	3,445	63	1,010 D	41.0%	58.0%	41.4%	58.6%
21,390	HENDERSON	7,926	5,108	2,702	116	2,406 R	64.4%	34.1%	65.4%	34.6%
28,656	HENRY	11,168	4,299	6,601	268	2,302 D	38.5%	59.1%	39.4%	60.6%
15,151	HICKMAN	5,230	1,903	3,225	102	1,322 D	36.4%	61.7%	37.1%	62.9%
6,871	HOUSTON	2,541	738	1,757	46	1,019 D	29.0%	69.1%	29.6%	70.4%
15,957	HUMPHREYS	5,966	1,897	3,974	95	2,077 D	31.8%	66.6%	32.3%	67.7%
9,398	JACKSON	3,535	995	2,480	60	1,485 D	28.1%	70.2%	28.6%	71.4%
31,284	JEFFERSON	10,392	6,944	3,180	268	3,764 R	66.8%	30.6%	68.6%	31.4%
13,745	JOHNSON	4,955	3,716	1,141	98	2,575 R	75.0%	23.0%	76.5%	23.5%
319,694	KNOX	117,585	66,153	45,634	5,798	20,519 R	56.3%	38.8%	59.2%	40.8%
7,455	LAKE	2,563	823	1,718	22	895 D	32.1%	67.0%	32.4%	67.6%
24,555	LAUDERDALE	7,235	2,818	4,318	99	1,500 D	38.9%	59.7%	39.5%	60.5%
34,110	LAWRENCE	13,477	6,532	6,082	863	450 R	48.5%	45.1%	51.8%	48.2%
9,700	LEWIS	3,309	1,076	2,190	43	1,114 D	32.5%	66.2%	32.9%	67.1%
26,483	LINCOLN	8,409	2,856	5,387	166	2,531 D	34.0%	64.1%	34.6%	65.4%
28,553	LOUDON	10,376	6,382	3,699	295	2,683 R	61.5%	35.6%	63.3%	36.7%
41,878	MCMINN	13,547	7,825	5,460	262	2,365 R	57.8%	40.3%	58.9%	41.1%
22,525	MCNAIRY	8,514	4,603	3,801	110	802 R	54.1%	44.6%	54.8%	45.2%
15,700	MACON	4,961	2,925	1,947	89	978 R	59.0%	39.2%	60.0%	40.0%
74,546	MADISON	27,187	13,667	12,986	534	681 R	50.3%	47.8%	51.3%	48.7%
24,416	MARION	8,651	3,902	4,623	126	721 D	45.1%	53.4%	45.8%	54.2%
19,698	MARSHALL	6,666	2,282	4,277	107	1,995 D	34.2%	64.2%	34.8%	65.2%
51,095	MAURY	15,030	6,637	7,957	436	1,320 D	44.2%	52.9%	45.5%	54.5%

TENNESSEE

PRESIDENT 1980

1980 Census Population	County	Total Vote	Republican	Democratic	Other	Rep.-Dem. Plurality	Percentage Total Vote Rep.	Total Vote Dem.	Major Vote Rep.	Major Vote Dem.
7,431	MEIGS	2,316	1,278	999	39	279 R	55.2%	43.1%	56.1%	43.9%
28,700	MONROE	11,065	6,246	4,612	207	1,634 R	56.4%	41.7%	57.5%	42.5%
83,342	MONTGOMERY	20,698	8,503	11,573	622	3,070 D	41.1%	55.9%	42.4%	57.6%
4,510	MOORE	1,595	551	993	51	442 D	34.5%	62.3%	35.7%	64.3%
16,604	MORGAN	5,015	2,823	2,094	98	729 R	56.3%	41.8%	57.4%	42.6%
32,781	OBION	11,365	5,397	5,766	202	369 D	47.5%	50.7%	48.3%	51.7%
17,575	OVERTON	5,267	1,869	3,343	55	1,474 D	35.5%	63.5%	35.9%	64.1%
6,111	PERRY	2,232	783	1,401	48	618 D	35.1%	62.8%	35.9%	64.1%
4,358	PICKETT	2,102	1,319	758	25	561 R	62.7%	36.1%	63.5%	36.5%
13,602	POLK	4,960	2,414	2,470	76	56 D	48.7%	49.8%	49.4%	50.6%
47,690	PUTNAM	14,753	6,235	8,084	434	1,849 D	42.3%	54.8%	43.5%	56.5%
24,235	RHEA	7,889	4,689	3,070	130	1,619 R	59.4%	38.9%	60.4%	39.6%
48,425	ROANE	18,182	11,096	6,473	613	4,623 R	61.0%	35.6%	63.2%	36.8%
37,021	ROBERTSON	11,126	3,560	7,381	185	3,821 D	32.0%	66.3%	32.5%	67.5%
84,058	RUTHERFORD	27,350	11,208	15,213	929	4,005 D	41.0%	55.6%	42.4%	57.6%
19,259	SCOTT	4,832	3,014	1,724	94	1,290 R	62.4%	35.7%	63.6%	36.4%
8,605	SEQUATCHIE	3,052	1,512	1,509	31	3 R	49.5%	49.4%	50.0%	50.0%
41,418	SEVIER	14,439	10,576	3,450	413	7,126 R	73.2%	23.9%	75.4%	24.6%
777,113	SHELBY	308,517	140,157	159,240	9,120	19,083 D	45.4%	51.6%	46.8%	53.2%
14,935	SMITH	5,531	1,755	3,674	102	1,919 D	31.7%	66.4%	32.3%	67.7%
8,665	STEWART	3,318	985	2,274	59	1,289 D	29.7%	68.5%	30.2%	69.8%
143,968	SULLIVAN	50,470	25,963	22,341	2,166	3,622 R	51.4%	44.3%	53.7%	46.3%
85,790	SUMNER	26,735	11,876	14,150	709	2,274 D	44.4%	52.9%	45.6%	54.4%
32,930	TIPTON	9,401	4,339	4,934	128	595 D	46.2%	52.5%	46.8%	53.2%
6,137	TROUSDALE	2,354	629	1,674	51	1,045 D	26.7%	71.1%	27.3%	72.7%
16,362	UNICOI	5,844	3,828	1,880	136	1,948 R	65.5%	32.2%	67.1%	32.9%
11,707	UNION	3,951	2,453	1,435	63	1,018 R	62.1%	36.3%	63.1%	36.9%
4,728	VAN BUREN	1,404	499	886	19	387 D	35.5%	63.1%	36.0%	64.0%
32,653	WARREN	9,904	3,680	6,021	203	2,341 D	37.2%	60.8%	37.9%	62.1%
88,755	WASHINGTON	30,249	17,457	11,599	1,193	5,858 R	57.7%	38.3%	60.1%	39.9%
13,946	WAYNE	5,297	3,418	1,633	246	1,785 R	64.5%	30.8%	67.7%	32.3%
32,896	WEAKLEY	11,771	5,668	5,910	193	242 D	48.2%	50.2%	49.0%	51.0%
19,567	WHITE	5,613	2,100	3,415	98	1,315 D	37.4%	60.8%	38.1%	61.9%
58,108	WILLIAMSON	21,095	11,597	8,815	683	2,782 R	55.0%	41.8%	56.8%	43.2%
56,064	WILSON	19,274	7,535	11,248	491	3,713 D	39.1%	58.4%	40.1%	59.9%
4,591,120	TOTAL	1,617,616	787,761	783,051	46,804	4,710 R	48.7%	48.4%	50.1%	49.9%

TENNESSEE

PRESIDENT 1976

1970 Census Population	County	Total Vote	Republican	Democratic	Other	Rep.-Dem. Plurality	Percentage Total Vote Rep.	Total Vote Dem.	Major Vote Rep.	Major Vote Dem.
60,300	ANDERSON	24,242	10,494	13,455	293	2,961 D	43.3%	55.5%	43.8%	56.2%
25,039	BEDFORD	10,357	3,023	7,228	106	4,205 D	29.2%	69.8%	29.5%	70.5%
12,126	BENTON	5,806	1,678	4,088	40	2,410 D	28.9%	70.4%	29.1%	70.9%
7,643	BLEDSOE	3,401	1,620	1,757	24	137 D	47.6%	51.7%	48.0%	52.0%
63,744	BLOUNT	26,240	13,851	12,096	293	1,755 R	52.8%	46.1%	53.4%	46.6%
50,686	BRADLEY	18,051	9,136	8,776	139	360 R	50.6%	48.6%	51.0%	49.0%
26,045	CAMPBELL	9,557	4,277	5,206	74	929 D	44.8%	54.5%	45.1%	54.9%
8,467	CANNON	3,399	908	2,463	28	1,555 D	26.7%	72.5%	26.9%	73.1%
25,741	CARROLL	9,721	4,031	5,581	109	1,550 D	41.5%	57.4%	41.9%	58.1%
43,259	CARTER	16,510	8,934	7,443	133	1,491 R	54.1%	45.1%	54.6%	45.4%
13,199	CHEATHAM	5,664	1,376	4,225	63	2,849 D	24.3%	74.6%	24.6%	75.4%
9,927	CHESTER	4,517	1,949	2,532	36	583 D	43.1%	56.1%	43.5%	56.5%
19,420	CLAIBORNE	6,743	3,227	3,461	55	234 D	47.9%	51.3%	48.3%	51.7%
6,624	CLAY	2,678	982	1,671	25	689 D	36.7%	62.4%	37.0%	63.0%
25,283	COCKE	8,219	5,004	3,141	74	1,863 R	60.9%	38.2%	61.4%	38.6%
32,572	COFFEE	12,005	3,848	8,017	140	4,169 D	32.1%	66.8%	32.4%	67.6%
14,402	CROCKETT	4,697	1,694	2,963	40	1,269 D	36.1%	63.1%	36.4%	63.6%
20,733	CUMBERLAND	8,763	4,119	4,543	101	424 D	47.0%	51.8%	47.6%	52.4%
447,877	DAVIDSON	161,598	60,662	99,007	1,929	38,345 D	37.5%	61.3%	38.0%	62.0%
9,457	DECATUR	4,116	1,637	2,432	47	795 D	39.8%	59.1%	40.2%	59.8%
11,151	DE KALB	4,702	1,443	3,222	37	1,779 D	30.7%	68.5%	30.9%	69.1%
21,977	DICKSON	8,922	2,285	6,551	86	4,266 D	25.6%	73.4%	25.9%	74.1%
30,427	DYER	10,478	4,391	5,937	150	1,546 D	41.9%	56.7%	42.5%	57.5%
22,692	FAYETTE	6,040	2,133	3,853	54	1,720 D	35.3%	63.8%	35.6%	64.4%
12,593	FENTRESS	3,758	1,767	1,953	38	186 D	47.0%	52.0%	47.5%	52.5%
27,244	FRANKLIN	9,524	2,619	6,788	117	4,169 D	27.5%	71.3%	27.8%	72.2%
47,871	GIBSON	16,031	5,563	10,356	112	4,793 D	34.7%	64.6%	34.9%	65.1%
22,138	GILES	7,248	1,952	5,225	71	3,273 D	26.9%	72.1%	27.2%	72.8%
13,948	GRAINGER	4,863	2,805	2,018	40	787 R	57.7%	41.5%	58.2%	41.8%
47,630	GREENE	15,880	8,664	7,070	146	1,594 R	54.6%	44.5%	55.1%	44.9%
10,631	GRUNDY	3,721	850	2,850	21	2,000 D	22.8%	76.6%	23.0%	77.0%
38,696	HAMBLEN	14,628	6,989	7,504	135	515 D	47.8%	51.3%	48.2%	51.8%
254,236	HAMILTON	94,421	47,969	45,348	1,104	2,621 R	50.8%	48.0%	51.4%	48.6%
6,719	HANCOCK	2,090	1,309	764	17	545 R	62.6%	36.6%	63.1%	36.9%
22,435	HARDEMAN	6,270	2,254	3,934	82	1,680 D	35.9%	62.7%	36.4%	63.6%
18,212	HARDIN	6,852	3,362	3,438	52	76 D	49.1%	50.2%	49.4%	50.6%
33,726	HAWKINS	12,412	6,407	5,931	74	476 R	51.6%	47.8%	51.9%	48.1%
19,596	HAYWOOD	5,661	1,952	3,681	28	1,729 D	34.5%	65.0%	34.7%	65.3%
17,291	HENDERSON	7,586	4,152	3,366	68	786 R	54.7%	44.4%	55.2%	44.8%
23,749	HENRY	9,881	2,585	7,162	134	4,577 D	26.2%	72.5%	26.5%	73.5%
12,096	HICKMAN	4,787	1,154	3,590	43	2,436 D	24.1%	75.0%	24.3%	75.7%
5,845	HOUSTON	2,427	407	1,990	30	1,583 D	16.8%	82.0%	17.0%	83.0%
13,560	HUMPHREYS	5,413	1,338	4,021	54	2,683 D	24.7%	74.3%	25.0%	75.0%
8,141	JACKSON	3,569	591	2,959	19	2,368 D	16.6%	82.9%	16.6%	83.4%
24,940	JEFFERSON	9,538	5,459	3,995	84	1,464 R	57.2%	41.9%	57.7%	42.3%
11,569	JOHNSON	4,478	2,986	1,464	28	1,522 R	66.7%	32.7%	67.1%	32.9%
276,293	KNOX	110,409	56,013	53,034	1,362	2,979 R	50.7%	48.0%	51.4%	48.6%
7,896	LAKE	2,549	591	1,933	25	1,342 D	23.2%	75.8%	23.4%	76.6%
20,271	LAUDERDALE	6,877	2,105	4,747	25	2,642 D	30.6%	69.0%	30.7%	69.3%
29,097	LAWRENCE	12,190	4,967	7,140	83	2,173 D	40.7%	58.6%	41.0%	59.0%
6,761	LEWIS	3,036	617	2,391	28	1,774 D	20.3%	78.8%	20.5%	79.5%
24,318	LINCOLN	7,518	1,724	5,732	62	4,008 D	22.9%	76.2%	23.1%	76.9%
24,266	LOUDON	9,233	4,458	4,683	92	225 D	48.3%	50.7%	48.8%	51.2%
35,462	MCMINN	13,732	6,638	7,020	74	382 D	48.3%	51.1%	48.6%	51.4%
18,369	MCNAIRY	7,736	3,388	4,293	55	905 D	43.8%	55.5%	44.1%	55.9%
12,315	MACON	4,051	2,063	1,951	37	112 R	50.9%	48.2%	51.4%	48.6%
65,727	MADISON	24,659	11,364	12,989	306	1,625 D	46.1%	52.7%	46.7%	53.3%
20,577	MARION	7,642	2,965	4,615	62	1,650 D	38.8%	60.4%	39.1%	60.9%
17,319	MARSHALL	6,209	1,674	4,457	78	2,783 D	27.0%	71.8%	27.3%	72.7%
44,028	MAURY	14,265	5,327	8,747	191	3,420 D	37.3%	61.3%	37.8%	62.2%

TENNESSEE

PRESIDENT 1976

1970 Census Population	County	Total Vote	Republican	Democratic	Other	Rep.-Dem. Plurality	Percentage Total Vote Rep.	Percentage Total Vote Dem.	Percentage Major Vote Rep.	Percentage Major Vote Dem.
5,219	MEIGS	2,242	975	1,254	13	279 D	43.5%	55.9%	43.7%	56.3%
23,475	MONROE	10,756	5,335	5,368	53	33 D	49.6%	49.9%	49.8%	50.2%
62,721	MONTGOMERY	18,448	5,923	12,310	215	6,387 D	32.1%	66.7%	32.5%	67.5%
3,568	MOORE	1,448	331	1,101	16	770 D	22.9%	76.0%	23.1%	76.9%
13,619	MORGAN	4,939	1,949	2,953	37	1,004 D	39.5%	59.8%	39.8%	60.2%
29,936	OBION	10,320	2,986	7,204	130	4,218 D	28.9%	69.8%	29.3%	70.7%
14,866	OVERTON	5,047	1,115	3,897	35	2,782 D	22.1%	77.2%	22.2%	77.8%
5,238	PERRY	2,201	520	1,660	21	1,140 D	23.6%	75.4%	23.9%	76.1%
3,774	PICKETT	1,944	986	948	10	38 R	50.7%	48.8%	51.0%	49.0%
11,669	POLK	5,155	1,835	3,284	36	1,449 D	35.6%	63.7%	35.8%	64.2%
35,487	PUTNAM	12,708	4,079	8,485	144	4,406 D	32.1%	66.8%	32.5%	67.5%
17,202	RHEA	7,241	3,449	3,735	57	286 D	47.6%	51.6%	48.0%	52.0%
38,881	ROANE	16,491	7,121	9,216	154	2,095 D	43.2%	55.9%	43.6%	56.4%
29,102	ROBERTSON	10,114	2,505	7,547	62	5,042 D	24.8%	74.6%	24.9%	75.1%
59,428	RUTHERFORD	23,082	7,921	14,854	307	6,933 D	34.3%	64.4%	34.8%	65.2%
14,762	SCOTT	4,730	2,432	2,260	38	172 R	51.4%	47.8%	51.8%	48.2%
6,331	SEQUATCHIE	2,842	1,065	1,733	44	668 D	37.5%	61.0%	38.1%	61.9%
28,241	SEVIER	11,814	7,608	3,993	213	3,615 R	64.4%	33.8%	65.6%	34.4%
722,014	SHELBY	279,601	128,646	147,893	3,062	19,247 D	46.0%	52.9%	46.5%	53.5%
12,509	SMITH	5,136	1,332	3,753	51	2,421 D	25.9%	73.1%	26.2%	73.8%
7,319	STEWART	2,972	510	2,442	20	1,932 D	17.2%	82.2%	17.3%	82.7%
127,329	SULLIVAN	46,762	22,087	23,353	1,322	1,266 D	47.2%	49.9%	48.6%	51.4%
56,106	SUMNER	22,007	7,946	13,848	213	5,902 D	36.1%	62.9%	36.5%	63.5%
28,001	TIPTON	9,072	3,329	5,667	76	2,338 D	36.7%	62.5%	37.0%	63.0%
5,155	TROUSDALE	1,726	332	1,385	9	1,053 D	19.2%	80.2%	19.3%	80.7%
15,254	UNICOI	5,782	3,211	2,526	45	685 R	55.5%	43.7%	56.0%	44.0%
9,072	UNION	3,457	1,801	1,631	25	170 R	52.1%	47.2%	52.5%	47.5%
3,758	VAN BUREN	1,442	346	1,085	11	739 D	24.0%	75.2%	24.2%	75.8%
26,972	WARREN	9,115	2,364	6,666	85	4,302 D	25.9%	73.1%	26.2%	73.8%
73,924	WASHINGTON	29,032	14,770	13,951	311	819 R	50.9%	48.1%	51.4%	48.6%
12,365	WAYNE	4,511	2,597	1,891	23	706 R	57.6%	41.9%	57.9%	42.1%
28,827	WEAKLEY	9,696	2,875	6,605	216	3,730 D	29.7%	68.1%	30.3%	69.7%
16,355	WHITE	5,314	1,382	3,874	58	2,492 D	26.0%	72.9%	26.3%	73.7%
34,330	WILLIAMSON	16,266	7,880	8,183	203	303 D	48.4%	50.3%	49.1%	50.9%
36,999	WILSON	15,362	4,696	10,537	129	5,841 D	30.6%	68.6%	30.8%	69.2%
3,924,164	TOTAL	1,476,345	633,969	825,879	16,497	191,910 D	42.9%	55.9%	43.4%	56.6%

TENNESSEE

PRESIDENT 1972

1970 Census Population	County	Total Vote	Republican	Democratic	Other	Rep.-Dem. Plurality	Percentage Total Vote Rep.	Percentage Total Vote Dem.	Percentage Major Vote Rep.	Percentage Major Vote Dem.
60,300	ANDERSON	20,999	13,865	6,713	421	7,152 R	66.0%	32.0%	67.4%	32.6%
25,039	BEDFORD	7,135	4,262	2,565	308	1,697 R	59.7%	35.9%	62.4%	37.6%
12,126	BENTON	4,228	2,614	1,479	135	1,135 R	61.8%	35.0%	63.9%	36.1%
7,643	BLEDSOE	2,962	1,952	899	111	1,053 R	65.9%	30.4%	68.5%	31.5%
63,744	BLOUNT	21,771	16,078	5,303	390	10,775 R	73.9%	24.4%	75.2%	24.8%
50,686	BRADLEY	13,513	10,440	2,804	269	7,636 R	77.3%	20.8%	78.8%	21.2%
26,045	CAMPBELL	6,687	4,909	1,629	149	3,280 R	73.4%	24.4%	75.1%	24.9%
8,467	CANNON	2,589	1,615	911	63	704 R	62.4%	35.2%	63.9%	36.1%
25,741	CARROLL	8,349	5,784	2,290	275	3,494 R	69.3%	27.4%	71.6%	28.4%
43,259	CARTER	13,514	11,102	2,191	221	8,911 R	82.2%	16.2%	83.5%	16.5%
13,199	CHEATHAM	3,719	2,235	1,321	163	914 R	60.1%	35.5%	62.9%	37.1%
9,927	CHESTER	3,887	2,787	961	139	1,826 R	71.7%	24.7%	74.4%	25.6%
19,420	CLAIBORNE	4,912	3,632	1,230	50	2,402 R	73.9%	25.0%	74.7%	25.3%
6,624	CLAY	1,664	982	648	34	334 R	59.0%	38.9%	60.2%	39.8%
25,283	COCKE	6,153	5,268	805	80	4,463 R	85.6%	13.1%	86.7%	13.3%
32,572	COFFEE	9,695	6,416	2,973	306	3,443 R	66.2%	30.7%	68.3%	31.7%
14,402	CROCKETT	3,504	2,642	735	127	1,907 R	75.4%	21.0%	78.2%	21.8%
20,733	CUMBERLAND	6,225	4,593	1,482	150	3,111 R	73.8%	23.8%	75.6%	24.4%
447,877	DAVIDSON	134,797	82,636	48,869	3,292	33,767 R	61.3%	36.3%	62.8%	37.2%
9,457	DECATUR	3,655	2,368	1,187	100	1,181 R	64.8%	32.5%	66.6%	33.4%
11,151	DE KALB	3,320	2,014	1,243	63	771 R	60.7%	37.4%	61.8%	38.2%
21,977	DICKSON	6,446	3,645	2,619	182	1,026 R	56.5%	40.6%	58.2%	41.8%
30,427	DYER	7,988	6,066	1,600	322	4,466 R	75.9%	20.0%	79.1%	20.9%
22,692	FAYETTE	5,463	3,264	2,067	132	1,197 R	59.7%	37.8%	61.2%	38.8%
12,593	FENTRESS	2,853	2,154	665	34	1,489 R	75.5%	23.3%	76.4%	23.6%
27,244	FRANKLIN	7,192	4,136	2,896	160	1,240 R	57.5%	40.3%	58.8%	41.2%
47,871	GIBSON	13,934	9,900	3,625	409	6,275 R	71.0%	26.0%	73.2%	26.8%
22,138	GILES	5,051	2,914	1,875	262	1,039 R	57.7%	37.1%	60.8%	39.2%
13,948	GRAINGER	3,713	2,842	828	43	2,014 R	76.5%	22.3%	77.4%	22.6%
47,630	GREENE	12,709	9,772	2,764	173	7,008 R	76.9%	21.7%	78.0%	22.0%
10,631	GRUNDY	2,503	1,364	1,005	134	359 R	54.5%	40.2%	57.6%	42.4%
38,696	HAMBLEN	11,624	8,879	2,563	182	6,316 R	76.4%	22.0%	77.6%	22.4%
254,236	HAMILTON	82,794	58,469	20,657	3,668	37,812 R	70.6%	24.9%	73.9%	26.1%
6,719	HANCOCK	2,222	1,813	393	16	1,420 R	81.6%	17.7%	82.2%	17.8%
22,435	HARDEMAN	5,294	3,494	1,550	250	1,944 R	66.0%	29.3%	69.3%	30.7%
18,212	HARDIN	5,769	4,401	1,202	166	3,199 R	76.3%	20.8%	78.5%	21.5%
33,726	HAWKINS	10,775	7,791	2,608	376	5,183 R	72.3%	24.2%	74.9%	25.1%
19,596	HAYWOOD	5,253	3,123	1,966	164	1,157 R	59.5%	37.4%	61.4%	38.6%
17,291	HENDERSON	6,597	5,122	1,313	162	3,809 R	77.6%	19.9%	79.6%	20.4%
23,749	HENRY	7,611	4,613	2,694	304	1,919 R	60.6%	35.4%	63.1%	36.9%
12,096	HICKMAN	3,466	1,943	1,393	130	550 R	56.1%	40.2%	58.2%	41.8%
5,845	HOUSTON	1,725	800	870	55	70 D	46.4%	50.4%	47.9%	52.1%
13,560	HUMPHREYS	4,338	2,263	1,973	102	290 R	52.2%	45.5%	53.4%	46.6%
8,141	JACKSON	2,079	956	1,085	38	129 D	46.0%	52.2%	46.8%	53.2%
24,940	JEFFERSON	7,382	5,925	1,357	100	4,568 R	80.3%	18.4%	81.4%	18.6%
11,569	JOHNSON	3,861	3,362	450	49	2,912 R	87.1%	11.7%	88.2%	11.8%
276,293	KNOX	90,484	64,747	24,076	1,661	40,671 R	71.6%	26.6%	72.9%	27.1%
7,896	LAKE	1,746	1,147	536	63	611 R	65.7%	30.7%	68.2%	31.8%
20,271	LAUDERDALE	5,585	3,597	1,771	217	1,826 R	64.4%	31.7%	67.0%	33.0%
29,097	LAWRENCE	9,482	6,438	2,824	220	3,614 R	67.9%	29.8%	69.5%	30.5%
6,761	LEWIS	2,248	1,056	1,138	54	82 D	47.0%	50.6%	48.1%	51.9%
24,318	LINCOLN	5,281	3,266	1,867	148	1,399 R	61.8%	35.4%	63.6%	36.4%
24,266	LOUDON	7,131	5,357	1,604	170	3,753 R	75.1%	22.5%	77.0%	23.0%
35,462	MCMINN	10,520	7,423	2,838	259	4,585 R	70.6%	27.0%	72.3%	27.7%
18,369	MCNAIRY	6,519	4,774	1,610	135	3,164 R	73.2%	24.7%	74.8%	25.2%
12,315	MACON	3,033	2,295	653	85	1,642 R	75.7%	21.5%	77.8%	22.2%
65,727	MADISON	21,409	15,481	5,203	725	10,278 R	72.3%	24.3%	74.8%	25.2%
20,577	MARION	5,839	3,711	1,929	199	1,782 R	63.6%	33.0%	65.8%	34.2%
17,319	MARSHALL	4,378	2,593	1,526	259	1,067 R	59.2%	34.9%	63.0%	37.0%
44,028	MAURY	11,121	7,371	3,262	488	4,109 R	66.3%	29.3%	69.3%	30.7%

TENNESSEE

PRESIDENT 1972

1970 Census Population	County	Total Vote	Republican	Democratic	Other	Rep.-Dem. Plurality	Percentage Total Vote Rep.	Percentage Total Vote Dem.	Percentage Major Vote Rep.	Percentage Major Vote Dem.
5,219	MEIGS	1,635	1,052	539	44	513 R	64.3%	33.0%	66.1%	33.9%
23,475	MONROE	8,634	5,657	2,870	107	2,787 R	65.5%	33.2%	66.3%	33.7%
62,721	MONTGOMERY	13,899	7,839	5,691	369	2,148 R	56.4%	40.9%	57.9%	42.1%
3,568	MOORE	996	608	356	32	252 R	61.0%	35.7%	63.1%	36.9%
13,619	MORGAN	3,703	2,531	1,084	88	1,447 R	68.3%	29.3%	70.0%	30.0%
29,936	OBION	8,243	5,800	2,243	200	3,557 R	70.4%	27.2%	72.1%	27.9%
14,866	OVERTON	3,594	1,947	1,573	74	374 R	54.2%	43.8%	55.3%	44.7%
5,238	PERRY	1,871	900	937	34	37 D	48.1%	50.1%	49.0%	51.0%
3,774	PICKETT	1,325	957	357	11	600 R	72.2%	26.9%	72.8%	27.2%
11,669	POLK	3,772	2,285	1,431	56	854 R	60.6%	37.9%	61.5%	38.5%
35,487	PUTNAM	9,999	6,038	3,738	223	2,300 R	60.4%	37.4%	61.8%	38.2%
17,202	RHEA	5,299	3,842	1,312	145	2,530 R	72.5%	24.8%	74.5%	25.5%
38,881	ROANE	12,470	8,742	3,433	295	5,309 R	70.1%	27.5%	71.8%	28.2%
29,102	ROBERTSON	7,399	4,175	2,985	239	1,190 R	56.4%	40.3%	58.3%	41.7%
59,428	RUTHERFORD	17,554	11,256	5,811	487	5,445 R	64.1%	33.1%	66.0%	34.0%
14,762	SCOTT	3,502	2,775	679	48	2,096 R	79.2%	19.4%	80.3%	19.7%
6,331	SEQUATCHIE	2,010	1,298	629	83	669 R	64.6%	31.3%	67.4%	32.6%
28,241	SEVIER	9,578	8,273	1,128	177	7,145 R	86.4%	11.8%	88.0%	12.0%
722,014	SHELBY	247,882	161,922	81,089	4,871	80,833 R	65.3%	32.7%	66.6%	33.4%
12,509	SMITH	3,188	1,812	1,260	116	552 R	56.8%	39.5%	59.0%	41.0%
7,319	STEWART	1,935	790	1,098	47	308 D	40.8%	56.7%	41.8%	58.2%
127,329	SULLIVAN	38,517	27,593	10,007	917	17,586 R	71.6%	26.0%	73.4%	26.6%
56,106	SUMNER	15,157	10,020	4,596	541	5,424 R	66.1%	30.3%	68.6%	31.4%
28,001	TIPTON	7,749	5,542	1,853	354	3,689 R	71.5%	23.9%	74.9%	25.1%
5,155	TROUSDALE	1,230	663	539	28	124 R	53.9%	43.8%	55.2%	44.8%
15,254	UNICOI	4,766	3,877	822	67	3,055 R	81.3%	17.2%	82.5%	17.5%
9,072	UNION	2,527	1,927	570	30	1,357 R	76.3%	22.6%	77.2%	22.8%
3,758	VAN BUREN	1,021	629	364	28	265 R	61.6%	35.7%	63.3%	36.7%
26,972	WARREN	5,894	3,565	2,118	211	1,447 R	60.5%	35.9%	62.7%	37.3%
73,924	WASHINGTON	23,188	17,343	5,284	561	12,059 R	74.8%	22.8%	76.6%	23.4%
12,365	WAYNE	3,632	2,898	673	61	2,225 R	79.8%	18.5%	81.2%	18.8%
28,827	WEAKLEY	8,165	5,836	2,027	302	3,809 R	71.5%	24.8%	74.2%	25.8%
16,355	WHITE	3,727	2,252	1,392	83	860 R	60.4%	37.3%	61.8%	38.2%
34,330	WILLIAMSON	10,564	7,556	2,616	392	4,940 R	71.5%	24.8%	74.3%	25.7%
36,999	WILSON	9,861	6,486	3,096	279	3,390 R	65.8%	31.4%	67.7%	32.3%
3,924,164	TOTAL	1,201,182	813,147	357,293	30,742	455,854 R	67.7%	29.7%	69.5%	30.5%

TENNESSEE

PRESIDENT 1968

1960 Census Population	County	Total Vote	Republican	Democratic	AIP	Other	Plurality	Percentage Rep.	Dem.	AIP
60,032	ANDERSON	21,754	10,233	7,198	4,323		3,035 R	47.0%	33.1%	19.9%
23,150	BEDFORD	8,385	1,870	2,416	4,099		1,683 A	22.3%	28.8%	48.9%
10,662	BENTON	4,782	1,468	1,059	2,255		787 A	30.7%	22.1%	47.2%
7,811	BLEDSOE	3,166	1,477	957	732		520 R	46.7%	30.2%	23.1%
57,525	BLOUNT	22,336	12,753	5,176	4,407		7,577 R	57.1%	23.2%	19.7%
38,324	BRADLEY	13,845	6,924	2,762	4,159		2,765 R	50.0%	19.9%	30.0%
27,936	CAMPBELL	7,659	4,024	2,268	1,367		1,756 R	52.5%	29.6%	17.8%
8,537	CANNON	3,053	780	809	1,464		655 A	25.5%	26.5%	48.0%
23,476	CARROLL	8,987	3,757	1,932	3,298		459 R	41.8%	21.5%	36.7%
41,578	CARTER	14,636	9,467	2,160	3,009		6,458 R	64.7%	14.8%	20.6%
9,428	CHEATHAM	3,944	669	778	2,497		1,719 A	17.0%	19.7%	63.3%
9,569	CHESTER	4,294	1,408	849	2,037		629 A	32.8%	19.8%	47.4%
19,067	CLAIBORNE	5,190	3,101	1,314	775		1,787 R	59.7%	25.3%	14.9%
7,289	CLAY	1,932	814	667	451		147 R	42.1%	34.5%	23.3%
23,390	COCKE	7,754	5,645	950	1,159		4,486 R	72.8%	12.3%	14.9%
28,603	COFFEE	11,171	3,337	3,040	4,794		1,457 A	29.9%	27.2%	42.9%
14,594	CROCKETT	4,500	932	703	2,865		1,933 A	20.7%	15.6%	63.7%
19,135	CUMBERLAND	6,012	3,115	1,428	1,469		1,646 R	51.8%	23.8%	24.4%
399,743	DAVIDSON	136,607	44,175	44,543	47,889		3,346 A	32.3%	32.6%	35.1%
8,324	DECATUR	3,830	1,409	877	1,544		135 A	36.8%	22.9%	40.3%
10,774	DE KALB	3,895	1,532	847	1,516		16 R	39.3%	21.7%	38.9%
18,839	DICKSON	6,800	1,291	2,034	3,475		1,441 A	19.0%	29.9%	51.1%
29,537	DYER	10,701	2,826	2,033	5,842		3,016 A	26.4%	19.0%	54.6%
24,577	FAYETTE	5,546	740	2,236	2,570		334 A	13.3%	40.3%	46.3%
13,288	FENTRESS	3,505	2,026	671	808		1,218 R	57.8%	19.1%	23.1%
25,528	FRANKLIN	9,128	1,700	2,489	4,939		2,450 A	18.6%	27.3%	54.1%
44,699	GIBSON	15,288	4,093	3,962	7,233		3,140 A	26.8%	25.9%	47.3%
22,410	GILES	7,433	1,264	2,203	3,966		1,763 A	17.0%	29.6%	53.4%
12,506	GRAINGER	4,145	2,788	761	596		2,027 R	67.3%	18.4%	14.4%
42,163	GREENE	13,657	7,957	2,947	2,753		5,010 R	58.3%	21.6%	20.2%
11,512	GRUNDY	3,567	618	1,307	1,642		335 A	17.3%	36.6%	46.0%
33,092	HAMBLEN	11,031	6,382	2,390	2,259		3,992 R	57.9%	21.7%	20.5%
237,905	HAMILTON	84,823	29,302	23,441	32,080		2,778 A	34.5%	27.6%	37.8%
7,757	HANCOCK	2,043	1,489	318	236		1,171 R	72.9%	15.6%	11.6%
21,517	HARDEMAN	5,804	1,171	1,709	2,924		1,215 A	20.2%	29.4%	50.4%
17,397	HARDIN	6,388	2,910	1,153	2,325		585 R	45.6%	18.0%	36.4%
30,468	HAWKINS	10,228	6,217	2,213	1,798		4,004 R	60.8%	21.6%	17.6%
23,393	HAYWOOD	5,618	1,152	1,709	2,757		1,048 A	20.5%	30.4%	49.1%
16,115	HENDERSON	6,907	3,591	1,230	2,086		1,505 R	52.0%	17.8%	30.2%
22,275	HENRY	8,656	2,068	3,149	3,439		290 A	23.9%	36.4%	39.7%
11,862	HICKMAN	4,385	760	1,152	2,473		1,321 A	17.3%	26.3%	56.4%
4,794	HOUSTON	1,809	232	636	941		305 A	12.8%	35.2%	52.0%
11,511	HUMPHREYS	4,352	866	1,391	2,095		704 A	19.9%	32.0%	48.1%
9,233	JACKSON	2,703	673	1,122	908		214 D	24.9%	41.5%	33.6%
21,493	JEFFERSON	8,187	5,494	1,494	1,199		4,000 R	67.1%	18.2%	14.6%
10,765	JOHNSON	3,932	3,107	450	375		2,657 R	79.0%	11.4%	9.5%
250,523	KNOX	90,007	47,202	24,528	18,277		22,674 R	52.4%	27.3%	20.3%
9,572	LAKE	2,408	409	737	1,262		525 A	17.0%	30.6%	52.4%
21,844	LAUDERDALE	6,754	1,080	2,108	3,566		1,458 A	16.0%	31.2%	52.8%
28,049	LAWRENCE	10,527	4,343	2,191	3,993		350 R	41.3%	20.8%	37.9%
6,269	LEWIS	2,540	455	1,088	997		91 D	17.9%	42.8%	39.3%
23,829	LINCOLN	7,229	1,167	1,848	4,214		2,366 A	16.1%	25.6%	58.3%
23,757	LOUDON	7,876	4,299	1,581	1,996		2,303 R	54.6%	20.1%	25.3%
33,662	MCMINN	11,522	6,098	2,889	2,535		3,209 R	52.9%	25.1%	22.0%
18,085	MCNAIRY	7,228	2,979	1,377	2,872		107 R	41.2%	19.1%	39.7%
12,197	MACON	3,744	2,173	530	1,041		1,132 R	58.0%	14.2%	27.8%
60,655	MADISON	21,080	6,143	5,517	9,420		3,277 A	29.1%	26.2%	44.7%
21,036	MARION	6,404	1,959	1,661	2,784		825 A	30.6%	25.9%	43.5%
16,859	MARSHALL	6,108	1,202	1,527	3,379		1,852 A	19.7%	25.0%	55.3%
41,699	MAURY	14,597	3,048	3,401	8,148		4,747 A	20.9%	23.3%	55.8%

TENNESSEE

PRESIDENT 1968

1960 Census Population	County	Total Vote	Republican	Democratic	AIP	Other	Plurality	Percentage Rep.	Dem.	AIP
5,160	MEIGS	1,664	729	493	442		236 R	43.8%	29.6%	26.6%
23,316	MONROE	8,897	4,749	2,926	1,222		1,823 R	53.4%	32.9%	13.7%
55,645	MONTGOMERY	14,424	3,248	5,538	5,638		100 A	22.5%	38.4%	39.1%
3,454	MOORE	1,426	224	346	856		510 A	15.7%	24.3%	60.0%
14,304	MORGAN	3,799	1,803	968	1,028		775 R	47.5%	25.5%	27.1%
26,957	OBION	9,335	2,420	2,235	4,680		2,260 A	25.9%	23.9%	50.1%
14,661	OVERTON	4,026	1,258	1,592	1,176		334 D	31.2%	39.5%	29.2%
5,273	PERRY	2,029	519	726	784		58 A	25.6%	35.8%	38.6%
4,431	PICKETT	1,488	884	405	199		479 R	59.4%	27.2%	13.4%
12,160	POLK	4,016	1,808	1,454	754		354 R	45.0%	36.2%	18.8%
29,236	PUTNAM	10,307	3,693	3,541	3,073		152 R	35.8%	34.4%	29.8%
15,863	RHEA	5,966	2,428	1,301	2,237		191 R	40.7%	21.8%	37.5%
39,133	ROANE	13,189	6,033	3,258	3,898		2,135 R	45.7%	24.7%	29.6%
27,335	ROBERTSON	8,021	1,802	2,315	3,904		1,589 A	22.5%	28.9%	48.7%
52,368	RUTHERFORD	16,862	4,168	4,921	7,773		2,852 A	24.7%	29.2%	46.1%
15,413	SCOTT	4,131	2,406	991	734		1,415 R	58.2%	24.0%	17.8%
5,915	SEQUATCHIE	2,223	663	549	1,011		348 A	29.8%	24.7%	45.5%
24,251	SEVIER	10,217	7,629	1,112	1,476		6,153 R	74.7%	10.9%	14.4%
627,019	SHELBY	231,898	73,416	81,486	76,996		4,490 D	31.7%	35.1%	33.2%
12,059	SMITH	4,363	1,089	1,443	1,831		388 A	25.0%	33.1%	42.0%
7,851	STEWART	2,541	443	1,041	1,057		16 A	17.4%	41.0%	41.6%
114,139	SULLIVAN	40,025	20,251	9,783	9,991		10,260 R	50.6%	24.4%	25.0%
36,217	SUMNER	16,487	4,519	4,376	7,592		3,073 A	27.4%	26.5%	46.0%
28,564	TIPTON	8,436	1,422	2,071	4,943		2,872 A	16.9%	24.5%	58.6%
4,914	TROUSDALE	1,595	252	694	649		45 D	15.8%	43.5%	40.7%
15,082	UNICOI	5,080	3,327	910	843		2,417 R	65.5%	17.9%	16.6%
8,498	UNION	2,932	1,956	527	449		1,429 R	66.7%	18.0%	15.3%
3,671	VAN BUREN	1,116	327	282	507		180 A	29.3%	25.3%	45.4%
23,102	WARREN	7,718	1,858	2,046	3,814		1,768 A	24.1%	26.5%	49.4%
64,832	WASHINGTON	22,737	12,882	4,930	4,925		7,952 R	56.7%	21.7%	21.7%
11,908	WAYNE	4,131	2,417	506	1,208		1,209 R	58.5%	12.2%	29.2%
24,227	WEAKLEY	9,371	2,858	1,988	4,525		1,667 A	30.5%	21.2%	48.3%
15,577	WHITE	4,757	1,423	1,584	1,750		166 A	29.9%	33.3%	36.8%
25,267	WILLIAMSON	9,718	2,788	2,063	4,867		2,079 A	28.7%	21.2%	50.1%
27,668	WILSON	11,300	2,736	2,916	5,648		2,732 A	24.2%	25.8%	50.0%
3,567,089	TOTAL	1,248,617	472,592	351,233	424,792		47,800 R	37.8%	28.1%	34.0%

TENNESSEE

ELECTION NOTES

1984 Other vote was 3,072 Bergland (Independent); 1,852 LaRouche (Independent); 1,763 Richards (Independent); 1,036 Hall (Independent); 978 Johnson (Independent); 715 Mason (Independent); 524 Serrette (Independent); 4 Anderson (write-in); 7 Dennis (write-in); 117 scattered write-in.

1980 Other vote was 35,991 Anderson (Independent); 7,116 Clark (Independent); 1,112 Commoner (Independent); 521 Bubar (Independent); 519 McReynolds (Independent); 503 Hall (Independent); 490 DeBerry (Independent); 400 Griswold (Independent); 152 scattered write-in.

1976 Other vote was 5,769 Anderson (Independent); 5,004 McCarthy (Independent); 2,303 Maddox (Independent); 1,375 MacBride (Independent); 547 Hall (Independent); 512 LaRouche (Independent); 442 Bubar (Independent); 316 Miller (Independent); 229 scattered write-in. Early unamended canvass gave the scattered write-in vote total as 230.

1972 Other vote was 30,373 Schmitz (American); 369 scattered write-in.

1968 Wallace on the ballot as American.

TEXAS

POPULAR VOTE FOR PRESIDENT 1920 TO 1984

Year	Total Vote	Republican Vote	Republican Candidate	Democratic Vote	Democratic Candidate	Other Vote	Plurality	Percentage Total Vote Rep.	Percentage Total Vote Dem.	Percentage Major Vote Rep.	Percentage Major Vote Dem.
1984	5,397,571	3,433,428	Reagan, Ronald	1,949,276	Mondale, Walter F.	14,867	1,484,152 R	63.6%	36.1%	63.8%	36.2%
1980	4,541,636	2,510,705	Reagan, Ronald	1,881,147	Carter, Jimmy	149,784	629,558 R	55.3%	41.4%	57.2%	42.8%
1976	4,071,884	1,953,300	Ford, Gerald R.	2,082,319	Carter, Jimmy	36,265	129,019 D	48.0%	51.1%	48.4%	51.6%
1972	3,471,281	2,298,896	Nixon, Richard M.	1,154,289	McGovern, George S.	18,096	1,144,607 R	66.2%	33.3%	66.6%	33.4%
1968 **	3,079,216	1,227,844	Nixon, Richard M.	1,266,804	Humphrey, Hubert H.	584,568	38,960 D	39.9%	41.1%	49.2%	50.8%
1964	2,626,811	958,566	Goldwater, Barry M.	1,663,185	Johnson, Lyndon B.	5,060	704,619 D	36.5%	63.3%	36.6%	63.4%
1960	2,311,084	1,121,310	Nixon, Richard M.	1,167,567	Kennedy, John F.	22,207	46,257 D	48.5%	50.5%	49.0%	51.0%
1956	1,955,168	1,080,619	Eisenhower, Dwight D.	859,958	Stevenson, Adlai E.	14,591	220,661 R	55.3%	44.0%	55.7%	44.3%
1952	2,075,946	1,102,878	Eisenhower, Dwight D.	969,228	Stevenson, Adlai E.	3,840	133,650 R	53.1%	46.7%	53.2%	46.8%
1948	1,249,577	303,467	Dewey, Thomas E.	824,235	Truman, Harry S.	121,875	520,768 D	24.3%	66.0%	26.9%	73.1%
1944	1,150,334	191,423	Dewey, Thomas E.	821,605	Roosevelt, Franklin D.	137,306	630,182 D	16.6%	71.4%	18.9%	81.1%
1940	1,124,437	212,692	Willkie, Wendell	909,974	Roosevelt, Franklin D.	1,771	697,282 D	18.9%	80.9%	18.9%	81.1%
1936	849,701	104,661	Landon, Alfred M.	739,952	Roosevelt, Franklin D.	5,088	635,291 D	12.3%	87.1%	12.4%	87.6%
1932	874,382	98,218	Hoover, Herbert C.	771,109	Roosevelt, Franklin D.	5,055	672,891 D	11.2%	88.2%	11.3%	88.7%
1928	717,733	372,324	Hoover, Herbert C.	344,542	Smith, Alfred E.	867	27,782 R	51.9%	48.0%	51.9%	48.1%
1924	657,054	130,794	Coolidge, Calvin	483,381	Davis, John W.	42,879	352,587 D	19.9%	73.6%	21.3%	78.7%
1920	486,109	114,658	Harding, Warren G.	287,920	Cox, James M.	83,531	173,262 D	23.6%	59.2%	28.5%	71.5%

In 1968 other vote was 584,269 American (Wallace) and 299 scattered.

ELECTORAL COLLEGE VOTE 1920 TO 1984

Year	Total	Republican	Democratic	Other
1984	29	29	—	—
1980	26	26	—	—
1976	26	—	26	—
1972	26	26	—	—
1968	25	—	25	—
1964	25	—	25	—
1960	24	—	24	—
1956	24	24	—	—
1952	24	24	—	—
1948	23	—	23	—
1944	23	—	23	—
1940	23	—	23	—
1936	23	—	23	—
1932	23	—	23	—
1928	20	20	—	—
1924	20	—	20	—
1920	20	—	20	—

TEXAS

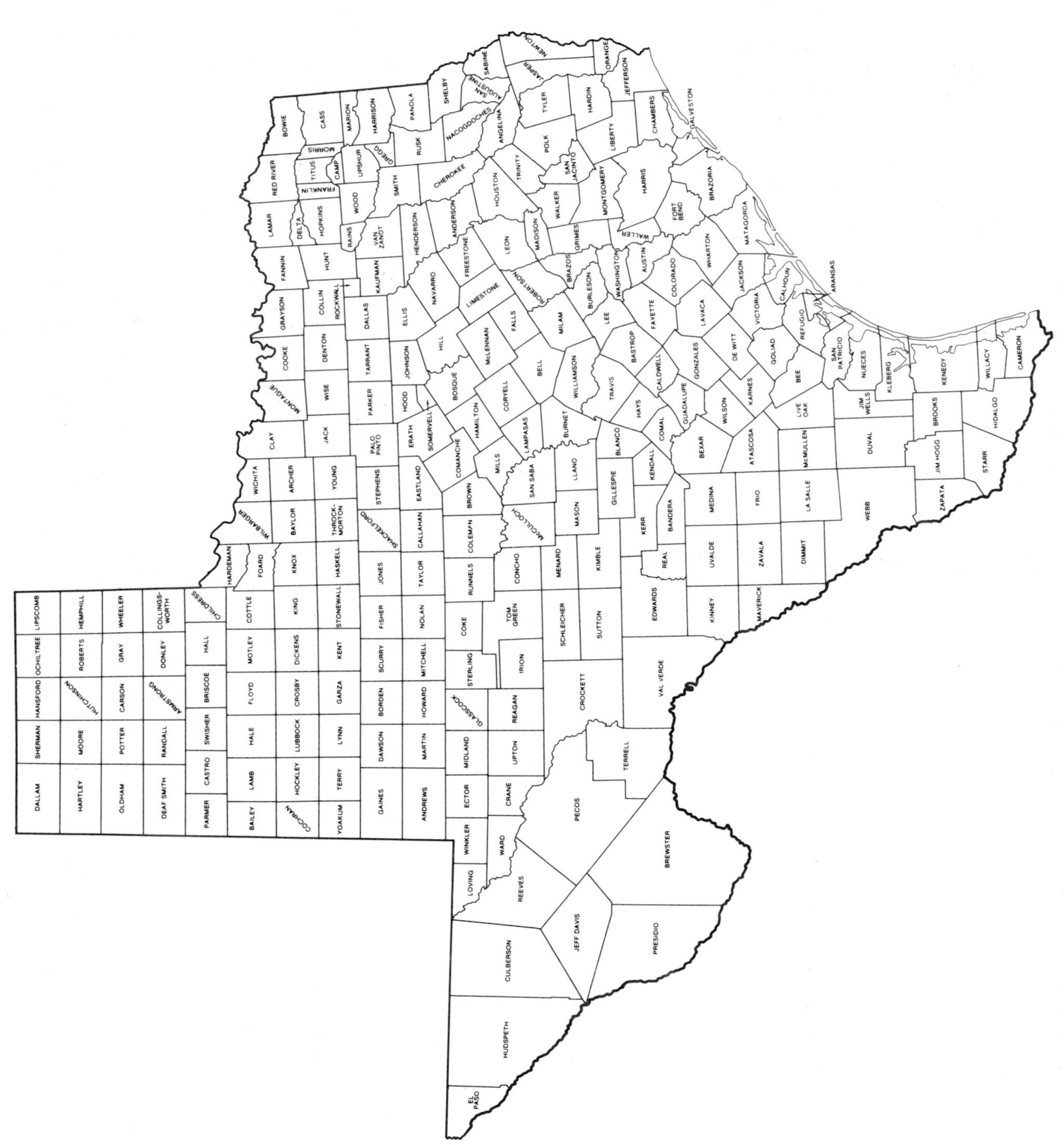
NEWTON
ORANGE
JEFFERSON
SABINE
JASPER
SAN AUGUSTINE
SHELBY
PANOLA
HARRISON
MARION
CASS
BOWIE
RED RIVER
MORRIS
TITUS
CAMP
UPSHUR
GREGG
RUSK
NACOGDOCHES
ANGELINA
TYLER
HARDIN
CHAMBERS
GALVESTON
LIBERTY
POLK
SAN JACINTO
TRINITY
HOUSTON
CHEROKEE
SMITH
WOOD
FRANKLIN
HOPKINS
DELTA
LAMAR
FANNIN
HUNT
RAINS
VAN ZANDT
HENDERSON
ANDERSON
FREESTONE
LEON
MADISON
WALKER
MONTGOMERY
HARRIS
BRAZORIA
FORT BEND
WALLER
GRIMES
BRAZOS
ROBERTSON
LIMESTONE
NAVARRO
KAUFMAN
ROCKWALL
COLLIN
GRAYSON
COOKE
DENTON
DALLAS
ELLIS
TARRANT
JOHNSON
HILL
McLENNAN
FALLS
MILAM
BURLESON
WASHINGTON
AUSTIN
WHARTON
MATAGORDA
COLORADO
FAYETTE
LEE
BASTROP
LAVACA
JACKSON
CALHOUN
ARANSAS
VICTORIA
DE WITT
GONZALES
CALDWELL
REFUGIO
GOLIAD
BEE
SAN PATRICIO
NUECES
KLEBERG
KENEDY
WILLACY
CAMERON
HIDALGO
BROOKS
JIM WELLS
LIVE OAK
KARNES
WILSON
GUADALUPE
COMAL
HAYS
TRAVIS
WILLIAMSON
BELL
CORYELL
BOSQUE
HOOD
SOMERVELL
ERATH
HAMILTON
LAMPASAS
BURNET
BLANCO
KENDALL
BEXAR
ATASCOSA
McMULLEN
DUVAL
JIM HOGG
STARR
ZAPATA
WEBB
LA SALLE
FRIO
MEDINA
BANDERA
KERR
GILLESPIE
LLANO
MASON
SAN SABA
MILLS
COMANCHE
BROWN
EASTLAND
PALO PINTO
PARKER
WISE
MONTAGUE
CLAY
JACK
YOUNG
ARCHER
WICHITA
WILBARGER
BAYLOR
THROCK-MORTON
STEPHENS
SHACKELFORD
CALLAHAN
COLEMAN
McCULLOCH
MENARD
KIMBLE
REAL
UVALDE
ZAVALA
DIMMIT
MAVERICK
KINNEY
EDWARDS
SUTTON
SCHLEICHER
CONCHO
RUNNELS
TAYLOR
JONES
HASKELL
KNOX
FOARD
HARDEMAN
CHILDRESS
COTTLE
KING
STONEWALL
FISHER
NOLAN
COKE
TOM GREEN
IRION
STERLING
MITCHELL
SCURRY
KENT
DICKENS
MOTLEY
HALL
COLLINGS-WORTH
WHEELER
HEMPHILL
LIPSCOMB
OCHILTREE
ROBERTS
GRAY
DONLEY
BRISCOE
FLOYD
CROSBY
GARZA
BORDEN
HOWARD
GLASSCOCK
REAGAN
CROCKETT
VAL VERDE
TERRELL
UPTON
MIDLAND
MARTIN
DAWSON
LYNN
LUBBOCK
HALE
SWISHER
ARMSTRONG
CARSON
HUTCHINSON
HANSFORD
SHERMAN
MOORE
POTTER
RANDALL
CASTRO
LAMB
HOCKLEY
TERRY
GAINES
ANDREWS
ECTOR
CRANE
PECOS
BREWSTER
PRESIDIO
JEFF DAVIS
REEVES
WARD
WINKLER
LOVING
CULBERSON
HUDSPETH
EL PASO
YOAKUM
COCHRAN
BAILEY
PARMER
DEAF SMITH
OLDHAM
HARTLEY
DALLAM

TEXAS

PRESIDENT 1984

1980 Census Population	County	Total Vote	Republican	Democratic	Other	Rep.-Dem. Plurality	Percentage: Total Vote Rep.	Total Vote Dem.	Major Vote Rep.	Major Vote Dem.
38,381	ANDERSON	13,423	8,634	4,747	42	3,887 R	64.3%	35.4%	64.5%	35.5%
13,323	ANDREWS	4,750	3,918	820	12	3,098 R	82.5%	17.3%	82.7%	17.3%
64,172	ANGELINA	23,831	14,685	9,054	92	5,631 R	61.6%	38.0%	61.9%	38.1%
14,260	ARANSAS	6,067	4,352	1,696	19	2,656 R	71.7%	28.0%	72.0%	28.0%
7,266	ARCHER	3,587	2,487	1,089	11	1,398 R	69.3%	30.4%	69.5%	30.5%
1,994	ARMSTRONG	1,034	791	238	5	553 R	76.5%	23.0%	76.9%	23.1%
25,055	ATASCOSA	8,845	5,279	3,547	19	1,732 R	59.7%	40.1%	59.8%	40.2%
17,726	AUSTIN	6,834	4,872	1,941	21	2,931 R	71.3%	28.4%	71.5%	28.5%
8,168	BAILEY	2,586	1,888	684	14	1,204 R	73.0%	26.5%	73.4%	26.6%
7,084	BANDERA	3,938	3,152	771	15	2,381 R	80.0%	19.6%	80.3%	19.7%
24,726	BASTROP	11,221	6,439	4,744	38	1,695 R	57.4%	42.3%	57.6%	42.4%
4,919	BAYLOR	2,346	1,314	1,019	13	295 R	56.0%	43.4%	56.3%	43.7%
26,030	BEE	9,064	5,377	3,659	28	1,718 R	59.3%	40.4%	59.5%	40.5%
157,889	BELL	44,762	31,117	13,322	323	17,795 R	69.5%	29.8%	70.0%	30.0%
988,800	BEXAR	340,826	203,319	136,947	560	66,372 R	59.7%	40.2%	59.8%	40.2%
4,681	BLANCO	2,665	1,957	700	8	1,257 R	73.4%	26.3%	73.7%	26.3%
859	BORDEN	468	325	140	3	185 R	69.4%	29.9%	69.9%	30.1%
13,401	BOSQUE	5,983	3,923	2,046	14	1,877 R	65.6%	34.2%	65.7%	34.3%
75,301	BOWIE	28,409	18,244	10,077	88	8,167 R	64.2%	35.5%	64.4%	35.6%
169,587	BRAZORIA	58,009	39,166	18,609	234	20,557 R	67.5%	32.1%	67.8%	32.2%
93,588	BRAZOS	47,221	34,733	12,348	140	22,385 R	73.6%	26.1%	73.8%	26.2%
7,573	BREWSTER	3,545	2,066	1,462	17	604 R	58.3%	41.2%	58.6%	41.4%
2,579	BRISCOE	1,017	538	471	8	67 R	52.9%	46.3%	53.3%	46.7%
8,428	BROOKS	3,614	896	2,702	16	1,806 D	24.8%	74.8%	24.9%	75.1%
33,057	BROWN	12,585	8,468	4,070	47	4,398 R	67.3%	32.3%	67.5%	32.5%
12,313	BURLESON	5,666	3,076	2,578	12	498 R	54.3%	45.5%	54.4%	45.6%
17,803	BURNET	8,907	5,895	2,983	29	2,912 R	66.2%	33.5%	66.4%	33.6%
23,637	CALDWELL	7,732	4,315	3,401	16	914 R	55.8%	44.0%	55.9%	44.1%
19,574	CALHOUN	7,039	4,434	2,586	19	1,848 R	63.0%	36.7%	63.2%	36.8%
10,992	CALLAHAN	4,867	3,538	1,305	24	2,233 R	72.7%	26.8%	73.1%	26.9%
209,727	CAMERON	56,126	29,545	26,394	187	3,151 R	52.6%	47.0%	52.8%	47.2%
9,275	CAMP	4,168	2,238	1,917	13	321 R	53.7%	46.0%	53.9%	46.1%
6,672	CARSON	3,254	2,412	826	16	1,586 R	74.1%	25.4%	74.5%	25.5%
29,430	CASS	11,760	6,677	5,053	30	1,624 R	56.8%	43.0%	56.9%	43.1%
10,556	CASTRO	3,056	2,026	1,009	21	1,017 R	66.3%	33.0%	66.8%	33.2%
18,538	CHAMBERS	6,989	4,322	2,632	35	1,690 R	61.8%	37.7%	62.2%	37.8%
38,127	CHEROKEE	12,711	8,187	4,494	30	3,693 R	64.4%	35.4%	64.6%	35.4%
6,950	CHILDRESS	2,481	1,574	900	7	674 R	63.4%	36.3%	63.6%	36.4%
9,582	CLAY	4,426	2,569	1,844	13	725 R	58.0%	41.7%	58.2%	41.8%
4,825	COCHRAN	1,689	1,117	557	15	560 R	66.1%	33.0%	66.7%	33.3%
3,196	COKE	1,600	1,060	532	8	528 R	66.3%	33.3%	66.6%	33.4%
10,439	COLEMAN	4,217	2,790	1,420	7	1,370 R	66.2%	33.7%	66.3%	33.7%
144,576	COLLIN	74,838	61,095	13,604	139	47,491 R	81.6%	18.2%	81.8%	18.2%
4,648	COLLINGSWORTH	2,149	1,396	742	11	654 R	65.0%	34.5%	65.3%	34.7%
18,823	COLORADO	6,971	4,528	2,428	15	2,100 R	65.0%	34.8%	65.1%	34.9%
36,446	COMAL	17,683	13,452	4,179	52	9,273 R	76.1%	23.6%	76.3%	23.7%
12,617	COMANCHE	4,948	2,678	2,248	22	430 R	54.1%	45.4%	54.4%	45.6%
2,915	CONCHO	1,408	821	580	7	241 R	58.3%	41.2%	58.6%	41.4%
27,656	COOKE	11,564	8,260	3,278	26	4,982 R	71.4%	28.3%	71.6%	28.4%
56,767	CORYELL	12,199	9,056	3,113	30	5,943 R	74.2%	25.5%	74.4%	25.6%
2,947	COTTLE	1,150	507	623	20	116 D	44.1%	54.2%	44.9%	55.1%
4,600	CRANE	1,874	1,473	392	9	1,081 R	78.6%	20.9%	79.0%	21.0%
4,608	CROCKETT	1,684	1,094	589	1	505 R	65.0%	35.0%	65.0%	35.0%
8,859	CROSBY	2,599	1,376	1,212	11	164 R	52.9%	46.6%	53.2%	46.8%
3,315	CULBERSON	917	509	407	1	102 R	55.5%	44.4%	55.6%	44.4%
6,531	DALLAM	2,103	1,594	496	13	1,098 R	75.8%	23.6%	76.3%	23.7%
1,556,390	DALLAS	610,496	405,444	203,592	1,460	201,852 R	66.4%	33.3%	66.6%	33.4%
16,184	DAWSON	5,483	3,685	1,781	17	1,904 R	67.2%	32.5%	67.4%	32.6%
21,165	DEAF SMITH	6,283	4,762	1,485	36	3,277 R	75.8%	23.6%	76.2%	23.8%
4,839	DELTA	2,001	1,024	973	4	51 R	51.2%	48.6%	51.3%	48.7%

TEXAS

PRESIDENT 1984

1980 Census Population	County	Total Vote	Republican	Democratic	Other	Rep.-Dem. Plurality	Percentage Total Vote		Percentage Major Vote	
							Rep.	Dem.	Rep.	Dem.
143,126	DENTON	69,796	52,865	16,772	159	36,093 R	75.7%	24.0%	75.9%	24.1%
18,903	DE WITT	6,292	4,401	1,882	9	2,519 R	69.9%	29.9%	70.0%	30.0%
3,539	DICKENS	1,294	594	692	8	98 D	45.9%	53.5%	46.2%	53.8%
11,367	DIMMIT	3,892	1,338	2,546	8	1,208 D	34.4%	65.4%	34.4%	65.6%
4,075	DONLEY	1,831	1,297	529	5	768 R	70.8%	28.9%	71.0%	29.0%
12,517	DUVAL	4,959	1,201	3,748	10	2,547 D	24.2%	75.6%	24.3%	75.7%
19,480	EASTLAND	7,389	4,841	2,522	26	2,319 R	65.5%	34.1%	65.7%	34.3%
115,374	ECTOR	40,342	31,228	8,913	201	22,315 R	77.4%	22.1%	77.8%	22.2%
2,033	EDWARDS	786	626	159	1	467 R	79.6%	20.2%	79.7%	20.3%
59,743	ELLIS	24,945	16,873	8,029	43	8,844 R	67.6%	32.2%	67.8%	32.2%
479,899	EL PASO	118,459	66,114	51,917	428	14,197 R	55.8%	43.8%	56.0%	44.0%
22,560	ERATH	9,395	6,122	3,234	39	2,888 R	65.2%	34.4%	65.4%	34.6%
17,946	FALLS	5,986	3,133	2,834	19	299 R	52.3%	47.3%	52.5%	47.5%
24,285	FANNIN	9,106	4,692	4,399	15	293 R	51.5%	48.3%	51.6%	48.4%
18,832	FAYETTE	8,112	5,711	2,379	22	3,332 R	70.4%	29.3%	70.6%	29.4%
5,891	FISHER	2,357	965	1,384	8	419 D	40.9%	58.7%	41.1%	58.9%
9,834	FLOYD	3,134	2,092	1,023	19	1,069 R	66.8%	32.6%	67.2%	32.8%
2,158	FOARD	925	472	448	5	24 R	51.0%	48.4%	51.3%	48.7%
130,846	FORT BEND	60,209	41,370	18,729	110	22,641 R	68.7%	31.1%	68.8%	31.2%
6,893	FRANKLIN	2,948	1,836	1,104	8	732 R	62.3%	37.4%	62.4%	37.6%
14,830	FREESTONE	6,122	3,624	2,489	9	1,135 R	59.2%	40.7%	59.3%	40.7%
13,785	FRIO	4,669	2,003	2,656	10	653 D	42.9%	56.9%	43.0%	57.0%
13,150	GAINES	3,533	2,714	797	22	1,917 R	76.8%	22.6%	77.3%	22.7%
195,940	GALVESTON	76,836	40,262	36,092	482	4,170 R	52.4%	47.0%	52.7%	47.3%
5,336	GARZA	1,750	1,219	521	10	698 R	69.7%	29.8%	70.1%	29.9%
13,532	GILLESPIE	6,651	5,496	1,137	18	4,359 R	82.6%	17.1%	82.9%	17.1%
1,304	GLASSCOCK	536	403	128	5	275 R	75.2%	23.9%	75.9%	24.1%
5,193	GOLIAD	2,377	1,540	836	1	704 R	64.8%	35.2%	64.8%	35.2%
16,883	GONZALES	6,172	3,962	2,196	14	1,766 R	64.2%	35.6%	64.3%	35.7%
26,386	GRAY	10,988	8,955	2,003	30	6,952 R	81.5%	18.2%	81.7%	18.3%
89,796	GRAYSON	34,450	22,554	11,803	93	10,751 R	65.5%	34.3%	65.6%	34.4%
99,487	GREGG	40,643	29,697	10,700	246	18,997 R	73.1%	26.3%	73.5%	26.5%
13,580	GRIMES	5,752	3,365	2,370	17	995 R	58.5%	41.2%	58.7%	41.3%
46,708	GUADALUPE	19,488	14,382	5,060	46	9,322 R	73.8%	26.0%	74.0%	26.0%
37,592	HALE	10,891	7,670	3,202	19	4,468 R	70.4%	29.4%	70.5%	29.5%
5,594	HALL	2,045	1,058	984	3	74 R	51.7%	48.1%	51.8%	48.2%
8,297	HAMILTON	3,258	2,118	1,130	10	988 R	65.0%	34.7%	65.2%	34.8%
6,209	HANSFORD	2,476	2,213	259	4	1,954 R	89.4%	10.5%	89.5%	10.5%
6,368	HARDEMAN	2,173	1,238	927	8	311 R	57.0%	42.7%	57.2%	42.8%
40,721	HARDIN	15,206	8,380	6,782	44	1,598 R	55.1%	44.6%	55.3%	44.7%
2,409,547	HARRIS	872,167	536,029	334,135	2,003	201,894 R	61.5%	38.3%	61.6%	38.4%
52,265	HARRISON	20,509	12,618	7,773	118	4,845 R	61.5%	37.9%	61.9%	38.1%
3,987	HARTLEY	1,786	1,419	356	11	1,063 R	79.5%	19.9%	79.9%	20.1%
7,725	HASKELL	3,151	1,701	1,434	16	267 R	54.0%	45.5%	54.3%	45.7%
40,594	HAYS	19,187	12,467	6,663	57	5,804 R	65.0%	34.7%	65.2%	34.8%
5,304	HEMPHILL	2,067	1,650	413	4	1,237 R	79.8%	20.0%	80.0%	20.0%
42,606	HENDERSON	20,076	12,725	7,302	49	5,423 R	63.4%	36.4%	63.5%	36.5%
283,229	HIDALGO	79,432	35,059	44,147	226	9,088 D	44.1%	55.6%	44.3%	55.7%
25,024	HILL	8,790	5,344	3,420	26	1,924 R	60.8%	38.9%	61.0%	39.0%
23,230	HOCKLEY	7,545	5,462	2,044	39	3,418 R	72.4%	27.1%	72.8%	27.2%
17,714	HOOD	9,921	6,817	3,063	41	3,754 R	68.7%	30.9%	69.0%	31.0%
25,247	HOPKINS	9,493	5,772	3,707	14	2,065 R	60.8%	39.0%	60.9%	39.1%
22,299	HOUSTON	7,834	4,542	3,275	17	1,267 R	58.0%	41.8%	58.1%	41.9%
33,142	HOWARD	11,691	7,519	4,115	57	3,404 R	64.3%	35.2%	64.6%	35.4%
2,728	HUDSPETH	923	557	362	4	195 R	60.3%	39.2%	60.6%	39.4%
55,248	HUNT	21,322	14,303	6,971	48	7,332 R	67.1%	32.7%	67.2%	32.8%
26,304	HUTCHINSON	11,171	9,078	2,052	41	7,026 R	81.3%	18.4%	81.6%	18.4%
1,386	IRION	822	619	199	4	420 R	75.3%	24.2%	75.7%	24.3%
7,408	JACK	2,779	1,825	945	9	880 R	65.7%	34.0%	65.9%	34.1%
13,352	JACKSON	5,478	3,661	1,804	13	1,857 R	66.8%	32.9%	67.0%	33.0%

TEXAS

PRESIDENT 1984

1980 Census Population	County	Total Vote	Republican	Democratic	Other	Rep.-Dem. Plurality	Percentage: Total Vote Rep.	Percentage: Total Vote Dem.	Percentage: Major Vote Rep.	Percentage: Major Vote Dem.
30,781	JASPER	11,779	5,965	5,787	27	178 R	50.6%	49.1%	50.8%	49.2%
1,647	JEFF DAVIS	815	511	299	5	212 R	62.7%	36.7%	63.1%	36.9%
250,938	JEFFERSON	100,215	45,124	54,846	245	9,722 D	45.0%	54.7%	45.1%	54.9%
5,168	JIM HOGG	2,313	608	1,703	2	1,095 D	26.3%	73.6%	26.3%	73.7%
36,498	JIM WELLS	13,715	5,896	7,795	24	1,899 D	43.0%	56.8%	43.1%	56.9%
67,649	JOHNSON	27,474	18,254	9,148	72	9,106 R	66.4%	33.3%	66.6%	33.4%
17,268	JONES	6,383	4,017	2,343	23	1,674 R	62.9%	36.7%	63.2%	36.8%
13,593	KARNES	4,882	3,068	1,802	12	1,266 R	62.8%	36.9%	63.0%	37.0%
39,015	KAUFMAN	14,938	9,343	5,554	41	3,789 R	62.5%	37.2%	62.7%	37.3%
10,635	KENDALL	5,522	4,568	938	16	3,630 R	82.7%	17.0%	83.0%	17.0%
543	KENEDY	207	96	110	1	14 D	46.4%	53.1%	46.6%	53.4%
1,145	KENT	588	332	253	3	79 R	56.5%	43.0%	56.8%	43.2%
28,780	KERR	14,974	11,829	3,102	43	8,727 R	79.0%	20.7%	79.2%	20.8%
4,063	KIMBLE	1,784	1,333	442	9	891 R	74.7%	24.8%	75.1%	24.9%
425	KING	194	141	53		88 R	72.7%	27.3%	72.7%	27.3%
2,279	KINNEY	1,263	774	486	3	288 R	61.3%	38.5%	61.4%	38.6%
33,358	KLEBERG	10,681	5,712	4,924	45	788 R	53.5%	46.1%	53.7%	46.3%
5,329	KNOX	1,952	1,027	921	4	106 R	52.6%	47.2%	52.7%	47.3%
42,156	LAMAR	14,820	9,273	5,504	43	3,769 R	62.6%	37.1%	62.8%	37.2%
18,669	LAMB	5,828	3,892	1,919	17	1,973 R	66.8%	32.9%	67.0%	33.0%
12,005	LAMPASAS	4,653	3,285	1,356	12	1,929 R	70.6%	29.1%	70.8%	29.2%
5,514	LA SALLE	2,514	1,007	1,504	3	497 D	40.1%	59.8%	40.1%	59.9%
19,004	LAVACA	7,532	5,058	2,464	10	2,594 R	67.2%	32.7%	67.2%	32.8%
10,952	LEE	4,632	2,967	1,659	6	1,308 R	64.1%	35.8%	64.1%	35.9%
9,594	LEON	5,038	3,207	1,821	10	1,386 R	63.7%	36.1%	63.8%	36.2%
47,088	LIBERTY	16,866	10,504	6,292	70	4,212 R	62.3%	37.3%	62.5%	37.5%
20,224	LIMESTONE	7,305	4,063	3,228	14	835 R	55.6%	44.2%	55.7%	44.3%
3,766	LIPSCOMB	1,708	1,461	241	6	1,220 R	85.5%	14.1%	85.8%	14.2%
9,606	LIVE OAK	3,759	2,481	1,260	18	1,221 R	66.0%	33.5%	66.3%	33.7%
10,144	LLANO	5,954	4,042	1,894	18	2,148 R	67.9%	31.8%	68.1%	31.9%
91	LOVING	73	57	16		41 R	78.1%	21.9%	78.1%	21.9%
211,651	LUBBOCK	76,219	57,151	18,793	275	38,358 R	75.0%	24.7%	75.3%	24.7%
8,605	LYNN	2,630	1,617	1,009	4	608 R	61.5%	38.4%	61.6%	38.4%
8,735	MCCULLOCH	3,502	2,060	1,433	9	627 R	58.8%	40.9%	59.0%	41.0%
170,755	MCLENNAN	65,578	42,232	23,206	140	19,026 R	64.4%	35.4%	64.5%	35.5%
789	MCMULLEN	398	337	61		276 R	84.7%	15.3%	84.7%	15.3%
10,649	MADISON	3,553	2,158	1,384	11	774 R	60.7%	39.0%	60.9%	39.1%
10,360	MARION	4,463	2,336	2,111	16	225 R	52.3%	47.3%	52.5%	47.5%
4,684	MARTIN	1,740	1,218	512	10	706 R	70.0%	29.4%	70.4%	29.6%
3,683	MASON	1,743	1,168	570	5	598 R	67.0%	32.7%	67.2%	32.8%
37,828	MATAGORDA	13,694	8,452	5,201	41	3,251 R	61.7%	38.0%	61.9%	38.1%
31,398	MAVERICK	4,861	1,783	3,063	15	1,280 D	36.7%	63.0%	36.8%	63.2%
23,164	MEDINA	8,803	5,737	3,053	13	2,684 R	65.2%	34.7%	65.3%	34.7%
2,346	MENARD	1,125	725	394	6	331 R	64.4%	35.0%	64.8%	35.2%
82,636	MIDLAND	41,039	33,706	7,214	119	26,492 R	82.1%	17.6%	82.4%	17.6%
22,732	MILAM	8,140	4,384	3,734	22	650 R	53.9%	45.9%	54.0%	46.0%
4,477	MILLS	1,960	1,262	688	10	574 R	64.4%	35.1%	64.7%	35.3%
9,088	MITCHELL	3,357	2,007	1,332	18	675 R	59.8%	39.7%	60.1%	39.9%
17,410	MONTAGUE	7,030	4,406	2,602	22	1,804 R	62.7%	37.0%	62.9%	37.1%
128,487	MONTGOMERY	54,690	41,230	13,293	167	27,937 R	75.4%	24.3%	75.6%	24.4%
16,575	MOORE	5,796	4,649	1,129	18	3,520 R	80.2%	19.5%	80.5%	19.5%
14,629	MORRIS	5,727	2,778	2,925	24	147 D	48.5%	51.1%	48.7%	51.3%
1,950	MOTLEY	819	533	282	4	251 R	65.1%	34.4%	65.4%	34.6%
46,786	NACOGDOCHES	18,812	13,063	5,694	55	7,369 R	69.4%	30.3%	69.6%	30.4%
35,323	NAVARRO	13,509	7,816	5,672	21	2,144 R	57.9%	42.0%	57.9%	42.1%
13,254	NEWTON	5,439	2,123	3,296	20	1,173 D	39.0%	60.6%	39.2%	60.8%
17,359	NOLAN	6,136	3,608	2,524	4	1,084 R	58.8%	41.1%	58.8%	41.2%
268,215	NUECES	101,213	54,333	46,721	159	7,612 R	53.7%	46.2%	53.8%	46.2%
9,588	OCHILTREE	3,917	3,492	419	6	3,073 R	89.1%	10.7%	89.3%	10.7%
2,283	OLDHAM	990	762	226	2	536 R	77.0%	22.8%	77.1%	22.9%

TEXAS

PRESIDENT 1984

1980 Census Population	County	Total Vote	Republican	Democratic	Other	Rep.-Dem. Plurality	Percentage Total Vote Rep.	Total Vote Dem.	Major Vote Rep.	Major Vote Dem.
83,838	ORANGE	32,303	15,386	16,816	101	1,430 D	47.6%	52.1%	47.8%	52.2%
24,062	PALO PINTO	9,077	5,701	3,349	27	2,352 R	62.8%	36.9%	63.0%	37.0%
20,724	PANOLA	8,885	5,676	3,179	30	2,497 R	63.9%	35.8%	64.1%	35.9%
44,609	PARKER	19,759	13,647	6,050	62	7,597 R	69.1%	30.6%	69.3%	30.7%
11,038	PARMER	3,102	2,524	567	11	1,957 R	81.4%	18.3%	81.7%	18.3%
14,618	PECOS	5,080	3,451	1,596	33	1,855 R	67.9%	31.4%	68.4%	31.6%
24,407	POLK	9,918	5,987	3,898	33	2,089 R	60.4%	39.3%	60.6%	39.4%
98,637	POTTER	28,902	20,396	8,365	141	12,031 R	70.6%	28.9%	70.9%	29.1%
5,188	PRESIDIO	1,902	837	992	73	155 D	44.0%	52.2%	45.8%	54.2%
4,839	RAINS	2,591	1,560	1,027	4	533 R	60.2%	39.6%	60.3%	39.7%
75,062	RANDALL	36,409	30,249	6,044	116	24,205 R	83.1%	16.6%	83.3%	16.7%
4,135	REAGAN	1,324	1,079	243	2	836 R	81.5%	18.4%	81.6%	18.4%
2,469	REAL	1,369	1,004	360	5	644 R	73.3%	26.3%	73.6%	26.4%
16,101	RED RIVER	5,512	2,979	2,518	15	461 R	54.0%	45.7%	54.2%	45.8%
15,801	REEVES	4,872	2,461	2,396	15	65 R	50.5%	49.2%	50.7%	49.3%
9,289	REFUGIO	3,988	2,421	1,559	8	862 R	60.7%	39.1%	60.8%	39.2%
1,187	ROBERTS	645	539	106		433 R	83.6%	16.4%	83.6%	16.4%
14,653	ROBERTSON	6,016	2,663	3,339	14	676 D	44.3%	55.5%	44.4%	55.6%
14,528	ROCKWALL	8,349	6,688	1,639	22	5,049 R	80.1%	19.6%	80.3%	19.7%
11,872	RUNNELS	4,177	2,968	1,179	30	1,789 R	71.1%	28.2%	71.6%	28.4%
41,382	RUSK	15,741	11,081	4,599	61	6,482 R	70.4%	29.2%	70.7%	29.3%
8,702	SABINE	3,993	2,045	1,940	8	105 R	51.2%	48.6%	51.3%	48.7%
8,785	SAN AUGUSTINE	3,529	1,937	1,583	9	354 R	54.9%	44.9%	55.0%	45.0%
11,434	SAN JACINTO	5,659	3,174	2,466	19	708 R	56.1%	43.6%	56.3%	43.7%
58,013	SAN PATRICIO	19,962	11,074	8,838	50	2,236 R	55.5%	44.3%	55.6%	44.4%
6,204	SAN SABA	2,647	1,566	1,070	11	496 R	59.2%	40.4%	59.4%	40.6%
2,820	SCHLEICHER	1,187	854	326	7	528 R	71.9%	27.5%	72.4%	27.6%
18,192	SCURRY	6,629	5,028	1,564	37	3,464 R	75.8%	23.6%	76.3%	23.7%
3,915	SHACKELFORD	1,604	1,181	415	8	766 R	73.6%	25.9%	74.0%	26.0%
23,084	SHELBY	8,501	4,863	3,610	28	1,253 R	57.2%	42.5%	57.4%	42.6%
3,174	SHERMAN	1,524	1,269	246	9	1,023 R	83.3%	16.1%	83.8%	16.2%
128,366	SMITH	56,119	40,740	15,227	152	25,513 R	72.6%	27.1%	72.8%	27.2%
4,154	SOMERVELL	2,061	1,422	635	4	787 R	69.0%	30.8%	69.1%	30.9%
27,266	STARR	6,713	1,658	5,047	8	3,389 D	24.7%	75.2%	24.7%	75.3%
9,926	STEPHENS	3,955	2,898	1,046	11	1,852 R	73.3%	26.4%	73.5%	26.5%
1,206	STERLING	710	577	129	4	448 R	81.3%	18.2%	81.7%	18.3%
2,406	STONEWALL	1,244	599	643	2	44 D	48.2%	51.7%	48.2%	51.8%
5,130	SUTTON	1,721	1,251	465	5	786 R	72.7%	27.0%	72.9%	27.1%
9,723	SWISHER	3,261	1,611	1,642	8	31 D	49.4%	50.4%	49.5%	50.5%
860,880	TARRANT	368,862	248,050	120,147	665	127,903 R	67.2%	32.6%	67.4%	32.6%
110,932	TAYLOR	44,202	34,444	9,628	130	24,816 R	77.9%	21.8%	78.2%	21.8%
1,595	TERRELL	698	407	289	2	118 R	58.3%	41.4%	58.5%	41.5%
14,581	TERRY	4,724	3,181	1,535	8	1,646 R	67.3%	32.5%	67.5%	32.5%
2,053	THROCKMORTON	979	586	388	5	198 R	59.9%	39.6%	60.2%	39.8%
21,442	TITUS	8,727	5,069	3,631	27	1,438 R	58.1%	41.6%	58.3%	41.7%
84,784	TOM GREEN	32,910	23,847	8,981	82	14,866 R	72.5%	27.3%	72.6%	27.4%
419,573	TRAVIS	219,813	124,944	94,124	745	30,820 R	56.8%	42.8%	57.0%	43.0%
9,450	TRINITY	4,735	2,599	2,115	21	484 R	54.9%	44.7%	55.1%	44.9%
16,223	TYLER	6,785	3,638	3,119	28	519 R	53.6%	46.0%	53.8%	46.2%
28,595	UPSHUR	11,976	7,325	4,614	37	2,711 R	61.2%	38.5%	61.4%	38.6%
4,619	UPTON	1,994	1,603	380	11	1,223 R	80.4%	19.1%	80.8%	19.2%
22,441	UVALDE	7,287	4,790	2,482	15	2,308 R	65.7%	34.1%	65.9%	34.1%
35,910	VAL VERDE	9,787	5,909	3,857	21	2,052 R	60.4%	39.4%	60.5%	39.5%
31,426	VAN ZANDT	13,003	8,474	4,506	23	3,968 R	65.2%	34.7%	65.3%	34.7%
68,807	VICTORIA	25,945	18,787	7,037	121	11,750 R	72.4%	27.1%	72.8%	27.2%
41,789	WALKER	13,100	8,809	4,263	28	4,546 R	67.2%	32.5%	67.4%	32.6%
19,798	WALLER	7,963	4,116	3,828	19	288 R	51.7%	48.1%	51.8%	48.2%
13,976	WARD	4,693	3,474	1,188	31	2,286 R	74.0%	25.3%	74.5%	25.5%
21,998	WASHINGTON	8,996	6,506	2,483	7	4,023 R	72.3%	27.6%	72.4%	27.6%
99,258	WEBB	20,936	8,582	12,308	46	3,726 D	41.0%	58.8%	41.1%	58.9%

TEXAS

PRESIDENT 1984

1980 Census Population	County	Total Vote	Republican	Democratic	Other	Rep.-Dem. Plurality	Percentage Total Vote Rep.	Total Vote Dem.	Major Vote Rep.	Major Vote Dem.
40,242	WHARTON	13,584	8,495	5,072	17	3,423 R	62.5%	37.3%	62.6%	37.4%
7,137	WHEELER	3,062	2,251	805	6	1,446 R	73.5%	26.3%	73.7%	26.3%
121,082	WICHITA	45,080	28,932	16,009	139	12,923 R	64.2%	35.5%	64.4%	35.6%
15,931	WILBARGER	5,673	3,644	2,011	18	1,633 R	64.2%	35.4%	64.4%	35.6%
17,495	WILLACY	5,391	2,340	3,037	14	697 D	43.4%	56.3%	43.5%	56.5%
76,521	WILLIAMSON	35,784	25,774	9,911	99	15,863 R	72.0%	27.7%	72.2%	27.8%
16,756	WILSON	7,434	4,588	2,829	17	1,759 R	61.7%	38.1%	61.9%	38.1%
9,944	WINKLER	2,974	2,213	752	9	1,461 R	74.4%	25.3%	74.6%	25.4%
26,575	WISE	10,853	6,958	3,856	39	3,102 R	64.1%	35.5%	64.3%	35.7%
24,697	WOOD	10,612	7,144	3,449	19	3,695 R	67.3%	32.5%	67.4%	32.6%
8,299	YOAKUM	2,668	2,204	456	8	1,748 R	82.6%	17.1%	82.9%	17.1%
19,083	YOUNG	7,503	5,282	2,203	18	3,079 R	70.4%	29.4%	70.6%	29.4%
6,628	ZAPATA	2,801	1,214	1,577	10	363 D	43.3%	56.3%	43.5%	56.5%
11,666	ZAVALA	3,868	924	2,937	7	2,013 D	23.9%	75.9%	23.9%	76.1%
14,229,191	TOTAL	5,397,571	3,433,428	1,949,276	14,867	1,484,152 R	63.6%	36.1%	63.8%	36.2%

TEXAS

PRESIDENT 1980

1980 Census Population	County	Total Vote	Republican	Democratic	Other	Rep.-Dem. Plurality	Percentage Total Vote Rep.	Percentage Total Vote Dem.	Percentage Major Vote Rep.	Percentage Major Vote Dem.
38,381	ANDERSON	11,330	5,970	5,163	197	807 R	52.7%	45.6%	53.6%	46.4%
13,323	ANDREWS	4,013	2,800	1,155	58	1,645 R	69.8%	28.8%	70.8%	29.2%
64,172	ANGELINA	20,394	9,900	10,140	354	240 D	48.5%	49.7%	49.4%	50.6%
14,260	ARANSAS	5,068	3,081	1,800	187	1,281 R	60.8%	35.5%	63.1%	36.9%
7,266	ARCHER	3,289	1,804	1,444	41	360 R	54.8%	43.9%	55.5%	44.5%
1,994	ARMSTRONG	1,065	709	333	23	376 R	66.6%	31.3%	68.0%	32.0%
25,055	ATASCOSA	8,469	4,364	3,980	125	384 R	51.5%	47.0%	52.3%	47.7%
17,726	AUSTIN	5,753	3,734	1,893	126	1,841 R	64.9%	32.9%	66.4%	33.6%
8,168	BAILEY	2,655	1,809	800	46	1,009 R	68.1%	30.1%	69.3%	30.7%
7,084	BANDERA	3,360	2,373	894	93	1,479 R	70.6%	26.6%	72.6%	27.4%
24,726	BASTROP	8,748	3,768	4,716	264	948 D	43.1%	53.9%	44.4%	55.6%
4,919	BAYLOR	2,306	1,098	1,183	25	85 D	47.6%	51.3%	48.1%	51.9%
26,030	BEE	7,931	4,171	3,606	154	565 R	52.6%	45.5%	53.6%	46.4%
157,889	BELL	37,885	20,729	15,823	1,333	4,906 R	54.7%	41.8%	56.7%	43.3%
988,800	BEXAR	308,474	159,578	137,729	11,167	21,849 R	51.7%	44.6%	53.7%	46.3%
4,681	BLANCO	2,301	1,434	794	73	640 R	62.3%	34.5%	64.4%	35.6%
859	BORDEN	415	279	131	5	148 R	67.2%	31.6%	68.0%	32.0%
13,401	BOSQUE	5,437	2,908	2,431	98	477 R	53.5%	44.7%	54.5%	45.5%
75,301	BOWIE	25,650	13,942	11,339	369	2,603 R	54.4%	44.2%	55.1%	44.9%
169,587	BRAZORIA	47,544	27,614	18,253	1,677	9,361 R	58.1%	38.4%	60.2%	39.8%
93,588	BRAZOS	29,539	17,798	9,856	1,885	7,942 R	60.3%	33.4%	64.4%	35.6%
7,573	BREWSTER	2,892	1,496	1,271	125	225 R	51.7%	43.9%	54.1%	45.9%
2,579	BRISCOE	1,150	562	561	27	1 R	48.9%	48.8%	50.0%	50.0%
8,428	BROOKS	3,333	780	2,488	65	1,708 D	23.4%	74.6%	23.9%	76.1%
33,057	BROWN	11,549	6,515	4,867	167	1,648 R	56.4%	42.1%	57.2%	42.8%
12,313	BURLESON	4,609	1,943	2,615	51	672 D	42.2%	56.7%	42.6%	57.4%
17,803	BURNET	7,933	4,033	3,711	189	322 R	50.8%	46.8%	52.1%	47.9%
23,637	CALDWELL	6,184	2,879	3,155	150	276 D	46.6%	51.0%	47.7%	52.3%
19,574	CALHOUN	6,549	3,312	3,034	203	278 R	50.6%	46.3%	52.2%	47.8%
10,992	CALLAHAN	4,331	2,284	2,002	45	282 R	52.7%	46.2%	53.3%	46.7%
209,727	CAMERON	46,285	22,041	23,200	1,044	1,159 D	47.6%	50.1%	48.7%	51.3%
9,275	CAMP	3,618	1,531	2,052	35	521 D	42.3%	56.7%	42.7%	57.3%
6,672	CARSON	2,942	1,888	1,006	48	882 R	64.2%	34.2%	65.2%	34.8%
29,430	CASS	10,672	4,993	5,578	101	585 D	46.8%	52.3%	47.2%	52.8%
10,556	CASTRO	3,218	1,955	1,199	64	756 R	60.8%	37.3%	62.0%	38.0%
18,538	CHAMBERS	5,806	3,140	2,517	149	623 R	54.1%	43.4%	55.5%	44.5%
38,127	CHEROKEE	11,486	5,629	5,726	131	97 D	49.0%	49.9%	49.6%	50.4%
6,950	CHILDRESS	2,713	1,443	1,222	48	221 R	53.2%	45.0%	54.1%	45.9%
9,582	CLAY	4,109	1,824	2,233	52	409 D	44.4%	54.3%	45.0%	55.0%
4,825	COCHRAN	1,607	1,064	513	30	551 R	66.2%	31.9%	67.5%	32.5%
3,196	COKE	1,558	708	838	12	130 D	45.4%	53.8%	45.8%	54.2%
10,439	COLEMAN	3,994	2,228	1,719	47	509 R	55.8%	43.0%	56.4%	43.6%
144,576	COLLIN	53,861	36,559	15,187	2,115	21,372 R	67.9%	28.2%	70.7%	29.3%
4,648	COLLINGSWORTH	1,851	1,020	798	33	222 R	55.1%	43.1%	56.1%	43.9%
18,823	COLORADO	5,991	3,520	2,377	94	1,143 R	58.8%	39.7%	59.7%	40.3%
36,446	COMAL	13,714	9,758	3,554	402	6,204 R	71.2%	25.9%	73.3%	26.7%
12,617	COMANCHE	4,588	1,977	2,550	61	573 D	43.1%	55.6%	43.7%	56.3%
2,915	CONCHO	1,417	700	702	15	2 D	49.4%	49.5%	49.9%	50.1%
27,656	COOKE	10,802	6,760	3,842	200	2,918 R	62.6%	35.6%	63.8%	36.2%
56,767	CORYELL	9,920	5,494	4,097	329	1,397 R	55.4%	41.3%	57.3%	42.7%
2,947	COTTLE	1,266	511	732	23	221 D	40.4%	57.8%	41.1%	58.9%
4,600	CRANE	1,951	1,310	607	34	703 R	67.1%	31.1%	68.3%	31.7%
4,608	CROCKETT	1,494	885	595	14	290 R	59.2%	39.8%	59.8%	40.2%
8,859	CROSBY	2,806	1,361	1,408	37	47 D	48.5%	50.2%	49.2%	50.8%
3,315	CULBERSON	976	541	423	12	118 R	55.4%	43.3%	56.1%	43.9%
6,531	DALLAM	1,639	965	632	42	333 R	58.9%	38.6%	60.4%	39.6%
1,556,390	DALLAS	518,213	306,682	190,459	21,072	116,223 R	59.2%	36.8%	61.7%	38.3%
16,184	DAWSON	5,205	3,267	1,867	71	1,400 R	62.8%	35.9%	63.6%	36.4%
21,165	DEAF SMITH	5,864	4,073	1,666	125	2,407 R	69.5%	28.4%	71.0%	29.0%
4,839	DELTA	2,142	767	1,347	28	580 D	35.8%	62.9%	36.3%	63.7%

TEXAS

PRESIDENT 1980

1980 Census Population	County	Total Vote	Republican	Democratic	Other	Rep.-Dem. Plurality	Percentage Total Vote Rep.	Total Vote Dem.	Major Vote Rep.	Major Vote Dem.
143,126	DENTON	49,908	29,908	17,381	2,619	12,527 R	59.9%	34.8%	63.2%	36.8%
18,903	DE WITT	5,580	3,450	2,044	86	1,406 R	61.8%	36.6%	62.8%	37.2%
3,539	DICKENS	1,481	554	912	15	358 D	37.4%	61.6%	37.8%	62.2%
11,367	DIMMIT	3,323	1,173	2,102	48	929 D	35.3%	63.3%	35.8%	64.2%
4,075	DONLEY	1,888	1,106	751	31	355 R	58.6%	39.8%	59.6%	40.4%
12,517	DUVAL	4,757	1,012	3,706	39	2,694 D	21.3%	77.9%	21.4%	78.6%
19,480	EASTLAND	6,877	3,442	3,346	89	96 R	50.1%	48.7%	50.7%	49.3%
115,374	ECTOR	36,179	26,188	9,069	922	17,119 R	72.4%	25.1%	74.3%	25.7%
2,033	EDWARDS	824	575	237	12	338 R	69.8%	28.8%	70.8%	29.2%
59,743	ELLIS	19,580	10,046	9,219	315	827 R	51.3%	47.1%	52.1%	47.9%
479,899	EL PASO	99,526	53,276	40,082	6,168	13,194 R	53.5%	40.3%	57.1%	42.9%
22,560	ERATH	8,306	3,981	4,156	169	175 D	47.9%	50.0%	48.9%	51.1%
17,946	FALLS	6,007	2,606	3,328	73	722 D	43.4%	55.4%	43.9%	56.1%
24,285	FANNIN	8,611	3,196	5,284	131	2,088 D	37.1%	61.4%	37.7%	62.3%
18,832	FAYETTE	6,804	4,104	2,590	110	1,514 R	60.3%	38.1%	61.3%	38.7%
5,891	FISHER	2,437	838	1,564	35	726 D	34.4%	64.2%	34.9%	65.1%
9,834	FLOYD	3,556	2,043	1,477	36	566 R	57.5%	41.5%	58.0%	42.0%
2,158	FOARD	978	349	617	12	268 D	35.7%	63.1%	36.1%	63.9%
130,846	FORT BEND	38,286	25,366	11,583	1,337	13,783 R	66.3%	30.3%	68.7%	31.3%
6,893	FRANKLIN	2,633	1,105	1,487	41	382 D	42.0%	56.5%	42.6%	57.4%
14,830	FREESTONE	5,265	2,468	2,739	58	271 D	46.9%	52.0%	47.4%	52.6%
13,785	FRIO	4,668	1,753	2,849	66	1,096 D	37.6%	61.0%	38.1%	61.9%
13,150	GAINES	3,656	2,390	1,182	84	1,208 R	65.4%	32.3%	66.9%	33.1%
195,940	GALVESTON	63,297	29,527	30,778	2,992	1,251 D	46.6%	48.6%	49.0%	51.0%
5,336	GARZA	1,897	1,188	677	32	511 R	62.6%	35.7%	63.7%	36.3%
13,532	GILLESPIE	6,018	4,736	1,170	112	3,566 R	78.7%	19.4%	80.2%	19.8%
1,304	GLASSCOCK	535	416	116	3	300 R	77.8%	21.7%	78.2%	21.8%
5,193	GOLIAD	2,287	1,170	1,081	36	89 R	51.2%	47.3%	52.0%	48.0%
16,883	GONZALES	5,922	2,931	2,896	95	35 R	49.5%	48.9%	50.3%	49.7%
26,386	GRAY	10,149	7,187	2,786	176	4,401 R	70.8%	27.5%	72.1%	27.9%
89,796	GRAYSON	31,326	16,811	13,807	708	3,004 R	53.7%	44.1%	54.9%	45.1%
99,487	GREGG	34,190	23,399	10,219	572	13,180 R	68.4%	29.9%	69.6%	30.4%
13,580	GRIMES	4,602	2,087	2,440	75	353 D	45.3%	53.0%	46.1%	53.9%
46,708	GUADALUPE	15,428	9,901	5,049	478	4,852 R	64.2%	32.7%	66.2%	33.8%
37,592	HALE	11,050	7,277	3,610	163	3,667 R	65.9%	32.7%	66.8%	33.2%
5,594	HALL	2,220	1,141	1,057	22	84 R	51.4%	47.6%	51.9%	48.1%
8,297	HAMILTON	3,267	1,683	1,526	58	157 R	51.5%	46.7%	52.4%	47.6%
6,209	HANSFORD	2,596	2,046	518	32	1,528 R	78.8%	20.0%	79.8%	20.2%
6,368	HARDEMAN	2,273	1,056	1,174	43	118 D	46.5%	51.6%	47.4%	52.6%
40,721	HARDIN	13,732	6,087	7,358	287	1,271 D	44.3%	53.6%	45.3%	54.7%
2,409,547	HARRIS	720,014	416,655	274,061	29,298	142,594 R	57.9%	38.1%	60.3%	39.7%
52,265	HARRISON	17,493	9,328	7,746	419	1,582 R	53.3%	44.3%	54.6%	45.4%
3,987	HARTLEY	1,757	1,248	470	39	778 R	71.0%	26.8%	72.6%	27.4%
7,725	HASKELL	3,436	1,447	1,951	38	504 D	42.1%	56.8%	42.6%	57.4%
40,594	HAYS	13,289	6,517	6,013	759	504 R	49.0%	45.2%	52.0%	48.0%
5,304	HEMPHILL	1,780	1,152	592	36	560 R	64.7%	33.3%	66.1%	33.9%
42,606	HENDERSON	16,305	7,903	8,199	203	296 D	48.5%	50.3%	49.1%	50.9%
283,229	HIDALGO	61,717	25,808	34,542	1,367	8,734 D	41.8%	56.0%	42.8%	57.2%
25,024	HILL	8,936	4,113	4,688	135	575 D	46.0%	52.5%	46.7%	53.3%
23,230	HOCKLEY	7,183	4,599	2,447	137	2,152 R	64.0%	34.1%	65.3%	34.7%
17,714	HOOD	6,940	3,755	3,001	184	754 R	54.1%	43.2%	55.6%	44.4%
25,247	HOPKINS	8,318	3,834	4,344	140	510 D	46.1%	52.2%	46.9%	53.1%
22,299	HOUSTON	7,144	2,889	4,181	74	1,292 D	40.4%	58.5%	40.9%	59.1%
33,142	HOWARD	11,312	6,658	4,451	203	2,207 R	58.9%	39.3%	59.9%	40.1%
2,728	HUDSPETH	884	471	394	19	77 R	53.3%	44.6%	54.5%	45.5%
55,248	HUNT	18,501	9,283	8,773	445	510 R	50.2%	47.4%	51.4%	48.6%
26,304	HUTCHINSON	10,632	7,439	2,935	258	4,504 R	70.0%	27.6%	71.7%	28.3%
1,386	IRION	670	427	239	4	188 R	63.7%	35.7%	64.1%	35.9%
7,408	JACK	2,877	1,482	1,349	46	133 R	51.5%	46.9%	52.3%	47.7%
13,352	JACKSON	4,463	2,540	1,826	97	714 R	56.9%	40.9%	58.2%	41.8%

TEXAS

PRESIDENT 1980

1980 Census Population	County	Total Vote	Republican	Democratic	Other	Rep.-Dem. Plurality	Percentage Total Vote Rep.	Total Vote Dem.	Major Vote Rep.	Major Vote Dem.
30,781	JASPER	10,257	4,396	5,707	154	1,311 D	42.9%	55.6%	43.5%	56.5%
1,647	JEFF DAVIS	729	409	300	20	109 R	56.1%	41.2%	57.7%	42.3%
250,938	JEFFERSON	84,602	36,763	45,642	2,197	8,879 D	43.5%	53.9%	44.6%	55.4%
5,168	JIM HOGG	1,997	535	1,437	25	902 D	26.8%	72.0%	27.1%	72.9%
36,498	JIM WELLS	12,013	4,606	7,267	140	2,661 D	38.3%	60.5%	38.8%	61.2%
67,649	JOHNSON	22,454	11,411	10,542	501	869 R	50.8%	46.9%	52.0%	48.0%
17,268	JONES	5,874	2,765	3,043	66	278 D	47.1%	51.8%	47.6%	52.4%
13,593	KARNES	5,074	2,719	2,284	71	435 R	53.6%	45.0%	54.3%	45.7%
39,015	KAUFMAN	12,287	5,852	6,266	169	414 D	47.6%	51.0%	48.3%	51.7%
10,635	KENDALL	5,086	3,890	1,075	121	2,815 R	76.5%	21.1%	78.3%	21.7%
543	KENEDY	187	76	106	5	30 D	40.6%	56.7%	41.8%	58.2%
1,145	KENT	694	339	351	4	12 D	48.8%	50.6%	49.1%	50.9%
28,780	KERR	12,855	9,090	3,387	378	5,703 R	70.7%	26.3%	72.9%	27.1%
4,063	KIMBLE	1,651	1,011	608	32	403 R	61.2%	36.8%	62.4%	37.6%
425	KING	205	144	55	6	89 R	70.2%	26.8%	72.4%	27.6%
2,279	KINNEY	1,046	543	472	31	71 R	51.9%	45.1%	53.5%	46.5%
33,358	KLEBERG	10,053	4,608	5,125	320	517 D	45.8%	51.0%	47.3%	52.7%
5,329	KNOX	1,968	783	1,163	22	380 D	39.8%	59.1%	40.2%	59.8%
42,156	LAMAR	13,490	6,094	7,178	218	1,084 D	45.2%	53.2%	45.9%	54.1%
18,669	LAMB	5,933	3,723	2,132	78	1,591 R	62.8%	35.9%	63.6%	36.4%
12,005	LAMPASAS	4,381	2,323	1,979	79	344 R	53.0%	45.2%	54.0%	46.0%
5,514	LA SALLE	2,248	773	1,442	33	669 D	34.4%	64.1%	34.9%	65.1%
19,004	LAVACA	5,999	3,254	2,678	67	576 R	54.2%	44.6%	54.9%	45.1%
10,952	LEE	3,462	1,803	1,581	78	222 R	52.1%	45.7%	53.3%	46.7%
9,594	LEON	4,053	1,821	2,190	42	369 D	44.9%	54.0%	45.4%	54.6%
47,088	LIBERTY	13,561	6,470	6,810	281	340 D	47.7%	50.2%	48.7%	51.3%
20,224	LIMESTONE	6,319	2,835	3,403	81	568 D	44.9%	53.9%	45.4%	54.6%
3,766	LIPSCOMB	1,733	1,343	338	52	1,005 R	77.5%	19.5%	79.9%	20.1%
9,606	LIVE OAK	3,618	2,193	1,380	45	813 R	60.6%	38.1%	61.4%	38.6%
10,144	LLANO	5,097	2,866	2,130	101	736 R	56.2%	41.8%	57.4%	42.6%
91	LOVING	72	50	22		28 R	69.4%	30.6%	69.4%	30.6%
211,651	LUBBOCK	67,867	46,711	18,732	2,424	27,979 R	68.8%	27.6%	71.4%	28.6%
8,605	LYNN	2,874	1,603	1,236	35	367 R	55.8%	43.0%	56.5%	43.5%
8,735	MCCULLOCH	3,366	1,572	1,750	44	178 D	46.7%	52.0%	47.3%	52.7%
170,755	MCLENNAN	59,515	31,968	26,305	1,242	5,663 R	53.7%	44.2%	54.9%	45.1%
789	MCMULLEN	398	271	122	5	149 R	68.1%	30.7%	69.0%	31.0%
10,649	MADISON	3,018	1,389	1,583	46	194 D	46.0%	52.5%	46.7%	53.3%
10,360	MARION	3,730	1,666	2,015	49	349 D	44.7%	54.0%	45.3%	54.7%
4,684	MARTIN	1,716	1,093	605	18	488 R	63.7%	35.3%	64.4%	35.6%
3,683	MASON	1,621	966	630	25	336 R	59.6%	38.9%	60.5%	39.5%
37,828	MATAGORDA	10,382	5,545	4,585	252	960 R	53.4%	44.2%	54.7%	45.3%
31,398	MAVERICK	4,367	1,370	2,932	65	1,562 D	31.4%	67.1%	31.8%	68.2%
23,164	MEDINA	7,888	4,742	3,034	112	1,708 R	60.1%	38.5%	61.0%	39.0%
2,346	MENARD	1,050	548	489	13	59 R	52.2%	46.6%	52.8%	47.2%
82,636	MIDLAND	32,692	25,027	6,839	826	18,188 R	76.6%	20.9%	78.5%	21.5%
22,732	MILAM	7,627	3,251	4,230	146	979 D	42.6%	55.5%	43.5%	56.5%
4,477	MILLS	2,059	985	1,028	46	43 D	47.8%	49.9%	48.9%	51.1%
9,088	MITCHELL	2,926	1,455	1,446	25	9 R	49.7%	49.4%	50.2%	49.8%
17,410	MONTAGUE	6,472	3,143	3,233	96	90 D	48.6%	50.0%	49.3%	50.7%
128,487	MONTGOMERY	39,971	26,237	12,593	1,141	13,644 R	65.6%	31.5%	67.6%	32.4%
16,575	MOORE	5,583	3,736	1,743	104	1,993 R	66.9%	31.2%	68.2%	31.8%
14,629	MORRIS	5,280	2,133	3,105	42	972 D	40.4%	58.8%	40.7%	59.3%
1,950	MOTLEY	929	573	341	15	232 R	61.7%	36.7%	62.7%	37.3%
46,786	NACOGDOCHES	15,150	8,626	5,981	543	2,645 R	56.9%	39.5%	59.1%	40.9%
35,323	NAVARRO	12,591	5,400	6,988	203	1,588 D	42.9%	55.5%	43.6%	56.4%
13,254	NEWTON	4,714	1,379	3,284	51	1,905 D	29.3%	69.7%	29.6%	70.4%
17,359	NOLAN	5,695	2,781	2,796	118	15 D	48.8%	49.1%	49.9%	50.1%
268,215	NUECES	86,644	40,586	43,424	2,634	2,838 D	46.8%	50.1%	48.3%	51.7%
9,588	OCHILTREE	3,702	3,032	594	76	2,438 R	81.9%	16.0%	83.6%	16.4%
2,283	OLDHAM	874	557	290	27	267 R	63.7%	33.2%	65.8%	34.2%

TEXAS

PRESIDENT 1980

1980 Census Population	County	Total Vote	Republican	Democratic	Other	Rep.-Dem. Plurality	Percentage Total Vote Rep.	Percentage Total Vote Dem.	Percentage Major Vote Rep.	Percentage Major Vote Dem.
83,838	ORANGE	27,887	12,389	14,928	570	2,539 D	44.4%	53.5%	45.4%	54.6%
24,062	PALO PINTO	8,484	4,068	4,244	172	176 D	47.9%	50.0%	48.9%	51.1%
20,724	PANOLA	7,747	4,022	3,637	88	385 R	51.9%	46.9%	52.5%	47.5%
44,609	PARKER	16,155	8,505	7,336	314	1,169 R	52.6%	45.4%	53.7%	46.3%
11,038	PARMER	3,398	2,640	707	51	1,933 R	77.7%	20.8%	78.9%	21.1%
14,618	PECOS	4,395	2,723	1,602	70	1,121 R	62.0%	36.5%	63.0%	37.0%
24,407	POLK	8,108	3,771	4,213	124	442 D	46.5%	52.0%	47.2%	52.8%
98,637	POTTER	26,831	16,327	9,633	871	6,694 R	60.9%	35.9%	62.9%	37.1%
5,188	PRESIDIO	1,799	723	1,039	37	316 D	40.2%	57.8%	41.0%	59.0%
4,839	RAINS	2,022	813	1,174	35	361 D	40.2%	58.1%	40.9%	59.1%
75,062	RANDALL	31,382	23,136	7,323	923	15,813 R	73.7%	23.3%	76.0%	24.0%
4,135	REAGAN	1,351	917	414	20	503 R	67.9%	30.6%	68.9%	31.1%
2,469	REAL	1,453	832	603	18	229 R	57.3%	41.5%	58.0%	42.0%
16,101	RED RIVER	5,773	2,225	3,501	47	1,276 D	38.5%	60.6%	38.9%	61.1%
15,801	REEVES	4,544	2,315	2,138	91	177 R	50.9%	47.1%	52.0%	48.0%
9,289	REFUGIO	4,251	1,944	2,224	83	280 D	45.7%	52.3%	46.6%	53.4%
1,187	ROBERTS	642	482	150	10	332 R	75.1%	23.4%	76.3%	23.7%
14,653	ROBERTSON	5,310	1,661	3,572	77	1,911 D	31.3%	67.3%	31.7%	68.3%
14,528	ROCKWALL	6,184	4,036	1,985	163	2,051 R	65.3%	32.1%	67.0%	33.0%
11,872	RUNNELS	4,233	2,532	1,648	53	884 R	59.8%	38.9%	60.6%	39.4%
41,382	RUSK	14,467	8,705	5,582	180	3,123 R	60.2%	38.6%	60.9%	39.1%
8,702	SABINE	3,398	1,387	1,983	28	596 D	40.8%	58.4%	41.2%	58.8%
8,785	SAN AUGUSTINE	3,091	1,397	1,674	20	277 D	45.2%	54.2%	45.5%	54.5%
11,434	SAN JACINTO	4,193	1,726	2,376	91	650 D	41.2%	56.7%	42.1%	57.9%
58,013	SAN PATRICIO	17,494	8,326	8,627	541	301 D	47.6%	49.3%	49.1%	50.9%
6,204	SAN SABA	2,385	948	1,405	32	457 D	39.7%	58.9%	40.3%	59.7%
2,820	SCHLEICHER	1,131	672	444	15	228 R	59.4%	39.3%	60.2%	39.8%
18,192	SCURRY	5,846	3,745	2,003	98	1,742 R	64.1%	34.3%	65.2%	34.8%
3,915	SHACKELFORD	1,581	959	606	16	353 R	60.7%	38.3%	61.3%	38.7%
23,084	SHELBY	7,804	3,500	4,215	89	715 D	44.8%	54.0%	45.4%	54.6%
3,174	SHERMAN	1,456	1,128	286	42	842 R	77.5%	19.6%	79.8%	20.2%
128,366	SMITH	43,700	28,236	14,838	626	13,398 R	64.6%	34.0%	65.6%	34.4%
4,154	SOMERVELL	1,852	792	1,015	45	223 D	42.8%	54.8%	43.8%	56.2%
27,266	STARR	6,253	1,389	4,782	82	3,393 D	22.2%	76.5%	22.5%	77.5%
9,926	STEPHENS	3,608	2,161	1,372	75	789 R	59.9%	38.0%	61.2%	38.8%
1,206	STERLING	586	364	218	4	146 R	62.1%	37.2%	62.5%	37.5%
2,406	STONEWALL	1,219	488	719	12	231 D	40.0%	59.0%	40.4%	59.6%
5,130	SUTTON	1,511	1,000	485	26	515 R	66.2%	32.1%	67.3%	32.7%
9,723	SWISHER	3,366	1,450	1,854	62	404 D	43.1%	55.1%	43.9%	56.1%
860,880	TARRANT	305,066	173,466	121,068	10,532	52,398 R	56.9%	39.7%	58.9%	41.1%
110,932	TAYLOR	37,032	22,961	13,245	826	9,716 R	62.0%	35.8%	63.4%	36.6%
1,595	TERRELL	686	411	260	15	151 R	59.9%	37.9%	61.3%	38.7%
14,581	TERRY	5,195	3,178	1,945	72	1,233 R	61.2%	37.4%	62.0%	38.0%
2,053	THROCKMORTON	908	444	455	9	11 D	48.9%	50.1%	49.4%	50.6%
21,442	TITUS	7,700	3,747	3,872	81	125 D	48.7%	50.3%	49.2%	50.8%
84,784	TOM GREEN	27,271	16,555	9,892	824	6,663 R	60.7%	36.3%	62.6%	37.4%
419,573	TRAVIS	160,093	73,151	75,028	11,914	1,877 D	45.7%	46.9%	49.4%	50.6%
9,450	TRINITY	4,068	1,503	2,510	55	1,007 D	36.9%	61.7%	37.5%	62.5%
16,223	TYLER	6,195	2,545	3,540	110	995 D	41.1%	57.1%	41.8%	58.2%
28,595	UPSHUR	9,852	4,836	4,894	122	58 D	49.1%	49.7%	49.7%	50.3%
4,619	UPTON	1,684	1,169	485	30	684 R	69.4%	28.8%	70.7%	29.3%
22,441	UVALDE	6,366	3,887	2,402	77	1,485 R	61.1%	37.7%	61.8%	38.2%
35,910	VAL VERDE	9,353	5,055	4,116	182	939 R	54.0%	44.0%	55.1%	44.9%
31,426	VAN ZANDT	11,340	5,495	5,707	138	212 D	48.5%	50.3%	49.1%	50.9%
68,807	VICTORIA	21,269	13,392	7,382	495	6,010 R	63.0%	34.7%	64.5%	35.5%
41,789	WALKER	10,906	5,657	4,869	380	788 R	51.9%	44.6%	53.7%	46.3%
19,798	WALLER	6,463	3,019	3,329	115	310 D	46.7%	51.5%	47.6%	52.4%
13,976	WARD	4,396	2,912	1,405	79	1,507 R	66.2%	32.0%	67.5%	32.5%
21,998	WASHINGTON	7,495	4,821	2,518	156	2,303 R	64.3%	33.6%	65.7%	34.3%
99,258	WEBB	17,593	5,421	11,856	316	6,435 D	30.8%	67.4%	31.4%	68.6%

TEXAS

PRESIDENT 1980

1980 Census Population	County	Total Vote	Republican	Democratic	Other	Rep.-Dem. Plurality	Percentage Total Vote Rep.	Percentage Total Vote Dem.	Percentage Major Vote Rep.	Percentage Major Vote Dem.
40,242	WHARTON	11,958	6,598	5,138	222	1,460 R	55.2%	43.0%	56.2%	43.8%
7,137	WHEELER	2,743	1,626	1,090	27	536 R	59.3%	39.7%	59.9%	40.1%
121,082	WICHITA	41,625	22,884	17,657	1,084	5,227 R	55.0%	42.4%	56.4%	43.6%
15,931	WILBARGER	5,463	3,031	2,347	85	684 R	55.5%	43.0%	56.4%	43.6%
17,495	WILLACY	5,108	1,995	3,047	66	1,052 D	39.1%	59.7%	39.6%	60.4%
76,521	WILLIAMSON	26,661	15,035	10,408	1,218	4,627 R	56.4%	39.0%	59.1%	40.9%
16,756	WILSON	6,632	3,443	3,097	92	346 R	51.9%	46.7%	52.6%	47.4%
9,944	WINKLER	3,232	2,160	1,021	51	1,139 R	66.8%	31.6%	67.9%	32.1%
26,575	WISE	9,205	4,350	4,674	181	324 D	47.3%	50.8%	48.2%	51.8%
24,697	WOOD	8,671	4,515	4,033	123	482 R	52.1%	46.5%	52.8%	47.2%
8,299	YOAKUM	2,694	1,937	715	42	1,222 R	71.9%	26.5%	73.0%	27.0%
19,083	YOUNG	7,022	4,153	2,740	129	1,413 R	59.1%	39.0%	60.2%	39.8%
6,628	ZAPATA	2,131	874	1,218	39	344 D	41.0%	57.2%	41.8%	58.2%
11,666	ZAVALA	3,538	831	2,621	86	1,790 D	23.5%	74.1%	24.1%	75.9%
14,229,191	TOTAL	4,541,636	2,510,705	1,881,147	149,784	629,558 R	55.3%	41.4%	57.2%	42.8%

TEXAS

PRESIDENT 1976

1970 Census Population	County	Total Vote	Republican	Democratic	Other	Rep.-Dem. Plurality	Percentage Total Vote Rep.	Percentage Total Vote Dem.	Percentage Major Vote Rep.	Percentage Major Vote Dem.
27,789	ANDERSON	9,715	4,172	5,499	44	1,327 D	42.9%	56.6%	43.1%	56.9%
10,372	ANDREWS	3,937	2,127	1,777	33	350 R	54.0%	45.1%	54.5%	45.5%
49,349	ANGELINA	17,112	7,223	9,750	139	2,527 D	42.2%	57.0%	42.6%	57.4%
8,902	ARANSAS	4,181	1,985	2,136	60	151 D	47.5%	51.1%	48.2%	51.8%
5,759	ARCHER	2,561	966	1,577	18	611 D	37.7%	61.6%	38.0%	62.0%
1,895	ARMSTRONG	1,027	506	513	8	7 D	49.3%	50.0%	49.7%	50.3%
18,696	ATASCOSA	7,072	2,415	4,565	92	2,150 D	34.1%	64.6%	34.6%	65.4%
13,831	AUSTIN	5,033	2,686	2,313	34	373 R	53.4%	46.0%	53.7%	46.3%
8,487	BAILEY	2,627	1,255	1,356	16	101 D	47.8%	51.6%	48.1%	51.9%
4,747	BANDERA	2,766	1,554	1,183	29	371 R	56.2%	42.8%	56.8%	43.2%
17,297	BASTROP	7,204	2,383	4,788	33	2,405 D	33.1%	66.5%	33.2%	66.8%
5,221	BAYLOR	2,130	783	1,335	12	552 D	36.8%	62.7%	37.0%	63.0%
22,737	BEE	6,722	2,953	3,690	79	737 D	43.9%	54.9%	44.5%	55.5%
124,483	BELL	32,912	15,126	17,499	287	2,373 D	46.0%	53.2%	46.4%	53.6%
830,460	BEXAR	271,430	121,176	146,581	3,673	25,405 D	44.6%	54.0%	45.3%	54.7%
3,567	BLANCO	1,956	1,015	923	18	92 R	51.9%	47.2%	52.4%	47.6%
888	BORDEN	390	150	234	6	84 D	38.5%	60.0%	39.1%	60.9%
10,966	BOSQUE	4,883	1,912	2,954	17	1,042 D	39.2%	60.5%	39.3%	60.7%
67,813	BOWIE	22,214	9,590	12,445	179	2,855 D	43.2%	56.0%	43.5%	56.5%
108,312	BRAZORIA	41,744	19,475	21,711	558	2,236 D	46.7%	52.0%	47.3%	52.7%
57,978	BRAZOS	26,700	15,685	10,628	387	5,057 R	58.7%	39.8%	59.6%	40.4%
7,780	BREWSTER	2,624	1,368	1,227	29	141 R	52.1%	46.8%	52.7%	47.3%
2,794	BRISCOE	1,119	285	823	11	538 D	25.5%	73.5%	25.7%	74.3%
8,005	BROOKS	3,429	641	2,782	6	2,141 D	18.7%	81.1%	18.7%	81.3%
25,877	BROWN	10,095	4,483	5,577	35	1,094 D	44.4%	55.2%	44.6%	55.4%
9,999	BURLESON	4,081	1,142	2,924	15	1,782 D	28.0%	71.6%	28.1%	71.9%
11,420	BURNET	6,636	2,777	3,818	41	1,041 D	41.8%	57.5%	42.1%	57.9%
21,178	CALDWELL	5,921	2,235	3,647	39	1,412 D	37.7%	61.6%	38.0%	62.0%
17,831	CALHOUN	6,061	2,377	3,642	42	1,265 D	39.2%	60.1%	39.5%	60.5%
8,205	CALLAHAN	3,864	1,581	2,241	42	660 D	40.9%	58.0%	41.4%	58.6%
140,368	CAMERON	42,111	16,448	25,310	353	8,862 D	39.1%	60.1%	39.4%	60.6%
8,005	CAMP	3,285	1,133	2,146	6	1,013 D	34.5%	65.3%	34.6%	65.4%
6,358	CARSON	2,824	1,269	1,542	13	273 D	44.9%	54.6%	45.1%	54.9%
24,133	CASS	8,875	3,712	5,134	29	1,422 D	41.8%	57.8%	42.0%	58.0%
10,394	CASTRO	3,076	1,007	2,033	36	1,026 D	32.7%	66.1%	33.1%	66.9%
12,187	CHAMBERS	4,852	1,835	2,927	90	1,092 D	37.8%	60.3%	38.5%	61.5%
32,008	CHEROKEE	10,465	3,921	6,509	35	2,588 D	37.5%	62.2%	37.6%	62.4%
6,605	CHILDRESS	2,626	1,043	1,578	5	535 D	39.7%	60.1%	39.8%	60.2%
8,079	CLAY	3,783	1,200	2,568	15	1,368 D	31.7%	67.9%	31.8%	68.2%
5,326	COCHRAN	1,739	701	1,031	7	330 D	40.3%	59.3%	40.5%	59.5%
3,087	COKE	1,377	517	844	16	327 D	37.5%	61.3%	38.0%	62.0%
10,288	COLEMAN	3,955	1,669	2,264	22	595 D	42.2%	57.2%	42.4%	57.6%
66,920	COLLIN	36,000	21,608	14,039	353	7,569 R	60.0%	39.0%	60.6%	39.4%
4,755	COLLINGSWORTH	1,804	629	1,169	6	540 D	34.9%	64.8%	35.0%	65.0%
17,638	COLORADO	6,075	2,991	3,028	56	37 D	49.2%	49.8%	49.7%	50.3%
24,165	COMAL	10,554	6,377	4,068	109	2,309 R	60.4%	38.5%	61.1%	38.9%
11,898	COMANCHE	4,731	1,297	3,414	20	2,117 D	27.4%	72.2%	27.5%	72.5%
2,937	CONCHO	1,195	474	715	6	241 D	39.7%	59.8%	39.9%	60.1%
23,471	COOKE	9,329	4,804	4,483	42	321 R	51.5%	48.1%	51.7%	48.3%
35,311	CORYELL	8,929	4,140	4,710	79	570 D	46.4%	52.7%	46.8%	53.2%
3,204	COTTLE	1,361	311	1,047	3	736 D	22.9%	76.9%	22.9%	77.1%
4,172	CRANE	1,680	963	664	53	299 R	57.3%	39.5%	59.2%	40.8%
3,885	CROCKETT	1,608	802	804	2	2 D	49.9%	50.0%	49.9%	50.1%
9,085	CROSBY	3,092	897	2,176	19	1,279 D	29.0%	70.4%	29.2%	70.8%
3,429	CULBERSON	787	373	407	7	34 D	47.4%	51.7%	47.8%	52.2%
6,012	DALLAM	2,007	936	1,029	42	93 D	46.6%	51.3%	47.6%	52.4%
1,327,321	DALLAS	464,385	263,081	196,303	5,001	66,778 R	56.7%	42.3%	57.3%	42.7%
16,604	DAWSON	4,653	2,474	2,162	17	312 R	53.2%	46.5%	53.4%	46.6%
18,999	DEAF SMITH	5,435	2,776	2,613	46	163 R	51.1%	48.1%	51.5%	48.5%
4,927	DELTA	1,991	421	1,563	7	1,142 D	21.1%	78.5%	21.2%	78.8%

TEXAS

PRESIDENT 1976

1970 Census Population	County	Total Vote	Republican	Democratic	Other	Rep.-Dem. Plurality	Percentage: Total Vote Rep.	Total Vote Dem.	Major Vote Rep.	Major Vote Dem.
75,633	DENTON	39,692	20,440	18,887	365	1,553 R	51.5%	47.6%	52.0%	48.0%
18,660	DE WITT	5,327	2,754	2,540	33	214 R	51.7%	47.7%	52.0%	48.0%
3,737	DICKENS	1,571	343	1,222	6	879 D	21.8%	77.8%	21.9%	78.1%
9,039	DIMMIT	2,624	890	1,721	13	831 D	33.9%	65.6%	34.1%	65.9%
3,641	DONLEY	1,804	704	1,095	5	391 D	39.0%	60.7%	39.1%	60.9%
11,722	DUVAL	4,941	661	4,267	13	3,606 D	13.4%	86.4%	13.4%	86.6%
18,092	EASTLAND	6,695	2,340	4,320	35	1,980 D	35.0%	64.5%	35.1%	64.9%
91,805	ECTOR	30,328	18,973	10,802	553	8,171 R	62.6%	35.6%	63.7%	36.3%
2,107	EDWARDS	672	412	258	2	154 R	61.3%	38.4%	61.5%	38.5%
46,638	ELLIS	17,055	6,996	9,991	68	2,995 D	41.0%	58.6%	41.2%	58.8%
359,291	EL PASO	89,465	42,697	45,477	1,291	2,780 D	47.7%	50.8%	48.4%	51.6%
18,141	ERATH	7,790	2,925	4,821	44	1,896 D	37.5%	61.9%	37.8%	62.2%
17,300	FALLS	6,567	2,261	4,277	29	2,016 D	34.4%	65.1%	34.6%	65.4%
22,705	FANNIN	7,985	2,102	5,845	38	3,743 D	26.3%	73.2%	26.5%	73.5%
17,650	FAYETTE	6,493	3,030	3,428	35	398 D	46.7%	52.8%	46.9%	53.1%
6,344	FISHER	2,576	573	1,993	10	1,420 D	22.2%	77.4%	22.3%	77.7%
11,044	FLOYD	3,414	1,402	1,991	21	589 D	41.1%	58.3%	41.3%	58.7%
2,211	FOARD	950	240	706	4	466 D	25.3%	74.3%	25.4%	74.6%
52,314	FORT BEND	28,787	17,354	11,264	169	6,090 R	60.3%	39.1%	60.6%	39.4%
5,291	FRANKLIN	2,404	758	1,636	10	878 D	31.5%	68.1%	31.7%	68.3%
11,116	FREESTONE	4,361	1,674	2,679	8	1,005 D	38.4%	61.4%	38.5%	61.5%
11,159	FRIO	3,908	1,280	2,598	30	1,318 D	32.8%	66.5%	33.0%	67.0%
11,593	GAINES	3,544	1,643	1,880	21	237 D	46.4%	53.0%	46.6%	53.4%
169,812	GALVESTON	63,735	25,251	37,873	611	12,622 D	39.6%	59.4%	40.0%	60.0%
5,289	GARZA	1,725	755	957	13	202 D	43.8%	55.5%	44.1%	55.9%
10,553	GILLESPIE	4,885	3,541	1,260	84	2,281 R	72.5%	25.8%	73.8%	26.2%
1,155	GLASSCOCK	413	218	190	5	28 R	52.8%	46.0%	53.4%	46.6%
4,869	GOLIAD	1,731	846	875	10	29 D	48.9%	50.5%	49.2%	50.8%
16,375	GONZALES	5,026	1,789	3,219	18	1,430 D	35.6%	64.0%	35.7%	64.3%
26,949	GRAY	9,962	6,010	3,872	80	2,138 R	60.3%	38.9%	60.8%	39.2%
83,225	GRAYSON	29,095	11,981	17,015	99	5,034 D	41.2%	58.5%	41.3%	58.7%
75,929	GREGG	27,612	17,582	9,827	203	7,755 R	63.7%	35.6%	64.1%	35.9%
11,855	GRIMES	4,148	1,473	2,656	19	1,183 D	35.5%	64.0%	35.7%	64.3%
33,554	GUADALUPE	12,935	6,766	6,054	115	712 R	52.3%	46.8%	52.8%	47.2%
34,137	HALE	11,007	5,390	5,580	37	190 D	49.0%	50.7%	49.1%	50.9%
6,015	HALL	2,314	671	1,633	10	962 D	29.0%	70.6%	29.1%	70.9%
7,198	HAMILTON	3,189	1,176	1,981	32	805 D	36.9%	62.1%	37.3%	62.7%
6,351	HANSFORD	2,406	1,401	983	22	418 R	58.2%	40.9%	58.8%	41.2%
6,795	HARDEMAN	2,225	805	1,403	17	598 D	36.2%	63.1%	36.5%	63.5%
29,996	HARDIN	10,688	4,046	6,558	84	2,512 D	37.9%	61.4%	38.2%	61.8%
1,741,912	HARRIS	685,264	357,536	321,897	5,831	35,639 R	52.2%	47.0%	52.6%	47.4%
44,841	HARRISON	15,639	7,787	7,796	56	9 D	49.8%	49.8%	50.0%	50.0%
2,782	HARTLEY	1,597	811	774	12	37 R	50.8%	48.5%	51.2%	48.8%
8,512	HASKELL	3,359	838	2,512	9	1,674 D	24.9%	74.8%	25.0%	75.0%
27,642	HAYS	12,875	5,714	7,005	156	1,291 D	44.4%	54.4%	44.9%	55.1%
3,084	HEMPHILL	1,578	858	707	13	151 R	54.4%	44.8%	54.8%	45.2%
26,466	HENDERSON	12,937	4,658	8,245	34	3,587 D	36.0%	63.7%	36.1%	63.9%
181,535	HIDALGO	54,593	19,199	35,021	373	15,822 D	35.2%	64.1%	35.4%	64.6%
22,596	HILL	8,032	2,680	5,327	25	2,647 D	33.4%	66.3%	33.5%	66.5%
20,396	HOCKLEY	7,130	3,137	3,949	44	812 D	44.0%	55.4%	44.3%	55.7%
6,368	HOOD	5,061	1,857	3,181	23	1,324 D	36.7%	62.9%	36.9%	63.1%
20,710	HOPKINS	7,592	2,556	4,992	44	2,436 D	33.7%	65.8%	33.9%	66.1%
17,855	HOUSTON	5,421	2,229	3,179	13	950 D	41.1%	58.6%	41.2%	58.8%
37,796	HOWARD	11,972	4,899	6,984	89	2,085 D	40.9%	58.3%	41.2%	58.8%
2,392	HUDSPETH	881	395	479	7	84 D	44.8%	54.4%	45.2%	54.8%
47,948	HUNT	15,314	6,676	8,543	95	1,867 D	43.6%	55.8%	43.9%	56.1%
24,443	HUTCHINSON	9,933	6,137	3,691	105	2,446 R	61.8%	37.2%	62.4%	37.6%
1,070	IRION	604	302	297	5	5 R	50.0%	49.2%	50.4%	49.6%
6,711	JACK	2,871	1,049	1,814	8	765 D	36.5%	63.2%	36.6%	63.4%
12,975	JACKSON	4,433	1,884	2,524	25	640 D	42.5%	56.9%	42.7%	57.3%

TEXAS

PRESIDENT 1976

1970 Census Population	County	Total Vote	Republican	Democratic	Other	Rep.-Dem. Plurality	Percentage Total Vote Rep.	Total Vote Dem.	Major Vote Rep.	Major Vote Dem.
24,692	JASPER	8,607	3,167	5,422	18	2,255 D	36.8%	63.0%	36.9%	63.1%
1,527	JEFF DAVIS	607	288	309	10	21 D	47.4%	50.9%	48.2%	51.8%
244,773	JEFFERSON	80,546	32,451	47,581	514	15,130 D	40.3%	59.1%	40.5%	59.5%
4,654	JIM HOGG	2,074	429	1,645		1,216 D	20.7%	79.3%	20.7%	79.3%
33,032	JIM WELLS	11,550	3,547	7,961	42	4,414 D	30.7%	68.9%	30.8%	69.2%
45,769	JOHNSON	18,127	7,194	10,864	69	3,670 D	39.7%	59.9%	39.8%	60.2%
16,106	JONES	5,416	2,072	3,318	26	1,246 D	38.3%	61.3%	38.4%	61.6%
13,462	KARNES	4,718	1,675	2,996	47	1,321 D	35.5%	63.5%	35.9%	64.1%
32,392	KAUFMAN	10,204	3,867	6,302	35	2,435 D	37.9%	61.8%	38.0%	62.0%
6,964	KENDALL	3,793	2,543	1,190	60	1,353 R	67.0%	31.4%	68.1%	31.9%
678	KENEDY	205	65	139	1	74 D	31.7%	67.8%	31.9%	68.1%
1,434	KENT	647	171	474	2	303 D	26.4%	73.3%	26.5%	73.5%
19,454	KERR	9,978	6,021	3,767	190	2,254 R	60.3%	37.8%	61.5%	38.5%
3,904	KIMBLE	1,632	846	759	27	87 R	51.8%	46.5%	52.7%	47.3%
464	KING	197	96	100	1	4 D	48.7%	50.8%	49.0%	51.0%
2,006	KINNEY	843	318	516	9	198 D	37.7%	61.2%	38.1%	61.9%
33,166	KLEBERG	9,647	3,771	5,803	73	2,032 D	39.1%	60.2%	39.4%	60.6%
5,972	KNOX	2,060	551	1,498	11	947 D	26.7%	72.7%	26.9%	73.1%
36,062	LAMAR	13,076	4,443	8,601	32	4,158 D	34.0%	65.8%	34.1%	65.9%
17,770	LAMB	5,815	2,413	3,374	28	961 D	41.5%	58.0%	41.7%	58.3%
9,323	LAMPASAS	3,982	1,563	2,376	43	813 D	39.3%	59.7%	39.7%	60.3%
5,014	LA SALLE	1,983	677	1,294	12	617 D	34.1%	65.3%	34.3%	65.7%
17,903	LAVACA	5,964	2,466	3,458	40	992 D	41.3%	58.0%	41.6%	58.4%
8,048	LEE	3,303	1,348	1,937	18	589 D	40.8%	58.6%	41.0%	59.0%
8,738	LEON	3,261	1,161	2,085	15	924 D	35.6%	63.9%	35.8%	64.2%
33,014	LIBERTY	11,704	4,552	7,086	66	2,534 D	38.9%	60.5%	39.1%	60.9%
18,100	LIMESTONE	5,900	2,045	3,825	30	1,780 D	34.7%	64.8%	34.8%	65.2%
3,486	LIPSCOMB	1,569	911	644	14	267 R	58.1%	41.0%	58.6%	41.4%
6,697	LIVE OAK	2,961	1,287	1,656	18	369 D	43.5%	55.9%	43.7%	56.3%
6,979	LLANO	4,324	1,947	2,361	16	414 D	45.0%	54.6%	45.2%	54.8%
164	LOVING	86	47	35	4	12 R	54.7%	40.7%	57.3%	42.7%
179,295	LUBBOCK	63,707	38,478	24,797	432	13,681 R	60.4%	38.9%	60.8%	39.2%
9,107	LYNN	2,757	1,166	1,575	16	409 D	42.3%	57.1%	42.5%	57.5%
8,571	MCCULLOCH	3,207	1,300	1,888	19	588 D	40.5%	58.9%	40.8%	59.2%
147,553	MCLENNAN	55,970	25,370	30,091	509	4,721 D	45.3%	53.8%	45.7%	54.3%
1,095	MCMULLEN	411	217	194		23 R	52.8%	47.2%	52.8%	47.2%
7,693	MADISON	2,961	1,062	1,885	14	823 D	35.9%	63.7%	36.0%	64.0%
8,517	MARION	3,167	1,291	1,860	16	569 D	40.8%	58.7%	41.0%	59.0%
4,774	MARTIN	1,618	698	907	13	209 D	43.1%	56.1%	43.5%	56.5%
3,356	MASON	1,640	805	814	21	9 D	49.1%	49.6%	49.7%	50.3%
27,913	MATAGORDA	8,731	3,679	4,971	81	1,292 D	42.1%	56.9%	42.5%	57.5%
18,093	MAVERICK	3,802	924	2,840	38	1,916 D	24.3%	74.7%	24.5%	75.5%
20,249	MEDINA	6,988	3,252	3,681	55	429 D	46.5%	52.7%	46.9%	53.1%
2,646	MENARD	1,000	441	543	16	102 D	44.1%	54.3%	44.8%	55.2%
65,433	MIDLAND	27,195	19,178	7,725	292	11,453 R	70.5%	28.4%	71.3%	28.7%
20,028	MILAM	7,315	2,404	4,871	40	2,467 D	32.9%	66.6%	33.0%	67.0%
4,212	MILLS	1,710	684	1,012	14	328 D	40.0%	59.2%	40.3%	59.7%
9,073	MITCHELL	2,804	1,058	1,730	16	672 D	37.7%	61.7%	37.9%	62.1%
15,326	MONTAGUE	6,294	2,182	4,087	25	1,905 D	34.7%	64.9%	34.8%	65.2%
49,479	MONTGOMERY	29,659	15,739	13,718	202	2,021 R	53.1%	46.3%	53.4%	46.6%
14,060	MOORE	5,575	2,759	2,767	49	8 D	49.5%	49.6%	49.9%	50.1%
12,310	MORRIS	4,931	1,843	3,071	17	1,228 D	37.4%	62.3%	37.5%	62.5%
2,178	MOTLEY	961	428	522	11	94 D	44.5%	54.3%	45.1%	54.9%
36,362	NACOGDOCHES	14,141	7,315	6,697	129	618 R	51.7%	47.4%	52.2%	47.8%
31,150	NAVARRO	11,068	4,012	6,995	61	2,983 D	36.2%	63.2%	36.4%	63.6%
11,657	NEWTON	4,502	1,011	3,468	23	2,457 D	22.5%	77.0%	22.6%	77.4%
16,220	NOLAN	5,545	2,431	3,094	20	663 D	43.8%	55.8%	44.0%	56.0%
237,544	NUECES	86,325	32,797	52,755	773	19,958 D	38.0%	61.1%	38.3%	61.7%
9,704	OCHILTREE	3,587	2,471	1,084	32	1,387 R	68.9%	30.2%	69.5%	30.5%
2,258	OLDHAM	911	354	554	3	200 D	38.9%	60.8%	39.0%	61.0%

TEXAS

PRESIDENT 1976

1970 Census Population	County	Total Vote	Republican	Democratic	Other	Rep.-Dem. Plurality	Percentage Total Vote Rep.	Total Vote Dem.	Major Vote Rep.	Major Vote Dem.
71,170	ORANGE	24,484	9,147	15,177	160	6,030 D	37.4%	62.0%	37.6%	62.4%
28,962	PALO PINTO	7,905	2,684	5,170	51	2,486 D	34.0%	65.4%	34.2%	65.8%
15,894	PANOLA	6,977	3,218	3,731	28	513 D	46.1%	53.5%	46.3%	53.7%
33,888	PARKER	12,969	4,692	8,186	91	3,494 D	36.2%	63.1%	36.4%	63.6%
10,509	PARMER	3,417	1,487	1,914	16	427 D	43.5%	56.0%	43.7%	56.3%
13,748	PECOS	4,233	2,234	1,971	28	263 R	52.8%	46.6%	53.1%	46.9%
14,457	POLK	6,967	2,529	4,384	54	1,855 D	36.3%	62.9%	36.6%	63.4%
90,511	POTTER	26,036	13,819	11,917	300	1,902 R	53.1%	45.8%	53.7%	46.3%
4,842	PRESIDIO	1,936	687	1,232	17	545 D	35.5%	63.6%	35.8%	64.2%
3,752	RAINS	1,855	510	1,339	6	829 D	27.5%	72.2%	27.6%	72.4%
53,885	RANDALL	26,524	17,115	9,074	335	8,041 R	64.5%	34.2%	65.4%	34.6%
3,239	REAGAN	1,234	666	563	5	103 R	54.0%	45.6%	54.2%	45.8%
2,013	REAL	969	448	510	11	62 D	46.2%	52.6%	46.8%	53.2%
14,298	RED RIVER	5,533	1,852	3,670	11	1,818 D	33.5%	66.3%	33.5%	66.5%
16,526	REEVES	4,342	1,711	2,613	18	902 D	39.4%	60.2%	39.6%	60.4%
9,494	REFUGIO	3,765	1,537	2,218	10	681 D	40.8%	58.9%	40.9%	59.1%
967	ROBERTS	562	350	202	10	148 R	62.3%	35.9%	63.4%	36.6%
14,389	ROBERTSON	4,996	1,244	3,741	11	2,497 D	24.9%	74.9%	25.0%	75.0%
7,046	ROCKWALL	3,936	2,087	1,828	21	259 R	53.0%	46.4%	53.3%	46.7%
12,108	RUNNELS	4,282	2,203	2,068	11	135 R	51.4%	48.3%	51.6%	48.4%
34,102	RUSK	12,915	6,800	6,063	52	737 R	52.7%	46.9%	52.9%	47.1%
7,187	SABINE	3,296	904	2,391	1	1,487 D	27.4%	72.5%	27.4%	72.6%
7,858	SAN AUGUSTINE	2,870	1,047	1,817	6	770 D	36.5%	63.3%	36.6%	63.4%
6,702	SAN JACINTO	3,529	1,094	2,406	29	1,312 D	31.0%	68.2%	31.3%	68.7%
47,288	SAN PATRICIO	15,395	5,853	9,469	73	3,616 D	38.0%	61.5%	38.2%	61.8%
5,540	SAN SABA	2,005	582	1,408	15	826 D	29.0%	70.2%	29.2%	70.8%
2,277	SCHLEICHER	993	516	468	9	48 R	52.0%	47.1%	52.4%	47.6%
15,760	SCURRY	5,459	2,797	2,639	23	158 R	51.2%	48.3%	51.5%	48.5%
3,323	SHACKELFORD	1,518	748	764	6	16 D	49.3%	50.3%	49.5%	50.5%
19,672	SHELBY	7,387	2,695	4,680	12	1,985 D	36.5%	63.4%	36.5%	63.5%
3,657	SHERMAN	1,416	679	718	19	39 D	48.0%	50.7%	48.6%	51.4%
97,096	SMITH	39,275	22,238	16,856	181	5,382 R	56.6%	42.9%	56.9%	43.1%
2,793	SOMERVELL	1,391	332	1,054	5	722 D	23.9%	75.8%	24.0%	76.0%
17,707	STARR	5,325	664	4,646	15	3,982 D	12.5%	87.2%	12.5%	87.5%
8,414	STEPHENS	3,429	1,621	1,796	12	175 D	47.3%	52.4%	47.4%	52.6%
1,056	STERLING	381	202	174	5	28 R	53.0%	45.7%	53.7%	46.3%
2,397	STONEWALL	1,070	252	812	6	560 D	23.6%	75.9%	23.7%	76.3%
3,175	SUTTON	1,609	831	768	10	63 R	51.6%	47.7%	52.0%	48.0%
10,373	SWISHER	3,577	753	2,811	13	2,058 D	21.1%	78.6%	21.1%	78.9%
716,317	TARRANT	248,631	124,433	122,287	1,911	2,146 R	50.0%	49.2%	50.4%	49.6%
97,853	TAYLOR	34,543	19,822	14,453	268	5,369 R	57.4%	41.8%	57.8%	42.2%
1,940	TERRELL	642	317	321	4	4 D	49.4%	50.0%	49.7%	50.3%
14,118	TERRY	5,001	2,113	2,859	29	746 D	42.3%	57.2%	42.5%	57.5%
2,205	THROCKMORTON	1,016	356	658	2	302 D	35.0%	64.8%	35.1%	64.9%
16,702	TITUS	6,822	2,603	4,205	14	1,602 D	38.2%	61.6%	38.2%	61.8%
71,047	TOM GREEN	23,554	12,316	11,064	174	1,252 R	52.3%	47.0%	52.7%	47.3%
295,516	TRAVIS	152,213	71,031	78,585	2,597	7,554 D	46.7%	51.6%	47.5%	52.5%
7,628	TRINITY	3,154	1,042	2,100	12	1,058 D	33.0%	66.6%	33.2%	66.8%
12,417	TYLER	5,318	1,965	3,322	31	1,357 D	36.9%	62.5%	37.2%	62.8%
20,976	UPSHUR	8,211	3,272	4,902	37	1,630 D	39.8%	59.7%	40.0%	60.0%
4,697	UPTON	1,561	869	686	6	183 R	55.7%	43.9%	55.9%	44.1%
17,348	UVALDE	5,449	3,103	2,299	47	804 R	56.9%	42.2%	57.4%	42.6%
27,471	VAL VERDE	8,152	3,476	4,603	73	1,127 D	42.6%	56.5%	43.0%	57.0%
22,155	VAN ZANDT	9,898	3,385	6,449	64	3,064 D	34.2%	65.2%	34.4%	65.6%
53,766	VICTORIA	17,028	9,594	7,326	108	2,268 R	56.3%	43.0%	56.7%	43.3%
27,680	WALKER	10,171	4,974	5,105	92	131 D	48.9%	50.2%	49.4%	50.6%
14,285	WALLER	4,862	1,992	2,828	42	836 D	41.0%	58.2%	41.3%	58.7%
13,019	WARD	4,218	2,123	2,046	49	77 R	50.3%	48.5%	50.9%	49.1%
18,842	WASHINGTON	6,500	3,820	2,635	45	1,185 R	58.8%	40.5%	59.2%	40.8%
72,859	WEBB	14,698	4,222	10,362	114	6,140 D	28.7%	70.5%	28.9%	71.1%

TEXAS

PRESIDENT 1976

1970 Census Population	County	Total Vote	Republican	Democratic	Other	Rep.-Dem. Plurality	Percentage Total Vote Rep.	Total Vote Dem.	Major Vote Rep.	Major Vote Dem.
36,729	WHARTON	10,644	4,682	5,914	48	1,232 D	44.0%	55.6%	44.2%	55.8%
6,434	WHEELER	2,888	1,273	1,598	17	325 D	44.1%	55.3%	44.3%	55.7%
121,862	WICHITA	41,266	19,024	22,017	225	2,993 D	46.1%	53.4%	46.4%	53.6%
15,355	WILBARGER	5,476	2,145	3,280	51	1,135 D	39.2%	59.9%	39.5%	60.5%
15,570	WILLACY	4,557	1,542	2,984	31	1,442 D	33.8%	65.5%	34.1%	65.9%
37,305	WILLIAMSON	17,010	7,481	9,355	174	1,874 D	44.0%	55.0%	44.4%	55.6%
13,041	WILSON	5,902	1,926	3,973	3	2,047 D	32.6%	67.3%	32.6%	67.4%
9,640	WINKLER	3,266	1,842	1,382	42	460 R	56.4%	42.3%	57.1%	42.9%
19,687	WISE	8,013	2,856	5,133	24	2,277 D	35.6%	64.1%	35.7%	64.3%
18,589	WOOD	7,226	3,076	4,107	43	1,031 D	42.6%	56.8%	42.8%	57.2%
7,344	YOAKUM	2,680	1,477	1,181	22	296 R	55.1%	44.1%	55.6%	44.4%
15,400	YOUNG	6,166	2,652	3,473	41	821 D	43.0%	56.3%	43.3%	56.7%
4,352	ZAPATA	1,682	462	1,216	4	754 D	27.5%	72.3%	27.5%	72.5%
11,370	ZAVALA	2,578	735	1,822	21	1,087 D	28.5%	70.7%	28.7%	71.3%
11,196,730	TOTAL	4,071,884	1,953,300	2,082,319	36,265	129,019 D	48.0%	51.1%	48.4%	51.6%

TEXAS

PRESIDENT 1972

1970 Census Population	County	Total Vote	Republican	Democratic	Other	Rep.-Dem. Plurality	Percentage Total Vote Rep.	Total Vote Dem.	Major Vote Rep.	Major Vote Dem.
27,789	ANDERSON	8,065	5,826	2,233	6	3,593 R	72.2%	27.7%	72.3%	27.7%
10,372	ANDREWS	3,310	2,615	677	18	1,938 R	79.0%	20.5%	79.4%	20.6%
49,349	ANGELINA	16,589	11,453	4,970	166	6,483 R	69.0%	30.0%	69.7%	30.3%
8,902	ARANSAS	2,890	2,037	844	9	1,193 R	70.5%	29.2%	70.7%	29.3%
5,759	ARCHER	2,152	1,494	632	26	862 R	69.4%	29.4%	70.3%	29.7%
1,895	ARMSTRONG	951	768	177	6	591 R	80.8%	18.6%	81.3%	18.7%
18,696	ATASCOSA	5,208	3,400	1,804	4	1,596 R	65.3%	34.6%	65.3%	34.7%
13,831	AUSTIN	4,154	3,084	1,043	27	2,041 R	74.2%	25.1%	74.7%	25.3%
8,487	BAILEY	2,305	1,837	465	3	1,372 R	79.7%	20.2%	79.8%	20.2%
4,747	BANDERA	2,259	1,796	434	29	1,362 R	79.5%	19.2%	80.5%	19.5%
17,297	BASTROP	5,010	3,097	1,906	7	1,191 R	61.8%	38.0%	61.9%	38.1%
5,221	BAYLOR	1,789	1,190	598	1	592 R	66.5%	33.4%	66.6%	33.4%
22,737	BEE	5,866	3,779	2,067	20	1,712 R	64.4%	35.2%	64.6%	35.4%
124,483	BELL	24,411	17,525	6,848	38	10,677 R	71.8%	28.1%	71.9%	28.1%
830,460	BEXAR	230,193	137,572	91,662	959	45,910 R	59.8%	39.8%	60.0%	40.0%
3,567	BLANCO	1,695	1,215	460	20	755 R	71.7%	27.1%	72.5%	27.5%
888	BORDEN	433	330	96	7	234 R	76.2%	22.2%	77.5%	22.5%
10,966	BOSQUE	3,976	2,947	1,014	15	1,933 R	74.1%	25.5%	74.4%	25.6%
67,813	BOWIE	20,015	14,722	5,227	66	9,495 R	73.6%	26.1%	73.8%	26.2%
108,312	BRAZORIA	32,432	21,045	11,350	37	9,695 R	64.9%	35.0%	65.0%	35.0%
57,978	BRAZOS	20,051	14,243	5,692	116	8,551 R	71.0%	28.4%	71.4%	28.6%
7,780	BREWSTER	2,446	1,524	904	18	620 R	62.3%	37.0%	62.8%	37.2%
2,794	BRISCOE	1,000	642	349	9	293 R	64.2%	34.9%	64.8%	35.2%
8,005	BROOKS	2,781	1,117	1,657	7	540 D	40.2%	59.6%	40.3%	59.7%
25,877	BROWN	8,233	5,990	2,171	72	3,819 R	72.8%	26.4%	73.4%	26.6%
9,999	BURLESON	3,125	1,762	1,361	2	401 R	56.4%	43.6%	56.4%	43.6%
11,420	BURNET	4,688	3,438	1,227	23	2,211 R	73.3%	26.2%	73.7%	26.3%
21,178	CALDWELL	5,160	3,171	1,974	15	1,197 R	61.5%	38.3%	61.6%	38.4%
17,831	CALHOUN	5,566	3,614	1,936	16	1,678 R	64.9%	34.8%	65.1%	34.9%
8,205	CALLAHAN	2,939	2,223	665	51	1,558 R	75.6%	22.6%	77.0%	23.0%
140,368	CAMERON	34,300	20,816	13,340	144	7,476 R	60.7%	38.9%	60.9%	39.1%
8,005	CAMP	2,641	1,599	1,041	1	558 R	60.5%	39.4%	60.6%	39.4%
6,358	CARSON	2,466	1,868	561	37	1,307 R	75.8%	22.7%	76.9%	23.1%
24,133	CASS	7,288	5,303	1,981	4	3,322 R	72.8%	27.2%	72.8%	27.2%
10,394	CASTRO	2,451	1,685	751	15	934 R	68.7%	30.6%	69.2%	30.8%
12,187	CHAMBERS	3,602	2,390	1,206	6	1,184 R	66.4%	33.5%	66.5%	33.5%
32,008	CHEROKEE	8,288	5,743	2,467	78	3,276 R	69.3%	29.8%	70.0%	30.0%
6,605	CHILDRESS	2,458	1,716	729	13	987 R	69.8%	29.7%	70.2%	29.8%
8,079	CLAY	2,945	1,893	1,023	29	870 R	64.3%	34.7%	64.9%	35.1%
5,326	COCHRAN	1,536	1,106	415	15	691 R	72.0%	27.0%	72.7%	27.3%
3,087	COKE	1,134	761	358	15	403 R	67.1%	31.6%	68.0%	32.0%
10,288	COLEMAN	3,112	2,386	721	5	1,665 R	76.7%	23.2%	76.8%	23.2%
66,920	COLLIN	22,637	17,667	4,783	187	12,884 R	78.0%	21.1%	78.7%	21.3%
4,755	COLLINGSWORTH	1,751	1,250	501		749 R	71.4%	28.6%	71.4%	28.6%
17,638	COLORADO	5,017	3,495	1,502	20	1,993 R	69.7%	29.9%	69.9%	30.1%
24,165	COMAL	8,628	6,761	1,823	44	4,938 R	78.4%	21.1%	78.8%	21.2%
11,898	COMANCHE	3,818	2,608	1,176	34	1,432 R	68.3%	30.8%	68.9%	31.1%
2,937	CONCHO	1,059	709	350		359 R	66.9%	33.1%	66.9%	33.1%
23,471	COOKE	8,070	6,317	1,702	51	4,615 R	78.3%	21.1%	78.8%	21.2%
35,311	CORYELL	6,366	5,077	1,235	54	3,842 R	79.8%	19.4%	80.4%	19.6%
3,204	COTTLE	1,135	564	571		7 D	49.7%	50.3%	49.7%	50.3%
4,172	CRANE	1,522	1,123	349	50	774 R	73.8%	22.9%	76.3%	23.7%
3,885	CROCKETT	1,180	851	329		522 R	72.1%	27.9%	72.1%	27.9%
9,085	CROSBY	2,541	1,503	1,021	17	482 R	59.1%	40.2%	59.5%	40.5%
3,429	CULBERSON	803	555	238	10	317 R	69.1%	29.6%	70.0%	30.0%
6,012	DALLAM	1,629	1,271	327	31	944 R	78.0%	20.1%	79.5%	20.5%
1,327,321	DALLAS	438,795	305,112	129,662	4,021	175,450 R	69.5%	29.5%	70.2%	29.8%
16,604	DAWSON	4,095	3,247	846	2	2,401 R	79.3%	20.7%	79.3%	20.7%
18,999	DEAF SMITH	5,009	3,690	1,240	79	2,450 R	73.7%	24.8%	74.8%	25.2%
4,927	DELTA	1,546	957	581	8	376 R	61.9%	37.6%	62.2%	37.8%

TEXAS

PRESIDENT 1972

1970 Census Population	County	Total Vote	Republican	Democratic	Other	Rep.-Dem. Plurality	Percentage Total Vote Rep.	Total Vote Dem.	Major Vote Rep.	Major Vote Dem.
75,633	DENTON	28,920	19,138	9,720	62	9,418 R	66.2%	33.6%	66.3%	33.7%
18,660	DE WITT	5,147	3,755	1,357	35	2,398 R	73.0%	26.4%	73.5%	26.5%
3,737	DICKENS	1,245	708	534	3	174 R	56.9%	42.9%	57.0%	43.0%
9,039	DIMMIT	2,262	1,172	1,078	12	94 R	51.8%	47.7%	52.1%	47.9%
3,641	DONLEY	1,581	1,229	350	2	879 R	77.7%	22.1%	77.8%	22.2%
11,722	DUVAL	4,352	623	3,729		3,106 D	14.3%	85.7%	14.3%	85.7%
18,092	EASTLAND	5,743	4,106	1,630	7	2,476 R	71.5%	28.4%	71.6%	28.4%
91,805	ECTOR	26,960	21,386	5,449	125	15,937 R	79.3%	20.2%	79.7%	20.3%
2,107	EDWARDS	634	520	109	5	411 R	82.0%	17.2%	82.7%	17.3%
46,638	ELLIS	12,626	8,779	3,839	8	4,940 R	69.5%	30.4%	69.6%	30.4%
359,291	EL PASO	83,090	49,981	32,435	674	17,546 R	60.2%	39.0%	60.6%	39.4%
18,141	ERATH	6,433	4,777	1,648	8	3,129 R	74.3%	25.6%	74.4%	25.6%
17,300	FALLS	4,857	3,017	1,825	15	1,192 R	62.1%	37.6%	62.3%	37.7%
22,705	FANNIN	6,181	3,826	2,295	60	1,531 R	61.9%	37.1%	62.5%	37.5%
17,650	FAYETTE	5,291	3,882	1,400	9	2,482 R	73.4%	26.5%	73.5%	26.5%
6,344	FISHER	2,147	1,207	933	7	274 R	56.2%	43.5%	56.4%	43.6%
11,044	FLOYD	3,022	2,181	841		1,340 R	72.2%	27.8%	72.2%	27.8%
2,211	FOARD	685	369	312	4	57 R	53.9%	45.5%	54.2%	45.8%
52,314	FORT BEND	15,089	10,475	4,541	73	5,934 R	69.4%	30.1%	69.8%	30.2%
5,291	FRANKLIN	1,607	1,059	546	2	513 R	65.9%	34.0%	66.0%	34.0%
11,116	FREESTONE	3,748	2,459	1,283	6	1,176 R	65.6%	34.2%	65.7%	34.3%
11,159	FRIO	3,511	1,904	1,588	19	316 R	54.2%	45.2%	54.5%	45.5%
11,593	GAINES	2,625	1,923	669	33	1,254 R	73.3%	25.5%	74.2%	25.8%
169,812	GALVESTON	53,811	30,936	22,565	310	8,371 R	57.5%	41.9%	57.8%	42.2%
5,289	GARZA	1,599	1,153	446		707 R	72.1%	27.9%	72.1%	27.9%
10,553	GILLESPIE	4,074	3,490	526	58	2,964 R	85.7%	12.9%	86.9%	13.1%
1,155	GLASSCOCK	369	288	75	6	213 R	78.0%	20.3%	79.3%	20.7%
4,869	GOLIAD	1,484	1,018	464	2	554 R	68.6%	31.3%	68.7%	31.3%
16,375	GONZALES	3,876	2,707	1,164	5	1,543 R	69.8%	30.0%	69.9%	30.1%
26,949	GRAY	9,444	7,968	1,367	109	6,601 R	84.4%	14.5%	85.4%	14.6%
83,225	GRAYSON	23,734	16,769	6,952	13	9,817 R	70.7%	29.3%	70.7%	29.3%
75,929	GREGG	25,716	19,927	5,325	464	14,602 R	77.5%	20.7%	78.9%	21.1%
11,855	GRIMES	3,376	2,243	1,116	17	1,127 R	66.4%	33.1%	66.8%	33.2%
33,554	GUADALUPE	11,698	8,287	3,404	7	4,883 R	70.8%	29.1%	70.9%	29.1%
34,137	HALE	9,273	7,051	2,135	87	4,916 R	76.0%	23.0%	76.8%	23.2%
6,015	HALL	1,934	1,303	607	24	696 R	67.4%	31.4%	68.2%	31.8%
7,198	HAMILTON	2,617	1,931	685	1	1,246 R	73.8%	26.2%	73.8%	26.2%
6,351	HANSFORD	2,190	1,947	202	41	1,745 R	88.9%	9.2%	90.6%	9.4%
6,795	HARDEMAN	1,987	1,357	614	16	743 R	68.3%	30.9%	68.8%	31.2%
29,996	HARDIN	8,157	5,190	2,952	15	2,238 R	63.6%	36.2%	63.7%	36.3%
1,741,912	HARRIS	584,531	365,672	215,916	2,943	149,756 R	62.6%	36.9%	62.9%	37.1%
44,841	HARRISON	14,060	9,600	4,333	127	5,267 R	68.3%	30.8%	68.9%	31.1%
2,782	HARTLEY	1,180	946	206	28	740 R	80.2%	17.5%	82.1%	17.9%
8,512	HASKELL	2,694	1,744	950		794 R	64.7%	35.3%	64.7%	35.3%
27,642	HAYS	9,519	5,406	4,068	45	1,338 R	56.8%	42.7%	57.1%	42.9%
3,084	HEMPHILL	1,157	942	214	1	728 R	81.4%	18.5%	81.5%	18.5%
26,466	HENDERSON	9,013	6,263	2,741	9	3,522 R	69.5%	30.4%	69.6%	30.4%
181,535	HIDALGO	41,499	22,920	18,366	213	4,554 R	55.2%	44.3%	55.5%	44.5%
22,596	HILL	6,379	4,481	1,882	16	2,599 R	70.2%	29.5%	70.4%	29.6%
20,396	HOCKLEY	5,765	4,084	1,625	56	2,459 R	70.8%	28.2%	71.5%	28.5%
6,368	HOOD	2,710	1,743	949	18	794 R	64.3%	35.0%	64.7%	35.3%
20,710	HOPKINS	5,640	3,903	1,710	27	2,193 R	69.2%	30.3%	69.5%	30.5%
17,855	HOUSTON	5,187	3,317	1,844	26	1,473 R	63.9%	35.6%	64.3%	35.7%
37,796	HOWARD	10,080	7,343	2,714	23	4,629 R	72.8%	26.9%	73.0%	27.0%
2,392	HUDSPETH	727	467	250	10	217 R	64.2%	34.4%	65.1%	34.9%
47,948	HUNT	13,239	9,535	3,655	49	5,880 R	72.0%	27.6%	72.3%	27.7%
24,443	HUTCHINSON	9,121	7,411	1,405	305	6,006 R	81.3%	15.4%	84.1%	15.9%
1,070	IRION	477	363	111	3	252 R	76.1%	23.3%	76.6%	23.4%
6,711	JACK	2,507	1,719	775	13	944 R	68.6%	30.9%	68.9%	31.1%
12,975	JACKSON	3,929	2,743	1,163	23	1,580 R	69.8%	29.6%	70.2%	29.8%

TEXAS

PRESIDENT 1972

1970 Census Population	County	Total Vote	Republican	Democratic	Other	Rep.-Dem. Plurality	Percentage Total Vote Rep.	Total Vote Dem.	Major Vote Rep.	Major Vote Dem.
24,692	JASPER	7,325	4,575	2,746	4	1,829 R	62.5%	37.5%	62.5%	37.5%
1,527	JEFF DAVIS	595	382	202	11	180 R	64.2%	33.9%	65.4%	34.6%
244,773	JEFFERSON	75,837	45,819	29,909	109	15,910 R	60.4%	39.4%	60.5%	39.5%
4,654	JIM HOGG	1,618	765	848	5	83 D	47.3%	52.4%	47.4%	52.6%
33,032	JIM WELLS	9,698	5,283	4,404	11	879 R	54.5%	45.4%	54.5%	45.5%
45,769	JOHNSON	14,136	10,042	3,968	126	6,074 R	71.0%	28.1%	71.7%	28.3%
16,106	JONES	4,263	3,202	1,050	11	2,152 R	75.1%	24.6%	75.3%	24.7%
13,462	KARNES	4,428	2,639	1,780	9	859 R	59.6%	40.2%	59.7%	40.3%
32,392	KAUFMAN	7,906	5,100	2,795	11	2,305 R	64.5%	35.4%	64.6%	35.4%
6,964	KENDALL	3,183	2,681	484	18	2,197 R	84.2%	15.2%	84.7%	15.3%
678	KENEDY	213	124	88	1	36 R	58.2%	41.3%	58.5%	41.5%
1,434	KENT	688	465	223		242 R	67.6%	32.4%	67.6%	32.4%
19,454	KERR	7,760	6,039	1,511	210	4,528 R	77.8%	19.5%	80.0%	20.0%
3,904	KIMBLE	1,243	971	266	6	705 R	78.1%	21.4%	78.5%	21.5%
464	KING	219	143	75	1	68 R	65.3%	34.2%	65.6%	34.4%
2,006	KINNEY	660	425	234	1	191 R	64.4%	35.5%	64.5%	35.5%
33,166	KLEBERG	9,803	5,312	4,481	10	831 R	54.2%	45.7%	54.2%	45.8%
5,972	KNOX	1,800	1,148	638	14	510 R	63.8%	35.4%	64.3%	35.7%
36,062	LAMAR	10,652	7,736	2,865	51	4,871 R	72.6%	26.9%	73.0%	27.0%
17,770	LAMB	5,366	3,981	1,350	35	2,631 R	74.2%	25.2%	74.7%	25.3%
9,323	LAMPASAS	2,949	2,251	688	10	1,563 R	76.3%	23.3%	76.6%	23.4%
5,014	LA SALLE	1,648	1,073	567	8	506 R	65.1%	34.4%	65.4%	34.6%
17,903	LAVACA	4,721	3,288	1,429	4	1,859 R	69.6%	30.3%	69.7%	30.3%
8,048	LEE	2,814	1,877	920	17	957 R	66.7%	32.7%	67.1%	32.9%
8,738	LEON	2,568	1,699	863	6	836 R	66.2%	33.6%	66.3%	33.7%
33,014	LIBERTY	9,432	6,111	3,311	10	2,800 R	64.8%	35.1%	64.9%	35.1%
18,100	LIMESTONE	4,423	2,949	1,452	22	1,497 R	66.7%	32.8%	67.0%	33.0%
3,486	LIPSCOMB	1,400	1,226	156	18	1,070 R	87.6%	11.1%	88.7%	11.3%
6,697	LIVE OAK	2,359	1,745	610	4	1,135 R	74.0%	25.9%	74.1%	25.9%
6,979	LLANO	2,943	2,164	766	13	1,398 R	73.5%	26.0%	73.9%	26.1%
164	LOVING	62	55	7		48 R	88.7%	11.3%	88.7%	11.3%
179,295	LUBBOCK	59,296	43,564	15,353	379	28,211 R	73.5%	25.9%	73.9%	26.1%
9,107	LYNN	2,471	1,766	697	8	1,069 R	71.5%	28.2%	71.7%	28.3%
8,571	MCCULLOCH	2,525	1,769	753	3	1,016 R	70.1%	29.8%	70.1%	29.9%
147,553	MCLENNAN	49,485	33,377	15,947	161	17,430 R	67.4%	32.2%	67.7%	32.3%
1,095	MCMULLEN	396	304	88	4	216 R	76.8%	22.2%	77.6%	22.4%
7,693	MADISON	2,101	1,540	561		979 R	73.3%	26.7%	73.3%	26.7%
8,517	MARION	2,790	1,680	1,106	4	574 R	60.2%	39.6%	60.3%	39.7%
4,774	MARTIN	1,243	935	287	21	648 R	75.2%	23.1%	76.5%	23.5%
3,356	MASON	1,487	1,096	369	22	727 R	73.7%	24.8%	74.8%	25.2%
27,913	MATAGORDA	7,495	5,003	2,473	19	2,530 R	66.8%	33.0%	66.9%	33.1%
18,093	MAVERICK	3,197	1,477	1,710	10	233 D	46.2%	53.5%	46.3%	53.7%
20,249	MEDINA	5,649	4,059	1,507	83	2,552 R	71.9%	26.7%	72.9%	27.1%
2,646	MENARD	921	644	273	4	371 R	69.9%	29.6%	70.2%	29.8%
65,433	MIDLAND	23,750	18,905	4,388	457	14,517 R	79.6%	18.5%	81.2%	18.8%
20,028	MILAM	5,719	3,554	2,159	6	1,395 R	62.1%	37.8%	62.2%	37.8%
4,212	MILLS	1,483	1,089	388	6	701 R	73.4%	26.2%	73.7%	26.3%
9,073	MITCHELL	2,492	1,790	699	3	1,091 R	71.8%	28.0%	71.9%	28.1%
15,326	MONTAGUE	4,768	3,463	1,286	19	2,177 R	72.6%	27.0%	72.9%	27.1%
49,479	MONTGOMERY	19,447	15,067	4,358	22	10,709 R	77.5%	22.4%	77.6%	22.4%
14,060	MOORE	4,538	3,620	863	55	2,757 R	79.8%	19.0%	80.7%	19.3%
12,310	MORRIS	3,885	2,699	1,162	24	1,537 R	69.5%	29.9%	69.9%	30.1%
2,178	MOTLEY	906	657	230	19	427 R	72.5%	25.4%	74.1%	25.9%
36,362	NACOGDOCHES	12,437	8,757	3,656	24	5,101 R	70.4%	29.4%	70.5%	29.5%
31,150	NAVARRO	9,303	6,039	3,246	18	2,793 R	64.9%	34.9%	65.0%	35.0%
11,657	NEWTON	3,605	1,946	1,636	23	310 R	54.0%	45.4%	54.3%	45.7%
16,220	NOLAN	4,976	3,634	1,338	4	2,296 R	73.0%	26.9%	73.1%	26.9%
237,544	NUECES	75,250	41,682	33,277	291	8,405 R	55.4%	44.2%	55.6%	44.4%
9,704	OCHILTREE	3,202	2,861	298	43	2,563 R	89.4%	9.3%	90.6%	9.4%
2,258	OLDHAM	863	666	173	24	493 R	77.2%	20.0%	79.4%	20.6%

TEXAS

PRESIDENT 1972

1970 Census Population	County	Total Vote	Republican	Democratic	Other	Rep.-Dem. Plurality	Percentage			
							Total Vote		Major Vote	
							Rep.	Dem.	Rep.	Dem.
71,170	ORANGE	20,478	13,234	7,172	72	6,062 R	64.6%	35.0%	64.9%	35.1%
28,962	PALO PINTO	7,247	5,058	2,181	8	2,877 R	69.8%	30.1%	69.9%	30.1%
15,894	PANOLA	5,864	4,324	1,511	29	2,813 R	73.7%	25.8%	74.1%	25.9%
33,888	PARKER	10,349	7,152	3,184	13	3,968 R	69.1%	30.8%	69.2%	30.8%
10,509	PARMER	2,823	2,304	495	24	1,809 R	81.6%	17.5%	82.3%	17.7%
13,748	PECOS	3,309	2,419	847	43	1,572 R	73.1%	25.6%	74.1%	25.9%
14,457	POLK	4,828	3,048	1,760	20	1,288 R	63.1%	36.5%	63.4%	36.6%
90,511	POTTER	25,335	18,891	6,264	180	12,627 R	74.6%	24.7%	75.1%	24.9%
4,842	PRESIDIO	1,462	785	674	3	111 R	53.7%	46.1%	53.8%	46.2%
3,752	RAINS	1,404	865	532	7	333 R	61.6%	37.9%	61.9%	38.1%
53,885	RANDALL	22,323	18,557	3,470	296	15,087 R	83.1%	15.5%	84.2%	15.8%
3,239	REAGAN	955	703	244	8	459 R	73.6%	25.5%	74.2%	25.8%
2,013	REAL	642	483	150	9	333 R	75.2%	23.4%	76.3%	23.7%
14,298	RED RIVER	4,475	3,112	1,361	2	1,751 R	69.5%	30.4%	69.6%	30.4%
16,526	REEVES	3,942	2,427	1,510	5	917 R	61.6%	38.3%	61.6%	38.4%
9,494	REFUGIO	3,000	1,937	1,060	3	877 R	64.6%	35.3%	64.6%	35.4%
967	ROBERTS	550	467	71	12	396 R	84.9%	12.9%	86.8%	13.2%
14,389	ROBERTSON	3,953	1,977	1,976		1 R	50.0%	50.0%	50.0%	50.0%
7,046	ROCKWALL	2,518	1,890	610	18	1,280 R	75.1%	24.2%	75.6%	24.4%
12,108	RUNNELS	3,491	2,752	739		2,013 R	78.8%	21.2%	78.8%	21.2%
34,102	RUSK	11,072	8,179	2,867	26	5,312 R	73.9%	25.9%	74.0%	26.0%
7,187	SABINE	2,273	1,333	936	4	397 R	58.6%	41.2%	58.7%	41.3%
7,858	SAN AUGUSTINE	2,268	1,508	753	7	755 R	66.5%	33.2%	66.7%	33.3%
6,702	SAN JACINTO	2,322	1,296	1,020	6	276 R	55.8%	43.9%	56.0%	44.0%
47,288	SAN PATRICIO	12,502	7,179	5,097	226	2,082 R	57.4%	40.8%	58.5%	41.5%
5,540	SAN SABA	1,681	1,106	567	8	539 R	65.8%	33.7%	66.1%	33.9%
2,277	SCHLEICHER	881	630	250	1	380 R	71.5%	28.4%	71.6%	28.4%
15,760	SCURRY	5,050	3,777	1,223	50	2,554 R	74.8%	24.2%	75.5%	24.5%
3,323	SHACKELFORD	1,244	909	331	4	578 R	73.1%	26.6%	73.3%	26.7%
19,672	SHELBY	6,092	4,292	1,792	8	2,500 R	70.5%	29.4%	70.5%	29.5%
3,657	SHERMAN	1,181	996	169	16	827 R	84.3%	14.3%	85.5%	14.5%
97,096	SMITH	31,827	23,671	8,041	115	15,630 R	74.4%	25.3%	74.6%	25.4%
2,793	SOMERVELL	987	703	284		419 R	71.2%	28.8%	71.2%	28.8%
17,707	STARR	5,713	2,389	3,320	4	931 D	41.8%	58.1%	41.8%	58.2%
8,414	STEPHENS	2,944	2,259	678	7	1,581 R	76.7%	23.0%	76.9%	23.1%
1,056	STERLING	383	286	94	3	192 R	74.7%	24.5%	75.3%	24.7%
2,397	STONEWALL	1,075	662	394	19	268 R	61.6%	36.7%	62.7%	37.3%
3,175	SUTTON	957	705	245	7	460 R	73.7%	25.6%	74.2%	25.8%
10,373	SWISHER	3,122	1,790	1,300	32	490 R	57.3%	41.6%	57.9%	42.1%
716,317	TARRANT	221,138	151,596	69,187	355	82,409 R	68.6%	31.3%	68.7%	31.3%
97,853	TAYLOR	28,731	22,417	6,024	290	16,393 R	78.0%	21.0%	78.8%	21.2%
1,940	TERRELL	591	467	124		343 R	79.0%	21.0%	79.0%	21.0%
14,118	TERRY	4,190	3,057	1,099	34	1,958 R	73.0%	26.2%	73.6%	26.4%
2,205	THROCKMORTON	919	568	348	3	220 R	61.8%	37.9%	62.0%	38.0%
16,702	TITUS	5,393	3,671	1,703	19	1,968 R	68.1%	31.6%	68.3%	31.7%
71,047	TOM GREEN	21,961	15,784	6,082	95	9,702 R	71.9%	27.7%	72.2%	27.8%
295,516	TRAVIS	125,329	70,561	54,157	611	16,404 R	56.3%	43.2%	56.6%	43.4%
7,628	TRINITY	2,295	1,467	826	2	641 R	63.9%	36.0%	64.0%	36.0%
12,417	TYLER	4,290	2,955	1,321	14	1,634 R	68.9%	30.8%	69.1%	30.9%
20,976	UPSHUR	6,624	4,736	1,879	9	2,857 R	71.5%	28.4%	71.6%	28.4%
4,697	UPTON	1,463	1,186	256	21	930 R	81.1%	17.5%	82.2%	17.8%
17,348	UVALDE	5,327	3,883	1,438	6	2,445 R	72.9%	27.0%	73.0%	27.0%
27,471	VAL VERDE	6,124	4,052	2,049	23	2,003 R	66.2%	33.5%	66.4%	33.6%
22,155	VAN ZANDT	6,784	4,839	1,939	6	2,900 R	71.3%	28.6%	71.4%	28.6%
53,766	VICTORIA	15,498	11,246	4,226	26	7,020 R	72.6%	27.3%	72.7%	27.3%
27,680	WALKER	8,041	5,082	2,940	19	2,142 R	63.2%	36.6%	63.4%	36.6%
14,285	WALLER	3,839	2,263	1,538	38	725 R	58.9%	40.1%	59.5%	40.5%
13,019	WARD	3,792	2,687	1,049	56	1,638 R	70.9%	27.7%	71.9%	28.1%
18,842	WASHINGTON	5,198	3,862	1,323	13	2,539 R	74.3%	25.5%	74.5%	25.5%
72,859	WEBB	14,458	6,011	8,435	12	2,424 D	41.6%	58.3%	41.6%	58.4%

TEXAS

PRESIDENT 1972

1970 Census Population	County	Total Vote	Republican	Democratic	Other	Rep.-Dem. Plurality	Percentage Total Vote Rep.	Percentage Total Vote Dem.	Percentage Major Vote Rep.	Percentage Major Vote Dem.
36,729	WHARTON	9,757	6,271	3,481	5	2,790 R	64.3%	35.7%	64.3%	35.7%
6,434	WHEELER	2,268	1,766	502		1,264 R	77.9%	22.1%	77.9%	22.1%
121,862	WICHITA	36,682	25,197	10,948	537	14,249 R	68.7%	29.8%	69.7%	30.3%
15,355	WILBARGER	4,519	3,183	1,139	197	2,044 R	70.4%	25.2%	73.6%	26.4%
15,570	WILLACY	3,730	2,317	1,384	29	933 R	62.1%	37.1%	62.6%	37.4%
37,305	WILLIAMSON	10,867	6,998	3,806	63	3,192 R	64.4%	35.0%	64.8%	35.2%
13,041	WILSON	5,032	2,953	2,072	7	881 R	58.7%	41.2%	58.8%	41.2%
9,640	WINKLER	3,095	2,467	602	26	1,865 R	79.7%	19.5%	80.4%	19.6%
19,687	WISE	6,006	4,230	1,741	35	2,489 R	70.4%	29.0%	70.8%	29.2%
18,589	WOOD	6,658	4,746	1,842	70	2,904 R	71.3%	27.7%	72.0%	28.0%
7,344	YOAKUM	2,443	1,952	457	34	1,495 R	79.9%	18.7%	81.0%	19.0%
15,400	YOUNG	4,840	3,353	1,486	1	1,867 R	69.3%	30.7%	69.3%	30.7%
4,352	ZAPATA	1,463	695	768		73 D	47.5%	52.5%	47.5%	52.5%
11,370	ZAVALA	2,432	1,288	1,122	22	166 R	53.0%	46.1%	53.4%	46.6%
11,196,730	TOTAL	3,471,281	2,298,896	1,154,289	18,096	1,144,607 R	66.2%	33.3%	66.6%	33.4%

TEXAS

PRESIDENT 1968

1960 Census Population	County	Total Vote	Republican	Democratic	AIP	Other	Plurality	Percentage Rep.	Dem.	AIP
28,162	ANDERSON	9,471	2,828	3,447	3,196		251 D	29.9%	36.4%	33.7%
13,450	ANDREWS	3,634	1,400	922	1,312		88 R	38.5%	25.4%	36.1%
39,814	ANGELINA	15,930	4,645	5,174	6,111		937 A	29.2%	32.5%	38.4%
7,006	ARANSAS	2,715	1,076	1,222	417		146 D	39.6%	45.0%	15.4%
6,110	ARCHER	2,357	636	1,308	413		672 D	27.0%	55.5%	17.5%
1,966	ARMSTRONG	941	434	301	206		133 R	46.1%	32.0%	21.9%
18,828	ATASCOSA	5,098	1,805	2,522	771		717 D	35.4%	49.5%	15.1%
13,777	AUSTIN	4,354	1,971	1,299	1,084		672 R	45.3%	29.8%	24.9%
9,090	BAILEY	2,558	1,174	820	563	1	354 R	45.9%	32.1%	22.0%
3,892	BANDERA	1,800	842	535	423		307 R	46.8%	29.7%	23.5%
16,925	BASTROP	5,117	1,455	2,687	975		1,232 D	28.4%	52.5%	19.1%
5,893	BAYLOR	2,164	657	1,064	443		407 D	30.4%	49.2%	20.5%
23,755	BEE	5,544	1,995	2,957	589	3	962 D	36.0%	53.3%	10.6%
94,097	BELL	21,145	5,705	11,893	3,547		6,188 D	27.0%	56.2%	16.8%
687,151	BEXAR	184,874	72,951	95,325	16,598		22,374 D	39.5%	51.6%	9.0%
3,657	BLANCO	1,457	614	620	223		6 D	42.1%	42.6%	15.3%
1,076	BORDEN	386	117	157	112		40 D	30.3%	40.7%	29.0%
10,809	BOSQUE	3,921	1,377	1,817	727		440 D	35.1%	46.3%	18.5%
59,971	BOWIE	19,599	5,966	6,468	7,165		697 A	30.4%	33.0%	36.6%
76,204	BRAZORIA	30,103	10,631	11,439	8,026	7	808 D	35.3%	38.0%	26.7%
44,895	BRAZOS	15,579	6,839	6,299	2,437	4	540 R	43.9%	40.4%	15.6%
6,434	BREWSTER	2,091	790	958	342	1	168 D	37.8%	45.8%	16.4%
3,577	BRISCOE	1,158	411	528	219		117 D	35.5%	45.6%	18.9%
8,609	BROOKS	2,604	534	1,904	166		1,370 D	20.5%	73.1%	6.4%
24,728	BROWN	8,602	2,997	3,999	1,606		1,002 D	34.8%	46.5%	18.7%
11,177	BURLESON	3,263	891	1,678	694		787 D	27.3%	51.4%	21.3%
9,265	BURNET	3,978	1,459	1,876	643		417 D	36.7%	47.2%	16.2%
17,222	CALDWELL	5,130	1,402	2,889	837	2	1,487 D	27.3%	56.3%	16.3%
16,592	CALHOUN	5,350	1,672	2,612	1,065	1	940 D	31.3%	48.8%	19.9%
7,929	CALLAHAN	3,096	921	1,437	737	1	516 D	29.7%	46.4%	23.8%
151,098	CAMERON	29,527	11,759	15,726	2,042		3,967 D	39.8%	53.3%	6.9%
7,849	CAMP	2,901	555	1,272	1,074		198 D	19.1%	43.8%	37.0%
7,781	CARSON	2,685	1,211	904	570		307 R	45.1%	33.7%	21.2%
23,496	CASS	7,350	1,930	2,536	2,883	1	347 A	26.3%	34.5%	39.2%
8,923	CASTRO	2,838	1,033	1,181	623	1	148 D	36.4%	41.6%	22.0%
10,379	CHAMBERS	3,607	1,061	1,217	1,329		112 A	29.4%	33.7%	36.8%
33,120	CHEROKEE	9,608	2,575	3,242	3,791		549 A	26.8%	33.7%	39.5%
8,421	CHILDRESS	2,759	1,045	1,093	621		48 D	37.9%	39.6%	22.5%
8,351	CLAY	3,174	936	1,573	665		637 D	29.5%	49.6%	21.0%
6,417	COCHRAN	1,630	548	633	449		85 D	33.6%	38.8%	27.5%
3,589	COKE	1,159	387	563	208	1	176 D	33.4%	48.6%	17.9%
12,458	COLEMAN	4,109	1,507	1,449	1,153		58 R	36.7%	35.3%	28.1%
41,247	COLLIN	16,262	6,494	5,918	3,850		576 R	39.9%	36.4%	23.7%
6,276	COLLINGSWORTH	1,933	712	746	475		34 D	36.8%	38.6%	24.6%
18,463	COLORADO	5,438	2,296	1,976	1,163	3	320 R	42.2%	36.3%	21.4%
19,844	COMAL	6,710	3,646	2,338	724	2	1,308 R	54.3%	34.8%	10.8%
11,865	COMANCHE	4,125	1,436	1,980	708	1	544 D	34.8%	48.0%	17.2%
3,672	CONCHO	1,110	411	502	197		91 D	37.0%	45.2%	17.7%
22,560	COOKE	7,922	3,799	2,711	1,412		1,088 R	48.0%	34.2%	17.8%
23,961	CORYELL	5,857	1,698	2,987	1,172		1,289 D	29.0%	51.0%	20.0%
4,207	COTTLE	1,276	268	742	266		474 D	21.0%	58.2%	20.8%
4,699	CRANE	1,703	493	498	712		214 A	28.9%	29.2%	41.8%
4,209	CROCKETT	1,359	509	571	279		62 D	37.5%	42.0%	20.5%
10,347	CROSBY	2,840	865	1,574	401		709 D	30.5%	55.4%	14.1%
2,794	CULBERSON	773	298	330	145		32 D	38.6%	42.7%	18.8%
6,302	DALLAM	2,008	990	588	430		402 R	49.3%	29.3%	21.4%
951,527	DALLAS	363,554	184,193	123,809	55,552		60,384 R	50.7%	34.1%	15.3%
19,185	DAWSON	4,513	2,091	1,522	900		569 R	46.3%	33.7%	19.9%
13,187	DEAF SMITH	4,713	2,474	1,545	691	3	929 R	52.5%	32.8%	14.7%
5,860	DELTA	1,882	370	1,037	475		562 D	19.7%	55.1%	25.2%

TEXAS

PRESIDENT 1968

1960 Census Population	County	Total Vote	Republican	Democratic	AIP	Other	Plurality	Percentage Rep.	Dem.	AIP
47,432	DENTON	18,863	8,222	7,463	3,178		759 R	43.6%	39.6%	16.8%
20,683	DE WITT	5,244	2,589	1,871	784		718 R	49.4%	35.7%	15.0%
4,963	DICKENS	1,534	428	811	295		383 D	27.9%	52.9%	19.2%
10,095	DIMMIT	1,660	584	896	177	3	312 D	35.2%	54.0%	10.7%
4,449	DONLEY	1,627	816	543	268		273 R	50.2%	33.4%	16.5%
13,398	DUVAL	4,483	384	3,978	121		3,594 D	8.6%	88.7%	2.7%
19,526	EASTLAND	6,350	2,453	2,884	1,013		431 D	38.6%	45.4%	16.0%
90,995	ECTOR	24,540	10,557	5,312	8,671		1,886 R	43.0%	21.6%	35.3%
2,317	EDWARDS	639	409	148	82		261 R	64.0%	23.2%	12.8%
43,395	ELLIS	12,067	3,794	5,431	2,838	4	1,637 D	31.4%	45.0%	23.5%
314,070	EL PASO	68,116	30,347	32,658	5,111		2,311 D	44.6%	47.9%	7.5%
16,236	ERATH	6,059	2,209	2,915	935		706 D	36.5%	48.1%	15.4%
21,263	FALLS	5,699	1,345	2,990	1,364		1,626 D	23.6%	52.5%	23.9%
23,880	FANNIN	7,177	1,585	3,931	1,661		2,270 D	22.1%	54.8%	23.1%
20,384	FAYETTE	5,775	2,380	1,833	1,562		547 R	41.2%	31.7%	27.0%
7,865	FISHER	2,385	555	1,560	268	2	1,005 D	23.3%	65.4%	11.2%
12,369	FLOYD	3,617	1,465	1,305	847		160 R	40.5%	36.1%	23.4%
3,125	FOARD	978	216	594	168		378 D	22.1%	60.7%	17.2%
40,527	FORT BEND	11,514	4,573	4,493	2,447	1	80 R	39.7%	39.0%	21.3%
5,101	FRANKLIN	1,989	481	1,001	507		494 D	24.2%	50.3%	25.5%
12,525	FREESTONE	4,093	958	2,066	1,069		997 D	23.4%	50.5%	26.1%
10,112	FRIO	2,432	795	1,330	307		535 D	32.7%	54.7%	12.6%
12,267	GAINES	3,525	1,401	1,087	1,037		314 R	39.7%	30.8%	29.4%
140,364	GALVESTON	52,598	16,229	26,041	10,322	6	9,812 D	30.9%	49.5%	19.6%
6,611	GARZA	1,660	615	662	383		47 D	37.0%	39.9%	23.1%
10,048	GILLESPIE	4,105	2,945	725	432	3	2,220 R	71.7%	17.7%	10.5%
1,118	GLASSCOCK	447	169	106	172		3 A	37.8%	23.7%	38.5%
5,429	GOLIAD	1,553	707	690	156		17 R	45.5%	44.4%	10.0%
17,845	GONZALES	4,389	1,476	1,930	983		454 D	33.6%	44.0%	22.4%
31,535	GRAY	10,795	5,994	2,374	2,427		3,567 R	55.5%	22.0%	22.5%
73,043	GRAYSON	23,001	8,007	10,379	4,615		2,372 D	34.8%	45.1%	20.1%
69,436	GREGG	23,120	9,278	5,733	8,109		1,169 R	40.1%	24.8%	35.1%
12,709	GRIMES	3,525	1,076	1,473	976		397 D	30.5%	41.8%	27.7%
29,017	GUADALUPE	9,102	4,332	3,529	1,241		803 R	47.6%	38.8%	13.6%
36,798	HALE	10,298	4,696	3,293	2,309		1,403 R	45.6%	32.0%	22.4%
7,322	HALL	2,225	753	1,038	434		285 D	33.8%	46.7%	19.5%
8,488	HAMILTON	2,834	1,266	1,116	452		150 R	44.7%	39.4%	15.9%
6,208	HANSFORD	2,188	1,359	392	437		922 R	62.1%	17.9%	20.0%
8,275	HARDEMAN	2,549	873	1,145	531		272 D	34.2%	44.9%	20.8%
24,629	HARDIN	8,862	1,986	2,894	3,979	3	1,085 A	22.4%	32.7%	44.9%
1,243,158	HARRIS	471,037	202,079	182,546	86,412		19,533 R	42.9%	38.8%	18.3%
45,594	HARRISON	13,951	3,668	4,959	5,324		365 A	26.3%	35.5%	38.2%
2,171	HARTLEY	1,160	597	299	264		298 R	51.5%	25.8%	22.8%
11,174	HASKELL	3,211	713	1,888	610		1,175 D	22.2%	58.8%	19.0%
19,934	HAYS	6,183	1,993	3,546	643	1	1,553 D	32.2%	57.4%	10.4%
3,185	HEMPHILL	1,300	699	400	201		299 R	53.8%	30.8%	15.5%
21,786	HENDERSON	7,932	2,315	3,119	2,497	1	622 D	29.2%	39.3%	31.5%
180,904	HIDALGO	37,111	14,455	20,087	2,569		5,632 D	39.0%	54.1%	6.9%
23,650	HILL	6,977	1,809	3,415	1,751	2	1,606 D	25.9%	48.9%	25.1%
22,340	HOCKLEY	6,147	2,265	2,426	1,456		161 D	36.8%	39.5%	23.7%
5,443	HOOD	2,161	593	1,155	411	2	562 D	27.4%	53.4%	19.0%
18,594	HOPKINS	6,492	1,860	2,700	1,932		768 D	28.7%	41.6%	29.8%
19,376	HOUSTON	6,237	1,391	2,782	2,062	2	720 D	22.3%	44.6%	33.1%
40,139	HOWARD	10,501	3,812	3,897	2,789	3	85 D	36.3%	37.1%	26.6%
3,343	HUDSPETH	707	285	289	132	1	4 D	40.3%	40.9%	18.7%
39,399	HUNT	12,905	4,651	4,785	3,469		134 D	36.0%	37.1%	26.9%
34,419	HUTCHINSON	10,148	4,813	2,416	2,919		1,894 R	47.4%	23.8%	28.8%
1,183	IRION	490	211	187	92		24 R	43.1%	38.2%	18.8%
7,418	JACK	2,611	966	1,133	512		167 D	37.0%	43.4%	19.6%
14,040	JACKSON	4,286	1,438	1,698	1,145	5	260 D	33.6%	39.6%	26.7%

TEXAS

PRESIDENT 1968

1960 Census Population	County	Total Vote	Republican	Democratic	AIP	Other	Plurality	Percentage Rep.	Dem.	AIP
22,100	JASPER	7,183	1,839	2,438	2,906		468 A	25.6%	33.9%	40.5%
1,582	JEFF DAVIS	496	191	239	66		48 D	38.5%	48.2%	13.3%
245,659	JEFFERSON	77,868	26,007	30,032	21,824	5	4,025 D	33.4%	38.6%	28.0%
5,022	JIM HOGG	1,552	223	1,276	53		1,053 D	14.4%	82.2%	3.4%
34,548	JIM WELLS	10,047	2,827	6,304	913	3	3,477 D	28.1%	62.7%	9.1%
34,720	JOHNSON	12,417	4,372	5,330	2,709	6	958 D	35.2%	42.9%	21.8%
19,299	JONES	4,979	1,676	2,372	931		696 D	33.7%	47.6%	18.7%
14,995	KARNES	4,299	1,342	2,271	686		929 D	31.2%	52.8%	16.0%
29,931	KAUFMAN	8,092	2,431	3,311	2,350		880 D	30.0%	40.9%	29.0%
5,889	KENDALL	2,471	1,569	538	364		1,031 R	63.5%	21.8%	14.7%
884	KENEDY	183	76	100	7		24 D	41.5%	54.6%	3.8%
1,727	KENT	634	143	303	188		115 D	22.6%	47.8%	29.7%
16,800	KERR	6,643	3,692	1,878	1,073		1,814 R	55.6%	28.3%	16.2%
3,943	KIMBLE	1,368	640	463	264	1	177 R	46.8%	33.8%	19.3%
640	KING	224	44	109	71		38 D	19.6%	48.7%	31.7%
2,452	KINNEY	599	198	333	68		135 D	33.1%	55.6%	11.4%
30,052	KLEBERG	8,016	2,713	4,633	670		1,920 D	33.8%	57.8%	8.4%
7,857	KNOX	2,127	580	1,222	325		642 D	27.3%	57.5%	15.3%
34,234	LAMAR	10,933	3,395	4,635	2,903		1,240 D	31.1%	42.4%	26.6%
21,896	LAMB	6,322	2,595	2,267	1,460		328 R	41.0%	35.9%	23.1%
9,418	LAMPASAS	2,818	935	1,423	460		488 D	33.2%	50.5%	16.3%
5,972	LA SALLE	1,081	324	645	112		321 D	30.0%	59.7%	10.4%
20,174	LAVACA	5,314	1,698	2,165	1,451		467 D	32.0%	40.7%	27.3%
8,949	LEE	2,989	1,075	1,283	631		208 D	36.0%	42.9%	21.1%
9,951	LEON	3,075	659	1,536	880		656 D	21.4%	50.0%	28.6%
31,595	LIBERTY	9,608	2,746	3,469	3,393		76 D	28.6%	36.1%	35.3%
20,413	LIMESTONE	5,683	1,485	2,796	1,402		1,311 D	26.1%	49.2%	24.7%
3,406	LIPSCOMB	1,545	1,079	279	187		800 R	69.8%	18.1%	12.1%
7,846	LIVE OAK	2,344	938	922	484		16 R	40.0%	39.3%	20.6%
5,240	LLANO	2,825	1,079	1,282	464		203 D	38.2%	45.4%	16.4%
226	LOVING	81	23	18	40		17 A	28.4%	22.2%	49.4%
156,271	LUBBOCK	50,154	25,646	15,430	9,078		10,216 R	51.1%	30.8%	18.1%
10,914	LYNN	2,882	1,005	1,333	544		328 D	34.9%	46.3%	18.9%
8,815	MCCULLOCH	2,659	947	1,353	359		406 D	35.6%	50.9%	13.5%
150,091	MCLENNAN	46,639	15,958	22,388	8,268	25	6,430 D	34.2%	48.0%	17.7%
1,116	MCMULLEN	428	169	160	99		9 R	39.5%	37.4%	23.1%
6,749	MADISON	2,367	608	994	765		229 D	25.7%	42.0%	32.3%
8,049	MARION	2,854	637	1,260	957		303 D	22.3%	44.1%	33.5%
5,068	MARTIN	1,255	343	373	539		166 A	27.3%	29.7%	42.9%
3,780	MASON	1,518	789	560	169		229 R	52.0%	36.9%	11.1%
25,744	MATAGORDA	8,466	3,094	3,595	1,777		501 D	36.5%	42.5%	21.0%
14,508	MAVERICK	2,506	771	1,570	165		799 D	30.8%	62.6%	6.6%
18,904	MEDINA	5,251	2,058	2,471	722		413 D	39.2%	47.1%	13.7%
2,964	MENARD	971	491	362	118		129 R	50.6%	37.3%	12.2%
67,717	MIDLAND	23,222	12,789	4,756	5,675	2	7,114 R	55.1%	20.5%	24.4%
22,263	MILAM	6,409	1,614	3,269	1,525	1	1,655 D	25.2%	51.0%	23.8%
4,467	MILLS	1,663	645	722	296		77 D	38.8%	43.4%	17.8%
11,255	MITCHELL	2,981	893	1,589	499		696 D	30.0%	53.3%	16.7%
14,893	MONTAGUE	5,205	1,736	2,555	914		819 D	33.4%	49.1%	17.6%
26,839	MONTGOMERY	13,255	4,353	4,021	4,879	2	526 A	32.8%	30.3%	36.8%
14,773	MOORE	4,996	2,378	1,359	1,258	1	1,019 R	47.6%	27.2%	25.2%
12,576	MORRIS	4,088	1,064	1,701	1,323		378 D	26.0%	41.6%	32.4%
2,870	MOTLEY	1,107	415	397	295		18 R	37.5%	35.9%	26.6%
28,046	NACOGDOCHES	9,880	3,235	3,449	3,196		214 D	32.7%	34.9%	32.3%
34,423	NAVARRO	10,388	2,845	5,296	2,245	2	2,451 D	27.4%	51.0%	21.6%
10,372	NEWTON	3,541	555	1,476	1,509	1	33 A	15.7%	41.7%	42.6%
18,963	NOLAN	5,938	1,969	2,784	1,185		815 D	33.2%	46.9%	20.0%
221,573	NUECES	67,491	21,307	39,025	7,159		17,718 D	31.6%	57.8%	10.6%
9,380	OCHILTREE	3,132	2,208	432	492		1,716 R	70.5%	13.8%	15.7%
1,928	OLDHAM	788	320	237	230	1	83 R	40.6%	30.1%	29.2%

TEXAS

PRESIDENT 1968

1960 Census Population	County	Total Vote	Republican	Democratic	AIP	Other	Plurality	Percentage Rep.	Dem.	AIP
60,357	ORANGE	21,216	5,886	6,485	8,845		2,360 A	27.7%	30.6%	41.7%
20,516	PALO PINTO	7,436	2,627	3,552	1,257		925 D	35.3%	47.8%	16.9%
16,870	PANOLA	5,947	1,586	1,711	2,650		939 A	26.7%	28.8%	44.6%
22,880	PARKER	9,303	3,068	4,301	1,934		1,233 D	33.0%	46.2%	20.8%
9,583	PARMER	3,102	1,539	833	730		706 R	49.6%	26.9%	23.5%
11,957	PECOS	4,019	1,524	1,592	900	3	68 D	37.9%	39.6%	22.4%
13,861	POLK	4,567	1,013	1,841	1,712	1	129 D	22.2%	40.3%	37.5%
115,580	POTTER	27,072	13,338	8,238	5,486	10	5,100 R	49.3%	30.4%	20.3%
5,460	PRESIDIO	1,582	481	969	132		488 D	30.4%	61.3%	8.3%
2,993	RAINS	1,204	340	558	306		218 D	28.2%	46.3%	25.4%
33,913	RANDALL	18,592	11,400	4,060	3,128	4	7,340 R	61.3%	21.8%	16.8%
3,782	REAGAN	1,112	454	370	288		84 R	40.8%	33.3%	25.9%
2,079	REAL	703	290	277	136		13 R	41.3%	39.4%	19.3%
15,682	RED RIVER	5,104	1,305	2,245	1,554		691 D	25.6%	44.0%	30.4%
17,644	REEVES	3,509	1,310	1,456	743		146 D	37.3%	41.5%	21.2%
10,975	REFUGIO	3,299	1,114	1,699	486		585 D	33.8%	51.5%	14.7%
1,075	ROBERTS	514	311	90	113		198 R	60.5%	17.5%	22.0%
16,157	ROBERTSON	4,742	965	2,833	944		1,868 D	20.4%	59.7%	19.9%
5,878	ROCKWALL	1,975	614	778	582	1	164 D	31.1%	39.4%	29.5%
15,016	RUNNELS	3,823	1,707	1,448	668		259 R	44.7%	37.9%	17.5%
36,421	RUSK	12,546	3,739	4,078	4,729		651 A	29.8%	32.5%	37.7%
7,302	SABINE	2,468	455	1,078	935		143 D	18.4%	43.7%	37.9%
7,722	SAN AUGUSTINE	2,460	506	817	1,137		320 A	20.6%	33.2%	46.2%
6,153	SAN JACINTO	2,309	381	1,235	693		542 D	16.5%	53.5%	30.0%
45,021	SAN PATRICIO	12,411	3,717	6,818	1,876		3,101 D	29.9%	54.9%	15.1%
6,381	SAN SABA	2,140	535	1,140	465		605 D	25.0%	53.3%	21.7%
2,791	SCHLEICHER	952	396	378	178		18 R	41.6%	39.7%	18.7%
20,369	SCURRY	4,861	1,745	2,031	1,084	1	286 D	35.9%	41.8%	22.3%
3,990	SHACKELFORD	1,507	557	673	277		116 D	37.0%	44.7%	18.4%
20,479	SHELBY	6,923	1,127	2,511	3,285		774 A	16.3%	36.3%	47.5%
2,605	SHERMAN	1,396	723	297	376		347 R	51.8%	21.3%	26.9%
86,350	SMITH	30,571	12,079	8,897	9,595		2,484 R	39.5%	29.1%	31.4%
2,577	SOMERVELL	901	313	384	204		71 D	34.7%	42.6%	22.6%
17,137	STARR	5,367	1,374	3,922	71		2,548 D	25.6%	73.1%	1.3%
8,885	STEPHENS	3,051	1,287	1,239	525		48 R	42.2%	40.6%	17.2%
1,177	STERLING	375	170	151	54		19 R	45.3%	40.3%	14.4%
3,017	STONEWALL	1,110	213	635	262		373 D	19.2%	57.2%	23.6%
3,738	SUTTON	910	412	351	147		61 R	45.3%	38.6%	16.2%
10,607	SWISHER	3,560	1,177	1,760	623		583 D	33.1%	49.4%	17.5%
538,495	TARRANT	190,747	81,786	79,705	29,256		2,081 R	42.9%	41.8%	15.3%
101,078	TAYLOR	25,626	12,218	9,107	4,289	12	3,111 R	47.7%	35.5%	16.7%
2,600	TERRELL	601	250	201	149	1	49 R	41.6%	33.4%	24.8%
16,286	TERRY	4,427	1,948	1,625	854		323 R	44.0%	36.7%	19.3%
2,767	THROCKMORTON	1,061	317	618	126		301 D	29.9%	58.2%	11.9%
16,785	TITUS	5,775	1,572	2,317	1,886		431 D	27.2%	40.1%	32.7%
64,630	TOM GREEN	19,536	9,682	6,774	3,074	6	2,908 R	49.6%	34.7%	15.7%
212,136	TRAVIS	82,520	34,309	39,667	8,424	120	5,358 D	41.6%	48.1%	10.2%
7,539	TRINITY	2,779	636	1,146	997		149 D	22.9%	41.2%	35.9%
10,666	TYLER	3,786	1,120	1,204	1,462		258 A	29.6%	31.8%	38.6%
19,793	UPSHUR	6,885	1,519	2,480	2,886		406 A	22.1%	36.0%	41.9%
6,239	UPTON	1,586	664	463	459		201 R	41.9%	29.2%	28.9%
16,814	UVALDE	4,759	2,252	1,736	768	3	516 R	47.3%	36.5%	16.1%
24,461	VAL VERDE	5,698	1,914	3,205	573	6	1,291 D	33.6%	56.2%	10.1%
19,091	VAN ZANDT	6,751	1,954	2,706	2,091		615 D	28.9%	40.1%	31.0%
46,475	VICTORIA	14,730	6,352	6,042	2,336		310 R	43.1%	41.0%	15.9%
21,475	WALKER	5,789	1,946	2,391	1,452		445 D	33.6%	41.3%	25.1%
12,071	WALLER	3,439	958	1,684	797		726 D	27.9%	49.0%	23.2%
14,917	WARD	4,265	1,552	1,331	1,382		170 R	36.4%	31.2%	32.4%
19,145	WASHINGTON	5,607	3,244	1,686	677		1,558 R	57.9%	30.1%	12.1%
64,791	WEBB	11,826	2,103	9,419	304		7,316 D	17.8%	79.6%	2.6%

TEXAS

PRESIDENT 1968

1960 Census Population	County	Total Vote	Republican	Democratic	AIP	Other	Plurality	Percentage Rep.	Dem.	AIP
38,152	WHARTON	9,959	3,773	4,304	1,882		531 D	37.9%	43.2%	18.9%
7,947	WHEELER	2,558	1,176	812	570		364 R	46.0%	31.7%	22.3%
123,528	WICHITA	33,414	11,937	15,387	6,087	3	3,450 D	35.7%	46.0%	18.2%
17,748	WILBARGER	5,198	1,909	1,996	1,292	1	87 D	36.7%	38.4%	24.9%
20,084	WILLACY	3,638	1,243	1,930	465		687 D	34.2%	53.1%	12.8%
35,044	WILLIAMSON	10,123	2,923	5,528	1,669	3	2,605 D	28.9%	54.6%	16.5%
13,267	WILSON	4,199	1,321	2,336	542		1,015 D	31.5%	55.6%	12.9%
13,652	WINKLER	3,579	1,391	938	1,249	1	142 R	38.9%	26.2%	34.9%
17,012	WISE	5,864	1,983	2,774	1,107		791 D	33.8%	47.3%	18.9%
17,653	WOOD	6,259	2,046	2,192	2,020	1	146 D	32.7%	35.0%	32.3%
8,032	YOAKUM	2,462	1,123	615	724		399 R	45.6%	25.0%	29.4%
17,254	YOUNG	5,346	1,860	2,482	1,004		622 D	34.8%	46.4%	18.8%
4,393	ZAPATA	1,212	251	909	52		658 D	20.7%	75.0%	4.3%
12,696	ZAVALA	2,215	693	1,307	214	1	614 D	31.3%	59.0%	9.7%
9,579,677	TOTAL	3,079,216	1,227,844	1,266,804	584,269	299	38,960 D	39.9%	41.1%	19.0%

TEXAS

ELECTION NOTES

1984 Other vote was 14,613 LaRouche (Independent); 126 Hall (write-in); 87 Johnson (write-in); 41 Serrette (write-in).

1980 Other vote was 111,613 Anderson (Independent); 37,643 Clark (Libertarian); 453 Commoner (write-in); 49 Hall (write-in); 15 Perkins (write-in); 11 Griswold (write-in). There is a discrepancy of one vote in the total of the other vote column.

1976 Other vote was 20,118 McCarthy (Independent); 11,442 Anderson (American); 1,723 Camejo (Socialist Workers); 189 MacBride (write-in); 41 Maddox (write-in); 2,752 scattered write-in. Early unamended canvass gave the Republican vote in Lamar county as 4,437 and the Republican state-wide total vote as 1,953,294.

1972 Other vote was 8,664 Jenness (Socialist Workers); 6,039 Schmitz (write-in); 3,393 scattered write-in. Although the the addition of the various county totals for the Democratic and other vote columns shows a small discrepancy, the official state certified totals are used here.

1968 Wallace on the ballot as American. Other vote was scattered write-in. Early unamended canvass gave the scattered write-in vote as 489.

UTAH

POPULAR VOTE FOR PRESIDENT 1920 TO 1984

Year	Total Vote	Republican Vote	Republican Candidate	Democratic Vote	Democratic Candidate	Other Vote	Plurality	Percentage Total Vote Rep.	Percentage Total Vote Dem.	Percentage Major Vote Rep.	Percentage Major Vote Dem.
1984	629,656	469,105	Reagan, Ronald	155,369	Mondale, Walter F.	5,182	313,736 R	74.5%	24.7%	75.1%	24.9%
1980	604,222	439,687	Reagan, Ronald	124,266	Carter, Jimmy	40,269	315,421 R	72.8%	20.6%	78.0%	22.0%
1976	541,198	337,908	Ford, Gerald R.	182,110	Carter, Jimmy	21,180	155,798 R	62.4%	33.6%	65.0%	35.0%
1972	478,476	323,643	Nixon, Richard M.	126,284	McGovern, George S.	28,549	197,359 R	67.6%	26.4%	71.9%	28.1%
1968	422,568	238,728	Nixon, Richard M.	156,665	Humphrey, Hubert H.	27,175	82,063 R	56.5%	37.1%	60.4%	39.6%
1964	401,413	181,785	Goldwater, Barry M.	219,628	Johnson, Lyndon B.		37,843 D	45.3%	54.7%	45.3%	54.7%
1960	374,709	205,361	Nixon, Richard M.	169,248	Kennedy, John F.	100	36,113 R	54.8%	45.2%	54.8%	45.2%
1956	333,995	215,631	Eisenhower, Dwight D.	118,364	Stevenson, Adlai E.		97,267 R	64.6%	35.4%	64.6%	35.4%
1952	329,554	194,190	Eisenhower, Dwight D.	135,364	Stevenson, Adlai E.		58,826 R	58.9%	41.1%	58.9%	41.1%
1948	276,306	124,402	Dewey, Thomas E.	149,151	Truman, Harry S.	2,753	24,749 D	45.0%	54.0%	45.5%	54.5%
1944	248,319	97,891	Dewey, Thomas E.	150,088	Roosevelt, Franklin D.	340	52,197 D	39.4%	60.4%	39.5%	60.5%
1940	247,819	93,151	Willkie, Wendell	154,277	Roosevelt, Franklin D.	391	61,126 D	37.6%	62.3%	37.6%	62.4%
1936	216,679	64,555	Landon, Alfred M.	150,248	Roosevelt, Franklin D.	1,876	85,693 D	29.8%	69.3%	30.1%	69.9%
1932	206,578	84,795	Hoover, Herbert C.	116,750	Roosevelt, Franklin D.	5,033	31,955 D	41.0%	56.5%	42.1%	57.9%
1928	176,603	94,618	Hoover, Herbert C.	80,985	Smith, Alfred E.	1,000	13,633 R	53.6%	45.9%	53.9%	46.1%
1924 **	156,990	77,327	Coolidge, Calvin	47,001	Davis, John W.	32,662	30,326 R	49.3%	29.9%	62.2%	37.8%
1920	145,828	81,555	Harding, Warren G.	56,639	Cox, James M.	7,634	24,916 R	55.9%	38.8%	59.0%	41.0%

In 1924 other vote was Progressive.

ELECTORAL COLLEGE VOTE 1920 TO 1984

Year	Total	Republican	Democratic	Other
1984	5	5	—	—
1980	4	4		—
1976	4	4	—	—
1972	4	4	—	—
1968	4	4	—	—
1964	4	—	4	—
1960	4	4	—	—
1956	4	4	—	—
1952	4	4	—	—
1948	4	—	4	—
1944	4	—	4	—
1940	4	—	4	—
1936	4	—	4	—
1932	4	—	4	—
1928	4	4	—	—
1924	4	4	—	—
1920	4	4	—	—

UTAH

CACHE
RICH
BOX ELDER
WEBER
MORGAN
DAVIS
DAGGETT
SUMMIT
SALT LAKE
TOOELE
WASATCH
DUCHESNE
UINTAH
UTAH
JUAB
CARBON
SANPETE
MILLARD
EMERY
GRAND
SEVIER
BEAVER
PIUTE
WAYNE
IRON
GARFIELD
SAN JUAN
WASHINGTON
KANE

UTAH

PRESIDENT 1984

1980 Census Population	County	Total Vote	Republican	Democratic	Other	Rep.-Dem. Plurality	Percentage Total Vote Rep.	Percentage Total Vote Dem.	Percentage Major Vote Rep.	Percentage Major Vote Dem.
4,378	BEAVER	2,231	1,516	708	7	808 R	68.0%	31.7%	68.2%	31.8%
33,222	BOX ELDER	15,283	13,243	1,983	57	11,260 R	86.7%	13.0%	87.0%	13.0%
57,176	CACHE	26,442	22,127	4,123	192	18,004 R	83.7%	15.6%	84.3%	15.7%
22,179	CARBON	8,818	4,393	4,357	68	36 R	49.8%	49.4%	50.2%	49.8%
769	DAGGETT	525	296	227	2	69 R	56.4%	43.2%	56.6%	43.4%
146,540	DAVIS	62,102	49,863	11,727	512	38,136 R	80.3%	18.9%	81.0%	19.0%
12,565	DUCHESNE	5,210	4,437	746	27	3,691 R	85.2%	14.3%	85.6%	14.4%
11,451	EMERY	4,439	3,081	1,326	32	1,755 R	69.4%	29.9%	69.9%	30.1%
3,673	GARFIELD	1,935	1,609	315	11	1,294 R	83.2%	16.3%	83.6%	16.4%
8,241	GRAND	3,367	2,463	876	28	1,587 R	73.2%	26.0%	73.8%	26.2%
17,349	IRON	8,251	6,856	1,342	53	5,514 R	83.1%	16.3%	83.6%	16.4%
5,530	JUAB	2,829	1,902	917	10	985 R	67.2%	32.4%	67.5%	32.5%
4,024	KANE	2,009	1,710	294	5	1,416 R	85.1%	14.6%	85.3%	14.7%
8,970	MILLARD	5,563	4,345	1,192	26	3,153 R	78.1%	21.4%	78.5%	21.5%
4,917	MORGAN	2,430	1,934	481	15	1,453 R	79.6%	19.8%	80.1%	19.9%
1,329	PIUTE	757	606	151		455 R	80.1%	19.9%	80.1%	19.9%
2,100	RICH	931	797	131	3	666 R	85.6%	14.1%	85.9%	14.1%
619,066	SALT LAKE	264,926	183,536	78,488	2,902	105,048 R	69.3%	29.6%	70.0%	30.0%
12,253	SAN JUAN	3,758	2,598	1,145	15	1,453 R	69.1%	30.5%	69.4%	30.6%
14,620	SANPETE	6,777	5,507	1,227	43	4,280 R	81.3%	18.1%	81.8%	18.2%
14,727	SEVIER	6,870	5,736	1,072	62	4,664 R	83.5%	15.6%	84.3%	15.7%
10,198	SUMMIT	5,701	4,093	1,539	69	2,554 R	71.8%	27.0%	72.7%	27.3%
26,033	TOOELE	10,130	6,478	3,584	68	2,894 R	63.9%	35.4%	64.4%	35.6%
20,506	UINTAH	8,574	7,337	1,186	51	6,151 R	85.6%	13.8%	86.1%	13.9%
218,106	UTAH	87,504	72,284	14,801	419	57,483 R	82.6%	16.9%	83.0%	17.0%
8,523	WASATCH	3,824	2,789	1,015	20	1,774 R	72.9%	26.5%	73.3%	26.7%
26,065	WASHINGTON	13,977	12,049	1,846	82	10,203 R	86.2%	13.2%	86.7%	13.3%
1,911	WAYNE	1,159	930	224	5	706 R	80.2%	19.3%	80.6%	19.4%
144,616	WEBER	63,334	44,590	18,346	398	26,244 R	70.4%	29.0%	70.8%	29.2%
1,461,037	TOTAL	629,656	469,105	155,369	5,182	313,736 R	74.5%	24.7%	75.1%	24.9%

UTAH

PRESIDENT 1980

1980 Census Population	County	Total Vote	Republican	Democratic	Other	Rep.-Dem. Plurality	Percentage Total Vote Rep.	Total Vote Dem.	Major Vote Rep.	Major Vote Dem.
4,378	BEAVER	2,157	1,477	621	59	856 R	68.5%	28.8%	70.4%	29.6%
33,222	BOX ELDER	15,111	12,500	2,142	469	10,358 R	82.7%	14.2%	85.4%	14.6%
57,176	CACHE	25,735	20,251	3,639	1,845	16,612 R	78.7%	14.1%	84.8%	15.2%
22,179	CARBON	9,063	4,320	4,317	426	3 R	47.7%	47.6%	50.0%	50.0%
769	DAGGETT	415	290	109	16	181 R	69.9%	26.3%	72.7%	27.3%
146,540	DAVIS	57,859	45,695	9,065	3,099	36,630 R	79.0%	15.7%	83.4%	16.6%
12,565	DUCHESNE	4,819	3,827	854	138	2,973 R	79.4%	17.7%	81.8%	18.2%
11,451	EMERY	4,579	3,076	1,315	188	1,761 R	67.2%	28.7%	70.1%	29.9%
3,673	GARFIELD	2,015	1,578	375	62	1,203 R	78.3%	18.6%	80.8%	19.2%
8,241	GRAND	3,354	2,362	703	289	1,659 R	70.4%	21.0%	77.1%	22.9%
17,349	IRON	7,804	6,207	1,242	355	4,965 R	79.5%	15.9%	83.3%	16.7%
5,530	JUAB	2,701	1,872	720	109	1,152 R	69.3%	26.7%	72.2%	27.8%
4,024	KANE	1,834	1,492	256	86	1,236 R	81.4%	14.0%	85.4%	14.6%
8,970	MILLARD	4,537	3,620	795	122	2,825 R	79.8%	17.5%	82.0%	18.0%
4,917	MORGAN	2,435	1,985	373	77	1,612 R	81.5%	15.3%	84.2%	15.8%
1,329	PIUTE	719	551	157	11	394 R	76.6%	21.8%	77.8%	22.2%
2,100	RICH	939	762	143	34	619 R	81.2%	15.2%	84.2%	15.8%
619,066	SALT LAKE	252,835	169,411	58,472	24,952	110,939 R	67.0%	23.1%	74.3%	25.7%
12,253	SAN JUAN	3,650	2,774	763	113	2,011 R	76.0%	20.9%	78.4%	21.6%
14,620	SANPETE	6,614	5,143	1,260	211	3,883 R	77.8%	19.1%	80.3%	19.7%
14,727	SEVIER	6,949	5,614	1,112	223	4,502 R	80.8%	16.0%	83.5%	16.5%
10,198	SUMMIT	5,093	3,330	1,184	579	2,146 R	65.4%	23.2%	73.8%	26.2%
26,033	TOOELE	9,712	6,024	3,132	556	2,892 R	62.0%	32.2%	65.8%	34.2%
20,506	UINTAH	7,332	6,045	1,049	238	4,996 R	82.4%	14.3%	85.2%	14.8%
218,106	UTAH	86,121	71,859	12,166	2,096	59,693 R	83.4%	14.1%	85.5%	14.5%
8,523	WASATCH	3,946	2,799	994	153	1,805 R	70.9%	25.2%	73.8%	26.2%
26,065	WASHINGTON	12,197	10,181	1,678	338	8,503 R	83.5%	13.8%	85.9%	14.1%
1,911	WAYNE	1,098	835	226	37	609 R	76.0%	20.6%	78.7%	21.3%
144,616	WEBER	62,599	43,807	15,404	3,388	28,403 R	70.0%	24.6%	74.0%	26.0%
1,461,037	TOTAL	604,222	439,687	124,266	40,269	315,421 R	72.8%	20.6%	78.0%	22.0%

UTAH

PRESIDENT 1976

1970 Census Population	County	Total Vote	Republican	Democratic	Other	Rep.-Dem. Plurality	Percentage Total Vote Rep.	Percentage Total Vote Dem.	Percentage Major Vote Rep.	Percentage Major Vote Dem.
3,800	BEAVER	2,076	1,088	963	25	125 R	52.4%	46.4%	53.0%	47.0%
28,129	BOX ELDER	13,501	9,319	3,353	829	5,966 R	69.0%	24.8%	73.5%	26.5%
42,331	CACHE	23,194	16,636	5,430	1,128	11,206 R	71.7%	23.4%	75.4%	24.6%
15,647	CARBON	8,683	3,360	5,157	166	1,797 D	38.7%	59.4%	39.5%	60.5%
666	DAGGETT	365	217	131	17	86 R	59.5%	35.9%	62.4%	37.6%
99,028	DAVIS	47,097	31,216	14,084	1,797	17,132 R	66.3%	29.9%	68.9%	31.1%
7,299	DUCHESNE	3,982	2,619	1,110	253	1,509 R	65.8%	27.9%	70.2%	29.8%
5,137	EMERY	3,643	1,717	1,771	155	54 D	47.1%	48.6%	49.2%	50.8%
3,157	GARFIELD	1,776	1,163	539	74	624 R	65.5%	30.3%	68.3%	31.7%
6,688	GRAND	2,855	1,781	931	143	850 R	62.4%	32.6%	65.7%	34.3%
12,177	IRON	6,833	4,757	1,700	376	3,057 R	69.6%	24.9%	73.7%	26.3%
4,574	JUAB	2,501	1,290	1,091	120	199 R	51.6%	43.6%	54.2%	45.8%
2,421	KANE	1,509	1,094	330	85	764 R	72.5%	21.9%	76.8%	23.2%
6,988	MILLARD	3,963	2,484	1,224	255	1,260 R	62.7%	30.9%	67.0%	33.0%
3,983	MORGAN	2,154	1,356	701	97	655 R	63.0%	32.5%	65.9%	34.1%
1,164	PIUTE	675	377	265	33	112 R	55.9%	39.3%	58.7%	41.3%
1,615	RICH	806	541	248	17	293 R	67.1%	30.8%	68.6%	31.4%
458,607	SALT LAKE	238,777	144,100	86,659	8,018	57,441 R	60.3%	36.3%	62.4%	37.6%
9,606	SAN JUAN	3,222	1,856	1,182	184	674 R	57.6%	36.7%	61.1%	38.9%
10,976	SANPETE	5,935	3,683	1,925	327	1,758 R	62.1%	32.4%	65.7%	34.3%
10,103	SEVIER	5,650	3,686	1,564	400	2,122 R	65.2%	27.7%	70.2%	29.8%
5,879	SUMMIT	3,763	2,316	1,282	165	1,034 R	61.5%	34.1%	64.4%	35.6%
21,545	TOOELE	9,251	4,657	4,371	223	286 R	50.3%	47.2%	51.6%	48.4%
12,684	UINTAH	5,807	4,017	1,342	448	2,675 R	69.2%	23.1%	75.0%	25.0%
137,776	UTAH	70,993	49,328	18,327	3,338	31,001 R	69.5%	25.8%	72.9%	27.1%
5,863	WASATCH	3,150	1,940	1,092	118	848 R	61.6%	34.7%	64.0%	36.0%
13,669	WASHINGTON	8,414	5,944	1,893	577	4,051 R	70.6%	22.5%	75.8%	24.2%
1,483	WAYNE	939	555	334	50	221 R	59.1%	35.6%	62.4%	37.6%
126,278	WEBER	59,684	34,811	23,111	1,762	11,700 R	58.3%	38.7%	60.1%	39.9%
1,059,273	TOTAL	541,198	337,908	182,110	21,180	155,798 R	62.4%	33.6%	65.0%	35.0%

UTAH

PRESIDENT 1972

1970 Census Population	County	Total Vote	Republican	Democratic	Other	Rep.-Dem. Plurality	Percentage Total Vote Rep.	Percentage Total Vote Dem.	Percentage Major Vote Rep.	Percentage Major Vote Dem.
3,800	BEAVER	2,053	1,332	682	39	650 R	64.9%	33.2%	66.1%	33.9%
28,129	BOX ELDER	12,794	9,880	2,134	780	7,746 R	77.2%	16.7%	82.2%	17.8%
42,331	CACHE	21,525	16,538	4,018	969	12,520 R	76.8%	18.7%	80.5%	19.5%
15,647	CARBON	7,438	3,956	3,335	147	621 R	53.2%	44.8%	54.3%	45.7%
666	DAGGETT	280	204	50	26	154 R	72.9%	17.9%	80.3%	19.7%
99,028	DAVIS	40,911	29,706	7,954	3,251	21,752 R	72.6%	19.4%	78.9%	21.1%
7,299	DUCHESNE	3,097	2,183	629	285	1,554 R	70.5%	20.3%	77.6%	22.4%
5,137	EMERY	2,550	1,666	769	115	897 R	65.3%	30.2%	68.4%	31.6%
3,157	GARFIELD	1,603	1,290	242	71	1,048 R	80.5%	15.1%	84.2%	15.8%
6,688	GRAND	2,546	1,837	560	149	1,277 R	72.2%	22.0%	76.6%	23.4%
12,177	IRON	6,648	5,085	1,098	465	3,987 R	76.5%	16.5%	82.2%	17.8%
4,574	JUAB	2,429	1,629	691	109	938 R	67.1%	28.4%	70.2%	29.8%
2,421	KANE	1,454	1,146	218	90	928 R	78.8%	15.0%	84.0%	16.0%
6,988	MILLARD	3,815	2,689	777	349	1,912 R	70.5%	20.4%	77.6%	22.4%
3,983	MORGAN	2,036	1,456	363	217	1,093 R	71.5%	17.8%	80.0%	20.0%
1,164	PIUTE	603	475	102	26	373 R	78.8%	16.9%	82.3%	17.7%
1,615	RICH	759	604	120	35	484 R	79.6%	15.8%	83.4%	16.6%
458,607	SALT LAKE	209,666	132,066	68,489	9,111	63,577 R	63.0%	32.7%	65.9%	34.1%
9,606	SAN JUAN	2,773	1,893	677	203	1,216 R	68.3%	24.4%	73.7%	26.3%
10,976	SANPETE	5,652	3,995	1,220	437	2,775 R	70.7%	21.6%	76.6%	23.4%
10,103	SEVIER	5,071	3,700	820	551	2,880 R	73.0%	16.2%	81.9%	18.1%
5,879	SUMMIT	3,158	2,209	836	113	1,373 R	69.9%	26.5%	72.5%	27.5%
21,545	TOOELE	8,545	5,641	2,621	283	3,020 R	66.0%	30.7%	68.3%	31.7%
12,684	UINTAH	5,868	4,712	716	440	3,996 R	80.3%	12.2%	86.8%	13.2%
137,776	UTAH	59,460	42,179	10,828	6,453	31,351 R	70.9%	18.2%	79.6%	20.4%
5,863	WASATCH	2,914	2,046	693	175	1,353 R	70.2%	23.8%	74.7%	25.3%
13,669	WASHINGTON	6,662	5,176	956	530	4,220 R	77.7%	14.4%	84.4%	15.6%
1,483	WAYNE	832	597	183	52	414 R	71.8%	22.0%	76.5%	23.5%
126,278	WEBER	55,334	37,753	14,503	3,078	23,250 R	68.2%	26.2%	72.2%	27.8%
1,059,273	TOTAL	478,476	323,643	126,284	28,549	197,359 R	67.6%	26.4%	71.9%	28.1%

UTAH

PRESIDENT 1968

1960 Census Population	County	Total Vote	Republican	Democratic	AIP	Other	Plurality	Percentage Rep.	Dem.	AIP
4,331	BEAVER	1,944	989	795	158	2	194 R	50.9%	40.9%	8.1%
25,061	BOX ELDER	11,688	7,680	3,093	907	8	4,587 R	65.7%	26.5%	7.8%
35,788	CACHE	17,303	11,906	4,327	1,050	20	7,579 R	68.8%	25.0%	6.1%
21,135	CARBON	7,239	2,618	4,344	271	6	1,726 D	36.2%	60.0%	3.7%
1,164	DAGGETT	291	152	97	42		55 R	52.2%	33.3%	14.4%
64,760	DAVIS	34,087	20,658	10,624	2,787	18	10,034 R	60.6%	31.2%	8.2%
7,179	DUCHESNE	2,834	1,733	858	243		875 R	61.2%	30.3%	8.6%
5,546	EMERY	2,403	1,223	1,019	161		204 R	50.9%	42.4%	6.7%
3,577	GARFIELD	1,487	1,033	314	139	1	719 R	69.5%	21.1%	9.3%
6,345	GRAND	2,357	1,435	707	215		728 R	60.9%	30.0%	9.1%
10,795	IRON	5,011	3,337	1,157	514	3	2,180 R	66.6%	23.1%	10.3%
4,597	JUAB	2,226	1,201	907	118		294 R	54.0%	40.7%	5.3%
2,667	KANE	1,135	814	147	174		640 R	71.7%	13.0%	15.3%
7,866	MILLARD	3,509	2,318	971	220		1,347 R	66.1%	27.7%	6.3%
2,837	MORGAN	1,703	1,020	551	130	2	469 R	59.9%	32.4%	7.6%
1,436	PIUTE	638	411	167	60		244 R	64.4%	26.2%	9.4%
1,685	RICH	747	525	183	39		342 R	70.3%	24.5%	5.2%
383,035	SALT LAKE	188,663	101,942	77,247	9,323	151	24,695 R	54.0%	40.9%	4.9%
9,040	SAN JUAN	2,335	1,393	680	262		713 R	59.7%	29.1%	11.2%
11,053	SANPETE	5,312	3,304	1,696	307	5	1,608 R	62.2%	31.9%	5.8%
10,565	SEVIER	4,744	3,190	1,167	384	3	2,023 R	67.2%	24.6%	8.1%
5,673	SUMMIT	2,857	1,782	961	113	1	821 R	62.4%	33.6%	4.0%
17,868	TOOELE	8,267	3,422	4,250	592	3	828 D	41.4%	51.4%	7.2%
11,582	UINTAH	4,622	3,034	1,145	437	6	1,889 R	65.6%	24.8%	9.5%
106,991	UTAH	49,528	29,226	16,629	3,666	7	12,597 R	59.0%	33.6%	7.4%
5,308	WASATCH	2,643	1,611	941	86	5	670 R	61.0%	35.6%	3.3%
10,271	WASHINGTON	5,000	3,226	975	796	3	2,251 R	64.5%	19.5%	15.9%
1,728	WAYNE	813	511	248	54		263 R	62.9%	30.5%	6.6%
110,744	WEBER	51,182	27,034	20,465	3,658	25	6,569 R	52.8%	40.0%	7.1%
890,627	TOTAL	422,568	238,728	156,665	26,906	269	82,063 R	56.5%	37.1%	6.4%

UTAH

ELECTION NOTES

1984 Other vote was 2,447 Bergland (Libertarian); 1,345 Dennis (American); 844 Johnson (Citizens); 220 Serrette (Independent Alliance); 184 Hall (Communist); 142 Mason (Socialist Workers).

1980 Other vote was 30,284 Anderson (Independent); 7,226 Clark (Libertarian); 1,009 Commoner (Independent); 965 Greaves (American); 522 Rarick (Independent American); 139 Hall (Independent); 124 DeBerry (Socialist Workers). Early unamended canvass gave the Libertarian state-wide total vote as 7,156.

1976 Other vote was 13,284 Anderson (American); 3,907 McCarthy (Independent); 2,438 MacBride (Libertarian); 1,162 Maddox (Concerned Citizens); 268 Camejo (Independent); 121 Hall (Independent). Early unamended canvass gave the American state-wide total vote as 13,304.

1972 Other vote was Schmitz (American Independent).

1968 Wallace on the ballot as American Independent. Other vote was 180 no candidate indicated for President but Gonzales for Vice-President (Peace and Freedom); 89 Halstead (Socialist Workers). Early unamended canvass incorrectly listed 54 Socialist Workers votes for San Juan county which should have been listed as cast in Salt Lake county.

VERMONT

POPULAR VOTE FOR PRESIDENT 1920 TO 1984

Year	Total Vote	Republican Vote	Republican Candidate	Democratic Vote	Democratic Candidate	Other Vote	Plurality	Percentage Total Vote Rep.	Percentage Total Vote Dem.	Percentage Major Vote Rep.	Percentage Major Vote Dem.
1984	234,561	135,865	Reagan, Ronald	95,730	Mondale, Walter F.	2,966	40,135 R	57.9%	40.8%	58.7%	41.3%
1980	213,299	94,628	Reagan, Ronald	81,952	Carter, Jimmy	36,719	12,676 R	44.4%	38.4%	53.6%	46.4%
1976	187,765	102,085	Ford, Gerald R.	80,954	Carter, Jimmy	4,726	21,131 R	54.4%	43.1%	55.8%	44.2%
1972	186,947	117,149	Nixon, Richard M.	68,174	McGovern, George S.	1,624	48,975 R	62.7%	36.5%	63.2%	36.8%
1968	161,404	85,142	Nixon, Richard M.	70,255	Humphrey, Hubert H.	6,007	14,887 R	52.8%	43.5%	54.8%	45.2%
1964	163,089	54,942	Goldwater, Barry M.	108,127	Johnson, Lyndon B.	20	53,185 D	33.7%	66.3%	33.7%	66.3%
1960	167,324	98,131	Nixon, Richard M.	69,186	Kennedy, John F.	7	28,945 R	58.6%	41.3%	58.6%	41.4%
1956	152,978	110,390	Eisenhower, Dwight D.	42,549	Stevenson, Adlai E.	39	67,841 R	72.2%	27.8%	72.2%	27.8%
1952	153,557	109,717	Eisenhower, Dwight D.	43,355	Stevenson, Adlai E.	485	66,362 R	71.5%	28.2%	71.7%	28.3%
1948	123,382	75,926	Dewey, Thomas E.	45,557	Truman, Harry S.	1,899	30,369 R	61.5%	36.9%	62.5%	37.5%
1944	125,361	71,527	Dewey, Thomas E.	53,820	Roosevelt, Franklin D.	14	17,707 R	57.1%	42.9%	57.1%	42.9%
1940	143,062	78,371	Willkie, Wendell	64,269	Roosevelt, Franklin D.	422	14,102 R	54.8%	44.9%	54.9%	45.1%
1936	143,689	81,023	Landon, Alfred M.	62,124	Roosevelt, Franklin D.	542	18,899 R	56.4%	43.2%	56.6%	43.4%
1932	136,980	78,984	Hoover, Herbert C.	56,266	Roosevelt, Franklin D.	1,730	22,718 R	57.7%	41.1%	58.4%	41.6%
1928	135,191	90,404	Hoover, Herbert C.	44,440	Smith, Alfred E.	347	45,964 R	66.9%	32.9%	67.0%	33.0%
1924	102,917	80,498	Coolidge, Calvin	16,124	Davis, John W.	6,295	64,374 R	78.2%	15.7%	83.3%	16.7%
1920	89,961	68,212	Harding, Warren G.	20,919	Cox, James M.	830	47,293 R	75.8%	23.3%	76.5%	23.5%

ELECTORAL COLLEGE VOTE 1920 TO 1984

Year	Total	Republican	Democratic	Other
1984	3	3	—	—
1980	3	3	—	—
1976	3	3	—	—
1972	3	3	—	—
1968	3	3	—	—
1964	3	—	3	—
1960	3	3	—	—
1956	3	3	—	—
1952	3	3	—	—
1948	3	3	—	—
1944	3	3	—	—
1940	3	3	—	—
1936	3	3	—	—
1932	3	3	—	—
1928	4	4	—	—
1924	4	4	—	—
1920	4	4	—	—

VERMONT

GRAND ISLE
FRANKLIN
ORLEANS
ESSEX
LAMOILLE
CHITTENDEN
CALEDONIA
WASHINGTON
ADDISON
ORANGE
RUTLAND
WINDSOR
BENNINGTON
WINDHAM

VERMONT

PRESIDENT 1984

1980 Census Population	County	Total Vote	Republican	Democratic	Other	Rep.-Dem. Plurality	Percentage Total Vote Rep.	Percentage Total Vote Dem.	Percentage Major Vote Rep.	Percentage Major Vote Dem.
29,406	ADDISON	13,030	7,589	5,299	142	2,290 R	58.2%	40.7%	58.9%	41.1%
33,345	BENNINGTON	15,304	9,035	6,039	230	2,996 R	59.0%	39.5%	59.9%	40.1%
25,808	CALEDONIA	10,614	7,249	3,223	142	4,026 R	68.3%	30.4%	69.2%	30.8%
115,534	CHITTENDEN	55,869	30,217	24,830	822	5,387 R	54.1%	44.4%	54.9%	45.1%
6,313	ESSEX	2,349	1,632	693	24	939 R	69.5%	29.5%	70.2%	29.8%
34,788	FRANKLIN	14,574	8,683	5,755	136	2,928 R	59.6%	39.5%	60.1%	39.9%
4,613	GRAND ISLE	2,551	1,537	980	34	557 R	60.3%	38.4%	61.1%	38.9%
16,767	LAMOILLE	7,528	4,674	2,746	108	1,928 R	62.1%	36.5%	63.0%	37.0%
22,739	ORANGE	10,645	6,407	4,088	150	2,319 R	60.2%	38.4%	61.0%	39.0%
23,440	ORLEANS	9,395	5,966	3,294	135	2,672 R	63.5%	35.1%	64.4%	35.6%
58,347	RUTLAND	24,991	15,236	9,545	210	5,691 R	61.0%	38.2%	61.5%	38.5%
52,393	WASHINGTON	25,168	13,706	11,163	299	2,543 R	54.5%	44.4%	55.1%	44.9%
36,933	WINDHAM	18,283	9,880	8,206	197	1,674 R	54.0%	44.9%	54.6%	45.4%
51,030	WINDSOR	24,260	14,054	9,869	337	4,185 R	57.9%	40.7%	58.7%	41.3%
511,456	TOTAL	234,561	135,865	95,730	2,966	40,135 R	57.9%	40.8%	58.7%	41.3%

VERMONT

PRESIDENT 1980

1980 Census Population	County	Total Vote	Republican	Democratic	Other	Rep.-Dem. Plurality	Percentage Total Vote Rep.	Percentage Total Vote Dem.	Percentage Major Vote Rep.	Percentage Major Vote Dem.
29,406	ADDISON	11,630	5,216	4,351	2,063	865 R	44.8%	37.4%	54.5%	45.5%
33,345	BENNINGTON	13,721	6,091	5,361	2,269	730 R	44.4%	39.1%	53.2%	46.8%
25,808	CALEDONIA	10,523	5,986	3,284	1,253	2,702 R	56.9%	31.2%	64.6%	35.4%
115,534	CHITTENDEN	47,003	18,310	19,027	9,666	717 D	39.0%	40.5%	49.0%	51.0%
6,313	ESSEX	2,340	1,305	799	236	506 R	55.8%	34.1%	62.0%	38.0%
34,788	FRANKLIN	13,445	5,998	5,914	1,533	84 R	44.6%	44.0%	50.4%	49.6%
4,613	GRAND ISLE	2,240	947	999	294	52 D	42.3%	44.6%	48.7%	51.3%
16,767	LAMOILLE	6,890	3,228	2,414	1,248	814 R	46.9%	35.0%	57.2%	42.8%
22,739	ORANGE	9,402	4,656	3,079	1,667	1,577 R	49.5%	32.7%	60.2%	39.8%
23,440	ORLEANS	9,217	4,503	3,671	1,043	832 R	48.9%	39.8%	55.1%	44.9%
58,347	RUTLAND	24,236	11,142	9,597	3,497	1,545 R	46.0%	39.6%	53.7%	46.3%
52,393	WASHINGTON	23,151	9,714	9,559	3,878	155 R	42.0%	41.3%	50.4%	49.6%
36,933	WINDHAM	16,598	7,062	5,830	3,706	1,232 R	42.5%	35.1%	54.8%	45.2%
51,030	WINDSOR	22,903	10,470	8,067	4,366	2,403 R	45.7%	35.2%	56.5%	43.5%
511,456	TOTAL	213,299	94,628	81,952	36,719	12,676 R	44.4%	38.4%	53.6%	46.4%

VERMONT

PRESIDENT 1976

1970 Census Population	County	Total Vote	Republican	Democratic	Other	Rep.-Dem. Plurality	Percentage Total Vote Rep.	Total Vote Dem.	Major Vote Rep.	Major Vote Dem.
24,266	ADDISON	10,129	5,726	4,164	239	1,562 R	56.5%	41.1%	57.9%	42.1%
29,282	BENNINGTON	12,387	6,712	5,443	232	1,269 R	54.2%	43.9%	55.2%	44.8%
22,789	CALEDONIA	9,193	5,488	3,511	194	1,977 R	59.7%	38.2%	61.0%	39.0%
99,131	CHITTENDEN	41,348	22,013	17,992	1,343	4,021 R	53.2%	43.5%	55.0%	45.0%
5,416	ESSEX	2,188	1,161	1,002	25	159 R	53.1%	45.8%	53.7%	46.3%
31,282	FRANKLIN	11,977	6,190	5,610	177	580 R	51.7%	46.8%	52.5%	47.5%
3,574	GRAND ISLE	1,908	1,004	866	38	138 R	52.6%	45.4%	53.7%	46.3%
13,309	LAMOILLE	5,740	3,535	2,016	189	1,519 R	61.6%	35.1%	63.7%	36.3%
17,676	ORANGE	8,132	4,768	3,171	193	1,597 R	58.6%	39.0%	60.1%	39.9%
20,153	ORLEANS	7,772	4,075	3,561	136	514 R	52.4%	45.8%	53.4%	46.6%
52,637	RUTLAND	21,724	11,565	9,778	381	1,787 R	53.2%	45.0%	54.2%	45.8%
47,659	WASHINGTON	20,254	10,919	8,764	571	2,155 R	53.9%	43.3%	55.5%	44.5%
33,476	WINDHAM	15,223	7,928	6,794	501	1,134 R	52.1%	44.6%	53.9%	46.1%
44,082	WINDSOR	19,691	11,001	8,282	408	2,719 R	55.9%	42.1%	57.1%	42.9%
444,732	TOTAL	187,765	102,085	80,954	4,726	21,131 R	54.4%	43.1%	55.8%	44.2%

VERMONT

PRESIDENT 1972

1970 Census Population	County	Total Vote	Republican	Democratic	Other	Rep.-Dem. Plurality	Percentage Total Vote Rep.	Total Vote Dem.	Major Vote Rep.	Major Vote Dem.
24,266	ADDISON	9,800	6,467	3,262	71	3,205 R	66.0%	33.3%	66.5%	33.5%
29,282	BENNINGTON	12,453	7,542	4,804	107	2,738 R	60.6%	38.6%	61.1%	38.9%
22,789	CALEDONIA	9,939	6,762	3,094	83	3,668 R	68.0%	31.1%	68.6%	31.4%
99,131	CHITTENDEN	39,704	23,063	16,163	478	6,900 R	58.1%	40.7%	58.8%	41.2%
5,416	ESSEX	2,110	1,441	655	14	786 R	68.3%	31.0%	68.8%	31.3%
31,282	FRANKLIN	12,065	8,109	3,898	58	4,211 R	67.2%	32.3%	67.5%	32.5%
3,574	GRAND ISLE	2,018	1,259	743	16	516 R	62.4%	36.8%	62.9%	37.1%
13,309	LAMOILLE	5,935	4,164	1,659	112	2,505 R	70.2%	28.0%	71.5%	28.5%
17,676	ORANGE	7,797	5,389	2,332	76	3,057 R	69.1%	29.9%	69.8%	30.2%
20,153	ORLEANS	7,762	4,906	2,793	63	2,113 R	63.2%	36.0%	63.7%	36.3%
52,637	RUTLAND	22,563	14,143	8,261	159	5,882 R	62.7%	36.6%	63.1%	36.9%
47,659	WASHINGTON	20,169	12,421	7,596	152	4,825 R	61.6%	37.7%	62.1%	37.9%
33,476	WINDHAM	15,100	9,062	5,925	113	3,137 R	60.0%	39.2%	60.5%	39.5%
44,082	WINDSOR	19,532	12,421	6,989	122	5,432 R	63.6%	35.8%	64.0%	36.0%
444,732	TOTAL	186,947	117,149	68,174	1,624	48,975 R	62.7%	36.5%	63.2%	36.8%

VERMONT

PRESIDENT 1968

1960 Census Population	County	Total Vote	Republican	Democratic	AIP	Other	Plurality	Percentage Rep.	Percentage Dem.	Percentage AIP
20,076	ADDISON	8,228	5,006	2,914	278	30	2,092 R	60.8%	35.4%	3.4%
25,088	BENNINGTON	11,416	5,967	4,966	401	82	1,001 R	52.3%	43.5%	3.5%
22,786	CALEDONIA	8,485	4,996	3,201	250	38	1,795 R	58.9%	37.7%	2.9%
74,425	CHITTENDEN	32,250	14,621	16,420	1,000	209	1,799 D	45.3%	50.9%	3.1%
6,083	ESSEX	2,025	1,009	952	57	7	57 R	49.8%	47.0%	2.8%
29,474	FRANKLIN	11,681	5,218	6,027	398	38	809 D	44.7%	51.6%	3.4%
2,927	GRAND ISLE	1,559	754	730	73	2	24 R	48.4%	46.8%	4.7%
11,027	LAMOILLE	4,358	2,965	1,239	140	14	1,726 R	68.0%	28.4%	3.2%
16,014	ORANGE	6,250	4,135	1,879	200	36	2,256 R	66.2%	30.1%	3.2%
20,143	ORLEANS	7,118	4,055	2,762	269	32	1,293 R	57.0%	38.8%	3.8%
46,719	RUTLAND	20,127	10,318	9,000	699	110	1,318 R	51.3%	44.7%	3.5%
42,860	WASHINGTON	17,839	9,387	7,826	497	129	1,561 R	52.6%	43.9%	2.8%
29,776	WINDHAM	12,721	6,916	5,353	374	78	1,563 R	54.4%	42.1%	2.9%
42,483	WINDSOR	17,347	9,795	6,986	468	98	2,809 R	56.5%	40.3%	2.7%
389,881	TOTAL	161,404	85,142	70,255	5,104	903	14,887 R	52.8%	43.5%	3.2%

VERMONT

ELECTION NOTES

1984 Other vote was 1,002 Bergland (Libertarian); 423 LaRouche (Independent); 323 Serrette (Liberty Union); 264 Johnson (Citizens); 127 Mason (Socialist Workers); 115 Hall (Communist); 712 scattered write-in.

1980 Other vote was 31,761 Anderson (Independent); 2,316 Commoner (Citizens); 1,900 Clark (Libertarian); 136 McReynolds (Liberty Union); 118 Hall (Communist); 75 DeBerry (Socialist Workers); 413 scattered write-in.

1976 Other vote was 4,001 McCarthy (McCarthy '76); 430 Camejo (Socialist Workers); 196 LaRouche (U.S. Labor); 99 scattered write-in. The Democratic candidate was also the Independent Vermonters nominee and 991 of his votes were received as the IV candidate. Early unamended canvass gave the Rutland county vote as 9,867 Republican; 7,440 Democratic/Independent Vermonters; the canvass was amended to correct an undercount in the votes from Rutland City.

1972 Other vote was 1,010 Spock (Liberty Union); 296 Jenness (Socialist Workers); 318 scattered write-in.

1968 Wallace on the ballot as George Wallace party. Other vote was 579 no Presidential candidate indicated (New Party); 295 Halstead (Socialist Workers); 29 scattered write-in.

VIRGINIA

POPULAR VOTE FOR PRESIDENT 1920 TO 1984

		Republican		Democratic				Percentage			
								Total Vote		Major Vote	
Year	Total Vote	Vote	Candidate	Vote	Candidate	Other Vote	Plurality	Rep.	Dem.	Rep.	Dem.
1984	2,146,635	1,337,078	Reagan, Ronald	796,250	Mondale, Walter F.	13,307	540,828 R	62.3%	37.1%	62.7%	37.3%
1980	1,866,032	989,609	Reagan, Ronald	752,174	Carter, Jimmy	124,249	237,435 R	53.0%	40.3%	56.8%	43.2%
1976	1,697,094	836,554	Ford, Gerald R.	813,896	Carter, Jimmy	46,644	22,658 R	49.3%	48.0%	50.7%	49.3%
1972	1,457,019	988,493	Nixon, Richard M.	438,887	McGovern, George S.	29,639	549,606 R	67.8%	30.1%	69.3%	30.7%
1968 **	1,361,491	590,319	Nixon, Richard M.	442,387	Humphrey, Hubert H.	328,785	147,932 R	43.4%	32.5%	57.2%	42.8%
1964	1,042,267	481,334	Goldwater, Barry M.	558,038	Johnson, Lyndon B.	2,895	76,704 D	46.2%	53.5%	46.3%	53.7%
1960	771,449	404,521	Nixon, Richard M.	362,327	Kennedy, John F.	4,601	42,194 R	52.4%	47.0%	52.8%	47.2%
1956	697,978	386,459	Eisenhower, Dwight D.	267,760	Stevenson, Adlai E.	43,759	118,699 R	55.4%	38.4%	59.1%	40.9%
1952	619,689	349,037	Eisenhower, Dwight D.	268,677	Stevenson, Adlai E.	1,975	80,360 R	56.3%	43.4%	56.5%	43.5%
1948	419,256	172,070	Dewey, Thomas E.	200,786	Truman, Harry S.	46,400	28,716 D	41.0%	47.9%	46.1%	53.9%
1944	388,485	145,243	Dewey, Thomas E.	242,276	Roosevelt, Franklin D.	966	97,033 D	37.4%	62.4%	37.5%	62.5%
1940	346,608	109,363	Willkie, Wendell	235,961	Roosevelt, Franklin D.	1,284	126,598 D	31.6%	68.1%	31.7%	68.3%
1936	334,590	98,336	Landon, Alfred M.	234,980	Roosevelt, Franklin D.	1,274	136,644 D	29.4%	70.2%	29.5%	70.5%
1932	297,942	89,637	Hoover, Herbert C.	203,979	Roosevelt, Franklin D.	4,326	114,342 D	30.1%	68.5%	30.5%	69.5%
1928	305,364	164,609	Hoover, Herbert C.	140,146	Smith, Alfred E.	609	24,463 R	53.9%	45.9%	54.0%	46.0%
1924	223,603	73,328	Coolidge, Calvin	139,717	Davis, John W.	10,558	66,389 D	32.8%	62.5%	34.4%	65.6%
1920	231,000	87,456	Harding, Warren G.	141,670	Cox, James M.	1,874	54,214 D	37.9%	61.3%	38.2%	61.8%

In 1968 other vote was 321,833 American Independent (Wallace); 4,671 Socialist Labor; 1,680 Peace and Freedom and 601 Prohibition.

ELECTORAL COLLEGE VOTE 1920 TO 1984

Year	Total	Republican	Democratic	Other
1984	12	12	—	—
1980	12	12	—	—
1976	12	12	—	—
1972 **	12	11	—	1 LIBERTARIAN
1968	12	12	—	—
1964	12	—	12	—
1960	12	12	—	—
1956	12	12	—	—
1952	12	12	—	—
1948	11	—	11	—
1944	11	—	11	—
1940	11	—	11	—
1936	11	—	11	—
1932	11	—	11	—
1928	12	12	—	—
1924	12	—	12	—
1920	12	—	12	—

In 1972 one of the twelve Republican electors voted in the Electoral College for the Libertarian candidates rather than for the national Republican candidates.

VIRGINIA

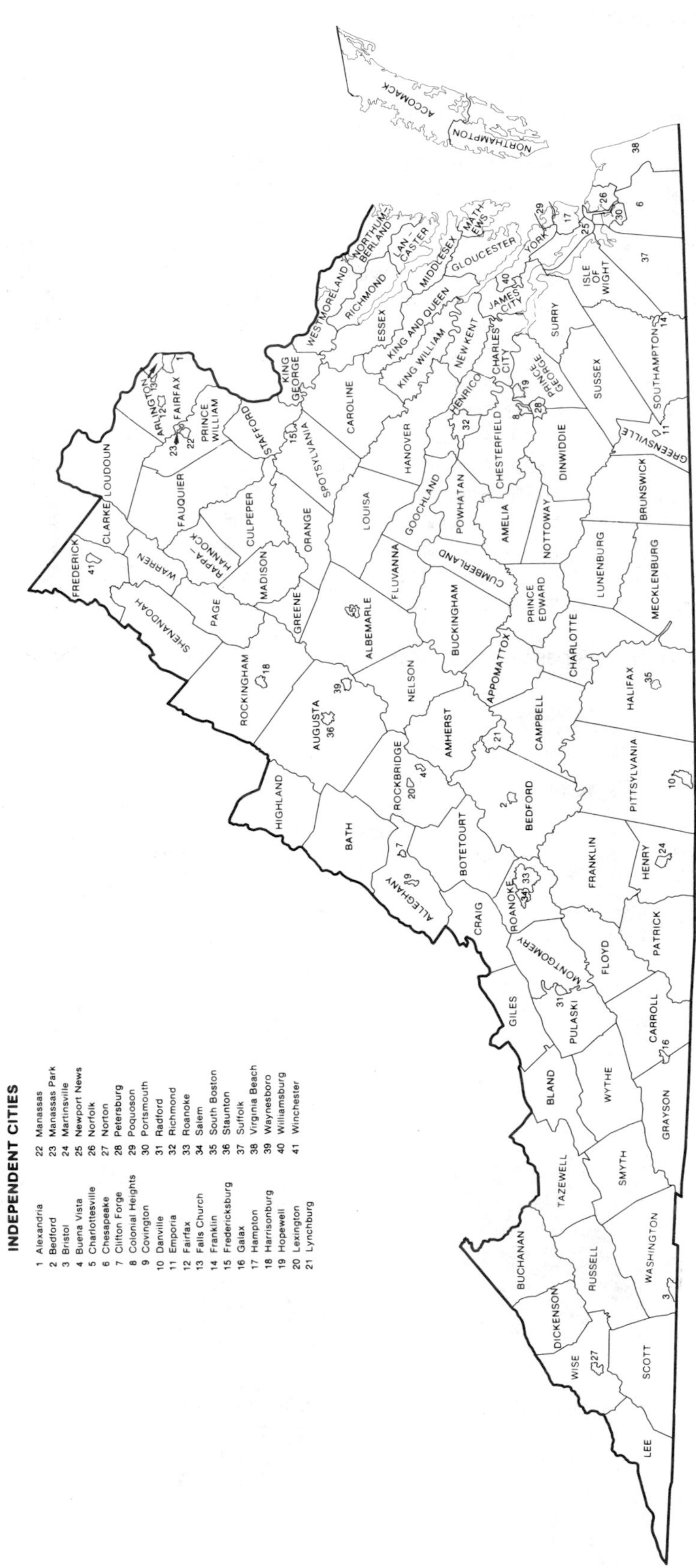
INDEPENDENT CITIES
1 Alexandria
2 Bedford
3 Bristol
4 Buena Vista
5 Charlottesville
6 Chesapeake
7 Clifton Forge
8 Colonial Heights
9 Covington
10 Danville
11 Emporia
12 Fairfax
13 Falls Church
14 Franklin
15 Fredericksburg
16 Galax
17 Hampton
18 Harrisonburg
19 Hopewell
20 Lexington
21 Lynchburg
22 Manassas
23 Manassas Park
24 Martinsville
25 Newport News
26 Norfolk
27 Norton
28 Petersburg
29 Poquoson
30 Portsmouth
31 Radford
32 Richmond
33 Roanoke
34 Salem
35 South Boston
36 Staunton
37 Suffolk
38 Virginia Beach
39 Waynesboro
40 Williamsburg
41 Winchester
FREDERICK
CLARKE
LOUDOUN
ARLINGTON
FAIRFAX
PRINCE WILLIAM
FAUQUIER
SHENANDOAH
WARREN
PAGE
RAPPA-HANNOCK
CULPEPER
MADISON
STAFFORD
KING GEORGE
ROCKINGHAM
HIGHLAND
GREENE
ORANGE
SPOTSYLVANIA
AUGUSTA
ALBEMARLE
LOUISA
CAROLINE
WESTMORELAND
NORTHUM-BERLAND
RICHMOND
ESSEX
LAN-CASTER
KING AND QUEEN
KING WILLIAM
MIDDLESEX
MATH-EWS
GLOUCESTER
BATH
ALLEGHANY
ROCKBRIDGE
NELSON
FLUVANNA
GOOCHLAND
HANOVER
NEW KENT
HENRICO
CHARLES CITY
JAMES CITY
YORK
AMHERST
BUCKINGHAM
CUMBERLAND
POWHATAN
CHESTERFIELD
AMELIA
CRAIG
BOTETOURT
APPOMATTOX
PRINCE EDWARD
NOTTOWAY
DINWIDDIE
PRINCE GEORGE
SURRY
ISLE OF WIGHT
GILES
ROANOKE
BEDFORD
CAMPBELL
CHARLOTTE
LUNENBURG
SUSSEX
BUCHANAN
DICKENSON
WISE
TAZEWELL
BLAND
PULASKI
MONTGOMERY
FLOYD
FRANKLIN
RUSSELL
SMYTH
WYTHE
LEE
SCOTT
WASHINGTON
GRAYSON
CARROLL
PATRICK
HENRY
PITTSYLVANIA
HALIFAX
MECKLENBURG
BRUNSWICK
GREENSVILLE
SOUTHAMPTON
ACCOMACK
NORTHAMPTON

VIRGINIA

PRESIDENT 1984

1980 Census Population	County	Total Vote	Republican	Democratic	Other	Rep.-Dem. Plurality	Percentage Total Vote Rep.	Percentage Total Vote Dem.	Percentage Major Vote Rep.	Percentage Major Vote Dem.
31,268	ACCOMACK	12,466	8,047	4,355	64	3,692 R	64.6%	34.9%	64.9%	35.1%
55,783	ALBEMARLE	22,530	14,455	7,982	93	6,473 R	64.2%	35.4%	64.4%	35.6%
14,333	ALLEGHANY	5,037	3,067	1,932	38	1,135 R	60.9%	38.4%	61.4%	38.6%
8,405	AMELIA	3,804	2,336	1,432	36	904 R	61.4%	37.6%	62.0%	38.0%
29,122	AMHERST	10,530	7,004	3,409	117	3,595 R	66.5%	32.4%	67.3%	32.7%
11,971	APPOMATTOX	4,932	3,386	1,498	48	1,888 R	68.7%	30.4%	69.3%	30.7%
152,599	ARLINGTON	72,242	34,848	37,031	363	2,183 D	48.2%	51.3%	48.5%	51.5%
53,732	AUGUSTA	19,323	15,308	3,899	116	11,409 R	79.2%	20.2%	79.7%	20.3%
5,860	BATH	2,175	1,434	727	14	707 R	65.9%	33.4%	66.4%	33.6%
34,927	BEDFORD COUNTY	15,217	10,371	4,754	92	5,617 R	68.2%	31.2%	68.6%	31.4%
6,349	BLAND	2,693	1,812	867	14	945 R	67.3%	32.2%	67.6%	32.4%
23,270	BOTETOURT	9,289	5,959	3,243	87	2,716 R	64.2%	34.9%	64.8%	35.2%
15,632	BRUNSWICK	6,073	2,950	3,040	83	90 D	48.6%	50.1%	49.2%	50.8%
37,989	BUCHANAN	13,053	5,053	7,828	172	2,775 D	38.7%	60.0%	39.2%	60.8%
11,751	BUCKINGHAM	4,580	2,627	1,879	74	748 R	57.4%	41.0%	58.3%	41.7%
45,424	CAMPBELL	17,924	13,388	4,380	156	9,008 R	74.7%	24.4%	75.3%	24.7%
17,904	CAROLINE	6,138	2,949	3,111	78	162 D	48.0%	50.7%	48.7%	51.3%
27,270	CARROLL	10,042	7,056	2,914	72	4,142 R	70.3%	29.0%	70.8%	29.2%
6,692	CHARLES CITY	2,584	776	1,776	32	1,000 D	30.0%	68.7%	30.4%	69.6%
12,266	CHARLOTTE	4,856	2,999	1,811	46	1,188 R	61.8%	37.3%	62.3%	37.7%
141,372	CHESTERFIELD	68,811	54,896	13,739	176	41,157 R	79.8%	20.0%	80.0%	20.0%
9,965	CLARKE	3,763	2,529	1,215	19	1,314 R	67.2%	32.3%	67.5%	32.5%
3,948	CRAIG	2,033	1,173	845	15	328 R	57.7%	41.6%	58.1%	41.9%
22,620	CULPEPER	7,926	5,596	2,255	75	3,341 R	70.6%	28.5%	71.3%	28.7%
7,881	CUMBERLAND	3,329	2,027	1,237	65	790 R	60.9%	37.2%	62.1%	37.9%
19,806	DICKENSON	8,844	3,921	4,848	75	927 D	44.3%	54.8%	44.7%	55.3%
22,602	DINWIDDIE	8,114	4,547	3,485	82	1,062 R	56.0%	43.0%	56.6%	43.4%
8,864	ESSEX	3,440	2,120	1,300	20	820 R	61.6%	37.8%	62.0%	38.0%
596,901	FAIRFAX COUNTY	291,298	183,181	107,295	822	75,886 R	62.9%	36.8%	63.1%	36.9%
35,889	FAUQUIER	14,451	10,319	4,056	76	6,263 R	71.4%	28.1%	71.8%	28.2%
11,563	FLOYD	5,069	3,431	1,599	39	1,832 R	67.7%	31.5%	68.2%	31.8%
10,244	FLUVANNA	3,612	2,247	1,332	33	915 R	62.2%	36.9%	62.8%	37.2%
35,740	FRANKLIN COUNTY	12,762	7,684	4,903	175	2,781 R	60.2%	38.4%	61.0%	39.0%
34,150	FREDERICK	12,267	9,542	2,671	54	6,871 R	77.8%	21.8%	78.1%	21.9%
17,810	GILES	7,460	4,340	3,047	73	1,293 R	58.2%	40.8%	58.8%	41.2%
20,107	GLOUCESTER	10,025	7,109	2,830	86	4,279 R	70.9%	28.2%	71.5%	28.5%
11,761	GOOCHLAND	5,617	3,404	2,178	35	1,226 R	60.6%	38.8%	61.0%	39.0%
16,579	GRAYSON	6,890	4,508	2,319	63	2,189 R	65.4%	33.7%	66.0%	34.0%
7,625	GREENE	3,000	2,216	760	24	1,456 R	73.9%	25.3%	74.5%	25.5%
10,903	GREENSVILLE	4,772	2,304	2,352	116	48 D	48.3%	49.3%	49.5%	50.5%
30,599	HALIFAX	11,103	6,726	4,231	146	2,495 R	60.6%	38.1%	61.4%	38.6%
50,398	HANOVER	23,718	18,800	4,831	87	13,969 R	79.3%	20.4%	79.6%	20.4%
180,735	HENRICO	85,448	63,864	21,336	248	42,528 R	74.7%	25.0%	75.0%	25.0%
57,654	HENRY	19,906	12,693	6,976	237	5,717 R	63.8%	35.0%	64.5%	35.5%
2,937	HIGHLAND	1,406	997	398	11	599 R	70.9%	28.3%	71.5%	28.5%
21,603	ISLE OF WIGHT	9,412	5,664	3,650	98	2,014 R	60.2%	38.8%	60.8%	39.2%
22,763	JAMES CITY	10,677	7,104	3,486	87	3,618 R	66.5%	32.6%	67.1%	32.9%
5,968	KING AND QUEEN	2,664	1,449	1,201	14	248 R	54.4%	45.1%	54.7%	45.3%
10,543	KING GEORGE	3,841	2,356	1,450	35	906 R	61.3%	37.8%	61.9%	38.1%
9,334	KING WILLIAM	4,284	2,803	1,448	33	1,355 R	65.4%	33.8%	65.9%	34.1%
10,129	LANCASTER	5,044	3,416	1,559	69	1,857 R	67.7%	30.9%	68.7%	31.3%
25,956	LEE	10,554	5,365	5,085	104	280 R	50.8%	48.2%	51.3%	48.7%
57,427	LOUDOUN	26,128	17,765	8,227	136	9,538 R	68.0%	31.5%	68.3%	31.7%
17,825	LOUISA	6,543	3,789	2,703	51	1,086 R	57.9%	41.3%	58.4%	41.6%
12,124	LUNENBURG	4,526	2,713	1,754	59	959 R	59.9%	38.8%	60.7%	39.3%
10,232	MADISON	4,055	2,723	1,302	30	1,421 R	67.2%	32.1%	67.7%	32.3%
7,995	MATHEWS	4,005	2,868	1,106	31	1,762 R	71.6%	27.6%	72.2%	27.8%
29,444	MECKLENBURG	10,316	6,777	3,438	101	3,339 R	65.7%	33.3%	66.3%	33.7%
7,719	MIDDLESEX	3,885	2,612	1,206	67	1,406 R	67.2%	31.0%	68.4%	31.6%
63,516	MONTGOMERY	19,765	12,428	7,202	135	5,226 R	62.9%	36.4%	63.3%	36.7%

VIRGINIA

PRESIDENT 1984

1980 Census Population	County	Total Vote	Republican	Democratic	Other	Rep.-Dem. Plurality	Percentage Total Vote Rep.	Total Vote Dem.	Major Vote Rep.	Major Vote Dem.
	NANSEMOND COUNTY									
12,204	NELSON	4,853	2,777	2,021	55	756 R	57.2%	41.6%	57.9%	42.1%
8,781	NEW KENT	3,899	2,679	1,204	16	1,475 R	68.7%	30.9%	69.0%	31.0%
14,625	NORTHAMPTON	5,207	2,906	2,226	75	680 R	55.8%	42.8%	56.6%	43.4%
9,828	NORTHUMBERLAND	4,628	3,166	1,407	55	1,759 R	68.4%	30.4%	69.2%	30.8%
14,666	NOTTOWAY	5,793	3,418	2,296	79	1,122 R	59.0%	39.6%	59.8%	40.2%
18,063	ORANGE	6,821	4,483	2,285	53	2,198 R	65.7%	33.5%	66.2%	33.8%
19,401	PAGE	7,519	5,021	2,437	61	2,584 R	66.8%	32.4%	67.3%	32.7%
17,647	PATRICK	6,674	4,703	1,908	63	2,795 R	70.5%	28.6%	71.1%	28.9%
66,147	PITTSYLVANIA	23,824	15,743	7,791	290	7,952 R	66.1%	32.7%	66.9%	33.1%
13,062	POWHATAN	5,327	3,921	1,381	25	2,540 R	73.6%	25.9%	74.0%	26.0%
16,456	PRINCE EDWARD	6,156	3,454	2,589	113	865 R	56.1%	42.1%	57.2%	42.8%
25,733	PRINCE GEORGE	7,178	4,999	2,136	43	2,863 R	69.6%	29.8%	70.1%	29.9%
144,703	PRINCE WILLIAM	50,803	34,992	15,631	180	19,361 R	68.9%	30.8%	69.1%	30.9%
35,229	PULASKI	12,699	8,242	4,364	93	3,878 R	64.9%	34.4%	65.4%	34.6%
6,093	RAPPAHANNOCK	2,707	1,696	999	12	697 R	62.7%	36.9%	62.9%	37.1%
6,952	RICHMOND COUNTY	2,730	1,869	830	31	1,039 R	68.5%	30.4%	69.2%	30.8%
72,945	ROANOKE COUNTY	34,054	23,348	10,569	137	12,779 R	68.6%	31.0%	68.8%	31.2%
17,911	ROCKBRIDGE	6,194	4,067	2,098	29	1,969 R	65.7%	33.9%	66.0%	34.0%
57,038	ROCKINGHAM	17,807	13,480	4,220	107	9,260 R	75.7%	23.7%	76.2%	23.8%
31,761	RUSSELL	12,599	5,738	6,760	101	1,022 D	45.5%	53.7%	45.9%	54.1%
25,068	SCOTT	9,821	5,804	3,904	113	1,900 R	59.1%	39.8%	59.8%	40.2%
27,559	SHENANDOAH	11,900	9,048	2,771	81	6,277 R	76.0%	23.3%	76.6%	23.4%
33,366	SMYTH	12,811	8,593	4,102	116	4,491 R	67.1%	32.0%	67.7%	32.3%
18,731	SOUTHAMPTON	8,051	4,669	3,300	82	1,369 R	58.0%	41.0%	58.6%	41.4%
34,435	SPOTSYLVANIA	12,297	8,207	4,012	78	4,195 R	66.7%	32.6%	67.2%	32.8%
40,470	STAFFORD	14,782	10,293	4,429	60	5,864 R	69.6%	30.0%	69.9%	30.1%
6,046	SURRY	3,370	1,462	1,875	33	413 D	43.4%	55.6%	43.8%	56.2%
10,874	SUSSEX	4,731	2,183	2,408	140	225 D	46.1%	50.9%	47.5%	52.5%
50,511	TAZEWELL	17,896	9,645	8,014	237	1,631 R	53.9%	44.8%	54.6%	45.4%
21,200	WARREN	7,631	5,016	2,551	64	2,465 R	65.7%	33.4%	66.3%	33.7%
46,487	WASHINGTON	17,826	12,132	5,573	121	6,559 R	68.1%	31.3%	68.5%	31.5%
14,041	WESTMORELAND	5,663	3,219	2,363	81	856 R	56.8%	41.7%	57.7%	42.3%
43,863	WISE	15,399	7,909	7,303	187	606 R	51.4%	47.4%	52.0%	48.0%
25,522	WYTHE	9,866	6,773	2,996	97	3,777 R	68.6%	30.4%	69.3%	30.7%
35,463	YORK	14,337	10,214	4,063	60	6,151 R	71.2%	28.3%	71.5%	28.5%
	City									
103,217	ALEXANDRIA	45,253	21,166	23,552	535	2,386 D	46.8%	52.0%	47.3%	52.7%
5,991	BEDFORD CITY	2,573	1,553	997	23	556 R	60.4%	38.7%	60.9%	39.1%
19,042	BRISTOL	7,468	5,012	2,429	27	2,583 R	67.1%	32.5%	67.4%	32.6%
6,717	BUENA VISTA	2,073	1,335	724	14	611 R	64.4%	34.9%	64.8%	35.2%
39,916	CHARLOTTESVILLE	14,306	6,947	7,317	42	370 D	48.6%	51.1%	48.7%	51.3%
114,486	CHESAPEAKE	44,684	27,542	16,740	402	10,802 R	61.6%	37.5%	62.2%	37.8%
5,046	CLIFTON FORGE	1,876	965	896	15	69 R	51.4%	47.8%	51.9%	48.1%
16,509	COLONIAL HEIGHTS	7,630	6,387	1,218	25	5,169 R	83.7%	16.0%	84.0%	16.0%
9,063	COVINGTON	3,162	1,722	1,391	49	331 R	54.5%	44.0%	55.3%	44.7%
45,642	DANVILLE	18,161	12,141	5,846	174	6,295 R	66.9%	32.2%	67.5%	32.5%
4,840	EMPORIA	2,078	1,252	807	19	445 R	60.3%	38.8%	60.8%	39.2%
19,390	FAIRFAX CITY	9,538	6,234	3,263	41	2,971 R	65.4%	34.2%	65.6%	34.4%
9,515	FALLS CHURCH	5,101	2,684	2,398	19	286 R	52.6%	47.0%	52.8%	47.2%
7,308	FRANKLIN CITY	3,130	1,561	1,537	32	24 R	49.9%	49.1%	50.4%	49.6%
15,322	FREDERICKSBURG	5,973	3,500	2,439	34	1,061 R	58.6%	40.8%	58.9%	41.1%
6,524	GALAX	2,375	1,548	814	13	734 R	65.2%	34.3%	65.5%	34.5%
122,617	HAMPTON	44,068	25,537	18,180	351	7,357 R	57.9%	41.3%	58.4%	41.6%
19,671	HARRISONBURG	7,661	5,221	2,384	56	2,837 R	68.2%	31.1%	68.7%	31.3%
23,397	HOPEWELL	8,292	5,661	2,564	67	3,097 R	68.3%	30.9%	68.8%	31.2%
7,292	LEXINGTON	2,163	1,197	946	20	251 R	55.3%	43.7%	55.9%	44.1%

VIRGINIA

PRESIDENT 1984

1980 Census Population	City	Total Vote	Republican	Democratic	Other	Rep.-Dem. Plurality	Percentage Total Vote Rep.	Total Vote Dem.	Major Vote Rep.	Major Vote Dem.
66,743	LYNCHBURG	26,772	18,047	8,542	183	9,505 R	67.4%	31.9%	67.9%	32.1%
15,438	MANASSAS	6,466	4,613	1,824	29	2,789 R	71.3%	28.2%	71.7%	28.3%
6,524	MANASSAS PARK	1,355	975	375	5	600 R	72.0%	27.7%	72.2%	27.8%
18,149	MARTINSVILLE	7,254	4,234	2,942	78	1,292 R	58.4%	40.6%	59.0%	41.0%
	NANSEMOND CITY									
144,903	NEWPORT NEWS	55,698	33,614	21,834	250	11,780 R	60.4%	39.2%	60.6%	39.4%
266,979	NORFOLK	75,516	36,360	38,913	243	2,553 D	48.1%	51.5%	48.3%	51.7%
4,757	NORTON	1,668	806	842	20	36 D	48.3%	50.5%	48.9%	51.1%
41,055	PETERSBURG	15,074	5,753	9,248	73	3,495 D	38.2%	61.4%	38.4%	61.6%
8,726	POQUOSON	4,328	3,667	647	14	3,020 R	84.7%	14.9%	85.0%	15.0%
104,577	PORTSMOUTH	40,801	18,940	21,623	238	2,683 D	46.4%	53.0%	46.7%	53.3%
13,225	RADFORD	4,669	2,855	1,781	33	1,074 R	61.1%	38.1%	61.6%	38.4%
219,214	RICHMOND CITY	88,628	38,754	49,408	466	10,654 D	43.7%	55.7%	44.0%	56.0%
100,220	ROANOKE CITY	36,492	19,008	17,300	184	1,708 R	52.1%	47.4%	52.4%	47.6%
23,958	SALEM	9,810	6,419	3,347	44	3,072 R	65.4%	34.1%	65.7%	34.3%
7,093	SOUTH BOSTON	2,893	1,899	974	20	925 R	65.6%	33.7%	66.1%	33.9%
21,857	STAUNTON	8,196	6,137	2,012	47	4,125 R	74.9%	24.5%	75.3%	24.7%
47,621	SUFFOLK	19,119	10,128	8,842	149	1,286 R	53.0%	46.2%	53.4%	46.6%
262,199	VIRGINIA BEACH	97,594	72,571	24,703	320	47,868 R	74.4%	25.3%	74.6%	25.4%
15,329	WAYNESBORO	6,079	4,465	1,579	35	2,886 R	73.4%	26.0%	73.9%	26.1%
9,870	WILLIAMSBURG	3,402	1,913	1,469	20	444 R	56.2%	43.2%	56.6%	43.4%
20,217	WINCHESTER	7,152	5,055	2,064	33	2,991 R	70.7%	28.9%	71.0%	29.0%
5,346,818	TOTAL	2,146,635	1,337,078	796,250	13,307	540,828 R	62.3%	37.1%	62.7%	37.3%

VIRGINIA

PRESIDENT 1980

1980 Census Population	County	Total Vote	Republican	Democratic	Other	Rep.-Dem. Plurality	Percentage Total Vote Rep.	Percentage Total Vote Dem.	Percentage Major Vote Rep.	Percentage Major Vote Dem.
31,268	ACCOMACK	10,698	5,371	4,872	455	499 R	50.2%	45.5%	52.4%	47.6%
55,783	ALBEMARLE	19,582	10,424	7,293	1,865	3,131 R	53.2%	37.2%	58.8%	41.2%
14,333	ALLEGHANY	4,756	2,185	2,411	160	226 D	45.9%	50.7%	47.5%	52.5%
8,405	AMELIA	3,701	1,969	1,643	89	326 R	53.2%	44.4%	54.5%	45.5%
29,122	AMHERST	8,840	5,088	3,476	276	1,612 R	57.6%	39.3%	59.4%	40.6%
11,971	APPOMATTOX	4,217	2,548	1,492	177	1,056 R	60.4%	35.4%	63.1%	36.9%
152,599	ARLINGTON	66,861	30,854	26,502	9,505	4,352 R	46.1%	39.6%	53.8%	46.2%
53,732	AUGUSTA	17,120	11,011	5,202	907	5,809 R	64.3%	30.4%	67.9%	32.1%
5,860	BATH	2,007	921	999	87	78 D	45.9%	49.8%	48.0%	52.0%
34,927	BEDFORD COUNTY	11,840	6,608	4,721	511	1,887 R	55.8%	39.9%	58.3%	41.7%
6,349	BLAND	2,345	1,278	1,002	65	276 R	54.5%	42.7%	56.1%	43.9%
23,270	BOTETOURT	8,602	4,408	3,698	496	710 R	51.2%	43.0%	54.4%	45.6%
15,632	BRUNSWICK	5,864	2,310	3,430	124	1,120 D	39.4%	58.5%	40.2%	59.8%
37,989	BUCHANAN	10,629	4,554	5,768	307	1,214 D	42.8%	54.3%	44.1%	55.9%
11,751	BUCKINGHAM	3,923	1,864	1,933	126	69 D	47.5%	49.3%	49.1%	50.9%
45,424	CAMPBELL	14,721	9,592	4,473	656	5,119 R	65.2%	30.4%	68.2%	31.8%
17,904	CAROLINE	5,154	2,071	2,924	159	853 D	40.2%	56.7%	41.5%	58.5%
27,270	CARROLL	9,634	5,905	3,437	292	2,468 R	61.3%	35.7%	63.2%	36.8%
6,692	CHARLES CITY	2,131	506	1,564	61	1,058 D	23.7%	73.4%	24.4%	75.6%
12,266	CHARLOTTE	4,530	2,322	2,108	100	214 R	51.3%	46.5%	52.4%	47.6%
141,372	CHESTERFIELD	53,613	37,908	13,060	2,645	24,848 R	70.7%	24.4%	74.4%	25.6%
9,965	CLARKE	3,266	1,876	1,156	234	720 R	57.4%	35.4%	61.9%	38.1%
3,948	CRAIG	1,779	768	946	65	178 D	43.2%	53.2%	44.8%	55.2%
22,620	CULPEPER	7,255	4,312	2,519	424	1,793 R	59.4%	34.7%	63.1%	36.9%
7,881	CUMBERLAND	3,024	1,515	1,355	154	160 R	50.1%	44.8%	52.8%	47.2%
19,806	DICKENSON	7,995	3,687	4,177	131	490 D	46.1%	52.2%	46.9%	53.1%
22,602	DINWIDDIE	7,018	3,369	3,475	174	106 D	48.0%	49.5%	49.2%	50.8%
8,864	ESSEX	2,987	1,581	1,280	126	301 R	52.9%	42.9%	55.3%	44.7%
596,901	FAIRFAX COUNTY	239,705	137,620	73,734	28,351	63,886 R	57.4%	30.8%	65.1%	34.9%
35,889	FAUQUIER	11,670	6,782	4,119	769	2,663 R	58.1%	35.3%	62.2%	37.8%
11,563	FLOYD	4,323	2,447	1,642	234	805 R	56.6%	38.0%	59.8%	40.2%
10,244	FLUVANNA	3,184	1,605	1,424	155	181 R	50.4%	44.7%	53.0%	47.0%
35,740	FRANKLIN COUNTY	11,090	4,993	5,685	412	692 D	45.0%	51.3%	46.8%	53.2%
34,150	FREDERICK	10,787	7,293	2,948	546	4,345 R	67.6%	27.3%	71.2%	28.8%
17,810	GILES	6,940	2,978	3,627	335	649 D	42.9%	52.3%	45.1%	54.9%
20,107	GLOUCESTER	7,897	4,261	3,138	498	1,123 R	54.0%	39.7%	57.6%	42.4%
11,761	GOOCHLAND	4,877	2,423	2,290	164	133 R	49.7%	47.0%	51.4%	48.6%
16,579	GRAYSON	6,547	3,494	2,875	178	619 R	53.4%	43.9%	54.9%	45.1%
7,625	GREENE	2,811	1,702	925	184	777 R	60.5%	32.9%	64.8%	35.2%
10,903	GREENSVILLE	3,800	1,583	2,142	75	559 D	41.7%	56.4%	42.5%	57.5%
30,599	HALIFAX	9,836	5,088	4,528	220	560 R	51.7%	46.0%	52.9%	47.1%
50,398	HANOVER	20,368	14,262	5,383	723	8,879 R	70.0%	26.4%	72.6%	27.4%
180,735	HENRICO	75,551	50,505	21,023	4,023	29,482 R	66.8%	27.8%	70.6%	29.4%
57,654	HENRY	17,783	8,258	8,800	725	542 D	46.4%	49.5%	48.4%	51.6%
2,937	HIGHLAND	1,278	751	487	40	264 R	58.8%	38.1%	60.7%	39.3%
21,603	ISLE OF WIGHT	7,784	3,526	3,951	307	425 D	45.3%	50.8%	47.2%	52.8%
22,763	JAMES CITY	8,048	4,289	3,068	691	1,221 R	53.3%	38.1%	58.3%	41.7%
5,968	KING AND QUEEN	2,150	949	1,128	73	179 D	44.1%	52.5%	45.7%	54.3%
10,543	KING GEORGE	3,332	1,784	1,318	230	466 R	53.5%	39.6%	57.5%	42.5%
9,334	KING WILLIAM	3,601	2,036	1,446	119	590 R	56.5%	40.2%	58.5%	41.5%
10,129	LANCASTER	4,557	2,780	1,567	210	1,213 R	61.0%	34.4%	64.0%	36.0%
25,956	LEE	9,377	4,417	4,758	202	341 D	47.1%	50.7%	48.1%	51.9%
57,427	LOUDOUN	20,492	12,076	6,694	1,722	5,382 R	58.9%	32.7%	64.3%	35.7%
17,825	LOUISA	5,706	2,633	2,809	264	176 D	46.1%	49.2%	48.4%	51.6%
12,124	LUNENBURG	4,136	2,045	1,958	133	87 R	49.4%	47.3%	51.1%	48.9%
10,232	MADISON	3,521	1,959	1,351	211	608 R	55.6%	38.4%	59.2%	40.8%
7,995	MATHEWS	3,716	2,204	1,300	212	904 R	59.3%	35.0%	62.9%	37.1%
29,444	MECKLENBURG	8,913	4,853	3,790	270	1,063 R	54.4%	42.5%	56.1%	43.9%
7,719	MIDDLESEX	3,344	1,810	1,395	139	415 R	54.1%	41.7%	56.5%	43.5%
63,516	MONTGOMERY	17,344	8,222	7,455	1,667	767 R	47.4%	43.0%	52.4%	47.6%

VIRGINIA

PRESIDENT 1980

1980 Census Population	County	Total Vote	Republican	Democratic	Other	Rep.-Dem. Plurality	Percentage Total Vote Rep.	Total Vote Dem.	Major Vote Rep.	Major Vote Dem.
	NANSEMOND COUNTY									
12,204	NELSON	4,496	1,866	2,410	220	544 D	41.5%	53.6%	43.6%	56.4%
8,781	NEW KENT	3,035	1,739	1,204	92	535 R	57.3%	39.7%	59.1%	40.9%
14,625	NORTHAMPTON	4,743	2,165	2,363	215	198 D	45.6%	49.8%	47.8%	52.2%
9,828	NORTHUMBERLAND	4,330	2,598	1,551	181	1,047 R	60.0%	35.8%	62.6%	37.4%
14,666	NOTTOWAY	5,611	2,813	2,593	205	220 R	50.1%	46.2%	52.0%	48.0%
18,063	ORANGE	6,158	3,381	2,420	357	961 R	54.9%	39.3%	58.3%	41.7%
19,401	PAGE	7,138	4,297	2,607	234	1,690 R	60.2%	36.5%	62.2%	37.8%
17,647	PATRICK	6,123	3,436	2,382	305	1,054 R	56.1%	38.9%	59.1%	40.9%
66,147	PITTSYLVANIA	20,280	12,022	7,653	605	4,369 R	59.3%	37.7%	61.1%	38.9%
13,062	POWHATAN	4,570	2,933	1,484	153	1,449 R	64.2%	32.5%	66.4%	33.6%
16,456	PRINCE EDWARD	5,598	2,774	2,553	271	221 R	49.6%	45.6%	52.1%	47.9%
25,733	PRINCE GEORGE	5,888	3,389	2,310	189	1,079 R	57.6%	39.2%	59.5%	40.5%
144,703	PRINCE WILLIAM	39,119	23,061	12,787	3,271	10,274 R	59.0%	32.7%	64.3%	35.7%
35,229	PULASKI	12,040	5,747	5,769	524	22 D	47.7%	47.9%	49.9%	50.1%
6,093	RAPPAHANNOCK	2,367	1,179	1,055	133	124 R	49.8%	44.6%	52.8%	47.2%
6,952	RICHMOND COUNTY	2,495	1,567	854	74	713 R	62.8%	34.2%	64.7%	35.3%
72,945	ROANOKE COUNTY	30,814	17,182	12,114	1,518	5,068 R	55.8%	39.3%	58.6%	41.4%
17,911	ROCKBRIDGE	5,677	2,784	2,475	418	309 R	49.0%	43.6%	52.9%	47.1%
57,038	ROCKINGHAM	17,859	11,397	5,294	1,168	6,103 R	63.8%	29.6%	68.3%	31.7%
31,761	RUSSELL	10,874	4,778	5,764	332	986 D	43.9%	53.0%	45.3%	54.7%
25,068	SCOTT	9,387	4,744	4,314	329	430 R	50.5%	46.0%	52.4%	47.6%
27,559	SHENANDOAH	11,203	7,517	3,137	549	4,380 R	67.1%	28.0%	70.6%	29.4%
33,366	SMYTH	11,861	6,033	5,335	493	698 R	50.9%	45.0%	53.1%	46.9%
18,731	SOUTHAMPTON	6,587	2,997	3,347	243	350 D	45.5%	50.8%	47.2%	52.8%
34,435	SPOTSYLVANIA	10,005	5,385	4,039	581	1,346 R	53.8%	40.4%	57.1%	42.9%
40,470	STAFFORD	12,075	7,106	4,211	758	2,895 R	58.8%	34.9%	62.8%	37.2%
6,046	SURRY	2,821	962	1,756	103	794 D	34.1%	62.2%	35.4%	64.6%
10,874	SUSSEX	4,273	1,664	2,447	162	783 D	38.9%	57.3%	40.5%	59.5%
50,511	TAZEWELL	14,425	7,021	7,003	401	18 R	48.7%	48.5%	50.1%	49.9%
21,200	WARREN	6,920	3,861	2,597	462	1,264 R	55.8%	37.5%	59.8%	40.2%
46,487	WASHINGTON	15,597	8,402	6,390	805	2,012 R	53.9%	41.0%	56.8%	43.2%
14,041	WESTMORELAND	4,989	2,510	2,271	208	239 R	50.3%	45.5%	52.5%	47.5%
43,863	WISE	13,141	5,767	6,779	595	1,012 D	43.9%	51.6%	46.0%	54.0%
25,522	WYTHE	8,766	4,758	3,677	331	1,081 R	54.3%	41.9%	56.4%	43.6%
35,463	YORK	12,133	6,744	4,532	857	2,212 R	55.6%	37.4%	59.8%	40.2%
	City									
103,217	ALEXANDRIA	40,388	17,865	17,134	5,389	731 R	44.2%	42.4%	51.0%	49.0%
5,991	BEDFORD CITY	2,423	1,145	1,149	129	4 D	47.3%	47.4%	49.9%	50.1%
19,042	BRISTOL	6,515	3,432	2,889	194	543 R	52.7%	44.3%	54.3%	45.7%
6,717	BUENA VISTA	2,089	942	1,031	116	89 D	45.1%	49.4%	47.7%	52.3%
39,916	CHARLOTTESVILLE	14,562	5,907	6,866	1,789	959 D	40.6%	47.2%	46.2%	53.8%
114,486	CHESAPEAKE	36,904	17,888	17,155	1,861	733 R	48.5%	46.5%	51.0%	49.0%
5,046	CLIFTON FORGE	1,825	716	1,012	97	296 D	39.2%	55.5%	41.4%	58.6%
16,509	COLONIAL HEIGHTS	7,063	5,012	1,692	359	3,320 R	71.0%	24.0%	74.8%	25.2%
9,063	COVINGTON	3,150	1,187	1,813	150	626 D	37.7%	57.6%	39.6%	60.4%
45,642	DANVILLE	17,362	10,665	6,138	559	4,527 R	61.4%	35.4%	63.5%	36.5%
4,840	EMPORIA	1,902	988	855	59	133 R	51.9%	45.0%	53.6%	46.4%
19,390	FAIRFAX CITY	8,004	4,475	2,614	915	1,861 R	55.9%	32.7%	63.1%	36.9%
9,515	FALLS CHURCH	4,758	2,485	1,703	570	782 R	52.2%	35.8%	59.3%	40.7%
7,308	FRANKLIN CITY	2,456	1,045	1,324	87	279 D	42.5%	53.9%	44.1%	55.9%
15,322	FREDERICKSBURG	4,968	2,502	2,174	292	328 R	50.4%	43.8%	53.5%	46.5%
6,524	GALAX	2,293	1,188	1,061	44	127 R	51.8%	46.3%	52.8%	47.2%
122,617	HAMPTON	37,765	17,023	18,517	2,225	1,494 D	45.1%	49.0%	47.9%	52.1%
19,671	HARRISONBURG	5,796	3,388	1,896	512	1,492 R	58.5%	32.7%	64.1%	35.9%
23,397	HOPEWELL	7,872	4,423	3,102	347	1,321 R	56.2%	39.4%	58.8%	41.2%
7,292	LEXINGTON	2,083	956	963	164	7 D	45.9%	46.2%	49.8%	50.2%

VIRGINIA

PRESIDENT 1980

1980 Census Population	City	Total Vote	Republican	Democratic	Other	Rep.-Dem. Plurality	Percentage Total Vote Rep.	Total Vote Dem.	Major Vote Rep.	Major Vote Dem.
66,743	LYNCHBURG	24,417	15,245	7,783	1,389	7,462 R	62.4%	31.9%	66.2%	33.8%
15,438	MANASSAS	4,952	3,009	1,565	378	1,444 R	60.8%	31.6%	65.8%	34.2%
6,524	MANASSAS PARK	1,254	729	447	78	282 R	58.1%	35.6%	62.0%	38.0%
18,149	MARTINSVILLE	7,032	3,433	3,337	262	96 R	48.8%	47.5%	50.7%	49.3%
	NANSEMOND CITY									
144,903	NEWPORT NEWS	46,982	22,423	22,066	2,493	357 R	47.7%	47.0%	50.4%	49.6%
266,979	NORFOLK	67,200	27,506	35,118	4,576	7,612 D	40.9%	52.3%	43.9%	56.1%
4,757	NORTON	1,400	572	762	66	190 D	40.9%	54.4%	42.9%	57.1%
41,055	PETERSBURG	13,277	5,001	7,931	345	2,930 D	37.7%	59.7%	38.7%	61.3%
8,726	POQUOSON	3,399	2,338	877	184	1,461 R	68.8%	25.8%	72.7%	27.3%
104,577	PORTSMOUTH	35,949	13,660	20,900	1,389	7,240 D	38.0%	58.1%	39.5%	60.5%
13,225	RADFORD	4,463	1,964	2,225	274	261 D	44.0%	49.9%	46.9%	53.1%
219,214	RICHMOND CITY	87,106	34,629	47,975	4,502	13,346 D	39.8%	55.1%	41.9%	58.1%
100,220	ROANOKE CITY	34,946	15,164	18,139	1,643	2,975 D	43.4%	51.9%	45.5%	54.5%
23,958	SALEM	9,389	4,862	4,091	436	771 R	51.8%	43.6%	54.3%	45.7%
7,093	SOUTH BOSTON	2,649	1,615	971	63	644 R	61.0%	36.7%	62.5%	37.5%
21,857	STAUNTON	7,927	4,819	2,658	450	2,161 R	60.8%	33.5%	64.5%	35.5%
47,621	SUFFOLK	16,765	7,179	9,064	522	1,885 D	42.8%	54.1%	44.2%	55.8%
262,199	VIRGINIA BEACH	79,235	47,936	24,895	6,404	23,041 R	60.5%	31.4%	65.8%	34.2%
15,329	WAYNESBORO	5,978	3,697	1,926	355	1,771 R	61.8%	32.2%	65.7%	34.3%
9,870	WILLIAMSBURG	2,953	1,344	1,199	410	145 R	45.5%	40.6%	52.9%	47.1%
20,217	WINCHESTER	6,623	4,240	2,006	377	2,234 R	64.0%	30.3%	67.9%	32.1%
5,346,818	TOTAL	1,866,032	989,609	752,174	124,249	237,435 R	53.0%	40.3%	56.8%	43.2%

VIRGINIA

PRESIDENT 1976

1970 Census Population	County	Total Vote	Republican	Democratic	Other	Rep.-Dem. Plurality	Percentage Total Vote Rep.	Percentage Total Vote Dem.	Percentage Major Vote Rep.	Percentage Major Vote Dem.
29,004	ACCOMACK	9,536	4,494	4,807	235	313 D	47.1%	50.4%	48.3%	51.7%
37,780	ALBEMARLE	16,632	9,084	7,310	238	1,774 R	54.6%	44.0%	55.4%	44.6%
12,461	ALLEGHANY	4,265	1,756	2,462	47	706 D	41.2%	57.7%	41.6%	58.4%
7,592	AMELIA	3,458	1,634	1,715	109	81 D	47.3%	49.6%	48.8%	51.2%
26,072	AMHERST	7,776	3,956	3,675	145	281 R	50.9%	47.3%	51.8%	48.2%
9,784	APPOMATTOX	3,863	1,964	1,702	197	262 R	50.8%	44.1%	53.6%	46.4%
174,284	ARLINGTON	64,599	30,972	32,536	1,091	1,564 D	47.9%	50.4%	48.8%	51.2%
44,220	AUGUSTA	14,692	8,452	5,626	614	2,826 R	57.5%	38.3%	60.0%	40.0%
5,192	BATH	1,932	888	1,029	15	141 D	46.0%	53.3%	46.3%	53.7%
26,728	BEDFORD COUNTY	9,246	4,189	4,766	291	577 D	45.3%	51.5%	46.8%	53.2%
5,423	BLAND	2,017	1,047	961	9	86 R	51.9%	47.6%	52.1%	47.9%
18,193	BOTETOURT	7,573	3,343	4,021	209	678 D	44.1%	53.1%	45.4%	54.6%
16,172	BRUNSWICK	5,668	2,387	3,071	210	684 D	42.1%	54.2%	43.7%	56.3%
32,071	BUCHANAN	10,728	3,850	5,791	1,087	1,941 D	35.9%	54.0%	39.9%	60.1%
10,597	BUCKINGHAM	3,758	1,487	2,179	92	692 D	39.6%	58.0%	40.6%	59.4%
43,319	CAMPBELL	12,245	7,442	4,354	449	3,088 R	60.8%	35.6%	63.1%	36.9%
13,925	CAROLINE	4,796	1,648	3,064	84	1,416 D	34.4%	63.9%	35.0%	65.0%
23,092	CARROLL	8,968	4,820	4,010	138	810 R	53.7%	44.7%	54.6%	45.4%
6,158	CHARLES CITY	1,951	439	1,455	57	1,016 D	22.5%	74.6%	23.2%	76.8%
11,551	CHARLOTTE	4,394	2,023	2,312	59	289 D	46.0%	52.6%	46.7%	53.3%
76,855	CHESTERFIELD	42,436	27,812	14,126	498	13,686 R	65.5%	33.3%	66.3%	33.7%
8,102	CLARKE	2,794	1,440	1,276	78	164 R	51.5%	45.7%	53.0%	47.0%
3,524	CRAIG	1,667	546	1,103	18	557 D	32.8%	66.2%	33.1%	66.9%
18,218	CULPEPER	6,696	3,659	2,892	145	767 R	54.6%	43.2%	55.9%	44.1%
6,179	CUMBERLAND	2,757	1,284	1,302	171	18 D	46.6%	47.2%	49.7%	50.3%
16,077	DICKENSON	8,209	3,471	4,583	155	1,112 D	42.3%	55.8%	43.1%	56.9%
25,046	DINWIDDIE	6,473	2,413	3,873	187	1,460 D	37.3%	59.8%	38.4%	61.6%
7,099	ESSEX	2,730	1,380	1,306	44	74 R	50.5%	47.8%	51.4%	48.6%
455,021	FAIRFAX COUNTY	205,957	110,424	92,037	3,496	18,387 R	53.6%	44.7%	54.5%	45.5%
26,375	FAUQUIER	9,111	4,715	4,002	394	713 R	51.8%	43.9%	54.1%	45.9%
9,775	FLOYD	3,925	2,071	1,728	126	343 R	52.8%	44.0%	54.5%	45.5%
7,621	FLUVANNA	2,770	1,296	1,415	59	119 D	46.8%	51.1%	47.8%	52.2%
26,858	FRANKLIN COUNTY	10,199	3,532	6,439	228	2,907 D	34.6%	63.1%	35.4%	64.6%
28,893	FREDERICK	8,672	5,162	3,389	121	1,773 R	59.5%	39.1%	60.4%	39.6%
16,741	GILES	6,739	2,731	3,779	229	1,048 D	40.5%	56.1%	42.0%	58.0%
14,059	GLOUCESTER	6,404	3,025	3,156	223	131 D	47.2%	49.3%	48.9%	51.1%
10,069	GOOCHLAND	4,455	2,104	2,259	92	155 D	47.2%	50.7%	48.2%	51.8%
15,439	GRAYSON	6,251	3,021	3,146	84	125 D	48.3%	50.3%	49.0%	51.0%
5,248	GREENE	2,130	1,095	895	140	200 R	51.4%	42.0%	55.0%	45.0%
9,604	GREENSVILLE	3,646	1,137	2,413	96	1,276 D	31.2%	66.2%	32.0%	68.0%
30,076	HALIFAX	8,697	4,045	4,352	300	307 D	46.5%	50.0%	48.2%	51.8%
37,479	HANOVER	17,859	11,559	6,069	231	5,490 R	64.7%	34.0%	65.6%	34.4%
154,364	HENRICO	68,981	45,405	21,729	1,847	23,676 R	65.8%	31.5%	67.6%	32.4%
50,901	HENRY	16,024	5,612	9,680	732	4,068 D	35.0%	60.4%	36.7%	63.3%
2,529	HIGHLAND	1,132	629	493	10	136 R	55.6%	43.6%	56.1%	43.9%
18,285	ISLE OF WIGHT	7,009	2,718	4,145	146	1,427 D	38.8%	59.1%	39.6%	60.4%
17,853	JAMES CITY	6,454	3,186	3,000	268	186 R	49.4%	46.5%	51.5%	48.5%
5,491	KING AND QUEEN	1,992	778	1,111	103	333 D	39.1%	55.8%	41.2%	58.8%
8,039	KING GEORGE	2,958	1,383	1,513	62	130 D	46.8%	51.1%	47.8%	52.2%
7,497	KING WILLIAM	3,156	1,597	1,501	58	96 R	50.6%	47.6%	51.5%	48.5%
9,126	LANCASTER	4,074	2,381	1,581	112	800 R	58.4%	38.8%	60.1%	39.9%
20,321	LEE	10,284	4,679	5,415	190	736 D	45.5%	52.7%	46.4%	53.6%
37,150	LOUDOUN	17,748	9,192	7,995	561	1,197 R	51.8%	45.0%	53.5%	46.5%
14,004	LOUISA	5,135	2,151	2,857	127	706 D	41.9%	55.6%	43.0%	57.0%
11,687	LUNENBURG	3,652	1,816	1,739	97	77 R	49.7%	47.6%	51.1%	48.9%
8,638	MADISON	3,228	1,710	1,466	52	244 R	53.0%	45.4%	53.8%	46.2%
7,168	MATHEWS	3,303	1,908	1,309	86	599 R	57.8%	39.6%	59.3%	40.7%
29,426	MECKLENBURG	8,769	4,423	4,076	270	347 R	50.4%	46.5%	52.0%	48.0%
6,295	MIDDLESEX	3,039	1,608	1,312	119	296 R	52.9%	43.2%	55.1%	44.9%
47,157	MONTGOMERY	15,742	7,971	7,539	232	432 R	50.6%	47.9%	51.4%	48.6%

VIRGINIA

PRESIDENT 1976

1970 Census Population	County	Total Vote	Republican	Democratic	Other	Rep.-Dem. Plurality	Percentage Total Vote Rep.	Total Vote Dem.	Major Vote Rep.	Major Vote Dem.
	NANSEMOND COUNTY									
11,702	NELSON	4,027	1,516	2,426	85	910 D	37.6%	60.2%	38.5%	61.5%
5,300	NEW KENT	2,644	1,259	1,338	47	79 D	47.6%	50.6%	48.5%	51.5%
14,442	NORTHAMPTON	4,735	2,043	2,459	233	416 D	43.1%	51.9%	45.4%	54.6%
9,239	NORTHUMBERLAND	4,126	2,167	1,814	145	353 R	52.5%	44.0%	54.4%	45.6%
14,260	NOTTOWAY	5,222	2,486	2,558	178	72 D	47.6%	49.0%	49.3%	50.7%
13,792	ORANGE	5,161	2,549	2,309	303	240 R	49.4%	44.7%	52.5%	47.5%
16,581	PAGE	7,337	3,780	3,401	156	379 R	51.5%	46.4%	52.6%	47.4%
15,282	PATRICK	5,377	2,349	2,740	288	391 D	43.7%	51.0%	46.2%	53.8%
58,789	PITTSYLVANIA	17,913	9,173	7,929	811	1,244 R	51.2%	44.3%	53.6%	46.4%
7,696	POWHATAN	3,636	2,010	1,528	98	482 R	55.3%	42.0%	56.8%	43.2%
14,379	PRINCE EDWARD	5,429	2,734	2,448	247	286 R	50.4%	45.1%	52.8%	47.2%
29,092	PRINCE GEORGE	4,960	2,254	2,630	76	376 D	45.4%	53.0%	46.2%	53.8%
95,094	PRINCE WILLIAM	31,524	15,446	15,215	863	231 R	49.0%	48.3%	50.4%	49.6%
29,564	PULASKI	10,624	4,764	5,546	314	782 D	44.8%	52.2%	46.2%	53.8%
5,199	RAPPAHANNOCK	1,981	881	1,071	29	190 D	44.5%	54.1%	45.1%	54.9%
5,841	RICHMOND COUNTY	2,288	1,391	864	33	527 R	60.8%	37.8%	61.7%	38.3%
67,339	ROANOKE COUNTY	26,948	13,587	13,120	241	467 R	50.4%	48.7%	50.9%	49.1%
16,637	ROCKBRIDGE	4,940	2,157	2,525	258	368 D	43.7%	51.1%	46.1%	53.9%
47,890	ROCKINGHAM	15,789	9,768	5,349	672	4,419 R	61.9%	33.9%	64.6%	35.4%
24,533	RUSSELL	10,667	4,287	6,014	366	1,727 D	40.2%	56.4%	41.6%	58.4%
24,376	SCOTT	9,494	4,313	4,496	685	183 D	45.4%	47.4%	49.0%	51.0%
22,852	SHENANDOAH	9,830	6,296	3,364	170	2,932 R	64.0%	34.2%	65.2%	34.8%
31,349	SMYTH	10,641	5,032	5,246	363	214 D	47.3%	49.3%	49.0%	51.0%
18,582	SOUTHAMPTON	5,889	2,366	3,399	124	1,033 D	40.2%	57.7%	41.0%	59.0%
16,424	SPOTSYLVANIA	7,560	3,210	4,210	140	1,000 D	42.5%	55.7%	43.3%	56.7%
24,587	STAFFORD	9,502	4,451	4,900	151	449 D	46.8%	51.6%	47.6%	52.4%
5,882	SURRY	2,833	929	1,829	75	900 D	32.8%	64.6%	33.7%	66.3%
11,464	SUSSEX	4,094	1,360	2,497	237	1,137 D	33.2%	61.0%	35.3%	64.7%
39,816	TAZEWELL	13,439	5,565	7,565	309	2,000 D	41.4%	56.3%	42.4%	57.6%
15,301	WARREN	6,517	2,985	3,221	311	236 D	45.8%	49.4%	48.1%	51.9%
40,835	WASHINGTON	14,015	6,865	6,547	603	318 R	49.0%	46.7%	51.2%	48.8%
12,142	WESTMORELAND	4,568	1,909	2,355	304	446 D	41.8%	51.6%	44.8%	55.2%
35,947	WISE	13,351	5,691	7,134	526	1,443 D	42.6%	53.4%	44.4%	55.6%
22,139	WYTHE	8,241	4,231	3,578	432	653 R	51.3%	43.4%	54.2%	45.8%
27,762	YORK	10,451	5,603	4,736	112	867 R	53.6%	45.3%	54.2%	45.8%
	City									
110,938	ALEXANDRIA	37,910	16,880	19,858	1,172	2,978 D	44.5%	52.4%	45.9%	54.1%
6,011	BEDFORD CITY	2,294	1,043	1,122	129	79 D	45.5%	48.9%	48.2%	51.8%
14,857	BRISTOL	6,361	2,943	3,343	75	400 D	46.3%	52.6%	46.8%	53.2%
6,425	BUENA VISTA	1,853	771	993	89	222 D	41.6%	53.6%	43.7%	56.3%
38,880	CHARLOTTESVILLE	13,869	6,673	6,846	350	173 D	48.1%	49.4%	49.4%	50.6%
89,580	CHESAPEAKE	32,157	12,851	17,651	1,655	4,800 D	40.0%	54.9%	42.1%	57.9%
5,501	CLIFTON FORGE	1,893	770	993	130	223 D	40.7%	52.5%	43.7%	56.3%
15,097	COLONIAL HEIGHTS	6,934	4,291	2,409	234	1,882 R	61.9%	34.7%	64.0%	36.0%
10,060	COVINGTON	3,165	1,173	1,820	172	647 D	37.1%	57.5%	39.2%	60.8%
46,391	DANVILLE	17,212	10,235	6,425	552	3,810 R	59.5%	37.3%	61.4%	38.6%
5,300	EMPORIA	2,020	1,055	899	66	156 R	52.2%	44.5%	54.0%	46.0%
21,970	FAIRFAX CITY	7,823	4,174	3,464	185	710 R	53.4%	44.3%	54.6%	45.4%
10,772	FALLS CHURCH	4,588	2,323	2,202	63	121 R	50.6%	48.0%	51.3%	48.7%
6,880	FRANKLIN CITY	2,290	1,127	1,116	47	11 R	49.2%	48.7%	50.2%	49.8%
14,450	FREDERICKSBURG	5,150	2,527	2,550	73	23 D	49.1%	49.5%	49.8%	50.2%
6,278	GALAX	2,370	1,128	1,218	24	90 D	47.6%	51.4%	48.1%	51.9%
120,779	HAMPTON	36,048	15,021	19,202	1,825	4,181 D	41.7%	53.3%	43.9%	56.1%
14,605	HARRISONBURG	5,358	3,376	1,803	179	1,573 R	63.0%	33.7%	65.2%	34.8%
23,471	HOPEWELL	7,807	3,764	3,691	352	73 R	48.2%	47.3%	50.5%	49.5%
7,597	LEXINGTON	2,035	1,027	945	63	82 R	50.5%	46.4%	52.1%	47.9%

VIRGINIA

PRESIDENT 1976

1980 Census Population	City	Total Vote	Republican	Democratic	Other	Rep.-Dem. Plurality	Percentage Total Vote Rep.	Percentage Total Vote Dem.	Percentage Major Vote Rep.	Percentage Major Vote Dem.
54,083	LYNCHBURG	23,804	14,564	8,227	1,013	6,337 R	61.2%	34.6%	63.9%	36.1%
9,164	MANASSAS	3,737	1,992	1,646	99	346 R	53.3%	44.0%	54.8%	45.2%
6,844	MANASSAS PARK	1,189	444	709	36	265 D	37.3%	59.6%	38.5%	61.5%
19,653	MARTINSVILLE	6,935	3,147	3,491	297	344 D	45.4%	50.3%	47.4%	52.6%
	NANSEMOND CITY									
138,177	NEWPORT NEWS	44,492	20,914	23,058	520	2,144 D	47.0%	51.8%	47.6%	52.4%
307,951	NORFOLK	70,402	28,099	39,295	3,008	11,196 D	39.9%	55.8%	41.7%	58.3%
4,001	NORTON	1,430	577	811	42	234 D	40.3%	56.7%	41.6%	58.4%
36,103	PETERSBURG	13,082	5,041	7,852	189	2,811 D	38.5%	60.0%	39.1%	60.9%
5,441	POQUOSON	2,640	1,461	1,140	39	321 R	55.3%	43.2%	56.2%	43.8%
110,963	PORTSMOUTH	36,246	12,872	22,837	537	9,965 D	35.5%	63.0%	36.0%	64.0%
11,596	RADFORD	4,122	1,844	2,240	38	396 D	44.7%	54.3%	45.2%	54.8%
249,621	RICHMOND CITY	83,110	37,176	44,687	1,247	7,511 D	44.7%	53.8%	45.4%	54.6%
92,115	ROANOKE CITY	35,949	14,738	20,696	515	5,958 D	41.0%	57.6%	41.6%	58.4%
21,982	SALEM	8,690	4,196	4,404	90	208 D	48.3%	50.7%	48.8%	51.2%
6,889	SOUTH BOSTON	2,438	1,389	1,001	48	388 R	57.0%	41.1%	58.1%	41.9%
24,504	STAUNTON	7,863	4,681	2,951	231	1,730 R	59.5%	37.5%	61.3%	38.7%
45,024	SUFFOLK	15,609	6,066	9,246	297	3,180 D	38.9%	59.2%	39.6%	60.4%
172,106	VIRGINIA BEACH	63,518	34,593	25,824	3,101	8,769 R	54.5%	40.7%	57.3%	42.7%
16,707	WAYNESBORO	5,915	3,528	2,209	178	1,319 R	59.6%	37.3%	61.5%	38.5%
9,069	WILLIAMSBURG	3,195	1,654	1,468	73	186 R	51.8%	45.9%	53.0%	47.0%
14,643	WINCHESTER	6,484	4,075	2,346	63	1,729 R	62.8%	36.2%	63.5%	36.5%
4,648,494	TOTAL	1,697,094	836,554	813,896	46,644	22,658 R	49.3%	48.0%	50.7%	49.3%

VIRGINIA

PRESIDENT 1972

1970 Census Population	County	Total Vote	Republican	Democratic	Other	Rep.-Dem. Plurality	Percentage Total Vote Rep.	Total Vote Dem.	Major Vote Rep.	Major Vote Dem.
29,004	ACCOMACK	9,026	6,496	2,406	124	4,090 R	72.0%	26.7%	73.0%	27.0%
37,780	ALBEMARLE	12,951	8,447	4,303	201	4,144 R	65.2%	33.2%	66.3%	33.7%
12,461	ALLEGHANY	3,830	2,584	1,069	177	1,515 R	67.5%	27.9%	70.7%	29.3%
7,592	AMELIA	2,471	1,606	778	87	828 R	65.0%	31.5%	67.4%	32.6%
26,072	AMHERST	6,639	4,909	1,512	218	3,397 R	73.9%	22.8%	76.5%	23.5%
9,784	APPOMATTOX	3,565	2,788	684	93	2,104 R	78.2%	19.2%	80.3%	19.7%
174,284	ARLINGTON	66,383	39,406	25,877	1,100	13,529 R	59.4%	39.0%	60.4%	39.6%
44,220	AUGUSTA	11,181	9,106	1,766	309	7,340 R	81.4%	15.8%	83.8%	16.2%
5,192	BATH	1,636	1,127	462	47	665 R	68.9%	28.2%	70.9%	29.1%
26,728	BEDFORD COUNTY	7,199	5,286	1,501	412	3,785 R	73.4%	20.9%	77.9%	22.1%
5,423	BLAND	1,914	1,352	527	35	825 R	70.6%	27.5%	72.0%	28.0%
18,193	BOTETOURT	5,481	3,806	1,519	156	2,287 R	69.4%	27.7%	71.5%	28.5%
16,172	BRUNSWICK	5,281	3,072	2,130	79	942 R	58.2%	40.3%	59.1%	40.9%
32,071	BUCHANAN	8,554	4,801	3,566	187	1,235 R	56.1%	41.7%	57.4%	42.6%
10,597	BUCKINGHAM	3,352	2,107	1,186	59	921 R	62.9%	35.4%	64.0%	36.0%
43,319	CAMPBELL	14,157	11,676	2,055	426	9,621 R	82.5%	14.5%	85.0%	15.0%
13,925	CAROLINE	3,951	2,086	1,814	51	272 R	52.8%	45.9%	53.5%	46.5%
23,092	CARROLL	6,989	5,247	1,583	159	3,664 R	75.1%	22.6%	76.8%	23.2%
6,158	CHARLES CITY	1,735	535	1,177	23	642 D	30.8%	67.8%	31.3%	68.8%
11,551	CHARLOTTE	3,777	2,501	1,182	94	1,319 R	66.2%	31.3%	67.9%	32.1%
76,855	CHESTERFIELD	29,253	24,934	3,823	496	21,111 R	85.2%	13.1%	86.7%	13.3%
8,102	CLARKE	2,627	1,816	715	96	1,101 R	69.1%	27.2%	71.8%	28.2%
3,524	CRAIG	1,220	774	425	21	349 R	63.4%	34.8%	64.6%	35.4%
18,218	CULPEPER	5,092	3,707	1,316	69	2,391 R	72.8%	25.8%	73.8%	26.2%
6,179	CUMBERLAND	2,374	1,371	969	34	402 R	57.8%	40.8%	58.6%	41.4%
16,077	DICKENSON	6,462	3,633	2,711	118	922 R	56.2%	42.0%	57.3%	42.7%
25,046	DINWIDDIE	5,305	3,314	1,901	90	1,413 R	62.5%	35.8%	63.5%	36.5%
7,099	ESSEX	2,368	1,482	808	78	674 R	62.6%	34.1%	64.7%	35.3%
455,021	FAIRFAX COUNTY	169,246	112,135	54,844	2,267	57,291 R	66.3%	32.4%	67.2%	32.8%
26,375	FAUQUIER	6,873	4,654	2,039	180	2,615 R	67.7%	29.7%	69.5%	30.5%
9,775	FLOYD	3,211	2,444	708	59	1,736 R	76.1%	22.0%	77.5%	22.5%
7,621	FLUVANNA	2,137	1,438	637	62	801 R	67.3%	29.8%	69.3%	30.7%
26,858	FRANKLIN COUNTY	7,110	4,674	2,273	163	2,401 R	65.7%	32.0%	67.3%	32.7%
28,893	FREDERICK	7,139	5,367	1,604	168	3,763 R	75.2%	22.5%	77.0%	23.0%
16,741	GILES	5,706	3,671	1,869	166	1,802 R	64.3%	32.8%	66.3%	33.7%
14,059	GLOUCESTER	5,064	3,642	1,292	130	2,350 R	71.9%	25.5%	73.8%	26.2%
10,069	GOOCHLAND	3,488	2,127	1,254	107	873 R	61.0%	36.0%	62.9%	37.1%
15,439	GRAYSON	5,283	3,565	1,603	115	1,962 R	67.5%	30.3%	69.0%	31.0%
5,248	GREENE	1,544	1,208	318	18	890 R	78.2%	20.6%	79.2%	20.8%
9,604	GREENSVILLE	2,869	1,608	1,197	64	411 R	56.0%	41.7%	57.3%	42.7%
30,076	HALIFAX	7,959	5,469	2,384	106	3,085 R	68.7%	30.0%	69.6%	30.4%
37,479	HANOVER	13,663	11,095	2,200	368	8,895 R	81.2%	16.1%	83.5%	16.5%
154,364	HENRICO	61,904	52,536	8,420	948	44,116 R	84.9%	13.6%	86.2%	13.8%
50,901	HENRY	12,024	7,556	4,042	426	3,514 R	62.8%	33.6%	65.1%	34.9%
2,529	HIGHLAND	997	774	206	17	568 R	77.6%	20.7%	79.0%	21.0%
18,285	ISLE OF WIGHT	5,998	3,555	2,305	138	1,250 R	59.3%	38.4%	60.7%	39.3%
17,853	JAMES CITY	5,441	3,372	1,992	77	1,380 R	62.0%	36.6%	62.9%	37.1%
5,491	KING AND QUEEN	1,772	1,033	708	31	325 R	58.3%	40.0%	59.3%	40.7%
8,039	KING GEORGE	2,391	1,675	658	58	1,017 R	70.1%	27.5%	71.8%	28.2%
7,497	KING WILLIAM	2,660	1,839	797	24	1,042 R	69.1%	30.0%	69.8%	30.2%
9,126	LANCASTER	3,745	2,683	1,009	53	1,674 R	71.6%	26.9%	72.7%	27.3%
20,321	LEE	7,945	4,957	2,825	163	2,132 R	62.4%	35.6%	63.7%	36.3%
37,150	LOUDOUN	13,557	9,417	3,941	199	5,476 R	69.5%	29.1%	70.5%	29.5%
14,004	LOUISA	4,005	2,545	1,338	122	1,207 R	63.5%	33.4%	65.5%	34.5%
11,687	LUNENBURG	3,564	2,464	1,044	56	1,420 R	69.1%	29.3%	70.2%	29.8%
8,638	MADISON	2,539	1,864	639	36	1,225 R	73.4%	25.2%	74.5%	25.5%
7,168	MATHEWS	2,987	2,164	730	93	1,434 R	72.4%	24.4%	74.8%	25.2%
29,426	MECKLENBURG	9,309	6,381	2,804	124	3,577 R	68.5%	30.1%	69.5%	30.5%
6,295	MIDDLESEX	2,449	1,697	724	28	973 R	69.3%	29.6%	70.1%	29.9%
47,157	MONTGOMERY	13,248	9,348	3,692	208	5,656 R	70.6%	27.9%	71.7%	28.3%

VIRGINIA

PRESIDENT 1972

1970 Census Population	County	Total Vote	Republican	Democratic	Other	Rep.-Dem. Plurality	Percentage Total Vote Rep.	Percentage Total Vote Dem.	Percentage Major Vote Rep.	Percentage Major Vote Dem.
	NANSEMOND COUNTY									
11,702	NELSON	3,191	2,145	954	92	1,191 R	67.2%	29.9%	69.2%	30.8%
5,300	NEW KENT	2,029	1,370	633	26	737 R	67.5%	31.2%	68.4%	31.6%
14,442	NORTHAMPTON	3,893	2,587	1,246	60	1,341 R	66.5%	32.0%	67.5%	32.5%
9,239	NORTHUMBERLAND	3,258	2,332	884	42	1,448 R	71.6%	27.1%	72.5%	27.5%
14,260	NOTTOWAY	4,367	2,979	1,308	80	1,671 R	68.2%	30.0%	69.5%	30.5%
13,792	ORANGE	3,869	2,758	1,032	79	1,726 R	71.3%	26.7%	72.8%	27.2%
16,581	PAGE	5,980	4,326	1,585	69	2,741 R	72.3%	26.5%	73.2%	26.8%
15,282	PATRICK	4,023	2,951	942	130	2,009 R	73.4%	23.4%	75.8%	24.2%
58,789	PITTSYLVANIA	16,737	12,108	4,429	200	7,679 R	72.3%	26.5%	73.2%	26.8%
7,696	POWHATAN	2,636	1,751	810	75	941 R	66.4%	30.7%	68.4%	31.6%
14,379	PRINCE EDWARD	4,850	3,199	1,585	66	1,614 R	66.0%	32.7%	66.9%	33.1%
29,092	PRINCE GEORGE	3,552	2,405	1,084	63	1,321 R	67.7%	30.5%	68.9%	31.1%
111,102	PRINCE WILLIAM	27,884	20,149	7,266	469	12,883 R	72.3%	26.1%	73.5%	26.5%
29,564	PULASKI	8,722	6,281	2,311	130	3,970 R	72.0%	26.5%	73.1%	26.9%
5,199	RAPPAHANNOCK	1,547	1,055	471	21	584 R	68.2%	30.4%	69.1%	30.9%
5,841	RICHMOND COUNTY	2,018	1,565	435	18	1,130 R	77.6%	21.6%	78.3%	21.8%
67,339	ROANOKE COUNTY	25,778	19,920	5,318	540	14,602 R	77.3%	20.6%	78.9%	21.1%
16,637	ROCKBRIDGE	4,051	3,009	956	86	2,053 R	74.3%	23.6%	75.9%	24.1%
47,890	ROCKINGHAM	12,275	10,025	2,026	224	7,999 R	81.7%	16.5%	83.2%	16.8%
24,533	RUSSELL	8,502	5,010	3,367	125	1,643 R	58.9%	39.6%	59.8%	40.2%
24,376	SCOTT	7,744	5,125	2,474	145	2,651 R	66.2%	31.9%	67.4%	32.6%
22,852	SHENANDOAH	8,644	7,128	1,422	94	5,706 R	82.5%	16.5%	83.4%	16.6%
31,349	SMYTH	8,868	6,409	2,280	179	4,129 R	72.3%	25.7%	73.8%	26.2%
18,582	SOUTHAMPTON	4,807	3,225	1,498	84	1,727 R	67.1%	31.2%	68.3%	31.7%
16,424	SPOTSYLVANIA	5,442	3,577	1,775	90	1,802 R	65.7%	32.6%	66.8%	33.2%
24,587	STAFFORD	7,214	5,222	1,901	91	3,321 R	72.4%	26.4%	73.3%	26.7%
5,882	SURRY	2,117	1,067	988	62	79 R	50.4%	46.7%	51.9%	48.1%
11,464	SUSSEX	3,855	2,120	1,645	90	475 R	55.0%	42.7%	56.3%	43.7%
39,816	TAZEWELL	10,667	7,233	3,181	253	4,052 R	67.8%	29.8%	69.5%	30.5%
15,301	WARREN	5,357	3,718	1,508	131	2,210 R	69.4%	28.2%	71.1%	28.9%
40,835	WASHINGTON	12,111	8,805	3,028	278	5,777 R	72.7%	25.0%	74.4%	25.6%
12,142	WESTMORELAND	3,532	2,331	1,113	88	1,218 R	66.0%	31.5%	67.7%	32.3%
35,947	WISE	11,242	6,739	4,402	101	2,337 R	59.9%	39.2%	60.5%	39.5%
22,139	WYTHE	6,156	4,553	1,431	172	3,122 R	74.0%	23.2%	76.1%	23.9%
33,203	YORK	10,341	7,745	2,302	294	5,443 R	74.9%	22.3%	77.1%	22.9%
	City									
110,938	ALEXANDRIA	36,169	20,235	15,409	525	4,826 R	55.9%	42.6%	56.8%	43.2%
6,011	BEDFORD CITY	2,063	1,407	529	127	878 R	68.2%	25.6%	72.7%	27.3%
14,857	BRISTOL	3,893	2,665	1,157	71	1,508 R	68.5%	29.7%	69.7%	30.3%
6,425	BUENA VISTA	1,409	990	373	46	617 R	70.3%	26.5%	72.6%	27.4%
38,880	CHARLOTTESVILLE	13,353	7,935	5,240	178	2,695 R	59.4%	39.2%	60.2%	39.8%
89,580	CHESAPEAKE	26,080	17,722	7,289	1,069	10,433 R	68.0%	27.9%	70.9%	29.1%
5,501	CLIFTON FORGE	1,784	1,127	575	82	552 R	63.2%	32.2%	66.2%	33.8%
15,097	COLONIAL HEIGHTS	6,028	5,304	541	183	4,763 R	88.0%	9.0%	90.7%	9.3%
10,060	COVINGTON	2,998	1,910	948	140	962 R	63.7%	31.6%	66.8%	33.2%
46,391	DANVILLE	16,916	12,463	4,148	305	8,315 R	73.7%	24.5%	75.0%	25.0%
5,300	EMPORIA	1,947	1,340	565	42	775 R	68.8%	29.0%	70.3%	29.7%
21,970	FAIRFAX CITY	7,475	5,063	2,274	138	2,789 R	67.7%	30.4%	69.0%	31.0%
10,772	FALLS CHURCH	4,943	2,967	1,895	81	1,072 R	60.0%	38.3%	61.0%	39.0%
6,880	FRANKLIN CITY	2,179	1,416	738	25	678 R	65.0%	33.9%	65.7%	34.3%
14,450	FREDERICKSBURG	4,976	3,211	1,702	63	1,509 R	64.5%	34.2%	65.4%	34.6%
6,278	GALAX	2,061	1,497	524	40	973 R	72.6%	25.4%	74.1%	25.9%
120,779	HAMPTON	33,435	21,897	10,648	890	11,249 R	65.5%	31.8%	67.3%	32.7%
14,605	HARRISONBURG	4,693	3,626	992	75	2,634 R	77.3%	21.1%	78.5%	21.5%
23,471	HOPEWELL	6,891	5,229	1,485	177	3,744 R	75.9%	21.5%	77.9%	22.1%
7,597	LEXINGTON	2,070	1,345	695	30	650 R	65.0%	33.6%	65.9%	34.1%

VIRGINIA

PRESIDENT 1972

1980 Census Population	City	Total Vote	Republican	Democratic	Other	Rep.-Dem. Plurality	Percentage Total Vote Rep.	Total Vote Dem.	Major Vote Rep.	Major Vote Dem.
54,083	LYNCHBURG	17,890	13,259	4,208	423	9,051 R	74.1%	23.5%	75.9%	24.1%
	MANASSAS									
	MANASSAS PARK									
19,653	MARTINSVILLE	6,326	3,879	2,292	155	1,587 R	61.3%	36.2%	62.9%	37.1%
35,166	NANSEMOND CITY	9,966	5,767	3,929	270	1,838 R	57.9%	39.4%	59.5%	40.5%
138,177	NEWPORT NEWS	40,312	27,169	12,233	910	14,936 R	67.4%	30.3%	69.0%	31.0%
307,951	NORFOLK	66,217	38,385	25,737	2,095	12,648 R	58.0%	38.9%	59.9%	40.1%
4,001	NORTON	1,313	823	463	27	360 R	62.7%	35.3%	64.0%	36.0%
36,103	PETERSBURG	12,053	6,710	5,156	187	1,554 R	55.7%	42.8%	56.5%	43.5%
	POQUOSON									
110,963	PORTSMOUTH	34,350	20,090	13,124	1,136	6,966 R	58.5%	38.2%	60.5%	39.5%
11,596	RADFORD	3,752	2,577	1,121	54	1,456 R	68.7%	29.9%	69.7%	30.3%
249,621	RICHMOND CITY	80,302	46,244	33,055	1,003	13,189 R	57.6%	41.2%	58.3%	41.7%
92,115	ROANOKE CITY	28,671	18,541	9,498	632	9,043 R	64.7%	33.1%	66.1%	33.9%
21,982	SALEM	7,553	5,649	1,744	160	3,905 R	74.8%	23.1%	76.4%	23.6%
6,889	SOUTH BOSTON	2,605	1,865	709	31	1,156 R	71.6%	27.2%	72.5%	27.5%
24,504	STAUNTON	7,068	5,531	1,416	121	4,115 R	78.3%	20.0%	79.6%	20.4%
9,858	SUFFOLK	3,073	2,137	898	38	1,239 R	69.5%	29.2%	70.4%	29.6%
172,106	VIRGINIA BEACH	49,733	38,074	10,373	1,286	27,701 R	76.6%	20.9%	78.6%	21.4%
16,707	WAYNESBORO	5,354	4,163	1,061	130	3,102 R	77.8%	19.8%	79.7%	20.3%
9,069	WILLIAMSBURG	3,108	1,786	1,274	48	512 R	57.5%	41.0%	58.4%	41.6%
14,643	WINCHESTER	6,151	4,647	1,418	86	3,229 R	75.5%	23.1%	76.6%	23.4%
4,648,494	TOTAL	1,457,019	988,493	438,887	29,639	549,606 R	67.8%	30.1%	69.3%	30.7%

VIRGINIA

PRESIDENT 1968

1960 Census Population	County	Total Vote	Republican	Democratic	AIP	Other	Plurality	Percentage Rep.	Dem.	AIP
30,635	ACCOMACK	9,181	3,231	2,467	3,460	23	229 A	35.2%	26.9%	37.7%
30,969	ALBEMARLE	8,441	4,512	2,255	1,657	17	2,257 R	53.5%	26.7%	19.6%
12,128	ALLEGHANY	3,793	1,649	988	1,153	3	496 R	43.5%	26.0%	30.4%
7,815	AMELIA	2,528	857	830	832	9	25 R	33.9%	32.8%	32.9%
22,953	AMHERST	6,674	2,656	1,543	2,449	26	207 R	39.8%	23.1%	36.7%
9,148	APPOMATTOX	4,037	1,753	756	1,512	16	241 R	43.4%	18.7%	37.5%
163,401	ARLINGTON	61,326	28,163	26,107	6,746	310	2,056 R	45.9%	42.6%	11.0%
37,363	AUGUSTA	10,900	6,313	2,028	2,483	76	3,830 R	57.9%	18.6%	22.8%
5,335	BATH	1,897	872	494	529	2	343 R	46.0%	26.0%	27.9%
25,107	BEDFORD COUNTY	7,840	2,807	1,574	3,316	143	509 A	35.8%	20.1%	42.3%
5,982	BLAND	1,862	938	560	361	3	378 R	50.4%	30.1%	19.4%
16,715	BOTETOURT	5,140	2,598	1,272	1,267	3	1,326 R	50.5%	24.7%	24.6%
17,779	BRUNSWICK	5,147	1,139	1,910	2,088	10	178 A	22.1%	37.1%	40.6%
36,724	BUCHANAN	9,816	3,699	5,003	1,067	47	1,304 D	37.7%	51.0%	10.9%
10,877	BUCKINGHAM	3,204	1,027	984	1,185	8	158 A	32.1%	30.7%	37.0%
32,958	CAMPBELL	12,811	5,731	1,996	4,425	659	1,306 R	44.7%	15.6%	34.5%
12,725	CAROLINE	4,426	1,162	2,165	1,084	15	1,003 D	26.3%	48.9%	24.5%
23,178	CARROLL	7,651	4,909	1,773	958	11	3,136 R	64.2%	23.2%	12.5%
5,492	CHARLES CITY	1,960	320	1,457	176	7	1,137 D	16.3%	74.3%	9.0%
13,368	CHARLOTTE	4,265	1,042	1,045	2,163	15	1,118 A	24.4%	24.5%	50.7%
71,197	CHESTERFIELD	39,292	22,015	5,715	11,504	58	10,511 R	56.0%	14.5%	29.3%
7,942	CLARKE	2,644	1,127	768	742	7	359 R	42.6%	29.0%	28.1%
3,356	CRAIG	1,258	581	419	256	2	162 R	46.2%	33.3%	20.3%
15,088	CULPEPER	4,694	2,229	1,239	1,217	9	990 R	47.5%	26.4%	25.9%
6,360	CUMBERLAND	2,432	844	978	602	8	134 D	34.7%	40.2%	24.8%
20,211	DICKENSON	7,415	3,412	3,355	639	9	57 R	46.0%	45.2%	8.6%
22,183	DINWIDDIE	5,257	1,451	1,551	2,245	10	694 A	27.6%	29.5%	42.7%
6,690	ESSEX	2,164	791	897	468	8	106 D	36.6%	41.5%	21.6%
261,417	FAIRFAX COUNTY	117,319	57,462	44,796	14,805	256	12,666 R	49.0%	38.2%	12.6%
24,066	FAUQUIER	6,501	2,845	2,099	1,536	21	746 R	43.8%	32.3%	23.6%
10,462	FLOYD	3,537	2,275	715	537	10	1,560 R	64.3%	20.2%	15.2%
7,227	FLUVANNA	2,145	913	569	660	3	253 R	42.6%	26.5%	30.8%
25,925	FRANKLIN COUNTY	8,308	3,036	2,025	3,219	28	183 A	36.5%	24.4%	38.7%
21,941	FREDERICK	7,454	3,696	1,612	2,137	9	1,559 R	49.6%	21.6%	28.7%
17,219	GILES	6,277	2,722	2,045	1,372	138	677 R	43.4%	32.6%	21.9%
11,919	GLOUCESTER	4,364	1,619	1,210	1,526	9	93 R	37.1%	27.7%	35.0%
9,206	GOOCHLAND	3,461	1,216	1,389	836	20	173 D	35.1%	40.1%	24.2%
17,390	GRAYSON	6,587	3,563	1,926	1,090	8	1,637 R	54.1%	29.2%	16.5%
4,715	GREENE	1,549	856	255	433	5	423 R	55.3%	16.5%	28.0%
10,620	GREENSVILLE	3,165	529	1,367	1,256	13	111 D	16.7%	43.2%	39.7%
33,637	HALIFAX	9,102	2,634	2,199	4,235	34	1,601 A	28.9%	24.2%	46.5%
27,550	HANOVER	10,847	5,425	2,079	3,330	13	2,095 R	50.0%	19.2%	30.7%
117,339	HENRICO	54,726	34,212	8,600	11,868	46	22,344 R	62.5%	15.7%	21.7%
40,335	HENRY	15,224	3,946	4,175	6,802	301	2,627 A	25.9%	27.4%	44.7%
3,221	HIGHLAND	1,069	619	284	166		335 R	57.9%	26.6%	15.5%
17,164	ISLE OF WIGHT	5,635	1,312	1,977	2,328	18	351 A	23.3%	35.1%	41.3%
11,539	JAMES CITY	4,065	1,443	1,521	1,083	18	78 D	35.5%	37.4%	26.6%
5,889	KING AND QUEEN	2,073	568	882	614	9	268 D	27.4%	42.5%	29.6%
7,243	KING GEORGE	2,195	829	730	632	4	99 R	37.8%	33.3%	28.8%
7,563	KING WILLIAM	2,431	1,046	764	615	6	282 R	43.0%	31.4%	25.3%
9,174	LANCASTER	3,650	1,640	1,134	876		506 R	44.9%	31.1%	24.0%
25,824	LEE	9,399	4,450	4,105	827	17	345 R	47.3%	43.7%	8.8%
24,549	LOUDOUN	9,970	4,577	3,262	2,117	14	1,315 R	45.9%	32.7%	21.2%
12,959	LOUISA	3,964	1,510	1,290	1,149	15	220 R	38.1%	32.5%	29.0%
12,523	LUNENBURG	4,012	1,181	1,180	1,630	21	449 A	29.4%	29.4%	40.6%
8,187	MADISON	2,439	1,188	478	763	10	425 R	48.7%	19.6%	31.3%
7,121	MATHEWS	2,777	1,309	691	773	4	536 R	47.1%	24.9%	27.8%
31,428	MECKLENBURG	9,478	2,750	2,667	4,022	39	1,272 A	29.0%	28.1%	42.4%
6,319	MIDDLESEX	2,042	809	575	655	3	154 R	39.6%	28.2%	32.1%
32,923	MONTGOMERY	11,547	7,098	2,700	1,712	37	4,398 R	61.5%	23.4%	14.8%

VIRGINIA

PRESIDENT 1968

1960 Census Population	County	Total Vote	Republican	Democratic	AIP	Other	Plurality	Percentage Rep.	Dem.	AIP
31,366	NANSEMOND COUNTY	10,033	2,101	4,174	3,723	35	451 D	20.9%	41.6%	37.1%
12,752	NELSON	3,426	1,130	1,120	1,163	13	33 A	33.0%	32.7%	33.9%
4,504	NEW KENT	1,904	526	765	609	4	156 D	27.6%	40.2%	32.0%
16,966	NORTHAMPTON	3,974	1,410	1,418	1,129	17	8 D	35.5%	35.7%	28.4%
10,185	NORTHUMBERLAND	3,492	1,438	1,077	968	9	361 R	41.2%	30.8%	27.7%
15,141	NOTTOWAY	4,830	1,614	1,529	1,673	14	59 A	33.4%	31.7%	34.6%
12,900	ORANGE	3,661	1,727	879	1,050	5	677 R	47.2%	24.0%	28.7%
15,572	PAGE	6,800	3,667	2,125	995	13	1,542 R	53.9%	31.3%	14.6%
15,282	PATRICK	5,275	2,187	1,105	1,974	9	213 R	41.5%	20.9%	37.4%
58,296	PITTSYLVANIA	19,890	5,096	5,427	9,302	65	3,875 A	25.6%	27.3%	46.8%
6,747	POWHATAN	2,663	722	1,004	929	8	75 D	27.1%	37.7%	34.9%
14,121	PRINCE EDWARD	4,666	1,857	1,567	1,224	18	290 R	39.8%	33.6%	26.2%
20,270	PRINCE GEORGE	4,761	1,559	1,272	1,920	10	361 A	32.7%	26.7%	40.3%
50,164	PRINCE WILLIAM	18,686	7,944	5,566	5,160	16	2,378 R	42.5%	29.8%	27.6%
27,258	PULASKI	8,265	4,409	2,497	1,346	13	1,912 R	53.3%	30.2%	16.3%
5,368	RAPPAHANNOCK	1,363	594	394	372	3	200 R	43.6%	28.9%	27.3%
6,375	RICHMOND COUNTY	2,069	1,011	490	563	5	448 R	48.9%	23.7%	27.2%
45,635	ROANOKE COUNTY	21,124	12,439	3,902	4,745	38	7,694 R	58.9%	18.5%	22.5%
16,502	ROCKBRIDGE	4,014	2,280	845	885	4	1,395 R	56.8%	21.1%	22.0%
40,485	ROCKINGHAM	11,715	7,779	2,111	1,817	8	5,668 R	66.4%	18.0%	15.5%
26,290	RUSSELL	8,872	3,858	3,554	1,369	91	304 R	43.5%	40.1%	15.4%
25,813	SCOTT	9,984	5,345	3,144	1,474	21	2,201 R	53.5%	31.5%	14.8%
21,825	SHENANDOAH	8,681	5,461	1,654	1,561	5	3,807 R	62.9%	19.1%	18.0%
31,066	SMYTH	9,751	5,297	2,631	1,808	15	2,666 R	54.3%	27.0%	18.5%
19,931	SOUTHAMPTON	5,262	1,376	1,803	2,070	13	267 A	26.1%	34.3%	39.3%
13,819	SPOTSYLVANIA	4,926	1,675	1,647	1,589	15	28 R	34.0%	33.4%	32.3%
16,876	STAFFORD	6,482	2,572	1,698	2,197	15	375 R	39.7%	26.2%	33.9%
6,220	SURRY	2,366	523	1,126	708	9	418 D	22.1%	47.6%	29.9%
12,411	SUSSEX	3,794	1,105	1,541	1,135	13	406 D	29.1%	40.6%	29.9%
44,791	TAZEWELL	11,338	4,434	4,734	2,023	147	300 D	39.1%	41.8%	17.8%
14,655	WARREN	5,296	2,297	1,513	1,479	7	784 R	43.4%	28.6%	27.9%
38,076	WASHINGTON	13,029	6,665	3,243	3,092	29	3,422 R	51.2%	24.9%	23.7%
11,042	WESTMORELAND	3,506	1,402	1,156	943	5	246 R	40.0%	33.0%	26.9%
43,579	WISE	12,606	5,004	5,942	1,635	25	938 D	39.7%	47.1%	13.0%
21,975	WYTHE	6,963	3,638	1,765	1,377	183	1,873 R	52.2%	25.3%	19.8%
21,583	YORK	9,088	3,356	2,370	3,330	32	26 R	36.9%	26.1%	36.6%
	City									
91,023	ALEXANDRIA	31,816	13,265	14,351	4,131	69	1,086 D	41.7%	45.1%	13.0%
5,921	BEDFORD CITY	2,380	1,047	569	679	85	368 R	44.0%	23.9%	28.5%
17,144	BRISTOL	4,377	1,930	1,531	911	5	399 R	44.1%	35.0%	20.8%
6,300	BUENA VISTA	1,660	814	387	456	3	358 R	49.0%	23.3%	27.5%
29,427	CHARLOTTESVILLE	11,335	5,601	3,831	1,781	122	1,770 R	49.4%	33.8%	15.7%
73,647	CHESAPEAKE	24,760	6,234	6,843	11,084	599	4,241 A	25.2%	27.6%	44.8%
5,268	CLIFTON FORGE	2,122	925	734	462	1	191 R	43.6%	34.6%	21.8%
9,587	COLONIAL HEIGHTS	5,413	2,650	650	2,106	7	544 R	49.0%	12.0%	38.9%
11,062	COVINGTON	3,595	1,551	1,195	846	3	356 R	43.1%	33.2%	23.5%
46,577	DANVILLE	16,874	6,796	4,495	5,391	192	1,405 R	40.3%	26.6%	31.9%
5,535	EMPORIA	2,191	812	657	716	6	96 R	37.1%	30.0%	32.7%
13,585	FAIRFAX CITY	6,084	2,963	2,153	959	9	810 R	48.7%	35.4%	15.8%
10,192	FALLS CHURCH	4,382	2,005	1,860	504	13	145 R	45.8%	42.4%	11.5%
7,264	FRANKLIN CITY	2,256	951	792	511	2	159 R	42.2%	35.1%	22.7%
13,639	FREDERICKSBURG	5,068	2,142	2,036	878	12	106 R	42.3%	40.2%	17.3%
5,254	GALAX	2,309	1,257	748	304		509 R	54.4%	32.4%	13.2%
89,258	HAMPTON	32,606	10,532	11,308	10,690	76	618 D	32.3%	34.7%	32.8%
11,916	HARRISONBURG	4,352	2,859	1,036	453	4	1,823 R	65.7%	23.8%	10.4%
17,895	HOPEWELL	6,743	2,942	1,568	2,092	141	850 R	43.6%	23.3%	31.0%
7,537	LEXINGTON	2,085	1,170	734	177	4	436 R	56.1%	35.2%	8.5%

VIRGINIA

PRESIDENT 1968

1960 Census Population	City	Total Vote	Republican	Democratic	AIP	Other	Plurality	Percentage Rep.	Percentage Dem.	Percentage AIP
54,790	LYNCHBURG	18,299	9,943	4,305	3,649	402	5,638 R	54.3%	23.5%	19.9%
	MANASSAS									
	MANASSAS PARK									
18,798	MARTINSVILLE	7,276	2,618	2,727	1,856	75	109 D	36.0%	37.5%	25.5%
	NANSEMOND CITY									
113,662	NEWPORT NEWS	37,069	12,774	13,370	10,763	162	596 D	34.5%	36.1%	29.0%
304,869	NORFOLK	65,829	22,302	28,477	14,500	550	6,175 D	33.9%	43.3%	22.0%
4,996	NORTON	1,267	495	555	215	2	60 D	39.1%	43.8%	17.0%
36,750	PETERSBURG	11,169	3,478	5,519	2,158	14	2,041 D	31.1%	49.4%	19.3%
	POQUOSON									
114,773	PORTSMOUTH	37,381	9,402	15,734	12,127	118	3,607 D	25.2%	42.1%	32.4%
9,371	RADFORD	3,749	2,077	1,206	461	5	871 R	55.4%	32.2%	12.3%
219,958	RICHMOND CITY	66,668	26,380	32,857	7,325	106	6,477 D	39.6%	49.3%	11.0%
97,110	ROANOKE CITY	30,008	15,368	9,281	5,269	90	6,087 R	51.2%	30.9%	17.6%
16,058	SALEM	6,846	3,955	1,369	1,507	15	2,448 R	57.8%	20.0%	22.0%
5,974	SOUTH BOSTON	2,587	1,298	620	662	7	636 R	50.2%	24.0%	25.6%
22,232	STAUNTON	7,221	4,434	1,729	1,054	4	2,705 R	61.4%	23.9%	14.6%
12,609	SUFFOLK	3,365	1,277	1,044	1,039	5	233 R	37.9%	31.0%	30.9%
85,218	VIRGINIA BEACH	37,742	16,316	10,101	10,962	363	5,354 R	43.2%	26.8%	29.0%
15,694	WAYNESBORO	5,378	3,301	1,446	613	18	1,855 R	61.4%	26.9%	11.4%
6,832	WILLIAMSBURG	2,474	1,156	991	247	80	165 R	46.7%	40.1%	10.0%
15,110	WINCHESTER	4,833	2,695	1,360	770	8	1,335 R	55.8%	28.1%	15.9%
3,966,949	TOTAL	1,361,491	590,319	442,387	321,833	6,952	147,932 R	43.4%	32.5%	23.6%

VIRGINIA

Under Virginia's local government system a number of urban areas are organized as cities independent of county authority. The number of these cities is subject to change and their boundaries alter from year to year. There were 38 of these independent cities in 1968, 39 in 1972, 41 in 1976, 1980 and 1984. All cities and counties that voted in any one of the election years covered in this volume are carried in all the tables so the user will find the voting data in the same order for each election. In 1972 the independent city of Nansemond was created from Nansemond county. In 1974 Nansemond city and Suffolk city merged and became the new Suffolk city. In 1975 Manassas and Manassas Park cities were created out of parts of Prince William county and Poquoson city was created out of part of York county.

ELECTION NOTES

1984 Other vote was LaRouche (Independent).

1980 Other vote was 95,418 Anderson (Independent); 14,024 Commoner (Independent); 12,821 Clark (Libertarian); 1,986 DeBerry (Independent).

1976 Other vote was 17,802 Camejo (Socialist Workers); 16,686 Anderson (American); 7,508 LaRouche (U.S. Labor); 4,648 MacBride (Libertarian).

1972 Other vote was 19,721 Schmitz (American); 9,918 Fisher (Socialist Labor).

1968 Wallace on the ballot as American Independent. Other vote was 4,671 Blomen (Socialist Labor); 1,680 Gregory (Peace and Freedom); 601 Munn (Prohibition). Data table includes 1,561 American Independent votes cast in Shenandoah county not reported on state canvass.

WASHINGTON

POPULAR VOTE FOR PRESIDENT 1920 TO 1984

Year	Total Vote	Republican Vote	Republican Candidate	Democratic Vote	Democratic Candidate	Other Vote	Plurality	Percentage Total Vote Rep.	Percentage Total Vote Dem.	Percentage Major Vote Rep.	Percentage Major Vote Dem.
1984	1,883,910	1,051,670	Reagan, Ronald	807,352	Mondale, Walter F.	24,888	244,318 R	55.8%	42.9%	56.6%	43.4%
1980	1,742,394	865,244	Reagan, Ronald	650,193	Carter, Jimmy	226,957	215,051 R	49.7%	37.3%	57.1%	42.9%
1976	1,555,534	777,732	Ford, Gerald R.	717,323	Carter, Jimmy	60,479	60,409 R	50.0%	46.1%	52.0%	48.0%
1972	1,470,847	837,135	Nixon, Richard M.	568,334	McGovern, George S.	65,378	268,801 R	56.9%	38.6%	59.6%	40.4%
1968	1,304,281	588,510	Nixon, Richard M.	616,037	Humphrey, Hubert H.	99,734	27,527 D	45.1%	47.2%	48.9%	51.1%
1964	1,258,556	470,366	Goldwater, Barry M.	779,881	Johnson, Lyndon B.	8,309	309,515 D	37.4%	62.0%	37.6%	62.4%
1960	1,241,572	629,273	Nixon, Richard M.	599,298	Kennedy, John F.	13,001	29,975 R	50.7%	48.3%	51.2%	48.8%
1956	1,150,889	620,430	Eisenhower, Dwight D.	523,002	Stevenson, Adlai E.	7,457	97,428 R	53.9%	45.4%	54.3%	45.7%
1952	1,102,708	599,107	Eisenhower, Dwight D.	492,845	Stevenson, Adlai E.	10,756	106,262 R	54.3%	44.7%	54.9%	45.1%
1948	905,058	386,314	Dewey, Thomas E.	476,165	Truman, Harry S.	42,579	89,851 D	42.7%	52.6%	44.8%	55.2%
1944	856,328	361,689	Dewey, Thomas E.	486,774	Roosevelt, Franklin D.	7,865	125,085 D	42.2%	56.8%	42.6%	57.4%
1940	793,833	322,123	Willkie, Wendell	462,145	Roosevelt, Franklin D.	9,565	140,022 D	40.6%	58.2%	41.1%	58.9%
1936	692,338	206,892	Landon, Alfred M.	459,579	Roosevelt, Franklin D.	25,867	252,687 D	29.9%	66.4%	31.0%	69.0%
1932	614,814	208,645	Hoover, Herbert C.	353,260	Roosevelt, Franklin D.	52,909	144,615 D	33.9%	57.5%	37.1%	62.9%
1928	500,840	335,844	Hoover, Herbert C.	156,772	Smith, Alfred E.	8,224	179,072 R	67.1%	31.3%	68.2%	31.8%
1924 **	421,549	220,224	Coolidge, Calvin	42,842	Davis, John W.	158,483	69,497 R	52.2%	10.2%	83.7%	16.3%
1920 **	398,715	223,137	Harding, Warren G.	84,298	Cox, James M.	91,280	138,839 R	56.0%	21.1%	72.6%	27.4%

In 1924 other vote was 150,727 Progressive; 5,991 American; 1,004 Socialist Labor and 761 Communist. In 1920 other vote was 77,246 Farmer-Labor; 8,913 Socialist; 3,800 Prohibition and 1,321 Socialist Labor.

ELECTORAL COLLEGE VOTE 1920 TO 1984

Year	Total	Republican	Democratic	Other
1984	10	10	—	—
1980	9	9	—	—
1976 **	9	8	—	1 REAGAN
1972	9	9	—	—
1968	9	—	9	—
1964	9	—	9	—
1960	9	9	—	—
1956	9	9	—	—
1952	9	9	—	—
1948	8	—	8	—
1944	8	—	8	—
1940	8	—	8	—
1936	8	—	8	—
1932	8	—	8	—
1928	7	7	—	—
1924	7	7	—	—
1920	7	7	—	—

In 1976 one of the nine Republican electors voted in the Electoral College for Ronald Reagan for President rather than for the national Republican candidate.

WASHINGTON

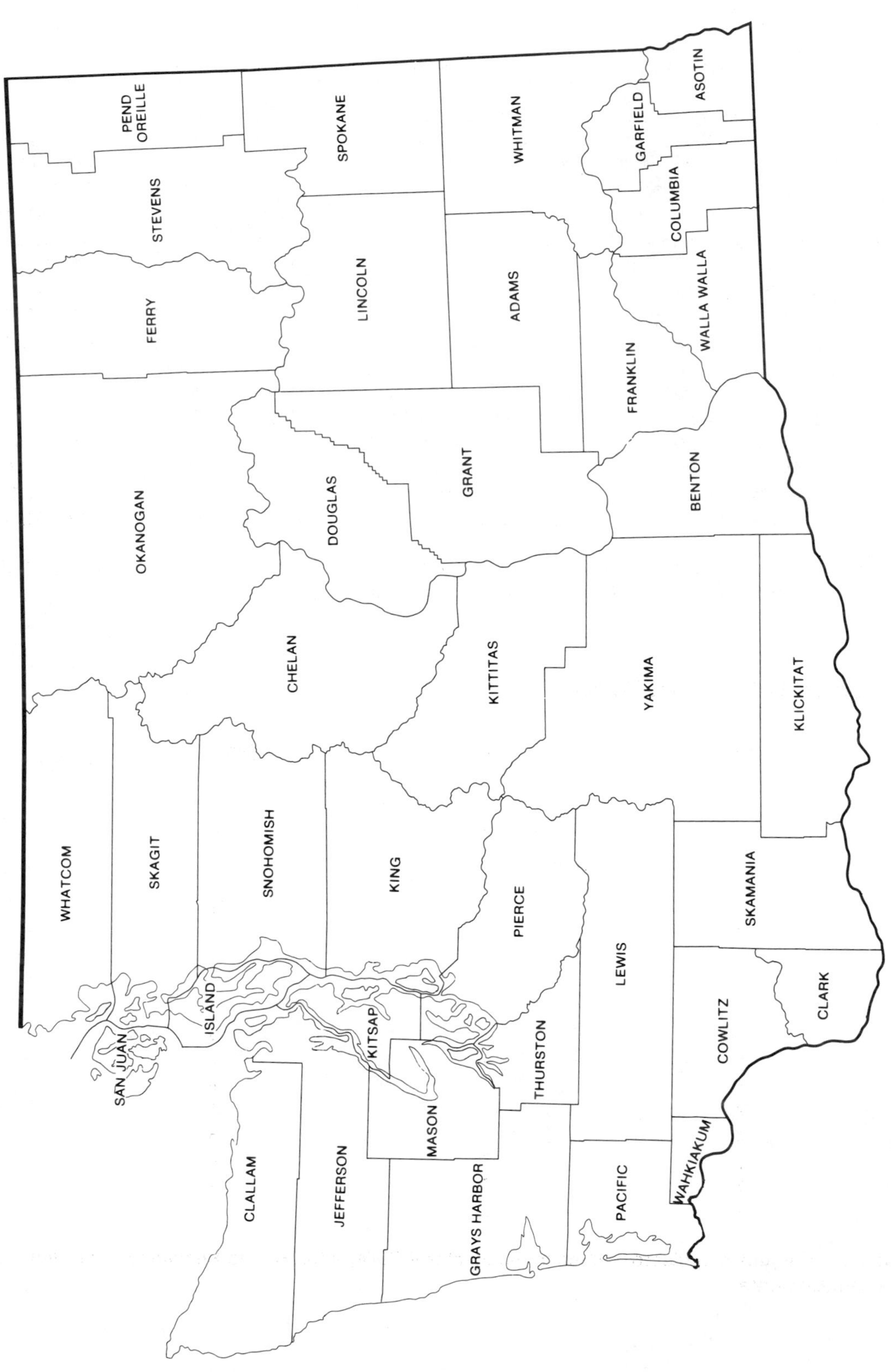
PEND OREILLE
SPOKANE
WHITMAN
ASOTIN
GARFIELD
STEVENS
COLUMBIA
LINCOLN
ADAMS
WALLA WALLA
FERRY
FRANKLIN
OKANOGAN
DOUGLAS
GRANT
BENTON
CHELAN
KITTITAS
YAKIMA
KLICKITAT
WHATCOM
SKAGIT
SNOHOMISH
KING
PIERCE
LEWIS
SKAMANIA
ISLAND
SAN JUAN
KITSAP
CLARK
COWLITZ
THURSTON
MASON
CLALLAM
JEFFERSON
GRAYS HARBOR
PACIFIC
WAHKIAKUM

WASHINGTON

PRESIDENT 1984

1980 Census Population	County	Total Vote	Republican	Democratic	Other	Rep.-Dem. Plurality	Percentage Total Vote Rep.	Percentage Total Vote Dem.	Percentage Major Vote Rep.	Percentage Major Vote Dem.
13,267	ADAMS	4,809	3,449	1,311	49	2,138 R	71.7%	27.3%	72.5%	27.5%
16,823	ASOTIN	7,021	3,876	3,042	103	834 R	55.2%	43.3%	56.0%	44.0%
109,444	BENTON	46,631	32,307	13,784	540	18,523 R	69.3%	29.6%	70.1%	29.9%
45,061	CHELAN	20,994	13,667	6,978	349	6,689 R	65.1%	33.2%	66.2%	33.8%
51,648	CLALLAM	23,735	13,605	9,701	429	3,904 R	57.3%	40.9%	58.4%	41.6%
192,227	CLARK	76,957	40,681	35,248	1,028	5,433 R	52.9%	45.8%	53.6%	46.4%
4,057	COLUMBIA	2,095	1,404	673	18	731 R	67.0%	32.1%	67.6%	32.4%
79,548	COWLITZ	30,968	14,858	15,361	749	503 D	48.0%	49.6%	49.2%	50.8%
22,144	DOUGLAS	9,698	6,443	3,127	128	3,316 R	66.4%	32.2%	67.3%	32.7%
5,811	FERRY	2,210	1,232	935	43	297 R	55.7%	42.3%	56.9%	43.1%
35,025	FRANKLIN	12,268	7,724	4,328	216	3,396 R	63.0%	35.3%	64.1%	35.9%
2,468	GARFIELD	1,428	913	493	22	420 R	63.9%	34.5%	64.9%	35.1%
48,522	GRANT	19,584	12,888	6,298	398	6,590 R	65.8%	32.2%	67.2%	32.8%
66,314	GRAYS HARBOR	25,671	11,286	14,050	335	2,764 D	44.0%	54.7%	44.5%	55.5%
44,048	ISLAND	20,616	13,548	6,850	218	6,698 R	65.7%	33.2%	66.4%	33.6%
15,965	JEFFERSON	9,334	4,543	4,602	189	59 D	48.7%	49.3%	49.7%	50.3%
1,269,749	KING	639,261	332,987	298,620	7,654	34,367 R	52.1%	46.7%	52.7%	47.3%
147,152	KITSAP	66,713	36,101	29,681	931	6,420 R	54.1%	44.5%	54.9%	45.1%
24,877	KITTITAS	11,531	6,580	4,830	121	1,750 R	57.1%	41.9%	57.7%	42.3%
15,822	KLICKITAT	6,757	3,910	2,712	135	1,198 R	57.9%	40.1%	59.0%	41.0%
56,025	LEWIS	23,931	15,846	7,634	451	8,212 R	66.2%	31.9%	67.5%	32.5%
9,604	LINCOLN	5,193	3,474	1,671	48	1,803 R	66.9%	32.2%	67.5%	32.5%
31,184	MASON	15,650	8,410	7,007	233	1,403 R	53.7%	44.8%	54.6%	45.4%
30,639	OKANOGAN	13,059	7,476	5,330	253	2,146 R	57.2%	40.8%	58.4%	41.6%
17,237	PACIFIC	8,421	3,613	4,679	129	1,066 D	42.9%	55.6%	43.6%	56.4%
8,580	PEND OREILLE	4,075	2,374	1,655	46	719 R	58.3%	40.6%	58.9%	41.1%
485,643	PIERCE	195,108	112,877	79,498	2,733	33,379 R	57.9%	40.7%	58.7%	41.3%
7,838	SAN JUAN	5,526	2,900	2,514	112	386 R	52.5%	45.5%	53.6%	46.4%
64,138	SKAGIT	33,326	18,840	13,947	539	4,893 R	56.5%	41.9%	57.5%	42.5%
7,919	SKAMANIA	3,339	1,736	1,552	51	184 R	52.0%	46.5%	52.8%	47.2%
337,720	SNOHOMISH	158,995	90,362	66,728	1,905	23,634 R	56.8%	42.0%	57.5%	42.5%
341,835	SPOKANE	149,336	88,043	59,620	1,673	28,423 R	59.0%	39.9%	59.6%	40.4%
28,979	STEVENS	12,771	8,211	4,304	256	3,907 R	64.3%	33.7%	65.6%	34.4%
124,264	THURSTON	62,045	34,442	26,840	763	7,602 R	55.5%	43.3%	56.2%	43.8%
3,832	WAHKIAKUM	1,739	776	930	33	154 D	44.6%	53.5%	45.5%	54.5%
47,435	WALLA WALLA	19,398	12,361	6,804	233	5,557 R	63.7%	35.1%	64.5%	35.5%
106,701	WHATCOM	50,686	27,228	22,670	788	4,558 R	53.7%	44.7%	54.6%	45.4%
40,103	WHITMAN	16,849	10,021	6,621	207	3,400 R	59.5%	39.3%	60.2%	39.8%
172,508	YAKIMA	66,182	40,678	24,724	780	15,954 R	61.5%	37.4%	62.2%	37.8%
4,132,156	TOTAL	1,883,910	1,051,670	807,352	24,888	244,318 R	55.8%	42.9%	56.6%	43.4%

WASHINGTON

PRESIDENT 1980

1980 Census Population	County	Total Vote	Republican	Democratic	Other	Rep.-Dem. Plurality	Percentage Total Vote Rep.	Total Vote Dem.	Major Vote Rep.	Major Vote Dem.
13,267	ADAMS	4,776	3,248	1,223	305	2,025 R	68.0%	25.6%	72.6%	27.4%
16,823	ASOTIN	6,659	3,275	2,724	660	551 R	49.2%	40.9%	54.6%	45.4%
109,444	BENTON	44,413	28,728	11,561	4,124	17,167 R	64.7%	26.0%	71.3%	28.7%
45,061	CHELAN	19,850	11,299	6,483	2,068	4,816 R	56.9%	32.7%	63.5%	36.5%
51,648	CLALLAM	22,296	11,515	8,029	2,752	3,486 R	51.6%	36.0%	58.9%	41.1%
192,227	CLARK	72,075	33,223	30,584	8,268	2,639 R	46.1%	42.4%	52.1%	47.9%
4,057	COLUMBIA	2,086	1,349	587	150	762 R	64.7%	28.1%	69.7%	30.3%
79,548	COWLITZ	28,639	13,154	12,560	2,925	594 R	45.9%	43.9%	51.2%	48.8%
22,144	DOUGLAS	8,709	5,171	2,833	705	2,338 R	59.4%	32.5%	64.6%	35.4%
5,811	FERRY	2,100	1,108	802	190	306 R	52.8%	38.2%	58.0%	42.0%
35,025	FRANKLIN	11,961	7,327	3,719	915	3,608 R	61.3%	31.1%	66.3%	33.7%
2,468	GARFIELD	1,519	875	509	135	366 R	57.6%	33.5%	63.2%	36.8%
48,522	GRANT	18,196	11,152	5,673	1,371	5,479 R	61.3%	31.2%	66.3%	33.7%
66,314	GRAYS HARBOR	25,444	10,226	11,290	3,928	1,064 D	40.2%	44.4%	47.5%	52.5%
44,048	ISLAND	18,559	10,926	5,422	2,211	5,504 R	58.9%	29.2%	66.8%	33.2%
15,965	JEFFERSON	8,170	3,645	3,279	1,246	366 R	44.6%	40.1%	52.6%	47.4%
1,269,749	KING	600,157	272,567	235,046	92,544	37,521 R	45.4%	39.2%	53.7%	46.3%
147,152	KITSAP	60,296	29,420	20,893	9,983	8,527 R	48.8%	34.7%	58.5%	41.5%
24,877	KITTITAS	10,748	5,359	4,075	1,314	1,284 R	49.9%	37.9%	56.8%	43.2%
15,822	KLICKITAT	6,284	3,113	2,596	575	517 R	49.5%	41.3%	54.5%	45.5%
56,025	LEWIS	22,749	13,636	6,962	2,151	6,674 R	59.9%	30.6%	66.2%	33.8%
9,604	LINCOLN	5,337	3,324	1,597	416	1,727 R	62.3%	29.9%	67.5%	32.5%
31,184	MASON	13,737	6,745	5,241	1,751	1,504 R	49.1%	38.2%	56.3%	43.7%
30,639	OKANOGAN	12,493	6,460	4,634	1,399	1,826 R	51.7%	37.1%	58.2%	41.8%
17,237	PACIFIC	8,012	3,132	3,727	1,153	595 D	39.1%	46.5%	45.7%	54.3%
8,580	PEND OREILLE	3,835	2,136	1,399	300	737 R	55.7%	36.5%	60.4%	39.6%
485,643	PIERCE	176,511	90,247	64,444	21,820	25,803 R	51.1%	36.5%	58.3%	41.7%
7,838	SAN JUAN	5,031	2,363	1,666	1,002	697 R	47.0%	33.1%	58.6%	41.4%
64,138	SKAGIT	30,623	15,520	11,299	3,804	4,221 R	50.7%	36.9%	57.9%	42.1%
7,919	SKAMANIA	3,095	1,416	1,373	306	43 R	45.8%	44.4%	50.8%	49.2%
337,720	SNOHOMISH	135,907	66,153	52,003	17,751	14,150 R	48.7%	38.3%	56.0%	44.0%
341,835	SPOKANE	140,685	78,096	49,263	13,326	28,833 R	55.5%	35.0%	61.3%	38.7%
28,979	STEVENS	11,530	7,094	3,584	852	3,510 R	61.5%	31.1%	66.4%	33.6%
124,264	THURSTON	54,823	26,369	20,508	7,946	5,861 R	48.1%	37.4%	56.3%	43.7%
3,832	WAHKIAKUM	1,778	828	751	199	77 R	46.6%	42.2%	52.4%	47.6%
47,435	WALLA WALLA	18,977	11,223	5,825	1,929	5,398 R	59.1%	30.7%	65.8%	34.2%
106,701	WHATCOM	46,057	21,371	18,430	6,256	2,941 R	46.4%	40.0%	53.7%	46.3%
40,103	WHITMAN	17,024	8,636	5,726	2,662	2,910 R	50.7%	33.6%	60.1%	39.9%
172,508	YAKIMA	61,253	33,815	21,873	5,565	11,942 R	55.2%	35.7%	60.7%	39.3%
4,132,156	TOTAL	1,742,394	865,244	650,193	226,957	215,051 R	49.7%	37.3%	57.1%	42.9%

WASHINGTON

PRESIDENT 1976

1970 Census Population	County	Total Vote	Republican	Democratic	Other	Rep.-Dem. Plurality	Percentage: Total Vote Rep.	Percentage: Total Vote Dem.	Percentage: Major Vote Rep.	Percentage: Major Vote Dem.
12,014	ADAMS	4,773	2,795	1,790	188	1,005 R	58.6%	37.5%	61.0%	39.0%
13,799	ASOTIN	5,828	2,752	2,898	178	146 D	47.2%	49.7%	48.7%	51.3%
67,540	BENTON	34,611	22,135	11,306	1,170	10,829 R	64.0%	32.7%	66.2%	33.8%
41,355	CHELAN	18,692	10,492	7,623	577	2,869 R	56.1%	40.8%	57.9%	42.1%
34,770	CLALLAM	18,386	9,132	8,268	986	864 R	49.7%	45.0%	52.5%	47.5%
128,454	CLARK	61,201	27,938	31,080	2,183	3,142 D	45.6%	50.8%	47.3%	52.7%
4,439	COLUMBIA	2,034	1,153	829	52	324 R	56.7%	40.8%	58.2%	41.8%
68,616	COWLITZ	28,406	12,531	14,958	917	2,427 D	44.1%	52.7%	45.6%	54.4%
16,787	DOUGLAS	8,564	4,547	3,809	208	738 R	53.1%	44.5%	54.4%	45.6%
3,655	FERRY	1,692	776	814	102	38 D	45.9%	48.1%	48.8%	51.2%
25,816	FRANKLIN	10,403	5,671	4,369	363	1,302 R	54.5%	42.0%	56.5%	43.5%
2,911	GARFIELD	1,560	892	616	52	276 R	57.2%	39.5%	59.2%	40.8%
41,881	GRANT	17,721	9,192	7,777	752	1,415 R	51.9%	43.9%	54.2%	45.8%
59,553	GRAYS HARBOR	23,893	9,464	13,478	951	4,014 D	39.6%	56.4%	41.3%	58.7%
27,011	ISLAND	14,104	7,804	5,859	441	1,945 R	55.3%	41.5%	57.1%	42.9%
10,661	JEFFERSON	6,092	2,794	2,913	385	119 D	45.9%	47.8%	49.0%	51.0%
1,156,633	KING	550,119	279,382	248,743	21,994	30,639 R	50.8%	45.2%	52.9%	47.1%
101,732	KITSAP	50,750	23,124	25,701	1,925	2,577 D	45.6%	50.6%	47.4%	52.6%
25,039	KITTITAS	10,017	4,765	4,858	394	93 D	47.6%	48.5%	49.5%	50.5%
12,138	KLICKITAT	5,719	2,573	2,890	256	317 D	45.0%	50.5%	47.1%	52.9%
45,467	LEWIS	21,167	10,933	9,026	1,208	1,907 R	51.7%	42.6%	54.8%	45.2%
9,572	LINCOLN	5,081	2,925	1,978	178	947 R	57.6%	38.9%	59.7%	40.3%
20,918	MASON	11,291	4,758	6,060	473	1,302 D	42.1%	53.7%	44.0%	56.0%
25,867	OKANOGAN	11,595	5,455	5,543	597	88 D	47.0%	47.8%	49.6%	50.4%
15,796	PACIFIC	7,350	2,781	4,278	291	1,497 D	37.8%	58.2%	39.4%	60.6%
6,025	PEND OREILLE	3,170	1,516	1,533	121	17 D	47.8%	48.4%	49.7%	50.3%
411,027	PIERCE	159,148	74,668	78,238	6,242	3,570 D	46.9%	49.2%	48.8%	51.2%
3,856	SAN JUAN	3,722	1,998	1,467	257	531 R	53.7%	39.4%	57.7%	42.3%
52,381	SKAGIT	26,837	13,060	12,718	1,059	342 R	48.7%	47.4%	50.7%	49.3%
5,845	SKAMANIA	2,652	1,102	1,436	114	334 D	41.6%	54.1%	43.4%	56.6%
265,236	SNOHOMISH	115,488	55,375	55,623	4,490	248 D	47.9%	48.2%	49.9%	50.1%
287,487	SPOKANE	127,954	68,290	55,660	4,004	12,630 R	53.4%	43.5%	55.1%	44.9%
17,405	STEVENS	9,109	4,719	3,824	566	895 R	51.8%	42.0%	55.2%	44.8%
76,894	THURSTON	44,056	21,000	21,247	1,809	247 D	47.7%	48.2%	49.7%	50.3%
3,592	WAHKIAKUM	1,710	704	942	64	238 D	41.2%	55.1%	42.8%	57.2%
42,176	WALLA WALLA	18,400	10,883	7,012	505	3,871 R	59.1%	38.1%	60.8%	39.2%
81,950	WHATCOM	41,679	20,007	19,739	1,933	268 R	48.0%	47.4%	50.3%	49.7%
37,900	WHITMAN	15,068	8,168	6,197	703	1,971 R	54.2%	41.1%	56.9%	43.1%
144,971	YAKIMA	55,492	29,478	24,223	1,791	5,255 R	53.1%	43.7%	54.9%	45.1%
3,409,169	TOTAL	1,555,534	777,732	717,323	60,479	60,409 R	50.0%	46.1%	52.0%	48.0%

WASHINGTON

PRESIDENT 1972

1970 Census Population	County	Total Vote	Republican	Democratic	Other	Rep.-Dem. Plurality	Percentage Total Vote Rep.	Percentage Total Vote Dem.	Percentage Major Vote Rep.	Percentage Major Vote Dem.
12,014	ADAMS	4,519	3,083	1,110	326	1,973 R	68.2%	24.6%	73.5%	26.5%
13,799	ASOTIN	5,780	2,911	2,559	310	352 R	50.4%	44.3%	53.2%	46.8%
67,540	BENTON	30,346	18,517	9,824	2,005	8,693 R	61.0%	32.4%	65.3%	34.7%
41,355	CHELAN	17,413	10,470	5,889	1,054	4,581 R	60.1%	33.8%	64.0%	36.0%
34,770	CLALLAM	16,089	9,372	5,620	1,097	3,752 R	58.3%	34.9%	62.5%	37.5%
128,454	CLARK	58,569	28,775	27,179	2,615	1,596 R	49.1%	46.4%	51.4%	48.6%
4,439	COLUMBIA	2,080	1,445	533	102	912 R	69.5%	25.6%	73.1%	26.9%
68,616	COWLITZ	28,182	14,431	12,682	1,069	1,749 R	51.2%	45.0%	53.2%	46.8%
16,787	DOUGLAS	7,481	4,512	2,420	549	2,092 R	60.3%	32.3%	65.1%	34.9%
3,655	FERRY	1,527	815	560	152	255 R	53.4%	36.7%	59.3%	40.7%
25,816	FRANKLIN	10,523	5,972	3,867	684	2,105 R	56.8%	36.7%	60.7%	39.3%
2,911	GARFIELD	1,534	1,004	481	49	523 R	65.4%	31.4%	67.6%	32.4%
41,881	GRANT	15,814	9,370	5,487	957	3,883 R	59.3%	34.7%	63.1%	36.9%
59,553	GRAYS HARBOR	23,745	10,839	11,786	1,120	947 D	45.6%	49.6%	47.9%	52.1%
27,011	ISLAND	11,003	7,495	3,149	359	4,346 R	68.1%	28.6%	70.4%	29.6%
10,661	JEFFERSON	5,179	2,770	2,096	313	674 R	53.5%	40.5%	56.9%	43.1%
1,156,633	KING	529,694	298,707	212,509	18,478	86,198 R	56.4%	40.1%	58.4%	41.6%
101,732	KITSAP	45,446	25,831	17,011	2,604	8,820 R	56.8%	37.4%	60.3%	39.7%
25,039	KITTITAS	10,126	5,464	4,299	363	1,165 R	54.0%	42.5%	56.0%	44.0%
12,138	KLICKITAT	5,648	3,061	2,293	294	768 R	54.2%	40.6%	57.2%	42.8%
45,467	LEWIS	20,585	12,071	6,946	1,568	5,125 R	58.6%	33.7%	63.5%	36.5%
9,572	LINCOLN	5,275	3,647	1,453	175	2,194 R	69.1%	27.5%	71.5%	28.5%
20,918	MASON	9,177	4,873	3,907	397	966 R	53.1%	42.6%	55.5%	44.5%
25,867	OKANOGAN	10,334	5,796	3,835	703	1,961 R	56.1%	37.1%	60.2%	39.8%
15,796	PACIFIC	7,166	3,349	3,585	232	236 D	46.7%	50.0%	48.3%	51.7%
6,025	PEND OREILLE	2,931	1,746	1,071	114	675 R	59.6%	36.5%	62.0%	38.0%
411,027	PIERCE	148,065	84,265	56,933	6,867	27,332 R	56.9%	38.5%	59.7%	40.3%
3,856	SAN JUAN	2,795	1,786	906	103	880 R	63.9%	32.4%	66.3%	33.7%
52,381	SKAGIT	24,448	14,212	9,233	1,003	4,979 R	58.1%	37.8%	60.6%	39.4%
5,845	SKAMANIA	2,645	1,288	1,153	204	135 R	48.7%	43.6%	52.8%	47.2%
265,236	SNOHOMISH	104,821	60,032	39,471	5,318	20,561 R	57.3%	37.7%	60.3%	39.7%
287,487	SPOKANE	125,185	74,320	44,337	6,528	29,983 R	59.4%	35.4%	62.6%	37.4%
17,405	STEVENS	7,899	4,839	2,390	670	2,449 R	61.3%	30.3%	66.9%	33.1%
76,894	THURSTON	38,792	22,297	14,596	1,899	7,701 R	57.5%	37.6%	60.4%	39.6%
3,592	WAHKIAKUM	1,726	818	796	112	22 R	47.4%	46.1%	50.7%	49.3%
42,176	WALLA WALLA	18,533	12,579	5,364	590	7,215 R	67.9%	28.9%	70.1%	29.9%
81,950	WHATCOM	38,801	22,585	15,027	1,189	7,558 R	58.2%	38.7%	60.0%	40.0%
37,900	WHITMAN	16,266	9,548	6,248	470	3,300 R	58.7%	38.4%	60.4%	39.6%
144,971	YAKIMA	54,705	32,240	19,729	2,736	12,511 R	58.9%	36.1%	62.0%	38.0%
3,409,169	TOTAL	1,470,847	837,135	568,334	65,378	268,801 R	56.9%	38.6%	59.6%	40.4%

WASHINGTON

PRESIDENT 1968

1960 Census Population	County	Total Vote	Republican	Democratic	AIP	Other	Plurality	Percentage Rep.	Dem.	AIP
9,929	ADAMS	4,141	2,572	1,270	299		1,302 R	62.1%	30.7%	7.2%
12,909	ASOTIN	5,434	2,307	2,693	433	1	386 D	42.5%	49.6%	8.0%
62,070	BENTON	28,579	14,659	10,878	3,024	18	3,781 R	51.3%	38.1%	10.6%
40,744	CHELAN	17,230	9,093	6,787	1,324	26	2,306 R	52.8%	39.4%	7.7%
30,022	CLALLAM	14,234	5,921	7,030	1,248	35	1,109 D	41.6%	49.4%	8.8%
93,809	CLARK	44,474	18,858	23,046	2,514	56	4,188 D	42.4%	51.8%	5.7%
4,569	COLUMBIA	2,152	1,221	754	175	2	467 R	56.7%	35.0%	8.1%
57,801	COWLITZ	25,750	10,842	13,363	1,507	38	2,521 D	42.1%	51.9%	5.9%
14,890	DOUGLAS	6,665	3,234	2,764	663	4	470 R	48.5%	41.5%	9.9%
3,889	FERRY	1,387	608	596	182	1	12 R	43.8%	43.0%	13.1%
23,342	FRANKLIN	9,575	4,234	4,038	1,299	4	196 R	44.2%	42.2%	13.6%
2,976	GARFIELD	1,586	841	602	143		239 R	53.0%	38.0%	9.0%
46,477	GRANT	14,367	7,007	5,773	1,574	13	1,234 R	48.8%	40.2%	11.0%
54,465	GRAYS HARBOR	22,684	7,720	13,480	1,426	58	5,760 D	34.0%	59.4%	6.3%
19,638	ISLAND	8,000	4,077	3,238	677	8	839 R	51.0%	40.5%	8.5%
9,639	JEFFERSON	4,505	1,827	2,251	407	20	424 D	40.6%	50.0%	9.0%
935,014	KING	474,935	218,457	223,469	31,450	1,559	5,012 D	46.0%	47.1%	6.6%
84,176	KITSAP	39,815	14,520	22,273	2,986	36	7,753 D	36.5%	55.9%	7.5%
20,467	KITTITAS	8,729	4,212	3,921	579	17	291 R	48.3%	44.9%	6.6%
13,455	KLICKITAT	5,173	2,355	2,454	357	7	99 D	45.5%	47.4%	6.9%
41,858	LEWIS	18,668	8,779	8,444	1,428	17	335 R	47.0%	45.2%	7.6%
10,919	LINCOLN	5,053	2,994	1,721	337	1	1,273 R	59.3%	34.1%	6.7%
16,251	MASON	8,590	3,397	4,540	638	15	1,143 D	39.5%	52.9%	7.4%
25,520	OKANOGAN	9,935	4,490	4,379	1,064	2	111 R	45.2%	44.1%	10.7%
14,674	PACIFIC	6,605	2,491	3,740	364	10	1,249 D	37.7%	56.6%	5.5%
6,914	PEND OREILLE	2,714	1,117	1,350	245	2	233 D	41.2%	49.7%	9.0%
321,590	PIERCE	135,718	51,436	72,670	11,391	221	21,234 D	37.9%	53.5%	8.4%
2,872	SAN JUAN	1,963	1,164	685	108	6	479 R	59.3%	34.9%	5.5%
51,350	SKAGIT	22,594	10,354	10,529	1,667	44	175 D	45.8%	46.6%	7.4%
5,207	SKAMANIA	2,380	968	1,221	189	2	253 D	40.7%	51.3%	7.9%
172,199	SNOHOMISH	87,424	36,252	44,019	7,005	148	7,767 D	41.5%	50.4%	8.0%
278,333	SPOKANE	110,594	52,650	49,423	8,420	101	3,227 R	47.6%	44.7%	7.6%
17,884	STEVENS	7,345	3,435	2,948	957	5	487 R	46.8%	40.1%	13.0%
55,049	THURSTON	30,499	13,742	14,228	2,493	36	486 D	45.1%	46.7%	8.2%
3,426	WAHKIAKUM	1,675	641	899	131	4	258 D	38.3%	53.7%	7.8%
42,195	WALLA WALLA	16,923	10,042	5,841	1,028	12	4,201 R	59.3%	34.5%	6.1%
70,317	WHATCOM	31,199	14,695	14,003	2,387	114	692 R	47.1%	44.9%	7.7%
31,263	WHITMAN	13,789	7,810	5,218	710	51	2,592 R	56.6%	37.8%	5.1%
145,112	YAKIMA	51,198	27,488	19,499	4,161	50	7,989 R	53.7%	38.1%	8.1%
2,853,214	TOTAL	1,304,281	588,510	616,037	96,990	2,744	27,527 D	45.1%	47.2%	7.4%

WASHINGTON

ELECTION NOTES

1984 Other vote was 8,844 Bergland (Libertarian); 5,724 Richards (Populist); 4,712 LaRouche (Independent); 1,891 Johnson (Citizens); 1,654 Serrette (New Alliance); 814 Hall (Communist); 641 Holmes (Workers World); 608 Mason (Socialist Workers). The Democratic vote in King county and the Democratic state-wide total vote have been adjusted to correct a 9,000 vote undercount in King county.

1980 Other vote was 185,073 Anderson (Independent); 29,213 Clark (Libertarian); 9,403 Commoner (Citizens); 1,137 DeBerry (Socialist Workers); 956 McReynolds (Socialist); 834 Hall (Communist); 341 Griswold (Workers World).

1976 Other vote was 36,986 McCarthy (Independent); 8,585 Maddox (American Independent); 5,046 Anderson (American Constitution); 5,042 MacBride (Libertarian); 1,124 Wright (Bicentennial Reality); 905 Camejo (Socialist Workers); 903 LaRouche (U.S. Labor); 817 Hall (Communist); 713 Levin (Socialist Labor); 358 Zeidler (Socialist).

1972 Other vote was 58,906 Schmitz (Independent); 2,644 Spock (People's); 1,537 Hospers (Libertarian); 1,102 Fisher (Socialist Labor); 623 Jenness (Socialist Workers); 566 Hall (Communist).

1968 Wallace on the ballot as American. Other vote was 1,609 Cleaver (Peace and Freedom); 488 Blomen (Socialist Labor); 377 Mitchell (Free Ballot); 270 Halstead (Socialist Workers).

WEST VIRGINIA

POPULAR VOTE FOR PRESIDENT 1920 TO 1984

Year	Total Vote	Republican Vote	Republican Candidate	Democratic Vote	Democratic Candidate	Other Vote	Plurality	Percentage Total Vote Rep.	Percentage Total Vote Dem.	Percentage Major Vote Rep.	Percentage Major Vote Dem.
1984	735,742	405,483	Reagan, Ronald	328,125	Mondale, Walter F.	2,134	77,358 R	55.1%	44.6%	55.3%	44.7%
1980	737,715	334,206	Reagan, Ronald	367,462	Carter, Jimmy	36,047	33,256 D	45.3%	49.8%	47.6%	52.4%
1976	750,964	314,760	Ford, Gerald R.	435,914	Carter, Jimmy	290	121,154 D	41.9%	58.0%	41.9%	58.1%
1972	762,399	484,964	Nixon, Richard M.	277,435	McGovern, George S.		207,529 R	63.6%	36.4%	63.6%	36.4%
1968	754,206	307,555	Nixon, Richard M.	374,091	Humphrey, Hubert H.	72,560	66,536 D	40.8%	49.6%	45.1%	54.9%
1964	792,040	253,953	Goldwater, Barry M.	538,087	Johnson, Lyndon B.		284,134 D	32.1%	67.9%	32.1%	67.9%
1960	837,781	395,995	Nixon, Richard M.	441,786	Kennedy, John F.		45,791 D	47.3%	52.7%	47.3%	52.7%
1956	830,831	449,297	Eisenhower, Dwight D.	381,534	Stevenson, Adlai E.		67,763 R	54.1%	45.9%	54.1%	45.9%
1952	873,548	419,970	Eisenhower, Dwight D.	453,578	Stevenson, Adlai E.		33,608 D	48.1%	51.9%	48.1%	51.9%
1948	748,750	316,251	Dewey, Thomas E.	429,188	Truman, Harry S.	3,311	112,937 D	42.2%	57.3%	42.4%	57.6%
1944	715,596	322,819	Dewey, Thomas E.	392,777	Roosevelt, Franklin D.		69,958 D	45.1%	54.9%	45.1%	54.9%
1940	868,076	372,414	Willkie, Wendell	495,662	Roosevelt, Franklin D.		123,248 D	42.9%	57.1%	42.9%	57.1%
1936	829,945	325,358	Landon, Alfred M.	502,582	Roosevelt, Franklin D.	2,005	177,224 D	39.2%	60.6%	39.3%	60.7%
1932	743,774	330,731	Hoover, Herbert C.	405,124	Roosevelt, Franklin D.	7,919	74,393 D	44.5%	54.5%	44.9%	55.1%
1928	642,752	375,551	Hoover, Herbert C.	263,784	Smith, Alfred E.	3,417	111,767 R	58.4%	41.0%	58.7%	41.3%
1924	583,662	288,635	Coolidge, Calvin	257,232	Davis, John W.	37,795	31,403 R	49.5%	44.1%	52.9%	47.1%
1920	509,936	282,007	Harding, Warren G.	220,785	Cox, James M.	7,144	61,222 R	55.3%	43.3%	56.1%	43.9%

ELECTORAL COLLEGE VOTE 1920 TO 1984

Year	Total	Republican	Democratic	Other
1984	6	6	—	—
1980	6	—	6	—
1976	6	—	6	—
1972	6	6	—	—
1968	7	—	7	—
1964	7	—	7	—
1960	8	—	8	—
1956	8	8	—	—
1952	8	—	8	—
1948	8	—	8	—
1944	8	—	8	—
1940	8	—	8	—
1936	8	—	8	—
1932	8	—	8	—
1928	8	8	—	—
1924	8	8	—	—
1920	8	8	—	—

WEST VIRGINIA

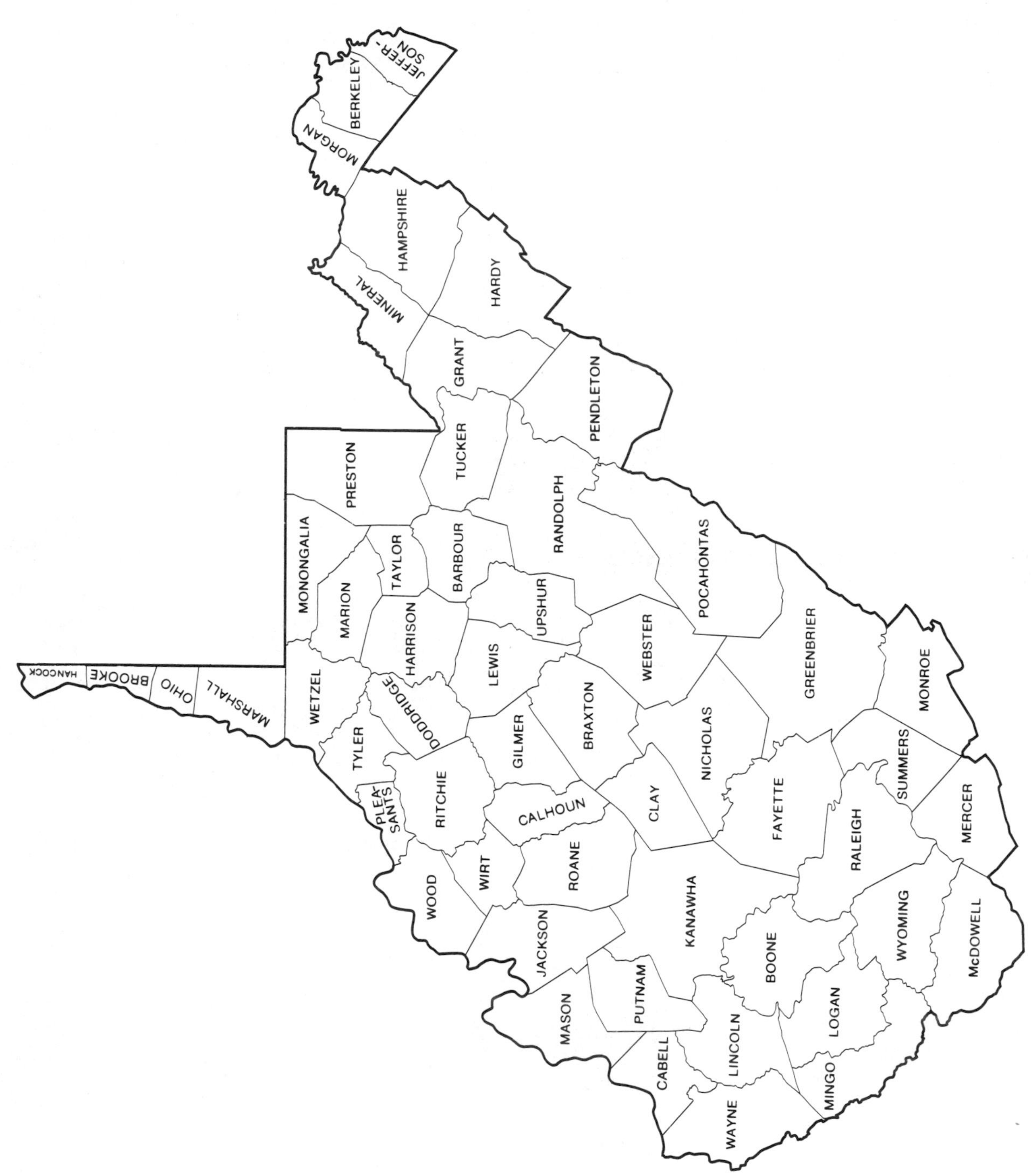

WEST VIRGINIA

PRESIDENT 1984

1980 Census Population	County	Total Vote	Republican	Democratic	Other	Rep.-Dem. Plurality	Percentage Total Vote Rep.	Percentage Total Vote Dem.	Percentage Major Vote Rep.	Percentage Major Vote Dem.
16,639	BARBOUR	6,995	3,877	3,108	10	769 R	55.4%	44.4%	55.5%	44.5%
46,775	BERKELEY	19,092	12,887	6,181	24	6,706 R	67.5%	32.4%	67.6%	32.4%
30,447	BOONE	11,821	4,656	7,121	44	2,465 D	39.4%	60.2%	39.5%	60.5%
13,894	BRAXTON	6,265	2,902	3,350	13	448 D	46.3%	53.5%	46.4%	53.6%
31,117	BROOKE	11,498	4,819	6,636	43	1,817 D	41.9%	57.7%	42.1%	57.9%
106,835	CABELL	37,445	21,815	15,513	117	6,302 R	58.3%	41.4%	58.4%	41.6%
8,250	CALHOUN	3,276	1,765	1,473	38	292 R	53.9%	45.0%	54.5%	45.5%
11,265	CLAY	3,796	1,667	2,117	12	450 D	43.9%	55.8%	44.1%	55.9%
7,433	DODDRIDGE	3,195	2,343	836	16	1,507 R	73.3%	26.2%	73.7%	26.3%
57,863	FAYETTE	19,086	7,360	11,650	76	4,290 D	38.6%	61.0%	38.7%	61.3%
8,334	GILMER	3,452	1,953	1,494	5	459 R	56.6%	43.3%	56.7%	43.3%
10,210	GRANT	4,554	3,715	828	11	2,887 R	81.6%	18.2%	81.8%	18.2%
37,665	GREENBRIER	12,974	7,337	5,599	38	1,738 R	56.6%	43.2%	56.7%	43.3%
14,867	HAMPSHIRE	6,187	4,065	2,102	20	1,963 R	65.7%	34.0%	65.9%	34.1%
40,418	HANCOCK	16,124	7,326	8,708	90	1,382 D	45.4%	54.0%	45.7%	54.3%
10,030	HARDY	4,587	2,938	1,641	8	1,297 R	64.1%	35.8%	64.2%	35.8%
77,710	HARRISON	34,437	19,400	14,969	68	4,431 R	56.3%	43.5%	56.4%	43.6%
25,794	JACKSON	11,310	7,117	4,147	46	2,970 R	62.9%	36.7%	63.2%	36.8%
30,302	JEFFERSON	10,134	5,884	4,216	34	1,668 R	58.1%	41.6%	58.3%	41.7%
231,414	KANAWHA	89,542	51,499	37,832	211	13,667 R	57.5%	42.3%	57.6%	42.4%
18,813	LEWIS	8,031	5,297	2,693	41	2,604 R	66.0%	33.5%	66.3%	33.7%
23,675	LINCOLN	9,902	4,405	5,467	30	1,062 D	44.5%	55.2%	44.6%	55.4%
50,679	LOGAN	17,382	6,425	10,892	65	4,467 D	37.0%	62.7%	37.1%	62.9%
49,899	MCDOWELL	12,883	4,284	8,546	53	4,262 D	33.3%	66.3%	33.4%	66.6%
65,789	MARION	27,020	13,106	13,833	81	727 D	48.5%	51.2%	48.7%	51.3%
41,608	MARSHALL	16,616	8,615	7,947	54	668 R	51.8%	47.8%	52.0%	48.0%
27,045	MASON	12,393	6,648	5,701	44	947 R	53.6%	46.0%	53.8%	46.2%
73,942	MERCER	23,155	13,910	9,164	81	4,746 R	60.1%	39.6%	60.3%	39.7%
27,234	MINERAL	11,138	7,291	3,832	15	3,459 R	65.5%	34.4%	65.5%	34.5%
37,336	MINGO	12,726	4,275	8,434	17	4,159 D	33.6%	66.3%	33.6%	66.4%
75,024	MONONGALIA	28,274	14,972	13,236	66	1,736 R	53.0%	46.8%	53.1%	46.9%
12,873	MONROE	5,954	3,612	2,333	9	1,279 R	60.7%	39.2%	60.8%	39.2%
10,711	MORGAN	4,932	3,469	1,457	6	2,012 R	70.3%	29.5%	70.4%	29.6%
28,126	NICHOLAS	9,273	4,656	4,588	29	68 R	50.2%	49.5%	50.4%	49.6%
61,389	OHIO	23,662	13,447	10,163	52	3,284 R	56.8%	43.0%	57.0%	43.0%
7,910	PENDLETON	3,518	2,047	1,464	7	583 R	58.2%	41.6%	58.3%	41.7%
8,236	PLEASANTS	3,725	2,265	1,458	12	797 R	60.5%	39.1%	60.7%	39.3%
9,919	POCAHONTAS	4,386	2,479	1,903	4	576 R	56.5%	43.4%	56.6%	43.4%
30,460	PRESTON	11,031	6,955	4,054	22	2,901 R	63.0%	36.8%	63.2%	36.8%
38,181	PUTNAM	14,492	9,238	5,208	46	4,030 R	63.7%	35.9%	63.9%	36.1%
86,821	RALEIGH	29,122	14,571	14,442	109	129 R	50.0%	49.6%	50.2%	49.8%
28,734	RANDOLPH	10,964	6,100	4,839	25	1,261 R	55.6%	44.1%	55.8%	44.2%
11,442	RITCHIE	4,609	3,355	1,231	23	2,124 R	72.8%	26.7%	73.2%	26.8%
15,952	ROANE	6,240	3,751	2,468	21	1,283 R	60.1%	39.6%	60.3%	39.7%
15,875	SUMMERS	5,659	2,975	2,670	14	305 R	52.6%	47.2%	52.7%	47.3%
16,584	TAYLOR	6,765	4,007	2,754	4	1,253 R	59.2%	40.7%	59.3%	40.7%
8,675	TUCKER	4,014	2,240	1,766	8	474 R	55.8%	44.0%	55.9%	44.1%
11,320	TYLER	4,575	3,170	1,395	10	1,775 R	69.3%	30.5%	69.4%	30.6%
23,427	UPSHUR	8,466	5,951	2,468	47	3,483 R	70.3%	29.2%	70.7%	29.3%
46,021	WAYNE	17,236	8,811	8,378	47	433 R	51.1%	48.6%	51.3%	48.7%
12,245	WEBSTER	3,926	1,565	2,355	6	790 D	39.9%	60.0%	39.9%	60.1%
21,874	WETZEL	8,207	4,626	3,549	32	1,077 R	56.4%	43.2%	56.6%	43.4%
4,922	WIRT	2,322	1,450	868	4	582 R	62.4%	37.4%	62.6%	37.4%
93,648	WOOD	36,279	24,821	11,357	101	13,464 R	68.4%	31.3%	68.6%	31.4%
35,993	WYOMING	11,095	5,379	5,691	25	312 D	48.5%	51.3%	48.6%	51.4%
1,949,644	TOTAL	735,742	405,483	328,125	2,134	77,358 R	55.1%	44.6%	55.3%	44.7%

WEST VIRGINIA

PRESIDENT 1980

1980 Census Population	County	Total Vote	Republican	Democratic	Other	Rep.-Dem. Plurality	Percentage: Total Vote		Percentage: Major Vote	
							Rep.	Dem.	Rep.	Dem.
16,639	BARBOUR	7,086	3,311	3,451	324	140 D	46.7%	48.7%	49.0%	51.0%
46,775	BERKELEY	17,454	9,955	6,783	716	3,172 R	57.0%	38.9%	59.5%	40.5%
30,447	BOONE	12,000	4,164	7,515	321	3,351 D	34.7%	62.6%	35.7%	64.3%
13,894	BRAXTON	6,408	2,403	3,795	210	1,392 D	37.5%	59.2%	38.8%	61.2%
31,117	BROOKE	11,795	4,622	6,430	743	1,808 D	39.2%	54.5%	41.8%	58.2%
106,835	CABELL	39,588	19,482	17,732	2,374	1,750 R	49.2%	44.8%	52.4%	47.6%
8,250	CALHOUN	3,441	1,606	1,717	118	111 D	46.7%	49.9%	48.3%	51.7%
11,265	CLAY	3,762	1,452	2,185	125	733 D	38.6%	58.1%	39.9%	60.1%
7,433	DODDRIDGE	3,051	1,888	1,043	120	845 R	61.9%	34.2%	64.4%	35.6%
57,863	FAYETTE	19,774	5,784	13,175	815	7,391 D	29.3%	66.6%	30.5%	69.5%
8,334	GILMER	3,486	1,452	1,854	180	402 D	41.7%	53.2%	43.9%	56.1%
10,210	GRANT	4,591	3,452	1,041	98	2,411 R	75.2%	22.7%	76.8%	23.2%
37,665	GREENBRIER	14,004	6,221	7,128	655	907 D	44.4%	50.9%	46.6%	53.4%
14,867	HAMPSHIRE	5,585	2,879	2,522	184	357 R	51.5%	45.2%	53.3%	46.7%
40,418	HANCOCK	16,475	6,610	8,784	1,081	2,174 D	40.1%	53.3%	42.9%	57.1%
10,030	HARDY	4,499	2,329	2,050	120	279 R	51.8%	45.6%	53.2%	46.8%
77,710	HARRISON	34,602	14,251	18,813	1,538	4,562 D	41.2%	54.4%	43.1%	56.9%
25,794	JACKSON	10,581	6,041	4,120	420	1,921 R	57.1%	38.9%	59.5%	40.5%
30,302	JEFFERSON	9,818	4,454	4,679	685	225 D	45.4%	47.7%	48.8%	51.2%
231,414	KANAWHA	91,760	42,604	42,829	6,327	225 D	46.4%	46.7%	49.9%	50.1%
18,813	LEWIS	7,611	3,747	3,455	409	292 R	49.2%	45.4%	52.0%	48.0%
23,675	LINCOLN	9,490	4,009	5,317	164	1,308 D	42.2%	56.0%	43.0%	57.0%
50,679	LOGAN	17,428	4,945	12,024	459	7,079 D	28.4%	69.0%	29.1%	70.9%
49,899	MCDOWELL	13,943	3,862	9,822	259	5,960 D	27.7%	70.4%	28.2%	71.8%
65,789	MARION	26,471	10,952	14,189	1,330	3,237 D	41.4%	53.6%	43.6%	56.4%
41,608	MARSHALL	15,916	7,252	7,832	832	580 D	45.6%	49.2%	48.1%	51.9%
27,045	MASON	12,108	6,040	5,683	385	357 R	49.9%	46.9%	51.5%	48.5%
73,942	MERCER	24,741	12,273	11,804	664	469 R	49.6%	47.7%	51.0%	49.0%
27,234	MINERAL	11,274	6,125	4,671	478	1,454 R	54.3%	41.4%	56.7%	43.3%
37,336	MINGO	13,280	3,716	9,328	236	5,612 D	28.0%	70.2%	28.5%	71.5%
75,024	MONONGALIA	27,826	11,972	12,883	2,971	911 D	43.0%	46.3%	48.2%	51.8%
12,873	MONROE	6,072	2,999	2,877	196	122 R	49.4%	47.4%	51.0%	49.0%
10,711	MORGAN	4,627	2,833	1,594	200	1,239 R	61.2%	34.4%	64.0%	36.0%
28,126	NICHOLAS	9,516	3,885	5,265	366	1,380 D	40.8%	55.3%	42.5%	57.5%
61,389	OHIO	23,873	11,414	10,973	1,486	441 R	47.8%	46.0%	51.0%	49.0%
7,910	PENDLETON	3,504	1,677	1,724	103	47 D	47.9%	49.2%	49.3%	50.7%
8,236	PLEASANTS	3,447	1,852	1,494	101	358 R	53.7%	43.3%	55.3%	44.7%
9,919	POCAHONTAS	4,355	2,011	2,170	174	159 D	46.2%	49.8%	48.1%	51.9%
30,460	PRESTON	10,746	5,828	4,317	601	1,511 R	54.2%	40.2%	57.4%	42.6%
38,181	PUTNAM	14,686	7,561	6,409	716	1,152 R	51.5%	43.6%	54.1%	45.9%
86,821	RALEIGH	28,831	10,713	16,955	1,163	6,242 D	37.2%	58.8%	38.7%	61.3%
28,734	RANDOLPH	10,921	4,374	5,937	610	1,563 D	40.1%	54.4%	42.4%	57.6%
11,442	RITCHIE	4,691	3,081	1,450	160	1,631 R	65.7%	30.9%	68.0%	32.0%
15,952	ROANE	5,953	3,219	2,498	236	721 R	54.1%	42.0%	56.3%	43.7%
15,875	SUMMERS	5,797	2,456	3,114	227	658 D	42.4%	53.7%	44.1%	55.9%
16,584	TAYLOR	6,487	3,010	3,216	261	206 D	46.4%	49.6%	48.3%	51.7%
8,675	TUCKER	3,855	1,798	1,862	195	64 D	46.6%	48.3%	49.1%	50.9%
11,320	TYLER	4,382	2,707	1,482	193	1,225 R	61.8%	33.8%	64.6%	35.4%
23,427	UPSHUR	8,099	4,751	2,867	481	1,884 R	58.7%	35.4%	62.4%	37.6%
46,021	WAYNE	16,719	7,541	8,687	491	1,146 D	45.1%	52.0%	46.5%	53.5%
12,245	WEBSTER	3,974	1,262	2,578	134	1,316 D	31.8%	64.9%	32.9%	67.1%
21,874	WETZEL	8,015	3,588	4,035	392	447 D	44.8%	50.3%	47.1%	52.9%
4,922	WIRT	2,293	1,176	1,058	59	118 R	51.3%	46.1%	52.6%	47.4%
93,648	WOOD	35,512	20,080	13,622	1,810	6,458 R	56.5%	38.4%	59.6%	40.4%
35,993	WYOMING	11,512	4,537	6,624	351	2,087 D	39.4%	57.5%	40.7%	59.3%
1,949,644	TOTAL	737,715	334,206	367,462	36,047	33,256 D	45.3%	49.8%	47.6%	52.4%

WEST VIRGINIA

PRESIDENT 1976

1970 Census Population	County	Total Vote	Republican	Democratic	Other	Rep.-Dem. Plurality	Percentage Total Vote Rep.	Percentage Total Vote Dem.	Percentage Major Vote Rep.	Percentage Major Vote Dem.
14,030	BARBOUR	6,882	3,235	3,647		412 D	47.0%	53.0%	47.0%	53.0%
36,356	BERKELEY	17,151	8,935	8,216		719 R	52.1%	47.9%	52.1%	47.9%
25,118	BOONE	11,604	3,072	8,528	4	5,456 D	26.5%	73.5%	26.5%	73.5%
12,666	BRAXTON	5,928	1,913	4,012	3	2,099 D	32.3%	67.7%	32.3%	67.7%
29,685	BROOKE	13,007	4,792	8,197	18	3,405 D	36.8%	63.0%	36.9%	63.1%
106,918	CABELL	40,455	19,644	20,811		1,167 D	48.6%	51.4%	48.6%	51.4%
7,046	CALHOUN	3,457	1,283	2,173	1	890 D	37.1%	62.9%	37.1%	62.9%
9,330	CLAY	3,944	1,282	2,662		1,380 D	32.5%	67.5%	32.5%	67.5%
6,389	DODDRIDGE	3,049	1,804	1,245		559 R	59.2%	40.8%	59.2%	40.8%
49,332	FAYETTE	20,955	5,459	15,496		10,037 D	26.1%	73.9%	26.1%	73.9%
7,782	GILMER	3,616	1,371	2,245		874 D	37.9%	62.1%	37.9%	62.1%
8,607	GRANT	4,302	2,976	1,323	3	1,653 R	69.2%	30.8%	69.2%	30.8%
32,090	GREENBRIER	14,153	5,862	8,291		2,429 D	41.4%	58.6%	41.4%	58.6%
11,710	HAMPSHIRE	5,201	2,097	3,104		1,007 D	40.3%	59.7%	40.3%	59.7%
39,749	HANCOCK	17,398	6,771	10,627		3,856 D	38.9%	61.1%	38.9%	61.1%
8,855	HARDY	4,851	1,858	2,993		1,135 D	38.3%	61.7%	38.3%	61.7%
73,028	HARRISON	36,687	15,172	21,467	48	6,295 D	41.4%	58.5%	41.4%	58.6%
20,903	JACKSON	10,694	5,360	5,334		26 R	50.1%	49.9%	50.1%	49.9%
21,280	JEFFERSON	9,030	3,864	5,166		1,302 D	42.8%	57.2%	42.8%	57.2%
229,515	KANAWHA	95,991	42,213	53,602	176	11,389 D	44.0%	55.8%	44.1%	55.9%
17,847	LEWIS	7,696	3,736	3,960		224 D	48.5%	51.5%	48.5%	51.5%
18,912	LINCOLN	8,257	2,997	5,260		2,263 D	36.3%	63.7%	36.3%	63.7%
46,269	LOGAN	17,143	4,021	13,122		9,101 D	23.5%	76.5%	23.5%	76.5%
50,666	MCDOWELL	14,688	4,107	10,557	24	6,450 D	28.0%	71.9%	28.0%	72.0%
61,356	MARION	28,191	10,391	17,800		7,409 D	36.9%	63.1%	36.9%	63.1%
37,598	MARSHALL	15,346	6,705	8,641		1,936 D	43.7%	56.3%	43.7%	56.3%
24,306	MASON	11,974	5,205	6,769		1,564 D	43.5%	56.5%	43.5%	56.5%
63,206	MERCER	25,552	10,791	14,761		3,970 D	42.2%	57.8%	42.2%	57.8%
23,109	MINERAL	11,028	5,130	5,898		768 D	46.5%	53.5%	46.5%	53.5%
32,780	MINGO	11,666	3,010	8,655	1	5,645 D	25.8%	74.2%	25.8%	74.2%
63,714	MONONGALIA	27,990	11,827	16,163		4,336 D	42.3%	57.7%	42.3%	57.7%
11,272	MONROE	6,047	2,750	3,297		547 D	45.5%	54.5%	45.5%	54.5%
8,547	MORGAN	4,298	2,369	1,929		440 R	55.1%	44.9%	55.1%	44.9%
22,552	NICHOLAS	9,697	3,462	6,235		2,773 D	35.7%	64.3%	35.7%	64.3%
64,197	OHIO	24,293	12,476	11,817		659 R	51.4%	48.6%	51.4%	48.6%
7,031	PENDLETON	3,658	1,554	2,104		550 D	42.5%	57.5%	42.5%	57.5%
7,274	PLEASANTS	3,307	1,608	1,699		91 D	48.6%	51.4%	48.6%	51.4%
8,870	POCAHONTAS	4,075	1,740	2,330	5	590 D	42.7%	57.2%	42.8%	57.2%
25,455	PRESTON	11,314	5,719	5,595		124 R	50.5%	49.5%	50.5%	49.5%
27,625	PUTNAM	14,560	6,334	8,226		1,892 D	43.5%	56.5%	43.5%	56.5%
70,080	RALEIGH	30,405	10,637	19,768		9,131 D	35.0%	65.0%	35.0%	65.0%
24,596	RANDOLPH	12,087	4,822	7,265		2,443 D	39.9%	60.1%	39.9%	60.1%
10,145	RITCHIE	4,815	2,874	1,941		933 R	59.7%	40.3%	59.7%	40.3%
14,111	ROANE	6,736	3,216	3,519	1	303 D	47.7%	52.2%	47.8%	52.2%
13,213	SUMMERS	6,197	2,254	3,943		1,689 D	36.4%	63.6%	36.4%	63.6%
13,878	TAYLOR	6,796	2,891	3,905		1,014 D	42.5%	57.5%	42.5%	57.5%
7,447	TUCKER	3,719	1,396	2,323		927 D	37.5%	62.5%	37.5%	62.5%
9,929	TYLER	4,331	2,514	1,817		697 R	58.0%	42.0%	58.0%	42.0%
19,092	UPSHUR	8,302	4,789	3,513		1,276 R	57.7%	42.3%	57.7%	42.3%
37,581	WAYNE	15,967	6,009	9,958		3,949 D	37.6%	62.4%	37.6%	62.4%
9,809	WEBSTER	3,908	971	2,931	6	1,960 D	24.8%	75.0%	24.9%	75.1%
20,314	WETZEL	8,835	3,793	5,042		1,249 D	42.9%	57.1%	42.9%	57.1%
4,154	WIRT	2,213	1,031	1,182		151 D	46.6%	53.4%	46.6%	53.4%
86,818	WOOD	35,457	18,382	17,075		1,307 R	51.8%	48.2%	51.8%	48.2%
30,095	WYOMING	12,061	4,286	7,775		3,489 D	35.5%	64.5%	35.5%	64.5%
1,744,237	TOTAL	750,964	314,760	435,914	290	121,154 D	41.9%	58.0%	41.9%	58.1%

WEST VIRGINIA

PRESIDENT 1972

1970 Census Population	County	Total Vote	Republican	Democratic	Other	Rep.-Dem. Plurality	Percentage: Total Vote		Percentage: Major Vote	
							Rep.	Dem.	Rep.	Dem.
14,030	BARBOUR	6,690	4,432	2,258		2,174 R	66.2%	33.8%	66.2%	33.8%
36,356	BERKELEY	15,477	10,954	4,523		6,431 R	70.8%	29.2%	70.8%	29.2%
25,118	BOONE	11,327	5,985	5,342		643 R	52.8%	47.2%	52.8%	47.2%
12,666	BRAXTON	5,926	3,155	2,771		384 R	53.2%	46.8%	53.2%	46.8%
29,685	BROOKE	12,770	7,544	5,226		2,318 R	59.1%	40.9%	59.1%	40.9%
106,918	CABELL	43,894	29,582	14,312		15,270 R	67.4%	32.6%	67.4%	32.6%
7,046	CALHOUN	3,520	1,992	1,528		464 R	56.6%	43.4%	56.6%	43.4%
9,330	CLAY	3,998	2,168	1,830		338 R	54.2%	45.8%	54.2%	45.8%
6,389	DODDRIDGE	2,929	2,284	645		1,639 R	78.0%	22.0%	78.0%	22.0%
49,332	FAYETTE	21,842	11,876	9,966		1,910 R	54.4%	45.6%	54.4%	45.6%
7,782	GILMER	3,415	2,056	1,359		697 R	60.2%	39.8%	60.2%	39.8%
8,607	GRANT	4,170	3,556	614		2,942 R	85.3%	14.7%	85.3%	14.7%
32,090	GREENBRIER	13,250	8,827	4,423		4,404 R	66.6%	33.4%	66.6%	33.4%
11,710	HAMPSHIRE	4,721	3,084	1,637		1,447 R	65.3%	34.7%	65.3%	34.7%
39,749	HANCOCK	17,361	10,634	6,727		3,907 R	61.3%	38.7%	61.3%	38.7%
8,855	HARDY	4,119	2,609	1,510		1,099 R	63.3%	36.7%	63.3%	36.7%
73,028	HARRISON	35,106	22,196	12,910		9,286 R	63.2%	36.8%	63.2%	36.8%
20,903	JACKSON	10,233	7,226	3,007		4,219 R	70.6%	29.4%	70.6%	29.4%
21,280	JEFFERSON	7,604	4,822	2,782		2,040 R	63.4%	36.6%	63.4%	36.6%
229,515	KANAWHA	103,053	65,021	38,032		26,989 R	63.1%	36.9%	63.1%	36.9%
17,847	LEWIS	7,840	5,778	2,062		3,716 R	73.7%	26.3%	73.7%	26.3%
18,912	LINCOLN	8,549	4,673	3,876		797 R	54.7%	45.3%	54.7%	45.3%
46,269	LOGAN	19,578	9,533	10,045		512 D	48.7%	51.3%	48.7%	51.3%
50,666	MCDOWELL	15,753	8,942	6,811		2,131 R	56.8%	43.2%	56.8%	43.2%
61,356	MARION	27,959	16,095	11,864		4,231 R	57.6%	42.4%	57.6%	42.4%
37,598	MARSHALL	17,344	10,966	6,378		4,588 R	63.2%	36.8%	63.2%	36.8%
24,306	MASON	11,137	7,129	4,008		3,121 R	64.0%	36.0%	64.0%	36.0%
63,206	MERCER	25,672	17,846	7,826		10,020 R	69.5%	30.5%	69.5%	30.5%
23,109	MINERAL	10,433	7,157	3,276		3,881 R	68.6%	31.4%	68.6%	31.4%
32,780	MINGO	13,069	7,484	5,585		1,899 R	57.3%	42.7%	57.3%	42.7%
63,714	MONONGALIA	27,479	16,758	10,721		6,037 R	61.0%	39.0%	61.0%	39.0%
11,272	MONROE	5,830	3,716	2,114		1,602 R	63.7%	36.3%	63.7%	36.3%
8,547	MORGAN	4,132	3,014	1,118		1,896 R	72.9%	27.1%	72.9%	27.1%
22,552	NICHOLAS	9,535	5,907	3,628		2,279 R	62.0%	38.0%	62.0%	38.0%
64,197	OHIO	28,926	18,435	10,491		7,944 R	63.7%	36.3%	63.7%	36.3%
7,031	PENDLETON	3,455	2,207	1,248		959 R	63.9%	36.1%	63.9%	36.1%
7,274	PLEASANTS	3,232	2,025	1,207		818 R	62.7%	37.3%	62.7%	37.3%
8,870	POCAHONTAS	4,026	2,391	1,635		756 R	59.4%	40.6%	59.4%	40.6%
25,455	PRESTON	10,784	7,807	2,977		4,830 R	72.4%	27.6%	72.4%	27.6%
27,625	PUTNAM	13,036	8,265	4,771		3,494 R	63.4%	36.6%	63.4%	36.6%
70,080	RALEIGH	29,736	19,150	10,586		8,564 R	64.4%	35.6%	64.4%	35.6%
24,596	RANDOLPH	10,732	6,923	3,809		3,114 R	64.5%	35.5%	64.5%	35.5%
10,145	RITCHIE	4,625	3,635	990		2,645 R	78.6%	21.4%	78.6%	21.4%
14,111	ROANE	6,639	4,253	2,386		1,867 R	64.1%	35.9%	64.1%	35.9%
13,213	SUMMERS	6,413	3,895	2,518		1,377 R	60.7%	39.3%	60.7%	39.3%
13,878	TAYLOR	6,470	4,385	2,085		2,300 R	67.8%	32.2%	67.8%	32.2%
7,447	TUCKER	3,620	2,163	1,457		706 R	59.8%	40.2%	59.8%	40.2%
9,929	TYLER	4,487	3,362	1,125		2,237 R	74.9%	25.1%	74.9%	25.1%
19,092	UPSHUR	8,244	6,449	1,795		4,654 R	78.2%	21.8%	78.2%	21.8%
37,581	WAYNE	16,026	9,775	6,251		3,524 R	61.0%	39.0%	61.0%	39.0%
9,809	WEBSTER	4,183	2,114	2,069		45 R	50.5%	49.5%	50.5%	49.5%
20,314	WETZEL	9,322	6,046	3,276		2,770 R	64.9%	35.1%	64.9%	35.1%
4,154	WIRT	2,133	1,442	691		751 R	67.6%	32.4%	67.6%	32.4%
86,818	WOOD	38,201	27,315	10,886		16,429 R	71.5%	28.5%	71.5%	28.5%
30,095	WYOMING	12,394	7,926	4,468		3,458 R	64.0%	36.0%	64.0%	36.0%
1,744,237	TOTAL	762,399	484,964	277,435		207,529 R	63.6%	36.4%	63.6%	36.4%

WEST VIRGINIA

PRESIDENT 1968

1960 Census Population	County	Total Vote	Republican	Democratic	AIP	Other	Plurality	Percentage Rep.	Percentage Dem.	AIP
15,474	BARBOUR	6,781	3,206	3,210	365		4 D	47.3%	47.3%	5.4%
33,791	BERKELEY	14,473	7,223	4,929	2,321		2,294 R	49.9%	34.1%	16.0%
28,764	BOONE	10,287	2,970	6,391	926		3,421 D	28.9%	62.1%	9.0%
15,152	BRAXTON	6,050	2,441	3,268	341		827 D	40.3%	54.0%	5.6%
28,940	BROOKE	13,141	4,191	7,506	1,444		3,315 D	31.9%	57.1%	11.0%
108,202	CABELL	43,102	19,418	19,018	4,666		400 R	45.1%	44.1%	10.8%
7,948	CALHOUN	3,612	1,612	1,682	318		70 D	44.6%	46.6%	8.8%
11,942	CLAY	3,739	1,474	1,916	349		442 D	39.4%	51.2%	9.3%
6,970	DODDRIDGE	2,851	1,861	844	146		1,017 R	65.3%	29.6%	5.1%
61,731	FAYETTE	21,723	5,246	14,546	1,931		9,300 D	24.1%	67.0%	8.9%
8,050	GILMER	3,197	1,401	1,582	214		181 D	43.8%	49.5%	6.7%
8,304	GRANT	3,978	2,936	786	256		2,150 R	73.8%	19.8%	6.4%
34,446	GREENBRIER	13,599	5,559	6,318	1,722		759 D	40.9%	46.5%	12.7%
11,705	HAMPSHIRE	4,444	1,959	1,791	694		168 R	44.1%	40.3%	15.6%
39,615	HANCOCK	18,831	6,181	10,174	2,476		3,993 D	32.8%	54.0%	13.1%
9,308	HARDY	4,025	1,768	1,767	490		1 R	43.9%	43.9%	12.2%
77,856	HARRISON	34,809	13,703	18,872	2,234		5,169 D	39.4%	54.2%	6.4%
18,541	JACKSON	9,582	5,173	3,462	947		1,711 R	54.0%	36.1%	9.9%
18,665	JEFFERSON	6,929	2,718	3,129	1,082		411 D	39.2%	45.2%	15.6%
252,925	KANAWHA	99,886	41,712	46,650	11,524		4,938 D	41.8%	46.7%	11.5%
19,711	LEWIS	7,835	4,027	3,168	640		859 R	51.4%	40.4%	8.2%
20,267	LINCOLN	8,631	3,662	4,386	583		724 D	42.4%	50.8%	6.8%
61,570	LOGAN	20,301	4,754	13,686	1,861		8,932 D	23.4%	67.4%	9.2%
71,359	MCDOWELL	18,937	4,020	12,842	2,075		8,822 D	21.2%	67.8%	11.0%
63,717	MARION	29,261	10,177	17,246	1,838		7,069 D	34.8%	58.9%	6.3%
38,041	MARSHALL	17,080	7,252	8,449	1,379		1,197 D	42.5%	49.5%	8.1%
24,459	MASON	10,636	5,208	4,549	879		659 R	49.0%	42.8%	8.3%
68,206	MERCER	26,087	9,985	12,739	3,363		2,754 D	38.3%	48.8%	12.9%
22,354	MINERAL	10,043	4,545	4,225	1,273		320 R	45.3%	42.1%	12.7%
39,742	MINGO	13,798	3,988	8,677	1,133		4,689 D	28.9%	62.9%	8.2%
55,617	MONONGALIA	23,945	9,261	13,128	1,556		3,867 D	38.7%	54.8%	6.5%
11,584	MONROE	5,890	2,925	2,412	553		513 R	49.7%	41.0%	9.4%
8,376	MORGAN	3,720	2,244	1,015	461		1,229 R	60.3%	27.3%	12.4%
25,414	NICHOLAS	9,377	3,678	4,858	841		1,180 D	39.2%	51.8%	9.0%
68,437	OHIO	30,263	13,073	15,026	2,164		1,953 D	43.2%	49.7%	7.2%
8,093	PENDLETON	3,628	1,687	1,643	298		44 R	46.5%	45.3%	8.2%
7,124	PLEASANTS	3,260	1,534	1,522	204		12 R	47.1%	46.7%	6.3%
10,136	POCAHONTAS	4,434	2,040	1,948	446		92 R	46.0%	43.9%	10.1%
27,233	PRESTON	10,217	5,636	4,020	561		1,616 R	55.2%	39.3%	5.5%
23,561	PUTNAM	11,601	5,252	5,009	1,340		243 R	45.3%	43.2%	11.6%
77,826	RALEIGH	29,506	8,775	17,744	2,987		8,969 D	29.7%	60.1%	10.1%
26,349	RANDOLPH	10,967	4,508	5,562	897		1,054 D	41.1%	50.7%	8.2%
10,877	RITCHIE	4,671	3,106	1,281	284		1,825 R	66.5%	27.4%	6.1%
15,720	ROANE	6,914	3,851	2,639	424		1,212 R	55.7%	38.2%	6.1%
15,640	SUMMERS	6,675	2,305	3,521	849		1,216 D	34.5%	52.7%	12.7%
15,010	TAYLOR	6,431	3,012	2,953	466		59 R	46.8%	45.9%	7.2%
7,750	TUCKER	3,601	1,511	1,758	332		247 D	42.0%	48.8%	9.2%
10,026	TYLER	4,534	2,897	1,324	313		1,573 R	63.9%	29.2%	6.9%
18,292	UPSHUR	7,311	4,565	2,319	427		2,246 R	62.4%	31.7%	5.8%
38,977	WAYNE	16,319	6,004	8,227	2,088		2,223 D	36.8%	50.4%	12.8%
13,719	WEBSTER	4,107	1,241	2,582	284		1,341 D	30.2%	62.9%	6.9%
19,347	WETZEL	8,949	4,122	4,038	789		84 R	46.1%	45.1%	8.8%
4,391	WIRT	2,011	1,051	820	140		231 R	52.3%	40.8%	7.0%
78,331	WOOD	36,632	18,960	14,293	3,379		4,667 R	51.8%	39.0%	9.2%
34,836	WYOMING	11,595	3,947	6,641	1,007		2,694 D	34.0%	57.3%	8.7%
1,860,421	TOTAL	754,206	307,555	374,091	72,560		66,536 D	40.8%	49.6%	9.6%

WEST VIRGINIA

ELECTION NOTES

1984 Other vote was 996 Richards (Populist); 645 Mason (Socialist Workers); 493 Serrette (Alliance). Early unamended canvass gave the Democratic vote in Jackson county as 4,179.

1980 Other vote was 31,691 Anderson (Independent); 4,356 Clark (Libertarian).

1976 Other vote was 113 McCarthy (write-in); 17 Anderson (write-in); 16 MacBride (write-in); 12 Maddox (write-in); 5 Hall (write-in); 2 Camejo (write-in); 125 scattered write-in. Early unamended canvass gave the Republican state-wide total vote as 314,726 and the Democratic state-wide total vote as 435,864; both the Republican and Democratic votes were amended in Wood county.

1972

1968 Wallace on the ballot as American.

WISCONSIN

POPULAR VOTE FOR PRESIDENT 1920 TO 1984

Year	Total Vote	Republican Vote	Republican Candidate	Democratic Vote	Democratic Candidate	Other Vote	Plurality	Percentage Total Vote Rep.	Percentage Total Vote Dem.	Percentage Major Vote Rep.	Percentage Major Vote Dem.
1984	2,211,689	1,198,584	Reagan, Ronald	995,740	Mondale, Walter F.	17,365	202,844 R	54.2%	45.0%	54.6%	45.4%
1980	2,273,221	1,088,845	Reagan, Ronald	981,584	Carter, Jimmy	202,792	107,261 R	47.9%	43.2%	52.6%	47.4%
1976	2,104,175	1,004,987	Ford, Gerald R.	1,040,232	Carter, Jimmy	58,956	35,245 D	47.8%	49.4%	49.1%	50.9%
1972	1,852,890	989,430	Nixon, Richard M.	810,174	McGovern, George S.	53,286	179,256 R	53.4%	43.7%	55.0%	45.0%
1968	1,691,538	809,997	Nixon, Richard M.	748,804	Humphrey, Hubert H.	132,737	61,193 R	47.9%	44.3%	52.0%	48.0%
1964	1,691,815	638,495	Goldwater, Barry M.	1,050,424	Johnson, Lyndon B.	2,896	411,929 D	37.7%	62.1%	37.8%	62.2%
1960	1,729,082	895,175	Nixon, Richard M.	830,805	Kennedy, John F.	3,102	64,370 R	51.8%	48.0%	51.9%	48.1%
1956	1,550,558	954,844	Eisenhower, Dwight D.	586,768	Stevenson, Adlai E.	8,946	368,076 R	61.6%	37.8%	61.9%	38.1%
1952	1,607,370	979,744	Eisenhower, Dwight D.	622,175	Stevenson, Adlai E.	5,451	357,569 R	61.0%	38.7%	61.2%	38.8%
1948	1,276,800	590,959	Dewey, Thomas E.	647,310	Truman, Harry S.	38,531	56,351 D	46.3%	50.7%	47.7%	52.3%
1944	1,339,152	674,532	Dewey, Thomas E.	650,413	Roosevelt, Franklin D.	14,207	24,119 R	50.4%	48.6%	50.9%	49.1%
1940	1,405,522	679,206	Willkie, Wendell	704,821	Roosevelt, Franklin D.	21,495	25,615 D	48.3%	50.1%	49.1%	50.9%
1936	1,258,560	380,828	Landon, Alfred M.	802,984	Roosevelt, Franklin D.	74,748	422,156 D	30.3%	63.8%	32.2%	67.8%
1932	1,114,814	347,741	Hoover, Herbert C.	707,410	Roosevelt, Franklin D.	59,663	359,669 D	31.2%	63.5%	33.0%	67.0%
1928	1,016,831	544,205	Hoover, Herbert C.	450,259	Smith, Alfred E.	22,367	93,946 R	53.5%	44.3%	54.7%	45.3%
1924 **	840,827	311,614	Coolidge, Calvin	68,115	Davis, John W.	461,098	142,064 P	37.1%	8.1%	82.1%	17.9%
1920	701,281	498,576	Harding, Warren G.	113,422	Cox, James M.	89,283	385,154 R	71.1%	16.2%	81.5%	18.5%

In 1924 other vote was 453,678 Progressive; 3,773 Communist; 2,918 Prohibition; 458 Socialist Labor and 271 Commonwealth Land.

ELECTORAL COLLEGE VOTE 1920 TO 1984

Year	Total	Republican	Democratic	Other
1984	11	11	—	—
1980	11	11	—	—
1976	11	—	11	—
1972	11	11	—	—
1968	12	12	—	—
1964	12	—	12	—
1960	12	12	—	—
1956	12	12	—	—
1952	12	12	—	—
1948	12	—	12	—
1944	12	12	—	—
1940	12	—	12	—
1936	12	—	12	—
1932	12	—	12	—
1928	13	13	—	—
1924	13	—	—	13 PROGRESSIVE
1920	13	13	—	—

WISCONSIN

DOUGLAS
BAYFIELD
ASHLAND
IRON
VILAS
BURNETT
WASHBURN
SAWYER
PRICE
ONEIDA
FLORENCE
FOREST
POLK
BARRON
RUSK
LINCOLN
LANGLADE
MARINETTE
TAYLOR
ST. CROIX
DUNN
CHIPPEWA
MENOM-
INEE
OCONTO
MARATHON
CLARK
PIERCE
EAU CLAIRE
SHAWANO
DOOR
PEPIN
BUFFALO
TREMPEALEAU
WOOD
PORTAGE
WAUPACA
OUTAGAMIE
BROWN
KEWAUNEE
JACKSON
WAUSHARA
WINNE-
BAGO
CALUMET
MANITOWOC
ADAMS
LA
CROSSE
MONROE
JUNEAU
MARQUETTE
GREEN
LAKE
FOND DU LAC
SHEBOY-
GAN
VERNON
COLUMBIA
SAUK
DODGE
WASHING-
TON
OZAUKEE
CRAWFORD
RICHLAND
DANE
JEFFERSON
WAUSHARA
MILWAUKEE
IOWA
GRANT
LAFAYETTE
GREEN
ROCK
WALWORTH
RACINE
KENOSHA

WISCONSIN

PRESIDENT 1984

1980 Census Population	County	Total Vote	Republican	Democratic	Other	Rep.-Dem. Plurality	Percentage Total Vote Rep.	Percentage Total Vote Dem.	Percentage Major Vote Rep.	Percentage Major Vote Dem.
13,457	ADAMS	6,413	3,644	2,713	56	931 R	56.8%	42.3%	57.3%	42.7%
16,783	ASHLAND	8,271	3,517	4,680	74	1,163 D	42.5%	56.6%	42.9%	57.1%
38,730	BARRON	17,784	9,587	8,060	137	1,527 R	53.9%	45.3%	54.3%	45.7%
13,822	BAYFIELD	7,567	3,474	4,034	59	560 D	45.9%	53.3%	46.3%	53.7%
175,280	BROWN	81,976	51,186	30,208	582	20,978 R	62.4%	36.8%	62.9%	37.1%
14,309	BUFFALO	6,308	3,325	2,921	62	404 R	52.7%	46.3%	53.2%	46.8%
12,340	BURNETT	6,918	3,528	3,328	62	200 R	51.0%	48.1%	51.5%	48.5%
30,867	CALUMET	13,898	8,969	4,735	194	4,234 R	64.5%	34.1%	65.4%	34.6%
52,127	CHIPPEWA	21,350	10,983	10,200	167	783 R	51.4%	47.8%	51.8%	48.2%
32,910	CLARK	13,918	8,098	5,647	173	2,451 R	58.2%	40.6%	58.9%	41.1%
43,222	COLUMBIA	19,941	11,658	8,124	159	3,534 R	58.5%	40.7%	58.9%	41.1%
16,556	CRAWFORD	7,906	4,411	3,435	60	976 R	55.8%	43.4%	56.2%	43.8%
323,545	DANE	169,978	74,009	94,638	1,331	20,629 D	43.5%	55.7%	43.9%	56.1%
75,064	DODGE	31,758	20,455	11,052	251	9,403 R	64.4%	34.8%	64.9%	35.1%
25,029	DOOR	12,270	8,264	3,915	91	4,349 R	67.4%	31.9%	67.9%	32.1%
44,421	DOUGLAS	21,467	7,066	14,290	111	7,224 D	32.9%	66.6%	33.1%	66.9%
34,314	DUNN	16,364	8,472	7,709	183	763 R	51.8%	47.1%	52.4%	47.6%
78,805	EAU CLAIRE	39,931	20,394	19,344	193	1,050 R	51.1%	48.4%	51.3%	48.7%
4,172	FLORENCE	2,115	1,227	870	18	357 R	58.0%	41.1%	58.5%	41.5%
88,964	FOND DU LAC	40,361	26,067	13,982	312	12,085 R	64.6%	34.6%	65.1%	34.9%
9,044	FOREST	4,546	2,296	2,213	37	83 R	50.5%	48.7%	50.9%	49.1%
51,736	GRANT	21,471	13,427	7,890	154	5,537 R	62.5%	36.7%	63.0%	37.0%
30,012	GREEN	12,299	7,826	4,367	106	3,459 R	63.6%	35.5%	64.2%	35.8%
18,370	GREEN LAKE	8,721	6,198	2,441	82	3,757 R	71.1%	28.0%	71.7%	28.3%
19,802	IOWA	8,902	4,982	3,842	78	1,140 R	56.0%	43.2%	56.5%	43.5%
6,730	IRON	3,653	1,667	1,967	19	300 D	45.6%	53.8%	45.9%	54.1%
16,831	JACKSON	7,856	4,383	3,427	46	956 R	55.8%	43.6%	56.1%	43.9%
66,152	JEFFERSON	28,783	17,779	10,788	216	6,991 R	61.8%	37.5%	62.2%	37.8%
21,039	JUNEAU	8,855	5,627	3,151	77	2,476 R	63.5%	35.6%	64.1%	35.9%
123,137	KENOSHA	55,697	26,112	29,233	352	3,121 D	46.9%	52.5%	47.2%	52.8%
19,539	KEWAUNEE	9,213	5,705	3,444	64	2,261 R	61.9%	37.4%	62.4%	37.6%
91,056	LA CROSSE	43,765	25,717	17,787	261	7,930 R	58.8%	40.6%	59.1%	40.9%
17,412	LAFAYETTE	7,592	4,582	2,959	51	1,623 R	60.4%	39.0%	60.8%	39.2%
19,978	LANGLADE	9,582	5,828	3,675	79	2,153 R	60.8%	38.4%	61.3%	38.7%
26,555	LINCOLN	12,134	6,681	5,352	101	1,329 R	55.1%	44.1%	55.5%	44.5%
82,918	MANITOWOC	37,390	19,635	17,249	506	2,386 R	52.5%	46.1%	53.2%	46.8%
111,270	MARATHON	48,672	27,077	20,126	1,469	6,951 R	55.6%	41.4%	57.4%	42.6%
39,314	MARINETTE	18,365	11,439	6,798	128	4,641 R	62.3%	37.0%	62.7%	37.3%
11,672	MARQUETTE	5,512	3,404	2,031	77	1,373 R	61.8%	36.8%	62.6%	37.4%
3,373	MENOMINEE	1,231	392	832	7	440 D	31.8%	67.6%	32.0%	68.0%
964,988	MILWAUKEE	458,042	196,259	259,134	2,649	62,875 D	42.8%	56.6%	43.1%	56.9%
35,074	MONROE	13,884	8,225	5,564	95	2,661 R	59.2%	40.1%	59.6%	40.4%
28,947	OCONTO	14,140	8,713	5,288	139	3,425 R	61.6%	37.4%	62.2%	37.8%
31,216	ONEIDA	16,384	9,782	6,416	186	3,366 R	59.7%	39.2%	60.4%	39.6%
128,799	OUTAGAMIE	56,971	36,765	19,789	417	16,976 R	64.5%	34.7%	65.0%	35.0%
66,981	OZAUKEE	34,892	23,896	10,763	233	13,133 R	68.5%	30.8%	68.9%	31.1%
7,477	PEPIN	3,203	1,555	1,629	19	74 D	48.5%	50.9%	48.8%	51.2%
31,149	PIERCE	15,022	7,611	7,285	126	326 R	50.7%	48.5%	51.1%	48.9%
32,351	POLK	16,263	8,101	8,033	129	68 R	49.8%	49.4%	50.2%	49.8%
57,420	PORTAGE	28,192	13,603	14,399	190	796 D	48.3%	51.1%	48.6%	51.4%
15,788	PRICE	7,856	4,286	3,479	91	807 R	54.6%	44.3%	55.2%	44.8%
173,132	RACINE	79,654	42,085	36,953	616	5,132 R	52.8%	46.4%	53.2%	46.8%
17,476	RICHLAND	7,760	4,857	2,844	59	2,013 R	62.6%	36.6%	63.1%	36.9%
139,420	ROCK	59,329	32,483	26,430	416	6,053 R	54.8%	44.5%	55.1%	44.9%
15,589	RUSK	7,985	4,061	3,843	81	218 R	50.9%	48.1%	51.4%	48.6%
43,262	ST. CROIX	21,644	11,365	10,126	153	1,239 R	52.5%	46.8%	52.9%	47.1%
43,469	SAUK	18,310	11,067	7,157	86	3,910 R	60.4%	39.1%	60.7%	39.3%
12,843	SAWYER	6,971	3,911	2,981	79	930 R	56.1%	42.8%	56.7%	43.3%
35,928	SHAWANO	16,235	10,635	5,469	131	5,166 R	65.5%	33.7%	66.0%	34.0%
100,935	SHEBOYGAN	47,876	26,343	21,111	422	5,232 R	55.0%	44.1%	55.5%	44.5%

WISCONSIN

PRESIDENT 1984

1980 Census Population	County	Total Vote	Republican	Democratic	Other	Rep.-Dem. Plurality	Percentage Total Vote Rep.	Percentage Total Vote Dem.	Percentage Major Vote Rep.	Percentage Major Vote Dem.
18,817	TAYLOR	8,276	4,918	3,271	87	1,647 R	59.4%	39.5%	60.1%	39.9%
26,158	TREMPEALEAU	11,522	6,007	5,405	110	602 R	52.1%	46.9%	52.6%	47.4%
25,642	VERNON	11,608	6,468	5,051	89	1,417 R	55.7%	43.5%	56.2%	43.8%
16,535	VILAS	9,024	5,963	2,940	121	3,023 R	66.1%	32.6%	67.0%	33.0%
71,507	WALWORTH	30,715	20,590	9,876	249	10,714 R	67.0%	32.2%	67.6%	32.4%
13,174	WASHBURN	7,078	3,847	3,188	43	659 R	54.4%	45.0%	54.7%	45.3%
84,848	WASHINGTON	38,572	25,278	12,966	328	12,312 R	65.5%	33.6%	66.1%	33.9%
280,326	WAUKESHA	140,663	92,415	47,308	940	45,107 R	65.7%	33.6%	66.1%	33.9%
42,831	WAUPACA	19,184	13,097	5,894	193	7,203 R	68.3%	30.7%	69.0%	31.0%
18,526	WAUSHARA	8,636	5,768	2,782	86	2,986 R	66.8%	32.2%	67.5%	32.5%
131,703	WINNEBAGO	62,183	39,014	22,791	378	16,223 R	62.7%	36.7%	63.1%	36.9%
72,799	WOOD	32,882	20,525	12,118	239	8,407 R	62.4%	36.9%	62.9%	37.1%
4,705,767	TOTAL	2,211,689	1,198,584	995,740	17,365	202,844 R	54.2%	45.0%	54.6%	45.4%

WISCONSIN

PRESIDENT 1980

1980 Census Population	County	Total Vote	Republican	Democratic	Other	Rep.-Dem. Plurality	Percentage Total Vote Rep.	Percentage Total Vote Dem.	Percentage Major Vote Rep.	Percentage Major Vote Dem.
13,457	ADAMS	6,527	3,304	2,773	450	531 R	50.6%	42.5%	54.4%	45.6%
16,783	ASHLAND	8,685	3,262	4,469	954	1,207 D	37.6%	51.5%	42.2%	57.8%
38,730	BARRON	18,698	8,791	8,654	1,253	137 R	47.0%	46.3%	50.4%	49.6%
13,822	BAYFIELD	7,802	3,278	3,705	819	427 D	42.0%	47.5%	46.9%	53.1%
175,280	BROWN	82,997	47,067	29,796	6,134	17,271 R	56.7%	35.9%	61.2%	38.8%
14,309	BUFFALO	7,428	3,569	3,276	583	293 R	48.0%	44.1%	52.1%	47.9%
12,340	BURNETT	6,757	3,027	3,200	530	173 D	44.8%	47.4%	48.6%	51.4%
30,867	CALUMET	14,321	7,885	5,036	1,400	2,849 R	55.1%	35.2%	61.0%	39.0%
52,127	CHIPPEWA	21,921	10,531	9,836	1,554	695 R	48.0%	44.9%	51.7%	48.3%
32,910	CLARK	15,039	7,921	6,091	1,027	1,830 R	52.7%	40.5%	56.5%	43.5%
43,222	COLUMBIA	21,031	10,478	8,715	1,838	1,763 R	49.8%	41.4%	54.6%	45.4%
16,556	CRAWFORD	7,861	3,934	3,392	535	542 R	50.0%	43.1%	53.7%	46.3%
323,545	DANE	168,563	57,545	85,609	25,409	28,064 D	34.1%	50.8%	40.2%	59.8%
75,064	DODGE	33,682	19,435	11,966	2,281	7,469 R	57.7%	35.5%	61.9%	38.1%
25,029	DOOR	13,006	7,170	4,961	875	2,209 R	55.1%	38.1%	59.1%	40.9%
44,421	DOUGLAS	21,219	7,258	11,703	2,258	4,445 D	34.2%	55.2%	38.3%	61.7%
34,314	DUNN	17,095	7,428	7,743	1,924	315 D	43.5%	45.3%	49.0%	51.0%
78,805	EAU CLAIRE	38,943	17,304	17,602	4,037	298 D	44.4%	45.2%	49.6%	50.4%
4,172	FLORENCE	2,261	1,187	943	131	244 R	52.5%	41.7%	55.7%	44.3%
88,964	FOND DU LAC	42,497	24,196	15,293	3,008	8,903 R	56.9%	36.0%	61.3%	38.7%
9,044	FOREST	4,680	2,070	2,402	208	332 D	44.2%	51.3%	46.3%	53.7%
51,736	GRANT	23,830	13,298	8,406	2,126	4,892 R	55.8%	35.3%	61.3%	38.7%
30,012	GREEN	14,296	7,714	5,336	1,246	2,378 R	54.0%	37.3%	59.1%	40.9%
18,370	GREEN LAKE	9,262	5,868	2,851	543	3,017 R	63.4%	30.8%	67.3%	32.7%
19,802	IOWA	9,001	4,068	4,154	779	86 D	45.2%	46.2%	49.5%	50.5%
6,730	IRON	4,021	1,811	1,941	269	130 D	45.0%	48.3%	48.3%	51.7%
16,831	JACKSON	8,524	4,327	3,629	568	698 R	50.8%	42.6%	54.4%	45.6%
66,152	JEFFERSON	30,016	16,174	11,335	2,507	4,839 R	53.9%	37.8%	58.8%	41.2%
21,039	JUNEAU	10,146	5,591	3,884	671	1,707 R	55.1%	38.3%	59.0%	41.0%
123,137	KENOSHA	55,893	24,481	26,738	4,674	2,257 D	43.8%	47.8%	47.8%	52.2%
19,539	KEWAUNEE	9,794	5,577	3,706	511	1,871 R	56.9%	37.8%	60.1%	39.9%
91,056	LA CROSSE	45,293	23,427	17,304	4,562	6,123 R	51.7%	38.2%	57.5%	42.5%
17,412	LAFAYETTE	8,597	4,421	3,598	578	823 R	51.4%	41.9%	55.1%	44.9%
19,978	LANGLADE	9,883	4,866	4,498	519	368 R	49.2%	45.5%	52.0%	48.0%
26,555	LINCOLN	12,755	6,473	5,438	844	1,035 R	50.7%	42.6%	54.3%	45.7%
82,918	MANITOWOC	38,754	18,591	17,330	2,833	1,261 R	48.0%	44.7%	51.8%	48.2%
111,270	MARATHON	53,549	25,868	23,281	4,400	2,587 R	48.3%	43.5%	52.6%	47.4%
39,314	MARINETTE	19,182	10,444	7,718	1,020	2,726 R	54.4%	40.2%	57.5%	42.5%
11,672	MARQUETTE	5,789	3,166	2,180	443	986 R	54.7%	37.7%	59.2%	40.8%
3,373	MENOMINEE	936	302	544	90	242 D	32.3%	58.1%	35.7%	64.3%
964,988	MILWAUKEE	464,160	183,450	240,174	40,536	56,724 D	39.5%	51.7%	43.3%	56.7%
35,074	MONROE	15,689	8,136	6,521	1,032	1,615 R	51.9%	41.6%	55.5%	44.5%
28,947	OCONTO	14,314	8,292	5,352	670	2,940 R	57.9%	37.4%	60.8%	39.2%
31,216	ONEIDA	16,867	8,602	7,008	1,257	1,594 R	51.0%	41.5%	55.1%	44.9%
128,799	OUTAGAMIE	59,456	31,500	21,284	6,672	10,216 R	53.0%	35.8%	59.7%	40.3%
66,981	OZAUKEE	35,040	21,371	10,779	2,890	10,592 R	61.0%	30.8%	66.5%	33.5%
7,477	PEPIN	3,473	1,541	1,673	259	132 D	44.4%	48.2%	47.9%	52.1%
31,149	PIERCE	15,662	6,209	7,312	2,141	1,103 D	39.6%	46.7%	45.9%	54.1%
32,351	POLK	16,313	7,207	7,607	1,499	400 D	44.2%	46.6%	48.6%	51.4%
57,420	PORTAGE	30,708	10,465	16,443	3,800	5,978 D	34.1%	53.5%	38.9%	61.1%
15,788	PRICE	8,172	4,028	3,595	549	433 R	49.3%	44.0%	52.8%	47.2%
173,132	RACINE	79,775	39,683	33,565	6,527	6,118 R	49.7%	42.1%	54.2%	45.8%
17,476	RICHLAND	8,594	4,601	3,413	580	1,188 R	53.5%	39.7%	57.4%	42.6%
139,420	ROCK	61,218	30,960	24,740	5,518	6,220 R	50.6%	40.4%	55.6%	44.4%
15,589	RUSK	7,800	3,704	3,584	512	120 R	47.5%	45.9%	50.8%	49.2%
43,262	ST. CROIX	21,792	9,265	10,203	2,324	938 D	42.5%	46.8%	47.6%	52.4%
43,469	SAUK	20,208	9,992	8,456	1,760	1,536 R	49.4%	41.8%	54.2%	45.8%
12,843	SAWYER	7,089	3,548	3,065	476	483 R	50.0%	43.2%	53.7%	46.3%
35,928	SHAWANO	16,283	9,922	5,410	951	4,512 R	60.9%	33.2%	64.7%	35.3%
100,935	SHEBOYGAN	48,600	23,036	20,974	4,590	2,062 R	47.4%	43.2%	52.3%	47.7%

WISCONSIN

PRESIDENT 1980

1980 Census Population	County	Total Vote	Republican	Democratic	Other	Rep.-Dem. Plurality	Percentage Total Vote Rep.	Percentage Total Vote Dem.	Percentage Major Vote Rep.	Percentage Major Vote Dem.
18,817	TAYLOR	8,972	4,596	3,739	637	857 R	51.2%	41.7%	55.1%	44.9%
26,158	TREMPEALEAU	12,133	5,992	5,390	751	602 R	49.4%	44.4%	52.6%	47.4%
25,642	VERNON	12,774	6,528	5,501	745	1,027 R	51.1%	43.1%	54.3%	45.7%
16,535	VILAS	9,932	6,034	3,293	605	2,741 R	60.8%	33.2%	64.7%	35.3%
71,507	WALWORTH	33,730	19,194	11,344	3,192	7,850 R	56.9%	33.6%	62.9%	37.1%
13,174	WASHBURN	6,887	3,193	3,172	522	21 R	46.4%	46.1%	50.2%	49.8%
84,848	WASHINGTON	39,493	23,213	12,944	3,336	10,269 R	58.8%	32.8%	64.2%	35.8%
280,326	WAUKESHA	139,236	81,059	46,612	11,565	34,447 R	58.2%	33.5%	63.5%	36.5%
42,831	WAUPACA	20,397	12,568	6,401	1,428	6,167 R	61.6%	31.4%	66.3%	33.7%
18,526	WAUSHARA	9,077	5,576	2,987	514	2,589 R	61.4%	32.9%	65.1%	34.9%
131,703	WINNEBAGO	64,360	34,286	24,203	5,871	10,083 R	53.3%	37.6%	58.6%	41.4%
72,799	WOOD	34,483	17,987	13,804	2,692	4,183 R	52.2%	40.0%	56.6%	43.4%
4,705,767	TOTAL	2,273,221	1,088,845	981,584	202,792	107,261 R	47.9%	43.2%	52.6%	47.4%

WISCONSIN

PRESIDENT 1976

1970 Census Population	County	Total Vote	Republican	Democratic	Other	Rep.-Dem. Plurality	Percentage: Total Vote Rep.	Total Vote Dem.	Major Vote Rep.	Major Vote Dem.
9,234	ADAMS	5,594	2,377	3,089	128	712 D	42.5%	55.2%	43.5%	56.5%
16,743	ASHLAND	7,961	3,045	4,688	228	1,643 D	38.2%	58.9%	39.4%	60.6%
33,955	BARRON	16,406	7,393	8,678	335	1,285 D	45.1%	52.9%	46.0%	54.0%
11,683	BAYFIELD	6,706	2,624	3,885	197	1,261 D	39.1%	57.9%	40.3%	59.7%
158,244	BROWN	72,318	36,571	33,572	2,175	2,999 R	50.6%	46.4%	52.1%	47.9%
13,743	BUFFALO	6,441	2,844	3,448	149	604 D	44.2%	53.5%	45.2%	54.8%
9,276	BURNETT	6,469	2,573	3,720	176	1,147 D	39.8%	57.5%	40.9%	59.1%
27,604	CALUMET	13,157	6,589	6,241	327	348 R	50.1%	47.4%	51.4%	48.6%
47,717	CHIPPEWA	20,155	8,137	11,538	480	3,401 D	40.4%	57.2%	41.4%	58.6%
30,361	CLARK	13,784	6,095	7,238	451	1,143 D	44.2%	52.5%	45.7%	54.3%
40,150	COLUMBIA	19,933	10,075	9,457	401	618 R	50.5%	47.4%	51.6%	48.4%
15,252	CRAWFORD	7,226	3,393	3,629	204	236 D	47.0%	50.2%	48.3%	51.7%
290,272	DANE	152,756	63,466	82,321	6,969	18,855 D	41.5%	53.9%	43.5%	56.5%
69,004	DODGE	31,674	17,335	13,643	696	3,692 R	54.7%	43.1%	56.0%	44.0%
20,106	DOOR	11,420	6,557	4,553	310	2,004 R	57.4%	39.9%	59.0%	41.0%
44,657	DOUGLAS	20,989	6,999	13,478	512	6,479 D	33.3%	64.2%	34.2%	65.8%
29,154	DUNN	15,040	6,751	7,882	407	1,131 D	44.9%	52.4%	46.1%	53.9%
67,219	EAU CLAIRE	35,386	16,388	18,263	735	1,875 D	46.3%	51.6%	47.3%	52.7%
3,298	FLORENCE	1,925	922	965	38	43 D	47.9%	50.1%	48.9%	51.1%
84,567	FOND DU LAC	39,895	22,226	16,571	1,098	5,655 R	55.7%	41.5%	57.3%	42.7%
7,691	FOREST	4,245	1,604	2,574	67	970 D	37.8%	60.6%	38.4%	61.6%
48,398	GRANT	22,220	12,016	9,639	565	2,377 R	54.1%	43.4%	55.5%	44.5%
26,714	GREEN	13,076	7,085	5,632	359	1,453 R	54.2%	43.1%	55.7%	44.3%
16,878	GREEN LAKE	8,612	5,020	3,411	181	1,609 R	58.3%	39.6%	59.5%	40.5%
19,306	IOWA	8,685	4,195	4,252	238	57 D	48.3%	49.0%	49.7%	50.3%
6,533	IRON	3,805	1,340	2,399	66	1,059 D	35.2%	63.0%	35.8%	64.2%
15,325	JACKSON	7,276	3,406	3,735	135	329 D	46.8%	51.3%	47.7%	52.3%
60,060	JEFFERSON	28,876	15,528	12,577	771	2,951 R	53.8%	43.6%	55.2%	44.8%
18,455	JUNEAU	9,087	4,242	4,512	333	270 D	46.7%	49.7%	48.5%	51.5%
117,917	KENOSHA	51,338	22,349	27,585	1,404	5,236 D	43.5%	53.7%	44.8%	55.2%
18,961	KEWAUNEE	9,322	4,447	4,607	268	160 D	47.7%	49.4%	49.1%	50.9%
80,468	LA CROSSE	41,704	24,188	16,674	842	7,514 R	58.0%	40.0%	59.2%	40.8%
17,456	LAFAYETTE	8,195	4,131	3,839	225	292 R	50.4%	46.8%	51.8%	48.2%
19,220	LANGLADE	8,936	4,630	4,134	172	496 R	51.8%	46.3%	52.8%	47.2%
23,499	LINCOLN	11,738	5,672	5,800	266	128 D	48.3%	49.4%	49.4%	50.6%
82,294	MANITOWOC	36,798	16,039	19,819	940	3,780 D	43.6%	53.9%	44.7%	55.3%
97,457	MARATHON	48,054	21,898	24,934	1,222	3,036 D	45.6%	51.9%	46.8%	53.2%
35,810	MARINETTE	17,439	8,591	8,482	366	109 R	49.3%	48.6%	50.3%	49.7%
8,865	MARQUETTE	5,217	2,607	2,516	94	91 R	50.0%	48.2%	50.9%	49.1%
2,607	MENOMINEE	1,122	324	766	32	442 D	28.9%	68.3%	29.7%	70.3%
1,054,262	MILWAUKEE	456,545	192,008	249,739	14,798	57,731 D	42.1%	54.7%	43.5%	56.5%
31,610	MONROE	13,998	7,242	6,465	291	777 R	51.7%	46.2%	52.8%	47.2%
25,553	OCONTO	13,048	6,232	6,541	275	309 D	47.8%	50.1%	48.8%	51.2%
24,427	ONEIDA	14,947	7,347	7,216	384	131 R	49.2%	48.3%	50.4%	49.6%
119,356	OUTAGAMIE	52,568	28,363	23,079	1,126	5,284 R	54.0%	43.9%	55.1%	44.9%
54,421	OZAUKEE	31,961	19,817	11,271	873	8,546 R	62.0%	35.3%	63.7%	36.3%
7,319	PEPIN	3,338	1,312	1,955	71	643 D	39.3%	58.6%	40.2%	59.8%
26,652	PIERCE	14,112	5,676	8,039	397	2,363 D	40.2%	57.0%	41.4%	58.6%
26,666	POLK	14,924	6,159	8,485	280	2,326 D	41.3%	56.9%	42.1%	57.9%
47,541	PORTAGE	26,269	9,520	15,912	837	6,392 D	36.2%	60.6%	37.4%	62.6%
14,520	PRICE	7,428	3,204	4,028	196	824 D	43.1%	54.2%	44.3%	55.7%
170,838	RACINE	75,787	37,088	36,740	1,959	348 R	48.9%	48.5%	50.2%	49.8%
17,079	RICHLAND	8,258	4,466	3,634	158	832 R	54.1%	44.0%	55.1%	44.9%
131,970	ROCK	57,860	28,325	28,048	1,487	277 R	49.0%	48.5%	50.2%	49.8%
14,238	RUSK	6,989	2,724	4,050	215	1,326 D	39.0%	57.9%	40.2%	59.8%
34,354	ST. CROIX	18,715	7,685	10,601	429	2,916 D	41.1%	56.6%	42.0%	58.0%
39,057	SAUK	19,220	9,577	9,204	439	373 R	49.8%	47.9%	51.0%	49.0%
9,670	SAWYER	5,918	2,720	3,055	143	335 D	46.0%	51.6%	47.1%	52.9%
32,650	SHAWANO	15,584	8,505	6,751	328	1,754 R	54.6%	43.3%	55.7%	44.3%
96,660	SHEBOYGAN	47,413	22,332	24,226	855	1,894 D	47.1%	51.1%	48.0%	52.0%

WISCONSIN

PRESIDENT 1976

1970 Census Population	County	Total Vote	Republican	Democratic	Other	Rep.-Dem. Plurality	Percentage Total Vote Rep.	Percentage Total Vote Dem.	Percentage Major Vote Rep.	Percentage Major Vote Dem.
16,958	TAYLOR	7,921	3,591	4,101	229	510 D	45.3%	51.8%	46.7%	53.3%
23,344	TREMPEALEAU	11,740	5,341	6,218	181	877 D	45.5%	53.0%	46.2%	53.8%
24,557	VERNON	11,914	6,132	5,534	248	598 R	51.5%	46.4%	52.6%	47.4%
10,958	VILAS	8,350	4,929	3,209	212	1,720 R	59.0%	38.4%	60.6%	39.4%
63,444	WALWORTH	31,365	18,091	12,418	856	5,673 R	57.7%	39.6%	59.3%	40.7%
10,601	WASHBURN	6,467	2,787	3,503	177	716 D	43.1%	54.2%	44.3%	55.7%
63,839	WASHINGTON	34,120	18,798	14,422	900	4,376 R	55.1%	42.3%	56.6%	43.4%
231,365	WAUKESHA	121,133	70,418	47,487	3,228	22,931 R	58.1%	39.2%	59.7%	40.3%
37,780	WAUPACA	18,086	10,849	6,857	380	3,992 R	60.0%	37.9%	61.3%	38.7%
14,795	WAUSHARA	8,098	4,449	3,485	164	964 R	54.9%	43.0%	56.1%	43.9%
129,934	WINNEBAGO	58,127	32,149	24,485	1,493	7,664 R	55.3%	42.1%	56.8%	43.2%
65,362	WOOD	30,992	15,479	14,728	785	751 R	49.9%	47.5%	51.2%	48.8%
4,417,933	TOTAL	2,104,175	1,004,987	1,040,232	58,956	35,245 D	47.8%	49.4%	49.1%	50.9%

WISCONSIN

PRESIDENT 1972

1970 Census Population	County	Total Vote	Republican	Democratic	Other	Rep.-Dem. Plurality	Percentage Total Vote Rep.	Percentage Total Vote Dem.	Percentage Major Vote Rep.	Percentage Major Vote Dem.
9,234	ADAMS	4,137	2,200	1,833	104	367 R	53.2%	44.3%	54.5%	45.5%
16,743	ASHLAND	7,414	3,478	3,771	165	293 D	46.9%	50.9%	48.0%	52.0%
33,955	BARRON	14,055	8,418	5,376	261	3,042 R	59.9%	38.2%	61.0%	39.0%
11,683	BAYFIELD	5,879	3,045	2,736	98	309 R	51.8%	46.5%	52.7%	47.3%
158,244	BROWN	65,675	37,101	26,511	2,063	10,590 R	56.5%	40.4%	58.3%	41.7%
13,743	BUFFALO	5,672	3,079	2,461	132	618 R	54.3%	43.4%	55.6%	44.4%
9,276	BURNETT	5,466	2,972	2,389	105	583 R	54.4%	43.7%	55.4%	44.6%
27,604	CALUMET	11,542	6,446	4,804	292	1,642 R	55.8%	41.6%	57.3%	42.7%
47,717	CHIPPEWA	17,123	8,451	8,210	462	241 R	49.4%	47.9%	50.7%	49.3%
30,361	CLARK	12,641	7,138	4,617	886	2,521 R	56.5%	36.5%	60.7%	39.3%
40,150	COLUMBIA	17,447	10,122	7,083	242	3,039 R	58.0%	40.6%	58.8%	41.2%
15,252	CRAWFORD	6,315	3,705	2,487	123	1,218 R	58.7%	39.4%	59.8%	40.2%
290,272	DANE	137,177	56,020	79,567	1,590	23,547 D	40.8%	58.0%	41.3%	58.7%
69,004	DODGE	27,737	17,068	9,898	771	7,170 R	61.5%	35.7%	63.3%	36.7%
20,106	DOOR	10,121	6,503	3,430	188	3,073 R	64.3%	33.9%	65.5%	34.5%
44,657	DOUGLAS	19,771	8,419	11,054	298	2,635 D	42.6%	55.9%	43.2%	56.8%
29,154	DUNN	12,565	6,660	5,681	224	979 R	53.0%	45.2%	54.0%	46.0%
67,219	EAU CLAIRE	30,971	15,883	14,300	788	1,583 R	51.3%	46.2%	52.6%	47.4%
3,298	FLORENCE	1,796	971	757	68	214 R	54.1%	42.1%	56.2%	43.8%
84,567	FOND DU LAC	34,470	21,007	12,050	1,413	8,957 R	60.9%	35.0%	63.5%	36.5%
7,691	FOREST	3,729	1,856	1,678	195	178 R	49.8%	45.0%	52.5%	47.5%
48,398	GRANT	19,061	11,873	6,915	273	4,958 R	62.3%	36.3%	63.2%	36.8%
26,714	GREEN	11,222	7,422	3,634	166	3,788 R	66.1%	32.4%	67.1%	32.9%
16,878	GREEN LAKE	7,457	5,046	2,174	237	2,872 R	67.7%	29.2%	69.9%	30.1%
19,306	IOWA	7,626	4,387	3,131	108	1,256 R	57.5%	41.1%	58.4%	41.6%
6,533	IRON	3,451	1,723	1,648	80	75 R	49.9%	47.8%	51.1%	48.9%
15,325	JACKSON	6,476	3,937	2,445	94	1,492 R	60.8%	37.8%	61.7%	38.3%
60,060	JEFFERSON	24,648	14,621	9,303	724	5,318 R	59.3%	37.7%	61.1%	38.9%
18,455	JUNEAU	8,030	4,833	2,943	254	1,890 R	60.2%	36.7%	62.2%	37.8%
117,917	KENOSHA	44,576	24,041	19,441	1,094	4,600 R	53.9%	43.6%	55.3%	44.7%
18,961	KEWAUNEE	8,403	4,802	3,360	241	1,442 R	57.1%	40.0%	58.8%	41.2%
80,468	LA CROSSE	34,746	21,992	12,152	602	9,840 R	63.3%	35.0%	64.4%	35.6%
17,456	LAFAYETTE	7,786	4,898	2,804	84	2,094 R	62.9%	36.0%	63.6%	36.4%
19,220	LANGLADE	7,629	4,368	3,011	250	1,357 R	57.3%	39.5%	59.2%	40.8%
23,499	LINCOLN	10,840	6,206	4,175	459	2,031 R	57.3%	38.5%	59.8%	40.2%
82,294	MANITOWOC	34,237	16,599	16,489	1,149	110 R	48.5%	48.2%	50.2%	49.8%
97,457	MARATHON	41,872	21,454	18,500	1,918	2,954 R	51.2%	44.2%	53.7%	46.3%
35,810	MARINETTE	15,238	8,740	5,900	598	2,840 R	57.4%	38.7%	59.7%	40.3%
8,865	MARQUETTE	4,289	2,682	1,537	70	1,145 R	62.5%	35.8%	63.6%	36.4%
2,607	MENOMINEE	976	355	608	13	253 D	36.4%	62.3%	36.9%	63.1%
1,054,262	MILWAUKEE	416,977	191,874	210,802	14,301	18,928 D	46.0%	50.6%	47.6%	52.4%
31,610	MONROE	11,436	7,625	3,640	171	3,985 R	66.7%	31.8%	67.7%	32.3%
25,553	OCONTO	10,965	6,511	4,041	413	2,470 R	59.4%	36.9%	61.7%	38.3%
24,427	ONEIDA	11,577	6,811	4,262	504	2,549 R	58.8%	36.8%	61.5%	38.5%
119,356	OUTAGAMIE	46,044	27,533	17,447	1,064	10,086 R	59.8%	37.9%	61.2%	38.8%
54,421	OZAUKEE	25,466	15,759	8,503	1,204	7,256 R	61.9%	33.4%	65.0%	35.0%
7,319	PEPIN	2,963	1,458	1,409	96	49 R	49.2%	47.6%	50.9%	49.1%
26,652	PIERCE	11,716	5,899	5,611	206	288 R	50.3%	47.9%	51.3%	48.7%
26,666	POLK	12,533	6,567	5,738	228	829 R	52.4%	45.8%	53.4%	46.6%
47,541	PORTAGE	23,341	9,346	13,564	431	4,218 D	40.0%	58.1%	40.8%	59.2%
14,520	PRICE	6,792	3,694	2,831	267	863 R	54.4%	41.7%	56.6%	43.4%
170,838	RACINE	68,236	38,490	27,778	1,968	10,712 R	56.4%	40.7%	58.1%	41.9%
17,079	RICHLAND	7,654	5,062	2,492	100	2,570 R	66.1%	32.6%	67.0%	33.0%
131,970	ROCK	52,319	30,361	21,033	925	9,328 R	58.0%	40.2%	59.1%	40.9%
14,238	RUSK	6,279	3,007	3,075	197	68 D	47.9%	49.0%	49.4%	50.6%
34,354	ST. CROIX	16,291	8,553	7,488	250	1,065 R	52.5%	46.0%	53.3%	46.7%
39,057	SAUK	17,522	10,285	6,980	257	3,305 R	58.7%	39.8%	59.6%	40.4%
9,670	SAWYER	4,928	3,081	1,765	82	1,316 R	62.5%	35.8%	63.6%	36.4%
32,650	SHAWANO	13,154	8,807	3,940	407	4,867 R	67.0%	30.0%	69.1%	30.9%
96,660	SHEBOYGAN	43,537	21,500	21,114	923	386 R	49.4%	48.5%	50.5%	49.5%

WISCONSIN

PRESIDENT 1972

1970 Census Population	County	Total Vote	Republican	Democratic	Other	Rep.-Dem. Plurality	Percentage Total Vote Rep.	Percentage Total Vote Dem.	Percentage Major Vote Rep.	Percentage Major Vote Dem.
16,958	TAYLOR	7,398	4,125	2,934	339	1,191 R	55.8%	39.7%	58.4%	41.6%
23,344	TREMPEALEAU	10,095	5,723	4,232	140	1,491 R	56.7%	41.9%	57.5%	42.5%
24,557	VERNON	10,403	6,836	3,407	160	3,429 R	65.7%	32.8%	66.7%	33.3%
10,958	VILAS	6,708	4,422	1,907	379	2,515 R	65.9%	28.4%	69.9%	30.1%
63,444	WALWORTH	27,023	17,823	8,598	602	9,225 R	66.0%	31.8%	67.5%	32.5%
10,601	WASHBURN	5,665	3,220	2,336	109	884 R	56.8%	41.2%	58.0%	42.0%
63,839	WASHINGTON	27,024	15,338	10,434	1,252	4,904 R	56.8%	38.6%	59.5%	40.5%
231,365	WAUKESHA	97,622	59,399	34,573	3,650	24,826 R	60.8%	35.4%	63.2%	36.8%
37,780	WAUPACA	15,755	11,040	4,418	297	6,622 R	70.1%	28.0%	71.4%	28.6%
14,795	WAUSHARA	6,739	4,466	2,094	179	2,372 R	66.3%	31.1%	68.1%	31.9%
129,934	WINNEBAGO	51,482	29,488	20,450	1,544	9,038 R	57.3%	39.7%	59.0%	41.0%
65,362	WOOD	26,980	14,806	10,415	1,759	4,391 R	54.9%	38.6%	58.7%	41.3%
4,417,933	TOTAL	1,852,890	989,430	810,174	53,286	179,256 R	53.4%	43.7%	55.0%	45.0%

WISCONSIN

PRESIDENT 1968

1960 Census Population	County	Total Vote	Republican	Democratic	AIP	Other	Plurality	Percentage Rep.	Dem.	AIP
7,566	ADAMS	3,774	1,691	1,614	461	8	77 R	44.8%	42.8%	12.2%
17,375	ASHLAND	7,155	2,557	4,147	401	50	1,590 D	35.7%	58.0%	5.6%
34,270	BARRON	13,589	7,526	5,183	867	13	2,343 R	55.4%	38.1%	6.4%
11,910	BAYFIELD	5,703	2,333	3,036	323	11	703 D	40.9%	53.2%	5.7%
125,082	BROWN	56,165	30,133	21,615	4,341	76	8,518 R	53.7%	38.5%	7.7%
14,202	BUFFALO	5,520	2,992	2,112	413	3	880 R	54.2%	38.3%	7.5%
9,214	BURNETT	4,488	2,056	2,010	414	8	46 R	45.8%	44.8%	9.2%
22,268	CALUMET	10,209	5,792	3,609	792	16	2,183 R	56.7%	35.4%	7.8%
45,096	CHIPPEWA	16,407	7,772	7,335	1,282	18	437 R	47.4%	44.7%	7.8%
31,527	CLARK	12,358	6,325	4,601	1,398	34	1,724 R	51.2%	37.2%	11.3%
36,708	COLUMBIA	16,447	8,633	6,698	1,067	49	1,935 R	52.5%	40.7%	6.5%
16,351	CRAWFORD	6,135	3,316	2,391	419	9	925 R	54.1%	39.0%	6.8%
222,095	DANE	104,904	39,917	59,951	3,771	1,265	20,034 D	38.1%	57.1%	3.6%
63,170	DODGE	25,763	14,909	8,948	1,875	31	5,961 R	57.9%	34.7%	7.3%
20,685	DOOR	8,924	5,647	2,728	535	14	2,919 R	63.3%	30.6%	6.0%
45,008	DOUGLAS	19,131	5,656	12,506	930	39	6,850 D	29.6%	65.4%	4.9%
26,156	DUNN	10,530	5,415	4,392	709	14	1,023 R	51.4%	41.7%	6.7%
58,300	EAU CLAIRE	25,299	11,799	12,302	1,169	29	503 D	46.6%	48.6%	4.6%
3,437	FLORENCE	1,699	821	718	157	3	103 R	48.3%	42.3%	9.2%
75,085	FOND DU LAC	32,743	18,184	12,563	1,934	62	5,621 R	55.5%	38.4%	5.9%
7,542	FOREST	3,149	1,264	1,470	412	3	206 D	40.1%	46.7%	13.1%
44,419	GRANT	17,264	10,789	5,414	1,054	7	5,375 R	62.5%	31.4%	6.1%
25,851	GREEN	10,664	6,502	3,501	641	20	3,001 R	61.0%	32.8%	6.0%
15,418	GREEN LAKE	7,687	4,893	2,299	488	7	2,594 R	63.7%	29.9%	6.3%
19,631	IOWA	7,422	4,005	2,897	509	11	1,108 R	54.0%	39.0%	6.9%
7,830	IRON	3,319	1,137	1,913	262	7	776 D	34.3%	57.6%	7.9%
15,151	JACKSON	6,002	3,172	2,293	529	8	879 R	52.8%	38.2%	8.8%
50,094	JEFFERSON	22,726	12,478	8,716	1,470	62	3,762 R	54.9%	38.4%	6.5%
17,490	JUNEAU	7,148	3,828	2,595	712	13	1,233 R	53.6%	36.3%	10.0%
100,615	KENOSHA	42,158	17,089	21,427	3,548	94	4,338 D	40.5%	50.8%	8.4%
18,282	KEWAUNEE	7,804	4,467	2,622	703	12	1,845 R	57.2%	33.6%	9.0%
72,465	LA CROSSE	31,280	17,433	11,570	2,214	63	5,863 R	55.7%	37.0%	7.1%
18,142	LAFAYETTE	7,425	4,084	2,853	470	18	1,231 R	55.0%	38.4%	6.3%
19,916	LANGLADE	7,513	3,712	3,064	718	19	648 R	49.4%	40.8%	9.6%
22,338	LINCOLN	9,330	4,793	3,858	670	9	935 R	51.4%	41.4%	7.2%
75,215	MANITOWOC	30,680	13,562	15,298	1,790	30	1,736 D	44.2%	49.9%	5.8%
88,874	MARATHON	38,115	16,907	18,063	3,051	94	1,156 D	44.4%	47.4%	8.0%
34,660	MARINETTE	14,797	7,134	6,415	1,223	25	719 R	48.2%	43.4%	8.3%
8,516	MARQUETTE	3,882	2,374	1,228	279	1	1,146 R	61.2%	31.6%	7.2%
2,606	MENOMINEE	740	179	531	30		352 D	24.2%	71.8%	4.1%
1,036,041	MILWAUKEE	402,575	160,022	206,027	35,056	1,470	46,005 D	39.7%	51.2%	8.7%
31,241	MONROE	12,024	6,938	4,012	1,056	18	2,926 R	57.7%	33.4%	8.8%
24,849	OCONTO	10,569	5,680	3,737	1,141	11	1,943 R	53.7%	35.4%	10.8%
22,112	ONEIDA	10,467	5,077	4,435	941	14	642 R	48.5%	42.4%	9.0%
101,794	OUTAGAMIE	42,327	25,080	14,224	2,956	67	10,856 R	59.3%	33.6%	7.0%
38,441	OZAUKEE	20,942	12,155	7,246	1,505	36	4,909 R	58.0%	34.6%	7.2%
7,332	PEPIN	2,989	1,493	1,263	231	2	230 R	49.9%	42.3%	7.7%
22,503	PIERCE	10,240	4,990	4,783	453	14	207 R	48.7%	46.7%	4.4%
24,968	POLK	11,442	5,583	5,179	656	24	404 R	48.8%	45.3%	5.7%
36,964	PORTAGE	17,158	6,180	10,014	900	64	3,834 D	36.0%	58.4%	5.2%
14,370	PRICE	6,528	3,096	2,794	621	17	302 R	47.4%	42.8%	9.5%
141,781	RACINE	62,639	28,028	27,045	7,457	109	983 R	44.7%	43.2%	11.9%
17,684	RICHLAND	6,929	4,141	2,288	485	15	1,853 R	59.8%	33.0%	7.0%
113,913	ROCK	49,551	25,229	20,567	3,655	100	4,662 R	50.9%	41.5%	7.4%
14,794	RUSK	5,963	2,666	2,559	726	12	107 R	44.7%	42.9%	12.2%
29,164	ST. CROIX	14,157	6,595	6,807	735	20	212 D	46.6%	48.1%	5.2%
36,179	SAUK	16,078	8,608	6,406	1,019	45	2,202 R	53.5%	39.8%	6.3%
9,475	SAWYER	4,745	2,475	1,830	435	5	645 R	52.2%	38.6%	9.2%
32,006	SHAWANO	13,245	8,444	3,602	1,181	18	4,842 R	63.8%	27.2%	8.9%
86,484	SHEBOYGAN	39,634	17,764	20,170	1,592	108	2,406 D	44.8%	50.9%	4.0%

WISCONSIN

PRESIDENT 1968

1960 Census Population	County	Total Vote	Republican	Democratic	AIP	Other	Plurality	Percentage Rep.	Dem.	AIP
17,843	TAYLOR	6,923	3,043	2,910	959	11	133 R	44.0%	42.0%	13.9%
23,377	TREMPEALEAU	9,593	4,861	3,971	747	14	890 R	50.7%	41.4%	7.8%
25,663	VERNON	10,560	5,824	3,666	1,062	8	2,158 R	55.2%	34.7%	10.1%
9,332	VILAS	5,748	3,339	1,798	598	13	1,541 R	58.1%	31.3%	10.4%
52,368	WALWORTH	24,328	15,040	7,505	1,755	28	7,535 R	61.8%	30.8%	7.2%
10,301	WASHBURN	5,092	2,425	2,273	384	10	152 R	47.6%	44.6%	7.5%
46,119	WASHINGTON	22,661	12,439	8,104	2,065	53	4,335 R	54.9%	35.8%	9.1%
158,249	WAUKESHA	86,585	47,557	31,947	6,921	160	15,610 R	54.9%	36.9%	8.0%
35,340	WAUPACA	15,807	10,606	3,978	1,206	17	6,628 R	67.1%	25.2%	7.6%
13,497	WAUSHARA	6,407	4,187	1,652	566	2	2,535 R	65.4%	25.8%	8.8%
107,928	WINNEBAGO	47,139	25,361	18,605	3,045	128	6,756 R	53.8%	39.5%	6.5%
59,105	WOOD	24,445	11,795	10,921	1,695	34	874 R	48.3%	44.7%	6.9%
3,951,777	TOTAL	1,691,538	809,997	748,804	127,835	4,902	61,193 R	47.9%	44.3%	7.6%

WISCONSIN

ELECTION NOTES

1984 Other vote was 4,883 Bergland (Libertarian); 3,864 Richards (Constitution); 3,791 LaRouche (Independent); 1,456 Johnson (Citizens); 1,006 Serrette (Independent Alliance); 619 Holmes (Workers World); 596 Hall (Communist); 444 Mason (Socialist Workers); 706 scattered write-in.

1980 Other vote was 160,657 Anderson (Independent); 29,135 Clark (Libertarian); 7,767 Commoner (Citizens); 1,519 Rarick (Constitution); 808 McReynolds (Socialist); 772 Hall (Communist); 414 Griswold (Workers World); 383 DeBerry (Socialist Workers); 1,337 scattered write-in.

1976 Other vote was 34,943 McCarthy (Independent); 8,552 Maddox (American); 4,298 Zeidler (Democratic Socialist); 3,814 MacBride (Libertarian); 1,691 Camejo (Socialist Workers); 943 Wright (People's); 749 Hall (Communist); 738 LaRouche (U.S. Labor); 389 Levin (Socialist Labor); 2,839 scattered write-in.

1972 Other vote was 47,525 Schmitz (American); 2,701 Spock (People's); 998 Fisher (Socialist Labor); 663 Hall (Communist); 506 Reed (Socialist Workers); 893 scattered write-in.

1968 Wallace on the ballot as Independent. Other vote was 1,338 Blomen (Socialist Labor); 1,222 Halstead (Socialist Workers); 2,342 scattered write-in.

WYOMING

POPULAR VOTE FOR PRESIDENT 1920 TO 1984

Year	Total Vote	Republican Vote	Republican Candidate	Democratic Vote	Democratic Candidate	Other Vote	Plurality	Percentage Total Vote Rep.	Percentage Total Vote Dem.	Percentage Major Vote Rep.	Percentage Major Vote Dem.
1984	188,968	133,241	Reagan, Ronald	53,370	Mondale, Walter F.	2,357	79,871 R	70.5%	28.2%	71.4%	28.6%
1980	176,713	110,700	Reagan, Ronald	49,427	Carter, Jimmy	16,586	61,273 R	62.6%	28.0%	69.1%	30.9%
1976	156,343	92,717	Ford, Gerald R.	62,239	Carter, Jimmy	1,387	30,478 R	59.3%	39.8%	59.8%	40.2%
1972	145,570	100,464	Nixon, Richard M.	44,358	McGovern, George S.	748	56,106 R	69.0%	30.5%	69.4%	30.6%
1968	127,205	70,927	Nixon, Richard M.	45,173	Humphrey, Hubert H.	11,105	25,754 R	55.8%	35.5%	61.1%	38.9%
1964	142,716	61,998	Goldwater, Barry M.	80,718	Johnson, Lyndon B.		18,720 D	43.4%	56.6%	43.4%	56.6%
1960	140,782	77,451	Nixon, Richard M.	63,331	Kennedy, John F.		14,120 R	55.0%	45.0%	55.0%	45.0%
1956	124,127	74,573	Eisenhower, Dwight D.	49,554	Stevenson, Adlai E.		25,019 R	60.1%	39.9%	60.1%	39.9%
1952	129,253	81,049	Eisenhower, Dwight D.	47,934	Stevenson, Adlai E.	270	33,115 R	62.7%	37.1%	62.8%	37.2%
1948	101,425	47,947	Dewey, Thomas E.	52,354	Truman, Harry S.	1,124	4,407 D	47.3%	51.6%	47.8%	52.2%
1944	101,340	51,921	Dewey, Thomas E.	49,419	Roosevelt, Franklin D.		2,502 R	51.2%	48.8%	51.2%	48.8%
1940	112,240	52,633	Willkie, Wendell	59,287	Roosevelt, Franklin D.	320	6,654 D	46.9%	52.8%	47.0%	53.0%
1936	103,382	38,739	Landon, Alfred M.	62,624	Roosevelt, Franklin D.	2,019	23,885 D	37.5%	60.6%	38.2%	61.8%
1932	96,962	39,583	Hoover, Herbert C.	54,370	Roosevelt, Franklin D.	3,009	14,787 D	40.8%	56.1%	42.1%	57.9%
1928	82,835	52,748	Hoover, Herbert C.	29,299	Smith, Alfred E.	788	23,449 R	63.7%	35.4%	64.3%	35.7%
1924 **	79,900	41,858	Coolidge, Calvin	12,868	Davis, John W.	25,174	16,684 R	52.4%	16.1%	76.5%	23.5%
1920	56,253	35,091	Harding, Warren G.	17,429	Cox, James M.	3,733	17,662 R	62.4%	31.0%	66.8%	33.2%

In 1924 other vote was Progressive.

ELECTORAL COLLEGE VOTE 1920 TO 1984

Year	Total	Republican	Democratic	Other
1984	3	3	—	—
1980	3	3	—	—
1976	3	3	—	—
1972	3	3	—	—
1968	3	3	—	—
1964	3	—	3	—
1960	3	3	—	—
1956	3	3	—	—
1952	3	3	—	—
1948	3	—	3	—
1944	3	3	—	—
1940	3	—	3	—
1936	3	—	3	—
1932	3	—	3	—
1928	3	3	—	—
1924	3	3	—	—
1920	3	3	—	—

WYOMING

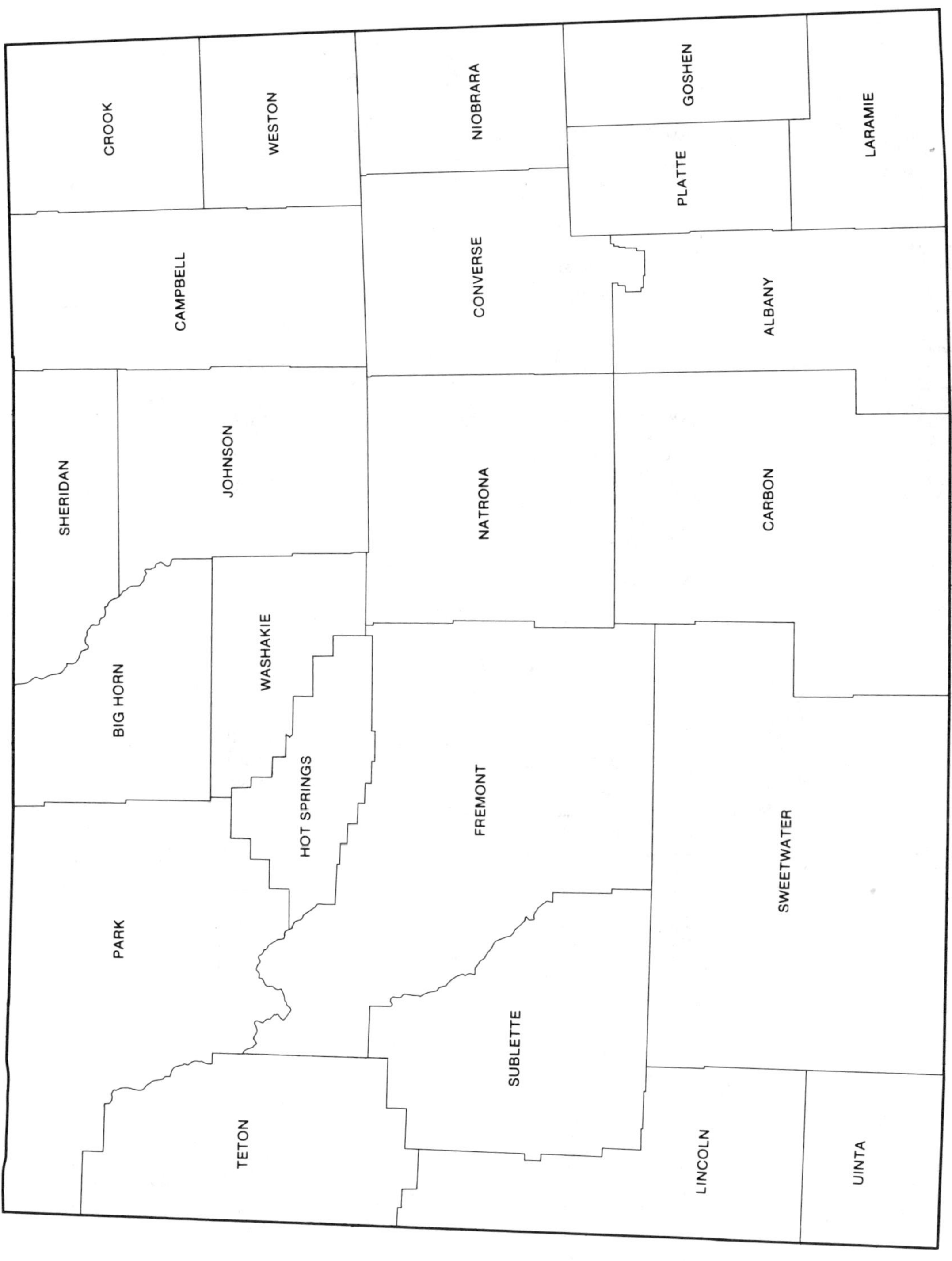
CROOK
WESTON
NIOBRARA
GOSHEN
LARAMIE
PLATTE
CAMPBELL
CONVERSE
ALBANY
SHERIDAN
JOHNSON
NATRONA
CARBON
WASHAKIE
BIG HORN
HOT SPRINGS
FREMONT
SWEETWATER
PARK
SUBLETTE
TETON
LINCOLN
UINTA

WYOMING

PRESIDENT 1984

1980 Census Population	County	Total Vote	Republican	Democratic	Other	Rep.-Dem. Plurality	Percentage Total Vote		Percentage Major Vote	
							Rep.	Dem.	Rep.	Dem.
29,062	ALBANY	12,346	7,452	4,708	186	2,744 R	60.4%	38.1%	61.3%	38.7%
11,896	BIG HORN	5,253	4,019	1,175	59	2,844 R	76.5%	22.4%	77.4%	22.6%
24,367	CAMPBELL	9,995	8,387	1,525	83	6,862 R	83.9%	15.3%	84.6%	15.4%
21,896	CARBON	6,952	4,557	2,295	100	2,262 R	65.5%	33.0%	66.5%	33.5%
14,069	CONVERSE	4,523	3,542	929	52	2,613 R	78.3%	20.5%	79.2%	20.8%
5,308	CROOK	2,754	2,286	450	18	1,836 R	83.0%	16.3%	83.6%	16.4%
38,992	FREMONT	13,999	9,885	3,969	145	5,916 R	70.6%	28.4%	71.4%	28.6%
12,040	GOSHEN	5,184	3,776	1,364	44	2,412 R	72.8%	26.3%	73.5%	26.5%
5,710	HOT SPRINGS	2,646	1,943	672	31	1,271 R	73.4%	25.4%	74.3%	25.7%
6,700	JOHNSON	3,241	2,634	558	49	2,076 R	81.3%	17.2%	82.5%	17.5%
68,649	LARAMIE	29,799	19,348	10,110	341	9,238 R	64.9%	33.9%	65.7%	34.3%
12,177	LINCOLN	4,921	3,854	1,021	46	2,833 R	78.3%	20.7%	79.1%	20.9%
71,856	NATRONA	26,464	18,488	7,598	378	10,890 R	69.9%	28.7%	70.9%	29.1%
2,924	NIOBRARA	1,359	1,098	239	22	859 R	80.8%	17.6%	82.1%	17.9%
21,639	PARK	10,095	7,994	1,965	136	6,029 R	79.2%	19.5%	80.3%	19.7%
11,975	PLATTE	4,120	2,813	1,232	75	1,581 R	68.3%	29.9%	69.5%	30.5%
25,048	SHERIDAN	11,279	7,460	3,648	171	3,812 R	66.1%	32.3%	67.2%	32.8%
4,548	SUBLETTE	2,396	1,976	389	31	1,587 R	82.5%	16.2%	83.6%	16.4%
41,723	SWEETWATER	13,712	8,308	5,230	174	3,078 R	60.6%	38.1%	61.4%	38.6%
9,355	TETON	5,139	3,487	1,565	87	1,922 R	67.9%	30.5%	69.0%	31.0%
13,021	UINTA	5,411	4,075	1,276	60	2,799 R	75.3%	23.6%	76.2%	23.8%
9,496	WASHAKIE	4,253	3,245	970	38	2,275 R	76.3%	22.8%	77.0%	23.0%
7,106	WESTON	3,127	2,614	482	31	2,132 R	83.6%	15.4%	84.4%	15.6%
469,557	TOTAL	188,968	133,241	53,370	2,357	79,871 R	70.5%	28.2%	71.4%	28.6%

WYOMING

PRESIDENT 1980

1980 Census Population	County	Total Vote	Republican	Democratic	Other	Rep.-Dem. Plurality	Percentage Total Vote		Percentage Major Vote	
							Rep.	Dem.	Rep.	Dem.
29,062	ALBANY	11,527	5,830	3,772	1,925	2,058 R	50.6%	32.7%	60.7%	39.3%
11,896	BIG HORN	5,223	3,709	1,212	302	2,497 R	71.0%	23.2%	75.4%	24.6%
24,367	CAMPBELL	7,669	5,613	1,400	656	4,213 R	73.2%	18.3%	80.0%	20.0%
21,896	CARBON	7,283	4,337	2,272	674	2,065 R	59.5%	31.2%	65.6%	34.4%
14,069	CONVERSE	4,229	2,987	922	320	2,065 R	70.6%	21.8%	76.4%	23.6%
5,308	CROOK	2,416	1,909	413	94	1,496 R	79.0%	17.1%	82.2%	17.8%
38,992	FREEMONT	13,403	9,077	3,307	1,019	5,770 R	67.7%	24.7%	73.3%	26.7%
12,040	GOSHEN	5,315	3,572	1,373	370	2,199 R	67.2%	25.8%	72.2%	27.8%
5,710	HOT SPRINGS	2,555	1,602	745	208	857 R	62.7%	29.2%	68.3%	31.7%
6,700	JOHNSON	3,148	2,291	635	222	1,656 R	72.8%	20.2%	78.3%	21.7%
68,649	LARAMIE	27,713	15,361	9,512	2,840	5,849 R	55.4%	34.3%	61.8%	38.2%
12,177	LINCOLN	4,694	3,412	1,063	219	2,349 R	72.7%	22.6%	76.2%	23.8%
71,856	NATRONA	26,672	16,801	7,111	2,760	9,690 R	63.0%	26.7%	70.3%	29.7%
2,924	NIOBRARA	1,412	1,075	270	67	805 R	76.1%	19.1%	79.9%	20.1%
21,639	PARK	8,811	6,435	1,718	658	4,717 R	73.0%	19.5%	78.9%	21.1%
11,975	PLATTE	4,618	2,642	1,555	421	1,087 R	57.2%	33.7%	62.9%	37.1%
25,048	SHERIDAN	9,646	5,649	3,034	963	2,615 R	58.6%	31.5%	65.1%	34.9%
4,548	SUBLETTE	2,082	1,538	357	187	1,181 R	73.9%	17.1%	81.2%	18.8%
41,723	SWEETWATER	12,067	6,265	4,728	1,074	1,537 R	51.9%	39.2%	57.0%	43.0%
9,355	TETON	5,212	3,004	1,361	847	1,643 R	57.6%	26.1%	68.8%	31.2%
13,021	UINTA	4,151	2,738	1,138	275	1,600 R	66.0%	27.4%	70.6%	29.4%
9,496	WASHAKIE	3,897	2,634	945	318	1,689 R	67.6%	24.2%	73.6%	26.4%
7,106	WESTON	2,970	2,219	584	167	1,635 R	74.7%	19.7%	79.2%	20.8%
469,557	TOTAL	176,713	110,700	49,427	16,586	61,273 R	62.6%	28.0%	69.1%	30.9%

WYOMING

PRESIDENT 1976

1970 Census Population	County	Total Vote	Republican	Democratic	Other	Rep.-Dem. Plurality	Percentage Total Vote Rep.	Percentage Total Vote Dem.	Percentage Major Vote Rep.	Percentage Major Vote Dem.
26,431	ALBANY	11,622	6,734	4,663	225	2,071 R	57.9%	40.1%	59.1%	40.9%
10,202	BIG HORN	4,747	3,117	1,618	12	1,499 R	65.7%	34.1%	65.8%	34.2%
12,957	CAMPBELL	4,995	3,306	1,620	69	1,686 R	66.2%	32.4%	67.1%	32.9%
13,354	CARBON	6,584	3,556	3,010	18	546 R	54.0%	45.7%	54.2%	45.8%
5,938	CONVERSE	3,347	2,188	1,150	9	1,038 R	65.4%	34.4%	65.5%	34.5%
4,535	CROOK	2,139	1,438	653	48	785 R	67.2%	30.5%	68.8%	31.2%
28,352	FREEMONT	11,063	6,584	4,423	56	2,161 R	59.5%	40.0%	59.8%	40.2%
10,885	GOSHEN	5,038	2,764	2,262	12	502 R	54.9%	44.9%	55.0%	45.0%
4,952	HOT SPRINGS	2,379	1,413	958	8	455 R	59.4%	40.3%	59.6%	40.4%
5,587	JOHNSON	2,866	2,042	797	27	1,245 R	71.2%	27.8%	71.9%	28.1%
56,360	LARAMIE	26,294	14,061	12,040	193	2,021 R	53.5%	45.8%	53.9%	46.1%
8,640	LINCOLN	4,044	2,464	1,555	25	909 R	60.9%	38.5%	61.3%	38.7%
51,264	NATRONA	22,621	13,761	8,640	220	5,121 R	60.8%	38.2%	61.4%	38.6%
2,924	NIOBRARA	1,477	1,042	427	8	615 R	70.5%	28.9%	70.9%	29.1%
17,752	PARK	8,602	5,878	2,656	68	3,222 R	68.3%	30.9%	68.9%	31.1%
6,486	PLATTE	3,450	1,844	1,593	13	251 R	53.4%	46.2%	53.7%	46.3%
17,852	SHERIDAN	8,652	5,382	3,206	64	2,176 R	62.2%	37.1%	62.7%	37.3%
3,755	SUBLETTE	1,826	1,284	528	14	756 R	70.3%	28.9%	70.9%	29.1%
18,391	SWEETWATER	10,574	4,937	5,575	62	638 D	46.7%	52.7%	47.0%	53.0%
4,823	TETON	3,957	2,667	1,204	86	1,463 R	67.4%	30.4%	68.9%	31.1%
7,100	UINTA	3,811	2,124	1,559	128	565 R	55.7%	40.9%	57.7%	42.3%
7,569	WASHAKIE	3,541	2,361	1,168	12	1,193 R	66.7%	33.0%	66.9%	33.1%
6,307	WESTON	2,714	1,770	934	10	836 R	65.2%	34.4%	65.5%	34.5%
332,416	TOTAL	156,343	92,717	62,239	1,387	30,478 R	59.3%	39.8%	59.8%	40.2%

WYOMING

PRESIDENT 1972

1970 Census Population	County	Total Vote	Republican	Democratic	Other	Rep.-Dem. Plurality	Percentage Total Vote Rep.	Percentage Total Vote Dem.	Percentage Major Vote Rep.	Percentage Major Vote Dem.
26,431	ALBANY	11,917	7,021	4,873	23	2,148 R	58.9%	40.9%	59.0%	41.0%
10,202	BIG HORN	4,300	3,244	1,049	7	2,195 R	75.4%	24.4%	75.6%	24.4%
12,957	CAMPBELL	3,755	2,953	783	19	2,170 R	78.6%	20.9%	79.0%	21.0%
13,354	CARBON	6,339	4,037	2,292	10	1,745 R	63.7%	36.2%	63.8%	36.2%
5,938	CONVERSE	3,000	2,312	682	6	1,630 R	77.1%	22.7%	77.2%	22.8%
4,535	CROOK	2,110	1,760	339	11	1,421 R	83.4%	16.1%	83.8%	16.2%
28,352	FREEMONT	10,647	7,359	3,248	40	4,111 R	69.1%	30.5%	69.4%	30.6%
10,885	GOSHEN	5,164	3,629	1,515	20	2,114 R	70.3%	29.3%	70.5%	29.5%
4,952	HOT SPRINGS	2,367	1,678	689		989 R	70.9%	29.1%	70.9%	29.1%
5,587	JOHNSON	2,650	2,203	436	11	1,767 R	83.1%	16.5%	83.5%	16.5%
56,360	LARAMIE	22,855	15,010	7,791	54	7,219 R	65.7%	34.1%	65.8%	34.2%
8,640	LINCOLN	3,666	2,459	969	238	1,490 R	67.1%	26.4%	71.7%	28.3%
51,264	NATRONA	22,200	15,649	6,514	37	9,135 R	70.5%	29.3%	70.6%	29.4%
2,924	NIOBRARA	1,537	1,245	289	3	956 R	81.0%	18.8%	81.2%	18.8%
17,752	PARK	7,875	5,890	1,950	35	3,940 R	74.8%	24.8%	75.1%	24.9%
6,486	PLATTE	3,127	2,200	925	2	1,275 R	70.4%	29.6%	70.4%	29.6%
17,852	SHERIDAN	9,318	6,432	2,874	12	3,558 R	69.0%	30.8%	69.1%	30.9%
3,755	SUBLETTE	1,653	1,348	304	1	1,044 R	81.5%	18.4%	81.6%	18.4%
18,391	SWEETWATER	8,915	5,175	3,713	27	1,462 R	58.0%	41.6%	58.2%	41.8%
4,823	TETON	3,116	2,182	810	124	1,372 R	70.0%	26.0%	72.9%	27.1%
7,100	UINTA	3,000	2,011	968	21	1,043 R	67.0%	32.3%	67.5%	32.5%
7,569	WASHAKIE	3,430	2,604	825	1	1,779 R	75.9%	24.1%	75.9%	24.1%
6,307	WESTON	2,629	2,063	520	46	1,543 R	78.5%	19.8%	79.9%	20.1%
332,416	TOTAL	145,570	100,464	44,358	748	56,106 R	69.0%	30.5%	69.4%	30.6%

WYOMING

PRESIDENT 1968

1960 Census Population	County	Total Vote	Republican	Democratic	AIP	Other	Plurality	Percentage Rep.	Dem.	AIP
21,290	ALBANY	9,079	4,422	4,079	578		343 R	48.7%	44.9%	6.4%
11,898	BIG HORN	4,325	2,771	1,201	353		1,570 R	64.1%	27.8%	8.2%
5,861	CAMPBELL	2,541	1,694	558	289		1,136 R	66.7%	22.0%	11.4%
14,937	CARBON	5,656	2,532	2,725	399		193 D	44.8%	48.2%	7.1%
6,366	CONVERSE	2,382	1,658	492	232		1,166 R	69.6%	20.7%	9.7%
4,691	CROOK	1,733	1,240	318	175		922 R	71.6%	18.3%	10.1%
26,168	FREEMONT	9,398	5,417	3,093	888		2,324 R	57.6%	32.9%	9.4%
11,941	GOSHEN	4,716	2,719	1,529	468		1,190 R	57.7%	32.4%	9.9%
6,365	HOT SPRINGS	2,144	1,273	705	166		568 R	59.4%	32.9%	7.7%
5,475	JOHNSON	2,352	1,737	398	217		1,339 R	73.9%	16.9%	9.2%
60,149	LARAMIE	20,992	9,824	9,519	1,649		305 R	46.8%	45.3%	7.9%
9,018	LINCOLN	3,561	2,030	1,246	285		784 R	57.0%	35.0%	8.0%
49,623	NATRONA	18,674	10,679	5,900	2,095		4,779 R	57.2%	31.6%	11.2%
3,750	NIOBRARA	1,490	1,136	250	104		886 R	76.2%	16.8%	7.0%
16,874	PARK	7,134	4,677	1,852	605		2,825 R	65.6%	26.0%	8.5%
7,195	PLATTE	2,967	1,613	1,035	319		578 R	54.4%	34.9%	10.8%
18,989	SHERIDAN	8,434	5,163	2,659	612		2,504 R	61.2%	31.5%	7.3%
3,778	SUBLETTE	1,688	1,152	310	226		842 R	68.2%	18.4%	13.4%
17,920	SWEETWATER	7,449	2,726	4,086	637		1,360 D	36.6%	54.9%	8.6%
3,062	TETON	2,049	1,419	461	169		958 R	69.3%	22.5%	8.2%
7,484	UINTA	2,884	1,510	1,199	175		311 R	52.4%	41.6%	6.1%
8,883	WASHAKIE	3,184	2,038	948	198		1,090 R	64.0%	29.8%	6.2%
7,929	WESTON	2,373	1,497	610	266		887 R	63.1%	25.7%	11.2%
330,066	TOTAL	127,205	70,927	45,173	11,105		25,754 R	55.8%	35.5%	8.7%

WYOMING

ELECTION NOTES

1984 Other vote was Bergland (Libertarian).

1980 Other vote was 12,072 Anderson (Independent); 4,514 Clark (Independent).

1976 Other vote was 624 McCarthy (write-in); 290 Anderson (write-in); 89 MacBride (write-in); 30 Maddox (write-in); 354 scattered write-in.

1972 Other vote was Schmitz (write-in).

1968 Wallace on the ballot as Independent.

DISTRICT OF COLUMBIA

POPULAR VOTE FOR PRESIDENT 1964 TO 1984

Year	Total Vote	Republican Vote	Republican Candidate	Democratic Vote	Democratic Candidate	Other Vote	Plurality	Percentage Total Vote Rep.	Percentage Total Vote Dem.	Percentage Major Vote Rep.	Percentage Major Vote Dem.
1984	211,288	29,009	Reagan, Ronald	180,408	Mondale, Walter F.	1,871	151,399 D	13.7%	85.4%	13.9%	86.1%
1980	175,237	23,545	Reagan, Ronald	131,113	Carter, Jimmy	20,579	107,568 D	13.4%	74.8%	15.2%	84.8%
1976	168,830	27,873	Ford, Gerald R.	137,818	Carter, Jimmy	3,139	109,945 D	16.5%	81.6%	16.8%	83.2%
1972	163,421	35,226	Nixon, Richard M.	127,627	McGovern, George S.	568	92,401 D	21.6%	78.1%	21.6%	78.4%
1968	170,578	31,012	Nixon, Richard M.	139,566	Humphrey, Hubert H.		108,554 D	18.2%	81.8%	18.2%	81.8%
1964	198,597	28,801	Goldwater, Barry M.	169,796	Johnson, Lyndon B.		140,995 D	14.5%	85.5%	14.5%	85.5%

Under the 23rd Amendment to the Constitution, the District of Columbia became entitled to choose Electors beginning with the 1964 election.

ELECTORAL COLLEGE VOTE 1964 TO 1984

Year	Total	Republican	Democratic	Other
1984	3	—	3	—
1980	3	—	3	—
1976	3	—	3	—
1972	3	—	3	—
1968	3	—	3	—
1964	3	—	3	—

DISTRICT OF COLUMBIA

1984

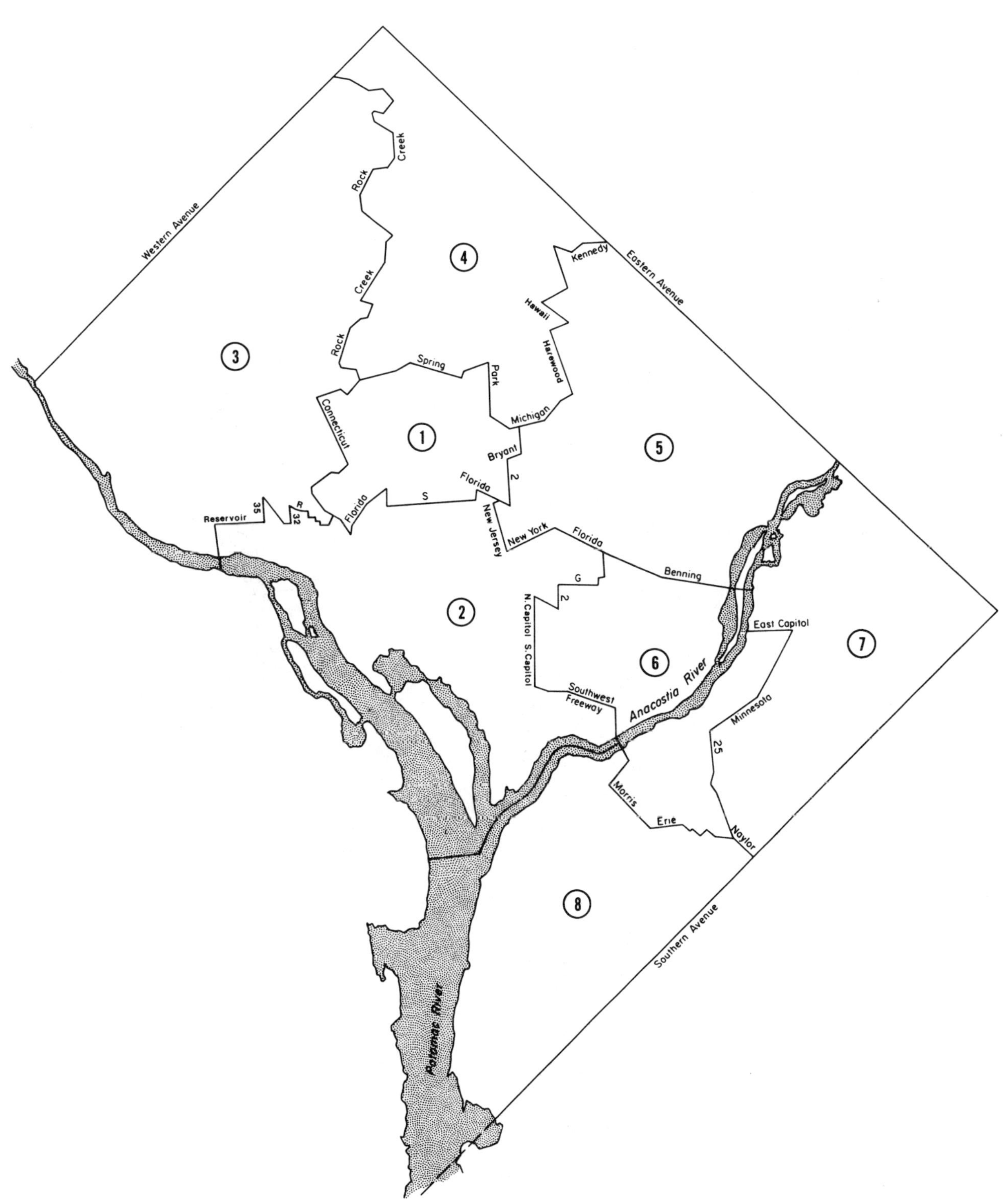

DISTRICT OF COLUMBIA

1972-1976-1980

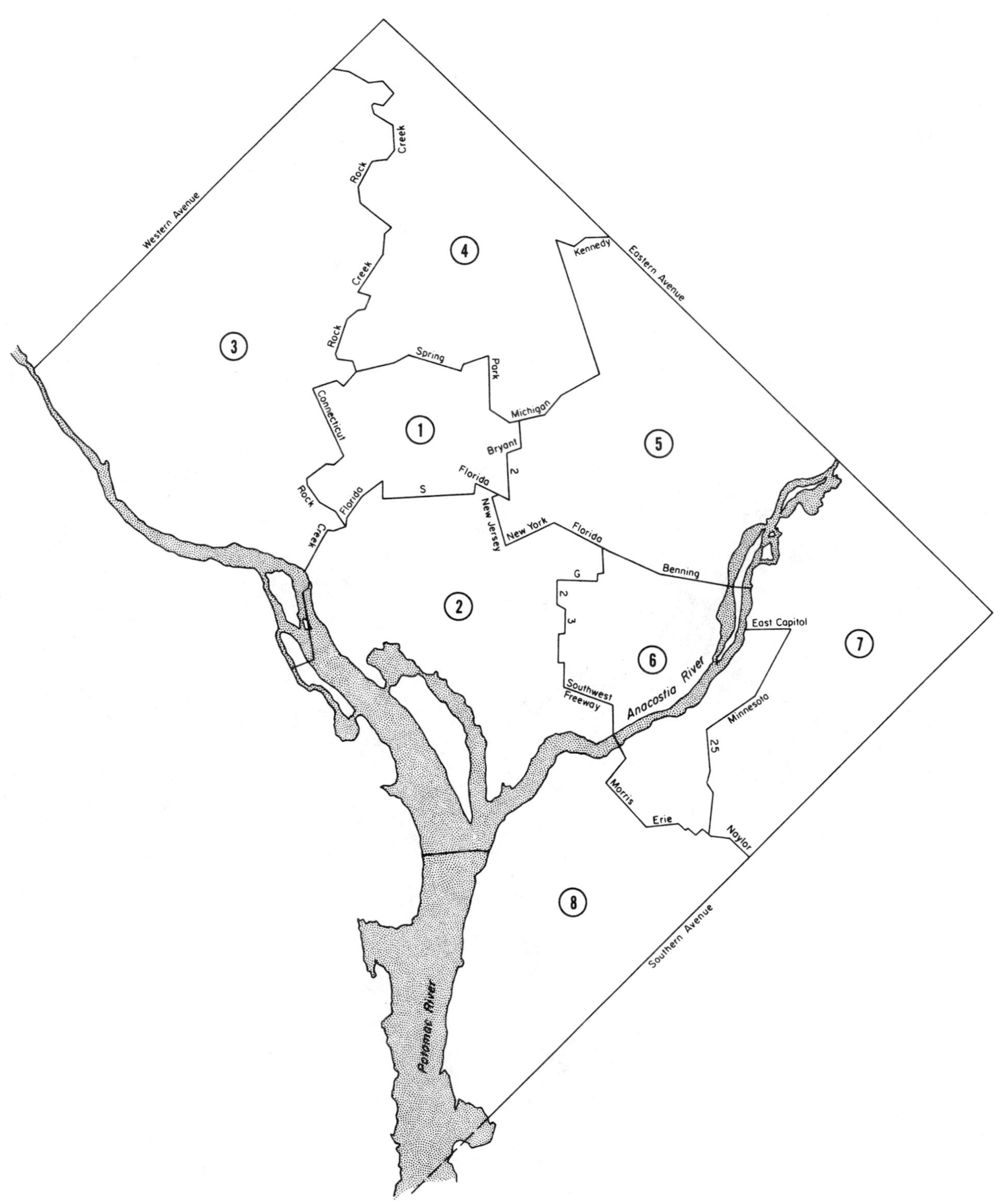

DISTRICT OF COLUMBIA

1968

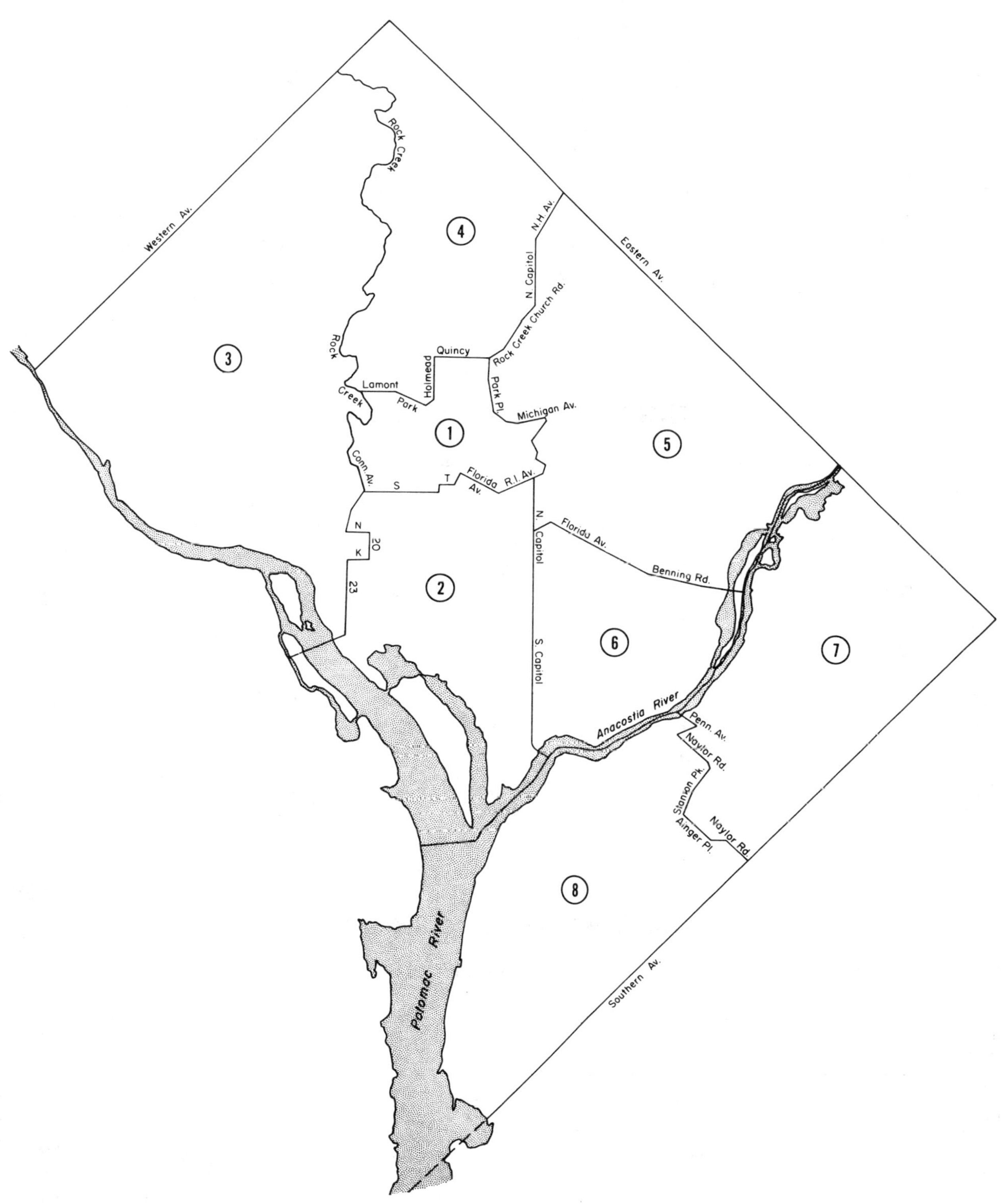

DISTRICT OF COLUMBIA

PRESIDENT 1984

1980 Census Population	Ward	Total Vote	Republican	Democratic	Other	Rep.-Dem. Plurality	Percentage Total Vote Rep.	Percentage Total Vote Dem.	Percentage Major Vote Rep.	Percentage Major Vote Dem.
78,700	WARD 1	23,501	2,550	20,638	313	18,088 D	10.9%	87.8%	11.0%	89.0%
81,400	WARD 2	25,393	5,435	19,677	281	14,242 D	21.4%	77.5%	21.6%	78.4%
77,800	WARD 3	35,047	12,496	22,234	317	9,738 D	35.7%	63.4%	36.0%	64.0%
81,900	WARD 4	32,084	2,264	29,551	269	27,287 D	7.1%	92.1%	7.1%	92.9%
82,600	WARD 5	28,112	1,523	26,394	195	24,871 D	5.4%	93.9%	5.5%	94.5%
75,700	WARD 6	25,239	2,589	22,415	235	19,826 D	10.3%	88.8%	10.4%	89.6%
82,400	WARD 7	25,195	1,303	23,734	158	22,431 D	5.2%	94.2%	5.2%	94.8%
77,900	WARD 8	16,101	628	15,377	96	14,749 D	3.9%	95.5%	3.9%	96.1%
	SPECIAL BALLOTS	616	221	388	7	167 D	35.9%	63.0%	36.3%	63.7%
638,400	TOTAL	211,288	29,009	180,408	1,871	151,399 D	13.7%	85.4%	13.9%	86.1%

DISTRICT OF COLUMBIA

PRESIDENT 1980

1980 Census Population	Ward	Total Vote	Republican	Democratic	Other	Rep.-Dem. Plurality	Percentage Total Vote Rep.	Percentage Total Vote Dem.	Percentage Major Vote Rep.	Percentage Major Vote Dem.
77,400	WARD 1	18,804	1,870	14,060	2,874	12,190 D	9.9%	74.8%	11.7%	88.3%
72,700	WARD 2	20,194	3,409	13,156	3,629	9,747 D	16.9%	65.1%	20.6%	79.4%
88,300	WARD 3	35,759	12,654	15,258	7,847	2,604 D	35.4%	42.7%	45.3%	54.7%
82,900	WARD 4	27,273	1,734	23,993	1,546	22,259 D	6.4%	88.0%	6.7%	93.3%
81,700	WARD 5	22,562	1,040	20,497	1,025	19,457 D	4.6%	90.8%	4.8%	95.2%
73,400	WARD 6	19,064	1,550	15,022	2,492	13,472 D	8.1%	78.8%	9.4%	90.6%
83,400	WARD 7	20,857	935	19,138	784	18,203 D	4.5%	91.8%	4.7%	95.3%
77,900	WARD 8	10,622	336	9,918	368	9,582 D	3.2%	93.4%	3.3%	96.7%
	SPECIAL BALLOTS	102	17	71	14	54 D	16.7%	69.6%	19.3%	80.7%
637,700	TOTAL	175,237	23,545	131,113	20,579	107,568 D	13.4%	74.8%	15.2%	84.8%

DISTRICT OF COLUMBIA

PRESIDENT 1976

1970 Census Population	Ward	Total Vote	Republican	Democratic	Other	Rep.-Dem. Plurality	Percentage Total Vote Rep.	Percentage Total Vote Dem.	Percentage Major Vote Rep.	Percentage Major Vote Dem.
94,215	WARD 1	16,577	2,064	13,982	531	11,918 D	12.5%	84.3%	12.9%	87.1%
94,076	WARD 2	19,245	4,019	14,638	588	10,619 D	20.9%	76.1%	21.5%	78.5%
94,719	WARD 3	35,729	15,184	19,583	962	4,399 D	42.5%	54.8%	43.7%	56.3%
94,193	WARD 4	26,785	2,064	24,432	289	22,368 D	7.7%	91.2%	7.8%	92.2%
94,679	WARD 5	21,503	1,365	19,932	206	18,567 D	6.3%	92.7%	6.4%	93.6%
95,192	WARD 6	16,947	1,575	15,032	340	13,457 D	9.3%	88.7%	9.5%	90.5%
95,019	WARD 7	20,641	1,136	19,372	133	18,236 D	5.5%	93.9%	5.5%	94.5%
94,417	WARD 8	11,403	466	10,847	90	10,381 D	4.1%	95.1%	4.1%	95.9%
756,510	TOTAL	168,830	27,873	137,818	3,139	109,945 D	16.5%	81.6%	16.8%	83.2%

DISTRICT OF COLUMBIA

PRESIDENT 1972

1970 Census Population	Ward	Total Vote	Republican	Democratic	Other	Rep.-Dem. Plurality	Percentage Total Vote Rep.	Total Vote Dem.	Major Vote Rep.	Major Vote Dem.
94,215	WARD 1	16,944	2,994	13,860	90	10,866 D	17.7%	81.8%	17.8%	82.2%
94,076	WARD 2	19,080	4,985	13,999	96	9,014 D	26.1%	73.4%	26.3%	73.7%
94,719	WARD 3	36,994	18,269	18,608	117	339 D	49.4%	50.3%	49.5%	50.5%
94,193	WARD 4	25,547	3,106	22,366	75	19,260 D	12.2%	87.5%	12.2%	87.8%
94,679	WARD 5	19,392	1,830	17,507	55	15,677 D	9.4%	90.3%	9.5%	90.5%
95,192	WARD 6	16,020	1,686	14,278	56	12,592 D	10.5%	89.1%	10.6%	89.4%
95,019	WARD 7	18,418	1,641	16,730	47	15,089 D	8.9%	90.8%	8.9%	91.1%
94,417	WARD 8	11,026	715	10,279	32	9,564 D	6.5%	93.2%	6.5%	93.5%
756,510	TOTAL	163,421	35,226	127,627	568	92,401 D	21.6%	78.1%	21.6%	78.4%

DISTRICT OF COLUMBIA

PRESIDENT 1968

1960 Census Population	Ward	Total Vote	Republican	Democratic	AIP	Other	Plurality	Percentage Rep.	Dem.	AIP
	WARD 1	14,563	1,692	12,871			11,179 D	11.6%	88.4%	
	WARD 2	13,604	3,031	10,573			7,542 D	22.3%	77.7%	
	WARD 3	37,151	17,169	19,982			2,813 D	46.2%	53.8%	
	WARD 4	26,082	2,568	23,514			20,946 D	9.8%	90.2%	
	WARD 5	22,489	1,209	21,280			20,071 D	5.4%	94.6%	
	WARD 6	14,046	1,217	12,829			11,612 D	8.7%	91.3%	
	WARD 7	21,997	1,626	20,371			18,745 D	7.4%	92.6%	
	WARD 8	15,187	995	14,192			13,197 D	6.6%	93.4%	
	SPECIAL BALLOTS	5,459	1,505	3,954			2,449 D	27.6%	72.4%	
763,956	TOTAL	170,578	31,012	139,566			108,554 D	18.2%	81.8%	

DISTRICT OF COLUMBIA

Data for the District of Columbia are carried by wards. Included are three ward maps, with election years noted, so the user can relate data to geography. Population by wards is not available for the 1968 election and the population by wards given with the 1980 and 1984 elections data is from the Office of Planning and Development of the District of Columbia and represents rounded-off figures.

ELECTION NOTES

1984 Other vote was 279 Bergland (Libertarian); 257 Hall (Communist); 165 Serrette (Independent); 127 LaRouche (Independent); 127 Mason (Socialist Workers); 107 Holmes (Workers World); 809 scattered write-in. Special ballots listed in the table are those classed by the District election authorities as Federal Voters.

1980 Other vote was 16,337 Anderson (Independent); 1,840 Commoner (Citizens); 1,114 Clark (Libertarian); 371 Hall (Communist); 173 DeBerry (Socialist Workers); 52 Griswold (Workers World); 692 scattered write-in. Early unamended canvass gave the vote as 23,313 Republican; 130,231 Democratic; 16,131 Anderson (Independent); 1,826 Citizens; 1,104 Libertarian; 369 Communist; 690 scattered write-in. Special ballots listed in the table are those classed by District election authorities as Federal Voters.

1976 Other vote was 545 Camejo (Socialist Workers); 274 MacBride (Libertarian); 219 Hall (Communist); 157 LaRouche (U.S. Labor); 1,944 scattered write-in.

1972 Other vote was 316 Reed (Socialist Workers); 252 Hall (Communist).

1968

1984 PRESIDENTIAL PRIMARIES

In 1984 twenty-nine states and the District of Columbia held Presidential primaries though there was no Republican voting in Alabama, Connecticut, New York, North Carolina and South Dakota, and no Democratic voting in Texas.

In some jurisdictions balloting was for delegate groups linked to specific Presidential candidates, in others electors indicated only a personal preference as to their party's nominee. The votes listed in California for the Democratic primary are the sum of the highest delegate vote for each candidate in each of the state's forty-five Congressional Districts.

The tables included here give the major party primary vote in each state for those candidates who polled at least 100,000 votes. An asterisk in the table indicates votes written-in for a candidate not on the ballot.

Republican candidates on the ballot in at least one state were Gary R. Arnold, Benjamin Fernandez, David M. Kelley, Ronald Reagan, Harold E. Stassen.

Democratic candidates on the ballot in at least one state were Reubin Askew, Hugh G. Bagley, Martin J. Beckman, Bob Brewster, Walter R. Buchanan, Raymond J. Caplette, Roy J. Clendenan, Alan Cranston, John H. Glenn, Robert K. Griser, Gary W. Hart, Ernest F. Hollings, Jesse L. Jackson, Richard B. Kay, William King, Claude R. Kirk, Stephen A. Koczak, William P. Kreml, Lyndon H. LaRouche, George S. McGovern, Walter F. Mondale, Edward T. O'Donnell, Chester M. Rudnicki, Cyril E. Sagan, Alfred Timinski, Betty J. Williams, Gerald Willis.

ALABAMA MARCH 13

Republican No Presidential primary held.

Democratic 148,165 Mondale; 89,286 Glenn; 88,465 Hart; 83,787 Jackson; 6,153 Willis; 4,759 Hollings; 4,464 Uncommitted; 1,827 Askew; 1,377 Cranston.

CALIFORNIA JUNE 5

Republican 1,874,897 Reagan; 78 scattered.

Democratic 1,155,499 Hart; 1,049,342 Mondale; 546,693 Jackson; 96,770 Glenn; 69,926 McGovern; 52,647 LaRouche; 26 scattered.

American Independent 7,374 Charles R. Glenn; 3,567 Lowery; 3,052 Mohr; 2,507 Willis; 4 scattered.

Peace & Freedom 3,171 Johnson; 1,160 Condit; 731 Serrette; 651 Holmes; 2 scattered.

Libertarian 34 scattered.

CONNECTICUT MARCH 27

Republican No Presidential primary held.

Democratic 116,286 Hart; 64,230 Mondale; 26,395 Jackson; 6,098 Askew; 2,426 McGovern; 2,283 Hollings; 1,973 Uncommitted; 955 Glenn; 196 Cranston.

1984 PRESIDENTIAL PRIMARIES

FLORIDA MARCH 13

Republican 344,150 Reagan.

Democratic 463,799 Hart; 394,350 Mondale; 144,263 Jackson; 128,209 Glenn; 26,258 Askew; 17,614 McGovern; 3,115 Hollings; 2,097 Cranston; 1,328 Kay; 1,157 Koczak.

GEORGIA MARCH 13

Republican 50,793 Reagan.

Democratic 208,588 Mondale; 186,903 Hart; 143,730 Jackson; 122,744 Glenn; 11,321 McGovern; 3,800 Hollings; 3,068 Uncommitted; 1,804 Willis; 1,660 Askew; 923 Cranston.

IDAHO MAY 22

Republican 97,450 Reagan; 8,237 "None of the Names Shown".

Democratic 31,737 Hart; 16,460 Mondale; 3,104 Jackson; 2,225 "None of the Names Shown"; 1,196 LaRouche.

ILLINOIS MARCH 20

Republican 594,742 Reagan; 336 scattered.

Democratic 670,951 Mondale; 584,579 Hart; 348,843 Jackson; 25,336 McGovern; 19,800 Glenn; 4,797 Williams; 2,786 Cranston; 2,182 Askew; 151 scattered.

INDIANA MAY 8

Republican 428,559 Reagan.

Democratic 299,491 Hart; 293,413 Mondale; 98,190 Jackson; 16,046 Glenn; 9,815 Brewster.

LOUISIANA MAY 5

Republican 14,964 Reagan; 1,723 Uncommitted.

Democratic 136,707 Jackson; 79,593 Hart; 71,162 Mondale; 19,409 Uncommitted; 4,970 LaRouche; 3,158 McGovern; 1,924 Griser; 1,344 Kay; 543 Koczak.

MARYLAND MAY 8

Republican 73,663 Reagan.

Democratic 215,222 Mondale; 129,387 Jackson; 123,365 Hart; 15,807 Uncommitted; 7,836 LaRouche; 5,796 McGovern; 6,238 Glenn; 1,768 Cranston; 1,467 Hollings.

MASSACHUSETTS MARCH 13

Republican 58,996 Reagan; 5,005 No Preference; 1,936 scattered.

Democratic 245,943 Hart; 160,893 Mondale; 134,341 McGovern; 45,456 Glenn; 31,824 Jackson; 5,080 No Preference; 1,394 Askew; 1,203 Hollings; 853 Cranston; 3,975 scattered.

1984 PRESIDENTIAL PRIMARIES

MONTANA JUNE 5

Republican 66,432 Reagan; 5,378 No Preference; 77 scattered.

Democratic 28,385 No Preference; 3,080 Hart (write-in); 2,026 Mondale (write-in); 388 Jackson (write-in); 335 scattered.

NEBRASKA MAY 15

Republican 145,245 Reagan; 1,403 scattered.

Democratic 86,582 Hart; 39,635 Mondale; 13,495 Jackson; 4,631 Uncommitted; 1,561 McGovern; 1,227 LaRouche; 538 Cranston; 450 Hollings; 736 scattered.

NEW HAMPSHIRE FEBRUARY 28

Republican 65,033 Reagan; 1,543 Stassen; 360 Kelley; 252 Arnold; 202 Fernandez; 8,180 scattered.

Democratic 37,702 Hart; 28,173 Mondale; 12,088 Glenn; 5,311 Jackson; 5,217 McGovern; 3,583 Hollings; 2,136 Cranston; 1,025 Askew; 155 Koczak; 132 Buchanan; 127 Beckman; 74 O'Donnell; 50 Willis; 34 King; 27 Kay; 25 Kreml; 24 Bagley; 24 Kirk; 21 Rudnicki; 20 Clendenan; 20 Sagan; 19 Caplette; 5,144 scattered.

NEW JERSEY JUNE 5

Republican 240,054 Reagan.

Democratic 305,516 Mondale; 200,948 Hart; 159,788 Jackson; 10,309 LaRouche.

NEW MEXICO JUNE 5

Republican 40,805 Reagan; 2,189 Uncommitted.

Democratic 87,610 Hart; 67,675 Mondale; 22,168 Jackson; 5,143 McGovern; 3,330 LaRouche; 1,477 Uncommitted.

NEW YORK APRIL 3

Republican No Presidential primary held.

Democratic 621,581 Mondale; 380,564 Hart; 355.541 Jackson; 15,941 Glenn; 6,815 Cranston; 4,547 McGovern; 2,877 Askew; 84scattered.

NORTH CAROLINA MAY 8

Republican No Presidential primary held.

Democratic 342,324 Mondale; 289,877 Hart; 243,945 Jackson; 44,232 No Preference; 17,659 Glenn; 10,149 McGovern; 8,318 Hollings; 3,144 Askew; 1,209 Cranston.

1984 PRESIDENTIAL PRIMARIES

NORTH DAKOTA JUNE 12

Republican 44,109 Reagan.

Democratic 28,603 Hart; 4,018 LaRouche; 934 Mondale (write-in).

OHIO MAY 8

Republican 658,169 Reagan.

Democratic 608,528 Hart; 583,595 Mondale; 237,133 Jackson; 8,991 McGovern; 4,653 Cranston; 4,336 LaRouche.

OREGON MAY 15

Republican 238,594 Reagan; 4,752 scattered.

Democratic 233,638 Hart; 110,374 Mondale; 37,106 Jackson; 10,831 Glenn; 5,943 LaRouche; 1,787 scattered.

PENNSYLVANIA APRIL 10

Republican 616,916 Reagan; 4,290 scattered.

Democratic 747,267 Mondale; 551,335 Hart; 264,463 Jackson; 22,829 Cranston; 22,605 Glenn; 19,180 LaRouche; 13,139 McGovern; 6,090 Griser; 5,071 Askew; 2,972 Hollings; 1,343 scattered.

RHODE ISLAND MARCH 13

Republican 2,028 Reagan; 207 Uncommitted.

Democratic 20,011 Hart; 15,338 Mondale; 3,875 Jackson; 2,249 Glenn; 2,146 McGovern; 439 Uncommitted; 273 Cranston; 96 Askew; 84 Hollings.

SOUTH DAKOTA JUNE 5

Republican No Presidential primary held.

Democratic 26,641 Hart; 20,495 Mondale; 2,738 Jackson; 1,383 LaRouche; 1,304 Uncommitted.

TENNESSEE MAY 1

Republican 75,367 Reagan; 7,546 Uncommitted; 8 scattered.

Democratic 132,201 Mondale; 93,710 Hart; 81,418 Jackson; 6,682 Uncommitted; 4,198 Glenn; 3,824 McGovern; 30 scattered.

TEXAS MAY 5

Republican 308,713 Reagan; 11,126 Uncommitted.

Democratic No Presidential primary held.

1984 PRESIDENTIAL PRIMARIES

VERMONT MARCH 6

Republican 33,218 Reagan; 425 scattered.

Democratic 51,873 Hart; 14,834 Mondale; 5,761 Jackson; 444 Askew; 1,147 scattered.

Liberty Union 276 Serrette; 33 scattered.

WEST VIRGINIA JUNE 5

Republican 125,790 Reagan; 11,206 Stassen.

Democratic 198,776 Mondale; 137,866 Hart; 24,697 Jackson; 7,274 LaRouche; 632 Timinski.

WISCONSIN APRIL 3

Republican 280,608 "Ronald Reagan Yes"; 14,047 "Ronald Reagan No"; 158 scattered.

Democratic 282,435 Hart; 261,374 Mondale; 62,524 Jackson; 10,166 McGovern; 7,036 "None of the Names Shown"; 6,398 Glenn; 2,984 Cranston; 1,650 Hollings; 683 Askew; 518 scattered.

Constitution 1,391 Uninstructed Delegation; 56 scattered.

Labor and Farm 13,840 "William O. Hart Yes"; 1,769 "William O. Hart No"; 67 scattered.

Libertarian 3,513 "David P. Bergland Yes"; 857 "David P. Bergland No"; 15 scattered.

DISTRICT OF COLUMBIA MAY 1

Republican 5,692 Reagan.

Democratic 69,106 Jackson; 26,320 Mondale; 7,305 Hart.

1984 REPUBLICAN PREFERENCE PRIMARIES

Date		State	Total Vote	Reagan	Other
Feb.	28	New Hampshire	75,570	65,033	10,537
Mar.	6	Vermont	33,643	33,218	425
	13	Alabama	No Primary Held		
	13	Florida	344,150	344,150	—
	13	Georgia	50,793	50,793	—
	13	Massachusetts	65,937	58,996	6,941
	13	Rhode Island	2,235	2,028	207
	20	Illinois	595,078	594,742	336
	27	Connecticut	No Primary Held		
April	3	New York	No Primary Held		
	3	Wisconsin	294,813	280,608	14,205
	10	Pennsylvania	621,206	616,916	4,290
May	1	District of Columbia	5,692	5,692	—
	1	Tennessee	82,921	75,367	7,554
	5	Louisiana	16,687	14,964	1,723
	5	Texas	319,839	308,713	11,126
	8	Indiana	428,559	428,559	—
	8	Maryland	73,663	73,663	—
	8	North Carolina	No Primary Held		
	8	Ohio	658,169	658,169	—
	15	Nebraksa	146,648	145,245	1,403
	15	Oregon	243,346	238,594	4,752
	22	Idaho	105,687	97,450	8,237
June	5	California	1,874,975	1,874,897	78
	5	Montana	71,887	66,432	5,455
	5	New Jersey	240,054	240,054	—
	5	New Mexico	42,994	40,805	2,189
	5	South Dakota	No Primary Held		
	5	West Virginia	136,996	125,790	11,206
	12	North Dakota	44,109	44,109	
			6,575,651	6,484,987	90,664

Other vote includes 22,791 Uncommitted; 14,047 "Ronald Reagan No"; 12,749 Stassen; 10,383 No Preference; 8,237 "None of the Names Shown"; 360 Kelley; 252 Arnold; 202 Fernandez; 21,643 scattered.

1984 DEMOCRATIC PREFERENCE PRIMARIES

Date		State	Total Vote	Glenn	Hart	Jackson	LaRouche	McGovern	Mondale	Other
Feb.	28	New Hampshire	101,131	12,088	37,702	5,311	—	5,217	28,173	12,640
Mar.	6	Vermont	74,059	—	51,873	5,761	—	—	14,834	1,591
	13	Alabama	428,283	89,286	88,465	83,787	—	—	148,165	18,580
	13	Florida	1,182,190	128,209	463,799	144,263	—	17,614	394,350	33,955
	13	Georgia	684,541	122,744	186,903	143,730	—	11,321	208,588	11,255
	13	Massachusetts	630,962	45,456	245,943	31,824	—	134,341	160,893	12,505
	13	Rhode Island	44,511	2,249	20,011	3,875	—	2,146	15,338	892
	20	Illinois	1,659,425	19,800	584,579	348,843	—	25,336	670,951	9,916
	27	Connecticut	220,842	955	116,286	26,395	—	2,426	64,230	10,550
April	3	New York	1,387,950	15,941	380,564	355,541	—	4,547	621,581	9,776
	3	Wisconsin	635,768	6,398	282,435	62,524	—	10,166	261,374	12,871
	10	Pennsylvania	1,656,294	22,605	551,335	264,463	19,180	13,139	747,267	38,305
May	1	District of Columbia	102,731	—	7,305	69,106	—	—	26,320	—
	1	Tennessee	322,063	4,198	93,710	81,418	—	3,824	132,201	6,712
	5	Louisiana	318,810	—	79,593	136,707	4,970	3,158	71,162	23,220
	5	Texas	No Primary held							
	8	Indiana	716,955	16,046	299,491	98,190	—	—	293,413	9,815
	8	Maryland	506,886	6,238	123,365	129,387	7,836	5,796	215,222	19,042
	8	North Carolina	960,857	17,659	289,877	243,945	—	10,149	342,324	56,903
	8	Ohio	1,447,236	—	608,528	237,133	4,336	8,991	583,595	4,653
	15	Nebraska	148,855	—	86,582	13,495	1,227	1,561	39,635	6,355
	15	Oregon	399,679	10,831	233,638	37,106	5,943	—	110,374	1,787
	22	Idaho	54,722	—	31,737	3,104	1,196	—	16,460	2,225
June	5	California	2,970,903	96,770	1,155,499	546,693	52,647	69,926	1,049,342	26
	5	Montana	34,214	—	3,080*	388*	—	—	2,026*	28,720
	5	New Jersey	676,561	—	200,948	159,788	10,309	—	305,516	—
	5	New Mexico	187,403	—	87,610	22,168	3,330	5,143	67,675	1,477
	5	South Dakota	52,561	—	26,641	2,738	1,383	—	20,495	1,304
	5	West Virginia	369,245	—	137,866	24,697	7,274	—	198,776	632
	12	North Dakota	33,555	—	28,603	—	4,018	—	934	—
			18,009,192	617,473	6,503,968	3,282,380	123,649	334,801	6,811,214	335,707

Other vote includes 77,697 No Preference; 59,254 Uncommitted; 52,759 Askew; 51,437 Cranston; 33,684 Hollings; 9,815 Brewster; 9,261 "None of the Names Shown"; 8,014 Griser; 7,957 Willis; 4,847 Williams; 2,699 Kay; 1,855 Koczak; 632 Timinski; 132 Buchanan; 127 Beckman; 74 O'Donnell; 34 King; 25 Kreml; 24 Bagley; 24 Kirk; 21 Rudnicki; 20 Clendenan; 20 Sagan; 19 Caplette; 15,276 scattered.

1980 PRESIDENTIAL PRIMARIES

In 1980 thirty-five states and the District of Columbia held Presidential primaries. California Democrats and South Dakota Republicans and Democrats held slate-type preferential primaries. In New York, Democrats had a Presidential preference, but Republicans held primaries for the selection of delegates only, without indication of Presidential preference. In Mississippi, Republicans elected delegates by Congressional Districts pledged to candidates and the vote indicated is for the highest of each slate's candidates in each CD. In Arkansas, the Republicans did not hold a primary although Democrats did. In South Carolina, the Democrats did not hold a primary but Republicans did. The vote in Ohio is for delegates at-large pledged to specific candidates and elected as a group.

The tables included here give the major party primary vote in each state for those candidates who were on the ballot in at least ten states and polled at least 25,000 votes.

Republican candidates on the ballot in at least one state were John B. Anderson, Donald Badgley, Howard H. Baker, Jr., Nick Belluso, George Bush, William E. Carlson, Alvin G. Carris, John B. Connally, Philip M. Crane, Robert Dole, Benjamin Fernandez, Alvin J. Jacobson, V. A. Kelley, C. Leon Pickett, Ronald Reagan, Harold E. Stassen, R. W. Yeager.

Democratic candidates on the ballot in at least one state were Frank Ahern, Edmund G. Brown, Jr., Jimmy Carter, Cliff Finch, Richard B. Kay, Edward M. Kennedy, Lyndon H. LaRouche, Bob Maddox, William L. Nuckols, Don Reaux, Ray Rollinson.

ALABAMA MARCH 11

Republican	147,352 Reagan; 54,730 Bush; 5,099 Crane; 1,963 Baker; 1,077 Connally; 544 Stassen; 447 Dole; 141 Belluso.
Democratic	193,734 Carter; 31,382 Kennedy; 9,529 Brown; 1,670 Uncommitted; 609 Nuckols; 540 Maddox.

ARKANSAS MAY 27

Republican	No Presidential primary held.
Democratic	269,375 Carter; 80,904 Uncommitted; 78,542 Kennedy; 19,469 Finch.

CALIFORNIA JUNE 3

Republican	2,057,923 Reagan; 349,315 Anderson; 125,113 Bush; 21,465 Crane; 10,242 Fernandez; 14 scattered.
Democratic	1,507,142 Kennedy slate; 1,266,276 Carter slate; 382,759 Unpledged slate; 135,962 Brown slate; 71,779 LaRouche slate; 51 scattered.
American Independent	10,838 Downey; 10,358 Rarick; 9 scattered.
Peace & Freedom	4,071 Spock; 2,494 Hall; 1,596 McReynolds; 1,330 Griswold; 3 scattered.

CONNECTICUT MARCH 25

Republican	70,367 Bush; 61,735 Reagan; 40,354 Anderson; 4,256 Uncommitted; 2,446 Baker; 1,887 Crane; 598 Connally; 333 Dole; 308 Fernandez.
Democratic	98,662 Kennedy; 87,207 Carter; 13,403 Uncommitted; 5,617 LaRouche; 5,386 Brown.

FLORIDA MARCH 11

Republican	345,699 Reagan; 185,996 Bush; 56,636 Anderson; 12,000 Crane; 6,345 Baker; 4,958 Connally, 1,377 Stassen; 1,086 Dole; 898 Fernandez.
Democratic	666,321 Carter; 254,727 Kennedy; 104,321 No Preference; 53,474 Brown; 19,160 Kay.

1980 PRESIDENTIAL PRIMARIES

GEORGIA MARCH 11

Republican 146,500 Reagan; 25,293 Bush; 16,853 Anderson; 6,308 Crane; 2,388 Connally; 1,571 Baker; 809 Fernandez; 249 Dole; 200 Stassen.

Democratic 338,772 Carter; 32,315 Kennedy; 7,255 Brown; 3,707 Uncommitted; 1,378 Finch; 840 Kay; 513 LaRouche.

IDAHO MAY 27

Republican 111,868 Reagan; 13,130 Anderson; 5,416 Bush; 3,441 Uncommitted; 1,024 Crane.

Democratic 31,383 Carter; 11,087 Kennedy; 5,934 Uncommitted; 2,078 Brown.

American 97 Rarick; 63 Uncommitted.

Libertarian 88 Clark; 39 Uncommitted.

ILLINOIS MARCH 18

Republican 547,355 Reagan; 415,193 Anderson; 124,057 Bush; 24,865 Crane; 7,051 Baker; 4,548 Connally; 3,757 Kelley; 1,843 Dole; 1,412 scattered.

Democratic 780,787 Carter; 359,875 Kennedy; 39,168 Brown; 19,192 LaRouche; 2,045 scattered.

INDIANA MAY 6

Republican 419,016 Reagan; 92,955 Bush; 56,342 Anderson.

Democratic 398,949 Carter; 190,492 Kennedy.

KANSAS APRIL 1

Republican 179,739 Reagan; 51,924 Anderson; 35,838 Bush; 3,603 Baker; 2,067 Connally; 1,650 Fernandez; 1,367 Crane; 1,063 Yeager; 483 Carris; 383 Stassen; 311 Carlson; 244 Badgley; 6,726 "None of the Names Shown".

Democratic 109,807 Carter; 61,318 Kennedy; 9,434 Brown; 632 Maddox; 629 Finch; 571 Ahern; 364 Rollinson; 11,163 "None of the Names Shown".

KENTUCKY MAY 27

Republican 78,072 Reagan; 6,861 Bush; 4,791 Anderson; 3,084 Uncommitted; 1,223 Stassen; 764 Fernandez.

Democratic 160,819 Carter; 55,167 Kennedy; 19,219 Uncommitted; 2,609 Kay; 2,517 Finch.

LOUISIANA APRIL 5

Republican 31,212 Reagan; 7,818 Bush; 2,221 Uncommitted; 155 Belluso; 126 Stassen; 84 Fernandez; 67 Pickett.

Democratic 199,956 Carter; 80,797 Kennedy; 41,614 Uncommitted; 16,774 Brown; 11,153 Finch; 3,362 Kay; 2,830 Maddox; 2,255 Reaux.

MARYLAND MAY 13

Republican 80,557 Reagan; 68,389 Bush; 16,244 Anderson; 2,113 Crane.

Democratic 226,528 Carter; 181,091 Kennedy; 45,879 Uncommitted; 14,313 Brown; 4,891 Finch; 4,388 LaRouche.

1980 PRESIDENTIAL PRIMARIES

MASSACHUSETTS MARCH 4

Republican 124,365 Bush; 122,987 Anderson; 115,334 Reagan; 19,366 Baker; 4,714 Connally; 4,669 Crane; 2,243 No Preference; 577 Dole; 374 Fernandez; 218 Stassen; 5,979 scattered.

Democratic 590,393 Kennedy; 260,401 Carter; 31,498 Brown; 19,663 No Preference; 5,368 scattered.

MICHIGAN MAY 20

Republican 341,998 Bush; 189,184 Reagan; 48,947 Anderson; 10,265 Uncommitted; 2,248 Fernandez; 1,938 Stassen; 596 scattered.

Democratic 36,385 Uncommitted; 23,043 Brown; 8,948 LaRouche; 10,048 scattered.

MISSISSIPPI JUNE 3

Republican 23,028 Reagan slate; 2,105 Bush slate; 618 Unslated (CD's 3 and 4 only).

Democratic No Presidential primary held.

MONTANA JUNE 3

Republican 68,744 Reagan; 7,665 Bush; 3,014 No Preference.

Democratic 66,922 Carter; 47,671 Kennedy; 15,466 No Preference.

NEBRASKA MAY 13

Republican 155,995 Reagan; 31,380 Bush; 11,879 Anderson; 1,420 Dole; 1,062 Crane; 799 Stassen; 400 Fernandez; 2,268 scattered.

Democratic 72,120 Carter; 57,826 Kennedy; 16,041 Uncommitted; 5,478 Brown; 1,169 LaRouche; 1,247 scattered.

NEVADA MAY 27

Republican 39,352 Reagan; 3,078 Bush; 4,965 "None of These Candidates".

Democratic 25,159 Carter; 19,296 Kennedy; 22,493 "None of These Candidates".

NEW HAMPSHIRE FEBRUARY 26

Republican 72,983 Reagan; 33,443 Bush; 18,943 Baker; 14,458 Anderson; 2,618 Crane; 2,239 Connally; 597 Dole; 1,876 scattered.

Democratic 52,692 Carter; 41,745 Kennedy; 10,743 Brown; 2,326 LaRouche; 566 Kay; 3,858 scattered.

NEW JERSEY JUNE 3

Republican 225,959 Reagan; 47,447 Bush; 4,571 Stassen.

Democratic 315,109 Kennedy; 212,387 Carter; 19,499 Uncommitted; 13,913 LaRouche.

1980 PRESIDENTIAL PRIMARIES

NEW MEXICO JUNE 3

Republican 37,982 Reagan; 7,171 Anderson; 5,892 Bush; 4,412 Crane, 1,795 Fernandez; 1,347 Uncommitted; 947 Stassen.

Democratic 73,721 Kennedy; 66,621 Carter; 9,734 Uncommitted; 4,798 LaRouche; 4,490 Finch.

NEW YORK MARCH 25

Republican No Presidential primary was held. Delegates were elected, but without indication of Presidential preference.

Democratic 582,757 Kennedy; 406,305 Carter.

NORTH CAROLINA MAY 6

Republican 113,854 Reagan; 36,631 Bush; 8,542 Anderson; 4,538 No Preference; 2,543 Baker; 1,107 Connally; 629 Dole; 547 Crane.

Democratic 516,778 Carter; 130,684 Kennedy; 68,380 No Preference; 21,420 Brown.

OHIO JUNE 3

Republican 692,288 Reagan; 164,485 Bush.

Democratic 605,744 Carter; 523,874 Kennedy; 35,268 LaRouche; 21,524 Kay.

OREGON MAY 20

Republican 170,449 Reagan; 109,210 Bush; 32,118 Anderson; 2,324 Crane; 1,265 scattered.

Democratic 208,693 Carter; 114,651 Kennedy; 34,409 Brown; 10,569 scattered.

PENNSYLVANIA APRIL 22

Republican 626,759 Bush; 527,916 Reagan; 30,846 Baker; 26,890 Anderson (write-in); 10,656 Connally, 6,767 Stassen; 4,357 Jacobson; 2,521 Fernandez; 4,699 scattered.

Democratic 736,854 Kennedy; 732,332 Carter; 93,865 No Preference; 37,669 Brown; 12,831 scattered.

RHODE ISLAND JUNE 3

Republican 3,839 Reagan; 993 Bush; 348 Uncommitted; 107 Stassen; 48 Fernandez.

Democratic 26,179 Kennedy; 9,907 Carter; 1,160 LaRouche; 771 Uncommitted; 310 Brown.

SOUTH CAROLINA MARCH 8

Republican 79,549 Reagan; 43,113 Connally; 21,569 Bush; 773 Baker; 171 Fernandez; 150 Stassen; 117 Dole; 59 Belluso.

Democratic No Presidential primary was held.

SOUTH DAKOTA JUNE 3

Republican 72,861 Reagan slate; 5,366 No Preference slate; 3,691 Bush slate; 987 Stassen slate.

Democratic 33,418 Kennedy slate; 31,251 Carter slate; 4,094 Uncommitted slate (in CD 1 only).

1980 PRESIDENTIAL PRIMARIES

TENNESSEE MAY 6

Republican 144,625 Reagan; 35,274 Bush; 8,722 Anderson; 4,976 Uncommitted; 1,574 Crane; 39 scattered.

Democratic 221,658 Carter; 53,258 Kennedy; 11,515 Uncommitted; 5,612 Brown; 1,663 Finch; 925 LaRouche; 49 scattered.

TEXAS MAY 3

Republican 268,798 Reagan; 249,819 Bush; 8,152 Uncommitted.

Democratic 770,390 Carter; 314,129 Kennedy; 257,250 Uncommitted; 35,585 Brown.

VERMONT MARCH 4

Republican 19,720 Reagan; 19,030 Anderson; 14,226 Bush; 8,055 Baker; 1,238 Crane; 884 Connally; 105 Stassen; 2,353 scattered.

Democratic 29,015 Carter; 10,135 Kennedy; 553 scattered.

Liberty Union 257 Gardner; 165 McReynolds; 76 Hall; 75 scattered.

WEST VIRGINIA JUNE 3

Republican 115,407 Reagan; 19,509 Bush; 3,100 Stassen.

Democratic 197,687 Carter; 120,247 Kennedy.

WISCONSIN APRIL 1

Republican 364,898 Reagan; 276,164 Bush; 248,623 Anderson; 3,298 Baker; 2,951 Crane; 2,312 Connally; 1,051 Fernandez; 1,010 Stassen; 2,595 "None of the Names Shown"; 4,951 scattered.

Democratic 353,662 Carter; 189,520 Kennedy; 74,496 Brown; 6,896 LaRouche; 1,842 Finch; 2,694 "None of the Names Shown"; 509 scattered.

DISTRICT OF COLUMBIA MAY 6

Republican 4,973 Bush; 2,025 Anderson; 270 Crane; 201 Stassen; 60 Fernandez.

Democratic 39,561 Kennedy; 23,697 Carter; 892 LaRouche.

1980 REPUBLICAN PREFERENCE PRIMARIES

Date		State	Total Vote	Anderson	Baker	Bush	Connally	Crane	Reagan	Other
Feb.	26	New Hampshire	147,157	14,458	18,943	33,443	2,239	2,618	72,983	2,473
Mar.	4	Massachusetts	400,826	122,987	19,366	124,365	4,714	4,669	115,334	9,391
	4	Vermont	65,611	19,030	8,055	14,226	884	1,238	19,720	2,458
	8	South Carolina	145,501	—	773	21,569	43,113	—	79,549	497
	11	Alabama	211,353	—	1,963	54,730	1,077	5,099	147,352	1,132
	11	Florida	614,995	56,636	6,345	185,996	4,958	12,000	345,699	3,361
	11	Georgia	200,171	16,853	1,571	25,293	2,388	6,308	146,500	1,258
	18	Illinois	1,130,081	415,193	7,051	124,057	4,548	24,865	547,355	7,012
	25	Connecticut	182,284	40,354	2,446	70,367	598	1,887	61,735	4,897
	25	New York	No Primary Held							
April	1	Kansas	285,398	51,924	3,603	35,838	2,067	1,367	179,739	10,860
	1	Wisconsin	907,853	248,623	3,298	276,164	2,312	2,951	364,898	9,607
	5	Louisiana	41,683	—	—	7,818	—	—	31,212	2,653
	22	Pennsylvania	1,241,411	26,890	30,846	626,759	10,656	—	527,916	18,344
May	3	Texas	526,769	—	—	249,819	—	—	268,798	8,152
	6	Indiana	568,313	56,342	—	92,955	—	—	419,016	—
	6	North Carolina	168,391	8,542	2,543	36,631	1,107	547	113,854	5,167
	6	Tennessee	195,210	8,722	—	35,274	—	1,574	144,625	5,015
	6	District of Columbia	7,529	2,025	—	4,973	—	270	—	261
	13	Maryland	167,303	16,244	—	68,389	—	2,113	80,557	—
	13	Nebraska	205,203	11,879	—	31,380	—	1,062	155,995	4,887
	20	Michigan	595,176	48,947	—	341,998	—	—	189,184	15,047
	20	Oregon	315,366	32,118	—	109,210	—	2,324	170,449	1,265
	27	Arkansas	No Primary Held							
	27	Idaho	134,879	13,130	5,416	—	—	1,024	111,868	3,441
	27	Kentucky	94,795	4,791	—	6,861	—	—	78,072	5,071
	27	Nevada	47,395	—	—	3,078	—	—	39,352	4,965
June	3	California	2,564,072	349,315	—	125,113	—	21,465	2,057,923	10,256
	3	Mississippi	25,751	—	—	2,105	—	—	23,028	618
	3	Montana	79,423	—	—	7,665	—	—	68,744	3,014
	3	New Jersey	277,977	—	—	47,447	—	—	225,959	4,571
	3	New Mexico	59,546	7,171	—	5,892	—	4,412	37,982	4,089
	3	Ohio	856,773	—	—	164,485	—	—	692,288	—
	3	Rhode Island	5,335	—	—	993	—	—	3,839	503
	3	South Dakota	82,905	—	—	3,691	—	—	72,861	6,353
	3	West Virginia	138,016	—	—	19,509	—	—	115,407	3,100
			12,690,451	1,572,174	112,219	2,958,093	80,661	97,793	7,709,793	159,718

Other vote includes 38,708 Uncommitted; 24,753 Stassen; 23,423 Fernandez; 15,161 No Preference; 9,321 "None of the Names Shown"; 7,298 Dole, 4,965 "None of These Candidates"; 4,357 Jacobson; 3,757 Kelley; 1,063 Yeager; 483 Carris; 355 Belluso; 311 Carlson; 244 Badgley; 67 Pickett; 25,452 scattered.

1980 DEMOCRATIC PREFERENCE PRIMARIES

Date		State	Total Vote	Brown	Carter	Kennedy	LaRouche	Other
Feb.	26	New Hampshire	111,930	10,743	52,692	41,745	2,326	4,424
Mar.	4	Massachusetts	907,323	31,498	260,401	590,393	—	25,031
	4	Vermont	39,703	—	29,015	10,135	—	553
	8	South Carolina	No Primary Held					
	11	Alabama	237,464	9,529	193,734	31,382	—	2,819
	11	Florida	1,098,003	53,474	666,321	254,727	—	123,481
	11	Georgia	384,780	7,255	338,772	32,315	513	5,925
	18	Illinois	1,201,067	39,168	780,787	359,875	19,192	2,045
	25	Connecticut	210,275	5,386	87,207	98,662	5,617	13,403
	25	New York	989,062	—	406,305	582,757	—	—
April	1	Kansas	193,918	9,434	109,807	61,318	—	13,359
	1	Wisconsin	629,619	74,496	353,662	189,520	6,896	5,045
	5	Louisiana	358,741	16,774	199,956	80,797	—	61,214
	22	Pennsylvania	1,613,551	37,669	732,332	736,854	—	106,696
May	3	Texas	1,377,354	35,585	770,390	314,129	—	257,250
	6	Indiana	589,441	—	398,949	190,492	—	—
	6	North Carolina	737,262	21,420	516,778	130,684	—	68,380
	6	Tennessee	294,680	5,612	221,658	53,258	925	13,227
	6	District of Columbia	64,150	—	23,697	39,561	892	—
	13	Maryland	477,090	14,313	226,528	181,091	4,388	50,770
	13	Nebraska	153,881	5,478	72,120	57,826	1,169	17,288
	20	Michigan	78,424	23,043	—	—	8,948	46,433
	20	Oregon	368,322	34,409	208,693	114,651	—	10,569
	27	Arkansas	448,290	—	269,375	78,542	—	100,373
	27	Idaho	50,482	2,078	31,383	11,087	—	5,934
	27	Kentucky	240,331	—	160,819	55,167	—	24,345
	27	Nevada	66,948	—	25,159	19,296	—	22,493
June	3	California	3,363,969	135,962	1,266,276	1,507,142	71,779	382,810
	3	Mississippi	No Primary Held					
	3	Montana	130,059	—	66,922	47,671	—	15,466
	3	New Jersey	560,908	—	212,387	315,109	13,913	19,499
	3	New Mexico	159,364	—	66,621	73,721	4,798	14,224
	3	Ohio	1,186,410	—	605,744	523,874	35,268	21,524
	3	Rhode Island	38,327	310	9,907	26,179	1,160	771
	3	South Dakota	68,763	—	31,251	33,418	—	4,094
	3	West Virginia	317,934	—	197,687	120,247	—	—
			18,747,825	573,636	9,593,335	6,963,625	177,784	1,439,445

Other vote includes 950,378 Uncommitted; 301,695 No Preference; 48,061 Kay; 48,032 Finch; 22,493 "None of These Candidates"; 13,857 "None of the Names Shown"; 4,002 Maddox; 2,255 Reaux; 609 Nuckols; 571 Ahern; 364 Rollinson; 47,128 Scattered.

1976 PRESIDENTIAL PRIMARIES

In 1976 twenty-six states and the District of Columbia held preferential primaries. California and South Dakota held slate-type preferential primaries. In the District and the other twenty-four states the voter marked his ballot for his preference among the candidates listed and in some states could write in his choice if the candidate he preferred was not on the ballot. In a few states the voter had an additional option for uncommitted, no preference or none. In Alabama, New York and Texas delegates to the national party conventions were elected in primaries, but none of these states provided for a specific expression of Presidential preference by the voter save by an indication of the Presidential preference of the candidates for convention delegates.

In each state the vote used is the preferential vote if there was such a vote. In Ohio, the vote is for delegates at-large pledged to specific candidates and elected as a group. In several states there were both a preference and a delegate vote. In such cases the preference vote is indicated here, even though the delegate contest was controlling in terms of individuals chosen to go to the party national conventions in Kansas City and New York City.

The tables included here give the major party primary vote in each state for those candidates who were on the ballot in at least ten states or who polled a minimum of one percent of their party's total national Presidential preference vote.

Republican candidates on the ballot in at least one state were Lar Daly, Gerald R. Ford, Tommy Klein and Ronald Reagan.

Democratic candidates on the ballot in at least one state were Frank Ahern, Stanley N. Arnold, Birch Bayh, Lloyd Bentsen, Arthur O. Blessitt, Frank Bona, Edmund G. Brown, Jr., Robert C. Byrd, Jimmy Carter, Frank Church, Billy Joe Clegg, Gertrude W. Donahey, Abram Eisenman, John S. Gonas, Jesse Gray, Fred R. Harris, Hubert H. Humphrey, Henry M. Jackson, Robert L. Kelleher, Edward M. Kennedy, Rick Loewenherz, Frank Lomento, Floyd L. Lunger, Ellen McCormack, Fifi Rockefeller, George Roden, Ray Rollinson, Terry Sanford, Bernard B. Schechter, Milton Shapp, R. Sargent Shriver, Morris K. Udall and George C. Wallace.

ARKANSAS MAY 25

Republican	20,628 Reagan; 11,430 Ford; 483 Uncommitted.
Democratic	314,306 Carter; 83,005 Wallace; 57,152 Uncommitted; 37,783 Udall; 9,554 Jackson. Original uncorrected canvass gave the Uncommitted vote as 57,067.

CALIFORNIA JUNE 8

Republican	1,604,836 Reagan; 845,655 Ford; 20 scattered write-ins.
Democratic	2,013,210 Brown slate; 697,092 Carter slate; 250,581 Church slate; 171,501 Udall slate; 102,292 Wallace slate; 78,595 Uncommitted slate; 38,634 Jackson slate; 29,242 McCormack slate; 16,920 Harris slate; 11,419 Bayh slate; 215 scattered write-ins.
American Independent	3,447 Shea; 2,922 Rarick; 2,447 Watson; 1,719 Procell; 1,523 Goodloe; 7 scattered write-ins.
Peace & Freedom	4,351 Wright; 1,372 Zeidler; 12 scattered write-ins.

FLORIDA MARCH 9

Republican	321,982 Ford; 287,837 Reagan.
Democratic	448,844 Carter; 396,820 Wallace; 310,944 Jackson; 37,626 No Preference; 32,198 Shapp; 27,235 Udall; 8,750 Bayh; 7,889 Blessitt; 7,595 McCormack; 7,084 Shriver; 5,397 Harris; 5,042 Byrd; 4,906 Church.

1976 PRESIDENTIAL PRIMARIES

GEORGIA MAY 4

Republican 128,671 Reagan; 59,801 Ford.

Democratic 419,272 Carter; 57,594 Wallace; 9,755 Udall; 3,628 Byrd; 3,358 Jackson; 2,477 Church; 1,487 Ahern; 1,378 Shriver; 824 Bayh; 699 Harris; 635 McCormack; 351 Eisenman; 277 Bentsen; 263 Bona; 181 Shapp; 153 Roden; 139 Kelleher.

IDAHO MAY 25

Republican 66,743 Reagan; 22,323 Ford; 727 Uncommitted.

Democratic 58,570 Church; 8,818 Carter; 1,700 Humphrey; 1,453 Brown (write-in); 1,115 Wallace; 981 Udall; 964 Uncommitted; 485 Jackson; 319 Harris.

American 409 Rarick; 261 Anderson; 92 Uncommitted.

ILLINOIS MARCH 16

Republican 456,750 Ford; 311,295 Reagan; 7,582 Daly; 266 scattered write-ins.

Democratic 630,915 Carter; 361,798 Wallace; 214,024 Shriver; 98,862 Harris; 6,315 scattered write-ins.

INDIANA MAY 4

Republican 323,779 Reagan; 307,513 Ford.

Democratic 417,480 Carter; 93,121 Wallace; 72,080 Jackson; 31,708 McCormack.

KENTUCKY MAY 25

Republican 67,976 Ford; 62,683 Reagan; 1,781 Uncommitted; 1,088 Klein.

Democratic 181,690 Carter; 51,540 Wallace; 33,262 Udall; 17,061 McCormack; 11,962 Uncommitted; 8,186 Jackson; 2,305 Fifi Rockefeller.

MARYLAND MAY 18

Republican 96,291 Ford; 69,680 Reagan.

Democratic 286,672 Brown; 219,404 Carter; 32,790 Udall; 24,176 Wallace; 13,956 Jackson; 7,907 McCormack; 6,841 Harris.

MASSACHUSETTS MARCH 2

Republican 115,375 Ford; 63,555 Reagan; 6,000 No Preference; 3,519 scattered write-ins.

Democratic 164,393 Jackson; 130,440 Udall; 123,112 Wallace; 101,948 Carter; 55,701 Harris; 53,252 Shriver; 34,963 Bayh; 25,772 McCormack; 21,693 Shapp; 9,804 No Preference; 7,851 Humphrey (write-in); 1,623 Kennedy (write-in); 1,603 Kelleher; 364 Bentsen; 351 Sanford; 2,951 scattered write-ins.

American No candidate names were printed on the ballot; there were 595 write-in votes including 86 for Wallace. In addition there were 98 No Preference votes.

1976 PRESIDENTIAL PRIMARIES

MICHIGAN MAY 18

Republican 690,180 Ford; 364,052 Reagan; 8,473 Uncommitted; 109 scattered write-ins.

Democratic 307,559 Carter; 305,134 Udall; 49,204 Wallace; 15,853 Uncommitted; 10,332 Jackson; 7,623 McCormack; 5,738 Shriver; 4,081 Harris; 3,142 scattered write-ins.

MONTANA JUNE 1

Republican 56,683 Reagan; 31,100 Ford; 1,996 No Preference.

Democratic 63,448 Church; 26,329 Carter; 6,708 Udall; 3,820 No Preference; 3,680 Wallace; 2,856 Jackson.

NEBRASKA MAY 11

Republican 113,493 Reagan; 94,542 Ford; 379 scattered write-ins.

Democratic 67,297 Church; 65,833 Carter; 12,685 Humphrey; 7,199 Kennedy; 6,033 McCormack; 5,567 Wallace; 4,688 Udall; 2,642 Jackson; 811 Harris; 407 Bayh; 384 Shriver; 1,467 scattered write-ins.

NEVADA MAY 25

Republican 31,637 Reagan; 13,747 Ford; 2,365 "None of these Candidates".

Democratic 39,671 Brown; 17,567 Carter; 6,778 Church; 4,603 "None of these Candidates"; 2,490 Wallace; 2,237 Udall; 1,896 Jackson.

NEW HAMPSHIRE FEBRUARY 24

Republican 55,156 Ford; 53,569 Reagan; 2,949 scattered write-ins.

Democratic 23,373 Carter; 18,710 Udall; 12,510 Bayh; 8,863 Harris; 6,743 Shriver; 4,596 Humphrey (write-in); 1,857 Jackson (write-in); 1,061 Wallace (write-in); 1,007 McCormack; 828 Blessitt; 371 Arnold; 174 Clegg; 173 Schechter; 135 Bona; 87 Kelleher; 53 Sanford; 49 Loewenherz; 1,791 scattered write-ins.

NEW JERSEY JUNE 8

Republican 242,122 Ford, unopposed.

Democratic 210,655 Carter; 49,034 Church; 31,820 Jackson; 31,183 Wallace; 21,774 McCormack; 3,935 Lunger; 3,574 Gray; 3,555 Lomento; 3,021 Rollinson; 2,288 Gonas.

NORTH CAROLINA MARCH 23

Republican 101,468 Reagan; 88,897 Ford; 3,362 No Preference.

Democratic 324,437 Carter; 210,166 Wallace; 25,749 Jackson; 22,850 No Preference; 14,032 Udall; 5,923 Harris; 1,675 Bentsen.

OHIO JUNE 8

Republican 516,111 Ford; 419,646 Reagan.

Democratic 593,130 Carter; 240,342 Udall; 157,884 Church; 63,953 Wallace; 43,661 Donahey; 35,404 Jackson.

1976 PRESIDENTIAL PRIMARIES

OREGON MAY 25

Republican 150,181 Ford; 136,691 Reagan; 11,663 scattered write-ins.

Democratic 145,394 Church; 115,310 Carter; 106,812 Brown (write-ins); 22,488 Humphrey; 11,747 Udall; 10,983 Kennedy; 5,797 Wallace; 5,298 Jackson; 3,753 McCormack; 1,344 Harris; 743 Bayh; 2,963 scattered write-ins.

PENNSYLVANIA APRIL 27

Republican 733,472 Ford; 40,510 Reagan (write-in); 22,678 scattered write-ins.

Democratic 511,905 Carter; 340,340 Jackson; 259,166 Udall; 155,902 Wallace; 38,800 McCormack; 32,947 Shapp; 15,320 Bayh; 13,067 Harris; 12,563 Humphrey (write-in); 5,032 scattered write-ins.

Constitutional 1,333 Cunningham; 87 scattered write-ins.

RHODE ISLAND JUNE 1

Republican 9,365 Ford; 4,480 Reagan; 507 Uncommitted.

Democratic 19,035 Uncommitted; 18,237 Carter; 16,423 Church; 2,543 Udall; 2,468 McCormack; 756 Jackson; 507 Wallace; 247 Bayh; 132 Shapp.

SOUTH DAKOTA JUNE 1

Republican 43,068 Reagan slate; 36,976 Ford slate; 4,033 No Preference slate.

Democratic 24,186 Carter slate; 19,510 Udall slate; 7,871 No Preference slate; 4,561 McCormack slate; 1,412 Wallace slate; 573 Harris slate; 558 Jackson slate.

TENNESSEE MAY 25

Republican 120,685 Ford; 118,997 Reagan; 2,756 Uncommitted; 97 scattered write-ins.

Democratic 259,243 Carter; 36,495 Wallace; 12,420 Udall; 8,026 Church; 6,148 Uncommitted; 5,672 Jackson; 1,782 McCormack; 1,628 Harris; 1,556 Brown (write-in); 507 Shapp; 109 Humphrey (write-in); 492 scattered write-ins, including all 424 write-ins in Shelby County. .

VERMONT MARCH 2

Republican 27,014 Ford; 4,892 Reagan (write-in); 251 scattered.

Democratic 16,335 Carter; 10,699 Shriver; 4,893 Harris; 3,324 McCormack; 3,463 scattered.

Liberty Union 965 Wright; 150 scattered.

WEST VIRGINIA MAY 11

Republican 88,386 Ford; 67,306 Reagan.

Democratic 331,639 Byrd; 40,938 Wallace.

1976 PRESIDENTIAL PRIMARIES

WISCONSIN APRIL 6

Republican 326,869 Ford; 262,126 Reagan; 2,234 "None of the Names Shown"; 583 scattered write-ins.

Democratic 271,220 Carter; 263,771 Udall; 92,460 Wallace; 47,605 Jackson; 26,982 McCormack; 8,185 Harris; 7,154 "None of the Names Shown"; 5,097 Shriver; 1,730 Bentsen; 1,255 Bayh; 596 Shapp; 14,473 scattered write-ins.

American No candidate names were printed on the ballot; there were 1,033 write-in votes.

DISTRICT OF COLUMBIA MAY 4

Republican No Presidential candidates on the ballot.

Democratic 10,521 Carter; 10,149 Uncommitted (Fauntroy slate); 6,999 Udall; 5,161 Uncommitted (Washington slate); 461 Harris.

1976 REPUBLICAN PREFERENCE PRIMARIES

Date		State	Total Vote	Ford	Reagan	Other
February	24	New Hampshire	111,674	55,156	53,569	2,949
March	2	Massachusetts	188,449	115,375	63,555	9,519
	2	Vermont	32,157	27,014	4,892	251
	9	Florida	609,819	321,982	287,837	–
	16	Illinois	775,893	456,750	311,295	7,848
	23	North Carolina	193,727	88,897	101,468	3,362
April	6	Wisconsin	591,812	326,869	262,126	2,817
	27	Pennsylvania	796,660	733,472	40,510	22,678
May	4	District of Columbia	No Primary			
	4	Georgia	188,472	59,801	128,671	–
	4	Indiana	631,292	307,513	323,779	–
	11	Nebraska	208,414	94,542	113,493	379
	11	West Virginia	155,692	88,386	67,306	–
	18	Maryland	165,971	96,291	69,680	–
	18	Michigan	1,062,814	690,180	364,052	8,582
	25	Arkansas	32,541	11,430	20,628	483
	25	Idaho	89,793	22,323	66,743	727
	25	Kentucky	133,528	67,976	62,683	2,869
	25	Nevada	47,749	13,747	31,637	2,365
	25	Oregon	298,535	150,181	136,691	11,663
	25	Tennessee	242,535	120,685	118,997	2,853
June	1	Montana	89,779	31,100	56,683	1,996
	1	Rhode Island	14,352	9,365	4,480	507
	1	South Dakota	84,077	36,976	43,068	4,033
	8	California	2,450,511	845,655	1,604,836	20
	8	New Jersey	242,122	242,122	–	–
	8	Ohio	935,757	516,111	419,646	–
			10,374,125	5,529,899	4,758,325	85,901

Other vote includes 7,582 Daly; 1,088 Klein; 42,514 scattered write-ins; 15,391 No Preference; 14,727 Uncommitted; 2,365 "None of These Candidates"; 2,234 "None of the Names Shown".

1976 DEMOCRATIC PREFERENCE PRIMARIES

Date	State	Total Vote	Bayh	Brown	Byrd	Carter	Church	Harris	Jackson	McCormack	Shriver	Udall	Wallace	Other
February 24	New Hampshire	82,381	12,510	–	–	23,373	–	8,863	1,857	1,007	6,743	18,710	1,061	8,257
March 2	Massachusetts	735,821	34,963	–	–	101,948	–	55,701	164,393	25,772	53,252	130,440	123,112	46,240
2	Vermont	38,714	–	–	–	16,335	–	4,893	–	3,324	10,699	–	–	3,463
9	Florida	1,300,330	8,750	–	5,042	448,844	4,906	5,397	310,944	7,595	7,084	27,235	396,820	77,713
16	Illinois	1,311,914	–	–	–	630,915	–	98,862	–	–	214,024	–	361,798	6,315
23	North Carolina	604,832	–	–	–	324,437	–	5,923	25,749	–	–	14,032	210,166	24,525
April 6	Wisconsin	740,528	1,255	–	–	271,220	–	8,185	47,605	26,982	5,097	263,771	92,460	23,953
27	Pennsylvania	1,385,042	15,320	–	–	511,905	–	13,067	340,340	38,800	–	259,166	155,902	50,542
May 4	District of Columbia	33,291	–	–	–	10,521	–	461	–	–	–	6,999	–	15,310
4	Georgia	502,471	824	–	3,628	419,272	2,477	699	3,358	635	1,378	9,755	57,594	2,851
4	Indiana	614,389	–	–	–	417,480	–	–	72,080	31,708	–	–	93,121	–
11	Nebraska	175,013	407	–	–	65,833	67,297	811	2,642	6,033	384	4,688	5,567	21,351
11	West Virginia	372,577	–	–	331,639	–	–	–	–	–	–	–	40,938	–
18	Maryland	591,746	–	286,372	–	219,404	–	6,841	13,956	7,907	–	32,790	24,176	–
18	Michigan	708,666	–	–	–	307,559	–	4,081	10,332	7,623	5,738	305,134	49,204	18,995
25	Arkansas	501,800	–	–	–	314,306	–	–	9,554	–	–	37,783	83,005	57,152
25	Idaho	74,405	–	1,453	–	8,818	58,570	319	485	–	–	981	1,115	2,664
25	Kentucky	306,006	–	–	–	181,690	–	–	8,186	17,061	–	33,262	51,540	14,267
25	Nevada	75,242	–	39,671	–	17,567	6,778	–	1,896	–	–	2,237	2,490	4,603
25	Oregon	432,632	743	106,812	–	115,310	145,394	1,344	5,298	3,753	–	11,747	5,797	36,434
25	Tennessee	334,078	–	1,556	–	259,243	8,026	1,628	5,672	1,782	–	12,420	36,495	7,256
June 1	Montana	106,841	–	–	–	26,329	63,448	–	2,856	–	–	6,708	3,680	3,820
1	Rhode Island	60,348	247	–	–	18,237	16,423	–	756	2,468	–	2,543	507	19,167
1	South Dakota	58,671	–	–	–	24,186	–	573	558	4,561	–	19,510	1,412	7,871
8	California	3,409,701	11,419	2,013 210	–	697,092	250,581	16,920	38,634	29,242	–	171,501	102,292	78,810
8	New Jersey	360,839	–	–	–	210,655	49,034	–	31,820	21,774	–	–	31,183	16,373
8	Ohio	1,134,374	–	–	–	593,130	157,884	–	35,404	–	–	240,342	63,953	43,561
		16,052,652	86,438	2,449 374	340,309	6,235,609	830,818	234,568	1,134,375	238,027	304,399	1,611,754	1,995,388	591,593

Other vote includes 88,254 Shapp; 61,992 Humphrey; 43,661 Donahey 19,805 Kennedy; 8,717 Blessitt; 4,046 Bentsen; 3,935 Lunger; 3,574 Gray; 3,555 Lomento; 3,021 Rollinson; 2,305 Fifi Rockefeller; 2,288 Gonas; 1,829 Kelleher; 1,487 Ahern; 404 Sanford; 398 Bona; 371 Arnold; 351 Eisenman; 174 Clegg; 173 Schechter; 153 Roden; 49 Loewenherz; 205,019 Uncommitted; 81,971 No Preference; 42,304 scattered write-ins; 7,154 "None of the Names Shown"; 4,603 "None of These Candidates".

1972 PRESIDENTIAL PRIMARIES

In 1972 twenty states and the District of Columbia held preferential primaries. California, South Dakota and the District of Columbia held slate-type preferential primaries. In the other eighteen states the voter marked his ballot for his preference among the candidates listed and in some states could write in his choice if the candidate he preferred was not on the ballot. In a few states the voter had an additional option for uncommitted or for none of the listed candidates. In Alabama and New York, delegates to the national party conventions were elected in primaries, but neither state provided for a specific expression of Presidential preference by the voter, nor printed on the ballot any indication of the Presidential preference of the candidates for convention delegates.

In each state the vote used is the preferential vote if there was such a vote. In Ohio, where no specific preference vote was authorized, the major candidates ran state-wide at-large blocks of delegate candidates, and the vote given is that for the highest vote winner in each of these blocks. In several states there were both a preference and a delegate vote. In such cases the preference vote is indicated here, even though the delegate contest was controlling in terms of individuals chosen to go to the party national conventions in Miami Beach.

The tables included here give the vote in each state for those candidates on the ballot in ten or more states. Other votes, for ballot candidates or written-in, are included in the general "Other" category.

Republican candidates on the ballot in at least one state were John M. Ashbrook, Paul N. McCloskey, Richard M. Nixon, Patrick Paulsen.

Democratic candidates on the ballot in at least one state were Shirley Chisholm, Edward T. Coll, Walter E. Fauntroy, R. Vance Hartke, Hubert H. Humphrey, Henry M. Jackson, Edward M. Kennedy, John V. Lindsay, Eugene J. McCarthy, George S. McGovern, Wilbur D. Mills, Patsy Mink, Edmund S. Muskie, Terry Sanford, George C. Wallace, Samuel W. Yorty.

CALIFORNIA JUNE 6

Republican — 2,058,825 Nixon slate; 224,922 Ashbrook slate; 175 scattered.

Democratic — 1,550,652 McGovern slate; 1,375,064 Humphrey slate; 268,551 Wallace (write-in); 157,435 Chisholm slate; 72,701 Muskie slate; 50,745 Yorty slate; 34,203 McCarthy slate; 28,901 Jackson slate; 26,246 Lindsay slate; 20 scattered.

FLORIDA MARCH 14

Republican — 360,278 Nixon; 36,617 Ashbrook; 17,312 McCloskey.

Democratic — 526,651 Wallace; 234,658 Humphrey; 170,156 Jackson; 112,523 Muskie; 82,386 Lindsay; 78,232 McGovern; 43,989 Chisholm; 5,847 McCarthy; 4,539 Mills; 3,009 Hartke; 2,564 Yorty.

ILLINOIS MARCH 21

Republican — No Presidential candidates on the ballot. Write-in votes were 32,550 Nixon; 170 Ashbrook; 47 McCloskey; 802 scattered.

Democratic — 766,914 Muskie; 444,260 McCarthy; 7,017 Wallace (write-in); 3,687 McGovern (write-in); 1,476 Humphrey (write-in); 777 Chisholm (write-in); 442 Jackson (write-in); 242 Kennedy (write-in); 118 Lindsay (write-in); 211 scattered.

INDIANA MAY 2

Republican — 417,069 Nixon, unopposed.

Democratic — 354,244 Humphrey; 309,495 Wallace; 87,719 Muskie.

1972 PRESIDENTIAL PRIMARIES

MARYLAND MAY 16

Republican 99,308 Nixon; 9,223 McCloskey; 6,718 Ashbrook.

Democratic 219,687 Wallace; 151,981 Humphrey; 126,978 McGovern; 17,728 Jackson; 13,584 Yorty; 13,363 Muskie; 12,602 Chisholm; 4,776 Mills; 4,691 McCarthy; 2,168 Lindsay; 573 Mink.

MASSACHUSETTS APRIL 25

Republican 99,150 Nixon; 16,435 McCloskey; 4,864 Ashbrook; 1,690 scattered.

Democratic 325,673 McGovern; 131,709 Muskie; 48,929 Humphrey; 45,807 Wallace; 22,398 Chisholm; 19,441 Mills; 8,736 McCarthy; 8,499 Jackson; 2,348 Kennedy (write-in); 2,107 Lindsay; 874 Hartke; 646 Yorty; 589 Coll; 760 scattered.

MICHIGAN MAY 16

Republican 321,652 Nixon; 9,691 McCloskey; 5,370 Uncommitted; 30 scattered.

Democratic 809,239 Wallace; 425,694 McGovern; 249,798 Humphrey; 44,090 Chisholm; 38,701 Muskie; 10,700 Uncommitted; 6,938 Jackson; 2,862 Hartke; 51 scattered.

NEBRASKA MAY 9

Republican 179,464 Nixon; 9,011 McCloskey; 4,996 Ashbrook; 801 scattered.

Democratic 79,309 McGovern; 65,968 Humphrey; 23,912 Wallace; 6,886 Muskie; 5,276 Jackson; 3,459 Yorty; 3,194 McCarthy; 1,763 Chisholm; 1,244 Lindsay; 377 Mills; 293 Kennedy (write-in); 249 Hartke; 207 scattered.

NEW HAMPSHIRE MARCH 7

Republican 79,239 Nixon; 23,190 McCloskey; 11,362 Ashbrook; 1,211 Paulsen; 2,206 scattered.

Democratic 41,235 Muskie; 33,007 McGovern; 5,401 Yorty; 3,563 Mills (write-in); 2,417 Hartke; 954 Kennedy (write-in); 348 Humphrey (write-in); 280 Coll; 197 Jackson (write-in); 175 Wallace (write-in); 1,277 scattered.

NEW JERSEY JUNE 6

Republican No Presidential candidates on the ballot.

Democratic 51,433 Chisholm; 25,401 Sanford.

NEW MEXICO JUNE 6

Republican 49,067 Nixon; 3,367 McCloskey; 3,035 None of the Names Shown.

Democratic 51,011 McGovern; 44,843 Wallace; 39,768 Humphrey; 6,411 Muskie; 4,236 Jackson; 3,819 None of the Names Shown; 3,205 Chisholm.

1972 PRESIDENTIAL PRIMARIES

NORTH CAROLINA MAY 6

Republican 159,167 Nixon; 8,732 McCloskey.

Democratic 413,518 Wallace; 306,014 Sanford; 61,723 Chisholm; 30,739 Muskie; 9,416 Jackson.

OHIO MAY 2

Republican 692,828 Nixon, unopposed.

Democratic 499,680 Humphrey; 480,320 McGovern; 107,806 Muskie; 98,498 Jackson; 26,026 McCarthy.

OREGON MAY 23

Republican 231,151 Nixon; 29,365 McCloskey; 16,696 Ashbrook; 4,798 scattered.

Democratic 205,328 McGovern; 81,868 Wallace; 51,163 Humphrey; 22,042 Jackson; 12,673 Kennedy; 10,244 Muskie; 8,943 McCarthy; 6,500 Mink; 5,082 Lindsay; 2,975 Chisholm; 1,208 Mills; 618 scattered.

PENNSYLVANIA APRIL 25

Republican No Presidential candidates on the ballot. Write-in votes were 153,886 Nixon; 30,915 scattered. Of the latter, most were for candidates for the Democratic nomination, including 20,472 Wallace.

Democratic 481,900 Humphrey; 292,437 Wallace; 280,861 McGovern; 279,983 Muskie; 38,767 Jackson; 306 Chisholm (write-in); 585 scattered.

RHODE ISLAND MAY 23

Republican 4,953 Nixon; 337 McCloskey; 175 Ashbrook; 146 Uncommitted.

Democratic 15,603 McGovern; 7,838 Muskie; 7,701 Humphrey; 5,802 Wallace; 490 Uncommitted; 245 McCarthy; 138 Jackson; 41 Mills; 6 Yorty.

SOUTH DAKOTA JUNE 6

Republican 52,820 Nixon slate, unopposed.

Democratic 28,017 McGovern slate, unopposed.

TENNESSEE MAY 4

Republican 109,696 Nixon; 2,419 Ashbrook; 2,370 McCloskey; 4 scattered.

Democratic 335,858 Wallace; 78,350 Humphrey; 35,551 McGovern; 18,809 Chisholm; 9,634 Muskie; 5,896 Jackson; 2,543 Mills; 2,267 McCarthy; 1,621 Hartke; 1,476 Lindsay; 692 Yorty; 24 scattered.

WEST VIRGINIA MAY 9

Republican No Presidential candidates on the ballot.

Democratic 246,596 Humphrey; 121,888 Wallace.

1972 PRESIDENTIAL PRIMARIES

WISCONSIN APRIL 4

Republican 277,601 Nixon; 3,651 McCloskey; 2,604 Ashbrook; 2,315 None of the Names Shown; 273 scattered.

Democratic 333,528 McGovern; 248,676 Wallace; 233,748 Humphrey; 115,811 Muskie; 88,068 Jackson; 75,579 Lindsay; 15,543 McCarthy; 9,198 Chisholm; 2,450 None of the Names Shown; 2,349 Yorty; 1,213 Mink; 913 Mills; 766 Hartke; 183 Kennedy (write-in); 559 scattered.

DISTRICT OF COLUMBIA MAY 2

Republican No slates entered.

Democratic 21,217 Fauntroy slate; 8,343 Uncommitted slate.

1972 REPUBLICAN PREFERENCE PRIMARIES

Date		State	Total Vote	Ashbrook	McCloskey	Nixon	Other
March	7	New Hampshire	117,208	11,362	23,190	79,239	3,417
	14	Florida	414,207	36,617	17,312	360,278	–
	21	Illinois	33,569	170	47	32,550	802
April	4	Wisconsin	286,444	2,604	3,651	277,601	2,588
	25	Massachusetts	122,139	4,864	16,435	99,150	1,690
	25	Pennsylvania	184,801	–	–	153,886	30,915
May	2	District of Columbia	No Slates Entered				
	2	Indiana	417,069	–	–	417,069	–
	2	Ohio	692,828	–	–	692,828	–
	4	Tennessee	114,489	2,419	2,370	109,696	4
	6	North Carolina	167,899	–	8,732	159,167	–
	9	Nebraska	194,272	4,996	9,011	179,464	801
	9	West Virginia	No Candidates Entered				
	16	Maryland	115,249	6,718	9,223	99,308	–
	16	Michigan	336,743	–	9,691	321,652	5,400
	23	Rhode Island	5,611	175	337	4,953	146
	23	Oregon	282,010	16,696	29,365	231,151	4,798
June	6	California	2,283,922	224,922	–	2,058,825	175
	6	New Jersey	No Candidates Entered				
	6	New Mexico	55,469	–	3,367	49,067	3,035
	6	South Dakota	52,820	–	–	52,820	–
			5,876,749	311,543	132,731	5,378,704	53,771

Other vote includes 1,211 Paulsen; 52,559 Uncommitted, None, and scattered.

1972 DEMOCRATIC PREFERENCE PRIMARIES

Date		State	Total Vote	Chisholm	Humphrey	Jackson	McCarthy	McGovern	Muskie	Wallace	Other
March	7	New Hampshire	88,854	–	348	197	–	33,007	41,235	175	13,892
	14	Florida	1,264,554	43,989	234,658	170,156	5,847	78,232	112,523	526,651	92,498
	21	Illinois	1,225,144	777	1,476	442	444,260	3,687	766,914	7,017	571
April	4	Wisconsin	1,128,584	9,198	233,748	88,068	15,543	333,528	115,811	248,676	84,012
	25	Massachusetts	618,516	22,398	48,929	8,499	8,736	325,673	131,709	45,807	26,765
	25	Pennsylvania	1,374,839	306	481,900	38,767	–	280,861	279,983	292,437	585
May	2	District of Columbia	29,560	–	–	–	–	–	–	–	29,560
	2	Indiana	751,458	–	354,244	–	–	–	87,719	309,495	–
	2	Ohio	1,212,330	–	499,680	98,498	26,026	480,320	107,806	–	–
	4	Tennessee	492,721	18,809	78,350	5,896	2,267	35,551	9,634	335,858	6,356
	6	North Carolina	821,410	61,723	–	9,416	–	–	30,739	413,518	306,014
	9	Nebraska	192,137	1,763	65,968	5,276	3,194	79,309	6,886	23,912	5,829
	9	West Virginia	368,484	–	246,596	–	–	–	–	121,888	–
	16	Maryland	568,131	12,602	151,981	17,728	4,691	126,978	13,363	219,687	21,101
	16	Michigan	1,588,073	44,090	249,798	6,938	–	425,694	38,701	809,239	13,613
	23	Rhode Island	37,864	–	7,701	138	245	15,603	7,838	5,802	537
	23	Oregon	408,644	2,975	51,163	22,042	8,943	205,328	10,244	81,868	26,081
June	6	California	3,564,518	157,435	1,375,064	28,901	34,203	1,550,652	72,701	268,551	77,011
	6	New Jersey	76,834	51,433	–	–	–	–	–	–	25,401
	6	New Mexico	153,293	3,205	39,768	4,236	–	51,011	6,411	44,843	3,819
	6	South Dakota	28,017	–	–	–	–	28,017	–	–	–
			15,993,965	430,703	4,121,372	505,198	553,955	4,053,451	1,840,217	3,755,424	733,645

Other vote includes 331,415 Sanford; 196,406 Lindsay; 79,446 Yorty; 37,401 Mills; 21,217 Fauntroy; 16,693 Kennedy; 11,798 Hartke; 8,286 Mink; 869 Coll; 30,114 Uncommitted, None, and scattered.

1968 PRESIDENTIAL PRIMARIES

In 1968 thirteen states held Presidential primaries. California, Florida, Ohio and South Dakota held slate-type preferential primaries and in the other states electors indicated personal preference as to their party's nominee. In Illinois and New Jersey for both the Republican and Democratic primaries and in Pennsylvania for the Republican primary only, no Presidential candidates names were on the ballot and votes listed for those primaries were all cast as write-ins. In addition to these thirteen, the District of Columbia held a primary in which delegate slate voting was permitted, but no Presidential candidates names appeared on the ballot. In West Virginia no Presidential candidates filed in either primary and write-in votes were not allowed.

The tables included here give the major party primary vote in each state for principal candidates. All votes listed in the Democratic preference primary table for Senator Humphrey were cast as write-in votes.

Republican candidates who were on the ballot in at least one state or who received substantial write-in votes were Elmer W. Coy, Don DuMont, William E. Evans, Herbert F. Hoover, Americus Liberator, Richard M. Nixon, Ronald Reagan, James A. Rhodes, Nelson A. Rockefeller, George W. Romney, Raymond P. Shafer, Harold E. Stassen, Willis E. Stone, John A. Volpe, David Watumull.

Democratic candidates who were on the ballot in at least one state or who received substantial write-in votes were Roger D. Branigin, John G. Crommelin, Jacob J. Gordon, Hubert H. Humphrey, Lyndon B. Johnson, Edward M. Kennedy, Robert F. Kennedy, Richard E. Lee, Eugene J. McCarthy, George A. Smathers, George C. Wallace, Stephen M. Young.

CALIFORNIA JUNE 4

Republican 1,525,091 Reagan slate, unopposed.

Democratic 1,472,166 Robert F. Kennedy slate; 1,329,301 McCarthy slate; 380,286 No Preference slate.

FLORIDA MAY 28

Republican 51,509 No Preference slate, unopposed.

Democratic 236,242 Smathers slate; 147,216 McCarthy slate; 128,899 No Preference slate.

ILLINOIS JUNE 11

Republican No Presidential candidates on the ballot. Write-in votes were 17,490 Nixon; 2,165 Rockefeller; 1,601 Reagan; 1,147 scattered.

Democratic No Presidential candidates on the ballot. Write-in votes were 4,646 McCarthy; 4,052 Edward M. Kennedy; 2,059 Humphrey; 1,281 scattered.

INDIANA MAY 7

Republican 508,362 Nixon, unopposed.

Democratic 328,118 Robert F. Kennedy; 238,700 Branigin; 209,695 McCarthy.

MASSACHUSETTS APRIL 30

Republican 31,964 Rockefeller (write-in); 31,465 Volpe; 27,447 Nixon (write-in); 1,770 Reagan (write-in); 13,875 scattered.

Democratic 122,697 McCarthy; 68,604 Robert F. Kennedy (write-in); 44,156 Humphrey (write-in); 6,890 Johnson (write-in); 1,688 Wallace (write-in); 4,868 scattered.

1968 PRESIDENTIAL PRIMARIES

NEBRASKA MAY 14

Republican 140,336 Nixon; 42,703 Reagan; 10,225 Rockefeller (write-in); 2,638 Stassen; 1,302 Liberator; 3,272 scattered.

Democratic 84,102 Robert F. Kennedy; 50,655 McCarthy; 12,087 Humphrey (write-in); 9,187 Johnson; 1,298 Wallace (write-in); 5,282 scattered.

NEW HAMPSHIRE MARCH 12

Republican 80,666 Nixon; 11,241 Rockefeller (write-in); 1,743 Romney; 527 Stone; 429 Stassen; 247 Hoover; 161 Watumull; 151 Evans; 73 Coy; 39 DuMont; 8,661 scattered.

Democratic 27,520 Johnson (write-in); 23,263 McCarthy; 186 Crommelin; 170 Lee; 77 Gordon; 4,248 scattered.

NEW JERSEY JUNE 4

Republican No Presidential candidates on the ballot. Write-in votes were 71,809 Nixon; 11,530 Rockefeller; 2,737 Reagan; 2,516 scattered.

Democratic No Presidential candidates on the ballot. Write-in votes were 9,906 McCarthy; 8,603 Robert F. Kennedy; 5,578 Humphrey; 1,399 Wallace; 1,960 scattered.

OHIO MAY 7

Republican 614,492 James A. Rhodes slate, unopposed.

Democratic 549,140 Stephen M. Young slate, unopposed.

OREGON MAY 28

Republican 203,037 Nixon; 63,707 Reagan; 36,305 Rockefeller (write-in); 9,110 scattered.

Democratic 163,990 McCarthy; 141,631 Robert F. Kennedy; 45,174 Johnson; 12,421 Humphrey (write-in); 957 Wallace (write-in); 8,897 scattered.

PENNSYLVANIA APRIL 23

Republican No Presidential candidates on the ballot. Write-in votes were 171,815 Nixon; 52,915 Rockefeller; 7,934 Reagan; 1,223 Shafer; 53,686 scattered.

Democratic 428,259 McCarthy; 65,430 Robert F. Kennedy (write-in); 51,998 Humphrey (write-in); 24,147 Wallace (write-in); 21,265 Johnson (write-in); 5,990 scattered.

SOUTH DAKOTA JUNE 4

Republican 68,113 Nixon slate, unopposed.

Democratic 31,826 Robert F. Kennedy slate; 19,316 Johnson slate; 13,145 McCarthy slate.

1968 PRESIDENTIAL PRIMARIES

WISCONSIN APRIL 2

Republican 390,368 Nixon; 50,727 Reagan; 28,531 Stassen; 7,995 Rockefeller (write-in); 6,763 No Preference; 2,087 Romney (write-in); 3,382 scattered.

Democratic 412,160 McCarthy; 253,696 Johnson; 46,507 Robert F. Kennedy (write-in); 11,861 No Preference; 4,031 Wallace (write-in); 3,605 Humphrey (write-in); 1,142 scattered.

1968 REPUBLICAN PREFERENCE PRIMARIES

Date		State	Total Vote	Nixon	Reagan	Other
March	12	New Hampshire	103,938	80,666	—	23,272
April	2	Wisconsin	489,853	390,368	50,727	48,758
	23	Pennsylvania	287,573	171,815	7,934	107,824
	30	Massachusetts	106,521	27,447	1,770	77,304
May	7	Indiana	508,362	508,362	—	—
	7	Ohio	614,492	—	—	614,492
	14	Nebraska	200,476	140,336	42,703	17,437
	28	Florida	51,509	—	—	51,509
	28	Oregon	312,159	203,037	63,707	45,415
June	4	California	1,525,091	—	1,525,091	—
	4	New Jersey	88,592	71,809	2,737	14,046
	4	South Dakota	68,113	68,113	—	—
	11	Illinois	22,403	17,490	1,601	3,312
			4,379,082	1,679,443	1,696,270	1,003,369

Other vote includes 614,492 Rhodes; 164,340 Rockefeller; 31,598 Stassen; 31,465 Volpe; 3,830 Romney; 1,302 Americus; 1,223 Shafer; 527 Stone; 247 Hoover; 161 Watumull; 151 Evans; 73 Coy; 39 DuMont; 58,272 No Preference and 95,649 scattered.

1968 DEMOCRATIC PREFERENCE PRIMARIES

Date		State	Total Vote	McCarthy	Kennedy	Johnson	Humphrey	Other
March	12	New Hampshire	55,464	23,263	—	27,520	—	4,681
April	2	Wisconsin	733,002	412,160	46,507	253,696	3,605	17,034
	23	Pennsylvania	597,089	428,259	65,430	21,265	51,998	30,137
	30	Massachusetts	248,903	122,697	68,604	6,890	44,156	6,556
May	7	Indiana	776,513	209,695	328,118	—	—	238,700
	7	Ohio	549,140	—	—	549,140		
	14	Nebraska	162,611	50,655	84,102	9,187	12,087	6,580
	28	Florida	512,357	147,216	—	—	—	365,141
	28	Oregon	373,070	163,990	141,631	45,174	12,421	9,854
June	4	California	3,181,753	1,329,301	1,472,166	—	—	380,286
	4	New Jersey	27,446	9,906	8,603	—	5,578	3,359
	4	South Dakota	64,287	13,145	31,826	19,316	—	—
	11	Illinois	12,038	4,646	—	—	2,059	5,333
			7,293,673	2,914,933	2,246,987	383,048	131,904	1,616,801

Other vote includes 549,140 Young; 238,700 Branigin; 236,242 Smathers; 33,520 Wallace; 4,052 Edward M. Kennedy; 186 Crommelin; 170 Lee; 77 Gordon; 521,046 No Preference and 33,668 scattered.